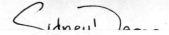

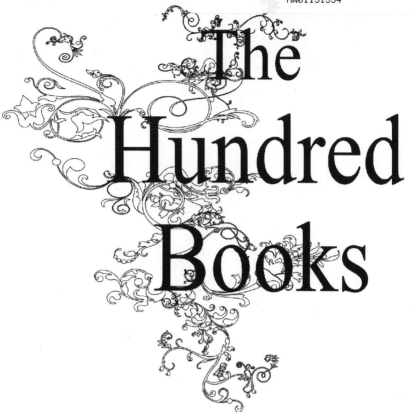

The Hundred Books

Edited and compiled
by
Glyn Lloyd-Hughes

PRINT DATA:
Crown Quarto 18.91cm x 24.59cm

For my beloved,
My Victoria

Ond ða swiðe lytle fiorme ðara boca wiston, for ðæm ðe hie hiora
nanwuht ongietan ne meahton, for ðæm ðe hie næron on hiora agen
geðeode awritene … Forðy me ðyncð betre, gif iow swæ ðyncð, ðæt we
eac sume bec, ða ðe niedbeðearfosta sien eallum monnum to wiotonne,
ðæt we ða on ðæt geðeode wenden ðe we ealle gecnawan mægen …
hwilum word be worde, hwilum andgit of andgiete …

Ælfred kyning

(And they had very little benefit from those books, for they could not
understand anything in them, because they were not written in their own
language … Therefore it seems better to me, if it seems so to you, that
we translate those certain books, which are most needful for all men to
know, into that language we all can understand, … sometimes word for
word, and sometimes sense for sense…)

King Alfred The Great of England, from the preface to
his translation of Pope Gregory's *Pastoral Care*

INTRODUCTION

You should listen to this story, for when we get to the end we shall know
more than we do now. The Snow Queen (p319)

There's a certain set of books which you're just supposed to know about, at least if you live in The West and want people to call you '*educated*'. Of course, hardly anyone has actually read them – they mostly look far too old, long or boring for that – but, still, the polite world expects its members to have a rough working relationship with The Bible and Shakespeare, to be able to spot Brobdingnag on a map, to know that Gaul is divided into three parts, that a line has no width and to be at least on nodding terms with Dr Jekyll, Tiny Tim, Starbuck, Socrates, Mr. Scrooge, Leopold Bloom, Raskolnikov, Einstein and Enkidu.

So here are those books. We could argue about precisely which ones should have been picked, but, for the most part, there just ain't no argument. The 'Gigamesh' *is* the oldest story book known, Newton's 'Principia' *is* the foundation of modern physics and so on. For the rest, they've not just someone's whim, they're the books which are most quoted, most copied and most sold.

True, this *Literary Canon,* is mostly made of dead white males, and looks rather like it might be the preserve of public schoolboys and curmudgeonly Oxbridge dons. But we can't change history; we have to take things as they are. Like it or not, the way our world is now has largely been built for us from the musings of Plato and Aristotle, from the stories of Homer, Chaucer, Milton, Dickens, from the ideas of Freud and Newton and the rest. And if you do want to change the future for better, you'll need to know how the past was made, and the task will be a whole lot easier if you know what people mean when they talk about things like Proust's cup of tea, or call something 'Kafkaesque'.

What's different this time is that they've been squashed up into nice little abridgements. Proper abridgements, mind, not those nasty, soulless, lists-of-facts you can buy from people who want to help you pass exams, nor the re-writing that Reader's Digest used to do. Here I've tried to give you the full beam of the story, the guts of the style and all those quotable quotes, in every word the words the original author wrote, in the order they wrote them. The original, just squeezed down to something like a readable short story. Here you're very likely to discover that ancient Greek theatre, medieval theology and even economics are all actually rather fascinating.

And something more – *The Hundred Books* makes it possible to read a whole lot as a single narrative, to discover a *Pisgah View* of the whole grand thing in way normally impossible to ordinary mortals.

You'll love it.

Glyn Lloyd-Hughes
Adlington, Lancashire
Spring 2011

Contents

The Epic of Gilgamesh
⊨𝍖 ⊨𝍖 ⫼ ⫟⊨𝍖 𝍖 ⊨𝍖

(Southern Mesopotamia, c2,100BCE)

Here is the oldest written story still known.

The real King Gilgamesh lived about 2,600BCE and was a leader of one of the first great human civilisations, at one of the first cities; Uruk, the ancient city of Babylonia, from which the modern name Iraq derives.

Several versions of this story have been discovered. This abridgement is based on the 1855 translation by George Smith of the clay tablets discovered in the library of Nineveh. The many missing portions are marked [...]. Abridged: GH

Tablet I

Of He who has seen all things, I will make known. Of the One who has done all things, I will tell. Anu-of-the-Sky granted him knowledge. He saw the Secrets, discovered the Hidden, and brought knowledge of time before the Flood. He returned to us from afar, and carved on stone the tale of his toils. He built walls for Uruk-Haven. See the walls of true-fired brick- did not the Seven Sages lay out its plan? One league for a city, one league for gardens, one league for courts of stone. Find the copper tablet box, loose its lock of bronze, take the tablet of lapis lazuli, and read-

Gilgamesh the King. Gilgamesh the mighty, son of the noble cow, Rimat-Ninsun. Gilgamesh the fine. Part god, part man. Gilgamesh the beautiful. Mighty as a bull, no man dare raise weapon against him. Gilgamesh the herdsman of his people! Gilgamesh leaves not the bride to her lover, Gilgamesh leaves not the girl to her mother, Gilgamesh takes the daughter even from the warrior!

And the people feared, and they prayed to Anu-the-Protector-of-the-Sky, and Anu told Aruru-the-Creator; "You created mankind! Create a match for Gilgamesh, that Uruk may find peace!" And Aruru cleaned her hands, and threw clay into the silent wilderness. And made Enkidu, the wild man, he of the shaggy hair. Enkidu ate grass with the gazelles, and jostled at the watering-hole with the animals.

A noble trapper came to the watering-hole and saw the strange man from the mountains, mighty as a meteorite that falls from the gods! The trapper's father spoke: "In Uruk lives Gilgamesh, strongest of the strong, mightier yet than the meteorite of Anu. Go! Tell Gilgamesh of this man. He will give you the harlot Shamhat, she can overcome the strong."

He made the journey, "Go, trapper, bring the harlot, Shamhat", said Gilgamesh, "and when the animals drink at the watering-hole have her put off her robe."

They travelled three days to the place, and the trapper and the harlot sat down. Then Enkidu, who eats grasses with the gazelles, came to drink with the beasts and Shamhat

released her robe. Enkidu saw her, saying "Spread out your robe so that we might lie together" and his lust groaned over her. For six days and seven nights did Enkidu stay uplifted by her charms. And understanding arrived, and wisdom came in him.

She said: "Enkidu, come you into Uruk-Haven, where Gilgamesh the wise struts over the people, where the folk dress in finery, where every day is a festival, where they play the lyre and drum and the harlots laugh and stand prettily. Enkidu, you do not know how to live!"

Gilgamesh, called to his mother: "I dreamed of a falling star, like the meteorite of Anu. I tried to lift it, but it was too mighty for me" The mother of Gilgamesh, the wise, all-knowing, Rimat-Ninsun, the wise, all-knowing, said to Gilgamesh: "The stone is a man. A man you will love and embrace as a wife, a mighty man, strong as the meteorite. A comrade who saves his friend."

Gilgamesh spoke to his mother saying: "By Enlil, the Great Counsellor, so may it be! may I have a friend and adviser, a friend and adviser may I have!"

Tablet II

[...] The harlot spoke to Enkidu, saying: "Eat bread, Enkidu, drink beer, it is our way." Enkidu ate, and drank beer- seven jugs! His face glowed, he sang with joy! He washed his shaggy body, rubbed himself with oil, and became human. He put on clothing, took up a weapon, and became a warrior. He routed the wolves, he chased the lions. With Enkidu as their guard, the herders could rest. [...]

Enkidu said; "Young man, why do you hurry?" "I go to a wedding, for me awaits a feast of delights, for Gilgamesh the King awaits the girl behind the veil, for Gilgamesh takes the wife before her husband. This is his holy destiny since the severing of his cord. This is his custom." Enkidu, flushed with anger, and walked away [...]

The young man is at the house, the marriage bed is ready, and Gilgamesh is ready to take what he has power to take. Enkidu stands before the bridal chamber, Enkidu stands before Gilgamesh. They grappled with each other at the door, they wrestle each other in the street. The doorposts tremble and the walls shake. [...]

Gilgamesh bent his knees, his anger fell away. Enkidu said to Gilgamesh: "Your mother bore you for kingship." [...]

They kissed each other and became friends. The mother of Gilgamesh, the wise, all-knowing, Rimat-Ninsun, the wise, all-knowing, said to Gilgamesh: "Enkidu has no father, no mother, his shaggy hair no one cuts. He was born alone in the wilderness." Enkidu sat and wept, his eyes filled with tears, his arms felt limp. They took each other by the hand, [...] and [...] their hands like [...] Enkidu made a declaration to Gilgamesh. [...]

"To protect the Great Cedar Forest Enlil made Humbaba, whose roar is flood, whose mouth is fire, whose breath is death! He can hear a rustling leaf 100 leagues away, who would go into his forest!"

Gilgamesh spoke to Enkidu: "I will do go- and I will cut down the Great Cedar. I will establish fame for eternity! Come, my friend, to the forge; a hatchet, a sword, and armour of one good talent weight."

Gilgamesh spoke to the men of Uruk: "I go to make my fame, grant me blessings! By the new year ceremonies, I will return!" The Counsellors of Uruk spoke; "Young Gilgamesh, your heart carries you off, who among even the Great Igigi Gods can confront Humbaba?"

Tablet III

"Let Enkidu go ahead, let his body urge him back to the wives, Enkidu! We trust our King to you!"

Gilgamesh and Enkidu together went to the Egalmah Temple, saying, "Mother Ninsun, Great Queen, wise, all-knowing, Intercede with Shamash for us". Ninsun washed herself with the purity plant, donned her jewels, donned her sash, donned her crown, sprinkled water onto the ground, went up to the roof and set incense in front of Shamash, spoke the ritual words. She laid a pendant on Enkidu's neck. [...] Gilgamesh [...] an offering of cuttings [...] sons of the king [...]

Tablet IV

At twenty leagues they broke for food, At thirty leagues they stopped for rest. Fifty leagues in a day, for one month and a half.

They dug a well facing Shamash-Of-The-Setting-Sun, and Gilgamesh climbed a mountain peak to offer flour, saying: "Mountain, bring me a dream from Shamash."

Gilgamesh slept, and woke afeared and calling; "My friend, did you touch me? Did a god pass by? Why are my muscles weak?" Enkidu, my friend, the dream has come- the mountain fell upon us, I fought a wild bull, I drank water from a waterskin."

"Your dream is good my friend, we will capture Humbaba, we will throw his corpse into the wasteland." [...] 'A slippery path is not feared by two people who help each other. ' 'A three-ply rope cannot be cut. ' "Take my hand, my friend, We will go together to the Cedar Forest. Heed not death, do not lose heart!"

Tablet V

They stood at the forest's edge, they saw the Cedar Mountain, the dwelling of the Gods, the throne of Imini. Enkidu spoke to Humbaba: "A slippery path is not feared by two people who help each other. A three-ply rope cannot be cut."

Humbaba spoke to Gilgamesh, saying: "Gilgamesh, why have you come? Give advice, Enkidu?, you son-of-a-fish, who does not even know his own father!"

Enkidu spoke to Gilgamesh, saying: "Why, my friend, do you whine and hide? Comfort, my friend [...] One hour [...] strike hard [...] flood [...] whip. They whirled around in circles as the mountains of Hermon and Lebanon split.

And then Shamash raised against Humbaba mighty tempests- Southwind, Northwind, Whistling Wind, Piercing Wind, Blizzard, Wind of Simurru, Demon Wind, Ice Wind, Sandstorm- thirteen winds against Humbaba's face.

Humbaba begged "Gilgamesh, offspring of Rimat-Nlnsun [...] Gilgamesh, let me go, I will be your servant. I have fine Myrtle wood for your palace!"

[...] Enkidu addressed Gilgamesh: "Grind him, kill him, Humbaba, Guardian of the Forest! Destroy him before the gods be filled with rage. But you sit there like a shepherd, while Enlil is in Nippur, Shamash is in Sippar!" [...] his friend [...] by his side [...] pulled out his insides including his tongue.

Enkidu addressed Gilgamesh: "My friend, we have cut down the towering cedar whose top scrapes the sky. Make from it a door 72 cubits high, 24 cubits wide, one cubit thick, its doorposts of a single piece. Let the Euphrates carry it to Nippur. They tied together a raft [...] Enkidu steered [...] While Gilgamesh held the head of Humbaba.

Tablet VI

Gilgamesh returned and placed his crown on his head, and Princess Ishtar raised her eyes; "Gilgamesh, be you my husband and you will have a chariot of lapis lazuli and gold, a house of fragrant cedar. Our doorpost will kiss your feet. All will worship you! Your she-goats will bear triplets, your ewes twins"

Gilgamesh addressed Princess Ishtar saying: "If I married you, I will have a half-door that keeps out no wind, an elephant who devours its own skin, a shoe that bites its owner's feet! You loved the colourful 'Little Shepherd' bird, yet you broke his wing. You loved the 'Mighty Lion', yet you dug for him seven pits. You loved the 'Stallion', yet gave him the whip. You loved Ishullanu, your father's date gardener, you said 'Here is my vulva.'"

Then Ishtar called in a rage to the heavens, "Father Anu, Gilgamesh has insulted me!" Send the Bull of Heaven, to kill Gilgamesh. Or else I will smash the doorposts of the Netherworld, and let the dead go up to eat the living!"

"If you demand the Bull of Heaven from me, There will be seven years of empty husks for Uruk."

Ishtar led the Bull of Heaven down to the earth. At Uruk it snorted, and a pit opened up, and one hundred, two hundred, men of Uruk fell in.

Enkidu seized the Bull of Heaven by its horns, saying to Gilgamesh: "My friend, be bold [...] I will rip out [...] I grasp the Bull [...] thrust your sword." Gilgamesh, like an expert butcher, in its neck he thrust his sword. They killed the Bull of Heaven, they ripped out its heart and presented it to Shamash, bowing humbly.

Ishtar stood upon the wall of Uruk-Haven, saying, "Woe unto Gilgamesh who slandered me and killed the Bull of Heaven!" The men of Uruk gathered, saying, "Gilgamesh is the bravest of men, boldest of males! Ishtar delights no one." Gilgamesh held a celebration in his palace. Enkidu slept and dreamed, and revealed his dream to his friend.

Tablet VII

"In my dream the Gods Anu, Enlil, and Shamash held council, saying; 'They killed the Bull of Heaven, they slew Humbaba, they pulled up the Cedar. One of them must die!' Enlil said: 'Let Enkidu die, Gilgamesh must not die!'"

Enkidu grew sick. Enkidu lay with sickness. His tears flowing like canals, Gilgamesh said: "O brother, dear brother, why are they absolving me?"

Enkidu said to Gilgamesh, his friend: "So now must I become a ghost, to sit with the dead, to see my dear brother nevermore!" Enkidu raised his eyes, [...] Spoke to the door as if it were human: "Idiot wooden door! I fashioned you, yet this is all your gratitude."

Gilgamesh listened, and his tears flowed, saying: "Friend, why do you utter such foolishness? I will appeal to your god. I will call on Enlil, the Father of Gods. I will fashion a statue of you, of gold without measure". At the first gleam of the sun his tears poured forth. "Hear me, O Shamash, on behalf of my precious life, may the trapper not get enough to feed himself. The harlot Shamhat I curse with a Great Curse; May you not be able to love your own child; May dregs of beer stain your beautiful lap; May a drunk soil your festival robe with vomit; May you never acquire anything of bright alabaster; May a crossroad be your home, a wasteland your bed; May owls nest in your walls; May you have no parties!"

Enkidu's bowels shuddered, Lying alone, he spoke as he felt, to his friend: "Listen, my friend, to my dream. I stood between heaven and earth, an a man of dark visage- a face like the Anzu, with paws of a lion, talons of an eagle-dragged me by my hair down to the House of Darkness, the dwelling of Irkalla-Queen-of-the-Netherworld, to the house of no return, to the house where they dwell without light, where dirt is their drink, clay is their food, where their garments are the feathers of fowl, where they dwell in darkness and dust.

In the House of Dust that I entered, everywhere royal crowns in heaps, and everywhere the bearers of crowns, once rulers of lands, served sweetmeats to Anu and Enlil.

There sat the high priest and acolyte, the purification priest and ecstatic, the anointed priests of the Great Gods. There sat Etana and Sumukan. There sat Ereshkigal-Queen-of-the-Netherworld, and Beletseri-Scribe-of-the-Netherworld knelt before her, she raised her head. [...]

Enkidu lies down a first day, a second day a tenth, [...] grew ever worse. Enkidu called out to Gilgamesh, "My friend hates me [...] My friend who saved me in battle has abandoned me!" [...]

At his noises Gilgamesh [...] Like a dove he moaned [...] "May he not be held, in death [...] I will mourn him [...] I at his side [...] "

Tablet VIII

As day began to dawn Gilgamesh addressed his friend: "May the road to the Cedar Forest mourn you. May the Elders of Uruk-Haven mourn you. May the men of the mountains mourn you. May the bear, the hyena, panther, tiger, lion, stag, ibex and the creatures of the plains mourn you. May the holy River Ulaja, along whose banks we grandly used to stroll, mourn you. May the pure Euphrates, from which we drank, mourn you. May the herder, who made butter and light beer for you, mourn you. May the harlot, who caressed you with oils, mourn you. May the brothers mourn over you like sisters; may the lamentation priests shave their heads for you."

"Hear me, O elders of Uruk, hear me, O men! Enkidu, my friend, the swift mule, fleet wild ass of the mountain, panther of the wilderness, we joined together and went to the mountain, we killed the Bull of Heaven, we overwhelmed Humbaba of the Cedar Forest, what now is this sleep which has seized you? You have turned dark and do not hear me!"

But Enkidu's eyes do not move. Gilgamesh touched his heart, it beat no longer. He covered his friend's face like a bride, swooping over him like an eagle, like a lioness deprived of her cubs

Gilgamesh shears off his curls, tears off his finery, and calls to the land: "You, blacksmith! You, lapidary! You, coppersmith! You, goldsmith! You, jeweler! Create 'My Friend', fashion a statue of him. His chest of lapis lazuli, his skin of gold." [...] I [...] carnelian [...] to my friend. [...] your dagger

A carnelian bowl he filled with honey. A lapis lazuli bowl he filled with butter. And displayed it before Shamash. [...]

Tablet IX

Gilgamesh cried bitterly, "I am too to die like Enkidu? Deep sadness penetrates my core, I fear my death. I will set out to the land of Utnapishtim son of Ubartutu." [...]

Then he reached Mount Mashu, which daily guards the rising and setting of the sun. Scorpion-beings watch its gate, the sight of them is death. The male scorpion-being called to his female: "He who comes to us, his body is the flesh of gods!" "Gilgamesh, why have you travelled so far, over treacherous rivers?" [...]

"I come to find my ancestor Utanapishtim, the man who joined the assembly of the Gods, and was given eternal life. Now! Open the Gate

The scorpion-being spoke to Gilgamesh, saying: "Go on, Gilgamesh, fear not! The Mashu mountains I give to you" [...]

Two leagues he travelled, dense was the darkness, light there was none. Nine leagues he travelled, the North Wind licked his face, dense was the darkness, light there was none.

Twelve leagues he travelled and it grew bright. Before him, the garden of bejewelled shrubs, their leaves of lapis lazuli. [...] cedar [...] agate [...] of the sea [...] lapis lazuli [...] like thorns and briars [...] carnelian [...] rubies hematite [...] like [...] emeralds [...] of the sea [...] Gilgamesh [...] walking [...] raised his eyes and saw [...]

Tablet X

By the seashore lives the veiled tavern-keeper Siduri, hers the golden fermenting vat. Gilgamesh wanders, his body is the flesh of gods! But sadness is within him.

The tavern-keeper saw him, bolted her door, locked her lock. Gilgamesh spoke, "Tavern-keeper, let me in, or I will break your door, smash your lock! I am Gilgamesh, I killed Humbaba of the Cedar Forest, I killed the Bull of Heaven."

The tavern-keeper spoke: "If you are Gilgamesh, Why is your heart wretched, your face haggard! Why is there such sadness deep within you?" "Should not I be so? Enkidu, my friend, swift mule of the mountain, panther of the wilderness, Enkidu, whom I love deeply, who went through every hardship with me, the fate of mankind has overtaken him.

Six days and seven nights I mourned over him, and would not allow him to be buried until a maggot fell out of his nose. I was terrified by his appearance, I learned to fear death. Tavern-keeper, what is the way to Utanapishtim?"

The tavern-keeper spoke to Gilgamesh: "The way to the Waters of Death is treacherous, go to Urshanabi, the ferryman, he has 'The Stone Things', cross with him, if you can, or turn back."

Urshanabi spoke to Gilgamesh: "Why is your heart wretched, your face haggard! Why is there such sadness deep within you?" "Should not I be so? Enkidu, my friend, swift mule of the mountain, panther of the wilderness, Enkidu, whom I love deeply, who went through every hardship with me, the fate of mankind has overtaken him."

"Now, Urshanabi! What is the way to Utanapishtim? Urshanabi spoke to Gilgamesh: "It is your hands, Gilgamesh, that prevent the crossing! You have smashed 'The Stone Things', pulled out their cords. Gilgamesh, take your axe, go into the woods, cut down 300 punting

poles each 60 cubits long." And Gilgamesh cut 300 punting poles each 60 cubits long.

They took to the boat and travelled three days, as far as a month's journey, and come at the Waters of Death. Urshanabi said to Gilgamesh: "Your hand must not pass over these Waters of Death, take a pole to press us on, then cast each pole away."

Utnapishtim was gazing off into the distance, The one who is coming is not a man of mine, [...] I keep looking but not [...] I keep looking but not [...]

Utnapishtim said to Gilgamesh: "Why is your heart wretched, your face haggard! Why is there such sadness deep within you?" "Should not I be so? Enkidu, my friend, swift mule of the mountain, panther of the wilderness, Enkidu, whom I love deeply, who went through every hardship with me, the fate of mankind has overtaken him. Six days and seven nights I mourned over him, And would not allow him to be buried, Until a maggot fell out of his nose. My friend whom I love has turned to clay"

Utnapishtim spoke to Gilgamesh: "Have you ever [...] Gilgamesh [...] the fool [...] [...] beer dregs instead of butter, [...] the temple of the holy gods [...] mankind [...] his fate. Your life is toil without cease, for what? Mankind is snapped off like a reed in a canebreak, To the fine youth and to the lovely girl [...] Death. No one can know Death, see the face of Death, hear the voice of Death.

Tablet XI

Utnapishtim spoke to Gilgamesh: "I will reveal to you a secret of the gods: at Shuruppak, beside the Euphrates was a city old, with gods inside it. And the hearts of the Great Gods moved them to inflict the Great Flood. Father Anu uttered the oath of secrecy, Valiant Enlil was their Adviser, Ninurta their Chamberlain, Ennugi their Minister of Canals."

"Prince Ea told their talk to the reed house: 'Reed house, reed house! Wall, wall! Man of Shuruppak, son of Ubartutu: tear down the house and build a boat! Abandon wealth and make all living beings go into the boat. Its length must be that of its width. Roof it over like the Apsu.' "

"I will do it. But what shall I say to the city, the people, the Elders!"

"Ea spoke: 'Say to them: Enlil spurns me, I cannot reside in your city, nor set foot on Enlil's earth. I will go down to the Apsu to live with Prince Ea, and upon you he will rain down abundance of fowl and fishes. In the morning he will shower down loaves of bread, And in the evening a rain of wheat!'"

The carpenter brought his adze, the reed worker his flattening stone, the child to carry the pitch, the weak to bring as they can. On the fifth day I laid out her hull. One field in area, walls of height each 10 times 12 cubits. I laid out six decks, each of nine compartments. I plugged it well against the water. Saw to the punting poles and laid in what was necessary. Three times 3,600 measures of pitch came from the kiln. I gave the workmen ale, oil, and wine, as if it were river water, so they could make a party like the New Year's Festival. The boat was finished by sunset. The launching was very difficult.

Whatever I had, I loaded on it: my gold and silver, I loaded on; my beasts, I loaded on; my kith and kin, I led into it. All the beasts and animals of the field, and the craftsmen, I had go up.

The time arrived, and loaves showered down, then a rain of wheat. Dawn began to glow and a black cloud came. Forth went Ninurta-Lord-of-The-Earth and made the dikes overflow. The Anunnaki lifted up the torches, setting the land ablaze.

The South Wind blew, and the mountain sank. No one could see his fellow. The gods themselves cowered like dogs by the walls. Ishtar shrieked like a woman in childbirth. Six days and seven nights came the wind and flood, then the sea fell calm.

I looked around, and all the human beings had become clay! I opened a window, I saw daylight, I fell to my knees and wept. I looked across the sea, and saw a land at twelve leagues off.

On Mount Nimush the boat rested. A second day, a third and fourth. A fifth, a sixth, and on the seventh, I sent forth a dove. But she found no rest for her foot, and circled back to me. I sent forth a swallow. But she found no rest for her foot, and circled back to me. I sent forth a raven. And the raven found dried earth, and circled not back.

Then I let out all that was in the boat, and sacrificed a sheep and incense by the mountain-ziggurat. Seven and seven holy vessels of reeds, of cedar, and myrtle. The gods smelled the savor, and gathered like flies.

Great Enlil came, he saw the boat, Was filled with rage at the Igigi gods: 'Where did a living being escape? No man was to survive the annihilation!'

Enlil went up inside the boat and grasped my hand and had my wife kneel by me. He touched our foreheads and he blessed us: 'Let Utnapishtim and his wife become immortal like us, like gods! Let them reside far away, at the Mouth of the Rivers.'

Now Gilgamesh, who will convene the gods on your behalf, to find the life eternal that you seek? Begin! You must not sleep for six days and seven nights." But as he sat down, sleep, like a fog, blew upon him.

The wife of Utanapishtim, baked day loaves and placed them by his head, The second stale, the third moist, the fourth turned white, The fifth mouldy, the sixth still fresh. The seventh- and suddenly he awoke.

Gilgamesh said to Utanapishtim: "As sleep began to pour over me you touched me and alerted me!" Utnapishtim spoke to Gilgamesh: "Look, Gilgamesh, count your day loaves!" Gilgamesh said to Utnapishtim the Faraway: "O woe! What shall I do, where shall I go! The Snatcher has taken hold of my flesh, I must return home empty-handed!"

Take him, let him wash, cast away his animal skins into the sea, soothe his body with oil, put on his royal robes! The wife of Utnapishtim said: "What can we give Gilgamesh that he may go home with honour?" Utnapishtim spoke: "Gilgamesh, I will disclose to you a hidden thing, there is a plant [...] like a boxthorn, whose thorns will prick like a rose. If you take that plant you will become young again."

So Gilgamesh fastened stones to his feet, to dive down to Apsu the Ocean of the Netherworld. He took the plant, though it pricked his hand, he cut away the stones, and returned to the shore.

Gilgamesh said: "This is a plant against decay, I will bring it to Uruk-Haven, have an old man eat it. The plant is called 'Old-Becomes-Young.' Then I will eat it and return to the condition of my youth."

At twenty leagues they broke for food, at thirty leagues they stopped for the night. By a spring Gilgamesh went to bathe. There a serpent smelled the fragrance, and silently came and took the plant. And going back, it threw off its old casing, and became new.

And Gilgamesh wept tears, "O ferryman! For whom have my arms laboured? For whom has my heart's blood roiled? Who now will remember me?"

At twenty leagues they broke for food, at thirty leagues they stopped for the night. They came in to Uruk-Haven. Gilgamesh said to Urshanabi the ferryman: "Go up, Urshanabi, onto the wall of Uruk and walk around.

See the walls of true-fired brick. Did not the Seven Sages lay out its plan? One league for a city, One league for gardens, One league for courts of stone."

The Book of The Dead

(Egypt, c1300BCE)

The 'Book of the Dead', or the 'Book of Coming Forth Into Day' is the modern name for the collections of prayers found on or near a deceased's sarcophagus. Though there are as many different versions as there are burials, they give some insight into the spiritual system behind the great Egyptian civilisation and prefigure later afterlives, such as that on p112. This is the famous Papyrus of Ani, a scribe from the city of Thebes, dating from 19th dynasty of the New Kingdom.

Abridged:GH from the translation by E.A. Wallis Budge

THE PLEA OF ANI THE SCRIBE FOR ADMISSION TO THE UNDERWORLD AND A SAFE RESURRECTION AT THE EVIT

Osiris in Ani the Scribe says: Praise be to thee, Osiris the Bull. O Amentet, the eternal king is here to put words into my mouth. I am Thoth, the great god in the sacred book, who fought for thee. I am one of the great gods that fought on behalf of Osiris. Ra, the sun-God, commanded me-Thoth-to do battle on the earth for the wronged Osiris, and I obeyed. I am among them moreover who wait over Osiris, now king of the underworld.

I am with Horus, son of Osiris, on the day when the great feast of Osiris is kept. I am the priest pouring forth libations at Tattu, I am the prophet in Abydos. I am here, O ye that bring perfected souls into the abode of Osiris, bring ye the perfected soul of Osiris in the Scribe Ani, into the blissful home of Osiris. Let him see, hear, stand, and sit as ye do in the home of Osiris.

O ye who give cakes and ale to perfected souls, give ye at morn and at eve cakes and ale to the soul of Ani the Scribe.

O ye who open the way and prepare the paths to the abode of Osiris, open the way and prepare the path that the soul of Osiris in Ani the Scribe may enter in confidence and come forth at the resurrection victoriously. May he not be turned back, may he enter and come forth; for his conscience has been weighed in the scales and is not found lacking.

THE PRAYER OF ANI THE SCRIBE

The chapter about coming forth by day and living after death: Says Osiris in Ani: O thou, only shining one of the moon; let me, departing from the crowd on earth, find entrance into the abode of shades. Open then for me the door to the underworld, and at length let me come back to earth and perform my part among men.

A chapter whereby the Shabti funeral statuettes may be made to work for a man in the underworld: O thou statuette there! If in the underworld I shall be called upon to perform any tasks, be thou my representative and act for me- planting and sowing fields, watering the soil and carrying the sands of East and West.

A chapter concerning the piercing of the back of Apepi: Tur, the overseer of the houses, says through his god Tmu : O thou wax one, thou image of Apepi, who takest thy victims captive and destroyest them, who preyest upon the weak and helpless, may I never be thy victim; may I never suffer collapse before thee. May the venom never enter my limbs, which are as those of the god Tmu. O let not the pains of death, which have reached thee; come upon me. I am the god Tmu, living in the foremost part of the Sky. I am the only one in the primordial water. I have many mysterious names, and provide myself a dwelling to endure millions of years. I was born of Tmu, and I am safe and sound.

About contending against fever with the shield of truth and good conduct: Says Osiris in Ani: I go forth against my foes endowed with the defence of truth and good conduct. I cross the heavens, and traverse the earth. Though a denizen of the underworld, I tread the earth like one alive, following in the footsteps of the blessed spirits. I have the gift of living a million years. I eat with my mouth and chew with my jaw, because I worship him who is master of the lower world.

THE SPIRIT OF THE SCRIBE MESEMNETER PRAYS THAT SOME OFFENDED GOD MAY BE CONCILIATED

About removing the anger of the god towards the departed one: The scribe Mesemneter, chief deputy of Amon, says: Praise be to thee, O God, who makest the moments to glide by, who guardest the secrets of the life beyond that of the earth, and guidest me when I utter words. The god is angered against me. But let my faults be wasted away, and let the god of Right and Truth bear them upon me. Remove them wholly from me, O god of Right and Truth. Let the offended one be at peace with me. Remove the wall of separation from before us.

A hymn to Ra at his rising and setting: Osiris in the scribe says: Praise to thee, O Ra, when thou risest. Shine thou upon my face. Let me arise with thee into the heavens, and travel with thee in the boat wherein thou sailest on the clouds.

Thou passest in peace across the heavens, and art victorious over all thy foes.

Praise to thee who art Ra when thou risest, and Tmu when in beauty thou settest. The dwellers in the land of night come forth to see thee ascend the sky. I, too, would join the throng; O let me not be held back.

A Hymn of praise to Osiris: Praise be unto thee, Osiris, lord of eternity, who appearest in many guises, and whose attributes are glorious.

Thou lookest towards the underworld and causest the earth to shine as with gold.

The dead rise up to gaze on thy face; their hearts are at peace if they but look on thee.

LITANY TO OSIRIS

Prayer: Praise to thee, O lord of the starry gods of Annu, more glorious than the gods hidden in Annu.

Answer to each prayer: Grant thou me a peaceful life, for I am truthful and just. I have uttered no falsehoods nor acted deceitfully.

Prayer: Praise to thee, O Ani; with thy long strides movest thou across the heavens.

Prayer: Praise to thee, O thou who art mighty in thy hour, great and mighty prince, lord and creator of eternity.

Prayer: Praise to those whose throne is Right and Truth, who hatest fraud and deceit.

Prayer: Praise to thee who bringest Hapi in thy boat from his place.

Prayer: Praise to thee, O creator of the gods, thou king of the North and the South. O Osiris, the all-conquering one, ruler of the world, lord of the heavens.

HYMN OF PRAISE TO THE SETTING SUN

About the mystery of the underworld and about travelling through the underworld.

When he sets on the underworld the gods adore him. The great god Ra rises with two eyes of sun and moon; all the seven gods welcome him in the evening into the underworld. They sing his praises, calling him Tmu. The deceased one says, "Praise be to thee, O Ra, praise be to thee, O Tmu. Thou hast risen and put on strength, and thou settest in glorious splendour into the underworld. Thou sailest in thy boat across the heavens, and thou established the earth. East and West adore thee, bowing and doing homage to thee day and night."

ABOUT THE COMING BACK INTO DAY OF DEPARTED SHADES.

Of the praises of entering the lower world and of coming out: Osiris in the scribe Ani says it is a good and profitable thing on earth for a man to recite this text, since all the words written herein shall come to pass.

I am Ra, who at my rising rule all things. I am the great self-made god.

I am yesterday and to-morrow. I gave the command, and a scene of strife among the gods arose. What is this? It is Amentet, the underworld.

What is this? The horizon of my father Tmu of the setting sun. All of my failings are now supplied, my sins cleansed as I pass through the two lakes which purify the offences which men offer the gods.

I advance on the path, descending to the realm of Osiris, passing through the gate Teser. O all ye who have passed this way in safety, let me grasp your hands and be brought to your abode.

O ye divine powers of Maert, the sworn foes of falsehood, may I come to you.

I am the great Cat of Ra himself, and therefore in his name which I bear, I can tread on all my enemies. O great Ra, who climbest the heavenly vaults and who sailest in thy boat across the firmament with undisputed authority, do thou save me from that austere god whose eyebrows are as menacing as the balance that weighs the deeds of men. Save me, I pray thee, from these guardians of the passages who will, if they-may, impede my progress. O Tmu, who livest in the august abode, god of gods, who thrivest upon damned souls, thou dog-faced, human-skinned one, devourer of shades, digester of human hearts, O fearful one, save me from the great soul-foe who gnaws and destroys shades of men.

O Chepera in thy bark, save me from the testing guardians into whose charge the glorious inviolate god has committed his foes; deliver thou me. May these never undo me, may I never fall helpless into the chambers of torture. O ye gods, in the presence of Osiris, reach, forth your arms, for I am one of the gods in your midst.

The Osiris in Ani flies away like a haw, he clucks like a goose, he is safe from destruction as the serpent Nehebkau . Avaunt, ye lions that obstruct my path. O Ra, thou ascending one, let me rise with thee, and have a triumphant arrival to my old earthly abode.

A LITANY ADDRESSED TO THOTH

If this chapter is recited over the deceased he shall come forth into the day and pass through the transformations which the departed one desires.

The speech of Ammautef, the priest: I have come to you, ye gods of heaven, earth, and the underworld, bringing with me Ani, the scribe, who has done no wrong against any gods, so that ye may protect him and give him good-speed to the underworld.

The speech of Ani himself: Praise be to thee, O thou ruler of Amenta, Unneferu, who presides in Abydos. I have come to thee with a pure heart, free from sin. I have told no falsehoods nor acted deceitfully. Give thou me in the tomb the food I need for the journey, so let me have a safe entrance to the underworld and a sure exit.

The speech of the priest Samerif: I come to the gods residing at Restau. I have brought you Osiris in Ani; grant him bread, water, and air, and also an abode in the Field of Peace called Sechithotepu.

The speech of Ani himself: Praise be to Osiris, everlasting lord, and to the gods of Restau. I come to thee knowing thy goodwill and having learned those rites which thou requirest for entrance into the lower world. May I have a safe arrival, and find food in thy presence.

Litany to Thoth: O thou who makest Osiris triumphant over his foes, make thou this scribe Nebenseri victorious over his foes. O Thoth, make Ani triumphant over his enemies, etc., etc.

OF MAGICAL PURPOSES

Chapter of the Crown of Triumph: Thy father Tmu has made thee this beautiful crown as a magical charm so that thou mayest live for ever. Thy father Seb gives thee his inheritance. Osiris, the prince of Amenta, makes thee victorious over thy foes. Go thou as Horus, son of Isis and Osiris, and triumph ever on thy way to the underworld.

Yea Osiris in Aufankh shall, through this recited text, live and triumph for ever and ever. Horus repeated these words four times, and his enemies fell headlong. And Osiris in Aufankh has repeated these words four times, so let him be victorious.

This chapter is to be recited over a consecrated crown placed over the face of the deceased, and thou shalt cast incense into the flame on behalf of Osiris in Aufankh, so securing triumph over all his foes. And food and drink shall in the underworld be reached him in the presence of Osiris its king.

Chapter about making the deceased remember his name in the underworld: Nu triumphant, son of Amen-hotep, says: Let me remember my name in the great House below on the night when years are counted and months are reckoned up. If any god come to me, let me at once be able to utter his name.

Chapter about not letting the heart of the deceased act against him in the underworld: My heart, received from my mother, my heart, without which life on earth was not possible, rise then not up against me in the presence of the gods in the great day of judgment when human thoughts, words, and acts shall all be weighed in a balance.

These words are to be inscribed on a hard green, gold-coated scarab, which is to be inserted through the mouth into the bosom of the deceased.

Chapter about repelling the ass-eater: Avaunt! serpent Hai, impure one, hater of Osiris. Get thee back, for Thoth has cut off thy head. Let alone the ass, that I may have clear skies when I cross to the underworld in the Neshmet boat. I am guiltless before the gods, and have wronged none. So avaunt! thou sun-beclouding one, and let me have a prosperous voyage.

Chapter about reserving for the deceased his seat in the underworld: Nu says: My seat, my throne, come ye to me, surround me, divine ones. I am a mummy-shaped person. O grant that I may become like the great god, successful, having seat and throne.

Chapter about coming forth into day from the underworld: He who knows this chapter by heart is safe against danger in this world and in all other abodes.

Nebseni, lord of reverence, says: I am yesterday and know to-morrow. I am able to be born again. Here is the invisible force which creates gods and gives food to denizens of the underworld. I go as a messenger to Osiris. O goddess Aucherit, grant that I may come forth from the underworld to see Ra's blazing orb. O thou conductor of shades, let me have a fair path to the underworld and a sure arrival. May I be defended against all opposing powers. May the cycle of gods listen to me and grant my request

---

The Bhagavad-Gita

भगवद्गीता

"The Song of God"
(India, c1000BCE)

In India's Epic *Mahabharat*, it is told how Holy Lord Krishna refused to bear arms in the great war between the Kaurava and the Pandava clans, but offered a choice of his personal attendance to one side and the loan of his army to the other. The Pandavas chose the former, and so Krishna became a charioteer for Prince Arjuna. The 'Yogas' (understandings) of the *Bhagavad Gita*, book 63 of the *Mahabharat*, are a central text of Hinduism, and deeply influenced the creation of the Sikh and Buddhist traditions.

Abridged: GH

1. The Anguish Of Arjuna

1: King Dhritaraashtra said to his charioteer: O Sanjaya, what did my people and the Pandavas do before the great battle of Kurukshetra? Sanjaya said: King Duryodhana approached his guru, Drona, and said: Behold this mighty army! Here are heroes such as Yuyudhaana and Viraata, Drupada, valiant Yudhaamanyu, the formidable Uttamauja and their noble commanders.

14: Then great kettledrums, cymbals and trumpets sounded. And Lord Krishna and Arjuna, in their chariot with white horses, blew their celestial conches.

19: Arjuna was shaken with compassion and sorrow, saying: O Krishna, these are my kinsmen, ready to fight and die. My limbs shake, my hairs stand on end. My great bow, Gaandeeva, falls from my hand. What is the use of killing? O Krishna. What is the use of victory, of kingdoms, of pleasure, even of life itself? I have no wish to kill my teachers, my brothers, my relatives, not even for the sovereignty of the three worlds. With the destruction of a family, the eternal traditions will fall, immorality will prevail, women will be dishonourable and social order will collapse. Hell will be the fate of the ancestors, deprived of the proper offerings of rice-balls and water. Arjuna sat down and wept.

THUS ENDS THE YOGA 'THE ANGUISH OF ARJUNA'

2. Transcendental Knowledge

2: The Blessed Lord said: O Arjuna, such dejection is not for a noble Aryan, it is no way heaven. Be strong and prepare for battle.

4: Arjuna said: O Krishna, how can I strike noble gurus, Bheeshma and Drona? My heart rages with weakness and pity. I cannot see here the eternal law of necessity, the eternal Dharma. Teach me, O Krishna.

10: Lord Krishna, smiled and said: Your grief is unneeded, yet your words are wise. You and I, and these kings have always existed, and always will. Just as the underlying self, the Atma, acquires a body as a child, and the child grows a new body to be a youth and so to old age, then the Atma acquires another body beyond death. Pleasure and pain, heat and cold are no more than the senses of the body meeting with sense-objects Such are transitory. Learn to endure them, O Arjuna.

17: Atma is never destroyed. No weapon cuts it, no fire burns it, water does not wet it wet, nor the wind make it dry. Atma is unchanging. Know this, and be at peace. Death is as necessary as is birth. So grieve not over the inevitable. You are a warrior, so do your duty as a warrior. If you do not fight this righteous war, then your disgrace will be famed forever, and to the honorable, dishonor is worse than death. So, get up and fight, O Arjuna.

39: O Arjuna. Listen to the wisdom of the discipline of action called Karma-Yoga, and learn to become free. The unwise delight in chanting hymns from the Vedas, and see nothing above them. They learn from the Vedas of three states or Gunas of mind. Rise above all three, and become Self-knowing, O Arjuna. To a Self-knowing person scriptures are as useful as a reservoir in the midst of a flood. So, do your duty, O Arjuna, with your mind given to the Lord, abandon worry, abandon care for consequence, keep calm in success and in failure. Become a Karma-yogi, O Arjuna!

51: The wise Karma-yogi, renounces all care for the fruits of work, is freed from the bondage of rebirth and attains the divine. When you have pierced the veil of delusion, then you can become indifferent to the voice of mere scriptures.

54: Arjuna said: O Krishna, this person whose understanding, whose Prajna, is truly conscious- how do they sit, how do they walk, how do they talk? Who are they?

55: The Blessed Lord said: When one is completely free from desires, when one is satisfied in the Self, has joy in the Self, then one has steady Prajna, O Arjuna. To have steady Prajna, learn to withdraw the senses from mere objects, as a tortoise withdraws into its shell.

59: Abstain from sensual pleasures, and desire fades. Touch the Supreme, and all cravings fall away. Sensual desires come from attachment to mere objects, and anger comes from unfulfilled desire. And from anger arises delusion, to bewilder the mind and destroy the reason.

66: There can be no peace without Self-knowledge, and no happiness without peace. It is the wandering senses which wreck the Prajna in sight of the spiritual shore.

69: A yogi is aware of Atma, of which others know nothing, but a yogi knows nothing of the sense objects about which others are aware. Peace comes when all and any desires can enter the mind without creating a disturbance, as the river calmly enters the ocean. One who desires material objects is never peaceful.

71: To abandon all desires and becomes free from longing, even of the feeling of 'I' and 'my', is to gain peace. O Arjuna, this is the Braahmee, the state above consciousness, above delusion. To reach this, even if only at the end of one's life, is to be one with the Supreme.

THUS ENDS THE YOGA 'TRANSCENDENTAL KNOWLEDGE'

3. On Action

1: Arjuna said: O Krishna, if detachment is so fine, then why must I fight?

3: The Blessed Lord said: O Arjuna, in this world there are two spiritual paths. For the contemplative there is the path of Self-knowledge or Samnyasa, called Jnana-yoga, for the active there is the path of unselfish work or Karma-yoga.

4: But no one attains perfection by merely giving up work. Just to keep your body alive needs some action. In the beginning Brahmaa, the creator, made human beings, and decreed the work of devout worship, called Yajna. Nourish the Devas with Yajna, and the Devas will nourish you, for as all life needs food, and food needs rain, so rain is assured by performing Yajna. It is your duty to keep the wheel of creation in motion by worship, O Arjuna. Just like King Janaka of old, perform your duty as a guide to your people, for whatever standard noble persons set, the world follows.

26: The ignorant may be attached to the mere fruits of work, but it is not for the wise to unsettle them, rather, inspire them by your example of calmness and detachment, for the wise and the foolish alike are followers of their nature.

36: Arjuna said: O Krishna, why do we commit sin against our own will?

37: The Blessed Lord said: It is the spirit of sensuousness, Kamma. Kamma is your enemy. Kamma is the passionate desire for material pleasures, and Kamma becomes anger if it is unfulfilled. As the fire is hidden by its smoke, so self-knowledge is obscured by Kamma. O Arjuna, kill this devil!.

THUS ENDS THE YOGA 'ON ACTION'

4. Knowing Renunciation

1:The Blessed Lord said: It was I who taught the knowledge of Karma-yoga to King Vivasvaan, and it was he who handed it down through the royal sages. After a long time the science was lost from this earth.

4: Arjuna said: But Vivasvaan was born in ancient time, long before you appeared. How can such be?

5: The Blessed Lord said: Both you and I have had many births. I remember them all, O Arjuna, but you do not remember. I am eternal, imperishable, the Lord of all. It is I who control my own great nature, my Yoga-Maya. Whenever the way of high truth, the Dharma, declines in the world, then, O Arjuna, do I manifest Myself to protect the good and transform the wicked.

11: Whatever way my people worship Me, I return to them accordingly. Those who long for earthly success worship the Devas, and success is granted easily in the human world.

14: Your human acts do not bind Me, for I desire not the fruits of work. To understand this is to be released from the bonds of Karma. The one who sees the inaction in action, and action in inaction, is a wise person, a yogi ready to accomplish everything. Those who abjure attachment, whose work is offered as a duty to the Lord, are liberated.

24: Supreme one and only God is Brahman, and Brahman is the offering itself. Brahman is the clarified butter, poured by Brahman into the fire of Brahman.

25: Some yogis perform the Yajna of worship to the Devas. Some offer the restraint of their hearing and their other senses as sacrifice. Others offer their wealth, their simplicity, their practice of yoga, others, their vows or their study of scripture. Those who follow the yogic way make a sacrifice of their every breath in and out. Others yet, of every bite they eat.

31: From Yajna comes the sweet nectar of wisdom, and union with the eternal Brahman. O Arjuna, if this this world is no happy place for those who do not make any sacrifice, then how can the other world be? But, O Arjuna, the knowledge of sacrifice is greater than any material sacrifice. So, grasp this knowledge by humble reverence, by honest inquiry, and by learning from a guru who has realized the truth. Even the most sinful of all sinners may cross over oceans of sin by the raft of knowledge. Truly, as the fire distills wood to ashes, the fire of Self-knowledge purifies like no other.

THUS ENDS THE YOGA 'KNOWING
RENUNCIATION'

5. Renunciation Of Action

1: Arjuna said: O Krishna, You praise the transcendental knowledge of Karma-Samnyasa, and you praise the disinterested action of Karma-Yoga. Which is the better?

2: The Blessed Lord said: Both lead to the Supreme. Karma-yoga may be the greater, but, though the childish see them as different, one who masters either gains the fruits of both.

6: O Arjuna, without Karma-yoga, Samnyasa is far away. A Karma-yogi performs action by body, mind, intellect, and senses, without desires beyond self-purification. Abandoning the fruits of work, they attain Supreme Bliss. Those who remain attached to the fruits of work become bound by selfishness. One who looks at a learned Braahmana, an outcast, even a cow, an elephant, or a dog with an equal eye has realized Brahman because Brahman is seamless and impartial.

27: Renouncing the pleasures of the senses, with eyes and mind fixed only at the point between the eyebrows, with gentle equal breathing through the nostrils, with senses, mind, and intellect under control, free from lust, anger, and fear, the sage becomes truly free.

THUS ENDS THE YOGA 'RENUNCIATION OF
ACTION'

6. Self-Control And Self-Knowledge

2: O Arjuna, know that no Karma-yogi becomes a Samnyasa who has not renounced the selfish motives behind action.

5: Know that the mind is your friend, and it is your enemy. If you can master your own mind you will be tranquil in heat and cold, in pleasure and in pain, impartial to friends and enemies, relatives, saints and sinners.

11: The yogi should sit in a clean place, on a firm seat, neither too high nor too low, covered with sacred Kusha grass, with a skin, and a cloth. Sitting comfortably and concentrating on a single object, let the yogi practice meditation for self-purification. Hold the waist, spine, chest, neck, and head erect, motionless and steady, fix the whole gaze steadily between the eye brows and nowhere else. Serene and fearless in mind, celibate in body, let the yogi have Me as the supreme goal.

16: This yoga is impossible for the one who eats too much, or too little, who sleeps too much, or too little. But for the one who is moderate, this meditation will take away all sorrow.

19: Steadfast as a lamp burning sheltered from the wind, so is the Yogi's mind shut from all sense-storms and burns bright to Heaven. A bliss arrives, the infinite bliss of contact with Brahman, which is beyond the reach of the senses. After realizing Brahman, one is never separated from absolute reality.

23: This yoga should be practised with firm determination, without any doubts, abandoning all selfishness, and completely restraining the senses. By a training of intellect, by keeping the mind fully absorbed in the Self one gradually attains tranquillity. If the restless mind wanders, one should gently bring it home to reflection of the Supreme.

30: Those who find Me in everything and everything in Me, are not separated from Me, nor I from them. Those who adore Me as abiding in all beings, abide in Me, whoever they are.

33: Arjuna said: But, O Krishna, my mind is restless, turbulent and strong. O Krishna, to restrain the mind is as difficult as restraining the wind.

35: The Blessed Lord said: O Arjuna, perseverance! Detachment!

37: Arjuna said: What of thy faithful failures- those who cannot keep to the path of the yogi? What of them, O Krishna? Do they disappear like clouds, O Krishna?

40: The Blessed Lord said: There is no destruction, O Arjuna. The unsuccessful yogi lives in the heaven, to be reborn into the house of the pure and prosperous, or into a family of the wise. The yogi is superior to the ascetic. The yogi is superior to the scholar of scripture. The yogi is superior to the ritualist. Therefore, O Arjuna, be a yogi.

THUS ENDS THE YOGA 'SELF-CONTROL AND SELF-KNOWLEDGE'

7. Wisdom And Self-Realisation

1: The Blessed Lord said: O Arjuna, listen well, and you shall learn to know me. Scarce one person in a thousand strives for perfection, and scarce any of the perfected truly understands Me.

4: Know, O Arjuna, that there are eight parts to my Prakriti, my Lower Nature- earth, water, fire, air, ether, mind, the understanding called buddhi, and the I-sense called ahamkara. My other, Higher Nature, is the Purusha by which the entire universe is sustained.

6: Know O Arjuna, that all life has grown from this two-part energy, and know that Brahman is the origin of the entire universe, and is as well its dissolution. Everything in the universe is strung on Brahman like jewels on the thread of a necklace.

8: O Arjuna, I am the freshness of water, I am the radiance of the sun and the moon, I am the sacred syllable OM in all the Vedas, I am the sound in the air, I am the strength in men, I am the fragrance of the earth, I am the heat in fire, the life in all beings, I am the intelligence of the intelligent, I am the strength of the strong, I am the lust in human beings that gives rise to life.

16: Know O Arjuna, that four types seek me; the distressed, the searching, the greedy and the wise. They are all indeed noble, but the wise are My very Self, it is they who realise that all things are a manifestation of Brahman.

21: Whosoever desires to worship, whatever deity, whatever name, whatever form, if they have faith, I make their faith steady. With steady faith in their way of devotion, it is I alone who grant their wishes.

24: The ignorant think of Me as being like a man, for they cannot comprehend My supreme and imperishable and incomparable existence. Veiled by Divine Power, My Yoga-Maya, they do not know Me as the unborn and eternal Brahman. O Arjuna, I know, the past, the present, and the future, but no one really knows Me.

THUS ENDS THE YOGA 'WISDOM AND SELF-REALISATION'

8. The Imperishable Brahman

1: Arjuna said: O Krishna, what is Brahman? What is the Spirit called Adhyaatma? What is Karma? What is Adhibhuta? Who is Adhiyajna, does He dwell in the body? How can You be remembered at the time of death?

3: The Blessed Lord said: Brahman is the Supreme imperishable. The individual self is called Adhyaatma or Jeevaatma. The creative power that causes the actions of beings is Karma. All transient things are called Adhibhuta, and the soul is Adhidaiva. I am Adhiyajna, the five elements of the body.

5: The One who leaves the abode of his body, at the hour of death, remembering Me attains My abode. Such is certain. If he keeps a mind steady with devotion, making the Pranic energy rise up between the eyebrows, controlling the nine doors of the body while meditating on Brahman and uttering the sacred sound OM, he will attain the Supreme. I am easily attainable, O Arjuna, by the steadfast yogi who thinks always of Me.

17: Those who know that the day of Brahman lasts one thousand ages, and his night lasts one thousand ages, begin to know the meaning of day and night.

23: Know, O Arjuna, that after your bodily death there are two paths. The path of light is the path of spiritual practice of yoga and of Self-knowledge, it leads to the heavenly bliss of nirvana. The path of darkness, of materialism, of ignorance, leads only to another birth. Therefore, O Arjuna, be steadfast in yoga.

THUS ENDS THE YOGA 'THE IMPERISHABLE BRAHMAN'

9. The Great Knowledge And The Great Mystery

1: The Blessed Lord said: I shall declare to you, who are endowed with reverence, the most profound secret of Self-knowledge, the way to freedom from all the miseries of worldly existence. This most kingly, most secret, and very sacred knowledge which can be known by instinct, is easy to practice, and is imperishable.

4: Know that this entire universe is pervaded by Me. All beings subsist in Me, I do not depend on them. And at the end of each Great Kalpa Cycle, O Arjuna, all things merge into me, and I create them again.

15: Some worship Me by knowledge, others worship in other ways. But I take care of all who worship me with steadfast devotion. Those who worship the Devas go to the Devas, those who worship the ancestors go to the ancestors, worshippers of the ghosts go to the ghosts, but My devotees come to Me and remain in me forever.

26: Whosoever makes a pure-hearted offering to Me with devotion, be it a leaf, a flower, fruit or water, I accept with joy.

27: O Arjuna, whatever you do, whatever you eat, whatever you offer to the sacred fire, whatever charity you give, whatever austerity you perform, do it unto Me. For if even the most weak and sinful person resolves to worship Me with single-minded loving devotion, such a person becomes a saint, even women, merchants, labourers, even the evil-minded. Fix your mind on Me, be devoted to Me, worship Me, and bow down to Me. Unite yourself with Me.

THUS ENDS THE YOGA 'THE GREAT KNOWLEDGE AND THE GREAT MYSTERY'

10. Divine Glories

1: The Blessed Lord said: O Arjuna, listen once again to My supreme word. Neither the Devas nor the great Maharishi sages know My origin, because I am the origin of all Devas and sages. Nonviolence, equanimity, contentment, austerity, charity, fame, and ill fame- all these traits arise from Me alone. I am the origin. Everything emanates from Me.

12: Arjuna said: How may I know You, O Lord?

19: The Blessed Lord said: I am the beginning, middle, and end of all. I am Vishnu. I am the radiant sun among luminaries. I am Maric among the gods of wind. I am the moon among the stars. I am the Sama Veda among the Vedas. I am Indra among the Devas. I am the mind among the senses. I am Shiva among the Rudras. I am Kubera among the Yakshas and demons. I am the fire among the Vasus. I am Meru among the mountain peaks. I am Bhrigu among the great sages. I am the monosyllable OM among the words. I am the Himalaya among the immovables. I am Varuna among the water gods. I am Lord Rama among the warriors. I am the shark among the fishes. I am the Ganges among the rivers. I am logic of the logician. I am the "A" among the alphabets. I am the tricks of the gambler. I am the splendor of the splendid. I am the victory of the winner. I am resolution of the strong-hearted. I am the goodness of the good. I am the power of rulers. I am the statesmanship of the seekers of victory. I am silence among the secrets. I am the Self-knowledge of the wise.

40. O great warrior! I am many, many, more things. Yet with but one tiny fragment of myself I hold up all this whole mighty universe.

THUS ENDS THE YOGA 'DIVINE GLORIES'

11. The Vision Of The Cosmic Form

1: Arjuna said: O Krishna, I hear of Your imperishable glory, yet I wish to see You. I wish to see Your form, O Supreme Being.

7: O Arjuna, you cannot see me with the eye of your body! Take here the gift of celestial sight, and Behold!

10: And Arjuna saw the Form of the Lord, with many mouths and many eyes, many divine jewels, and holding many divine weapons. Wearing divine garlands and divine cloth, anointed with celestial perfumes and ointments, full of all wonders, the limitless God with faces on all sides.

12: If the splendour of a thousands of suns were to blaze forth at once into the sky, even that would not resemble the splendour of that exalted being. Arjuna saw the entire universe, divided in many ways, but standing One in all in the body of Krishna, the God of gods.

15: Then Arjuna, filled with wonder, his hairs standing on end, bowed his head to the Lord and prayed with folded hands: O Lord of the universe, I see You everywhere. I see no beginning nor the middle nor any end. I see You with infinite power, with Your eyes the sun and moon, Your mouth a blazing fire scorching all the universe. I am frightened O Krishna. I find no peace nor any courage. I see Your mouths, with fearful teeth, glowing like fires of cosmic dissolution.

31: Who are You? O greatest of gods, have mercy on me! I wish to understand You, the primal Being, I wish to know Your mission.

32: The Blessed Lord said: Now, I am become Death, the destroyer of worlds. Even without your participation the warriors arrayed in the opposing armies shall cease to exist. Therefore, get up and attain your destiny. Conquer your enemies and enjoy a prosperous kingdom. All these men have already been destroyed by Me. You are only an instrument, O Arjuna. Therefore kill those who are already slain by Me. Do not fear. You will certainly conquer the enemies in the battle, therefore, fight!

35: Arjuna, trembling with folded hands, prostrated with fear and spoke to Krishna in a choked voice: You are Vaayu, Yama, Agni, Varuna, Shashaanka, and Brahmaa as well as the father of Brahmaa. Salutations to You a thousand times, and again and again salutations to You. If I have insulted you, if I have scorned you, O Krishna, I implore You for forgiveness.

45: I am honoured to behold that which has never been seen before, yet my mind is tormented with fear. O God of gods, the refuge of the universe have mercy! I wish to see You with a crown, holding mace and discus in Your hand. O Lord with a thousand arms, appear in the four-armed form.

47: The Blessed Lord said: O Arjuna, do not be perturbed. And Lord Krishna revealed His four-armed form, then His gentle human form, and the Great Soul Mahatma Krishna consoled Arjuna in his terror.

THUS ENDS THE YOGA 'THE VISION OF THE COSMIC FORM'

12. Devotion

1: Arjuna said: Some of your steadfast devotees worship You as a divine person, others worship you as formless or impersonal, which of these has the best understanding of yoga?

2: The Blessed Lord said: Those who worship with supreme faith by fixing their mind on Me as personal God, I consider the best yogis. But those who worship the imperishable, they also attain Me. For Humans, with their bodies, it is a hard task to fix on the formless, so such is a difficult path to Self-realization.

9: If you cannot meditate steadily on Me, then seek to reach Me by whatever spiritual discipline you may. If you cannot do such, then be intent on performing your duty for Me. If you cannot do such, then surrender unto My will with gentle mind, and renounce the fruits of work.

12: Knowledge is better than mere ritual, meditation is better than mere knowledge, renunciation is better than mere meditation, and peace always follows the renunciation of attachment to the fruits of work.

13: One who hates no creature, who is friendly and compassionate, free from the "I" and the "my", who is even-minded in pain and pleasure, forgiving, ever content, who has subdued the mind, whose resolve is firm, whose mind and intellect are engaged in dwelling upon Me; such a devotee is dear to Me.

20: But those devotees who have faith and who sincerely try to grow these immortal virtues, who set Me as their supreme goal, they are very dear to Me.

THUS ENDS THE YOGA 'DEVOTION'

13. The Knower And The Known

1: Arjuna said: I have heard of underlying form of matter called Prakriti, of the cosmic spirit called Purusha, and of the holy field called Kshetra, I wish to learn of these, O Krishna."

The Blessed Lord said: "This body is a holy field, a Kshetra, and he who knows it is called the Kshetrajna. Know that I am the creator of all creation, O Arjuna, the knower of all fields.

3: What the Kshetra is, hear from Me. It is the five great elements, it is the I-sense, it is the intellect, it is the Prakti of unformed matter, it is the ten organs of the body along and the mind as an eleventh, it is the five objects of the senses, it is the desire, and the will - such is Kshetra. With hands and feet everywhere, with eyes, head, and face everywhere; having ears everywhere, the creator exists in the creation by pervading everything. The light of all lights, He is the knowledge, the object of knowledge, and sits in the hearts of all beings. Such is Kshetra.

19. Know both Prakriti and Purusha are truly beginningless and eternal. Know that all things you know and see are sprung from Prakriti. Prakriti is the cause of the body and of the senses, while it is Purusha that experiences, joy and sorrow. Whoever understands Purusha and Prakriti will be released from the cycle of rebirth, no matter what be his mode of living.

24. There are some who seek to perceive the Atma within themselves through the Jnana-Yoga of pure-minded meditation, others who approach it through the discipline of knowledge or work called Karma-Yoga. Some do not understand Brahman, but having heard of it from others, take to worship. They too transcend death by their firm faith. They who understand the difference between the body of creation and the Atma of the creator and know the technique of liberation, attain the Supreme.

THUS ENDS THE YOGA 'THE KNOWER AND THE KNOWN'

14. The Three Gunas

3: The Great Nature Prakriti is like a womb to Me, O Arjuna, it is where I place the seed and the spirit called the Purusha from which all beings are born. Then the three Gunas bind down the immortal soul to the body and make it what it is.

9: The Guna called Saattva attaches to happiness, the Guna Raajas to action, and Guna Taamas to ignorance. Those who are established in Saattva go to heaven, When Raajas is predominant, then greed, restlessness, passion arises, such persons are reborn in the mortal world. The Taamasika one, abiding in the lowest Guna, goes to the hell of birth as a lower creature.

21: Arjuna said: What of those who transcend all three Gunas?

22: The Blessed Lord said: The one who serves Me with love and unswerving devotion transcends Gunas, and becomes fit to realise Brahman, for I am the abode of the immortal and eternal Brahman, of everlasting Dharma, and of the absolute bliss.

THUS ENDS THE YOGA 'THE THREE GUNAS'

15. Supreme Spirit

1: The Blessed Lord said: The wise speak of the eternal Ashvattha tree whose leaves are the hymns of the Veda, whose branches spread over all the cosmos. Nourished by the Gunas, its shoots are pleasures and its roots, desire. They enmesh the human world.

6: Invisible, that is My abode. I support all beings with My power, and with the sap-giving moon I nourish all the plants. I am in the body of all the living, I digest all four varieties of food.

16: In this world there are things perishable beings and the imperishable Atma. There is also the supreme spirit called Ishvara or Paramaatma, the indestructible Lord who pervades the three worlds and sustains them. Beyond the perishable body, and higher than the imperishable Atma, there am I, Purushottama the Supreme Spirit.

THUS ENDS THE YOGA 'SUPREME SPIRIT'

16. The Divine And The Demoniac

1: The Blessed Lord said: Fearlessness, purity, perseverance in yoga, charity, restraint, sacrifice, study of scripture, honesty, nonviolence, truthfulness, renunciation, equanimity, abstaining from malicious talk, compassion for all creatures, freedom from greed, gentleness, modesty, absence of fickleness, splendour, forgiveness, fortitude, cleanliness- these are the qualities of those with divine virtues.

4: Hypocrisy, arrogance, pride, anger, harshness, and ignorance- these are the marks of those born with demonic qualities, O Arjuna.

5: Do not grieve, O Arjuna, you are born with divine qualities.

6: In this world, all persons are either of the divine, or of the demonic. The demonic do not know what to do and what not to do. Forever anxious, certain that pleasures of the senses are the highest goal, they are bound by hundreds of ties of desire and enslaved by lust and anger. They search after wealth and think they are successful, powerful, and happy. They delude themselves that being born into a great family, giving to charity, or performing religious duties are all that is needed. Such hateful people I hurl into the wombs of demons again and time again, to sink to the lowest hell.

21: Lust, anger, and greed are the three gates of hell-, let scripture be your guide and learn to abjure them.

THUS ENDS THE YOGA 'THE DIVINE AND THE DEMONIAC'

17. Threefold Faith

1: Arjuna said: What of those who perform spiritual practices with faith, but do not follow the words of scripture?

2: The Blessed Lord said: Natural faith is determined by their Gunas. The Saattvika persons worship Devas, the Raajasika people worship demigods, and the Taamasika persons worship ghosts and spirits.

7: Just so with food. Saattvika persons prefer foods that promote health and virtue, such as are juicy, smooth, and agreeable to the stomach. Raajasika persons like foods which cause pain, such as are salty, spicy, and dry. Taamasika persons care for the half-cooked, tasteless, stale and impure.

17: Austerities practiced by the Saattvika are done with supreme faith, without a desire for the fruit. Raajasik austerity is unsteady and done for the sake of respect and for show. Austerity performed without proper understanding, or with self-torture, or for harming others, is Taamasik.

20: The Saattvika performs charity as a duty to the deserving, without care for return. Raajasik charity is given unwillingly, or to get some reward. Charity given wrongly, or to the unworthy, without respect, is said to be Taamasik.

23: OM TAT SAT

24: Good acts of charity and austerity, as are prescribed in the scriptures, are always commenced by uttering "OM" by those who know Brahman, or by uttering "TAT" by those who seek nirvana. The word "SAT" is used for any faithful or auspicious act, O Arjuna.

28: Whatever is done without faith; whether it is sacrifice, charity, austerity, or any other act; is called Asat. It has no value here or hereafter, O Arjuna.

THUS ENDS THE YOGA 'THREEFOLD FAITH'

18. Liberation By Renunciation

1: Arjuna said: What is the nature of Samnyasa and Tyaaga, O Lord Krishna?

2: The Blessed Lord said: The wise sages call Samnyasa the renunciation of selfish work, and Tyaaga the renunciation of attachment to the fruits of work.

4: O Arjuna, to renounce obligatory work is not proper, it is your duty, for human beings can never completely abstain from work.

13: Learn from Me, O Arjuna, the Saamkhya doctrine of five causes of action. The physical body is the seat of Karma, the doer of the Guna, the root of the Prajna, the place of natural impulses and the home of the ruling deities. Thus, the fool who considers himself as the sole agent, does not understand. Free from the notion of doership, he knows that even if he kills all these warriors he kills them not and he is free.

29: Now hear of the Buddhi, the threefold division of the intellect, based on Gunas, O Arjuna. The Buddhi which brings understanding of proper work, of right and wrong action, fear and bravery, bondage and liberty, which allows proper regulation of the mind, that Buddhi is Saattvika. It is by the Raajasika Buddhi that one incorrectly distinguishes between Dharma and Adharma, between right and wrong action. Weak resolve, sleep, fear, grief, despair, and arrogance are Taamasika, O Arjuna.

36: Hear now of the threefold pleasure. The pleasure of spiritual practice which makes sorrow fall away, that which is as poison in the beginning but like nectar in the end, is Saattvika. Sensual pleasures come as nectars at first, but turn to poison in the end, are Raajasika pleasures. The pleasure that delude from beginning to end, which come from laziness and confusion; such are Taamasika pleasures.

41: The proper division into the four castes - Braahmana, Kshatriya, Vaishya, and Shudra - is also based on the Gunas of peoples' natures, O Arjuna. Those who have serenity, self control, austerity, purity, patience, honesty, knowledge, Self-realization, and belief in God are Braahmanas, the intellectuals. Those who have heroism, vigour, firmness, dexterity, charity, and administrative skills are Kshatriyas, the protectors. Those who excel in growing and rearing, in commerce and industry are Vaishyas. Those who labour for others are Shudras.

45: The highest perfection is found in accordance with one's natural work. Even one's inferior natural work is better than superior unnatural work.

50: Learn from Me, O Arjuna, how living in solitude, eating modestly, controlling thought, word, and deed, ever absorbed in meditation, and in detachment, relinquishing egotism, violence, pride, lust, anger, and desire for possessions, freed from the "my", and peaceful, one becomes fit for attaining oneness with Brahman.

55: By devotion to Me one learns my essence. Knowing my essence, one immediately merges into Me. Setting aside all noble deeds, just surrender completely to the will of God, I will free you from all sins. Keep this knowledge close to yourself, it is not for those who cannot practice austerity, who have no devotion, who cannot listen, or who speaks ill of Me. But the one who can teach this supreme secret to My devotees is performing the highest service to Me and shall certainly attain Me.

72. Have you heard, O Arjuna? Have you understood?

73: Arjuna said: I have learned, and I have understood. By Thy grace my doubts are gone. I am ready to do my duty.

74: Sanjaya said: Thus, O King, did I hear this wonderful secret and supreme yoga from Krishna himself. O King, I stand amazed. O King, I rejoice again and again. Wherever is Krishna, the lord of yoga; and wherever is Arjuna, the archer; there will be everlasting prosperity, victory, happiness, and morality. Such I know.

THUS ENDS THE YOGA 'LIBERATION BY RENUNCIATION'

The Torah

תּוֹרָה

The Five Books of Moses
(The Levant Desert, c650BCE?)

This is the foundation of the Hebrew Bible, and the basic text of the Jewish, Christian and Muslim religious traditions. It is known to Christians as the *Pentateuch,* The First Books of The Old Testament, and to Muslims as the *Tawrat* (توراة). The Torah has a long history of being very faithfully copied, so that there are now negligible differences between versions maintained by different communities. However, there is also a strong tradition of worn-out Torah scrolls being destroyed, making it difficult to date its first writing.

Based on the 1616 'King James' translation, substantially based on Tyndale's (see p77) of 1530. Abridged:GH.

Genesis or Bereshit (בראשית), The First Book of Moses

1 In the beginning God created the heaven and the earth. And God said, Let there be light, let there be a firmament of Heaven and waters under it, and a dry land called Earth. [11] And God said, Let the earth bring forth grass, and herbs and trees yielding fruit. [16] And God made two great lights to rule the day and night and the stars also in the firmament of the heaven [21] And God created great whales, and every living creature and every winged fowl, and God blessed them, saying, Be fruitful, and multiply. [26] And God said, Let us make man in our image: to have dominion over all the earth, and over every living thing. [27] So man and woman created he them. [31] And God saw every thing that he had made, and it was very good.

2 And on the seventh day God rested from all his work. And God blessed the seventh day, and sanctified it. [5] Then the LORD God caused it to rain upon the earth, yet there was no man to till the ground. [7] And the LORD God formed man of the dust of the ground, and breathed into his nostrils the breath of life. And the LORD planted a garden eastward in Eden; and there he put the man, saying, Of the tree of the knowledge of good and evil, which is in the garden, thou shalt not eat. [20] And Adam gave names to all cattle, and the fowl, and every beast; but found not an help meet for him. [21] And the LORD God caused a sleep to fall upon Adam: and he took one of his ribs, and made he a woman. And Adam said, This is now bone of my bones, and flesh of my flesh: she shall be called Woman, because she was taken out of Man. [24] Therefore shall a man leave his father and his mother, and shall cleave unto his wife: and they shall be one flesh. [25] And they were both naked and were not ashamed.

3 Now the serpent came unto the woman saying, Hath God said, Ye shall not eat of every tree of the garden? [5] For God doth know that in the day ye eat thereof, then your eyes shall be opened, and ye shall be as gods, knowing good and evil. [6] And the woman told to Adam and they both ate of the tree of knowledge, and their eyes were opened, and they knew that they were naked; and sewed themselves aprons of fig leaves. [8] And the LORD God walking in the garden calling unto Adam, Where art thou? [10] And he said, I heard thy voice, and I was afraid, because I was naked; and I hid myself. And God said, Hast thou eaten of the tree? And the man said, The woman gave me of the tree, and I did eat. [13] And the woman said, The serpent beguiled me. [14] And the LORD God cursed the serpent above every beast; upon thy belly shalt thou go, and dust shalt thou eat all the days of thy life: And I will put enmity between thee and the woman, and between thy seed and her seed; it shall bruise thy head, and thou shalt bruise his heel. [16] Unto the woman he said; in sorrow thou shalt bring forth children; and thy husband shall rule over thee. And unto Adam he said, Because thou hast hearkened unto the voice of thy wife, and hast eaten of the tree, in the sweat of thy face shalt thou eat bread, till thou return unto the ground; for of it wast thou taken: for dust thou art, and unto dust shalt thou return. [20] And Adam called his wife's name Eve. And the LORD God sent him forth from the garden of Eden, to till the ground. [24] And he placed at the east of the garden of Eden Cherubims, and a flaming sword, to preserve the tree of life.

4 And Adam knew Eve his wife; and she conceived, and bare Cain, and again bare his brother Abel. And Abel was a keeper of sheep, but Cain was a tiller of the ground. [8] And it came to pass that Cain rose up against Abel, and slew him. And the LORD said unto Cain, Where is Abel thy brother? And he said, I know not: Am I my brother's keeper? [10] And he said, The voice of thy brother's blood crieth unto me from the ground. Now art thou cursed from the earth. And the LORD set a mark upon Cain. And Cain went out from the presence of the LORD, and dwelt in the land of Nod, on the east of Eden. [17] And Cain knew his wife; and she conceived, and bare Enoch: and he builded a city.

5 And Adam lived an hundred and thirty years, and begat Seth: and he begat sons and daughters. And Seth lived an hundred and five years, and begat Enos. And Enos begat Cainan, and the descendant of Cainan begat Methuselah. And all the days of Methuselah were nine hundred sixty and nine years: and he died.

6 There were giants in the earth in those days; when the sons of God came unto the daughters of men, and they bare children to them, the same became mighty men of renown. And God saw that the wickedness of man was great in the earth, and repented that he had made man, and it grieved him at his heart. [7] And the LORD said, I will destroy man. But Noah found grace in the eyes of the LORD. [13] And God said unto Noah, Make thee an ark of gopher wood; of length three hundred cubits. [17] And, behold I do bring a flood of waters upon the earth, to destroy all flesh, but thou shalt come into the ark, and thy sons with thee. [19] And of every living thing, two of every sort shalt thou bring into the ark, to keep them alive; they shall be male and female. Thus Noah did.

7 I will cause it to rain upon the earth forty days and forty nights; and every living substance that I have made will I destroy. And Noah went into the ark. [19] And the waters prevailed exceedingly upon the earth; and all the high hills were covered, and every living substance was destroyed.

8 And the ark rested in the seventh month, upon the mountains of Ararat. And Noah sent forth a dove. But the dove found no rest. And he stayed yet other seven days; and sent forth the dove; and, lo, in her mouth was an olive leaf pluckt off: so Noah knew that the waters were abated. And Noah went forth, and with him every beast, after their kinds. [20] And Noah builded an altar unto the LORD; and took of every clean beast, and of every clean fowl, and offered burnt offerings on the altar.

9 And God blessed Noah and his sons Shem, Ham, and Japheth, and said unto them, Be fruitful, and multiply, and replenish the earth. And Noah he planted a vineyard: and he drank of the wine, and was drunken.

10 By the families of the sons of Noah were the nations divided in the earth after the flood. And the whole earth was of one language, and of one speech.

11 And it came to pass, that they found a plain in the land of Shinar; and they dwelt there. And they said one to another, let us make brick, let us build us a city and a tower whose top may reach unto heaven. [5] And the LORD said, Behold, the people is one, and they have all one language; and now nothing will be restrained from them, which they have imagined to do. Let us go down, and confound their language, that they may not understand one another's speech. [8] So the LORD scattered them abroad from thence upon the face of all the earth: and they left off to build the city. [9] Therefore is the name of it called Babel.

These are the generations of Shem: Shem begat Arphaxad. And Arphaxad begat Salah: And Salah begat Eber: And Eber begat Peleg: And Peleg begat Reu: And Reu begat Serug: And Serug begat Nahor: And Nahor begat Terah: And Terah begat Abram, Nahor, and Haran. And Terah took Abram from Ur of the Chaldees into the land of Canaan, and dwelt there.

12 Now the LORD had said unto Abram, Go thee out of thy country, unto a land that I will shew thee: [2] And I will make of thee a great nation. [4] So Abram departed, and Lot his brother's son, and they went into the land of Canaan. And the LORD appeared unto Abram, and said, Unto thy seed will I give this land: and there builded he an altar unto the LORD, who appeared unto him.

13 And Abram was very rich in cattle, in silver, and in gold. And there was a strife between the herdmen of Abram's cattle and the herdmen of Lot's cattle. And Abram said unto Lot, Let there be no strife, separate thyself, I pray thee, from me. Then Lot chose him all the plain of Jordan and pitched his tent toward Sodom; and Abram dwelled in the land of Canaan. Then Abram removed his tent, and dwelt in Hebron. [8] And after years the kings of Sodom and of Gomorrah joined battle in the vale of Siddim with four kings. And the kings of Sodom and of Gomorrah fled, and they that conquered took Lot, Abram's brother's son, and his goods. [14] And when Abram heard that his brother was taken captive, he armed his servants, and he brought back all the goods, and brought his brother Lot, and the women also.

15 After these things the word of the LORD came unto Abram in a vision, saying, Fear not, Abram: I am thy shield. [2] And Abram said, LORD God, what wilt thou give me, seeing I go childless? [4] And, behold, the LORD said, Look now toward heaven, as the number of the stars, so shall thy seed be. Now Sarai Abram's wife bare him no children. And Sarai said unto Abram: I pray thee, go in unto my maid, Hagar; that I may obtain children by her. And Abram went in unto Hagar, and Hagar bare Abram a son: and Abram called his name, Ishmael. [16] And Abram was fourscore and six years old.

17 And when Abram was ninety years old and nine, the LORD appeared, and said unto him; I will make my covenant between me and thee, and will multiply thee exceedingly. [5] Neither shall thy name any more be called Abram, but Abraham; for a father of many nations. [10] Every man child among you shall circumcise the flesh of your foreskin; and it shall be a token of the covenant betwixt me and you. [15] As for Sarai thy wife, Sarah shall her name be, and she shall be a mother of nations. [17] Then Abraham laughed, and said in his heart, Shall a child be born unto her that is ninety years old?

18 The LORD appeared unto Abraham as he sat in the tent door in the heat of the day. For, lo, three men stood there: and Abraham bowed himself toward the ground, saying: Pass not away, I pray thee, from thy servant: I will fetch water, and wash your feet, and rest yourselves under the tree. And Abraham brought butter, and milk, and a calf dressed and set it before them, and they did eat. [17] And the LORD said, Because the sin of Sodom and Gomorrah is very grievous, I will go down now upon them. [23] And Abraham said, Wilt thou destroy the righteous with the wicked? [26] And the LORD said, If I find in Sodom fifty, or thirty, or ten righteous, then will I spare the place.

19 Then at even two angels came to Sodom; and Lot did greet them, and he made them a feast, and did bake unleavened bread, and they did eat and tarry at the house of Lot. [4] Then came the men of the city, calling to Lot, Where are the men which came in this night? bring them out, that we may know them. [6] And Lot said, Behold, I have two daughters which have not known man; let me bring them out unto you, and do ye to them as you wish: only unto these men do nothing. [15] And when the morning arose, then the angels hastened Lot, saying, Arise, take thy wife, and thy two daughters, which are here; lest thou be consumed in the iniquity of the city. Escape for thy life and look not behind thee. [24] Then the LORD rained upon Sodom and upon Gomorrah brimstone and fire out of heaven; And he overthrew those cities, and all the inhabitants of the cities. [26] But the wife of Lot looked back from behind him, and she became a pillar of salt. And Abraham gat up early in the morning and he looked toward Sodom and Gomorrah, and beheld smoke as the smoke of a furnace. [30] And Lot dwelt in a cave in the mountain, and his two daughters with him. And the firstborn said unto the younger, Come, let us make our father drink wine, and we will lie with him, that we may preserve seed of our father. [36] Thus were both the daughters of Lot with child by their own father. And the first born bare a son, and called his name Moab. And the younger, she also bare a son, and called his name Benammi.

21 And the LORD visited Sarah as he had said, for Sarah conceived, and bare Abraham a son in his old age. And Abraham called his name Isaac, and circumcised him as God had commanded.

22 And it came to pass, that God did tempt Abraham, saying; Behold, here I am. Take thy son, Isaac, whom thou lovest, and offer him there for a burnt offering upon the mountains. And Abraham rose up early in the morning, and saddled his ass, and took Isaac. [9] And Abraham built an altar, and laid wood in order, and bound Isaac his son, and laid him on the altar upon the wood. And Abraham stretched forth his hand, and took the knife to slay his son. [11] And the angel of the LORD called out of heaven, and said, Abraham, Abraham. Now I know that thou fearest God, seeing thou hast not withheld thy only son from me. And Abraham looked, and behold, a ram caught in a thicket by his horns: and Abraham took the ram, and offered him up in the stead of his son. [15] And the angel of the LORD called unto Abraham out of heaven: In thy seed shall all the nations of the earth be blessed; because thou hast obeyed my voice.

23 And Sarah was an hundred and seven and twenty years old, and died; and Abraham came to mourn for Sarah, and to weep for her. And Abraham bought with silver the cave of Machpelah for a buryingplace.

25 Then again Abraham took a wife, and her name was Keturah, and she bare him children. Then Abraham gave up the ghost, and died in a good old age, full of years. [9] And his sons Isaac and Ishmael buried him in the cave of Machpelah. [13] And the sons of Ishmael were twelve: twelve princes of nations. [20] Isaac took Rebekah to wife, and his wife conceived. And, behold, there were twins in her womb. And the first came out like an hairy garment; and they called his name Esau. And after that came his brother, and his name was Jacob. [27] Esau was a cunning hunter and Jacob was a plain man, dwelling in tents. And Isaac loved Esau: but Rebekah loved Jacob. [29] And it came to pass that Esau came from the field, and he was faint, and said to Jacob, Feed me, I pray. [31] And Jacob said, Sell me this day thy birthright. [32] And Esau said, Behold, I am at the point to die: and what profit this birthright to me? And he sold his birthright unto Jacob. [34] Then Jacob gave Esau bread and pottage of lentiles; and he did eat and drink.

28 And Isaac called Jacob, and said unto him, Arise, go to Padanaram, and take thee a wife from the daughers of Laban thy mother's brother. [10] And Jacob lighted upon a certain place, and lay down to sleep. And he dreamed, and behold a ladder set up on the earth, and the top of it reached to heaven: and behold the angels of God ascending and descending on it. And, behold, the LORD stood above it, and said, I am the LORD God of Abraham thy father, and the God of Isaac: the land whereon thou liest, to thee will I give it, and to thy seed.

29 Then Jacob went on his journey, and came upon a well, and sheep watering and there Rachel the daughter of Leban. [11] And Jacob kissed Rachel, and wept. [13] And Laban brought him to his house. [18] And Jacob said, I will serve thee seven years for Rachel thy younger daughter. [20] And Jacob served seven years; and they seemed unto him but a few days, for the love he had to Rachel, and said unto Laban, Give me my wife, for my days are fulfilled. [26] And Laban said, It must not be so done in our country, to give the younger before the firstborn. Take then first my daughter Leah. [32] And Leah conceived of Jacob, and bare sons. And Bilhah, the handmaid of Rachel, conceived of Jacob, and bare Jacob a son. [30] And Zilpah Leah's maid bare Jacob a son, and a second son. [22] And God remembered Rachel, and opened her womb. And she bare a son; and she called his name Joseph.

35 And God appeared unto Jacob again, saying; Thy name shall be called Israel. [11] Be fruitful and multiply; a nation shall be of thee, and kings shall come of thy loins. And the land which I gave Abraham and Isaac, to thee I give it. [17] And it came to pass that Rachel had hard labour of her second son, Benjamin, and died. And Jacob set a pillar upon her grave: that is there unto this day in Bethlehem. [22] Now the sons of Jacob were twelve: Of Leah; Reuben, Simeon, Levi, Judah, Issachar, Zebulun: Of Rachel; Joseph, and Benjamin: Of Bilhah; Dan, and Naphtali: Of Zilpah; Gad, and Asher. [28] And the days of Isaac were an hundred and fourscore years, and he gave up the ghost, being old and full of days.

37 Now Israel loved Joseph more than all his children, because he was the son of his old age: and he made him a coat of many colours. [4] And when his brethren saw that their father loved him more, they hated him. [5] And Joseph dreamed a dream, and he told it his brethren: behold, we were binding sheaves in the field, and, lo, my sheaf arose, and stood upright; and your sheaves made obeisance to mine. And his brethren conspired against him to slay him, and seeing him afar, they said one to another, Behold, this dreamer cometh. [23] And they stript Joseph out of his coat of many colours, and cast him into a pit. Then, behold, a company of Ishmeelites came from Gilead with their camels bearing spicery. And they sold Joseph to the Ishmeelites for twenty pieces of silver. And they took Joseph's coat, and killed a kid, and dipped the coat in the blood. [32] And they sent the coat to their father. And he knew it, and said, It is my son's coat; an evil beast hath devoured him. [34] And Jacob rent his clothes, and mourned for his son many days.

39 And Joseph was brought to Egypt; and Potiphar, an officer of Pharaoh, captain of the guard, bought him. And Joseph found grace in his sight, and he made him overseer over his house. [7] And it came to pass that his master's wife cast her eyes upon Joseph; and she said, Lie with me. But Joseph fled. [17] And she spake unto her lord, saying, The Hebrew servant does mock me. [20] And Joseph's master put him into the prison.

40 And after these things, the butler of the king of Egypt and his baker offended their lord. And Pharaoh put them into the prison, and Joseph made there interpretations of their dreams such as came to pass. [21] Upon Pharaoh's birthday he restored the chief butler, but he hanged the baker: as Joseph had interpreted to them.

41 And it came to pass that Pharaoh dreamed that he stood by the river, and there came seven well favoured kine and fatfleshed; and seven other kine, ill favoured and leanfleshed. And the ill favoured kine did eat up the well

favoured kine. So Pharaoh awoke, and he sent for the magicians, and told them his dream; but there was none that could interpret them. [9] Then spake the chief butler, saying, I do remember an Hebrew servant, and he interpreted to us our dreams. Then was Joseph brought hastily out of the dungeon: and he shaved, and changed his raiment, and came in unto Pharaoh. [25] And Joseph heard the dream of Pharaoh, and said: [28] What God is about to do he sheweth unto Pharaoh. Behold, there come seven years of great plenty throughout the land: And after them seven years of famine. [33] Therefore let Pharaoh appoint officers to lay up corn for store against famine. [38] And Pharaoh said, Can we find such a one in whom the Spirit of God is? [41] And Pharaoh set Joseph over all the land of Egypt, and gave Joseph to wife Asenath the daughter of Potipherah the priest of On. [54] And the seven years of dearth began to come; but in all the land of Egypt there was bread.

42 Now when Jacob saw that there was corn in Egypt, Jacob said unto his sons: get you down thither, and buy for us from thence; that we may not die. [6] And Joseph it was that sold to all the people of the land: and Joseph's brethren came, and bowed down themselves before him. And Joseph knew his brethren, but they knew not him. And Joseph sorely tested his brothers by trickery until they saw him for their brother that was sold.

45 Joseph said; Haste ye to my father, and say God hath made Joseph lord of all Egypt: come unto me, tarry not: [10] And thou shalt dwell in the land of Goshen, and thou shalt be near me: And there will I nourish thee.

50 And his brethren went and fell down before him; and said, We be thy servants. [19] And Joseph said unto them, Fear not: Ye thought evil against me; but God meant it unto good, to bring to pass, to save much people alive. And Joseph dwelt in Egypt, he, and his father's house: and Joseph lived an hundred and ten years and died: and they embalmed him in Egypt.

Exodus or Shemot (שמות)
The Second Book of Moses

1 The names of the children of Israel, which came into Egypt with Jacob were: Reuben, Simeon, Levi, and Judah, Issachar, Zebulun, Benjamin, Dan, Naphtali, Gad, and Asher. And they were fruitful, and multiplied, and waxed exceeding mighty; and the land was filled with them. [8] Now there arose a new king over Egypt, and he said, Behold, the children of Israel are more and mightier than we: let us deal with them. [11] Therefore he set over them taskmasters to afflict them with burdens and with hard bondage. And they built for Pharaoh treasure cities, Pithom and Raamses. [15] And the king of Egypt spake to the midwives of the Hebrews, and said, When ye do the office of a midwife, to the Hebrew women, and see them upon the stools; if it be a son, then ye shall kill him. But the midwives feared God, and saved the men children alive, and the people multiplied, and waxed very mighty. [20]

Therefore Pharaoh charged all his people, saying, Every son that is born ye shall cast into the river.

2 And there was a daughter of Levi who bare a son: and when she could not longer hide him, she put the child in an ark of bulrushes and laid it by the river's brink. [5] And the daughter of Pharaoh came down to wash herself and she saw the ark and she saw the child: and, behold, the babe wept. And she had compassion, and the child grew, and he became her son. And she called his name Moses. [11] And it came to pass, when Moses was grown, that he spied an Egyptian smiting an Hebrew, one of his brethren. And he slew the Egyptian, and hid him in the sand. And Moses fled from the face of Pharaoh, and dwelt in the land of Midian and took to wife Zipporah the daughter of Reuel. [22] And she bare him a son, and he called his name Gershom: for he said, I have been a stranger in a strange land. And in time, the king of Egypt died: and the children of Israel sighed by reason of the bondage, and God heard their groaning, and remembered his covenant with Abraham, with Isaac, and with Jacob.

3 Now Moses kept the flock of Jethro his father in law, the priest of Midian. And the angel of the LORD appeared unto him in a flame of fire out of the midst of a bush: and behold the bush was not burned up. And God called and said, Moses, Moses, I am the God of thy father, the God of Abraham, the God of Isaac, I have seen the affliction of my people in Egypt, and I am come down to deliver them, and to bring them unto a land flowing with milk and honey; the place of the Canaanites, the Hittites, the Amorites, the Perizzites, the Hivites, and the Jebusites. [16] Now I will send thee to gather the elders of Israel and to go unto Pharaoh, that thou mayest bring forth the children of Israel. [21] And when ye go, ye shall not go empty, but every woman shall borrow of her neighbour jewels of silver, and jewels of gold, and raiment: and ye shall put them upon your sons, and upon your daughters; and ye shall spoil the Egyptians.

4 And Moses answered and said, But they will not hearken unto me: for they will say, The LORD hath not appeared unto thee. And the LORD said, Cast thine rod to the ground. And he cast it on the ground, and it became a serpent. And he put forth his hand, and caught it, and it became a rod in his hand. [6] And the LORD said; Put now thine hand into thy bosom. And he put his hand into his bosom: and behold, his hand was leprous as snow. And he put his hand to his bosom again, and, behold, it was turned again as flesh. And the LORD said, If they will not hearken to the voice of these signs, thou shalt take water of the river, and pour it upon the dry land: and the water shall become blood. [10] And Moses said, O my LORD, I am not eloquent, but I am slow of speech. And the LORD said unto him, Who hath made man's mouth? Now therefore go, and I will be with thy mouth. Yet take Aaron the Levite, thy brother, I know he can speak well, he shall be thy spokesman. [29] And Moses and Aaron gathered together all the elders of the children of Israel, and Aaron spake the words which the LORD had spoken unto Moses, and did the signs in the sight of the people. And the people believed: and they bowed their heads and worshipped.

5 And afterward Moses and Aaron went and told Pharaoh: let us go, we pray thee, three days' into the desert, and sacrifice unto the LORD our God; lest he fall upon us with pestilence, or with the sword. [4] And the king of Egypt said unto them, go you back to your works. And Pharaoh commanded the taskmasters to no more give the people straw to make brick, but let them go and gather straw for themselves, yet shall they deliver the same tale of bricks. [22] And Moses returned unto the LORD, and said, Wherefore hast thou so evil entreated this people?

6 Then the LORD said unto Moses, Now shalt thou see what I will do to Pharaoh, I am the LORD. I appeared unto Abraham, unto Isaac, and unto Jacob, but by my name JEHOVAH was I not known to them.

7 And the LORD spake unto Moses and unto Aaron, saying, go unto Pharaoh, let him ask for a miracle of you. And Moses and Aaron went unto Pharaoh, and Aaron cast down the rod before Pharaoh, and it became a serpent. Then Pharaoh called the magicians of Egypt, they also did cast down every man his rod, and they became serpents: but Aaron's rod swallowed up their rods. [13] And Pharaoh's heart hardened, that he hearkened not unto them. And the LORD spake unto Moses, Say unto Aaron, Take thy rod, and stretch out thine hand upon the waters of Egypt, that they may become blood. [20] And Moses and Aaron did so, and the fish in the river died; and the river stank, and the Egyptians could not drink of the water; and there was blood throughout all the land of Egypt. And Pharaoh's heart was hardened.

8 And the LORD spake unto Moses, Go unto Pharaoh, and say unto him, Thus saith the LORD, Let my people go. But the heart of Pharaoh was hardened. So the LORD did smite the land with frogs. And the frogs went up into their houses, and into their bedchambers, and upon their bed. [16] And many times did Moses ask of Pharaoh, and in each was Pharaoh's heart hardened, and in each did the LORD bring down pestilences on the people of Egypt. The earth became lice in man and in beast throughout all the land. And there came a grievous swarm of flies, and the land was corrupted by the flies. And all the cattle of Egypt died: but the cattle of the children of Israel died not. And there were boils breaking forth with blains upon man and upon beast. And Moses stretched forth his rod toward heaven: and the LORD sent fire mingled with thunder and hail very grievous. Only in the land of Goshen, where the children of Israel were, was there no hail. And the heart of Pharaoh was hardened, neither would he let the children of Israel go.

10 And the LORD brought an east wind upon the land and the east wind brought locusts. [14] And the locust were very grievous; before them there were no such locusts as they, neither after them shall be such. And they did eat every herb of the land, and all the fruit of the trees which the hail had left: and there remained not any green thing in all the land of Egypt.

11 And the LORD said unto Moses, Yet will I bring one plague more upon Pharaoh, and upon Egypt. Speak ye unto all Israel, saying that every man shall take of the blood of a lamb, and strike it on his door post. And therein shall they eat the flesh of the lamb this night, roast with fire, and unleavened bread, and bitter herbs. And ye shall eat it with your loins girded, your shoes on your feet, and your staff in your hand; and ye shall eat it in haste: it is the LORD's passover.

12 For I will this night smite all the firstborn of Egypt; and against all the gods of Egypt I will execute judgment. And the blood shall be a token upon the houses where ye are: I will pass over you. [14] And this day shall be unto you a memorial; and ye shall keep it throughout your generations for ever. Seven days shall there be no leaven in your houses; in all your habitations shall ye eat unleavened bread. [28] And the children of Israel did as the LORD had commanded. [29] And it came to pass, that at midnight the LORD smote all the firstborn in the land of Egypt, from the firstborn of Pharaoh on his throne unto the firstborn of the captive in the dungeon; and all the firstborn of cattle. And among the Egyptians there was not a house where there was not one dead. [31] And Pharaoh called for Moses and Aaron, and said, Rise up, both ye and the children of Israel; and go. Take your flocks and your herds, and be gone. [37] And the children of Israel journeyed from Rameses to Succoth, about six hundred thousand men, even the selfsame day as it came to pass that the children of Israel had been in Egypt for four hundred and thirty years. [39] And they baked unleavened bread, for it was not leavened because they were thrust out of Egypt in haste.

13 And God led the people about, through the way of the wilderness of the Red sea. [19] And Moses took the bones of Joseph with him. And the LORD went before them by day in a pillar of a cloud, and by night in a pillar of fire, to lead them the way.

14 And when it was told the king of Egypt that the people fled: then the heart of Pharaoh was turned, Why have we let Israel go from serving us? And he took six hundred chariots, and he pursued after the children of Israel. [10] And when Pharaoh drew nigh, the children of Israel were sore afraid, and they said unto Moses, it had been better for us to serve the Egyptians, than that we should die in the wilderness. [15] And the LORD said unto Moses, Lift thou up thy rod, and stretch out thine hand over the sea, and divide it. And, behold, the LORD caused the sea to go back by a strong east wind all that night, and made the sea dry land, and the waters were divided. [22] And the children of Israel went into the midst of the sea upon the dry ground: and the waters were a wall on their right hand, and on their left. And the Egyptians pursued them, and the waters came again, upon their chariots, and upon their horsemen. [31] And Israel saw that great work which the LORD did upon the Egyptians: and the people feared the LORD, and believed the LORD, and his servant Moses.

15 Then sang Moses and the children of Israel with timbrels and with dances unto the LORD, saying, I will sing unto the LORD, for he hath triumphed gloriously: Pharaoh's chariots and his host hath he cast into the Red sea: his chosen captains also are drowned. Who is like unto thee, O LORD, among the gods? who is like thee, glorious in holiness, fearful in praises, doing wonders? And Miriam the prophetess, the sister of Aaron, took a timbrel in her hand; and all the women went out after her with timbrels and with dances and with singing. [22] So Moses brought Israel from the Red sea, and they went out into the wilderness; and found no sustenance. And the people murmured against Moses, saying, What shall we eat, and what shall we drink? And they came to wells of water, then said the LORD unto Moses, Behold, I will rain bread from heaven for you; and the people shall go out and gather.

16 And it came to pass, that quails came up: and in the morning, behold, upon the face of the wilderness there lay a small round thing, as small as the hoar frost on the ground. And Moses said unto them, This is the bread which the LORD hath given you to eat. And the house of Israel called the name thereof Manna: and it was like coriander seed, white; and the taste of it was like wafers made with honey.

17 And the children of Israel journeyed in the wilderness, and pitched in Rephidim: and the people thirsted there for water [5] And the LORD said unto Moses, Go and with thy rod smite the rock, and there shall come water out of it. And Moses did so in the sight of the elders of Israel.

18 And Jethro, Moses' father in law, came unto Moses saw all that he did judge the people between one and another. And Jethro said unto him, this thing is too heavy for thee alone. So Moses hearkened to his father in law, and did choose able men, and made them heads over the people.

19 In the third month the children of Israel came into the wilderness of Sinai and there camped before the mount. [3] And Moses went up unto God in the mountain, and the LORD said, Ye have seen how I bare you on eagles' wings, and brought you unto myself. If ye will obey my voice, then ye shall be a peculiar treasure above all people: ye shall be an holy nation. [16] And it came to pass on the third day, that there were thunders and lightnings, and a smoke upon the mount, and a trumpet exceeding loud and the whole mount quaked greatly.

20 And God spake, saying, I am the LORD thy God, thou shalt have no other gods before me; Thou shalt not make unto thee any graven image, or any likeness of any thing. Thou shalt not bow down to them: for I the LORD thy God am a jealous God; Thou shalt not take the name of the LORD thy God in vain; Remember the sabbath day, to keep it holy. Six days only shalt thou labour; Honour thy father and thy mother; Thou shalt not kill; Thou shalt not commit adultery; Thou shalt not steal; Thou shalt not bear false witness against thy neighbour; Thou shalt not covet thy neighbour's house, thy neighbour's wife, nor his manservant, his maidservant, his ox, his ass, nor any thing that is thy neighbour's. [18] And all the people saw the thunderings, and the lightnings, and the noise, and the mountain smoking: and when the people saw it, they removed afar off. And they said unto Moses, let not God speak with us, lest we die. [22] And the LORD said unto Moses, Thus thou shalt say unto the children of Israel; [23] Ye shall not make gods of silver, nor of gold. [24] An altar of earth thou shalt make unto me, and shalt sacrifice burnt offerings thereon.

24 And Moses wrote all the words of the LORD, and rose up early in the morning, and builded an altar under the hill, and twelve pillars, according to the twelve tribes of Israel. And Moses sacrificed peace offerings of oxen unto the LORD, and read of the covenant to the people: and they said, All that the LORD hath said will we do. [9] Then went up Moses, and the elders of Israel: And they saw the God of Israel. [12] And the LORD said unto Moses, Come up to me into the mount: and I will give thee tables of stone, and a law, and commandments which I have written. [15] And Moses went up into the midst of a cloud, and was in the mount forty days and forty nights. And the LORD gave unto Moses two tables of testimony of stone, written with the finger of God.

32 And when the people saw that Moses delayed to come down out of the mount, the people said unto Aaron, Make us gods. And Aaron fashioned of molten gold a calf: and they said, These be thy gods, O Israel, which brought thee up out of the land of Egypt. And they offered burnt offerings. [7] And the LORD said unto Moses, Go, get thee down; for thy people have turned aside quickly from me. [15] And Moses turned, and went down from the mount, the two tables of the testimony in his hand: And as he came unto the camp, he saw the calf: and Moses' anger waxed hot, and he cast the tables down, and brake them. [20] And he took the calf, and ground it to powder. [26] Then Moses said, Who is on the LORD's side? And the sons of Levi gathered together unto him. And he said unto them, Go throughout the camp, and slay every man. And there fell that day about three thousand.

33 And Moses took the holy tabernacle, and pitched it afar off from the camp. And as Moses entered into the tabernacle, a cloudy pillar descended, and stood at the door, and there the Lord talked with Moses as a man speaketh unto his friend. And Moses made plea for his people.

34 And the LORD said unto Moses, Hew thee two more tables of stone: and I will write upon these tables as the first, which thou brakest. And he hewed two tables of stone; and Moses went up mount Sinai. And the LORD descended in the cloud, and stood with him there. And he said, Behold, I make a covenant: before all thy people I will do marvels: behold, I drive out before thee the Amorite, the Canaanite, the Hittite, the Perizzite, the Hivite, and the Jebusite. Make no covenant with the inhabitants of the land whither thou goest, but destroy their altars, break their images, and cut down their groves. And Moses came down from mount Sinai with the two tables of testimony, and the skin of Moses' face shone.

35 And Moses spake unto all the congregation of the children of Israel, saying, This the LORD has commanded, Whosoever is willing, let him bring gold, silver, and brass, blue, purple, and scarlet, and fine cloths and skins, and oil and sweet incense, and Onyx stones.

36 And all the wise men wrought the work of a sanctuary, ten curtains of fine linen, with cherubims of cunning make, and boards for the tabernacle of shittim wood, and four pillars overlaid with gold. And an ark to carry the tables of stone. And a candlestick of pure gold with three branches out of the one side, and three of the other side. And Bezaleel of the tribe of Judah, made all that the LORD commanded Moses.

40 And the LORD spake unto Moses, saying, On the first day of the first month shalt thou set up the tabernacle of the tent of the congregation. And thou shalt put therein the ark of the testimony. And thou shalt bring Aaron and his sons unto the tabernacle, and anoint him; that he may minister unto me in the priest's office. Then did he set the bread in order, and light the lamps before the LORD, and burn sweet incense upon the altar. [34] Then a cloud covered the tent of the congregation, and the glory of the LORD filled the tabernacle, and fire was on it by night, in the sight of all the house of Israel, throughout all their journeys.

Leviticus or Vayyiqra (ויקרא)
The Third Book of Moses

1 And the LORD called unto Moses, and spake unto him out of the tabernacle of the congregation, saying, If any man bring an offering of a beast or a fowl unto the LORD, let him offer a male without blemish, of his own voluntary will at the door of the tabernacle.

4 And the LORD spake unto Moses, saying, If a soul shall sin through ignorance against any of the commandments; then let him bring a young bullock without blemish. And the priest shall take of the bullock's blood, and dip his finger in the blood, and sprinkle of the blood seven times before the LORD. [27] And if any one of the common people sin through ignorance, he shall bring a kid of the goats, a female without blemish.

7 In the place where they kill the burnt offering shall they kill the trespass offering: and the blood thereof shall he sprinkle round about upon the altar. And he shall offer of it all the fat thereof, and the two kidneys, and the caul. And the priest shall burn them upon the altar for an offering unto the LORD. [6] Every male among the priests shall eat thereof: it shall be eaten in the holy place: it is most holy.

9 And it came to pass on the eighth day, that Moses called Aaron and his sons, and the elders of Israel; And he said unto Aaron, Take a young calf for a sin offering, and a ram for a burnt offering, and offer them before the LORD. [8] Aaron therefore went unto the altar, and made the offerings. [24] And there came a fire out from before the LORD, and consumed upon the altar the burnt offering and the fat: which when all the people saw, they shouted, and fell on their faces.

10 And Nadab and Abihu, the sons of Aaron, took either of them his censer, and put fire therein, and put incense thereon, and offered strange fire before the LORD, which he commanded them not. And there went out fire from the LORD, and devoured them, and they died before the LORD.

11 And the LORD spake, saying, These are the beasts which ye shall eat. Whatsoever is clovenfooted, and cheweth the cud, that shall ye eat. Ye shall not eat of the camel, coney, hare, nor the swine, nor their carcase shall ye touch; they are unclean to you. [9] These shall ye eat of all that are in the waters: whatsoever hath fins and scales. [13] And these among the fowls shall not be eaten, they are an abomination: the eagle, ossifrage, ospray, vulture, kites, ravens, owls, cuckow, hawks, cormorant, pelican, stork, the lapwing, and the bat. [21] Yet ye may eat of the locust, beetle and the grasshopper after their kind. [29] Unclean unto you among the creeping things are; the weasel, mouse, tortoises, ferret, chameleon, lizard, snail, and the mole. This is the law of the beasts.

12 And the LORD spake unto Moses, saying, If a woman have conceived seed, and born a man child: then she shall be unclean seven days; and in the eighth day the flesh of his foreskin shall be circumcised. But if she bear a maid child, then she shall be unclean two weeks. And when the days of her purifying are fulfilled, she shall bring a burnt offering, unto the door of the tabernacle.

13 And the LORD spake unto Moses and Aaron, saying, When a man shall have in the skin of his flesh a rising, a scab, or bright spot, then he shall be brought unto the priest and if it is a plague of leprosy: the priest shall pronounce him unclean. [45] And the leper his clothes shall be rent, and his head bare, and he shall put a covering upon his upper lip, and shall cry, Unclean, unclean. And he shall dwell alone.

17 And the LORD spake unto Moses, saying, What man of the house of Israel, that killeth a beast and bringeth it not unto the tabernacle, that man shall be cut off from among his people. [7] And they shall no more offer their sacrifices unto devils, after whom they have gone a whoring. [11] And for the life of the flesh is in the blood, No soul of you shall eat blood, neither shall any stranger that sojourneth among you.

18 Ye shall do my judgments, and keep mine ordinances: I am the LORD your God. [6] None of you shall approach to any that is near of kin to him, to uncover their nakedness, neither thy father, nor thy mother, nor thy sister. [20] Moreover thou shalt not lie carnally with thy neighbour's wife. [22] Thou shalt not lie with mankind, as with womankind: it is abomination. Neither shalt thou lie with any beast to defile thyself therewith: neither shall any woman stand before a beast to lie down thereto: it is confusion.

19 And the LORD spake unto Moses, saying, say unto the congregation of the children of Israel, Ye shall be holy: for I the LORD your God am holy. Ye shall fear every man his mother, and his father, and keep my sabbaths: I am the LORD your God. Turn ye not unto idols, nor make to yourselves molten gods. [9] And when ye reap the harvest of your land, reap not the corners of thy field nor thy vineyard; thou shalt leave them for the poor and stranger. Ye shall not steal, neither deal falsely, neither lie. And ye shall not swear by my name falsely, I am the LORD. Thou shalt not curse the deaf, nor put a stumblingblock before the blind. Thou shalt not go up and down as a talebearer among thy people. Thou shalt not avenge, nor bear any grudge against the children of thy people, but thou shalt love thy neighbour as thyself: I am the LORD. [27] Ye shall not round the corners of your heads, nor mar the corners of thy beard. [29] Do not prostitute thy daughter; lest the land fall to whoredom. Regard not them that have familiar spirits, neither seek after wizards. Honour the old man, and fear thy God. Ye shall do no unrighteousness in judgment, in meteyard, in weight, or in measure.

20 And the LORD spake unto Moses, saying, say to the children of Israel, Ye shall keep my statutes, I am the LORD. Every one that curseth his father or his mother shall be surely put to death. And the man that lieth with his father's wife: both of them shall surely be put to death. And if a man lie with his daughter in law, both of them shall surely be put to death. If a man also lie with mankind, as he lieth with a woman, both of them have committed an abomination: they shall surely be put to death. And if a man take a wife and her mother, it is wickedness: they shall be burnt with fire, both he and they; that there be no wickedness among you. [27] A man also or woman that hath a familiar spirit, or that is a wizard, shall surely be put to death: they shall stone them with stones.

22 What man soever of the seed of Aaron is a leper, or hath a running issue; he shall not eat of the holy things. [10] There shall no stranger eat of the holy thing: a sojourner of the priest, or an hired servant, shall not eat of the holy thing. [23] Either a bullock or a lamb that hath any thing superfluous or lacking in his parts, that mayest thou offer for a freewill offering; but for a vow it shall not be accepted. Ye shall not offer unto the LORD that which is bruised, or crushed, or broken, or cut. Keep ye my commandments: I am the LORD.

23 Six days shall work be done: but the seventh day is the sabbath of rest, an holy convocation; ye shall do no work therein. These are the feasts of the LORD: In the fourteenth day of the first month at even is the LORD's passover. And on the fifteenth day of the same month is the feast of unleavened bread. Also in the fifteenth day of the seventh month, when ye have gathered in the fruit of the land, ye shall keep a feast unto the LORD seven days: And ye shall take the boughs of goodly trees and branches of palm trees and ye shall rejoice before the LORD your God seven days.

24 And the LORD spake unto Moses, saying, command the children of Israel, that they bring pure olive oil, to cause the lamps to burn continually. And thou shalt bake twelve cakes, set in two rows, six on a row, upon the pure table before the LORD. And thou shalt put frankincense upon each row, that it may be on the bread for a memorial. Every sabbath he shall set it in order before the LORD, and it shall be Aaron's and his sons'; and they shall eat it in the holy place. [10] And the son of Shelomith an Israelitish woman, whose father was an Egyptian, went out among and blasphemed the name of the Lord, and cursed. And they brought him unto Moses. And the LORD spake unto Moses, saying, Let all that heard him lay their hands upon his head, and let all the congregation stone him. [16] He that blasphemeth the name of the LORD shall surely be put to death, and all the congregation shall certainly stone him. And he that killeth any man shall surely be put to death. And he that killeth a beast shall make it good; beast for beast. [19] And if a man cause a blemish in his neighbour, so shall it be done to him; Breach for breach, eye for eye, tooth for tooth.

25 And the LORD spake unto Moses in mount Sinai, saying, Six years thou shalt sow thy field and prune thy vineyard. But in the seventh year shall be a sabbath of rest unto the land. And ye shall hallow too, the fiftieth year, and proclaim liberty throughout all the land. [23] For the land shall not be sold for ever: for the land is mine, for ye are strangers and sojourners with me. And if thy brother be waxen poor; then thou shalt relieve him. Take thou no usury of him, or increase: but fear thy God. [39] And if thy brother that dwelleth by thee be waxen poor, and be sold unto thee; thou shalt not compel him to serve as a bondservant: but as an hired servant, unto the year of jubile. And then shall he depart from thee, he and his children with him [44] Thy bondmen, and thy bondmaids, which thou shalt have, shall be of the heathen that are round about you; of them shall ye buy bondmen and bondmaids. Of the children of the strangers that do sojourn among you, of them shall ye buy, and of their families that are with you, which they begat in your land: and they shall be your possession.

26 Ye shall make you no idols nor graven image, Ye shall keep my sabbaths, and reverence my sanctuary: I am the LORD. If ye keep my commandments, then I will give you rain in due season, and the land shall yield her increase, and the trees shall yield fruit. And I will give peace in the land, and I will rid evil beasts out of the land, neither shall the sword go through your land. And ye shall chase your enemies, and they shall fall before you by the sword. And five of you shall chase an hundred, and an hundred of you shall put ten thousand to flight. And I will walk among you, and will be your God, and ye shall be my people.

Numbers or Bamidbar (במדבר)
The Fourth Book of Moses

1 And the LORD spake unto Moses in the wilderness of Sinai, in the second year after they were come out of Egypt, saying, Take ye the sum of men that are able to go forth to war. And of the families of Reuben, Simeon, Judah, Dan, Naphtali, Gad, Asher, Issachar, Zebulun, Joseph, Menasheh, Ephraim and Benjamin were numbered six hundred thousand and three thousand and five hundred

and fifty. But the Levites were not numbered. For the LORD had spoken, saying, Thou shalt appoint the Levites over the tabernacle. And so did they.

5 And the LORD spake unto Moses, saying, Command the children of Israel, that they put out of the camp every leper, and every one that is defiled by the dead. [11] And the LORD spake unto Moses, saying, If any man's wife go aside, and a man lie with her carnally, and it be hid from the eyes of her husband, then shall the man bring his wife unto the priest, and an offering of barley meal. And the priest shall take holy water mixed with the dust of the floor of the tabernacle, and charge the woman to say if man have lain with her, and to drink the water, that, if she have done trespass against her husband, that the water shall become bitter, and her belly shall swell, and her thigh shall rot.

6 And the LORD spake unto Moses, saying, When either man or woman shall take the vow of a Nazarite: He shall separate himself from wine and strong drink, no razor shall come upon his head. And he shall consecrate unto the LORD his days.

9 And the LORD spake unto Moses in the wilderness of Sinai, saying, Let the children of Israel keep the passover. And on the day the cloud covered the tabernacle: and at even there was upon the tabernacle the appearance of fire. Then after that the children of Israel journeyed: and in the place where the cloud abode, there the children of Israel pitched their tents.

10 And the LORD spake unto Moses, saying, Make thee two trumpets of silver, and when they shall blow them, all shall assemble themselves to thee. [11] And the children of Israel departed from the mount of the LORD three days' journey: and the ark of the covenant of the LORD went before them, to search out a resting place.

11 And when the people complained: and the LORD heard it; and was displeased; and a fire of the LORD burnt them. And the people cried unto Moses; and when Moses prayed unto the LORD, the fire was quenched. And the children of Israel wept again, and said, Who shall give us flesh to eat? We remember in Egypt the fish; cucumbers, melons, leeks, and garlick: But now there is nothing beside this manna. And the people gathered it and made cakes of it: and the taste was as fresh oil. [23] And the LORD said unto Moses, thou shalt see now whether my word shall come to pass unto thee or not. [31] And there went forth a wind from the LORD, and brought quails from the sea, and let them fall by the camp. And the people gathered the quails. And while the flesh was yet between their teeth, the wrath of the LORD was kindled against the people, and the LORD smote them with a great plague. [35] And the people journeyed from Kibrothhattaavah unto Hazeroth; and abode at Hazeroth.

12 And Miriam and Aaron spake against Moses because of the Ethiopian woman whom he had married: for he had married an Ethiopian woman. (Now Moses was very meek, above all men.) And the LORD came down in the pillar of the cloud; and, behold, Miriam became leprous. And Moses cried unto the LORD, saying, Heal her now, O God. And Miriam was shut out from the camp seven days. And afterward the people removed from Hazeroth, and pitched in the wilderness of Paran.

13 And Moses sent them to spy out the land of Canaan. And they returned, saying; Surely it floweth with milk and honey, nevertheless the people be strong, and the cities are walled. The Amalekites, the Hittites, the Jebusites, the Amorites and the Canaanites dwell there. And all the men are of a great stature, and there we saw giants, and we were in their sight as grasshoppers.

15 [32] And while the children of Israel were in the wilderness, they found a man that gathered sticks upon the sabbath day. And the LORD said unto Moses, The man shall be surely put to death: all the congregation shall stone him with stones without the camp. And all the congregation brought him without the camp, and stoned him with stones, and he died; as the LORD commanded. [37] And the LORD spake unto Moses, saying, Bid the children of Israel make them fringes in the borders of their garments with a ribband of blue.

16 Now Korah, the son of Izhar, rose with certain of the children of Israel, and they took every man his censer, and laid incense thereon, and stood in the door of the tabernacle. And the LORD spake unto Moses and unto Aaron, saying, Separate yourselves from among this congregation, that I may consume them. And Moses spake unto, saying, Depart, I pray you, lest ye be consumed. And Moses said unto Aaron, Take a censer, and put fire therein from off the altar, and go unto the congregation. And Aaron took as Moses commanded; and, behold, a plague was begun among the people: and they that died in the plague were fourteen thousand and seven hundred

20 Then came the children of Israel into the desert of Zin: and Miriam died, and was buried there. And the people gathered together against Moses and Aaron saying, Why have ye brought us unto this evil place of no seed, or figs, or vines, or pomegranates; neither is there any water. And the LORD spake unto Moses, saying, [8] Take the rod and speak ye unto the rock before their eyes; and it shall give forth his water. And Moses with his rod he smote the rock twice: and the water came out abundantly. And the LORD spake unto Moses and Aaron, Because ye believed me not, therefore ye shall not go into the land which I have given. [20] And the children of Israel journeyed unto mount Hor. And the LORD spake, saying, Aaron shall be gathered unto his people. And Moses did as the LORD commanded: and stripped Aaron of his garments, and put them upon Eleazar his son; and Aaron died. And Aaron was an hundred and twenty and three years old. And the congregation mourned for thirty days.

27 Then came the daughters of Zelophehad, before Moses, saying, Our father died in the wilderness, but had no sons. And Moses brought their cause before the LORD. And the LORD said; If a man die, and have no son, then ye shall cause his inheritance to pass unto his daughter. And if he

have no daughter, then unto his brethren. [12] And the LORD said unto Moses, Get thee up into this mount Abarim, and see the land which I have given unto the children of Israel. And when thou hast seen it, thou also shalt be gathered unto thy people, as Aaron thy brother was gathered.

28 And the LORD spake unto Moses, saying, Command the children of Israel, and say unto them, My offering, and my bread for my sacrifices made by fire, for a sweet savour unto me, shall ye observe to offer unto me in their due season. [7] And the drink offering thereof shall be the fourth part of an hin for the one lamb: in the holy place shalt thou cause the strong wine to be poured unto the LORD for a drink offering.

30 And Moses spake unto the heads of the tribes concerning the children of Israel, saying, This is the thing which the LORD hath commanded. If a man vow a vow; he shall not break his word, he shall do according to all that proceedeth out of his mouth. [3] If a woman also vow a vow, and her father shall hold his peace at her; then all her vows shall stand. [5] But if her father disallow her in the day that he heareth; not any of her vows, shall stand: and the LORD shall forgive her, because her father disallowed her, and so of her husband. [16] These are the statutes, which the LORD commanded Moses.

31 And the LORD spake unto Moses, saying, arm some of yourselves unto the war, and go against the Midianites, and avenge the LORD of Midian. [5] So they warred against the Midianites, as the LORD commanded Moses; and they slew all the males. And they burnt all their cities, and all their castles. And they took all the spoil, and all the prey, both of men and of beasts. [15] And Moses said unto them, Now therefore kill every male among the little ones, and kill every woman that hath known man by lying with him. [18] But all the women children, that have not known a man by lying with him, keep alive for yourselves. [32] And the booty was six hundred thousand and seventy thousand and five thousand sheep, and threescore and twelve thousand beeves, and threescore and one thousand asses, [35] And thirty and two thousand persons in all. [54] And Moses and Eleazar the priest took the gold, and brought it into the tabernacle of the congregation, for a memorial for the children of Israel before the LORD.

33 These are the journeys of the children of Israel, which went forth out of the land of Egypt with their armies under the hand of Moses and Aaron. And Moses wrote their goings out according to their journeys. And they departed from Rameses, and travelled and encamped by the Red sea. And they travelled by way of the wilderness of Sin, even unto the plains of Moab by Jordan near Jericho. [50] And the LORD spake unto Moses, saying, When ye are passed over Jordan into the land of Canaan; Then ye shall drive out all the inhabitants of the land from before you, and destroy all their pictures, and their images, and their high places. And ye shall dispossess the inhabitants of the land, and dwell therein: for I have given you the land to possess. [54] And ye shall divide the land by lot among your families. But if ye will not drive out the inhabitants of the land from before you; then it shall come to pass, that those which ye let remain shall be pricks in your eyes, and thorns in your sides, and shall vex you in the land. [56] Moreover it shall come to pass, that I shall do unto you, as I thought to do unto them.

34 And the LORD spake unto Moses; Say unto the children of Israel, When ye come into the land of Canaan which is your inheritance, then your south border shall be the salt sea. And the great sea shall be your west border. And the North to Ziphron, and the east to Jordan. This is the land which the LORD commanded to give unto the tribes of the children of Israel.

Deuteronomy or **Devarim (דברים)**
The Fifth Book of Moses

1 These be the words which Moses spake unto all Israel in the wilderness: The LORD our God spake unto us saying: Turn you, and take journey, and go to the land of the Canaanites, unto Lebanon, unto the great river Euphrates. Go and possess the land which the LORD sware unto your fathers, Abraham, Isaac, and Jacob.

2 Then we turned, and took our journey into the wilderness. And the LORD said, Pass through the coast of your brethren the children of Esau: Meddle not with them. But [33] the LORD our God delivered Sihon king of Heshbon before us; and we smote him. And we took all his cities and utterly destroyed the men, and the women, and the little ones, of every city, we left none to remain: [35] Only the cattle and the spoil we took for a prey.

3 And then Og the king of Bashan came out against us. But the LORD our God delivered him to our hands, and we took his threescore cities and his towns, and we utterly destroyed the men, the women, and the children. For king Og was of the giants; behold his bedstead was of iron; is it not in Rabbath yet? nine cubits was the length thereof. [23] And I besought the LORD, saying, O Lord GOD, thou hast shew thy greatness: for what God is there in heaven or in earth, that can do thy works? [25] I pray thee, let me go over, and see the good land that is beyond Jordan. But the LORD was wroth with me for your sakes, and would not hear me: and the LORD said unto me, Get thee up into the top of Pisgah, and behold: for thou shalt not go over Jordan, but charge Joshua, and encourage him: for he shall go over.

4 [25] When thou shalt beget children, and ye shall have remained long in the land, and shall do evil in the sight of the LORD thy God. [27] And the LORD shall scatter you among the nations, and ye shall be left few in number. But if from thence thou shalt seek the LORD thy God, thou shalt find him. [40] Thou shalt keep therefore his statutes, and his commandments, which I command thee this day. And this is the law which Moses set before the children of Israel:

5 Thou shalt have none other gods before me. Thou shalt not make thee any graven image. [11] Thou shalt not take the name of the LORD thy God in vain. [12] Six days thou shalt labour, and do all thy work. [16] Honour thy father and thy mother. [17] Thou shalt not kill. Neither shalt thou commit adultery. Neither shalt thou steal. [20] Neither shalt thou bear false witness against thy neighbour. [21] Neither shalt thou desire thy neighbour's wife, or any thing that is thy neighbour's. [32] Ye shall observe therefore as the LORD your God hath commanded you.

6 And these words shall be in thine heart: And thou shalt teach them diligently unto thy children. And thou shalt write them upon the posts of thy house, and on thy gates.

13 Thou shalt not hearken unto the words of that prophet, or that dreamer of dreams who is found saying, Let us go after other gods, and let us serve them. And that prophet, or that dreamer of dreams, shall be put to death

14 Ye are the children of the LORD your God: ye shall not cut yourselves, nor make any baldness between your eyes for the dead. [3] Thou shalt not eat any abominable thing.

17 Thou shalt not sacrifice unto the LORD thy God any beast wherein is blemish, or any evilfavouredness: for that is an abomination. If there be found among you, man or woman, that hath gone and served other gods, and worshipped them, either the sun, or moon, or any of the host of heaven, thou shalt stone them with stones till they die. [14] When thou art come unto the land which the LORD thy God giveth thee, I will set a king over thee. But he shall not multiply horses to himself, neither shall he multiply wives to himself. And he shall write him a copy of this law in a book: And it shall be with him all the days of his life.

19 Thou shalt divide thy land into into parts, that every slayer may flee thither. Every slayer that killeth his neighbour ignorantly, whom he hated not; As when a man goeth with his neighbour to hew wood, and his axe head slippeth and slay his neighbour; he shall flee unto a city of refuge and live. [14] Thou shalt not remove thy neighbour's landmark, [15] One witness shall not rise up against a man: at the mouth of two witnesses shall the matter be established. [21] And thine eye shall not pity; but life shall go for life, eye for eye, tooth for tooth, hand for hand, foot for foot.

21 If one be found slain, lying in the field, and it be not known who hath slain him: Then shall the elders of the near city strike off an heifer's neck, and shall wash their hands over the heifer, saying, Our hands have not shed this blood.

22 Thou shalt not see thy brother's ox or his sheep or his ass or his raiment go astray, thou shalt bring them again unto thy brother. [5] The woman shall not wear that which pertaineth unto a man, neither shall a man put on a woman's garment: for all that do so are abomination. If a bird's nest chance to be before thee thou shalt not take the dam with the young: But thou shalt let the dam go. When thou buildest a new house, then thou shalt make a battlement for thy roof, that no man fall from thence. [9] Thou shalt not sow thy vineyard with divers seeds. Thou shalt not plow with an ox and an ass together. Thou shalt not wear a garment of divers sorts, as of woollen and linen together. [12] Thou shalt make thee fringes upon thy vesture. [13] If any man take a wife, and bring an evil name upon her, saying, I found her not a maid: Then if the tokens of virginity be not found: then the men of her city shall stone her with stones that she die. [22] If a man be found lying with a woman married to an husband, then they shall both of them die. If a damsel that is a virgin be betrothed unto an husband, and a man find her in the city, and lie with her; Then ye shall stone them with stones that they die. But if a man find a betrothed damsel, and force her: then the man only shall die.

23 He that is wounded in the stones, or hath his privy member cut off, shall not enter into the congregation of the LORD. A bastard shall not enter into the congregation of the LORD; even to his tenth generation. An Ammonite or Moabite shall not enter into the congregation of the LORD; even to their tenth generation. [10] If there be among you any man, that is not clean by reason of uncleanness that chanceth him by night, then shall he wash himself with water. [17] There shall be no whore of the daughters of Israel, nor a sodomite of the sons of Israel. Unto a stranger thou mayest lend upon usury; but unto thy brother thou shalt not. [21] When thou shalt vow a vow unto the LORD thy God, thou shalt not slack to pay it. That which is gone out of thy lips thou shalt keep and perform. When thou comest into thy neighbour's vineyard, then thou mayest eat grapes thy fill; but thou shalt not put any in thy vessel. Of thy neighbour's standing corn of thy neighbour thou mayest pluck the ears with thine hand.

24 When a man hath taken a wife, and it come to pass that she find no favour in his eyes: then let him write her a bill of divorcement, and send her out of his house that she may go and be another man's wife. [6] No man shall take a millstone to pledge: for he taketh a man's life to pledge. [14] Thou shalt not oppress an hired servant. [16] The fathers shall not be put to death for the children, neither shall the children be put to death for the fathers. [19] When thou cuttest thine harvest, and hast forgot a sheaf in the field, when thou beatest thine olive tree, thou shalt not go over the boughs again, when thou gatherest the grapes of thy vineyard, thou shalt not glean it afterward. Such will be for the stranger, the fatherless, and the widow.

25 If there be a controversy between men, the judges may condemn the wicked to be beaten, then forty stripes, and not exceed. [4] Thou shalt not muzzle the ox when he treadeth the corn. [5] If brethren dwell together, and one of them die with no child, the wife of the dead shall not marry unto a stranger, her husband's brother shall take her to him to wife, and perform the duty of an husband's brother unto her. [13] Thou shalt not have in thy bag divers weights, a great and a small. But thou shalt have a perfect and just weight.

27 And Moses with the elders of Israel commanded the people, saying, Keep all the commandments. And it shall be that ye shall pass over Jordan unto the land that floweth with milk and honey.

28 If thou shalt hearken diligently unto the voice of the LORD thy God, to observe and to do all his commandments which I command thee this day, that the LORD thy God will set thee on high above all nations of the earth.

31 And Moses went and spake these words unto all Israel. I am an hundred and twenty years old this day; I can no more go out and come in: also the LORD hath said unto me, Thou shalt not go over the Jordan. The LORD thy God, he will go over before thee, and he will destroy nations before thee, and thou shalt possess them: and Joshua shall go over with thee. [13] And the LORD appeared in the tabernacle in a pillar of a cloud: And the LORD said unto Moses, Behold, thou shalt sleep with thy fathers; and this people will rise up, and go a whoring after the gods of the strangers, and will forsake me. Then my anger shall be kindled against them. And it came to pass, when Moses had made an end of writing the words of this law in a book, that he commanded the Levites take the book, saying, [27] I know that after my death ye will utterly corrupt yourselves, and turn aside from the way which I have commanded you; and evil will befall you. And Moses spake in the ears of all the congregation of Israel the words of this song:

32 Give ear, O ye heavens, and I will speak;

And hear, O earth, my doctrine fall as rain, my speech distil'd as dew,

I will proclaim the name of the LORD. He is the Rock, his work is perfect,

His lot is his people, as an eagle fluttereth over her young, spreadeth her wings, taketh them, beareth them.

Our enemies I will heap mischiefs upon; The sword without, and terror within,

I shall destroy the young man and the virgin, the suckling with the man of gray hairs.

I whet my glittering sword, and mine hand will take hold on judgment; I will render vengeance.

I will make mine arrows drunk with blood, and my sword shall devour flesh.

Rejoice, O ye nations: he will avenge the blood of his servants, and will be merciful unto his land, and to his people.

34 And Moses went up from the plains of Moab to the top of Pisgah. And the LORD said unto him, This is the land which I sware unto Abraham, unto Isaac, and unto Jacob, but thou shalt not go over thither. So Moses the servant of the LORD died there in the land of Moab, and he buried him in a valley: but no man knoweth of his sepulchre unto this day. And the children of Israel wept for Moses thirty days. And there arose not a prophet since in Israel like unto Moses, whom the LORD knew face to face.

The Odyssey
(*ΟΔΎΣΣΕΙΑ*)
by Homer
(Greece, c600BCE)

The tales of the *Iliad*, telling of the Trojan wars, and the *Odyssey,* about Odysseus' (*Ulysses* to the Romans) long journey home from them, were treated as definitive sources of moral instruction by the Ancient Greeks, though it remains unclear who, if anyone, their supposed author 'Homer' was.

Based on the 1616 translation by George Chapman, of which the 19[th]cent. poet John Keats wrote the poem "On first looking into Chapman's Homer".

Abridged: JH/GH

YEARS after taking part with the Achaean Greeks in the great war against Troy, which saw the death of the warrior-heroes Hector and Patroclus, Ulysses had come not to his home in Ithaca. Therefore many suitors came to woo his wife Penelope, devouring his substance with riotous living, sorely grieving her heart and that of their young son, Telemachus. But the nymph Calypso had held Ulysses for seven years an unwilling guest in the island of Ogygia. Now the gods were minded to bring home the man...

I-HOW ULYSSES CAME TO PHAEACIA, AND OF NAUSICAA

ARGUMENT.
The Deities sit; The Man retired;
The Ulyssean wit; By Pallas fired.

That wandered wondrous far, when he the town
Of sacred Troy had sacked and shivered down;
The cities of a world of nations
With all their manners, minds and, fashions
He saw and knew; at sea felt many woes,
Much care sustained to save from overthrows
Himself and friends in their retreat for home;
But so their fates he could not overcome.

Then came Pallas Athene to Telemachus and bade him take ship that he might get tidings of his sire. And he spake words of reproach to the company of suitors. To whom...

Antinous only in this sort replied:
'High spoken, and of spirit unpacified,
How have you shamed us in this speech of yours!
Will you brand us for an offence not ours?
Your mother, first in craft, is first in cause.
Three years are past, and near the fourth now draws,
Since first she mocked the peers Achian;
All she made hope, and promised every man.'

The suitors suffered Telemachus to depart, though they repented after; and he came with Athene, in disguise of Mentor, to Nestor at Pylos. and thence to Menelaus at Sparta, who told him how he had laid hold on Proteus, the

seer, and learnt from him first of the slaying of his own brother Agamemnon; and, secondly, concerning Ulysses

Laertes' son; whom I beheld
In nymph Calypso's palace, who compelled
His stay with her, and since he could not see
His country earth, he mourned incessantly.

Laden with rich gifts, Telemachus set out on his return home, while the suitors sought to way-lay him. And, meantime, Calypso, warned by Hermes, let Ulysses depart from Ogygia on a raft. Which, being overwhelmed by storms, he yet made shore on the isle of Phaeacia; where, finding shelter, he fell asleep. But Pallas visited the Princess Nausicaa in a dream.

Straight rose the lovely morn, that up did raise
Fair-veiled Nausicaa, whose dream her praise
To admiration took.

She went with her maidens, with raiment for cleansing, to the river, where, having washed the garments,

They bathed themselves, and all with glittering oil
Smoothed their white skins, refreshing then their toil
With pleasant dinner. Then Nausicaa,
With other virgins did at stool-ball
Their shoulder-reaching head-tires laying by.
Nausicaa, with the wrists of ivory,
The liking stroke struck, singing first a song,
As custom ordered, and, amidst the throng.
Nausicaa, whom never husband tamed,
Above them all in all the beauties flamed.
The queen now for the upstroke, struck the ball
Quite wide off th' other maids, and made it fall
Amidst the whirlpools. At which, out shrieked all,
And with the shriek did wise Ulysses wake; .
Who, hearing maidish voices, from the brake
Put hasty head out; and his sight did press
The eyes of soft-haired virgins ... .
Horrid was His rough appearance to them; the hard pass
He had at sea struck by him. All in flight
The virgins scattered, frighted with this sight.
All but Nausicaa fled; but she fast stood;

Pallas had put a boldness in her breast,
And in her fair limbs tender fear compress'd.
And still she stood him, as resolved to know
What man he was, or out of what should grow
His strange repair to them. Then thus spake he:
'Let me beseech, O queen, this truth of thee,
Are you of mortal or the deified race?
If of the gods, that th' ample heavens embrace.
I can resemble you to none above
So near as Cynthia, chaste-born birth of Jove.
If sprung of humans that inhabit earth,
Thrice blest are both the authors of your birth;
But most blest he that hath the gift to engage
Your bright neck in the yoke of marriage.'

*He prayed her then for some garment, and that she would
show him the town. Then she, calling her maidens, they
brought for him food and oil and raiment, and went apart
while he should cleanse and array himself.*

And Pallas wrought in him a grace full great
From head to shoulders, and ashore did seat
His goodly presence. As he sat apart,
Nausicaa's eyes struck wonder through her heart;
He showed to her till now not worth the note;
But now he seemed as he had godhead got.

*Then, fearing the gossip of the market place, she bade him
follow afoot with her maidens, giving him direction how he
should find her father's palace, which entering,*

'Address suit to my mother, that her mean
May make the day of your redition seen.
For if she once be won to wish you well,
Your hope may instantly your passport seal,
And thenceforth sure abide to see your friends,
Fair house, and all to which your heart contends,'

*Nausicaa and her maidens went for ward, Ulysses
following after a time; whom Pallas met, and told him of
the King Alcinous and the Queen Arete. Then he, being
wrapped in a cloud which she had set about him, entered
unmarked; and, the cloud vanishing, embraced the knees of
Arete in supplication, as one distressed by many labours.
And they all received him graciously. Now, as they sat at
meat, a bard sang of the fall of Troy; and Alcinous, the
king, marked how Ulysses wept at the tale; and then
Ulysses told them who he was, and of his adventures, on
this wise:*

II-ULYSSES TELLS OF HIS WANDERINGS

*After many wanderings, we came to the isle of the giant
one-eyed Cyclops, and I, with twelve of my men, to his
cave. He coming home bespake us.*

'Ho! guests! What are ye! Whence sail ye these seas?
Traffic or rove ye, and, like thieves, oppress
Poor strange adventurers, exposing so

Your souls to danger, and your lives to woe?'
'Reverence the gods, thou greatest of all that live,
We suppliants are.' 'O thou fool,' answered he,
'To come so far, and to importune me
With any god's fear or observed love!
We Cyclops care not for your goat-fed Jove
Nor other blest ones; we are better far.
To Jove himself dare I bid open war.'

*The Cyclop devoured two sailors, and slept. I slew him not
sleeping-*

For there we all had perished, since it past
Our powers to lift aside a log so vast
As barred all outscape.

*At morn, he drove forth the flocks, but barred the entry
again, having devoured two more of my comrades. But we
made ready a great stake for thrusting out his one eye. And
when he came home at night, driving in all his sheep,*

Two of my soldiers more
At once he snatched up, and to supper went.
Then dared I words to him, and did present
A bowl of wine with these words: 'Cyclop! take
A bowl of wine.' 'Thy name, that I may make
A hospitable gift; for this rich wine
Fell from the river, that is mere divine,
Of nectar and ambrosia.' 'Cyclop, see,
My name is No-Man.' Cruel answered he.
'No-Man! I'll eat thee last of all thy friends.'
He slept; we took the spar, made keen before,
And plunged it in his eye. Then did he roar
In claps like thunder.

*Other Cyclops gathered, to inquire who had harmed him;
but he...*

'by craft not might
No-Man hath given me death.' They then said right,
'If no man hurt thee, and thyself alone,
That which is done to thee by Jove is done.'
Then groaning up and down, he groping tried
To find the stone, which found, he put aside,
But in the door sat, feeling if he could,
As the sheep issued, on some man lay hold.

*But we, ranging the sheep three abreast, were borne out
under their bellies, and drove them in haste down to our
ship; and having put out, I cried aloud:*

'Cyclop! if any ask thee who imposed
Th' unsightly blemish that thine eye enclosed,
Say that Ulysses, old Laertes' son,
Whose seat is Ithaca, and who hath won
Surname of city-raxer, bored it out.'
At this he brayed so loud that round about
He drove affrighted echoes through the air

In burning fury; and the top he tare
From off a huge rock, and so right a throw
Made at our ship that just before the prow
It overflew and fell, missed mast and all
Exceeding little; but about the fall
So fierce a wave it raised that back it bore
Our ship, so far it almost touched the shore.

*So we escaped; but the Cyclop stirred up against us the
wrath of his father Neptune. Thereafter we came to the
caves of Aeolus, lord of the winds, and then to the land of
the giants called Laestrygones, whence there escaped but
one ship of all our company.*

Then to the isle of Aeaea we attained,
Where fair-haired, dreadful, eloquent Circe reigned.

Then I sent Eurylochus, and a company, to search the land.

These in a dale did Circe's house descry;
Before her gates hill-wolves and lions lie;
Which, with her virtuous drugs, so tame she made
That wolf nor lion would no man invade
With any violence, but all arose,
Their huge, long tails wagged, and in fawns would close,
As loving dogs. Amaz'd they stay'd at gate.
And heard within the goddess elevate
A voice divine, as at her web she wrought,
Subtle and glorious and past earthly thought.

*She called them in, but Eurylochus, abiding without, saw
her feast them, and then turn them with her wand into
swine. From him hearing these things I hastened thither.
But Hermes met me, and gave me of the herb Moly, to be a
protection against her spells, and wise counsel withal. So
when she had feasted me she touched me with her wand.*

I drew my sword, and charged her, as I meant
To take her life. When out she cried, and bent
Beneath my sword her knees, embracing mine,
And full of tears, said, 'Who of what high line,
Art thou? Deep-souled Ulysses must thou be.'
Then I, 'O Circe, I indeed am he.
Dissolve the charms my friends' forced forms and enchain,
And show me here my honoured friends like men.'

*Now she restored them and, knowing the will of the gods,
made good cheer for us all, so that we abode with her for
one year. Nor might we depart hence till I had made
journey to the abode of Hades to get speech of Tiresias the
Seer. Whereby I saw many shades of famous folk, past
recounting. Thence returning Circe suffered us to be gone;
with warnings of perils before us, and of how we should
avoid them.*

First to the Sirens. Whoso hears the call
Of any Siren, he will so despise
Both wife and children, for their sorceries,
That never home turns his affection's stream,
Nor they take joy in him nor he in them.
Next, monstrous Scylla. Six long necks look out
Of her rank shoulders; every neck doth let
A ghastly head out; every head, three set,
Thick thrust together, of abhorred teeth,
And every tooth stuck with a sable death;
Charybdis, too, whose horrid throat did draw
The brackish sea up. These we saw

*And escaped only in part. Then came we to the island
where are fed the Oxen of the Sun; and because my
comrades would slay them, destruction came upon us. and
I alone came alive to the isle of Calypso.*

III-HOW ULYSSES CAME BACK TO ITHACA

*Now, when Ulysses had made an end, it pleased Alcinous
and all the Phaeacians that they should speed him home
with many rich gifts. So they set him in a ship, and bore
him to Ithaca, and laid him on the shore, yet sleeping, with
all the goodly gifts about him, and departed. But he,
waking, wist not where he was till Pallas came to him. Who
counselled him how he should deal with the Wooers, and
disguised him as a man ancient and worn. Then Ulysses
sought and found the faithful swine-herd Eumaeus, who
made him welcome, not knowing who he was, and told him
of the ill doing of the suitors. But Pallas went and brought
back Telemachus from Sparta, evading the Wooers'
ambush.*

Out rushed amazed Eumaeus, and let go
The cup to earth, that he had laboured so,
Cleansed for the neat wine, did the prince surprise
Kissed his fair forehead, both his lovely eyes,
And wept for joy. They entering, from his seat
His father rose to him; who would not let
The old man remove, but drew him back, and prest
With earnest terms his sitting, saying, 'Guest,
Take here your seat again.'

*Eumaeus departing, Pallas restored Ulysses to his own
likeness, and he made himself known to Telemachus, and
instructed him.*

'Go thou for home, and troop up with the Wooers,
Thy will,- with theirs joined, power with their rude powers;
And after shall the herdsman guide to town
Mv steps, my person wholly overgrown
With all appearance of a poor old swain,
Heavy and wretched. If their high disdain
Of my vile presence makes them my desert
Affect with contumelies, let thy loved heart
Beat in fixed confines of thy bosom still,
And see me suffer, patient of their ill.
But when I give the sign, all th' arms that are
Aloft thy roof in some near room prepare-
Two swords, two darts, two shields, left for us twain.
But let none know Ulysses near again.'

But when air's rosy birth, the morn arose
Telemachus did for the town dispose
His early steps; went on with spritely pace,
And to the Wooers studied little grace ...
And now the king and herdsman from the field
Drew nigh the town; when in the yard there lay
A dog called Argus, which before his way
Assumed for Ilion, Ulysses bred,
Yet stood his pleasure then in little stead,
As being too young, but, growing to his grace,
Young men made choice of him for every chase,
Or of their wild goats, of their hares or harts;
But, his king gone, and he, now past his parts,
Lay all abjectly on the stable's store,
Before the ox-stall, and mule's stable-door,
To keep the clothes cast from the peasants' hands
While they laid compass on Ulysses' lands;
The dog, with ticks (unlook'd to) overgrown.
But by this dog no sooner seen but known
Was wise Ulysses; who new enter'd there.
Up went his dog's laid ears, and, coming near,
Up he himself rose, fawned, and wagged his stern,
Couch'd close his ears, and lay so; nor discern
Could ever more his dearly-loved lord again.
Ulysses saw it, nor had power t' abstain
From shedding tears; but (far-off seeing his swain)
His grief dissembled ... Then they entered in,
And left poor Argus dead; his lord's first sight
Since that time twenty years bereft his sight.

Telemachus welcomed the way-worn suppliant; the feasting Wooers, too, sent him portions of meat, save Antinous, who...

Rapt up a stool, with which he smit
The king's right shoulder, twixt his neck and it.
He stood him like a rock. Antinous' dart
Stirred not Ulysses, who in his great heart
Deep ills projected.

The very Wooers were wroth. Which clamour Penelope hearing, she sent for Eumaeus, and bade him summon the stranger to her; but he would not come till evening, by reason of the suitors, from whom he had discourteous treatment. Now Ulysses, coming to Penelope, did not discover himself, but told her false tales of his doings. Then she bade call the ancient nurse Euryclea, that she might wash the stranger's feet. But by a scar he came to be discovered by the aged dame. Her he charged with silence and to let no ear in all the court more know his being there. As for Penelope, she told him of her intent to promise herself to the man who could wield Ulysses' bow, knowing well that none had the strength and skill.

IV-OF THE DOOM OF THE SUITORS

On the morrow came Penelope to the Wooers, bearing the bow of her lord.

Her maids on both sides stood; and thus she spake:
'Hear me, ye Wooers, that a pleasure take
To do me sorrow, and my house invade
To eat and drink, as if 'twere only made
To serve your rapines, striving who shall frame
Me for his wife. And since 'tis made a game,
I here propose divine Ulysses' bow
For that great master-piece, to which ye vow.
He that can draw it with least show to strive,
And through these twelve axe-heads an arrow drive,
Him will I follow, and this house forego'
Whereat the herd Eumaeus wept for woe.

Then Telemachus set up the axe-heads, and himself made vain essay, the more to tempt the Wooers. And while they after him strove all vainly, Ulysses went out and bespake Eumaeus and another herd, Philoetius.

I am your Lord; through many a sufferance tried
Arrived now here, whom twenty years have held
Forth from my home. Of all the company
Now serving here besides, not one but you
Mine ear hath witness willing to bestow
Their wishes of my life so long held dead.
The envious Wooers will by no means give
The offer of the bow and arrow leave
To come at me; spite then their pride, do thou,
My good Eumaeus, bring both shaft and bow
To my hand's proof; and charge the maids before
That instantly they shut in every door.
Do thou, Philoetius, keep their closure fast.'

Then Ulysses claiming to make trial of the bow, the Wooers would have denied him; but Penelope would not; whereas Telemachus made a vow that it was for himself and none other to decide, and the guest should make trial.

But when the wise Ulysses once had laid,
His fingers on it, and to proof survey
The still sound plight it held, as one of skill
In song. and of the harp. doth at his will,
In tuning of his instrument, extend
A string out with his pin, touch all, and lend
To every well-wreath'd string his perfect sound,
Strook all together; with such ease drew round
The king the bow. Then twang'd he up the string,
That as a swallow in the air doth sing,
So sharp the string sung when he gave it touch.
Once having bent and drawn it. Which so much
Amazed the Wooers, that their colours went
And came most grievously. And then Jove rent
The air with thunder; which at heart did cheer
The now-enough-sustaining traveller.
Then through the axes at the first hole flow
The steel-charged arrow. Straightway to him drew
His son in complete arms ... .
'Now for us There rests another mark more hard to hit,
And such as never man before hath smit;

Whose full point likewise my hands shall assay,
And try if Phoebus will give me his day.'
He said, and off his bitter arrow thrust
Right at Antinous, that struck him just
As he was lifting up the bowl, to show
That 'twixt the cup and lip much ill may grow.

Then the rest cried out upon him with threats, while they made vain search for weapons in the hall.

He, frowning, said, 'Dogs, see in me the man
Ye all held dead at Troy. My house it is
That thus ye spoil, and thus your luxuries
File with my women's rapes; in which ye woo
The wife of one that lives, and no thought show
Of man's fit fear, or gods', your present fame.
Or any fair sense of your future name;
And. therefore present and eternal death
Shall end your base life.'

Then the Wooers made at Ulysses and Telemachus, who smote down first Eurymachus and then Amphinomus. But way to the armoury having been left, the Wooers got arms by aid of a traitor; whom Eumaeus and Philoetius, smote, and then came to Ulysses and his son. Moreover. Pallas also came to their help; so that the Wooers, being routed-

Ulysses and his son the flyers chased
As when. with crooked beaks and seres, a cast
Of hill-bred eagles, cast off at some game,
That yet their strengths keep, but, put up in flame
The eagle stoops; from which, along the field
The poor fowls make wing this and that way yield
Their hard-flown pinions, then the clouds assay
For 'scape or shelter, their forlorn dismay
All spirit exhaling, all wings' strength to carry
Their bodies forth, and truss'd up, to the quarry
Their falconers ride in, and rejoice to see
Their hawks perform a flight so fervently ;
So in their flight Ulysses with his heir
Did stoop and cuff the Wooers, that the air
Broke in vast sighs, whose heads they shot and cleft,
The pavement boiling with the souls they reft.

Now all the Wooers were slain, and they of the household that were their accomplices; and the chamber was purified. Then the servants hastened to report all these things to Penelope who could hardly accord credence until Ulysses made himself known to her by undeniable proofs.

Then first did tears ensue
Her rapt assurance; then she ran and spread
Her arms about his neck, kiss'd oft his head.
He wept for joy. t'enjoy a wife so fit
For his grave mind, that knew his depth of wit.

But as for the Wooers, Hermes gathered the souls of them together, and, as bats gibbering in a cavern rise. so came they forth gibbering and went down to the House of Hades.

Cyllenian Hermes with his golden rod.
The Wooers' souls, that yet retain'd abode
Amidst their bodies, call'd in dreadful rout
Forth to th' Infernals; who came murmuring out.
And as amids the desolate retreat
Of some vast cavern, made the sacred seat
Of austere spirits, bats with breasts and wings
Clasp fast the walls, and each to other clings,
But. swept off from their coverts, up they rise
And fly with murmurs in amazeful guise
About the cavern; so these, grumbling rose
And flocked together. Down before them goes
None-hurting Mercury to Hell's broad ways,
And straight to those straits where the ocean stays
His lofty current in calm deeps, they flew.
Then to the snowy rock they next withdrew,
And to the close of Phoebus' orient gates.
The nation then of dreams, and then the states
Of those souls' idols that the weary dead
Gave up in earth, which in a flow'ry mead
Had habitable situation.
And there they saw the soul of Thetis' son,
Of good Patroclus, brave Antilochus,
And Ajax, the supremely strenuous
Of all the Greek host next Peleion
All which assembled about Maia's son.

The Fables of Aesop
(*ΟΙ ΜΥΘΟΙ ΤΟΥ ΑΙΣΩΠΟΥ*)
(Greece, c500BCE)

Tradition has it that Aesop was a slave in ancient Greece, though these moralising tales have been added to later many, many times. The Fables were translated into Latin by Phaedrus, a slave himself, around 25 BC.

Unless otherwise noted, all based on translations by Joseph Jacobs (1900) and GC Macaulay (1890). Abridged: GH

The Cock and The Jewel

A Cock was searching for food in the farmyard when suddenly he spied something shinning amid the straw. "Ho! ho!" said he, "that's for me," and soon rooted it out. It turned out to be a Jewel that had been lost in the yard. "You may be a treasure," said the Cock, "to men that prize you, but for me I would rather have a single barley-corn than a peck of Jewels."

Precious things are for those who prize them.

Of the Cok and of the precious stone

[William Caxton's version of 1484] As a Cok ones sought his pasture in the donghylle he fond a precious stone to whome the Cok sayd Ha a fayre stone and precious thow arte here in the fylth And yf he desyreth the had found the as I haue he should haue take the vp and sette the ageyne in thy fyrst estate but in vayne I haue found the For no thynge I haue to do with the ne no good I may doo to the ne thou to me

And thys fable sayd Esope to them that rede this book For by the cok is to vnderstond the fool whiche retcheth not of sapyence ne of wysedome as the Cok retcheth and setteth not by the precious stone And by the stone is to vnderstond this fayre and playsaunt book

The Tortoise and the Hare

The Hare was once boasting of his speed before the other animals. "I have never yet been beaten," said he, "when I put forth my full speed. I challenge any one here to race with me."

The Tortoise said quietly, "I accept your challenge."

"That is a good joke," said the Hare; "I could dance round you all the way."

"Keep your boasting till you've beaten," answered the Tortoise. "Shall we race?"

So a course was fixed and a start was made. The Hare

Woodcut from Steinhowel's edition of 1501

darted almost out of sight at once, but soon stopped and, to show his contempt for the Tortoise, lay down to have a nap. The Tortoise plodded on and plodded on, and when the Hare awoke from his nap, he saw the Tortoise just near the winning-post and could not run up in time to save the race. Then said the Tortoise:

Slow and certain wins the race.

The Lion's Share

The Lion went once a-hunting along with the Fox, the Jackal, and the Wolf. They hunted and they hunted till at last they surprised a Stag, and soon took its life. Then came the question how the spoil should be divided. "Quarter me this Stag," roared the Lion; so the other animals skinned it and cut it into four parts. Then the Lion took his stand in front of the carcass and pronounced judgement: The first quarter is for me in my capacity as King of Beasts; the second is mine as arbiter; another share comes to me for my part in the chase; and as for the fourth quarter, well, as for that, I should like to see which of you will dare to lay a paw upon it."

"Humph," grumbled the Fox as he walked away with his tail between his legs; but he spoke in a low growl .

You may share the labours of the great, but you will not share the spoil

A Fox and Grapes

[Sir Roger L'Estrange's version of 1692] There was a Time when a Fox would have ventur'd as far for a Bunch of Grapes as for a Shoulder of Mutton; and it was a Fox of those Days, and that Palate, that stood gaping under a Vine, and licking his Lips at a most delicious Cluster of Grapes that he had spy'd out there; he fetch'd a hundred and a hundred Leaps at it, till at last, when he was as weary as a Dog, and found that there was no Good to be done; Hang 'em (says he) they are as sour as Crabs; and so away he went, turning off the Disappointment with a Jest.

THE MORAL: 'Tis Matter of Skill and Address, when a Man cannot honestly compass what he would be at, to appear easy and indifferent upon all Repulses and Disappointments.

The Peacock and Juno

A Peacock once placed a petition before Juno desiring to have the voice of a nightingale in addition to his other attractions; but Juno refused his request. When he persisted, and pointed out that he was her favourite bird, she said:

Be content with your lot; one cannot be first in everything.

The Wolf in Sheep's Clothing

A Wolf found great difficulty in getting at the sheep owing to the vigilance of the shepherd and his dogs. But one day it found the skin of a sheep that had been flayed and thrown aside, so it put it on over its own pelt and strolled down among the sheep. The Lamb that belonged to the sheep, whose skin the Wolf was wearing, began to follow the Wolf in the Sheep's clothing; so, leading the Lamb a little apart, he soon made a meal off her, and for some time he succeeded in deceiving the sheep, and enjoying hearty meals.

Appearances are deceptive.

The Dog in the Manger

A Dog looking out for its afternoon nap jumped into the Manger of an Ox and lay there cosily upon the straw. But soon the Ox, returning from its afternoon work, came up to the Manger and wanted to eat some of the straw. The Dog in a rage, being awakened from its slumber, stood up and barked at the Ox, and whenever it came near attempted to bite it. At last the Ox had to give up the hope of getting at the straw, and went away muttering:

Ah, people often grudge others what they cannot enjoy themselves

The Ass in the Lion's Skin

An Ass once found a Lion's skin which the hunters had left out in the sun to dry. He put it on and went towards his native village. All fled at his approach, both men and animals, and he was a proud Ass that day. In his delight he lifted up his voice and brayed, but then every one knew him, and his owner came up and gave him a sound cudgelling for the fright he had caused. And shortly afterwards a Fox came up to him and said: "Ah, I knew you by your voice."

Fine clothes may disguise, but silly words disclose a fool.

The Two Pots

Two Pots had been left on the bank of a river, one of brass, and one of earthenware. When the tide rose they both floated off down the stream. Now the earthenware pot tried its best to keep aloof from the brass one, which cried out: "Fear nothing, friend, I will not strike you."

"But I may come in contact with you," said the other, "if I come too close; and whether I hit you, or you hit me, I shall suffer for it."

The strong and the weak cannot keep company.

Avaricious and Envious

Two neighbours came before Jupiter and prayed him to grant their hearts' desire. Now the one was full of avarice, and the other eaten up with envy. So to punish them both, Jupiter granted that each might have whatever he wished for himself, but only on condition that his neighbour had twice as much. The Avaricious man prayed to have a room full of gold. No sooner said than done; but all his joy was turned to grief when he found that his neighbour had two rooms full of the precious metal. Then came the turn of the Envious man, who could not bear to think that his neighbour had any joy at all. So he prayed that he might have one of his own eyes put out, by which means his companion would become totally blind.

Vices are their own punishment.

The Goose With the Golden Eggs

One day a countryman going to the nest of his Goose found there an egg all yellow and glittering. When he took it up it was as heavy as lead and he was going to throw it away, because he thought a trick had been played upon him. But he took it home on second thoughts, and soon found to his delight that it was an egg of pure gold. Every morning the same thing occurred, and he soon became rich by selling his eggs. As he grew rich he grew greedy; and thinking to get at once all the gold the Goose could give, he killed it and opened it only to find nothing.

Greed oft o'er reaches itself.

The Wind and the Sun

The Wind and the Sun were disputing which was the stronger. Suddenly they saw a traveller coming down the road, and the Sun said: "I see a way to decide our dispute. Whichever of us can cause that traveller to take off his cloak shall be regarded as the stronger. You begin." So the Sun retired behind a cloud, and the Wind began to blow as hard as it could upon the traveller. But the harder he blew the more closely did the traveller wrap his cloak round him, till at last the Wind had to give up in despair. Then the Sun came out and shone in all his glory upon the traveller, who soon found it too hot to walk with his cloak on.

Kindness effects more than severity.

Hercules and the Waggoner

A Waggoner was once driving a heavy load along a very muddy way. At last he came to a part of the road where the wheels sank half-way into the mire, and the more the horses pulled, the deeper sank the wheels. So the Waggoner threw down his whip, and knelt down and prayed to Hercules the Strong. "O Hercules, help me in this my hour of distress," quoth he. But Hercules appeared to him, and said:

"Tut, man, don't sprawl there. Get up and put your shoulder to the wheel."

The gods help them that help themselves.

The Miser and His Gold

Once upon a time there was a Miser who used to hide his gold at the foot of a tree in his garden; but every week he used to go and dig it up and gloat over his gains. A robber, who had noticed this, went and dug up the gold and decamped with it. When the Miser next came to gloat over his treasures, he found nothing but the empty hole. He tore his hair, and raised such an outcry that all the neighbours came around him, and he told them how he used to come and visit his gold. "Did you ever take any of it out?" asked one of them.

"Nay," said he, "I only came to look at it."

"Then come again and look at the hole," said a neighbour; "it will do you just as much good."

Wealth unused might as well not exist.

Belling the Cat

Long ago, the mice had a general council to consider what measures they could take to outwit their common enemy, the Cat. Some said this, and some said that; but at last a young mouse got up and said he had a proposal to make, which he thought would meet the case. "You will all agree," said he, "that our chief danger consists in the sly and treacherous manner in which the enemy approaches us. Now, if we could receive some signal of her approach, we could easily escape from her. I venture, therefore, to propose that a small bell be procured, and attached by a ribbon round the neck of the Cat. By this means we should always know when she was about, and could easily retire while she was in the neighbourhood."

This proposal met with general applause, until an old mouse got up and said: "That is all very well, but who is to bell the Cat?" The mice looked at one another and nobody spoke. Then the old mouse said:

It is easy to propose impossible remedies

The Old Man and Death

An old labourer, bent double with age and toil, was gathering sticks in a forest. At last he grew so tired and hopeless that he threw down the bundle of sticks, and cried out: "I cannot bear this life any longer. Ah, I wish Death would only come and take me!"

As he spoke, Death, a grisly skeleton, appeared saying: "What wouldst thou, Mortal? I heard thee call me."

"Please, sir," replied the woodcutter, "would you kindly help me to lift this faggot of sticks on to my shoulder?"

We would often be sorry if our wishes were gratified.

The Eagle and the Arrow

An Eagle was soaring through the air when suddenly it heard the whizz of an Arrow, and felt itself wounded to death. Slowly it fluttered down to the earth, with its life-blood pouring out of it. Looking down upon the Arrow with which it had been pierced, it found that the shaft of the Arrow had been feathered with one of its own plumes. "Alas!" it cried, as it died,

We often give our enemies the means for our own destruction

The Buffoon and the Countryman

At a country fair there was a Buffoon who made all the people laugh by imitating the cries of various animals. He finished off by squeaking so like a pig that the spectators thought that he had a porker concealed about him. But a Countryman who stood by said: "Call that a pig's squeak! Nothing like it. You give me till tomorrow and I will show you what it's like." The audience laughed, but next day, sure enough, the Countryman appeared on the stage, and putting his head down squealed so hideously that the spectators hissed and threw stones at him to make him stop. "You fools!" he cried, "see what you have been hissing," and held up a little pig whose ear he had been pinching to make him utter the squeals.

Men often applaud an imitation and hiss the real thing.

The Analects

論語

of Confucius

(Qufu, South-East China, c450BCE)

These are the sayings of 'The Great Teacher', collected by his students. '*Master*' Kong, (Kong *Fuzi*) was a public official whose social philosophy of harmony became the official ethical system of the State, a position it held until the 20th Century. In China, and much of South-East Asia, Confucius is still accorded a degree of respect so high that many a westerner has even assumed that 'Confucianism' is a religion.

Based on the 1861 translation by James Legge. Abridged: GH

1:1 The Master said, 'Is it not pleasant to learn learn with a constant perseverance and application? 'Is it not delightful to have friends coming from distant quarters?' 'Is he not a man of complete virtue[1], who feels no discomposure though men may take no note of him?'

1:3 The Master said, 'Fine words and an insinuating appearance are seldom associated with true virtue[2].'

1:4 Tsang said, 'I daily examine myself on three points:- whether, in transacting business for others, I may have been not faithful;- whether, in intercourse with friends, I

---

1   **Man of Virtue (君子 Jūnzǐ):** "The man who follows Rén", "The Superior Man", "Gentleman"

2   **Virtue (仁 Rén):** "Humaneness", "Virtue", "Benevolence", "Love", "Jen", "Goodness"

may have been not sincere;- whether I may have not mastered and practised the instructions of my teacher.

1:8 The Master said, 'If the scholar be not grave, he will not call forth any veneration, and his learning will not be solid. 'Hold faithfulness and sincerity as first principles. 'Have no friends not equal to yourself. 'When you have faults, do not fear to abandon them.'

1:13 Yu said, 'When agreements are made according to what is right, what is spoken can be made good. When respect is shown according to what is proper, one keeps far from shame and disgrace. When the parties upon whom a man leans are proper persons to be intimate with, he can make them his guides and masters.'

1:15 Tsze-kung said, 'What do you pronounce concerning the poor man who yet does not flatter, and the rich man who is not proud?' The Master replied, 'They will do; but they are not equal to him, who, though poor, is yet cheerful, and to him, who, though rich, loves the rules of propriety[3].'

1:16 The Master said, 'I will not be afflicted at men's not knowing me; I will be afflicted that I do not know men.'

2:2 The Master said, 'In the Book of Poetry are three hundred pieces, but the design of them all may be embraced in one sentence- "Having no depraved thoughts."'

2:4 The Master said, 'At fifteen, I had my mind bent on learning. 'At thirty, I stood firm. 'At forty, I had no doubts. 'At fifty, I knew the decrees of Heaven. 'At sixty, my ear was an obedient organ for the reception of truth. 'At seventy, I could follow what my heart desired, without transgressing what was right.'

2:5 Mang I asked what filial piety[4] was. The Master said, 'It is not being disobedient.'

2:7 Tsze-yu asked what filial piety was. The Master said, 'The filial piety of now-a-days means the support of one's parents. But dogs and horses likewise are able to do something in the way of support; without reverence, what is there to distinguish the one support given from the other?'

2:11 The Master said, 'If a man keeps cherishing his old knowledge, so as continually to be acquiring new, he may be a teacher of others.'

2:13 Tsze-kung asked what constituted the superior man. The Master said, 'He acts before he speaks, and afterwards speaks according to his actions.'

2:15 The Master said, 'Learning without thought is labour lost; thought without learning is perilous.'

2:20 Chi K'ang asked how to cause the people to reverence their ruler, to be faithful to him, and to go on to nerve themselves to virtue. The Master said, 'Let him preside over them with gravity;- then they will reverence him. Let him be filial and kind to all;- then they will be faithful to him. Let him advance the good and teach the incompetent;- then they will eagerly seek to be virtuous.'

2:24 'To see what is right and not to do it is want of courage.'

3:4 The Master said, 'In festive ceremonies, it is better to be sparing than extravagant. In ceremonies of mourning, it is better that there be deep sorrow than a minute attention to observances.'

3:32 The Master instructing the grand music-master of Lu said, 'How to play music may be known. At the commencement of the piece, all the parts should sound together. As it proceeds, they should be in harmony while severally distinct and flowing without break, and thus on to the conclusion.'

3:26 The Master said, 'High station filled without indulgent generosity; ceremonies performed without reverence; mourning conducted without sorrow;- how should I contemplate such ways?'

4:3 The Master said, 'It is only the (truly) virtuous man, who can love, or who can hate, others.'

4:5 The Master said, 'Riches and honours are what men desire. If it cannot be obtained in the proper way, they should not be held. Poverty and meanness are what men dislike. If it cannot be avoided in the proper way, they should not be avoided.

4:9 The Master said, 'A scholar, whose mind is set on truth, and who is ashamed of bad clothes and bad food, is not fit to be discoursed with. '

4:11 The Master said, 'The superior man thinks of virtue; the small man thinks of comfort. The superior man thinks of the sanctions of law; the small man thinks of favours which he may receive. '

4:16 The Master said, 'The mind of the superior man is conversant with righteousness; the mind of the mean man is conversant with gain.'

4:18 The Master said, 'In serving his parents, a son may remonstrate with them, but gently; when he sees that they do not incline to follow his advice, he shows an increased degree of reverence, but does not abandon his purpose; and should they punish him, he does not allow himself to murmur.'

4:25 The Master said, 'Virtue is not left to stand alone. He who practises it will have neighbours'

5:15 The Master said of Tsze-ch'an that he had four of the characteristics of a superior man:- in his conduct of himself, he was humble; in serving his superiors, he was respectful; in nourishing the people, he was kind; in ordering the people, he was just.'

---

3   **Propriety (礼 Li):** "Protocol", "The proper way", "The established rules", "Rites", "Decorum", "Manners", "Ritual", "Etiquette"

4   **Filial piety (孝 Xiào):** The long-established rules whereby in the 'The Five Constant Relationships' (parent/child, elder/younger siblings, husband/wife, elder/younger friends, rulers/subjects) the senior party owes care to the junior, who owes respect in return.

5:19 Chi Wan thought three times before taking action. When the Master was informed of it, he said, 'Twice will do.'

6:10 Yen Ch'iu said, 'It is not that I do not delight in your doctrines, but my strength is insufficient.' The Master said, 'Those whose strength is insufficient give over in the middle of the way but now you limit yourself.'

6:18 The Master said, 'They who know the truth are not equal to those who love it, and they who love it are not equal to those who delight in it.'

7:7 The Master said, 'From the man bringing his bundle of dried flesh for my teaching upwards, I have never refused instruction to any one.'

7:8 The Master said, 'I do not open up the truth to one who is not eager to get knowledge, nor help out any one who is not anxious to explain himself. When I have presented one corner of a subject to any one, and he cannot from it learn the other three, I do not repeat my lesson.'

7:15 The Master said, 'With coarse rice to eat, with water to drink, and my bended arm for a pillow;- I have still joy in the midst of these things. Riches and honours acquired by unrighteousness, are to me as a floating cloud.'

7:36 The Master said, 'The superior man is satisfied and composed; the mean man is always full of distress.'

8:2 The Master said, 'Respectfulness, without the rules of propriety, becomes laborious bustle; carefulness, without the rules of propriety, becomes timidity; boldness, without the rules of propriety, becomes insubordination; straightforwardness, without the rules of propriety, becomes rudeness.

8:9 The Master said, 'The people may be made to follow a path of action, but they may not be made to understand it.'

9:4 There were four things from which the Master was entirely free. He had no foregone conclusions, no arbitrary predeterminations, no obstinacy, and no egoism.

9:13 The Master was wishing to go and live among the nine wild tribes of the east. Some one said, 'They are rude. How can you do such a thing?' The Master said, 'If a superior man dwelt among them, what rudeness would there be?'

9:18 The Master said, 'The prosecution of learning may be compared to what may happen in raising a mound. If there want but one basket of earth to complete the work, and I stop, the stopping is my own work. It may be compared to throwing down the earth on the level ground. Though but one basketful is thrown at a time, the advancing with it is my own going forward.'

9:28 The Master said, 'The wise are free from perplexities; the virtuous from anxiety; and the bold from fear.'

10:12 The stable being burned down, when he was at court, on his return he said, 'Has any man been hurt?' He did not ask about the horses.

12:4 Sze-ma Niu asked about the superior man. The Master said, 'The superior man has neither anxiety nor fear.' 'Being without anxiety or fear!' said Nui;- 'does this constitute what we call the superior man?' The Master said, 'When internal examination discovers nothing wrong, what is there to be anxious about, what is there to fear?'

12:11 The Duke Ching, of Ch'i, asked Confucius about government. Confucius replied, 'There is government, when the prince is prince, and the minister is minister; when the father is father, and the son is son.' 'Good!' said the duke; 'if, indeed; the prince be not prince, the minister not minister, the father not father, and the son not son, although I have my revenue, can I enjoy it?'

12:13 The Master said, 'In hearing litigations, I am like any other body. What is necessary, however, is to cause the people to have no litigations.'

12:15 The Master said, 'By extensively studying all learning, and keeping himself under the restraint of the rules of propriety, one may thus likewise not err from what is right.'

12:17 Chi K'ang asked Confucius about government. Confucius replied, 'To govern means to rectify. If you lead on the people with correctness, who will dare not to be correct?'

12:19 Chi K'ang asked Confucius about government, saying, 'What do you say to killing the unprincipled for the good of the principled?' Confucius replied, 'Sir, in carrying on your government, why should you use killing at all? Let your evinced desires be for what is good, and the people will be good. The relation between superiors and inferiors, is like that between the wind and the grass. The grass must bend, when the wind blows across it.'

12:22 Fan Ch'ih asked about benevolence. The Master said, 'It is to love all men.' He asked about knowledge. The Master said, 'It is to know all men.'

12:23 Tsze-kung asked about friendship. The Master said, 'Faithfully admonish your friend, and skilfully lead him on. If you find him impracticable, stop. Do not disgrace yourself.'

13:3 Tsze-lu said, 'The ruler of Wei has been waiting for you, in order with you to administer the government. What will you consider the first thing to be done?' The Master replied, 'What is necessary is to rectify names[5].' 'So, indeed!' said Tsze-lu. 'You are wide of the mark! Why must there be such rectification?' The Master said, 'How uncultivated you are, Yu! A superior man, in regard to what he does not know, shows a cautious reserve. 'If names be not correct, language is not in accordance with the truth of things. If language be not in accordance with the truth of things, affairs cannot be carried on to success. 'When affairs cannot be carried on to success, proprieties and music will not flourish. When proprieties and music do not flourish, punishments will not be properly awarded. When punishments are not properly awarded, the people do not

---

5   **Rectification of Names (正名 Zhengming)**: "Correct descriptions", "Defining terms" A central message of Confucianism.

know how to move hand or foot. 'Therefore a superior man considers it necessary that the names he uses may be spoken appropriately, and also that what he speaks may be carried out appropriately. What the superior man requires, is just that in his words there may be nothing incorrect.'

13:5 The Master said, 'Though a man may be able to recite the three hundred odes, yet if, when intrusted with a governmental charge, he knows not how to act, or if, when sent to any quarter on a mission, he cannot give his replies unassisted, notwithstanding the extent of his learning, of what practical use is it?'

13:6 The Master said, 'When a prince's personal conduct is correct, his government is effective without the issuing of orders. If his personal conduct is not correct, he may issue orders, but they will not be followed.'

14:1 Hsien asked what was shameful. The Master said, 'When good government prevails in a state, to be thinking only of salary; and, when bad government prevails, to be thinking, in the same way, only of salary;- this is shameful.'

14:23 Tsze-lu asked how a ruler should be served. The Master said, 'Do not impose on him, and, moreover, withstand him to his face.'

14:24 The Master said, 'The progress of the superior man is upwards; the progress of the mean man is downwards.'

14:29 The Master said, 'The superior man is modest in his speech, but exceeds in his actions.'

14:36 Some one said, 'What do you say concerning the principle that injury should be recompensed with kindness?' The Master said, 'With what then will you recompense kindness? 'Recompense injury with justice, and recompense kindness with kindness.'

15:2 The Master said, 'Ts'ze, you think, I suppose, that I am one who learns many things and keeps them in memory?' Tsze-kung replied, 'Yes,- but perhaps it is not so?' 'No,' was the answer; 'I seek a unity all-pervading.'

15:18 The Master said, 'The superior man is distressed by his want of ability. He is not distressed by men's not knowing him.'

15:19 The Master said, 'The superior man dislikes the thought of his name not being mentioned after his death.'

15:20 The Master said, 'What the superior man seeks, is in himself. What the mean man seeks, is in others.'

15:21 The Master said, 'The superior man is dignified, but does not wrangle. He is sociable, but not a partisan.'

15:22 The Master said, 'The superior man does not promote a man simply on account of his words, nor does he put aside good words because of the man.'

15:23 Tsze-kung asked, saying, 'Is there one word which may serve as a rule of practice for all one's life?' The Master said, 'Is not Reciprocity such a word? What you do not want done to yourself, do not do to others.'

15:31 The Master said, 'The object of the superior man is truth. Food is not his object. There is ploughing;- even in that there is sometimes want. So with learning;- emolument

may be found in it. The superior man is anxious lest he should not get truth; he is not anxious lest poverty should come upon him.'

15:36 The Master said, 'The superior man is correctly firm, and not firm merely.'

15:38 The Master said, 'In teaching there should be no distinction of classes.'

15:40 The Master said, 'In language it is simply required that it convey the meaning.'

16:6 Confucius said, 'There are three errors to which they who stand in the presence of a man of virtue and station are liable. They may speak when it does not come to them to speak;- this is called rashness. They may not speak when it comes to them to speak;- this is called concealment. They may speak without looking at the countenance of their superior;- this is called blindness.'

16:8 Confucius said, 'There are three things of which the superior man stands in awe. He stands in awe of the ordinances of Heaven. He stands in awe of great men. He stands in awe of the words of sages. 'The mean man does not know the ordinances of Heaven, and consequently does not stand in awe of them. He is disrespectful to great men. He makes sport of the words of sages.'

16:9 Confucius said, 'Those who are born with the possession of knowledge are the highest class of men. Those who learn, and so, readily, get possession of knowledge, are the next. Those who are dull and stupid, and yet compass the learning, are another class next to these. As to those who are dull and stupid and yet do not learn;- they are the lowest of the people.'

17:2 The Master said, 'By their natures, men are nearly alike; it is by their habits they get to be wide apart.'

17:3 The Master said, 'There are only the wise of the highest class, and the stupid of the lowest class, who cannot be changed.'

17:6 Tsze-chang asked Confucius about perfect virtue. Confucius said, 'To be able to practise five things everywhere under heaven constitutes perfect virtue.' He begged to ask what they were, and was told, 'Gravity, generosity of soul, sincerity, earnestness, and kindness. If you are grave, you will not be treated with disrespect. If you are generous, you will win all. If you are sincere, people will repose trust in you. If you are earnest, you will accomplish much. If you are kind, this will enable you to employ the services of others.

17:24 Tsze-kung said, 'Has the superior man his hatreds also?' The Master said, 'He has his hatreds. He hates those who proclaim the evil of others. He hates the man who, being in a low station, slanders his superiors. He hates those who have valour merely, and are unobservant of propriety. He hates those who are forward and determined, and, at the same time, of contracted understanding.'

19:9 Tsze-hsia said, 'The superior man undergoes three changes. Looked at from a distance, he appears stern; when approached, he is mild; when he is heard to speak, his language is firm and decided.'

20:3 The Master said, 'Without recognising the ordinances of Heaven, it is impossible to be a superior man. 'Without an acquaintance with the rules of Propriety, it is impossible

for the character to be established. 'Without knowing the force of words, it is impossible to know men.'

The Histories of Herodotus
(*ΗΙΣΤΟΡΙΑ ΤΟΥ ΗΡΟΔΟΤΟΥ*)
by Herodotus of Halicarnassos
(Greece, c450BCE)

Herodotus, the 'Father of History', set about trying to find out the cause and course of the great war between Greeks and Persians. The result was either the first ever researched history book in a European language, or the first travel book. His more than occasional lack of precision, though, has also earned him the title 'Father of Lies'.

Based on the 1890 translation by GC Macaulay. The chapter headings named after the Muses - spirits of the Arts – are medieval additions.

Abridged: JH/GH

THIS is the Showing forth of the Inquiry of Herodotus of Halicarnassos, to the end that neither the deeds of men may be forgotten by lapse of time, nor the works great and marvellous, of both Greeks and Barbarians, may lose their renown; and especially that the causes may be remembered for which these waged war with one another.

Book I (*Clio*)

I will not dispute whether those ancient tales be true, of the divine Io and of Helen, and the like, which one or another have called the sources of the war between the Greek Hellenes and the barbarians of Asia; but I will begin with those wrongs whereof I myself have knowledge.

In the days of Sadyattes, king of Lydia, and his son Alyattes, there was war between Lydia and Miletus. And Croesus, the son of Alyattes, made himself master of the lands which are bounded by the river Halys, and he waxed in power and wealth, so that there was none like to him. To him came Solon, the statesman of Athens, of whom Croesus asked, "Much report we have of thy wisdom. Look upon our treasuries and our palace and tell us, who is the happiest of men?" To this the Athenian replied that the happiest man he had known was Tellos of Athens, a modest man, who had died a most fair death when yet a grandfather in defending his city. By which Solon meant that good fortune is not to be found in wealth, but that none may be judged so until his life's end.

Thereafter trouble fell upon Croesus by the slaying of his son when he was a-hunting. Then Cyrus the Persian rose up and made himself master of the Medes and Persians, and Croesus, fearing his power, made offerings to the Oracles and asked of them whether he should march against the Persians. The Oracles all agreed, declaring to Croesus that if he should march against the Persians he should destroy a great empire.

So he sought to make alliance with the chief of the states of Hellas. In those days, Pisistratus was despot of Athens; but Sparta was mighty, by the laws of Lycurgus. Therefore Croesus sent envoys to the Spartans to make alliance with them, which was done very willingly.

But when Croesus went up against Cyrus, his army was put to flight, and Cyrus besieged him in the city of Sardis, and took it, and made himself lord of Lydia. Thus the prophecy of the Oracle was fulfilled, yet it was the empire of Croesus himself which fell. Cyrus was to have burned Croesus alive, but heard him, when yet upon the pyre, calling upon Solon in remembrance of the vagaries of fortune, so that Cyrus, finding him wise and pious, he made him his counsellor.

Now, this Cyrus had before overthrown the Median king, Astyages, whose daughter was his own mother. For her father, fearing a dream, wedded her to a Persian, and when she bore a child, he gave order for its slaying. But the babe was taken away and brought up by a herdsman of the hill-folk. But in course of time the truth became known to Astyages, and to Harpagus, the officer who had been bidden to slay the babe, and to Cyrus himself. Then Harpagus, fearing the wrath of Astyages, bade Cyrus gather together the Persians - who in those days were a hardy people of the mountains - and made himself king over the Medians; which things Cyrus did, overthrowing his grandfather Astyages. And in this wise began the dominion of the Persians.

The Ionian cities of Asia were zealous to make alliance with Cyrus when he had overthrown Croesus. But he held them of little account, and threatened them, and the Lacedæmonians also, who sent him messengers warning him to let the Ionians alone. And he sent Harpagus against the cities of the Ionians, of whom certain Phocæans and Teians sailed away to Rhegium and Abdera rather than become the slaves of the barbarians; but the rest, though they fought valiantly enough, were brought to submission by Harpagus.

While Harpagus was completing the subjugation of the West, Cyrus was making conquest of Upper Asia, and overthrew the kingdom of Assyria, of which the chief city was Babylon, a very wonderful city, wherein there had ruled two famous queens, Semiramis and Nitocris. Now, this queen had made the city wondrous by having the course of the river changed, and many other things, yet Cyrus took it by a shrewd device, drawing off the water of the river so as to gain a passage. Thus Babylon also fell under the sway of the Persian.

The Babylonians use no oil of olives, but only that of sesame seed; they have date-palms of which they make food and wine and honey, and their boats are very ingenious, being made of straw. They wear their hair long, anoint their body with perfumes and every man carries a carved staff. They had a custom of gathering their maidens and placing them together for sale in the market. Those of beautiful form were soon sold, which provided dowries for those unshapely or crippled, so that every young woman was provided for. This good custom does not now exist, instead the common people, when wanting livelihood, prostitute their female children. Next in their wisdom, is this: of physicians they make no use, but rather they bear out the sick into the marketplace, that people who have known the same might come up and give advice.

Then Cyrus would have made war upon Tomyris, the queen of the Massagetæ, who dwelt to the eastward.

There the people have discovered a certain fruit of such a kind that when they have assembled together in companies around the fire, they throw some of it into the fire, and they are intoxicated by the smoke as Greeks are with wine, until at last they rise up to dance and begin to sing.

There was a very great battle, and Cyrus himself was slain and the most part of his host. And Cambyses, his son, reigned in his stead.

Book II (*Euterpe*)

Cambyses set out to conquer Egypt, taking in his army certain of the Greeks. Of all that I shall tell about that land, the most was told to me by the priests whom I myself visited at Memphis and Thebes and Heliopolis.

They Egyptians are wont to account themselves a most ancient people, to prove which their king Psammetichus had two new-born children brought up by a shepherd never to hear human voice. When they were two years old they were heard to say "beats" which is the Phrygian word for 'bread', so Psammetichus   concluded that only the Phrygians were a more ancient people than themselves.

The Egyptians were the first of mankind to determine the annual revolution of the sun and first to designate the twelve gods, which the Greeks borrowed from them. Moreover, they first dedicated to these deities altars, statues, and temples; and first also sculptured animals in stone. Egypt has wonders more in number than any other land.

The Ionians reckon that Egypt is only the Nile Delta, but I reckon that the whole Egyptian territory is from the cataracts and Elephantiné down to the sea, parted into the Asiatic part and the Libyan part by the Nile.

As for the causes of the rising and falling of the Nile, the reasons that men give are of no account. And of the sources whence the river springs are strange stories told of which I say not whether they be true or false: but the course of it is known for four months' journey by land and water, and in my opinion it is a river comparable to the Ister.

The crocodile of the Nile has four feet and is an animal belonging to the land and the water both; he has eyes like those of a pig and teeth large and tusky. Now for some of the Egyptians the crocodiles are sacred, and they train them to tameness, and put ornaments upon their feet and ears, and after they are dead they bury them in sacred tombs, embalming them. But others catch them by using as bait a pig: and the hunter forthwith plasters up its eyes with mud, and very easily gets the mastery of him.

There is also a sacred bird called the phœnix, with feathers red and gold, which I did not myself see except in painting. This bird they say (though I cannot believe) contrives to carry his father, in an egg fashioned of myrrh, to the temple of the Sun.

Their ways of burial are these: whenever a man of regard dies, they go to the embalmers who, with a crooked iron tool, draw out the brain through the nostrils. They take out the whole contents of the belly, and fill it with myrrh and cassia. Having so done they keep it covered up in natron for seventy days, then is wrapped in fine linen cut into bands, smeared with gum. Then the kinsfolk receive it, and have a wooden figure made in the shape of a man, and with this they enclose the corpse, and store it in a sepulchral chamber, setting it to stand upright against the wall.

The priests tell that the first ruler of Egypt was Menes, and after him were three hundred and thirty kings, counting one queen, who was called Nitocris. After them came Sesostris, who carried his conquest as far as the Thracians and Scythians; and later was Rhampsinitus, who married his daughter to the clever thief who robbed his treasure-house; and after him Cheops, who built the pyramid, drawing the stones from the Arabian mountain down to the Nile. Chephren also, and Mycerinus built pyramids, and the Greeks have a story - which is not true - that another was built by Rhodopis. And in the reign of Sethon, Egypt was invaded by Sennacherib the Assyrian, whose army's bowstrings were eaten by field-mice.

A thing more wonderful than the pyramids is the labyrinth near Lake Moeris, and still more wonderful is Lake Moeris itself, all which were made by the twelve kings who ruled at once after Sethon. And after them, Psammetichus made himself the monarch; and after him his great grandson Apries prospered greatly, till he was overthrown by Amasis. And Amasis also prospered, and showed favour to the Greeks. But for whatever reason, in his day Cambyses made his expedition against Egypt, invading it just when Amasis had died, and his son Psammenitus was reigning.

Book III (*Thalia*)

Cambyses put the Egyptian army to rout in a great battle, and conquered the country, making Psammenitus prisoner. Yet he would have set him up as governor of the province, according to the Persian custom, but that Psammenitus was stirred up to revolt, and, being discovered, was put to death. Thereafter Cambyses would have made war upon Carthage, but that the Phoenicians would not aid him; and against the Ethiopians, who are called "long-lived," but his army could get no food; and against the Ammonians, but the troops that went were seen no more.

Now, madness came upon Cambyses, and he died, having committed many crimes, among which was the slaying of his brother Smerdis. And there rose up one among the Magi who pretended to be Smerdis, and was proclaimed king. But this false Smerdis was one whose ears had been cut off, and he was thus found out by one of his wives, the daughter of a Persian nobleman, Otanes. Then seven nobles conspired together, since they would not be ruled over by one of the Magi; and having determined that it was best to have one man for ruler, rather than the rule of the people or of the nobles, they slew Smerdis and made Darius, the son of Hystaspes, their king.

Then Darius divided the Persian empire into twenty satrapies, whereof each one paid its own tribute, save Persia itself, and he was lord of all Asia, and Egypt also.

In the days of Cambyses, Polycrates was despot of Samos, being the first who ever thought to make himself a ruler of the seas. And he had prospered marvellously. But Oroetes, the satrap of Sardis, compassed his death by foul treachery, and wrought many other crimes; whom Darius in turn put to death by guile, fearing to make open war upon him. And not long afterwards, he sent Otanes to make conquest of Samos. And during the same days there was a revolt of the Babylonians; and Darius went up against Babylon, yet for twenty months he could not take it. Howbeit, it was taken by the act of Zopyrus, who, having mutilated himself, went to the Babylonians and told them that Darius had thus evilly entreated him, and so winning their trust, he made easy entry for the Persian army, and so Babylon was taken the second time.

Book IV (*Melpomene*)

Now, Darius was minded to make conquest of the Scythians - concerning which people, and the lands beyond, there are many marvels told, as of a bald-headed folk called Argippæi; and the Arimaspians or one-eyed people; and the Hyperborean land where it is said that the air is, at a certain season, full of feathers such that men are not able either to see or pass. But the opinion I have is this; that it is not feathers, but snow: for whomsoever has seen snow falling, knows what I mean. It will be for this reason that, I think, the most Northern lands are uninhabitable.

Of these lands are legends only; nothing is known. But concerning the earth's surface, this much is known, that Libya is surrounded by water, certain Phoenicians having sailed round it. And of the unknown regions of Asia much was searched out by order of Darius.

Of the Indians the number is far greater than that of any other race of men; and they brought in a tribute of three hundred and sixty talents of gold-dust. Which gold they got in a curious fashion: In the deserts they have a race of ants, which are in size smaller than dogs but larger than foxes, and which dwell under ground and carry up the sand which contains gold.

The Scythians have no cities; but there are great rivers in Scythia, whereof the Ister is the greatest of all known streams, being greater even than the Nile, if we reckon its tributaries. The great god of the Scythians is Ares; and their war customs are savage exceedingly, and all their ways barbarous.

Against this folk Darius resolved to march. His plan was to convey his army across the Bosphorus on a bridge of boats, while the Ionian fleet should sail up to the Ister and bridge that, and await him. So he crossed the Bosphorus and marched through Thrace, subduing on his way the Getse, who believe that there is no true death. But when he passed the Ister, he would have taken the Ionians along with him; but by counsel of Coes of Mitylene, he resolved to leave them in charge of the bridge, giving order that, after sixty days, they might depart home, but no sooner.

Then the Scythians, fearing that they could not match the great king's army, summoned the other barbaric peoples to their aid; among whom were the Sauromatians, who are fabled to be the offspring of the Amazons. And some were willing, but others not. Therefore the Scythians retired before Darius, first towards those peoples who would not come to their help; and so enticed him into desert regions, yet would in no wise come to battle with him.

Book V (*Terpsichore*)

Now, at length, Darius found himself in so evil a plight that he began to march back to the Ister. And certain Scythians came to the Ionians, and counselled them to destroy the bridge, the sixty days being passed. And this Miltiades, the Athenian despot of the Chersonese, would have had them do, so that Darius might perish with all his army; but Histiæus of Miletus dissuaded them, because the rule of the despots was upheld by Darius. And thus the Persian army was saved, Megabazus being left in Europe to subdue the Hellespontines. When Megabazus had subdued many of the Thracian peoples, who, indeed, lack only union with each other to make them the mightiest of all nations, he sent an embassy to Amyntas, the king of Macedon, to demand earth and water. But because those envoys insulted the ladies of the court, Alexander, the son of Amyntas, slew them all, and of them or all their train was never aught heard more.

Now Darius, with fair words, bade Histiseus of Miletus abide with him at the royal town of Susa. Then Aristagoras, the brother of Histiæus, having failed in an attempt to subdue Naxos, and fearing both Artaphernes, the satrap of Sardis, and the Persian general Megabazus, with whom he had quarrelled, sought to stir up a revolt of the Ionian cities; being incited thereto by secret messages from Histiseus.

Book VI (*Erato*)

To this end, he sought alliance with the Lacedæmonians; but they would have nothing to do with him, deeming the venture too remote. Then he went to Athens, whence the sons of Pisistratus had been driven forth just before. For Hipparchus had been slain by Harmodius and Aristogiton, and afterwards Hippias would hardly have been expelled but that his enemies captured his children and so could make with him what terms they chose. But the Pisistratidse having been expelled, the city grew in might, and changes were made in the government of it by Cleisthenes the Alcmæonid. But the party that was against Cleisthenes got aid from Cleomenes of Sparta; yet the party of Cleisthenes won.

Then, since they reckoned that there would be war with Sparta, the Athenians had sought friendship with Artaphernes at Sardis; but since he demanded earth and water they broke off. But because Athens was waxing in strength, the Spartans bethought them of restoring the despotism of the Pisistratidæ. But Sosicles, the Corinthian, dissuaded the allies of Sparta from taking part in so evil a deed. Then Hippias sought to stir up against the Athenians the ill-will of Artaphernes, who bade them take back the Pisistratidæ, which they would not do.

Therefore, when Aristagoras came thither, the Athenians were readily persuaded to promise him aid. And he, having gathered the troops of the Ionians, who were at one with him, marched with them and the Athenians against Sardis and took the city, which by a chance was set on fire. But after that the Athenians refused further help to the Ionians, who were worsted by the Persians. But the ruin of the Ionians was at the sea-fight of Lade, where the men of Chios fought stoutly; but they of Samos and Lesbos deserting, there was a great rout.

Thereafter King Darius, being very wroth with the Athenians for their share in the burning of Sardis, sent a great army across the waters of the Hellespont to march through Thrace against Athens, under his young kinsman Mardonius. But disaster befell these at the hands of the Thracians, and the fleet that was to aid them was shattered in a storm; so that they returned to Asia without honour. Then Darius sent envoys to demand earth and water from the Greek states; and of the islanders the most gave them, and some also of the cities on the mainland; and among these were the Aeginetans, who were at feud with Athens.

But of those who would not give the earth and water were the Eretrians of Eubcea. So Darius sent a great armament by sea against Eretria and Athens, led by Datis and Artaphernes, which sailed first against Eretria. The Athenians, indeed, sent aid; but when they found that the counsels of the Eretrians were divided, so that no firm stand might be made, they withdrew. Nevertheless, the Eretrians fought valiantly behind their walls, till they were betrayed on the seventh day. But the Persians, counselled by Hippias, sailed to the bay of Marathon, from where the Athenian generals sent off a herald, namely Pheidippides, who practised running as his profession, to Sparta for aid. Pheidippides said that he had met the God Pan along the way and so the Spartans promised aid, yet for sacred reasons they would not move until the full moon. Years later the Athenians thus established a temple to Pan and an annual race in his honour.

So the Athenian host had none to aid them save the loyal Platæans, valiant though few. Yet in the council of their generals the word of Miltiades was given for battle, whereto the rest consented. Then the Athenians and Platæans, being drawn up in a long line, charged across the plain nigh a mile, running upon the masses of the Persians; and, breaking them upon the wings, turned and routed the centre also after long fighting, and drove them down to the ships, slaying as they went; and of the ships they took seven. And of the barbarians there fell 6,400 men, and of the Athenians. But as for the story that the Alcmæonidæ hoisted a friendly signal to the Persians, I credit it not at all.

Book VII (*Polymnia*)

Now, Darius was very wroth with the Greeks when he heard of these things, and made preparation for a mighty armament to overthrow them, and also the Egyptians, who revolted soon afterwards. But he died before he was ready, and Xerxes, his son, reigned in his stead. Then, having first crushed the Egyptians, he, being ruled by Mardonius, gathered a council and declared his intent of marching against the Hellenes; which resolution was commended by Mardonius, but Artabanus, the king's uncle, spoke wise words of warning. Then Xerxes would have changed his mind, but for a dream which came to him twice, and to Artabanus also, threatening disaster if he ceased from his project; so that Artabanus was won over to favour it.

Then Xerxes made vast provision for his invasion for the building of a bridge over the Hellespont, and the cutting of a canal through the peninsula of Athos, where the fleet of Mardonius had been shattered. And from all parts of his huge empire he mustered his hosts first in Cappadocia, and marched thence by way of Sardis to the waters of the Hellespont. But because, when the bridge was a building, a great storm wrecked it, he bade flog the naughty waves three hundred times and had fetters thrown into the water. Thereafter a bridge was built and he passed over with his host, which took seven days to accomplish.

And when they were come to Doriscus he numbered them, and found them to be 1,700,000 men, besides his fleets. And in the fleet were 1,207 great ships, manned chiefly by the Phoenicians and the Greeks of Asia, having also Persian and Scythian fighting men on board. But when

Demaratus, an exiled king of Sparta, warned Xerxes of the valour of all the Greeks, but chiefly of the Spartans, who would give battle, however few they might be, against any foe, however many, his words seemed to Xerxes a jest, seeing how huge his own army was.

Now, Xerxes had sent to many of the Greek states heralds to demand earth and water, which many had given; but to Athens and Sparta he had not sent, because there the heralds of his father Darius had been evilly entreated. And if it had not been for the resolution of the Athenians at this time, all Hellas would have been forced to submit to the Great King; for they, in despite of threatening oracles, held fast to their defiance, being urged thereto by Themistocles of Athens, who showed them how those oracles must mean that, although they would suffer evil things, they would be victorious by means of wooden bulwarks, which is to say, ships; and thus they were encouraged to rely upon building and manning a mighty fleet. And all the other cities of Greece resolved to stand by them, except the Argives, who would not submit to the leadership of the Spartans. And in like manner Gelon, the despot of Syracuse in Sicily, would not send aid unless he were accepted as leader. Nor were the men of Thessaly willing to join, since the other Greeks could not help them to guard Thessaly itself.

Therefore the Greeks resolved to make their stand at the strait of Artemisium by sea and some three hundred only of the Spartans commanded by king Leonidas at the "Hot Gates" of Thermopylæ on land, where, as they gathered, Xerxes sent a scout on horseback to see how many they were. The spy saw the men practising athletic exercises and combing their long hair. Hearing this Xerxes was not able to conjecture the truth, namely that they were preparing to die; but thought them merely ridiculous.

Yet when the Persians sought to storm the pass, they were beaten back with ease, until a track was found by which they might take the defenders in the rear. Then Leonidas bade the rest of the army, and his soothsayer, depart except his Spartans. I am of opinion that Leonidas desired to lay up glory for himself, but the Thespians also would not go. Thus those Spartans and Thespians went out into the open and died gloriously. A stone lion has now been erected there in their memory.

Book VIII (*Urania*)

During these same days the Greek fleet at Artemisium fought several engagements with the Persian fleet, in which neither side had much the better. And thereafter the Greek fleet withdrew, but was persuaded to remain undispersed in the bay of Salamis. The Peloponnesians were no longer minded to attempt the defence of Attica, but to fortify their isthmus, so that the Athenians had no choice but either to submit or to evacuate Athens, removing their families and their goods to Troezen or Aegina or Salamis. In the fleet, their contingent was by far the largest and best, but the commanding admiral was the Spartan Eurybiades. Then the Persians, passing through Boeotia, but, being dispersed before Delphi by thunderbolts and other portents, took

possession of Athens, after a fierce fight with the garrison in the Acropolis.

Then the rest of the Greek fleet was fain to withdraw from Salamis, and look to the safety of the Peloponnese only. But Themistocles warned them that if they did so, the Athenians would leave them and sail to new lands and make themselves a new Athens; and thus the fleet was persuaded to hold together at Salamis. Yet he did not trust only to their goodwill, but sent a messenger to the Persian fleet that the way of retreat might be intercepted. For the Persian fleet had gathered at Phalerum, and now looked to overwhelm the Grecian fleet altogether, despite the council of Queen Artemisia of Halicarnassus, who would have had them not fight by sea at all. When Aristides, called the Just, the great rival of Themistocles, came to the Greeks with the news that their retreat by sea was cut off, then they were no longer divided, but resolved to fight it out.

In the battle, the Aeginetans and the Athenians did the best of all the Greeks, and Themistocles best among the commanders; nor was ever any fleet more utterly put to rout than that of the Persians, among whom Queen Artemisia won praise unmerited. As for King Xerxes, panic seized him when he saw the disaster to his fleet, and he made haste to flee. He consented, however, to leave Mardonius behind with 300,000 troops in Thessaly, he being still assured that he could crush the Greeks. And it was well for him that Themistocles was over-ruled in his desire to pursue and annihilate the fleet, then sail to the Hellespont and destroy the bridge.

Book IX (*Calliope*)

When the winter and spring were passed, Mardonius marched from Thessaly and again occupied Athens, which the Athenians had again evacuated, the Spartans having failed to send succour. But when at length the Lacedæmonians, fearing to lose the Athenian fleet, sent forth an army, the Persians fell back to Boeotia. So the Greek hosts gathered near Platæa to the number of 108,000 men, but the troops of Mardonius were about 350,000. Yet, by reason of doubtful auguries, both armies held back, till Mardonius resolved to attack, whereof warning was brought to the Athenians by Alexander of Macedon. But when the Spartan Pausanias, the general of the Greeks, heard of this, he did what caused no little wonder, for he proposed that the Athenians instead of the Lacedæmonians should face the picked troops of the Persians, as having fought them at Marathon. But Mardonius, seeing them move, moved his picked troops also. Then Mardonius sent some light horse against the Greeks by a fountain whence flowed the water for the army; which, becoming choked, it was needful to move to a new position. But the move being made by night, most of the allies withdrew into the town. But the Spartans, and Tegeans and Athenians, perceiving this, held each their ground till dawn.

Now, in the morning the picked Persian troops fell on the Spartans, and their Grecian allies attacked the Athenians. But, Mardonius being slain, the Persians fled to their camp, which was stormed by the Spartans and Tegeans, and the Athenians, who also had routed their foes; and there the barbarians were slaughtered, so that of 300,000 men not 3,000 were left alive. But Artabazus, who, before the battle, had withdrawn with 40,000 men, escaped by forced marches to the Hellespont.

And on that same day was fought another fight by sea at Mycale in Ionia, where also the barbarians were utterly routed, for the fleet had sailed thither. And thence the Greeks sailed to Sestos, captured the place, and so went home.

Lysistrata
(*ΛΥΣΙΣΤΡΆΤΑ*)
by Aristophanes of Athens
(Greece, 411BCE)

The comic play *Lysistrata* was first performed as popular unrest against the Peloponnesian War (p46) intensified after Athens suffered the loss of her whole navy and much of her army. The play was forbidden by the Nazis, by the Greek military junta in 1960s, and it remains banned *de jure* in the USA. It has been revived many times over the centuries, often as an message against war, notably in the 'Lysistrata Project' of 2002.

Abridged: GH, largely based on an uncredited translation published in 1912, possibly by Oscar Wilde (p418).

A public square at Athens

Lysistrata: Ah! if only they had been invited to a Bacchic revelling, or a feast of Pan or Aphrodité, why! the streets would have been impassable for the thronging tambourines! Now there's never a woman here - ah! except my neighbour Calonicé, approaching yonder... Good day, Calonicé.

Calonicé: Good day, Lysistrata; but pray, why this dark face, my dear? It does not make you look pretty.

Lysistrata: Oh, Calonicé, my heart is on fire; I blush for our sex. Men will have it we are tricky and sly....

Calonicé: And they are quite right!

Lysistrata: Yet, look you, when the women are summoned to meet for a matter of importance, they lie abed instead of coming.

Calonicé: And why do you summon us, dear Lysistrata? What is it all about?

Lysistrata: Something big.

Calonicé: And thick too?

Lysistrata: Oh! No that. If that was all, I would have no difficulty collecting our women. But now, our country's fortunes depend on us - it is for us to exterminate the Peloponnesian and the Boeotian threat! .

Calonicé: But how? When we women mostly lie in our households, wearing silky yellow gowns?

Lysistrata: Nay, those gowns, those scents and slippers, those cosmetics and transparent robes are our weapons!

Calonicé: How so, pray?

Lysistrata: There is not a man will resist ...

Calonicé: Quick, I will get me a yellow gown from the dyer's. But look! here are some arrivals.

Calonicé: Yes! 'Tis Myrrhiné and all the female population of Anagyra!

Myrrhiné: Are we late, Lysistrata? I could not find my girdle in the dark. Ah! here comes Lampito.

Lysistrata: Good day, Lampito, dear friend from Lacedaemon. How handsome you look! and how strong! You could strangle a bull surely!

Lampito: Yes, indeed, I really think I could. It is only because I do gymnastics and kick dancing.

Calonicé: Superb bosoms!

Lampito: La! You are not feeling a beast for the sacrifice. So, who has called together this council of women, pray?

Myrrhiné: What is the most important business you wish to inform us about?

Lysistrata: I will tell you. Is there is not one of you whose husband is not abroad at this moment.

Calonicé: Mine has been the last five months in Thrace.

Myrrhiné: 'Tis seven long months since mine left me for Pylos.

Lampito: As for mine, if he ever does return from service, he's no sooner back than he takes down his shield again and flies back to the wars.

Lysistrata: And I have been without a man too. Not even one of those eight-inch leather ones. Now tell me, if I know how to bring an end to this war, are you with me?

Myrrhiné: Yes verily, by all the goddesses, I swear I will, though I have to put my gown in pawn, and drink the money the same day.

Calonicé: And so will I, though I must be split in two like a flat-fish, and have half myself removed.

Lysistrata: Then I will out with it at last, my mighty secret! Oh! sister women, if we would compel our husbands to make peace, we must refrain...

Myrrhiné: Refrain from what? tell us, tell us!

Lysistrata: We must refrain from men altogether... Nay, why do you turn your backs on me? Where are you going?

Calonicé: Bah! This is idle talk....What if our husbands drag us by force into the bedchamber?

Lysistrata: Hold on to the door posts.

Calonicé: But if they beat us?

Lysistrata: Then yield to their wishes, but with a bad grace. There's no satisfaction for a man, unless the woman shares it.

Lampito: Maybe, but what about persuading everyone else? How are we to cure folk of their warlike frenzy?

Lysistrata: Ah! but we have seen to that; this very day the Acropolis will be in our hands. While we speak, our older sisters, are, even now, going, under pretence of offering sacrifice, to seize the citadel.

Lampito: This is clever!

Lysistrata: Come, quick, Lampito, and let us bind ourselves by an inviolable oath. Let us sacrifice a sheep!

Calonicé: No, Lysistrata, that is not right. Let's take a white horse, and sacrifice it, and swear on its entrails.

Lysistrata: But where get a white horse from?

Lysistrata: Listen to me. Let's sacrifice a skin of Thasian wine into it.

Lampito: Ah! that oath pleases me more than I can say.

Lysistrata: Let them bring me a bowl and a skin of wine.

Calonicé: Ah! my dears, what a noble big bowl! 'Twill be fun to empty that!

Lysistrata: Set the bowl down on the ground, and lay your hands on the victim... Almighty goddess, Persuasion, and thou, bowl, boon comrade of joy and merriment, receive this our sacrifice, and be propitious to us poor women!

Calonicé: Oh! the fine red blood! how well it flows!

Lampito: A splendid bouquet!

Lysistrata: Come, then, Lampito, and all of you, - I will have naught to do with lover or husband...

Calonicé: I will have naught to do with lover or husband...

Lysistrata: Albeit he come to me with strength and passion...

Calonicé: Albeit he come to me with strength and passion... Oh! Lysistrata, I cannot bear it!

Lysistrata: I will live at home in perfect chastity...

Calonicé: I will live at home in perfect chastity...

Lysistrata: And if I keep my oath, may I be suffered to drink of this wine.

Calonicé: And if I keep my oath, may I be suffered to drink of this wine.

Lysistrata: Will ye all take this oath?

All: Yes, yes!

Lysistrata: Then lo! I'll now consume this remnant. (She drinks.)

Calonicé: Yes, yes, by Aphrodité; let us keep up our old-time repute for obstinacy and spite.

Before the gates of the Acropolis

Chorus of Old Men: Forward men, as needs must. Ah! Come, all, let us lay our faggots about the citadel, and on the blazing pile burn these vile conspiratresses, one and all - and that Lysistrata, first and foremost! Come, by, Demeter, they will not laugh at me! Phew! phew! (blows the fire.) Oh! dear! what a dreadful smoke! It bites my eyes like a mad dog.

Chorus of Women: Oh! my dears, methinks I see fire and smoke; can it be a conflagration? Let's pick up our water-jars, for We are going to put out your fire.

Chorus of Old Men: Put out my fire - you!

Chorus of Women: Water, do your office! (The women pitch the water in their water-pots over the old men.)

Chorus of Old Men: Oh, dear! oh, dear! oh, dear!

Magistrate: These women, have they made din enough, I wonder, with their tambourines?

Chorus of Old Men: But you don't know all their effrontery yet! They abused and insulted us; then soused us with the water in their water-pots, and have set us wringing out our clothes, for all the world as if we had bepissed ourselves.

Magistrate: And 'tis well done too, by Posidon! We men must share the blame of their ill conduct; it is we who teach them to love riot and dissoluteness. We give them jemelery and shoes. I only came here to raise money for the navy, and what happens? Those women clap the door in my face. Ho! there, my fine fellow! (addressing one of his officers) what are you gaping at the crows about? looking for a tavern, I suppose, eh? Come, crowbars here, and force open the gates.

Lysistrata: No need to force the gates, here I am.

Magistrate: (to the officer) Seize her!

First Woman: By Pandrosos! if you lay a hand on her, I'll trample you underfoot till you spill your guts!

Magistrate: What do you mean? Officer, where are you got to? Lay hold of her.

Lysistrata: Forward, my gallant companions; march forth, ye vendors of grain and eggs, garlic and vegetables, keepers of taverns and bakeries, wrench and strike and tear; come, a torrent of invective and insult! (They beat the officers.) Enough, enough!

Magistrate: Here's a fine exploit for my officers!

Lysistrata: Ah, ha! You did not know the ardour that fills the bosom of free-born dames.

Chorus of Old Men: Sir, sir! what use of words? they are of no avail with wild beasts of this sort. Don't you know how they have just washed us down - and with no very fragrant soap!

Magistrate: (addressing the women) I would ask you first why ye have barred our gates.

Lysistrata: To seize the treasury.

Magistrate: What do you propose to do then, pray?

Lysistrata: You ask me that! Why, we propose to administer the treasury ourselves.

Magistrate: You do?

Lysistrata: Do we not administer the budget of household expenses?

Magistrate: But that is not the same thing.

Lysistrata: How so - not the same thing?

Magistrate: The treasury supplies the expenses of war.

Lysistrata: That's our first principle - no war!

Magistrate: Stop your croaking, old crow, you!

Lysistrata: Too long we have endured in modest silence all you men did, with the usual, "Just weave your web; else your cheeks will smart for hours. War is men's business!"

Magistrate: Bravo! well said indeed! May I die a thousand deaths ere I obey one who wears a veil!

Lysistrata: If that's all that troubles you, here, take my veil, wrap it round your head, and hold your tongue. Then take this basket; put on a girdle, card wool, munch beans. The War shall be women's business.

Chorus of Women: Lay aside your water-pots, we will help our friends.

Lysistrata: If only we may stir amorous feelings among the men that they stand as firm as sticks, we shall indeed deserve the name of peace-makers among the Greeks.

Magistrate: And how, pray, would you propose to restore peace and order in all the countries of Greece?

Lysistrata: 'Tis the easiest thing in the world! When we are winding thread, and it is tangled, we pass the spool across and through the skein, now this way, now that way; even so, to finish off the War, we shall send embassies hither and thither and everywhere, to disentangle matters.

Magistrate: And 'tis with your yarn you think to appease so many bitter enmities, you silly women?

Lysistrata: If only you had common sense, you would always do in politics the same as we do with our yarn.

Magistrate: Come, how is that, eh?

Lysistrata: We wash the yarn to separate the grease and filth; do the same with all bad citizens, sort them out and drive them forth with rods.

Magistrate: Enough said!

Lysistrata: Say no more, but what afflicts me is to see our girls growing old in lonely grief.

Magistrate: Don't the men grow old too?

Lysistrata: That is not the same thing. When the soldier returns from the wars, even though he has white hair, he very soon finds a young wife. But a woman has only one summer; if she does not make hay while the sun shines, no one will afterwards have anything to say to her, and she

spends her days consulting oracles that never send her a husband.

Magistrate: But the old man who can still do it...

Lysistrata: Go buy yourself a bier, and I will knead you a honey-cake for Cerberus[1]. Here, take this garland. (Drenching him with water.)

First Woman: And this one too. (Drenching him)

Second Woman: And these fillets. (Drenching him.)

Magistrate: To treat me so scurvily! What an insult! I will go show myself to my fellow-magistrates!

Chorus of Old Men: Awake, friends of freedom; let us hold ourselves aye ready to act. Is this not the beginning of Tyranny?

Chorus of Women: What matters that I was born a woman, if I can cure your misfortunes? I pay my share of tolls and taxes, by giving men to the State. But you, you miserable greybeards, you contribute nothing to the public charges; on the contrary, you have wasted the treasure of our forefathers, as it was called, the treasure amassed in the days of the Persian Wars[2]. Have you one word to say for yourselves? Ah! don't irritate me, you there, or I'll lay my slipper across your jaws; and it's pretty heavy.

Chorus of Old Men: Outrage upon outrage! Let us punish the minxes, every one of us that has a shaft to boast of. Come, off with our tunics, let us strip naked, and, if they wish to be knights, let's give them a good ride!

Chorus of Women: By the blessed goddesses, just you dare to measure strength with me, old greybeard, and I warrant you you'll never eat garlic or black beans more.

Several days later, inside the citadel.

Chorus of Women: You, Lysistrata, you who are leader of our glorious enterprise, why do I see you coming towards me with so gloomy an air?

Lysistrata: 'Tis the behaviour of these naughty women, 'tis the female heart and female weakness so discourages me. I cannot stop them any longer from lusting after the men. They are all for deserting. The first I caught was slipping out by the postern gate near the cave of Pan; another was letting herself down by a rope and pulley. One and all, they are inventing excuses to be off home. Look! there goes one, trying to get out! Halloa there! whither away so fast?

First Woman: I want to go home; I have some Miletus wool in the house, which is getting all eaten up by the worms.

Lysistrata: Bah! you and your worms! go back, I say!

Second Woman: Unhappy woman that I am! I've left some flax at home unstript! I will come straight back.

Lysistrata: You shall do nothing of the kind!

Third Woman: I am going to have a child - now, this minute.

---

1   **Cerberus:** see p112
2   **Persian Wars:** see p46

Lysistrata: But you were not pregnant yesterday!

Third Woman: Well, I am to-day. Oh! let me go in search of the midwife, Lysistrata, quick, quick!

Lysistrata: A fable!

Fourth Woman: I cannot sleep any more in the Acropolis, now I have seen the snake that guards the Temple. Ah! and those confounded owls with their dismal hooting! I cannot get a wink of rest, and I'm just dying of fatigue.

Lysistrata: You wicked women, have done with your falsehoods! You want your husbands, that's plain enough. But hold out, my dears, hold out! A little more patience, and the victory will be ours. An oracle promises us success, if only we remain united. Shall I repeat the words?

First Woman: Yes, tell us what the Oracle declares.

Lysistrata: Silence then! Now - "When as the swallows, fleeing before the hoopoes, shall have all flocked together in one place, and shall refrain them from all amorous commerce, then will be the end of all the ills of life; yea, and Zeus, which doth thunder in the skies, shall set above what was erst below...."

Chorus of Women: What! shall the men be underneath?

Chorus of Old Men: I want to tell you a fable they used to relate to me when I was a little boy. This is it...

Lysistrata: A man! a man! I see him approaching all afire with the flames of love.

Myrrhiné: It's my husband Cinesias.

Lysistrata: Ah! good day, my dear friend. Your name is not unknown amongst us. Your wife has it forever on her lips; and she never touches an egg or an apple without saying: "'Twill be for Cinesias."

Cinesias: Oh! I beseech you, go and call her to me! Myrrhiné, my little darling Myrrhiné! Come down to me quick.

Myrrhiné: No indeed, not I.

Cinesias: Oh! Myrrhiné, in our child's name, hear me; at any rate hear the child! Little lad, call your mother.

Child: Mammy, mammy, mammy!

Cinesias: There, listen! Don't you pity the poor child? It's six days now since he was washed and fed.

Myrrhiné: Poor darling, your father takes mighty little care of you!

Cinesias: Everything is going to rack and ruin in the house. Oh! won't you come back home?

Myrrhiné: No, at least, not till a sound Treaty puts an end to the War.

Cinesias: Well, if you wish it so much, it will be done.

Myrrhiné: Well and good! When that's done, I will come home. Till then, I am bound by an oath.

Cinesias: At any rate, let's have a short time together. In the cave of Pan; nothing could be better.

Myrrhiné: But how shall I purify myself, before going back into the citadel?

Cinesias: Nothing easier! you can wash at the Clepsydra.

Myrrhiné: (coming back with a bed) Come, get to bed quick; I am going to undress.

Cinesias: Ah! great Zeus, may she soon be done!

Myrrhiné: (coming back with a flask of perfume) Hold out your hand; now rub it in.

Cinesias: Oh! in Apollo's name, I don't much like the smell of it; but perhaps 'twill improve when it's well rubbed in.

Myrrhiné: There, what a scatterbrain I am; if I have not brought Rhodian perfumes!

Myrrhiné: (coming back with another flask) Here, take this bottle.

Cinesias: Come, you provoking creature, to bed with you, and don't bring another thing.

Myrrhiné: Coming, coming; I'm just slipping off my shoes. Dear boy, will you vote for peace?

Cinesias: I'll think about it. (Myrrhiné runs away.) I'm a dead man, she is killing me! She has gone, and left me in torment!

Chorus of Old Men: Poor, miserable wretch, baulked in your amorousness!

Cinesias: Ye gods in heaven, what pains I suffer!

Herald: Say, where shall I find the Senate and the Prytanes? I am a herald, come from Sparta about making peace.

Magistrate: But look, you are hiding a lance under your clothes, surely.

Herald: No, nothing of the sort.

Magistrate: Then why do you turn away like that, and hold your cloak out from your body? Have you gotten swellings in the groin with your journey?

Herald: No, but the Spartan women have kicked the men all access to them.

Magistrate: But whatever do you do?

Herald: We are at our wits' end; we walk bent double, just as if we were carrying lanterns in a wind. The jades have sworn we shall not so much as touch them till we have all agreed to conclude peace.

Magistrate: Ha, ha! So I see now, 'tis a general conspiracy embracing all Greece. Go you back to Sparta and bid them send Envoys to treat for peace.

Herald: What could be better? I fly at your command.

Chorus of Old Men: No wild beast is there, no flame of fire, more fierce and untamable than woman; the leopard is less savage and shameless.

Chorus of Women: And yet you dare to make war upon me, wretch, when you might have me for your most faithful friend and ally.

Chorus of Old Men: Never, never can my hatred cease towards women.

Chorus of Women: Well, please yourself. Still I cannot bear to leave you all naked as you are; folks would laugh at you. Come, I am going to put this tunic on you.

Chorus of Old Men: You are right, upon my word! it was only in my confounded fit of rage I took it off. Ah! here come the Envoys from Sparta with their long flowing beards; why, you would think they wore a cage between their thighs. (Enter the Lacedaemonian Envoys.) Hail to you, Laconians; tell us how you fare.

A Laconian: No need for many words; you can see what a state we are in.

An Athenian: Can anybody tell us where Lysistrata is? Surely she will have some compassion on our condition. Lo! the foremost men in Hellas, seduced by your fascinations, are agreed to entrust you with the task of ending their quarrels.

Lysistrata: 'Twill be an easy task - if only they refrain from mutual indulgence in masculine love; if they do, I shall know the fact at once. Now, where is the gentle goddess Peace? You Athenians, you Laconians, approach! At Olympia, and Thermopylae, and Delphi, and a score of other places, you celebrate before the same altars; yet you go cutting each other's throats, when all the while the Barbarian is yonder threatening you!

Laconian: Look upon the goddess of Peace! I have never see a woman of more gracious dignity.

Athenian: I have never seen a woman with a finer body!

A Laconian: My dear, sweet friend, come, take your flute in hand; I would fain dance and sing my best in honour of the Athenians and our noble selves.

An Athenian: Yes, take your flute, i' the gods' name. What a delight to dance!

Lysistrata: All is for the best; and now, Laconians, take your wives away home with you, and you, Athenians, yours. May husband live happily with wife, and wife with husband. Dance, dance, to celebrate our bliss, and let us be heedful to avoid like mistakes for the future.

The Republic
(*ΠΟΛΙΤΕΊΑ*)
by Plato of Athens
(Greece, c355BCE)

Socrates, the belligerent street-corner philosopher of the city of Athens, refused to write anything down, so that it was left to his pupil Plato to record his many discussions, of which *The Republic* is one. While its conclusions may seem, with two-and-a-half thousand years of hindsight, either silly or dangerous, the step-by-step ('dialectic') process of searching for answers which are thought to be waiting for us 'out there' is considered to be the foundation of the *Western* way of thinking, in contrast to the harmonious certainties of the *East* (see p42).

Based on the 1871 translation by Benjamin Jowett. Abridged: GH. Numbers in [SQUARE] brackets are page numbers of the 1578 Stephanus edition, commonly used as a reference.

---

[327] YESTERDAY I went down with my friends to the harbour at Piraeus to see the festival of the Goddess. It was the first time it has been held here in Athens, the processions really were wonderful, especially the new type of race where runners passed batons to each other.

Afterwards we went to Polemarchus' house and found his old father Cephalus, garlanded as if for a glorification, who said to me, "You don't visit us as often as you should, Socrates. I may be too old for physical pleasures, but I enjoy intelligent conversation all the more." "Actually," I said, "I enjoy talking to old men, for you have already trod the long road. Tell me, is old age a difficult time of life, or not?"

"You know, Socrates, when we old men get together, most of them just grumble. They complain that they don't make love or go to parties, and that their families don't respect them. But I remember someone asking the old poet Sophocles whether he still enjoyed sex, he replied that he was glad to have left that frenzy behind him. A good reply I thought, for it is not age that matters but character. For a sensible, good-tempered man, old age is easy- otherwise youth as well as age is a burden."

[330] "I am afraid," I said, "that people will say you are content because you are rich."

"Riches won't make a bad man happy, though wealth has its uses. It makes it easier to avoid cheating and lying, or the fear that one has left some sacrifice to God or debt to man unpaid.

"But surely, goodness is more than just..."

"You can continue this discussion with Polemarchus, I must go to the sacrifice."

"Well then Polemarchus," said I, "what do you think it is to do right."

"Simonides the poet says 'to give every man his due', so I think goodness, or justice, is helping your friends and harming your enemies."

"Tell me, if we harm a horse or a dog, do we make the creature better or worse?"

"Worse, certainly."

"So that cannot be justice?"

[337] Eventually Thrasymachus exploded at us; "Childish nonsense Socrates! Justice, or 'right', is nothing more nor less than what is in the interest of those in power. What our rulers call 'justice' is simply making a profit from the people. Who comes off best in business? Always the unjust man, and he'll pay less tax too."

"But don't we agree," I said, "that justice is an excellence of the mind, and injustice a defect?"

"I admit that."

"Then, my blessed Thrasymachus, injustice can never be more profitable than justice."

Glaucon did not seem satisfied. "Men make laws to protect themselves from each other, and they call these laws 'right'. Imagine how a man would behave with no laws to restrain him. You know the story of the Lydian shepherd who found a magic ring which made him invisible?"

"Yes."

[361] "Could anyone have the iron will to resist using the ring to take whatever he wanted? I think not, no man is just of his own will, but only from fear of the law. The unjust man, if he is skilled, will always appear to be in the right, while what will happen to the just man? He'll end up being blamed for others crimes, and like as not end up being scourged and crucified. What we need from you, Socrates, is a proof that justice is better than injustice, irrespective of what Gods or men may think.

I was delighted, "How can I refuse? But we are short-sighted creatures, perhaps we might easier see the answer in a bigger thing, like a whole community."

"I dare say."

"So, let us invent a community. Society originates because individuals can't supply all their own needs. We need food and clothing and shelter, so, at least, we need a farmer, a weaver and a builder. And should each work at just one job, or should they split the work between them?"

"Stick to one specialised skill, they'll be better at it."

"We'll need more citizens then, and we'll need imports, so ships and sailors and merchants. And retailers, labourers, a market and a currency. Will that do? They'll produce wheat and barley, wine, clothes, shoes and houses. They will serve fine cakes on leaves and relax on beds of myrtle."

"No luxuries?"

"I forgot; they'll have cheese and figs, and nuts to roast by the fire."

[373] "Really!" said Glaucon, "that might do for pigs; we need things like furniture, sweets and prostitutes."

"That'll need more people; painters, musicians, seamstresses and such. And that'll mean more land, and trying to get it from our neighbours will mean war, so we'll need an army."

"Can't the citizens fight for themselves?"

"Haven't we already agreed that people work best if they stick to one trade? The Guardians of our city must be professionals."

"They'll need to be like well-bred dogs; strong, courageous and high-spirited."

"But Glaucon," I said "Won't that make them aggressive? Don't you think that they also need the spirit of a philosopher?"

"What?"

"A dog knows friend from foe by using knowledge, and is not philosophy the love of knowledge?"

"So we must give our Guardians a philosophical spirit."

"Quite so, and that means we must educate them, beginning when they are very young and every impression makes its mark."

"How?"

[380] "We'll persuade their mothers and nurses to tell them stories. But none of those traditional tales that portray Gods and heroes as dishonest. God must always be represented as perfect in goodness and beauty, so that our Guardians can grow up pious and honest. And we absolutely can't permit them to take part in any plays and readings other than those which present good and noble people. We'll only allow brave and noble music: Lydian music is too miserable, even for women. Then, with simple arts we will get honest, natural, beauty and goodness in character.

[403] "Certainly. But such keen understanding of beauty, Socrates, leads to sexual desire, with all its madness."

"So it does. We will make a law that a man may embrace and kiss his boyfriend, but no more."

"I agree."

"Physical education is next, which begins with diet. No drunkenness, of course, and every athlete knows to abstain from spices, so no rich Syracusan cooking. And definitely no Corinthian girlfriends. Elaborate food causes disease, just as elaborate music causes indiscipline. And indiscipline and disease lead to law-courts and surgeries."

"It is bound to happen."

"And when people start to need lawyers and doctors, we have conclusive proof that the education system is worthless. Men in the courts before snoozing juries, trying to get remedies by legal trickery, is a proof positive that they don't have enough education to arrange their own lives properly. Just as disgraceful is going to the doctor, not with any real malady, but because they've filled their bodies with garbage, which the pompous medical profession manages to name as some new-fangled disease."

"I agree."

[411] "So? What next?" I said, "We must decide who among the Guardians is to govern our State. They'll need to be intelligent, capable and willing to devote their lives to the interests of the community. And we'll have to make sure that their high principles can't be spirited away."

"What do you mean by that?"

[414] "If we want to see if a colt is nervous, we expose him to alarming noises. We must do the same with our young Guardians; expose them to pleasure and fear, testing them like gold is tested in the furnace. That is how we will choose which is to be a ruler and which ruled. We'd have to convince the whole community that it was in their interests to be ruled of course. I wonder if we could contrive some sort of 'glorious myth'?"

"What sort of myth."

[415] "We shall tell our citizens this tale; Ye citizens are brothers all, but God fashioned gold to some, silver to others, iron, and bronze to the rest. The Rulers have gold; the Auxiliaries silver, farmers and artisans have iron and bronze. This is as nature has ordered, for prophecy tells that when men of iron or bronze guard the State, it will be destroyed. That is the story. Do you think they will believe it?"

"Not in the first generation," he said, "but the next may."

"That will do, even a rumour can inspire people. But, let us return to earth. Our Guardians will have no private property. They will eat together, and their houses will be open to all. We'll tell them that they have no need of earthly gold or silver because they have gold in their hearts."

"I think not, Socrates." Said Adeimantus; "They're hardly going to be happy, living like that."

[421] "Yes." I replied. "They won't be able to afford holidays abroad or fancy women. But I am trying to promote the happiness of the whole community. You know, wealth makes men careless; poverty makes them slovenly."

"I agree," he replied, "but how will a community with no wealth fight a war if they need to?"

"Adeimantus," I said, "don't you think our well-trained soldiers will be a match for any number of podgy conscripts?" But there is one further matter."

"What is that?"

"How we should order our places of worship, our rites for the dead and our prayers to the powers of the otherworld, that is something we can leave to tradition. So, with that, Adeimantus, I think we have a city founded for you, and I think you will see that it surely must contain the four virtues of wisdom, courage, self-discipline and justice. The Guardians will have wisdom, so even if they are the smallest class, their rule will make the whole State wise. Courage will come because they will have knowledge of what is worth fearing. Self-discipline, or 'mastering yourself', as people say, is a bit of a puzzle as if you are master of yourself, then, presumably, you must also be subject to yourself, which is ridiculous. I think what is meant is that there is good and bad in everyone and the good part should control of the bad, so in our State the mean desires of children, slaves, women and the lower

classes will be controlled by the wisdom of the superior rulers."

"So where is justice hiding?"

[432] "Oh, our quarry is right in front of us. Justice is keeping what is properly one's own, and didn't we agree that in our State each person was to stick to their own job?"

"True."

[435] "And just as our State had populace, auxiliaries and rulers working in harmony, doesn't it begin to look as if the mind has three similar elements; desire, reason, and spirit."

"I think so."

"Good." I said. "And can we agree that injustice is like war between the parts of the mind, a sort of disease?"

"So our citizens must all work together."

"Absolutely. And that means something I dare hardly mention."

Glaucon laughed. "We absolve you, do go on."

[452] "I am going to suggest that we educate and train women the same as men, even as soldiers. Does that seem ridiculous?

"People would think it absurd."

"This is not a joke. Women bear children, of course, and are generally better at cooking and weaving, but don't some men cook and weave? The sort of skills needed for administering a State are found as often in women as in men. Just as the Guardians will be the best citizens, the women Guardians will be the best women. Even if we might have to give women lighter duties, they can still play a full part."

"A singular idea!"

"Wait until you hear the next one! As the Guardians, men and women, are allowed them to mix freely, what will happen?"

"Sex- it is a bigger inspiration than any logic."

[459] "Now, Glaucon, I know that you keep pet dogs and birds. How do you breed from them?"

"Are you going to suggest that we breed people just as I breed dogs, by selecting the finest to mate?"

"Indeed. We need a real pedigree herd of Guardians, so we will have an annual festival to bring our brides and grooms together. There will be ceremonies and songs and a cunning lottery, fixed by the Rulers, to decide who is fit to mate. In this way, the inferior Guardians will blame the lottery instead of the Rulers. The children can be taken away to be educated, and any inferior, or deformed, ones can be quietly disposed of. They'll have to be in the prime of life to breed, say from twenty-five to fifty-five for men and twenty to forty for woman. Past those ages they can have sex with whoever they want, unless they're closely related, but they had better take precautions to avoid children."

"But they won't know who they are related to."

"They should be able to work it out from their ages, or something. Our State will have no 'yours' and 'mine'. It will have rulers and subjects, not as master and slave, but like brothers. There will be no reason for anyone to think of their own success or failure, only that of the State. And, most of all, everyone will feel they are one family because they have wives and children in common. Any little arguments can be settled with fists, there and then."

"Good. It will help our men keep fit."

"Children will go, carefully protected, to watch battles, so that they'll learn about warfare, and their parents will fight all the harder."

[468] "What about the actual fighting?"

"War should be conducted decently; no stripping of corpses, no burning of houses, our enemies should be treated with respect and no Greek should ever be taken into slavery. Any soldier who deserts should be demoted, but the brave should be honoured with feasts and crowns, and, you may not agree with this, given something extra."

"What?"

"Be allowed to kiss whichever boy or girl they fancy- that would encourage bravery! Those who die in battle will, we will say, become holy spirits to guard the earth, but we won't dirty our temples by dedicating weapons in them."

"This is all fine, Socrates," said Glaucon, "but you still haven't shown that such a State would be possible in practice."

[472] "We've been painting a word-picture of an ideal state. Is our portrait any the worse if that state can't be found? Until philosophers are kings, or the kings and princes of this world have the spirit and power of philosophy, and political greatness and wisdom meet in one, cities will never have rest from their evils, nor humanity itself I believe. Only then will this our State have a possibility of life and behold the light of day."

"Explain."

"Some people are naturally fitted for philosophy and leadership. Let me explain. If a man loves something, he must feel affection for all of it, not love one part to the exclusion of the rest."

"I'm not quite with you."

"Really Glaucon!" I said, "Whenever you fancy a pretty boy you call a small nose charming and a big one noble, a dark complexion manly and a fair one divine. You always manage to find beauty in the whole."

"Its true."

"So, the Philosopher's passion is for wisdom of every kind- he's ready to learn and never satisfied. If philosophers understand the eternal and immutable, while non-philosophers are lost in multiplicity and change, which of the two should be Guardians of the State, able to guard its laws and customs?"

[485] "It would be absurd not to choose the philosophers. But what other characteristics should he have?"

"Truthfulness. And hatred of untruth. Is there anything closer to wisdom than truth? And if a man has greatness of mind and breadth of vision to contemplate all reality, can he regard human life as anything of any great consequence?"

"No."

"So he won't think death anything to be afraid of."

"No."

Adeimantus interrupted, "Socrates! Your arguments are like a game of draughts where the expert hems in the ordinary player. You know that people who study philosophy too long become both weird and useless to society."

[488] "There is some truth in that, but let me give you an illustration. Imagine the master of a ship- larger and stronger than his crewmen, but a bit deaf and short-sighted and no great seaman. The crew quarrel as to who is to control the ship, the factions attack each other and even attack the master. They don't know that there is an art of navigation, they've never learned it and don't even consider it something that can be taught. They don't know that a true navigator must study the seasons, the sky and the winds. So they fight for who should take control, and call the true navigator a useless star gazer. I'm trying to show the attitude of society towards the true philosopher, and you won't be wrong if you compare our politicians with the sailors."

"Yes, I understand."

[492] "There are many influences which destroy the best of natures. Some people say our youngsters are corrupted by learning speech-making from the Sophist lawyers, but isn't it really public opinion which ruins them?

[493] "How."

"Like the person who feeds a wild beast every day and becomes familiar with its noises and actions, those Sophist talkers teach nothing but popular opinion, they learn how to recognise what the crowd like, and they pander to it. They call what annoys the beast 'bad', and what pleases it 'good', but they've no knowledge of the beast's real nature. [496] Abused as it is, philosophy still has a high reputation- so that stunted minds crave it. Like the bald tinker who has got out of prison and come into money. True philosophers survive only if circumstances keep them away from politics and public, like our disabled friend Theages. Perhaps I shouldn't mention it, because it is so odd, but my own saviour is an inner voice[1] that tells me what not to do. And, nowadays philosophy is taught too young. The better way is to learn a little philosophy in youth, then in later life, when they've done with politics and war, they can devote their energies to it. The philosophers eyes should be turned away from the petty quarrels of men, to the realm of fixed realities, where all is order and justice. Like an artist, our philosopher must begin by wiping the slate of human habits and society clean."

---

1   See Cyrano de Bergerac, page 180

"That sounds impossible."

[502] "Difficult, I admit, but if just one individual achieved it in the whole of time, might that not be good enough?"

"So, what is 'good'?"

"Do you really want a blind, halting display from me when you can have nice clear accounts from other people?"

"Now, don't give up Socrates!"

"I shall try, but I fear it is beyond me. But I will tell you, if you like, about something which seems to me to be like a child of the Good."

[507] "Go on..."

"Have you noticed that sight and visible objects need something?"

"What is that?"

"It is light. And which of the heavenly bodies is responsible for that?"

"You mean the sun."

[509] "Yes. The sun is not itself sight, it is the cause of sight. And the sun, you will agree, also causes the process of generation, growth and nourishment, without itself being such a process. Let me sketch out this diagram.

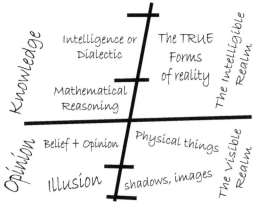

The vertical line divides what we know of from how we know it. In the Visible Realm are the things we can observe, the lowest of which are mere shadows or reflections which we know to be illusions. Physical things we comprehend through belief or opinion. In the higher Realm of the Intelligible, we have knowledge of the true essences, the 'Forms' of reality, which are not built on opinion, but are necessary."

"I see."

[515] "I want to go on to picture the enlightenment or ignorance of the human condition as follows: Imagine an underground chamber in which are prisoners who have been chained since childhood with their legs and necks fastened so that they can only look straight ahead. Behind them is a road along which all sorts of men pass, and behind that a fire so that the prisoners see in front of them the shadows cast by the passers-by and the things they carry. "

"An odd sort of prisoners."

"They are like us. Wouldn't they assume that the shadows were the real thing and that any voices they hear belonged to the shadows?"

"Inevitably."

[516] "Suppose one of them were let loose and was dragged up, probably unwillingly, into the sunlight. He would be so dazzled by the glare that he wouldn't be able to see a thing. But he would grow accustomed to the light and come to see shadows, then reflections, and at last objects themselves and finally the sun. And if he then went back to the cave, wouldn't he be blinded by the darkness? And if he told of what he had seen, wouldn't the other prisoners think him mad?

"They certainly would."

"Now, my dear Glaucon, you won't go wrong if you connect the upper world of sight with the upward progress of the mind into the reason.

"I agree, so far as I can understand you."

"You see, people can be blinded by light as much as by darkness. We must dismiss the idea of some teachers that they can put into the mind knowledge that wasn't already there- as if they could put sight into blind eyes. There could be a better skill- to make the mind turn away from the world of change and look straight at reality, at the brightest of all realities which we call the Good. Isn't that so?"

"Yes."

"Most societies today are shadow battles and struggles for power, as if it were some great prize. The better is quite different; the State is best ruled and most tranquil when leaders come to their duties with least enthusiasm. We ought now to consider how such men should be trained, how they can be led up to the light. And it's not something we can toss an oyster-shell to decide."

[522] "Haven't we already decided on physical training, music and such?"

"Yes, but they'll need the ability to count and calculate. Few people see how it can draw men towards reality."

"By measuring distances?"

"No, you don't understand. Look at my three fingers here. Each one is just a finger. But as soon as we ask 'is it fat or thin' or 'pale or dark' we are confronted by opposites, like soft or hard, light or heavy, and we have to decide between them, and arithmetic is useful there. Not that our students will be concerned with accountancy or commerce, they are above that, but arithmetic will fit them for war."

"That's true."

"The next subject is geometry."

"That is certainly useful in war, for pitching camp and organising manoeuvres."

"True, but that is the mere geometry of everyday life. We are concerned with the squares and other shapes which pure geometry contemplates as perfect and eternal."

"I see."

"The third subject should be astronomy, do you agree?"

"Certainly, knowledge of the seasons is valuable to the farmer, sailor and soldier alike."

[528] "Really, Glaucon! You want to seem practical. How amusing!"

"Even I can see that astronomy makes the mind look upwards."

"You haven't understood. Do you think that staring at the ceiling develops the mind? The beautiful stars are the finest visible things. But they are far inferior to the true reality of the heavens which is found in the mathematics of their motion."

"Explain."

"I'm afraid, Glaucon, that you won't be able to follow. All I can talk about is an image of the truth, not the reality, only dialectic can reveal that- and only to someone already experienced. Dialectic begins by grinding down assumptions to the first basic principles they are founded on. Dialectic is the very coping-stone that tops-off our education system."

"I agree, as far as I can understand you."

[535] "Good. Do you remember the kind of people we picked to rule? We want the bravest, toughest, most honest and, if possible, the best-looking."

"Undoubtedly."

"Arithmetic and other studies can begin in childhood, but we mustn't use compulsion."

"Why not?"

"Compulsory learning never sticks in the mind. Instead, we'll let children learn through play. We'll have compulsory schooling for, say, five years. After that they can be sent down to the Cave to hold some minor public office until they are fifty. Then they will be ready to become full-time philosophers, and, when their turn comes, act, reluctantly, as Rulers."

"They will be fine men indeed."

"And women. Don't forget the women."

"Of course."

"Well, that is our society, with political power in the hands of philosophers."

[544] "That may be our perfect society, but what about the real societies we have now. What of them?"

"There are four types: timarchy, oligarchy, democracy and tyranny. There are hereditary monarchies and other types, but they are all really crosses between these. But, you know, societies aren't made of timber and stone, but out of men whose characters determine the direction of the whole, so we need to look at men as well."

"That would be logical."

"Our ideal state turns into timarchy when the ruling class become disunited, usually when the lower classes begin to crave profit and land and while upper classes urge traditional values. Society becomes envious, greedy, competitive and frightened of having intelligent people in office. The Timarchic man will be harsh to his slaves and crave power, not through intelligent discussion, but by showing might."

"What's next?"

"Oligarchy, where power belongs to those with wealth. And when men get richer, they get less honourable and they keep the populace down by force. Let me ask you, what would happen if we chose the richest man as captain of a ship?"

"We would be shipwrecked."

"Exactly. Worse, the wealthy live on investments, without trade or skill, worthless to their city."

"True."

"Next, I suppose, we have democracy. It rises when oligarchy reduces to poverty men born for better things; they grow angry and crave a revolution. The money makers themselves fuel such desire with poisoned loans and exorbitant interest rates. I suppose many people would think democracy the best of societies, there's no compulsion, so there's a profusion of opinions. But its diversity of ideas is only like a decorated cloak, the sort of thing that women and children crave. But that means that the best aren't forced to rule, so democracies get worthless politicians who just pretend to be the people's friends. The excessive desire for liberty is the downfall of democracies into the most powerful society and man; tyranny and the tyrant."

"How?"

[566] "A leader arises with the mob at his disposal, he brings false accusations and is not afraid of murder, he hints at debts cancelled and land redistributed. He begins a class-war against property owners. If he is exiled, he returns all the stronger. Then he demands bodyguards and uses then to grasp the reigns of state. At first he smiles and makes grand promises. He stirs up war to show that people need a leader, and taxes them to pay for it. He seeks out men of courage and purges his state of them."

"An odd kind of purge."

"True, a doctor gives a purgative to remove poison while the tyrant does the opposite."

"And yet supporters will flock to him."

[569] "Certainly. Then, when the people discover what a beast they've created, he'll be too strong to depose."

"Exactly."

[572] "You know, I think that inside even the best of us have a terrible bestial and lawless side."

"I agree."

"Would you say that the people of a tyrannical state are miserable slaves?"

"Certainly. Only the tyrant himself has any happiness."

"You think so? Consider this; does a wealthy slave-owner live in fear of his slaves?"

"No, because society protects his way of life."

[579] "Now, imagine he was surrounded by neighbours who considered slave-owning a crime."

"He would be in constant fear."

"Exactly the predicament of the tyrant. His life is haunted by fear, he's a source of misery to himself as well as others."

"I see."

[582] "So we can't compare these lives on the amount of pleasure each one gives, for each takes its own pleasure in knowledge, success or gain. We must look to the goodness or badness in them. True pleasure is only known to the true philosopher, who, through reason, knows the highest, but can also see the lowest. Do you know how many times happier a philosopher is?"

"No, tell me."

"There are three types of pleasure, and there are five types of man, from the tyrant to the democrat, to the oligarch, to the timarch to the philosopher-king. So that's 3x3x3x3x3x3, which is 729. The philosopher is 729 times happier than the tyrant. It is quite obvious."

[588] "Obvious to you perhaps."

"The human personality is like a creature in the old stories. A beast with dozens of heads, some wild, some tame, which it can change at will, all wrapped up inside a human's skin."

"So I doubt if our perfect society could ever exist on this earth."

"Perhaps you are right. But perhaps it already exists in some supposed otherworld of the mind. Maybe it is already now there, so that any man with a heart fit for justice can become one of its citizens."

"That may be right."

[595] "You know, I've been brought up to respect writers, especially Homer, but of all the things in our State, I do think the most important might be to reject imitative art."

"Explain."

"You agree that there are many beds and tables, but only one idea, one absolute form, of a bed, or a table. The craftsman follows the form to make a bed, but he can't make the idea itself. Yet an artist can make the mere appearance of a bed, or of anything he wants, and artists and poets listen to advice from no one."

"Apparently not."

"The decent man always hides his emotions, but poets and artists are always representing these unreasonable shows. They appeal to the ignorant multitude, and worse, the poet indulges our lowest desires. They don't realise how these infect our reasoning. Theatre is full of dirty jokes, anger, erotic passion, pleasure and pain, when such things should be allowed to perish."

"I can't deny it."

[607] "So, Glaucon, all the poetry we can allow in our State is hymns of praise to good men. Anyway, we haven't mentioned the greatest prize that awaits a good man."

"It must be something very big."

"Don't you realise, " I asked, "that the soul is immortal and imperishable?"

"Can you really believe that?"

"It is easy to demonstrate. You agree that each thing has its own specific evil which can destroy it, like ophthalmia to the eyes, mildew to grain, rust to iron?"

"True."

"So what is the specific evil of the soul?"

"What we've discussed; injustice, indiscipline, cowardice, ignorance and so on."

"But do they actually destroy the soul?"

"Far from it, wickedness tends to destroy other people and protect the soul that has it."

"So if even its own evil cannot destroy the soul, surely it cannot die, and if souls exist forever, there must always be the same number of them."

"I suppose so."

[613] "You will grant that the Gods see a man's true character."

"Yes."

"So we may assume that a man receives just rewards from the Gods?"

"But what are they?"

[614] "Let me tell you the story of Er of Pamphylia. He was killed in battle, and on the tenth day, on his funeral pyre, he came to life again and told this story of what he'd seen in the other world.

He travelled a strange journey and arrived with many others in great lawn, where two great chasms lead towards the inner earth and the sky, and another two lead back. In the centre sat stern judges who fixed a sign to each arriving soul telling of what it had done in its time on earth before sending it off to the heavens or the inner earth as was its merit.[618] Those who have caused deaths or slavery gain the same treatment themselves, just as those who have been good and just and god-fearing are treated in that way. He did explain what happened to those who died in infancy, but it was not very interesting. After seven days in the meadow, he set out with souls who had served their times below, by the great Spindle of Necessity, where Lachesis of the Fates scattered lots upon the ground, saying "Souls, it is time to choose your life for tomorrow". And the lots were of every kind of life; poverty, riches, exile, tyranny of both men and animals.

This is the moment, my dear Glaucon, when knowledge of good and ill is all. An iron will is needed to choose the honest course.

> The first soul chose the life of a tyrant. He had come from a life in a peaceful state, and did not understand the horrors that awaited him. Er was filled with pity and laughter and wonder to see so many choose evil when they thought it good. Thamyris the singer chose to be a nightingale, Ajax the warrior picked a lion's life. The jester Thersites put on the form of a monkey. Odysseus, remembering his trials, searched for the uneventful life of an ordinary man, and found it lying neglected, and chose it with great joy as the greatest prize of all.[621] Lachesis allotted to each a guardian spirit, and the souls walked to rest by the river of Lethe-the-ever-forgetting. They drank the waters and slept, and as they slept, a great storm arose and each soul, like a shooting star, was swept away to their birth. Er awoke at dawn lying upon his funeral pyre.

So, Glaucon, this tale is preserved, and if we remember it well it will preserve us. If we keep peace with ourselves and the Gods and seek forever wisdom and justice, then, like victors at the Olympiad, we will receive our prize in this life and in our next journey of a thousand years all will be well."

The Ethics
(*ΔΕΟΝΤΟΛΟΓΊΑ*)
known as the Nicomachean Ethics
by Aristotle of Stagira
(Greece, c320BCE)

Aristotle was a pupil of Plato (p55) at the Academy of Athens, the first European university. He wrote more than twenty books, on subjects from politics and logic to animal diseases, with a boldness and certainly which was far removed from the free and open discussions of his mentor. Forgotten in the West, his writings were preserved by Islamic (p92) scholars to be re-discovered by the mediaeval Christian church, who liked his no-disagreement style, and to whom Aristotle became *The Philosopher*.

Based on WD Ross's translation of 1908 and DP Chase's of 1911. Abridged: GH.

Book One

Every art, every enquiry, every pursuit, is thought to aim at some good. Medicine aims at health, shipbuilding, a vessel and economics, wealth. So, will not the knowledge of whatever 'the good' is have great influences on life? Furthermore, men judge best the things they have long experience of, so the young, (whether young in years or youthful in passions), will profit little from what is taught here.

Both philosophers and common men agree that by 'good' we mean happiness. The vulgar, like beasts, identify happiness with pleasure. Superior, refined, people tend to identify it with honour and virtue. We can say that, as a lyre-player plays the lyre, and a good player plays it well, so the function of a good man is noble use of his rational abilities. We must ask if happiness can be learned, or comes from divine providence, or by chance.

Though a man may have many changes of fortune, the best man makes good use of what chance throws at him, though his happiness depends, somewhat, on one's friends. Yet is 'goodness' a thing praised or prized? Things are praised for their relationship to something else; we praise the good man, the good athlete etc. because their actions relate to something we call good. Eudoxus was right to say that pleasure, like god, is not praised but prized.

We can say that happiness is an activity of the soul according to virtue, the student of politics must examine human virtue, for his duty is to perfect it.

Book Two

Intellectual virtue comes largely from learning, while ethical virtues come mainly from habit. We wish to know not what virtue is, but how to practice it.

The soul consists of three things- passions, faculties and character, so virtue must be in one of these. Passions are feelings accompanied by pleasure or pain if they are too little or too great, such as appetite, fear, confidence or joy. We are not called good because of our passions, for we do not choose them, but virtue is by choice. If, then virtue is neither a passion nor a faculty, it must be found with character.

But what state of character is virtue? By the excellence of the eye we see well, by the excellence of a horse it runs well, so the virtue of man is that which makes his work good. The master of any art avoids excess, avoids deficit and seeks the middle, the intermediate. Too much confidence is rashness, too little is cowardliness. Too much liberality is prodigality, too little is meanness. Too much honour is vanity, too little is undue humility. Each is in a sense opposed to the others, as when the brave man seems rash to the coward, and cowardly to the rash man. Even finding the middle of a circle takes skill.

Anyone can get angry, or be generous, but to do so to the right person, to the right extent, at the right time with the right motive in the right way is not easy. Especially, we must guard against pleasure, because pleasure cannot be judged impartially.

Book Three

Only voluntary actions are praised or blamed, while involuntary actions receive pardon or pity. So, we must discuss choice, for it shows up character better than actions do. Both children and animals share voluntary action, as they share appetite and anger, but they cannot be said to make rational choices. Wishes relate to the ends, choice to the means, and opinion precedes them both.

Our virtue is of means, so if it is in our power to act nobly, it is also in our power to do evil. We do not punish ignorance, unless the man is the cause of his own ignorance, as when we double the penalty for crimes committed while drunk, since man has the power not to get drunk. Yet, some men voluntarily make their own ignorance, by being unjust or self-indulgent. Let us consider the several virtues, beginning with courage.

The brave man should always fear disgrace, he who does not is shameless. Poverty and disease we perhaps ought not to fear, for they are not due to man himself. The truly brave man has conquered the greatest fear of all, fear of death. Surely the noblest; death in battle, is indeed honoured by the state.

The brave man is he who nobly faces what he fears for the right reason, in the right manner and at the right time. First is the courage of citizen-soldiers. This is nearest to true courage, for it comes from virtue, desire for honour and fear of disgrace, which is noble. Second, there is Socrates' idea that courage is knowledge. Third, passionate enthusiasm is often thought a form of courage. Fourth, the sanguine man resembles the brave man. Fifth, men who are ignorant of danger appear to be brave, but only by their ignorance. The brave man fears death and wounds, yet still choose the noble deeds of war, for it is not the exercise of virtue, which is pleasant, but its end.

Now, temperance is concerned with bodily pleasures. But we do not call the music-lover, the art-lover or the lover of perfumes intemperate. The grossest pleasures are those of touch and taste, for even dogs enjoy the taste of the hare.

Some desires seem to be universal, such as desire for food and sex. But different people desire different foods and have differing sexual preferences. The temperate man finds the middle position, he desires the right things in moderation.

Self-indulgence is a more voluntary fault than cowardice, for the first is actuated by pleasure, the second by pain. Self-indulgence is childish, and just as the obedient child should live as his tutor directs, so the temperate man should be guided in his passions by his rational intellect.

Book Four

Liberality is concerned with the use of wealth, prodigality is an excess of liberality, while meanness is its deficiency.

A deficiency in magnificence is niggardliness, excess is tasteless vulgarity. Giving grandly requires artistic skill to choose the fitting expenditure that will bring honour without seeming to show-off. To err in magnificence is a vice, if a harmless ones.

Proper pride and self-respect seems a worthy thing. The man who thinks himself worthy of less than his real worth is unduly humble. The man with proper pride has nobility and goodness of character. The vain man, on the other hand, will adorn himself in fancy clothes and expect praise for mere good-luck. The man of undue humility robs himself of what he truly deserves, but cannot be thought bad, only mistaken.

We blame both the ambitious man for seeking honour more than is right, and the unambitious man as not willing to be honoured even for noble reasons. The man who is angry at the right things, with the right people, in the right way, is praiseworthy. If he errs at all, it is to have too little anger at things worthy of anger. Bitter, sulky people, repress their angry passions, making them troublesome to themselves and to their friends.

In daily life, some people obsequiously agree with everyone, while others churlishly oppose everything. Truthfulness is noble, but is only praiseworthy when a man practices it equally regarding tiny things as well as when much is at stake. The mock-modest man seems more attractive. The man who finds the middle state can listen well and talk with cultured wit. Let us now discuss justice.

Book Five

By justice, men generally mean that character that disposes men to act justly, and injustice the opposite. Lawlessness and avarice are thought unjust, so that law-abiding and fairness is thought just. Since avarice is though unjust, so, to some extent, justice is concerned with goods. Justice itself is complete virtue in its fullest sense, and alone of the virtues, is directed towards others.

It is clear that a man who commits adultery from desire is merely licentious, but one who does so for gain is unjust. We see that particular injustices are concerned with gain of money or honour, while universal justice is found in the virtuous conduct. Particular acts of justice are concerned with the division of money or honour, or with rectifying errors of distribution.

Political justice is either natural or legal. The natural is that which is the same everywhere, independent of people's opinions, while laws can differ greatly. If a man seized the hand of another and used it to strike a third man, then the second man would not have acted voluntarily. Mistakes committed in ignorance and from ignorance are pardonable; but those committed in ignorance but through some unnatural passion are inexcusable.

Can a man treat himself unjustly? If a man kills himself, he is acting unjustly. It is towards the State that man owes duty, so if he takes his own life the State properly dishonours him. This completes our analysis of justice.

Book Six

We have already said that one should aim at the mean between deficiency and excess, as right principle dictates. But if you grasped only this, you would have no knowledge of how to apply it. Hence, we must discover what the right principle is.

In the soul three things control actions; sensation, intellect and appetite. Since moral virtue involves choice, and choice is deliberate appetite then, if the choice is to be good, the reasoning behind it must be true and the desire right. The origin of action is choice, and the origin of choice is appetite and purposive reasoning. Judgement and opinion need not be included as they can often err. Science aims at knowledge of the eternal and is supposed to be teachable. Since production is different to action, art is not concerned with action but has an element of chance, as Agathon says: Art loves chance, and chance loves art.

To understand prudence, or practical wisdom, we may consider what type of person we call prudent. A prudent man is able to deliberate rightly, not just about particular things like health, but about the good life generally. Prudence, then, is a virtue, and one which is of the calculative, reasoning part of the soul. But it is not merely a rational state, for such can be forgotten while prudence cannot.

Wisdom seems the most finished form of knowledge. Wisdom is scientific and intuitive knowledge of what is by nature most precious.

Prudence and political science are the same state of mind, but they are realised differently. The man who knows and provides for his own interests is called prudent, but politicians are considered meddling busybodies.

What is called judgement is the faculty of judging correctly what is equitable. And equitable judgement is sympathetic judgement.

What is the use of the intellectual virtues? Wisdom and prudence, being virtues, must be desirable in themselves, even without any result. But the aim can be noble or base, which is why we may call both prudent and unscrupulous people clever. Prudence is not quite the same, for insight cannot lead to prudence without some virtue.

If we have a disposition towards justice or temperance or courage, then we have it from our birth, but moral qualities are acquired.

Book Seven

There are three states of character to be avoided: vice, indiscipline and brutishness. The contrary of vice is virtue and of indiscipline is discipline.

We must consider whether indisciplined people act knowingly or unknowingly- whether the indisciplined man is so because of his circumstances or his attitude. Firstly, for a man to do wrong without reflecting on his own knowledge is very different from acting with that knowledge. Secondly, there are two types of practical knowledge that act as the starting-point to actions. Thirdly, we may assume that indisciplined people are like those asleep, or drunk, or mentally disturbed or in the grip of temper or sexual craving, who speak and act without knowledge. Fourth, even if a man knows both the universal and particular premises his natural desires may sway his scientific judgement.

It is obvious that indiscipline or discipline are concerned with pleasures and pains. Now, certain pleasures, such as food and sex, are necessary, others, like victory or honour or wealth are merely desirable. Also, morbid states, like nail-biting or homosexuality, may come naturally to some people, or may have been acquired by habit, for instance if someone has been sexually misused as a child. Where nature is the cause, we do not blame people as indisciplined. But those congenitally incapable of reason we call brutish, and those troubled by illness we call morbid.

Indiscipline of temper, which is anger, is different to indiscipline of desire, because a bad man can do much more harm than a brute.

The man who pursues excessive pleasures is licentious, because he is unrepentant. On the other hand, the man deficient in the appreciation of pleasures is the opposite of licentious, while the temperate man is between the two.

Some people cling doggedly to their opinion, whom we call obstinate. The opinionated are motivated by pleasure and pain and enjoy a sense of superiority. Thus they resemble the indisciplined. The indisciplined and the licentious man both pursue bodily pleasures, but the first thinks it is wrong while the second does not.

The prudent man is morally good. But simply knowing what is right does not make a man prudent, he must be inclined to actually do it,. The indisciplined man is not so disposed. He is like a State which has good laws, but fails to implement them, while the bad man is like a State that actually does implement its bad laws.

So is pleasure good? Some say that pleasure is not a good because it hinders thinking. Others that some pleasures are disgraceful or harmful, and others that pleasure cannot be the supreme good because it is not an end but a process. This does not prove that pleasure is not a good.

The argument that there must be something better than pleasure because the end is better than the process is not conclusive because pleasures are a species of activity, and therefore an end. Pain is clearly an evil to be avoided. Now, the opposite of pain is pleasure, so it must be good. When Speusippus argued that good is contrary to both pleasure and pain, he cannot be correct, for he refused to allow that pleasure is an evil.

Different people may pursue different pleasures, but it is always pleasure which they pursue. Those who think that some noble pleasures are highly desirable, but bodily pleasures are not, ought to consider why, in that case, the pains which are contrary to them are bad, for the contrary of a bad thing is a good one. The bad man shuns, not just excessive pain, but all pain. Now, pleasure drives out pain. Only God could enjoy one simple pleasure forever.

Book Eight

Friendship is a kind of virtue, or implies virtue. It is necessary for living, for nobody would choose to live without friends. When we are young, friends keep us from mistakes, and later, friendship is the bond that holds communities together. It might help if we could define what an object of affection is. Is it the good that people love, or only what is good for them? It would be absurd for a man to wish for the good of his wine.

There are three kinds of friendship. Some, especially the old or the ambitious, love from utility, to derive benefit from the friendship. Sometimes such people do not even like each other, as with friendship with foreigners. Those who love on the grounds of pleasure are motivated by their own pleasure. Only the friendship of those who are similarly truly good is perfect, but it is rare, as good man are rare.

With friendship for the sake of pleasure, as beauty wanes, so often the friendship wanes too. Pleasure or utility friendship is possible between two bad men, but obviously only good men can be friends for their own sakes.

Friends who spend their time together confer mutual benefit. Friendship arises less readily among sour and elderly people, while young men become friends much more quickly and easily than older men, although the latter may still be well-disposed toward others. However, to have many perfect friends is no more possible than to be in love with many people at once, for love is a kind of excess of friendship.

Another kind of friendship involves superiority, as the affection of father for son, husband for wife or master for servant. In such cases, affection is proportionate to merit; the better person must be loved more than he loves. There is a great gulf in the form of affection between ordinary people and gods or royalty. This raises a problem as to whether friends do actually wish each other the greatest of goods, ie. to be a god, because they will no longer have them as friends.

Most people seem to want to be loved rather than to love. For honour is men's confirmation of their own opinion of themselves. But people enjoy being loved for its own sake, so it may be supposed that being loved is better than being honoured. Friendship seems to consist more in giving than in receiving affection, as we see in the joy that mothers show in loving their children.

There is a similarity between friendship and justice, as is seen in the wider community. There is the friendship of a king for his subjects. In perverted constitutions, where there is nothing in common between ruler and ruled, friendship and justice are rarely found.

Friendship between relatives appears to be derived from parental affection. Parents love their children from the moment of birth, but children only come to understand this later. Hence mothers love their children more than fathers do. This love of children for parents, or of men for the gods, implies a relation to an object superior to oneself. Man is by his nature a pairing rather than a social creature and the family is an older and more necessary thing than the state. Humans cohabit not merely to produce children, but, as the functions of husband and wife are different they supply each other's deficiencies to secure the necessities of life. Children, too, form a bond between parents, which is why childless marriages so often break up.

Quarrels occur most of all in friendships based on usefulness because each is only using the other for his own benefit, but in friendships based on virtue, quarrels are rare because the friends are eager to treat each other well.

Book Nine

In all dissimilar friendships, there is equitable exchange. Quarrels occur when the outcome of the friendship differs from the parties' desires. If both wanted pleasure, all would be satisfactory. But if one wants pleasure, and the other gain, all fails, for it is what a man actually needs that he is anxious to get, and it is only for its sake that he is prepared to give what he has.

When the association was one of utility or pleasure there seems nothing odd in dissolving it if they no longer have the attributes we sought. When a person is mistaken in thinking he has been loved for his character, though his friend has done nothing to suggest it, he has only himself to blame. To remain friends would seem impossible. Perhaps, as often with boyhood friendships, one should show a little more favour to former friends for old time's sake.

Goodwill differs somewhat from either friendship or affection, for we can feel it towards people we do not even know. Does a happy man need friends? Hesiod's principle that "neither let many share thy table, or none" may be true for friends through utility, and a few friends for amusement are enough, like a pinch of seasoning in food. But, with friends of good character, they must also be friends of one another, if they are to live together, and this is difficult if the numbers are large. Do we need friends the more in good times of in bad? Those who are in misfortune need help, while in good times they need companionship. Thus friendship is more needed in adversity, where friends can lighten ones grief. But a resolute man will invite friends to share success, but hesitate to involve them in misfortunes. Everyone wishes to share their pleasures, be it in drinking, playing dice, or going in for athletics or hunting, or philosophy.

So much for friendship.

Book Ten

Next, we must discuss pleasure, for it is very closely bound up with human nature. Now, some philosophers say that pleasure is the Good. Eudoxus thought that pleasure is the ultimate Good. Plato refutes the view that pleasure is the ultimate Good by pointing out that a pleasant life is more desirable with wisdom than without, and that if the mixture is better, pleasure is not The Good, for the good cannot become more desirable by adding anything to it. If only irrational creatures sought pleasure, there might be some truth in the idea that what creatures seek is not a good, but as thinking men are attracted to it also, then plainly those who hold such a view are talking nonsense. Some say that pleasure is not a good as its opposite, evil, can be opposed as well by another evil as by a good. This argument has some merit, but need not concern us here. Others claim that the good and pleasures cannot be the same thing for pleasures vary in degree, which the ultimate good cannot. Again, they claim that pain is a deficiency and pleasure its replenishment. This might be true of food, but the pleasure of, say, learning, is not preceded by any pain. Some people take pleasure in disreputable things, but we may be sure this only applies to people of an unhealthy disposition.

Probably, we cannot feel pleasure continuously because the senses become fatigued, and pleasures of the intellect differ from those of the senses. Those who work with pleasure show better judgement and greater precision. This is clear when we see how activities are hindered by competing pleasures. Since activities differ in goodness, each has a pleasure proper to it. The pleasure proper to a worthy activity is good and that proper to an unworthy activity bad. Further, intellectual pleasures are superior sensual ones. Clearly, disgraceful pleasures are not really pleasures, except to the depraved. But what are the good pleasures of a good man?

Happiness is not a state, but an activity of some sort which is chosen for its own sake and is self-sufficient. If true happiness is an activity in accordance with virtue, it must be in accordance with the highest virtue and with the very best part of man. Life lived with moral virtue is happy in a secondary way, since justice and bravery are purely human concerns. Some hold that people can be good by nature, others that it must be taught. A temperate way of life is not easy for most people, which is why the State should encourage goodness by appealing to finer feelings, and discourage evil by penalties.

Elements of Geometry
(ΣΤΟΙΧΕῖΑ)
by Euclid of Alexandria
(Greece, c300BCE)

This is the most successful textbook of all time. It is not just that Euclid established the system by which we still build and measure, but his method of writing down *rules*, then *propositions* and then *proofs* is the model even now for all the exact sciences.

If you find it difficult to follow, then as Euclid himself said when King Ptolemy asked if there was no easier way of learning, "There is no royal road to geometry".

Book 1 only, on plane geometry, abridged, GH.

Definitions

Definition 1. A point is that which has no size.

Definition 2. A line is a length without any breadth

Definition 3. The ends of a line are points.

Definition 4. A straight line is a line which lies evenly with the points on itself.

Definition 5. A surface is that which has length and breadth only.

Definition 6. The edges of a surface are lines.

Definition 7. A plane surface is a surface which lies evenly with the straight lines on itself.

Definition 8. A plane angle is the inclination to one another of two lines in a plane which meet one another and do not lie in a straight line.

Definition 9. And when the lines containing the angle are straight, the angle is called rectilinear.

Definition 10. When a straight line standing on a straight line makes the adjacent angles equal to one another, each of the equal angles is a right angle, and the straight line standing on the other is called a perpendicular to that on which it stands.

Definition 11. An obtuse angle is an angle greater than a right angle.

Definition 12. An acute angle is an angle less than a right angle.

Definition 13. A boundary is that which is an extremity of anything.

Definition 14. A figure is that which is contained by any boundary or boundaries.

Definition 15. A circle is a plane figure contained by one single line such that all the straight lines radiating towards than line from one single point lying within the figure are equal to one another.

Definition 16. And the point is called the centre of the circle.

Definition 19. Rectilinear figures are those which are contained by straight lines, trilateral figures being those contained by three, quadrilateral those contained by four, and multilateral those contained by more than four straight lines.

Definition 20. Of trilateral figures, an equilateral triangle is that which has its three sides equal, an isosceles triangle that which has two of its sides alone equal, and a scalene triangle that which has its three sides unequal.

Definition 21. Further, of trilateral figures, a right-angled triangle is that which has a right angle, an obtuse-angled triangle that which has an obtuse angle, and an acute-angled triangle that which has its three angles acute.

Definition 22. Of quadrilateral figures, a square is that which is both equilateral and right-angled; an oblong that which is right-angled but not equilateral; a rhombus that which is equilateral but not right-angled; and a rhomboid that which has its opposite sides and angles equal to one another but is neither equilateral nor right-angled. And let quadrilaterals other than these be called trapezia.

Definition 23. Parallel straight lines are straight lines which, being in the same plane and being produced indefinitely in both directions, do not meet one another in either direction.

Postulates

Let the following be postulated, which is to say to be granted as known without need of proof.

Postulate 1. How to draw a straight line from any point to any point.

Postulate 2. How to produce a finite straight line continuously in a straight line.

Postulate 3. How to draw a circle with any centre and radius.

Postulate 4. That all right angles equal one another.

Postulate 5. That, if a straight line falling on two straight lines makes the interior angles on the same side less than

Postulate 5

two right angles, the two straight lines, if produced indefinitely, meet on that side on which the angles are less than two right angles.

Common Notions

Common notion 1. Things which equal the same thing also equal one another.

Common notion 2. If equals are added to equals, then the wholes are equal.

Common notion 3. If equals are subtracted from equals, then the remainders are equal.

Common notion 4. Things which coincide with one another equal one another.

Common notion 5. The whole is greater than the part.

Propositions

Proposition 1. To construct an equilateral triangle on a

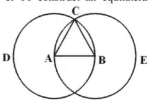

given finite straight line. Let AB be the given finite straight line on which it is required to construct an equilateral triangle. Describe the circle BCD with centre at A and radius AB. Again describe the circle ACE with centre B and radius BA. Join the straight lines CA and CB from the point C at which the circles cut one another to the points A and B. Now, since the point A is the center of the circle CDB, therefore AC equals AB. Again, since the point B is the center of the circle CAE, therefore BC equals BA. But AC was proved equal to AB, therefore each of the straight lines AC and BC equals AB. And things which equal the same thing also equal one another, therefore AC also equals BC. Therefore the three straight lines AC, AB, and BC equal one another. Therefore the triangle ABC is equilateral, and it has been constructed on the given finite straight line AB.

Proposition 9. To bisect or cut a given rectilinear angle precisely in half: Let BAC be the angle it is required to bisect. Take an arbitrary point D on AB. Cut off AE from AC equal to AD, and join DE. Construct the equilateral triangle DEF on DE, and join AF. I say that the angle BAC is bisected by the straight line AF. Since AD equals AE, and AF is common, therefore the two sides AD and AF equal the two sides EA and AF respectively. And the base DF equals the base EF, therefore the angle DAF equals the angle EAF. Therefore the given rectilinear angle BAC is halved by the straight line AF, which is thevery thing which was required.

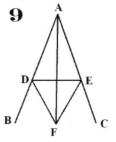

Proposition 10. To cut a straight line in half: Let AB be the given straight line. Construct the equilateral triangle ABC on it, and bisect the angle ACB by the straight line CD. I say that the straight line AB is bisected at the point D.

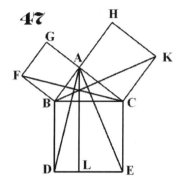

Proposition 47. In right-angled triangles the square on the side opposite the right angle equals the sum of the squares on the sides containing the right angle.

Sovran Maxims
by Epicurus of Samos
(Greece, c300BCE)

Epicurus was born in 341BC on the Greek island of Samos. He studied philosophy under the successors of Plato, and eventually founded his own school and community at the 'garden' in Athens. Epicureanism, a philosophy of refined and calculated pleasure-seeking (in contrast to the rival creed of Stoicism (see p84) with its watchword of 'duty'), flourished for centuries, spawning colonies and followers throughout Europe, only to fade with the coming of Christianity.

This summary, by unknown abridger, was reproduced in Diogenes Laertius' *Lives of the Eminent Philosophers,* 3rd Century AD.

1. A blessed and indestructible being has no trouble himself and brings no trouble upon any other being; so he is free from anger and partiality, for all such things imply weakness.

2. Death is nothing to us; for that which has been dissolved into its elements experiences no sensations, and that which has no sensation is nothing to us.

3. The magnitude of pleasure reaches its limit in the removal of all pain. When such pleasure is present, so long as it is uninterrupted, there is no pain either of body or of mind or of both together.

4. Continuous bodily pain does not last long; instead, pain, if extreme, is present a very short time, and even that degree of pain which slightly exceeds bodily pleasure does not last for many days at once. Diseases of long duration allow an excess of bodily pleasure over pain.

5. It is impossible to live a pleasant life without living wisely and honourably and justly, and it is impossible to live wisely and honourably and justly without living pleasantly. Whenever any one of these is lacking, when, for instance, the man is not able to live wisely, though he lives honourably and justly, it is impossible for him to live a pleasant life.

6. In order to obtain protection from other men, any means for attaining this end is a natural good.

7. Some men want fame and status, thinking that they would thus make themselves secure against other men. If the life of such men really were secure, they have attained a natural good; if, however, it is insecure, they have not attained the end which by nature's own prompting they originally sought.

8. No pleasure is a bad thing in itself, but the things which produce certain pleasures entail disturbances many times greater than the pleasures themselves.

9. If every pleasure had been capable of accumulation, not only over time but also over the entire body or at least over the principal parts of our nature, then pleasures would never differ from one another.

10. If the things that produce the pleasures of profligate men really freed them from fears of the mind concerning celestial and atmospheric phenomena, the fear of death, and the fear of pain; if, further, they taught them to limit their desires, we should never have any fault to find with such persons, for they would then be filled with pleasures from every source and would never have pain of body or mind, which is what is bad.

11. If we had never been troubled by celestial and atmospheric phenomena, nor by fears about death, nor by our ignorance of the limits of pains and desires, we should have had no need of natural science.

12. It is impossible for someone to dispel his fears about the most important matters if he doesn't know the nature of the universe but still gives some credence to myths. So without the study of nature there is no enjoyment of pure pleasure.

13. There is no advantage to obtaining protection from other men so long as we are alarmed by events above or below the earth or in general by whatever happens in the boundless universe.

14. Protection from other men, secured to some extent by the power to expel and by material prosperity, in its purest form comes from a quiet life withdrawn from the multitude.

15. The wealth required by nature is limited and is easy to procure; but the wealth required by vain ideals extends to infinity.

16. Chance seldom interferes with the wise man; his greatest and highest interests have been, are, and will be, directed by reason throughout his whole life.

17. The just man is most free from disturbance, while the unjust is full of the utmost disturbance.

18. Bodily pleasure does not increase when the pain of want has been removed; after that it only admits of variation. The limit of mental pleasure, however, is reached when we reflect on these bodily pleasures and their related emotions, which used to cause the mind the greatest alarms.

19. Unlimited time and limited time afford an equal amount of pleasure, if we measure the limits of that pleasure by reason.

20. The flesh receives as unlimited the limits of pleasure; and to provide it requires unlimited time. But the mind, intellectually grasping what the end and limit of the flesh is, and banishing the terrors of the future, procures a complete and perfect life, and we have no longer any need of unlimited time. Nevertheless the mind does not shun pleasure, and even when death is close, the mind still knows the pleasures of a good life.

21. He who understands the limits of life knows that it is easy to obtain that which removes the pain of want and makes the whole of life complete and perfect. Thus he has no longer any need of things which involve struggle.

22. We must consider both the ultimate end and all clear sensory evidence, to which we refer our opinions; for otherwise everything will be full of uncertainty and confusion.

23. If you fight against all your sensations, you will have no standard to which to refer, and thus no means of judging even those sensations which you claim are false.

24. If you reject absolutely any single sensation without stopping to distinguish between opinion about things awaiting confirmation and that which is already confirmed to be present, whether in sensation or in feelings or in any application of intellect to the presentations, you will confuse the rest of your sensations by your groundless opinion and so you will reject every standard of truth. If in your ideas based upon opinion you hastily affirm as true all that awaits confirmation as well as that which does not, you will not avoid error, as you will be maintaining the entire basis for doubt in every judgement between correct and incorrect opinion.

25. If you do not on every occasion refer each of your actions to the ultimate end prescribed by nature, but instead of this in the act of choice or avoidance turn to some other end, your actions will not be consistent with your theories.

26. All desires that do not lead to pain when they remain unsatisfied are unnecessary, but the desire is easily got rid of, when the thing desired is difficult to obtain or the desires seem likely to produce harm.

27. Of all the means which wisdom acquires to ensure happiness throughout the whole of life, by far the most important is friendship.

28. The same conviction which inspires confidence that nothing we have to fear is eternal or even of long duration, also enables us to see that in this life nothing enhances our security so much as friendship.

29. Of our desires some are natural and necessary, others are natural but not necessary; and others are neither natural nor necessary, but are due to groundless opinion.

30. Those natural desires which entail no pain when unsatisfied, though pursued with an intense effort, are also due to groundless opinion; and it is not because of their own nature they are not got rid of but because of man's groundless opinions.

31. Natural justice is a pledge of reciprocal benefit, to prevent one man from harming or being harmed by another.

32. Those animals which are incapable of making binding agreements with one another not to inflict nor suffer harm are without either justice or injustice; and likewise for those peoples who either could not or would not form binding agreements not to inflict nor suffer harm.

33. There never was such a thing as absolute justice, but only agreements made in mutual dealings among men providing against the infliction or suffering of harm.

34. Injustice is not an evil in itself, but only in consequence of the fear which is associated with the apprehension of being discovered.

35. It is impossible for a man who secretly violates the terms of the agreement not to harm or be harmed to feel confident that he will remain undiscovered, even if he has already escaped ten thousand times; for until his death he is never sure that he will not be detected.

36. In general justice is the same for all, for it is something found mutually beneficial in men's dealings, but in its application to particular places or other circumstances the same thing is not necessarily just for everyone.

37. Among the things held to be just by law, whatever is proved to be of advantage in men's dealings has the stamp of justice, whether or not it be the same for all; but if a man makes a law and it does not prove to be mutually advantageous, then this is no longer just.

And if what is mutually advantageous varies and only for a time corresponds to our concept of justice, nevertheless for that time it is just for those who do not trouble themselves about empty words, but look simply at the facts.

38. Where without any change in circumstances the things held to be just by law are seen not to correspond with the concept of justice in actual practice, such laws are not really just; but wherever the laws have ceased to be advantageous because of a change in circumstances, in that case the laws were for that time just when they were advantageous for the mutual dealings of the citizens, and subsequently ceased to be just when they were no longer advantageous.

39. The man who best knows how to meet external threats makes into one family all the creatures he can; and those he can not, he at any rate does not treat as aliens; and where he finds even this impossible, he avoids all dealings, and, so far as is advantageous, excludes them from his life.

40. Those who possess the power to defend themselves against threats by their neighbours, being thus in possession of the surest guarantee of security, live the most pleasant life with one another; and their enjoyment of the fullest intimacy is such that if one of them dies prematurely, the others do not lament his death as though it called for pity.

On Old Age
by Marcus Tullius Cicero
(Rome, c50BCE)

Marcus Tullius Cicero was a poet, philosopher, humorist, and one of the greatest legal orators Rome ever produced. True to his belief that *res publica* ('the public affair') was a citizen's highest duty, he successfully fought both corruption and the corrupt through the courts. Late in life he led the Senate against the brutality of Antony, and was, not surprisingly, rewarded by being murdered. This essay imagines a conversation between three of Cicero's friends.
Abridged: JH/GH

Concerning Old Age

SCIPIO: I have often admired your consummate wisdom, O Cato. It is shown in many ways, but in none more perfectly than in the singular ease and cheerfulness with which you bear the weight of years.

CATO: There is really nothing to wonder at in that. Those who have no interior source of happiness are afflicted by miseries at every stage of their life; but nothing that is in the course of nature is troublesome to the man who seeks his felicity within himself. It is usual for men to complain, at this season of life, that old age has stolen upon them before they had expected it; but they would feel its burden as heavily if they had hundreds of years in which to prepare it. As for the wisdom of which you speak, if I have any, it is no more than this- that I follow nature as the surest guide, and resign myself, with implicit obedience to all her sacred ordinances.

LAELIUS: Will you not then tell us how we ought to prepare for our declining years? For Scipio and I must grow old, too.

CATO: Willingly. It is certain that the true grievance, when there is one, lies in the man, and not in the age. Those whose desires are properly regulated, and who have nothing morose or petulant in their temper and manners, will find old age a very tolerable state indeed; but unsubdued passions and a forward disposition will embitter this, as they embitter every other stage of life. Therefore cultivate, throughout your life, the virtues; and they will yield an astonishing harvest for your latest years, besides the pleasures of memory.

When I was a lad I conceived a strong affection for Quintus Maximus, the veteran who recovered Tarentum. He had a noble, courteous dignity which age never impaired. You know what splendid service he did in politics and in the field, but I can assure you he appeared even greater in his private life. How rich was his conversation! How profound his knowledge of history! How skilled he was in the laws of augury! Well, it would be simply monstrous to suppose that the old man was not happy. A quiet, upright, cultivated life may also have a serene old age, as was the case of Plato, and again of Isocrates, and of Gorgias, who lived a hundred and seven years, and said, "I have no complaint to bring against old age."

When I consider the various disadvantages which old age is generally supposed to bring with it, I find that they may all be reduced to four general charges. The first is that it incapacitates a man for taking part in the affairs of the world. The second, that it produces bodily infirmities. Thirdly, it disqualifies him for the enjoyment of sensual pleasures. And, lastly, it brings him to the threshold of death. Let us examine these in order.

Old age disqualifies us from taking an active part in affairs. Certainly, in so far as the strength and vivacity of youth are required; but yet there are public services which can be rendered only in advanced life. Was Quintus Maximus idle in old age? Is the pilot useless in the ship because, while the crew are running about and sweating at their tasks, the old man sits quietly at the helm? Why is our supreme council called the senate, or why is the highest magistracy of the Lacedaemonians called the Elders, but because age qualifies a man for public affairs, and not disqualifies him?

You will find many an instance in history of a flourishing community well-nigh ruined by young and impetuous politicians, and then restored by the more sober administration of the aged.

It is often said that old age impairs the memory; and so doubtless it does in those who have not exercised their faculty. I have not found it so, and I never heard of any aged person who forgot where he had concealed his treasure. Mental powers become blunted chiefly when they are disused. Sophocles wrote tragedies in extreme old age, and I could give many similar instances. Among my friends in the country there are several of great age who are so keenly interested in farming that they never let any important operation be carried out without being themselves present to superintend it.

Examples might be given of men who have applied themselves at an advanced period of life to an art or science of which they had no previous knowledge. Solon used to say that he learnt something new every day. Old as I am, it is only lately that I took up the study of Greek, and you will remember that Socrates learned to play the lyre when he was past middle life.

The second complaint is that old age impairs our strength, and this, it must be acknowledged, is true enough. But for my part, I no more regret the vigour of my youth than I regretted then that I had not the strength of a bull or of an elephant. It is enough if we exert with spirit, on every proper occasion, the degree of strength which still remains to us.

It is said that Milo of Croton, watching athletes in the public arena, burst into tears because his muscles were wasted and impotent. The frivolous old man should have deplored the weakness rather of his mind than of his body, and that he had made his reputation by merely animal feats and not by the nobler excellences of man.

It is true that oratorical power is enfeebled by age: yet there is a certain melody of utterance which is not impaired by years. There is a calm and composed delivery that is exceedingly gracious, and I have often seen an eloquent old man captivating an audience. But even when he can no longer speak in public, the aged orator may form young men of genius to a manly eloquence.

After all, however, weakness of body is more often the result of dissipations than of long life. If a man be temperate, the decay of his strength will be gentle and not intolerable. Mine has remained sufficient for my duties in the senate and in public assemblies, and for the service of my friends. I am not as strong as you young men; but neither are you as strong as Pontius the athlete, yet you do not think him a more valuable man on that account. Nature leads us almost insensibly through the different seasons of human life.

Then, too, we must combat the infirmities of old age as we resist the onset of a disease. We have to attend somewhat to our health, take moderate exercise, and be somewhat abstemious; we have to take care not to let our minds fall into sloth, dullness and dotage. Believe me, dotage is not a weakness incidental to old age, but is the nemesis of frivolous days spent in idleness and folly. Age is truly worthy of respect in the man who guards himself from becoming the property of others, vindicates his just rights and maintains his authority to his dying day.

Just as I like to see a young man touched a little with the gravity of age, I am pleased with any youthful quality that I find in the old. That is why I am working at the seventh book of my Origins, revising all my old speeches, and writing a treatise on the augural, pontifical and civil law. To practise my memory, I run over, every evening, all that I have done, said, and heard during the day. I still plead for my friends in the courts, and make mature speeches in the senate. And even if I could not do these things I would lie on my couch at home and meditate on them. Thus the candle burns down to the last flicker and is not prematurely extinguished.

We come to the third disadvantage. Old age is without pleasures. Oh! what an admirable advantage, that we should at length be free from these temptations! I have never forgotten the sayings of the wise Archytas of Tarentum on this point. He said that no more deadly pestilence had been inflicted on man than these physical pleasures; that their insatiable appetite was the source of political treachery and of civil catastrophes; and that there was no crime to which sensual passions do not lead. He said that while reason was the noblest property of man, sensuality was reason's most fatal enemy. He said that there was nothing so detestable as sensuality, because in proportion as it increased it extinguished the light of the soul. If is from these dangers that old age delivers us, and very grateful we ought to be to old age.

But an old man need not be without his convivial pleasures. I have always been a member of clubs, and have enjoyed their festivities rather because of the conversation of my friends than for the pleasure of banqueting. I like to have a few of my neighbours every evening, when I am in the country, and we generally keep up the conversation to a very late hour.

But old men are not, like the young, nervously sensitive to pleasure. Although the spectator in the front row of the stalls enters more keenly into the acting, yet another, sitting away at the back, enjoys it too in his way; and though youth has a closer view of pleasure, old age, more detached from it, gets quite as much pleasure as it desires.

I do not know any part of life that is passed more agreeably than the learned leisure of a virtuous old age. When I think of many learned and studious old men who have carried on their literary and scientific labours through calm and happy years to the very end of life, I wonder that the gaiety of the theatre, the luxury of feasts, or the caresses of a mistress, can be compared for pleasure with these serene delights!

The occupations, of the country, too, are open even to the oldest; they seem to me to be particularly suited to the wise man, and delight me more than I can say. The work of the vineyard, the woodlands, arable ground and pastures, orchards, kitchen garden and flower garden, the feeding of cattle and tending of bees, the operations of grafting, are pleasure enough, for me. There is not a more delightful scene than that of a well-cultivated farm.

But remember, I am praising only that old age which has been built on the foundations of a well-spent life. That is no true old age which deserves not reverence; but where that reverence exists, what bodily advantages can be compared with the rewards which it brings? Those who deserve and attain it seem to me to have consummated the drama of life.

But there remains a fourth reason why men are often filled with anxiety at the approach of old age. Death is coming nearer and nearer.

Quite true; but the man is unhappy indeed who has not learnt in all his many years that there is nothing to be afraid of in death. If it means extinction, it is not worth troubling about; if, on the other hand, it means a transition to immortality, then it is only to be desired.

Again, death is as common to other periods of life as it is to old age, and there is no young man who can promise himself that he shall live until sunset. Again, though the young may only hope for long life, the old have already possessed it, and if long life be an advantage, the advantage is with the old.

But who are we, to speak of long life? A wise and good man will be content with the allotted measure, remembering that an actor may be equally approved though his part runs not to the end of the play; it is enough that he support the character assigned him with dignity. A very short time is quite enough for the purposes of honour and virtue. But as youth is the time of flower, so old age is the harvest of the fruit, the autumnal season which the wise will welcome and not lament.

Every event that is agreeable to nature is a real good, and nothing is more natural than for an old man to die. The fire goes out because the fuel is all burnt away. The aged should reasonably be indifferent to the continuance of their existence, and so attain a fortitude unknown to earlier years. Death is a change which we must undergo, perhaps at this very moment; and we can only secure an undisturbed repose and serenity of mind by heartily accepting it. Youth does not regret the toys of infancy nor manhood the amusements of childhood.

It has its own appropriate interests, and these, too, become in their turn languid and insipid. And when relish of it has wholly gone, then this present life goes, too.

The nearer death comes to me, the more clearly I seem to discern its real nature. I believe that your great fathers have not ceased to live, but that the state which they now enjoy is the only one that can truly be called life. The native seat of the soul is in heaven; confined within this prison of a body she is doomed to a severe penance. But I am persuaded that the gods have thus widely disseminated immortal spirits, and clothed them with human bodies, in order that there may be a race of intelligent creatures to contemplate the host of heaven, and to imitate in their conduct the same beautiful order and harmony.

I cannot believe that our ancestors would have so ardently endeavoured to deserve honourable remembrance if they had not been persuaded that they had a real interest in the verdict of future generations. For my own part, I am transported with impatience to join the society of my departed friends, and to be with other mighty men of the past of whom I have read. To this glorious assembly I am quickly advancing; and if some divinity should offer me my life over again. I would utterly reject the offer. This world is a place which nature never designed for my permanent abode; and I look upon my departure, not as being driven from my home, but as leaving my inn.

The Six Mistakes of Man

1 The delusion that personal gain is made by crushing others.
2 The tendency to worry about things that cannot be changed or corrected.
3 Insisting that a thing is impossible because we cannot accomplish it.
4 Refusing to set aside trivial preferences.
5 Neglecting development and refinement of the mind, and not acquiring the habit of reading and studying.
6 Attempting to compel others to believe and live as we do.

Commentaries on the Gallic Wars
(*Commentarii de Bello Gallico*)
by Julius Caesar
(Rome, c48BCE)

This is the book which helped make Rome into an Empire, and is the source for much of what we know about the Britons and the Celts. It is also the book rammed-into generations of reluctant juvenile Latin-learners which has spawned parodies from Ronald Searle to Asterix.

Gaius Julius was a member of the three-fold 'triumvirate' leadership of the Roman Republic when he began his campaigns against what is now France, Belgium and Britain. As leaders do, he portrayed his invasions as a necessary defensive action, but almost certainly wanted to to advance his own career. He helped the reality along by providing the public with this, somewhat imaginative, tale of Roman, and his own, mightiness - it worked, Julius soon became sole ruler of the Roman *Empire*.

Based on the 1915 translation by by W. A. Macdevitt. Abridged: JH/GH

I: THE WAR IN GAUL

(*Gallia est omnis divisa in partes tres...*)

Gaul is divided into three parts, one of which the Belgæ inhabit; the Aquitani another; those who in their own language are called Celts, in ours Gauls, the third. All these differ from each other in language, customs, and laws. Among the Gauls the Helvetii surpass the rest in valour, as they constantly contend in battle with the Germans. When Messala and Piso were consuls, Orgetorix, the most distinguished of the Helvetii, formed a conspiracy among the nobility, persuading them that, since they excelled all in valour, it would be very easy to acquire the supremacy of the whole of Gaul. They made great preparations for the expedition, but suddenly Orgetorix died, nor was suspicion lacking that he committed suicide.

After his death, the Helvetii nevertheless attempted the exodus from their territories. When it was reported to Caesar that they were attempting to make their route through our province, he gathered as great a force as possible, and by forced marches arrived at Geneva.

The Helvetii now sent ambassadors to Caesar, requesting permission to pass through the province, which he refused, inasmuch as he remembered that Lucius Cassius, the consul, had been slain and his army routed, and made to pass under the yoke by the Helvetii. Disappointed in their hope, the Helvetii attempted to force a passage across the Rhone, but, being resisted by the soldier, desisted.

After the war with the Helvetii was concluded, ambassadors from almost all parts of Gaul assembled to congratulate Caesar, and to declare that his victory had happened no less to the benefit of the land of Gaul than of the Roman people, because the Helvetii had quitted their country with the design of subduing the whole of Gaul.

When the assembly was dismissed, the chiefs' of the Ædui and of the Sequani waited upon Caesar to complain that Ariovistus, the king of the Germans, had seized a third of their land, which was the best in Gaul, and was now ordering them to depart from another third part.

To ambassadors sent by Caesar, demanding an appointment of some spot for a conference, Ariovistus gave an insolent reply, which was repeated on a second overture. Hearing that the king of the Germans was threatening to seize Vesontio, the capital of the Sequani, Caesar, by a forced march, arrived there and took possession of the city. Apprised of this event, Ariovistus changed his attitude, and sent messengers intimating that he agreed to meet Caesar, as they were now nearer to each other, and could meet without danger.

The conference took place, but it led to no successful result, for Ariovistus demanded that the Romans should withdraw from Gaul and his conduct became afterwards so hostile that it led to war. A battle took place about fifty miles from the Rhine. The Germans were routed and fled to the river, across which many escaped, the rest being slain in pursuit. Caesar, having concluded two very important wars in one campaign, conducted his army into winter quarters.

II: THE BELGAE

While Caesar was in winter quarters in Hither Gaul frequent reports were brought to him that all the Belgæ were entering into a confederacy against the Roman people, because they feared that, after all Celtic Gaul was subdued, our army would be led against them. Caesar, alarmed, levied two new legions in Hither Gaul, and proceeded to the territory of the Belgæ. As he arrived there unexpectedly, and sooner than anyone anticipated, the Remi, who are the nearest of the Belgæ to Celtic Gaul, sent messages of submission and gave Caesar full information about the other Belgæ.

Caesar next learned that the Nervii, a savage and very brave people, whose territories bordered those just conquered, had upbraided the rest of the Belgæ who had surrendered themselves to the Roman people, and had declared that they themselves would neither send ambassadors nor accept any condition of peace. He was informed concerning them that they allowed no access of any merchants, and that they suffered no wine and other things tending to luxury to be imported, because they thought that by their use the mind is enervated and the courage impaired.

After he had made three days' march into their territory, Caesar discovered that all the Nervii had stationed themselves on the other side of the River Sambre, not more than ten miles from his camp, and that they had persuaded the Atrebates and the Veromandui to join with them, and that likewise the Aduatuci were expected by them, and were on the march. The Roman army proceeded to encamp in front of the river, on a site sloping towards it. Here they were fiercely attacked by the Nervii, the assault being so sudden that Caesar had to do all things at one time. The standard as the sign to run to arms had to be displayed, the soldiers were to be called from the works on the rampart, the order of battle was to be formed, and a great part of these arrangements was prevented by the shortness of time and the sudden charge of the enemy.

Time was lacking even for putting on helmets and uncovering shields. In such an unfavorable state of affairs, various events of fortune followed. The soldiers of the ninth and tenth legions speedily drove back the Atrebates, who were breathless with running and fatigue. Many of them were slain. In like manner the Veromandui were routed by the eighth and eleventh legions; but as part of the camp was very exposed, the Nervii hastened in a very close body, under Boduagnatus, their leader, to rush against that quarter. Our horsemen and light-armed infantry were by the first assault routed, and the enemy, rushing into our camp in great numbers, pressed hard on the legions. But Caesar, seizing a shield and encouraging the soldiers, many of whose centurions had been slain, ordering them to extend their companies that they might more freely use their swords.

So great a change was soon effected that, though the enemy displayed great courage, the battle was ended so disastrously for them that the Nervii were almost annihilated. Scarcely five hundred were left who could bear arms. Their old men sent ambassadors to Caesar by the consent of all who remained, surrendering themselves. The Aduatuci, before mentioned, who were coming to the help of the Nervii, returned home when they heard of this battle.

All Gaul being now subdued, so high an opinion of this war was spread among the barbarians that ambassadors were sent to Caesar by those nations that dwelt beyond the Rhine, to promise that they would give hostages and execute his commands. He ordered these embassies to return to him at the beginning of the following summer, because he was hastening into Italy and Illyricum. Having led his legions into winter quarters among the Carnutes, the Andes, and the Turones, which states were close to those in which he had waged war, he set out for Italy, and a public thanksgiving of fifteen days was decreed for these achievements, an honour which before that time had been conferred on none.

III: WAR BY LAND AND SEA

When Caesar was setting out for Italy, he sent Servius Galba with the twelfth legion and part of the cavalry against the Nantuates, the Veragri, and the Seduni, who extend from the territories of the Allobroges and the Lake of Geneva and the River Rhone to the top of the Alps. The reason for sending him was that he desired that the pass along the Alps, through which the Roman merchants had been accustomed to travel with great danger, should be opened.

Galba fought several successful battles, stormed some of their forts, and concluded a peace. He then determined to winter in a village of the Veragri, which is called Octodurus. But before the winter camp could be completed the tops of the mountains were seen to be crowded with armed men, and soon these rushed down from all parts and discharged stones and darts on the ramparts.

The fierce battle that followed lasted for more than six hours. During the fight more than a third part of the army of 30,000 men of the Seduni and the Veragri were slain, and the rest were put to flight, panic-stricken. Then Galba, unwilling to tempt fortune again, after having burned all the buildings in that village, hastened to return into the province, urged chiefly by the want of corn and provision. As no enemy opposed his march, he brought his forces safely into the country of the Allobroges, and there wintered.

These things being achieved, Caesar, who was visiting Illyricum to gain a knowledge of that country, had every reason to suppose that Gaul was reduced to a state of tranquillity. For the Belgæ had been overcome, the Germans had been expelled, and the Seduni and the Veragri among the Alps defeated. But a sudden war sprang up in Gaul.

The occasion of that war was this. P. Crassus, a young man, had taken up his winter quarters with the seventh legion among the Andes, who border on the Atlantic Ocean. As corn was scarce, he sent out officers among the neighbouring states for the purpose of procuring supplies. The most considerable of these states was the Veneti, who have a very great number of ships with which they have been accustomed to sail into Britain, and thus they excel the rest of the states in nautical affairs. With them arose the beginning of the revolt.

The Veneti detained Silius and Velanius, who had been sent among them, for they thought they should recover by their means the hostages which they had given Crassus. The neighbouring people, the Essui and the Curiosolitæ, led on by the influence of the Veneti (as the measures of the Gauls are sudden and hasty) detained other officers for the same motive. All the sea-coast being quickly brought over to the sentiments of these states, they sent a common embassy to P. Crassus to say "If he wished to receive back his officers, let him send back to them their hostages."

Caesar, being informed of these things, since he was himself so far distant, ordered ships of war to be built on the River Loire; rowers to be raised from the province; sailors and pilots to be provided. These matters being quickly executed, he hastened to the army as soon as the season of the year admitted.

Caesar at once ordered his army, divided into several detachments, to attack the towns of the enemy in different districts. Many were stormed, yet much of the warfare was vain and much labour was lost, because the Veneti, having numerous ships specially adapted for such a purpose, their keels being flatter than those of our ships, could easily navigate the shallows and estuaries, and thus their flight hither and thither could not be prevented.

At length, in a naval fight, our fleet, being fully assembled, gained a victory so signal that, by that one battle, the war with the Veneti and the whole sea-coast was finished. Caesar thought that severe punishment should be inflicted, in order that for the future the rights of ambassadors should be respected by barbarians; he therefore put to death all their senate, and sold the rest for slaves.

About the same time P. Crassus arrived in Aquitania, which, as was already said, is, both from its extent and its number of population, a third part of Gaul. Here, a few years before, L. Valerius Præconius, the lieutenant, had been killed and his army routed, so that Crassus understood no ordinary care must be used. On his arrival being known, the Sotiates assembled great forces, and the battle that followed was long and vigorously contested. The Sotiates being routed, they retired to their principal stronghold, but it was stormed, and they submitted. Crassus then marched into the territories of the Vocates and the Tarusites, who raised a great host of men to carry on the war, but suffered total defeat, after which the greater part of Aquitania of its own accord surrendered to the Romans, sending hostages of their own accord from different tribes. A few only - and those remote nations - relying on the time of year, neglected to do this.

IV: BRITAIN

The following winter, this being the year in which Cn. Pompey and M. Crassus were consuls, the Germans, called the Usipetes, and likewise the Tenchtheri, with a great number of men, crossed the Rhine, not far from the place at which that river falls into the sea. The motive was to escape from the Suevi, the largest and strongest nation in Germany, by whom they had been for several years harassed and hindered from agricultural pursuits.

The Suevi are said to possess a hundred cantons, from each of which they send forth for war a thousand armed men yearly, the others remaining at home, and going forth in their turn in other years.

Caesar, hearing that various messages had been sent to them by the Gauls (whose fickle disposition he knew) asking them to come forward from the Rhine, and promising them all that they needed, set forward for the army earlier in the year than usual. When he had arrived in the region, he discovered that those things which he had

suspected would occur, had taken place, and that, allured by the hopes held out to them, the Germans were then making excursions to greater distances, and had advanced to the territories of the Euburones and the Condrusi, who are under the protection of the Treviri. After summoning the chiefs of Gaul, Caesar thought proper to pretend ignorance of the things which he had discovered, and, having conciliated and confirmed their minds, and ordered some cavalry to be raised, resolved to make war against the Germans.

When he had advanced some distance, the Germans sent ambassadors, begging him not to advance further, as they had come hither reluctantly, having been expelled from their country. But Caesar, knowing that they wished for delay only to make further secret preparations, refused the overtures. Marshalling his army in three lines, and marching eight miles, he took them by surprise, and the Romans rushed their camp. Many of the enemy were slain, the rest being either scattered or drowned in attempting to escape by crossing the Meuse in the flight.

The conflict with the Germans being finished, Caesar thought it expedient to cross the Rhine. Since the Germans were so easily urged to go into Gaul, he desired they should have fears for their own territories. Therefore, notwithstanding the difficulty of constructing a bridge, owing to the breadth, rapidity, and depth of the river, he devised and built one of timber and of great strength, piles being first driven in on which to erect it.

The army was led over into Germany, advanced some distance, and burnt some villages of the hostile Sigambri, who had concealed themselves in the woods after conveying away all their possessions. Then Caesar, having done enough to strike fear into the Germans and to serve both honour and interest, after a stay of eighteen days across the Rhine, returned into Gaul and cut down the bridge.

During the short part of the summer which remained he resolved to proceed into Britain, because succours had been constantly furnished to the Gauls from that country. He thought it expedient, if he only entered the island, to see into the character of the people, and to gain knowledge of their localities, harbours, and landing-places. Having collected about eighty transport ships, he set sail with two legions in fair weather, and the soldiers were attacked instantly on landing by the cavalry and charioteers of the barbarians. The enemy were vanquished, but could not be pursued, because the Roman horse had not been able to maintain their course at sea and to reach the island. This alone was wanting to Caesar's accustomed success.

V: ON THE THAMES

During the winter Caesar commanded as many ships as possible to be constructed, and the old repaired. About six hundred transports and twenty ships of war were built, and, after settling some disputes in Gaul among the chiefs, Caesar went to Port Itius with the legions. He took with him several of the leading chiefs of the Gauls, determined to retain them as hostages and to keep them with him during his next expedition to Britain, lest a commotion should arise in Gaul during his absence.

Caesar, having crossed to the shore of Britain and disembarked his army at a convenient spot advanced about twelve miles and repelled all attacks of the cavalry and charioteers of the enemy. Then he led his forces into the territories of Cassivellaunus to the River Thames, which river can be forded in one place only. Here an engagement took place which resulted in the flight of the Britons. But Cassivellaunus had sent messengers to the four kings who reigned over Kent and the districts by the sea, Cingetorix, Carvilius, Taximaquilus, and Segonax, commanding them to collect all their forces and assail the naval camp.

In the battle which ensued the Romans were victorious, and when Cassivellaunus heard of this disaster he sent ambassadors to Caesar to treat about a surrender. Caesar, since he had resolved to pass the winter on the continent, on account of sudden revolts in Gaul, demanded hostages and prescribed what tribute Britain should pay each year to the Roman people. Caesar, expecting for many reasons greater commotion in Gaul, levied additional forces. He saw that war was being prepared on all sides, that the Nervii, Aduatuci, and Menapii, with the addition of all the Germans on this side of the Rhine, were under arms; that the Senones did not assemble according to his command, and were concerting measures with Carnutes and the neighbouring states; and that the Germans were importuned by the Treviri in frequent embassies. Therefore he thought that he ought to take prompt measures for the war.

Accordingly, before the winter was ended, he marched with four legions unexpectedly into the territories of the Nervii, captured many men and much cattle, wasted their lands, and forced them to surrender and give hostages. He followed up his success by worsting the Senones, Carnutes, and Menapii, while Labienus defeated the Treviri.

VI: ON THE MANNERS OF MEN

Now it is proper to give an account of the manners of Gaul and Germany.

Throughout all Gaul there are two orders of men who are of rank and dignity, for the commoners are held almost as slaves, one is the Druids, the other the knights. The Druids are engaged in things sacred, conduct the public and the private sacrifices, instruct the young and are held in great honour. They determine respecting almost all controversies, public, private and of crimes, and are under one Druid who possesses supreme authority. This institution is supposed to have been devised in Britain, and those who desire to gain a more accurate knowledge of it generally proceed thither. The Druids do not go to war, and learn by heart a great number of verses, such that some remain in training twenty years. Nor do they regard it lawful to commit these to writing, though in other matters they use Greek characters. That practice they seem to me to have adopted because they do not desire their doctrines to be divulged among the mass of the people.

All the Gauls are extremely devoted to superstitious rites; and employ the Druids as the performers of sacrifices. They think that unless the life of a man be offered for the life of a man, the mind of the immortal gods cannot be rendered propitious. Thus, they have figures of vast size, the limbs of which formed of osiers they fill with living men, which being set on fire, the men perish enveloped in the flames.

They worship as their divinity, Mercury in particular, and Apollo, and Mars, and Jupiter, and Minerva. In many states you may see piles of things heaped up in consecrated spots; nor does any man dare take away those things for the most severe punishment, with torture, has been established for such a deed. All the Gauls assert that they are descended from the god Dis, which tradition has been handed down by the Druids.

Husbands have power of life and death over their wives and their children. Their funerals, considering the state of civilization among the Gauls, are magnificent and costly; and they cast into the fire all things, including living creatures, which they suppose to have been dear to them when alive; and, a little before this period, slaves and dependants, who were ascertained to have been beloved by them, were burnt together with them.

The Germans have neither Druids, nor do they pay great regard to sacrifices. They rank as gods; the sun, fire, and the moon; and have not heard of the other deities even by report. Their whole life is occupied in hunting and the military arts; and they hold in highest regard those who have remained chaste for the longest time. They do not pay much attention to agriculture, and a large portion of their food consists in milk, cheese, and flesh

The Hercynian forest is in breadth a journey of nine days, and has many kinds of wild beasts not seen in other parts; There is an ox of the shape of a stag, with great horns. There are animals called elks, much like roes, but of greater size, which never do they lie down for the purpose of rest, nor, if they have been thrown down by any accident, can they raise themselves up. There is a third animal which is called uri. These are a little below the elephant in size, and of the appearance, colour, and shape of a bull. Their strength and speed are extraordinary; and these the Germans take with much pains in pits and kill them, anxious for their horns, which they bind at the tips with silver, and use as cups at their most sumptuous entertainments.

Gaul being tranquil, Caesar, as he had determined, set out for Italy to hold the provincial assizes. There he was informed of the decree of the senate that all the youth of Italy should take the military oath, and he determined to hold a levy throughout the entire province. The Gauls, animated by the opportunity afforded through his absence, and indignant that they were reduced beneath the dominion of Rome, began to organise their plans for war openly.

Many of the nations confederated and selected as their commander Vercingetorix, a young Avernian. On hearing what had happened, Caesar set out from Italy for Transalpine Gaul, and began the campaign by marching into the country of the Helvii, although it was the severest time of the year, and the country was covered with deep snow.

The armies met, and Vercingetorix sustained a series of losses at Vellaunodunum, Genabum, and Noviodunum. The Gauls then threw a strong garrison into Avaricum, which Caesar besieged, and at length Caesar's soldiers took it by storm. All the Gauls, with few exceptions, joined in the revolt; and the united forces, under Vercingetorix, attacked the Roman army while it was marching into the country of the Sequani, but they suffered complete defeat. After struggling vainly to continue the war, Vercingetorix surrendered, and the Gallic chieftains laid down their arms. Caesar demanded a great number of hostages, sent his lieutenants with various legions to different stations in Gaul, and determined himself to winter at Bibracte. A supplication of twenty days was decreed at Rome by the senate on hearing of these successes.

The Gospels of Jesus Christ
(c70)

After the execution of the Jewish religious teacher Jesus of Nazareth (known to his followers as the 'Christ' - the 'Anointed One'), many biographies appeared. More than a dozen of these 'Gospels' (Greek for 'Good News') are still known, though the council of Christians held at Rome in 382, under their leader, Pope Damasus, settled on just four; the books of Matthew, Mark, Luke and John, to form, with the Torah (p23), the centrepieces of the Christian Bible.

For many centuries reading the Gospels was 'for learned persons only'. William Tyndale's vernacular translation which he hoped might "cause the boy that drives the plough in England to know more of the Scriptures than the Pope himself", brought him the reward of being strangled and burned at the stake in 1536.

Even now, they can be surprising, for the Jesus described here, by his near-contemporaries, is a more radical and complex character than the simple rabbi of popular devotion.

Based on the 1616 'King James' translation, substantially based on Tyndale's of 1535. Abridged: GH.

John 1 In the beginning was the Word, and the Word was with God, and the Word was God. All things were made by him; and without him was not any thing made that was made. In him was life; and the life was the light of men. And the light shineth in darkness; and the darkness comprehended it not. There was a man sent from God, whose name was John.

Luke 1 [5] In the days of Herod, king of Judaea, there was a certain priest named Zacharias, and his wife, who were stricken in years yet had no child. And it came to pass that an angel of the Lord appeared saying, I am Gabriel. Fear not, Zacharias: thy wife shall bear thee a son, and thus his wife Elisabeth conceived.

[26] And in the sixth month, Gabriel was sent from God unto a city of Galilee, named Nazareth, to Mary, a virgin espoused to Joseph. And the angel said, Hail, blessed art thou among women. Thou shalt conceive and bring forth a son, and shalt call his name JESUS. He shall be great, and of his kingdom there shall be no end.

Then said Mary, How shall this be, seeing I know not a man? [35] And the angel answered; The Holy Ghost shall come upon thee; for thy cousin Elisabeth hath also conceived. With God nothing shall be impossible. [46] And Mary said, My soul doth magnify the Lord. [57] Now Elisabeth's time came and she brought forth a son. And they called his name John.

Luke 2 And it came to pass, that there went out a decree from Caesar Augustus that all the world should be taxed, every one into his own city. And Joseph went into Bethlehem with Mary, being great with child. And there she brought forth her firstborn son, and wrapped him in swaddling clothes, and laid him in a manger, because there was no room in the inn.

And in that same country the angel of the Lord came upon shepherds, saying, Fear not: I bring you good tidings of great joy, for unto you is born this day a Saviour, Christ the Lord. And they found the babe, and they made known abroad that which was told them.

Matthew 2 Now when Jesus was born, behold, there came wise men from the east to Jerusalem, saying, Where is he that is born King of the Jews? for we have seen his star in the east, and are come to worship him.

And Herod the king enquired of them, saying, Go and search diligently for the child, that I may worship him also. [9] And, lo, the star went over where the young child was. And they were come into the house, and saw the child with Mary his mother, and fell down, and worshipped him: and presented unto him gifts; gold, and frankincense and myrrh.

[13] And when they were departed, behold, an angel appeareth to Joseph in a dream, saying, Arise, and take the child and his mother, and flee. And they departed into Egypt. [16] And Herod was exceeding wroth, and slew all the children that were in Bethlehem, from two years old and under. [19] But when Herod was dead, they arose, and came and dwelt in a city called Nazareth.

Luke 2 [21] And when eight days were accomplished for the circumcising, his name was called JESUS and they brought him to Jerusalem, to present him to the Lord.

[42] And, again, when he was twelve years old, they went up to Jerusalem for the feast. And, as they returned, the child Jesus tarried behind; and Joseph and his mother knew not of it supposing him to be in the company. And when they turned back again they found him in the temple, in the midst of the doctors, asking questions such that all were astonished.

Luke 3 Now in the fifteenth year of the reign of Tiberius Caesar, the word of God came unto John the son of Zacharias in the wilderness, he preaching baptism of repentance, as it is written in the book of Esaias saying, The voice of one crying in the wilderness, Prepare ye the way of the Lord. And John said, I baptize you with water; but one mightier than I cometh, the latchet of whose shoes I am not worthy to unloose: he shall baptize you with the Holy Ghost and with fire. [19] But Herod the tetrarch, had shut up John in prison.

[21] Now it came to pass, that Jesus was baptized of John, and the heaven was opened, and the Holy Ghost descended like a dove upon him, and a voice came from heaven, saying, Thou art my beloved Son; in thee I am well pleased.

Luke 4 And Jesus being full of the Holy Ghost was led by the Spirit into the wilderness, being forty days fasting and tempted of the devil. And the devil said, If thou be the Son of God, command this stone be made bread, and Jesus answered, It is written, Man shall not live by bread alone, but by every word of God. And the devil shewed unto him the kingdoms of the world, saying, All this will I give thee, if thou wilt worship me. And Jesus answered, Get thee behind me, Satan.

[14] And Jesus returned into Galilee. And in Nazareth, where he had been brought up, he went into the synagogue on the sabbath day to preach the gospel. And they said, Is not this Joseph's son? And he said unto them, Verily, no prophet is accepted in his own country. And they were filled with wrath, and rose up, and thrust him out of the city.

John 2 And there was a marriage in Cana of Galilee; and Jesus was called, and his disciples. And when they wanted wine, the mother of Jesus saith unto him, They have no wine. Jesus saith, Woman, mine hour is not yet come. And there were set there six waterpots of stone, and Jesus saith unto the servants, Fill the waterpots with water. And he saith, Draw out now, and bear unto the governor of the feast. And they bare it. When the ruler of the feast had tasted the water that was made wine, and knew not whence it was: he called the bridegroom, saying, Every man at the beginning doth set forth good wine; and when men have well drunk, then that which is worse: but thou hast kept the good wine until now. This beginning of miracles did Jesus in Cana of Galilee, and manifested forth his glory.

Luke 4 [31] And in Capernaum, he taught them, and they were astonished at his doctrine.

[33] And in the synagogue there was a man which had a spirit of an unclean devil, and cried out with a loud voice, saying, Jesus of Nazareth? Art thou come to destroy us? Thou Holy One of God. And Jesus threw the devil out of him. And they were all amazed, and the fame of him went out into every place round about. [40] Now when the sun was setting, all they that had any sick with divers diseases brought them unto him; and he laid his hands on every one of them, and healed them.

Luke 5 And it came to pass that he taught the people out of the ship belonging to Simon, upon the lake of Gennesaret. And when he had left speaking, he said unto Simon, Launch out into the deep, and let down your nets. And Simon said, Master, we have toiled all the night, and have taken nothing: nevertheless I will let down the net. And they were astonished, at the draught of the fishes which they had taken.

And Jesus said unto them, From henceforth thou shalt catch men. And they forsook all, and followed him. And much went fame abroad of him, and great multitudes came to hear, and to be healed.

[17] And when he was teaching, behold, men brought in a bed a man which was taken with a palsy. And, because of the multitude, they went upon the housetop, and let him down through the tiling into the midst before Jesus. [21] And the scribes and the Pharisees said; Who speaketh blasphemies? Who can forgive sins, but God alone?

But Jesus answered, Know ye that the Son of man hath power upon earth to forgive sins, and unto the sick of the palsy, Arise, and take up thy couch, and go into thine house. And he rose up, glorifying God.

[27] And after these things one Levi, who was a publican, made him a great feast in his own house with a company of publicans and others. But the scribes and Pharisees murmured, saying, Why do ye eat with publicans and sinners? And Jesus answered, They that are whole need not a physician; but they that are sick. I came not to call the righteous, but sinners to repentance.

Luke 6 And it came to pass on the sabbath that his disciples plucked ears of corn in the fields, and did eat, rubbing them in their hands. And certain Pharisees said unto them, Why do ye that which is not lawful on sabbath days? And Jesus answered, Have ye not read that king David, when hungred, even went into the house of God, and did eat the holy bread?

And it came to pass on another sabbath, that he entered the synagogue and there was a man whose hand was withered. And the scribes and Pharisees watched him, whether he would heal on the sabbath day. But he said unto them, Is it lawful on the sabbath to do good, or evil? to save life, or to destroy it? And looking round about upon them all, he said unto the man, Stretch forth thy hand, and his hand was restored whole.

And it came to pass that he went into a mountain to pray all night. And when it was day, he called unto him twelve disciples, whom he named apostles; Simon, (also named Peter,) and Andrew his brother, James, John, Philip, Bartholomew, Matthew and Thomas, James the son of Alphaeus, and Simon called Zelotes, Judas the brother of James, and Judas Iscariot, the traitor.

[22] And the whole multitude of Judaea and Jerusalem sought him out. And he lifted up his eyes on his disciples, and said, Blessed be ye poor: for yours is the kingdom of God. Blessed are ye that hunger: for ye shall be filled. Blessed are ye that weep: for ye shall laugh. Your reward is great in heaven, but woe unto you that are rich! for ye have received your consolation. [26] I say unto you, Love your enemies, do good to them which hate you, bless them that curse you, and pray for them which despitefully use you. And unto him that smiteth thee on one cheek offer also the other; and him that taketh away thy cloak forbid not to take thy coat also. Give to every man that asketh of thee; and as ye would that men should do to you, do ye also to them likewise. For if ye love them which love you, what thank have ye? But do good, and your reward shall be great. Judge not, and ye shall not be judged: condemn not, and ye shall not be condemned: forgive, and ye shall be forgiven: Give, and it shall be given unto you.

[39] And he spake a parable; Can the blind lead the blind? shall they not both fall into the ditch? And why beholdest thou the mote in thy brother's eye, but perceivest not the beam in thine own eye?

Luke 7 Now he entered Capernaum. And healed a certain centurion's beloved servant. [36] And he went into a Pharisee's house, and sat down to meat. And, behold, a woman in the city, a sinner, brought an alabaster box of ointment, and stood at his feet, and began to wash his feet with tears, and anointed them with the ointment. Now the Pharisee spake within himself, saying, if he were a prophet, he would know this woman is a sinner.

And Jesus answered, saying, Simon, There was a certain creditor which had two debtors: the one owed five hundred pence, and the other fifty. And when they had nothing to pay, he forgave them both. Tell me which of them will love him most? Simon answered, I suppose he to whom he forgave most. And he said, Thou rightly judged. Wherefore I say unto the woman, Her sins, which are many, are forgiven; for she loved much: but to whom little is forgiven, the same loveth little.

Luke 8 And he went throughout every city and village, preaching and shewing the glad tidings of the kingdom of God: and the twelve were with him, and certain women, which had been healed of evil spirits, Mary called Magdalene, and Joanna, and Susanna, and many others, which ministered unto him of their substance.

[4] And he spake by a parable: A sower went out to sow his seed: and some fell by the way side; and it was trodden down, and fowls devoured it. And some fell upon rock; and as soon as it was sprung up, it withered away, because it lacked moisture. And some fell among thorns; and the thorns choked it. And other fell on good ground, and sprang up, and bare fruit an hundredfold. Now; The seed is the word of God. Those by the way side are they that hear; then cometh the devil, and taketh away the word out of their hearts. They on the rock are they, which, when they hear, receive the word with joy; and these have no root, which for a while believe, and in time of temptation fall away. And that which fell among thorns are they, which, when they have heard, go forth, and are choked with cares and riches and pleasures of this life, and bring no fruit to perfection. But that on the good ground are they, which hear the word, and keep it, and bring forth fruit. [19] Then came to him his mother and his brethren, desiring to see him. And he said unto them, My mother and my brethren are these which hear the word of God, and do it.

[22] Now it came to pass that he went into a ship with his disciples: and there came down a storm. And they awoke him, saying, Master, master, we perish. Then he rebuked the wind: and there was calm. And they being afraid wondered, What manner of man is this! [26] And at Gadarenes, by Galile, they met a certain man, which had devils long time, and ware no clothes, and abode in the tombs. And Jesus asked him, What is thy name? And he said, Legion: because many devils were in him. And Jesus bade the devils enter into a herd of swine feeding on the mountain, and the herd ran violently down a steep place into the lake, and were choked. And the man published throughout the whole city how great things Jesus had done unto him.

[41] And, behold, there came a man named Jairus, who was a ruler of the synagogue: and he fell down before Jesus' that he would come into his house, for his only daughter lay a dying. But the people thronged him, and a woman having an issue of blood twelve years, which had spent all her living upon physicians, came behind, and touched the border of his garment: and immediately her issue of blood staunched. And Jesus said, Somebody hath touched me: for I perceive that virtue is gone out of me. And the woman came trembling, and he said unto her, Daughter, thy faith hath made thee whole; go in peace. Then cometh one from Jairus' house, saying; Thy daughter is dead; trouble not the Master. But Jesus said; Fear not: believe only. And when he came into the house, he said, Weep not; she is not dead, but sleepeth, and took her by the hand, and called, saying, Maid, arise. And her parents were astonished.

Luke 9 Then he called his twelve disciples together, and gave them power and authority over all devils, and to cure diseases, and sent them to preach the kingdom of God. And he said, Take neither staves, nor scrip, neither bread, neither money; neither have two coats apiece. And whosoever will not receive you, shake off the very dust of that city from your feet.

[7] Now Herod the tetrarch heard of all that was done by him: and he was perplexed. And Herod said, John have I now beheaded: but who is this? And he desired to see him.

[10] And the apostles, went into a desert place, and the people followed: and he spake unto them of the kingdom of God. And when the day began to wear, he said, Give ye them to eat. And they said, We have but five loaves and two fishes. And he took the loaves and the fishes, and looking up to heaven, he blessed them, and brake, and gave to the disciples to set before the multitude. And all did eat, and were filled: and there was taken up of fragments that remained, twelve baskets.

Mark 6 [45] And he constrained his disciples to get into a ship, and to go to the other side, while he sent away the people. And he departed into a mountain to pray. And when even was come, the ship was in the midst of the sea, and he alone on the land. And he saw them toiling in rowing, for the wind was against them: and about the fourth watch of the night he cometh unto them, walking upon the sea. But when they all saw him walking upon the sea, they supposed it had been a spirit, and cried out, and were troubled. And immediately he talked with them, saying, Be not afraid. And he went unto the ship; and the wind ceased: and they were sore amazed beyond measure.

Matthew 16 [13] When Jesus came into the coasts of Caesarea Philippi, he asked his disciples, Whom do men say that I am? And they said, Some say John the Baptist: some, Elias or one of the prophets. He saith unto them, But whom say ye that I am? And Simon Peter answered, Thou art the Christ, the Son of the living God. And Jesus said unto him, Blessed art thou, Simon Barjona: for flesh and blood hath not revealed it unto thee, but my Father which is in heaven. Thou art Peter, and upon this rock I will build my church; and the gates of hell shall not prevail against it. And I will give unto thee the keys of the kingdom of heaven: and whatsoever thou shalt bind on earth shall be bound in heaven: and whatsoever thou shalt loose on earth shall be loosed in heaven.

Then charged he his disciples that they should tell no man that he was the Christ. [24] Then said Jesus unto his disciples, If any man will come after me, let him deny himself, and take up his cross, and follow me. For whosoever will save his life shall lose it: and whosoever will lose his life for my sake shall find it. For what is a man profited, if he shall gain the whole world, and lose his own soul?

The Son of man shall come in the glory of his Father with his angels; and then he shall reward every man according to his works. Verily I say unto you, There be some standing here, which shall not taste of death, till they see the Son of man coming in his kingdom.

Matthew 17 And after six days Jesus taketh Peter, James, and John into an high mountain, and he was transfigured before them: and his face did shine as the sun, and his raiment was white as the light. And, behold, there appeared unto them Moses and Elias talking with him. And, behold, a bright cloud overshadowed them: and behold a voice out of the cloud, which said, This is my beloved Son, in whom I am well pleased; hear ye him. And as they came down from the mountain, Jesus charged them, saying, Tell the vision to no man, until the Son of man be risen again from the dead.

[24] And when they were come to Capernaum, they that received tribute money came to Peter. Jesus saith unto him, lest we should offend them, go thou to the sea, and cast an hook, and take up the fish that first cometh up; and when thou hast opened his mouth, thou shalt find a piece of money: that take, and give unto them for me and thee.

Luke 10 After these things the LORD appointed another seventy, and sent them two and two into every city and place. Saying, The harvest is great, but the labourers are few: Behold, I send you forth as lambs among wolves. Whatsoever city will receive you not, wipe even their dust off you, at the judgment it shall be more tolerable for Sodom[1] than for that city. Behold, I give unto you power to tread on serpents and scorpions, and over all the power of the enemy: and nothing shall by any means hurt you.

[25] And a certain lawyer tempted him, saying, Master, what shall I do to inherit eternal life? He said unto him, What is written in the law? And he answered, Thou shalt love the Lord thy God, and thy neighbour as thyself, but who is my neighbour? And Jesus answering said, A certain man went down from Jerusalem to Jericho, and fell among thieves, which left him half dead. And there came a priest that way: and he passed by on the other side, and likewise a Levite. But a certain Samaritan saw him and had compassion, and bound up his wounds, and set him on his own beast, and brought him to an inn, and took care of him. Which now of these three was neighbour unto him that fell among the thieves? And he said, He that shewed mercy on him. Then said Jesus unto him, Go, and do likewise.

Luke 11 And he said unto them, When ye pray, say, Our Father which art in heaven, Hallowed be thy name. Thy kingdom come. Thy will be done, as in heaven, so in earth. Give us day by day our daily bread. And forgive us our sins; for we also forgive every one that is indebted to us. And lead us not into temptation; but deliver us from evil.

[14] And he cast out a devil, and some of them said, He casteth out devils through Beelzebub the chief of the devils. But he said unto them, Every kingdom divided against itself is brought to desolation; and a house divided against a house falleth. He that is not with me is against me: and he that gathereth not with me scattereth.

Luke 12 He said unto his disciples; Whosoever shall confess me before men, him shall the Son of man confess before the angels of God: But he that denieth me before men shall be denied before the angels of God.

[14] Take heed, beware of covetousness: for a man's life consisteth not in the abundance of the things which he possesseth, and like unto the rich farmer, thou knowest not when thy soul shall be required of thee. Therefore take no thought for your life, what ye shall eat; neither for the body, what ye shall put on. The life is more than meat, and

---

1   **Sodom:** see Genesis 19 p23

the body is more than raiment. [24] Consider the lilies how they grow: they toil not, they spin not; and yet I say unto you, that Solomon in all his glory was not arrayed like one of these. If then God so clothe the grass, how much more will he clothe you, O ye of little faith?

[33] Sell that ye have, and give alms; provide yourselves with a treasure in the heavens, where no thief approacheth, neither moth corrupteth.

[49] I am come to send fire on the earth. Suppose ye that I am come to give peace on earth? I tell you, Nay; but rather division: The father shall be divided against the son, the mother against the daughter.

Luke 14 And it came to pass, as he went into the house of one of the chief Pharisees to eat bread on the sabbath day, that they watched him. And, behold, there was a man before him which had the dropsy, and he healed him.

And Jesus spake unto the lawyers and Pharisees, saying, Is it lawful to heal on the sabbath day? Which of you shall have an ass or an ox fallen into a pit, and will not straightway pull him out on the sabbath? And they could not answer him. [7] And he put forth a parable saying; when thou makest a dinner, call not thy friends, but call the poor, the maimed, the lame, the blind. For I say unto you, not all that were bidden shall taste of my supper. If any man come to me, and hate not his father, and mother, and wife, and children, and brethren, and sisters, yea, and his own life also, he cannot be my disciple. And whosoever doth not bear his cross, and come after me, cannot be my disciple. He that hath ears to hear, let him hear.

Luke 15 Then drew near unto him all the publicans and sinners for to hear him. And the Pharisees and scribes murmured, saying, This man receiveth sinners, and eateth with them.

[3] And he spake this parable saying, What man, having an hundred sheep, if he lose one, doth not leave the ninety and nine, and go find that which is lost? Likewise joy shall be in heaven over one sinner that repenteth, more than over ninety and nine just persons, which need no repentance. [11] And he said, A certain man had two sons. And the younger said to his father, Give me the portion of goods that falleth to me, and took his journey into a far country, and there wasted his substance with riotous living. And when he had spent all, there arose a mighty famine in that land; and he was sent him into the fields to feed swine. And he would fain have filled his belly with the husks that the swine did eat. And to himself he said, How many servants of my father's have bread enough to spare, and I perish with hunger! And he arose, and came to his father, and said unto him, Father, I have sinned, and am no more worthy to be called thy son. But the father said to his servants, Bring forth the best robe, bring hither the fatted calf, let us eat, and be merry: for this my son is found. Now his elder son was angry, saying; Father, these many years do I serve thee, yet thou never gavest me such: And he said unto him, Son, thou art ever with me, and all that I have is thine. Be

glad: for this thy brother was dead, and is alive again; and was lost, and is found.

Luke 16 And he said also unto his disciples, There was a certain rich man, which had a steward who he accused that he had wasted his goods. And he called him to give account. Then the steward said within himself, What shall I do when I am put out of this stewardship, that others may receive me? So he called his lord's debtors, and said unto the first, How much owest thou? And he said, An hundred measures of oil. And the steward said, Take thy bill, and and write fifty. Then to another, for an hundred measures of wheat, write fourscore. And the lord commended the unjust steward, because he had done wisely: for the children of this world are in their generation wiser than the children of light. So I say unto you, Make to yourselves friends of the mammon of unrighteousness; that, when ye fail, they may receive you into everlasting habitations.

No servant can serve two masters: for either he will hate the one, and love the other; or else he will hold to the one, and despise the other. Ye cannot serve God and mammon.

[19] There was a rich man and there was a beggar named Lazarus. And the beggar died, and was carried by the angels into Abraham's[2] bosom: the rich man also died, and was buried. And in hell he lift up his eyes, being in torments, and seeth Abraham afar off, and Lazarus in his bosom. And he cried, Father Abraham, have mercy, send Lazarus with water, for I am tormented in this flame. But Abraham said, Son, remember that thou in thy lifetime receivedst thy good things, and likewise Lazarus evil things: but now he is comforted, and thou art tormented.

Luke 17 Then said he unto the disciples, It is impossible but that offences will come: but woe unto him, through whom they come! It were better for him that a millstone were hanged about his neck, and he cast into the sea, than that he should offend one of the little ones.

Take heed to yourselves: If thy brother trespass against thee, rebuke him; and if he repent, forgive him. And if he trespass against thee seven times in a day, and seven times say, I repent; thou shalt forgive him.

[11] And he entered into a village of Samaria, and there cleansed ten lepers. And one of them glorified God, and fell down on his face, giving him thanks: and he was a Samaritan. And Jesus said, Were not ten cleansed? where are the nine? Only this stranger returned to give glory to God. Arise, go thy way: thy faith hath made thee whole.

[20] And the Pharisees asked when the kingdom of God should come, he answered them; The kingdom of God cometh not with observation. I tell you, in that night there shall be two men in one bed; the one shall be taken, and the other shall be left. Two women shall be grinding together; the one shall be taken, and the other left.

Luke 18 And he spake a parable unto them to this end, that men ought always to pray, Saying, [10] Two men went into the temple to pray; one a Pharisee, and the other a publican.

---

2   **Abraham:** see The Torah (p23), Genesis 17

The Pharisee prayed, God, I thank thee that I am not as other men are, extortioners, adulterers, even as this publican. I fast twice in the week and I give tithes. And the publican, standing afar off, would not lift up so much as his eyes unto heaven, but smote his breast, saying, God be merciful to me a sinner. I tell you: every one that exalteth himself shall be abased; and he that humbleth himself shall be exalted.

[15] And they brought unto him also infants, and Jesus said, Suffer little children to come unto me, and forbid them not: for of such is the kingdom of God.

[18] And a certain ruler asked him, Good Master, how shall I inherit eternal life? And Jesus said, if thou follow the commandments, yet lackest thou one thing: sell all that thou hast, and distribute unto the poor, and come, follow me. And when he heard this, he was very sorrowful: for he was rich. It is easier for a camel to go through a needle's eye, than for a rich man to enter into the kingdom of God.

[31] Then said unto the twelve, We go to Jerusalem, and as the prophets have written concerning the Son of man, he shall be mocked, and spitefully entreated, and put to death: and the third day he shall rise again. And they understood none of these things.

Luke 19 And Jesus passed through Jericho. And Zacchaeus the chief publican, sought to see Jesus and could not for the press, because he was little of stature. Therefore he climbed into a sycomore tree, and when Jesus came, he looked up, and said, Zacchaeus, come down, for to day I must abide at thy house.

[11] And he spake a parable, because they thought that the kingdom of God should immediately appear. He said, A certain nobleman was called into a far country, and he delivered to his servants each ten pounds, saying, Occupy till I come. And when he returned, the one said; Lord, thy pound hath earned ten. And another sayeth, Lord, thy pound hath gained five pounds. And he said to them; Good servants. And another came, saying, Lord, behold, here is thy pound, which I have kept laid up in a napkin; And he saith, thou wicked servant, wherefore gavest not thou my money into the bank, that I might have gained usury? Take from him the one pound, and give it to him that hath ten.

[26] For I say unto you, That unto every one which hath shall be given; and from him that hath not, even that he hath shall be taken away from him. [27] And those mine enemies, which would not that I should reign over them, bring hither, and slay them before me.

And when he had thus spoken, he came nigh to Bethphage and Bethany, at the mount of Olives, and sent two of his disciples, saying, Go ye into the village, ye shall find a colt tied, and bring him hither. And they found even as he had said: and they set Jesus thereon. And as he went, they spread their clothes in the way and he came into Jerusalem.

[45] And he went into the temple, and began to cast out them that sold therein, saying, My house is the house of prayer: but ye have made it a den of thieves. And he taught daily in the temple. But the chief priests and scribes sought to destroy him, but all the people were very attentive to hear him.

Luke 20 And it came to pass as he taught the people in the temple, the chief priests spake unto him, Tell us, by what authority doest thou these things?

And he answered, I will also ask you one thing; The baptisms of John, was it from heaven, or of men? And they reasoned, If we say, From heaven; he will say, Why then believed ye him not? But if we say, Of men; the people will stone us: for they hold John a prophet. And they answered, that they could not tell whence it was. And Jesus said, Neither then do I tell you by what authority I do these things.

[9] Then began he to speak to the people this parable; A certain man planted a vineyard, and let it forth to husbandmen, and went away. And at the season he sent a servant to the husbandmen, for the fruit of the vineyard: but the husbandmen beat him, and sent him away empty. And he sent another servant, and again a third. Then said the lord of the vineyard, I will send my beloved son: they will reverence him. But when the husbandmen saw him, they saw their inheritence, and killed him. What therefore shall the lord of the vineyard do? He shall come and destroy these husbandmen, and shall give the vineyard to others.

[17] And he said, It is written, The stone which the builders rejected, is become the cornerstone. [19] And they asked him, Master, is it lawful to give tribute unto Caesar? But he said, Shew me a penny. Whose image and superscription hath it? Therefore render unto Caesar the things which be Caesar's, and unto God the things which be God's. And they marvelled at his answer.

[27] Then came certain of the Sadducees, which deny that there is any resurrection; and asked, Master, Moses wrote, If any man die, his brother should take his wife. Therefore in the resurrection whose wife is she? And Jesus answered, They which obtain the resurrection from the dead, neither marry, nor are given in marriage: for they are equal unto the angels; and are the children of God. Then they durst not ask him any more.

Luke 21 And he looked up, and saw the rich men casting their gifts into the treasury, and also a certain poor widow casting in two mites. And he said, Truly, this poor widow hath cast in more than all: for she hath cast in all her living.

[5] And as some spake of the temple, how it was adorned with goodly stones and gifts, he said, All these things will one day be thrown down. And they asked him, When shall these things be? And he said, Many shall come in my name, saying, I am Christ; go ye not after them. Ye shall hear of wars and commotions, nation shall rise against nation, great earthquakes shall be in divers places, and famines, and pestilences; and fearful sights and great signs from heaven. And they shall persecute you for my name's sake. Settle not to meditate before ye shall answer: For I will give you a mouth and wisdom, which your adversaries shall not be able to gainsay nor resist. And ye shall be betrayed both by parents, and kinsfolks, and friends; And

ye shall be hated of all men for my name's sake. But there shall not an hair of your head perish.

And there shall be great distress in the land: and Jerusalem shall be trodden down of the Gentiles. And there shall be signs in the sun, and in the moon, and in the stars. And then shall they see the Son of man coming in a cloud with power and great glory. Watch ye therefore, and pray always.

Luke 22 Then entered Satan into Judas Iscariot, being of the number of the twelve. And he communed with the chief priests and captains, how he might betray him, and they were glad, and covenanted to give him money. [7] Then came the day of unleavened bread. And he sent Peter and John, saying, Go and prepare us the passover. Enter in the city and get you to an upper room furnished. And when the hour was come, he sat down, and the twelve apostles with him. And he took the cup, and gave thanks, and said, Take this, and divide it among yourselves: For I will not drink of the fruit of the vine, until the kingdom of God shall come.

And he took bread, and gave thanks, and brake it, and gave unto them, saying, This is my body which is given for you: this do in remembrance of me. Likewise also the cup after supper, saying, This cup is the new testament in my blood, which is shed for you. But, behold, the hand of him that betrayeth me is with me on the table.

[31] And the Lord said, Simon, Simon, behold, Satan hath desired to have you, and he replied, Lord, I am ready to go with thee unto death. And he said, I tell thee, Peter, the cock shall not crow this day, before that thou shalt thrice deny me.

[35] And he said unto them, When I sent you without purse, and scrip, and shoes, lacked ye any thing? And they said, Nothing. Then said he unto them, But now, he that hath no sword, let him sell his garment, and buy one. [39] And he went out, as he was wont, to the mount of Olives; and his disciples followed.

And he was withdrawn from them and prayed, Saying, Father, if thou be willing, remove this cup from me. And there appeared an angel from heaven, strengthening him. And his sweat was as drops of blood.

And, behold a multitude, and he that was called Judas, one of the twelve, went before them, and drew near unto Jesus to kiss him. But Jesus said unto him, Judas, betrayest thou the Son of man with a kiss? And one of them smote the servant of the high priest, and cut off his right ear. But Jesus touched his ear, and healed him. And then took they him into the high priest's house. And Peter followed afar off.

But a certain maid beheld Peter, saying; This man was also with him. And he denied it. And another said so, and another, yet Peter denied it. And while he yet spake, the cock crew, and Peter wept bitterly. [63] And the men that held Jesus mocked him, and smote him.

And as soon as it was day, the elders and the chief priests and scribes came together, and led him into their council, saying, Art thou the Son of God? And he said unto them,

Ye say that I am. And they said, What need we further witness? for we have heard of his own mouth.

Matthew 27 Then Judas, which had betrayed him, repented himself, and brought his thirty pieces of silver to the temple, saying; I have betrayed innocent blood, and departed, and went and hanged himself.

[11] And they brought Jesus before Pontius Pilate the governor: and the governor asked him, Art thou the King of the Jews? And Jesus said unto him, Thou sayest.

[15] Now at that feast the governor was wont to release a prisoner. Therefore when the people were gathered together, Pilate said unto them, Whom will ye that I release unto you? But the chief priests and elders persuaded the multitude that they should ask for one Barabbas, and destroy Jesus.

And the governor said, What evil hath he done? But they cried out, Let him be crucified. [24] When Pilate saw that he could prevail nothing, he took water, and washed his hands before the multitude, saying, I am innocent of the blood of this just person.

[26] Then released he Barabbas: and scourged Jesus, and delivered him to be crucified. And the soldierrs stripped him, and put on him a scarlet robe. And they platted a crown of thorns, and put it upon his head, and a reed in his right hand: and they mocked him, saying, Hail, King of the Jews!

[32] And as they came out, they found a man of Cyrene, Simon by name: him they compelled to bear his cross unto a place called Golgotha, that is to say, a place of a skull. And they crucified him, and parted his garments among them by casting lots. And set up over his head his accusation written, THIS IS JESUS THE KING OF THE JEWS. Then were there two thieves crucified with him, one on the right hand, and another on the left. And they that passed by reviled him, saying, If thou be the Son of God, come down from the cross.

[45] Now there was darkness over all the land and about the ninth hour Jesus cried with a loud voice, Eli, Eli, lama sabachthani? that is to say, My God, my God, why hast thou forsaken me? And Jesus yielded up the ghost. And, behold, the veil of the temple was rent in twain; and the earth did quake; And the graves were opened; and many saints which slept arose.

Now when the centurion watching Jesus saw those things, he said, Truly this was the Son of God. [57] When the even was come Joseph of Arimathaea went to Pilate, and begged the body of Jesus. And Joseph had the body wrapped in clean linen, and laid it in a new tomb hewn out in the rock: and he rolled a great stone to the door, and departed.

Luke 24 Now upon the first day of the week Mary Magdalene and Joanna, and Mary the mother of James came unto the sepulchre, and found the stone rolled away from the sepulchre. And they entered in, and found not the body of the Lord Jesus.

And as they were much perplexed thereabout, behold, two men stood by them in shining garments: Why seek ye the living among the dead? He is not here, but is risen. And they returned unto the eleven. [11] But their words seemed as idle tales.

Then Peter ran unto the sepulchre; and beheld the grave clothes. And two disciples went that day to a village called Emmaus. And Jesus himself drew near, and went with them, but they knew him not.

And at the village, they said, take meat with us. And he took bread, and blessed it, and brake it, and gave to them. And their eyes were opened, and they knew him; and he vanished from their sight.

[24] And they returned to Jerusalem, and found the eleven gathered together, saying, The Lord is risen indeed, and hath appeared to Simon. And as they spake, Jesus himself stood in the midst of them, and saith unto them, Peace be unto you.

But they were terrified and supposed that they had seen a spirit. And he said, Behold my hands and my feet: handle me, and see. Have ye here any meat? And they gave him a piece of a broiled fish, and an honeycomb. And he took it, and did eat before them.

John 20 [22] And he breathed on them, saying; Receive ye the Holy Ghost: Whose soever sins ye remit, they are remitted; and whose soever sins ye retain, they are retained.

[24] But Thomas, one of the twelve, called Didymus, was not with them when Jesus came. The other disciples therefore said unto him, We have seen the LORD. But he said, Except I shall see in his hands the print of the nails, and thrust my hand into his side, I will not believe. And after eight days again his disciples were within, and Thomas with them: then came Jesus, the doors being shut, and stood in the midst, and said, Peace be unto you. Then saith he to Thomas, Behold my hands; and reach thy hand into my side: and be not faithless, but believing.

And Thomas said unto him, My LORD and my God. Jesus saith: blessed are they that have not seen, and yet have believed.

Luke 24 [44] And he said unto them, All things must be fulfilled, which were written in the prophets concerning me. And ye are witnesses of these things.

And he led them out, and lifted up his hands, and blessed them. And he was carried up into heaven. And they were continually in the temple, praising and blessing God.

Amen.

The Meditations
of Marcus Aurelius (Antoninus), Emperor of Rome
(Written on campaign in modern-day Serbia and Hungary, c180)

Marcus Aurelius was known as one of the 'Five Good Emperors'. His 'Meditations' are a collections of notes on the stern and solid philosophy of *Stoicism*, founded by Zeno of the Stoa Poikile (Painted Colonnades) in 3rd century BC Cyprus. It was much favoured by the Roman elite, in contrast to the easy-going rival creed of Epicurius (p68)

Based on the 1862 translation by George Long. Abridged: GH

The Meditations of Marcus Aurelius

Marcus Aurelius Antoninus, Emperor of Rome, his First Book, concerning himself. Wherein he recordeth, what and of whom, whether Parents, Friends, or Masters; by their good examples, or good advice and counsel, he had learned:

I – OF THE CULTIVATION OF THE MIND

THE example of my grandfather Verus taught me to be candid and to control my temper. By the memory of my father's character I learnt to be modest and manly. My mother taught me regard for religion, to be generous and open-handed, and neither to do an ill turn to anyone nor even to think of it. She bred me also to a plain and inexpensive way of living.

I thank the gods that my grandfathers, parents, sister, preceptors, relatives, friends and domestics were almost all persons of probity and that I never happened to disoblige

any of them. By the goodness of the gods I was not provoked to expose my infirmities. I owe it to them also that my wife is so deferential, affectionate and frugal; and that when I had a mind to look into philosophy I did not spend too much time in reading or logic-chopping. All these points could never have been guarded without a protection from above.

II – OF PHILOSOPHY, THE MIND'S GREATEST SOLACE

PUT yourself in mind, every morning, that before that night you will meet with some meddlesome, ungrateful and abusive fellow, with some envious or unsociable churl. Remember that their perversity proceeds from ignorance of good and evil; and that since it has fallen to my share to understand the natural beauty of a good action and the deformity of an ill one; since I am satisfied that the disobliging person is of kin to me, our minds being coming from the Deity; since no man can do me a real injury because no man can force me to misbehave myself; I cannot therefore hate or be angry with one of my own nature and family. For we are all made for mutual assistance, no less than the parts of the body are for the service of the whole; whence it follows that clashing and opposition are utterly unnatural.

This being of mine consists of body, breath and that part which governs. Put away your books and face the matter itself. As for your body, value it no more than if you were just expiring; it is nothing but a little blood and bones. Your breath is but a little air pumped in and out. But the third part is your mind. Here make a stand. Consider that you are an old man, and do not let this noble part of you languish in slavery any longer. Let it not be overborne with selfish passions; let it not quarrel with fate, or be uneasy at the present, or afraid of the future. Providence shines clearly through the work of the gods. Let these reflections satisfy you, and make them your rule to live by. As for books, cease to be eager for them, that you may die in good humour heartily thanking the gods for what you have had.

Remember that you are a man and a Roman, and let your actions be done with dignity, gravity, humanity, freedom and justice; let every action be done as though it were your last. Have neither insincerity nor self-love. Man has to gain but few points in order to live a happy and godlike life.

And what, after all, is there to be afraid of in death? If the gods exist, you can suffer no harm; and if they do not exist, or take no care of us mortals, a world without gods or Providence is not worth a man's while to live in. But the being of the gods, and their concern in human affairs, is beyond dispute; and they have put it in every man's power not to fall into any calamity properly so called.

Living and dying, honour and infamy. Pleasure and pain, riches and poverty - all these are common to the virtuous and the depraved, and therefore intrinsically neither good not evil. We live but for a moment; our being is in a perpetual flux, our faculties are dim, our bodies tend ever to corruption; the soul is an eddy, fortune is not to be guessed at and posthumous fame is oblivion. To what, then, may we trust? Why, to nothing but philosophy. This is, to keep the interior divinity from injury and disgrace, and superior to pleasure and pain, without any dissembling and pretence, and to acquiesce in one's appointed lot.

III - OF RESOLUTENESS

OBSERVE that the least things and effects in nature are not without charm and beauty, as the little cracks in the crust of a loaf, though not intended by the baker, are agreeable and invite the appetite. Thus figs, when they are ripest, open and gape; and olives, when they are near decaying, are peculiarly attractive. The bending of an ear of corn, the frown of a lion, the foam of a boar, and many other like things, if you take them singly, are far from beautiful; but seen in their natural relations are characteristic and effective. So if a man have but inclination and thought to examine the product of the universe, he will find that the most unpromising appearances have their own appropriate charm.

Do not spend your thoughts upon other people, nor pry into the talk, fancies and projects of another, nor guess at what he is about, or why he is doing it. Think upon nothing but what you could willingly tell about, so that if your soul were laid open there would appear nothing but what was sincere, good-natured and public-spirited. A man thus qualified is a sort of priest and minister of the gods, and makes a right use of the divinity within him. Be cheerful; depend not at all on foreign supports, nor beg your happiness of another; do not throw away your legs to stand upon crutches.

If, in the whole compass of human life, you find anything preferable to justice and truth, temperance and fortitude, or to a mind self-satisfied with its own rational conduct and entirely resigned to fate, then turn to it as to your supreme happiness. But if there be nothing more valuable than the divinity within you, if all things are trifles in comparison with this, then do not divide your allegiance. Let your choice run all one way, and be resolute for that which is best. As for other speculations, throw them once for all out of your head.

IV - OF LOYALTY TO THE PRINCIPLES OF WISDOM

IT is the custom of people to go to unfrequented places and to the seashore and to the hills for retirement; and you yourself have often desired this solitude. But, after all, this is only a vulgar fancy, for it is in your power to withdraw into yourself whenever you have a mind to it. One's own heart is a place the most free from crowd and noise in the world if only one's thoughts are serene and the mind well ordered. Make, therefore, frequent use of this retirement, therein to refresh your virtue. And to this end be always provided with a few short, uncontested notions, to keep your understanding true. Do not forget to retire to this solitude of yours; let there be no straining or struggling in the matter, but move at ease.

If understanding be common to us all, then reason, its cause, must be common, too. And so also must the reason which governs conduct by commands and prohibitions be common to us all. Mankind is therefore under one common law and so are fellow-citizens; and the whole world is but one commonwealth, for there is no other society in which mankind can be incorporated.

Do not suppose that you are hurt, and your complaint will cease. If a man affronts you, do not defer to his opinion, or think just as he would have you do. No; look upon things as reality presents them. When incense is thrown upon the altar, one grain usually falls before another; but it matters not. Adhere to the principles of wisdom, and those who now take you for a monkey or a beast will make a god of you in a week.

A thing is neither better nor worse for being praised. Do virtues stand in need of a good word, or are they the worse for a bad one? An emerald will shine none the less though its worth be not spoken of.

Whatever is agreeable to You, O Universe, is so to me, too. Your operations are never mis-timed. Whatever Your seasons bring is fruit for me, O Nature. From You all things proceed, subsist in You, and return to You.

The greater part of what we say and do is unnecessary; and if this were only retrenched we should have more leisure and less disturbance. This applies to our thoughts also, for impertinence of thought leads to unnecessary action.

Mankind are poor, transitory things; one day in life, and the next turned to ashes. Therefore manage this minute wisely and part with it cheerfully; and like a ripe fruit, when you drop, make your acknowledgments to the tree that bore you.

V - OF SINCERITY IN ACTIONS

WHEN you feel unwilling to rise early in the morning, make this short speech to yourself: 'I am getting up now to do the business of a man; and am I out of humour for going about that I was made for, and for the sake of which I was sent into the world? Was I then designed for nothing but to doze beneath the counterpane?' Surely action is the end of your being. Look upon the plants and birds, the ants, spiders and bees, and you will see that they are all exerting their nature and busy in their station. Shall not a man act like a man?

Be not ashamed of any action which is in accordance with nature, and never be misled by the fear of censure or reproach. Where honesty prompts you to say or do anything, let not the opinion of others hold you back. Go straight forward, pursuing your own and the common interest.

Some men, when they do you a kindness, ask for the payment of gratitude; others, more modest, remember the favour and look upon you as their debtor. But there are yet other benefactors who forget their good deeds; and these are like the vine, which is satisfied by being fruitful in its kind and bears a bunch of grapes without expecting any thanks for it. A truly kind man never talks of a good turn that he has done, but does another as soon as he can, just like a vine that bears again the next season.

We commonly say that Aesculapius the healer has prescribed riding for one patient, walking for another, a cold bath for a third. In the same way we may say that the nature of the universe has ordered this or that person a disease, loss of limbs or estate, or some such other calamity; For as, in the first case, the word 'prescribed' means a direction for the health of the patient, so, in the latter, it means an application suitable for his constitution and destiny.

Be not uneasy, discouraged or out of humour, because practice falls short of precept in some particulars. If you happen to be vanquished, come on again, and be glad if most of what you do is worthy of a man.

We ought to live with the gods. This is done by being contented with the appointment of providence and by obeying the orders of that divinity which is God's deputy; and this divine authority is no more or less than that soul and reason which every man carries within him.

VI - OF LIBERALITY IN OUTLOOK

THE best way of revenge is not to imitate the injury. Be always doing something serviceable to mankind; and let this constant generosity be your pleasure, not forgetting a due regard to God.

The world is either an aggregation of atoms, or it is a unity ruled by law and providence. If the first, what should I stay for, where nature is a chaos and things are blindly jumbled together? But if there is a providence, I adore the great Governor of the world, and am at ease and cheerful in the prospect of protection.

Suppose you had a stepmother and a mother at the same time; though you would pay regard to the first, your converse would be principally with the latter. Let the court and philosophy represent these two relations to me.

If an antagonist in the circus tears our flesh with his nails, or tilts against us with his head, we do not cry out foul play, nor are we offended, nor do we suspect him afterwards as a dangerous person. Let us act thus in the other instances of life. When we receive a blow, let us think that we are but at a trial of skill and depart without malice or ill will.

It is enough to do my duty; as for other things, I will not be disturbed about them.

The vast continents of Europe and of Asia are but corners of the creation; the ocean is but a drop, and Mount Athos but a grain in respect of the universe; and the present instant of time is but a point to the extent of eternity.

When you have a mind to divert your fancy, try to consider the good qualities of your acquaintance - such as the enterprising vigour of this man, the modesty of another, the liberality of a third, and so on. Let this practice be always at hand.

VII - OF PATIENCE AND TOLERATION

WHAT is wickedness? It is nothing new. When you are in danger of being shocked, consider that the sight is nothing but what you have frequently seen already. All ages and histories towns and families, are full of the same stories; there is nothing new to be met with, but all things are common and quickly over.

Nature works up the matter of the universe like wax; now it is a horse; soon you will find it melted down and run into the figure of a tree, then a man, then something else. Only for a brief time is it fixed in any species. Consider the course of the stars as if you were driving through the sky and kept them company. Such contemplations as these scour off the rust contracted by conversing here below.

Rational creatures are designed for the advantage of each other. A sociable temper is that for which human nature was principally intended. It is a saying of Plato's that no one misses the truth by his own goodwill. The same may be said of honesty, sobriety, good nature and the like. Remember this for it will help to sweeten your temper.

Though the gods are immortal, and have had their patience tried through so many ages, yet they even provide liberally for us. And are you tired with evil men already, who are an unhappy mortal yourself?

VIII - OF THE TRIPLE RESPONSIBILITY

EVERY man has three relations to acquit himself in; his body, God, and his neighbours.

Have you seen a hand or a foot cut off and removed from the body? Just such a thing is the man who is discontented with destiny or cuts himself off by selfishness from the interest of mankind. But here is the fortunate aspect of the case - it lies in his power to set the limb on again. Consider the peculiar bounty of God to man in this privilege: He has set him above the necessity of breaking off from nature and providence at all; but supposing this misfortune to have occurred, it is in man's power to rejoin the body, and grow together again.

Do not take your whole life into your head at a time, nor burden yourself with the weight of the future. Neither what is past nor what is to come need afflict you, for you have only to deal with the present; and this is strangely lessened if you take it singly and by itself. Chide your fancy, therefore, if it grow faint.

Throw me into what climate or state your please, for all that I will keep my soul content. Is any misadventure big enough to ruffle my peace, or to make my mind mean, craving and servile? What is there that can justify such disorders?

Be not heavy in business, nor disturbed in conversation, nor rambling in thought. Do not burden yourself with too much employment. Do men curse you? This cannot prevent you from keeping a wise, temperature and upright mind. If a man standing by a lovely spring should rail at it, the water is none the worse for his foul language; and if he throw in dirt it will soon disappear and the fountain will be as wholesome as ever. How are you to keep your springs always running, that they may never stagnate into a pool? You must preserve in in the virtues of freedom, sincerity, moderation and good nature.

IX - OF MODERATION IN DEED AND WISH

DO not drudge like a galley-slave, nor do business in a laborious manner, as if you wish to be pitied or wondered at. As virtue and vice consist in action, and not in the impressions of the senses, so it is not what they feel, but what they do, that makes mankind happy or miserable.

X - OF SINCERITY AND ITS REWARDS

O MY soul, are you ever to be rightly good, sincere and uniform, and made more visible to yourself than the body that hangs about you? Are you ever likely to relish good nature and general kindness as you ought? Will you ever be fully satisfied, rise above wanting and wishing, and never desire to obtain your pleasure out of anything foreign,

either living or inanimate? Are you ever likely to be so happily qualified as to converse with the gods and men in such a manner as neither to complaint of them nor to be condemned by them?

Put it out of the power of all men to give you a bad name, and if anyone reports you not to be an honest or a good man let your practice give him the lie. This is quite feasible; for who can hinder you from being just and sincere?

There is no one so happy in his family and friends but that some of them, when they see him going, will rejoice at a good riddance. Let him be a person of never so much probity and prudence, yet someone will say at his grave: Well, our man of order and gravity is gone; we shall be no more troubled with his discipline.' This is the best treatment a good man must expect.

XI - OF CALMNESS UNDER ILL USAGE

WHAT a brave soul it is that is always ready to depart from the body and is unconcerned as to whether she will be extinguished, scattered, or removed! But she must be prepared upon reasonable grounds, and not out of mere obstinacy like the Christians; her fortitude must have nothing of noise or of tragic ostentation, but must be grave and seemly.

How fulsome and hollow does that man seem who cries: 'I'm resolved to deal sincerely with you!' Hark you, friend, what need of all this flourish? Let your actions speak. Your face ought to vouch for you. I would have virtue look out of the eye no less apparently than love does. A man of integrity and good nature can never be concealed, for his character is wrought into his countenance.

Gentleness and good humour are invincible, provided they are of the right stamp and without hypocrisy. This is the way to disarm the most outrageous person - to continue kind and unmoved under ill usage and to strike in at the right opportunity with advice. But let all be done out of mere love and kindness.

XII – OF ROMAN FORTITUDE

I HAVE often wondered how it is that everyone should love himself best and yet value his neighbour's opinion of him more than his own. If any man should be ordered to turn his inside outwards and publish every thought and fancy as fast as they came into his head, he would not submit to so much as a day of this discipline. Thus it is that we dread our neighbour's judgement more than our own.

What a mighty privilege man is born to, since it is in his power not to do anything but what God Almighty approves, and to be satisfied with all the distributions of providence!

Reflect upon those who have made the most glorious figure or have met with the greatest misfortunes. Where are they all now? They are vanished like a little smoke; they are nothing but ashes, and a tale - or not even a tale. The prize is insignificant and the game not worth the candle. It is much more becoming to a philosopher to stand clear of affectation, to be honest and moderate upon all occasions and to follow cheerfully wherever the gods lead on, remembering that nothing is more scandalous than a man who is proud of his humility.

Listen, friend! You have been a burgher of this great city. What matter though you have lived in it fewer years or more? If you have kept the laws of the corporation, the length or shortness of the time makes no difference. Where is the hardship, then, if nature, that planted you here, orders your removal? You cannot say you are sent off by an unjust tyrant. No! You quit the stage as fairly as a player does who has his discharge from the master of the revels.

'But I have only gone through three acts, and not held out to the end of the fifth!'

True; but in life three acts may complete the play. He is the only judge of completeness who first ordered your entrance and now orders your exit; you are accountable for neither the one nor the other. Retire, therefore, in serenity, as He who dismisses you is serene.

The Confessions
of Saint Augustine of Hippo
(Hippo Regius, modern Annaba, Algeria, c390)

Jesus Christ (p77) laid down certain principles, but his teachings were made into a Religion by others – most notably Paul of Tarsus and, here, Augustine of Hippo. Amongst Western Christians, Augustine is considered the Patron of Religious Thinkers, a saint and doctor of the Church, his feast celebrated on August 28th. To the Eastern church he is the Blessed Augustine, remembered on the 15th of June.

Based on the 1882 translation by EB Pusey. Abridged: GH

My son, here take the books of my Confessions. Take and use them as a Christian should, and with the charity of a Christian. Here find me as I am, and praise me for no more than I am. And if something in me pleases you, here praise Him with me. "For it is he that hath made us and not we ourselves." As, then, you find me in these pages, pray for me that I may go on to be perfected. Pray for me, my son, pray for me.

From Augustine's final letter to his son Darius

I

"Great art thou, O Lord, great is thy power, infinite thy wisdom. But how shall I call upon my God? Do the heavens and the earth contain thee? Though thou fill many vessels, none confine thee. Still, dust and ashes as I am, allow me to speak before thy mercy. From whence came I to this life-in-death? Or is it death-in-life? I grew out of infancy, or rather boyhood grew into me (for where would infancy go?); and I was no longer an infant who could not speak, but became a chattering boy. O my God! I was sent to a school, to learn tricks of speech for the sake of honour and foolish wealth. And when I learned not, I was flogged, as our forefathers thought proper. And I was punished for playing. And why? So that I might learn as a man play more shameful games. But about this time, O Lord, I observed men praying, and I began to pray. And yet, O Lord my God, creator of all, I sinned against my parents and teachers. Even as a boy I had heard of eternal life promised to us through the Lord our God. My mother Monica and the whole household, except my father, did acknowledge thee. But it was her desire, O my God, that I should take thee as my true Father. O my God, why was I not baptised into thee at that time? I had no love of learning, and hated to be driven to it, for no man does well against his will. I learned to read. Yet, O God, light of my heart, I did not love thee, and thus committed fornication against thee while those around me cried out "Well done!" The friendship of this world is indeed fornication against thee! I was driven to Greek by the rod, yet I loved to learn Latin. Oh, that men might see how better curiosity leads to learning than threats and fear! But I survived my boyhood to learn to take pleasure in truth. I had a good memory and spoke with vigour. Thanks be to thee, my joy, my pride, my confidence, my God.

II

What delighted me save love? Yet I shunned the bright path of friendship and pursued the fleshly passion of fornication. O! If I had heeded that voice from the clouds "It is good for a man not to touch a woman," and with joy become "a eunuch for the Kingdom of Heaven's sake". But it was my father who, at the baths, saw that I was becoming a man, and took pleasure in it, as if drunk with wine I ignored the counsel of thy handmaiden, my mother, "not to commit fornication". Instead, I rolled in the mire of Babylon as if on a bed of spices. Theft, too, is punished by thy law and by man's. Yet, a group of young scoundrels, I among them, did steal away a load of pears from our neighbour's tree. Poor fruit they were, which we dumped to the hogs. It was an evil act, and I loved it for being evil. Who can explain such a twisted and tangled knottiness? O my God, how I wandered far from thee, and made of myself a wasteland.

III

I came to Carthage, where a cauldron of unholy loves was seething and bubbling around me. And I took joy with the body of my lover, and so polluted the spring of friendship with the slime of lust. I became a master in the School of rhetoric, a craft which praises highest the lawyer with greatest deviousness. I even took companionship with the jeering club called 'The Wreckers', though thou knowest I took no part in their worst excesses. In my studies, I chanced upon Cicero's 'Hortensius', and it flamed in me the love of wisdom the Greeks call "philosophy". But I did not then know the words of thy apostle "Beware lest any man spoil you through philosophy and vain deceit" I studied, too, the Holy Scripture, and behold, I saw something sublime and veiled in mysteries. Thus, I fell among the followers of Mani, men who spoke of our Lord Jesus Christ and of the Paraclete and cried "Truth, Truth." The fables of poets I can make a food for the mind, but what nonsense were these men's snares! I came to hang on their foolish questions; "Whence comes evil?" "Has God hair and nails?" I did not yet know that evil is but privation of good, nor that God is spirit. I was blind. But my faithful mother, that chaste, pious and sober widow, wept for me. And thou gave to her an answer, by thy bishop, who told her that I was inflated with the novelty of heresy, "Let him alone. Pray for him. He will come, he will come".

IV

I had a mistress, without lawful marriage. I did repel a filthy sorcerer who offered fame in return for sacrifices, yet I happily consulted with astrologers who said, "Your sin is the doing of Venus, or Mars", that man may regard himself blameless. In those years a dear friend of childhood, who I had turned away from true faith, was taken unto thee after a fever. My heart was utterly darkened by this sorrow and everywhere I looked, I saw death. I should have raised my spirit to thee, O Lord, for thee to lighten my load. What did it profit me to untangle knotty volumes of rhetoric, without pious faith? O, those of lesser wit are easier fledged! O God, let thy wings bear us up when we are little and even down to our grey hairs, carry us.

V

Lord! Accept my confession! In my twenty-ninth year, thou didst so deal with me that I was persuaded to go to teach in Rome. So, with sadness, I lied to my sweet mother and slipped away unseen. Didst thou, O God, not hear my mother's tearful prayers that I stay? Thou, O Lord, had a greater purpose. Lo, in Rome, I was struck with grievous illness and would have fallen into fiery torment from my sins. Yet thou heard my mother's prayers and saved me, to carry out thy plan. Still I met with the deluded and deluding "saints" of Mani. Yet I now was half inclined to join the "Academic" philosophers in doubting everything, and denying man the power of comprehending certainty. Still I thought of God as like a huge man, and of evil as some solid thing. I began my work teaching rhetoric, yet found that some students would conspire to transfer to another teacher before their course was over, to evade their master's fees, an unfaithfulness I never had to bear in Africa. Such people are base indeed; they fornicate against thee. So I applied to work in Milan, and went there, to Ambrose thy bishop, whose eloquent discourse abundantly provided thy

people with the flour of thy wheat and the sober intoxication of thy wine. That man of God received me as a father would. I was drawing closer. He showed me how parts of the Old Testament were allegorical, where my literal interpretation had killed me spiritually. I resolved, at last, to become a catechumen; to take instruction in the faith of Christ.

VI

My mother joined me, assured in a dream that she would have safe passage. And she brought to the oratories offerings of porridge, bread, and wine, as had been her custom in Africa. But Ambrose forbade these earthly gifts, so that she learned to bring instead a heart full of purer petitions, and to give all she could to the poor. Ambrose seemed a happy man, only his celibacy appeared a burden, and I longed to discourse with him. I began to see how honestly the Catholic Church accepted thy teachings, without need of the Manicheans absurd proofs. I remember seeing a poor drunk laughing in the streets. He bought his contentment with a few coins, and would lose it the same night. But I lived on with my confusions. I remember too, how my good student Alypius took to following the madness of the gladiators' fights. I failed to persuade him the better, but thou showed me how to. I was teaching a text, when a simile occurred to me from the gladiatorial circus. Thou hast written in thy Book, "Rebuke a wise man, and he will love you." Now Alypius, took this to mean himself, and soon abandoned the bloody pastime. My friend Nebridius also come to Milan, so there were three begging mouths, waiting for thy food. I wooed, and became engaged to a girl two years too young to marry, and I agreed to wait for her. We were weary of the turbulent vexations of life. We considered making a community of ten, holding a purse in common, and each taking a turn to manage. But considering our wives, or our betrothed, the plan was cast aside. I sent my old lover back to Africa, still vowing to thee that she would know no other man, and leaving with me my son by her. But, slave of lust, I procured another mistress. Thus, Alypius, Nebridius, and myself whiled our time in discussions of good and evil. But I could not hear you near, calling "Run, I will carry you; yea, I will lead you home and then I will set you free."

VII

I now saw that thou, O God, has no body. But still I thought of thee as an infinity interpenetrating the whole mass of the world, so that a greater part of the earth would contain a greater part of thee; a smaller part, a smaller fraction of thee. But thou art not such a one. But still I did not know the cause of evil, but began to realise that evil doing comes from free will. I had seen a light, for I knew that I had free will. At last, thy light entered my inward soul! Not this earthly light, but as if the light of day were grown brighter and brighter, to flood all space. Love knows it, O Eternal Truth and True Love and Beloved Eternity!

VIII

O my God, let my bones be bathed in thy love. Of thy eternal life I was now certain, although I had seen it "through a glass darkly." I no longer craved certainty about thee, but rather greater steadfastness in thee. I went, therefore, to Simplicianus, the spiritual father of Bishop Ambrose and made a proud and public profession of Christ. At this time, one Ponticianus, a fellow African and high official of the emperor's, came to visit us. He was a Christian, and told us of many things we knew not before. He told of Anthony, the Egyptian monk, and of monasteries full of good brothers. But while he was speaking, thou, O Lord, turned me toward myself, that I might see how ugly I was, and how crooked and sordid, bespotted and ulcerous. I had long desired wisdom, yet here I was, still postponing the abandonment of this world and praying "Grant me chastity and continence, but not yet." I cried; "And thou, O Lord, how long? How long, O Lord? Wilt thou be angry forever? "How long, how long? Suddenly I heard the voice of a boy or a girl, I know not which, coming from the neighbouring house, chanting over and over again, "Pick it up, read it; pick it up, read it." I could not but think that this was a divine command to open the Bible and read the first passage I should light upon. So I opened the Apostle's book and read "Not in rioting and drunkenness, not in chambering and wantonness, not in strife and envying, but in the Lord Jesus Christ." I had no need to read further. My heart was infused with something like the light of full certainty and all the gloom of doubt vanished away.

IX

My plan became clear; to wait while harvest holiday was over, and then resign my position. Friend Verecundus, a heathen, was distressed by my choice, but gave us the use of his country house. And behold! Soon afterwards, he was taken with a sickness and chose to be baptised to depart this life to thy resurrection. Nebridius, too, became a faithful member of the Catholic Church, serving thee in perfect continence among his own people in Africa. Then thou didst release him from the flesh, and, my sweet friend, he now he lives in Abraham's bosom. So, I left my professorship, and retired with my friends and my beloved mother to the villa. During that time thou didst torture me with a terrible toothache, so that, God of all health, we bowed our knees in supplication, and the pain was gone. We returned to Milan, myself, Alypius, and Adeodatus (my son from my sinning) and were baptised. We were made free by the voices of thy sweet-speaking Church! The truth was poured forth into us, and my tears ran down, and I was happy. Thou, O Lord, also brought to us Evodius, a young man who had served as a secret service agent. He had converted to thee and baptised. We planned to return together to Africa, but, reaching Ostia, my mother died. That sober matron had, in her youth, slipped into the habit of drink. What could prevail against that secret disease but thy medicine, O Lord? A slave girl called her "a drunkard",

and, stung by this taunt, she saw her vileness and was cured. For, as the flattery of friends corrupts, so often do the taunts of enemies instruct. Thou, O Lord, ruler of heaven and earth, healest one soul by the unsoundness of another. Thus modestly and soberly brought up, she was given to a husband, and she busied herself to gain him to thee, She endured with patience his infidelity and his violent anger. While other matrons equally bore the marks of blows on their disfigured faces, she would admonish them for blaming their husbands, for they ought not to oppose their lords. Such gifts, O my God, my Mercy, did though bestow upon that good handmaid of thine, in whose womb thou didst create me. But, O God of my heart, I now beseech thee, forgive her sins, O Lord, "enter not into judgement" with her.

X

Let me know thee, O my Knower; let me know thee as I am known. Let me be taken to thee, O Strength of my soul. May the fruit of my confessions be refreshment to other men. But I will soar above even this, and closer yet to my God. I will enter the fields and spacious halls of memory, to ask what should be brought forth. Oh men! Ye marvel at the mountains and the seas and the skies, and yet neglect to marvel at yourselves. But these are not the things themselves. How can this be? I remember many things which I know now as false, yet it is not false that I remember them. I can remember fears without fear, and desires without desire. The memory seems as the belly of the mind, and joy and sadness are like sweet and bitter food. But look, it is from my memory that I say that there are four basic emotions; desire, joy, fear, sadness. It is a profound marvel, O my God, let me leap toward thee and find what I am. Oh, too late have I loved thee, beauty so ancient and so new, too late have I loved thee. Behold, thou wast within me and I was searching outside, among the beauty of thy creation. At last, didst thou call out loud, didst thou force open my deafness and didst chase away my blindness. Thou didst breathe fragrant odours and I drew in my breath; and now I pant for thee. Lord, have pity on me. Thou art the Physician, I am the sick man; thou art merciful, I need mercy. O Love, O my God, enkindle me! Lord, let my soul be free from the sticky glue of lust. Until then, I confess my filthy wickedness unto my good Lord, trembling with joy at thy gifts and grieving over my imperfections. Drunkenness is far from me, but "surfeiting" sometimes creeps upon thy servant. Verily Thou enjoinest me continency from the lust of the flesh, the lust of the eyes, and the ambition of the world. Thou enjoinest continency from concubinage; and for wedlock itself, Thou hast counselled something better than what Thou hast permitted. But there yet live in my memory (whereof I have much spoken) the images of such things as my ill custom there fixed. O Lord, my God, give ear, look and see, have mercy upon me; and heal me. I am not much troubled by the allurement of perfumes, though I may deceive myself in this. I am free from the allure of beautiful sounds, though I confess I find some repose in thy sweet hymns. The pleasures of sight confront me everywhere as daylight, the queen of colours, floods so many beautiful forms. From this, thou will rescue me, thou will. There is yet another temptation more perilous still- the foolish pursuit of knowledge and learning. True, the theatres do not now carry me away, nor care I to know the courses of the stars, and I detest sacrilegious mysteries. But how I take interest in idle tales! How I can be diverted by the sight of a dog chasing a rabbit, or a lizard catching flies! Such vanities interrupt our prayers. But, O Lord, there is yet a temptation left me; the desire to be feared and loved of men. There is one more evil temptation; the empty desire to please ourselves, taking pleasure in thy good things as if they were our own and not truly thine. Should I ask the angels? Should I pray? Should I invoke a ritual? The true Mediator between God and man is the man Christ Jesus Christ. Without thy son, I should utterly despair.

XI

Dost thou hear me from thy infinity O Lord? Dost thou see events in time? Let thy Scriptures be my chaste delight. Perfect me, O Lord, and reveal them unto me. But how didst thou make the heaven and the earth? Not like a craft-worker, imposing form on something that already existed, according to the fancy of the mind thou gave him. But how didst thou speak? Only from a body comes a voice. Didst thou then make a body? Thou dost call us to understand the eternal Word. But, my Lord, I know not how to ask. Some sinners dare to ask, "What was God doing before he made heaven and earth?" How shall I reply to such people? I will not answer, as one is did "He was preparing hell for those who pry too deep." For what is time? I know that there would be no past time if nothing had fallen away, and if nothing were still coming there would be no future time; and if there were nothing at all there would be no present time. What is the manner by which seers foretell secret things? O Lord my God, O good Father, I beseech thee through Christ, do not close off these things. Let their light dawn by thy enlightening mercy, O Lord. I once heard a learned man say that the motions of the sun and moon are time. But thou dost not command me to believe that time is motion, for no body is moved but in time. Yet I do measure intervals of time, but what is it that I thus measure, O my God? I ask thee. O my God, what is it that I am measuring? From the beginning thou didst know of all things, at all times. Time is thine, but thou art not in time. Let him who understands this confess to thee; and let him who does not understand also confess to thee!

XII

My heart is deeply stirred, O Lord, when words of thy Holy Scripture strike upon it. I humbly praise thee that madest heaven, and made the earth that made me. But where is thy heaven of heavens, O Lord? O Lord, when I first heard of such things, I did not understand it, for I could not conceive of matter without form. Yet, in the beginning, Holy, Holy, Holy, Lord God Almighty, through thy Wisdom, which is born of thy substance, thou didst create something out of

nothing. O my God, thy Scripture says that thou madest heaven and earth, but it does not say on what day. I understand that thy "heaven of heavens" is where all things are known, not "in part," not "through a glass darkly," but as a simultaneous whole. Let those who deny these things bark and crow with as much clamour as they please. I will beseech them to be quiet and to listen to they word. As for myself, I will sing to thee the songs of love in my pilgrimage to Jerusalem, my mother country. And I will say of them, "Be thou, O God, the judge between my confessions and their gainsaying." Some say that by 'heaven' Moses did not mean that spiritual creation which always beholds the face of God. Let all of us honour Moses, full of thy Spirit, O fountain of truth, and believe that thou didst reveal thyself to him. Thus, when one man says, "Moses meant such," and another says, "No, he meant this other," then why might not both be true, or there be a third or fourth truth, and it might be that Moses saw all of them. For cannot the one God so temper his Holy Scriptures that they speak many truths to many different people? What strength of mind, what length of time, would suffice for all thy books to be interpreted?

XIII

I call on thee, my God, my Mercy, who madest me and didst not forget me. I call thee into my soul. Now what thou saidst in the beginning "Let there be light, and there was light", I interpret, as referring to the spiritual creation, as it had a life which thou couldst illuminate. But why, O truth-speaking Light? Disperse the shadows and tell me, I beseech thee, why thy Scripture should only at last refer to thy Spirit? Was it inappropriate to tell of him "moving over the waters", unless something had first been mentioned over which he could move? As thy Apostle tells us, "Thy love is shed abroad in our hearts by the Holy Spirit" who teacheth us about spiritual gifts and showeth us the excellent way of love, that we may come to the surpassing knowledge of the love of Christ. The uncleanness of our own spirit flows downward with the love of worldly care; and the sanctity of thy Spirit raises us upward by the love of release from anxiety. Thus the angels fell, and the soul of man fell, that we might know the depth of the abyss over which thou decreed "Let there be light". Who can understand the omnipotent Trinity? Rare is the soul who, when he speaks of it, knows of what he speaks. Let thy works praise thee, that we may love thee; and let us love thee that thy works may praise thee. O Lord God, Grant us the peace of quietness, the peace of thy Sabbath, the peace without an evening. That we might find beautiful rest in thee in the Sabbath of life eternal. O Lord, our works are thy works through us. Thou seest not in time, thou movest not in time, thou resteth not in time. We can see those things which thou hast made because thou seest them. Thou, O the one good God, hast never ceased to do good! And we have accomplished some good works by thy good gifts, and even though they are not eternal, still we hope, after these things here, to find our rest in thy great sanctification. What man or what angel can teach men to understand this? We must ask it of thee; we must seek it in thee; we must knock for it at thy door. Only thus shall we find. Only thus shall the door be opened. Amen

FOR THE SAKE OF MY LORD

The Noble Quran
القرآن

(Mecca and Medina, modern Saudi Arabia, c632)

The Qur'ān, or 'recitation' is the central text of Islam, said to have been revealed by God to Muhammad bin Abdullah through the angel Gabriel over some twenty years and written down by Muhammad's companions. It consists of 114 *suras*, customarily arranged not chronologically or thematically, but, apart from the opening, simply in order of decreasing length. Each, except one, begins with the 'Bismala' *In the name of Allah...* and is typically divided into numbered *ayahs*. The meaning of the letter groups at the beginning of some suras remains obscure.

NOTE: This is not a devotional text, but a short abridgement for private study. It is traditionally taken that The Quran is a complete book in Arabic, and if it is not complete or not in Arabic, as with this and other abridgements or selections, then it is not the Quran, and is not due the high reverence usually accorded to the physical text.

Paraphrased from the translations by Abdullah Yusuf Ali and Mohammad Habib Shakir. Abridged: GH.

1: THE OPENING (Al-Fatehah)

In the name of Allah, the Beneficent, the Merciful

Praise be to Allah, the Cherisher and Sustainer of the worlds; The Beneficent, the Merciful. Master of the Day of Judgment. Thee do we serve and Thee do we beseech for help. Show us the straight way, the way of those who receive Thy Grace, not the way of those who gain Thy wrath or go astray.

2: THE COW (Al-Baqarah)

In the name of Allah, the Beneficent, the Merciful

1 A.L.M.

2 This is the definitive Scripture; honest guidance to those who guard against evil. Those who believe in the Unseen, are steadfast in prayer, and spend out of what We have granted them; They are truly guided by their Lord, they will prosper. As for the Disbelievers, whether thou warn them or not; they will not believe. Allah hath sealed their hearts, their hearing, and on their eyes is a veil. Theirs will be an awful punishment.

30 Thy Lord said, "I will create a vicegerent on earth." "O Adam! dwell thou and thy wife in the Garden; but approach not the tree, or ye transgress." Yet Satan made them fall. And we said, "Earth will be your dwelling-place- for a time."

40 O Children of Israel! Remember the favours I have bestowed upon you! We divided the sea for you, and drowned Pharaoh's people for you. We gave Moses the Scripture and the Commandments[1]. But the transgressors altered the words from that which had been given. [60] And remember ye beseeched Moses for water. And ye beseeched Moses for pot-herbs, and cucumbers, garlic, lentils, and onions. Those who believe in the Qur'an, and those who follow the scriptures of the Jews, the Christians

and the Sabians, any who believe in Allah and the Last Day, and work righteousness, shall have their reward with their Lord; on them shall be no fear.

67 And remember Moses said to his people, "Allah commands that ye sacrifice a heifer." Then they offered her in sacrifice, but not with good-will. Remember ye slew a man and fell into a dispute among yourselves as to a crime: But Allah was to bring forth what ye did hide. So We said, "Strike the body with a piece of the heifer." Thus Allah bringeth the dead to life and showeth you His Signs: Perchance ye may understand.

83 And remember We took a covenant from the Children of Israel: Worship none but Allah; treat with kindness your parents and kindred, and orphans and those in need; speak fair to the people; be steadfast in prayer; and practise regular charity. Then did ye turn back, except a few among you, and ye backslide even now. Whoever is an enemy to Allah and His angels and messengers, to Gabriel and Michael, Lo! Allah is an enemy to those who reject Faith. Be steadfast in prayer and regular in charity: And whatever good ye send forth for your souls before you, ye shall find it with Allah: for Allah sees well all that ye do.

113 The Jews say, "The Christians have naught to stand upon"; and the Christians say, "The Jews have naught to stand upon." Yet they profess to study the same Book. Allah will judge between them on the Day of Judgment. Say ye, "We believe in Allah, and the revelation given to us, and to Abraham and Moses[2] and Jesus[3]. Our religion is the Baptism of Allah: it is He Whom we worship". Those who reject Faith, and die rejecting, on them is Allah's curse, and the curse of angels, and of all mankind; Your Allah is One Allah: There is no god but He, Most Gracious, Most Merciful.

---

1   **The Scripture and Commandments:** see p23

2   **Abraham:** see The Torah (p23), Genesis 17
3   **Jesus:** see p77

164 Behold! the creation of the heavens and the earth; the night and the day; the rain which Allah Sends down, the life which He gives to an earth that is dead; the beasts, the winds, and the clouds. Here are Signs for the wise. O ye people! Eat of what is on earth, Lawful and good. He hath only forbidden you dead meat, blood, and the flesh of swine, and that on which any name hath been invoked other than that of Allah. But if one is forced by necessity, then is he guiltless. For Allah is Most Merciful.

178 O ye who believe! equality is prescribed to you in cases of murder: the free for the free, the slave for the slave, the woman for the woman. But if any remission is made by the brother of the slain, then grant any reasonable demand. It is prescribed, when death approaches you, to make a reasonable bequest to parents and next of kin.

183 O ye who believe! Ramadhan is the month every one of you should spend in fasting. But if one is ill, or travelling, the period should be made up later. Allah does not want to make difficulties. Permitted to you, on the night of the fasts, is the approach to your wives. They are your garments and ye are their garments. And you may eat and drink until the white thread of dawn appear to you distinct from its black thread. Those are Limits set by Allah: that you may learn self-restraint.

190 Fight in the cause of Allah those who fight you, but do not transgress limits; for Allah loveth not transgressors. Slay them wherever ye catch them, but fight them not at the Sacred Mosque. And fight on until there is no more Tumult or oppression, and there prevails justice and faith in Allah.

196 Perform the pilgrimage of Hajj and the visit to Mecca for Allah. And if ye are prevented, then send such gifts as can be obtained with ease, and shave not your heads until the gifts have reached their destination. Let there be no obscenity, nor wickedness, nor wrangling in the Hajj. Whatever good ye do, Allah knoweth it.

219 When they ask thee concerning wine and gambling. Say, "In them is some sin, and some gain; but the sin is greater than the gain." When they ask thee concerning orphans. Say, "The best thing to do is what is for their good."

221 Do not marry unbelieving women, until they believe: A slave woman who believes is better than an unbelieving woman, even though she allures you. A man slave who believes is better than an unbeliever, even though he allures you. Unbelievers do but beckon you to the Fire. But Allah beckons by His Grace to the Garden of bliss and forgiveness. When they ask thee concerning women's courses. Say: They are a hurt and a pollution: So keep away from women in their courses, for Allah loves those who keep themselves clean. A divorce is only permissible twice: after that, the parties should either hold together on equitable terms, or separate with kindness. So if a husband divorces his wife irrevocably, he cannot then re-marry her until after she has married and divorced another husband. Mothers shall give suck to their offspring for two whole years, if the father desire, but he shall bear the cost of food

and clothing. No soul shall have a burden laid on it greater than it can bear. No mother nor father shall be treated unfairly on account of their child.

255 [4]Allah! There is no god but He, the Living, the Self-subsisting, Eternal. No slumber can seize Him nor sleep. His are all things in the heavens and on earth. Who is there can intercede in His presence except as He permitteth? He knoweth what appeareth to His creatures as before or after or behind them. Nor shall they compass aught of His knowledge except as He willeth. His Throne extends over the heavens and the earth, and He feeleth no fatigue in guarding and preserving them for He is the Most High, the Supreme in glory.

256 Let there be no compulsion in religion. Truth stands out clear from error: whoever rejects evil and believes in Allah hath grasped the most trustworthy hand-hold, that never breaks. Allah is the Protector of those who have faith: from the depths of darkness He will lead them forth into light. Those who reject faith are the patrons are the evil ones. They will be companions of the fire, to dwell therein for ever. The parable of those who spend their substance in the way of Allah is that of a grain of corn: it groweth seven ears, and each ear Hath a hundred grains. Allah giveth manifold increase to whom He pleaseth: And Allah careth for all and He knoweth all things. O ye who believe! Give of the good things which ye have earned, and of the fruits of the earth which We have produced for you. Those who in charity spend of their goods by night and by day in secret or in public have great reward with their Lord.

275 Allah hath permitted trade and forbidden usury. If a debtor is in a difficulty, grant him time. But if ye remit it by way of charity, it is best if ye only knew. O ye who believe! When ye do business with each other, reduce your contracts to writing. Let a scribe write down faithfully, the one who takes liability to dictate. Allah knoweth all that ye do. On no soul doth Allah place a burden greater than it can bear.

3: THE FAMILY OF IMRAN (Ali-'Imran)

In the name of Allah, the Beneficent, the Merciful

1 A. L. M.

2 Allah! There is no god but He, the living, the Self-Subsisting, Eternal. He has sent down the Book, confirming what went before it. He sent down the Law of Moses and the Gospel of Jesus as a guide to mankind, and He sent down the Commandments for judgment between right and wrong. Say to those who reject Faith, "Soon will ye be vanquished and gathered together to Hell!"

35 Behold! a woman of Imran said, "O my Lord! I dedicate to Thee what is in my womb." And she was delivered of a female child, Mary, commended her and her offspring to Thy protection from the Evil One. Behold! the angels said, "O Mary! Allah hath chosen thee above the women of all nations. O Mary! Allah giveth thee glad tidings: his name will be Christ Jesus, held in honour in this world and the

---

4   Ayah 255 of sura 2 is known as the 'Throne Verse'.

Heavens." Mary said, "O my Lord! How shall I have a son when no man hath touched me?" He said, "Allah createth what He willeth. And Allah will teach him wisdom, and appoint him a messenger to the Children of Israel, to heal the blind, and the lepers, and to quicken the dead, by Allah's leave."

110 If only the People of the Book had faith! Some have faith, but most are perverted transgressors. They who believe in Allah and the Last Day; enjoin what is right, and forbid what is wrong; and hasten in good works: They are in the ranks of the righteous. Those who reject Faith will dwell in the Fire for ever.

118 Ye who believe! Take not into your intimacy those outside your ranks: They will not fail to corrupt you. They only desire your ruin: Rank hatred has already appeared from their mouths: What their hearts conceal is far worse.

149 O ye who believe! If ye obey the Unbelievers, they will drive you back on your heels, and ye will turn from Faith to your own loss. Soon shall We cast terror into the hearts of the Unbelievers, their abode will be the Fire!. Evil indeed is the home of the wrong-doers! Allah did indeed fulfil His promise to you when ye with His permission were about to annihilate your enemy, -until ye flinched and fell to disputing. Those of you who turned back on the day the two hosts met, were guided by Satan because of past actions. But Allah Has blotted out their fault: For Allah is Oft-Forgiving, Most Forbearing.

189 To Allah belongeth the dominion of the heavens and the earth; and Allah hath power over all things. Let not the strutting Unbelievers deceive thee: Their ultimate abode is Hell: what an evil bed to lie on! Yet, for those who fear their Lord, are Gardens, with rivers flowing beneath; therein are they to dwell for ever, a gift from the presence of Allah.

4: THE WOMEN (Al-Nesa')

In the name of Allah, the Beneficent, the Merciful

1 O mankind! reverence your Guardian-Lord, who created you from a single person, created, of like nature, his mate, and from them twain scattered like seeds countless men and women. Reverence Allah, through whom ye demand your mutual rights, and reverence the wombs that bore you, for Allah ever watches over you.

3 If ye fear that ye shall not be able to deal justly with orphans, marry women of your choice, two or three or four. But if ye fear that ye shall not be able to deal justly with them, then only one, or a slave-girl that your right hands possess. To those weak of understanding, feed and clothe them, and speak to them words of kindness and justice.

11 Allah directs you as regards your Children's inheritance: to the male, a portion equal to that of two females: if only daughters, two or more, their share is two-thirds of the inheritance; if only one, her share is a half. These are settled portions ordained by Allah, the All-Knowing, All-Wise.

19 O ye who believe! Ye are forbidden to inherit women against their will. Nor should ye treat them with harshness, but live with them in kindness and equity. Prohibited to you in marriage are your female relatives and your step-daughters born of your wives to whom ye have gone in, no prohibition if ye have not gone in. Allah doth wish to lighten your difficulties: For man was created weak in flesh.

34 Men are the protectors and maintainers of women, because Allah has given the one more strength than the other, and because they support them from their means. Therefore, righteous women are devoutly obedient. Of women on whose part ye fear disloyalty and ill-conduct, admonish them first, next, refuse to share their beds, and last, beat them lightly; but if they return to obedience, seek not against them means of annoyance: For Allah is Most High and great.

43 O ye who believe! Approach not prayers with a mind befogged, nor in a state of impurity. If ye are ill, or on a journey, or come from offices of nature, or ye have been in contact with women, and ye find no water, then take for yourselves clean sand or earth, and rub therewith your faces and hands. For Allah doth blot out sins and forgive again and again.

56 Those who reject our Signs, We shall soon cast into the Fire: as often as their skins are roasted through, We shall change them for fresh skins, that they may taste the penalty: for Allah is Exalted in Power. O ye who believe! Obey Allah, and obey the Messenger. Let those fight in the cause of Allah who sell the life of this world for the hereafter. To him who fighteth in the cause of Allah, whether he is slain or gets victory - We give him a great reward. And why should ye not fight in the cause of Allah and of those who, being weak, are ill-treated and oppressed?

86 When a courteous greeting is offered you, meet it with a greeting still more courteous. Allah takes careful account of all things.

92 Never should a believer kill a believer; but if it happens by mistake, it is ordained that he should free a believing slave, and pay compensation to the deceased's family. If a man kills a believer intentionally, his recompense is Hell, the curse of Allah is upon him.

100 He who forsakes his home in the cause of Allah, finds in the earth Many a refuge, wide and spacious: Should he die as a refugee from home for Allah and His Messenger, His reward becomes due and sure with Allah: And Allah is Oft-Forgiving, Most Merciful. When ye travel through the earth, there is no blame on you if ye shorten your prayers, for fear the Unbelievers may attack you. The Unbelievers are your open enemies.

129 Ye are never able to be fair and just between women, even if it is your ardent desire. But turn not away from a woman altogether, so as to leave her unsupported. If ye come to a friendly understanding, and practise self-restraint, Allah is oft-forgiving, Most Merciful.

156 That they rejected Faith uttered a grave false charge against Mary; they said, "We killed Christ Jesus the son of Mary, the Messenger of Allah", but they killed him not, nor crucified him, but so it was made to appear. Allah raised him up unto Himself; and Allah is Exalted in Power, Wise.

160 For the iniquity of the Jews We made unlawful for them certain foods which are good and wholesome. We have sent inspiration through Noah[5] and the Messengers. O People of the Book! Commit no excesses in your religion: Nor say of Allah aught but the truth. Christ Jesus was a messenger of Allah, say not "Trinity": for Allah is one Allah, He is above having a son. To Him belong all things in the heavens and on earth. Then those who believe in Allah, and hold fast to Him, soon will He admit them to mercy and grace.

5: THE TABLE SPREAD (Al-Ma'edah)

In the name of Allah, the Beneficent, the Merciful

1 O ye who believe! Fulfil your obligations. Lawful unto you for food are most four-footed animals, but animals of the chase are forbidden while ye are on pilgrimage.

6 O ye who believe! when ye prepare for prayer, wash yourselves.

12 Allah did make a covenant with the Children of Israel, From those, too, who call themselves Christians, We took a covenant, but they forgot. So We estranged them, with enmity and hatred to the Day of Judgment.

32 We ordained for the Children of Israel that if any one slew a person, unless for murder or for spreading mischief, it would be as if he slew the whole people: and if any one saved a life, it would be as if he saved a whole people. The punishment of those who wage war against Allah and His Messenger is execution, or crucifixion, or the cutting off of hands and feet, or exile. As to the thief, cut off their hands. But if the thief repents, Allah turneth to him in forgiveness. Allah is Oft-Forgiving, Most Merciful.

44 It was We who revealed the Law to Moses, "Life for life, eye for eye, tooth for tooth, and wound for wound." But if any one remits the retaliation from charity, it is an act of atonement.

46: And We sent Jesus the son of Mary, and the Gospel, as guidance and light, and confirmation of the Law of old. But O ye who believe! take not Jews and the Christians for your friends and protectors, they are but friends and protectors to each other. Your real friends are Allah, His Messenger, and the fellowship of believers. Strongest in enmity to the believers are the Jews and Pagans, and nearest in love to the believers are those who say, "We are Christians".

90 O ye who believe! Intoxicants and gambling, dedication of stones, and divination by arrows, are an abomination of Satan. Eschew such abomination, that ye may prosper. Satan's plan is to excite enmity and hatred between you, with intoxicants and gambling, and hinder you from the remembrance of Allah, and from prayer: will ye not then abstain?

97 Allah made the Ka'ba, the Sacred House, the Sacred Months, the animals for offerings, and the garlands that mark them. It was not Allah who instituted the superstitions of a slit-ear she-camel, or idol sacrifices for twin-births in animals.

109 One day will Allah gather the messengers together, and say, "O Jesus the son of Mary! Thou madest of clay the figure of a bird, and thou breathest upon it and it becometh a living bird, and thou healest those born blind, and the lepers, and thou bringest forth the dead, all by My leave. O Jesus son of Mary! Didst thou say unto men, worship me and my mother as gods?" And he will say, "Glory to Thee! never could I say what I had no right to say."

7: THE HEIGHTS (Al-A'araf)

In the name of Allah, the Beneficent, the Merciful

1 A.L.M.S.

4 How many towns have We destroyed? Our punishment took them while they slept or in their afternoon rest. Remember how we threw Adam and his wife from the garden when they transgressed. Let not Satan seduce you in the same manner. He and his tribe watch you from where ye cannot see, they are the friends to those without faith. O Children of Adam! wear your beautiful apparel for prayer. Eat and drink, but waste not, for Allah loveth not the wasters.

80 We sent Lut to his people, saying, "Do ye commit a new lewdness? For ye practise your lusts on men in preference to women." And we rained down on them a shower of brimstone. See what was the end of those who indulged in sin and crime! To the Madyan people We sent Shu'aib, saying, "O my people! worship Allah." But the earthquake took them unawares! We sent Moses with Our signs to Pharaoh, but they rejected them: So we punished the people with droughts and plagues.

137 And We made a people, considered weak and of no account, inheritors of lands in both east and west. The fair promise of thy Lord was fulfilled for the Children of Israel, because they had patience and constancy. And we ordained for them laws, yet the people of Moses made the image of calf for worship. Thus did we divide them into twelve nations.

180 The most beautiful names belong to Allah: so call on him by them and shun profanity. When the Qur'an is read, listen to it with attention, celebrate His praises, and prostrate before Him.

8: SPOILS OF WAR (Al-Anfal)

In the name of Allah, the Beneficent, the Merciful

1 The spoils of war are at the disposal of Allah and the Messenger. Remember your Lord assisted you with angels, saying, "I am with you, to strengthen the Believers. I will instil terror into the hearts of the Unbelievers- smite ye above their necks and smite all their finger-tips off them."

---

5 **Noah:** see The Torah (p23), Genesis 6

O ye who believe! it is not ye who slew the Unbelievers, it was Allah. When thou threwest dust, it was not thy act, but Allah's.

41 Know ye that of the booty ye acquire in war, a fifth share is for Allah, and his Messenger, and to near relatives, orphans, the needy, and the wayfarer. Yea, enjoy now what ye took in war, lawful and good, but fear Allah. He is Oft-Forgiving, Most Merciful.

9: THE DISPENSATION (Bara'ah)

3 An announcement from Allah and His Messenger, to the people on the day of the Great Pilgrimage! That Allah and His Messenger dissolve all treaty obligations with the dishonest among the Pagans. But when the proscribed months are past, then fight and slay the Pagans wherever ye find them, seize them, beleaguer them, and lie in wait for them with all cunning. If they repent, and establish regular prayers and practise regular charity, then open the way for them. Allah is Oft-Forgiving, Most Merciful. If a Pagan ask thee for asylum, grant it, that he may hear the word of Allah, for they are ignorant men. Oh ye who believe! Truly the Pagans are unclean, so let them not, after this year of theirs, approach the Sacred Mosque. Fight those who believe not in Allah nor acknowledge the religion of Truth, even if they are People of the Book, until they pay the Jizya tax and feel themselves subdued. The Jews call 'Uzair [Ezra] a son of Allah, and the Christians call Christ the son of Allah. Allah's curse be on them!

72 Allah hath promised to Believers, men and women, gardens of everlasting bliss. But the greatest bliss is the good pleasure of Allah. O Prophet! strive hard and firm against the unbelievers and the Hypocrites. Their abode is Hell, an evil refuge indeed.

10: JONAH (Younus)

In the name of Allah, the Beneficent, the Merciful

1 A.L.R. These are the verses of the Book of Wisdom.

2 Is it a wonderment that We have sent Our inspiration to a man among you? Say the Unbelievers, "Here is a sorcerer!" Those who believe will cry, "Glory to Allah! Cherisher and Sustainer of worlds!" Mankind was first but one nation. Had it not been for a word sent from thy Lord, their differences would have been settled. But most of them follow nothing but fancy, which availeth naught against truth.

37 This Qur'an is not such as can be produced by other than Allah, it is a confirmation of the revelations before it, and a fuller explanation of the Book. To those who say, "He forged it", say, "Bring a Sura like unto it, and call to your aid anyone you can besides Allah, if ye speak the truth!"

98 Why was there not a single township among those We warned, which believed, except the people of Jonah? When they believed, We permitted them to enjoy their life for a while. Follow thou the inspiration sent unto thee, and be patient and constant, till Allah do decide: for He is the best to decide.

12: JOSEPH (Yousuf)

In the name of Allah, the Beneficent, the Merciful

1 A.L.R. These are the verses of scripture sent down in plain Arabic, that ye may understand.

3 Here We relate the most beautiful of stories. Behold! The brothers of Joseph said, "Truly Joseph is loved more by our father than we! Let us throw him into a well." So they did, saying to their father, "Lo, the wolf devoured him." But Allah knoweth all they do! And the brethren sold Joseph for a few dirhams to a man of Egypt, who treated him well. But the wife of the house sought to seduce him, yet said he "Allah forbid! truly thy husband is my lord!" So she cast him into prison.

36 Now in the prison, two young men. Said one "I dream of pressing wine." said the other "I dream of birds eating bread from my head." "Tell us the meaning thereof." "O my companions! One of you will pour wine for his lord, the other will hang from the cross."

43 The king of Egypt said "I see in a vision seven fat kine, whom seven lean ones devour, and seven green ears of corn, and seven withered. O ye chiefs! Expound to me my vision" They said "We know not." But the companion of the prison, now released, said "Ask, O King, of Joseph." Joseph said "Seven years shall ye sow, then will come seven years of want." Said the King "I take thee to myself, an honoured man."

58 Came Joseph's brethren, to buy corn, and he knew them, but they knew him not. And by a trick he put a gold drinking-cup into his brother's saddle-bag, so that some shouted "Ye thieves! Slavery is the reward of the thief. Turn back to your father, and say, 'O father! Thy son committed theft! we bear witness!'"

83 And so, Jacob the father said "O my sons! go ye to enquire about Joseph and his brother, and never give up hope of Allah's Soothing." And when they returned into Joseph's presence they said "O exalted one! distress has seized our family, grant us some bushells, for Allah doth reward the charitable." He said "Know ye how ye dealt with Joseph and his brother? I am Joseph, and this is our brother, behold, never will Allah suffer the reward to be lost of those who do right." They said "Indeed we have sinned!" He said "Allah will forgive you! Take my old shirt, and cast it over the face of my father, and his old eyes will become clear." And so did they, and Joseph gave a home for them with himself in Egypt. Here is a true story of wise instruction, a guide and a mercy to such as believe.

16: THE BEE (Al-Nahl)

In the name of Allah, the Beneficent, the Merciful

1 Inevitable are the Command of Allah, seek ye not then to hasten them. He has created the heavens and the earth for just ends. He has created man from a sperm-drop, yet this same man disputes Him! Cattle He has created for you, that ye have pride in as ye drive them home in the evening, and to pasture in the morning, and who carry your heavy loads to far lands. He has created horses, mules, and donkeys, for you to ride and for show. He has created other things of which ye have no knowledge. He produces for you corn, olives, date-palms, grapes and fruit. He has made the Night and the Day, sun and moon. Allah sends down life-giving rain from the skies. And thy Lord taught the Bee to build its cells in hills, on trees, and in men's habitations. There issues from their bodies a drink of varying colours, wherein is healing for men. Truly, this is a Sign.

70 It is Allah who creates you and takes your souls at death, and who sends some back to an age where they know nothing after having known much. Allah is All-Knowing, All-Powerful. Allah has bestowed His gifts of sustenance more freely on some of you than on others.

127 Do thou be patient, for thy patience is from Allah; For Allah is with those who restrain themselves, and those who do good.

17: THE NIGHT JOURNEY or THE CHILDREN OF ISRAEL (Bani Israel)

In the name of Allah, the Beneficent, the Merciful

1 Glory to Allah Who did take His servant for a Journey by night from the Sacred Mosque to the farthest Mosque. He is the One Who heareth and seeth all. The One who gave Clear Warning to the Children of Israel, that twice would they do mischief and twice be punished!

13 On the Day of Judgment each man shall be brought to account. Therefore be kind to your parents. render to kindred their dues, and to those in want, and to the wayfarer. Kill not your children for fear of want, for We shall provide. Nor come to adultery, nor take life except for just cause. Come not to the orphan's property except to improve it, for all will be known to Allah.

35 Give full measure, and weigh with a balance true. Pursue not that of which thou hast no knowledge. Walk not on the earth with insolence, for thou canst not rend the earth asunder, nor approach the mountains in height.

45 Recite the Qur'an with respect and call upon Allah, or call upon Rahman, for all his names are Most Beautiful.

18: THE CAVE (Al-Kahf)

In the name of Allah, the Beneficent, the Merciful

1 Praise be to Allah, Who hath sent to His Servant the Book, and hath allowed therein no Crookedness. Those who say, "Allah hath a son" say falsehood!

10 Behold, some youthful companions betook themselves to a Cave, then We drew a veil over their ears, for a number of years. Then We roused them from sleep, and one said, "We have stayed perhaps a day." Some say they were five, some say seven and their dog. Enter not into controversies concerning the affair of the Sleepers. They stayed in their Cave three hundred years, and some say nine more.

83 When they ask thee concerning Zul-Qarnain[6], say, We granted him strength, that he followed clear roads to the place where the sun sets, and found there a pool of dark water and a People living. We said, "O Zul-qarnain! thou hast authority, to punish, or to protect." He said, "Whoever believes, and works righteousness, shall have a goodly reward." Then he came to the land where the sun rises, and found there a naked people. Then did he reach a place between two mountains, and found a people who scarcely understood a word. They said, "O Zul-qarnain! the Gog and Magog People do great mischief, make up a barrier between us and them." And he filled up the space between the mountains with iron and molten lead, saying, "In proper time my Lord will make it dust." Then shall We leave them to surge like waves on one another, the trumpet will blow, and We shall collect them together. The Unbelievers shall see Hell, and the righteous will have the Gardens of Paradise,

109 Say, "If the ocean were ink to write out the words of my Lord, sooner would the ocean be exhausted than would the words of my Lord."

19: MARY (Maryam)

In the name of Allah, the Beneficent, the Merciful

16 Tell now the story of Mary, how she withdrew from her family to a place in the East. She veiled herself and We sent to her Our Spirit, appearing as a handsome man. He said, "I am a messenger from thy Lord, to announce to thee the gift of a holy son." She said, "How shall I have a son, seeing that no man has touched me?" So she conceived him, and when the pains of childbirth came, a voice cried to her from beneath a palm-tree, "Grieve not! for thy Lord hath provided. Shake the trunk of the palm-tree, ripe dates will fall into stream beneath, so eat and drink and cool thine eye." Such was born Jesus the son of Mary, this is a statement of truth.

20: TA-HA

In the name of Allah, the Beneficent, the Merciful

1 Ta-Ha.

2 We have not sent down the Qur'an to be an occasion for distress, but only as an admonition to those who fear Allah.

9 Has the story of Moses reached thee? Behold, he saw a fire, and said to his family, "Tarry ye, perhaps I can bring you some burning brand therefrom." But from the fire a voice was heard, "I am thy Lord! in My presence put off thy shoes. And what is that in the right hand, O Moses?" He said, "It is my rod, on it I lean, with it I beat down fodder, and in it I find other uses." Allah said, "Throw it!" And behold! It became a snake, alive!

21 Allah said, "Go thou to Pharaoh." And Pharaoh said, "Hast thou come to drive us out of our land with magic, O Moses? We can surely produce magic also!" Than did Pharoh's magicians make, by trickery, rods and ropes to

---

6   **Zul-Qarnain:** 'The Two-Horned Lord', supposed to be Alexander the Great of Macedon

move like snakes, but the snakes of Moses' rod devoured them. And then Pharaoh pursued them with his forces, but the waters overcame him.

80 O ye Children of Israel! We delivered you from your enemy, and made a Covenant with you on the side of Mount Sinai, and We sent to you Manna and quails and brought you away from the worship of the image of a calf. Thus do We relate to thee some old stories: and for now have We sent an Arabic Qur'an.

132 Be constant in prayer. Say, "Wait ye, and soon shall ye know who it is that is on the straight way, and who it is that has received Guidance."

21: THE PROPHETS (Al-Anbya')

In the name of Allah, the Beneficent, the Merciful

1 Closer and closer to mankind comes their Reckoning, yet they heed not.

16 Not for idle sport did We create the heavens and the earth! We hurl the Truth against falsehood, and it knocks out its brain, and behold, falsehood doth perish! We granted to Moses and Aaron the Commandments, We bestowed on Abraham his proper course.

76 Remember Noah, when he cried to Us aforetime- We listened to his prayer and delivered him and his family from great distress. The people given to Evil We drowned in the Flood all together. And remember David and Solomon, Isma'il, Idris, and Zul-kifl, Zun-nun and Zakariya.

96 When the Gog and Magog people are let through their barrier, and they swarm from every hill. Then will the true promise draw nigh! Verily ye, unbelievers, and the false gods ye worship, are but fuel for Hell! Allah is One, therefore bow to His Will in Islam.

22 THE PILGRIMAGE (Al-Hajj)

In the name of Allah, the Beneficent, the Merciful

1 O mankind! fear your Lord! For at the Hour of Judgment Allah will admit those who believe and work righteous deeds to Gardens beneath which rivers flow, and they shall be adorned with gold and pearls, and their garments will be silk.

26 Behold! We gave to Abraham the Sacred House, saying, "Sanctify My House for those who walk it round, or present themselves therein in prayer. And proclaim the Pilgrimage among men, they will come to thee on foot and on every kind of camel."

34 To every people did We appoint rites of sacrifice; Then pronounce the name of Allah over the camels, and when they are killed, eat ye thereof, and feed the poor who beg with due humility. We have made animals subject to you, that ye may be grateful.

39 To those against whom war is made, permission is given to fight, because they are wronged, and verily, Allah is powerful for their aid. They are those who have been expelled from their homes for no cause but sayong, "Our Lord is Allah". Did not Allah check one set of people by means of another, so that the churches, synagogues and mosques, wherein Allah is honoured, do not fall. Allah will aid those who aid Him, for Allah is Mighty. Yet they ask thee to hasten the Punishment! But Allah will not fail in His Promise. Verily a Day in the sight of thy Lord is like a thousand years of your reckoning.

77 O ye who believe! Worship and do good. It is He who has chosen you, and has imposed no difficulties on you in religion, the faith of your father Abraham.

23: THE BELIEVERS (Al-Mu'minun)

In the name of Allah, the Beneficent, the Merciful

1 The believers must eventually succeed- Those who humble themselves in prayer, who avoid vain talk, who are active in deeds of charity, who abstain from sex except in marriage, or with the slaves whom their right hands possess. These will be the heirs, who will inherit Paradise, to dwell therein for ever.

12 Man We did create from a quintessence of clay, and all the good things of the earth. We sent prophets like to Noah, saying "O my people! worship Allah! Ye have no other god but Him." We inspired him to construct the Ark, then when at our Command, the fountains of the earth gushed forth, to take of every species, male and female, and his family- except the wrong-doers. We sent Moses and Aaron, and We made the son of Mary.

52 Verily this Brotherhood of yours is a single Brotherhood, therefore fear Me and no other.

24: THE LIGHT (Al-Noor)

In the name of Allah, the Beneficent, the Merciful

2 The woman and the man guilty of adultery or fornication- flog each of them with a hundred stripes Let not compassion move you, it is a matter prescribed by Allah, and let a party of Believers witness their punishment. And those who accuse a chaste women, and produce not four witnesses- flog them with eighty stripes. Unless they repent; for Allah is Oft-Forgiving, Most Merciful. Women impure are for men impure.

30 Say to the believing men that they should lower their gaze and guard their modesty. And say to the believing women that they should lower their gaze and guard their modesty. They should not display their beauty and ornaments without need. They should draw their veils over their bosoms and display their beauty only to their husbands, their close relatives, their slaves, or male servants who have no need of women. O ye Believers! turn ye towards Allah, that ye may attain Bliss. Let those who find not the wherewithal for marriage keep themselves chaste. If your goodly slave ask for their freedom, give them such, yea, and something more. But force not your maids to prostitution.

56 Pray, give Charity; and obey the Messenger; that ye may receive mercy. Never think that the Unbelievers will frustrate Allah's Plan. Their abode is Fire!

58 Let those whom your right hands possess, and children not of age, ask your permission before they come to your presence, on three occasions- before morning prayer, while ye doff your clothes for the noonday heat, and after late-night prayer.

60 Elderly women may lay aside their outer garments, provided they make not a wanton display. Allah sees and knows all things.

64 To Allah is heaven and earth. He knows your intention. One day ye will be brought back to Him.

27: THE ANT (Al-Naml)

In the name of Allah, the Beneficent, the Merciful

1 These are verses of the Qur'an- a book that makes things clear;

17 King Sulayman [Solomon] with his hosts, of jinns and men and birds, came to a valley of ants. And one of the ants said, "O ants, get into your habitations, lest ye be crushed under foot." And Soloman took a muster of the Birds, and said, "Where is the Hoopoe? And the Hoopoe came, saying, "I have have travelled from Saba [Sheba], where a woman rules from a magnificent throne, she and her people worshipping the sun." Sulayman said, "Go thou, and say to her, "In the name of Allah, Most Gracious, Most Merciful - come to me in submission." And she received the message and sent ambassadors with gifts. But Sulayman said, "This wealth is naught to what Allah has given me. Which of us can bring me her throne?" "I will", said an Ifrit [strong spirit]". Then said one who knew of the Book, "I will bring it in a wink", and Lo! Sulayman saw the throne before him, and said, "Let us disguise it, to see if she can recognise truth."

42 So when she arrived, she was asked, "Is this thy throne?" She said, "We know it to be so, for we have submitted to Allah." And in the great palace, she saw a lake of water, and lifted her skirts to walk over. He said, "This is but a paving of smooth glass." She said, "O my Lord! I indeed do now submit in Islam."

88 Thou seest the mountains and thinkest them firmly fixed, but they shall pass away as the clouds pass away, such is the artistry of Allah. So rehearse the Qur'an, for the good of thine own souls.

29: THE SPIDER (Al-'Ankaboot)

In the name of Allah, the Beneficent, the Merciful

1 A.L.M.

2 Do men think that saying, "We believe", will suffice? Remember the 'Ad and the Thamud people, whose fate ye may read in their ruins. Those who take protectors other than Allah are like the spider, who builds to itself a house; but truly the flimsiest of houses- if they but knew.

45 Recite the Book, and establish regular Prayer, for Prayer restrains from improper deeds. And dispute not with the People of the Book. Say, "Our Allah and your Allah is one, to Him we bow in Islam."

30: THE ROMANS (Al-Room)

In the name of Allah, the Beneficent, the Merciful

1 A. L. M.

2 The Roman Empire has been defeated, in a land close by, but soon they will be victorious again. With Allah is the Decision, in the past and in the Future.

33: THE CLANS (Al-Ahzab)

In the name of Allah, the Beneficent, the Merciful

1 O Prophet! Fear Allah, and hearken not to the Unbelievers and Hypocrites.

6 The Prophet is closer to the Believers than their own selves, and his wives are their mothers.

28 O ye wives of the Prophet! Whosoever of you committeth lewdness, her punishment will be doubled. But any that is devout, her reward will be doubled. O wives of the Prophet! Ye are not like other women!

50 O Prophet! We have made lawful to thee wives to whom thou hast paid dowry, and those whom thy right hand possesses from the prisoners of war, and daughters of thy uncles and aunts who migrated from Makka with thee, and any believing woman who dedicates her soul to the Prophet if the Prophet wishes her. This is only for thee, and not for the Believers at large.

53 O ye who believe! Enter not the Prophet's houses, unless ye are invited, and when ye have taken your meal, disperse, without seeking familiar talk. Such behaviour annoys the Prophet. And when ye ask his ladies for anything, ask them from before a screen- that makes for greater purity. Nor is it right for you that ye should annoy Allah's Messenger, or that ye should marry his widows after him. Those who annoy Allah and His Messenger – are cursed in this World and in the Hereafter will have a humiliating Punishment.

59 O Prophet! Tell thy wives and daughters, and the women of the believers, that they should cast their outer garments over their persons when abroad, that they should be able to be recognised and not molested. And Allah is Oft-Forgiving, Most Merciful.

64 Verily Allah has cursed the Unbelievers and prepared for them a Blazing Fire. O ye who believe! Fear Allah, and speak rightly.

36: YA-SEEN

In the name of Allah, the Beneficent, the Merciful

1 Ya Sin.Ya Sin. Ya Seen.

2 By the Qur'an, full of Wisdom, the wise Qur'an, thou art most surely among the messengers of the Straight Way, to warn a folk whose fathers were not warned. Verily We shall give life to the dead, and make record of all things.

14 We sent to them two messengers, and they rejected them: We sent a third: and they said, "Ye are only men; for Allah Most Gracious sends no sort of revelation." Then there came running, from the farthest part of the City, a man, saying, "O my people! Obey the messenger. I have faith in the Lord, listen, then, to me!" It was said: "Enter thou the Garden." But! Alas! There comes not a messenger, but they mock him!

33 A Sign is sent; the dead earth We do give life, and produce grain therefrom, and the orchard with date-palms and vines, that they may enjoy the fruits, not of their hands. Glory to Allah, Who created all things. We made a sign in the Night and the Day. We made the Moon to traverse her mansions till she returns like a withered date-stalk. We made the Sun to swim in its orbit. We bore their peoples through the Flood in the Ark. Not a Sign comes to them, but they turn away therefrom.

51 The trumpet shall be sounded, when behold! They from the tombs will rush forth to their Lord! Saying "Woe unto us! Who hath disturbed our rest?" Lo! they will be brought before Us! Then, shall ye be repaid of your past Deeds. Verily the Companions of the Garden shall that Day have joy in groves of cool shade, reclining on Thrones, every joyous fruit will be theirs. And O ye in sin! Did I not enjoin on you, O ye Children of Adam, that ye should not worship Satan and go the Straight Way? Here now is Hell of which ye were warned! Embrace ye the fire!."

69 We have not taught the Prophet poetry, the Qur'an is clear, that it may give warning to any who reject Truth.

37: THE RANKS (As-Saaffat)

In the name of Allah, the Beneficent, the Merciful

1 By those who range themselves in ranks, and so are strong in repelling evil, and thus proclaim the Message, verily, verily, your Allah is one!

40 The sincere servants of Allah are promised fruits of delight, and honour and dignity, in Gardens of Felicity. Facing each other on Thrones, round will be passed a Cup from a clear-flowing fountain, crystal-white of a taste delicious, free from headiness or intoxication. Beside them will be chaste women; restraining their glances with big eyes. Then they will turn to one another and question one another and one of them will say: "I had an intimate companion on the earth who did not accept the Message." Then a voice will say: "Would ye like to look down?" And he saw him in the midst of the Fire.

42: THE CONSULTATION (Al-Shoora)

In the name of Allah, the Beneficent, the Merciful

1 H.M

8 If Allah had so willed, He could have made all a single people, but He admits whom He will to His Mercy. To Him belong the keys of the heavens and the earth. The same religion has He established for you as that which He enjoined on Noah on Abraham, Moses, and Jesus. Namely, that ye should remain steadfast in religion, and make no divisions therein. They became divided only after Knowledge reached them, through selfish envy between themselves. The blame is only against those who oppress men and wrong-doing and insolently transgress beyond bounds through the land, defying right and justice: for such there will be a penalty grievous.

43: THE ORNAMENTS OF GOLD (Az-Zukhruf)

In the name of Allah, the Beneficent, the Merciful

1 H.M

2 By the Book that makes things clear, a Qur'an in Arabic. How many were the prophets We sent amongst the peoples of old? And never came there a prophet to them but they mocked him.

18 Is then one brought up among trinkets, truly to be associated with Allah? Nay! they say, "Our fathers followed a certain religion, and we follow their footsteps." But when the Truth came to them, they said: "We reject this sorcery!" But the Mercy of thy Lord is better than the wealth which they amass. Were everyone that blasphemes against Allah to have silver roofs for their houses and silver stair-ways, and silver doors and thrones and adornments of gold, this would be nothing but conveniences of the present life.

51 And Pharaoh proclaimed among his people, saying: "O my people! Does not the dominion of Egypt belong to me? Am I not better than this Moses, a contemptible wretch who can scarcely express himself clearly? Then why are not gold bracelets bestowed on him, or angels accompany him in procession?" Then when the son of Mary is held up as an example, behold, thy people raise a clamour in ridicule!

68 My devotees! No fear shall be on you that Day, nor shall ye grieve, - Enter ye the Garden, ye and your wives, rejoicing. To them will be passed round, dishes and goblets of gold: there will be there all that souls could desire, all that ayes could delight in.

47: MUHAMMAD (Muhammad)

In the name of Allah, the Beneficent, the Merciful

1 Those who reject Allah and hinder men from the Path, their deeds will Allah render vain. Those who reject Allah follow vanities, while those who believe follow the Truth. Therefore, when ye meet the Unbelievers in fight, smite at their necks. And when ye have bound them, then is the time for generosity or ransom, until the war lays down its burdens. Those who are slain in the Way of Allah, soon will He admit to the Garden.

15 The Garden for the righteous has rivers of water incorruptible, rivers of milk, rivers of wine, a joy to those who drink, and rivers of pure honey, and fruit of all kinds, and the Grace from their Lord. Can those in such Bliss be compared to such as dwell for ever in the Fire, drinking boiling water which cuts up their bowels to pieces?

49: THE PRIVATE APARTMENTS (Al-Hujurat)

In the name of Allah, the Beneficent, the Merciful.

2 O you who believe! do not raise your voices above the voice of the Prophet, and do not speak loud to him as you speak loud to one another, lest your deeds became null while you do not perceive.

11 O you who believe! let not one people laugh at another people perchance they may be better than they, nor let women laugh at other women, perchance they may be better than they; and do not find fault with your own people nor call one another by nicknames; evil is a bad name after faith, and whoever does not turn, these it is that are the unjust.

13 O you men! surely We have created you of a male and a female, and made you tribes and families that you may know each other; surely the most honourable of you with Allah is the one among you most careful of his duty; surely Allah is Knowing, Aware.

53: THE STAR (An-Najm)

In the name of Allah, the Beneficent, the Merciful

3 Truly the Prophet saw signs of his Lord near to the Lote-tree in the garden! Yet has anyone seen Lat and Uzza?[1] And the goddess, Manat? What! Sons for you, and for Allah, only daughters? These are but names which ye have invented!*

27 Those who believe not in the Hereafter, give the angels female names. But they have no knowledge. Shun those who turn away from Our Message.

49 Allah is the Lord of Sirius the Mighty Star, He who destroyed many peoples. Why then waste your time in vanities? But fall ye down in prostration to Allah, and adore Him!

97: THE NIGHT OF DESTINY (Al-Qadr)

In the name of Allah, the Beneficent, the Merciful

3 The Night of Power** is better than a thousand months. Therein come down the angels and the Spirit by Allah's permission, on every errand.

98: PROOF (Al-Bayyinah)

In the name of Allah, the Beneficent, the Merciful

5 To worship Allah, offering Him sincere devotion, being true in faith; to establish regular prayer; and to practise regular charity; and that is the Religion Right and Straight

6 Those who reject Truth, among the People of the Book and among the Polytheists, will be in Hell-Fire, to dwell therein for aye. They are the worst of creatures. Those who have faith and do righteous deeds, they are the best of creatures. Their reward is with Allah: Gardens of Eternity, beneath which rivers flow; they will dwell therein for ever; Allah well pleased with them, and they with Him: all this for such as fear their Lord and Cherisher.

105: THE ELEPHANT (Al-Feel)

In the name of Allah, the Beneficent, the Merciful

Seest thou not how thy Lord dealt with the Companions of the Elephant? Did He not make their treacherous plan go astray? And He sent against them Flights of Birds, striking them with stones of baked clay. Then did He make them like an empty field of stalks and straw, of which the corn has been eaten up.

109: THE DISBELIEVERS (Al-Kaaferoon)

In the name of Allah, the Beneficent, the Merciful

Say: O ye that reject Faith! I worship not that which ye worship, nor will ye worship that which I worship. To you be your Way, and to me mine.

114: MANKIND (Al-Naas)

In the name of Allah, the Beneficent, the Merciful

Say: I seek refuge with the Lord and Cherisher of Mankind, The King of Mankind, The God of Man, From the mischief of Shaitan, who whispers and hides, The one who whispers to the hearts of Mankind, Among jinns and among men.

---

*   **The 'Satanic Verse'.** Legend has it that, in order to appease the devotees of Lat, Uzza and Manat, Mohammed was tempted by Satan to add a verse here describing the goddesses as 'exalted birds, whose intercession is to be hoped for'.

**   The 27th night of Ramadan

Béowulf

(England, Northumberland?, c850)

Here is the beginning of English. Maybe the oldest story known in the mixture of Frisian, Nordic and Germanic dialects, which eventually became this language. 'Maybe', because it is far from clear where, when, for who or by whom it was written.

Translated: GH. Abridged: GH. Numbers are approximate positions of the customary chapters.

Hwæt! Wé Gárdena - in géardagum
Hú ðá æþelingas - ellen fremedon.

Listen! Of we Spear-Danes - in past times,
How great men - made great deeds.

Often Scyld, Scef's son, - from enemy hosts
Seized mead-benches; - and terrorised Heruli.
Oh! A good king! - To him an heir was born,

Béowulf! Of renown - in Northern Lands.
Then Scyld departed - at destiny's time,
Into the hands of Lord Frea. - His comrades all,
As he himself had bid, - a hero's vessel made,
To lay their prince - among his riches,
No finer keel, I've heard - ever sat on waves,
To drift off far - to gift the ocean.
Yet no hero knows - who landed that cargo.

1   Béowulf the elder, - beloved king,
To him in turn was born - sons: Heorogar and Hrothgar
And good Halga; - And to Hrothgar
Success in warcraft came, - to be remembered
By a grand mead-hall, - Thus craftsmen fine,
Over all middle-earth, - came, built, and named it:
'Heorot'! Towering high - and horn-gabled!
Yet a dark spirit - listened to its sounds,
Of revelry and harp - and poet's song.
Grendel was the listener - a hellish monster,
Marsh-stalker, - kith of Cain[1],
And friend of ogres, - friend of elves.

2   And when night came - the listener went,
To see that high house - full of slumbering knights.
And from their rest - seized thirty thanes
As plunder taken home - for a banquet of blood.
And the nother night - he came again, again.
Empty stood proud Heorot - twelve long winters

3   Of Grendel's deeds - fame was spread,
So that far, among the Geats - a strong man heard,
Ordered a wave-crosser - fine fit for a Chief,
And king, and men - bold champions all.
Fifteen together thrust off - from sand and cliffs
Bright arms and armour, - over the water-waves
Flying as the wind, - like birds, until,
They sighted a land - of bright sea-cliffs,
Where the coast guard-man - asked 'What are you?'
Where your lineage? - Where your quest?

4   Comrades of Higlac, - my father was Edgethow,
Among the Scyldings, - we seek a dark foe,
A hidden and hiding - despoiler of men.
Then led them he - to the Court of Great Men,
With 'May the Father - All-ruling protect you!'

5   Trod they stone-paved streets - to a noble hall,
Set they down sea-weary - their shields again the wall.
Strong soldiers came - to ask their reasons,
Saying they had not - seen from a foreign land,
So many men - So brave of face.
Béowulf am I of name - I have an errand to tell.

6   Hrothgar spoke, - Helm of the Scyldings.
'I knew your father Edgethow. - Welcome young Béowulf.

7   Know well that Grendel, - mocks me and mine
Hall Heorot is wasted, - my noble war-bands wane.
Know too that other - battle-men fired with beer
Have vowed vengeance - on Grendel. Only for us,
To find again the hall - stained with bitter gore.
Then bench was brought - and ale and pure sweet mead.

---

1   **Cain:** see Genesis 4, p23

And there was the joy of heroes, - all Danes and Wederas.

8 Unferth son of Edgelaf, - Spoke out to Béowulf,
'Are you the one of foolish boast - who swam the ocean sound?
Against Breca. And failed. - So 'gainst Grendel you will.'
Béowulf spoke, 'some truth - but I did battle there,
With sea-beasts - and there won.'

9 Came then Wealthow - Hrothgar's queen,
Adorned in gold - to give full cups.

10 Then in sleeping-time - a hall-guard posted:
On Grendel ogre-watch. - Yet in the colourless night
The shadow-wanderer - came slinking.

11 Grendel walking, - under clouds,
To the gold-hall of men - the door rushed in,
Fiend's feet - on floor mosaic
Around sleeping company - a life to be stolen.
Grasped he a sleeping warrior - bit into the bone-locks,
From veins drank blood, - swallowed great chunks;
Devoured all - hands and feet.
Then the hall aroused - in ghastly horror,

12 Earls all fighting - the murderous guest
A great wound apparent, - sinews sprang asunder,
Before the clash - of Béowulf
Grendel flees sick unto death - to seek his stinking home
All of him but - a hand and arm left
Under the gaping roof. - The grip of Grendel

13 Then in the morning, - as I heard tell,
Folk-chiefs arrived - from far and near
To behold the wonder. - And the king's own bard
Béowulf's glory proclaimed - under the sky's expanse
Like Sigmund - of old

14 Hrothgar spoke, the Hall - adorned with gold and Grendel's hand
'Now Béowulf, - like to me a son,
We will keep new kinship - through courage-works.
The monster is gone - save this hand only.
With nails - like steel
The war-creature's - heathenish hand-spurs.'

15 Then within Heorot - order was declaimed,
The stone gold-glittering - woven tapestries on walls,
Many wondrous sights. - And filled up with friends.
To Béowulf ; a golden banner - the treasure-sword, and helm;
A helm renowned that which - no mortal tools can harm
And to each man - from the chief of earls,
Bestowed possession, - horses and weapons.

18 To Béowulf from Wealthow - a full cup of wine,
And brought the largest necklet - of which on earth I have heard.
In gold, and rings - given with blessings.
The warriors cheered by drink - drank to heroes,
Cleared off the benches - set down to sleep.

19 Yet an avenger still lived; - Grendel's mother, troll-wife,
Lived in dreadful water - and remembered misery.
She came then to Heorot, - and the Ring-Danes sleeping.
Quickly stole away a knight, - beloved Æschere, to her fen
So Béowulf was called, - from sleeping elsewhere.

20 Hrothgar spoke, - 'My people say
That they saw two such - alien marchers in wasted lands
Far over the marsh waters.' - There must we go.

21 Béowulf spoke, - Do not sorrow, wise man
Better a friend do avenge, - than sorrow too-much.

Horses were bridled, - and foot-soldiers brought.
To follow the tracks - over forest and moor,
To great waters - of serpents.
Béowulf clothed in strong arms - carried no fear for his life.

22 Béowulf the son of Edgethow spoke; - 'Wise chieftain, if I for you
Should be parted from life, - to join my father;
Be you the hand-bearer - to my young retainers.'
And Béowulf the - man of the Geats
Into the surging-lake - drove down below
For half a long day - to the cave of the mere-wife.
Who snatched at the warrior - with her loathsome claws.

23 Spied among her cache of arms - a firm edged victory-tool,
A giant-forged sword, - he seized the ring-hilt,
Angrily struck, - through her neck
Broke bone - struck through
The ogre-woman fell dead - the warrior rejoiced.
And there saw he - Grendel lying,
Lifeless burst corpse. - Then with a sword blow
He cut its head away. - As those above with Hrothgar
Saw blood rise - on the turgid lake
And lost hope - for Béowulf.
Then that sword began - to heat with battle-gore
A great wonder! - Melted all away!
Straightaway Béowulf - dove up through water,
From his borrowed world - he came then to the land,
They thanking God - to see their friend,
Four had to carry - that dreadful head.

25 To Edgethow: - And the sword's hilt
Only left hot gold - to the old king given
The ancient work of giants; - an heirloom of ancient strife,

27 Béowulf spoke, - 'We sea-farers
Have come far to find fame - and are not disappointed.'
Hrothgar spoke: 'Between - our peoples now be peace.'

28 They came then to the flood - the young warriors;
Returning heroes, - to their Wederas,
Laden with horses - and much treasure.

29 Béowulf - for fifty winters
Was a wise king, - fatherland's father
Until one dark night - a dragon was awoke
A man, I know not who - chanced upon a heathen hoard
In a stark stone barrow - stole he some ornamented gold
From one who would - have his reply.

32 The hoarder was dragon - that flies by night,
33 Spewing flames - to burn bright houses.
Then was Béowulf - filled with gloom,
Unusual for him. - The fire-drake had
The strongest fortress of the coast - crushed down with hard flames.
Then that war-king - of the Wederas,
Ordered a shield - not of wood
Made of iron. - For tree-wood
No flame would stay. - Then with a troop
Set out to find - the hateful wyrm.

34 Then he went, - with the first thief
To the cairn under the ground - near the surging of the sea,
Filled inside - with jewels

35 Béowulf declared, - for the last time:
The noble vow-words - and saluted all his men
Bidding them wait; - 'It is not your adventure.'

The serpent rose, - the lord raised up his hand
And struck with his - ancestral sword,
Bright on bone, - as nobles' sons,
Not 'fraid of human battle, - ran to hide in woods.

36   Only Wiglaf son of Weohstan, - held his heart and said
'remember how we took our mead - together. Now our man
Has need of sturdy warriors.' - Running in to aid his lord
Flames came forth in waves - burned shield to the boss;
Then again the war-king - remembered his strength,
Into the serpent's head - hacked with iron sword
As the fierce fire-drake - clamped on Béowulf's neck
And gushed his life-blood. - As Wiglaf smote its belly

37   So his lord attacked - and felled the foe.
The wyrm lay dead - and Béowulf soon to follow
Asking boon to see for last - the sparkling treasure-wealth.

38   'I cannot stay here long. - After my fire is died
Order me a mound - at the ocean's cape;
On headland of whales, - to remind my people.
The Fates have chosen - to take up all
Of my kinsmen - to their destiny
Now I must after them.' - Then words no more.

42   So Wiglaf ordered - pyre-wood
And sent the dragon - over the cliff-wall,
For the waves to take - the keeper of baubles

43   With battle-shields they laid - their master on the wood
While smoke arose - and warriors wept
And a Geatish woman alone - wove for Béowulf a song
Then around the mound - rode the battle-brave
To speak of the man - and of his deeds
Of world-kings - the most generous,
Protector of people - most eager for honour.
Wyruldcyning - manna mildust,
Léodum líðost - ond lofgeornost

The Rubáiyát Of Omar Khayyám
رباعيات عمر خيام
(Persia, modern Iraq, c1120)

The Rubáiyát (meaning 'four lines') is a collection of Persian poems, attributed to the mathematician Omar Khayyám. It is one of the very few works which have been translated into pretty much *every* language. This abridgement is taken from the beautiful, popular, and wildly inaccurate, Edward Fitzgerald translation of 1859.

Abridged: GH

AWAKE! for Morning in the Bowl of Night
Has flung the Stone which puts the Stars to Flight:
  And Lo! the Hunter of the East has caught
The Sultán's Turret in a noose of light

Come, fill the Cup, and in the Fire of Spring
The Winter Garment of Repentance fling:
  The bird of Time has but a little way
To fly - and Lo! the Bird is on the Wing.

So come with old Khayyam and leave the Lot
  Of Kaikobad and Kaikhosru forgot:

With me along some Strip of Herbage strown
That just divides the desert from the sown,

Here with a Loaf of Bread beneath the Bough,
A Flask of Wine, a Book of Verse - and Thou
  Beside me singing in the Wilderness -
And Wilderness is Paradise Enough.

I sometimes think that never blows so red
The rose as where some buried Caesar bled.
  Ah, my Beloved, fill the cup that clears
To-day of Past Regrets and Future Fears -

To-morrow? - Why, To-morrow I may be
Myself with Yesterdays, seven thousand years.
  And this was all the harvest that I reaped -
'I came like water, and like Wind I go.'

'Tis all a Chequer-board of Nights and Days
Where Destiny with Men for Pieces plays:
  Hither and Thither moves, and mates and slays,
And one by one back in the Closet lays.
The Moving Finger writes; and, having writ,
Moves on: nor all thy Piety nor Wit

Shall lure it back to cancel half a Line,
Nor all thy Tears wash out a Word of it.

And that inverted Bowl we call The Sky,
Wherunder crawling coop't we live and die,
  Lift not thy hands to It for help - for It
Rolls impotently on as Thou or I.

So to this earthen Bowl I do adjourn
My Lip the Secret Well of Life to learn:
  And Lip to Lip it murmur'd - 'While you live
Drink! - for once dead you never shall return.'

The Magna Carta
The *Great Charter* of England
(Runnymede Meadow, near London, 1215)

John of England was so unjust and incompetent a king that his barons revolted and forced him to sign this agreement, solemnly guaranteeing for all time; religious independence, fixed courts, elected representatives and a rule of law which was to apply to king, officials and commoners alike. Although the charter has been altered and re-issued many times (The passage numbers vary a lot, and all but the sections marked '*' have been rescinded in England, item XXXIX as recently as June 2009.) the *Great Charter* remains the grand founding document of constitutional governments.

Abridged: GH

JOHN, by the grace of God King of England, Lord of Ireland, Duke of Normandy and Aquitaine, and Count of Anjou, to his archbishops, bishops, abbots, earls, barons, justices, foresters, sheriffs, stewards, servants, and to all his officials and loyal subjects, Greeting.

KNOW THAT BEFORE GOD, for the health of our soul and those of our ancestors and heirs, to the honour of God, the exaltation of the holy Church, and the better ordering of our kingdom, at the advice of our reverend fathers Stephen, archbishop of Canterbury, primate of all England, and cardinal of the holy Roman Church, Henry archbishop of Dublin, William bishop of London, Peter bishop of Winchester, Master Pandulf subdeacon and member of the papal household, Brother Aymeric master of the knighthood of the Temple in England, Alan de Galloway constable of Scotland, and other loyal subjects:

*I FIRST, THAT WE HAVE GRANTED TO GOD, and by this present charter have confirmed for us and our heirs in perpetuity, that the English Church shall be free, and shall have its rights undiminished, and its liberties unimpaired. That we wish this so to be observed, appears from the fact that of our own free will, before the outbreak of the present dispute between us and our barons, we granted and confirmed by charter the freedom of the Church's elections - a right reckoned to be of the greatest necessity and importance to it - and caused this to be confirmed by Pope Innocent III. This freedom we shall observe ourselves, and desire to be observed in good faith by our heirs in perpetuity.

*TO ALL FREE MEN OF OUR KINGDOM we have also granted, for us and our heirs for ever, all the liberties written out below, to have and to keep for them and their heirs, of us and our heirs:

II If any earl, baron, or other person that holds lands directly of the Crown, for military service, shall die, and at his death his heir shall be of full age and owe a 'relief', the heir shall have his inheritance on payment of the ancient scale of 'relief'. That is to say, the heir or heirs of an earl shall pay 100 for the entire earl's barony, the heir or heirs of a knight l00s. at most for the entire knight's 'fee', and any man that owes less shall pay less, in accordance with the ancient usage of 'fees'

III But if the heir of such a person is under age and a ward, when he comes of age he shall have his inheritance without 'relief' or fine.

V For so long as a guardian has guardianship of such land, he shall maintain the houses, parks, fish preserves, ponds, mills, and everything else pertaining to it, from the revenues of the land itself. When the heir comes of age, he shall restore the whole land to him, stocked with plough teams and such implements of husbandry as the season demands and the revenues from the land can reasonably bear.

VI Heirs may be given in marriage, but not to someone of lower social standing.

VII At her husband's death, a widow may have her marriage portion and inheritance at once and without trouble.

VIII No widow shall be compelled to marry, so long as she wishes to remain without a husband. But she must give security that she will not marry without royal consent, if she holds her lands of the Crown, or without the consent of whatever other lord she may hold them of.

IX Neither we nor our officials will seize any land or rent in payment of a debt, so long as the debtor has movable goods sufficient to discharge the debt.

X If anyone who has borrowed a sum of money from Jews dies before the debt has been repaid, his heir shall pay no interest on the debt for so long as he remains under age, irrespective of whom he holds his lands.

XII No 'scutage' or 'aid' may be levied in our kingdom without its general consent, unless it is for the ransom of our person, to make our eldest son a knight, and once

*XIII The city of London shall enjoy all its ancient liberties and free customs, both by land and by water. We also will and grant that all other cities, boroughs, towns, and ports shall enjoy all their liberties and free customs.

XV In future we will allow no one to levy an 'aid' from his free men, except to ransom his person, to make his eldest son a knight, and (once) to marry our eldest daughter. For these purposes only a reasonable 'aid' may be levied. 'Aids' from the city of London are to be treated similarly.

XVII Ordinary lawsuits shall not follow the royal court around, but shall be held in a fixed place.

XVIII Inquests of *novel disseisin, mort d'ancestor,* and *darrein presentment* shall be taken only in their proper county court. We ourselves, or in our absence abroad our chief justice, will send two justices to each county four times a year, and these justices, with four knights of the county elected by the county itself, shall hold the assizes in the county court, on the day and in the place where the court meets.

XIX If any assizes cannot be taken on the day of the county court, as many knights and freeholders shall afterwards remain behind, of those who have attended the court, as will suffice for the administration of justice, having regard to the volume of business to be done.

XX For a trivial offence, a free man shall be fined only in proportion to the degree of his offence, and for a serious offence correspondingly, but not so heavily as to deprive him of his livelihood. In the same way, a merchant shall be spared his merchandise, and a husbandman the implements of his husbandry, if they fall upon the mercy of a royal court. None of these fines shall be imposed except by the assessment on oath of reputable men of the neighbourhood.

XXI Earls and barons shall be fined only by their equals, and in proportion to the gravity of their offence.

XXIII No town or person shall be forced to build bridges over rivers except those with an ancient obligation to do so.

XXIV No sheriff, constable, coroners, or other royal officials are to hold lawsuits that should be held by the royal justices.

XXVII If a free man dies intestate, his movable goods are to be distributed by his next-of-kin and friends, under the supervision of the Church. The rights of his debtors are to be preserved.

XXVIII No constable or other royal official shall take corn or other movable goods from any man without immediate payment, unless the seller voluntarily offers postponement of this.

XXIX No constable may compel a knight to pay money for castle-guard if the knight is willing to undertake the guard in person, or with reasonable excuse to supply some other fit man to do it. A knight taken or sent on military service shall be excused from castle-guard for the period of this service.

XXX No sheriff, royal official, or other person shall take horses or carts for transport from any free man, without his consent.

XXXI Neither we nor any royal official will take wood for our castle, or for any other purpose, without the consent of the owner.

XXXIII All fish-weirs shall be removed from the Thames, the Medway, and throughout the whole of England, except on the sea coast.

XXXV There shall be standard measures of wine, ale, and corn (the London quarter), throughout the kingdom. There shall also be a standard width of dyed cloth, russett, and haberject, namely two ells within the selvedges. Weights are to be standardised similarly.

XXXVIII In future no official shall place a man on trial upon his own unsupported statement, without producing credible witnesses to the truth of it.

XXXIX No free man shall be seized or imprisoned, or stripped of his rights or possessions, or outlawed or exiled, or deprived of his standing in any other way, nor will we proceed with force against him, or send others to do so, except by the lawful judgement of his equals or by the law of the land.

XL To no one will we sell, to no one deny or delay right or justice.

XLI All merchants may enter or leave England unharmed and without fear, and may stay or travel within it, by land or water, for purposes of trade, free from all illegal exactions, in accordance with ancient and lawful customs. This, however, does not apply in time of war to merchants from a country that is at war with us. Any such merchants found in our country at the outbreak of war shall be detained without injury to their persons or property, until we or our chief justice have discovered how our own merchants are being treated in the country at war with us. If our own merchants are safe they shall be safe too.

XLII In future it shall be lawful for any man to leave and return to our kingdom unharmed and without fear, by land or water, preserving his allegiance to us, except in time of war, for some short period, for the common benefit of the realm.

XLV We will appoint as justices, constables, sheriffs, or other officials, only men that know the law of the realm and are minded to keep it well.

XLVIII All evil customs relating to forests and warrens, foresters, warreners, sheriffs and their servants, or riverbanks and their wardens, are at once to be investigated in every county by twelve sworn knights of the county, and within forty days of their enquiry the evil customs are to be abolished completely and irrevocably. But we, or our chief justice if we are not in England, are first to be informed.

XLIX We will at once return all hostages and charters delivered up to us by Englishmen as security for peace or for loyal service.

We have remitted and pardoned fully to all men any illwill, hurt, or grudges that have arisen between us and our subjects, whether clergy or laymen, since the beginning of the dispute. In addition we have caused letters patent to be made for the barons, bearing witness to this over the seals of Stephen archbishop of Canterbury, Henry archbishop of Dublin, the other bishops named above, and Master Pandulf.

IT IS ACCORDINGLY OUR WISH AND COMMAND that the English Church shall be free, and that men in our kingdom shall have and keep all these liberties, rights, and concessions, well and peaceably in their fullness and entirety for them and their heirs, of us and our heirs, in all things and all places for ever.

Both we and the barons have sworn that all this shall be observed in good faith and without deceit. Witness the above mentioned people and many others.

Given by our hand in the meadow that is called Runnymede, between Windsor and Staines, on the fifteenth day of June in the seventeenth year of our reign.

The Travels of Marco Polo of Venice
(*Il Milione: Le divisament dou monde / The Million: A Description of The World*)
by Rustichello of Pisa
(Genoa, c1298)

This book is famous as the first European description of China, the book which inspired Christopher Columbus to try to reach Asia by sailing into the west. But even if Marco Polo travelled as widely as he claims, he would not by any means have been the first European merchant to reach the Far East. His fame comes rather from his luck in being on the wrong side during a minor war between Venice and Genoa, and thereby finding himself in prison with the novelist Rustichello, a writer known to be not above a little embellishment.

Abridged: GH

PROLOGUE.

Great Princes, Kings, Knights and People of all degrees who desire to get knowledge of the sundry regions of the World, take this Book and cause it to be read to you. Ye shall find therein all kinds of wonderful things, for no person hath had so much experience of the divers parts of the World as hath had Messer Marco! Who being thereafter an inmate of the Prison at Genoa, he caused Messer Rusticiano of Pisa, who was in the said Prison likewise, to reduce the whole to writing; and this befell in the year 1298 from the birth of Jesus.

IN the middle of our century, two merchants of Venice, Nicolo and Matteo Polo, voyaged with a rich cargo of merchandise in their own ship, to Constantinople, and thence to the Black Sea. From the Crimea they travelled on horseback into Western Tartary, where they resided in business for a year, gaining by their politic behaviour the cordial friendship of the paramount chief of the tribes, named Barka.

Prevented from returning to Europe through the outbreak of a tribal war in Tartary, the travellers proceeded to Bokhara.

There they stayed three years. Here they made the acquaintance of the ambassador of the famous Kublai Khan. This potentate is called of all 'grand khan,' or supreme prince of all the Tartar tribes. The ambassador invited the merchants to visit his master.

Acceding to his request, they set out on the difficult journey, and on reaching their destination were cordially received by Kublai, for they were the first persons from Italy who had ever arrived in his dominions. He begged them to take with them to their country a commissioner from himself to the Pope of Rome. The result was unfortunate, for in a few days the commissioner fell ill on the way through Tartary, and was left behind. At Acre, the travellers heard that Pope Clement IV was dead. Arrived at Venice, Nicolo Polo found that his wife had died soon after his departure in giving birth to a son, the Marco of this history, who was now fifteen years of age.

Waiting for two years in Venice, the election of a new pope being delayed by successive obstacles, and fearing that the grand khan would be disappointed or might despair of their return, they set out again for the East, taking with them young Marco Polo. But at Jerusalem they heard of the accession of Gregory X to the pontifical throne, and hastened back to Italy. The new pope welcomed them with great honour, furnished them with credentials and commissioned to accompany them to the East two friars of great learning and talent, Fra Guglielmo da Tripoli and Fra Nicolo de Vicenza.

The party, entrusted with handsome presents from the pontiff to the grand khan, voyaged forth, and reached Armenia to find that region embroiled in war. The two friars, in terror, returned to the coast under the care of certain knight templars; but the three Venetians, accustomed to danger, continued their journey, which, on account of slow winter progress, lasted altogether three and a half years.

Kublai had removed to a splendid city named Cle Men Fu, and on arriving, a gracious reception awaited the three merchants, who narrated events and delivered the messages from Rome with the papal presents. Taking special notice of young Marco Polo, the grand khan enrolled him among his attendants of honour.

Marco soon became proficient in four languages, and displayed such extraordinary talents that he was sent on a mission to Karazan, a city six month's journey distant. On this mission he distinguished himself by his tact and success, and during the seventeen years spent in the service of the khan executed many similar tasks in every part of the empire.

The Venetians remained many years at the Tartar court, and at length, after amassing much wealth, felt constrained to return home. They were permitted to depart, taking with them, at the khan's request, a maiden named Kogatin, a relative of the khan, whom they were to conduct to the court of Arghun, a sovereign in India, to become his wife, The travellers were not fortunate, for they were compelled, through fresh wars among the Tartar princes, to return. But about this time Marco Polo happened to arrive after a long voyage in the East Indies, giving a most favourable report of the safety of the seas he had navigated. Accordingly it was arranged that the party should go by sea; and fourteen ships were prepared, each having four masts and nine sails, and some crews of over 200 men. On these embarked the three Venetians, the Indian ambassadors and the queen. In three months Java was reached, and India in eighteen more.

On landing, the travellers learnt that the King of Arghun had died some time before, and his son Kiakato was reigning in his stead, and that the lady was to be presented to Kiasan, another son, then on the borders of Persia guarding the frontier with an army of 60,000. This was done, and then the party returned to the residence, and there rested nine months before taking their leave.

While on their way they heard of the death of Kublai, this intelligence putting an end to their plan of revisiting those regions. Pursuing therefore, their intended route, they at length reached Trebizond, whence they proceeded to Negropont, and finally to Venice, at which place, in the enjoyment of health and abundant riches, they safely arrived in the year 1295.

The foregoing record enables the reader to judge of the opportunities Marco Polo had of acquiring a knowledge of the things he describes during a residence of many years in the eastern parts of the world.

PERSIA

Persia was anciently a great province, but it is now in great part destroyed by the Tartars. From the city called Saba came the three magi who adored Christ at Bethlehem. They are buried in Saba, and are all three entire with their beards and hair. They were Baldasar, Gaspar, and Melchior. After three days' journey you come to Palasata, the castle of the fire-worshippers. The people say that the three magi, when they adored Christ, were by Him presented with a closed box, which they carried with them for several days, and then, being curious to see what it contained, were constrained to open. In it was a stone signifying that they should remain firm to the faith they had received.

Thinking themselves deluded, they threw the stone into a pit, whence instantly fire flamed forth. Bitterly repenting, they took home with them some of the fire, and placed it in a church, where it is adored as a god, the sacrifices all being performed before it. Therefore, the people of Persia worship fire.

In the north of Persia the people tell of the Old Man of the Mountain. He was named Alo-eddin[1], and was a Moslem. In a lovely valley he had planted a magnificent garden and built a cluster of gorgeous palaces, supplied by means of conduits with streams of wine, milk, honey and pure water. Beautiful girls, skilled in music and dancing, and richly dressed, were among the inhabitants of this retreat.

The chief object of Alo-eddin in forming this fascinating garden was to persuade his followers that, as Mahomed had promised to the Moslems the enjoyments of Paradise, with every species of sensual gratification, so he was also a prophet and the compeer of Mahomed, and had the power of admitting to Paradise whom he pleased. An impregnable castle guarded the entrance to the enchanting valley, the entrance to this being through a secret passage.

At his court this chief entertained many youths, selected from the people of the mountains for their apparent courage and martial disposition. To these he daily preached on Paradise and his prerogative of granting admission; and at certain times he caused opium to be administered to a dozen of the youths, who, when half dead with sleep, were conveyed to apartments in the palaces in the gardens.

On awakening, each person found himself surrounded by lovely damsels, who sang, played, served delicate viands and exquisite wines, till the youth, intoxicated with, excess of enjoyment, believed himself to be assuredly in Paradise, and felt unwilling to quit it.

After four or five days the youths were again thrown into somnolency and carried out of the garden; and when asked by Alo-eddin where they had been, declared that by his favour they had been in Paradise, the whole court listening

---

1 **Alo-eddin:** see also, p206

with amazement to their recital. The consequence was that his followers were so devoted to his service that if any neighbouring princes gave him umbrage they were put to death by these disciplined assassins, and his tyranny made him dreaded through all the surrounding provinces.

At length the grand khan grew weary of hearing of his atrocious practices, and an army was sent in the year 1262 to besiege him in his castle. It was so strong that it held out for three years, until Alo-eddin was forced through lack of provisions to surrender, and was put to death. Thus perished Alo-eddin, the Old Man of the Mountain.

THE TARTARS

Now that I have begun to speak of the Tartars, I will tell you more about them. They never remain long anywhere, but when winter approaches remove to the plains of a warmer region, in order to find sufficient pasture for their cattle. Their flocks and herds are multitudinous. Their tents are formed of rods covered with felt, and being exactly round, and nicely put together, they can gather them together into one bundle and make them up as packages to carry about.

When they set them up again, they always make the entrance front to the south. Their travelling-cars are drawn by oxen and camels. The women do all the business of trading, buying and selling, and provide everything necessary for their husbands and families, the time of the men being entirely devoted to hunting, hawking and matters that relate to military life. They have the best falcons and also the best dogs in the world. They subsist entirely on flesh and milk, consuming horses, camels, dogs and animals of every description. They drink mares' milk, preparing it so that it has the qualities and flavour of white wine, and this beverage they call kemurs.

The Tartars believe in a supreme deity, to whom they offer incense and prayers; while they also worship another, called Natigay, whose image, covered with felt, is kept in every house. This god, who has a wife and children, and who, they consider, presides over their terrestrial concerns, protects their children and guards their cattle and grain. They show him great respect, and at their meals they never omit to take a fat morsel of the flesh and with it grease the mouth of the idol. Rich Tartars dress in cloth of gold and silks, with skins of the sable, the ermine and other animals. All their accoutrements are of the most expensive kind.

They are specially skilful in the use of the bow, and they are very brave in battle, but are cruel in disposition. Their martial qualities and their wonderful powers of endurance make them fitted to subdue the world, as, in fact, they have done with regard to a considerable portion of it.

When these Tartars engage in battle they never mingle with the enemy, but keep hovering about him, discharging their arrows first from one side and then from the other, occasionally pretending to fly, and during their flight shooting arrows backwards at their pursuers, killing men and horses as if they were combating face to face. In this sort of warfare the adversary imagines he has gained the victory, when in fact he has lost the battle. For the Tartars, observing the mischief they have done him, wheel about and, renewing the fight, overpower his remaining troops, and make them prisoners in spite of their utmost exertions.

Kublai is the sixth grand khan, and began his reign as grand khan in the year 1246 and commenced his reign as Emperor of China in 1280. It is forty-two years since he began his reign in Tartary and he is fully eighty-five years of age. It was his ancestor, Jenghiz, who first assumed the title of Khan.

Kublai is considered the most able and successful commander that ever led the Tartars to battle. He it was who completed the conquest of China by subduing the southern provinces and destroying the ancient dynasty. After this period he ceased to take the field in person. His first campaign was against rebels, of whom there were many both in Cathay and Nanji [North and South China].

The Tartars date the beginning of their Year from the beginning of February, and It ii their custom on that occasion to dress in white. Great numbers of beautiful white horses are presented to the grand khan. On the day of the White Feast all his elephants, amounting to five thousand, are exhibited in procession, covered with rich housings. It is a time of Splendid ceremonials and of sumptuous feasting.

The grand khan has many leopards and lynxes kept for the purpose of chasing deer, and also many lions, which are active in seizing boars, wild oxen, and asses, Stags, roebucks and other animals that are objects of sport. It is an admirable sight, when the lion is let loose in pursuit of the animal, to observe the savage eagerness and speed with which he overtakes it. His majesty has them conveyed for this purpose in cages placed on cars, and along with them is confined a little dog, with which they become familiarised. The grand khan has eagles also, which are trained to stoop at wolves, and such is their size and strength that none, however large, can escape from their talons.

Before we proceed further we shall speak of a memorable battle that was fought in the kingdom of Yun-chang. When the king of Myan [Myanmar] heard that an army of Tartars had arrived at Yun-chang, he resolved to attack it, in order that by its destruction the grand khan might be deterred from again attempting to station a force on the borders of his dominions.

For this purpose he assembled a very large army, including a multitude of elephants (an animal with which the country abounds), on whose backs were placed battlements, or castles of wood, capable of containing to the number of twelve or sixteen in each. With these, and a numerous army of horse and foot, he took the road to Yun-chang, where the grand khan's army lay, and, encamping at no great distance from it, intended to give his troops a few days of rest.

The Tartars, chiefly by their wonderful skill in archery, inflicted a terrible defeat on their foes; and the King of Mien, though he fought with the most undaunted courage, was compelled to flee, leaving the greater part of his troops killed or wounded.

In the northern parts of the world there dwell many Tartars, under a chief of the name of Kaidu, nearly related to Kublai, the grand khan. These Tartars are idolaters. They possess vast herds of horses, cows, sheep and other domestic animals. In these northern districts are found prodigious white bears, black foxes, wild asses in great numbers, and swarms of sables and martens. During the long and severe winters the Tartars travel in sledges drawn by great dogs.

Beyond the country of these northern Tartars is another region, which extends to the utmost bounds of the north and is called the Region of Darkness, because during most part of the winter months the sun is invisible, and the atmosphere is obscured to the same degree as that in which we find it just about the dawn of day, when we may be said to see and not to see. The intellects of the people are dull, and they have an air of stupidity. The Tartars often proceed on plundering expeditions against them to rob them of their cattle and goods, availing themselves for this purpose of those months in which the darkness prevails.

OF CEYLON AND MALABAR

The Island of Zeilan [Ceylon] is better circumstanced than any other in the world. It is governed by a king named Sendernaz. The people worship idols, and are independent of every other state. Both men and women go nearly nude. Their food is milk, rice and flesh, and they drink wine drawn from trees. Here is the best sappan-wood that can anywhere be met with.

The island produces more beautiful and valuable rubies than can be found in any other part of the world, and also many other precious stones. The king is reported to possess the grandest ruby that ever was seen, being a span in length, and the thickness of a man's arm, brilliant beyond description and without a single flaw. The grand khan, Kublai, sent ambassadors to this monarch, with a request that he would yield to him possession of this ruby; in return for which he should receive the value of a city. The answer was that he would not sell it for all the treasure of the universe. The grand khan, therefore, failed to acquire it.

Leaving the island of Zeilan, you reach the great province of Malabar, which is part of the continent of the greater India, the noblest and richest country in the world. It is governed by four kings, of whom the principal is named Senderbandi.

Within his district is a fishery for pearls. The pearl oysters are brought up in bags by divers. The king wears many jewels of immense value, and among them is a fine string containing one hundred and four splendid pearls and rubies.

In the province of Malabar is the body of St. Thomas the Apostle, who there suffered martyrdom. It rests in a small city to which vast numbers of Christians and Saracens resort. The latter regard him as a great prophet, and name him Ananias, signifying a holy personage.

In the year 1288 a powerful prince of the country, who at the time of harvest had accumulated as his portion an enormous quantity of rice, and whose granaries could not hold the vast store, used for that purpose a religious house belonging to the church of St. Thomas, although the guardians of the shrine begged him not thus to occupy the place. He persisted, and on the next night the holy apostle appeared to him, holding a small lance in his hand, which he held at his throat, threatening him with death if he should not immediately evacuate the house. The prince awoke in terror, and obeyed.

Various miracles are daily wrought here through the interposition of the blessed saint. The Christians who have the care of the church possess groves of coconut trees, and from these derive their means of subsistence.

The death of this most holy apostle took place in this wise. Having retired to a hermitage where he was engaged in prayer, and being surrounded by a number of pea-fowls, with which bird the country abounds, an idolater who happened to be passing, and did not perceive the holy man, shot an arrow at a pea-cock, which struck St. Thomas in his side. He only had time to thank the Lord for all His mercies, and into His hands resigned his spirit.

In the kingdom of Golkonda, which you enter upon leaving Malabar, after proceeding five hundred miles northward, are the best and most honourable merchants that can be found. No consideration whatever can induce them to speak an untruth. They have also an abhorrence of robbery, and likewise are remarkable for the virtue of continence, being satisfied with the possession of one wife. The Brahmans are distinguished by a badge, a thick cotton thread passed over the shoulder and tied under the arm.

The people are gross idolaters and much addicted to sorcery and divination When they are about to make a purchase of goods, they observe the shadow cast of their own bodies in the sunshine, and if the shadow be as large as it should be, they make the purchase that day. More over, when they are in a shop for the purchase of anything, if they see a tarantula, of which there are many there, they take notice from which side it comes, and regulate their business accordingly. Again, if they are going out of their houses and they hear anyone sneeze they return to the house and stay at home.

The Divine Comedy
(*La Divina Comèdia*)
By Dante Alighieri
(Verona, c1320)

The Jewish (p23) and Christian (p77) scriptures say almost nothing about what an afterlife may be like. Written by a minor politician exiled from Florence, this allegorical interpretation of heaven – with elements of Ancient Greek and Islamic (p92) tradition – has come to define what Christians should expect after death. The *Divine Comedy* was publicly burned in the infamous 'Bonfire of the vanities' in Florence in 1497.

Based on the verse translation by H. F. Cary, c1838. Abridged: JH

I: Inferno

[Dante loses his way in a gloomy forest, and is hindered by wild beasts from ascending a mountain. He is met by the ancient Roman poet Virgil, who promises to show him the punishments of hell, and afterwards of purgatory; and that he will be conducted by his lost beloved Beatrice into paradise. He follows the poet, and the two come to the gate of hell, where they read dread words:]

Through me you pass into the city of woe,
Through me you pass into eternal pain;
Through me among the people lost for aye.
Justice the founder of my fabric moved;
To rear me was the task of power divine,
Supremest wisdom and primeval love.
Before me things create were none, save things
Eternal, and eternal I endure.
All hope abandon, ye who enter here.

[They enter. Here, as Dante understands from Virgil, those were punished who had spent their time (for it could not be called living) in apathetic indifference to good and evil. Arriving at the river Acheron, they there find the old ferryman Charon, who takes the spirits to the opposite shore. As they reach it Dante, seized with terror, falls into a trance. Roused by thunder, and following his guide, he descends into Limbo, the first circle of the Inferno. Here are the souls of those who, though they have lived virtuously and suffer not for great sins, nevertheless, through lack of baptism, merit not the bliss of paradise. They pass on to the second circle. Here at the entrance is Minos, the infernal judge, by whom Dante is admonished to beware how he enters those regions. He faints, and on his recovery finds himself in the third circle, where the gluttonous are punished.]

Cerberus, cruel monster, fierce, strange,
Through his wide three-fold throat barks as a dog.
Over a multitude immersed beneath.
His eyes glare crimson, black his unctuous beard,
His belly large, and clawed the hands, with which
He tears the spirits, flays them, and their limbs
Piecemeal disports.

[They descend into the fourth circle, past Pluto, guradian of the caves. Here the same doom awaits the prodigal and the avaricious- everlastingly to meet in direful conflict, rolling great weights against each other with mutual curses. In the fifth circle they find the wrathful and gloomy, tormented by the Stygian lake.]

We the circle crossed
To the next steep, arriving at a well,
That boiling pours itself down to a foss
Sluiced from its source. Far murkier was the wave
Than sablest grain; and we in company
Of th' inky waters, journeying by their side,
Entered, though by a different track, beneath.
Into a lake, the Stygian named, expands
The dismal stream, when it hath reached the foot
Of the grey, withered cliffs. Intent I stood
To gaze, and in the marish sunk descried
A miry tribe, all naked, and with looks
Betokening rage. They with their hands alone
Struck not, but with the head, the breast, the feet,
Cutting each other piecemeal with their fangs.

[Phlegyas, ferryman of the lake, conveys Virgil and Dante across, and they arrive at the city of Dis, where demons close the portals against them. They enter by the help of an angel and discover that heretics are punished in tombs burning with fierce fire. Going forward between the sepulchres, the pilgrims arrive at the verge of a rocky precipice, which encloses the seventh circle, where the violent who have committed crimes against their neighbours are punished by being tormented in a river of blood. When the tormented souls try to emerge, a troop of centaurs aim arrows at them. One of these instructs the two pilgrims.]

"These are the souls of tyrants, who were given
To blood and rapine. Here they wail aloud
Their merciless wrongs. Here Alexander dwells,
And Dionysius fell, who many a year
Of woe wrought for fair Sicily. That brow,
Whereon the hair so jetty clustering hangs,
Is Azzolino; that with flaxen locks
Oliizzo of Este, in the world destroyed
By his foul stepson ... .

There Heaven's stern justice lays chastising hand
On Attila. who was the scourge of the earth,
On Sextus, and on Pyrrhus, and extracts
Tears ever by the seething flood unlocked
From the Rinieri; of Corneto this,
Pazzo the other named, who filled the ways
With violence and war."

[Still in the seventh circle, Dante enters the second compartment, which contains those who have done violence on their own persons and those who have violently consumed their goods. The first become trees, which bleed when a twig is broken, whereon the harpies build their nests; the latter are chased and torn by black mastiffs. The third compartment of this seventh circle is a plain of hot, dry sand, over which fall flakes of fire, slowly waiting down as flakes of snow; here are punished those who have committed sins of violence against God, against nature and against art. And in the eighth circle, among other lost ones are punished those who are guilty of simony. They are fixed with the head downwards in certain apertures, so that no more than the legs can be seen from without, and on the soles of the feet are seen burning flames. Dante is taken down by his guide to the bottom of the gulf, and there finds Pope Nicholas the Fifth, whose evil deeds, together with those of other pontiffs, are bitterly reprehended. The punishment of hypocrites is witnessed. Caiaphas is seen fixed to a cross on the ground so that all tread on him in passing. In the seventh gulf is seen robbers tormented by venomous serpents.]

We from the bridge's head descended, where
To the eighth mound it joins; and then, the chasm
Opening to view, I saw a crowd within
Of serpents terrible, so strange of shape
And hideous, that remembrance in my veins
Yet shrinks the vital current.
Amid the dread exuberance of woe
Ran naked spirits winged with horrid fear,
Nor hope had they of crevice where to hide,
Or heliotrope to charm them out of view.
With serpents were their hands behind them bound,
Which through their reins enfixed the tail and head
Twisted in folds before. And lo! on one
Near to our side, darted an adder up,
And, where the neck is on the shoulders tied,
Transpierced him.

[The two go forward to the arch that stretches over the eighth gulf, and behold numberless flames wherein are punished the evil counsellors, each flame containing a sinner, save one, in which were Diomede and Ulysses. Ulysses relates the manner of his death.]

"When I escaped
From Circe, who beyond a circling year
Had held me near Caieta by her charms,

Ere thus Aeneas had named the shore;
Nor fondness for my son, nor reverence
Of my old father, nor return of love,
That should have crowned Penelope with Joy,
Could overcome in me the zeal I had
To explore the world, and search the ways of life,
Man's evil and his virtue. Forth I sailed
In. to the deep illimitable main,
'With but one bark, and the small faithful band
That yet cleaved to me. As Iberia far,
Far as Morocco, either shore I saw.
And the Sardinian and each isle beside
'Which round that ocean bathes.
Tardy with age were I and my companions when we came
To the straight pass, where Hercules ordained
The boundaries not to be o'erstepped by man.
'O brothers!" I began, "who to the west
Through perils without number now have reached
To this the short remaining watch, that yet
Our senses have to wake, refuse not proof
Of the unpeopled world, following the track
Of Phoebus. Call to mind from whence we sprang;
Ye were not formed to live the life of brutes,
But virtue to pursue and knowledge high."
With these few words I sharpened for the voyage
The mind of my associates, that I then
Could scarcely have withheld them. To the dawn
Our poop we turned, and for the witless flight
Made our oars wings, still gaining on the left.
Each star of th' other pole night now beheld;
And ours so low that from the ocean floor
It rose not. Five times re-illum'd, as oft
Vanished the light from underneath the moon,
Since the deep way we entered, when from far
Appeared a mountain dim, loftiest methought
Of all I e'er beheld. Joy seized us straight,
But soon to mourning changed. From the new land
A whirlwind sprang, and at her foremost side
Did strike the vessel. Thrice it whiri'd her round
With all the waves; the fourth time lifted up
The poop, and sank the prow; so fate decreed,
And over us the booming billow closed"

[In the ninth gulf are seen sowers of scandal, schismatics and heretics, with their limbs miserably maimed or divided in different ways. Amongst these the poet finds Mahomet. After witnessing the tortures of forgers in the tenth gulf. the poets see the agonies of traitors in the ninth circle, which is a frozen realm. In the midst of this is Lucifer, at whose back Dante and Virgil ascend, till by a secret path they reach the surface of the other hemisphere and once more obtain sight of the stars.]

"The banners of Hell's Monarch do come forth
Towards us; therefore look,' so spake my guide,
'If thou discern him.' As, when breathes a cloud
Heavy and dense, or when the shades of night
Fall on our hemisphere, seems viewed from far

A windmill, which the blast stirs briskly round;
Such was the fabric then methought I saw.
To shield me from the wind, forthwith I drew
Behind my guide; no covert else was there.
Now came I (and with fear I bid my strain
But night now record the marvel) where the souls were all
Whelm'd underneath, transparent, as through glass.
Pellucid the frail stem. Some prone were laid
Others stood upright, this upon the soles,
That on his head, a third with face to feet
Arched like a bow. When to the point we came,
Whereat my guide was pleased that I should see
The creature eminent in beauty once.
He from before me stepped and made me pause.
'Lo!' he exclaimed, 'lo, Dis! and lo, the place,
Where thou hast need to arm thy heart with strength.'
Then stood forth that emperor, who sways
The realm of sorrow, at mid-breast from th' ice.
How passing strange it seemed, when I did spy
Upon his head three faces: one in front
Of hue vermilion, th' other two with this
Midway each shoulder joined and at the crest;
The right 'twixt wan and yellow seemed; the left
To look on, such as come from whence old Nile
Stoops to the lowlands. Under each shot forth
Two mighty wings, enormous as became
A bird so vast. Sails never such I saw
Outstretched on the wide sea. No plumes had they,
But were in texture like a bat; and these
He flapped i' th' air, that from him issued still
Three winds, wherewith Cocytus to its depth
Was frozen. At six eyes he wept; the tears
Adown three chins distili'd with bloody foam.
At every mouth his teeth a sinner champed,
Bruised as with ponderous engine; so that three
Were in this guise tormented. But far more
Than from that gnawing was the foremost pang'd
By the fierce rending, whence oft-times the back
Was stript of all its skin. 'That upper spirit
Who hath worst punishment,' so spake my guide,
'Is Judas, he that hath his head within
And plies the feet without. Of th' other two,
Whose heads are under, from the murky jaw
Who hangs, is Brutus; lo! how he doth writhe
And speaks not..... But night now reascends,
And it is time for parting. All is seen."

II: Purgatory

O'er better waves to speed her rapid course
The light barque of my genius lifts the sail,
Well pleased to leave so cruel sea behind
And of the second region I will sing,
In which the human spirit from sinful blot
Is purged, and for ascent to Heaven prepares.

*[The poet describes his rapturous delight at escaping a
little before daybreak from the infernal regions. He finds
himself breathing the pure air of the region round the Isle
of Purgatory. The shade of Cato of Utica appears and
admonishes the two pilgrims what is needful to be done
before they proceed on the way to Purgatory. He then
disappears. After having encountered many hovering
spirits, they reach the entrance and are admitted by the
angel deputed by St. Peter.[1]
Passing along a pathway, they reach an open and level
space that extends each way round the mountain. A while
marble cornice, on the side that rises, is covered with
engravings of many stories of humility. To this approach
the souls of those who expiate the sin of pride, bent down
beneath the weight of many stones. Dante tells how sin is
cancelled by suffering in Purgatory.]*

'What I see hither tending bears no trace
Of human semblance, nor of aught beside
That my foiled sight can guess!' He answering thus:
'So bent to earth, beneath their heavy terms
Of torment stoop they, that mine eye at first
Struggled as thine. But look intently thither:
And disentangle with thy labouring view
What, underneath those stones, approacheth; now,
E'en now, mayst thou discern the pangs of each.'
Christians and proud'. O poor and wretched ones!
That, feeble in the mind's eye, lean your trust
Upon unstaid perverseness! Know ye not
That we are worms, yet made at last to form
The winged insect, imp'd with angel plumes,
That to Heaven's Justice unobstructed soars?
Why buoy ye up aloft your unfledged souls?
Abortive then and shapeless ye remain.
Like the untimely embryon of a worm.
As, to support incumbent floor or roof,
For corbel is a figure sometimes seen.
That crumples up its knees unto its breast,
With the feigned posture stirring ruth unfeigned
In the beholder's fancy: so I saw
These fashioned when I noted well their guise.
Each, as his back was laden, came indeed.
Or more or less contracted; and it seemed
As he who showed most patience in his look,
Wailing, exclaimed, 'I can endure no more.'

*[They gain a second cornice and an angel invites the poets
to ascend the next steep. At the next cornice, where the sin
of anger is being purged, Dante witnesses remarkable
instances of patience. One of these is described.]*

After that I saw
A multitude, in fury burning, slay
With stones a stripling youth, and shout amain
'Destroy, destroy!' And him I saw, who. bowed
Heavy with death unto the ground, yet made
His eyes, unfolded upward, gates to heaven,
Praying forgiveness of the Almighty Sire.
Amidst that cruel conflict, on his foes,

---

1   **St Peter:** (as gatekeeper) See Gospels (p77), Matt. 16

114

With looks that win compassion to their aim.

[A thick mist envelops the pilgrims. and through the fog the voices are heard of spirits piteously praying. An angel marshals them to the fourth cornice, on which the sin of indifference is purged. Multitudes of spirits rush by, shouting forth memorable examples of the sin for which they are made to suffer. At the summoning of an angel, Virgil and Dante ascend the fifth cornice, where they find Pope Adrian the Fifth, who thus speaks:]

"Late, alas!
Was my conversion; but when I became
Rome's pastor I discerned at once the dream
And cozenage of life; saw that the heart
Rested not there, and yet no prouder height
Lured on the climber; wherefore, of that life
No more enamoured, in my bosom love
Of purer being kindled. For till then
I was a soul in misery; alienate
From God, and covetous of all earthly things;
Now, as thou seest, here punished for my doting.
Such cleansing from the taint of avarice
Do spirits, converted, need."

[Presently the mountain shakes, and all the spirits shout, 'Glory to God!' The poets mount to the sixth cornice, where the sin of gluttony is cleansed. Turning, they find a tree hung with sweet-smelling fruit, and watered by a shower that gushes from the rock. Voices are heard to proceed from the rock, recording examples of temperance.]

"The women of old Rome were satisfied
With water for their beverage. Daniel fed
On pulse, and wisdom gained The primal age
Was beautiful as gold; and hunger then
Made acorns tasteful, thirst each rivulet
Run nectar. Honey and locusts were the food
Whereon the Baptist in the wilderness
Fed, and that eminence of glory reached
And greatness, which th' Evangelist records."

[They arrive on the seventh and last cornice, where the sin of incontinence is purged in fire. An angel sends the two pilgrims forward to the last ascent, which leads to the celestial Paradise, situated on the summit of the mountains. Virgil gives Dante full liberty to use his own pleasure and judgement in the choice of his way till he shall meet. with Beatrice. Dante wanders through the forest of the terrestrial Paradise, till he is stopped by a stream. On the other side he beholds Matilda, culling flowers. He speaks with her, and learns that the water, Lethe or Eunoe, flowing between them has power, on her side to take away remembrance of offence, and on the other to bring back remembrance of all good deeds. Matilda moves along the side of the stream, in the opposite direction to the current, and Dante keeps equal pace with her on the opposite bank. A marvellous sight appears,

preceded by music. Beatrice descends from heaven, and rebukes the poet.]

I have beheld, ere now, at break of day,
The eastern clime all roseate; and the sky
Opposed, one deep and beautiful serene;
And the sun's face so shaded, and with mists
Attemper'd, at his rising, that the eye
Long while endured the sight; thus, in a cloud
Of flowers, that from those hands angelic rose,
And down within and outside of the car
Fell showering, in white veil with olive wreathed,
A virgin in my view appeared, beneath
Green mantle, robed in hue of living flame;
And o'er my spirit, that so long a time
Had from her presence felt no shuddering dread,
Albeit mine eyes discerned her not, there moved
A hidden virtue from her, at whose touch
The power of ancient love was strong within me.

[Beatrice thus addresses Dante:]

"Observe me well. I am, in sooth, I am
Beatrice. What! and hast thou deigned at last
Approach the mountain? Knewest not, O man!
Thy happiness is here?"

[To the virgins accompanying her Beatrice explains the reason of her rebukes administered to Dante. After she left the mortal vale he languished in his devotion for her whom he had adulated while she lived within his ken on earth. She says:]

"Soon as I had reached
The threshold of my second age. And changed
My mortal for immortal; then he left. me.
And gave himself to others. When from flesh
To spirit I had risen, and increase
Of beauty and of virtue circled me
I was less dear to him, and valued less,
His steps were turned into deceitful ways.
Following false images of good, that make
No promise perfect."

[Dante falls to the ground. Coming to himself again, he is by Matilda drawn through the waters of Lethe, and presented first to the four virgins who figure the cardinal virtues. These in turn lead him to the Gryphon, a symbol of our Saviour: and three virgins representing the evangelical virtues intercede for him with Beatrice, that she would display to him her second beauty. She relents, and her virgins lead Dante up to where she stands gazing at the sacred symbol. But they warn him not to gaze on her too fixedly.]

Mine eyes with such an eager coveting
Were bent to rid them of their ten years' thirst,
No other sense was waking, and e'en they

Were fenced on either side from heed of aught;
So tangled, in its customed toils, that smile
Of saintly brightness drew me to itself;
When forcibly, toward my left, my sight
The sacred virgins turned; for from their lips
I heard the warning sounds, 'Too fixed a gaze!'
Awhile my vision laboured; as when late
Upon the overstrained eyes the sun hath smote.
But soon, to lesser object, as the view
Was now recovered (lesser in respect
To that excess of sensible, whence late
I had perforce been sundered), on their right
I marked that glorious army wheel, and turn
Against the sun and sevenfold lights, their front.

[Beatrice darkly predicts to Dante some future events.
Lastly, the whole band arrive at a fountain, from which
point the streams, Lethe and Eunoe, separating, flow
different ways. Matilda, at the desire of Beatrice, causes
Dante to drink of the latter stream.]

And, where they stood, before them, as it seemed
I, Tigris and Euphrates both beheld
Forth from one fountain issue; and, like friends,
Linger at parting. '0 enlightening beam!
0 glory of our kind! beseech thee say
What water this, which from one source derived
Itself removes to distance from itself?'
To such entreaty answer thus was made:
'Entreat Matilda, that she teach thee this.'
And here, as one who clears himself of blame
Imputed, the fair dame returned, 'Of me
He this and more hath learnt; and I am safe
That Lethe's water hath not hid it from him.'
And Beatrice: 'Some more pressing care,
That oft the memory leaves, perchance hath made
His mind's eye dark. But lo, where Eunoe flows
Lead thither; and, as thou art wont, revive
His fainting virtue.' As a courteous spirit,
That proffers no excuses, but as soon
As he hath token of another's will.
Makes it his own; when she had taken me thus
The lovely maiden moved her on ....

III: Paradise

[Beatrice, whose glorious spirit has disclosed its grace and
beauty to Dante in the mountain of Purgatory, where she
had admonished him concerning his errors, and had
brought him to acknowledge them, leads him in an ascent
towards the first heaven. She also ministers to his soul
profound consolation and high enlightenment by relieving
him of some of his most perplexing and distressing doubts.
Dante and his celestial guide enter the moon. The cause of
the spots or shadows which appear in that satellite is
explained to him.]

'The virtue and motion of the sacred orbs,
A mallet by the workman's hand. Must needs

By blessed movers be inspired. This heaven,
Made beauteous by so many luminaries,
From the deep spirit that moves its circling sphere
Its image takes an impress as a seal:
And as the soul, that dwells within your dust,
Through members different, yet together formed,
In different powers resolves itself; e'en so
The intellectual efficacy unfolds
Its goodness multiplied throughout the stars.
On its own unity revolving still.
Different virtue compact different
Makes with the precious body it enlivens,
With which it knits, as life in you is knit.
From its original nature full of joy.
The virtue mingled through the body shines.
As joy through pupil of the living eye,
From hence proceeds that which from light to light
Seems different, and not from dense or rare.
This is the formal cause, that generates,
Proportioned to its power, the dusk or clear.'

[In the moon Dante learns that this satellite is allotted to
those who, after having made profession of chastity and a
religious life, had been compelled to violate their vows.
Dante ascends with Beatrice to the planet Mercury, which
is the second heaven, and here he finds a multitude of
spirits, one of whom offers to satisfy him of anything he
may wish to know from him. This spirit declares himself to
be the Emperor Justinian, and after speaking of his own
actions, recounts the victories, before him, gained under
the Roman Eagle, after which Justinian proceeds:]

"This little star is furnished with good spirits,
Whose mortal lives were busied to that end,
That honour and renown might wait on them;
And, when desires thus err in their intention,
True love must needs ascend with slacker beam
But it is part of our delight to measure
Our wages with the merit; and admire
The close proportion. Hence doth heavenly justice
Temper so evenly affection in us.
It never can warp to any wrongfulness."

[Beatrice then conducts the poet to the third heaven, the
planet Venus. Here he finds the soul of Charles Martel,
King of Hungary, who had been his friend on earth, and
who now, after speaking of the realms to which he had
been heir, unfolds the cause why children differ in
disposition from their parents.]

"The roots from whence your operation come
Must differ. Therefore one is Solon born;
Another, Xerxes; and Melchisedec
A third; and he a fourth whose airy voyage
Cost him his son. In her circuitous course,
Nature, that is the seal to mortal wax,
Doth well her art, but no distinction owns
'Twixt one or other household. Hence befalls

That Esau is so wide of Jacob; hence
Quirinus of so base a father springs,
He dates from Mars his lineage. Were it not
That Providence celestial over-rul'd,
Nature, in generation, must the path
Traced by the generator still pursue
Unswervingly. Thus place I in thy sight
That which was late behind thee."

[In this planet of Venus various spirits speak to Dante. Foico, the Provençal bard, tells him that the spirit of Rahab the harlot is there.]

"Inquire thou wouldst,
Who of this light is denizen, that here
Beside me sparkles, as the sunbeam doth
On the clear wave. Know, then, the soul of Rahab
Is in that gladsome harbour; to our tribe
United, and the foremost rank assigned.
She to this heaven, at which the shadow ends
Of your sublunar world, was taken up
First in Christ's triumph, of all souls redeemed;
For well behoved that in some part of heaven
She should remain a trophy, to declare
The mighty conquest won with either palm
For that she favoured first the high exploit
Of Joshua on the Holy Land, whereof
The Pope recks little now."

[The next ascent carries them into the sun, which is the fourth heaven. Dante describes the first sight.]

Then I saw a bright band, in liveliness
Surpassing, who themselves did make the crown,
And thus the centre; yet more sweet in voice
Than in their visage, beaming. Cinctured thus,
Sometime Latona's daughter we behold,
When the impregnate air retains the thread
That weaves her zone. In the celestial court,
Whence I return, are many jewels found,
So dear and beautiful they cannot brook
Transporting from that realm; and of these lights
Such was the song.

[Dante penetrates various circles of glorified spirits. Then with Beatrice he is translated into the fifth heaven, the planet Mars; and here behold the souls of those who had died fighting for the true faith. ranged as a cross, athwart which the spirits move to the sound of a melodious hymn.]

O genuine glitter of eternal Beam!
With what a sudden whiteness did it flow,
Overpowering vision in me. But so fair,
So passing lovely, Beatrice showed
Her infinite sweetness. Then mine eyes regained
Power to look up; and I beheld myself,
Sole with my lady, to more lofty bliss Translated.

[Dante ascends with Beatrice to the planet Jupiter, the sixth heaven, where he finds the souls of those who administered justice rightly to the world. There appears an eagle, formed of heavenly spirits.]

Before my sight appeared, with open wings,
The beauteous image, in fruition sweet,
Gladdening the thronged spirits. That which next
Befalls me to portray voice hath not uttered,
Nor hath ink written, nor in fantasy
Was e'er conceived. For I beheld and heard
The beak discourse; and what intention formed
Of many, singly as of one express,
Beginning, "For that I was just and piteous,
I am exalted to this height of glory,
The which no wish exceeds."

[Dante ascends with Beatrice to the seventh heaven, the planet Saturn, abode of souls who passed their life in holy contemplation. Next they mount to the eighth heaven of the fixed stars; and look back upon the earth. He sees Christ triumphing. The Saviour ascends, followed by His virgin mother, and Dante in the ninth heaven is permitted to behold the divine essence. He is taken up with Beatrice into the empyrean, to see the triumph of the angels and saintly multitude of the souls of the blessed as snow-white roses. Lastly, he is admitted a glimpse of the mystery of the Trinity, and the Union of Man with God.]

In that abyss
Of radiance, clear and lofty, seemed, methought,
Three orbs of triple hue, dipt in one 'bound;
And, from another, one reflected seemed,
As rainbow is from rainbow; and the third
Seemed fire breathed equally from both.
0 speech!
How feeble and how faint art thou to give
Conception birth. Yet this to what I saw
Is less than little. O eternal light!
Sole in thyself thou dwell'st; and of thyself
Sole understood, past, present, or to come;
Thou smiledst on that. circling, which in thee
Seemed as reflected splendour, while I mused;
For I therein, methought, in its own hue
Beheld our image painted; steadfastly
I therefore pored upon the view. As one
Who, versed in geometric lore, would fain
Measure the circle; and, though pondering long
And deeply, that beginning, which he needs,
Finds not; e'en such was I, intent to scan
The novel wonder, and trace out the form.
How to the circle fitted, and therein
How placed: but the flight was not for my wing.
Here vigour fail'd the tow'ring fantasy;
But yet the will roli'd onward, like a wheel
In even motion, by the Love impelled,
That moves the sun in heaven and all the stars.

The Decameron
or, Prince Galeotto

By Giovanni Boccaccio

(Florence?, c1350)

This collection of tales by an Italian lawyer is often held to be one of the first to try and depict realistic, spirited, characters. His stories have been re-used by, among others, Shakespeare, George Eliot, Keats and Tennyson. Decameron is meant to mean '100', but, this being an abridgement, you only get six of them.

Possession of *The Decameron* is still forbidden by federal law in the USA following an 1873 ruling on obscenity brought by the 'New York Society for the Suppression of Vice'. It has also been banned in South Africa and Australia.

Abridged: GH

BEGINNETH here the book wherein are contained one hundred tales told in ten days by seven ladies and three men.

The Seven Beautiful Maidens

In the year of our Lord 1348 a terrible plague broke out in Florence, which, from being the finest city in Italy, became the most desolate. It was a strange malady that no drugs could cure; and it was communicated, not merely by conversing with those strickened by the pestilence, but even by touching their clothes, or anything they had worn. As soon as the purple spots, which were the sign of the disease, appeared on the body, death was certain to ensue within three days.

So great were the terror and disorder and distress, that all laws, human and divine, were disregarded. Everybody in Florence did just as he pleased. The wilder sort broke into the houses of rich persons, and gave themselves over to riotous living, exclaiming that, since it was impossible to avoid dying from the plague, they would at least die merrily. Others shut themselves up from the rest of the world, and lived on spare diet, and many thousands fled from their houses into the open country, leaving behind them all their goods and wealth, and all their relatives and friends. Brother fled from brother, wife from husband, and, what was more cruel, even parents forsook their own children. It was perilous to walk the streets, for they were strewn with the bodies of plague-strickened wretches, and I have seen with my own eyes the very dogs perish that touched their rags.

Between March and July a hundred thousand persons died in Florence, though, before the calamity, the city was not supposed to have contained so many inhabitants. But I am weary of recounting out late miseries, and, passing by everything that I can well omit, I shall only observe that, when the city was almost depopulated, seven beautiful young ladies, in deep mourning, met one Tuesday evening in Saint Mary's Church, where indeed they composed the whole of the congregation. They were all related to each other, either by the ties of birth, or by the more generous bonds of friendship. Pampinea, the eldest, was twenty-eight years of age; Fiammetta was a little younger; Filomena, Emilia, Lauretta, and Neifile were still more youthful; and Elisa was only eighteen years old.

After the service was over, they got into a corner of the church, and began to devise what they should do, for they were now alone in the world.

"I would advise," said Pampinea, "that we should leave Florence, for the city is now dangerous to live in, not merely by reason of the plague, but because of the lawless men that prowl about the streets and break into our houses. Let us retire together into the country, where the air is pleasanter, and the green hills and the waving corn-fields afford a much more agreeable prospect than these desolate walls."

"I doubt," said Filomena, "if we could do this unless we got some man to help us."

"But how can we?" exclaimed Elisa. "Nearly all the men of our circle are dead, and the rest have gone away."

While they were talking, three handsome young cavaliers- Pamfilo, Filostrato, and Dioneo- came into the church, looking for their sweethearts, who by chance were Neifile, Pampinea, and Filomena.

"See," said Pampinea with a smile, "fortune is on our side. She has thrown in our way three worthy gentlemen, who, I am sure, will come with us if we care to invite them."

She then acquainted the cavaliers with her design, and begged them to help her to carry it out. At first they took it all for a jest; but when they found that the ladies were in earnest, they made arrangements to accompany them. So the next morning, at the break of day, the ladies and their maids, and the cavaliers and their men-servants, set out from Florence, and after travelling for two miles they came to the appointed place. It was a little wooded hill, remote from the highway, on the top of which was a stately palace with a beautiful court, and fine galleries, and splendid rooms adorned with excellent paintings. And around it were fair green meadows, a delightful garden, fountains of water, and pleasant trees.

Finding that everything in the palace had been set in order for their reception, the ladies and their cavaliers took a walk in the garden, and diverted themselves by singing love-songs, and weaving garlands of flowers. At three o'clock, dinner was laid in the banqueting hall, and when this was over, Dioneo took a lute and Fiammetta a viol, and played a merry air, while the rest of the company danced to the music. When the dance was ended, they began to sing, and so continued dancing and singing until nightfall. The cavaliers then retired to their chambers, and the ladies to theirs, after arranging that Pampinea should be the queen of their company for the following day, and direct all their feasts and amusements.

The next morning Queen Pampinea called them all up at nine o'clock, saying it was unwholesome to sleep in the daytime, and led them into a meadow of deep grass shadowed by tall trees.

"As the sun is high and hot," she continued, "and nothing is to be heard but the chirping of grasshoppers among the olives, it would be folly to think of walking. So let us sit down in a circle and tell stories. By the time the tales have gone round, the heat of the sun will have abated, and we can then divert ourselves as best we like. Now, Pamfilo," she said, turning to the cavalier on her right hand, "pray begin."

Cymon and Iphigenia: A Tale of Love

Of all the stories that have come into my mind, said Pamfilo, there is one which I am sure you will all like, for it shows how strange and wonderful is the power of love. Some time ago, there lived in the island of Cyprus a man of great rank and wealth, called Aristippus, who was very unhappy because his son Cymon, though very tall and handsome, was feeble in intellect. Finding that the most skilful teacher could not beat the least spark of knowledge into the head of his son, Aristippus made Cymon live out of his sight, among the slaves in his country-house.

There Cymon used to drudge like one of the slaves, whom, indeed, he resembled in the harshness of his voice and the uncouthness of his manners. But one day as he was tramping round the farm, with his staff upon his shoulder, he came upon a beautiful maiden sleeping in the deep grass of a meadow, with two women and a manservant slumbering at her feet. Cymon had never seen the face of a woman before, and, leaning upon his staff, he gazed in blank wonder at the lovely girl, and strange thoughts and feelings began to work within him. After watching her for a long time, he saw her eyes slowly open, and there was a sweetness about them that filled him with joy.

"Why are you looking at me like that?" she said. "Please go away. You frighten me!"

"I will not go away," he answered; "I cannot!"

And though she was afraid of him, he would not leave her until he had led her to her own house. He then went to his father and said he wanted to live like a gentleman, and not like a slave. His father was surprised to find that his voice had grown soft and musical, and his manners winning and courteous. So he dressed him in clothes suitable to his high station, and let him go to school. Four years after he had fallen in love, Cymon became the most accomplished

young gentleman in Cyprus. He then went to the father of Iphigenia, for such was her name, and asked for her in marriage. But her father replied that she was already promised to Pasimondas, a young nobleman of Rhodes, and that their nuptials were about to be celebrated.

"O Iphigenia," said Cymon to himself, on hearing the unhappy news, "it is now time for me to show you how I love you! Love for you has made a man of me, and marriage with you would make me as happy and as glorious as a god! Have you I will, or else I will die!"

He at once prevailed upon some young noblemen, who were his friends, to help him in fitting out a ship of war. With this he waylaid the vessel in which Iphigenia embarked for Rhodes. Throwing a grappling iron upon this ship, Cymon drew it close to his own. Then, without waiting for anyone to second him, he jumped among his enemies, and drove them like sheep before him, till they threw down their arms.

"I have not come to plunder you," said Cymon, "but to win the noble maiden, Iphigenia, whom I love more than aught else in the world. Resign her to me, and I will do you no harm!"

Iphigenia came to him all in tears.

"Do not weep, my sweet lady," he said to her tenderly. "I am your Cymon, and my long and constant love is worth more than all Pasimondas's promises."

She smiled at him through her tears, and he led her on board his ship, and sailed away to Crete, where he and his friends had relations and acquaintances. But in the night a violent tempest arose, and blotted out all the stars of heaven, and whirled the ship about, and drove it into a little bay upon the island of Rhodes, a bow-shot from the place where the Rhodian ship had just arrived.

Before they could put out to sea again, Pasimondas came with an armed host and took Cymon a prisoner, and led him to the chief magistrate of the Rhodians for that year, Lysimachus, who sentenced him and his friends to perpetual imprisonment, on the charge of piracy and abduction.

While Cymon was languishing in prison, with no hope of ever obtaining his liberty, Pasimondas prepared for his nuptials with Iphigenia. Now Pasimondas had a younger brother called Hormisdas, who wanted to marry a beautiful lady, Cassandra, with whom the chief magistrate Lysimachus was also in love. Pasimondas thought it would save a good deal of trouble and expense if he and his brother were to marry at the same time. So he arranged that this should be done. Thereupon Lysimachus was greatly angered. After a long debate with himself, honour gave way to love, and he resolved at all hazards to carry off Cassandra.

But whom should he get as companions in this wild enterprise? He at once thought of Cymon and his friends, and he fetched them out of prison and armed them, and concealed them in his house. On the wedding-day he divided them into three parties. One went down to the shore and secured a ship; one watched at the gate of Pasimondas's house; and the third party, headed by Cymon and Lysimachus, rushed with drawn swords into the bridal chamber and killed the two bridegrooms, and bore the tearful but by no means unwilling brides to the ship, and sailed joyfully away for Crete.

There they espoused their ladies, amidst the congratulations of their relatives and friends; and though, by reason of their actions, a great quarrel ensued between the two islands of Cyprus and Rhodes, everything was at last amicably adjusted. Cymon then returned with Iphigenia to Cyprus, and Lysimachus carried Cassandra back to Rhodes, and all of them lived very happily to the end of their days.

Alibech and Rustico: A Tale of the Devil

Dioneo began to speak as follows: "Charming ladies, maybe you have never heard tell how one putteth the devil in hell; wherefore, I will tell it you.

In the city of Capsa there was a rich man, who had a fair young daughter, by name Alibech. She, being a heathen, one day asked of a Christian how one might best serve God. The Christian answered that the great happiness of serving God best came to those who eschewed the things of the world. So, the girl, being but very simple and no more than fourteen years old, set off next morning all alone, to go to the desert of Thebais.

After some days, she reached the cell of a young hermit, a very devout and good man, named Rustico. He received her, and bade her to rest. But temptations tarried not, and laying aside devout thoughts, he fell to bethinking what course he should take so as to bring her to his pleasures, without her taking him for a debauched fellow.

Accordingly, he gave her to understand that the most acceptable service that could be rendered to God was to put back the devil into hell. The girl asked him how this might be done; 'Thou shalt soon know; do thou as thou shalt see me do.' So saying, he proceeded to put off his garments and abode stark naked, as likewise did the girl.

Whereupon Rustico, seeing her so fair, felt an accession of desire, and therewith came a certain insurgence of the flesh, which Alibech marking with surprise, saying: "Rustico, what is this, which I see thee have, that so protrudes, and which I have not?" "Oh! my daughter," said Rustico, "'tis the Devil: he is tormenting me most grievously." "Praise be to God," said the girl, "I see that I am in better case than thou, for no such Devil have I." "But instead," returned Rustico, "thou hast somewhat else that I have not." "Oh!" said Alibech, "what may that be?" "Hell," answered Rustico, "wilt thou have compassion on me and permit me to put my devil in hell, such wilt afford me great solace, and render to God a most acceptable service." Which said, he took the girl to one of the beds and taught her how to incarcerate this spirit accursed of God.

She began to find the game agreeable, and said to Rustico: "Now see I plainly that 'twas true, what the worthy men said at Capsa, of the service of God being so delightful: indeed I cannot remember that ever I had so much pleasure as in putting the Devil in hell."

But when she saw that Rustico had no more occasion for her to put the Devil in hell, she said to him one day: "Rustico, if thy Devil is chastened and gives thee no more trouble, my hell, on the other hand, gives me no peace; so thou wouldst do well to lend me the aid of thy Devil to allay the fervent heat of it." Rustico, accordingly satisfied her bytimes, but, overmuch desire on the one part was matched to a lack of power on the other.

It befell that a fire broke out in Capsa and burnt Alibech's father and his family in his own house. Thereupon, a young man called Neerbale, hearing that Alibech was alive, set out in search of her before the court laid hands upon her father's estate. To Rustico's great satisfaction he brought her back to Capsa, where he took her to wife and succeeded, in her right, to the ample inheritance of her father.

There, being asked by the women as to how she had served God in the desert, she answered that she served Him at putting the devil in hell, and with words and gestures, expounded it to them. Thereafter, telling it from one to another they brought it to a common saying that the most acceptable service one could render to God was to put the devil in hell, which byword is yet current there.

Gisippus and Titus: A Tale of Friendship

As we have learned of love, said Filomena, I will now relate a story showing the great power of friendship.

At the time when Octavius Caesar, who afterwards became the Emperor Augustus, was governing Rome as a triumvir, a young Roman gentleman, Titus Quintius Fulvus, went to Athens to study philosophy. There he became acquainted with a noble young Athenian named Gisippus, and a brotherly affection sprang up between them, and for three years they studied together and lived under the same roof.

In the meantime, Gisippus fell in love with a young and beautiful Athenian maiden named Sophronia, and a marriage was arranged between them. Some days before the marriage, Gisippus took his friend with him on a visit to his lady. It was the first time that Titus had seen Sophronia, and as he looked upon her beauty he grew as much enamoured as ever a man in the world was with a woman. So great was his passion that he could neither eat nor sleep, and he grew so sick that at last he was unable to rise from his bed. Gisippus was extremely grieved at his illness, and knowing that it must have been caused by some secret malady of the mind, he pressed him to reveal the cause of his grief. At length Titus, unable to restrain himself any longer, said, with his face streaming with tears:

"O Gisippus, I am unworthy of the name of friend! I have fallen in love with Sophronia, and it is killing me. How base I am! But pardon me, my dear friend, for I feel that I shall soon be punished for my disloyalty by death!"

Gisippus stood for some time in suspense by the bed side of Titus, divided between the claims of love and the claims of friendship. But at last he resolved to save his friend's life at the cost of his own happiness. Some days afterwards, Sophronia was brought to his house for the bridal ceremony to be consummated. Going softly into the bridal chamber where the bride was lying, he put out the candles, and then went silently to Titus, and told him that he might be the bridegroom. Titus was so overcome with shame that he refused to go; but Gisippus so passionately entreated him, that at last he consented. Going into the dark bridal chamber, he softly asked Sophronia if she would be his wife. She, thinking it was Gisippus, replied, "Yes." Then, taking a ring of value, and putting it upon her finger, Titus said: "And I will be your husband."

In the morning, Sophronia discovered the trick that had been put upon her. Stealing out of the house, she went to her father and mother, and told them that Gisippus had deceived her, and married her to Titus. Great was the resentment against Gisippus throughout Athens, for Sophronia came of a very ancient and noble family.

But seeing that what had been done could not be undone, the parents of the bride at last allowed Titus to lead her to Rome, where the scandal would not be known. But when Titus was gone, they resolved to take vengeance upon Gisippus. A powerful party was formed against him, who succeeded in getting him stripped of all his possessions, driven from Athens, and condemned to perpetual exile.

Friendless and beggared, Gisippus slowly travelled on foot to Rome, intending to ask Titus to help him. He found that his friend was now a rich and powerful man, enjoying the favour of the young Prince Octavius, and living in a splendid palace. Gisippus did not dare to enter it, as his clothes were now worn to rags, so he stood humbly by the gate like a beggar, hoping that his friend would recognise him and speak to him. But Titus came out in a hurry, and never even stopped to look at him; and Gisippus, thinking that he was now despised, went away confounded with grief and despair.

Wandering at random about the streets, he came at nightfall to a cavern where thieves were wont to gather, and laid down on the hard ground and wept himself to sleep. While he was sleeping, two thieves entered with their booty and began to quarrel about it, whereupon one killed the other and fled. In the morning some watchmen found Gisippus sleeping beside the dead body, and arrested him.

"Yes, I killed him," said Gisippus, who was now resolved to die, and thought that this would be a better way than taking his own life. Thereupon, the judge sentenced him to be crucified, which was the usual manner of death in these cases. By a strange chance, however, Titus came into the hall to defend a poor client. He instantly recognised Gisippus, and, wondering greatly at the sad change of his fortune, he determined at all costs to save him. But the case had gone so far that there was only one way of doing this.

And Titus took it. Stepping resolutely up to the judge, he greatly astonished everyone by exclaiming:

"Recall thy sentence. This person is innocent; I killed the man!"

Gisippus turned round in astonishment, and seeing Titus, he concluded that he was trying to save him for friendship's sake. But he was determined that he would not accept the sacrifice.

"Do not believe him, sir. I was the murderer. Let the punishment fall on me," he said to the judge.

The judge was amazed to see two men contending for the torture of crucifixion with as much eagerness as if it had been the highest honour in the world; and suddenly a notorious thief, who had been standing in the court, came forward and made this surprising declaration:

"This strange debate has so moved me that I will confess everything," he said. "You cannot believe, sir, that either of these men committed the murder. What should a man of the rank and wealth of Titus have to do in a thieves' cavern? He was never there. But this poor, ragged stranger was sleeping in a corner when I and my fellow entered. Thieves, you know, sometimes fall out, especially over their booty. This was what happened last night; and, to put an end to the quarrel, I used a knife."

The appearance of a third self-accuser so perplexed the judge that he put the case before Octavius Caesar, and Caesar called the three men up before him. Thereupon Titus and Gisippus related to him at length the strange story of their friendship, and he set the two friends at liberty, and even pardoned the thief for their sakes.

Titus then took Gisippus to his house and forced him to accept a half of his great wealth, and married him to his sister Fulvia, a very charming and lovely young noblewoman.

For the rest of their lives Titus and Sophronia, and Gisippus and Fulvia, lived very happily together in the same palace in Rome, and every day added something to their contentment and felicity.

The Three Rings: A Tale of Ingenuity

It was now Neifile's turn to tell a story, and she said that as there had been much controversy at Florence during the plague concerning religion, this had put her in mind of the tale of Melchizedeck.

This man was a very rich Jew, who lived at Alexandria in the reign of great Sultan Saladin. Saladin, being much impoverished by his wars, had a mind to rob Melchizedeck. In order to get a pretext for plundering the Jew, he sent for him.

"I hear that thou art very wise in religious matters," said Saladin, "and I wish to know which religion thou judgest to be the true one-the Jewish, the Mohammedan, or the Christian?"

The Jew saw that Saladin wanted to trap him. If he said that the Jewish or the Christian faith was the true one, he would be condemned as an infidel. If, on the other hand, he agreed that the Mohammedan religion was preferable to the others, the sultan would say that a wealthy believer ought to contribute largely to the expenses of the state. After considering how best to avoid the snare, the wise Jew replied:

"Some time ago, your majesty, there was a man who had a ring of great beauty and value. And he declared in his will that the son to whom this ring was bequeathed should be the head of the family, and that his descendants should rule over the descendants of the other sons. For many generations his wishes were carried out; but at last the ring came into the possession of a man who had three sons, all virtuous and dutiful to their father, and equally beloved by him.

"Being at a loss which son to prefer above the others, the good man got a skilful craftsman to make two rings, which were so like the first that he himself scarcely knew the true one. On his deathbed he gave one of these rings privately to each of his sons. Each of them afterwards laid claim to the government of the family, and produced the ring which his father had given him. But the rings were so much alike that it was impossible to tell which was the true one, and even to this day no one has been able to decide upon the matter. Thus has it happened, sire, in regard to the three laws of faith derived from God-Jew, Mohammedan, and Christian. Each believes that he is the true heir of the Almighty; but it is just as uncertain which has received the true law as it is which has received the true ring."

Saladin was mightily pleased at the ingenious way in which Melchizedeck escaped from the snare that had been spread for him. Instead of taking by force the money that he wanted from the Jew, he desired him to advance it on loan. This Melchizedeck did, and Saladin soon afterwards repaid the money and gave him presents, besides maintaining him nobly at court and making him his life-long friend.

For some days the ladies and cavaliers entertained one another with dancing and singing and story-telling. And then, as the plague had abated in Florence, they returned to the city. But before they went Dioneo told them a very strange and moving tale.

Griselda: A Tale of Wifely Patience

Men, said Dioneo, are wont to charge women with fickleness and inconstancy; but there comes into my mind a story of a woman's constancy and a man's cruelty which, I think you will agree, is worth the telling. Gualtieri, the young Marquis of Saluzzo, was a man who did not believe that any woman could be true and constant all her life. And for this reason he would not marry, but spent his whole time in hawking and hunting. His subjects, however, did not want him to die without an heir, and leave them without a lord, and they were always pressing him to marry. They went so far at last as to offer to provide a lady for him. This made him very angry.

"If I want a wife, my friends," he said, "I will choose one myself. And, look you, whatever her birth and upbringing are, pay her the respect due to her as my lady, or you shall know to your cost how grievous it is to me to have taken a wife when I did not want one."

A few days afterwards he was riding through a village, not far from his palace, when he saw a comely shepherd girl carrying water from a well to her father's house.

"What is your name?" said the young marquis.

"Griselda," said the shepherd girl.

"Well, Griselda," said the Marquis of Saluzzo, "I am looking for a wife. If I marry you, will you study to please me and carry out all my demands, whatever they are, without a murmur or a sullen look?"

"Yes, my lord," said Griselda.

Thereupon, the marquis sent his servants to fetch some rich and costly robes, and, leading Griselda out by the hand, he clothed her in gorgeous apparel, and set a coronet upon her head, and putting her on a palfrey, he led her to his palace. And there he celebrated his nuptials with as much pomp and grandeur as if he had been marrying the daughter of the King of France.

Griselda proved to be a good wife. She was so sweet-natured, and so gentle and kind in her manners, that her husband thought himself the happiest man in the world; and her subjects honoured her and loved her very dearly. In a very short time, her winning behaviour and her good works were the common subject of talk throughout the country, and great were the rejoicings when a daughter was born to her.

Unfortunately, her husband got a strange fancy into his head. He imagined she was good and gentle merely because everything went well with her; and, with great harshness, he resolved to try her patience by suffering. So he told her that the people were greatly displeased with her by reason of her mean parentage, and murmured because she had given birth to a daughter.

"My lord," said Griselda, "I know I am meaner than the meanest of my subjects, and that I am unworthy of the dignity to which you have advanced me. Deal with me, I pray, as you think best for your honour and happiness, and waste no thought upon me."

Soon afterwards one of his servants came to Griselda, and said: "Madam, I must either lose my own life, or obey my lord's commands. He has ordered me to take your daughter, and-"

He would not say anything more, and Griselda thought that he had orders to kill the child. Taking it out of the cradle, she kissed it, and tenderly laid it in the servant's arms. The marquis sent the little girl to one of his relatives at Bologna, to be brought up and educated. Some years afterwards Griselda gave birth to a boy. The marquis, naturally enough, was mightily pleased to have an heir; but he took also this child away from his wife.

"I am not able to live any longer with my people," he said. "They say they will not have a grandson of a poor shepherd as their future lord. I must dispose of this child as I did the other."

"My lord," replied Griselda, "study your own ease and happiness without the least care for me. Nothing is pleasing to me that is not pleasing to you."

The next day the marquis sent for his son in the same way as he had sent for his daughter, and had him brought up with her at Bologna. His people thought that the children had been put to death, and blamed him for his cruelty, and showed great pity for his wife. But Griselda would not allow them to attack her husband, but found excuses for him.

In spite of this, the marquis did not yet believe in the constancy and fidelity of his wife, and about sixteen years after their marriage he resolved to put her to a test.

"Woman," he said, "I am going to take another wife. I shall send you back to your father's cottage in the same state as I brought you from it, and choose a young lady of my own rank in life."

With the utmost difficulty Griselda kept back her tears, and humbly consented to be divorced. The marquis stripped her of her fine raiment, and sent her back to her father's hut dressed in a smock. Her husband then gave it out that he was about to espouse the daughter of the Count of Panago; and, sending for Griselda, he said:

"I am about to bring home my new bride, but I have no woman with me to set out the rooms and order the ceremony. As you are well acquainted with the government of my palace, I wish you to act as mistress for a day or two. Get everything in order, and invite what ladies you will to the festival. When the marriage is over, you must return to your father's hut."

These words pierced like daggers to the heart of Griselda. She was unable to part with her love for her husband as easily as she had parted with her high rank and great fortune.

"My lord," said Griselda, "I swore that I would be obedient to you, and I am ready to fulfil all your commands."

She went into the palace in her coarse attire and worked with the servants, sweeping the rooms and cleaning the furniture. After this was done, she invited all the ladies in the country to come to the festival. And on the day appointed for the marriage she received them, still clad in her coarse attire, but with smiling and gentle looks. At dinner-time the marquis arrived with his new lady-who was indeed a very beautiful girl. After presenting her to all the guests, many of whom congratulated him on making so good an exchange, he said, with a smile, to Griselda:

"What do you think of my bride?"

"My lord," she replied, "I like her extremely well. If she is as wise as she is fair, you may be the happiest man in the world with her. But I very humbly beg that you will not take with this lady the same heart-breaking measures you took with your last wife, because she is young and tenderly educated, while the other was from a child used to hardship."

"Pardon me! Pardon me! Pardon me!" said the marquis. "I know I have tried you harshly, Griselda. But I did not believe in the goodness and constancy of woman, and I would not believe in them until you proved me in the wrong. Let me restore, in one sweet minute, all the happiness that I have spent years in taking away from you. This young lady, my dear Griselda, is your daughter and mine! And look! Here is our son waiting behind her."

He led Griselda, weeping for joy, to her children. Then all the ladies in the hall rose up from the tables, and taking Griselda into a chamber, they clothed her in fine and noble raiment, and stayed with her many days, feasting and rejoicing. And the marquis sent for Griselda's father, the poor shepherd, and gave him a suite of rooms in the palace, where he lived in great happiness with his daughter and his grandchildren and his noble son-in-law.

The Canterbury Tales
By Geoffrey Chaucer
(London, c1388)

Geoffrey Chaucer was a civil servant, sufficiently highly thought of that King Edward III granted him a gallon of wine daily for life. This unfinished 'frame narrative' was one of the first popular books ever printed by the pioneer English printer William Caxton, and Chaucer "the firste fyndere of our fair langage."

Based on the modernised versions by Dryden and Wordsworth (p294): Abridged:GH

PROLOGUE

Original text:
WHEN that Aprilis, with his showers swoot,
The drought of March hath pierced to the root,
And bathed every vein in such licour,
Of which virtue engender'd is the flower... ...

Modernised version:
When droughty March is gone, and April showers
Freshen the earth and quicken all the flowers,
And little birds upon the budding trees
Wake in the night and sing their melodies,

Then moved by the sweet spring time, folks incline,
To go on pilgrimage to some great shrine;
And men of all degrees, from end to end
Of England, unto Canterbury wend,
To pray before the tomb of our great Saint,
For peace of soul, or cure of some complaint.
It happened in this season on a day,
In Southwark, at the Tabard, as I lay,
Ready to wend upon my pilgrim route
To Canterbury with a heart devout,
At night there came into that hostelry,
Full nine-and-twenty folk in company.
Good pilgrims were they all, I quickly found,
Who were, like me, to Canterbury bound;
And having spoken unto every one
Over the evening meal, I was anon
Admitted to their goodly company.
And then the keeper of our hostelry,
A merry, bright-eyed man, said he would ride
At his own cost with us. and be our guide;
Saying we were the merriest pilgrim band
That he had seen that year in all the land.
And now, I think, 'tis time to stay my verse,
And tell you of my fellow-travellers.
A knight came first, a very worthy man.
Who, from the earliest time when he began
To ride, had vowed himself to chivalry,
Honour and truth, freedom and courtesy.
And nobly had he fought in Holy Land
In fifteen battles, and had held command
To him a seat of honour all men gave;
For he was very wise as well as brave,
Yet in his port as meek as is a maid.
He never a discourteous word had said
In all his life to any living wight.
He was a very perfect, gentle knight.
Beside him rode his son, a handsome Squire
Of twenty years, in glittering attire.
At night his songs of love rang down the dale;
One servant only by his side was seen,
A Yeoman, in a coat and hood of green.
A Prioress rode behind this gallant boy;
A smiling, simple nun was she, and coy.
Her face was pleasant, and her voice was sweet,
And French she spoke right gracefully and neat
So tender was her heart, that she was stirred
To tears by a dead mouse or wounded bird.
A Monk behind this kind, sweet Prioress came
Who loved right well to ride and hunt for game.
A manly man he was, and strong and able,
And many a good horse had he in his stable.
The saintly rules of Maur and Benedict
He held were over-old and over-strict;
He cared not for that text a moulting hen,
Which says that hunters are not holy men;
I hold that his opinion was not bad.
Why should he study till he was half-mad,
Great joy he had in hunting down the hare.

And fat he was, and well he loved rich fare.
And next there came a Friar, in worsted gown,
Who knew right well each tavern in each town.
Familiar and well-beloved was he
With all the farming men and yeomanry;
Well could he sing, and play upon the harp,
And turn a merry saying or a sharp;
His eyes, they twinkled in his head as bright
As stars do on a clear and frosty night.
Beside a Franklin, jolly, plump and ruddy,
Who made good food and drink his only study,
There rode a Clerk from Oxford-one who took
No pleasure save in reading in a book.
Lean was his horse, as lean as is a rake;
And he, too, was not fat, I undertake.
No benefice had he obtained as yet,
And on no worldly place his mind was set;
For he would rather have at his bed's head
A score of volumes, bound in black or red,
On Aristotle[1] and philosophy,
Than splendid robes, fiddle and psaltery.
A Sergeant of the Law came next- a man
Who seemed to know all that a lawyer can.
Right well could he advise, and judge, and plead,
And draw up wisely every sort of deed.
A Good-wife who had come from Bath rode next-
A witty woman, but with deafness vexed.
Bold was her face, and red and very fair.
And so much glittering finery did she wear
That she was rather vulgarly overdressed,
Though everything she wore was of the best.
But still, as women go, she was not bad;
And though in turn five husbands she had had,
And worried them to death, she was full fain
To find a sixth and go to church again.
Close to the good-wife a Physician rode,
Whose rich habiliments of crimson showed
What profit he had made in those two years
When the great plague filled all men's minds with fears.
Some say gold is a sovran remedy,
And this physician loved it certainly.
But by him came a Parson, poor in dress,
But rich in learning and in holiness.
Wide was his parish, scattered was his flock,
But neither rain, nor snow, nor thunder shock
Prevented him from going to relieve
The sick, the poor, and all who mourn and grieve.
Some way behind this poor and godly priest,
A Pardoner rode upon an ambling beast,
Singing, 'Come hither, love, to me.' From Rome
Loaded with red-hot pardons, had he come.
His equal was not to be found, I swear,
For trickery, from Berwick unto Ware.
Among the relics which he had for sale
There was a fragment of Our Lady's veil,
A cross of common metal set with stones,

---

1   **Aristotle:** see p62

And a glass case containing a pig's bones.
These he would sell to some poor, foolish priest
As something worth their weight in gold at least.
Such was the rubbish that he trafficked in:
A greater rogue than he was never seen.
A Steward and a Miller too. were there,
A Haberdasher and a Carpenter,
A Weaver, and a Dyer, and a Cook
Who, on our pilgrimage, great trouble took
To roast our meat and make and bake our pies;
A right good cook he was for savouries.
With us to Canterbury now he came,
To cure his leg, for he had fallen lame.
The Miller was a man of brawn and might,
As ready for a frolic as a fight.
When to his mill the farmer's corn was sent,
It came back ground much smaller than it went.
No wheat he bought, no fields he ever tilled,
But all the year his corn bins were well filled.
And yet he was a jolly soul, I trow,
And honest in his way-as millers go.
Riding in front of all our company,
And blowing on a bagpipe merrily,
With puffing cheeks, and bagpipe strongly blown,
Gaily he played us out of Southwark town.
"Now," said the keeper of the Tabard Inn,
"I think, Sir Knight, you kindly might begin
A round of tales, to keep us blithe and merry
As we go riding on to Canterbury.
Let each of us now tell a tale in turn,
And then, when we to Southwark town return,
The teller of the tale that pleases most
Shall have a supper at the others' cost."
To this we all agreed with much delight.
And being wise and courteous, the old knight,
Sitting upon his horse, erect and bold,
Began to tell the tale that here is told.

The Knight's Tale

When Theseus, the Athenian monarch
To Thebes, and put the town to sword and flame,
Two brave young Thebans of the royal blood,
Arcite and Palamon, his power withstood.
Kinsmen they were and friends, and side by side
They fought, but could not turn the battle's tide;
And so they fell at last, still combating,
Into the hands of the Athenian king.
And Theseus, fearing that the brave young knights
Would struggle to regain their royal rights,
Resolved to make them prisoners for life,
And keep the Thebans from renewing strife.
So, in a tower beside his palace wall
Arcite and Palamon were put, and all
The doors were bolted; and a year went by
And still in prison they were forced to lie.
And then as Palamon, upon a day,
At morning in the pleasant month of May,
Was gazing from the window of the tower,

He saw a maiden, fairer than a flower,
Walking in beauty in the garden ground
Below the tower, and singing as she bound
A garland of sweet roses white and red,
To place upon her shining golden head.
"Ye gods!" cried Palamon, "captivity
Is in itself a bitter thing to dree!
Now love, now hopeless love, has come to fill
My heart with greater grief and misery still!"
Hearing his cries. Arcite ran up in haste
To comfort him, but as his arms embraced
His friend he saw the maiden like a flower
Walking **in** beauty underneath the tower.
There was a silence. And Arcite then said,
"Unless she love me I shall soon be dead!"
"I saw and loved her first," cried Palamon.
"I swear she shall be mine, and mine alone!
And you, Arcite, my kinsman and my friend,
Are you not sworn to serve me to the end,
As I am sworn to serve you all my life?
Then help me win this maiden for my wife."
"That will I not," Arcite replied; "above
All power of friendship is the power of love.
Stronger than yours my passion is, and I
Must win her for myself, or fail and die.
And I am very like to die," said he,
"For there's no hope that our captivity
Will ever end." But by strange hap, Arcite
Was set at liberty that very night.
A friend this favour from the king obtained,
Upon condition that Arcite remained
Away from Athens. "If Arcite is found,"
Said Theseus sternly, "on Athenian ground
He shall at once be killed." At this Arcite
Cried unto Palamon, "Oh, bitter spile!
Why was I born to such a cruel fate?
Happier are you, my friend, in your sad state.
Liberty only doubles all my pain;
For I shall never see her face again.
While you can sit and watch her from the tower.
And may, by change of fortune, get the power
Of winning her. Farewell, Oh, Palamon.
Think kindly on me now that I am gone!"
The god of love, the god of love! ah me!
How mighty, and how great a lord is he!
There is no power on earth that can withstand
The miracles men work at his command.
Seven years went by, and Palamon still strove
To free himself, and follow his sweet love.
Though now he knew that she was Emily,
The sister of King Theseus-enemy
Of him and all his race-he loved her more
Each time he chanced to see her than before.
Finding at last a friend in his distress,
He broke out of the tower, and donned the dress
And armour of a man of his degree,
And waited in the fields where Emily
Was riding with her maids at break of day.

To pluck green boughs and flowers, for it was May.
As he was hiding in the grass, a knight
Came singing down the road. It was Arcite!
Exile from Emily to him had seemed
Far worse than death, and now at length he deemed
That he had won her heart; for he had come
In strange disguise, bold and adventuresome,
And won renown at the Athenian court.
Sweetly he sang of Emily; but short
His song was. Springing fiercely to his side,
Palamon seized his bridle rein and cried,
"Down, traitor, down! And if you are a man
Fight for your life, and then sing if you can!"
Arcite got down, and drew his sword, and then
They fought more like to tigers than to men.
Neither gave way, but still warred where he stood;
And then, when all their armour streamed with blood.
Emily came riding by, arrayed in green,
And by her side was Theseus with his queen.
"Down with your swords!" the king cried. "If you give
Another stroke, neither of you shall live.
Are you both mad?" "May be," said Palamon,
"Seeing the thing that we are set upon.
We are your mortal foes. He is Arcite,
The Theban lord you vowed that you would smite
Dead if you ever found him in your lands.
And I deserve no pity at your hands,
For I am Palamon, your prisoner,
Broke out of prison, and now fighting here
With my dear friend and kinsman, as you see,
Instead of flying from captivity."
"Why do you fight?" the king said, with a frown.
"Love," Palamon replied, "has broken down
And utterly destroyed all friendly ties
Between us. Emily, since we were brought
Prisoners to Athens, love for you has wrought
Such rapture, misery, gladness, and despair
In our sad hearts, that we have ceased to care
Whether we lived or died. And now that I
Can never hope to win you, I would die."
Struck by his passion and sincerity,
Theseus said, turning unto Emily-
Who, with the queen, was kneeling at his feet,
And crying, "Pardon! Pardon them!" "My sweet,
I pardon them right willingly, and now
It lies with you to reconcile them. How
Will you decide, fair sister, which to take
Of these two knights? For both you cannot make
Blest with your love in happy married life.
But hold! There is a way to end this strife
According to the rules of courtesy.
Arcite and Palamon must come to me,
Each with a hundred lords at his command,
And joust in knightly wise for Emily's hand."
At this, bold Palamon and brave Arcite
Were filled with hope and ardour and delight.
Great joy was there in Greece. Who would not ride
The lists, and help to win so fair a bride?

Crowds of great kings and conquerors were bent
On fighting in the famous tournament.
So when the knights their bannerets unfurled
The flower of all the chivalry of the world
Rode at their side; and the earth seemed to rock
When the two hosts met in terrific shock.
Too close it grew for spears; and swords then flashed,
And down on helm and armour maces crashed.
Oh, what a havoc Palamon then made
To reach Arcite! But as he drove his blade
Clean at his foe, full twenty hostile lords
Closed in on him, and lashed him with their swords
And struck him to the earth. "Have done! have done!"
Cried Theseus, seeing the fall of Palamon.
"Arcite of Thebes has got the victory;
Arcite of Thebes shall now have Emily!"
But as Arcite rode up, with shining eyes
Fixed upon Emily, his lovely prize.
Holding his battered helmet in his hand,
His war-horse swerved close to the royal stand,
And down he fell on his uncovered head;
And where he fell he lay like one stone dead.
"What is this world?" he then began to moan.
When Emily came to him, and Palamon,
"What is this world? What joy in it men have?
Now with their love, and now in the cold grave
Alone, and with no kindly company.
Farewell, my life, my love, my Emily!
Now take me gently in your arms, I pray,
For love of God, and list to what I say.
Here is my friend and kinsman, Palamon;
And now I say, there is not any one-
Though I have fought with him in jealousy-
More worthy to be loved by you than he.
If you will be his true and loving wife,
Loyally will he serve you all his life,
In honour, knighthood, wisdom, truth and worth.
Noble he is by nature and by birth."
Then darkness fell upon him, and the breath
Of life went from his body; but in death
Still on his lady did he fix his eye;
His last word was, "Ah, mercy, Emily!"
Some time, both Emily and Palamon
Mourned for Arcite, but when a year had gone,
King Theseus in solemnity and state
United them in marriage. And thus fate
Gave, in the end, the bride Arcite had won
Unto his friend and kinsman. Palamon.

The Wife of Bath's Tale

In ancient times, in good King Arthur's[2] days,
Our merry England was a faerie place.
The elf-queen with her jolly company-
Then danced at night on manv a flowery lea,
And rings of darker grass at morn were found
In every field where she had led a round.
But now the begging friars have chased away

2   **King Arthur:** see p129

Each pretty sprite and each delightful fay;
In every spot haunted of old by elves,
You now will find the begging friars themselves.
But in King Arthur's reign this was not so.
One of his knights was riding, sad and slow,
At evening through a meadow, and he spied
Some fairies dancing by a forest side.
Boldly he galloped up to them, to ask
Their help; for he was troubled with a task
Beyond the power of man; but all the fays
Vanished before he reached their dancing-place.
Only a woman, ugly, old and grim,
He found there. And she rose, and said to him,
"No path is here, Sir Knight. But can I be
Of help to you?" "Yes, Granny," then said he,
"And I must perish if you cannot aid.
For my unknightly conduct to a maid
I have been sentenced by Queen Guinevere
To come before her throne within a year.
And tell her and her angry damoiselles
What thing a woman wants above all else.
Long has this question set the court at strife,
And if I solve it not, I lose my life.
The year has now gone by; and I have laid
The case before each mother, bride, and maid
Whom I have met in my long wandering.
But none of them agrees upon the thing
They most desire. For some want flattery,
Some love, some marriage, and some jollity;
And others honour, wealth or rich array-
What is their secret wish I cannot say.
Reveal it, granny, and you shall not want
Aught that I have it in my power to grant."
"Sir Knight," she answered, "will you swear to do
Anything in the world I ask of you
If now I rede the riddle to you aright?"
"Yes, on my honour, granny!" said the knight.
"Take me to court," she said, "and on the way
I then will tell you what you have to say."
When they to court were come. Queen Guinevere
Summoned the knight that evening to appear
And tell her, at the peril of his life,
What thing it was that widow, maid and wife
Desired most in the world. "Great Queen," said he,
"What women most desire is- sovereignty.
Fain would each wife obtain complete command
Over her husband, house, and wealth and land.
Single or wed, your sex aspire to sway;
They to rule all, while men, like slaves, obey."
At this there was no widow, wife or maid,
Who disagreed with what the knight had said.
Even the queen, with blushing cheeks, confessed
That he had found what women love the best.
And then, as still before the throne he stood,
The beldam he had met beside the wood
Said to the queen, " 'Twas I who taught this knight
In what it is we women most delight.
W^hen he had sworn that I should never want

Aught that he had it in his power to grant.
And now I ask him, as I saved his life,
To keep his word, and take me for his wife."
In vain the knight endeavoured to escape,
And tried to treat the matter as a jape;
In vain he offered gold, and land beside,
To free himself from such a withered bride.
The beldam firmly held him to his oath.
And even though Queen Guinevere was loath
To see a young knight in King Arthur's court
Married unto a woman of this sort,
Rather than let him tarnish his fair name
She ordered him to wed the wretched dame.
I cannot tell the mirth and rich array,
And joy and feasting of their marriage day.
And all the splendour of the festival.
In sober truth, there was no feast at all.
II was the saddest moment in his life
When the young knight took home his aged wife.
"Never was knight," he said, "in such disgrace.
Medea's magic could not mend your face.
Not only are you ugly, old and lean;
But, in your birth, a creature poor and mean.
Were you but nobly born, at least I might
Bear my misfortune bravely like a knight."
"Is that," said she, "what vexes you so sore?
Nobility of blood is nothing more
Than ancient wealthiness. Your pride of birth.
I hold it for a thing of little worth.
If your ancestors by their virtues won
High honour, this belongs to them alone.
Nothing of price do you derive from them
But rank and wealth, on which to base your claim
To greatness and nobility of soul;
Which things no wealth can purchase or control.
Low-born and poor and old I am, and yet
I do not think myself the worse for it.
Christ is our pattern of nobility,
And where was there a poorer man than He?
He only is a true-born gentleman
Who always does what gentle deeds he can.
As for my ugliness and my old age,
Choose now, if you would have me old and sage,
Or young and inexperienced in life."
"Nay, choose yourself," he said. "my wise, old wife."
"Then have I got the mastery of you."
She'said, "since you permit me now to do
What I desire. Look, look, my love!" said she,
"And grieve and wonder at the change in me!"
The knight turned, and discovered at his side
The sweetest, loveliest and tenderest bride
That ever. since the race of men began.
Brought love and happiness unto a man.

The Prioress's Tale

There was in Asia. in a mighty town
Of Christian folk, a street for Jews to be.
Which had been given to them for their own

By a great lord, for gain and usury.
Hateful to Christ and to His company;
And through this street all men might walk or ride;
Free was it, and unbarred at either side.
A little school of Christian people stood
Down at the farther end, in which there were
Some little children come of Christian blood,
Who studied in the school, from year to year,
The simple learning which was given there;
That is to say, reading and singing too,
As little children in their childhood do.
Among these children was a widow's son,
A little scholar scarcely seven years old,
Who through the street of Jewry used to run
Daily to school, with lightsome heart and bold;
And having by his mother oft been told
To pray unto Our Lady, he would say,
'Hail, Mary!' as he went upon his way.
Great joy this little child in singing took,
And though he was too young to join the choir,
When older children from their anthem book
Sang *Alma Redemptoris,* nigh and nigher
He used to creep, his little heart on fire,
Listening to every word and every note,
Until he got the anthem all by rote.
'0 Alma Redemptoris,' then he sang,
As home he went, with childish voice and sweet.
'0 Alma Redemptoris,' loud it rang
And echoed down the darksome Jewish street.
Day after day he sang it. and his feet
Moved lightly to each clear and liquid note
That sounded from his little tender throat.
Meeting this little child upon his path,
A Jew was filled with bitterness. "Oh, woe!
Woe upon Lsrael!" cried he in his wrath,
"That we should suffer this thing to be so!
What! shall this boy along our own street go
Singing, day after day, his hymns and saws,
Clean against our religion and our laws?"
With evil thoughts his fellows he inspired,
And filled their hearts with wickedness and hate;
Until at last a murderer they hired,
Who in a lonely alley lay in wait;
And as the child one evening, dark and late,
Came singing down the street, the villain slit
His throat, and threw his body in a pit.
The widowed mother waited all that night
After her little child, and he came not.
Then, at the earliest glimpse of morning light,
With face made pale by fear and anxious thought,
For her sweet child through all the town she sought,
Till in the end she learnt that he had been
In the Jews' street, and there he was last seen.
With woe and pity moving in her breast,
And working like to madness in her mind,
She wandered down the street, like one possessed.
Hoping in vain her little child to find:
And ever on Christ's Mother, meek and kind,

She cried for help; and then at last she prayed
The Jews to come in pity to her aid.
Yes. piteously and sadly did she pray
To every Jew and Jewess in that place
To tell her if her child had passed that
"No!" said they all. But Jesu of His grace
Guided her wandering steps, in little space,
Close to the pit in which her child was thrown;
And as she called on him with many a moan-
Oh, Thou great God that dost reveal Thy power
And wisdom by the mouth of Innocence!-
This jewel of chastity, this glorious flower
Of martyrdom, this child of excellence.
Raised from the pit his mangled throat, and thence
'0 Alma Redemptoris,' loudly sang.
Till with the sound the street of Jewry rang.
Full soon all Christian folk from far and near
Came to the pit to wonder at this thing.
They placed the murdered child upon a bier;
And all the time he never ceased to sing.
When to the church the body they did bring,
And blessed and sprinkled it with holy water,
It still sang, *'Alma Redemptoris Mater.'*
All wonder-stricken at this miracle,
The priest, cried, "By the Holy Trinity,
I summon you, 0 little child, to tell
The reason of this wondrous mystery!
How can you still keep singing, clear and free,
The *Alma Redemptoris* with your head
Nigh severed from your body? Are you dead?"
"My throat is cut unto the bone, I trow,"
Said the young child, "Yea, right unto the bone.
And by the law of nature, long ago
I should have died. But Jesus now has shown
His power, and made in me His glory known;
Letting me sing, *0 Alma Redemptoris,*
In praise and worship of His Mother's glories.
"This was the hymn I sang when I was slain.
Then in the pit to me there did appear
Sweet Jesu's Mother, and she put a grain
Upon my tongue, and said, 'Have thou no fear,
My child, but sing my praises loud and clear,
Till from thy tongue the grain is taken, then
In Heaven thou shalt sing to me again.' "
Then, in the silence of the wondering host,
From off his tongue the priest removed the grain;
And peacefully the child gave up the ghost,
While down his widowed mother's face like rain
The salt tears fell, and with a cry of pain
She dropped upon her face flat on the ground,
And lay as still as if she had been bound.
Then, having praised the Lord with solemn cheer,
For the great miracle that He had wrought,
The people knelt beside the little bier,
On which the child still lay; and having bought
A tomb for him of precious marble wrought.
His sweet and uncorrupted body, they
Enclosed therein, and then began to pray.

"0 Martyr wedded to virginity!
Before the white-milk Lamb of Paradise,
Thou goest singing now eternally;
The light of innocence in thy young eyes.

And in thy heart the fire of sacrifice!
Pray, pray, that unto us it may be given
To hear thee singing by the Throne in heaven."

Le Morte D'Arthur
(*The Death of Arthur*)
By Sir Thomas Mallory
(Wales?, c1460)

The real King Arthur, if he existed, was probably a leader of the Britons against the immigrant Angles (who became the *English*) some nine-hundred years before this, one of the first popular printed books in English. This is the version of King Arthur and his knights which spawned all those movies and musicals. Mallory himself was an odd character, an MP who was prosecuted for burglary, rape and sheep stealing, but managed to fight his way out of prison.

Adapted into modern English. Abridged: JH/GH

I PRAY you all, gentlemen and gentlewomen that readeth this book of Arthur and his knights, from the beginning to the ending, pray for me while I am alive, that God send me good deliverance, and when I am dead, I pray you all pray for my soul.

By Sir Thomas Maleore, knight, as Jesu help him.

I. The Coming of Arthur

It befell in the days of the noble Utherpendragon, when he was King of England, there was a mighty and noble duke in Cornwall, named the Duke of Tintagil, that held long war against him. And the duke's wife was called a right fair lady, and passing wise, and Igraine was her name. And the duke, issuing out of the castle at a postern to distress the king's host, was slain. Then all the barons, by one assent, prayed the king of accord between the Lady Igraine and himself. And the king gave them leave, for fain would he have accorded with her; and they were married in a morning with great mirth and joy.

When the Queen Igraine grew daily nearer the time when the child Arthur should be born, Merlin, by whose counsel the king had taken her to wife, came to the king and said: "Sir, you must provide for the nourishing of your child. I know a lord of yours that is a passing true man, and faithful, and he shall have the nourishing of your child. His name is Sir Ector, and he is a lord of fair livelihood." "As thou wilt," said the king, "be it." So the child was delivered unto Merlin, and he bare it forth unto Sir Ector, and made a holy man to christen him, and named him Arthur.

But, within two years, King Uther fell sick of a great malady, and therewith yielded up the ghost, and was interred as belonged unto a king; wherefore Igraine the queen made great sorrow, and all the barons.

Then stood the realm in great jeopardy a long while, for many weened to have been king. And Merlin went to the Archbishop of Canterbury, and counselled him to send for all the lords of the realm, and all the gentlemen of arms, to London before Christmas, upon pain of cursing, that Jesus, of His great mercy, should show some miracle who should be rightwise king. So in the greatest church of London there was seen against the high altar a great stone and in the midst thereof there was an anvil of steel, and therein stuck a fair sword, naked by the point, and letters of gold were written about the sword that said, "Whoso pulleth out this sword of this stone and anvil is rightwise king born of England."

And many essayed, but none might stir the sword.

And on New Year's Day the barons made a joust, and Sir Ector rode to the jousts; and with him rode Sir Kaye, his son, and young Arthur, that was his nourished brother.

And Sir Kaye, who was made knight at Allhallowmas afore, had left his sword at his father's lodging, and so prayed young Arthur to ride for it. Then Arthur said to himself, "I will ride to the churchyard and take the sword that sticketh in the stone for my brother Kaye." And so, lightly and fiercely, he pulled it out of the stone, and took horse and delivered to Sir Kaye the sword. "How got you this sword?" said Sir Ector to Arthur. "Sir, I will tell you," said Arthur; "I pulled it out of the stone without any pain." "Now," said Sir Ector, "I understand you must be king of this land." "Wherefore I?" said Arthur. "And for what cause?" "Sir," said Sir Ector, "for God will have it so." And therewithal Sir Ector kneeled down to the earth, and Sir Kaye also.

Then Sir Ector told him all how he had betaken him to nourish him; and Arthur made great moan when he understood that Sir Ector was not his father.

And at the Feast of Pentecost all manner of men essayed to pull out the sword, and none might prevail but Arthur, who pulled it out before all the lords and commons. And the commons cried, "We will have Arthur unto our king." And so anon was the coronation made.

And Merlin said to King Arthur, "Fight not with the sword that you had by miracle till you see that you go to the worst, then draw it out and do your best." And the sword, Excalibur, was so bright that it gave light like thirty torches.

II. The Marriage of Arthur

In the beginning of King Arthur, after that he was chosen king by adventure and by grace, for the most part the barons knew not that he was Utherpendragon's son but as Merlin made it openly known. And many kings and lords made great war against him for that cause, but King Arthur full well overcame them all; for the most part of the days of his life he was much ruled by the counsel of Merlin. So it befell on a time that he said unto Merlin, "My barons will let me have no rest, but needs they will have that I take a wife, and I will none take but by thy advice."

"It is well done," said Merlin, "for a man of your bounty and nobleness should not be without a wife. Now, is there any fair lady that ye love better than another?"

"Yea," said Arthur; "I love Guinever, the king's daughter, of the land of Cameliard. This damsel is the gentlest and fairest lady I ever could find."

"Sir," said Merlin, "she is one of the fairest that live, and as a man's heart is set he will be loth to return."

But Merlin warned the king privily that Guinever was not wholesome for him to take to wife, for he warned him that Launcelot should love her, and she him again. And Merlin went forth to King Leodegraunce, of Cameliard, and told him of the desire of the king that he would have to his wife Guinever, his daughter. "That is to me," said King Leodegraunce, "the best tidings that ever I heard; and I shall send him a gift that shall please him, for I shall give him the Table Round, the which Utherpendragon gave me; and when it is full complete there is a place for a hundred and fifty knights; and a hundred good knights I have myself, but I lack fifty, for so many have been slain in my days."

And so King Leodegraunce delivered his daughter, Guinever, to Merlin, and the Table Round, with the hundred knights, and they rode freshly and with great royalty, what by water and what by land.

And when Arthur heard of the coming of Guinever and the hundred knights of the Round Table he made great joy; and in all haste did ordain for the marriage and coronation in the most honourable wise that could be devised. And Merlin found twenty-eight good knights of prowess and worship, but no more could he find. And the Archbishop of Canterbury was sent for, and blessed the seats of the Round Table with great devotion.

Then was the high feast made ready, and the king was wedded at Camelot unto Dame Guinever, in the Church of St. Steven's, with great solemnity.

III. Sir Launcelot and the King

And here I leave off this tale, and overskip great books of Merlin, and Morgan le Fay, and Sir Balin le Savage, and Sir Launcelot du Lake, and Sir Galahad, and the Book of the Holy Grail, and the Book of Elaine, and come to the tale of Sir Launcelot, and the breaking up of the Round Table.

In the merry month of May, when every heart flourisheth and rejoiceth, it happened there befel a great misfortune, the which stinted not till the flower of the chivalry of all the world was destroyed and slain.

And all was along of two unhappy knights named Sir Agravaine and Sir Mordred, that were brethren unto Sir Gawaine. For these two knights had ever privy hate unto the queen, and unto Sir Launcelot. And Sir Agravaine said openly, and not in counsel, "I marvel that we all be not ashamed to see and know how Sir Launcelot cometh daily and nightly to the queen, and it is shameful that we suffer so noble a king to be ashamed." Then spake Sir Gawaine, "I pray you have no such matter any way before me, for I will not be of your counsel." And so said his brothers, Sir Gaheris and Sir Gareth. "Then will I," said Sir Mordred. And with these words they came to King Arthur, and told him they could suffer it no longer, but must tell him, and prove to him that Sir Launcelot was a traitor to his person.

"I would be loth to begin such a thing," said King Arthur, "for I tell you Sir Launcelot is the best knight among you all." For Sir Launcelot had done much for him and for his queen many times, and King Arthur loved him passing well.

Then Sir Agravaine advised that the king go hunting, and send word that he should be out all that night, and he and Sir Mordred, with twelve knights of the Round Table should watch the queen. So on the morrow King Arthur rode out hunting.

And Sir Launcelot told Sir Bors that night he would speak with the queen. "You shall not go this night by my counsel," said Sir Bors.

"Fair nephew," said Sir Launcelot, "I marvel me much why ye say this, sithence the queen hath sent for me." And he departed, and when he had passed to the queen's chamber, Sir Agravaine and Sir Mordred, with twelve knights, cried aloud without, "Traitor knight, now art thou taken!"

But Sir Launcelot after he had armed himself, set the chamber door wide open, and mightily and knightly strode among them, and slew Sir Agravaine and twelve of his fellows, and wounded Sir Mordred, who fled with all his might, and came straight to King Arthur, wounded and beaten, and all be-bled.

"Alas!" said the king, "now am I sure the noble fellowship of the Round Table is broken for ever, for with Launcelot will hold many a noble knight."

And the queen was adjudged to death by fire, for there was none other remedy but death for treason in those days. Then was Queen Guinever led forth without Carlisle, and despoiled unto her smock, and her ghostly father was brought to her to shrive her of her misdeeds; and there was weeping and wailing and wringing of hands.

But anon there was spurring and plucking up of horses, for Sir Launcelot and many a noble knight rode up to the fire, and none might withstand him. And a kirtle and gown were cast upon the queen, and Sir Launcelot rode his way with her to Joyous Gard, and kept her as a noble knight should.

Then came King Arthur and Sir Gawaine, whose brothers, Sir Gaheris and Sir Gareth, had been slain by Sir Launcelot unawares, and laid a siege to Joyous Gard. And Launcelot had no heart to fight against his lord, King Arthur; and Arthur would have taken his queen again, and would have accorded with Sir Launcelot, but Sir Gawaine would not suffer him. Then the Pope called unto him a noble clerk, the Bishop of Rochester, and gave him bulls, under lead, unto King Arthur, charging him that he take his queen, Dame Guinever, to him again, and accord with Sir Launcelot. And as for the queen, she assented. And the bishop had of the king assurance that Sir Launcelot should come and go safe. So Sir Launcelot delivered the queen to the king, who assented that Sir Launcelot should not abide in the land past fifteen days.

Then Sir Launcelot sighed, and said these words, "Truly me repenteth that ever I came into this realm, that I should be thus shamefully banished, undeserved, and causeless." And unto Queen Guinever he said, "Madam, now I must depart from you and this noble fellowship for ever; and since it is so, I beseech you pray for me, and send me word if ye be noised with any false tongues." And therewith Launcelot kissed the queen, and said openly, "Now let me see what he be that dare say the queen is not true to King Arthur-let who will speak, and he dare!" And he took his leave and departed, and all the people wept.

IV. The Passing of Arthur

Now, to say the truth, Sir Launcelot and his nephews were lords of the realm of France, and King Arthur and Sir Gawaine made a great host ready and shipped at Cardiff, and made great destruction and waste on his lands. And Arthur left the governance of all England to Sir Mordred. And Sir Mordred caused letters to be made that specified that King Arthur was slain in battle with Sir Launcelot; wherefore Sir Mordred made a parliament, and they chose him king, and he was crowned at Canterbury. But Queen Guinever came to London, and stuffed it with victuals, and garnished it with men, and kept it.

Then King Arthur raised the siege on Sir Launcelot, and came homeward with a great host to be avenged on Sir Mordred. And Sir Mordred drew towards Dover to meet him, and most of England held with Sir Mordred, the people were so new-fangled.

Then was there launching of great boats and small, and all were full of noble men of arms, and there was much slaughter of gentle knights; but King Arthur was so courageous none might let him to land; and his knights fiercely followed him, and put back Sir Mordred, and he fled.

But Sir Gawaine was laid low with a blow smitten on an old wound given him by Sir Launcelot. Then Sir Gawaine, after he had been shriven, wrote with his own hand to Sir Launcelot, flower of all noble knights: "I beseech thee, Sir Launcelot, return again to this realm, and see my tomb, and pray some prayer more or less for my soul. Make no tarrying but come with thy noble knights and rescue that noble king that made thee knight, for he is straitly bestood with a false traitor." And so Sir Gawaine betook his soul into the hands of our Lord God.

And many a knight drew unto Sir Mordred and many unto King Arthur, and never was there seen a dolefuller battle in a Christian land. And they fought till it was nigh night, and there were a hundred thousand laid dead upon the down.

"Alas! that ever I should see this doleful day," said King Arthur, "for now I come unto mine end. But would to God that I wist where that traitor Sir Mordred is, which hath caused all this mischief."

Then was King Arthur aware where Sir Mordred leaned upon his sword, and there King Arthur smote Sir Mordred throughout the body more than a fathom, and Sir Mordred smote King Arthur with his sword held in both hands on the side of the head, that the sword pierced the helmet and the brain-pan. And Sir Mordred fell dead; and the noble King Arthur fell in a swoon, and Sir Lucan and Sir Bedivere laid him in a little chapel not far from the sea-side.

And when he came to himself again, he said unto Sir Bedivere, "Take thou Excalibur, my good sword, and throw it into that water." And when Sir Bedivere (at the third essay) threw the sword into the water, as far as he might, there came an arm and a hand above the water, and met and caught it, and so shook and brandished it thrice; and then the hand vanished away with the sword in the water.

Then Sir Bedivere bore King Arthur to the water's edge, and fast by the bank hovered a little barge, and there received him three queens with great mourning. And Arthur said, "I will unto the vale of Avillon for to heal me of my grievous wound, and if thou never hear more of me, pray for my soul." And evermore the ladies wept.

And in the morning Sir Bedivere was aware between two hills of a chapel and a hermitage; and he saw there a hermit fast by a tomb newly graven. And the hermit said, "My son, here came ladies which brought this corpse and prayed me to bury him."

"Alas," said Sir Bedivere, "that was my lord, King Arthur."

And when Queen Guinever understood that her lord, King Arthur, was slain, she stole away and went to Almesbury, and made herself a nun, and was abbess and ruler as reason would.

And Sir Launcelot passed over into England, and prayed full heartily at the tomb of Sir Gawaine, and then rode alone to find Queen Guinever. And when Sir Launcelot was brought unto her, she said: "Through this knight and me all the wars were wrought, and through our love is my noble lord slain; therefore, Sir Launcelot, I require thee that thou never look me more in the visage."

And Sir Launcelot said: "The same destiny ye have taken you unto I will take me unto." And he besought the bishop that he might be his brother; then he put a habit on Sir Launcelot, and there he served God day and night, with prayers and fastings.

And when Queen Guinever died Sir Launcelot buried her beside her lord, King Arthur. Then mourned he continually until he was dead, so within six weeks after they found him stark dead, and he lay as he had smiled. Then there was weeping and dolor out of measure. And they buried Sir Launcelot with great devotion.

The Notebooks
of Leonardo Da Vinci
(Florence, Milan, Rome, Bologna & Venice, c1490)

A contemporary writer described Leonardo as being "endowed by Heaven with beauty, grace and talent in such abundance that he leaves other men far behind". His fame as a painter rests on the dozen or so of his surviving works, including the *Mona Lisa, The Last Supper* and the *Creation of Adam,* but the notes and fragments found in his many diaries mark him out as the definitive ever-enquiring and multi-talented 'Renaissance man'.

Abridged GH, from the 1883 translation by Jean Paul Richter.

Of Lines and of Perspective: The line has in itself neither matter nor substance and may rather be called an imaginary idea than a real object; and this being its nature it occupies no space. Therefore an infinite number of lines may be conceived of as intersecting each other at a point, which has no dimensions and is only of the thickness (if thickness it

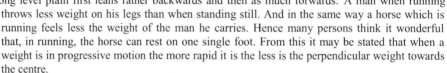

may be called) of one single line. Wherefore O painter! do not surround your bodies with lines.

Perspective is a rational demonstration by which experience confirms that every object sends its image to the eye by a pyramid of lines; and bodies of equal size will result in a pyramid of larger or smaller size, according to the difference in their distance, one

from the other. Shadow is the absence of light, merely the obstruction of the luminous rays by an opaque body. Shadow is of the nature of darkness. The difference between light and lustre: High-light or lustre on any object is not situated necessarily in the middle of an illuminated object, but moves as and where the eye moves in looking at it.

The movement of the human figure: A man when walking has his head in advance of his feet. A man when walking across a long level plain first leans rather backwards and then as much forwards. A man when running

throws less weight on his legs than when standing still. And in the same way a horse which is running feels less the weight of the man he carries. Hence many persons think it wonderful that, in running, the horse can rest on one single foot. From this it may be stated that when a weight is in progressive motion the more rapid it is the less is the perpendicular weight towards the centre.

Diving apparatus and Skating: Of walking under water. Method of walking on water.

On draperies: Painters ought not to give to drapery a great confusion of many folds, but rather only introduce them where they are held by the hands or the arms; the rest you may let fall simply where it is its nature to flow; and do not let the nude forms be broken by too many details and interrupted folds. How draperies should be drawn from nature: that is to say if you want to represent woollen cloth draw the folds from that; and if it is to be silk, or fine cloth or coarse, or of linen or of crape, vary the folds in each and do not represent dresses, as many do, from models covered with paper or thin leather which will deceive you greatly.

The use of swimming belts as a method of escaping in a tempest and shipwreck at sea: Have a coat made of leather, which must be double across the breast, and the leather must be quite air-tight. When you want to leap into the sea, blow out the skirt of your coat through the double hems of the breast; and jump into the sea, and allow yourself to be carried by the waves; when you see no shore near, give your attention to the sea you are in, and always keep in your mouth the air-tube which leads down into the coat; and if now and again you require to take a breath of fresh air, and the foam prevents you, you may draw a breath of the air within the coat.

On Flying machines: Man when flying must stand free from the waist upwards so as to be able to balance himself as he does in a boat so that the centre of gravity in himself and in the machine may counterbalance each other, and be shifted as necessity demands for the changes of its centre of resistance

Remember that your flying machine must imitate no other than the bat, because the web is what by its union gives the armour, or strength to the wings. If you imitate the wings of feathered birds, you will find a much stronger structure, because they are pervious; that is, their feathers are separate and the air passes through them. But the bat is aided by the web that connects the whole and is not pervious.

To escape the peril of destruction whilst in a Flying Machine. Destruction to such a machine may occur in two ways; of which the first is the breaking of the machine. The second would be when the machine should turn on its edge or nearly on its edge, because it ought always to descend in a highly oblique direction, and almost exactly balanced on its centre. As regards the breaking of the machine, that may be prevented by making it as strong as possible; and in whichever direction it may tend to turn over, one centre must be very far from the other; that is, in a machine 30 braccia long the centres must be 4 braccia one from the other.

Bags by which a man falling from a height of 6 braccia may avoid hurting himself, by a fall whether into water or on the ground; and these bags, strung together like a rosary, are to be fixed on one's back.

On Flying machines: An object offers as much resistance to the air as the air does to the object. You may see that the beating of its wings against the air supports a heavy eagle in the highest and rarest atmosphere, close to the sphere of elemental fire. Again you may see the air in motion over the sea, fill the swelling sails and drive heavily laden ships. From these instances, and the reasons given, a man with wings large enough and duly connected might learn to overcome the resistance of the air, and by conquering it, succeed in subjugating it and rising above it.

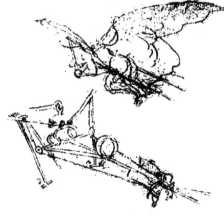

Of Greek fire: Take charcoal of willow, and saltpetre, and sulphuric acid, and sulphur, and pitch, with frankincense and camphor, and Ethiopian wool, and boil them all together. This fire is so ready to burn that it clings to the timbers even under water. And add to this composition liquid varnish, and bituminous oil, and turpentine and strong vinegar, and mix all together and dry it in the sun, or in an oven when the bread is taken out; and then stick it round hempen or other tow, moulding it into a round form, and studding it all over with very sharp nails. You must leave in this ball an opening to serve as a fusee, and cover it with rosin and sulphur.

Again, this fire, stuck at the top of a long plank which has one braccio length of the end pointed with iron that it may not be burnt by the said fire, is good for avoiding and keeping off the ships, so as not to be overwhelmed by their onset.

Again throw vessels of glass full of pitch on to the enemy's ships when the men in them are intent on the battle; and then by throwing similar burning balls upon them you have it in your power to burn all their ships.

Suggestions for a book on anatomy: This work must begin with the conception of man, and describe the nature of the womb and how the foetus lives in it, up to what stage it resides there, and in what way it quickens into life and feeds. Also its growth and what interval there is between one stage of growth and another. What it is that forces it out from the body of the mother, and for what reasons it sometimes comes out of the mother's womb before the due time.

You must show all the motions of the bones with their joints to follow the demonstration of the first three figures of the bones, and this should be done in the first book.

First draw the spine of the back; then clothe it by degrees, one after the other, with each of its muscles and put in the nerves and arteries and veins to each muscle by itself; and besides these note the vertebrae to which they are attached; which of the intestines come in contact with them; and which bones and other organs &c.

The most prominent parts of lean people are most prominent in the muscular, and equally so in fat persons. But concerning the difference in the forms of the muscles in fat persons as compared with muscular persons, it shall be described below.

There are eleven elementary tissues:— Cartilage, bones, nerves, veins, arteries, fascia, ligament and sinews, skin, muscle and fat.

The divisions of the head are 10, viz. 5 external and 5 internal, the external are the hair, skin, muscle, fascia and the skull; the internal are the dura mater, the pia mater, which enclose the brain. The pia mater and the dura mater come again underneath and enclose the brain; then the rete mirabile, and the occipital bone, which supports the brain from which the nerves spring.

The laws of nutrition and the support of life, or how the body of animals is constantly dying and being renewed: The body of any thing whatever that takes nourishment constantly dies and is constantly renewed; because nourishment can only enter into places where the former nourishment has expired, and if it has expired it no longer has life. And if you do not supply nourishment equal to the nourishment which is gone, life will fail in vigour, and if you take away this nourishment, the life is entirely destroyed. But if you restore as much is destroyed day by day, then as much of the life is renewed as is consumed, just as the flame of the candle is fed by the nourishment afforded by the liquid of this candle, which flame continually with a rapid supply restores to it from below as much as is consumed in dying above: and from a brilliant light is converted in dying into murky smoke; and this death is continuous, as the smoke is continuous; and the continuance of the smoke is equal to the continuance of the nourishment, and in the same instant all the flame is dead and all regenerated, simultaneously with the movement of its own nourishment.

On the origin of the soul: Though human ingenuity may make various inventions which, by the help of various machines answering the same end, it will never devise any inventions more beautiful, nor more simple, nor more to the purpose than Nature does; because in her inventions nothing is wanting, and nothing is superfluous, and she needs no counterpoise when she makes limbs proper for motion in the bodies of animals. But she puts into them the soul of the body, which forms them that is the soul of the mother which first constructs in the womb the form of the man and in due time awakens the soul that is to inhabit it. And this at first lies dormant and under the tutelage of the soul of the mother, who nourishes and vivifies it by the umbilical vein, with all its spiritual parts, and this happens because this umbilicus is joined to the placenta and the cotyledons, by which the child is attached to the mother. And these are the reason why a wish, a strong craving or a fright or any other mental suffering in the mother, has more influence on the child than on the mother; for there are many cases when the child loses its life from them, &c.

The rest of the definition of the soul I leave to the imaginations of friars, those fathers of the people who know all secrets by inspiration.

The Common Sense, is that which judges of things offered to it by the other senses. The ancient speculators have concluded that that part of man which constitutes his judgement is caused by a central organ to which the other five senses refer everything by means of impressibility; and to this centre they have given the name Common Sense. And they say that this Sense is situated in the centre of the head between Sensation and Memory. This Common Sense is acted upon by means of Sensation which is placed as a medium between it and the senses. Surrounding things transmit their images to the senses and the senses transfer them to the Sensation. Sensation sends them to the Common Sense, and by it they are stamped upon the memory and are there more or less retained according to the importance or force of the impression. That sense is most rapid in its function which is nearest to the sensitive medium and the eye, being the highest is the chief of the others. Of this then only we will speak, and the others we will leave in order not to make our matter too long.

The earth's place in the universe: The earth is not in the centre of the Sun's orbit nor at the centre of the universe, but in the centre of its companion elements, and united with them. And any one standing on the moon, when it and the sun are both beneath us, would see this our earth and the element of water upon it just as we see the moon, and the earth would light it as it lights us.

On the luminosity of the Earth in the universal space: In my book I propose to show, how the ocean and the other seas must, by means of the sun, make our world shine with the appearance of a moon, and to the remoter worlds it looks like a star; and this I shall prove.

On moving houses: Let houses be first made in pieces on the open places, and can then be fitted together with their timbers in the site where they are to be permanent. Let the width of the streets be equal to the average height of the houses.

The Palace of the prince must have a piazza in front of it. Houses intended for dancing or any kind of jumping or any other movements with a multitude of people, must be on the ground-floor; for I have already witnessed the destruction of some, causing death to many persons, and above all let every wall, be it ever so thin, rest on the ground or on arches with a good foundation. Let the mezzanines of the dwellings be divided by walls made of very thin bricks, and without wood on account of fire. Let all the privies have ventilation by shafts in the thickness of the walls, so as to exhale by the roofs. The ties of oak must be enclosed in the walls in order to be protected from fire.

Vitruvius' scheme of proportions: Vitruvius, the architect, says in his work on architecture that the measurements of the human body are distributed by Nature as follows: that is that 4 fingers make 1 palm, and 4 palms make 1 foot, 6 palms make 1 cubit; 4 cubits make a man's height. And 4 cubits make one pace and 24 palms make a man; and these measures he used in his buildings. If you open your legs so much as to decrease your height 1/14 and spread and raise your arms till your middle fingers touch the level of the top of your head you must know that the centre of the outspread limbs will be in the navel and the space between the legs will be an equilateral triangle.

The length of a man's outspread arms is equal to his height.

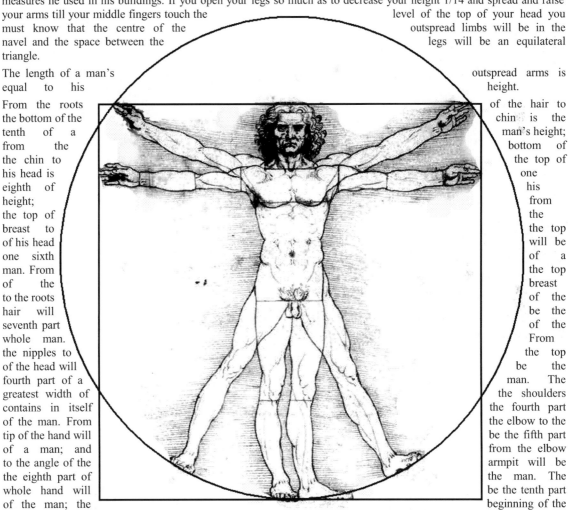

From the roots of the hair to the bottom of the chin is the tenth of a man's height; from the bottom of the chin to the top of his head is one eighth of his height; from the top of the breast to the top of his head will be one sixth of a man. From the top of the breast to the roots of the hair will be the seventh part of the whole man. From the nipples to the top of the head will be the fourth part of a man. The greatest width of the shoulders contains in itself the fourth part of the man. From the elbow to the tip of the hand will be the fifth part of a man; and from the elbow to the angle of the armpit will be the eighth part of the man. The whole hand will be the tenth part of the man; the beginning of the genitals marks the middle of the man. The foot is the seventh part of the man. From the sole of the foot to below the knee will be the fourth part of the man. From below the knee to the beginning of the genitals will be the fourth part of the man. The distance from the bottom of the chin to the nose and from the roots of the hair to the eyebrows is, in each case the same, and like the ear, a third of the face.

On the colour of the atmosphere: When the smoke from dry wood is seen between the eye of the spectator and some dark space or object, it will look blue. Thus the sky looks blue by reason of the darkness beyond it. And if you look towards the horizon of the sky, you will see the atmosphere is not blue, and this is caused by its density. And thus at each degree, as you raise your eyes above the horizon up to the sky over your head, you will see the atmosphere look darker and this is because a smaller density of air lies between your eye and the outer darkness. And if you go to the top of a high mountain the sky will look proportionately darker above you as the atmosphere becomes rarer between you and the darkness; and this will be more visible at each degree of increasing height till at last we should find darkness.

Utopia
By Sir Thomas More
(London, 1515)

Thomas More invented the word 'Utopia' for his perfect island, vaguely based Plato's (p55) idea of the perfect Republic, using a word which, from the Greek, could mean 'no-place' or 'good-place'. It has become the model for invented lands ever since. More was executed for disagreeing with King Henry VIII, but canonised a saint in 1935.

Based on the 1550 translation from Latin by Ralph Robinson. Abridged: GH

DEDICATION

To the Right Honourable Hieronymus Buslidius, Provost of Arienn -

Peter Giles, Citizen of Antwerp, wisheth health and felicity.

THOMAS MORE, the singular ornament of this our age, as you yourself can witness, sent unto me this other day of the Island of Utopia, to very few known, but far excelling Plato's[1]. Thus, O liberal supporter of good learning, and flower of this our time, I bid you most heartily well to fare.

At Antwerp, the first day of November.

THE FIRST BOOK,

OF THE COMMUNICATION OF RAPHAEL HYTHLODAY, CONCERNING THE BEST STATE OF A COMMONWEALTH

The most victorious and triumphant king of England, Henry VIII of that time, for the debatement of certain weighty matters sent me ambassador into Flanders, joined in commission with Cuthbert Tunstall, whose virtue and learning be of more excellency than that I am able to praise them. And whiles I was abiding at Antwerp, oftentimes among other did visit me one Peter Gyles, a citizen thereof whom one day I chanced to espy talking with a stranger, with whom he brought me to speech. Which Raphael Hythloday had voyaged with Master Amerigo Vespucci, but parting from him had returned home by way of Taprobane and Calicut.

Now, as he told us, he had found great and wide deserts and wildernesses inhabited with wild beasts and serpents, but also towns and cities and weal- publiques full of people governed by good and wholesome laws, beside many other that were fond and foolish. Then I urging him that, both by learning and experience, he might be any king's counsellor for the weal-publique -

"You be deceived," quoth he. "For the most part all princes have more delights in warlike matters and feats of chivalry than in the good feats of peace."

Then he speaking of England, "Have you been in our country, sir?" quoth I.

"Yea, forsooth," quoth he, "and there was I much bound and beholden to John Norton, at that time cardinal, archbishop and lord chancellor, in whose counsel the king put much trust.

"Now," quoth he, "one day as I sat at his table, there was a layman cunning in the law who began to praise the rigorous justice that was done upon felons, and to marvel how thieves were nevertheless so rife.

"'Nay, sir,' said I; 'but the punishment passeth the limits of justice. For simple theft is not so great an offence that it ought to be punished with death, nor doth that refrain them, since they cannot live but by thieving. There be many servitors of idle gentlemen who, when their master is dead, and they be thrust forth, have no craft whereby to earn their bread, nor can find other service, who must either starve for hunger or manfully play the thieves.

"'Moreover, look how your sheep do consume and devour whole fields, houses and cities. For noblemen and gentlemen, yea, and certain abbots, holy men, God wot, where groweth the finest wool, do enclose all in pastures, pluck down towns, and leave naught standing but only the church, to make it a sheep-house. Whereby the husbandmen are thrust out of their own; and then what can they do else but steal, and then justly, God wot, be hanged? Furthermore, victuals and other matters are dearer, seeing rich men buy up all, and with their monopoly keep the market as it please them. Unless you find a remedy for these enormities, you shall in vain vaunt yourselves of executing justice upon felons.

"'Beside, it is a pernicious thing that a thief and a murderer should suffer the like punishment, seeing that thereby the thief is rather provoked to kill. But among the polylerytes

---

1 Plato's Republic, see p55

in Persia there is a custom that they which be convict of felony are condemned to be common labourers, yet not harshly entreated, but condemned to death if they seek to run away. For they are also apparelled all alike, and to aid them is servitude for a free man.'

"Now the cardinal pronounced that this were a good order to take with vagabonds. But a certain parasite sayeth in jest that this were then an excellent order to take with the friars, seeing that they were the veriest vagabonds that be; a friar thereupon took the jest in very ill part, and could not refrain himself from calling the fellow ribald, villain and the son of perdition; whereat the jester became a scoffer indeed, for he could play a part in that play, no man better, making the friar more foolishly wroth than before.

"Now, none of them would have harkened to my counsel until the cardinal did approve it. So that if I were sitting in counsel with the French king, whose counsellors were all urging him to war; and should I counsel him not to meddle with Italy, but rather to tarry still at home; and should propose to him the decrees of the Achoriens which dwell over against the Island of Utopia, who, having by war conquered a new kingdom for their prince, constrained him to be content with, his old kingdom and give over the new one to one of his friends; this, mine advice, Master More, how think you it would be heard and taken?"

"So God help me, not very thankfully," quoth I.

"Howbeit, Master More," quoth he, "doubtless, wheresoever possessions be private, where money beareth all the stroke, it is almost impossible that the weal-publique may be justly governed and prosperously flourish. And when I consider the wise and goodly ordinances of the Utopians, among whom, all things being in common, every man hath abundance of everything, yet are there very few laws; I do fully persuade myself that until this property be exiled and banished, perfect wealth shall never be among men. Which, if you had lived with me in Utopia, you would doubtless grant."

"Therefore, Master Raphael," quoth I, "pray you describe unto us this land."

THE SECOND BOOK,

CONTAINING THE DESCRIPTION OF UTO- PIA, AND OF ALL THE GOOD LAWS AND ORDERS OF THE SAME ISLAND.

The island of Utopia is shaped like a new moon, in breadth at the middle 200 miles, narrowing to the tips, which fetch about a compass of 500 miles, and are sundered by eleven miles, having in the space between them a high rock; so that that whole coast is a great haven, but the way into it is securely guarded by hidden rocks. It hath fifty-four large and fair cities, all built in one fashion and having like manners, institutions and laws. The chief and head is Amaurote, being the midmost. Every city hath an equal shire, with farms thereon; and of the husbandmen, half

return each year to the city, their place being taken by a like number.

The city of Amaurote standeth four square, upon the River Anyder, and another lesser river floweth through it. The houses be fair and gorgeous, and the streets twenty foot broad; and at the back of each house a garden, whereby they set great store.

Each thirty families choose an officer, called a Siphogrant, and over every tenth siphogrant is a Tranibore. The prince is chosen for life by the siphogrants. All other offices are yearly, but the tranibores are not lightly changed. The prince and the tranibores hold council every third day, each day with two different siphogrants. They discuss no matter on the day that it is first brought forward. All the people are expert in husbandry, but each hath thereto his own proper craft of masonry or cloth-working, or some other; and, for the most part, that of his father. They work only six hours, which is enough - yea, and more for the store and abundance of things requisite, because all do work. There be none that are idle or busied about unprofitable occupations. In all that city and shire there be scarce 500 persons that be licensed from labour, that be neither too old nor too weak to work. Such be they that have license to learning in place of work. Out of which learned order be chosen ambassadors, priests, tranibores and the prince.

For their clothing, they wear garments of skins for work, and woollen cloaks of one fashion and of the natural colour; and for the linen, they care only for the whiteness, and not the fineness; wherefore their apparel is of small cost.

The city consisteth of families; and for each family the law is there be not fewer than ten children, nor more than sixteen of about thirteen years. Which numbers they maintain by taking from one family and adding to another, or one city and another, or by their foreign cities which they have in the waste places of neighbour lands. The eldest citizen ruleth the family. In each quarter of the city is a market-place whither is brought the work of each family, and each taketh away that he needeth, without money or exchange.

To every thirty families there is a hall, whither cometh the whole siphogranty at the set hour of dinner or supper; and a nursery thereto. But in the country they dine and sup in their own houses. If any desire to visit another city, the prince giveth letters of licence. But wherever he goeth he must work the allotted task. All be partners, so that none may be poor or needy; and all the cities do send to the common council at Amaurote, so that what one lacketh another maketh good out of its abundance.

Their superfluities they exchange with other lands for what they themselves lack, which is little but iron; or for money, which they use but seldom, and that for the hiring of soldiers. Of gold and silver they make not rich vessels, but mean utensils, fetters and gyves; and jewels and precious stones they make toys for children.

Although there be not many that are appointed only to learning, yet all in childhood be instructed therein; and the more part do bestow in learning their spare hours. In the course of the stars and movings of the heavenly sphere they be expert, but for the deceitful divination thereof they never dreamed of it.

They dispute of the qualities of the soul and reason of virtue, and of pleasure, wherein they think the felicity of man to rest; they believe that the soul is immortal, and by the goodness of God ordained to felicity, and that to our virtues and good deeds rewards be appointed hereafter, and to evil deeds punishments. Which principles, if they were disannulled, there is no man but would diligently pursue pleasure by right or wrong. But now felicity resteth only in that pleasure that is good and honest. Virtue they define to be life according to nature, which prescribeth us a joyful life.

But of what they call counterfeit pleasures they make naught; as of pride in apparel and gems, or in vain honours; or of dicing; or hunting, which they deem the most abject kind of butchery. But of true pleasures they give to the soul intelligence and that pleasure that cometh of contemplation of the truth, and the pleasant remembrance of the good life past. Of pleasures of the body they count first those that be sensibly felt and perceived, and thereto the body's health, which lacking, there is no place for any pleasure. But chiefest they hold the pleasures of the mind, the consciousness of virtue and the good life. Making little of the pleasures of appetite, they yet count it madness to reject the same for a vain shadow of virtue.

For bondmen, they have malefactors of their own people, criminals condemned to death in other lands, or poor labourers of other lands who, of their own free will, choose rather to be in bondage with them. The sick they tend with great affection; but, it the disease be not only incurable but full of anguish, the priests exhort them that they should willingly die, but cause him not to die against his will.

The women marry not before eighteen years, the men four years later. But if one have offended before marriage, he or she whether it be, is sharply punished. And before marriage the man and the woman are showed each to the other by discreet persons. To mock a man for his deformity is counted great reproach.

They do not only fear their people from doing evil by punishments, but also allure them to virtue by rewards of honour. They have but few laws, reproving other nations that innumerable books of law and expositions upon the same be not sufficient. Furthermore, they banish all such as do craftily handle the laws, but think it meet that every man should plead his own matter.

As touching leagues they never make one with any nation, putting no trust therein; seeing the more and holier ceremonies the league is knit up with, the sooner it is broken. Who perchance would change their minds if they lived here? But they be of opinion that no man should be counted an enemy who hath done no injury, and that the fellowship of nature is a strong league.

They count nothing so much against glory as glory gotten in war. And though they do daily practise themselves in the discipline of war, they go not to battle but in defence of their own country or their friends, or to right some assured wrong. They be ashamed to win the victory with much bloodshed, but rejoice if they vanquish their enemies by craft. They set a great price upon the life or person of the enemy's prince and of other chief adversaries, counting that they thereby save the lives of many of both parts that had otherwise been slain; and stir up neighbour peoples against them.

They lure soldiers out of all countries to do battle with them and especially a savage and fierce people called the Zapoletes, giving them greater wages than any other nation will. But of their own people they thrust not forth to battle any against his will; yet if women be willing, they do in set field stand every one by her husband's side, and each man is compassed about by his own kinsfolk; and they be themselves stout and hardy and disdainful to be conquered. It is hard to say whether they be craftier in laying ambush or wittier in avoiding the same. Their weapons be arrows, and at handstrokes not swords but pole-axes; and engines for war they devise and invent wondrous wittily.

There be divers kinds of religion. Some worship for God the sun, some the moon; some there be that give worship to a man that was once of the most excellent virtue; some believe that there is a certain godly power unknown, everlasting, incomprehensible; but all believe that there is one God, Maker and Ruler of the whole world. But after they heard us speak of Christ, with glad minds they agreed unto the same.

And this is one of their ancientest laws, that no man shall be blamed for reasoning in the maintenance of his own religion, giving to every man free liberty to believe what he would. Saving that none should conceive so base and vile an opinion as to think that souls do perish with the body, or that the world runneth at all adventures, governed by no divine providence.

They have priests of exceeding holiness, and therefore very few. Both childhood and youth are instructed of them, not more in learning than in good manners.

"This," quoth he, "is that order of the commonwealth which, in my judgement, is not only the best, but also that which alone of good right may claim and take upon it the name of a commonwealth or weal-publique."

Thus when Raphael had made an end of his tale, though many things came to my mind, which in the manners and laws of that people seemed to be instituted and founded of no good reason; yet because I knew he was weary of talking, I said that we would choose another time to weigh and examine the same matters. But, in the meantime, I, Thomas More, as I cannot agree and consent to all things that he said, so must I needs confess and grant that many things be in the Utopian weal-publique which in our cities I may rather wish for than hope after.

The Prince

(*Il Principe*)
By Niccolò Machiavelli
(Florence, 1532)

Here is possibly the most powerful book of all time. Oliver Cromwell owned a first edition, a copy was found in Napoleon's coach at Waterloo, Benito Mussolini wrote an essay about it and both Hitler and Stalin are said to have kept it by their bedsides. This handbook of subterfuge and deceit is *still* a standard work for politicians the world over. You can be pretty sure that *your* 'Prince', even if they call themselves President or Prime Minister, has read it.

Abridged: GH

DEDICATION

To the Magnificent Lorenzo Di Piero De' Medici

Those who strive to obtain the good graces of a prince generally bring precious things. I have nothing of value worthy of your magnificence, but bring this little work, trusting much to your benignity that it will not be considered presumptuous that a man of low and humble condition dare to discuss the concerns of princes.

I: OF THE KINDS OF PRINCIPALITIES

All states are either republics or principalities. Principalities are either hereditary, or are new. The new are either entirely new, as was Milan to Francesco Sforza or they are annexed to an existing hereditary state, as the kingdom of Naples was annexed by the King of Spain. Such dominions are accustomed either to live under a prince or to live in freedom; and are acquired by the arms of the prince himself, or of others, or else by fortune or by ability.

II: OF HEREDITARY PRINCIPALITIES

There are fewer difficulties in holding hereditary states than new ones; simply keeping the customs of his ancestors and acting prudently will allow a prince of average powers to maintain his state, only extraordinary force will deprive him of it, and whenever anything sinister happens to the usurper, he will regain it.

The Duke of Ferrara could not have withstood the attacks of the Venetians or of Pope Julius, unless he had been long established in his dominions. For the hereditary prince has less cause and less need to offend; hence he will be more loved, unless extraordinary vices cause him to be hated.

III: OF MIXED PRINCIPALITIES

A difficulty arises in new principalities; men change their rulers hoping to better themselves: only to discover they have worsened. You make enemies of those you have injured in seizing a principality, yet you cannot satisfy, but dare not injure, those friends who put you there. Strength in arms still needs the goodwill of the natives.

For these reasons Louis XII of France quickly occupied Milan, and quickly lost it, because those who had opened the gates to him gained no benefit and would not endure his maltreatment. However, rebellious provinces are not easily lost a second time, because the prince is willing to punish delinquents. Dominions of the same manners and language are easily held, for peoples alike in customs will live quietly together, as seen in Brittany and Normandy. He, who wishes to hold them, has only to extinguish their ruling family, and to maintain their laws and taxes.

But states differing in customs are less easily held. A great help is that the conqueror should reside there, as the Turk did in Greece, so that small disorders are quickly seen and remedied, and your officials kept in hand.

A better course is to establish colonies. This is inexpensive, and offends only the few citizens whose lands are taken; and those become poor and powerless, while those uninjured will be compliant, for fear it should happen to them. Men ought either to be well treated or crushed; they can avenge themselves of lighter injuries, therefore injury ought to be of such a kind that one does not fear revenge. However, a garrison in a colony is expensive, and the hard-pressed soldiery may become hostile.

Men always aim to acquire, which is natural, common, and praiseworthy. However, when they cannot do so, yet make the attempt, there is folly and blame. King Louis made five errors in obtaining Lombardy: he destroyed the minor powers, increased the strength of a greater power, brought in a foreign power, he did not settle in the country, he did not send colonies. There is a general rule here: he who makes another powerful is ruined.

IV: WHY THE KINGDOMS CONQUERED BY ALEXANDER, DID NOT REBEL

Alexander the Great mastered Asia in a few years, yet we must ask why, on his death, the empire did not rebel.

Principalities are governed either by a prince with a body of ministers, or by a prince and barons. The lord of the

Turks sends servants to administer different sanjaks, and shifts and changes them as he chooses. But the King of France is among an ancient body of lords, with their own prerogatives. There would be difficulties in seizing the kingdom of the Turk as the usurper cannot be called in or assisted by princes of the kingdom. But in kingdoms like France, one can always find malcontented barons to open the way into the state and render victory easy. However, to hold it will need their assistance, it is not enough to have exterminated the prince's family. When these things are remembered no one will marvel at the ease with which Alexander held his Empire.

V: THE WAY TO GOVERN LANDS WHICH FORMERLY LIVED UNDER THEIR OWN LAWS

On acquiring states accustomed to living in freedom under their own laws, there are three courses open; to ruin them, to reside there in person, or to permit them freedom under a friendly oligarchy, drawing a tribute. He who would keep a formerly free city will hold it more easily by means of its own citizens.

For example, the Spartans established oligarchy in Athens and Thebes, nevertheless they lost them. The Romans attempted to hold Greece as the Spartans held it, free with its own laws, and failed. For in truth he who becomes master of a city accustomed to freedom and does not destroy it, may expect to be destroyed by it, for it will always rally to the watchwords of liberty and its ancient privileges. When cities or countries are accustomed to live under a prince, and his family is exterminated, they, being accustomed to obey, cannot decide how to govern themselves. Such are very slow to take up arms, and a prince can secure them easily.

VI: OF NEW PRINCIPALITIES ACQUIRED BY ONE'S OWN ARMS AND ABILITY

A wise man ought to follow the paths beaten by great men. Now, becoming a prince from a private station presupposes sufficient ability or fortune to mitigate many difficulties. Nevertheless, he who has relied least on fortune is established the strongest.

Although Moses[1] merely executed the will of God, it was necessary that he should find the Israelites oppressed by the Egyptians, so that they should be disposed to follow him out of bondage. It was necessary that Cyrus should find the Persians discontented with the Medean government. The likes of these acquire a principality with difficulty, but keep it with ease.

To these, I add the example of Hiero, who rose from a private station to be Prince of Syracuse, after the oppressed Syracusans, chose him for their captain. He was of so great ability that it has been said he wanted nothing but a kingdom to be a king. He organised a new army, made new allies and on such foundations, he was able to build any

edifice. Thus, he endured much trouble in acquiring; he had but little in keeping.

VII: OF NEW PRINCIPALITIES ACQUIRED BY THE ARMS OF OTHERS OR BY GOOD FORTUNE

Those who rise from private citizen to prince by good fortune, rise easily, but struggle to stay there. Some gain states for money or by the favour of rulers, or by the corruption of soldiers. Such rely on the goodwill and fortune of others- two most inconstant and unstable things.

They do not know how to command, and have no friendly forces. States that rise suddenly, like all things which are born and grow rapidly, cannot have firm foundations to withstand the first storm. Unless, that is, they are prepared to lay the foundations afterwards.

To give two recent examples: Francesco Sforza, by great ability, rose from a private person to be Duke of Milan. On the other hand, Cesare Borgia, called Duke Valentino, acquired his state through his father, on whose decline he lost it, notwithstanding that he had done all possible to fix his roots.

The duke found Romagna under weak, plundering rulers. To bring back peace and authority, he promoted Ramiro d'Orco, a swift and cruel man. When the state was pacified, he replaced Ramiro with an equitable court of judgement, and had Ramiro executed and his body left on the piazza at Cesena beside a bloody knife. This barbarity showing the Duke to be the scourge, not the author, of evil-doing. He who believes that new benefits will cause great personages to forget old injuries is deceived.

VIII: OF THOSE WHO HAVE OBTAINED A PRINCIPALITY BY WICKEDNESS

A prince may rise from a private station either by wickedness, or by the favour of his fellow-citizens.

To illustrate the first method, consider how Agathocles, son of a potter, became King of Syracuse. Having rose through the military ranks to become Praetor, one morning he assembled the senators and leading citizens of Syracuse, as if to discuss state matters, and at a given signal had soldiers kill them all. Thus he seized the city and was even able to withstand the Carthaginian siege.

Yet it cannot be called talent to slay citizens, deceive friends, to be faithless, cruel and irreligious. Such methods may gain empires, but not glory. Still, the courage of Agathocles makes him admirable.

In our times, during the rule of Alexander VI, Oliverotto da Fermo, having been left an orphan, was brought up by his maternal uncle, Giovanni Fogliani, and sent into the military. But he disliked serving under others, so resolved to seize Fermo. He arranged to visit Giovanni Fogliani in his city, accompanied by one hundred retainers.

Oliverotto arranged a banquet for all the chiefs of Fermo. When the viands and entertainments were finished, Oliverotto began to talk of Pope Alexander and of Cesare,

---

1   **Moses:** see p23

saying that such matters ought to be discussed in private, betook them to a private chamber, where his soldiers slaughtered them all. Thus, Oliverotto forced the people and magistrates to make him prince. He killed all malcontents, and so strengthened himself that he held the city for a year, only being overthrown by Cesare Borgia.

Cruelty is well used, if one can say 'well' of such evil, when it is applied at one blow when necessary to one's security, and not persisted in afterwards. Cruelty is badly employed when it commences in a small way, to then multiply with time. Injuries ought to be done all at once, so that, being tasted less, they offend less. Benefits ought to be given little by little, so that the flavour of them may last longer.

IX: OF A CIVIL PRINCIPALITY

A prince is created either by the people or by the nobles, the one finding they cannot withstand the other, they set up a new power. Such a prince will find that one cannot, by fair dealing, satisfy the nobles, but you can satisfy the people as they desire only not to be oppressed. Furthermore, a prince can never secure himself against a hostile people, because they are too many, be he secure himself against the few nobles.

The worst a prince may expect from a hostile people is to be abandoned by them; but hostile nobles can rise against him. Further, the prince must live with the same people, but he can make and unmake nobles daily. Do not let any one accept the trite proverb "He who builds on the people, builds on the mud," for a prince who has courage, and who keeps the whole people encouraged, will have a secure foundation. A wise prince ought to ensure that his citizens will always have need of the state and of him, then he will find them faithful.

X: HOW THE STRENGTH OF PRINCIPALIT-IES OUGHT TO BE MEASURED

A prince needs always to know if he has power to support himself with his own resources, or whether he has need of the assistance of others. Those who have need of others are they who must defend themselves by sheltering behind walls.

The cities of Germany are absolutely free, and own but little country around them. They yield obedience to the emperor when it suits, nor do they fear any nearby power, because they are fortified with proper ditches and walls, and have sufficient artillery. Moreover, they always keep one year's food, drink and fuel in public depots, in which they always have the means of giving work to the community. They also have laws to encourage military exercises.

A strong city can withstand an army for a year or more, but few attackers could sustain a force for so long. And to whoever says that the citizens will rebel when they see their property outside the city burned, I say that such will only give them greater reason to fear the enemy. It will not be difficult for a wise prince to keep his citizens steadfast when he supports and defends them.

XI: OF ECCLESIASTICAL PRINCIPALITIES

It remains to speak of ecclesiastical principalities. Such states need no defence and alone are secure and happy. Being exalted and maintained by God, it would be presumptuous to discuss them.

XII: OF THE KINDS OF SOLDIERY, AND OF MERCENARIES

The chief foundations of all states are good laws and good arms. As there cannot be good laws where the state is not well armed, it follows that the well-armed state will have good laws.

A prince defends his state with his own arms, or mercenaries, auxiliaries, or a mixture. Mercenaries and auxiliaries are useless and dangerous. In peace one is robbed by them, and in war by the enemy. The fact is, they keep the field only for wages, which is not sufficient to make them willing to die for you. If Mercenary captains are capable men, then you cannot trust them, because they always aspire to their own greatness. But if the captain is not skilful, you are ruined in the usual way.

Italy has fallen into the power of mercenaries, first promoted by Alberigo da Conio, the Romagnian. After him came all the captains whose only success has been that Italy has been overrun by Charles, robbed by Louis, ravaged by Ferdinand, and insulted by the Switzers.

XIV: THAT WHICH CONCERNS A PRINCE ON THE ART OF WAR

A prince ought to have no other study than war; for this is the art of all rulers; it upholds born princes and enables others to become princes. Without its knowledge, many have lost their states.

Francesco Sforza became Duke of Milan through military skill. But to rise through war is not all, lack of military skill brings, among other evils, the abhorrence of all around you. Because, the armed and unarmed have disdain and suspicion against each other, they can never work well together. Therefore a prince who does not understand the art of war cannot be respected by his soldiers, nor can he rely on them.

He ought above all things to keep his men well organised and drilled, to pursue hunting, by which he learns to endure hardships, and gets to know the nature and lie of the mountains, the plains, the rivers and marshes- knowledge essential to success.

To exercise the intellect the prince should read history, and study there the actions of leaders, to examine the causes of their victories and defeat, just as Alexander the Great imitated Achilles, and Caesar, Alexander. A wise prince ought never to stand idle, but increase his resources with industry so that they may be available to him in adversity.

XV: OF THINGS FOR WHICH PRINCES ARE PRAISED OR BLAMED

Here I wish to give the real truth of the matter, not the fantasy of it, for a man who acts for good is likely to be ruined. It is necessary for a prince wishing to hold his own to know how to do wrong, and to make use of it when necessary.

Men may say that a prince is liberal or miserly, generous or rapacious, cruel or compassionate, faithless or faithful, cowardly or brave, affable or haughty, lascivious or chaste, sincere or cunning, grave or frivolous, religious or unbelieving, and the like. It would be praiseworthy if a prince exhibited all the good characters, but humanity being frail, it is sufficient that he be not reproached for the bad ones.

XVI: OF LIBERALITY AND MEANNESS

It is well that a prince be reputed liberal. Nevertheless, liberality exercised in secret brings no reputation. Therefore, any prince wishing to be thought liberal must do so with magnificence. But such requires money, the taxes for which will soon offend his subjects. Therefore, a prince ought not to fear being thought mean, for in time it will enhance his reputation as he can defend all attacks without burdening his people. It is one of those vices which will enable him to govern.

And if any should say: Caesar, and others, obtained empire by liberality, I answer; liberality is useful in becoming a prince, but worthless once in power. And an army must believe their prince liberal, otherwise that would not follow him.

A prince should guard, above all, against being despised and hated; and liberality leads to both. Therefore it is wiser to be reputed mean which brings reproach without hatred.

XVII: OF CRUELTY AND CLEMENCY, AND WHETHER IT IS BETTER TO BE LOVED THAN FEARED

Every prince may desire to be thought clement. But it was Cesare Borgia's cruelty which brought peace and unity to the Romagna. A prince who keeps his subjects united and loyal, ought not to mind the reproach of cruelty; for too much mercy will allow disorder to injure the whole people, whilst a few executions offend only individuals.

Is it better to be loved or feared? One might wish to be both, but they are not met in the same person. Because this is to be asserted in general of men, that they are ungrateful, fickle, false, cowardly, covetous, and as long as you succeed they are yours entirely. They will offer you their blood, property, life, and children when the need is far distant; but when it approaches they turn against you. The prince who relies on their promises is ruined; because friendships that are obtained by payments, and not by greatness or nobility of mind, may indeed be earned, but they are not secured, and in time of need cannot be relied upon. Men will readily offend a beloved, for love is preserved by the link of obligation which men will break at every opportunity for their advantage; but fear preserves you by a dread of punishment which never fails.

Nevertheless a prince ought to inspire fear in such a way that, if he does not win love, he avoids hatred. Which will always be as long as he abstains from the property and women of his subjects. But when it is necessary for him to proceed against the life of someone, he must do so with proper justification, but above all things he must keep his hands off the property of others, because men will quickly forget their father's death, but not the loss of their inheritance. But when a prince is with his army then it is necessary for him to disregard the reputation of cruelty, for without it he would never hold his army united.

How was it that Hannibal held together an enormous army composed of many various races of men? It was only his inhuman cruelty. Short-sighted are the writers who admire his deeds, and then condemn the principal cause of them.

I must conclude that, men love by their own will, but fear is from the will of their prince. A wise prince should always establish himself on that which is in his own control, only endeavouring to avoid hatred.

XVIII: OF THE WAY IN WHICH PRINCES SHOULD KEEP FAITH

It would be praiseworthy for a prince to keep faith, and to live with integrity and without guile. Nevertheless experience shows that princes who have done great things have held good faith of little account. You must know that there are two ways to dispute; law is proper to men, force to beasts. But law is frequently insufficient, so the prince must learn how to use the other method.

Like the old story of Achilles being educated by the Centaur Chiron, half beast and half man, so it is necessary for a prince to know how to make use of both natures. The lion is powerless against snares and the fox powerless against wolves. Therefore, it is necessary to be a fox to discover the snares and a lion to terrify the wolves. It is error to rely solely on the lion. A wise lord cannot keep faith when such may be turned against him. But it is necessary to know how to disguise this characteristic, and men are so simple, that he who seeks to deceive will always find someone willing to be deceived. Alexander the Sixth did nothing else but deceive, and his deceits were successful, because he well understood mankind.

It is not necessary for a prince to have all the good qualities, but it is very necessary to appear to have them. The prince should seem merciful, faithful, humane, religious, upright. The vulgar are always taken in by appearances and results; and this world consists of the vulgar. One prince of the present time, forever preaches peace and good faith, yet he is most hostile to both.

XIX: THAT ONE SHOULD AVOID BEING DESPISED AND HATED

When a prince is not hated, he need not fear other reproaches. It makes him hated above all, to be greedy, and to violate the property and women of his subjects. With their property and honour intact, the majority of men live content, and he has only to contend with the ambitious few. Thus a prince should guard against seeming fickle, frivolous, effeminate, mean-spirited or irresolute, and endeavour to show greatness, courage, gravity, and fortitude. Let his judgements be irrevocable, so that no one can hope to deceive him or to get round him.

Among the best-governed kingdoms of our times is France. He who founded the kingdom, knew that it was necessary to protect the people from the nobles and the nobles from the people. Yet not wishing for the king to be drawn into such disputes, he established a parliament as arbiter. There could be no better arrangement, for a prince ought to cherish the nobles, but not so as to make himself hated by the people.

Those emperors of Rome who succeeded had the difficulty of pleasing the people, the nobles and the army. Which three, being of opposing humours, they chose to satisfy the army, for if a prince cannot help being hated by some, he must avoid the hatred of the strongest. Both Pertinax and Alexander fell when the army conspired against them. Marcus lived and died honoured, because he owed nothing either to the soldiers or the people. Severus oppressed the people, but kept the soldiers friendly, so that he reigned successfully, well imitating the fox and the lion.

It will be seen that either hatred or contempt has been fatal to many emperors. But a prince, new to the principality, cannot imitate the actions of Marcus, nor, again, is it necessary to follow those of Severus, but he ought to take from Severus those parts which are necessary to found his state, and from Marcus those which are proper and glorious to keep a state that may already be stable and firm.

XX: ARE FORTRESSES, &c, ADVANTAGE-OUS OR HURTFUL?

To hold a state, some princes have disarmed their subjects, or kept their towns disunited, or have fostered enmities, some have built fortresses and some have overthrown them. There is no general rule.

A new prince cannot disarm his subjects, but he can arm some of them, who will become faithful, making the others easier to handle. But to attempt to disarm them shows your distrust, and breeds hatred. Therefore a new prince in a new principality has always distributed arms. But when a prince adds a new state to his old one, then he must disarm the men of that state, except those who have helped him acquire it; who, with time an opportunity, he should render soft and effeminate.

When mistress fortune desires to make a prince great, she brings him enemies, so that he may show his greatness by crushing them. For this reason, many consider that a wise prince might foster some animosity against himself, so that, having crushed it, his renown may rise.

Princes, especially new ones, often have more help from men who were, at first, distrusted than among those who were trusted. Pandolfo Petrucci, Prince of Siena, ruled largely by those who had been distrusted. But there is no general rule here; a prince must always consider why those who helped him did so. If they followed him only from disgust with the former power, then he will never satisfy them.

Only the prince who has more to fear from the people than from foreigners ought to build fortresses, but he who has more to fear from foreigners ought to leave them alone. That castle in Milan, built by Francesco Sforza, will make more trouble for the house of Sforza than anything else. The best possible fortress is not to be hated by the people, because, if you are hated, there will always be foreigners ready to assist the people against you.

XXI: HOW A PRINCE SHOULD CONDUCT HIMSELF SO AS TO GAIN RENOWN

A prince ought, above all things, always endeavour in every action to gain the reputation of being a great and remarkable man, as the King of Spain has done.

A prince is respected when he is clearly either a true friend or a downright enemy. If your powerful neighbours come to blows, it will always be more advantageous to declare yourself and make war strenuously. Irresolute princes who follow the neutral path are generally ruined. But when a prince declares himself gallantly in favour of one side, if his chosen ally conquers, then he becomes indebted to you. If your ally loses, he may shelter you until fortune rises again.

A prince ought never to make an alliance with one more powerful than himself for the purposes of attacking others; because if he conquers, you are at his discretion, which a prince ought never to be, as the Venetians were ruined by joining France against the Duke of Milan. Never let any Government imagine that it can choose perfectly safe courses; rather prudence consists in knowing how to distinguish the character of troubles, and to choose the lesser evil.

A prince ought to show himself a patron of the arts. He should also encourage peaceful crafts, commerce and agriculture, so that no one should be deterred from trade for fear of theft or excessive taxes. The prince should reward those who honour his state, and entertain the people with festivals and spectacles. And he ought to hold guilds or societies in esteem, and associate with them sometimes, to show his courtesy and liberality; while always maintaining the majesty of his rank.

XXII: OF THE SECRETARIES OF PRINCES

The first opinion which one forms of a prince is by observing the men he has around him; and foolish servants show the foolishness of their prince in choosing them.

Anyone who met Antonio da Venafro, servant of Pandolfo of Siena, would know the prince to be very clever in having such a servant. No man who seeks his own profit will make a good servant. To keep his servant honest the prince ought to study him, honouring him, enriching him, doing him kindnesses; and at the same time let him see that he cannot stand alone. When servants and princes do not trust each other, disaster will come to either one or the other.

XXIII: ON FLATTERERS

Flatterers, of whom courts are full, are a terrible pest and a terrible danger. One can guard against them only by letting men know that the truth does not offend you; but when every one may tell you the truth, respect is lost. Therefore, a wise prince ought to seek the honest council of only a few wise men, and afterwards form his own conclusions. Counsellors each have their own interests, and, like all men, will always prove untrue unless they are restrained.

XXV: OF DAME FORTUNE.

Many men believe the affairs of the world are governed by fortune and God, so that men cannot direct them. Fortune may direct one-half of our actions, but that she still leaves us to direct the other half. She may be like the raging flood, which sweeps away trees and buildings. But that does not mean that, when the waters settle, men cannot make barriers against such misfortune. In Italy, we have, unlike Germany, neglected these barriers, so that the recent invasions have found us without defence.

Fortune is changeful, yet mankind steadfast in their ways, success comes when the two are in agreement. For my part I consider that it is better to be adventurous than cautious, because fortune is a woman, and if you wish to control her it is necessary to beat and ill-use her; and she allows herself to be mastered by the adventurous.

XXVI: AN EXHORTATION TO LIBERATE ITALY FROM THE BARBARIANS

The present times seem fit for the arrival of a new prince, for like the Israelites, the Persians and the Medes, the present oppression of the Italians is such that their virtuous spirit may be shown. If, therefore, your illustrious house wishes to redeemed your country, it is necessary before all to have your own forces, commanded by their prince, honoured by him, and maintained at his expense. We cannot rely on Swiss and Spanish infantry, no matter how good they are.

This opportunity ought not to be missed for letting Italy see her liberator appear. What door would be closed to him? Who would refuse obedience to him? To all of us this barbarous dominion stinks. Let this just enterprise be undertaken, so that our native country may be ennobled, and verify that saying of Petrarch:

> *For old Roman valour is not dead,*
> *Nor in Italian hearts extinguish'ed.*

The Revolutions of the Celestial Orbs
By Nicolaus Copernicus
(Varmia, Poland, 1543)

Copernicus was not the first to realise that the earth goes round the sun (see Da Vinci p132), but he was among the first to try and prove it. This terrifying, and incontrovertible, idea meant that we humans, and our little home, were no longer the centre of everything. *The Revolutions* was placed on the Church's index of forbidden books, only being removed in 1835.

Book 1 only. Abridged: GH

Diligent reader,

in this new work you have the motions of the fixed stars and planets, reconstituted from ancient as well as recent observations, and embellished by new and marvellous hypotheses. Therefore buy, read, and enjoy this work.

TO HIS HOLINESS, POPE PAUL III,

From NICOLAUS COPERNICUS - A PREFACE TO HIS BOOKS ON THE REVOLUTIONS

Holy Father, some who discover that I here ascribe certain motions to the terrestrial globe will shout that I must be immediately repudiated. But a philosopher's ideas are not subject to the judgement of ordinary persons, because he endeavours to seek the truth in all things, to the extent permitted to human reason by God.

Yet many will still think my idea absurd, so I have dedicated my studies to Your Holiness. For even in my very remote country you are considered the highest authority by virtue of your lofty office and your love for literature and astronomy. Hence you can easily suppress attacks although, as the proverb has it, there is no remedy for a backbite.

Perhaps there will be ignorant babblers, who, twisting some passage of Scripture to their purpose, will find fault here. I disregard them. Astronomy is for astronomers, and most useful in correcting the ecclesiastical calendar. All else I leave to the judgement of Your Holiness and other learned astronomers. Lest I now seem to promise more than I can fulfil, I turn to the work itself.

INTRODUCTION

Among the many pursuits which invigorate men's minds, the strongest affection and zeal should, I think, be towards the most beautiful objects, and what is more beautiful than the heavens? Its very Latin names, caelum and mundus, denote sculpture and ornament. On account of heaven's transcendent perfection philosophers have called it a visible god. Such good arts draw men away from vices, as the Psalmist says. Even Plato shows the utility of astronomy, in dividing time into days and months and years, to keep the state alert to festivals and sacrifices.

However, this divine science's principles and assumptions, called "hypotheses" by the Greeks, have been a source of disagreement. To be sure, Claudius Ptolemy of Alexandria, has come close to perfecting our understanding, yet even the length of the year itself is not agreed.

But these difficulties are no excuse for indolence, so, by the grace of God, without whom we can accomplish nothing, I shall attempt to enquire into these matters differently from those who first opened the road to my investigations.

Chapter 1

THE UNIVERSE IS SPHERICAL

First of all, we must note that the universe is spherical. The reason is either that, of all forms, the sphere is the most perfect, needing no joint and being a complete whole; or that it is the most capacious of figures, best suited to enclose and retain all things. The sun, moon, planets and stars, are seen to be of this shape; and wholes strive to become spheres, as is apparent in drops of water. Hence no one will question the attribution of this form to the divine bodies.

Chapter 2

THE EARTH TOO IS SPHERICAL

The earth also is perfectly spherical, yet it is not immediately recognised as such. However, it is clear from the following considerations. A traveller going from any place toward the north, finds that pole of the daily rotation of the stars gradually climbs higher, while the opposite pole drops down. More stars in the north are seen not to set, while in the south certain stars are no longer seen to rise. Moreover, the elevations of the poles have the same ratio everywhere to the portions of the earth that have been traversed. This can happen on no figure other than a sphere. Furthermore, evening eclipses of the sun and moon are not seen by easterners, nor morning eclipses by westerners, while those occurring in between are seen later by easterners but earlier by westerners.

The waters also press down into the surface of the sphere, as sailors know, since land which is not seen from a ship is visible from the top of its mast. Likewise, if a light is attached to the top of the mast, as the ship draws away from land, those who remain ashore see the light drop down gradually until it finally disappears, as though setting.

Chapter 3

HOW EARTH FORMS A SINGLE SPHERE WITH WATER

It is clear that water, like earth, falls always downwards towards the centre, because of their heaviness. So it is clear that the earth does not have the form of a great uprising curve, as some have said, for if it were there could be no seas inland, nor any islands to be encountered on distant voyages. But it is well known that almost in the middle of the inhabited lands lie the Mediterranean and the Red Seas. Further, Ptolemy did not know of Cathay, a vast territory. We must add the many islands lately discovered, notably America, named after the ship's captain who found it, which may be a second group of inhabited countries.

From all these facts, finally, I think it is clear that land and water together press towards a single centre of gravity, and that there is little water in comparison with earth, even though more water perhaps appears on the surface.

The earth must in fact have the shape we see shadowed on the moon in eclipses, namely a perfect circle. Therefore the earth is not flat, as Empedocles and Anaximenes thought; nor drum-shaped, as Leucippus; nor bowl-shaped, as Heraclitus; nor hollow, as Democritus; nor cylindrical, as Ansaximander; nor does it extend infinitely downward, as Xenophanes taught; but it is perfectly round.

Chapter 4

THE MOTION OF THE HEAVENLY BODIES IS UNIFORM, ETERNAL, AND CIRCULAR

I shall now recall that the motion of heavenly bodies is circular, since the motion appropriate to a sphere is rotation in a circle, which is the simplest shape, wherein neither beginning nor end can be found.

The most conspicuous of the earth's motions is the daily rotation, which the Greeks call nuchthemeron, in which the skies are perceived as whirling from east to west. But we see the motions of the sun, moon, and the five planets as advancing in the opposite direction, that is, from west to east.

Yet these motions differ in many ways. In the first place, they do not swing around the same poles as the first motion, but run obliquely through the zodiac. Secondly, the sun and moon are observed to be sometimes slow, at other times faster in their course. Moreover, the other five planets at some times hold stationary then go backwards. Also, they wander in various ways, straying sometimes to the south and sometimes to the north; which is why they are called "planets" [wanderers]. Furthermore, they are at times nearer to the earth, when they are said to be in perigee; at other times they are farther away, when they are said to be in apogee.

We must acknowledge, however, that all these motions are circular, for they continually repeat themselves, and only a circle can bring back the past. To hold otherwise would be to infer some inconsistency or some imposition from without, which is impossible among bodies constituted so perfectly.

Yet it is clear that some of the motions of the celestial orbs seem, to us, not to be uniform. The cause may be either that their circles have poles different from the earth's or that the earth is not at the centre of the circles on which they revolve. Hence I deem it most necessary that we should carefully scrutinise the relation of the earth to the heavens.

Chapter 5

DOES CIRCULAR MOTION SUIT THE EARTH? WHAT IS ITS POSITION?

Authorities agree that the earth is at rest in the middle of the universe, and that any contrary view is inconceivable or entirely silly. Nevertheless, if we examine the matter more carefully, we shall see that this is by no means to be disregarded.

Every observed change of place is caused by a motion of either the observed object or of the observer or, of course, by an unequal displacement of each. It is the earth from which the celestial dance is beheld, therefore, if motion is ascribed to the earth, all things outside will appear as though they were moving past it. If you will allow that the heavens have no part in this motion but that the earth rotates daily from west to east, you will find that this accounts for the apparent rising and setting of the sun, moon, stars and planets.

An important question follows concerning the earth's position. Heretofore there has been virtually unanimous acceptance that the middle of the universe is the earth. But the fact that the same planets are observed nearer to the earth and farther away necessarily proves that the centre of the earth is not the centre of their circles.

It will occasion no surprise if, in addition to the daily rotation, some other motion is assigned to the earth. That the earth travels with several motions, and that it is one of the heavenly bodies are said to have been the opinions of Philolaus the Pythagorean. He was no ordinary astronomer,

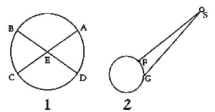

1   **2**

inasmuch as Plato did not delay going to Italy for the sake of visiting him, as Plato's biographers report.

Chapter 6

OF THE IMMENSITY OF THE HEAVENS COMPARED TO THE SIZE OF THE EARTH

The massive bulk of the earth does indeed shrink to insignificance in comparison with the size of the heavens. As can be demonstrated.

In the first diagram, let the circle ABCD be the circle of the horizon, and let E be the position from which we observe the motion of the stars. At a certain season the first point of the Crab will be seen to rise at C as the Goat is perceived to be setting at A. Yet at another season, as the Goat rises at B while the Crab is seen setting at D. From this it is very clear that the fixed stars appear to have the motion of a great circle.

Yet, to look at the second diagram, if two observers at different parts of the earth, F and G, were to draw a line towards a distant star, S, it is clear that each should measure a different angle between that line and the earth about them. It is also clear that if the star be farther away, the difference between the angles of F and G would be less, and that if the star was at an extraordinarily great distance then no difference would be observed. Such is the case. They become like parallel lines, because their terminus is enormously remote. This reasoning certainly makes it quite clear that the heavens are immense by comparison with the earth.

But it does not follow that the earth must be at rest in the middle of the universe. Indeed, it is less likely that the whole vast universe should rotate in just twenty-four hours, than the small earth do so.

If the heavens are a single sphere, revolving around the poles, then those parts nearest the pole will move most slowly, as we see happens when we observe the little bear. But if the earth had a motion with the whole celestial sphere, though in a smaller circle, then the daily risings and settings of the sun and other celestial bodies would not be seen.

But it is quite known that things travelling in a small orbit move faster than those in a larger one. Thus, saturn revolves in thirty years and the moon, undoubtedly nearest the earth, completes its course in one month, while the earth revolves in one day. But from this, we can know nothing of the earth's position, except to see that the heavens are of almost unlimited size compared to the earth.

Chapter 7

WHY THE ANCIENTS THOUGHT THAT THE EARTH REMAINED AT REST

The ancient philosophers argued that all things that have weight are, by nature, borne towards the very centre of the heaviest of them, and earth is the heaviest element of all, drawing things towards itself. It seems to follow that all heavy things come to rest at the middle. Thus, then, will the earth be at rest in the middle.

Further, according to Aristotle[1], the perfect motion of a single simple body is simple- either straight, being upward or downward, or circular. To be carried downward, that is, to seek the middle, is a property only of earth and water, which are considered heavy; on the other hand, air and fire, which are endowed with lightness, move upward and away from the middle. To these four elements it seems reasonable to assign straight motion, but to the heavenly bodies, circular motion around the middle. This is what Aristotle says.

Ptolemy of Alexandria remarks that, if the earth were to move in a daily rotation, its motion would have to be so exceedingly violent and fast that all things would be thrown off from its surface. The earth would long ago have burst asunder, he says, and dropped out of the skies (a quite preposterous notion). Objects would not be seen to fall perpendicularly, as their appointed place would meantime have been moved on. Moreover, clouds and things floating in the air would be seen drifting always westward.

Chapter 8

THE INADEQUACY OF PREVIOUS ARGUMENTS

For these and similar reasons the ancients insist that the earth remains at rest in the middle of the universe. Yet if anyone believes that the earth rotates, surely he will hold that its motion is natural, and what is brought into existence by nature cannot be violent for it will always be well-ordered so as to long endure. Ptolemy has no cause, then, to fear that the earth will be disrupted by a rotation created through natures handiwork, which is quite different from what art or human intelligence can accomplish. But why does he not feel this apprehension even more for the universe, whose motion must be the swifter, being much bigger than the earth? Many do regard that the earth is spherical, yet why do they hesitate to grant that it moves? The situation resembles what Virgil's Aeneas says:

> Forth from the harbour we sail, and the land and the cities slip backward

For when a ship is floating calmly along, the sailors suppose that they are stationary. In the same way, the motion of the earth can unquestionably produce the impression that the entire universe is rotating.

Then what about the clouds and the other things that hang in the air, or the bodies that fall down, or rise aloft? We would say that not only the earth rotates, but also the air with the earth. The air closest to the earth will accordingly seem to be still, and so will the things suspended in it.

Furthermore, bodies that are carried upward and downward do not execute a simple, uniform motion. For whatever falls moves slowly at first but increases its speed as it drops. On the other hand, we see that fire rises, then slackens all at once. Circular motion, however, always rolls along uniformly. But rectilinear motion quickly stops, bringing bodies to their own place, where their motion ends. Hence we can say that "circular" is with "rectilinear"

as "being alive" with "being sick". Surely Aristotle's division of simple motion into three types is merely a logical exercise.

Moreover, the quality of immobility is deemed more divine than change and instability, and therefore better suited to the earth than to the universe. But, it would seem quite absurd to attribute motion to the framework of space, and not, more appropriately, to that which occupies space, namely, the earth. Last of all, the planets clearly approach closer to the earth and recede farther from it. You see, then, that all these arguments make it more likely that the earth moves than that it is at rest. This is enough, in my opinion, about the first part of the question.

Chapter 9

CAN SEVERAL MOTIONS BE ATTRIBUTED TO THE EARTH?

Since nothing prevents the earth from moving, we should now consider whether it has one motion, or several, and whether it can be regarded as one of the planets. For, it is clear from the apparent non-uniform motion of the planets and the way that they vary in their distances from the earth, that these phenomena cannot be explained by circles concentric with the earth. Therefore, the further question arises whether the centre of the universe is identical with the centre of terrestrial gravity or with some other point. For my part I believe that gravity is nothing but a certain natural desire, implanted by the Creator, to gather all things towards the unity of a globe. This impulse is present, we may suppose, also in the sun, moon, and the other planets, so that through its operation they remain as spheres. But, they swing round their circuits in diverse ways. If, then, we accept that the sun is at rest, and the earth and other planets revolve around it, this will explain the risings and settings of the zodiacal signs and fixed stars. The positions of the planets, as well as their retrogradations and resumptions of forward motion will be recognised as being, not movements of the planets, but a mere appearance caused by the motion of the earth. All these facts are disclosed to us by observing the order in which the planets follow one another, and by the harmony of the entire universe, if only we look at the matter, as the saying goes, with both eyes.

Chapter 10

THE ORDER OF THE HEAVENLY SPHERES

Of all things visible, that the highest is the heaven of the fixed stars, is doubted by nobody. But the ancient philosophers, assuming that, among objects moving equally fast, those farther away seem to travel more slowly, as is proved in Euclid's[2] Optics. The moon revolves in the shortest period of time because, therefore, it runs on the smallest circle, nearest to the earth. The highest planet, on the other hand, is Saturn, which completes the biggest circuit in the longest time. Below it is Jupiter, followed by Mars.

---

1   **Aristotle:** see p62

2   **Euclid:** see p 66

According to Plato's followers, all the planets, being dark bodies, shine because they receive sunlight. Thus, they must be above the sun, otherwise we would see them sometimes obscured by shadows, which we do not.

In my judgement, therefore, we may look to the ideas of Martianus Capella, the author of an encyclopaedia, and other Latin writers, who thought that Venus and Mercury do not circle the earth, but have "other circles". And what other circle might there be, but that of the sun? If anyone

All these statements are difficult and almost inconceivable, being of course opposed to the beliefs of many people. Yet, as we proceed, with God's help I shall make them clearer than sunlight, at any rate to those who know some astronomy. So, if the size of the spheres is measured by the length of time of their rotation, the order of the spheres is the following:

The first and the highest sphere is of the fixed stars, which contains everything, and is therefore immovable. This is

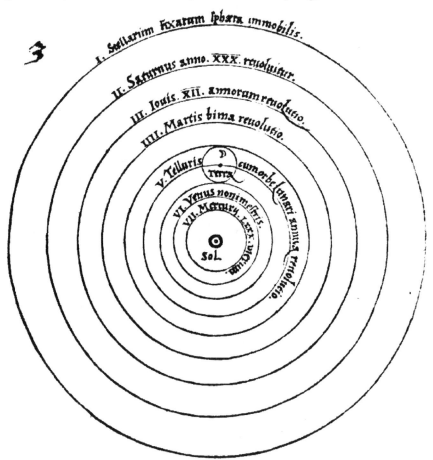

seizes on this notion, may he not also think likewise of Saturn, Jupiter, and Mars, and of the earth too?

Hence I feel no shame in asserting that the moon and the earth traverse a grand circle amid the rest of the planets in an annual revolution around the sun. Moreover, since the sun remains stationary, whatever appears as a motion of the sun is really due rather to the motion of the earth. This should be admitted, I believe, in preference to perplexing the mind with an almost infinite multitude of spheres, as must be done by those astronomers who try to fix the earth in the middle of the universe. On the contrary, we should rather heed the wisdom of nature, which especially avoids producing anything superfluous or useless, and frequently endows a single thing with many effects.

followed by the sphere of the first planet, Saturn, which completes its circuit in 30 years. After Saturn, Jupiter revolves in 12 years. Then Mars in 2 years. The fourth place is the earth, together with its moon. In the fifth place Venus in 9 months. Lastly, in the sixth place, Mercury, which revolves in 80 days.

At rest, however, in the middle of everything is the sun. For in this most beautiful temple, who would place this lamp in another or better position than that from which it can light up the whole thing at the same time? For, is not the sun called 'the lantern of the universe' and, 'its mind' and by others 'its ruler'? Hermes the Thrice Greatest calls it 'a visible god', and Sophocles' Electra, 'the all-seeing'. Thus indeed, as though upon a royal throne, the sun governs the family of planets revolving around it.

In this arrangement, therefore, we discover a marvellous symmetry of the universe, a harmonious linkage between the motion of the spheres and their size, such as can be found in no other way. From this, the attentive student may explain the many and curious motions of the planets.

Yet no such curiosities appear in the fixed stars. This proves their immense height, which makes the sphere of their annual motion vanish from before our eyes. For, every visible object has some measure of distance beyond which it is no longer seen, as is demonstrated in optics. From Saturn, the highest of the planets, to the sphere of the fixed stars there is an additional gap of the largest size. This is shown by the twinkling lights of the stars. By this token in particular they are distinguished from the planets, for there had to be a very great difference between what moves and what does not move. So vast, without any question, is the divine handiwork of the most excellent Almighty.

Romeo and Juliet
By William Shakespeare
(London, 1595)

Romeo and Juliet is the most popular love-story of all time, having been turned into at least 24 different operas, 14 orchestral works, 8 ballets, several musicals including *West Side Story,* and forming the inspiration for music by Duke Ellington, The Supremes, Bruce Springsteen, Lou Reed and Dire Straits. It has been filmed more often than any other play, from one of the first dramatic movies ever made to versions inspired by the story, such as *Shakespeare in Love* or *High School Musical.*

Abridged: GH

Dramatis Personae
Escalus, Prince of Verona.
Montague and Capulet, and their wives; heads of two houses at variance with each other.
Romeo, son to Montague.
Tybalt, nephew to Lady Capulet.
Mercutio, kinsman to the Prince.
Benvolio, nephew to Montague.

Friars Laurence and John.
Balthasar, servant to Romeo.
Peter, servant to Juliet's Nurse.
An Apothecary.
Juliet, daughter to Capulet.
Nurse to Juliet.
Citizens, Chorus, a page &c.

THE PROLOGUE

Chorus: Two households, both alike in dignity,
 In fair Verona, where we lay our scene,
 From ancient grudge break to new mutiny,
 Where civil blood makes civil hands unclean.
 From forth the fatal loins of these two foes
 A pair of star-cross'd lovers take their life;
 Whose misadventur'd piteous overthrows
 Doth with their death bury their parents' strife.

ACT I.

Scene I. *Verona. A public place with citizens. Enter Benvolio and Tybalt, fighting with swords*
Tybalt: Turn thee Benvolio! look upon thy death.
Benvolio: I do but keep the peace. Put up thy sword,
Tybalt: What, drawn, and talk of peace? I hate the word
 As I hate hell, all Montagues, and thee.
Enter an officer, and Citizens with clubs.
Citizens. Down with the Capulets! Down with the Montagues!
Enter Old Capulet in his gown, and his Wife.
Capulet: What noise is this? Give me my long sword, ho!
Wife. A crutch, a crutch! Why call you for a sword?

Capulet: My sword, I say! Old Montague is come
Enter Old Montague and his Wife.
Montague: Thou villain Capulet!- Hold me not, let me go.
M. Wife. Thou shalt not stir one foot to seek a foe.
Enter Prince Escalus, with his Train.
Prince Escalus: Rebellious subjects, enemies to peace,
 Throw your mistempered weapons to the ground
 And hear the sentence of your moved prince.
 If ever you disturb our streets again,
 Your lives shall pay the forfeit of the peace.
 For this time all the rest depart away.
 You, Capulet, shall go along with me;
 And, Montague, come you this afternoon,
 To know our farther pleasure in this case,
Exeunt, all but Montague, his Wife, and Benvolio.
M. Wife. O, where is Romeo? Saw you him to-day?
Benvolio: Madam, an hour before the worshipp'd sun
 Peer'd forth the golden window of the East,
 Underneath the grove of sycamore did I see your son.
Montague: Many a morning hath he there been seen,
 With tears augmenting the fresh morning's dew,
Benvolio: My noble uncle, do you know the cause?
Montague: I neither know it nor can learn of him
 But he is his own affections' counsellor.

Enter Romeo.

Benvolio: See, where he comes. So please you step aside,
  I'll know his grievance, or be much denied.
Montague: I would thou wert so happy by thy stay
  To hear true shrift. Come, madam, let's away,
  Exeunt Montague and Wife.
Benvolio: Good morrow, cousin.
Romeo: Is the day so young?
Benvolio: But new struck nine.
Romeo: Ay me! sad hours seem long.
Benvolio: What sadness lengthens Romeo's hours? In love?
Romeo: Out-
Benvolio: Of love?
Romeo: Out of her favour where I am in love.
Benvolio: Be rul'd by me: forget to think of her.
Romeo: O, teach me how I should forget to think!
Benvolio: By giving liberty unto thine eyes.
  Examine other beauties.
Romeo: Farewell. Thou canst not teach me to forget.
Exeunt.

Scene II. *A Street, Benvolio and Romeo. A servant enters*
Servant: God gi' go-den. I pray, sir, can you read?
Romeo: Ay, If I know the letters and the language.
Hands paper. Romeo reads.
  'Signior Martino and his wife and daughters;
  County Anselmo and his beauteous sisters;
  Signior Placentio and His lovely nieces;
  Mine uncle Capulet, his wife, and daughters;
  My fair niece Rosaline and Livia...'
  [Gives back the paper.] A fair assembly. Whither should
  they come?
Servant: To supper, to our house.
Romeo: Whose house?
Servant: Now I'll tell you without asking. My master is the
  great rich Capulet; and if you be not of the house of
  Montagues, I pray come and crush a cup of wine. Rest
  you merry! *Exit.*
Benvolio: At this same ancient feast of Capulet's
  Sups the fair Rosaline whom thou so lov'st;
  With all the admired beauties of Verona.
  Go thither, and with unattainted eye
  Compare her face with some that I shall show,
  And I will make thee think thy swan a crow.
Romeo: I'll go along, no such sight to be shown,
  But to rejoice in splendour of my own. *Exeunt.*

Scene IV. *A street. Enter Romeo, Mercutio, Benvolio, with
  five or six other Maskers; Torchbearers.*
Romeo: Give me a torch. I am not for this ambling.
  Being but heavy, I will bear the light.
Mercutio: Nay, gentle Romeo, we must have you dance.
Romeo: Not I, believe me. You have dancing shoes
  With nimble soles; I have a soul of lead
Mercutio: You are a lover. Borrow Cupid's wings
Romeo: Peace, peace, Mercutio, peace!
Benvolio: This wind you talk of blows us from ourselves.
  Supper is done, and we shall come too late.

They march about the stage. Exeunt.

Scene V. *At Capulet's house. Juliet, Tybalt, and all the
  Guests and Gentlewomen. The Maskers enter.*
Capulet: Welcome, gentlemen! Ladies that have their toes
  Unplagu'd with corns will have a bout with you.
  Ah ha, my mistresses! which of you all
  Will now deny to dance?
Romeo: *[to a Servingman]* What lady's that, which doth
  enrich the hand
  Of yonder knight?
Servant: I know not, sir.
Romeo: O, she doth teach the torches to burn bright!
  It seems she hangs upon the cheek of night
  Like a rich jewel in an Ethiop's ear-
  Beauty too rich for use, for earth too dear!
  Did my heart love till now? Forswear it, sight!
  For I ne'er saw true beauty till this night.
Tybalt: This, by his voice, should be a Montague.
Capulet: Why, how now, kinsman? Wherefore storm you
  so?
Tybalt: Uncle, this is a Montague, our foe;
  A villain, that is hither come in spite
  To scorn at our solemnity this night.
Capulet: Young Romeo is it?
Tybalt: 'Tis he, that villain Romeo.
Capulet: Content thee, gentle coz, let him alone.
  I'll make you quiet; what!- Cheerly, my hearts!
Tybalt: I will withdraw; but this intrusion shall,
  Now seeming sweet, convert to bitt'rest gall.
Exit. Romeo meets Juliet
Romeo: If I profane with my unworthiest hand
  This holy shrine, the gentle fine is this:
  My lips, two blushing pilgrims, ready stand
  To smooth that rough touch with a tender kiss.
Juliet: Good pilgrim, you do wrong your hand too much,
  Which mannerly devotion shows in this;
  For saints have hands that pilgrims' hands do touch,
  And palm to palm is holy palmers' kiss.
Romeo: Have not saints lips, and holy palmers too?
Juliet: Ay, pilgrim, lips that they must use in pray'r.
Romeo: Sin from my lips? O trespass sweetly urg'd!
  Give me my sin again. *[Kisses her.]*
Juliet: You kiss by th' book.
Nurse: Madam, your mother craves a word with you.
Romeo: What is her mother?
Nurse: Marry, bachelor,
  Her mother is the lady Capulet of the house.
Exeunt, all but Juliet and Nurse.
Juliet: Come hither, Nurse: What is yond gentleman?
  Go ask his name.- If he be married,
  My grave is like to be my wedding bed.
Nurse: His name is Romeo, and a Montague,
  The only son of your great enemy.
Juliet: My only love, sprung from my only hate!
  Too early seen unknown, and known too late!
Nurse: Anon, anon!
  Come, let's away; the strangers all are gone.

Exeunt.

ACT II.

Scene II. *Capulet's orchard. Enter Romeo. Enter Juliet above at a window.*

Romeo: But soft! What light through yonder window breaks?
　It is the East, and Juliet is the sun!
　Arise, fair sun, and kill the envious moon,
　It is my lady; O, it is my love!
　O that she knew she were!
　She speaks, yet she says nothing. What of that?
　Her eye discourses; I will answer it.
　I am too bold; 'tis not to me she speaks.
　Two of the fairest stars in all the heaven,
　Having some business, do entreat her eyes
　To twinkle in their spheres till they return.
　The brightness of her cheek would shame those stars
　As daylight doth a lamp; her eyes in heaven
　O that I were a glove upon that hand,
　That I might touch that cheek!
Juliet: O Romeo, Romeo! wherefore art thou Romeo?
　Deny thy father and refuse thy name!
　'Tis but thy name that is my enemy.
　Thou art thyself, though not a Montague.
　What's in a name? That which we call a rose
　By any other name would smell as sweet.
　Romeo, doff thy name; And for that name,
　Which is no part of thee, Take all myself.
Romeo: I take thee at thy word.
　Call me but love, and I'll be new baptiz'd;
　Henceforth I never will be Romeo.
Juliet: What man art thou that, thus bescreen'd in night,
　So stumblest on my counsel?
Romeo: My name, dear saint, is hateful to myself,
Juliet: How cam'st thou hither, tell me, and wherefore?
　The orchard walls are high and hard to climb,
　And the place death, considering who thou art,
　If any of my kinsmen find thee here.
Romeo: With love's light wings did I o'erperch these walls;
　Therefore thy kinsmen are no let to me.
Juliet: If they do see thee, they will murther thee.
Romeo: I have night's cloak to hide me from their sight;
Juliet: Thou knowest the mask of night is on my face;
　Dost thou love me, I know thou wilt say 'Ay';
Romeo: Lady, by yonder blessed moon I swear,
Romeo: What shall I swear by?
Juliet: Do not swear at all;
Or if thou wilt, swear by thy gracious self,
　Which is the god of my idolatry,
　And I'll believe thee.
Romeo: O, wilt thou leave me so unsatisfied?
Juliet: What satisfaction canst thou have to-night?
Nurse calls
　Anon, good nurse! Sweet Montague, be true.
　Stay but a little, I will come again. *Exit.*
Romeo: O blessed, blessed night! I am afeard,
　Being in night, all this is but a dream,

Enter Juliet above.

Juliet: Three words, dear Romeo, and good night indeed.
　If that thy bent of love be honourable,
　Thy purpose marriage, send me word to-morrow,
　By one that I'll procure to come to thee,
　Where and what time thou wilt perform the rite;
　And all my fortunes at thy foot I'll lay
　And follow thee my lord throughout the world.
Nurse: (*within*) Madam!
Juliet: Romeo!
Romeo: My dear?
Juliet: At what o'clock to-morrow
　Shall I send to thee?
Romeo: By the hour of nine.
Juliet: Good night, good night! Parting is such sweet sorrow,
　That I shall say good night till it be morrow.
Exit.

Scene III. *Friar Laurence's cell. Enter Friar, Laurence alone, with a basket.*

Friar: The grey-ey'd morn smiles on the frowning night,
　Check'ring the Eastern clouds with streaks of light;
　O, mickle is the powerful grace that lies
　In plants, herbs, stones, and their true qualities;
　For naught so vile that on the earth doth live
　But to the earth some special good doth give;
Enter Romeo.
Romeo: Good morrow, father.
Friar: Benedicite!
　What early tongue so sweet saluteth me?
　Our Romeo hath not been in bed to-night?
Romeo: That last is true-the sweeter rest was mine.
Friar: God pardon sin! Wast thou with Rosaline?
Romeo: With Rosaline, my ghostly father? No.
　I have forgot that name, and that name's woe.
Friar: That's my good son! But where hast thou been then?
Romeo: I'll tell thee ere thou ask it me again.
　I have been feasting with mine enemy,
　Where on a sudden one hath wounded me
　That's by me wounded. Both our remedies
　Within thy help and holy physic lies.
Friar: Be plain, good son, and homely in thy drift
　Riddling confession finds but riddling shrift.
Romeo: Then plainly know my heart's dear love is set
　On the fair daughter of rich Capulet;
　As mine on hers, so hers is set on mine,
　And all combin'd, save what thou must combine
　By holy marriage. When, and where, and how
　We met, we woo'd, and made exchange of vow,
　I'll tell thee as we pass; but this I pray,
　That thou consent to marry us to-day.
Friar: Holy Saint Francis! What a change is here!
　Is Rosaline, that thou didst love so dear,
　So soon forsaken? Young men's love then lies
　Not truly in their hearts, but in their eyes.
Romeo: I pray thee chide not. She whom I love now
　Doth grace for grace and love for love allow.

Friar: O, for this alliance may so happy prove
  To turn your households' rancour to pure love.
Exeunt.

Scene IV. *A street. Enter Benvolio and Mercutio.*

Mercutio: Where the devil should this Romeo be?
  Came he not home to-night?
Benvolio: Tybalt, the kinsman to old Capulet,
  Hath sent a letter to his father's house.
Enter Nurse and Peter her Man.
Mercutio: A sail, a sail!
Benvolio: Two, two! a shirt and a smock.
Nurse: My fan, Peter.
Mercutio: To hide her face; her fan's the fairer of the two.
Nurse: God ye good morrow, gentlemen.
Mercutio: God ye good-den, fair gentlewoman.
Nurse: Gentlemen, where I may find the young Romeo?
Romeo: Young Romeo will be older when you have found
  him. I am the youngest of that name.
Nurse: Sir, I desire some confidence with you.
Mercutio: Romeo, will you come to your father's? We'll to
  dinner thither.
Romeo: I will follow you.
Mercutio: Farewell, ancient lady. Farewell,
  [sings] lady, lady, lady.
Exeunt Mercutio, Benvolio.
Nurse: What saucy merchant was this that was so full of his
  ropery?
Romeo: Nurse, commend me to thy lady and mistress.
Nurse: Good heart, and i faith I will tell her as much.
  Lord! she will be a joyful woman.
Romeo: Bid her devise
  Some means to come to shrift this afternoon;
  And there she shall at Friar Laurence' cell
  Be shriv'd and married. Here is for thy pains.
Nurse: This afternoon, sir? Well, she shall be there.
Romeo: Commend me to thy lady.
Nurse: Ay, a thousand times. *[Exit Romeo.]* Peter!
Peter. Anon.
Nurse: Peter, take my fan, and go before, and apace.
Exeunt.

Scene V. *Capulet's orchard. Enter Juliet.*

Juliet: The clock struck nine when I did send the nurse;
  In half an hour she 'promis'd to return.
Enter Nurse and Peter.
  O God, she comes! O honey nurse, what news?
  Hast thou met with him? Send thy man away.
Nurse: Peter, stay at the gate. *Exit Peter.*
Juliet: What says he of our marriage? What of that?
Nurse: Lord, how my head aches!
  It beats as it would fall in twenty pieces.
Juliet: I' faith, I am sorry that thou art not well.
  Sweet, sweet, Sweet nurse, tell me, what says my love?
Nurse: Have you got leave to go to shrift to-day?
Juliet: I have.
Nurse: Then hie you hence to Friar Laurence' cell;
  There stays a husband to make you a wife.

Juliet: Hie to high fortune! Honest nurse, farewell.
Exeunt.

Scene VI. *Friar Laurence's cell. Enter Friar Laurence and Romeo.*

Friar: So smile the heavens upon this holy act.
Romeo: Amen, amen!
  It is enough I may but call her mine.
Enter Juliet.
Friar: Here comes the lady. O, so light a foot
  Come, come with me, and we will make short work;
  For, by your leaves, you shall not stay alone
  Till Holy Church incorporate two in one. *Exeunt.*

ACT III.

Scene I. *A public place. Enter Mercutio, Benvolio, and Men.*

Benvolio: I pray thee, good Mercutio, let's retire.
  The day is hot, the Capulets abroad.
Enter Romeo.
Tybalt: Well, peace be with you, sir. Here comes my man.
Mercutio: But I'll be hang'd, sir, if he wear your livery.
Tybalt: Romeo, the love I bear thee can afford
  No better term than this: thou art a villain.
Romeo: Tybalt, the reason that I have to love thee
  Doth much excuse the appertaining rage
Tybalt: Boy, this shall not excuse the injuries
  That thou hast done me; therefore turn and draw.
Romeo: I do protest I never injur'd thee,
  But love thee better than thou canst devise
Mercutio: O calm, dishonourable, vile submission!
Draws.
  Tybalt, you ratcatcher, will you walk?
Tybalt: What wouldst thou have with me?
Mercutio: Good King of Cats, nothing but one of your nine
  lives.
Tybalt: I am for you. *Draws.*
Mercutio: Come, sir, your passado! *They fight.*
Romeo: Gentlemen, for shame! forbear this outrage!
  Tybalt, Mercutio, the Prince expressly hath
  Forbid this bandying in Verona streets.
Tybalt under Romeo's arm thrusts Mercutio in, and flies
  with his Followers.
Mercutio: I am hurt.
  A plague o' both your houses! I am sped.
Benvolio: What, art thou hurt?
Mercutio: Ay, ay, a scratch, a scratch. Marry, 'tis enough.
  Where is my page? Go, villain, fetch a surgeon.
Exit Page.
Romeo: Courage, man. The hurt cannot be much.
Mercutio: No, 'tis not so deep as a well, nor so wide as a
  church door;   but 'tis enough, 'twill serve.
  I am peppered, I warrant, for this world. A plague o' both
  your houses! Why the devil came you between us? I was
  hurt under your arm.
Romeo: I thought all for the best.
Mercutio: They have made worms' meat of me!

Exit. supported by Benvolio.

Romeo: This gentleman, the Prince's near ally,
  My very friend, hath got this mortal hurt
  In my behalf- my reputation stain'd
  With Tybalt's slander- Tybalt, that an hour
  Hath been my kinsman. O sweet Juliet,
  Thy beauty hath made me effeminate
  And in my temper soft'ned valour's steel

Enter Benvolio.

Benvolio: O Romeo, Romeo, brave Mercutio's dead!

Enter Tybalt.

Tybalt: Thou, wretched boy, that didst consort him here,
  shalt with him hence.

They fight. Tybalt falls.

Benvolio: Romeo, away, be gone!
  The citizens are up, and Tybalt slain.
  Stand not amaz'd. The Prince will doom thee death
  If thou art taken. Hence, be gone, away!

Romeo: O, I am fortune's fool! *Exit Romeo.*

Scene III. *Friar Laurence's cell. Enter Friar Laurence.*
Enter Romeo.

Romeo: Father, what news? What is the Prince's doom

Friar: A gentler judgment vanish'd from his lips-
  Not body's death, but body's banishment.

Romeo: Ha, banishment? Be merciful, say 'death';
  For exile hath more terror in his look,

Friar: Hence from Verona art thou banished.
  Be patient, for the world is broad and wide.

Romeo: There is no world without Verona walls,
  But purgatory, torture, hell itself.

Friar: Thy fault our law calls death; but the kind Prince,
  Hath turn'd that black word death to banishment.
  This is dear mercy, and thou seest it not.

Romeo: 'Tis torture, and not mercy. Heaven is here,
  Where Juliet lives; and every cat and dog
  And little mouse, every unworthy thing,
  Live here in heaven and may look on her;
  But Romeo may not.

Knock

Friar: Arise; one knocks. Good Romeo, hide thyself.

Nurse: *[Enters]* Let me come in, and you shall know my
  errand.

Romeo: *[rises]* Nurse- Spakest thou of Juliet? How is it
  with her?
  Doth not she think me an old murtherer,
  Now I have stain'd the childhood of our joy
  With blood remov'd but little from her own?
  Where is she? and how doth she! and what says
  My conceal'd lady to our cancell'd love?

Nurse: O, she says nothing, sir, but weeps and weeps;

Romeo: As if that name did murther her;
  O, tell me, friar, tell me,
  In what vile part of this anatomy
  Doth my name lodge? Tell me, that I may sack
  The hateful mansion. *[Draws his dagger.]*

Friar: Hold thy desperate hand.
  Go get thee to thy love, as was decreed,

Ascend her chamber, hence and comfort her.

Nurse: Here is a ring she bid me give you, sir.
  Hie you, make haste, for it grows very late. *Exit.*

Friar: Go hence; good night;
  Sojourn in Mantua. I'll find out your man,
  And he shall signify from time to time
  Every good hap to you that chances here.

Romeo: Farewell. *Exeunt.*

Scene V. *Capulet's orchard. Enter Romeo and Juliet aloft,*
at the Window.

Juliet: Wilt thou be gone? It is not yet near day.
  It was the nightingale, and not the lark,

Romeo: It was the lark, the herald of the morn;
  I must be gone and live, or stay and die.

Juliet: Yond light is not daylight; I know it, I.
  It is some meteor that the sun exhales
  To be to thee this night a torchbearer
  And light thee on the way to Mantua.

Romeo: Let me be ta'en, let me be put to death.
  I am content, so thou wilt have it so.

Juliet: Hie hence, be gone, away!
  It is the lark that sings so out of tune,

Romeo: More light and light- more dark and dark

Enter Nurse:

Nurse: Madam! Your lady mother is coming!
  The day is broke; be wary, look about.

Juliet: Then, window, let day in, and let life out. *Exit.*

Romeo: Farewell, farewell! One kiss, and I'll descend.
He goeth down.

Juliet: Art thou gone so, my lord, my love, my friend?
  I must hear from thee every day in the hour,

Romeo: Farewell!
  I will omit no opportunity
  That may convey my greetings, love, to thee.

Juliet: O, think'st thou we shall ever meet again?

Romeo: I doubt it not; and all these woes shall serve
  For sweet discourses in our time to come.
  Adieu, adieu! *Exit.*

Enter Mother.

Lady. Why, how now, Juliet?

Juliet: Madam, I am not well.

Lady. Evermore weeping for your cousin's death?
  Well, well, thou hast a careful father, child;
  One who, to put thee from thy heaviness,
  Hath sorted out a sudden day of joy.

Juliet: Madam, in happy time! What day is that?

Lady. Marry, my child, early next Thursday morn
  The gallant, young, and noble gentleman,
  The County Paris, at Saint Peter's Church,
  Shall happily make thee there a joyful bride.

Juliet: Now by Saint Peter's Church, and Peter too,
  He shall not make me there a joyful bride!

Enter Capulet and Nurse:

Capulet: How now, wife?
  Have you delivered to her our decree?

Lady. Ay, sir; but she will none.

Capulet: How, how, choplogic? What is this?

Juliet: Good father, I beseech you on my knees,

Capulet: Hang thee, young baggage! disobedient wretch!
  I tell thee what- get thee to church a Thursday
  Or never after look me in the face! *Exit.*

Juliet: Is there no pity sitting in the clouds

Lady. Talk not to me, for I'll not speak a word.
  Do as thou wilt, for I have done with thee. *Exit.*

Juliet: O God!- O nurse, how shall this be prevented?
  My husband is on earth, my faith in heaven.
  What say'st thou? Hast thou not a word of joy?

Nurse: Romeo is banish'd;
  I think it best you married with the County.
  O, he's a lovely gentleman!

Juliet: Amen!

Nurse: What?

Juliet: Go in; and tell my lady I am gone,
  Having displeas'd my father, to Laurence' cell,
  To make confession and to be absolv'd. *Exeunt*

ACT IV.

Scene I. *Friar Laurence's cell. Enter Friar Laurence,*
Enter Juliet

Friar: Ah, Juliet, I already know thy grief;
  On Thursday next to be married to this County.

Juliet: God join'd my heart and Romeo's, thou our hands;
  And ere this hand, by thee to Romeo's seal'd,
  Shall be the label to another deed,
  Or my true heart with treacherous revolt
  Turn to another, this shall slay them both.

Friar: Hold, daughter. I do spy a kind of hope.
  Thou hast the strength of will to slay thyself,
  Then is it likely thou wilt undertake
  A thing like death to chide away this shame,
  Hold, then. Go home, be merry, give consent
  To marry Paris. Wednesday is to-morrow.
  To-morrow night look that thou lie alone;
  Let not the nurse lie with thee in thy chamber.
  Take thou this vial, being then in bed,
  And this distilled liquor drink thou off;
  When presently through all thy veins shall run
  A stiff and stark cold, like death;
  And in this borrowed likeness of shrunk death
  Thou shalt continue two-and-forty hours,
  And then awake as from a pleasant sleep.
  Now, when the bridegroom in the morning comes
  To rouse thee from thy bed, there art thou dead.
  Then, thou shalt be borne to that ancient vault
  Where all the kindred of the Capulets lie.
  In the mean time, against thou shalt awake,
  Shall Romeo by my letters know our drift;
  And hither shall he come; and he and I
  Will watch thy waking, and that very night
  Shall Romeo bear thee hence to Mantua.

Juliet: Give me, give me! O, tell not me of fear!

Friar: In this resolve. I'll send a friar with speed
  To Mantua, with my letters to thy lord. *Exeunt.*

ACT V.

Scene I. *Mantua. A street. Enter Romeo. Enter Romeo's*
Man Balthasar, booted.

Romeo: News from Verona! How now, Balthasar?
  How fares my Juliet? That I ask again,
  For nothing can be ill if she be well.

Man. Then she is well, and nothing can be ill.
  Her body sleeps in Capel's monument,
  And her immortal part with angels lives.

Romeo: Is it e'en so? Then I defy you, stars!
  Hire posthorses. I will hence to-night.

Exit [Balthasar].
  Well, Juliet, I will lie with thee to-night.
  And if a man did need a poison now,
  Whose sale is present death in Mantua,
  Here lives a caitiff wretch would sell it him.
  What, ho! apothecary!

Enter Apothecary.

Apoth. Who calls so loud?

Romeo: Come hither, man. I see that thou art poor.
  Hold, there is forty ducats. Let me have
  A dram of poison, such soon-speeding gear
  As will disperse itself through all the veins
  That the life-weary taker may fall dead. *Exeunt.*

Scene II. *Verona. Friar Laurence's cell. Enter Friar John*
to Friar Laurence.

Laur. Welcome from Mantua. What says Romeo?

John. Alas the searchers of the town,
  Suspecting that we both were in a house
  Where the infectious pestilence did reign,
  Seal'd up the doors, and would not let us forth,
  So that my speed to Mantua there was stay'd.

Laur. Who bare my letter, then, to Romeo?

John. I could not send it- here it is again. *Exit.*

Laur. Now, must I to the monument alone.
  Within this three hours will fair Juliet wake. *Exit.*

Scene III. *Verona. A churchyard; the monument of the*
Capulets. Enter Romeo, and Balthasar.

Romeo: Thou detestable maw, thou womb of death,

Romeo opens the tomb.

Romeo: O my love! my wife!
  Death, that hath suck'd the honey of thy breath,
  Hath had no power yet upon thy beauty.
  Thou art not conquer'd. Beauty's ensign yet
  Is crimson in thy lips and in thy cheeks,
  And death's pale flag is not advanced there.
  Tybalt, liest thou there in thy bloody sheet?
  Forgive me, cousin. Ah, dear Juliet,
  Here, here will I remain
  With worms that are thy chambermaids. O, here
  Will I set up my everlasting rest
  Eyes, look your last!
  Arms, take your last embrace! and, lips, O you
  The doors of breath, seal with a righteous kiss
  A dateless bargain to engrossing death!

Here's to my love! *[Drinks.]* O true apothecary!
Thy drugs are quick. Thus with a kiss I die. *Falls.*
Enter Friar Laurence, with lantern and spade.
Friar: Saint Francis be my speed! *[Enters the tomb.]*
  The lady stirs!   *Juliet rises.*
Juliet: O comfortable friar! where is my lord?
  I do remember well where I should be,
  And there I am. Where is my Romeo?
Friar: A greater power than we can contradict
  Hath thwarted our intents. Come, come away.
  Thy husband in thy bosom there lies dead;
Juliet: Go, get thee hence, for I will not away.
Exit Friar.
  What's here? Poison, I see.
  O churl! drunk all, and left no friendly drop
  To help me after? I will kiss thy lips.
  Haply some poison yet doth hang on them
[Kisses him.]
  Thy lips are warm! *[Sounds of the Watch without]*
  Yea, noise? Then I'll be brief. O happy dagger!
Snatches Romeo's dagger.

This is thy sheath; there rest, and let me die.
She stabs herself and falls on Romeo's body.
Enter Capulet, Montague, wives and others.
Prince: See what a scourge is laid upon your hate,
  That heaven finds means to kill your joys with love!
Capulet: O brother Montague, give me thy hand.
  This is my daughter's jointure, for no more
  Can I demand.
Montague: But I can give thee more;
  For I will raise her Statue in pure gold,
  That whiles Verona by that name is known,
  There shall no figure at such rate be set
  As that of true and faithful Juliet.
Capulet: As rich shall Romeo's by his lady's lie-
  Poor sacrifices of our enmity!
Prince: Never was a story of more woe
  Than this of Juliet and her Romeo.
Exeunt omnes.

THE END

Hamlet, Prince of Denmark
By William Shakespeare
(London, c1599)

Shakespeare's play is based on a legend retold by the 12th century Danish Chronicler 'Saxo Grammaticus'. The *Hamlet* story has been made into at least 26 operas, about a dozen films, and has inspired performance works as varied as *The Lion King*, *Hair* and Tom Stoppard's *Rosencrantz and Guildenstern Are Dead.*

Abridged: GH

Dramatis Personae
Claudius, King of Denmark.
Hamlet, son to the former, and nephew to the present king.
Polonius, Lord Chamberlain.
Horatio, friend to Hamlet.
Laertes, son to Polonius.
Marcellus, Bernardo, Francisco, officers.
Rosencrantz, Guildenstern, Osric, courtiers.

Gertrude, Queen of Denmark, mother to Hamlet.
Ophelia, daughter to Polonius.
Ghost of Hamlet's Father.
Two Clowns, gravediggers.
A **Priest.**
Group of **Players.**
Fortinbras, A Prince of Norway.

ACT I.

Scene I. *Elsinore Castle. A platform before the Castle.*
  Enter two Sentinels, Francisco, and Bernardo.
Ber. Have you had quiet guard Francisco?
Fran. Not a mouse stirring.
Enter Horatio and Marcellus.
Fran. Stand, ho! Who is there?
Ber. Welcome, Horatio. Welcome, good Marcellus.
Mar. What, has this thing appear'd again to-night?
  Horatio says 'tis but our fantasy,
Ber. Last night of all,
  When yond star...
Enter Ghost.
Mar. Peace! break thee off! Look where it comes again!
Ber. In the same figure, like the King that's dead.

Mar. Thou art a scholar; speak to it, Horatio.
Hor. Stay! Speak, speak! I charge thee speak!
Exit Ghost.
Mar. 'Tis gone and will not answer.
Ber. How now, Horatio? You tremble and look pale.
  Is not this something more than fantasy?
Hor. Before my God, I might not this believe
  Without the sensible and true avouch
  Of mine own eyes.
The cock crows.
Hor. Let us impart what we have seen to-night
  Unto young Hamlet; for, upon my life,
  This spirit, dumb to us, will speak to him.
Exeunt.

Scene II. *Elsinore. A room of state in the Castle.*

155

Musical flourish. Enter Claudius, King of Denmark, Gertrude the Queen, Hamlet, Polonius, Laertes and his sister Ophelia.

Laer. My dread lord,
    Your leave and favour to return to France;
    From whence though willingly I came to Denmark
    To show my duty in your coronation.
King. Have you your father's leave? What says Polonius?
Pol. He hath, my lord, wrung from me my slow leave
King. Take thy fair hour, Laertes. Time be thine,
    But now, my cousin Hamlet, and my son-
Ham. [*aside*] A little more than kin, and less than kind!
King. How is it that the clouds still hang on you?
Queen. Good Hamlet, cast thy nighted colour off,
    Do not for ever with thy vailed lids
    Seek for thy noble father in the dust.
    Thou know'st 'tis common. All that lives must die,
King. 'Tis sweet and commendable in your nature, Hamlet,
    To give these mourning duties to your father;
    But you must know, your father lost a father;
    That father lost, lost his. This must be so.
    We pray you throw to earth
    This unprevailing woe, and think of us
    As of a father; Come away.
Flourish. Exeunt all but Hamlet.
Ham. O that this too too solid flesh would melt,
    Thaw, and resolve itself into a dew!
    Frailty, thy name is woman!-
    A little month, or ere those shoes were old
    With which she followed my poor father's body
    Why she, even she married with my uncle;
    My father's brother, but no more like my father
    Than I to Hercules.
Enter Horatio, Marcellus, and Bernardo.
Hor. Hail to your lordship!
Ham. I am glad to see you well, Horatio!
    And what make you from Wittenberg?
Hor. My lord, I came to see your father's funeral.
Ham. I prithee do not mock me, fellow student.
    I think it was to see my mother's wedding.
Hor. Indeed, my lord, it followed hard upon.
Ham. The funeral bak'd meats
    Did coldly furnish forth the marriage tables.
    My father- methinks I see my father.
Hor. O, where, my lord?
Ham. In my mind's eye, Horatio.
Hor. I saw him once. He was a goodly king.
Ham. He was a man, take him for all in all.
    I shall not look upon his like again.
Hor. My lord, I think I saw him yesternight.
Ham. Saw? who?
Hor. My lord, the King your father.
Ham. The King my father?
Hor. Two nights together had these gentlemen
    Marcellus and Bernardo, on their watch
    Been thus encount'red. A figure like your father,
    Armed at point exactly, cap-a-pe,
Ham. I will watch to-night.

Perchance 'twill walk again.
Hor. I warr'nt it will.
Exeunt

Scene III. *Elsinore. A room in the house of Polonius.*
Enter Laertes and Ophelia.
Laer. My necessaries are embark'd. Farewell, sister.
    For Hamlet, and the trifling of his favour,
    Hold it a fashion, and a toy in blood;
    A violet in the youth of primy nature,
    No more.
Oph. No more but so?
Laer. Think it no more. But you must fear,
    His greatness weigh'd, his will is not his own;
    For he himself is subject to his birth.
Enter Polonius.
Pol. Yet here, Laertes? Aboard, aboard, for shame!
    The wind sits in the shoulder of your sail,
Laer. Farewell, Ophelia, and remember well
    What I have said to you.
Oph. 'Tis in my memory lock'd.
Laer. Farewell. *Exit.*
Pol. What is't, Ophelia, he hath said to you?
Oph. So please you, something touching the Lord Hamlet.
Pol. What is between you? Give me up the truth.
Oph. He hath, my lord, of late made many tenders
    Of his affection to me.
Pol. Affection? Pooh! You speak like a green girl,
    Ay, springes to catch woodcocks! I do know,
    I would not, in plain terms, from this time forth
    Have you so slander any moment leisure
    As to give words or talk with the Lord Hamlet.
    Look to't, I charge you. Come your ways.
Oph. I shall obey, my lord.
    Exeunt.

Scene IV. Elsinore. The platform before the Castle.
Enter Hamlet, Horatio, and Marcellus.
Ham. What hour now?
Hor. I think it lacks of twelve.
Enter Ghost.
Hor. Look, my lord, it comes!
Ham. Angels and ministers of grace defend us!
    Say, why is this? What should we do?
Ghost beckons Hamlet.
    I say, away!- Go on. I'll follow thee.
Mar. Let's follow. 'Tis not fit thus to obey him.
    Something is rotten in the state of Denmark.
Exit all but Ghost and Hamlet.
Ham. Whither wilt thou lead me? Speak!
Ghost. I am thy father's spirit,
    Doom'd for a certain term to walk the night,
    To ears of flesh and blood, list, list, O, list!
    Revenge his foul and most unnatural murther.
Ham. Murther?
Ghost. Murther most foul, as in the best it is;
    'Tis given out that, sleeping in my orchard,

A serpent stung me. But know, thou noble youth,
The serpent that did sting thy father's life
Now wears his crown.

Ham. My uncle?

Ghost. Ay, that incestuous, that adulterate beast,
With witchcraft of his wit, with traitorous gifts.
O wicked wit won to his shameful lust
The will of my most seeming-virtuous queen.
O Hamlet, let not the royal bed of Denmark be
A couch for luxury and damned incest.
Adieu, adieu, adieu! Remember me. *Exit Ghost.*

Ham. O most pernicious woman!
O villain, villain, smiling, damned villain!

Enter Horatio and Marcellus.

Mar. How is't, my noble lord?

Hor. What news, my lord?

Ham. There's neer a villain dwelling in all Denmark But
he's an arrant knave.

Hor. These are but wild and whirling words, my lord.

Ham. Consent to swear never to speak of this that you have
seen. Swear by my sword.

Ghost. [*beneath*] Swear by his sword.

Ham. There are more things in heaven and earth, Horatio,
Than are dreamt of in your philosophy.

Ghost. [*beneath*] Swear. [*They swear.*]

Ham. The time is out of joint. O cursed spite
That ever I was born to set it right!

Exeunt.

ACT II

Scene I. *Elsinore. A room in the house of Polonius.*
Enter Polonius and Ophelia.

Oph. O my lord, my lord, I have been so affrighted!

Pol. With what, i' th' name of God!

Oph. My lord, as I was sewing in my closet,
Lord Hamlet, with his doublet all unbrac'd,
And with a look so piteous in purport
As if he had been loosed out of hell
To speak of horrors- he comes before me.

Pol. Mad for thy love?

Oph. My lord, I do truly do fear it.

Pol. This is the very ecstasy of love,
What, have you given him any hard words of late?

Oph. No, my good lord; but, as you did command,
I did repel his letters and denied
His access to me.

Pol. That hath made him mad.
Come, go we to the King.

Exeunt.

Scene II. *Elsinore. A room in the Castle.*
Flourish. Enter King and Queen, Rosencrantz and Guildenstern, with others.

King. Welcome, dear Rosencrantz and Guildenstern.
Something have you heard of Hamlet's transformation.
I entreat you both, being brought up with him,
To draw him on to pleasures, and to gather

So much as from occasion you may glean.

Guil. We both obey.

Queen. Thanks, and I beseech you instantly to visit
My too much changed son.- Go!

Exeunt Rosencrantz and Guildenstern, with attendants.
Enter Polonius.

King. He tells me, my dear Gertrude, he hath found
The head and source of all your son's distemper.

Queen. I doubt it is no other but the main,
His father's death and our o'erhasty marriage.

Pol. Since brevity is the soul of wit,
I will be brief. Your noble son is mad.
And now remains to find the cause of this effect-
I have a daughter who hath given me this letter. [*Reads*]
'To the celestial, and my soul's idol, the most beautified
Ophelia,'-
('Beautified' is an ill phrase.)
'In her excellent white bosom, these, &c.
Thine evermore, most dear lady, HAMLET.'

King. But how hath she receiv'd his love?

Pol. When I had seen this hot love on the wing
Then my young mistress thus I did bespeak:
'Lord Hamlet is a prince, out of thy star.
This must not be.' And she took the fruits of my advice,
And he, repulsed, a short tale to make,
Fell into the madness wherein now he raves.

King. Do you think 'tis this?

Queen. it may be, very like.

King. How may we try it further?

Pol. You know sometimes he walks four hours together
Here in the lobby.
At such a time I'll loose my daughter to him.
Be you and I behind an arras then.
Mark the encounter. If he love her not,

King. We will try it.

Enter Hamlet, reading on a book.

Queen. But look where sadly the poor wretch comes
reading.

Pol. Away, I do beseech you, both away

Exeunt King and Queen, with Attendants.
How does my good Lord Hamlet?
Do you know me, my lord?

Ham. Excellent well. You are a fishmonger.
For if the sun breed maggots in a dead dog, being a god
kissing carrion- Have you a daughter?

Pol. I have, my lord.
[*aside*] Still harping on my daughter. Yet he said I was a
fishmonger. He is far gone, far gone! Truly in my youth
I suff'red much extremity for love- very near this.
Though this be madness, yet there is a method in't.

Enter Rosencrantz and Guildenstern.

Pol. You go to seek the Lord Hamlet. There he is.

Exit Polonius.

Guil. My honour'd lord!

Ros. My most dear lord!

Ham. My excellent good friends! How dost thou,
Guildenstern? Ah, Rosencrantz! Good lads, how do ye
both?

Guil. On Fortune's cap we are not the very button.

Ham. What have you, my good friends, deserved at the hands of Fortune that she sends you to prison?

Guil. Prison, my lord?

Ham. Denmark's a prison.

Ros. Then is the world one.

Ham. There is nothing either good or bad but thinking makes it so. To me it is a prison. I know the good King and Queen have sent for you.

Ros. To what end, my lord?

Ham. I have of late lost all my mirth, and indeed this most excellent canopy, the air appeareth no other thing to me than a foul and pestilent congregation of vapours. What a piece of work is a man! how noble in reason! how infinite in faculties! In action how like an angel! in apprehension how like a god! The beauty of the world, the paragon of animals! And yet to me what is this quintessence of dust? Man delights not me- no, nor woman neither.

Ros. To think, my lord, if you delight not in man, what lenten entertainment the players shall receive from you. We coted them on the way, and hither are they coming to offer you service.

Ham. What players are they?

Ros. Even those you were wont to take such delight in, the tragedians of the city.

Flourish for the Players.

Guil. There are the players.

Ham. Gentlemen, you are welcome to Elsinore. Your hands, come! But my uncle-father and aunt-mother are deceiv'd.

Guil. In what, my dear lord?

Ham. I am but mad north-north-west. When the wind is southerly I know a hawk from a handsaw.

Enter four or five Players.

Ham. You are welcome, masters; welcome. We'll have a speech straight. Come, give us a taste of your quality. Come, a passionate speech.

1st Play. What speech, my good lord?

Ham. I heard thee speak me a speech once, it, I remember, pleas'd not the million, 'twas caviary to the general. So, proceed you.

1st Play. 'O who, had seen the mobled queen-'

Ham. 'The mobled queen'?

1st Play. 'Run barefoot up and down, threat'ning the flames
    With bisson rheum; a clout upon that head
    Where late the diadem stood, and for a robe...

Ham. God's bodykins, man, much better! Take them in.

Ham. Along, friends. We'll hear a play to-morrow.

Exeunt the Players, with Rosencrantz and Guildenstern
    Now I am alone.
    O, vengeance!
    Why, what an ass am I! Fie upon't! foh!
    About, my brain! Hum, I have heard
    That guilty creatures, sitting at a play,
    Have by the very cunning of the scene
    Been struck so to the soul that presently
    They have proclaim'd their malefactions;

I'll have these Players
Play something like the murther of my father
Before mine uncle. I'll observe his looks;
The play's the thing wherein I'll catch the conscience of
the King. *Exit.*

ACT III

Scene I. *Elsinore. A room in the Castle.*
*Enter King, Queen, Polonius, Ophelia, Rosencrantz,
Guildenstern, and Lords.*

King. And can you by no drift of circumstance
    Get from him why he puts on this confusion?

Ros. He does confess he feels himself distracted,
    But from what cause he will by no means speak.

Queen. Did you assay him to any pastime?

Ros. Madam, it so fell out that certain players
    We o'erraught on the way. Of these we told him,
    And there did seem in him a kind of joy.

Pol. And he beseech'd me to entreat your Majesties
    To hear and see the matter.

King. Good gentlemen, give him a further edge
    And drive his purpose on to these delights.

Exeunt Rosencrantz and Guildenstern.

King. Sweet Gertrude, leave us too;
    For we have closely sent for Hamlet hither,
    That he, as 'twere by accident, may here
    Affront Ophelia.
    Her father and myself (lawful espials)
    Will so bestow ourselves that, seeing unseen,
    We may of their encounter frankly judge

Exit Queen.

Pol. Ophelia, walk you here.- Gracious, so please you,
    We will bestow ourselves.- [*To Ophelia*] Read on this
book,
    I hear him coming. Let's withdraw, my lord.

Exeunt King and Polonius, Enter Hamlet.

Ham. To be, or not to be- that is the question:
    Whether 'tis nobler in the mind to suffer
    The slings and arrows of outrageous fortune
    Or to take arms against a sea of troubles,
    And by opposing end them. To die- to sleep-
    No more; and by a sleep to say we end
    The heartache, and the thousand natural shocks
    That flesh is heir to. 'Tis a consummation
    Devoutly to be wish'd. To die- to sleep.
    To sleep- perchance to dream: ay, there's the rub!
    For in that sleep of death what dreams may come
    When we have shuffled off this mortal coil,
    Must give us pause. There's the respect
    That makes calamity of so long life.
    For who would bear the whips and scorns of time,
    Th' oppressor's wrong, the proud man's contumely,
    The pangs of despis'd love, the law's delay,
    When he himself might his quietus make
    With a bare bodkin? Who would these fardels bear,
    To grunt and sweat under a weary life,
    But that the dread of something after death-

The undiscover'd country, from whose bourn
No traveller returns- puzzles the will,
And makes us rather bear those ills we have
Than fly to others that we know not of?
Thus conscience does make cowards of us all,
And thus the native hue of resolution
Is sicklied o'er with the pale cast of thought,
And enterprises of great pith and moment
With this regard their currents turn awry
And lose the name of action.- Soft you now!
The fair Ophelia!

Oph. Good my lord,
How does your honour for this many a day?

Ham. I humbly thank you; well, well, well.

Oph. My lord, I have remembrances of yours
That I have longed long to re-deliver.
I pray you, now receive them.

Ham. No, not I!   I never gave you aught.

Oph. My honour'd lord, you know right well you did,

Ham. Get thee to a nunnery! I am very proud, revengeful,
ambitious; with more offences at my beck than I have
thoughts to put them in, imagination to give them shape,
or time to act them in. Where's your father?

Oph. At home, my lord.

Ham. Let the doors be shut upon him, that he may play the
fool nowhere but in's own house. Go, farewell. If thou
wilt needs marry, marry a fool; for wise men know well
enough what monsters you make of them. To a nunnery,
go; and quickly too. Farewell. *Exit.*

Oph. O, what a noble mind is here o'erthrown!
Enter King and Polonius.

King. Love? his affections do not that way tend;
Was not like madness. There's something in his soul
O'er which his melancholy sits on brood;
Thus set it down: he shall with speed to England
Haply the seas, and countries different,
With variable objects, shall expel
This something-settled matter in his heart.

Pol. To England send him.

King. Madness in great ones must not unwatch'd go.
Exeunt.

Scene II. *Elsinore. Hall in the Castle.*
Enter Hamlet and three of the Players.

Ham. Make the play, I pray you, as I gave it.

Player. I warrant your honour.

Ham. Bid the players make haste,
Exit Players

Ham. What, ho, Horatio!
Enter Horatio.

Hor. Here, sweet lord, at your service.

*Enter Trumpets and Kettledrums. Danish march. Enter
King, Queen, Polonius, Ophelia, Rosencrantz,
Guildenstern, and other Lords attendant, with the Guard
carrying torches.*

Ham. They are coming to the play. I must be idle.

King. How fares our cousin Hamlet?

Ham. Excellent, i' faith; of the chameleon's dish. I eat the
air, promise-cramm'd. You cannot feed capons so.

King. I have nothing with this answer, Hamlet.

Ham. No, nor mine now. [*To Polonius*] My lord, you play'd
once i' th' university, you say?

Pol. That did I, my lord, and was accounted a good actor. I
did enact Julius Caesar; Brutus kill'd me.

Queen. Come hither, my dear Hamlet, sit by me.

Ham. No, good mother. Lady, shall I lie in your lap? [*Sits
down at Ophelia's feet.*]

Oph. No, my lord.

Ham. What should a man do but be merry? For look you
how cheerfully my mother looks, and my father died
within 's two hours.

Oph. Nay 'tis twice two months, my lord.

Ham. So long? Nay then, let the devil wear black, for I'll
have a suit of sables. O heavens! die two months ago,
and not forgotten yet? Then there's hope a great man's
memory may outlive his life half a year.

Sound of hautboys playing. The dumb show enters.

*Enter a King and a Queen very lovingly; the Queen
embracing him and he her. He lays him down upon a
bank of flowers. She, seeing him asleep, leaves him.
Anon comes in a fellow, takes off his crown, kisses it,
pours poison in the sleeper's ears, and leaves him. The
Queen returns, finds the King dead, and makes
passionate action. The Poisoner with some three or four
Mutes, comes in again, seem to condole with her. The
dead body is carried away. The Poisoner wooes the
Queen with gifts; she seems harsh and unwilling awhile,
but in the end accepts his love. Exeunt.*

Ham. Madam, how like you this play?

Queen. The lady doth protest too much, methinks.

King. What do you call the play?

Ham. 'The Mousetrap.' This play is the image of a murther
done in Vienna. He poisons him i' th' garden for's estate.
His name's Gonzago.

Oph. The King rises.

Ham. What, frighted with false fire?

Queen. How fares my lord?

Pol. Give o'er the play.

King. Give me some light! Away!
Exeunt.

Scene IV. *The Queen's closet.*
Enter Queen and Polonius.

Pol. He will come straight. Look you lay home to him. Tell
him his pranks have been too broad to bear with,

Queen. I'll warrant you; fear me not. Withdraw; I hear him
coming.

Polonius hides behind the arras. Enter Hamlet.

Ham. Now, mother, what's the matter?

Queen. Hamlet, thou hast thy father much offended.

Ham. Mother, you have my father much offended.

Queen. What wilt thou do? Thou wilt not murther me?
Help, help, ho!

Pol. [*behind*] What, ho! help, help, help!

Ham. [*draws*] How now? a rat? Dead for a ducat, dead!
  [*Makes a pass through the arras and kills Polonius.*]
Pol. [*behind*] O, I am slain!
Queen. O me, what hast thou done?
Ham. Nay, I know not. Is it the King?
Queen. O, what a rash and bloody deed is this!
Ham. A bloody deed- almost as bad, good mother,
  As kill a king, and marry with his brother.
Queen. As kill a king?
Ham. [*Lifts up the arras and sees Polonius.*] Thou
  wretched, rash, intruding fool, farewell!
  I took thee for thy better.
Queen. O, speak to me no more!
  These words like daggers enter in mine ears.
  No more, sweet Hamlet!
Ham. A murtherer and a villain!
Enter the Ghost in his nightgown.
Ham. A king of shreds and patches!-
Queen. Alas, he's mad!
Ghost. Do not forget. This visitation
  Is but to whet thy almost blunted purpose.
Ham. How is it with you, lady?
Queen. Alas, how is't with you,
  That you do bend your eye on vacancy,
  And with th' encorporal air do hold discourse?
Ham. On him, on him! Look you how pale he glares!
  His form and cause conjoin'd, preaching to stones,
Queen. To whom do you speak this?
Ham. Do you see nothing there?
Queen. Nothing at all but ourselves.
Ham. Look how it steals away!
  My father, in his habit as he liv'd!
Exit Ghost.
Queen. This is the very coinage of your brain.
Ham. It is not madness that I have utt'red.
  I'll blessing beg of you.- For this same lord,
  I do repent; but heaven hath pleas'd it so,
  To punish me with this, and this with me,
  I must be cruel, only to be kind;
  Thus bad begins, and worse remains behind.
  Good night, mother.
Exit the Queen. Then Exit Hamlet, tugging in Polonius.

Scene V. *Elsinore. A room in the Castle.*
Enter Horatio, Queen, and a Gentleman.
Queen. I will not speak with her.
Gent. She speaks much of her father, and beats her heart.
Queen. Let her come in.
Exit Gentleman. Enter Ophelia distracted.
Oph. Where is the beauteous Majesty of Denmark?
Queen. How now, Ophelia?
Oph. Say you? Nay, pray You mark.
  (*Sings*) He is dead and gone, lady,
  He is dead and gone;
Queen. Nay, but Ophelia-
Oph. Pray you mark.
  (*Sings*) White his shroud as the mountain snow-
Enter King.

King. How do you, pretty lady?
Oph. Pray let's have no words of this; but when they ask,
  you what it means, say you this:
  (*Sings*) To-morrow is Saint Valentine's day,
King. How long hath she been thus?
Oph. I cannot choose but weep to think they would lay him
  i' th' cold ground. My brother shall know of it. Good
  night, ladies. Good night, sweet ladies.
Exit Ophelia
King. Follow her close; give her good watch, I pray you.
Exit Horatio.
  O, this is the poison of deep grief; it springs
  All from her father's death. O Gertrude, Gertrude,
  When sorrows come, they come not single spies.
  But in battalions!
Enter Laertes with others.
Laer. Where is this king? O thou vile king, Give me my
  father!
Queen. Calmly, good Laertes.
King. Let him go, Gertrude.
Laer. Where is my father?
King. Dead.
Queen. But not by him!
Laer. How came he dead? I'll not be juggled with:
Laer. To his good friends thus wide I'll ope my arms
  Like the kind life-rend'ring pelican.
  I am guiltless of your father's death.
Laer. How now? What noise is that?
Enter Ophelia.
  Dear maid, kind sister, sweet Ophelia!
  O heavens! is't possible a young maid's wits
  Should be as mortal as an old man's life?
Oph. (*sings*) (Hey non nony, nony, hey nony)
  There's rosemary, that's for remembrance.
  There's a daisy. I would give you some violets,
  But they wither'd all when my father died.
Exit Ophelia and Queen after
Laer. Do you see this, O God?
King. Laertes, I must commune with your grief.
  It was at Hamlet's hand your father met his end
  And where th' offence is let the great axe fall.
Laer. Have I a noble father lost;
  A sister driven into desp'rate terms,
  But my revenge will come.
King. I lov'd your father, as we love ourself;
Enter a Messenger with letters.
  How now? What news?
Mess. Letters, my lord, from Hamlet:
King. Laertes, you shall hear them.
  Leave us.
Exit Messenger.
  [*Reads*] 'High and Mighty, I am returned from England.
  To-morrow shall I beg leave to see your kingly eyes;
  when I shall (first asking your pardon thereunto) recount
  the occasion of my sudden and more strange return.
  'HAMLET.'
  What should this mean?
King. Will you be rul'd by me?

Laer. Ay my lord,

King. If he be now return'd, I will work him,
 And for his death no wind
 But even his mother shall call it accident.

Laer. My lord, I will be rul'd;
 The rather, if you could devise it so
 That I might be the organ.

King. He gave you such a masterly report
 For your rapier most especially,
 That he cried out 'twould be a sight indeed
 If one could match you.

Laer. To cut his throat i' th' church!

King. No place indeed should murther sanctuarize;
 Revenge should have no bounds. But, good Laertes,
 Will you do this? Keep close within your chamber.
 We'll put praise upon your excellence
 And set a double varnish on the fame
 And wager on your heads. He, being remiss,
 Will not peruse the foils; so that with ease,
 Or with a little shuffling, you may choose
 A sword unbated, and, in a pass of practice,
 Requite him for your father.

Laer. I will do't!
 And for that purpose I'll anoint my sword.
 I bought an unction of a mountebank,
 So mortal that, but dip a knife in it,
 Where it draws blood no cataplasm so rare,
 Collected from all simples that have virtue
 Under the moon, can save the thing from death

King. Let's further think of this,
 When he calls for drink, I'll have prepar'd him
 A chalice for the nonce; whereon but sipping,
 If he by chance escape your venom'd stuck,
 Our purpose may hold there.- But stay, what noise,

Enter Queen.
 How now, sweet queen?

Queen. One woe doth tread upon another's heel,
 So fast they follow. Your sister's drown'd, Laertes.

Laer. Drown'd! O, where?

Queen. There is a willow grows aslant a brook,
 There with fantastic garlands did she come
 Of crowflowers, nettles, daisies, and long purples,
 When down her weedy trophies and herself
 Fell in the weeping brook and unto that element,
 To muddy death.

Laer. Too much of water hast thou, poor Ophelia,
 And therefore I forbid my tears

Exeunt

ACT V

Scene I. *Elsinore. A churchyard.*

Enter two Clowns, with spades and pickaxes.

Clown. Is she to be buried in Christian burial when she
 wilfully seeks her own salvation?

Other. I tell thee she is; therefore make her grave straight.

Clown. How can that be, unless she drown'd herself in her
 own defence?

Other. Is't the crowner's quest law?

Clown. I'll put a question to thee.

Other. Go to!

Clown. What is he that builds stronger than either the
 mason, the shipwright, or the carpenter?

Other. The gallows-maker; for that frame outlives a
 thousand tenants.

Clown. I like thy wit well, in good faith. Go, fetch me a
 stoup of liquor.

Exit Second Clown. Enter Hamlet and Horatio afar off.
[Clown digs and sings.]
 In youth when I did love, did love,
  Methought it was very sweet;

Ham. Has this fellow no feeling of his business, that he
 sings at grave-making?

Hor. Custom hath made it in him a Property of easiness.
 What man dost thou dig it for?

Clown. For no man, sir.

Ham. What woman then?

Clown. One that was a woman, sir; but, rest her soul, she's
 dead.

Ham. How absolute the knave is! How long hast thou been
 a grave-maker?

Clown. Since the very day that young Hamlet was born- he
 that is mad, and sent into England.

Ham. How came he mad?

Clown. Very strangely, they say.

Ham. How long will a man lie i' th' earth ere he rot?

Clown. Faith, some eight year or nine year. Here's a skull
 now. This skull hath lien i' th' earth three-and-twenty
 years.

Ham. Whose was it?

Clown. This same skull, sir, was Yorick's skull, the King's
 jester.

Ham. *[Takes the skull.]* Alas, poor Yorick! I knew him,
 Horatio. A fellow of infinite jest, of most excellent
 fancy. He hath borne me on his back a thousand times.
 [Puts down the skull.]

Hor. E'en so, my lord.

Ham. To what base uses we may return, Horatio! Why may
 not imagination trace the noble dust of Alexander till he
 find it stopping a bunghole? But soft! aside! Here comes
 the King- *[Retires with Horatio.]*

Enter priests with a coffin in funeral procession, King,
 Queen, Laertes, with Lords attendant.

Laer. Lay her i' th' earth;
 And from her fair and unpolluted flesh
 May violets spring!

Ham. What, the fair Ophelia?

Queen. Sweets to the sweet! Farewell. *[Scatters flowers.]*
 I hop'd thou shouldst have been my Hamlet's wife;

Laer. Hold off the earth awhile,
 Till I have caught her once more in mine arms. *Leaps in*
 the grave.

Ham. *[comes forward]* What is he whose grief
 Bears such an emphasis? *[Leaps in after Laertes]*

Laer. The devil take thy soul! *[Grapples with him]*.

Ham. I lov'd Ophelia. Forty thousand brothers

Could not make up my sum.

King. O, he is mad, Laertes.

Queen. For love of God, forbear him!

Ham. Hear you, sir!

    Let Hercules himself do what he may,

    The cat will mew, and dog will have his day. *Exit.*

King. I pray thee, good Horatio, wait upon him.

    [*To Laertes*] Strengthen your patience

Exeunt.

Scene II. *Elsinore. A hall in the Castle.*

Enter Hamlet and Horatio.

Ham. So much for this, sir; now shall you see the other.

Hor. Remember it, my lord!

Ham. Sir, in my heart there was a kind of fighting

    And prais'd be rashness for it; let us know,

    Our indiscretion sometime serves us well

    When our deep plots do pall; and that should learn us

    There's a divinity that shapes our ends,

    Rough-hew them how we will-

Hor. If your mind dislike anything, obey it. I will forestall their

    repair hither and say you are not fit.

Ham. Not a whit, we defy augury; there's a special providence in the fall of a sparrow. Since no man knows aught of what he leaves, what is't to leave betimes? Let be.

Enter King, Queen, Laertes, Osric, and Lords, with other Attendants with foils and gauntlets. A table and flagons of wine on it.

King. Come, Hamlet, come, and take this hand from me.

    [*The King puts Laertes' hand into Hamlet's.*]

Ham. Give me your pardon, sir. I have done you wrong;

Laer. I stand aloof, and will no reconcilement

Ham. Give us the foils. Come on.

King. Give them the foils, young Osric. Cousin Hamlet,

    You know the wager?

Ham. Very well, my lord.

Laer. This is too heavy; let me see another.

Ham. This likes me well. These foils have all a length?

    Prepare to play.

Osr. Ay, my good lord.

King. Set me the stoups of wine upon that table.

Ham. Come on, sir.

Laer. Come, my lord.

They play.

Ham. One.

Laer. No.

Ham. Judgment!

Osr. A hit, a very palpable hit.

Laer. Well, again!

King. Stay, give me drink. Hamlet, this pearl is thine;

    Here's to thy health.

    [Drum; trumpets sound]

    Give him the cup.

Ham. I'll play this bout first; set it by awhile.

    Come. [*They play.*] Another hit. What say you?

Laer. A touch, a touch; I do confess't.

King. Our son shall win.

Queen. The Queen carouses to thy fortune, Hamlet.

Ham. Good madam!

King. Gertrude, do not drink.

Queen. I will, my lord; I pray you pardon me. *Drinks.*

King. [*aside*] It is the poison'd cup; it is too late.

Queen. Come, let me wipe thy face.

Laertes wounds Hamlet; then in scuffling, they change rapiers, and Hamlet wounds Laertes.

King. Part them! They are incens'd.

Ham. Nay come! Again!

The Queen falls.

Ham. How does the Queen?

King. She swoons to see them bleed.

Queen. No, no! The drink, the drink! I am poison'd. *Dies.*

Ham. O villany! Treachery! Seek it out.

Laertes falls.

Laer. Hamlet, thou art slain;

    No medicine in the world can do thee good.

    Unbated and envenom'd. The foul practice

    Hath turn'd itself on me. Lo, here I lie,

    Never to rise again. Thy mother's poison'd.

    I can no more. The King, the King's to blame.

Ham. The point envenom'd too?

    Then, venom, to thy work. *Hurts the King.*

All. Treason! treason!

King. O, yet defend me, friends! I am but hurt.

Ham. Here, thou incestuous, murd'rous, damned Dane,

    Drink off this potion! Is thy union here?

    Follow my mother. *King dies.*

Laer. He is justly serv'd.

    It is a poison temper'd by himself.

    Exchange forgiveness with me, noble Hamlet.

    Mine and my father's death come not upon thee,

    Nor thine on me! *Dies.*

Ham. Had I but time (as this fell sergeant, Death,

    Is strict in his arrest) O, I could tell you-

    But let it be. Horatio, I am dead;

    Thou liv'st; report me and my cause aright

    To the unsatisfied.

    Absent thee from felicity awhile,

    And in this harsh world draw thy breath in pain,

    To tell my story.

March afar off, and shot within.

    O, I die, Horatio!

    The rest is silence. *Dies.*

Hor. Good night, sweet prince,

    And flights of angels sing thee to thy rest!

Enter Fortinbras and others with Drum, Colours, and Attendants.

Fort. Where is this sight?

Hor. What is it you will see?

Fort. Let four captains

    Bear Hamlet like a soldier to the stage;

    For he was likely, had he been put on,

    To have prov'd most royally; and for his passage

    The soldiers' music and the rites of war

    Speak loudly for him.

Take up the bodies. Such a sight as this
Becomes the field but here shows much amiss.
Go, bid the soldiers shoot.

Exeunt marching; after the which a peal of ordnance are shot off.

THE END

Don Quixote
(*El ingenioso hidalgo don Quijote de la Mancha*)
By Miguel De Cervantes
(Madrid, 1604)

This is often considered to be the first modern novel, and the founding text of Spanish writing. In a poll of 2002 organised by the Nobel Institute, 100 leading authors including John le Carre, Doris Lessing, Seamus Heaney and Salman Rushdie selected *Don Quixote* as the best work of fiction *ever*.

Based on the translation by John Ormsby. Abridged: GH

I. Which treats of The Knight of La Mancha

In a certain village of La Mancha, which name I do not want to remember, there lived one of those old-fashioned gentlemen who keep a lance in the rack, an ancient target, a lean horse, and a greyhound for coursing. He had an olla of rather more beef than mutton, a salad on most nights, scraps on Saturdays, lentils on Fridays, and a pigeon or so extra on Sundays. His family consisted of a housekeeper turned forty, a niece not twenty, and a man who could saddle a horse, handle the pruning-hook, and also serve in the house. The master himself was nigh fifty years of age, lean-bodied and thin-faced, an early riser, and a great lover of hunting. His surname was Quixada, or Quesada.

You must know now that when our gentleman had nothing to do- which was almost all the year round- he read books on knight-errantry, and with such delight that he almost left off his sports, and even sold acres of land to buy these books. He would dispute with the curate of the parish, and with the barber, as to the best knight in the world. At nights he read these romances until it was day; a-day he would read until it was night. Thus, by reading much and sleeping little, he lost the use of his reason. His brain was full of nothing but enchantments, quarrels, battles, challenges, wounds, amorous plaints, torments, and abundance of impossible follies.

And, having lost his wits, he stumbled on the oddest fancy that ever entered madman's brain - to turn knight-errant himself, mount his steed, and ride through the world, redressing grievances, and exposing himself to every danger, that he might purchase everlasting honour and renown.

The first thing he did was to secure a suit of armour that had belonged to his great-grandfather. But he perceived one great defect in it, that it had no helmet. This deficiency his ingenuity supplied, by making one of pasteboard, which his sword demolished at the first stroke. After repairing this mischief, he went to visit his horse, whose bones stuck out, but who appeared to his master a finer beast than Alexander's Bucephalus. After four days of thought, he decided to call his horse Rozinante, and when the title was decided upon, he spent eight days more before he arrived at Don Quixote as a name for himself.

Now, he knew that a knight-errant needed a lady on whom he might bestow the empire of his heart. As he said to himself, "If, by my good fortune, I come across some giant, a common occurrence with knights-errant, and vanquish him, will it not be well to have some one I may send him to as a present, that he may fall on his knees before my sweet lady, and say, 'I am the giant Caraculiambro, lord of the island of Malindrania, vanquished in single combat by the never sufficiently extolled knight Don Quixote of La Mancha.

There lived close at hand a hard-working country lass, Aldonza Lorenzo, on whom sometimes he had cast an eye, but who was quite unmindful of the gentleman. Her he selected for his peerless lady, and dubbed her with the sweet-sounding name of Dulcinea del Toboso.

II. Which treats of an Adventure in a Courtyard

One morning, in the hottest part of July, with great secrecy, he armed himself, mounted Rozinante, and rode out of his backyard into the open fields. He was disturbed to think that the honour of knighthood had not yet been conferred upon him, but determined to rectify this matter at an early opportunity, and rode on soliloquising, after the manner of knight-errants, as happy as a man might be.

Towards evening he arrived at a common inn, before whose door sat two wenches, the companions of some carriers bound for Seville. Don Quixote instantly fancied the inn to be a castle, and the wenches to be fair ladies taking the air. He expected that some dwarf would show himself upon the battlements, and by sound of trumpet give notice that a knight was approaching the castle. But seeing that they were slow about it, he made for the inn door.

Raising his pasteboard visor, he addressed the wenches, "You high-born maidens need fear no rudeness, for that belongs not to the order of knighthood which I profess." The girls laughed to be called 'maidens', which was unusual in their line of work. Don Quixote rebuked them, whereat they laughed the more, and only the innkeeper's appearance prevented the knight's indignation from carrying him to extremities. This man was for peace, and welcomed the strange apparition to his inn with all civility, marvelling much to find himself addressed as Sir Castellan. So the knight sat down to supper with strange company, and discoursed of chivalry to the bewilderment of all present, treating the inn as a castle, the host as a noble gentleman, and the wenches as great ladies.

He presently sought the innkeeper alone in the stable, and, kneeling, requested to be dubbed a knight, vowing that he would not move from that place till 'twas done. The host guessed the distraction of his visitor and complied, counselling Don Quixote- who had never read of such things in books of chivalry- to provide himself henceforth with money and clean shirts, and no longer to ride penniless. That night Don Quixote watched his arms by moonlight, laying them upon the horse-trough in the yard of the inn, while from a distance the innkeeper and his guests watched the gaunt man, now leaning on his lance, and now walking to and fro, with his target on his arm.

It chanced that a carrier came to water his mules, and was about to remove the armour, when Don Quixote in a loud voice called him to desist. The man took no notice, and Don Quixote, calling upon his Dulcinea to assist him, lifted his lance and brought it down on the carrier's pate, laying him flat. A second carrier came, and was treated in like manner; but now all the company of them came, and with showers of stones made a terrible assault upon the knight. It was only the interference of the innkeeper that put an end to this battle, and by careful words he was able to appease Don Quixote's wrath and get him out of the inn.

On his way the now happy knight found a farmer beating a boy, and bidding him desist, inquired the reason of this chastisement. The man, afraid of the strange armoured figure, told how this boy did his work badly in the field, and deserved his flogging; but the boy declared that the farmer owed him wages, and that whenever he asked for them his master flogged him. Sternly did the Don command the man to pay the lad's wages, and when the fellow promised to do so directly he got home, and the boy protested that he would surely never keep that promise, Don Quixote threatened the farmer, saying, "I am the valorous Don Quixote of La Mancha, righter of wrongs, revenger and redresser of grievances; remember what you have promised and sworn, as you will answer the contrary at your peril." Convinced that the man dare not disobey, he rode forward, and the farmer very soon continued his flogging of the boy.

A company of merchants approaching caused Don Quixote to halt in the middle of the road, calling upon them to stand until they acknowledged Dulcinea del Toboso to be the peerless beauty of the world. This challenge was met with prevarication, which enraged Don Quixote, and clapping spurs to Rozinante he bore down upon the company with his lance couched.

A stumble of the horse threw him, and as he lay on the ground, unable to move, one of the servants of the company came up and broke the lance across Don Quixote's ribs. It was not until a countryman came by that the Don was extricated, and then he had to ride back to his own village on the ass of the poor labourer, being so stiff and sore as quite incapable to mount Rozinante.

The curate and the barber, seeing now what havoc romances of chivalry were making in the wits of this good gentleman, ran through his library while he lay wounded in bed, burned all his noxious works, and, securely locking the door, prepared the tale that enchantment had carried away the books and the very chamber itself.

None of the entreaties of his niece, nor the remonstrances of his housekeeper, could stay Don Quixote at home, and he soon prepared for a second sally. He persuaded a good, honest country labourer, Sancho Panza by name, to enter his service as squire, promising him for reward the first island or empire which his lance should happen to conquer. Thus did things happen in books of chivalry, and he did not doubt that thus it would happen with him.

III. Which treats of The Immortal Partnership

So it came to pass that one night Don Quixote stole away from his home, and Sancho Panza from his wife and children, and with the master on Rozinante, the servant on his ass, Dapple, hastened away under cover of darkness in search of adventures. As they travelled, "I beseech your worship," quoth Sancho, "be sure you forget not your promise of the island; for, I dare swear, I shall make shift to govern it, let it be never so big." The knight, in a rhapsody, foreshadowed the day when Sancho might be made even a king, for in romances of chivalry there is no limit to the gifts made by valorous knights to their faithful squires. But Sancho shook his head. "Though it rain kingdoms on the face of the earth, not one of them would fit well upon the head of my wife; for, I must needs tell you, she is not worth two brass-jacks to make a queen of."

As they were thus discoursing they espied some thirty windmills in the plain, which Don Quixote instantly took for giants. Nothing that Sancho said could dissuade him, and he must needs clap spurs to his horse and ride a-tilt at these great windmills, recommending himself to his lady Dulcinea. As he ran his lance into the sail of the first mill, the wind whirled about with such swiftness that the motion broke the lance into shivers, and hurled away both knight and horse along with it. When Sancho came upon his master the Don explained that some cursed necromancer had converted those giants into windmills to deprive him of the honour of victory.

When the knight was recovered they continued their way, and their next adventure was to meet two monks on mules riding before a coach, with four or five men on horseback, wherein sat a lady going to Seville to meet her husband. Don Quixote rode forward, addressed the monks as "cursed implements of hell," and bade them instantly release the lovely princess in the coach. The monks flew for their lives as Don Quixote charged down upon them, but Sancho was thrown down by the servants, who tore his beard, trampled his stomach, beat and mauled him in every part of his body, and then left him sprawling without breath or motion.

As for Don Quixote, he came off victor in this conflict, and only desisted from slaying his assailant on the plea of the lady in the coach, and on her promise that the conquered man should present himself before the peerless Dulcinea del Toboso. The recovered Sancho was surprised to find that his master had no island to bestow upon him after this incredible victory, wherein he himself had suffered so disastrously.

In a fierce encounter with some Yanguesian carriers, Don Quixote was wounded almost to death, and he explained to Sancho that his defeat he owed to fighting with common people, bidding Sancho in future to fight himself against such common fellows.

"Sir," said Sancho, "I am a peaceful man, a quiet fellow, do you see; I can make shift to forgive injuries as well as any man, as having a wife to maintain, and children to bring up. I freely forgive all mankind, high and low, lords and beggars, whatsoever wrongs they ever did or may do me, without the least exception."

At the next inn they came upon Don Quixote, who was lying prone on Sancho's ass, groaning in pain, vowed that here was a worthy castle. Sancho swore 'twas an inn. Their dispute lasted till they reached the door, where Sancho marched straight in, without troubling himself any further in the matter. It was here that surprising adventures took place. The knight, Sancho, and a carrier were obliged to share one chamber. The maid of the inn, entering this apartment, was mistaken by Don Quixote for the princess of the castle, and taking her in his arms, he poured out a rhapsody to the virtues of Dulcinea del Toboso. The carrier resented this, and in a moment the place was in an uproar. Such a fight never took place before, and when it was over both the knight and the squire were as near dead as men can be. To right himself, Don Quixote concocted a balsam of which he had read, and drinking it off, presently was so grievously ill that he was like to cast up his heart and liver.

Being got to bed again, he felt sure that he was now invulnerable, and he woke early next day, eager to sally forth. When the host asked for his reckoning, "How! Is this an inn?" quoth the Don. "Yes, and one of the best on the road." "How strangely have I been mistaken then! Upon my honour, I took it for a castle, and a considerable one, too." Saying which, he added that knights never yet paid for the honour they conferred in lying at any man's house, and so rode away. But poor Sancho Panza did not get off scot free, for they tossed him in a blanket in the backyard, where the Don could see the torture over the wall, but could by no means get to the rescue of his squire.

When they were together again, the gallant Don comforted poor Sancho Panza with hopes of an island, and explained away all their sufferings on the grounds of necromancy. All that had gone awry with them was the work of some cursed enchanters.

Their next adventure was begun by a cloud of dust on the horizon, which instantly made Don Quixote exclaim that a great battle was in progress. A nearer view revealed that the dust rose from a huge flock of sheep; but the knight's blood was up, and he rode forward as fast as poor Rozinante could carry him, and did frightful slaughter among the sheep, till the stones of the shepherd brought him to the earth. "Lord save us!" cried Sancho, as he assisted the Don to his feet. "Your worship has left on his lower side only two grinders, and on the upper not one."

Later, they came upon a company of priests, with lighted tapers, carrying a corpse through the night. Don Quixote charged them, brought one of the company to the ground, and scattered the rest. Sancho Panza, whose stomach cried cupboard, filled his wallet with the rich provisions of the priests, boasting to the wounded man that his master was the redoubtable Don Quixote of La Mancha, otherwise called the Knight of the Sorrowful Countenance. When the adventure was over, Don Quixote questioned his squire on this name, and Sancho replied, "I have been staring upon you this pretty while by the light of that unlucky priest's torch, and may I never stir if ever I set eyes on a more dismal countenance in my born days."

The next enterprise was with a barber, who carried his new brass basin on his head, so that it suggested to Don Quixote the famous helmet of Mambrino. Accordingly, he bore down upon the barber, put him to flight, and possessed himself of the basin, which he wore as a helmet. More serious was the following adventure, when Don Quixote released from the king's officers a gang of galley slaves, because they assured him that they travelled chained much against their will. So gallantly did the knight behave, that he conquered the officers and left them all but dead. Nevertheless, coming to an argument with the released convicts, whom he would have sent to his lady Dulcinea, he himself, and Sancho, too, were as mauled by the convicts as even those self-same officers.

It now came to Don Quixote that he must perform a penance in the mountains, and sending Sancho with a letter to Dulcinea, he divested himself of much of his armour and underwear, and performed the maddest gambols and self-tortures ever witnessed under a blue sky.

However, it chanced that Sancho Panza soon fell in with the curate and the barber of Don Quixote's village, and these good friends, by a cunning subterfuge, in which a beautiful young lady played a part, got Don Quixote safely home and into his own bed. The lady, affecting great distress, had made Don Quixote vow to enter upon no adventure until he had righted a wrong done against herself; and one night, as they journeyed on this mission, a great cage was made and placed over Don Quixote as he slept, and thus, persuaded that necromancy was at work against, him, the valiant knight was borne back a prisoner to his home.

IV. Which treats of Sancho and His Island

Nothing short of a prison cell could keep Don Quixote from his sallies, and soon he was on the road again, accompanied by his faithful squire. To Sancho, who believed his master mad, and whose chief aim in life was filling his own stomach, these adventures of the Don had but one end, the governorship of the promised island. While he thought the knight mad, he believed in him; and while he was selfish, he loved his master, as the tale tells.

It chanced that one day they came upon a frolicsome duke and duchess who had heard of their adventures, and who instantly set themselves to enjoy so rare a sport as that offered by the entertainment of the knight and his squire. The Don was invited to the duke's castle as a mighty hero, and there treated with all possible honour; but some tricks were played upon him which were certainly unworthy of the duke's courtesy. Nevertheless, this visit had the happiest culmination, since it was from the hands of the duke that Sancho at last received his governorship. Making pretence that a certain town on his estate, named Barataria, was an island, the duke dispatched Sancho to govern it; and after an affecting farewell with his master, who gave him the wisest possible advice on the subject of statecraft, Sancho set out in a glittering cavalcade to take up his governorship, with his beloved Dapple led behind.

After a magnificent entry into the city, Sancho Panza was called upon to give judgement in certain teasing disputes, and this he did with such wit and such wholesome common-sense that he delighted all who heard him. Well-pleased with himself, he sat down in a grand hall to a solitary banquet, with a physician standing by his side. No sooner had Sancho tasted a dish than the physician touched it with a wand, and a page bore it swiftly away. At first Sancho was confounded by this interference with his appetite, but presently he grew bold and expostulated; whereupon the physician said that his mission was to overlook the governor's health, and to see that he ate nothing which was prejudicial to his physical well-being, since the happiness of the state depended upon the health of its governor. Sancho bore it for some time, but at length, starting up, he bade the physician avaunt, saying, "By the sun's light, I'll get me a good cudgel, and beginning with your carcase, will so belabour all the physic-mongers in the island, that I will not leave one of the tribe. Let me eat, or let them take their government again; for an office that will not afford a man his victuals is not worth two horse beans."

At that moment there came a messenger from the duke, sweating, and with concern in his looks, who pulled a packet from his bosom and presented it to the governor. This message from the duke was to warn Sancho that a furious enemy intended to attack his island, and that he must be on his guard. "I have also the intelligence," wrote the duke, "from faithful spies, that there are four men got into the town in disguise to murder you, your abilities being regarded as a great obstacle to the enemy's design.

Take heed how you admit strangers to speak with you, and eat nothing that is laid before you."

Sancho set out to inspect his defences; but with every step he took he was confronted by some problem of government on which he was called upon to adjudicate. Harassed by these appeals, and half famished, our governor began to think that governorship was the sorriest trade on earth, and before a week was over he addressed to Don Quixote a letter, concluding, "Heaven preserve you from ill-minded enchanters, and send me safe and sound out of this government." One night he was awakened by the clanging of a great bell, and in came servants crying in affright that the enemy was approaching. Sancho rose, and was adjured by his subjects to lead them forth against their terrible foes. He asked for food, and declared that he knew nothing of arms. They rebuked him, and bringing him shields and a lance, proceeded to tie him up so tightly with shields behind and shields before that he could scarcely move. Then they bade him march, and lead on the army. "March!" quoth he. "These bonds stick so plaguey close that I cannot so much as bend my knees!" "For shame!" they answered. "It is fear and not armour that stiffens your legs." Thus rebuked, Sancho endeavoured to move, but fell flat on the earth like a great tortoise; while in the darkness the others made a clash with their swords and shields, and trampled upon the prone governor, who quite gave himself up for dead. But at break of day they raised a cry of "Victory!" and, lifting Sancho up, told him that their enemies were driven off.

To this he said nothing save to ask for his old clothes. And when he was dressed he went down to Dapple's stall, and embraced his faithful ass with tears in his eyes. "Come hither, my friend and true companion," quoth he; "happy were my days, my months, and years, when with thee I journeyed, and all my concern was to mend thy harness and find food for thy little stomach! But now that I have climbed to the towers of ambition, a thousand woes, a thousand torments, and four thousand tribulations have haunted my soul!" While he spoke he fitted on the pack-saddle, mounted his ass, bade farewell to the people, and departed in peace and great humility.

V. Which treats of The End of Don Quixote

Meanwhile, Don Quixote had been fooled to the top of his bent in the duke's castle, and had endured tribulations from maids and men sufficient to deject the finest fortitude. He was now in the mood to forsake that great castle, and to embrace once more the life of the open road, and so with Sancho Panza he started out to take up the threads of his old life. After adventures so miraculous as to seem incredible, Don Quixote was laid low in an encounter with a friend of his disguised as a knight, and by this defeat was so broken and humiliated that he thought to turn shepherd and to spend the remainder of his days in a pastoral life. Sancho cheered him, and kept his heart as high as it would reach in his misery, and together they turned their faces towards home, leaving the future to the disposition of Providence.

As they entered the village, two boys fighting in a field attracted the knight's attention, and he heard one of them cry, "Never fret yourself, you shall never see her while you have breath in your body!" The knight immediately applied these words to himself and Dulcinea, and nothing that Sancho could say had power to cheer his spirits. Moreover, the boys of the village, having seen them, raised a shout, and came laughing about them, saying, "Oh, law! here is Gaffer Sancho Panza's donkey as fine as a lady, and Don Quixote's beast thinner than ever!" The barber and the curate then came upon the scene and saw their old friend, and went with him to his house.

Here Don Quixote faithfully described his discomfiture in the encounter with another knight, and declared his intention honourably to observe the conditions laid upon him of being confined to his village for a year.

Melancholy increased with the poor knight, and he was seized with a violent fever. The physician and his friends conjectured that his sickness arose from regret for his defeat and disappointment of Dulcinea's disenchantment; they did all they could do to divert him, but in vain. One day he desired them to leave him, and for six hours he slept so profoundly that his niece thought he was dead. At the end of this time he wakened, and cried with a loud voice, "Blessed be Almighty God for this great benefit He has vouchsafed to me! His mercies are infinite; greater are they than the sins of men."

These rational words surprised his niece, and she asked what he meant by them. He answered that by God's mercy his judgment had returned, free and clear. "The cloud of ignorance," said he, "is now removed, which continuous reading of those noxious books of knight-errantry had laid upon me." He said that his great grief now was the lateness with which enlightenment had come, leaving him so little time to prepare his soul for death.

The others coming in, Don Quixote made his confession, and one went to fetch Sancho Panza. With tears in his eyes the squire sought his poor master's side, and when in the first clause of his will Don Quixote made mention of Sancho, saying afterwards, "Pardon me, my friend, that I brought upon you the shame of my madness," Sancho cried out, "Woe's me, your worship, do not die this bout; take my counsel, and live many a good year. For it is the maddest trick a man can play in his whole life to go out like the snuff of a candle, and die merely of the mulligrubs!"

The others admonished him in like spirit, but Don Quixote answered and said, "Gently, sirs! do not look in last year's nests for the birds of this year. I was mad, but now I have my reason. I was Don Quixote of La Mancha; but to-day I am Alonso Quixano the Good. I hope that my repentance and my sincerity will restore me to the esteem that once you had for me. And now let Master Notary proceed." So he finished writing his will, and then fell into a swooning fit, and lay full length in his bed. But he lingered some days, and when he did give up the ghost, or to speak more plainly, when he died, it was amidst the tears and lamentations of his family, and after he had received the last sacrament, and had expressed, in pathetic way, his horror at the books of chivalry.

The Advancement of Learning
By Sir Francis Bacon
(London, 1605)

Bacon entered Trinity College, Cambridge, at the age of 12, and became Lord Chancellor of England under James I. Here is the book in which he effectively founded the modern, experimental, scientific, approach to understanding. Before Bacon, 'learning' largely meant memorizing the classics, especially Aristotle (p62), and acceding to every diktat of established religion (p88). In *The Advancement of Learning*, he argued that the only knowledge of importance was that which could be discovered by observation- 'empirical' knowledge rooted in the natural world.

Abridged: GH

THE FIRST BOOK
To the King

THERE were under the law, excellent King, from their servants both tribute of duty and presents of affection. God hath given your Majesty a composition of understanding admirable, being able to compass and comprehend the greatest matters. Therefore I did conclude that I could not make unto your Majesty a better oblation than of some Treatise concerning the excellency of Learning and Knowledge.

Salomon gives a censure, HE THAT INCREASETH KNOWLEDGE INCREASETH ANXIETY, and St. Paul gives THAT WE BE NOT SPOILED THROUGH VAIN PHILOSOPHY.

To discover the error of this opinion, it was not the pure knowledge of nature which gave the occasion to the fall: but it was the proud knowledge of good and evil. There is no vexation or anxiety of mind which resulteth from knowledge, for all knowledge and wonder (which is the seed of knowledge) is an impression of pleasure in itself. And as for the conceit that too much knowledge should incline a man to Atheism, a little or superficial knowledge of Philosophy may incline man to Atheism, but a further proceeding therein doth bring the mind back again to Religion.

Let no man upon a weak conceit of sobriety or an ill-applied moderation think or maintain, that a man can search too far, or be too well studied in the book of God's word, or in the book of God's works; divinity or philosophy: but rather let men not mingle or confound these learnings together.

That Learning should dispose men to leisure, or undermine the reverence of laws, is assuredly without shadow of truth. There may be a sort of discredit that groweth unto Learning from learned men themselves, for no doubt there be amongst them, as in other professions, men of all temperatures.

Martin Luther was enforced to awake antiquity, so that the ancient authors, which had long time slept in libraries, began generally to be read and revolved, and thus did bring in an affectionate study of eloquence which grew speedily to an excess.

Yet the strength of all sciences is, as the strength of the old man's fagot of sticks, in the band that binds them. For the harmony of a science, supporting each part the other, is and ought to be the true confutation of all the smaller sort of objections. But, on the other side, if you take out every axiom, one by one, you may quarrel with them, and bend them, and break them at your pleasure.

Another error hath proceeded from a kind of adoration of the mind and understanding of man; by means whereof men have withdrawn themselves away from the contemplation of nature, and the observations of experience, and have tumbled up and down in their own reason and conceits. Upon these Heraclitus gave a just censure, saying, MEN SOUGHT TRUTH IN THEIR OWN LITTLE WORLDS, AND NOT IN THE GREAT AND COMMON WORLD.

Another error is impatience without mature suspension of judgement. If a man will begin with certainties, he shall end in doubts; but if he will be content to begin with doubts, he shall end in certainties. The end ought to be to preserve and augment whatsoever is solid and fruitful: that knowledge may not be, as a courtesan, for pleasure only, or as a **bondwoman**; but as a spouse, for generation, fruit, and comfort.

VI: First, let us seek the dignity of knowledge in the in the attributes and acts of God, as revealed to man.

Dionysius of Athens gives first place to the angels of Love, termed Seraphim; the second to the angels of Light, termed Cherubim; and the third to Thrones, Principalities, and the rest; so as the angels of Knowledge and Illumination are placed before the angels of Office and Domination.

We read the first Form that was created was Light. The first acts which man performed in Paradise consisted of the two summary parts of knowledge; the view of creatures, and the imposition of names.

In the age before the flood, the holy records honour the inventors and authors of music and works in metal. Moses the lawgiver[1] was learned in ALL THE LEARNING OF THE EGYPTIANS. Likewise that excellent book of Job will be found pregnant with natural philosophy; as, for example, cosmography, and the roundness of the world. So likewise Salomon the King became enabled not only to write Parables or Aphorisms concerning moral philosophy; but also to compile a Natural History of all verdure, from the cedar to the moss upon the wall, (which is but a rudiment between putrefaction and a herb,) and also of all things that breathe or move.

Our Saviour Himself did show His power to subdue ignorance by His conference with the priests and doctors of the law. Many of the ancient Bishops and Fathers of the Church were excellently read and studied in the learning of the heathen

Wherefore, there be two duties which philosophy and learning do perform to faith and religion. The one, because they are an effectual inducement to the exaltation of the glory of God: the other, because they minister a singular preservative against unbelief and error.

VII: According to that which the Grecians call APOTHEOSIS, inventors and authors of new arts were consecrated amongst the gods themselves; as were Ceres, Bacchus, Mercurius, Apollo, and others.

For although he might be thought partial to his own profession, he that said, THEN SHOULD PEOPLE AND ESTATES BE HAPPY, WHEN EITHER KINGS WERE PHILOSOPHERS, OR PHILOSOPHERS KINGS, yet so much is verified by experience, that under learned princes and governors there have been ever the best times.

Trajan was not learned: but was a great admirer and benefactor of learning; a founder of famous libraries. Adrian, his successor, was the most universal inquirer. But in my judgement the most excellent is that of Queen Elizabeth, your majestey's immediate predecessor. This lady was endued with learning great even amongst masculine princes; and unto the very last year of her life she was accustomed to appoint set hours for reading.

Alexander was bred and taught under Aristotle[2]. As for Julius Caesar, the excellency of his learning doth declare itself in his writings and works.

VIII: To proceed now to moral virtue: knowledge taketh away the wildness, barbarism and fierceness of men's minds. It taketh away levity, temerity, and insolency. It taketh away vain admiration, which is the root of all weakness. No man can marvel at the play of puppets, that goeth behind the curtain, and adviseth himself well of the motion.

So certainly, if a man meditate much upon the universal frame of nature, the earth with men upon it will not seem much other than an ant-hill, whereas some ants carry corn,

---

1   **Moses:** see p23
2   **Aristotle:** see p62

and some carry their young, and some go empty, and all to-and-fro a little heap of dust.

Knowledge investeth and crowneth man's nature. By learning man excelleth in that wherein man excelleth beasts; that by learning man ascendeth to the heavens, where in body he cannot come.

The dignity and excellency of knowledge and learning brings that whereunto man's nature doth most aspire, which is, immortality. For have not the verses of Homer continued twenty-five hundred years without the loss of a syllable; during which time infinite temples, castles and cities have decayed? The images of men's wits remain in books, exempted from the wrong of time, to cast their seeds in the minds of others, across the succeeding ages. If the invention of the ship was thought noble, which carrieth riches to the most remote regions, how much more are letters to be magnified, which, as ships, pass through the vast seas of time, that ages distant may participate of the wisdom and inventions, the one of the other?

Nevertheless it will be impossible for me to reverse the judgement of Aesop's Cock[3], that preferred the barleycorn before the gem. But: JUSTIFICATA EST SAPIENTIA A FILIIS SUIS[4].

THE SECOND BOOK

It remaineth to consider what kind of acts are to be performed by kings and others for the increase and advancement of learning.

The works towards learning are about three objects: the places of learning, the books of learning, and the persons of the learned.

The works concerning the places of learning are four; foundations and buildings, endowments with revenues, endowments with franchises and privileges, institutions and government.

The works touching books are two: first, libraries, which are the shrines where the relics of ancient saints are preserved and reposed: secondly, new editions of authors, with more correct impressions, more faithful translations, more profitable glosses, more diligent annotations, and the like.

The works pertaining to the persons of learned men are two: the reward and designation of readers in sciences already invented; and the reward and designation of inquirers concerning any parts of learning not sufficiently prosecuted.

First, amongst the colleges in Europe, I find it strange that they are all dedicated to professions, and none left free to arts and sciences at large, and this hath hindered the progression of learning. Hence it proceedeth that princes find no able men to serve them.

And because Founders of Colleges do plant, and Founders of Lectures do water, it followeth well to consider the smallness and meanness of the salary which is assigned unto them.

Another defect I note, that unto the deep and fruitful study of sciences, books be not the only instrumentals; for we see globes, astrolabes, maps, and the like, provided to astronomy: likewise some places have gardens for simples, and command the use of dead bodies for anatomies. In general, there will hardly be any disclosing of nature, except there be some allowance for experiments; whether they be appertaining to Vulcanus or Daedalus, furnace or engine. So you must allow the spials[5] and intelligencers of nature to bring in their bills; or else you shall be ill advertised.

I find the exercises used in the Universities do make too great a divorce between invention and memory; for their speeches are either premeditate, where nothing is left to invention, or merely extemporal, where little is left to memory: whereas in active life there is rather an intermixture of both.

Another defect which I note, ascendeth a little higher; knowledge would be yet more advanced, if there were more intelligence mutual between the Universities of Europe than now there is.

I: THE parts of human learning have reference to the three parts of man's understanding: history to his memory, poesy[6] to his imagination, and philosophy to his reason.

I am not ignorant that some sciences, as of the jurisconsults and the mathematicians, have set down memorials. But a just story of learning, the originals of knowledges and the sects, their inventions, traditions, their flourishings and decays throughout the ages, I may truly affirm to be wanting.

As to those histories of marvels, of sorceries, witchcrafts, and the like, I am not of the opinion that they be altogether excluded. But I hold fit that these narrations be sorted by themselves, and not be mingled with the narrations which are sincerely natural.

For history of nature wrought or mechanical, I find some collections made of agriculture, and of manual arts; but it is esteemed a kind of dishonour unto learning to descend to inquiry upon matters mechanical. But the truth is, it be not the highest instances that give the securest information. He that enquireth into the nature of a great Commonwealth, must find it first in a family, and the simple conjugations of man and wife, which are in every cottage. So we see how that secret of nature, of the turning of iron touched with the loadstone towards the north, was found out in needles of iron, not in bars of iron.

If my judgement be of any weight, the use of history mechanical is of all others the most radical and

---

3 **Aesop's Cock:** see p39
4 JUSTIFICATA EST SAPIENTIA A FILIIS SUIS: "Wisdom is justified of her children"

5 Spials: Spies, secret discoverers
6 Poesy: Poetry, imaginative writing.

fundamental towards natural philosophy and to the endowment and benefit of man's life.

II: As for civil history, it is not unfitly to be compared with the three kinds of pictures; some are unfinished, some are perfect, and some are defaced. History is of three kinds: for it either representeth a time, or a person, or an actions. The first we call chronicles, the second lives, and the third narrations. But for modern histories, the greater part are beneath mediocrity.

There is another portion of history, which Cornelius Tacitus maketh, namely, annals and journals. I cannot likewise be ignorant of a form of writing which some wise and grave men have used, containing a scattered history with politic discourse and observation; which kind of ruminated history I think more fit to place amongst books of policy.

IV: Poesy is a part of learning which doth truly refer to the imagination. Because the acts or events of true history have not that magnitude which satisfieth the mind of man, poesy feigneth acts and events greater and more heroical. In poesy I can report no deficience, for it is a plant which has sprung up and spread abroad more than any other kind. But it is not good to stay too long in the theatre. Let us now pass on to the palace of the mind, which we are to view with more reverence and attention.

V: In Philosophy, the contemplations of man do either penetrate unto God, or are reflected upon himself. Out of which does arise three forms; divine philosophy, natural philosophy, and human philosophy or humanity. These forms are like branches of a tree, that meet in a stem: therefore it is good that we erect and constitute one universal science, by the name of PHILOSOPHIA PRIMA[7], as the receptacle for all profitable observations and axioms as fall not within the compass of any of the special parts of philosophy or sciences, but are more common and of a higher stage.

This science I may justly report as deficient; for I see sometimes the profounder sort of wits now and then draw a bucket of water out of this well; but the spring-head thereof seemeth to me not to have been visited.

VI: Divine philosophy is that knowledge, or rudiment of knowledge, concerning God. In this part of knowledge, I am so far from noting any deficience, as I rather note an excess: where both religion and philosophy, being commixed together, will make an heretical religion, and an imaginary and fabulous philosophy.

VII: We will now proceed to natural philosophy.

If it be true that Democritus said, THAT THE TRUTH OF NATURE LIETH HID IN CERTAIN DEEP MINES AND CAVES, it were good to divide natural philosophy into the mine and the furnace: some to be pioneers and some smiths; some to dig, and some to refine and hammer.

Because all true and fruitful natural philosophy hath a double scale or ladder; ascending from experiments to the invention of causes, and descending from causes to the invention of new experiments; therefore I judge it that these two parts be severally considered.

Natural science or theory is divided into physique and metaphysique: and I intend PHILOSOPHIA PRIMA or Summary Philosophy to be the common principles and axioms which are promiscuous and indifferent to several sciences.

Physique should contemplate that which is inherent in matter, and therefore transitory; and Metaphysique that which is abstracted and fixed. Physique, inquireth and handleth the material and scient[8] causes; and Metaphysique handleth the formal and final causes.

There is some received and inveterate opinion that the inquisition of man is not competent to find out essential Forms or true differences. Yet, they are ill discoverers that think there is no land, when they can see nothing but sea.

VIII: There remaineth yet another part of Natural Philosophy, which is Mathematique; but I think it more agreeable to place it as a branch of Metaphysique.

In Mathematics I can report no deficience, except it be that men do not sufficiently understand the excellent use of the Pure Mathematics. As tennis is a game of no use in itself, but it maketh a quick eye and a supple body; so the Mathematics which is collateral and intervenient is no less worthy than that which is principal and intended. And as for the Mixed Mathematics, I may only make this prediction, that there cannot fail to be more kinds of them, as nature grows further disclosed.

As for Natural Magic, Alchemy, Astrology, and the like, containing certain credulous and superstitious conceits and frivolous experiments; it is as far differing from truth as the story of King Arthur is from Caesar's Commentaries.[9]

There ought be made a kalendar, or inventory, containing all the inventions, works or fruits of nature or art, which are now extant, and a note of what things are yet held impossible, or not invented. For the mariner's needle, which giveth the direction, is of no less benefit for navigation than the invention of the sails which give the motion.

IX: We come therefore now to that knowledge which is the KNOWLEDGE OF OURSELVES. This knowledge is but a portion of natural philosophy: and generally let this be a rule, that all partitions of knowledges be accepted; that the continuance and entireness of knowledge be preserved. The science of medicine, if it be forsaken by natural philosophy, it is not much better than an empirical practice.

X: The knowledge that concerneth the good of man's body is of four kinds, Health, Beauty, Strength, and Pleasure: so the knowledges are Medicine, or art of Cure; art of Decoration, which is called Cosmetic; art of Activity,

---

7   PHILOSOPHIA PRIMA: "First philosophy"

8   Scient: Knowing, skilful
9   Caesar's Commentaries, see p73

which is called Athletic; and art Voluptuary, which Tacitus truly calleth ERUDITUS LUXUS[10].

The ancient opinion that man was MICROCOSMUS, an abstract or model of the world, hath been fantastically strained by Paracelsus' and the alchemists. But thus much is evidently true, that of all substances which nature hath produced, man's body is the most extremely compounded. The Soul, on the other side, is the simplest of substances.

Medicine is a science which hath been more professed than laboured, and yet more laboured than advanced; the labour having been, in my judgement, rather in circle than in progression. Notably the discontinuance of the ancient diligence of Hippocrates, which used to set down a narrative of the cases of his patients, just as the lawyers are careful to report new cases for the direction of future judgments.

I esteem it the office of a physician not only to restore health, but to mitigate pain and dolors; and not only when such mitigation may conduce to recovery, but when it may serve to make a fair and easy passage. For Augustus Cæsar was wont to wish to himself that Euthanasia; and which was specially noted in Antoninus Pius, whose death was after the fashion of a kindly and pleasant sheep. But the physicians do make a kind of scruple and religion to stay with the patient after the disease is deplored; whereas in my judgement they ought to give the attendances for facilitating and assuaging of the pains and agonies of death.

For Cosmetic, it hath parts civil, and parts effeminate: for cleanness of body was ever esteemed. As for artificial decoration, it is neither fine enough to deceive, nor wholesome to please. For Athletic, I accept that the body of man may be brought, by activity, to hardness against wants and extremities. As for arts of pleasure sensual, the chief deficience is of laws to repress them.

XI: Knowledge of the Mind hath two parts; inquiries into the substance of the soul or mind, the other of the faculties or functions thereof. Such knowledge must be bounded by religion for the substance of the soul was not extracted out of the mass of heaven and earth, but was immediately inspired from God. Unto this part of knowledge there be two appendices; which have rather vapoured forth fables than kindled truth: divination and fascination.

Divination is superstitious; such as the heathen observations upon the inspection of sacrifices, the flights of birds, the swarming of bees; and Chaldean astrology, and the like. Fascination is the power and of imagination upon other bodies than the body of the imagination. Herein it may be pretended that Ceremonies and Charms, do work. Deficiencies in these knowledges I will report none, other than the general deficience, that it is not known how much of them is verity, and how much vanity.

XII: The Knowledge respecting the faculties of the mind of man is of two kinds; his Understanding and Reason, and the other his Will, Appetite, and Affection. The Arts intellectual are four in number: Art of Inquiry or Invention: Art of Examination or Judgment: Art of Custody or Memory: and Art of Elocution or Tradition.

XIII: Invention is of two kinds, much differing: the one of Arts and Sciences; and the other of Speech and Arguments. The former of these has such a deficience that there is in it NO READY MONEY. For as money will fetch all other commodities, so this knowledge is that which should purchase all the rest.

XIV: Now we pass unto the arts of Judgment, which handle the natures of Proofs and Demonstrations; which as to Induction hath a coincidence with Invention.

Although we think we govern our words, LOQUENDUM UT VULGUS, SENTIENDUM UT SAPIENTES*; yet words, as a Tartar's bow, do shoot back upon the understanding of the wisest, and mightily entangle and pervert the judgement So it is most necessary in all controversies to imitate the wisdom of the mathematicians, in setting down in the very beginning the definitions of our words and terms that others may know how we understand them.

XV: The custody or retaining of knowledge is either in writing or memoir; whereof writing hath two parts, the nature of the character, and the order of the entry.

XVI: Of the kind of transitive knowledge, concerning transferring our knowledge to others, the organ of tradition is either speech or writing: and we see the commerce of barbarous people, that understand not one another's language, and in the practice of divers that are dumb and deaf, that men's minds are expressed in gestures. And we understand that it is the use of China to write in characters which express neither letters nor words but things or notions; insomuch as provinces, which understand not one another's language, can nevertheless read one another's writings; and therefore they have a vast multitude of characters, as many, I suppose, as radical words.

Concerning the science of grammar, I cannot report it deficient.

XXIII: CIVIL knowledge hath three parts which are; conversation, negotiation, and government; and they be three wisdoms of divers natures: wisdom of the behaviour, wisdom of business, and wisdom of state. The first of these is well laboured, the second and third are deficient.

And it is not amiss for men in their race toward fortune, to cool themselves a little with that conceit which is elegantly expressed by the Emperor Charles the Fifth, THAT FORTUNE HATH SOMEWHAT OF THE NATURE OF A WOMAN, THAT IF SHE BE TOO MUCH WOOED, SHE IS THE FARTHER OFF.

Concerning Government, it is a part of knowledge secret and retired, some things are secret because they are hard to know, and some because they are not fit to utter.

XXIV: Now let us come to sacred and inspired divinity, the Sabbath and port of all men's labours and peregrinations.

---

10   ERUDITUS LUXUS: "The Refined Luxury"

XXV: The use of human reason in religion is of two sorts: the former, in the conception and apprehension of the mysteries of God to us revealed; the other, in the inferring and deriving of doctrine and direction thereupon. For the obtaining of the information, it resteth upon the true and sound interpretation of the Scriptures, which are the fountains of the water of life. These things I have passed over so briefly because I can report no deficience concerning them.

THUS have I made as it were a small globe of the intellectual world. The errors I claim as mine own: the good, if any be, is due TANQUM ADEPS SACRIFICII**,

to be incensed to the honour, first of the Divine Majesty, and next of your Majesty, to whom on earth I am most bounden.

DEO GLORIA***

---

*   LOQUENDUM UT VULGUS, SENTIENDUM UT SAPIENTES: "Speak like the commoners, think like the wise"

**   TANQUM ADEPS SACRIFICII: "As if obtained by a sacrifice"

*** DEO GLORIA: "To the glory of God"

On The Motion of the Heart and Blood
(*Exercitatio Anatomica de Motu Cordis et Sanguinis in Animalibus*)
By William Harvey
(London, 1628)

William Harvey of Folkestone studied medicine at Padua in Italy under the pioneering surgeon Hieronymus Fabricius, who had discovered the one-way valves in veins. Harvey solved the mystery of their function and succeeded in explaining the circulation of blood through the body by the heart through its alternate diastole (expansion) and systole (contraction). He was the first to suggest that mammals reproduced by the fertilisation of an egg by sperm. So accepted are his discoveries now that it seems remarkable that neither was universally believed in his own time.

Abridged: GH.

To The Most Illustrious And Indomitable Prince Charles King Of Great Britain, France, And Ireland Defender Of The Faith

Most Illustrious Prince!

The heart of animals is the foundation of their life, the sovereign of everything within them, the sun of their microcosm, from which all power proceeds. The King, in like manner, is the foundation of his kingdom, the heart of the republic, the fountain whence all power, all grace doth flow. The knowledge of his heart, therefore, will not be useless to a Prince, as embracing a kind of Divine example of his functions. Accept therefore this, my new Treatise on the Heart.

Your Majesty's most devoted servant,
William Harvey. London, 1628.

I: MOTIONS OF THE HEART IN LIVING AN- IMALS

When first I gave my mind to vivisections as a means of discovering the motions and uses of the heart, I found the task so truly arduous that I was almost tempted to think, with Fracastorius, that the motion of the heart was only to be comprehended by God. For I could neither rightly perceive at first when the systole and when the diastole took place, nor when and where dilation and contraction occurred, by reason of the rapidity of the motion, which, in

many animals, is accomplished in the twinkling of an eye, coming and going like a flash of lightning.

At least it appears that these things happen together or at the same instant: the tension of the heart, the pulse of its apex, which is felt externally by its striking against the chest, the thickening of its walls, and the forcible expulsion of the blood it contains by the constriction of its ventricles.

Hence the very opposite of the opinions commonly received appears to be true; inasmuch as it is generally believed that when the heart strikes the breast and the pulse is felt without, the heart is dilated in its ventricles and is filled with blood. But the contrary of this is the fact; that is to say, the heart is in the act of contracting and being emptied. Whence the motion, which is generally regarded as the diastole of the heart, is in truth its systole.

And in like manner the intrinsic motion of the heart is not the diastole but the systole; neither is it in the diastole that the heart grows firm and tense, but in the systole; for then alone when tense is it moved and made vigorous. When it acts and becomes tense the blood is expelled: when it relaxes and sinks together, it receives the blood in the manner and wise which will by and by be explained.

From divers facts it is also manifest in opposition to commonly received opinions, that the diastole of the arteries corresponds with the time of the heart's systole; and that the arteries are filled and distended by the blood forced into them by the contraction of the ventricles. It is in virtue of one and the same cause, therefore, that all the arteries of the body pulsate, viz. the contraction of the left ventricle in the same way as the pulmonary artery pulsates by the contraction of the right ventricle.

I am persuaded it will be found that the motion of the heart is as follows: First of all the auricle contracts and throws the blood into the ventricle, which being filled, the heart raises itself straightway, makes all its fibres tense, contracts the ventricles and performs a beat, by which beat it immediately sends the blood supplied to it by the auricle into the arteries ; the right ventricle sending its charge into the lungs by the vessel called the vena arteriosa, but which, in structure and function, and all things else is an artery; the left ventricle sending its charge into the aorta, and through this by the arteries to the body at large.

The grand cause of hesitation and error in this subject appears to me to have been the intimate connexion between the heart and the lungs. When men saw both the pulmonary artery and the pulmonary veins losing themselves in the lungs, of course it became a puzzle to them to know how the right ventricle should distribute the blood to the body or the left draw it from the venae cavae.

Or they have hesitated because they did not perceive the route by which the blood is transferred from the veins to the arteries, in consequence of the intimate connexion between the heart and lungs. And that this difficulty puzzled anatomists not a little when in their dissections they found the pulmonary artery and left ventricle full of black and clotted blood, plainly appears when they felt themselves compelled to affirm that the blood made its way from the right to the left ventricle by sweating through the septum of the heart.

Had anatomists only been as conversant with the dissection of the lower animals as they are with that of the human body, the matters that have hitherto kept them in perplexity of doubt would, in my opinion, have met them freed from every kind of difficulty. And first in fishes, in which the heart consists of but a single ventricle, they having no lungs, the thing is manifest. Here the sac, which is situated at the base of the heart, and is the part analogous to the auricle in man, plainly throws the blood into the heart, and the heart in its turn conspicuously transmits it by a pipe or artery, or vessel analogous to an artery; these are facts which are confirmed by simple ocular experiment. I have seen, further, that the same thing obtained most obviously.

And since we find that in the greater number of animals, in all indeed at a certain period of their existence, the channels for the transmission of the blood through the heart are so conspicuous, we have still to inquire wherefore in some creatures, those, namely, that have warm blood and that have attained to the adult age, man among the number, we should not conclude that the same thing is accomplished through the substance of the lungs, which, in the embryo, and at a time when the functions of these organs is in abeyance, nature effects by direct passages, and which indeed she seems compelled to adopt through want of a passage by the lungs; or wherefore it should be better (for nature always does that which is best) that she

should close up the various open routes which she had formerly made use of in the embryo, and still uses in all other animals; not only opening up no new apparent channels for the passage of the blood, therefore, but even entirely shutting up those which formerly existed in the embryos of those animals that have lungs.

For while the lungs are yet in a state of inaction, nature uses the two ventricles of the heart as if they formed but one for the transmission of the blood. The condition of the embryos of those animals which have lungs is the same as that of those animals which have no lungs.

Thus, by studying the structure of the animals who are nearer to and farther from ourselves in their modes of life and in the construction of their bodies, we can prepare ourselves to understand the nature of the pulmonary circulation in ourselves, and of the systemic circulation also.

II: SYSTEMIC CIRCULATION

What remains to be said is of so novel and unheard-of a character that I not only fear injury to myself from the envy of a few, but I tremble lest I have mankind at large for my enemies, so much do wont and custom that become as another nature, and doctrine once sown that hath struck deep root, and respect for antiquity, influence all men.

And, sooth to say, when I surveyed my mass of evidence, whether derived from vivisections, and my previous reflections on them, or from the ventricles of the heart and the vessels that enter into and issue from them, the symmetry and size of these conduits-for nature, doing nothing in vain. would never have given them so large a relative size without a purpose; or from the arrangement and intimate structure of the valves in particular and of the many other parts of the heart in general, with many things besides; and frequently and seriously bethought me and long revolved in my mind what might be the quantity of blood which was transmitted, in how short a time its passage might be effected and the like; and not finding it possible that this could be supplied by the juices of the ingested aliment without the veins on the one hand becoming drained, and the arteries on the other getting ruptured through the excessive charge of blood, unless the blood should somehow find its way from the arteries into the veins, and so return to the right side of the heart: when, I say, I surveyed all this evidence, I began to think whether there might not be a motion as it were in a circle.

Now this I afterwards found to be true; and I finally saw that the blood, forced by the action of the left ventricle into the arteries, was distributed to the body at large, and its several parts, in the same manner as it is sent through the lungs, impelled by the right ventricle into the pulmonary artery: and that it then passed through the veins and along the vena cava, and so round to the left ventricle in the manner already indicated.

For the moist earth, warmed by the sun, evaporates; the vapours drawn upwards are condensed, and descending in the form of rain moisten the earth again. And by this arrangement are generations of living things produced; in like manner, too, are tempests and meteors engendered by the circular motion of the sun. The various parts of the body are nourished and quickened by the warmer, more perfect, vaporous, spirituous and, as I may say, alimentive blood; which, on the contrary, in contact with these parts becomes cooled, coagulated and, so to speak, effete; whence it returns to its sovereign the heart, as if to its sources, or to the inmost home of the body, there to recover its state of excellence or perfection. Here it resumes its due fluidity, receives an infusion of natural heat and is impregnated with spirits, and hence it is again dispersed.

III: CONFIRMATIONS OF THE THEORY

Three points present themselves for confirmation, which, being established, I conceive that the truth I contend for will follow necessarily and appear as a thing obvious to all.

The first point is this. The blood is incessantly transmitted by the action of the heart from the vena cava to the arteries in such quantity that it cannot be supplied from the ingesta, and in such wise that the whole mass must very quickly pass through the organ. Let us assume the quantity of blood which the left ventricle of the heart will contain when distended to be, say, two ounces (in the dead body I have found it to contain upwards of two ounces); and let us suppose, as approaching the truth, that the fourth part of its charge is thrown into the artery at each contraction. Now, in the course of half an hour the heart will have made more than one thousand beats.

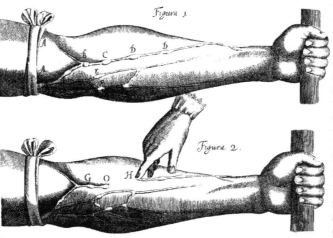

Figura 1.

Figura 2.

Multiplying the number of drachms propelled by the number of pulses, we have one thousand half-ounces sent from this organ into the artery; a larger quantity than is contained in the whole body.

This truth, indeed, presents itself obviously before us when we consider what happens in the dissection of living animals. The great artery need not be divided, but a very small branch only (as Galen even proves in regard to man), to have the whole of the blood in the body, as well that of the veins as of the arteries, drained away in the course of no long time-some half hour or less.

The second point is this. The blood, under the influence of the arterial pulse, enters, and is impelled in a continuous, equable and incessant stream through every part and member of the body in much larger quantity than were sufficient for nutrition, or than the whole mass of fluids could supply.

I have here to cite certain experiments. Ligatures are either very tight or of middling tightness. A ligature I designate as tight, or perfect, when it is drawn so close about an extremity that no vessel can be felt pulsating beyond it. Such ligatures are employed in the removal of tumours: and in these cases, all afflux of nutriment and heat being prevented by the ligature, we see the tumours dwindle and die, and finally drop off.

Now let anyone make an experiment upon the arm of a man, either using such a fillet as is employed in blood-letting, or grasping the limb lightly with his hand: let a ligature be thrown about the extremity and drawn as tightly as can be borne. It will be perceived that beyond the ligature the arteries do not pulsate, while above it the artery begins to rise higher at each diastole and to swell with a kind of tide as if it strove to break through and overcome the obstacle to its current. Then let the ligature be brought to that state of middling tightness which is used in bleeding, and it will be seen that the hand and arm will instantly become deeply suffused and extended, and the veins show themselves tumid and knotted.

Which is as much as to say that when the arteries pulsate the blood is flowing through them, but where they do not pulsate they cease from transmitting anything. The veins again being compressed, nothing can flow through them; the certain indication of which is that below the ligature they are much more tumid than above it.

Whence is this blood? It must needs arrive by the arteries. For that it cannot flow in by the veins appears from the fact that the blood cannot be forced towards the heart unless the ligature be removed.

Further, when we see the veins below the ligature instantly swell up and become gorged when from extreme tightness it is somewhat relaxed, the arteries meanwhile continuing unaffected, this is an obvious indication that the blood passes from the arteries into the veins and not from the veins into the arteries, and that there is either an anastomosis of the two orders of vessels, or pores in the flesh and solid parts that are permeable to the blood. And now we understand wherefore in phlebotomy we apply our fillet above the part that is punctured, not below it. Did the flow come from above, not from below, the bandage in this case would not only be of no service, but would prove a positive hindrance.

And further, we perceive that a circulation is absolutely necessary, seeing that the quantity of blood cannot be supplied immediately from the ingesta, and is vastly more than can he requisite for the mere nutrition of the parts.

That the veins return this blood to the heart incessantly from all parts and members of the body will be made clear from the valves which are found in the cavities of the veins themselves, from the uses of these and from experiments cognisable by the senses. The celebrated Hieronymus Fabricius first gave representations of the valves in the veins. Their office is by no means explained when we are told that it is to hinder the blood, by its weight, from flowing into inferior parts; for the edges of the valves in the jugular veins hang downwards, and are so contrived that they prevent the blood from rising. The valves, in a word, do not invariably look upwards, but always towards the trunks of the veins- towards the seat of the heart. They are solely made and instituted lest, instead of advancing from the extreme to the central parts of the body the blood should rather proceed along the veins from the centre to the extremities: but the delicate valves, while they readily open in the right direction, entirely prevent all such contrary motion, being so situated and arranged that if anything escapes, it is immediately received on the convexity of the one beneath, which is placed transversely with reference to the former, and so is hindered from getting any farther.

And this I have frequently experienced in my dissections of veins. If I attempted to pass a probe from the trunk of the veins into one of the smaller branches, whatever care I took I found it impossible to introduce it far any way by reason of the valves; whilst it was most easy to push it along in the opposite direction. from without inwards, or from the branches towards the trunks and roots. And now I may be allowed to give my view of the circulation of the blood, and to propose it for general adoption.

IV: THE CONCLUSION

Since all things, both argument and ocular demonstration, show that the blood passes through the lungs and heart by the action of the ventricles; and is sent for distribution to all parts of the body, where it makes its way into the veins and pores of the flesh; and then flows by the veins from the circumference on every side to the centre, from the lesser to the greater veins: and is by them finally discharged into the veini cuvii and right auricle of the heart, and this in such a quantity or in such a flux and reflux, thither by the arteries, hither by the veins, as cannot possibly be supplied by the ingesta, and is much greater than can be required for mere purposes of nutrition; therefore, it is absolutely necessary to conclude that the blood in the animal body is impelled in a circle and is in a state of ceaseless motion; and that this is the act, or function, which the heart performs by means of its pulse, and that it is the sole and only end of the motion and contraction of the heart. For it would be difficult to explain in any other way to what purpose all is constructed and arranged as we have seen it to be.

Meditations on First Philosophy
in which the Existence of God and the Distinction Between Mind and Body are Demonstrated.
By René Descartes
(Paris, 1641)

His leading work in physics, mathematics, optics, physiology, geometry and astronomy would have been quite enough to mark out Descartes as one of the founders of the Western way of thinking. But this petit bourgeois former soldier from La Haye in central France determined to round-off his career in science by presenting to the world his thoughts on how it is we construct truth. In it he expands the famous conclusion "I think, therefore I am" ('cogito ergo sum' in the original Latin) of his earlier *Discourse on Method* and so sets out the questions about the apparent two-part mind-body nature of humans which philosophy and psychology have been trying to answer ever since.

Based on the 1901 English translation by John Veitch, and the French of Duc de Luynes of 1647. Abridged: GH

DEDICATION

TO the Most Wise and Illustrious the Dean and Doctors of the Sacred Faculty of Theology in Paris.

We have faith that the human soul does not perish with the body, and that God exists, but it certainly does not seem possible to persuade infidels of any religion, or of any moral virtue, unless, to begin with, we prove these two facts by natural reason.

For the truth will easily cause all men of mind and learning to subscribe to your judgement; and your authority will cause the atheists, who are usually more arrogant than learned or judicious, to rid themselves of their contradictions. And, finally, all others will easily yield to such a mass of evidence, and there will be none who dares to doubt the existence of God and the real and true distinction between the human soul and the body.

It is for you now in your singular wisdom to judge of the importance of the establishment of such beliefs.

PREFACE to THE READER

I have already touched on the questions of God and the soul in the *Discourse on the Method of Rightly Conducting the Reason and Seeking Truth in the Sciences*, published in 1637. These questions appeared to me to be of such importance that I did not judge it proper to now write in French, in case it be read by feebler minds and they come to believe that it was permitted to them to attempt to follow the same path.

I expect no praise from common people, nor expect many readers. I ask no-one to hear what I have to say excepting those who desire to meditate seriously with me and can deliver themselves entirely from every sort of prejudice. I know too well that such men are rare. And while some have found here trivial complaint, they make no objection deserving of reply.

SYNOPSIS of THE SIX FOLLOWING MEDIT-ATIONS

In the following meditations I will show that doubt is possible, and that to doubt is proof of the existence of mind. I will provide a clear picture of the indivisible soul. I will prove that God exists without reference to the corporeal world. I will prove that what we perceive is true, and explain the origin of falsity. And I will prove that things exist.

MEDITATION ONE

Of the Things which may be brought within the Sphere of the Doubtful.

So many of the opinions I held so firmly in my youth I now know to be false, that I must admit how doubtful is everything I have since constructed. Thus, I have become convinced that, to establish firm structure for the sciences, I must build anew from the foundation. To-day, since I have a leisurely retirement, I shall at last seriously address myself to this problem. I shall begin by attacking those principles upon which all others rest.

I have formerly accepted as true and certain those things I learn through the senses. Like the fact that I am seated by this fire, in a dressing gown, with this paper in my hands. And how could I deny that this body is mine, unless I was as mad as those whose cerebella are so clouded by black bile that they believe they have an earthenware head or a glass body? Yet, I must remember that I have dreams, which are almost as insane. I have even dreamt of being here whilst I was lying undressed in bed! It seems to me that I am now awake, but I remind myself that I have dreamt that too. Yet even dreams are formed out of things real and true. Just as a painter represents sirens or satyrs from a medley of different animals; even quite novel images are still composed of real colours.

For the same reason, although general things may be imaginary, we are bound to confess that there are simpler objects which are certainly real; such as colours, quantity or magnitude and number. That is why Physics, Astronomy, Medicine and those sciences which consider composite things, are dubious; but Arithmetic, Geometry and sciences which treat of the very simple and general contain some certainty. For whether I am awake or asleep, two and three always form five, and a square has four sides. It does not seem possible that truths so clear and apparent can be uncertain.

Now, I have long believed in an all-powerful God who made me. I can imagine that other people deceive themselves, but how do I know that I am not deceived when I add two and three, or count the sides of a square? If God is good, how can it be that he sometimes permits me to be deceived?

I confess that there is nothing in all that I formerly believed, which I cannot doubt in some measure. So, I intend to attach myself to the idea that some evil genie is deceiving me; that the heavens, the earth, colours, figures, sound, even my body and senses are just illusions and dreams. This is difficult, for just as the prisoner who finds himself dreaming of liberty fears to awaken, so I may fall back into my former opinions.

MEDITATION TWO

Of the Nature of the Human Mind; and that it is more easily Known than the Body.

Yesterday's meditation left me all but drowning in doubts. Nonetheless, I will continue the journey in hope of finding, like Archimedes moving the earth, some fixed point of certainty.

It is not even necessary that God puts ideas into my mind, for it is possible that I am producing them myself. But am I myself something? I have chosen to deny that I have senses and body, but the deceiver can never cause me to be nothing so long as I think that I am something. So, we must definitely conclude that; 'I think, I exist', is necessarily true each time I conceive it.

But I do not yet know clearly what I am. I believed myself to be a man – a reasoning animal? But what is man, what is 'animal, and what means 'reasoning'? I know that I considered myself as having bones and flesh, that I was nourished, that I walked, that I felt, and that I thought, and I referred all these actions to the soul: but what is the soul?

Putting aside all which is not necessarily true: then I can accurately state that I am no more than a thing which thinks, that is to say a mind or a soul, which doubts, understands, affirms, denies, wills, refuses, imagines and feels.

I perceive things by the organs of sense, and seem to know them better than my own mind. But could these be but dreams?

Let us consider one simple corporeal thing- this piece of wax: fresh from the hive, with the sweetness of its honey and the aroma of flowers. It has its own colour, figure, size. It appears hard, cold, and if you strike it with the finger, it will emit a sound. But, I take it near to the fire; and it becomes liquid, its smell is lost and when one strikes it, no sound is made. All sensation is changed, yet we confess that it is the same wax. I can imagine that this wax might be made into a square or a triangle and still be the same wax. No! More! I imagine that it, or any piece of wax, could be formed into more shapes even that my mind can encompass. If the wax is properly to be known through appearance alone, might not the men I see outside my window be just automatic machines wearing hats and coats?

It is now manifest to me that things are not known from the fact that they are seen or touched, but because they are understood. I now see clearly that there is nothing which is easier for me to know than my mind. But it is difficult to rid oneself of a long-held view, so it will be well that I should rest at this point, to meditate on this new knowledge.

MEDITATION THREE

Of God: that He Exists.

I shall now close my eyes and ears, put away all thought of physical things, and try to better understand my own self. So far, my only assurance is to accept those things which I perceive very clearly and very distinctly as true, yet I know that I have often been mistaken. It remains possible that God might deceive me, therefore I must enquire as to whether God exists, and whether he is a deceiver.

If I hear sound, or see the sun, or feel heat, I judge that these sensations come from things outside of me. Just now, I feel heat, and judge that this feeling is produced by something different from me, ie. the fire. But I must doubt that it is nature which impels me to believe in material things, for there is often a great difference between knowledge and appearance. The sun, for instance, seems very small, yet we know from astronomical calculation that it is very great.

Those ideas which represent substances all seem more solid than those that represent modes or accidents; and that idea of a supreme God, eternal, infinite, omniscient, omnipotent, seems to have even more objective reality.

Now it is manifest that effects derive their reality from their causes, that something cannot proceed from nothing and that the perfect cannot proceed from something imperfect. The idea of heat, or stone, cannot exist in me unless it has been placed there by some cause at least as real as that which exists in the heat or stone. Thus I conclude that I cannot myself be the cause ideas, the cause must be outside me, and I seem to know so little about corporeal objects, as with the wax yesterday, that such ideas may well proceed from myself. There remains only the idea of God, whose attributes of infinity, independence, all-knowledge and all-power seem so exceptional that no idea of them could have come from within me; hence we must conclude that God exists.

The idea of substance could be from within me, as I am a substance, but, since I am finite, the idea of an infinite substance must proceed from elsewhere. We must say that the idea of God is very clear and distinct and more objectively real than others. Even if we can imagine that God does not exist, we cannot imagine that the idea of him means nothing.

Possibly the perfections of God are in some way already in me, yet I recognise that this cannot be, since it can never reach a point so high that it could not attain to yet greater increase, and where could such perfection have derived, from myself, or my parents, or some other source than God?

It is perfectly clear to all who consider the nature of time, that, in order to have existence at a particular moment, a substance must have the power to create itself anew in the next moment. But I am conscious of no such power in myself. There must be, as I have said, at least as much reality in the cause as in the effect; and since I am a thinking thing, it must be that the cause is likewise a thinking thing. But from what cause does God derive? If it derives from another cause, we must ask whether this second cause has a cause, for it is manifest that there can be no regression into infinity.

Finally, it is not my parents who conserve me, they are only the authors of the body in which the mind is implanted. Thus we must necessarily conclude from the simple fact that I exist, and that I have the idea of a perfect Being, that the proof of God's existence is grounded on the highest evidence.

It only remains to ask how I have acquired this idea of God. Not through the senses, nor as a fiction of my mind. The only alternative is that God, in creating me, placed this idea within me, like the mark of the workman on his work.

But before I go on, it seems right to pause to think on His majesty; at least as far as my dazzled mind will allow. For faith teaches us that the glory of this, and the other life, is contemplation of the Divine.

MEDITATION FOUR

Of the True and the False.

Over these past days I have found little certainty respecting corporeal objects, some respecting the mind, and more regarding God. I shall now go on to consider things purely intelligible.

I recognise it as impossible that God should ever deceive me; for fraud and deception testify to imperfection, malice or feebleness, which cannot be of God. So, my capacity for judgement, as it is from God, can never mislead me if I use it aright.

In the first place, knowing that I am feeble and limited, while God is infinite, I recognise that some of his ends, which seem imperfect, would be found to be perfect if we could but comprehend the whole. Considering my own errors, I find that they depend on my knowledge, and on my power of choice or free will. Though I recognise that my knowledge, memory and imagination are imperfect, in my free will I find power so great that I cannot conceive of any greater, and so see there the image of God.

Whence then come my errors? They come from the fact that my will is much wider in range than my understanding, and extending it to things which I do not understand I fall into error and sin. If I but abstain from giving judgement on things that I do not perceive with clearness and distinctness, it is plain that I act rightly. I have no cause to complain that God has not given me more powerful intelligence, since it is proper that a finite understanding should not comprehend all things. Nor have I reason to complain that He has given me a will larger than my understanding, since free-will must be complete if it is to exist at all. I perceive that God could have created me so that I never should err, although I remained free. Nevertheless, it seems that it is a greater perfection that parts of the universe should have error rather than all parts be the same.

In this day's Meditation, I have discovered that as long as I make judgements only on matters which I clearly and distinctly understand, I can never be deceived and will, without doubt, arrive at truth.

MEDITATION FIVE

Of the Essence of Material Things, and, again, of God, that he Exists.

Many questions about God and my own nature remain. But I must try to emerge from the state of doubt I have held to these last few days, and to see which of my ideas of the corporeal world are clear.

In the first place, I can clearly imagine extension in length, breadth or depth. For example, I have seen triangles; and I can form in my mind other shapes which have never been seen, yet still clearly know their properties. Hence they are something, for it is clear that what is true is something, and I have shown that what I know clearly is true. Indeed, I have always counted geometry and mathematics as the most certain.

When I think of this with care, I clearly see that existence can no more be separated from the essence of God than having three angles can be separated from the essence of triangle. Still, from the fact that I know, say, that a mountain must have a valley, it does not follow that there is a mountain. Similarly, I may conceive of God as having existence just as I can imagine a winged horse, although no such exists.

But this is mere sophism; for as the mountain and the valley cannot be separated from one another, I cannot conceive God without existence, it follows that existence is inseparable from Him, and hence that He exists.

It is not necessary that I should ever think of God, nevertheless, whenever I do, it is necessary that I attribute to Him every perfection, although I cannot enumerate them all. The idea of God, I discern, first, because I cannot conceive anything but God to whose essence existence necessarily pertains. Second, because it is not possible for me to conceive two or more Gods. Third, granted that such a God exists that He must exist eternally. Finally, because I know an infinitude of other properties in God, none of which I can either diminish or change.

For the rest, we must always return to the point that only those things that we conceive clearly and distinctly are true. If only my mind were not pre-occupied with prejudices, there would be nothing I could know more immediately and more easily than God. Once I recognise this, and see that He is not a deceiver, I can infer that what I perceive clearly and distinctly must be true. And so I very clearly recognise that the certainty and truth of all knowledge depends alone on the knowledge of the true God. Now that I know Him, I have the means of acquiring a perfect knowledge of many things.

MEDITATION SIX

Of the Existence of Material Things, and of the Real Distinction between the Soul and Body of Man

It now remains to inquire whether material things exist. I clearly and distinctly know of objects, inasmuch as they are represented by pure mathematics, and I know that my imagination is capable of persuading me of physical existence.

This is the more clear when we see the difference between imagination and pure intellection. For example, when I imagine a triangle, I conceive it, not only as a figure of three lines, but also by an inward vision, which I call imagining. But if I think of a chiliagon, a thousand-sided figure, I cannot in any way imagine it, as the imagination is a different power from understanding.

First I shall consider those matters perceived through the senses.

I perceived that I had this body - which I considered part, or possibly the whole, of myself. Further, I sensed that this body was amidst others, from which it could be affected with pain or pleasure. I also experienced appetites like hunger, thirst, and passions like joy, titillation, and anger. Outside myself, I beheld heat, light and colour, and scents and sounds, so that I could distinguish the sky, the earth, the sea and such. And, using my senses rather than my reason, I came to believe that all the ideas in my mind that had come to me through the senses.

But when I inquired, why painful sensation leads to sadness, and pleasurable sensation to joy, or a mysterious pinching of the stomach called hunger leads to desire to eat, and so on, I could only reason that nature taught me so. There is certainly no affinity (that I at least can understand) between the craving of the stomach and the desire to eat, any more than between pain and sadness.

But experience has gradually destroyed my faith in my senses. I have seen round towers from afar, which closely observed seemed square, and colossal statues, which appeared tiny. I found error in the external senses, and in the internal; for is there anything more internal than pain? And yet I learn that some persons seem to feel pain in an amputated part, which makes me doubt the sources of my own pain. I knew that my will did not control the ideas I received from the senses.

I can only explain my ability to make distinctions between one thing and another by concluding that my essence consists solely in the fact that I am a thinking thing. And although possibly I possess a body, because I have a clear and distinct idea of myself as only a thinking and un-extended thing, and it is thereby that I possess an idea of body as an extended and unthinking thing, it is certain that this soul, by which I am what I am, is entirely and absolutely distinct from my body, and can exist without it.

But there are many other things which nature seems to have taught me. For example; I hold the opinion that all space in which there is nothing that affects my senses is void. That a warm body contains heat. That a white or green body has in it the whiteness or greenness that I perceive. That bitter or sweet taste exists in bitter or sweet things. Or that the stars, towers, and other distant bodies are of the same figure as they appear to our eyes. Nature teaches me to flee from things that cause pain, and seek things that communicate pleasure. But it seems to me that it is mind alone, and not mind and body together, that is requisite to knowledge of the truth about such things. Thus, although a star makes no bigger impression on my eye than a tiny candle flame, yet I have always judged it larger.

This pursuit or avoidance things, taught me by nature, sometimes leads to error; as when the agreeable taste of some poisoned food may induce me to partake of the poison. Though here nature may be excused, for it only induces me to desire pleasant food, not poison. Thus, I can infer that I am not omniscient, which should not be astonishing, since man is finite in nature.

But we frequently deceive ourselves even in those things to which we are directly impelled by nature, as happens with those who when they are sick desire things hurtful to them. It might be said that sickness corrupts nature, but a sick man is as much God's creature as he who is in health. Just as a badly-made clock still follows the laws of nature, so it would be natural for a body, if it suffered the dropsy, to move the nerves and other parts to obtain drink, which is the feature of this disease although it is harmful to the sufferer. This comparison of a sick man to a faulty clock

may be a mere verbal quibble, but it remains to inquire how the goodness of God does not prevent the nature of man from being fallacious.

There is a great difference between mind and body, as body is by nature always divisible, and the mind is indivisible. For, if a foot or an arm is separated from my body, nothing has been taken away from my mind. I further notice that the mind does not receive impressions from the body directly, but only from the brain, or perhaps even from the small part of the brain where common sense resides. But because the nerves must pass through a long route, it may happen that some intervening part is excited, which may excite a mistaken movement in the brain. More usually, when, say nerves in the feet are violently moved, their movement, passing through the medulla of the spine to the inmost parts of the brain, gives a sign to the mind which makes it feel pain, as though in the foot. By this, the mind is excited to do its utmost to remove the cause of the evil as dangerous to the foot. It is true that God could have constituted the nature of man such that this movement would have conveyed something quite different to the mind, but nothing would have contributed so well to the conservation of the body.

Notwithstanding the supreme goodness of God, the nature of man, composed of mind and body, can sometimes be a source of deception.

This consideration helps me to recognise the errors to which my nature is subject, so as to avoid them, or correct them more easily. Knowing that my senses usually indicate to me truth respecting what is beneficial to the body, and being able almost always to avail myself of many of those senses in order to examine things, together with my memory to connect the present with the past, and my understanding of the causes errors, I ought no longer to fear the falsity of my everyday senses. So, I ought to set aside all the doubts of these past days as hyperbolical and ridiculous, particularly that very common uncertainty respecting dreams, for I now see that memory never connects dreams together as it unites waking events. I ought in never to doubt the truth of such matters, if having called up my senses, memory, and understanding to examine them, nothing is perceived by any one of them which is repugnant to that set forth by the others. For because God is no deceiver, it follows that I am not deceived in this.

But because the exigencies of action often oblige us to make up our minds before having leisure to examine matters carefully, we must confess that the life of man is frequently subject to error. We must in the end acknowledge the infirmity of our nature.

A Voyage to the Moon
By Cyrano de Bergerac
(Paris, 1647)

Cyrano the freethinking poet has become so famous, through plays, films, comic books, opera and novels, as the swashbuckler with the extraordinarily large nose, that it is easy to forget that he was also the more-or-less inventor of science fiction. If his ideas of the moon seem odd, consider those of a scientist of the same era on page 183.

Abridged: JH

I. Arrival on the Moon

After many experiments I constructed a flying machine, and, sitting on top of it, I boldly launched myself in the air from the crest of a mountain. I had scarcely risen more than half a mile when something went wrong with my machine, and it shot back to the earth. But, to my astonishment and joy, instead of descending with it, I continued to rise through the calm, moonlight air. For three-quarters of an hour I mounted higher and higher. Then suddenly all the weight of my body seemed to fall upon my head. I was no longer rising quietly from the Earth, but tumbling headlong on to the Moon. At last I crashed through a tree, and, breaking my fall among its leafy, yielding boughs, I landed gently on the grass below.

I found myself in the midst of a wild and beautiful forest, so full of the sweet music of singing-birds that it seemed as if every leaf on every tree had the tongue and figure of a nightingale. The ground was covered with unknown, lovely flowers, with a magical scent. As soon as I smelt it I became twenty years younger. My thin grey hairs changed into thick, brown, wavy tresses; my wrinkled face grew fresh and rosy; and my blood flowed through my veins with the speed and vigour of youth.

I was surprised to find no trace of human habitation in the forest. But in wandering about I came upon two strong, great animals, about twelve cubits long. One of them came towards me, and the other fled into the forest. But it quickly returned with seven hundred other beasts. As they approached me, I perceived that they were creatures with a human shape, who, however, went on all-fours like some gigantic kind of monkey. They shouted with admiration when they saw me; and one of them took me up by the neck and flung me on his back, and galloped with me into a great town.

When I saw the splendid buildings of the city I recognised my mistake. The four-footed creatures were really enormous men. Seeing that I went on two legs, they would not believe that I was a man like themselves. They thought I was an animal without any reasoning power, and they resolved to send me to their queen, who was fond of collecting strange and curious monsters.

All this, of course, I did not understand at the time. It took me some months to learn their language. These men of the Moon have two dialects; one for the nobility, the other for the common people. The language of the nobility is a kind of music; it is certainly a very pleasant means of expression. They are able to communicate their thoughts by lutes and other musical instruments quite as well as by the voice.

When twenty or thirty of them meet together to discuss some matter, they carry on the debate by the most harmonious concert it is possible to imagine.

The common people, however, talk by agitating different parts of their bodies. Certain movements constitute an entire speech. By shaking a finger, a hand, or an arm, for instance, they can say more than we can in a thousand words. Other motions, such as a wrinkle on the forehead, a shiver along a muscle, serve to design words. As they use all their body in speaking in this fashion, they have to go naked in order to make themselves clearly understood. When they are engaged in an exciting conversation they seem to be creatures shaken by some wild fever.

Instead of sending me at once to the Queen of the Moon, the man who had captured me earned a considerable amount of money by taking me every afternoon to the houses of the rich people. There I was compelled to jump and make grimaces, and stand in ridiculous attitudes in order to amuse the crowds of guests who had been invited to see the antics of the new animal.

But one day, as my master was pulling the rope around my neck to make me rise up and divert the company, a man came and asked me in Greek who I was. Full of joy at meeting someone with whom I could talk, I related to him the story of my voyage from the Earth.

"I cannot understand," I said, "how it was I rose up to the Moon when my machine broke down and fell to the Earth."

"That is easily explained," he said. "You had got within the circle of lunar influence, in which the Moon exerts a sort of sucking action on the fat of the body. The same thing often happens to me. Like you, I am a stranger on the Moon. I was born on the Sun, but, being of a roving disposition, I like to explore one planet after another. I have travelled a good deal in Europe, and conversed with several persons whose names you no doubt know. I remember that I was once famous in ancient Greece as the Demon of Socrates.[1]"

"Then you are a spirit?" I exclaimed.

"A kind of spirit," he replied. "I was one of the large company of the Men of the Sun who used to inhabit the

_____

1   Demon of Socrates: see The Republic (p55), line 496

Earth under the names of oracles, nymphs, woodland elves, and fairies. But we abandoned our world in the reign of the Emperor Augustus; your people then became so gross and stupid that we could no longer delight in their society. Since then I have stayed on the Moon. I find its inhabitants more enlightened than the inhabitants of the Earth."

"I don't!" I exclaimed. "Look how they treat me, as if I were a wild beast! I am sure that if one of their men of science voyaged to the Earth, he would be better received than I am here."

"I doubt it," said the Man of the Sun. "Your men of science would have him killed, stuffed, and put in a glass case in a museum."

II. The Garb of Shame

At this point our conversation was broken off by my keeper. He saw that the company was tired of my talk, which seemed to them mere grunting. So he pulled my rope, and made me dance and caper until the spectators ached with laughter.

Happily, the next morning the Man of the Sun opened my cage and put me on his back and carried me away.

"I have spoken to the King of the Moon," he said; "and he has commanded that you should be taken to his court and examined by his learned doctors."

As my companion went on four feet, he was able to travel as fast as a racehorse, and we soon arrived at another town, where we put up at an inn for dinner. I followed him into a magnificently furnished hall, and a servant asked me what I would begin with.

"Some soup," I replied.

I had scarcely pronounced the words when I smelt a very succulent broth. I rose up to look for the source of this agreeable smell; but my companion stopped me.

"What do you want to walk away for?" said he. "Stay and finish your soup."

"But where is the soup?" I said.

"Ah," he replied. "This is the first meal you have had on the Moon. You see, the people here only live on the smell of food. The fine, lunar art of cookery consists in collecting the exhalations that come from cooked meat, and bottling them up. Then, at meal-time, the various jars are uncorked, one after the other, until the appetites of the diners are satisfied."

"It is, no doubt, an exquisite way of eating," I said; "but I am afraid I shall starve on it."

"Oh, no, you will not," said he. "You will soon find that a man can nourish himself as well by his nose as by his mouth."

And so it was. After smelling for a quarter of an hour a variety of rich, appetising vapours, I rose up quite satisfied.

In the afternoon I was taken to the palace of the king, and examined by the greatest men of science on the Moon. In spite of all that my friend had said on my behalf, I was adjudged to be a mere animal, and again shut up in a cage. The king, queen, and courtiers spent a considerable time every day watching me, and with the help of the Man of the Sun I soon learned to speak a little of their, music-language. This caused a great deal of surprise. Several persons began to think that I was really a man who had been dwarfed and weakened from want of nourishment.

But the learned doctors again examined me, and decided that, as I did not walk on four legs, I must be a new kind of featherless parrot. Thereupon I was given a pole to perch on, instead of a nice warm bed to lie in; and every day the queen's fowler used to come and whistle tunes for me to learn. In the meantime, however, I improved my knowledge of the language, and at last I spoke so well and intelligibly that all the courtiers said that the learned doctors had been mistaken. One of the queen's maids of honour not only thought that I was a man, but fell in love with me. She often used to steal to my cage, and listen to my stories of the customs and amusements of our world. She was so interested that she begged me to take her with me if ever I found a way of returning to the Earth.

In my examination by the learned doctors I had stated that their world was but a Moon, and that the Moon from which I had come was really a world. It was this which had made them angry against me. But my friend, the Man of the Sun, at last prevailed upon the king to let me out of the cage on my retracting my wicked heresy. I was clad in splendid robes, and placed on a magnificent chariot to which four great noblemen were harnessed, and led to the centre of the city, where I had to make the following statement:

"People, I declare to you that this Moon is not a Moon but a world; and that the world I come from is not a world but a Moon. For this is what the Royal Council believe that you ought to believe."

The Man of the Sun then helped me to descend from the chariot, and took me quickly into a house, and stripped me of my gorgeous robes. "Why do you do that?" I asked. "This is the most splendid dress I have ever seen on the Moon."

"It is a garb of shame," said my companion. "You have this day undergone the lowest degradation that can be imposed on a man. You committed an awful crime in saying that the Moon was not a Moon. It is a great wonder you were not condemned to die of old age."

"Die of old age?" I said.

"Yes," replied my companion. "Usually, when a Man of the Moon comes to that time of life in which he feels that he is losing his strength of mind and body, he invites all his friends to a banquet. After explaining what little hope he has of adding anything to the fine actions of his life, he asks for permission to depart. If he has led a bad life, he is ordered to live; but if he has been a good man, his dearest friend kisses him, and plunges a dagger in his heart."

As he was talking, the son of the man in whose house we were staying entered the room. My companion quickly rose on his four feet, and made the young man a profound bow.

I asked him why he did this. He told me that on the Moon parents obey their children, and old men are compelled to show to young men the greatest respect.

"They are of opinion," said my companion, "that a strong and active young man is more capable of governing a family than a dull, infirm sexagenarian. I know that on your Earth old men are supposed to be wise and prudent. But, as a matter of fact, their wisdom and prudence consists merely of a timid frame of mind and a disinclination to take any risks."

The father then entered the room, and his son said to him in an angry voice:

"Why have you not got our house ready to sail away? You know the walls of the city have gone some hours ago. Bring me at once your image!"

The man brought a great wooden image of himself, and his son whipped it furiously for a quarter of an hour.

"And now," said the young man at last, "go and hoist the sails at once!"

III. Marvels of the Moon

There are two kinds of towns on the Moon: travelling towns and sedentary towns. In the travelling towns, each house is built of very light wood, and placed on a platform, beneath the four corners of which great wheels are fixed. When the time arrives for a voyage to the seaside or the forest, for a change of air, the townspeople hoist vast sails on the roofs of their dwellings, and sail away altogether towards the new site.

In the sedentary towns, on the other hand, the houses are made with great strong screws running from the cellars to the roofs, which enable them to be raised or lowered at discretion. The depth of the cellar is equal to the height of every house; in winter, the whole structure is lowered below the surface of the ground; in spring, it is lifted up again by means of the screw.

As, owing to the father's neglect, the house in which we were staying could not set sail until the next day, my companion and I accepted an invitation to stay the night there. Our host then sent for a doctor, who prescribed what foods I should smell, and what kind of bed I should lie in.

"But I am not sick!" I said to the Man of the Sun.

"If you were," he replied, "the doctor would not have been sent for. On the Moon, doctors are not paid to cure men, but to keep them in good health. They are officers of the state, and, once a day, they call at every house, and instruct the inmates how to preserve their natural vigour."

"I wish," I said, "you could get him to order me a dozen roasted larks instead of the mere smell of them. I should like to taste some solid food just for a change."

He spoke to the doctor, and at a sign from him, our host took a gun and led me into his garden.

"Are those the kind of birds you mean?" he said, pointing to a great swarm of larks singing high up in the sky.

I replied that they were, and he shot at them, and thirty larks tumbled over at our feet, not merely dead, but plucked, seasoned, and roasted.

"You see," said my host, "we mix with our gunpowder and shot a certain composition which cooks as well as kills."

I picked up one of the birds and ate it. In sober truth, I have never tasted on Earth anything so deliciously roasted.

When I had finished my repast, I was conducted to a little room, the floor of which was strewn with fine orange blossoms about three feet deep. The Men of the Moon always sleep on these thick, soft heaps of fragrant flowers, which are chosen for them every day by their doctors. Four servants came and undressed me, and gently rubbed my limbs and my body, and in a few moments I was fast asleep.

Early next morning I was awakened by the Man of the Sun, who said to me:

"I know you are anxious to return to your Earth and relate the story of all the strange and wonderful things you have seen on the Moon. If you care to while away an hour or two over this book, I will prepare for your return voyage."

The book which he put into my hand was an extraordinary object. It was a kind of machine, full of delicate springs, and it looked like a new kind of clock. In order to read it, you had to use, not your eyes, but your ears. For on touching one of the springs, it began to speak like a man. It was a history of the Sun, and I was still listening to it when my companion arrived.

"I am now ready," he said. "On what part of the Earth would you like to land?"

"In Italy," I replied. "That will save me the cost and trouble of travelling to Rome- a city I have always longed to see."

Taking me in his arms, the Man of the Sun rose swiftly up from the Moon and carried me across the intervening space, and dropped me rather roughly on a hill near Rome. When I turned to expostulate with him, I found that he had disappeared.

Micrographia
Or, Some Physiological Descriptions of Minute Bodies Made by Magnifying Glasses with Observations and Inquiries Thereupon
By Robert Hooke
(London, 1664)

The industrious Hooke was architect, chief surveyor of London and curator of experiments at the Royal Society. He investigated gasses, the law of elasticity is named after him, and he seems to have discovered how gravity acts long before Newton (p198). *Micrographia* was an astonishing success, bringing to the public (see Pepys, p194, Jan 20th 1665), as well as the scientific community, the tiny world in front of us, and observing cells for the first time.
Abridged: GH

TO THE KING.

SIR,

I do here most humbly lay this small Present at Your Majesties Royal feet. Amidst all those greater Designs, I here presume to bring in that which is more proportionable to the smalness of my Abilities, to that Mighty King, that has establisht an Empire over the best of all Invisible things of this World, the Minds of Men.

Your Majesties most humble and most obedient Subject and Servant, ROBERT HOOKE.

THE PREFACE.

It is the great prerogative of Mankind above other Creatures, that we are not only able to behold the works of Nature, but we have also the power of considering, comparing, altering, assisting, and improving them to various uses. Yet, not having a full sensation of an Object, we must be very lame and imperfect in our conceptions about it, hence, we often take the shadow of things for the substance.

These being the dangers of humane Reason, we may supply their infirmities with Instruments, with prodigious benefit to useful knowledge. By the means of Telescopes, there is

nothing so far distant but may be represented to our view; and by the help of Microscopes, there is nothing so small, as to escape our inquiry. What kind of mechanical way, and physical invention may yet be found out? The way of flying in the Air seems unpracticable, by reason of the want of strength in humane muscles; if that could be suppli'd, it were, I think, easie to make twenty contrivances to perform

the office of Wings: What Attempts I have made for the supplying that Defect, and my successes therein, which is not inconsiderable, I shall in another place relate.

The Microscope, which for the most part I made use of, was shap'd much like that in the Figure shown, the Tube being for the most part not above six or seven inches long.

I have made a Microscope with one piece of Glass, both whose surfaces were plains. I have made others of Waters, Gums, Resins, Salts, Arsenick, Oyls, and with divers other watery and oyly Liquors.

What the things I observ'd, the following descriptions will manifest; in brief, they were either exceeding small Bodies, some of which the Reader will find in the following Notes, and such, as I presume, (many of them at least) will be new, and perhaps not less strange

Of the Point of a sharp small Needle.

The Point of a Needle is commonly reckon'd sharp. But if view'd with a very good Microscope, we may find that the top of a Needle appears a broad, blunt, and very irregular end; not resembling a Cone, as is imagin'd, but onely a piece of a tapering body, with a great part of the top remov'd, or deficient. The Points of Pins are yet more blunt

Of the Edge of a Razor.

A Razor doth appear to be a Body of a very neat and curious aspect, till more closely viewed by the Microscope, and there we may observe its very Edge to be of all kind of shapes, except what it should be. For examining that of a very sharp one, I could not find that any part of it had any thing of sharpness in it; but it appeared a rough surface.

Of fine Lawn, or Linnen Cloth.

This is another product of Art, A piece of the finest Lawn I was able to get, so curious that the threads were scarce discernable by the naked eye, and yet through an ordinary Microscope you may perceive what a goodly piece of coarse Matting it is; what proportionable cords each of its threads are, being not unlike, both in shape and size, the bigger and coarser kind of single Rope-yarn, wherewith they usually make Cables.

Of several kindes of frozen Figures.

I have very often in a Morning, when there has been a great

discovery of them, presently hinted to me the true and intelligible reason of all the Phænomena of Cork. I have with my Microscope, plainly enough discover'd these Cells.

Schem XXXIV

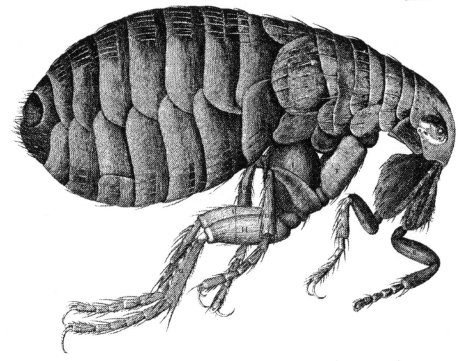

hoar-frost, with an indifferently magnifying Microscope, observ'd the small Stiriæ, or Crystalline beard, which then usually covers the face of most bodies that lie open to the cold air, and found them to be generally Hexangular prismatical bodies, much like the long Crystals of Salt-peter.

The parts of those curious branchings, or vortices, that usually in cold weather tarnish the surface of Glass, appear through the Microscope very rude and unshapen, as do most other kinds of frozen Figures, which to the naked eye seem exceeding neat and curious, such as the Figures of Snow, frozen Urine, Hail, several Figures frozen in common Water, &c.

Of the Schematisme or Texture of Cork, and of the Cells and Pores of some other such frothy Bodies.

I took a good clear piece of Cork, and with a Pen-knife sharpen'd as keen as a Razor, I cut a piece of it off, and thereby left the surface of it exceeding smooth, then examining it very diligently with a Microscope. I could exceeding plainly perceive it to be all perforated and porous, much like a Honey-comb. I no sooner discern'd these (which were indeed the first microscopical pores I ever saw, and perhaps, that were ever seen, for I had not met with any Writer or Person, that had made any mention of them before this) but me thought I had with the

Of a Plant growing in the blighted or yellow specks of Damask-rose-leaves, and some other kind of leaves.

I have for several years observ'd many of the leaves of the old shrubs of Damask Roses, all bespecked with yellow stains. Examining these with a Microscope, I was able plainly to distinguish, up and down the surface, several small yellow knobs, of a kind of yellowish red gummy substance, out of which I perceiv'd there sprung multitudes of little cases or black bodies like Seed-cods. I have often doubted whether they were the seed Cods of some little Plant, or some kind of small Buds, or the Eggs of some very small Insect, they appear'd of a dark brownish red, some almost quite black, and their stalks were of a very fine, which makes me to suppose them to be Vegetables, of a kind of Mildew or Blight

Of the Eyes and Head of a Grey drone-Fly.

I took a large grey Drone-Fly, (this I made choice of because I found this Fly to have the biggest clusters of eyes in proportion to his head, of any small kind of Fly) Then examining it according to my usual manner, by varying the degrees of light, and altering its position to each kinde of light, I drew that representation of it which is delineated here, and found these things to be as plain and evident, as notable and pleasant.

Of a Flea.

The strength and beauty of this small creature, had it no other relation at all to man, would deserve a description. For its strength, the Microscope is able to make no greater discoveries of it then the naked eye, but onely the curious contrivance of its leggs and joints, for the exerting that strength, is very plainly manifested, such as no other creature, I have yet observ'd. I could not perceive them tooth'd; but their jaws were shap'd very like the blades of a pair of round top'd Scizers, and were opened and shut just after the same manner; with these Instruments does this little busie Creature bite and pierce the skin.

Of a Louse.

This is a Creature so officious, that 'twill be known to every one at one time or other, so busie, and so impudent, that it will be intruding it self in every ones company, and so proud and aspiring withall, that it fears not to trample on the best, and affects nothing so much as a Crown. It feeds and lives very high, and that makes it so saucy, as to pull any one by the ears that comes in its way, and will never be quiet till it has drawn blood: it is troubled at nothing so much as at a man that scratches his head, as knowing that man is plotting and contriving some mischief against it.

Of multitudes of small Stars discoverable by the Telescope, and Of the Moon

'Ttis not unlikely, but that the meliorating of Telescopes will afford as great a variety of new Discoveries in the Heavens, as better Microscopes would among small terrestrial Bodies, and both would give us infinite cause, more and more to admire the omnipotence of the Creator.

In October 1664, just before the Moon was half inlightned, with a Glass of threescore foot long, I observed the Mountains of the Moon. I am not unapt to think, that the Vale may have Vegetables analogus to our Grass, Shrubs, and Trees; and most of these incompassing Hills may be covered with so thin a vegetable Coat, as we may observe the Hills with us to be, such as the short Sheep pasture which covers the Hills of Salisbury Plains.

Paradise Lost
By John Milton
(London, 1667)

Milton, a civil servant under England's brief period as a Republic, published his epic when he was becoming blind. Dryden, to whom it was shown, remarked, "This man cuts us all out, and the ancients too".

Abridged: JH

Of Man's First Disobedience, and the Fruit
Of that Forbidden Tree, whose mortal taste
Brought Death into the World, and all our woe,
With loss of EDEN, till one greater Man
Restore us, and regain the blissful Seat,
Sing Heav'nly Muse, that on the secret top
Of OREB, or of SINAI, didst inspire
That shepherd who first taught the chosen seed
In the beginning how the heavens and earth
Rose out of CHAOS; or, if SION's hill
Delight thee more, and Siloa's brook that flowed
Fast by the oracle of God, I thence
Invoke thy aid to my adventurous song,
That with no middle flight intends to soar
Above the Aonian mount, while it pursues
Things unattempted yet in prose or rhyme.
And chiefly thou, O Spirit, that dost prefer
Before all temples the upright heart and pure,
Instruct me, for thou know'st; thou from the first
Wast present, and, with mighty wings out-spread,
Dove-like sat'st brooding on the vast Abyss,
And mad'st it pregnant: what in me is dark
Illumine, what is low raise and support;
That, to the highth of this great argument.
I may assert th' Eternal Providence,
And justify the ways of God to men.
Say first, for Heaven hides nothing from thy view,
Nor the deep tract of Hell-say first what cause
Moved our grand parents, in that happy state,
Favoured of Heaven so highly, to fall off
From their Creator, and transgress His will
For one restraint, Lords of the World be-side?
Who first seduc'd them to that foul revolt?
The infernal Serpent; he it was whose guile,
Stirred up with envy and revenge, deceived
The mother of mankind, what time his pride
Had cast him out from Heaven, with all his host
Of rebel angels. ... Him the Almighty Power
Hurled headlong flaming from the ethereal sky,
With hideous ruin and combustion down
To bottomless perdition, there to dwell
In adamantine chains and penal fire,
Who durst defy the Omnipotent to arms.

[For nine days and nights the apostate Angel lay silent, 'rolling in the fiery gulf,' and then, looking round, he discerned by his side BEELZEBUB, 'one next himself in power and next in crime.' With him he took counsel, and rearing themselves from off the pool of fire they found footing on a dreary plain. Walking with uneasy steps the

burning vale, the lost Archangel made his way to the shore of 'that inflamed sea,' and called aloud to his associates to 'awake, arise, or be for ever fallen!' They heard, and gathered about him, all who were 'known to men by various names and various idols through the heathen world,' but with looks 'downcast and damp.']

Then straight commands that, at the warlike sound
Of trumpets loud and clarions, be upreared
His mighty standard. That proud honour claimed
Azazel as his right, a cherub tall,
Who forthwith from the glittering staff unfurled
The imperial ensign which full high advanc't
Shone like a Meteor streaming to the Wind
At which the universal host up-sent
A shout that tore Hell's conclave, and beyond
Frighted the reign of CHAOS and old Night.

[The mighty host now circled in orderly array about 'their dread commander.']

He, above the rest
In shape and gesture proudly eminent,
Stood like a tower. His form had yet not lost
All her original brightness, nor appeared
Less than Archangel ruined, and the excess
Of glory obscured: as when the sun newrisen
Looks through the horizontal misty air
Shorn of his beams, or, from behind the moon,
In dim eclipse, disastrous twilight sheds
On half the nations, and with fear of change
Perplexes monarchs. Darkened so, yet shone
Above them all the Archangel. But his face
Deep scars of thunder had intrenched, and care
Sat on his faded cheek, but under brows
Of dauntless courage and considerate pride,
Waiting revenge... He now prepared
To speak; whereat their doubled ranks they bend
From wing to wing, and half enclose him round
With all his peers. Attention held them mute.
Thrice he essayed, and thrice, in spite of scorn.
Tears, such as Angels weep, burst forth; at last
Words interwove with sighs found out their way:
"O myriads of immortal Spirits' O Powers,
Matchless, but with the Almighty!-and that strife
Was not inglorious, though the event was dire,
As this place testifies, and this dire change,
Hateful to utter. But what power of mind,
Foreseeing or presaging, from the depth
Of knowledge past or present, could have feared
How such united force of gods, how such
As stood like these, could ever know repulse?
He who reigns
Monarch in Heaven, till then as one secure
Sat on his throne, upheld by old repute,
Consent, or custom, and his regal state
Put forth at full, but still his strength concealed-
Which tempted our attempt, and wrought our fall.

Henceforth, his might we know, and know our own,
So as not either to provoke, or dread
New war, provoked. Our better part remains
To work in close design, by fraud or guile,
What force effected not; that he no less
At length from us may find who overcomes
By force hath overcome but half his foe.
Space may produce new Worlds, whereof so rife
There went a fame in Heaven that he ere long
Intended to create, and therein plant
A generation whom his choice regard
Should favour equal to the Sons of Heaven.
Thither, if but to pry, shall be perhaps
Our first eruption-thither, or elsewhere;
For this infernal pit shall never hold
Celestial Spirits in bondage, nor the abyss
Long under darkness cover. But these thoughts
Full counsel must mature. Peace is despaired;
For who can think submission? War, then war
Open or understood, must be resolved."
He spake; and to confirm his words, outflew
Millions of flaming swords, drawn from the thighs
Of mighty Cherubim. The sudden blaze
Far round illumined Hell. Highly they raged
Against the Highest, and fierce with grasped arms
Clashed on their sounding shields the din of war
Hurling defiance toward the vault of Heaven.

[The exiled host now led by Mammon, 'the least erected spirit that fell from Heaven,' proceeded to build Pandemonium. their architect being him whom 'men called Mulciber.' and...]

The great seraphic Lords and Cherubim
In close recess and secret conclave sat,
A thousand demi-gods on golden seats.
High on a throne of royal state, which far
Outshone the wealth of Ormus or of Ind,
Or where the gorgeous East with richest hand
Showers on her kings barbaric pearl and gold,
SATAN exalted sat, by merit raised
To that bad eminence, counselled war.

[Then uprose BELIAL- 'a fairer person lost not Heaven'- and reasoned that force was futile.]

The towers of Heaven are filled
With armed watch, that render all access
Impregnable.

[Besides, failure might lead to their annihilation, and who wished for that?]

Though full of pain, this intellectual being,
Those thoughts that wander through Eternity,
To perish rather, swallowd up and lost
In the wide womb of uncreated night,

[They were better now than when they were hurled from Heaven, or when they lay chained on the burning lake. Their Supreme Foe might in time remit His anger, and slacken those raging fires. Mammon also advised them to keep the peace, and make the best they could of Hell, a policy received with applause; but then BEELZEBUB, 'than whom. SATAN except, none higher sat,' rose, and with a look which 'drew audience and attention still as night,' developed the suggestion previously made by SATAN, that they should attack Heaven's High Arbitrator through His new-created Man, waste His creation, and 'drive as we are driven.']

"This would surpass
Common revenge, and interrupt His joy
In our confusion, and our joy upraise
In His disturbance."

[This proposal was gleefully received. But then the difficulty arose who should be sent in search of this new world? All sat mute, till SATAN declared that he would 'abroad through all the coasts of dark destruction,' a decision hailed with reverent applause. The council dissolved, the Infernal Peers disperse to their several employments: some to sports, some to warlike feats, some to argument, 'in wandering mazes lost,' some to adventurous discovery; while SATAN wings his way to the ninefold gate of Hell, guarded by Sin and her abortive offspring Death, and Sin, opening the gate for him to go out, cannot shut it again. The Fiend stands on the brink, 'pondering his voyage,' while before him appear...]

The secrets of the hoary Deep-a dark
Illimitable ocean, without bound,
Without dimensions; where length, breadth, and highth,
And time and place are lost; where eldest Night
And CHAOS, ancestors of Nature, hold Eternal anarchy.

[At last he spreads his 'sail-broad vans' for flight, and 'in the surging smoke, Uplifted spurns the ground.' He is directed by CHAOS and sable-vested Night, and comes to where he can see far off]

The empyreal Heaven, once his native seat,
And, fast by, hanging in a golden chain,
This pendent world, in bigness as a star
Of smallest magnitude close by the moon.

[As invocation to Light, and a lament for the poet's blindness now preludes a picture of Heaven, and the Almighty Father conferring with the only Son.]

Hail, holy Light, offspring of Heaven first-born!
Bright effluence of bright essence increate!
Whose fountain who shall tell? Before the Sun,
Before the Heavens, thou wert, and at the voice
Of God. as with a mantle, didst invest
The rising world of waters dark and deep,

Won from the void and formless Infinite!
But thou Revisit'st not these eyes, that roll in vain
To find thy piercing ray, and find no dawn.
With the year Seasons return; but not to me returns
Day, or the sweet approach of even or morn,
Or sight of vernal bloom, or summer's rose,
Or flocks, or herds, or human face divine;
But cloud instead, and ever-during dark
Surrounds me, from the cheerful ways of men
Cut off.

[God. observing the approach of SATAN to the world, foretells the fall of man to the Son, who listens while...]

In his face, Divine compassion visibly appeared,
Love without end, and without measure grace.

[The Father asks where such love can be found as will redeem man by satisfying eternal Justice.]

He asked, but all the Heavenly Quire stood mule,
And silence was in Heaven.

[Admiration seized All Heaven, and 'With solemn adoration down they cast, Their Crowns inwove with Amarant and Gold', when the Son replied:]

"Account me man. I for his sake will leave
Thy bosom, and this glory next to thee
Freely put off, and for him lastly die
Well pleased; on me let Death wreak all his rage.
Under his gloomy power I shall not long
Lie vanquish'd."

[While the immortal quires chanted their praise, SATAN drew near and sighted the world- the sun, earth, moon and companion planets.]

As when a scout,
Through dark and desert ways with peril gone
All night, at last by break of cheerful dawn
Obtains the brow of some high-climbing hill,
Which to his eye discovers unaware
The goodly prospect of some foreign land
First seen, or some renowned metropolis
With glistening spires and pinnacles adorned,
Which now the rising Sun gilds with his beams,
Such wonder seized, though after Heaven seen,
The Spirit malign, but much more envy seized.
At sight of all this world beheld so fair.

[Flying to the Sun, and taking the form of 'a stripling Cherub,' SATAN recognizes there the Archangel Uriel and accosts him.]

Brightest Seraph, tell
In which of all these shining orbs hath Man
His fixed seat, or fixed seat hath none,

But all these shining Orbs his choice to dwell;
That I may find him, and with secret gaze,
Or open admiration him behold
On whom the great Creator hath bestow'd
Worlds, and on whom hath all these graces pour'd.

[And Uriel, although held to be 'the sharpest-sighted spirit of all in Heaven,' was deceived, for angels cannot discern hypocrisy. So Uriel, pointing, answers:]

That place is earth, the seat of Man, that light
His day, which else as th'other hemisphere
Night would invade, but there the neighbouring moon
(So call that opposite fair star) her aid
Timely interposes, and her monthly round
Still ending, still renewing through mid-Heaven,
With borrowed light, her countenance triform
Hence fills and empties to enlighten the Earth.
And in her pale dominion checks the night.
That spot to which I point is Paradise,
Adam's abode; those lofty shades his bower.
Thy way thou canst not miss; me mine requires.'
Thus said. he turned: and SATAN, bowing low,
As to superior spirits is wont in Heaven,
Where honour due and reverence none neglects,
Took leave, and toward the coast of Earth beneath,
Down from the ecliptic, sped with hoped success,
Throws his steep flight in many an aery wheel,
Nor stayed till on Niphates' top he lights.

[Coming within sight of Paradise, SATAN's conscience is aroused, and lie grieves over the suffering his dire work will entail, exclaiming:]

"Me miserable! Which way shall I fly
Infinite wrath and infinite despair?
Which way I fly is Hell; myself am Hell."

[As he approaches Paradise more closely the deliciousness of the place affects even his senses.]

As when to them who sail
Beyond the Cape of Hope, and now are past
Mozambic, off at sea north-east winds blow
Sabean odours from the spicy shore
Of Araby the Blest, with such delay
Well pleased they slack (heir course, and many a league
Cheered with the grateful smell old Ocean smiles,
So entertained those odorous sweets the Fiend.

[At last, after sighting 'all kinds of living creatures new to sight and strange,' he descries Man.]

Two of far nobler shape, erect and tall,
God-like erect, with native honour clad
In naked majesty, seemed lords of all,
And worthy seemed: for in their looks divine
The image of their glorious Maker shone ....

For contemplation he, and valour, formed.
For softness she and sweet attractive grace;
He for God only. she for God in him ...
So hand in hand they passed, the loveliest pair
That ever since in love's embraces met-
Adam the goodliest man of men since born
His sons; the fairest of her daughters Eve.

[At the sight of the gentle pair. SATAN again almost relents. Taking the shape of various animals, he approaches to hear them talk. and finds from Adam that the only prohibition laid on them is partaking of the Tree of Knowledge. Eve, replying, tells Adam how she found herself alive, saw her form reflected in the water, and thought herself fairer even than he until...]

"Thy gentle hand
Seized mine; I yielded, and from that time see
How beauty is excelled by manly grace
And wisdom, which alone is truly fair."

[While SATAN roams through Paradise, with 'sly circumspection,' Uriel descends on an evening sunbeam to warn Gabriel, 'chief of the angelic guards,' that a suspected spirit with looks 'alien from Heaven,' had passed to earth, and Gabriel promises to find him before dawn.]

Now came still Evening on, and Twilight grey
Had in her sober livery all things clad;
Silence accompanied; for beast and bird,
They to their grassy couch, these to their nests
Were slunk, all but the wakeful nightingale.
She all night long her amorous descant sung.
Silence was pleased. Now glowed the firmament
With living sapphires: Hesperus, that led
The starry host, rode brightest, till the Moon.
Rising in clouded majesty, at length
Apparent queen, unveiled her peerless light.
And o'er the dark her silver mantle threw.

[Adam and Eve talk ere they retire to rest- she questioning him.]

"Sweet is the breath of Morn. her rising sweet
With charm of earliest birds; pleasant the Sun,
When first on this delightful land he spreads
His orient beams on herb, tree, fruit and flower,
Glistering with dew; fragrant the fertile earth
After soft showers; and sweet the coming on
Of grateful Evening mild; then silent Night,
With this her solemn bird, and this fair Moon,
And these the gems of Heaven, her starry train;
But neither breath of Morn, when she ascends
With charm of earliest birds; nor rising Sun
On this delightful land; nor herb. fruit, flower,
Glistering with dew; nor fragrance after showers;
Nor grateful Evening mild; nor silent Night,
With this her solemn bird; nor walk by moon,

Or glittering star-light, without thee is sweet.
But wherefore all night long shine these?
For whom This glorious sight,
When sleep hath shut all eyes?"

[Adam replies.]
"These have their course to finish round the Earth,
And they, though unbeheld in deep of night,
Shine not in vain. Nor think, though men were none,
That Heaven would want spectators, God want praise.
Millions of spiritual Creatures walk the earth
Unseen, both when we wake and when we sleep;
All these with ceaseless praise His works behold
Both day and night. ....."
Thus talking, hand in hand, alone they passed
On to their blissful bower.

[Gabriel then sends the Cherubim 'armed to their night watches.' and commands Ithuriel and Zephon to search the Garden, where they find SATAN; 'squat like a toad close to the ear of Eve,' seeking to taint her dreams.]

Him thus intent Ithuriel with his spear
Touched lightly; for no falsehood can endure
Touch of celestial temper, but returns
Of force to its own likeness.

[SATAN therefore starts up in his own person, and is conducted to Gabriel, who sees him coming with them, 'a third, of regal port, but faded splendour wan.' Gabriel and he engage in a heated altercation, and a fight seems imminent between the Fiend and the angelic squadrons that 'begin to hem him round,' when, by a sign in the sky, SATAN is reminded of his powerlessness in open fight, and flees, murmuring. 'And with him fled the shades of night.' Adam, waking in the morning, finds Eve flushed and distraught, and she tells him of her troublous dreams. He cheers her, and they pass out to the open field, and, adoring, raise their morning hymn of praise.]

"These are thy glorious works, Parent of good,
Almighty! thine this universal frame.
Thus wondrous fair-thyself how wondrous then!
Unspeakable! who sittest above these heavens
To us invisible, or dimly seen
In these thy lowest works; yet these declare
Thy goodness beyond thought, and power divine.
Speak, ye who best can tell, ye Sons of Light,
Angels-for ye behold him, and with songs
And choral symphonies, day without night,
Circle his throne rejoicing-ye in Heaven;
(In Earth join. all ye creatures, to extol
Him first, him last, him midst, and without end.
Fairest of Starrs, last in the train of Night,
If better thou belong not to the dawn,
Sure pledge of day, that crown'st the smiling morn
With thy bright circlet, praise him in thy sphere
While day arises, that sweet hour of prime.

Thou Son, of this great world both eye and soul,
Acknowledge him thy greater; sound his praise
In thy eternal course, both when thou climb'st
And when high noon hast gained, and when thou fall'st.
Moon, that now meet'st the orient Sun, now fliest,
With the fixed Stars, fixed in their orb that flies;
And ye five other wandering Fires, that move
In mystic dance, not without song, resound
His praise who out of Darkness called up Light. ...
Ye Mists and Exhalations, that now rise
From hill or steaming lake. dusky or grey,
Till the Sun paint your fleecy skirts with gold,
In honour to the World's great Author
Whether to deck with clouds the uncoloured sky,
Or wet the thirsty earth with falling showers,
Rising or falling, still advance his praise.
His praise, ye Winds, that from four quarters blow,
Breathe soft or loud; and wave your tops, ye Pines,
With every plant in sign of worship wave.
Fountains, and ye that warble as ye flow,
Melodious murmurs, warbling, tune his praise.
Join voices, all ye living souls. Ye birds,
That, singing, up to Heaven's gate ascend,
Bear on your wings and in your notes his praise. ....
Hail. universal Lord! Be bounteous still
To give us only good; and, if the night
Have gathered aught of evil. or concealed,
Disperse it, as now light dispels the dark."
So prayed they innocent, and to their thoughts
Firm peace recovered soon, and wonted calm.

[The Almighty now sends Raphael, 'the sociable Spirit,' from Heaven to warn Adam of his danger, and, alighting on the eastern cliff of Paradise, the Seraph shakes his plumes and diffuses heavenly fragrance around; then moving through the forest is seen by Adam, who, with Eve, entertains him, and seizes the occasion to ask him of 'their Being, who dwell in Heaven,' and further, what is meant by the angelic caution- 'if ye be found obedient.' Raphael thereupon tells of the disobedience, in Heaven, of SATAN, and his fall, 'from that high state of bliss into what woe.' He tells how the Divine decree of obedience to the Only Son was received by SATAN with envy, because he felt 'himself impaired'; and how, consulting with BEELZEBUB, he drew away all the spirits under their command to the 'spacious North,' and taunting them with being eclipsed, proposed that they should rebel. Only Abdiel remained faithful, and urged them to cease their 'impious rage,' and seek pardon in time, or they might find that he who had created them could uncreate them.]

So spake the Seraph Abdiel, faithful found;
Among the faithless, faithful only he;
Among innumerable false, unmoved,
Unshaken, unseduced, unterrified,
His loyalty he kept, his love, his zeal;
Nor number nor example with him wrought
To swerve from truth or change his constant mind

Though single.

[Raphael, continuing, tells Adam how Abdiel flew back to Heaven with the story of the revolt, but found it was known. The Sovran Voice, having welcomed the faithful messenger with 'Servant of God, well done!' orders the Arch- angels Michael and Gabriel to lead forth the celestial armies, while the banded powers of SATAN are hastening on to set the Proud Aspirer on the very Mount of God. 'Long time in even scale the battle hung,' but with the dawning of the third day, the Father directed the Messiah to ascend his chariot, and end the strife. 'Far off his coming shone.' and at his presence 'Heaven his wonted face renewed, and with fresh flowerets hill and valley smiled.' But nearing the foe, his countenance changed into a terror 'too severe to be beheld.']

Among them he arriv'd, in his right hand
Grasping ten thousand thunders, which he sent
Before him, such as in their souls infixed
Plagues; they, astonished, all resistance lost.
All courage; down their idle weapons, dropt.
The monstrous sigh, Struck them with horror;
headlong them selves they threw
Down from the verge of Heaven; eternal wrath
Burnt after them to the bottomless pit.

[A like fate, Raphael warns Adam, may befall mankind if they are guilty of disobedience. The 'affable Archangel,' at Adam's request, continues his talk by telling how the world began. Lest Lucifer should lake a pride in having 'dispeopled Heaven,' God announces to the Son that he will create another world, and a race to dwell in it who may]

They open to themselves at length the way
Up hither, under long obedience tri'd,
And Earth be chang'd to Heaven, & Heav'n to Earth,
One Kingdom, Joy and Union without end.
Mean while inhabit laxe, ye Powers of Heav'n,
And thou my Word, begotten Son, by thee
This I perform, speak thou, and be it done:
My overshadowing Spirit and might with thee
I send along; ride forth, and bid the Deep
Within appointed bounds be Heaven and Earth,
Boundless the deep, because I am who fill
Infinitude, nor vacuous the space.
Though I uncircumscrib'd myself retire,
And put not forth my goodness, which is free
To act or not; necessity and chance
Approach not me. and what I will is fate."
So spake th' Almighty, and to what he spake
His word, the Filial Godhead, gave effect.
Immediate are the acts of God, more swift
Than time or motion, but to human ears
Cannot without process of speech be told,
So (old as earthly notion can receive.
Great triumph and rejoicing was in Heaven
When such was heard declared th' Almighty's will;

Glory they sung to God most high.
Heaven opened wide
Her ever-during gates, harmonious sound
On golden hinges moving to let forth
The King of Glory, in his powerful Word
And Spirit coming to create new worlds.
On heavenly ground they stood, and from the shore
They viewed the vast immeasurable abyss,
Outrageous as a sea, dark, wasteful, wild,
Up from the bottom turned by furious winds
And surging waves, as mountains to assault
Heaven's highth, and with the centre mix the pole.
"Silence, ye troubled waves, and thou deep, peace!"
Said then the omnific Word. "Your discord end!"
Nor stayed; but on the wings of Cherubim,
Uplifted in paternal glory rode
Far into CHAOS and the World unborn;
For CHAOS heard his voice. ....
And Earth, self-balanced on her centre hung.

[The six days' creative work is then described in the order of Genesis[1]. Asked by Adam to tell him about the motions of the heavenly bodies, Raphael adjures him to refrain from thought on 'matters hid; to serve God and fear; and to be lowly wise.' He then asks Adam to tell him of his creation, he having at the time been absent on 'excursion towards the gates of Hell.' Adam complies, and relates how he appealed to God for a companion, and was answered in the fairest of God's gifts. Raphael warns Adam to beware lest passion for Eve sway his judgement, for on him depends the weal or woe of himself and all his sons. While Raphael was in Paradise, for seven nights SATAN hid himself in the shadow of the Earth. Then, rising as a mist, he crept into EDEN undetected, and entered the serpent as 'fittest imp of fraud,' but not until he had once more lamented that the environ of the earth was not for him. In the morning, when the human pair were at their pleasant labours, Eve decided they should work apart, for when near each other 'looks intervene and smiles,' and casual discourse. Adam replied, defending 'this sweet intercourse of looks and smiles,' because they had been made not for irksome toil, but for delight.]

But if much converse perhaps
Thee satiate, to short absence I could yield;
For solitude sometimes is best society,
And short retirement urges sweet return.
But other doubt possesses me, lest harm
Befall thee. ....

[Eve, 'with sweet austere composure,' replies.]

"That such an enemy we have, who seeks
Our ruin, both by thee informed I learn,
And from the parting Angel overheard.

---

1   **Genesis:** see p23

[She, however, repels the suggestion that she can be deceived. Adam replies that he does not wish her to be tempted, and that united they would be stronger and more watchful. Eve responds that if EDEN is so exposed that they are not secure apart, how can they be happy? Adam gives way.]

Her long with ardent look his eye pursued
Delighted, but desiring more her stay.
Oft he to her his charge of quick return
Repeated; she to him as oft engaged
To be returned by noon amid the bower,
And all things in best order to invite
Noontide repast, or afternoon's repose.
O much deceived, much failing, hapless Eve,
Of thy presumed return! Event perverse !
Thou never from that hour in Paradise
Found'st either sweet repast or sound repose.

[The Fiend, questing through the garden, finds her]

Veiled in a cloud of fragrance where she stood,
Half spied, so thick the roses bushing round
About her glowed. ... Then she upstays
Gently with myrtle band, mindless the while
Herself, though fairest unsupported flower,
From her best prop so far, and storm so nigh.

[Seeing her, SATAN 'much the place admired, the person more.']

As one who, long in populous city pent,
Forth issuing on a summer's morn to breathe
Among the pleasant villages and farms
Adjoined, from each thing met conceives delight-
The smell of grain, or tended grass, or kine,
Or dairy, each rural sight, each rural sound-
If chance with nymph-like step fair virgin pass,
What pleasing seemed, for her now pleases more,
She most, and in her looks sums all delight.
Such pleasure took the Serpent to behold
This flowery plat, the sweet recess of Eve
Thus early, thus alone.

[The original serpent did not creep on the ground, but was a handsome creature.]

With burnished neck of verdant gold, erect
Amidst his circling spires, that on the grass
Floated redundant. Pleasing was his shape
And lovely.

[Appearing before Eve with an air of worshipful admiration, and speaking in human language, the arch-deceiver gains her ear with flattery. 'Empress of this fair world, resplendent Eve.' She asks how it is that man's language is pronounced by 'tongue of brute.' The reply is that the power came through eating the fruit of a certain

tree, which gave him reason, and also constrained him to worship her as 'sovran of creatures.' Asked to show her the tree, he leads her swiftly to the Tree of Prohibition, and replying to her scruples and fears, declares]

Queen of this Universe! Do not believe
Those rigid threats of death. Ye shall not die.
How should ye? By the fruit? It gives you life
To knowledge. By the Threatener? Look on me-
Me who have touched and tasted, yet both live
And life more perfect have attained than Fate
Meant me, by venturing higher than my lot.
Shall that be shut to Man which to the Beast
Is open? or will God incense his ire
For such a pretty Trespass, and not praise
Rather your dauntless vertue, whom the pain
Of Death denounc't, whatever thing Death be,
Deterrd not from achieving what might leade
To happier life, knowledge of Good and Evil;
Of good, how just? of evil, if what is evil
Be real, why not known, since easier shunnd?
God therefore cannot hurt ye, and be just;
Goddess humane, reach, then, and freely taste!"
He ended; and his words, replete with guile.
Into her heart too easy entrance won.

[Eve herself then took up the argument and repeated admiringly the Serpent's persuasions.]

"In the day we eat
Of this fair fruit our doom is we shall die!
How dies the serpent? He hath eaten and lives,
And knows, and speaks, and reasons, and discerns.
Irrational till then. For us alone
Was death invented? Or to us denied
This intellectual food, for beasts reserved?
Here grows the cure of all, this fruit divine,
Fair to the eye, inviting to the taste,
Of virtue to make wise. What hinders then
To reach and feed at once both body and mind?"
... So saying, her rash hand in evil hour
Forth-reaching to the fruit, she plucked, she ate.
Earth felt the wound, and Nature from her seat,
Sighing through all her works, gave signs of woe
That all was lost. Back to the thicket slunk
The guilty serpent.

[At first elated by the fruit. Eve presently began to reflect, excuse herself, and wonder what the effect would be on Adam.]

"And I perhaps am secret. Heaven is high-
High. and remote to see from thence distinct.
Each thing on Earth; and other care perhaps
May have diverted from continual watch
Our great Forbidder, safe with all his spies
About him. But to Adam in what sort
Shall I appear? Shall I to him make known

As yet my change?
But what if God have seen,
And death ensue? Then I shall be no more;
And Adam, wedded to another Eve,
Shall live with her enjoying, I extinct!
A death to think! Confirmed then, I resolve
Adam shall share with me in bliss or woe;
So dear I love him that with him all deaths
I could endure, without him live no life."
Adam the while
Waiting desirous her return, had wove
Of choicest flowers a garland, to adorn
Her tresses. ... Soon as he heard
The fatal trespass done by Eve, amazed,
Astonished stood and blank.
From his slack hand the garland wreathed for Eve
Down dropt, and all the faded roses shed,
Speechless he stood and pale, till thus at length,
First to himself, he inward silence broke:
"O fairest of creation, last and best
Of all God's works, creature in whom excelled
Whatever can to sight or thought be formed,
Holy. divine, good, amiable, or sweet,
How art thou lost! How on a sudden lost!
Some cursed fraud
Of enemy hath beguiled thee, yet unknown.
And me with thee hath ruined; for with thee
Certain my resolution is to die.
How can I live without thee? How forego
Thy sweet converse, and love so dearly joined
To live again in these wild woods forlorn?"

[Then, turning to Eve, he tried to comfort her.]

Perhaps thou shalt not die ...
Now can I think that God. Creator wise,
Though threatening, will in earnest so destroy
Us. his prime creatures, dignified so high,
Set over all his works. ....
However, I with thee have fixed my lot,
Certain to undergo like doom. If death
Consort with thee, death is to me as life.
Our state cannot be severed; we are one."
So Adam; and thus Eve to him replied:
"O glorious trial of exceeding love,
Illustrious evidence, example high!"
So saying she embraced him, and for joy
Tenderly wept, much won that he his love
Had so ennobled as of choice to incur
Divine displeasure for her sake, or death.
In recompense ...
She gave him of that fair enticing fruit
With liberal hand. He scrupled not to eat
Against his better knowledge, not deceived,
But fondly overcome with female charm.

[The effect of the fruit on them is first to excite lust, with
guilty shame following, and realizing this after 'the

exhilarating vapour bland' had spent its force, Adam found
utterance for his remorse...]

"O Eve, in evil hour thou didst give ear
To that false Worm. ....
    ... How shall I behold the face
Henceforth of God or Angel, erst with joy
And rapture so oft beheld? Those Heavenly shapes
Will dazzle now this earthly, with their blaze
Insufferably bright. Oh, might I here
In solitude live savage, in some glade
Obscured, where highest woods, impenetrable
To star, or sunlight, spread their umbrage broad,
And brown as evening! Cover me, ye Pines!
Ye Cedars, with innumerable boughs
Hide me, where I may never see them more!"

[Then they cower in the woods, and clothe themselves with
leaves.]

Covered, but not at rest or ease of mind
They sat them down to weep.

[But passion also took possession of them, and they began
to taunt each other with recriminations, Adam, with
estranged look, exclaimed:]

"Would thou hadst hearkened to my words, and stayed
With me, as I besought thee, when that strange
Desire of wandering, this unhappy morn,
I know not whence possessed thee! We had then
Remained still happy!"

[Eve retorts:]
"Hadst thou been firm and fixed in thy dissent
Neither had I transgressed nor thou with me."

[Then Adam:]
"What could I more?
I warned thee, I admonished thee, foretold
The danger, and the lurking enemy
That lay in wait; beyond this had been force."
Thus they in mutual accusation spent
The fruitless hours, but neither self-condemning;
And of their vain contest appeared no end.

[The Angels left on guard now slowly return from Paradise
to Heaven to report their failure, but are reminded by God
that it was ordained; and the Son is sent down to judge the
guilty pair, after hearing their excuses, and to punish them
with the curses of toil and death. Meantime Sin and Death
'snuff the smell of mortal change' on Earth, and leaving
Hell-gate 'belching outrageous flame,' erect a broad road
from Hell to Earth through CHAOS, and as they come in
sight of the World meet SATAN steering his way back as an
angel 'between the Centaur and the Scorpion.' He makes
Sin and Death his plenipotentiaries on Earth, adjuring
them first to make man their thrall, and lastly kill; and as

they pass to the evil work 'the blasted stars look wan.' The return to Hell is received with loud acclaim, which comes in the form of a hiss, and SATAN and all his hosts are turned into grovelling snakes. Adam is sternly resentful against Eve, but both pass to 'sorrow unfeigned and humiliation meek.' The repentance of the pair is accepted by God, who sends down the Archangel Michael, with a cohort of Cherubim, to announce that death will not come until time has been given for repentance, but Paradise can no longer be their home. Whereupon Eve laments...]

"O unexpected stroke, worse than of Death!
Must I thus leave thee. Paradise? Thus leave
Thee, native soil? These happy walks and shades,
Fit haunt of gods, where I had hoped to spend
Quiet, though sad, the respite of that day
That must be mortal to us both? O flowers,
That never will in any other climate grow,
My early visitation and my last
At even, which I bred up with tender hand
From who now shall rear ye to the Sun, or rank
Your tribes, and water from the ambrosial fount?
Thee lastly, nuptial bower, by me adorned
With what to sight or smell was sweet; from thee
How shall I part, and whither wander down
Into the lower world, to this obscure
And wild, how shall we breathe in other air
Less pure, accustomed to immortal fruits?"

[The Angel counsels her...]
"Lament not, Eve, but patiently resign
What justly thou hast lost; nor set thy heart
Thus over-fond, on that which is not thine;
Thy going is not lonely; with thee goes
Thy husband; him to follow thou art bound;
Where he abides, think there thy native soil."

[Michael then ascending a hill with Adam shows him a vision of the world's history, and first of the ravages of death, while Eve sleeps.]
Adam wept,
Though not of woman born; compassion quelled
His best of Man, and gave him up to tears
A space, till firmer thoughts restrained excess,
And scarce recovering words his plaint renewed.
"O miserable Mankind, to what fall
Degraded, to what wretched state reserved!
.... Can thus
Th' Image of God in man created once
To such unsightly sufferings be debased?"

[The history is continued, with its promise of redemption, until Adam exclaims:]

"Full of doubt I stand
Whether I should repent me now in sin
By me done and occasioned, or rejoice

Much more that much more food thereof shall spring--
To God more glory, more good will to men
From God, and ever wrath grace shall abound.
But say, if our deliverer up to Heaven
Must re-ascend, what will betide the few
His faithful, left among th' unfaithful herd,
The enemies of truth; who then shall guide
His people, who defend? will they not deal
Worse with his followers than with him they dealt?"
"Be sure they will." said th' Angel; "but from Heav'n
He to his own a Comforter will send,
The promise of the Father, who shall dwell
His spirit within them, and the law of Faith
Working through love, upon their hearts shall write.
To guide them in all truth, and also arm
With spiritual armour, able to resist
SATAN's assaults, and quench his fiery darts.
What Man can do against them, not afraid,
Though to the death, against such cruelties
With inward consolations recompensed,
And oft supported so as shall amaze
Their proudest persecutors: for the Spirit
Pour'd first on his Apostles, whom he sends
To evangelise the nations, then on all
Baptiz'd shall them with wondrous gifts endue
To speak all tongues, and do all miracles,
As did their Lord before them. Thus they win
Great numbers of each nation to receive
With joy the tidings brought from Heav'n: at length
Their ministry perform'd, and race well run,
Their doctrine and their story written left,
They die."

[Eve awakens from propitious dreams, it having been shown to her that...]

"Though all by me is lost
Such favour I unworthy am vouchsafed.
By me the Promised Seed shall all restore."

[The time, however, has come when they must leave. A flaming sword, 'fierce as a comet,' advances towards them before the bright array of Cherubim.]

Whereat, in either hand the hastening Angel caught
Our lingering parents, and to the eastern gate
Led them direct, and down the cliff as fast
To the subjected plain-then disappeared.
They, looking back, all the eastern side beheld
Of Paradise, so late their happy seat,
Waved over by that flaming brand, the gate
With dreadful faces thronged and fiery arms.
Some natural tears they dropped, but wiped them soon;
The world was all before them, where to choose
Their place of rest, and Providence then guide.
They, hand in hand, with wandering steps and slow,
Through EDEN took their solitary way.

The Diary
of Samuel Pepys
(London 1669)

Pepys was an English naval administrator and MP. The private diary he kept from 1660 to 1669 was assumed to be written in code, but discovered to be in 'Shelton's shorthand' and transcribed in 1819. It records some of the most momentous events in the England of his age – the Restoration of King Charles after the republic, the Great Fire of London and the Plague - along with the lively personal detail which has made it a best seller ever since.

Abridged: GH

1660

January 1. Blessed be God, at the end of last year I was in very good health, without any sense of my old pain, but upon taking of cold. I lived in Axe Yard, having my wife and servant, Jane, and no other in family than us three.

The condition of the State was thus: the Rump [Parliament], after being disturbed by my Lord Lambert, was lately returned to sit again. The officers of the army all forced to yield. Lawson still lies in the river, and Monk is with his army in Scotland. The New Common Council of the City do speak very high; and had sent to Monk their sword-bearer, to acquaint him with their desires for a free and full parliament, which is at present the desires, and the hopes, and the expectations of all. My own private condition very handsome, and esteemed rich, but indeed very poor; besides my goods of my house, and my office, which at present is somewhat certain.

March 9. To my lord at his lodging, and came to Westminster with him in the coach; and I telling him that I was willing and ready to go with him to sea, he agreed that I should. I hear that it is resolved privately that a treaty be offered with the king.

March 26. This day it is two years since it pleased God that I was cut of the stone at Mrs. Turner's in Salisbury Court. And did resolve while I live to keep it a festival, as I did the last year at my house, and for ever to have Mrs. Turner and her company with me.

May 1. To-day I hear they were very merry at Deal, setting up the king's flag upon one of their maypoles, and drinking his health upon their knees in the streets, and firing the guns, which the soldiers of the castle threatened, but durst not oppose.

May 2. Welcome news of the parliament's votes yesterday, which will be remembered for the happiest May-day that hath been many a year to England. The king's letter was read in the house, wherein he submits himself and all things to them. The house, upon reading the letter, ordered £50,000 to be forthwith provided to send to his majesty for his present supply. The City of London have put out a declaration, wherein they do disclaim their owning any other government but that of a king, lords, and commons.

May 3. This morning my lord showed me the king's declaration to be communicated to the fleet. I went up to the quarter-deck with my lord and the commanders, and there read the papers; which done, the seamen did all of them cry out, "God bless King Charles!" with the greatest joy imaginable. After dinner to the rest of the ships quite through the fleet.

May 11. This morning we began to pull down all the state's arms in the fleet, having first sent to Dover for painters to come and set up the king's. After dinner we set sail from the Downs, but dropped anchor again over against Dover Castle.

May 12. My lord gave order for weighing anchor, which we did, and sailed all day.

May 14. In the morning the Hague was clearly to be seen by us. The weather bad; we were sadly washed when we come near the shore, it being very hard to land there.

May 23. Come infinity of people on board from the king to go along with him. The king, with the two dukes and Queen of Bohemia, Princess Royal, and Prince of Orange, come on board, where I, in their coming in, kissed the king's, queen's, and princess's hands, having done the other before. Infinite shooting of the runs, and that in a disorder on purpose, which was better than if it had been otherwise. We weighed anchor, and with a fresh gale and most happy weather we set sail for England.

May 24. Up, and made myself as fine as I could, with the stockings on and wide canons that I bought at Hague. Extraordinary press of noble company, and great mirth all day.

May 25. By the morning we were come close to the land, and everybody made ready to get on shore. I spoke to the Duke of York about business, who called me Pepys by name, and upon my desire did promise me his future favour. The king went in my lord's barge with the two dukes, and was received by General Monk with all love and respect at his entrance upon the land of Dover. The shouting and joy expressed by all is past imagination.

October 13. I went out to Charing Cross to see Major-Generall Harrison hanged, drawn, and quartered - which was done there - he looking as cheerfully as any man could do in that condition. He was presently cut down and his head and his heart shown to the people, at which there was great shouts of joy.

October 20. This morning one came to me to advise with me where to make me a window into my cellar in lieu of one that Sir W Batten had stopped up; and going down my cellar to look, I put my foot into a great heap of turds, by which I find that Mr Turner's house of office is full and comes into my cellar, which doth trouble me; but I will have it helped. '

December 30. At the end of the last and the beginning of this year, I do live in one of the houses belonging to the Navy Office, as one of the principal officers; my family being myself, my wife, Jane, Will Hewer, and Wayneman, my girl's brother. Myself in constant good health, and in a most handsome and thriving condition. Blessed be God for it. The king settled, and loved of all.

1662

May 4. Mr Holliard came to me and let me blood, about 16 ounces, I being exceedingly full of blood, and very good. I begun to be sick; but lying upon my back, I was presently well again and did give him 5s for his pains; and so we parted.

1663

April 4. We had a fricassee of rabbits and chicken, a leg of mutton boiled, three carps in a dish, a great dish of a side of lamb, a dish of roasted pigeons, a dish of four lobsters, three tarts, a most rare lamprey pie, - a dish of anchovies - good wine of several sorts; and all things mighty noble and to my great content.

1665

January 20. To the Swan at noon, for a bit of meat and dined. So took coach and to my Lady Sandwich's, and so to my bookseller's, and there took home Hooke's book of microscopy[1], a most excellent piece, and of which I am very proud. So home, and by and by again abroad with my wife about several businesses.

July 15. Up, and after all business done, though late, I to Deptford, but before I went out of the office saw there young Bagwell's wife returned, but could not stay to speak to her, though I had a great mind to it, and also another great lady, as to fine clothes, did attend there to have a ticket signed; which I did do, taking her through the garden to my office, where I signed it and had a salute of her. Mr. Carteret and I to the ferry-place at Greenwich. But, Lord! what silly discourse we had by the way as to love-matters, he being the most awkerd man I ever met with in my life as to that business.

July 31. I ended this month with the greatest joy that I ever did any in my life, because I have spent the greatest part of it with abundance of joy, and honour, and pleasant journeys, and brave entertainments, and without cost of money. We end this month after the greatest glut of content that ever I had, only under some difficulty because of the plague, which grows mightily upon us, the last week being about 1,700 or 1,800 of the plague. My Lord Sandwich at sea with a fleet of about one hundred sail, to the northward, expecting De Ruyter, or the Dutch East India fleet.

August 8. To my office a little, and then to the Duke of Albemarle's about some business. The streets empty all the way now, even in London, which is a sad sight. To Westminster Hall, where talking, hearing very sad stories. So home through the City again, wishing I may have taken no ill in going; but I will go, I think, no more thither. The news of De Ruyter's coming home is certain, and told to the great disadvantage of our fleet; but it cannot be helped.

August 10. To the office, where we sat all morning; in great trouble to see the bill this week rise so high, to above 4,000 in all, and of them above 3,000 of the plague. Home to draw over anew my will, which I had bound myself by oath to dispatch by to-morrow night; the town growing so unhealthy that a man cannot depend upon living two days.

August 12. The people die so that now it seems they are fain to carry the dead to be buried by daylight, the nights not sufficing to do it in. And my lord mayor commands people to be within at nine at night, that the sick may have liberty to go abroad for air. There is one also dead out of one of our ships at Deptford, which troubles us mightily. I am told, too, that a wife of one of the grooms at court is dead at Salisbury, so that the king and queen are speedily to be all gone to Milton. So God preserve us!

August 16. To the Exchange, where I have not been in a great while. But, Lord! how sad a sight it is to see the streets empty of people, and very few upon the 'Change. Jealous of every door that one sees shut up lest it should be the plague; and about two shops in three, if not more, generally shut up.

August 22. I walked to Greenwich, in my way seeing a coffin with a dead body therein, dead of the plague, which was carried out last night, and the parish have not appointed anybody to bury it; but only set a watch there all day and night, that nobody should go thither or come thence, this disease making us more cruel to one another than we are to dogs.

August 25. This day I am told that Dr. Burnett, my physician, is this morning dead of the plague, which is strange, his man dying so long ago, and his house this month open again. Now himself dead. Poor, unfortunate man!

August 30. I went forth and walked towards Moorfields to see (God forgive my presumption!) whether I could see any dead corpse going to the grave. But, Lord! how everybody looks, and discourse in the street is of death and nothing else, and few people going up and down, that the town is like a place distressed and forsaken.

September 3 (Lord's Day). Up; and put on my coloured silk suit very fine, and my new periwig, bought a good while since, but durst not wear, because the plague was in Westminster when I bought it; and it is a wonder what will be the fashion after the plague is done as to periwigs, for nobody will dare to buy any hair, for fear of the infection, that it has been cut off the heads of people dead of the plague. My Lord Brouncker, Sir J. Minnes, and I up to the vestry at the desire of the justices of the peace, in order to

1   **Hooke's book of microscopy,** see page 183

the doing something for the keeping of the plague from growing; but, Lord! to consider the madness of the people of the town, who will, because they are forbid, come in crowds along with the dead corpses to see them buried.

September 6. To London, to pack up more things; and there I saw fires burning in the streets, as it is through the whole city, by the lord mayor's order.

September 14. To the Duke of Albemarle, where I find a letter from my Lord Sandwich, of the fleet's meeting with about eighteen more of the Dutch fleet, and his taking of most of them; and the messenger says they had taken three after the letter was sealed, which being twenty-one, and those took the other day, is forty-five sail, some of which are good, and others rich ships. Having taken a copy of my lord's letter, I away toward the 'Change, the plague being all thereabouts. Here my news was highly welcome, and I did wonder to see the 'Change so full-I believe two hundred people. And, Lord! to see how I did endeavour to talk with as few as I could, there being now no shutting up of houses infected, that to be sure we do converse and meet with people that have the plague upon them. I spent some thought on the occurrences of this day, giving matter for as much content on one hand and melancholy on another, as any day in all my life. For the first, the finding of my money and plate all safe at London; the hearing of this good news after so great a despair of my lord's doing anything this year; and the decrease of 500 and more, which is the first decrease we have yet had in the sickness since it begun. Then, on the other side, my finding that though the bill in general is abated, yet in the City within the walls it is increased; my meeting dead corpses, carried close to me at noonday in Fenchurch Street.

One of my own watermen, that carried me daily, fell sick as soon as he had landed me on Friday last, when I had been all night upon the water, and is now dead of the plague. And, lastly, that both my servants, W. Hewer and Tom Edwards, have lost their fathers of the plague this week, do put me into great apprehension of melancholy, and with good reason.

November 15. The plague, blessed be God! is decreased 400, making the whole this week but 1,300 and odd, for which the Lord be praised!

December 25 (Christmas Day). To church in the morning, and there saw a wedding in the church, which I have not seen many a day, and the young people so merry with one another, and strange to see what delight we married people have to see these poor fools decoyed into our condition, every man and woman gazing and smiling at them.

December 31. Thus ends this year, to my great joy, in this manner. I have raised my estate from £1,300 in this year to £4,400. I have got myself greater interest, I think, by my diligence, and my employments increased by that of treasurer for Tangier and surveyor of the victuals. It is true we have gone through great melancholy because of the plague, and I put to great charges by it, by keeping my family long at Woolwich, and myself and my clerks at Greenwich, and a maid at London; but I hope the king will give us some satisfaction for that. But now the plague is abated almost to nothing, and I intending to get to London as fast as I can. To our great joy the town fills apace, and shops begin to be open again.

1666

September 2. Some of our maids sitting up late last night to get things ready against our feast to-day, Jane called us up about three in the morning to tell us of a great fire they saw in the City. So I rose, and slipped on my nightgown, and went to her window, and thought it to be on the back side of Mark Lane at the farthest, and so went to bed again. About seven rose again to dress myself, and there looked out at the window, and saw the fire not so much as it was, and further off. By-and-by Jane comes and tells me that above 300 houses have been burned down, and that it is now burning down all Fish Street, by London Bridge. So I made myself ready, and walked to the Tower, and there got up upon one of the high places; and there I did see the houses at that end of the bridge all on fire, and an infinite great fire on this and the other side of the bridge. So down with my heart full of trouble to the lieutenant of the Tower, who tells me that it begun this morning in the king's baker's house in Pudding Lane.

So I down to the waterside, and there got a boat, and through bridge, and there saw a lamentable fire. Everybody endeavouring to remove their goods, and flinging into the river, or bringing them into lighters that lay off; poor people staying in their houses till the very fire touched them, and then running into boats or clambering from one pair of stairs by the waterside to another. And among other things, the poor pigeons, I perceive, were loth to leave their houses, but hovered about the windows and balconies till they burned their wings and fell down. Having staid, and in an hour's time seen the fire rage every way, and nobody, to my sight, endeavouring to quench it, I to White Hall, and there up to the king's closet in the chapel, where people come about me, and I did give them an account which dismayed them all, and word was carried in to the king.

So I was called for, and did tell the king and Duke of York what I saw, and that unless his majesty did command houses to be pulled down, nothing could stop the fire. They seemed much troubled, and the king commanded me to go to my lord mayor from him and command him to spare no houses, but to pull down before the fire every way. Meeting with Captain Cocke, I in his coach, which he lent me, to Paul's, and there walked along Watling Street, as well as I could, every creature coming away loaded with goods to save, and here and there sick people carried away in beds. At last met my lord mayor in Canning Street, like a man spent. To the king's message, he cried, like a fainting woman, "Lord! what can I do? I am spent; people will not obey me. I have been pulling down houses; but the fire overtakes us faster than we can do it. " So I walked home, seeing people almost all distracted, and no manner of means used to quench the fire. The houses, too, so very thick thereabouts, and full of matter for burning, as pitch and tar in Thames Street, and warehouses of oil and wines and brandy.

Soon as I dined, I away, and walked through the City, the streets full of people, and horses and carts loaden with goods. To Paul's Wharf, where I took boat, and saw the fire was now got further, both below and above bridge, and no likelihood of stopping it. Met with the king and Duke of York in their barge. Their order was only to pull down houses apace; but little was or could be done, the fire coming so fast. Having seen as much as I could, I away to White Hall by appointment, and there walked to St. James's Park, and there met my wife, and Creed and Wood and his wife, and walked to my boat; and upon the water again, and to the fire, still increasing, and the wind great. So near the fire as we could for smoke, and all over the Thames you were almost burned with a shower of fire-drops.

When you could endure no more upon the water, we to a little ale-house on the Bankside, and there stayed till it was dark almost, and saw the fire grow; and as it grew darker, appeared more and more, and in corners and upon steeples, and between churches and houses, as far as we could see up the hill of the City, in a most horrid, malicious, bloody flame, not like the fine flame of an ordinary fire. We stayed till, it being darkish, we saw the fire as only one entire arch of fire from this to the other side of the bridge, and in a bow up the hill for an arch of above a mile long; it made me weep to see it. The churches, houses, and all on fire and flaming at once; and a horrid noise the flames made, and the cracking of houses at their ruin. So home with a sad heart.

March 27. I did go to the Swan; and there sent for Jervas my old periwig-maker and he did bring me a periwig; but it was full of nits, so as I was troubled to see it (it being his old fault) and did send him to make it clean.

April 26. To White Hall, and there saw the Duke of Albemarle, who is not well, and do grow crazy. Then I took a turn with Mr. Evelyn, with whom I walked two hours; talking of the badness of the government, where nothing but wickedness, and wicked men and women command the king; that it is not in his nature to gainsay anything that relates to his pleasures; that much of it arises from the sickliness of our ministers of state, who cannot be about him as the idle companions are, and therefore he gives way to the young rogues; and then from the negligence of the clergy, that a bishop shall never be seen about him, as the King of France hath always; that the king would fain have some of the same gang to be lord treasurer, which would be yet worse.

And Mr. Evelyn tells me of several of the menial servants of the court lacking bread, that have not received a farthing wages since the king's coming in. He tells me that now the Countess Castlemaine do carry all before her. He did tell me of the ridiculous humour of our king and knights of the Garter the other day, who, whereas heretofore their robes were only to be worn during their ceremonies, these, as proud of their coats, did wear them all day till night, and then rode in the park with them on. Nay, he tells me he did see my Lord Oxford and Duke of Monmouth in a hackney coach with two footmen in the park, with their robes on, which is a most scandalous thing, so as all gravity may be said to be lost among us.

August 18. Being weary, turned into St Dunstan's church, where I hear an able sermon of the minister of the place. And stood by a pretty, modest maid, whom I did labour to take by the hand and the body; but she would not, but got further and further from me, and at last I could perceive her to take pins out of her pocket to prick me if I should touch her again ...

1668

October 25. After supper, to have my head combed by Deb, which occasioned the greatest sorrow to me that ever I knew in this world; for my wife, coming up suddenly, did find me embracing the girl with my hand under her skirts; and indeed, I was with my hand in her cunny. I was at a wonderful loss upon it, and the girl also; and I endeavoured to put it off, but my wife was struck mute and grew angry, and as her voice came to her, grew quite out of order. But after her much crying and reproaching me with inconstancy and preferring a sorry girl before her, I did give her no provocations but did promise all fair usage to her, and love.

November 30. My wife after dinner went the first time abroad in her coach, calling on Roger Pepys, and visiting Mrs. Creed and my cousin Turner. Thus endeth this month with very good content, but most expenseful to my purse on things of pleasure, having furnished my wife's closet and the best chamber, and a coach and horses that ever I knew in the world; and I am put into the greatest condition of outward state that ever I was in, or hoped ever to be. But my eyes are come to that condition that I am not able to work. God do His will in it!

December 2. Abroad with my wife, the first time that ever I rode in my own coach, which do make my heart rejoice and praise God. So she and I to the king's playhouse, and there saw "The Usurper," a pretty good play. Then we to White Hall; where my wife stayed while I up to the duchess, to speak with the Duke of York; and here saw all the ladies, and heard the silly discourse of the king with his people about him.

December 21. To the Duke's playhouse, and saw "Macbeth." The king and court there, and we sat just under them and my Lady Castlemaine. And my wife, by my troth, appeared, I think, as pretty as any of them; I never thought so much before, and so did Talbot and W. Hewer. The king and Duke of York minded me, and smiled upon me; but it vexed me to see Moll Davis in the box over the king and my Lady Castlemaine, look down upon the king, and he up to her. And so did my Lady Castlemaine once; but when she saw Moll Davis she looked like fire, which troubled me.

1669

May 31. Up very betimes, and continued all the morning examining my accounts, in order to the fitting myself to go abroad beyond sea, which the ill-condition of my eyes and my neglect hath kept me behindhand in. Had another meeting with the Duke of York at White Hall on yesterday's work, and made a good advance; and so being called by my wife, we to the park, Mary Batelier and a Dutch gentleman, a friend of hers, being with us. Thence to "The World's End," a drinking house by the park; and there merry, and so home late.

And thus ends all that I doubt I shall ever be able to do with my own eyes in the keeping of my journal, having done now so long as to undo my eyes almost every time that I take a pen in my hand; and therefore resolve, from this time forward to have it kept by my people in longhand, and must be contented to set down no more than is fit for them and all the world to know. And so I betake myself to that course, which is almost as much as to see myself go into my grave; for which, and all the discomforts that will accompany my being blind, the good God prepare me!

S. P.

Mathematical Principles of Natural Philosophy
(*Philosophiæ Naturalis Principia Mathematica*)
by Sir Isaac Newton
(Cambridge, 1687)

Isaac shone at Grantham Grammar School, had a brief (and final, he never married) fling with an apothecary's stepdaughter, and went off to Cambridge University to produced tracts on literal interpretations of Scripture, to make major discoveries in optics and mathematics and to dabble in alchemy.

The *Principia* was a true revolution in human thinking- not only did it provide the famous explanation of gravity, but a method by which almost any physical event could be described in numbers. This was the beginning of modern science and engineering, and Newton's Laws are still the rules by which we build bridges and fly spacecraft.

Sadly, the story of his being inspired to study gravity by seeing an apple fall is almost certainly made-up, but it is probably true that, among his many great achievements, he invented the cat-flap - a device which, like everything else, can be understood through Newton's numbers, as its swinging is described by his Third Law.

Abridged: GH

An Ode
to the Splendid Ornament of Our Time and Nation:
the Treatise by the Eminent Isaac Newton
by Mr. Edmond Halley

Behold! the compass of the skies,
Jove's firm foundation for his works
The Sun in his throne moves the starry greats,
The comet's bearded star, and wandering Diana

Such vexed the philosophers of old,
And caused the schools to shout and shake,
Here, by simple numbers is cleared of dust and haze.

Celebrate now with nectars and with song,
NEWTON! Has opened the treasure-chest of truth!
NEWTON! Soars with Phoebus and the muses!
And has touched most near the mind of God.

PREFACE.

Since the ancients made great account of the science of mechanics in the investigation of natural things; and the moderns have endeavoured to subject the phænomena of nature to the laws of mathematics, I have in this treatise cultivated mathematics so far as it regards philosophy. For all the difficulty of philosophy seems to consist in this - from the phænomena of motions to investigate the forces of nature, and then from these forces to demonstrate the other phænomena.

I heartily beg that what I have here done may be read with candour; and that the defects in a subject so difficult be not so much reprehended as kindly supplied, and investigated by new endeavours of my readers.

ISAAC NEWTON. Cambridge, May 8, 1686.

BOOK I.
OF THE MOTION OF BODIES
DEFINITION I.

The quantity of matter is the measure of the same, arising from its density and bulk conjunctly.

THUS air of double density, in a double space, is quadruple in quantity; in a triple space, sextuple in quantity. And the same is known by the weight of each body.

DEFINITION II.

The quantity of motion is the measure of the same, arising from the velocity and quantity of matter conjunctly.

The motion of the whole is the sum of the motions of all the parts; and therefore in a body double in quantity, with equal velocity, the motion is double; with twice the velocity, it is quadruple.

DEFINITION III.

The *vis insita,* or innate force of matter, is a power of resisting, by which every body endeavours to persevere in its present state, whether it be of rest, or of moving uniformly forward in a right line.

DEFINITION IV.

An impressed force is an action exerted upon a body, in order to change its state, either of rest, or of moving uniformly forward in a right line.

DEFINITION V.

A centripetal force is that by which bodies are drawn or impelled, or any way tend, towards a point as a centre.

Of this sort is gravity, by which bodies tend to the centre of the earth; magnetism, by which iron tends to the load-stone; and that force, whatever it is, by which the planets are perpetually drawn aside from the rectilinear motions, which otherwise they would pursue, and made to revolve in curvilinear orbits. A stone whirled about in a sling, endeavours to recede from the hand that turns it; and by that endeavour, distends the sling.

DEFINITION VI.

The absolute quantity of a centripetal force is the measure of the same proportional to the efficacy of the cause that propagates it from the centre, through the spaces round about.

Thus the magnetic force is greater in one load-stone and less in another according to their sizes and strength of intensity.

DEFINITION VII.

The accelerative quantity of a centripetal force is the measure of the same, proportional to the velocity which it generates in a given time.

Thus the force of the same load-stone is greater at a less distance, and less at a greater: also the force of gravity is greater in valleys, less on tops of exceeding high mountains; and yet less at greater distances from the body of the earth; but at equal distances, it is the same everywhere; because (taking away, or allowing for the resistance of the air), it equally accelerates all falling bodies, whether heavy or light, great or small.

SCHOLIUM.

I do not define time, space, place and motion, as being well known to all. Only I must observe, that the vulgar conceive those quantities under no other notions but from the relation they bear to sensible objects. And thence arise certain prejudices.

AXIOMS, OR LAWS OF MOTION.

LAW I.

Every body perseveres in its state of rest, or of uniform motion in a right line, unless it is compelled to change that state by forces impressed thereon.

Projectiles persevere in their motions, so far as they are not retarded by the resistance of the air, or impelled downwards by the force of gravity. A top does not cease its rotation, otherwise than it is retarded by the air. The greater bodies of the planets and comets, meeting with less resistance in more free spaces, preserve their motions both progressive and circular for a much longer time.

LAW II.

The alteration of motion is ever proportional to the motive force impressed; and is made in the direction of the right line in which that force is impressed.

If any force generates a motion, a double force will generate double the motion, a triple force triple the motion, whether that force be impressed altogether and at once, or gradually and successively. And this motion (being always directed the same way with the generating force), if the body moved before, is added to or subtracted from the former motion, according as they directly conspire with or are directly contrary to each other; or obliquely joined, when they are oblique, so as to produce a new motion compounded from the determination of both.

LAW III.

To every action there is always opposed an equal reaction; or the mutual actions of two bodies upon each other are always equal, and directed to contrary parts.

Whatever draws or presses another is as much drawn or pressed by that other. If you press a stone with your finger, the finger is also pressed by the stone. If a horse draws a stone tied to a rope, the horse (if I may so say) will be equally drawn back towards the stone.

BOOK III- THE SYSTEM OF THE WORLD

IN the preceding Books I have laid down the principles of philosophy, principles not philosophical, but mathematical: such, to wit, as we may build our reasonings upon in philosophical inquiries. It is enough if one carefully read the Definitions, the Laws of Motion, and the first three Sections of the first Book. He may then pass on to this Book, and consult such of the remaining Propositions of the first Books as his occasions shall require.

RULES OF REASONING IN NATURAL PHILOSOPHY

RULE I.

We are to admit no more causes of natural things than are both true and sufficient to explain what is observed.

To this purpose the philosophers say that Nature does nothing in vain, and more is in vain when less will serve; for Nature is pleased with simplicity, and affects not the pomp of superfluous causes.

RULE II.

Therefore to the same natural effects we must, as far as possible, assign the same causes.

Such as respiration in a man being as that in a beast; the falling of stones in Europe being as in America; the light of our cooking fire and of the sun; the reflection of light in the earth, and in the planets.

RULE III.

The qualities of bodies, which admit neither intension nor remission of degrees, and which are found to belong to all bodies within the reach of our experiments, are to be esteemed the universal qualities of all bodies whatsoever.

We are certainly not to relinquish the evidence of experiments for the sake of dreams and vain fictions of our own devising; nor are we to recede from the analogy of Nature, which uses to be simple, and always consonant to itself. If it universally appears, by experiments and astronomical observations, that all bodies about the earth gravitate towards the earth, and that in proportion to the quantity of matter which they severally contain, that the moon likewise, according to the quantity of its matter, gravitates towards the earth; that, on the other hand, our sea gravitates towards the moon; and all the planets mutually one towards another; and the comets in like manner towards the sun; we must, in consequence of this rule, universally allow that all bodies whatsoever are endowed with a principle of mutual gravitation. For the argument from the appearances concludes with more force for the universal gravitation of all bodies that for their impenetrability; of which, among those in the celestial regions, we have no experiments, nor any manner of observation. Not that I affirm gravity to be essential to bodies: by their vis insita I mean nothing but their vis inertiæ. This is immutable. Their gravity is diminished as they recede from the earth.

RULE IV.

In experimental philosophy we are to look upon propositions collected by general induction from phænomena as accurately or very nearly true, notwithstanding any contrary hypotheses that may be imagined, till such time as other phænomena occur, by which they may either be made more accurate, or liable to exceptions.

This rule we must follow, that the argument of induction may not be evaded by hypotheses.

PROPOSITIONS

PROPOSITION I.

That the forces by which the moons around Jupiter are drawn off from a straight course and made to orbit the planet tend to Jupiter's centre; and are reciprocally as the squares of the distances of the places of those planets from that centre.

PROPOSITION II.

That the forces by which the primary planets are drawn off from a straight course and made to orbit, tends towards the sun; and are reciprocally as the squares of the distances of the places of those planets from the sun's centre.

PROPOSITION III

That the force by which the moon is retained in its orbit tends to the earth; and is reciprocally as the square of the distance of its place from the earth's centre.

PROPOSITION V.

That the moons around Jupiter gravitate towards Jupiter; those around Saturn, towards Saturn; those around the Sun, to the Sun; and by the forces of their gravity are drawn off from straight motions, and retained in curved orbits.

SCHOLIUM.

The force which retains the celestial bodies in their orbits we shall hereafter call gravity.

PROPOSITION VI.

That all bodies gravitate towards every planet; and that the weights of bodies towards any the same planet, at equal distances from the centre of the planet, are proportional to the quantities of matter which they severally contain.

Cor. 1. The weights of bodies do not depend upon their forms and textures.

Cor. 2. Universally, all bodies about the earth gravitate towards the earth; and the weights of all, at equal distances from the earth's centre, are as the quantities of matter which they severally contain.

Cor. 5. The power of gravity is of a different nature from the power of magnetism; for some bodies are attracted more by the magnet; others less; most bodies not at all.

PROPOSITION VII.

That there is a power of gravity tending to all bodies proportional to the quantity of matter which they contain.

Cor. 1. Therefore the force of gravity towards any whole planet arises from, and is compounded of, the forces of gravity towards all its parts.

Cor. 2. The force of gravity towards the several particles of any body is reciprocally as the square of the distance of places from the particles.

PROPOSITION IX.

That the force of gravity, considered downward from the surface of the planets, decreases nearly in the proportion of the distances from their centres.

PROPOSITION X.

That the motions of the planets in the heavens may subsist an exceedingly long time

It is shewn that at the height of 200 miles above the earth the air is more rare than it is at the superficies of the earth in the ratio of 30 to 0,0000000000003998, or as 75000000000000 to 1 nearly. And hence the planet Jupiter, revolving in a medium of the same density with that superior air, would not lose by the resistance of the medium the 1,000,000th part of its motion in 1,000,000 years. In the spaces near the earth the resistance is produced only by the air, exhalations, and vapours. When these are carefully exhausted by the air-pump from under the receiver, heavy bodies fall with perfect freedom, and without the least sensible resistance; gold itself, and the lightest down, let fall together, will descend with equal velocity.

HYPOTHESIS I.

That the centre of the system of the world is immovable.

This is acknowledged by all, while some contend that the earth, others that the sun, is fixed in that centre.

PROPOSITION XI.

That the common centre of gravity of the earth, the sun, and all the planets, is immovable.

For if that centre moved, the centre of the world would move also.

PROPOSITION XII.

That the sun is agitated by a perpetual motion, but never recedes far from the common centre of gravity of all the planets.

GENERAL SCHOLIUM.

The theory of swirling vortices, we cannot accept, for comets are carried with very eccentric motions with a freedom that is incompatible with the notion of a vortex.

Bodies projected in our air suffer no resistance but from the air. Withdraw the air, as is done in Mr. Boyle's vacuum, and the resistance ceases; for in this void a feather and a piece of solid gold descend with equal velocity. And as reason must place the celestial spaces above the earth's atmosphere, where there is no air to resist their motions, all bodies will move with the greatest freedom; and the planets and comets will constantly pursue their revolutions in orbits according to the mere laws of gravity, yet they could by no means have first derived their orbits from those laws.

This most beautiful system of the sun, planets, and comets, could only proceed from the counsel and dominion of an intelligent and powerful Being. This Being governs all things, not as the soul of the world, but as Lord over all; and on account of his dominion he is wont to be called Lord God pantokratwr, or Universal Ruler.

God is omnipresent not virtually only, but also substantially; for virtue cannot subsist without substance.

In him are all things contained and moved; yet neither affects the other. As a blind man has no idea of colours, so have we no idea of the manner by which the all-wise God perceives and understands all things. He is utterly void of all body and bodily figure, and can therefore neither be seen, nor heard, or touched; nor ought he to be worshiped under the representation of any corporeal thing. We have ideas of his attributes, but what the real substance of any thing is we know not. In bodies, we see only their figures and colours, we hear only the sounds, we touch only their outward surfaces, we smell only the smells, and taste the savours; but their inward substances are not to be known either by our senses, or by any reflex act of our minds: much less, then, have we any idea of the substance of God. We know him only by his most wise and excellent contrivances of things, and final cause: we admire him for his perfections; but we reverence and adore him on account of his dominion: for a god without dominion, providence, and final causes, is nothing else but Fate and Nature. Blind metaphysical necessity, which is certainly the same always and every where, could produce no variety of things. All that diversity of natural things which we find suited to different times and places could arise from nothing but the ideas and will of a Being necessarily existing. And thus much concerning God; to discourse of whom from the appearances of things, does certainly belong to Natural Philosophy.

Hitherto we have explained the phænomena of the heavens and of our sea by the power of gravity, but have not yet assigned the cause of this power. This is certain, that it must proceed from a cause that penetrates to the very centres of the sun and planets, without suffering the least diminution of its force; that operates not according to the quantity of the surfaces of the particles upon which it acts, but according to the quantity, of the solid matter which they contain, and propagates its virtue on all sides to immense distances, decreasing always in the duplicate proportion of the distances. Gravitation towards the sun is made up out of the gravitations towards the several particles of which the body of the sun is composed; but I have not been able to discover the cause of those properties of gravity from phænomena, and I frame no hypotheses; for whatever is not deduced from the phænomena is to have no place in experimental philosophy. To us it is enough that gravity does really exist, and acts according to the laws which we have explained.

And now we might add something concerning a certain most subtle Spirit which pervades and lies hid in all gross bodies; by the force and action of which Spirit the particles of bodies mutually attract one another, and cohere, and electric bodies operate, light is emitted, reflected, refracted, inflected, and heats bodies; and the members of animal bodies move at the command of the will by the vibrations of this Spirit, mutually propagated along the solid filaments of the nerves, from the outward organs of sense to the brain, and from the brain into the muscles.

The Pilgrim's Progress
From This World To That Which Is To Come
DELIVERED UNDER THE SIMILITUDE OF A DREAM
by John Bunyan
(London, 1678)

John Bunyan, the puritan of Elstow in Buckinghamshire, wrote *The Pilgrim's Progress* while imprisoned for preaching without a licence. It offers a story of salvation through personal effort, rather than by the favour of priests, which has made it an inspiration to the free churches ever since. It has been translated into more than 200 languages, and has never been out of print. In the English Church Bunyan is remembered with a Lesser Festival on 30 August.

Abridged: GH

The Author's Apology for his Book

When at the first I took my pen in hand
Thus for to write, I did not understand
To make another; which, when almost done,
Before I was aware, I this begun.
Thus, I set pen to paper with delight,
And quickly had my thoughts in black and white.
This book is writ in such a dialect
As may the minds of listless men affect:
It seems a novelty, and yet contains
Nothing but sound and honest gospel strains.
Wouldest thou lose thyself and catch no harm,
And find thyself again without a charm?
Wouldst read thyself, yet thou knowest not what,
And yet know whether thou art blest or not,
By reading the same lines? Oh, then come hither,
And lay my book, thy head, and heart together.

I. The Battle with Apollyon

As I walked through the wilderness of this world, I lighted on a certain place where there was a den, and laid me down in that place to sleep; and as I slept, I dreamed a dream. I dreamed I saw a man, clothed with rags, standing with his face from his own house, a book in his hand, and a great burden upon his back.

"O my dear wife and children!" he said, "I am informed that our city will be burnt with fire from heaven. We shall all come to ruin unless we can find a way of escape!"

His relations and friends thought that some distemper had got into his head; but he kept crying, in spite of all that they said to quieten him, "What shall I do to be saved?" He looked this way and that way, but could not tell which road to take. And a man named Evangelist came to him, and he said to Evangelist, "Whither must I fly?"

"Do you see yonder wicket gate?" said Evangelist, pointing with his finger over a very wide field. "Go there, and knock, and you will be told what to do."

I saw in my dream that the man began to run, and his wife and children cried after him to return, but the man ran on, crying, "Life! life! eternal life!"

Two of his neighbours pursued him and overtook him. Their names were Obstinate and Pliable.

"Come, come, friend Christian," said Obstinate. "Why are you hurrying away in this manner from the City of Destruction, in which you were born?"

"Because I have read in my book," replied Christian, "that it will be consumed with fire from heaven. I pray you, good neighbours, come with me, and seek for some way of escape."

After listening to all that Christian said, Pliable resolved to go with him, but Obstinate returned to the City of Destruction in scorn.

"What! Leave my friends and comforts for such a brain-sick fellow as you? No, I will go back to my own home."

Christian and Pliable walked on together, without looking whither they were going, and in the midst of the plain they fell into a very miry slough, which was called the Slough of Despond. Here they wallowed for a time, and Christian, because of the burden that was on his back, began to sink in the mire.

"Is this the happiness you told me of?" said Pliable. "If I get out again with my life, you shall make your journey alone."

With a desperate effort he got out of the mire, and went back, leaving Christian alone in the Slough of Despond. As Christian struggled under his burden towards the wicket gate, I saw in my dream that a man came to him, whose name was Help, and drew him out, and set him upon sound ground. But before Christian could get to the wicket gate, Mr. Worldly Wiseman came and spoke to him.

"How now, good fellow!" said Mr. Worldly Wiseman. "Where are you going with that heavy burden on your back?"

"To yonder wicket gate," said Christian. "For there, Evangelist told me, I shall be put into a way to be rid of my heavy burden."

"Evangelist is a dangerous and troublesome fellow," said Mr. Worldly Wiseman. "Do not follow his counsel. Hear me: I am older than you. I can tell you an easy way to get rid of your burden. You see the village on yonder high hill?"

"Yes," said Christian. "I remember the village is called Morality."

"It is," said Mr. Worldly Wiseman. "There you will find a very judicious gentleman whose name is Mr. Legality. If he is not in, inquire for his son, Mr. Civility. Both of them have great skill in helping men to get burdens off their shoulders."

Christian resolved to follow Mr. Worldly Wiseman's advice. But, as he was painfully climbing up the high hill, Evangelist came up to him, and said, "Are you not the man that I found crying in the City of Destruction, and directed to the little wicket gate? How is it that you have gone so far out of the way?"

Christian blushed for shame, and said that he had been led astray by Mr. Worldly Wiseman.

"Mr. Worldly Wiseman," said Evangelist, "is a wicked man. Mr. Legality is a cheat, and his son, Mr. Civility, is a hypocrite. If you listen to them they will beguile you of your salvation, and turn you from the right way."

Evangelist then set Christian in the true path which led to the wicket gate, over which was written, "Knock, and it shall be opened unto you." And Christian knocked, and a grave person, named Goodwill, opened the gate and let him in. I saw in my dream that Christian asked him to help him off with the burden that was upon his back, and Goodwill pointed to a narrow way running from the wicket gate, and said, "Do you see that narrow way? That is the way you must go. Keep to it, and do not turn down any of the wide and crooked roads, and you will soon come to the place of deliverance, where your burden will fall from your back of itself."

Christian then took his leave of Goodwill, and climbed up the narrow way till he came to a place upon which stood a cross. And I saw in my dream that as Christian came to the cross, his burden fell from off his back, and he became glad and lightsome. He gave three leaps for joy, and went on his way singing, and at nightfall he came to a very stately palace, the name of which was Beautiful. Four grave and lovely damsels, named Charity, Discretion, Prudence, and Piety, met him at the threshold, saying, "Come in, thou blessed of the Lord! This palace was built on purpose to entertain such pilgrims as thou."

Christian sat talking with the lovely damsels until supper was ready, and then they led him to a table that was furnished with fat things, and excellently fine wines. And after Christian had refreshed himself, the damsels showed him into a large chamber, whose window opened towards the sun-rising. The name of the chamber was Peace, and there Christian slept till break of day. Then he awoke, singing for joy, and the damsels took him into the armoury, and dressed him for battle. They harnessed him in armour

of proof, and gave him a stout shield and a good sword; for, they said, he would have to fight many a battle before he got to the Celestial City.

And I saw in my dream that Christian went down the hill on which the House Beautiful stood, and came to a valley, that was called the Valley of Humiliation, where he was met by a foul fiend, Apollyon.

"Prepare to die!" said Apollyon, straddling over the whole breadth of the narrow way. "I swear by my infernal den that thou shalt go no further. Here will I spill thy soul."

With that, he threw a flaming dart at his breast, but Christian caught it on his shield. Then Apollyon rushed upon him, throwing darts as thick as hail, and, notwithstanding all that Christian could do, Apollyon wounded him, and made him draw back. The sore combat lasted for half a day, and though Christian resisted as manfully as he could, he grew weaker and weaker by reason of his wounds. At last, Apollyon, espying his opportunity, closed in on Christian, and wrestling with him, gave him a dreadful fall, and Christian's sword flew out of his hand.

"Ah!" cried Apollyon, "I am sure of thee now!"

He pressed him almost to death, and Christian began to despair of life. But, as God would have it, while Apollyon was fetching his last blow, to make an end of this good man, Christian nimbly reached out his hand for his sword, and caught it, and gave him a deadly thrust. With that, Apollyon spread forth his wings, and sped him away, and Christian saw him no more.

Then, with some leaves from the tree of life, Christian healed his wounds, and with his sword drawn in his hand, he marched through the Valley of Humiliation, without meeting any more enemies.

But at the end of the valley was another, called the Valley of the Shadow of Death. On the right hand of this valley was a very deep ditch; it was the ditch into which the blind have led the blind in all ages, and have there miserably perished. And on the left hand was a dangerous quagmire, into which, if even a good man falls, he finds no bottom for his foot to stand on. The pathway here was exceeding narrow and very dark, and Christian was hard put to it to get through safely. And right by the wayside, in the midst of the valley, was the mouth of hell, and out of it came flame and smoke in great abundance, with sparks and hideous noises. But when the hosts of hell came at him, as he travelled on through the smoke and flame and dreadful noise, he cried out, "I will walk in the strength of the Lord God!"

Thereupon, the fiends gave over, and came no further; and suddenly the day broke, and Christian turned and saw all the hobgoblins, satyrs, and dragons of the pit far behind him, and though he was now got into the most dangerous part of the Valley of the Shadow of Death, he was no longer afraid. The place was so set, here with snares, traps, gins and nets, and there with pits and holes, and shelvings, that, had it been dark, he would surely have perished. But it was now clear day, and by walking warily Christian got safely to the end of the valley. And at the end of the valley, he saw another pilgrim marching on at some distance before him.

"Ho, ho!" shouted Christian. "Stay, and I will be your companion."

"No, I cannot stay," said the other pilgrim, whose name was Faithful. "I am upon my life, and the avenger of blood is behind me."

Putting out all his strength, Christian quickly got up with Faithful. Then I saw in my dream they went very lovingly on together, and had sweet discourse of all things that had happened to them in their pilgrimage; for they had been neighbours in the City of Destruction, and both of them were bound for the Delectable Mountains, and the Celestial City beyond. They were now in a great wilderness, and they walked on together till they came to the town of Vanity, at which a fair is kept all the year long, called Vanity Fair.

II. Vanity Fair

I saw in my dream that Christian and Faithful tried to avoid seeing Vanity Fair; but this they could not do, because the way to the Celestial City lies through the town where this lusty fair is kept. About 5,000 years ago, Beelzebub, Apollyon, and the rest of the fiends saw by the path which the pilgrims made, that their way lay through the town of Vanity. So they set up a fair there, in which all sorts of vanity should be sold every day in the year. Among the merchandise sold at this fair are lands, honours, titles, lusts, pleasures, and preferments; delights of all kinds, as servants, gold, silver, and precious stones; murders and thefts; blood and bodies, yea, and lives and souls. Moreover, at this fair, there are at all times to be seen jugglings, cheats, games, plays, fools, apes, knaves, and rogues, and that of every sort.

When Christian and Faithful came through Vanity Fair everybody began to stare and mock at them, for they were clothed in a raiment different from the raiment of the multitude that traded in the fair, and their speech also was different, and few could understand what they said. But what amused the townspeople most of all was that the pilgrims set light by all their wares.

"What will ye buy? What will ye buy?" said one merchant to them mockingly.

"We buy the truth," said Christian and Faithful, looking gravely upon him.

At this some men began to taunt the pilgrims, and some tried to strike them; and things at last came to a hubbub and great stir, and all the fair was thrown into disorder. Thereupon, Christian and Faithful were arrested as disturbers of the peace. After being beaten and rolled in the dirt, they were put into a cage, and made a spectacle to all the men of the fair. The next day they were again beaten, and led up and down the fair in heavy chains for an example and terror to others.

But some of the better sort were moved to take their part; and this so angered the chief men in the town that they resolved to put the pilgrims to death. They were therefore indicted before the Lord Chief Justice Hategood with having disturbed the trade of Vanity Fair, and won a party over to their own pernicious way of thinking, in contempt of the law of Prince Beelzebub. Mr. Envy, Mr. Superstition, and Mr. Pickthank bore witness against them; and the jurymen, on hearing Faithful affirm that the customs of their town of Vanity were opposed to the spirit of Christianity, brought him in guilty of high treason to Beelzebub. No doubt, they would have condemned Christian also; but, by the mercy of God, he escaped from prison, being assisted by one of the men of the town, named Hopeful, who had come over to his way of thinking.

Faithful was tied to a stake, and scourged, and stoned, and burnt to death. But I saw in my dream that the Shining Ones came with a chariot and horses, and made their way through the multitude to the flames in which Faithful was burning, and put him in the chariot, and, with the sound of trumpets, carried him up through the clouds, and on to the gate of the Celestial City.

So Christian was left alone to continue his journey; but I saw in my dream that, as he was going out of the town of Vanity, Hopeful came up to him and said that he would be his companion. And thus it ever is. Whenever a man dies to bear testimony to the truth, another rises out of his ashes to carry on his work.

Christian was in no wise cast down by the death of Faithful, but went on his way, singing,

Hail, Faithful, hail! Thy goodly works survive; And though they killed thee, thou art still alive.

And he was especially comforted by Hopeful telling him that there were a great many men of the better sort in Vanity Fair who were now resolved to undertake the pilgrimage to the Celestial City. Some way beyond Vanity Fair was a delicate plain, called Ease, where Christian and Hopeful went with much content. But at the farther side of that plain was a little hill, which was named Lucre. In this hill was a silver-mine which was very dangerous to enter, for many men who had gone to dig silver there had been smothered in the bottom by damps and noisome airs. Four men from Vanity Fair-Mr. Money-love, Mr. Hold-the-World, Mr. By-Ends, and Mr. Save-All-were going into the silver-mine as Christian and Hopeful passed by.

"Tarry for us," said Mr. Money-love; "and when we have got a little riches to take us on our journey, we will come with you."

Hopeful was willing to wait for his fellow-townsmen, but Christian told him that, having entered the mine, they would never come out; and, besides, that treasure is a snare to them that seek it, for it hindereth their pilgrimage. And he spoke truly; for I saw in my dream that some were killed by falling into the mine as they gazed from the brink, and the rest who went down to dig were poisoned by the vapours in the pit.

In the meantime, Christian and Hopeful came to the river of life, and walked along the bank with great delight. They drank of the water of the river, which was pleasant and enlivening to their weary spirits, and they ate of the fruit of the green trees that grew by the river side. Then, finding a fair meadow covered with lilies, they laid down and slept; and in the morning they rose up, wondrously refreshed, and continued their journey along the bank of the river. But the way soon grew rough and stony, and seeing on their left hand a stile across the meadow called By-Path Meadow, Christian leaped over it, and said to Hopeful, "Come, good Hopeful, let us go this way. It is much easier."

"I am afraid," said Hopeful, "that it will take us out of the right road."

But Christian persuaded him to jump over the stile, and there they got into a path which was very easy for their feet. But they had not gone very far when it began to rain and thunder and lighten in a most dreadful manner, and night came on apace, and stumbling along in the darkness, they reached Doubting Castle, and the lord thereof, Giant Despair, took them and threw them into a dark and dismal dungeon. Here they lay for three days without one bit of bread or drop of drink. On the third day Giant Despair came and flogged them with a great crabtree cudgel, and so disabled them that they were not even able to rise up from the mire of their dungeon floor. And indeed, they could scarcely keep their heads above the mud in which they lay.

Now Giant Despair had a wife, and her name was Diffidence; and when she found that, in spite of their flogging, Christian and Hopeful were still alive, she advised her husband to kill them outright. It happened, however, to be sunshiny weather, and sunshiny weather always made Giant Despair fall into a helpless fit, in which he lost for the time the use of his hands. So all he could do was to try and persuade his prisoners to kill themselves with knife or halter.

"Why," said he to Christian and Hopeful, "should you choose to live? You know you can never get out of Doubting Castle. What! Will you slowly starve to death like rats in a hole, instead of putting a sudden end to your misery, like men. I tell you again, you will never get out."

But when he was gone, Christian and Hopeful went down on their knees in their dungeon and prayed long and earnestly. Then Christian suddenly bethought himself, and after fumbling in his bosom, he drew out a key, saying, "What a fool am I to lie in a dismal dungeon when I can walk at liberty! Here is the key that I have been carrying in my bosom, called Promise, that will open every lock in Doubting Castle."

He at once tried it at the dungeon door, and turned the bolt with ease. He then led Hopeful to the iron gate of the castle, and though the lock went desperately hard, yet the key opened it. But as the gate moved, it made such a creaking that Giant Despair was aroused.

Hastily rising up, the giant set out to pursue the prisoners; but seeing that all the land was now flooded with sunshine, he fell into one of his helpless fits, and could not even get as far as the castle gate.

III. The Celestial City

Having thus got safely out of Doubting Castle, Christian and Hopeful made their way back to the banks of the river of life, and, following the rough and stony way, they came at last to the Delectable Mountains. And going up the mountains they beheld the gardens and orchards, the vineyards, the fountains of water; and here they drank and washed themselves, and freely ate of the pleasant grapes of the vineyards. Now, on top of the mountains there were four shepherds feeding their flocks, and the pilgrims went to them, and, leaning upon their staffs, they asked them the way to the Celestial City. And the shepherds took them by the hand and led them to the top of Clear, the highest of all the Delectable Mountains, and the pilgrims looked and saw, faintly and very far off, the gate and the glory of the Celestial City.

And I saw in my dream that the two pilgrims went down the Delectable Mountains along the narrow way, and after walking some distance they came to a place where the path branched. Here they stood still for a while, considering which way to take, for both ways seemed right. And as they were considering, behold, a man black of flesh and covered with a white robe, came up to them, and offered to lead them down the true way. But when they had followed him for some time they found that he had led them into a crooked road, and there they were entangled in a net.

Here they lay bewailing themselves, and at last they espied a Shining One coming toward them, with a whip in his hand.

"We are poor pilgrims going to the Celestial City," said Christian and Hopeful. "A black man clothed in white offered to lead us there, but entangled us instead in this net."

"It was Flatterer that did this," said the Shining One. "He is a false apostle that hath transformed himself into an angel."

I saw in my dream that he then rent the net and let the pilgrims out. Then he commanded them to lie down, and when they did so, he chastised them with his whip of cords, to teach them to walk in the good way, and refrain from following the advice of evil flatterers. And they thanked him for his kindness, and went softly along the right path, singing for very joy; and after passing through the Enchanted Land, which was full of vapours that made them dull and sleepy, they came to the sweet and pleasant country of Beulah. In this country the sun shone night and day, and the air was so bright and clear that they could see the Celestial City to which they were going. Yea, they met there some of the inhabitants, for the Shining Ones often walked in the Land of Beulah, because it was on the borders of Heaven.

As Christian and Hopeful drew near to the city their strength began to fail. It was builded of pearls and precious stones, and the streets were paved with gold; and what with the natural glory of the city, and the dazzling radiance of the sunbeams that fell upon it, Christian grew sick with desire as he beheld it; and Hopeful, too, was stricken with the same malady. And, walking on very slowly, full of the pain of longing, they came at last to the gate of the city. But between them and the gate there was a river, and the river was very deep, and no bridge went over it. And when Christian asked the Shining Ones how he could get to the gate of the city, they said to him, "You must go through the river, or you cannot come to the gate."

"Is the river very deep?" said Christian.

"You will find it deeper or shallower," said the Shining Ones, "according to the depth or shallowness of your belief in the King of our city."

The two pilgrims then entered the river. Christian at once began to sink, and, crying out to his good friend Hopeful, he said, "I sink in deep waters! The billows go over my head! All the waves go over me."

"Be of good cheer, my brother," said Hopeful, "I feel the bottom, and it is good!"

With that a great darkness and horror fell upon Christian; he could no longer see before him, and he was in much fear that he would perish in the river, and never enter in at the gate. When he recovered, he found he had got to the other side, and Hopeful was already there waiting for him.

And I saw in my dream that the city stood upon a mighty hill; but the pilgrims went up with ease, because they had left their mortal garments behind them in the river.

While they were thus drawing to the gate, behold, a company of the heavenly host came out to meet them. With them were several of the King's trumpeters, clothed in white and shining raiment, who made even the heavens to echo with their shouting and the sound of their trumpets.

Then all the bells in the city began to ring welcome, and the gate was opened wide, and the two pilgrims entered. And lo! as they entered they were transfigured; and they had raiment put on that shone like gold. And Shining Ones gave them harps to praise their King with, and crowns in token of honour.

And as the gates were opened, I looked in, and behold, the streets were paved with gold; and in them walked many men, with crowns on their heads, palms in their hands, and golden harps to sing praises withal. There were also of them that had wings and they answered one another saying, "Holy, holy, holy is the Lord!" And after that they shut up the gates, which, when I had seen, I wished myself among them.

Then I awoke, and behold! it was a dream.

The Arabian Nights

(*Les Mille et une nuits / The Thousand and One Nights*)
by Antoine Galland
(Paris, 1704)

This is the book which made *Aladdin*, *Ali Baba*, and *Sinbad* famous in the West, though it might well owe at least as much to M. Galland's own imagination as to the 12th Century Arabic folk tales it purports to be a translation of.

Abridged: GH

I. The Voyages of Sindbad the Sailor

When the father of Sindbad was taken to Almighty Allah, much wealth came to the possession of his son; but soon did it dwindle in boon companionship, for the city of Baghdad is sweet to the youthful. Then did Sindbad bethink him how he might restore his fortune, saying to himself: "Three things are better than other three; the day of death is better than the day of birth, a live dog is better than a dead lion, and the grave is better than want"; and gathering merchandise together, he took ship and sailed away to foreign countries.

Now it came to pass that the captain of this ship sighted a strange island, whereon were grass and trees, very pleasant to the eyes. So they anchored, and many went ashore. When these had gathered fruits, they made a fire, and were about to warm themselves, when the captain cried out from the ship: "Ho there! passengers, run for your lives and hasten back to the ship and leave your gear and save

yourselves from destruction. Allah preserve you! For this island whereon ye stand is no true island, but a great fish stationary a-middlemost of the sea, whereon the sand hath settled and trees have sprung up of old time, so that it is become like unto an island; but when ye lighted fires on it, it felt the heat and moved; and in a moment it will sink with you into the depths of the sea and ye will be drowned."

When the fish moved, the captain did not wait for his passengers, but sailed away, and Sindbad, seizing a tub, floated helpless in the great waters. But by the mercy of Allah he was thrown upon a true island, where a beautiful mare lay upon the ground, who cried at his approach. Then a man started up at the mare's cry, and seeing Sindbad, bore him to an underground chamber, where he regaled the waif with plenteous food. To him did this man explain how he was a groom of King Mirjan, and that he brought the king's mares to pasture on the island, hiding underground while the stallions of the sea came up out of the waves unto the mares. Presently Sindbad saw this strange sight, and witnessed how the groom drove the stallions back to the waves when they would have dragged the mares with them. After that he was carried before King Mirjan, who entreated him kindly, and when he had amassed wealth, returned by ship to Bussorah, and so to Baghdad.

But becoming possessed with the thought of travelling about the ways of men, he set out on a second voyage. And it came to pass that he landed with others on a lovely island, and lay down to sleep, after he had eaten many delicious fruits. Awaking, he found the ship gone. Then, praying to Almighty Allah, like a man distracted, he roamed about the island, presently climbing a tree to see what he could see. And he saw a great dome afar, and journeyed to it.

There was no entrance to this white dome, and as he went round about it, the sun became suddenly darkened, so that he looked towards it in fear, and lo! a bird in the heavens whose wings blackened all light. Then did Sindbad know that the dome was an egg, and that the bird was the bird roc, which feeds its young upon elephants. Sore afraid, he hid himself, and the bird settled upon the egg, and brooded upon it. Then Sindbad unwound his turban, and, tying one end to the leg of the great bird and the other about his own middle, waited for the dawn.

When the dawn was come, the bird flew into the heavens, unaware of the weight at its foot, and Sindbad was borne across great seas and far countries. When at last the bird settled on land, Sindbad unfastened his turban, and was free.

But the place was filled with frightful serpents, and strewn with diamonds. Sindbad saw a dead sheep on the ground, with diamonds sticking to its carcase, and he knew that this was a device of merchants, for eagles come and carry away these carcases to places beyond the reach of the serpents, and merchants take the diamonds sticking to the flesh. So he hid himself under the carcase, and an eagle bore him with it to inhabited lands, and he was delivered.

Again it came to him to travel, and on this his third voyage the ship was driven to the mountain of Zughb, inhabited by hairy apes. These apes seized all the goods and gear, breaking the ship, but spared the men. Then they perceived a great house and entered it, but nobody was there. At nightfall, however, a frightful giant entered, and began to feel the men one by one, till he found the fattest, and him the giant roasted over a fire and ate like a chicken. This happened many days, till Sindbad encouraged his friends, and they heated two iron spits in the fire, and while the giant slept put out his eyes. While they ran to the shore, where they had built a raft, the giant, bellowing with rage, returned with two ghuls, and pelted the raft with rocks, killing some, but the rest escaped. However, three only were alive when they reached land.

The shore on which these three landed was occupied by an immense serpent, like a dragon, who instantly ate one of the three, while Sindbad and the other climbed up a tree.

Next day the serpent glided up the tree, and ate the second. Then Sindbad descended, and with planks bound himself all round so that he was a man surrounded by a fence. Thus did he abide safe from the serpent till a ship saved him.

Now on his fourth voyage Sindbad's ship was wrecked, and he fell among hairy men, cannibals, who fattened all that they caught like cattle, and consumed them. He being thin and wasted by all his misfortunes, escaped death, and saw all his comrades fattened and roasted, till they went mad, with cries of anguish. It chanced that the shepherd, who tended these men in the folds, took pity on Sindbad and showed him the road out of danger, which taking, he arrived, after divers adventures and difficulties, at the country of a great king. In this country all were horsemen, but the saddle was unknown, so Sindbad made first the king, and afterwards the vizir, both saddle and stirrups, which so delighted them that he was advanced to great fortune and honour.

Then was he married to a maiden most beautiful and chaste, so lovely to behold that she ravished the senses, and he lived like one in a dream. But it came to pass that she died, and when they buried her they took Sindbad and shut him in the Place of the Dead with her, giving him a little food and water till he should die. Such was the custom, that husband and wife should accompany the dead wife or husband in the Place of the Dead-a mighty cave strewn with dead bodies, dark as night, and littered with jewels.

While Sindbad bewailed his lot in this place the doors opened, a dead body of a man was brought in, and with it his live wife, to whom food was given. Then Sindbad killed this fair lady with the bone of a leg, took her food and jewels, and thus did he serve all the live people thrust into the cavern. One day he heard a strange sound far up the cavern, and perceived in the distance a wild beast. Then he knew that there must be some entrance at that far end, and journeying thither, found a hole in the mountain which led to the sea. On the shore Sindbad piled all his jewels, returning every day to the cavern to gather more, till a ship came and bore him away.

His fifth voyage was interrupted by rocs, whose egg the sailors had smashed open to see the interior of what they took to be a dome. These birds flew over the ship with rocks in their claws, and let them fall on to the ship, so that it was wrecked.

Sindbad reached shore on a plank, and wandering on this island perceived an old man, very sad, seated by a river. The old man signalled to Sindbad that he should carry him on his back to a certain point, and this Sindbad very willingly bent himself to do. But once upon his back, the legs over the shoulders and wound round about his flanks, the old man refused to get off, and drove Sindbad hither and thither with most cruel blows. At last Sindbad took a gourd, hollowed it out, filled it with grape juice, stopped the mouth, and set it in the sun. Then did he drink of this wine and get merry and forget his misery, dancing with the old man on his neck. So the old man asked for the gourd, and drank of it, and fell sleepy, and dropped from Sindbad's neck, and Sindbad slew him.

After that, Sindbad amassed treasure by pelting apes with pebbles, who threw back at him cocoanuts, which he sold for money.

On his sixth voyage Sindbad was wrecked on the most frightful mountain which no ship could pass. The sight of all the useless wealth strewn upon this terrible place of wreck and death drove all the other passengers mad, so that they died. But Sindbad, finding a stream, built a raft, and drifted with it, till, almost dead, he arrived among Indians and Abyssinians. Here he was well treated, grew rich, and returned in prosperity to Baghdad.

But once again did he travel, and this time his vessel encountered in the middle seas three vast fish-like islands, which lashed out and destroyed the ship, eating most, but Sindbad escaped. When he reached land he found himself well cared for among kind people, and he grew rich in an old man's house, who married him to his only daughter. One day after the old man's death, and when he was as rich as any in that land, lo! all the men grew into the likeness of birds, and Sindbad begged one of them to take him on his back on the mysterious flight to which they were now bent. After persuasion the man-bird agreed, and Sindbad was carried up into the firmament till he could hear the angels glorifying God in the heavenly dome. Carried away by ecstasy, he shouted praise of Allah into the holy place, and instantly the bird fell to the ground, for they were evil and incapable of praising God. But Sindbad returned to his wife, and she told him how evil were those people, and that her father was not of them, and induced him to carry her to his own land. So he sold all his possessions, took ship, and came to Baghdad, where he lived in great splendour and honour, and this was the seventh and last voyage of Sindbad the Sailor.

II. The Tale of the Three Apples

The Caliph Haroun al-Raschid, walking by night in the city, found a fisherman lamenting that he had caught nothing for his wife and children. "Cast again," said the caliph, "and I will give thee a hundred gold pieces for whatsoever cometh up." So the man cast his net, and there came up a box, wherein was found a young damsel foully murdered. Now, to this murder confessed two men, a youth and an old man; and this was the story of the youth.

His wife fell ill, and had a longing for apples, so that he made the journey to Bussorah, and bought three apples from the caliph's gardener. But his wife would not eat them. One day, as he sat in his shop, passed a slave, bearing one of the apples. The husband asked how he came by it, whereat replied the slave that his mistress gave it him, saying that her wittol of a husband had journeyed to Bussorah for it. Then in rage the young man returned and slew his wife. Presently his little son came home, saying that he was afraid of his mother; and when the father questioned him, replied the child that he had taken one of his mother's three apples to play with, and that a slave had

stolen it. Then did the husband know his wife to be innocent, and he told her father all, and they both mourned for her, and both offered themselves to the executioner- the one that he was guilty, the other to save his son-in-law whose guilt was innocence.

From this story followed that of Noureddin and his son Bedreddin Hassan, whose marriage to the Lady of Beauty was brought about by a genie, in spite of great difficulties. And it was after hearing this tale that Haroun al-Raschid declared to his vizir: "It behoves that these stories be written in letters of liquid gold."

III. Hassan, the Rope-Maker

Two men, so it chanced, disputing whether wealth could give happiness, came before the shop of a poor rope-maker. Said one of the men: "I will give this fellow two hundred pieces of gold, and see what he does with it." Hassan, amazed by this gift, put the gold in his turban, except ten pieces, and went forth to buy hemp for his trade and meat for his children.

As he journeyed, a famished vulture made a pounce at the meat, and Hassan's turban fell off, with which the vulture, balked of the meat, flew away, far out of sight.

When the two men returned they found Hassan very unhappy, and the same who had given before gave him another two hundred pieces, which Hassan hid carefully, all but ten pieces, in a pot of bran. While he was out buying hemp, his wife exchanged the pot of bran for some scouring sand with a sandman in the street. Hassan was maddened when he came home, and beat his wife, and tore her hair, and howled like an evil spirit. When his friends returned they were amazed by his tale, but the one who had as yet given nothing now gave Hassan a lump of lead picked up in the street, saying: "Good luck shall come of homely lead, where gold profits nothing."

Hassan thought but little of the lead, and when a fisherman sent among his neighbours that night for a piece of lead wherewith to mend his nets, very willingly did Hassan part with this gift, the fisherman promising him the first fish he should catch.

When Hassan's wife cut open this fish to cook it, she found within it a large piece of glass, crystal clear, which she threw to the children for a plaything. A Jewess who entered the shop saw this piece of glass, picked it up, and offered a few pieces of money for it. Hassan's wife dared not do anything now without her husband's leave, and Hassan, being summoned, refused all the offers of the Jewess, perceiving that the piece of glass was surely a precious diamond. At last the Jewess offered a hundred thousand pieces of gold, and, as this was wealth beyond wealth, Hassan very willingly agreed to the barter.

IV. Prince Ahmed and the Fairy

Once upon a time there was a sultan who had three sons, and all these young men loved their cousin, the fatherless and motherless Nouronnihar, who lived at their father's court.

To decide which should marry the princess the sultan bade them go forth, each a separate way, and, after a time, determined to end their travels by assembling at a certain place. "He of you who brings back from his travels the greatest of rarities," said the sultan, "he shall marry the princess, my niece." To Almighty Allah was confided the rest.

The eldest of the princes, Houssain by name, consorted with merchants in his travels, but saw nothing strange or wonderful till he encountered a man crying a piece of carpet for forty pieces of gold. "Such is the magic of this carpet," protested the man, "that he who sits himself upon it is instantly transported to whatsoever place he desires to visit, be it over wide seas or tall mountains." The prince bought this carpet, amused himself with it for some time, and then flew joyfully to the place of assembly.

Hither came the second prince, Ali, who brought from Persia an ivory tube, down which, if any man looked, he beheld the sight that most he desired to see; and the third prince, the young Ahmed, who had bought for thirty-five pieces of gold a magic apple, the smell of which would restore a soul almost passed through the gate of death.

The three princes, desiring to see their beloved princess, looked down Ali's ivory tube, and, lo! the tragic sight that met their gaze-for the princess lay at the point of death.

Swiftly did they seat themselves upon Houssain's magic carpet, and in a moment of time found themselves beside the princess, whom Ahmed instantly restored to life and beauty and health by his magic apple.

As it seemed impossible to decide which of these rare things was the rarest, the sultan commanded that each prince should shoot an arrow, and he whose arrow flew farthest should become the husband of Nouronnihar.

Houssain drew the first bow; then Ali, whose arrow sped much farther, and then Ahmed, whose arrow was not to be found.

Houssain, in despair, gave up his right of succession to the throne, and, with a blighted heart, went out into the wilderness to become a holy man. Ali was married to the princess, and Ahmed went forth into the world to seek his lost arrow.

After long wandering, Ahmed found his arrow among desolate rocks, too far for any man to have shot with the bow; and, while he looked about him, amazed and dumfounded, he beheld an iron door in the rocks, which yielded to his touch and led into a very sumptuous palace. There advanced towards him a lady of surpassing loveliness, who announced that she was a genie, that she knew well who he was, and had sent the carpet, the tube, and the apple, and had guided his arrow to her door. Furthermore, she confessed to the prince great love for him, and offered him all that she possessed, leading him to a vast and magnificent chamber, where a marriage-feast was prepared for them.

Prince Ahmed was happy for some while, and then he thought of his father, grieving for him, and at last obtained leave from the beautiful genie to go on a visit to his home. At first his father was glad to see him, but afterwards jealousy of his son and the son's secret place of dwelling, and suspicion that a son so rich and powerful might have designs on his throne, led his father to lay hard and cruel burdens on Prince Ahmed.

However, all that he commanded Ahmed performed by help of the genie, even things the most impossible. He brought a tent which would cover the sultan's army, and yet, folded up, lay in the hollow of a man's hand. This and many other wonderful things did Ahmed perform, till the sultan asked for a man one foot and a half in height, with a beard thirty feet long, who could carry a bar of iron weighing five hundredweight.

Such a man the genie found, and the sultan, beholding him, turned away in disgust; whereat the dwarf flew at him in a rage, and with his iron bar smote him to death.

Thus, too, did the little man treat all the wicked courtiers and sorcerers who had incensed the sultan against his son. And Ahmed and the genie became sultan and sultana of all that world, while Ali and Nouronnihar reigned over a great province bestowed upon them by Prince Ahmed.

As for Houssain, he forsook not the life of a holy man living in the wilderness.

V. The Hunchback

There lived long ago a poor tailor with a pretty wife to whom he was tenderly attached. One day there came to his door a hunchback, who played upon a musical instrument and sang to it so amusingly that the tailor straightway carried him to his wife. So delighted by the hunchback's singing was the tailor's wife that she cooked a dish of fish and the three sat down to be merry. But in the midst of the feast a bone stuck in the hunchback's throat, and before a man could stare he was dead. Afraid that they should be accused of murder, the tailor conspired with his wife what they should do. "I have it," said he, and getting a piece of money he sallied forth at dark with the hunchback's body and arrived before the house of a doctor.

Here knocked he on the door, and giving the maid a piece of money, bade her hasten the doctor to his need. So soon as the maid's back was turned, he placed the hunchback on the top stair and fled. Now the doctor, coming quickly, struck against the corpse so that it fell to the bottom of the stairs. "Woe is me, for I have killed a patient!" said he, and fearing to be accused of murder, carried the body in to his wife.

Now they had a neighbour who was absent from home, and going to his room they placed the corpse against the fireplace. This man, returning and crying out: "So it is not the rats who plunder my larder!" began to belabour the hunchback, till the body rolled over and lay still. Then in great fear of his deed, this Mussulman carried the corpse into the street, and placed it upright against a shop.

Came by a Christian merchant at dawn of day, and running against the hunchback tumbled him over; then thinking himself attacked he struck the body, and at that moment the watch came by and haled the merchant before the sultan.

Now the hunchback was a favourite of the sultan, and he ordered the Christian merchant to be executed.

To the scaffold, just when death was to be done, came the Mussulman, and confessed that he was the murderer. So the executioner released the Christian, and was about to hang the other, when the doctor came and confessed to being the murderer. So the doctor took the place of the Mussulman, when the tailor and his wife hastened to the scene, and confessed that they were guilty.

Now, when this story came to the ears of the sultan, he said: "Great is Allah, whose will must be done!" and he released all of them, and commanded this story of the hunchback to be written in a book.

VI. Aladdin, or the Wonderful Lamp

There was in the old time a bad and idle boy who lived with his mother, a poor widow, and gave her much unrest. And there came to him one day a wicked magician, who called himself the boy's uncle, and made rich presents to the mother, and one day he led Aladdin out to make him a merchant. Now, the magician knew by his magic of a vast hoard of wealth, together with a wonderful lamp, which lay in the earth buried in Aladdin's name. And he sent the boy to fetch the lamp, giving him a magic ring, and waited on the earth for his return. But Aladdin, his pockets full of jewels, refused to give up the lamp till his false uncle helped him to the surface of the earth, and in rage the magician caused the stone to fall upon the cave, and left Aladdin to die.

But as he wept, wringing his hands, the genie of the magic ring appeared, and by his aid Aladdin was restored to his mother. There, with the genie of the lamp to wait upon him, he lived, till, seeing the sultan's daughter pass on her way to the bath, he conceived violent love for her, and sent his mother to the sultan with all his wonderful jewels, asking the princess in marriage. The sultan, astonished by the gift of jewels, set Aladdin to perform prodigies of wonder, but all these he accomplished by aid of the genie, so that at last the sultan was obliged to give him the princess in marriage. And Aladdin caused a great pavilion to rise near the sultan's palace, and this was one of the wonders of the world, and there he abode in honour and fame.

Then the wicked magician, knowing by magic the glory of Aladdin, came disguised, crying "New Lamps for Old!" and one of the maids in the pavilion gave him the wonderful lamp, and received a new one from the coppersmith. The magician transplanted the pavilion to Africa, and Aladdin, coming home, found the sultan enraged against him and his palace vanished. But by means of the genie of the ring he discovered the whereabouts of his pavilion, and going thither, slew the magician, possessed himself anew of the lamp, and restored his pavilion to its former site.

But the magician's wicked brother, plotting revenge, obtained access to the princess in disguise of a holy woman he had foully murdered, and he would have certainly slain Aladdin but for a warning of the genie, by which Aladdin was enabled to kill the magician. After that Aladdin lived in glory and peace, and ascended in due course to the throne, and reigned with honour and mercy.

VII. Ali Baba and the Forty Thieves

Now, the father of Ali Baba left both his sons poor; but Kasim married a rich wife, and so he lived plenteously, while his poor brother, Ali Baba, worked in the wood. It came to pass that Ali Baba one day saw in the wood a company of forty robbers, the captain of whom cried, "Open, Sesame!" to a great rock, and lo! it opened, and the men disappeared. When they were gone out again, Ali Baba came from his hiding, and, addressing the rock in the same way, found that it obeyed him. Then went he in and took much of the treasure, which he drove home on his mule. Now, when his wife sent to the brother Kasim for scales, wherewith she might weigh all this treasure, the sister-in-law being suspicious that one so poor should have need of scales, smeared the bottom of the pan with wax and grease, and discovered on the return a gold piece. This she showed to Kasim, who made Ali Baba confess the tale. Then Kasim went to the cave, entered, loaded much treasure, and was about to depart, when he found he had forgotten the magic words whereby he entered. There was he found by the forty thieves, who slew and quartered him. Ali Baba found the quarters, took them home, got a blind tailor to sew them together, and gave his brother burial.

Now, the robbers discovered Ali Baba's house, and they hid themselves in oil-jars hung on the backs of mules, and the captain drove them. Thus came they to Ali Baba's house, and the captain craved lodging for himself and his beasts. Surely would Ali Baba have been captured, tortured, and put to death but for his maid, the faithful and astute Morgiana, who discovered men in the jars, and, boiling cans of oil, poured it upon them one by one, and so delivered her master. But the captain had escaped, and Ali Baba still went in great fear of his life. But when he returned, disguised so that he might have puzzled the wisest, Morgiana recognised the enemy of her master; and she was dancing before him and filling his eyes with pleasure; and when it came for her to take the tambourine and go round for largess, she strengthened her heart and, quick as the blinding lightning, plunged a dagger into his vitals. Thus did the faithful Morgiana save her master, and he married her to his nephew, the son of Kasim, and they lived long in great joy and blessing.

VIII. The Fisherman and the Genie

There was once a poor fisherman who every day cast his net four times into the sea. On a day he went forth, and casting in his net, drew up with great labour a dead jackass; casting again, an earthen pitcher full of sand; casting a third time vexatiously, potsherds and shattered glass; and at the last a jar of yellow copper, leaden-capped, and stamped with the seal-ring of Solomon, the son of David. His rage was silenced at sight of the sacred seal, and, removing the cap, smoke issued, which, taking vast shape, became a terrible genie frightful to see.

Said the genie: "By what manner of death wilt thou die, for I have sworn, by Allah, to slay the man who freed me!" He moreover explained how Solomon had placed him in the jar for heresy, and how he had lain all those years at the bottom of the sea. For a hundred years, he said, he swore that he would make rich for ever and ever the man who freed him; for the next hundred, that for such an one he would open the hoards of the earth; then, that he would perfectly fulfil such an one's three wishes; finally, in his rage, that he would kill the man who freed him.

Now, the fisherman, having pleaded in vain, said that he did not believe the tale, seeing that so huge a genie could never have got into so small a jar. Whereat the genie made smoke of himself, and re-entered the vase. Instantly then did the fisherman stopper it, nor would he let the genie free till that wicked one had promised to spare his life and do him service. Grudgingly and wrathfully did the genie issue forth, but being now under oath to Allah, he spared the fisherman and did him service.

He took him to a lake in the black mountains, bade him throw in his net, and bear the catch to the sultan. Now, by the fisherman's catching of four fish all of a different hue, the sultan discovered that this lake in the mountains was once a populous and mighty city, whereof the prince and all the inhabitants had been bewitched in ancient time. When the city was restored and all those many people called back to life, the sultan enriched the fisherman, who lived afterwards in wealth.

IX. The Enchanted Horse

In olden times there came to the Court of Persia a stranger from Ind, riding a horse made of wood, which, said he, could fly whithersoever its rider wished. When the sultan had seen the horse fly to a mountain and back, he asked the Hindu its price, and said the man: "Thy daughter's hand." Now the prince, standing by, was enraged at this insolence, but his father said: "Have no fear that I should do this thing. Howsoever, lest another king become possessed of the horse, I will bargain for it." But the impetuous prince, doubting the truth of the horse's power, jumped upon its back, turned the peg which he had observed the Hindu to turn, and instantly was borne far away.

The king, enraged that the Hindu could not bring back his son, had the man cast into prison, albeit the Hindu protested that soon the prince must discover the secret of

stopping the horse by means of a second peg, and therefore would soon return.

Now the prince did not discover this secret till he was far away, and it was night. He came to earth near a palace, and going in, found there an exquisite lady sleeping, and knew by her dress that she was of a rank equal with his own. Then he pleaded to her for succour, and she constrained him to stay, and for many weeks he abode as a guest. After that time he said, "Come to my father's court, that we may be married!" And early one dawn he bore her to Persia on the back of the enchanted horse.

So glad was the king at his son's return that he released the Hindu.

Now the Hindu, hearing what had happened, determined on revenge. He found where the horse was placed, and going to the palace where the foreign princess was housed, sent for her in the sultan's name, and she came to him. Then he seated her upon the horse, and mounting up in full view of the sultan and his royal son, flew far away with his lovely captive.

It was the Hindu's desire to marry this princess, but when they were come to earth, she withstood him, and cried for help and succour. To her came the sultan of that place, and slew the Hindu, and would have married her, but she was faithful to her lover and feigned madness.

Then the sultan offered rewards to any who should cure her of this frightful madness, and many physicians came and failed. Now, her lover, distracted at sight of seeing her in mid-air with the Hindu, had turned Holy Man, roaming the earth without hope like one who is doomed.

It happened that he came to the palace where the princess lay in her feigned madness, and hearing the tale of her, and of the enchanted horse, with new hope and a great joy in his heart, he went in, disguised as a physician, and in secret made himself known.

Then he stood before the sultan of that land, and said: "From the enchanted horse hath she contracted this madness, and by the enchanted horse shall she lose it." And he gave orders to dress her in glorious array, to crown her with jewels and gold, and to lead her forth to the palace square.

A vast concourse assembled there, and the prince set his beloved lady on the horse, and pretending incantations, leapt suddenly upon its back, turned the peg, and as the enchanted steed flew towards Persia, over his shoulder cried the glad prince: "When next, O sultan, thou wouldst marry a princess who implores thy protection, ask first for her consent."

Principles of Human Knowledge

WHEREIN THE CHIEF CAUSES OF ERROR AND DIFFICULTY IN THE SCIENCES, WITH THE GROUNDS OF
SCEPTICISM, ATHEISM, AND IRRELIGION, ARE INQUIRED INTO

by George Berkeley
(Dublin, 1710)

George Berkeley of Trinity College Dublin was, at various times (when not engaged in 'converting the savage Americans to Christianity'), Dean, Lecturer in Greek, Hebrew and Optics. His fame rests on this espousal of 'subjective idealism'- the idea that things might well have no existence at all outside our consciousness, a concept irritatingly difficult to refute, though Dr Johnson (page 257) famously kicked a stone, saying 'Sir, I refute it thus!'.

Abridged: GH

DEDICATION

To the Right Honourable THOMAS, EARL OF
PEMBROKE

My Lord,

 That a man who has written something with a design to promote Useful Knowledge and Religion in the world should make choice of your lordship for his patron, will not be thought strange by any one acquainted with the present state of the church and learning, and knowing how great an ornament and support you are to both. Thus I lay this treatise at your lordship's feet.

Your lordship's most humble and most devoted
servant,
GEORGE BERKELEY

INTRODUCTION

Philosophy being THE STUDY OF WISDOM AND TRUTH, it may be expected that those who have spent most time and pains in it should enjoy a greater calm and serenity of mind, and greater clearness of knowledge. Yet we see the illiterate bulk of mankind that walk the high-road of plain common sense, for the most part easy and undisturbed. But no sooner do we follow the light of a superior principle, but a thousand scruples spring up, and we are insensibly drawn into uncouth paradoxes and forlorn Scepticism.

Upon the whole, I am inclined to think that the far greater part, if not all, of those difficulties which have hitherto amused philosophers, and blocked up the way to knowledge, are entirely owing to ourselves - that we have first raised a dust and then complain we cannot see.

Unless we take care TO CLEAR THE FIRST PRINCIPLES OF KNOWLEDGE FROM THE embarras and DELUSION OF WORDS, we may make infinite reasonings upon them to no purpose; we may draw consequences from consequences, and be never the wiser.

OF THE PRINCIPLES OF HUMAN KNOW-LEDGE

OBJECTS OF HUMAN KNOWLEDGE. - It is evident to any one who takes a survey of the objects of human knowledge, that they are either IDEAS actually imprinted on the senses; or ideas formed by help of memory and imagination. By sight I have the ideas of light and colours. By touch I perceive hard and soft, heat and cold, motion and resistance. Smelling furnishes me with odours; the palate with tastes; and hearing conveys sounds to the mind. And as several of these are observed to accompany each other, they come to be marked by name, and so to be reputed as one thing. Thus, for example a certain colour, taste, smell, figure and consistence having been observed to go together, are accounted one distinct thing, signified by the name APPLE. Other collections of ideas constitute a stone, a tree, a book, and the like sensible things - which as they are pleasing or disagreeable excite the passions of love, hatred, joy, grief, and so forth.

MIND - SPIRIT - SOUL. - But, besides all that endless variety of ideas or objects of knowledge, there is likewise something which knows or perceives them, which I call MIND, SPIRIT, SOUL, or MYSELF.

HOW FAR THE ASSENT OF THE VULGAR CONCEDED. - That neither our thoughts, nor passions, nor ideas formed by the imagination, exist WITHOUT the mind, is what EVERYBODY WILL ALLOW. Their ESSE is PERCIPI, nor is it possible they should have any existence out of the minds or thinking things which perceive them.

Some truths are so obvious to the mind that a man need only open his eyes to see them. Such I take this important one to be, viz., that all the choir of heaven and furniture of the earth, in a word all those bodies which compose the mighty frame of the world, have not any subsistence without a mind; that consequently so long as they are not actually perceived by me, or do not exist in my mind or that of any other CREATED SPIRIT, they must either have no existence at all, OR ELSE SUBSIST IN THE MIND OF SOME ETERNAL SPIRIT.

THE PHILOSOPHICAL NOTION OF MATTER INVOLVES A CONTRADICTION. - Some make a DISTINCTION betwixt PRIMARY and SECONDARY qualities. By the former they mean extension, figure, motion, rest, solidity or impenetrability, and number; by the latter they denote all other sensible qualities, as colours, sounds, tastes, and so forth. But it is evident that extension, figure, and motion are ONLY IDEAS EXISTING IN THE MIND, and that an idea can be like nothing but another idea, and that consequently neither they nor their archetypes can exist in an UNPERCEIVING substance. Hence, it is plain that that the very notion of what is called MATTER or CORPOREAL SUBSTANCE, involves a contradiction in it.

ARGUMENT AD HOMINEM. - Again, GREAT and SMALL, SWIFT and SLOW, ARE ALLOWED TO EXIST NOWHERE WITHOUT THE MIND, being entirely RELATIVE, and changing as the frame or position of the organs of sense varies. Without the mind there is neither great nor small, the motion neither swift nor slow, that is, they are nothing at all. But, say you, there is extension in general, and motion in general. But without extension solidity cannot be conceived, the same must also be true of solidity.

That NUMBER is entirely THE CREATURE OF THE MIND, and dependent on men's understanding, that it is strange to think how any one should give it an absolute existence without the mind.

PHILOSOPHICAL MEANING OF "MATERIAL SUBSTANCE". - If we inquire into what the most accurate philosophers declare themselves to mean by MATERIAL SUBSTANCE, we shall find them acknowledge they have no other meaning annexed to those sounds but the idea of BEING IN GENERAL.

THE EXISTENCE OF EXTERNAL BODIES AFFORDS NO EXPLICATION OF THE MANNER IN WHICH OUR IDEAS ARE PROCUCED. - Though we give the materialists their external bodies, they by their own confession are never the nearer knowing how our ideas are produced. Hence it is evident the production of ideas or sensations in our minds can be no reason why we should suppose Matter or corporeal substances, SINCE THAT IS ACKNOWLEDGED TO REMAIN EQUALLY INEXPLICABLE WITH OR WITHOUT THIS SUPPOSITION.

Were it necessary to add any FURTHER PROOF AGAINST THE EXISTENCE OF MATTER after what has been said, I could instance several of those errors and difficulties (not to mention impieties) which have sprung from that tenet. It has occasioned numberless controversies and disputes in philosophy, and not a few in religion. But I shall not enter into the detail of them in this place.

CAUSE OF IDEAS. - We perceive a continual succession of ideas, some are anew excited, others are changed or totally disappear. There is therefore some cause of these ideas, whereon they depend, and which produces and changes them. That this cause cannot be any quality or idea or combination of ideas, is clear from the preceding section. I must therefore be a substance; but it has been

shown that there is no corporeal or material substance: it remains therefore that the CAUSE OF IDEAS is an incorporeal active substance or Spirit.

NO IDEA OF SPIRIT. - A spirit is one simple, undivided, active being - as it perceives ideas it is called the UNDERSTANDING, and as it produces or otherwise operates about them it is called the WILL. Such is the nature of SPIRIT that it cannot be of itself perceived, BUT ONLY BY THE EFFECTS WHICH IT PRODUCETH.

LAWS OF NATURE. - The ideas of Sense are more strong, lively, and DISTINCT than those of the imagination; they have likewise a steadiness, order, and coherence, and are not excited at random, as those which are the effects of human wills often are, but in a regular train or series, the admirable connexion whereof sufficiently testifies the wisdom and benevolence of its Author. Now THE SET RULES OR ESTABLISHED METHODS WHEREIN THE MIND WE DEPEND ON EXCITES IN US THE IDEAS OF SENSE, ARE CALLED THE LAWS OF NATURE; and these we learn by experience, which teaches us that such and such ideas are attended with such and such other ideas, in the ordinary course of things.

KNOWLEDGE NECESSARY FOR THE CONDUCT OF WORLDLY AFFAIRS. - This gives us a sort of foresight which enables us to regulate our actions for the benefit of life. That food nourishes, sleep refreshes, and fire warms us; that to sow in the seed-time is the way to reap in the harvest - all this we know, NOT BY DISCOVERING ANY NECESSARY CONNEXION BETWEEN OUR IDEAS, but only by the observation of the settled laws of nature, without which we should be all in uncertainty and confusion, and a grown man no more know how to manage himself in the affairs of life than an infant just born.

OF REAL THINGS AND IDEAS OR CHIMERAS. - The ideas imprinted on the Senses by the Author of nature are called REAL THINGS. The ideas of Sense are allowed to have more reality in them, that is, to be more (1) STRONG, (2) ORDERLY, and (3) COHERENT than the creatures of the mind; but this is no argument that they exist without the mind.

FIRST GENERAL OBJECTION. - ANSWER. We must now answer any objections, and if I seem too prolix to those of quick apprehensions, I hope it may be pardoned, since all men do not equally apprehend things of this nature, and I am willing to be understood by every one.

FIRST, it will be objected that by the foregoing principles ALL THAT IS REAL AND SUBSTANTIAL IN NATURE IS BANISHED OUT OF THE WORLD. I ANSWER, that by the principles premised we are not deprived of any one thing in nature. Whatever we see, feel, hear, or anywise conceive or understand remains as secure as ever.

SECOND OBJECTION. - It will be OBJECTED that there is a great difference betwixt imagining oneself burnt, and actually being so. To which the answer is that nobody will pretend that real pain can possibly be without the mind.

THIRD OBJECTION - It will be objected that we see things at distance which consequently do not exist in the mind. In answer that in a DREAM we do oft perceive things as existing, and yet those things are acknowledged to have their existence only in the mind.

FOURTH OBJECTION. - It will be objected that from the foregoing it follows things are every moment annihilated and created anew. The trees therefore are in the garden, or the chairs in the parlour, no longer than there is somebody to perceive them. Upon SHUTTING MY EYES all the furniture in the room is reduced to nothing, and upon opening them it is again created. In ANSWER to all which, I ask the reader whether he means anything by the actual existence of an idea distinct from its being perceived.

OBJECTIONS DERIVED FROM THE SCRIPTURES ANSWERED. - Some there are who think that the Holy Scriptures are so clear in the point as will sufficiently convince every good Christian that bodies do really exist; there being in Holy Writ innumerable facts related which evidently suppose the reality of timber and stone, mountains and rivers, and cities, and human bodies. To which I answer that no sort of writings whatever, sacred or profane, which use those and the like words in the vulgar acceptation, or so as to have a meaning in them, are in danger of having their truth called in question by our doctrine. And I do not think that what philosophers call Matter, or the existence of objects without the mind, is anywhere mentioned in Scripture. It will be urged that miracles do, at least, lose much of their stress and import by our principles. What must we think of Moses' rod?[1] was it not really turned into a serpent; or was there only a change of ideas in the minds of the spectators? And, can it be supposed that our Saviour did no more at the marriage-feast in Cana than impose on the sight, and smell, and taste of the guests, so as to create in them the appearance or idea only of wine? The same may be said of all other miracles; which, in consequence of the foregoing principles, must be looked upon only as so many cheats, or illusions of fancy. To this I reply, that the rod was changed into a real serpent, and the water into real wine. This does not in the least contradict what I have elsewhere said.

THE REMOVAL OF MATTER GIVES CERTAINTY TO KNOWLEDGE. - From the principles we have laid down it follows human knowledge may naturally be reduced to two heads - that of ideas and that of spirits. So long as we attribute a real existence to unthinking things, distinct from their being perceived, it is not only impossible for us to know with evidence the nature of any real unthinking being, but even that it exists. Hence it is that we see philosophers distrust their senses, and doubt of the existence of heaven and earth, of everything they see or feel, even of their own bodies. But, all this doubtfulness, which so bewilders and confounds the mind and makes

philosophy ridiculous in the eyes of the world, vanishes if we annex a meaning to our words.

SENSIBLE QUALITIES REAL. - It were a mistake to think that what is here said derogates in the least from the reality of things. All the difference is that, according to us, the unthinking beings perceived by sense have no existence distinct from being perceived, and cannot exist in any other substance than those unextended indivisible substances or spirits which act and think and perceive them.

OBJECTIONS OF ATHEISTS OVERTURNED. - For, as we have shown the doctrine of Matter or corporeal substance to have been the main pillar and support of Scepticism, and all the impious schemes of Atheism and Irreligion. All their monstrous systems have so visible and necessary a dependence on it that, when this corner-stone is once removed, the whole fabric cannot choose but fall to the ground.

OF IDOLATORS. - The existence of Matter, or bodies unperceived, has not only been the main support of Atheists and Fatalists, but on the same principle doth Idolatry likewise in all its various forms depend. Did men but consider that the sun, moon, and stars, and every other object of the senses are only so many sensations in their minds, which have no other existence but barely being perceived, doubtless they would never fall down and worship their own ideas, but rather address their homage to that ETERNAL INVISIBLE MIND which produces and sustains all things.

We next treat of SPIRITS. By the word spirit we mean only that which thinks, wills, and perceives; this, and this alone, constitutes the signification of the term. But it will be objected that, if there is no idea signified by the terms soul, spirit, and substance, they are wholly insignificant, or have no meaning in them. I answer, those words do mean or signify a real thing; that what I am myself, that which I denote by the term I, is the same with what is meant by soul or spiritual substance.

THE NATURAL IMMORTALITY OF THE SOUL IS A NECESSARY CONSEQUENCE OF THE FOREGOING DOCTRINE. - It must not be supposed that they who assert the natural immortality of the soul are of opinion that it is incapable of annihilation by the Creator, but only that it is not liable to be broken or dissolved by the ordinary laws of nature or motion. They indeed who hold the soul of man to be only a system of animal spirits, make it perishing and corruptible as the body; since such a being could not survive the ruin of the tabernacle wherein it is enclosed. And this notion has been greedily embraced and cherished by the worst part of mankind, as the most effectual antidote against all impressions of virtue and religion. But we have shown that the soul is indivisible, incorporeal, unextended, and it is consequently incorruptible; that is to say, "the soul of man is naturally immortal."

It is evident to every one that those things which are called the Works of Nature, that is, the far greater part of the ideas or sensations perceived by us, are not produced by, or

---

1   **Moses' rod:** see the Torah p23, Exodus 4 and 14

dependent on, the wills of men. There is therefore some other Spirit that causes them; I say if we consider all these things, and at the same time attend to the meaning and import of the attributes One, Eternal, Infinitely Wise, Good, and Perfect, we shall clearly perceive that they belong to the aforesaid Spirit, "who works all in all," and "by whom all things consist."

THE EXISTENCE OF GOD MORE EVIDENT THAN THAT OF MAN. - Hence, it is evident that God is known as certainly and immediately as any other mind or spirit whatsoever distinct from ourselves. It seems to be a general pretence of the unthinking herd that they cannot see God. Could we but see Him, say they, as we see a man, we should believe that He is, and believing obey His commands. But alas, we need only open our eyes to see the Sovereign Lord of all things, with a more full and clear view than we do any one of our fellow-creatures. But when we see the colour, size, figure, and motions of a man, we perceive only certain sensations or ideas excited in our own minds. And after the same manner we see God; whithersoever we direct our view, we do at all times and in all places perceive manifest tokens of the Divinity.

That the discovery of this great truth, which lies so near and obvious to the mind, should be attained to by the reason of so very few, is a sad instance of the stupidity and inattention of men, who, though they are surrounded with such clear manifestations of the Deity, are yet so little affected by them that they seem, as it were, blinded with excess of light.

The Life and Strange Surprising Adventures of Robinson Crusoe

by Daniel Defoe
(London, 1719)

Daniel Foe (he added the aristocratic 'De' himself) produced what is sometimes thought of as the first modern novel in English. It is likely that he based the story on the real-life Alexander Selkirk, who spent more than four years on the Pacific island known then as Más a Tierra, but which changed its name in 1966 to 'Robinson Crusoe Island'.

Abridged: JH

I. I Go to Sea

I was born of a good family in the city of York, where my father - a foreigner, of Bremen - settled after having retired from business. My father had given me a competent share of learning and designed me for the law; but I would be satisfied in nothing but going to sea. My mind was filled with thoughts of seeing the world, and nothing could persuade me to give up my desire.

At length, on September 1, 1651, I left home, and went on board a ship bound for London. The ship was no sooner out of the Humber than the wind began to blow and the sea to rise in a most frightful manner; and as I had never been at sea before, I was most inexpressibly sick in body and terrified in mind. The next day, however, the wind abated, and for several days the weather continued calm. My fears being forgotten, and the current of my desires returned, I entirely forgot the vows to return home that I made in my distress.

The sixth day of our being at sea we came into Yarmouth Roads and cast anchor. Our troubles were not yet over, however, for a few days later the wind increased till it blew a terrible storm indeed. I began to see terror in the faces even of the seamen themselves; and as the captain passed me, I could hear him softly to himself say, several times, "We shall be all lost!"

My horror of mind put me into such a condition that I can by no words describe it. The storm increased, and the seamen every now and then cried out the ship would founder. One of the men cried out that we had sprung a leak, and all hands were called to the pumps; but the water increasing in the hold, it was apparent that the ship would founder. We fired guns for help, and a ship who had rid it out just ahead of us ventured a boat out. It was with the utmost hazard the boat came near us, but at last we got all into it, and got into shore, though not without much difficulty, and walked afterwards on foot to Yarmouth.

Having some money in my pocket, I travelled to London, and there got acquainted with the master of a ship which traded on the coast of Guinea. This captain, taking a fancy to my conversation, told me if I would make a voyage with him I might do some trading on my own account. I embraced the offer, and went the voyage with him. With the help of some of my relations I raised L40, which I laid out in toys, beads, and such trifles as my friend the captain said were most in demand on the Guinea Coast. It was a prosperous voyage. It made me both a sailor and a merchant, for my adventure yielded me on my return to London almost £300, and this filled me with those aspiring thoughts which have since so completed my ruin.

I was now set up as a Guinea trader, and made up my mind to go the same voyage again in the same ship; but this was the unhappiest voyage ever man made, for as we were off the African shore we were surprised by a Moorish rover of Salee, who gave chase with all sail. About three in the afternoon he came up with us, and after a great fight we were forced to yield, and were carried all prisoners into the port of Salee, where we were sold as slaves.

I was fortunate enough to fall into the hands of a master who treated me with no little kindness. He frequently went fishing, and as I was dexterous in catching fish, he never went without me. One day he sent me out with a Moor to catch fish for him. Then notions of deliverance darted into my thoughts, and I prepared not for fishing, but for a voyage. When everything was ready, we sailed away to the fishing-grounds. Purposely catching nothing, I said we had better go farther out. The Moor agreed, and I ran the boat out near a league farther; then I brought to as if I would fish. Instead of that, however, I stepped forward, and, stooping behind the Moor, took him by surprise and tossed him overboard. He rose to the surface, and called on me to take him in. For reply I presented a gun at him, and told him if he came nearer the boat I would shoot him, and that as the sea was calm, he might easily swim ashore. So he turned about, and swam for the shore, and I make no doubt but he reached it with ease.

About ten days afterwards, as I was steering out to double a cape, I came in sight of a Portuguese ship. On coming nearer, they hailed me, but I understood not a word. At last a Scotch sailor called to me, and I answered I was an Englishman, and had made my escape from the Moors of Salee. They then bade me come on board, and very kindly took me in, with all my goods.

We had a very good voyage to the Brazils, and when we reached our destination the captain recommended me to an honest man who had a sugar plantation. Here I settled down for a while, and learned the planting of sugar. Then I took a piece of land, and became a planter myself. My affairs prospered, and had I continued in the station I was now in, I had room for many happy things to have yet befallen me; but I was still to be the agent of my own miseries.

II. Lord of an Island and Alone

Some of my neighbours, hearing that I had a knowledge of Guinea trading, proposed to fit out a vessel and send her to the coast of Guinea to purchase negroes to work in our plantations. I was well pleased with the idea; and when they asked me to go to manage the trading part, I forgot all the perils and hardships of the sea, and agreed to go. A ship being fitted out, we set sail on September 1, 1659.

We had very good weather for twelve days, but after crossing the line, violent hurricanes took us, and drove us out of the way of all human commerce. In this distress, one morning, there was a cry of "Land!" and almost at the same moment the ship struck against a sandbank. We took to a boat, and worked towards the land; but before we could reach it, a raging wave came rolling astern of us, and overset the boat. We were all thrown into the sea, and out of fifteen who were on board, none escaped but myself. I managed, somehow, to scramble to shore, and clambered up the cliffs, and sat me down on the grass half-dead. Night coming on me, I took up my lodging in a tree.

When I waked, it was broad day, the weather clear, and the storm abated. What surprised me most was that in the night the ship had been lifted from the bank by the swelling tide, and driven ashore almost as far as the place where I had landed. I saw that if we had all kept on board we had been all safe, and I had not been so miserable as to be left entirely destitute of all company as I now was.

I swam out to the ship, and found that her stern lay lifted up on the bank. All the ship's provisions were dry, and, being well disposed to eat, I filled my pockets and ate as I went about other things, for I had no time to lose. We had several spare yards and planks, and with these I made a raft. I emptied three of the seamen's chests, and let them down upon the raft, and filled them with provisions. I also let down the carpenter's chest, and some arms and ammunition-all of which, after much labour, I got safely to land.

My next work was to view the country. Where I was I yet knew not, but after I had with great labour got to the top of a hill which rose up very steep and high, I saw my fate, to my great affliction-/viz./, that I was in an island, uninhabited except by wild beasts.

I now began to consider that I might yet get a great many things out of the ship which would be useful to me; so every day at low water I went on board, and brought away something or other until I had the biggest magazine that was ever laid up, I believe, for one man. I verily believe, had the calm weather held, I should have brought away the whole ship piece by piece; but on the fourteenth day it blew a storm, and next morning, behold, no more ship was to be seen. I must not forget that I brought on shore two cats and a dog. He was a trusty servant to me many years. I wanted nothing that he could fetch me, nor any company. I only wanted him to talk to me, but that he could not do. Later, I managed to catch a parrot, which did much to cheer my loneliness. I taught him to speak, and it would have done your heart good to have heard the pitying tones in which he used to say, "Robin-poor Robin Crusoe!"

I now went in search of a place where to fix my dwelling. I found a little plain on the side of a rising hill, which was there as steep as a house-side, so that nothing could come down on me from the top. On the side of this rock was a hollow space like the entrance of a cave, before which I resolved to pitch my tent. Before I set up my tent, I drew a half-circle before the hollow place, which extended backwards about twenty yards. In this half-circle I planted two rows of strong stakes, driving them into the ground like piles, above five feet and a half high, and sharpened at the top. Then I took some pieces of cable I had found in the ship, and laid them in rows one upon another between the stakes; and this fence was so strong that neither man nor beast could get into it or over it. The entrance I made to be by a short ladder to go over the top, and when I was in I lifted the ladder after me.

Inside the fence, with infinite labour, I carried all my riches, provisions, ammunition, and stores. And I made me a large tent, also, to preserve me from the rains. When I had done this I began to work my way into the rock. All the earth and stones I dug out I laid up within my fence, and thus I made me a cave just behind my tent which served me like a cellar.

In the middle of my labours it happened that, rummaging in my things, I found a little bag with but husks of corn and dust in it. Wishing to make use of the bag, I shook it out on one side of my fortification. It was a little before the great rains that I threw this stuff away, not remembering that I had thrown anything there; about a month after, I saw some green stalks shooting up. I was perfectly astonished when, after a little longer time, I saw ten or twelve ears of barley. I knew not how it came there. At last it occurred to me that I had shaken out the bag there. Besides the barley there were also a few stalks of rice. I carefully saved the ears of this corn, you may be sure, and resolved to sow them all again. When my corn was ripe, I used a cutlass as a scythe, and cut off the ears, and rubbed them out with my hands. At the end of my harvesting I had nearly two bushels of rice, and two bushels and a half of barley. I kept all this for seed, and bore the want of bread with patience.

I soon found that I needed many things to make me comfortable. First I wanted a chair and a table, for without them I must live like a savage. So I set to work. I had never handled a tool in my life, but I had a saw, an axe, and several hatchets, and I soon learned to use them all. If I wanted a board, I had to chop down a tree. From the trunk of the tree I cut a log of the length my board was to be. Then I split the log, and, with infinite labour, hewed it flat till it was as thin as a board. I made myself a table and a chair out of short pieces of board, and from the large boards I made some wide shelves. On these I laid my tools and other things.

From time to time I made many useful things. From a piece of ironwood, cut in the forest with great labour, I made a spade to dig with. Then I wanted a pick-axe, but for long I could not think how I was to get one. At length I made use of crowbars from the wreck. These I heated in the fire, and, little by little, shaped them till I made a pick-axe, proper enough, though heavy.

At first I felt the need of baskets in which to carry things, so I set to work as a basket-maker. It came to my mind that the twigs of the tree whence I cut my stakes might serve. I found them to my purpose as much as I could desire, and, during the next rainy season, I employed myself in making a great many baskets. Though I did not finish them handsomely, yet I made them sufficiently serviceable.

I had, however, one want greater than all the others-bread. My barley was very fine, the grains were large and smooth; but before I could make bread I must grind the grains into flour. I spent many a day to find out a Stone to cut hollow and make fit for a mortar, and could find none; nor were the rocks of the island of hardness sufficient. So I gave it over and rounded a great block of hard wood and, with the

help of fire and great labour, made a hollow in it. I made a great heavy pestle of the wood called ironwood.

The baking part was the next thing to be considered; for, first, I had no yeast. As to that, there was no supplying the want, so I did not concern myself much about it. But for an oven I was indeed in great pain. At length I found out an experiment for that also. I made some earthen vessels, broad but not deep, about two feet across, and about nine inches deep. These I burned in the fire till they were as hard as nails and as red as tiles, and when I wanted to bake I made a great fire upon a hearth which I paved with some square tiles of my own making.

When the fire had all burned I drew the embers forward upon my hearth, and let them be there till the hearth was very hot. My loaves being ready, I swept the hearth and set them on the hottest part of it. Over each loaf I placed one of the large earthen pots, and drew the embers all round to keep in and add to the heat. And thus I baked my barley loaves and became, in a little time, a good pastrycook into the bargain.

It need not be wondered at if all these things took up most of the third year of my abode in the island. I had now brought my state of life to be much easier than it was at first, and I learned to look more upon the bright side of my condition and less on the dark.

Had anyone in England met such a man as I was, it must have frightened them, or raised great laughter. On my head I wore a great, high, shapeless cap of goat's skin. Stockings and shoes I had none, but I had made a pair of somethings, I scarce knew what to call them, to slip over my legs; a jacket, with the skirts coming down to the middle of my thighs, and a pair of open-kneed breeches of the same, completing my outfit. I had a broad belt of goat's skin, and in this I hung, on one side, a saw, on the other, a hatchet. Under my arm hung two pouches for shot and powder; at my back I carried my basket, on my shoulder my gun, and over my head a great clumsy goat's skin umbrella.

A stoic[1] would have smiled to have seen me at dinner. There was my majesty, prince and lord of the whole island. How like a king I dined, too, all alone, attended by my servants! Poll, my parrot, as if he had been my favourite, was the only person permitted to talk to me. My old dog sat at my right hand, and two cats on each side of the table, expecting a bit from my hand as a mark of special favour.

III. The Footprint

It was my custom to make daily excursions to some part of the island. One day, walking along the beach, I was exceedingly surprised with the print of a man's naked foot plainly impressed on the sand. I stood like one thunderstruck. I listened, I looked around, but I could hear nothing nor see anything. I went up to a rising ground to look further; I walked backwards and forwards on the shore, but I could see only that one impression.

---

1   **Stoicism** (see p84)

I went to it again. There was exactly a foot-toes, heel, and every part of a foot. How it came thither I knew not; but I hurried home, looking behind me at every two or three steps, and mistaking every bush and tree, fancying every stump to be a man. I had no sleep that night; but my terror gradually wore off, and after some days I ventured down to the beach to take measure of the footprint by my own.

I found it much larger! This filled me again with all manner of fears, and when I went home I began to prepare against an attack. I got out my muskets, loaded them, and went to an enormous amount of labour and trouble-all because I had seen the print of a naked foot on the sand. There seemed to me then no labour too great, no task too toilsome, and I made me a second fortification, and planted a vast number of stakes on the outside of my outer wall, which grew and became a thick grove of trees, entirely concealing the place of my retreat, and adding greatly to my security.

I had now been twenty-two years on the island, and had grown so accustomed to the place that, had I felt myself secure from the attack by savages, I fancied I could have been contented to remain there till I died of old age.

For many months the perturbation of my mind was very great; in the day great troubles overwhelmed me, and in the night I dreamed often of killing savages. About two years after I first knew these fears, I was surprised one morning by seeing five canoes on the shore. I could not tell what to think of it, so went and lay in my castle perplexed and discomforted. At length, becoming very impatient, I clambered up to the top of the hill and perceived, by the help of my perspective glass, no less than thirty men dancing round a fire with barbarous gestures. While I was looking, two miserable wretches were dragged from the boats. One was immediately knocked down, while the other, seeing himself a little at liberty, started away from them and ran along the sands directly towards me. I was dreadfully frightened, that I must acknowledge, when I perceived him run my way, especially when, as I thought, I saw him pursued by the whole body. But my spirits began to recover when I found that but three men followed him, and that he outstripped them exceedingly, in running.

Presently he came to a creek and, making nothing of it, plunged in, landed, and ran on with exceeding strength. Two of the pursuers swam the creek, but the third went no farther, and soon after went back again. I immediately took my two guns, ran down the hill and clapped myself in the way between the pursuers and the pursued, hallooing aloud to him that fled. Then, rushing on the foremost of the pursuers, I knocked him down with the stock of my piece. The other stopped, as if frightened, but as I came nearer, I perceived he was fitting a bow and arrow to shoot at me; so I was then obliged to shoot at him first, which I did and killed him.

The poor savage who fled was so frightened with the noise of my piece that he seemed inclined still to fly. I gave him all the signs of encouragement I could think of, and he came nearer, kneeling down every ten or twelve steps. I took him up and made much of him, and comforted him. Then, beckoning him to follow me, I took him to my cave on the farther part of the island. Here, having refreshed him, I made signs for him to lie down to sleep, which the poor creature did. After he had slumbered about half an hour, he came out of the cave, running to me, laying himself down and setting my foot upon his head to let me know he would serve me so long as he lived.

In a little time I began to speak to him and teach him to speak to me; and, first, I let him know his name should be Friday, which was the day I saved his life. I likewise taught him to say "Master," and then let him know that was to be my name. I made a little tent for him, and took in my ladders at night, so that he could no way come at me.

But I needed not this precaution, for never man had a more faithful, loving servant than Friday was to me. I made it my business to teach him everything that was proper to make him useful, especially to make him speak, and he was the aptest scholar that ever was. Indeed, this was the pleasantest year of all the life I led in this place. I began now to have some use for my tongue again, and, besides the pleasure of talking to Friday, I had a singular satisfaction in the fellow himself. His simple, unfeigned honesty appeared to me more and more every day, and I began really to love the creature; and I believe he loved me more than it was possible for him ever to love anything before.

IV. The End of Captivity

I was now entered on the seven-and-twentieth year of my captivity on the island. One morning I bade Friday go to the seashore and see if he could find a turtle. He had not been gone long when he came running back like one that felt not the ground, or the steps he set his feet on, and cries out to me, "O master! O sorrow! O bad!"

"What's the matter, Friday?" said I.

"O yonder, there," says he; "one, two, three canoes!"

"Well," says I, "do not be frightened."

However, I saw the poor fellow was most terribly scared, for nothing ran in his head but that the savages were come back to look for him, and would cut him in pieces and eat him. I comforted him, and told him I was in as much danger as he. Then I went up the hill and found quickly by my glass that there were one-and-twenty savages, whose business seemed to be a triumphant banquet upon three human bodies. I came down again to Friday and, going towards the wretches, sent Friday a little ahead to see what they were doing. He came back and told me that they were eating the flesh of one of their prisoners, and that a bearded man lay bound, whom he said they would kill next.

This fired the very soul within me, and, going to a little rising ground, I turned to Friday and said, "Now, Friday, do exactly as you see me do." So, with a musket, I took aim at the savages; Friday did the like, and we fired, killing three of them and wounding five more. They were in a dreadful consternation, and after we fired again among the amazed wretches, I made directly towards the poor victim who was lying upon the beach. Loosing him, I found he was a Spaniard. He took pistol and sword from me thankfully, and flew upon his murderers, and, Friday, pursuing the flying wretches, in the end but four of the twenty-one escaped in a canoe.

I was minded to pursue them lest they should return with a greater force and devour us by mere multitude. So, running to a canoe, I bade Friday follow me, but was surprised to find another poor creature lying therein, bound hand and foot. I immediately cut his fastenings and bade Friday tell him of his deliverance. But when Friday came to hear him speak and to look in his face, it would have moved anyone to tears to have seen how Friday kissed him, embraced him, hugged him, cried, danced, sung, and then cried again. It was a good while before I could make him tell me what was the matter, but when he came a little to himself, he told me it was his father. He sat down by the old man a long while, and took his arms and ankles, which were numbed with the binding, and chafed and rubbed them with his hands.

My island was now peopled, and I thought myself rich in subjects. The Spaniard and the old savage had been with us about seven months, sharing in our labours, when, being unable to keep means of deliverance out of my thoughts, I gave them leave to go over in one of the canoes to the mainland, where some of the Spaniard's shipmates were cast away, giving them provisions sufficient for themselves and all the Spaniards, for eight days.

It was no less than eight days I had waited for their return when Friday came to me and called aloud, "Master, master, they are come!" I jumped up and climbed to the top of the hill, and with my glass plainly made out an English ship, and its long-boat standing in for the shore. I cannot express the joy I was in at seeing a ship, and one that was manned by my own countrymen; but yet I had some secret doubts, bidding me keep on my guard. Presently the boat was run upon the beach, and in all eleven men landed, whereof three were unarmed and bound, whom I could perceive using passionate gestures of entreaty and despair. Presently the seamen were all gone straggling in the woods, leaving the three distressed men under a tree a little distance from me. I resolved to discover myself to them, and marched with Friday towards them, and called aloud in Spanish, "What are ye, gentlemen?" They started up at the noise, and I perceived them about to fly from me, when I spoke to them in English.

"Gentlemen," says I, "do not be surprised at me; perhaps you may have a friend near, when you did not expect it. Can you not put a stranger in the way to help you?"

One of them, looking like one astonished, returned, "Sir, I was captain of that ship; my men have mutinied against me, and have set me on shore in this desolate place with these two men-my mate and a passenger."

He then told me that if two among the mutineers, who were desperate villains, were secured, he believed the rest on shore would return to their duty. He anticipated my proposals in venturing their deliverance by telling me that both he and the ship, if recovered, should be wholly directed by me in everything. Then I gave them muskets, and the mutineers returning, the two villains were killed, and the rest begged for mercy, and joined us. More of them coming ashore, we fell upon them at night, so that at the captain's call they laid down their arms, trusting to the mercy of the governor of the island, for such they supposed me to be.

It now occurred to me that the time of my deliverance was come, and that it would be easy to bring these fellows in to be hearty in getting possession of the ship. And so it proved, for, the ship being boarded next morning, and the new rebel captain shot, the rest yielded without any more lives lost.

When I saw my deliverance then put visibly into my hands, I was ready to sink down with the surprise, and it was a good while before I could speak a word to the captain, who was in as great an ecstasy as I. After some time, I came dressed in a new habit of the captain's, being still called governor. Being all met, and the captain with me, I caused the prisoners to be brought before me, told them I had got a full account of their villainous behaviour to the captain, and asked of them what they had to say why I should not execute them as pirates. I told them I had resolved to quit the island, but that they, if they went, could only go as prisoners in irons; so that I could not tell what was the best for them, unless they had a mind to take their fate in the island. They seemed thankful for this, and said they would much rather venture to stay than be carried to England to be hanged. So I left it on that issue. When the captain was gone I sent for the men up to me in my apartment and let them into the story of my living there; showed them my fortifications, the way I made my bread, planted my corn; and, in a word, all that was necessary to make them easy. I told them the story, also of the Spaniards that were to be expected, and made them promise to treat them in common with themselves.

I left the next day and went on board the ship with Friday. And thus I left the island the 19th of December, in the year 1686, after eight and twenty years, and, after a long voyage, I arrived in England, the 11th of June, 1687, having been thirty-five years absent.

Gulliver's Travels
Into Several Remote Nations of the World
by Jonathan Swift
(Dublin, 1726)

Jonathan Swift was a political pamphleteer and Dean of St. Patrick's, Dublin. *Gulliver* is both a satire on human nature and a parody of the travellers' tales of the day. It was immensely popular, the poet John Gay said that "it is universally read, from the cabinet council to the nursery", yet it was denounced as "wicked and obscene" in his own land.

Abridged: GH/JH

THE PUBLISHER TO THE READER

The author of these travels, Mr. Lemuel Gulliver, is my ancient and intimate friend. It is with his permission that I now venture to send these papers of his into the world, hoping they may be, at least for some time, a better entertainment than the common scribbles about politics and party.

This volume would have been at least twice as large if I had not made bold to strike out innumerable passages relating to the winds and tides, likewise the account of longitudes and latitudes; wherein I have reason to apprehend that Mr. Gulliver may be a little dissatisfied; but I was resolved to fit the work as much as possible to the general capacity of readers.

As for any farther particulars relating to the author, the reader will receive satisfaction from the first pages of the book.

RICHARD SYMPSON.

PART I: A VOYAGE TO LILLIPUT

My father had a small estate in Nottinghamshire, but the charge of maintaining me at Cambridge being too great, after three years there I was bound apprentice to an eminent surgeon in London; in my spare time I studied navigation, and mathematics, useful to those who travel, as I always believed, at some time, it would be my fortune to do.

After studying physics in Leyden for two years, I became surgeon to the Swallow, and made a voyage or two in the Levant. I then settled in London, married, but after some years, my business beginning to fail, having consulted with my wife, I determined to go again to sea and made several voyages to the East and West Indies, by which I got some addition to my fortune.

In 1699, being on a voyage in the South Seas, we were driven on a rock, and the ship immediately split. I conclude my companions were all lost; for my part, I swam as fortune directed me, and being pushed forward by wind and tide, found myself at last within my depth, and had to wade near a mile before I got to shore. I was extremely tired, and lay down on the grass and slept soundly until daylight. I attempted to rise, but found myself strongly fastened to the ground, not able to turn even my head. I felt something moving gently up my leg, and over my breast, when

bending my eyes downward, I perceived a human creature, not six inches high, with a bow and arrows in his hand; and felt a number more following him. I roared so loud, they all fell off in a fright, but soon returned. I struggled, and broke the strings that fastened my left hand, but the creatures ran off before I could seize them, and I felt about a hundred arrows discharged into my left hand, which pricked like so many needles. I lay still, groaning with grief and pain, till some of the inhabitants came and cut the strings that fastened my head, when turning it a little I saw one, who seemed to be a person of quality, who made me a long speech, of which I understood not one word; but in which I could observe many periods of threatening, and others of pity and kindness.

I answered in the most submissive manner, and being famished with hunger (perhaps against the strict rules of decency), put my finger in my mouth, to signify I wanted food. He understood me very well. Several ladders were applied to my sides, and a hundred of the inhabitants mounted, laden with food and drink, and supplied me as fast as they could, with marks of wonder at my bulk and appetite.

It seems that at the first moment I was discovered, the Emperor had notice by an express, and it was determined in council that I should be secured and fed, and at once conveyed to the capital city.

A sleepy potion having been mingled with my wine, I again slept. These people have arrived to a great perfection in mechanics, and by means of cords and pulleys, in less than three hours, I was raised and slung on to the largest of their machines, used for the carriage of trees and other great weights. Fifteen hundred of the largest horses, each about four and a half inches high, were employed to draw me towards the metropolis. The Emperor and all his Court came out to meet us. In the largest temple in the kingdom, disused because polluted by a murder some years before, I was to be lodged, secured by fourscore and eleven chains locked to my left leg. They were about two yards long and being fixed within four inches of the gate of the temple, allowed me to creep in and lie on the ground at my full length.

The Emperor is taller, by almost the breadth of my nail, than any of his court, his features strong and masculine, and his deportment majestic. He had reigned for seven years in great felicity, and generally victorious. I lay on my side, for the better convenience of beholding him, but I have had him many times since in my hand, and therefore cannot be deceived in this description. He held his sword drawn in his hand to defend himself, if I should happen to break loose, and spoke to me many times, and I answered, but neither of us could understand a syllable.

The Emperor had frequent councils to debate what course should be taken with me; they apprehended I might break loose; or might cause a famine; but my behaviour had made a favourable impression, and his Majesty made provision for me out of his own Treasury, and coming frequently to see me, I soon learnt to express my desire for liberty, which was after a time granted on certain conditions.

I soon learnt, in spite of its flourishing appearance, this country laboured under two evils; a violent faction at home, and the danger of invasion, by a most potent enemy, from abroad. The two parties in the kingdom were distinguished by the high or low heels of their shoes. The high heels were most agreeable to their ancient constitution, but the present Emperor was determined only to make use of low heels in the administration of the government-but the heir apparent seemed to have some tendency to high heels.

They were threatened with an invasion from the Island of Blefusco, which had been engaged in an obstinate war with Lilliput for a long time, on a question of a schism in religion. They had now prepared a numerous fleet, and were about to descend upon us, and his Majesty, in his confidence in my strength and valour, laid this account of his affairs before me.

I Depart from Blefusco

Having ascertained the depth of the channel between the two countries, and viewed the enemy's fleet through my perspective glass, I obtained a great quantity of cable and bars of iron. I twisted the bars into hooks which I fixed to fifty cables, and walked into the sea, wading with what haste I could, swam about thirty yards in the middle, and arrived at the fleet in about half an hour.

The enemy were so frightened when they saw me that they fled, and swam to shore. I then took my tackling, fixed a hook to each vessel, and tied all my cords together at the end; but not a ship would stir, they were held too fast by their anchors. The enemy's arrows disturbed me much, but I resolutely cut all the cables, and with the greatest ease drew fifty of the largest men of war with me. The tide had now fallen, and I waded safe to the royal port of Lilliput, where the Emperor received me with the highest honour. So immeasurable is the ambition of princes, that he thought now of nothing less than the complete submission of Blefusco; but I plainly protested "that I would never be an instrument of bringing a free and brave people into slavery"; and the wisest part of the Council were of my opinion.

His Majesty never forgave me, and an intrigue began which had like to have been my utter ruin; but a considerable person at Court informed me of the schemes against me,

and I resolved at once to pay a visit to Blefusco, whose Emperor had sent a solemn embassy to Lilliput with humble offers of peace, and who received me with the generosity suitable to so great a Prince.

Three days after my arrival I observed a boat overturned on the coast, which with great difficulty I managed to get to the royal port of Blefusco; I told the Emperor that my good fortune had thrown this boat in my way, to carry me towards my native country, and begged his orders for materials to fit it up, together with his license to depart, which, after some kind expostulation, he was pleased to grant.

His Majesty of Lilliput had sent an envoy, to ask his brother of Blefusco to have me sent back to be punished as a traitor with the loss of my eyes; so that I resolved to "venture myself on the ocean rather than be an occasion of difference between two such mighty monarchs."

I stored the boat with the carcasses of sheep and oxen, and with bread and drink proportionable, and as much ready-dressed meat as four-hundred cooks could provide. I took with me cows and bulls, and rams and ewes, intending to propagate the breed in my own country; and would gladly have taken a dozen or two of the natives, but this his Majesty would not permit. Besides making a diligent search in my pockets, his Majesty engaged my honour "not to carry away any of his subjects, although by their own desire."

I set sail, and on the third day descried a sail steering to the south-east. I made all the sail I could, and in half an hour she espied me and flung out her flag and fired a gun.

My heart leaped within me to see her English colours, and putting my cows and sheep into my pockets, I soon got on board with all my provisions.

The Captain, a very civil man, and an excellent sailor, treated me with kindness, and we arrived in England with only one misfortune: the rats carried off one of my sheep. The rest I got safely ashore, and made a considerable profit in showing them to persons of quality, and before I began my second voyage I sold them for six hundred pounds.

I stayed but two months with my wife and family, for my insatiable desire of seeing foreign countries would suffer me to stay no longer. I left fifteen hundred pounds with my wife; my uncle had left me a small estate near Epping of about thirty pounds a year, and I had a long lease of the Black Bull in Fetter Lane; so that I was in no danger of leaving my wife and family upon the parish. My son Johnny was at the grammar school, and a towardly child. My daughter Betty (who is now well married) was then at her needlework.

I took leave of them with tears on both sides, and went on board the Adventure, a merchant ship of 300 tons, bound for Surat.

PART II: A VOYAGE TO BROBDINGNAG

We made a good voyage, until we had passed the Straits of Madagascar, when the southern monsoon set in, and we were driven many leagues out of our course. Being in distress for water, and coming in sight of land, some of us went on shore in search of it. I walked alone about a mile, when, seeing nothing to satisfy my curiosity, I was returning when I saw our men already in the boat, and rowing for life to the ship, with a huge creature walking after them, the sea up his knees.

I ran off as fast as I could, up a hill, and along what I took for a highroad, but could see little, on either side the corn rising at least forty feet, until I came to a stone stile, which it was impossible for me to climb. I was looking for a gap in the hedge, when I saw one of the inhabitants in the next field. He seemed as high as an ordinary spire steeple, and took about ten yards at each step. I ran to hide myself in the corn, whence I saw him at the stile calling out in a voice which at first I certainly took for thunder. Seven monsters like himself then came, and began to reap the field where I lay. I made a shift to get away, squeezing myself between the stalks, till I came to a part laid by the rain and wind. It was impossible to advance a step, and I heard the reapers not a hundred yards behind me. Being quite dispirited with toil, I lay down and began to bemoan my widow and fatherless children, when one of the reapers came quite near me, and I screamed as loud as I could, fearing I should be squashed to death by his foot. He looked about, and at last espying me, took me carefully behind, between his finger and thumb, as I myself had done with a weasel in England.

I resolved not to struggle, but ventured to put my hands together in a supplicating manner, and say some words in a humble, melancholy tone, and letting him know by my gestures how grievously he pinched my sides. He seemed to apprehend my meaning, and put me gently in the lapel of his coat, and ran along to show me to his master, the substantial farmer I had first seen in the field.

He placed me gently on all fours on the ground, but I immediately got up, and walked slowly backwards and forwards to let those people see I had no intent to run away. They all sat down in a circle round me, and the farmer was soon convinced I was a rational creature, but we were quite unintelligible to one another. He put me gently in his handkerchief and took me to show to his wife. She at first screamed, as women do at a toad, but seeing how well I observed the signs her husband made, she, by degrees, grew extremely fond of me.

A servant brought in dinner, and the farmer put me on the table. The wife minced some bread and meat and placed it before me. I made her a low bow, took out my knife and fork, and fell to eating, which gave them great delight. The farmer's youngest son, an arch boy of ten, took me up by the legs and held me so high in the air, that I trembled in every limb; but the farmer snatched me from him and gave him such a box on the ear, as would have felled a European troop of horse to the earth.

I fell on my knees, and pointing to the boy made my master understand I desired his son to be pardoned. The lad took

his seat again and I went and kissed his hand, which my master took and made him stroke me gently with it.

When dinner was almost done, the nurse came in with a child of a year old in her arms, who at once began to squall to get me for a plaything.

The mother, out of pure indulgence, held me up to the child, who seized me by the middle and got my head into his mouth, where I roared so loud, the urchin was frightened, and let me drop, and I should have infallibly broke my neck, if the mother had not held her apron underneath.

My mistress, perceiving I was very tired, put me on her own bed after dinner, and covered me with a clean white handkerchief; I slept, and dreamed I was at home with my wife and children, which aggravated my sorrows when I awoke, to find myself alone in a bed twenty feet wide. Two rats had crept up the curtains, and had the boldness to attack me, but I had the good fortune to rip one up with my hanger, before he could do me any mischief, and the other ran away; though not without one good wound. These creatures were the size of a large mastiff, and infinitely more nimble and fierce. My mistress was extremely rejoiced to find I was not hurt, and with her little daughter fitted me up the baby's cradle against night, which was then placed on a shelf for fear of rats.

The daughter, nine years old, and not above forty feet high, was very good natured, became my schoolmistress, and called me Grildrig, which imports in English, mannikin. To her I chiefly owe my preservation: I called her Glumdalclitch, or Little Nurse, and I heartily wish it was in my power to requite her care and affection as she deserves, instead of being, as I have reason to fear, the innocent unhappy instrument of her disgrace.

My master, being advised to show me as a sight in the next town, I was carried there in a box by Glumdalclitch on a pillion behind her father, who, after consulting the inn-keeper, hired the crier to give notice to the town of a strange creature to be seen not six feet long, resembling in every part a human creature, could speak several words, and perform a hundred diverting tricks.

I was shown that day till I was half dead with weariness and vexation, for those who had seen me made such wonderful reports that the people were ready to break down the doors to come in.

My master, finding how profitable I was likely to be, showed me in all the considerable towns in the kingdom, till observing that I was almost reduced to a skeleton, concluded I must soon die, and sold me to the Queen for a thousand pieces of gold. Her Majesty asked me "whether I should be content to live at Court?" I bowed down to the table, and humbly answered, "I should be proud to devote my life to her Majesty's service," and begged the favour that Glumdalclitch might be admitted into her service and continue to be my nurse and instructor.

At the Court of Brobdingnag

Her Majesty agreed, and easily got the farmer's consent, and the poor girl herself was not able to hide her joy.

The Queen was surprised at so much wit and good sense in so small an animal, and took me in her own hand to the King, who, though as learned a person as any in his dominions, conceived I might be a piece of clockwork, until he heard me speak. He sent for three great scholars, who, after much debate, concluded that I was only lusus naturae; a determination agreeable to the modern philosophy of Europe, whose professors have invented this wonderful solution of all difficulties, to the unspeakable advancement of human knowledge.

I entreated to be heard a word or two, and assured them that I came from a country where everything was in proportion, and where, in consequence, I might defend myself and find sustenance. To which they only replied, with a smile of contempt, saying, "that the farmer had instructed me very well in my lesson." The King, who had a much better understanding, dismissed his learned men, and after some further examination, began to think what we told him might be true. A convenient apartment was provided for Glumdalclitch, a governess to attend to her education, a maid to dress her, and two other servants; but the care of me was wholly appropriated to herself. I soon became a great favourite with the King; my little chair and table were placed at his left hand, before the salt-cellar, and he took pleasure in conversing with me, inquiring into the laws, government, and learning of Europe. He made very wise observations upon all I said, but once when I had been a little too copious in talking of my beloved country, he took me up in his hand, and in a hearty fit of laughter asked me if I were a Whig or a Tory? Then, turning to his first minister, observed how contemptible a thing was human grandeur, which could be mimicked by such diminutive insects as I.

But as I was not in a condition to resent injuries, so upon mature thoughts I began to doubt whether I was injured or no. For after being accustomed to the sight of these people for some time, I really began to imagine myself dwindled many degrees below my usual size. My littleness exposed me to many ridiculous and troublesome accidents, which determined Glumdalclitch never to let me go abroad out of her sight. I was, indeed, treated with much kindness, the favourite of the King and Queen, and the delight of the whole Court. But I could never forget the domestic pledges I had left behind me, and longed to be again with people with whom I could converse on equal terms.

About the beginning of the third year of my stay in this country, Glumdalclitch and I attended the King and Queen in a progress round the south coast. I was carried as usual in my travelling box, a very convenient closet about twelve feet wide. I longed to see the ocean, which must be the only scene of my escape, and desired leave to take the air of the sea with a page who sometimes took charge of me.

I shall never forget with what unwillingness Glumdalclitch consented; we were both much tired with our journey, and the poor girl was so ill as to be confined to her chamber. The boy took me out in my box towards the seashore, when ordering him to set me down, I cast many a wistful glance toward the sea.

I found myself not very well, and hoping a nap would do me good soon fell asleep. I conjecture as I slept the page went off to look for birds' eggs, for I was awakened by finding myself raised high in the air and borne forward with prodigious speed. I called out, I looked out, but could see nothing but clouds and sky. I heard a great flapping of wings-they increased very fast, and my box was tossed up and down, and I felt myself falling with incredible swiftness. My fall was stopped by a terrible squash, I was quite in the dark for a minute, then I could see light from the tops of my windows. I had fallen into the sea. I did then, and do now, suppose that the eagle, that had flown away with me, was pursued by two or three others, and forced to let me drop. I was for four hours, under these circumstances, expecting, and, indeed, hoping, every moment to be my last.

I heard a grating sound on the side of my box, and soon felt I was being towed along the sea, and called for help until I was hoarse. In return I heard a great shout, giving me transports of joy, and somebody called in the English tongue that I was safe, for my box was fastened to their ship. The carpenter came, in a few minutes, and sawed a hole, through which I was taken into the ship in a very weak condition.

The Captain, a worthy Shropshire man, was returning to England, and we came into the Downs on the 3rd of June, 1706, about nine months after my escape.

When I came to my own house my wife protested I should never go to sea any more.

The History of Tom Jones, a Foundling
by Henry Fielding
(London, 1749)

The aristocratic Fielding of Glastonbury was a lawyer and playwright whose fiercely satirical pamphlets (some under the name of 'Hercules Vinegar') and plays were instrumental in an irritated government restricting them through the Theatrical Licensing Act of 1737.

Abridged: JH

Mr. Allworthy Makes a Discovery

In that part of the country which is commonly called Somersetshire there lately lived a gentleman whose name was Allworthy, and who might well be called the favourite of both nature and fortune. From the former of these he derived an agreeable person, a sound constitution, a solid understanding, and a benevolent heart; by the latter he was decreed to the inheritance of one of the largest estates in the country.

Mr. Allworthy lived, for the most part, retired in the country, with one sister, for whom he had a very tender affection. This lady, Miss Bridget Allworthy, now somewhat past the age of thirty, was of that species of women whom you commend rather for good qualities than beauty.

Mr. Allworthy had been absent a full quarter of a year in London on some very particular business, and having returned to his house very late in the evening, retired, much fatigued, to his chamber. Here, after he had spent some minutes on his knees - a custom which he never broke through on any account - he was preparing to step into bed, when, upon opening the clothes, to his great surprise, he beheld an infant wrapped up in some coarse linen, in a sweet and profound sleep, between his sheets. He stood for some time lost in astonishment at this sight; but soon began to be touched with sentiments of compassion for the little wretch before him. He then rang his bell, and ordered an elderly woman-servant to rise immediately and come to him.

The consternation of Mrs. Deborah Wilkins at the finding of the little infant was rather greater than her master's had been; nor could she refrain from crying out, with great horror, "My good sir, what's to be done?"

Mr. Allworthy answered she must take care of the child that evening, and in the morning he would give orders to provide it a nurse.

"Yes, sir," says she, "and I hope your worship will send out your warrant to take up the hussy its mother. Indeed, such wicked sluts cannot be too severely punished for laying their sins at honest men's doors; and though your worship knows your own innocence, yet the world is censorious, and if your worship should provide for the child it may make the people after to believe. If I might be so bold as to give my advice, I would have it put in a basket, and sent out and laid at the churchwarden's door. It is a good night,

only a little rainy and windy, and if it was well wrapped up and put in a warm basket, it is two to one but it lives till it is found in the morning. But if it should not, we have discharged our duty in taking care of it; and it is, perhaps, better for such creatures to die in a state of innocence than to grow up and imitate their mothers."

But Mr. Allworthy had now got one of his fingers into the infant's hand, which, by its gentle pressure, seeming to implore his assistance, certainly outpleaded the eloquence of Mrs. Deborah. Mr. Allworthy gave positive orders for the child to be taken away and provided with pap and other things against it waked. He likewise ordered that proper clothes should be procured for it early in the morning, and that it should be brought to himself as soon as he was stirring.

Such was the respect Mrs. Wilkins bore her master, under whom she enjoyed a most excellent place, that her scruples gave way to his peremptory commands, and, declaring the child was a sweet little infant, she walked off with it to her own chamber.

Allworthy betook himself to those pleasing slumbers which a heart that hungers after goodness is apt to enjoy when thoroughly satisfied.

In the morning Mr. Allworthy told his sister he had a present for her, and, when Mrs. Wilkins produced the little infant, told her the whole story of its appearance.

Miss Bridget took the good-natured side of the question, intimated some compassion for the helpless little creature, and commended her brother's charity in what he had done. The good lady subsequently gave orders for providing all necessaries for the child, and her orders were indeed so liberal that had it been a child of her own she could not have exceeded them.

The Foundling Achieves Manhood

Miss Bridget having been asked in marriage by one Captain Blifil, a half-pay officer, and the nuptials duly celebrated, Mrs. Blifil was in course of time delivered of a fine boy.

Though the birth of an heir to his beloved sister was a circumstance of great joy to Mr. Allworthy, yet it did not alienate his affections from the little foundling to whom he had been godfather, and had given his own name of Thomas; the surname of Jones being added because it was believed that was the mother's name.

He told his sister, if she pleased, the newborn infant should be bred up together with little Tommy, to which she consented, for she had truly a great complaisance for her brother.

The captain, however, could not so easily bring himself to bear what he condemned as a fault in Mr. Allworthy; for his meditations being chiefly employed on Mr. Allworthy's fortune, and on his hopes of succession, he looked on all the instances of his brother-in-law's generosity as diminutions of his own wealth.

But one day, while the captain was exulting in the happiness which would accrue to him by Mr. Allworthy's death, he himself died of apoplexy.

So the two boys grew up together under the care of Mr. Allworthy and Mrs. Blifil, and by the time he was fourteen Tom Jones-who, according to universal opinion, was certainly born to be hanged-had been already convicted of three robberies-viz., of robbing an orchard, of stealing a duck out of a farmer's yard, and of picking Master Blifil's pocket of a ball.

The vices of this young man were, moreover, heightened by the disadvantageous light in which they appeared when opposed to the virtues of Master Blifil, his companion. He was, indeed, a lad of remarkable disposition-sober, discreet, and pious beyond his age; and many expressed their wonder that Mr. Allworthy should suffer such a lad as Tom Jones to be educated with his nephew lest the morals of the latter should be corrupted by his example.

To say the truth, the whole duck, and great part of the apples, were converted to the use of Tom's friend, the gamekeeper, and his family; though, as Jones alone was discovered, the poor lad bore not only the whole smart, but the whole blame.

Mr. Allworthy had committed the instruction of the two boys to a learned divine, the Reverend Mr. Thwackum, who resided in the house; but though Mr. Allworthy had given him frequent orders to make no difference between the lads, yet was Thwackum altogether as kind and gentle to Master Blifil as he was harsh, nay, even barbarous, to the other. In truth, Blifil had greatly gained his master's affections; partly by the profound respect he always showed his person, but much more by the decent reverence with which he received his doctrine, for he had got by heart, and frequently repeated, his phrases, and maintained all his master's religious principles, with a zeal which was surprising in one so young.

Tom Jones, on the other hand, was not only deficient in outward tokens of respect, often forgetting to pull off his cap at his master's approach, but was altogether unmindful both of his master's precepts and example.

At the, age of twenty, however, Tom, for his love of hunting, had become a great favourite with Mr. Allworthy's neighbour, Squire Western; and Sophia, Mr. Western's only child, lost her heart irretrievably to him before she suspected it was in danger. On his side, Tom was truly sensible of the great worth of Sophia. He liked her person extremely, no less admired her accomplishments, and tenderly loved her goodness. In reality, as he had never once entertained any thoughts of possessing her, nor had ever given the least voluntary indulgence to his inclinations, he had a much stronger passion for her than he himself was acquainted with.

An accident occurred on the hunting-field in saving Sophia from her too mettlesome horse kept Jones a prisoner for some time in Mr. Western's house, and during those weeks he not only found that he loved Sophia with an unbounded passion, but he plainly saw the tender sentiments she had for him; yet could not this assurance lessen his despair of obtaining the consent of her father, nor the horrors which attended his pursuit of her by any base or treacherous method.

Hence, at the approach of the young lady, he grew pale; and, if this was sudden, started. If his eyes accidentally met hers, the blood rushed into his cheeks, and his countenance became all over scarlet. If he touched her, his hand, nay, his whole frame, trembled.

All these symptoms escaped the notice of the squire, but not so of Sophia. She soon perceived these agitations of mind in Jones, and was at no loss to discover the cause; for, indeed, she recognised it in her own breast. In a word, she was in love with him to distraction. It was not long before Jones was able to attend her to the harpsichord, where she would kindly condescend for hours together to charm him with the most delicious music.

The news that Mr. Allworthy was dangerously ill (for a servant had brought word that he was dying) broke off Tom's stay at Mr. Western's, and drove all the thoughts of love out of his head. He hurried instantly into the chariot which was sent for him, and ordered the coachman to drive with all imaginable haste; nor did the idea of Sophia once occur to him on the way.

Tom Jones Falls into Disgrace

On the night when the physician announced that Mr. Allworthy was out of danger Jones was thrown into such immoderate excess of rapture by the news that he might be truly said to be drunk with joy-an intoxication which greatly forwards the effects of wine; and as he was very free, too, with the bottle, on this occasion he became very soon literally drunk.

Jones had naturally violent animal spirits, and Thwackum, resenting his speeches, only the doctor's interposition prevented wrath kindling. After which, Jones gave loose to mirth, sang two or three amorous songs, and fell into every frantic disorder which unbridled joy is apt to inspire; but so far was he from any disposition to quarrel that he was ten times better-humoured, if possible, than when he was sober.

Blifil, whose mother had died during her brother's illness, was highly offended at a behaviour which was so inconsistent with the sober and prudent reserve of his own temper. The recent death of his mother, he declared, made such conduct very indecent.

"It would become them better," he said, "to express the exultations of their hearts at Mr. Allworthy's recovery in thanksgiving, than in drunkenness and riot."

Wine had not so totally overpowered Jones as to prevent him recollecting Blifil's loss the moment it was mentioned. He at once offered to shake Mr. Blifil by the hand, and begged his pardon, saying his excessive joy for Mr. Allworthy's recovery had driven every other thought out of his mind.

Blifil scornfully rejected his hand, and with an insulting illusion to the misfortune of Jones's birth provoked the latter to blows. The scuffle which ensued might have produced mischief had it not been for the interference of Thwackum and the physician.

Blifil, however, only waited for an opportunity to be revenged on Jones, and the occasion was soon forthcoming when Mr. Allworthy was fully recovered from his illness.

Mr. Western had found out that his daughter was in love with Tom Jones, and at once decided that she should marry Blifil, to whom Sophia professed great abhorrence.

As for Blifil, the success of Jones was much more grievous to him than the loss of Sophia, whose estate, indeed, was dearer to him than her person.

Mr. Western swore that his daughter shouldn't have a ha'penny, nor the twentieth part of a brass farthing, if she married Jones; and Blifil, with many sighs, professed to his uncle that he could not bear the thought of Sophia being ruined by her preference for Jones.

"This lady, I am sure, will be undone in every sense; for, besides the loss of most part of her own fortune, she will be married to a beggar. Nay, that is a trifle; for I know him to be one of the worst men in the world."

"How?" said Mr. All worthy. "I command you to tell me what you mean."

"You know, sir," said Blifil, "I never disobeyed you. In the very day of your utmost danger, when myself and all the family were in tears, he filled the house with riot and debauchery. He drank, and sang, and roared; and when I gave him a gentle hint of the indecency of his actions, he fell into a violent passion, swore many oaths, called me rascal, and struck me. I am sure I have forgiven him that long ago. I wish I could so easily forget his ingratitude to the best of benefactors."

Thwackum was now sent for, and corroborated every circumstance which the other had deposed.

Poor Jones was too full of grief at the thought that Western had discovered the whole affair between him and Sophia to make any adequate defence. He could not deny the charge of drunkenness, and out of modesty sunk everything that related particularly to himself.

Mr. Allworthy answered that he was now resolved to banish him from his sight for ever. "Your audacious attempt to steal away a young lady calls upon me to justify my own character in punishing you. And there is no part of your character which I resent more than your ill-treatment of that good young man (meaning Blifil), who hath behaved with so much tenderness and honour towards you."

A flood of tears now gushed from the eyes of Jones, and every faculty of speech and motion seemed to have deserted him. It was some time before he was able to obey Allworthy's peremptory commands of departing, which he at length did, having first kissed his hands with a passion difficult to be affected, and as difficult to be described.

Mr. Allworthy, however, did not permit him to leave the house penniless, but presented him with a note for £500. He then commanded him to go immediately, and told Jones that his clothes, and everything else, should be sent to him whithersoever he should order them.

Jones had hardly set out, which he did with feelings of agony and despair, before Sophia Western decided that only in flight could she be saved from marriage with the detested Blifil.

Mr. Western, in spite of tremendous love for his daughter, thought her inclinations of as little consequence as Blifil himself conceived them to be; and Mr. Allworthy, who said "he would on no account be accessory to forcing a young lady into a marriage contrary to her own will," was satisfied by his nephew's disingenuous statement that the young lady's behaviour to him was full as forward as he wished it.

Sophia, having appointed her maid to meet her at a certain place not far from the house, exactly at the ghostly and dreadful hour of twelve, began to prepare for her own departure.

But first she was obliged to give a painful audience to her father, and he treated her in so violent and outrageous a manner that he frightened her into an affected compliance with his will, which so highly pleased the good squire that he at once changed his frowns into smiles, and his menaces into promises.

He vowed his whole soul was wrapped in hers, that her consent had made him the happiest of mankind.

He then gave her a large bank-bill to dispose of in any trinkets she pleased, and kissed and embraced her in the fondest manner.

Sophia reverenced her father piously and loved him passionately, but the thoughts of her beloved Jones quickly destroyed all the regretful promptings of filial love.

Tom Jones's Restoration

After many adventures on the road Mr. Jones reached London; and as he had often heard Mr. Allworthy mention the gentlewoman at whose house in Bond Street he used to lodge when he was in town, he sought the house, and was soon provided with a room there on the second floor. Mrs. Miller, the person who let these lodgings, was the widow of a clergyman, and Mr. Allworthy had settled an annuity of £50 a year on her, "in consideration of always having her first floor when he was in town."

Tom Jones's fortunes were now very soon at the lowest. Having been forced into a quarrel in the streets with an acquaintance named Fitzpatrick, and having wounded him with his sword, a number of fellows rushed in and carried Jones off to the civil magistrate, who, being informed that the wound appeared to be mortal, straightway committed the prisoner to the Gatehouse.

Sophia Western was also in London at the house of her aunt; and soon afterwards Mr. Western, Mr. Allworthy, and Blifil all reached the city.

It was just at this time that Mr. Allworthy, consenting to his nephew once more offering himself to Sophia, came with Blifil to his accustomed lodgings in Bond Street. Mrs. Miller, to whom Jones had showed many kindnesses, at once put in a good word for the unfortunate young man; and, on Blifil exulting over the manslaughter Jones was alleged to have committed, declared that the wounded man, whoever he was, was in fault. This, indeed, was shortly afterwards corroborated by Fitzpatrick himself, who acknowledged his mistake.

But it was not till Mr. Allworthy discovered that Blifil had been arranging with a lawyer to get the men who had arrested Jones to bear false witness, and learnt further that Tom Jones was his sister Bridget's child, and that on her death-bed Mrs. Blifil's message to her brother confessing the fact had been suppressed by her son, that his old feelings of affection for Tom Jones returned. Before setting out to visit Jones in the prison Mr. Allworthy called on Sophia to inform her that he regretted Blifil had ever been encouraged to give her annoyance, and that Mr. Jones was his nephew and his heir.

Men over-violent in their dispositions are, for the most part, as changeable in them. No sooner was Western informed of Mr. Allworthy's intention to make Jones his heir than he joined heartily with the uncle in every commendation of the nephew, and became as eager for his daughter's marriage with Jones as he had before been to couple her to Blifil.

Fitzpatrick being recovered of his wound, and admitting the aggression, Jones was released from custody and returned to his lodgings to meet Mr. Allworthy.

It is impossible to conceive a more tender or moving scene than this meeting between the uncle and nephew. Allworthy received Jones into his arms. "O my child!" he cried, "how have I been to blame! How have I injured you! What amends can I ever make you for those unkind suspicions which I have entertained, and for all the sufferings they have occasioned you?"

"Am I not now made amends?" cried Jones. "Would not my sufferings, had they been ten times greater, have been now richly repaid?"

Here the conversation was interrupted by the arrival of Western, who could no longer be kept away even by the authority of Allworthy himself. Western immediately went up to Jones, crying out, "My old friend Tom, I am glad to see thee, with all my heart. All past must be forgotten. Come along with me; I'll carry thee to thy mistress this moment."

Here Allworthy interposed; and the squire was obliged to consent to delay introducing Jones to Sophia till the afternoon.

Blifil, now thoroughly exposed in his treachery, was at first sullen and silent, balancing in his mind whether he should yet deny all; but finding at last the evidence too strong against him, betook himself to confession, and was now as remarkably mean as he had been before remarkably wicked. Mr. Allworthy subsequently settled £200 a year upon him, to which Jones hath privately added a third. Upon this income Blifil lives in one of the northern counties. He is also lately turned Methodist, in hopes of marrying a very rich widow of that sect. Sophia would not at first permit any promise of an immediate engagement with Jones because of certain stories of his inconstancy, but Mr. Western refused to hear of any delay.

"To-morrow or next day?" says Western, bursting into the room where Sophia and Jones were alone.

"Indeed, sir," says she, "I have no such intention."

"But I can tell thee," replied he, "why hast not; only because thou dost love to be disobedient, and to plague and vex thy father. When I forbid her, then it was all nothing but sighing and whining, and languishing and writing; now I am for thee-(this to Jones)-she is against thee. All the spirit of contrary, that's all. She is above being guided and governed by her father, that is the whole truth on't. It is only to disoblige and contradict me."

"What would my papa have me do?" cries Sophia.

"What would I ha' thee do?" says he, "why gee un thy hand this moment."

"Well, sir," said Sophia, "I will obey you. There is my hand, Mr. Jones."

"Well, and will you consent to ha' un to-morrow morning?" says Western.

"I will be obedient to you, sir," cries she.

"Why, then, to-morrow morning be the day," cries he.

"Why, then, to-morrow morning shall be the day, papa, since you will have it so," said Sophia. Jones then fell upon his knees and kissed her hand in an agony of joy, while Western began to caper and dance about the room, presently crying out, "Where the devil is Allworthy?" He then sallied out in quest of him, and very opportunely left the lovers to enjoy a few tender minutes alone.

But he soon returned with Allworthy, saying, "If you won't believe me, you may ask her yourself. Hast not gin thy consent, Sophy, to be married to-morrow?"

"Such are your commands, sir," cries Sophia, "and I dare not be guilty of disobedience."

"I hope there is not the least constraint," cries Allworthy.

"Why, there," cried Western, "you may bid her unsay all again if you will. Dost repent heartily of thy promise, dost not, Sophy?"

"Indeed, papa," cried she. "I do not repent, nor do I believe I ever shall, of any promise in favour of Mr. Jones."

"Then, nephew," cries Allworthy, "I felicitate you most heartily, for I think you are the happiest of men."

Mr. Allworthy, Mr. Western, and Mrs. Miller were the only persons present at the wedding, and within two days of that event Mr. Jones and Sophia attended Mr. Western and Mr. Allworthy into the country.

There is not a neighbour or a servant, who doth not most gratefully bless the day when Mr. Jones was married to Sophia.

Of Miracles
by David Hume
(Edinburgh, 1751)

Of Miracles is part of a collection of essays by David Hume, the genial billiard-playing Scottish historian, journalist and philosopher. It is considered a foundation of the 'Enlightenment' – the time in the 18th Century when humans began to realise that reason and observation were probably better guides to living than tradition and deference.

Not just 'On Miracles', but *every single thing Hume ever wrote* has been prohibited by the Church.

Abridged: GH

Part I

Evidence for the truth of our Christian religion is founded on the testimony of eye-witnesses to the miracles of our saviour, by which he proved his divine mission. Our evidence is then less than that of our senses, it is external evidence and not brought home to everyone's breast by the immediate operation of the holy spirit.

I flatter myself that I have discovered an argument, which, if just, will, with the wise and learned, be an everlasting check to all kinds of superstitious delusion, and consequently will be useful as long as the world endures.

A miracle is a violation of the laws of nature. It is no miracle that a man, seemingly in good health, should die of a sudden; such a death, though unusual, has frequently been observed. But it is a miracle that a dead man should come to life; because that has never been observed. There must, therefore, be a uniform experience against every miraculous event, otherwise it would not merit the appellation.

The consequent general maxim is, "That no testimony is sufficient to establish a miracle, unless the testimony be of such kind, that its falsehood would be more miraculous than the fact which it endeavours to establish."

When anyone tells me that he saw a dead man restored to life, I consider whether it be more probable that this person deceive or be deceived, or that the fact should really have happened. I weigh the one miracle against the other. If the falsehood of his testimony would be more miraculous than the event which he relates; then, and not till then, can he pretend to command by belief or opinion.

Part II

In the foregoing we have supposed that testimony of a miracle may amount to a proof, but it is easy to shew that we have been too liberal.

First, there is not to be found in all history any chroniclers of a miracle who are entirely above suspicion.

Secondly. The passion of surprise or wonder, being an agreeable emotion, tends towards the belief in miracles, even among those who must hear only stories. Eloquence leaves little room for reflection.

Thirdly, it forms a strong presumption against supernatural revelations that they chiefly abound among ignorant and barbarous nations. It is strange a judicious reader is apt to say that such prodigious events never happen in our days.

Fourth. Testimony that a religion is proved by miracles, must confound itself. The religions of ancient Rome, Turkey, Siam or China abound in miracles. But to claim that the miracles of one's religion confound all others, must likewise destroy all credit in miracles.

I need not add the difficulty of detecting falsehoods. Even a court of judicature, with all the authority, accuracy and judgement it can employ, often finds itself at a loss to distinguish truth from falsehood. The wise and learned commonly think the infancy of new religions too small a matter to deserve regard, and when they would later detect a cheat, the season is past and the witnesses perished.

It is experience alone which gives authority to human testimony; and it is the same experience which assures us of the laws of nature. Our most holy religion is founded on Faith, not reason, and whoever assents to it is conscious of a continued miracle in his own person, which subverts all the principles of his understanding.

The Life and Opinions of Tristram Shandy, Gentleman
by Laurence Sterne
(London, 1757)

Laurence Sterne was a priest from Clonmel in Co. Tipperary, who wrote this stupendously popular comic novel during the year his mother died, his wife was gravely ill, and he was diagnosed with tuberculosis. It is the fount of the ingenious and bizarrely incoherent 'learned wit' which eventually caused the likes of Monty Python.

Abridged: JH/GH

I

On the fifth day of November, 1718, was I, Tristram Shandy, gentleman, brought forth into this scurvy and disastrous world of ours. I wish I had been born in the moon, or in any of the planets (except Jupiter or Saturn), because I never could bear cold weather; for it could not well have fared worse with me in any of them (though I will not answer for Venus) than it has in this vile dirty planet of ours, which of my conscience with reverence be it spoken I take to be made up of the shreds and clippings of the rest; not but the planet is well enough, provided a man could be born in it to a great title or to a great estate, or could anyhow contrive to be called up to public charges and employments of dignity and power; but that is not my case; and therefore every man will speak of the fair as his own market has gone in it; for which cause I affirm it over again to be one of the vilest worlds that ever was made; for I can truly say, that from the first hour I drew breath in it, to this - I can now scarce draw it at all, for an asthma I got in skating against the wind in Flanders - I have been the continual sport of what the world calls Fortune, and though I will not wrong her by saying she has ever made me feel the weight of any great and signal evil, yet with all the good temper in the world, I affirm it of her, that in every stage of my life, and at every turn and corner where she could get fairly at me, the ungracious duchess has pelted me with a set of as pitiful misadventures and cross accidents as ever small hero sustained.

II

"I wonder what's all that noise and running backwards and forwards for above stairs?" quoth my father, addressing himself after an hour and a half's silence to my Uncle Toby, who, you must know, was sitting on the opposite side of the fire, smoking his pipe all the time in mute contemplation of a new pair of black plush breeches which he had got on. "What can they be doing, brother?" quoth my father; "We can scarce hear ourselves talk."

"I think," replied my uncle Toby, taking his pipe from his mouth and striking the head of it two or three times upon the nail of his left thumb as he began his sentence; "I think," says he - but to enter rightly into my Uncle Toby's sentiments upon this matter, you must be made to enter just a little into his character.

III

The wound in my Uncle Toby's groin, which he received at the siege of Namur, rendering him unfit for the service, it was thought expedient he should return to England, in order, if possible, to be set to rights.

He was four years totally confined, partly to his bed and all of it to his room; and in the course of his cure, which was all that time in hand, suffered unspeakable misery.

My father at that time was just beginning business in London, and had taken a house, and as the truest friendship and cordiality subsisted between the two brothers, and as my father thought my Uncle Toby could nowhere be so well nursed and taken care of as in his own house, he assigned him the very best apartment in it. And what was a much more sincere mark of his affection still, he would never suffer a friend or acquaintance to step into the house, but he would take him by the hand, and lead him upstairs to see his brother Toby, and chat an hour by his bedside.

The history of a soldier's wound beguiles the pain of it - my uncle's visitors at least thought so, and they would frequently turn the discourse to that subject, and from that subject the discourse would generally roll on to the siege itself.

IV

When my Uncle Toby got his map of Namur to his mind he began immediately to apply himself, and with the utmost diligence, to the study of it. The more my Uncle Toby pored over the map, the more he took a liking to it.

In the latter end of the third year my Uncle began to break in upon daily regularity of a clean shirt, and to allow his surgeon scarce time sufficient to dress his wound, concerning himself so little about it as not to ask him once in seven times dressing how it went on, when, lo! all of a sudden - for the change was as quick as lightning - he began to sigh heavily for his recovery, complained to my father, grew impatient with the surgeon; and one morning, as he heard his foot coming upstairs, he shut up his books and thrust aside his instruments, in order to expostulate with him upon the protraction of his cure, which he told him might surely have been accomplished at least by that time.

Desire of life and health is implanted in man's nature; the love of liberty and enlargement is a sister - passion to it. These my Uncle Toby had in common with his species. But nothing wrought with our family after the common way.

V

When a man gives himself up to the government of a ruling passion, or, in other words, when his hobbyhorse grows headstrong, farewell cool reason and fair discretion. My Uncle Toby's wound was near well; he broiled with impatience to put his design in execution; and so, without consulting further, with any soul living, which, by the way, I think is right, when you are predetermined to take no one soul's advice, he privately ordered Trim, his man, to pack up a bundle of lint and dressings, and hire a chariot and four to be at the door exactly by twelve o'clock that day, when he knew my father would be upon change. So, leaving a banknote upon the table for the surgeon's care of him, and a letter of tender thanks for his brother's, he packed up his maps, his books of fortification, his instruments, and so forth, and by the help of a crutch on one side and Trim on the other, my Uncle Toby embarked for Shandy Hall.

The reason, or rather the rise, of this sudden demigration was as follows:

The table in my Uncle Toby's room, being somewhat of the smallest, for that infinity of great and small instruments of knowledge which usually lay crowded upon it, he had the accident in reaching over for his tobacco box to throw down his compasses, and in stooping to take the compasses up, with his sleeve he threw down his case of instruments and snuffers; and in his endeavouring to catch the snuffers in falling, he thrust his books off the table. 'Twas to no purpose for a man, lame as my Uncle Toby was, to think of redressing all these evils by himself; he rung his bell for his man Trim, - "Trim," quoth my Uncle Toby, "prithee see what confusion I have been making. I must have some better contrivance, Trim."

I must here inform you that this servant of my Uncle Toby's, who went by the name of Trim, had been a corporal in my Uncle's own company. His real name was James Butter, but having got the nickname of Trim in the regiment, my Uncle Toby, unless when he happened to be very angry with him, would never call him by any other name.

The poor fellow had been disabled for the service by a wound on his left knee by a musket bullet at the Battle of Landen, which was two years before the affair of Namur; and as the fellow was well - beloved in the regiment, and a handy fellow into the bargain, my Uncle Toby took him for his servant, and of excellent use was he, attending my Uncle Toby in the camp and in his quarters as valet, groom, barber, cook, sempster, and nurse; and indeed, from first to last, waited upon him and served him with great fidelity and affection.

My Uncle Toby loved the man in return, and what attached him more to him still, was the similitude of their knowledge; for Corporal Trim by four years occasional attention to his master's discourse upon fortified towns had become no mean proficient in the science, and was thought by the cook and chambermaid to know as much of the nature of strongholds as my Uncle Toby himself.

"If I durst presume," said Trim, "to give your honour my advice, and speak my opinion in this matter" - "Thou art welcome, Trim," quoth my Uncle Toby. "Why then," replied Trim, pointing with his right hand towards a map of Dunkirk: "I think with humble submission to your honour's better judgement, that the ravelins, bastions, and curtains, make but a poor, contemptible, fiddle - faddle piece of work of it here upon paper, compared to what your honour and I could make of it were we out in the country by ourselves, and had but a rood and a half of ground to do what we pleased with. As summer is coming on," continued Trim, "your honour might sit out of doors and give me the nography" - (call it icnography, quoth my uncle) - "of the town or citadel your honour was pleased to sit down before, and I will be shot by your honour upon the glacis of it if I did not fortify it to your honour's mind." - "I dare say thou wouldst, Trim," quoth my uncle. "I would throw out the earth," continued the corporal, "upon this hand towards the town for the scarp, and on the right hand towards the campaign for the counterscarp." - "Very right, Trim," quoth my Uncle Toby. "And when I had sloped them to your mind, an' please your honour, I would face the glacis, as the finest fortifications are done in Flanders, with sods, and as your honour knows they should be, and I would make the walls and parapets with sods too." - "The best engineers call them gazons, Trim," said my Uncle Toby.

"Your honour understands these matters," replied corporal Trim, "better than any officer in His Majesty's service; but would your honour please but let us go into the country, I would work under your honour's directions like a horse, and make fortifications for you something like a Tansy with all their batteries, saps, ditches, and pallisadoes, that it should be worth all the world to ride twenty miles to go and see it."

My Uncle Toby blushed as red as scarlet as Trim went on, but it was not a blush of guilt, of modesty, or of anger - it was a blush of joy; he was fired with Corporal Trim's project and description. "Trim," said my Uncle Toby, "say no more; but go down, Trim, this moment, my lad, and bring up my supper this instant."

Trim ran down and brought up his master's supper, to no purpose. Trim's plan of operation ran so in my Uncle Toby's head, he could not taste it. "Trim," quoth my Uncle Toby, "get me to bed." 'Twas all one. Corporal Trim's description had fired his imagination. My Uncle Toby could not shut his eyes. The more he considered it, the more bewitching the scene appeared to him; so that two full hours before daylight he had come to a final determination, and had concerted the whole plan of his and Corporal Trim's decampment.

My Uncle Toby had a neat little country house of his own in the village where my father's estate lay at Shandy. Behind this house was a kitchen garden of about half an acre; and at the bottom of the garden, and cut off from it by a tall yew hedge, was a bowling - green, containing just about as much ground as Corporal Trim wished for. So that as Trim uttered the words, "a rood and a half of ground, to do what they would with," this identical bowling - green instantly presented itself upon the retina of my Uncle Toby's fancy.

Never did lover post down to a beloved mistress with more heat and expectation than my Uncle Toby did to enjoy this self - same thing in private.

VI

"Then reach my breeches off the chair," said my father to Susanah. "There's not a moment's time to dress you, sir," cried Susanah; "bless me, sir, the child's in a fit. Mr. Yorick's curate's in the dressing room with the child upon his arm, waiting for the name; and my mistress bid me run as fast as I could to know, as Captain Shandy is the godfather, whether it should not be called after him."

"Were one sure," said my father to himself, scratching his eyebrow, "that the child was expiring, one might as well compliment my brother Toby as not, and 'twould be a pity in such a case to throw away so great a name as Trismegistus upon him. But he may recover."

"No, no," said my father to Susanah, "I'll get up." - "There's no time," cried Susanah, "the child's as black as my shoe." - "Trismegistus," said my father: "but stay; thou art a leaky vessel, Susanah; canst thou carry Trismegistus in thy head the length of the gallery without scattering?" - "Can I," cried Susanah, shutting the door in a huff. "If she can, I'll be shot," said my father, bouncing out of bed in the dark and groping for his breeches.

Susanah ran with all speed along the gallery.

My father made all possible speed to find his breeches. Susanah got the start and kept it. "'Tis Tris something," cried Susanah. "There is no Christian name in the world," said the curate, "beginning with Tris, but Tristram." - "Then 'tis Tristram - gistus," quoth Susanah.

"There is no gistus to it, noodle; 'tis my own name," replied the curate, dipping his hand as he spoke into the basin. "Tristram," said he, etc., etc. So Tristram was I called, and Tristram shall I be to the day of my death.

VII. The Story of Le Fevre

It was some time in the summer of that year in which Dendermond was taken by the Allies, which was about seven years after the time that my Uncle Toby and Trim had privately decamped from my father's house in town, in order to lay some of the finest sieges to some of the finest cities in Europe, when my Uncle Toby was one evening getting his supper, with Trim sitting behind him at a small sideboard, when the landlord of a little inn in the village came into the parlour with an empty phial in his hand, to beg a glass or two of sack: "'Tis for a poor gentleman, I think, of the Army," said the landlord, "who has been taken ill at my house four days ago, and has never held up his head since, or had a desire to taste anything, till just now, that he has a fancy for a glass of sack and a thin toast: 'I think,' says he, 'it would comfort me.' If I could neither beg, borrow nor buy such a thing," added the landlord, "I would almost steal it for the poor gentleman, he is so ill. I hope in God he will still mend, we are all of us concerned for him."

"Thou art a good - natured soul, I will answer for thee," cried my Uncle Toby, "and thou shalt drink the poor gentleman's health in a glass of sack thyself, and take a couple of bottles with my service and tell him he is heartily welcome to them, and to a dozen more if they will do him good."

"Though I am persuaded," said my Uncle Toby, as the landlord shut the door, "he is a very compassionate fellow, Trim, yet I cannot help entertaining a high opinion of his guest too; there must be something more than common in him, that in so short a time should win so much upon the affections of his host." - "And of his whole family," added the Corporal, "for they are all concerned for him." - "Step after him," said my Uncle Toby; "do, Trim, ask if he knows his name.

"I have quite forgot it truly," said the landlord, coming back to the parlour with the Corporal, "but I can ask his son again." - "Has he a son with him, then?" said my Uncle Toby. "A boy," replied the landlord, "of about eleven or twelve years of age; but the poor creature has tasted almost as little as his father; he does nothing but mourn and lament for him night and day. He has not stirred from the bedside these two days."

My Uncle Toby lay down his knife and fork, and thrust his plate from before him, as the landlord gave him the account; and Trim, without being ordered, took it away without saying one word, and in a few minutes after brought him his pipe and tobacco.

"Trim," said my Uncle Toby, after he had lighted his pipe and smoked about a dozen whiffs; "I have a project in my head, as it is a bad night, of wrapping myself up warm and paying a visit to this poor gentleman." "Leave it, an' please your honour, to me," quoth the Corporal; "I'll take my hat and stick and go to the house and reconnoitre, and act accordingly; and I will bring your honour a full account in an hour."

VIII. The Story of Le Fevre (continued)

It was not till my Uncle Toby had knocked the ashes out of his third pipe that Corporal Trim returned from the inn, and gave him the following account.

"I despaired at first," said the Corporal, "of being able to bring back any intelligence to your honour about the

Lieutenant and his son; for when I asked where his servant was, from whom I made myself sure of knowing everything which was proper to be asked," - ("that's a right distinction, Trim," said my Uncle Toby) - "I was answered, an' please your honour, that he had no servant with him; that he had come to the inn with hired horses, which, upon finding himself unable to proceed (to join, I suppose the regiment) he had dismissed the morning after he came. 'If I get better, my dear,' said he, as he gave his purse to his son to pay the man, 'we can hire horses from hence' - 'but, alas! the poor gentleman will never get from hence,' said the landlady to me, 'for I heard the deathwatch all night long; and when he dies, the youth, his son, will certainly die with him, for he's broken - hearted already.' I was hearing this account, when the youth came into the kitchen, to order the thin toast the landlord spoke of. 'But I will do it for my father myself,' said the youth. 'Pray let me save you the trouble, young gentleman,' said I, taking up a fork for that purpose. 'I believe, sir,' said he, very modestly, 'I can please him best myself.' - 'I am sure,' said I, 'his honour will not like the toast the worse for being toasted by an old soldier,' The youth took hold of my hand and instantly burst into tears." ("Poor youth," said my Uncle Toby, "he has been bred up from an infant in the army, and the name of a soldier, Trim, sounded in his ears like the name of a friend. I wish I had him here.")

"When I gave him the toast," continued the Corporal, "I thought it was proper to tell him I was Captain Shandy's servant, and that your honour (though a stranger) was extremely concerned for his father, and that if there was anything in your house or cellar," - ("And thou mightest have added my purse, too," said my Uncle Toby) - he was heartily welcome to it. He made a very low bow (which was meant to your honour) but no answer, for his heart was full; so he went upstairs with the toast. When the lieutenant had taken his glass of sack and toast, he felt himself a little revived, and sent down into the kitchen to let me know that he should be glad if I would step upstairs. He did not offer to speak to me till I had walked up close to his bedside. 'If you are Captain Shandy's servant,' said he, 'you must present my thanks to your master, with my little boy's thanks along with them, for his courtesy to me: if he was of Leven's,' said the Lieutenant, - I told him your honour was. 'Then,' said he, 'I served three campaigns with him in Flanders, and remember him; but 'tis most likely that he remembers nothing of me. You will tell him, however, that the person his good nature has laid under obligations to him is one Le Fevre, a lieutenant in Angus' - 'but he knows me not,' said he a second time, musing. 'Possibly he may know my story,' added he. 'Pray tell the Captain I was the ensign at Breda whose wife was most unfortunately killed with musket - shot as she lay in my arms in my tent'"

"I remember," said my Uncle Toby, sighing, "the story of the ensign and his wife. But finish the story thou art upon." - "'Tis finished already," said the Corporal, "for I could stay no longer, so wished his honour good night; young Le Fevre rose from off the bed, and saw me to the bottom of the stairs, and, as we went down, he told me they had come from Ireland and were on their route to join the regiment in Flanders. But, alas!" said the Corporal, "the lieutenant's last day's march is over."

IX. The Story of Le Fevre (concluded)

"Thou hast left this matter short," said my Uncle Toby to the Corporal, as he was putting him to bed, "and I will tell thee in what, Trim. When thou offeredst Le Fevre whatever was in my house, thou shouldst have offered him my house, too. A sick brother officer should have the best quarter's, Trim, and if we had him with us, we could tend and look to him. Thou art an excellent nurse thyself, Trim, and what with thy care of him, and the old woman's, and his boy's, and mine together, we might recruit him again at once and set him upon his legs. In a fortnight or three weeks he might march."

"He will never march, an' please your honour, in this world," said the Corporal. "He will march," said my Uncle Toby, rising up from the side of the bed with one shoe off. "An' please your honour," said the Corporal, "he will never march but to his grave." - "He shall march," cried my Uncle Toby, marching the foot which had a shoe on, though without advancing an inch, "he shall march to his regiment." "He cannot stand it," said the Corporal. "He shall be supported," said my Uncle Toby. "He'll drop at last," said the Corporal. "He shall not drop," said my Uncle Toby, firmly. "Ah, well - a - day, do what we can for him," said Trim, "the poor soul will die." - "He shall not die, by G -," cried my Uncle Toby.

The Accusing Spirit which flew up to Heaven's chancery with the oath, blushed as he gave it in; and the Recording Angel, as he wrote it down, dropped a tear upon the word, and blotted it out for ever.

* * *

The sun looked bright the morning after to every eye in the village but Le Fevre's and his afflicted son's. My Uncle Toby, who had rose up an hour before his wonted time, entered the lieutenant's room, and sat himself down upon the chair by the bedside, and opened the curtain in the manner an old friend and brother officer would have done it.

There was a frankness in my Uncle Toby - not the effect of familiarity, but the cause of it - which let you at once into his soul, and showed you the goodness of his nature. The blood and spirits of Le Fevre, which were waxing cold and slow within him, and were retreating to the last citadel, the heart, rallied back. The film forsook his eyes for a moment. He looked up wistfully in my Uncle Toby's face, then cast a look upon his boy. Nature instantly ebbed again. The film returned to its place: the pulse fluttered, stopped, went on - throbbed, stopped again - moved, stopped - .

My Uncle Toby, with young Le Fevre in his hand, attended the poor lieutenant as chief mourners to his grave.

On The Social Contract
or Principles of Political Right

by Jean-Jacques Rousseau
(Geneva, 1762)

Born in 1712 at Geneva, one of Europe's few enduring democratic enclaves, Rousseau, by way of spells as a notary, a coppersmith and a musical composer, fell in among the Enlightenment thinkers of Paris. His ideas on education angered the French parliament and his advocacy of freedom of religion led to physical attacks. But it was *The Social Contract* which presented the wild and dangerous idea that it is the *people* who make up a State, the *inalienable Sovereign Body Politic*, who, alone, should take responsibility for their own government. It played a great part in setting The West aflame in violent revolution, so that Napoleon, musing before Rousseau's tomb, is said to have wondered whether it might not have been better for the world if neither of them had ever been born.

Such espousal of individual freedom has not always made Rousseau popular – his books have been banned by the church from 1766, in the USA from 1929, and the Soviet Union from 1935.

Abridged: GH

Foederis æquas Dicamus leges.
[Let us set equal terms for the truce,
   - Virgil, The Æneid]

This little treatise is the least unworthy part of a longer work, which I began years ago, without then realising my limitations.

I MEAN to inquire if there can be any sure and legitimate method of civil administration, which will take men as they are, and laws as they might be; uniting justice and necessity. If I were a Prince or a Legislator, I should not waste time in words; I should do it. But, as I was born a citizen of a free State, I feel that my right to vote makes it my duty to study laws, and reflecting upon governments, I find always new reasons to love that of my own country.

Man is born free; and everywhere he is in irons. One thinks himself the master of others, and still remains a greater slave than they. How did this come about? If I took into account only the effects of force, I should say: "When a people is compelled to obey, and obeys, it does well; but when it can shake off the yoke, and shakes it off, it does still better." The social order is a sacred and basic right, but it does not come from nature, it is founded on convention.

The family may be called the natural model of political societies: the ruler being he father, the people, the children. Grotius and Hobbes, however, write about the human species as like herds of cattle, Caligula concluded that either kings were gods, or that men were beasts, and Aristotle[1] said that men are not equal naturally; some are born for slavery, and others for dominion.

But strength alone is never enough to make a man master, unless he transforms strength into right, and obedience into duty. To yield to physical force is an act of prudent necessity, not of will. If a brigand with a pistol demands my purse, I will surrender it. But if I could withstand him,

am I still conscience-bound to give it up? Force does not create right; we are obliged to obey only legitimate powers.

SLAVERY

SINCE no man has natural authority over his fellow, and force creates no right, we must conclude that legitimate authority comes only from agreed conventions between men. If an individual, says Grotius, can alienate his liberty and make himself a slave, why could not a whole people do the same and make itself subject to a king? But a man who becomes a slave does not give himself, he sells himself, at least for his subsistence: but what could a people sell itself for? Far from giving his subjects sustenance, a King takes his from them. Perhaps the despot offers security, but what when his ambition leads to wars? Tranquillity is found in dungeons; but does that make them desirable places to live? To say that a man gives himself gratuitously, is to say that he is mad, and madness creates no right.

Even if a man could alienate himself, he could not alienate his children. To renounce liberty is incompatible with man's nature; To subdue a multitude is not to rule a society.

THE SOCIAL CONTRACT

MEN, in the *State of Nature*, must have reached some point when the obstacles to maintaining their state exceeded the ability of each individual. The human race must then perish, or change. But, as men cannot create new forces, only unite and direct existing ones, they can preserve themselves only by combining.

The problem then is to find a form of association which "Will defend and protect the person and goods of each associate, yet in which each may still freely obey himself alone." The solution to this fundamental problem is the *Social Contract*. The clauses of this contract may be reduced to one- the total giving of all the rights of every individual to the community, in the knowledge that, because the same condition applies to everyone, no one has any interest in making them harsh, and no associate has anything more to demand.

---

1 **Aristotle:** see p62

Such an association creates a moral and collective body, composed of as many members as the people assembled. This public person, formed by the union of many, is called a city, or a Republic or Body Politic, its people citizens, the members of, and collective owners of, The Sovereign power.

But, in order then that the Social Contract may not be an empty formula, it asserts that whoever refuses to obey the General Will shall be compelled to do so by the whole body. This means nothing less than that he will be forced to be free. In this lies the key to the political machine, this alone legitimises civil undertaking.

The passage from the State of Nature to the civil state produces a very remarkable change in man; by substituting justice for instinct, and duty for physical impulses, it gives his actions a morality they formerly lacked. What man loses by the Social Contract is his natural liberty and an unlimited right to everything; what he gains is civil liberty and the proprietorship of his possessions.

SOVEREIGNTY

I hold then, that Sovereignty, being the exercise of the General Will, can never be alienated, and that the Sovereign, who is actually a collective being, cannot be represented except by himself.

The General Will is always right and tends to the public advantage; but it does not follow that the deliberations of the people are always correct. The people is never corrupted, but is often deceived.

It is therefore essential, if the General Will is to express itself, that there should be no partial factions within the State, that each citizen should think only his own thoughts. But if there are partial societies, it is best to have as many as possible and to prevent them from being unequal, as was done by Solon.

Each man alienates, by the Social Contract, only such of his powers, goods and liberty as it is important for the community to control. It is not a convention between a superior and an inferior, but a convention between the body and each of its members. It is legitimate, because it is based on the Social Contract. It is equitable, because it is common to all. It is useful, because it can have no other object than the general good, and it is stable, because it is guaranteed by the supreme power.

Thus it is clear that the Social Contract does not involve any real renunciation by individuals, rather, the contract gives them the advantage of security and protection.

RIGHT OF LIFE AND DEATH

There is not a single ill-doer who could not be turned to some good. The State has no right to put to death, even for the sake of making an example, any one whom it can leave alive without danger. But I feel my heart restraining my pen; let us leave these questions to the just man who has never offended.

LAW

All justice comes from God, and if we knew how to receive such high inspiration, we should need neither government nor laws.

In the State of Nature, where everything is common, I owe nothing to him whom I have promised nothing. But in a society, rights are fixed by law. But what, in society, is a law?

I give the name "Republic" to every State governed by laws, no matter what its form of administration. Now, the people, being subject to the laws, ought to be their author, but how? But how can a blind multitude, often ignorant even of its own good, carry out the great and difficult enterprise of legislation?

To discover the rules best suited to a nation would need an extraordinary intellect, able to understand human nature and human happiness, yet not be part of it, to be able to work in one century for the benefit of the next. In short, it would take gods to give men laws. Legislators therefore, in all ages, have claimed that the gods direct their wisdom. But it is not anybody who can make the gods speak. Any man may carve tablets of stone, or bribe an oracle. He may perhaps gather a band of fools; but he will never found an empire. We should not conclude that politics and religion have the same purpose, but that, when nations arise, the one is used as an instrument for the other.

THE PEOPLE

Just as an architect surveys the site to see if it will bear the weight of the building, so the wise Legislator begins by investigating the fitness of the people. Most peoples, like most men, are docile in youth; but become incorrigible as they grow old. Once customs have become inveterate, reform is dangerous or useless. Thus, Russia will never really be civilised, because Peter the Great tried to make his barbarous people into Germans or Englishmen, when he ought to have been making Russians. The period at which a State is first established is the moment when it is most vulnerable. Usurpers always choose troublous times to pass destructive laws, which is one of the surest means of distinguishing the Legislator from the tyrant.

What people are ready for new legislation? One bound by common or interests, but unaware of the yoke of law. One that is secure, but without ingrained superstitions. These conditions are rarely found united, thus few States have good constitutions.

If we ask what great good should be the end of legislation, we shall answer liberty and equality. To this end, every good legislative system need modifying to local situations. If, for instance, the soil is unproductive, or the land crowded, the people should turn to crafts, and exchange manufactures for the commodities they lack. If they dwell in fertile lands, or lack inhabitants, they should attend to agriculture. If a nation dwells on a convenient coast, let it cover the sea with ships and foster commerce and navigation. It will have a life that will be short, but glorious.

Thus, among the Jews and the Arabs, the chief object was religion; among the Athenians, letters; at Carthage, commerce; at Rhodes shipping; at Rome, virtue.

If the commonwealth is to be put into the best possible shape, there are various relations to be considered. There is the action of the Body Politic body upon itself, there is the civil law and the criminal law. With these three goes a fourth law, which is not graven on marble or brass, but on the hearts of the citizens. I am speaking of morality, of custom, above all of public opinion; a power unknown to political thinkers, yet on which everything else depends.

GOVERNMENT

Government is an intermediate body set up between the subjects and the Sovereign, whose members are called magistrates, kings or governors, and the whole body bears the name *Prince*. Good government should be proportionately stronger as the people is more numerous. But, as the State grows, the number of magistrates may increase to the extent that the relative force or activity of the government decreases. From this it follows that the larger the State, the more should the government be tightened, so that the number of the rulers diminish in proportion to the increase of that of the people.

DEMOCRACY

Strictly, there never has been a real democracy, and never will be. It is against nature for the many to govern the few, and it is unimaginable that the whole people should be forever assembled to consider public affairs. A true democratic government requires a very small, simple, State, where the people can readily be got together, where each citizen can know all the rest, and where there are few inequalities.

No government is so subject to civil wars and divisions as democratic government, because none is so prone to change. Under such a constitution the citizen should arm himself with strength and constancy, and say, every day of his life; "Better freedom with danger than peace with slavery". Were there a nation of gods, their government would be democratic. Such perfect government is not for men.

Hereditary aristocracy is the worst of all governments; but elective aristocracy is the best, and is an aristocracy properly so called. Assemblies are more easily held, and the credit of the State is better sustained. It is the best and most natural arrangement that the wisest should govern the many, as long as they govern for its profit, and not for their own.

Monarchy is really suitable only for large States, and Royal government is clearly the strongest. But if, according to Plato, the "king by nature" is such a rarity, and as royal education seems only to corrupt, what is to be hoped from men brought up to reign? Kings will come to the throne wicked or incompetent, or the throne will make them so.

FORMS OF GOVERNMENT

Liberty, as Montesquieu held, not being a fruit of all climates, is not within the reach of all peoples.

Government produces nothing; it takes only from the land and the people. Thus we find, in every climate, natural causes for the form of government; barren lands remain uncultivated, or are peopled by savages; lands yielding mere subsistence are inhabited by barbarians. Lands with a moderate surplus suit free peoples; those abundant and fertile call for monarchical government, with the surplus being consumed by the luxury of the Prince: which is preferable to it being dissipated among individuals.

Yet, to get an equal product, what a difference there must be in tillage: in Sicily, there is only need to scratch the ground; in England, how men must toil! Persia abounds less in commodities because the inhabitants need less. Chardin says that "They are very proud of their manner of life, pointing out how their complexion excels that of Christians. Their skins are fine and smooth; while their subjects, the Armenians, who live the European way, are rough and blotchy." In India, there are millions whose subsistence does not cost a halfpenny a day. Even in Europe, a Spaniard will live for a week on a German's dinner.

To all these points may be added another, that hot countries need inhabitants less than cold countries, yet can support more of them. Such a double surplus is all to the advantage of despotism.

DEGENERATION OF GOVERNMENT

AS the individual will acts against the General Will, so government continually opposes Sovereignty. This unavoidable defect tends ceaselessly to destroy it, as age and death destroy the human body.

If Sparta and Rome perished, what State can hope to endure for ever? We must not attempt the impossible in trying to set up eternal government, nor try to endow man with a stability which is beyond humans. The Body Politic begins to die as soon as it is born, and carries in itself the causes of its destruction.

THE SOVEREIGN AUTHORITY

IT is not enough for the assembled people to fix the constitution of the State; they must hold assemblies on fixed and known dates, properly summoned by the appointed magistrates in accordance with established laws.

Such assemblies, which are the aegis of the Body Politic and the curb on government, terrify rulers, who take any chance they can to stop them.

The people of England thinks itself free; but it is free only during the parliamentary elections. As soon as they are over, slavery overtakes them, and they are nothing. The use they make of the brief moments of liberty shows indeed that it deserves to lose it.

The idea of representation is modern. In Greece, all that the people had to do, it did for itself; by assembling in the public square; but they had a generous climate, no natural greed, and slaves to do their work for them. Without the same advantages, how can you preserve the same rights? Is liberty to be maintained only by slavery? It may be so. Extremes meet.

As for you, you modern peoples, you have no slaves, but you are slaves yourselves. I do not mean to encourage slavery, merely show why modern peoples, believing themselves to be free, have representatives, while ancient peoples had none.

GOVERNMENT IS NOT A CONTRACT

AS the citizens, by the Social Contract, are all equal, all can prescribe what all should do, but no one has a right to demand that another shall do what he does not do himself. There is only one contract with the State, and that is the act of association, which in itself excludes the existence of any other contract.

The institution of government is a law, not a contract. The holders of executive power are the people's officers, not its masters; for them there is no question of contract.

When therefore the people sets up an hereditary government, monarchical or aristocratic, the administration is provisional, until the people chooses to order it otherwise. But changes are always dangerous, established government should be touched only when it fails the public good. Change must be measured, lest the Prince, under the pretext of keeping the peace, tries to extend his powers,

The periodical assemblies of which I have spoken are designed to prevent or postpone this calamity, above all when they need no formal summoning; so the Prince cannot stop them without declaring himself a law-breaker.

VOTING

IT may be seen that the way in which general business is managed gives an indication of the health of the Body Politic. Long debates, dissension and tumult proclaim the ascendancy of individual interests and the decline of the State. At the other extreme, unanimity recurs when the citizens, having fallen into servitude, use their votes out of fear or flattery; deliberation ceases, and only worship or malediction is left.

Now, a difference of one vote destroys equality; but there are several grades of unequal division, which may be regulated by two general rules. First, the more grave and important the questions discussed, the nearer should opinion approach unanimity. Secondly, the more a matter calls for speed, the smaller the difference in the numbers of votes may be allowed; where an instant decision is needed, a majority of one should suffice.

There are two possible methods to choose the Prince and the magistrates; choice and lot. Both have been employed in various republics, and a mixture of the two still survives in the election of the Doge at Venice.

"Election by drawing lots is natural to democracy..." says Montesquieu, it is "unfair to nobody, and gives each citizen some hope of serving his country." Election by lot would have few disadvantages in a real democracy, but I have already said that real democracy is only an ideal. When choice and lot are combined, positions that require special talents, such as military posts, should be filled by the former; the lottery for cases such as judges, in which good sense, justice, and integrity are enough.

I should now speak of the methods of counting opinions in the assembly of the people; but perhaps an account of the Roman constitution will better illustrate my point.

THE ROMANS

Voting, among ancient Romans, was simple; each man declared himself aloud. But, when the people grew corrupt, each man was allowed to privately record his preference on a tablet, though the honesty of the counting officers remained suspect. Edicts were issued to prevent the buying of votes, but their very number proves how useless they were.

THE inflexibility of the laws, may, in certain cases, bring about, at a time of crisis, the ruin of the State. In these rare and obvious cases, provision is made for public security by a particular act entrusting it solely to one, worthy Dictator. Whenever this important trust is conferred, it is important that its duration should be fixed at a very brief period, incapable of being prolonged, lest the dictatorship become either tyrannical or idle. At Rome, the dictators held office for six months only; time enough to provide against the need that had caused him to be chosen; but insufficient to invent new tyrannies.

JUST as the law is the declaration of the General Will, so the Censorship is the declaration of public judgement. Men always love what is good; it is in judging what is good that they go wrong. A Censorship upholds morality by preventing opinion from growing corrupt, by preserving it through wise applications, and sometimes simply by defining it.

It is impossible to admire too much the art with which this resource, wholly lost today, was employed by the Romans and the Lacedæmonians. A man of bad morals having once presented a good proposal in the Spartan Council, the Ephors ignored it, and had a virtuous citizen make the same proposal. What an honour for the one, and what disgrace for the other, without praise or blame of either! No actual punishment would have been so severe.

CIVIL RELIGION

AT first men had no kings save gods, and no government save priests. But, when Jesus set up a spiritual kingdom, he separated the theological from the political; the State was no longer one, and thus began the divisions that trouble Christianity still.

We are told that true Christians would form a perfect society. Yet, if all the citizens were good Christians, a single self-seeker, a Catiline or a Cromwell, would soon get the better of them. To drive out the usurper, violence would have to be employed, which accords ill with Christian meekness. Christianity preaches servitude and dependence, a spirit entirely favourable to tyranny. True Christians are made to be slaves.

But, let us come back to our point. It is important to the community that each citizen should have a religion that will make him love his duty. There is a sort of purely non-religious faith, which the Sovereign should fix. While it can compel no one to believe, it can banish from the State whoever does not believe- not for impiety, but as an anti-social being.

The dogmas of this civil religion ought to be few and simple, without explanation or commentary: The existence of a mighty, intelligent and beneficent Divinity, possessed of foresight and providence, the life to come, the happiness of the just, the punishment of the wicked, the sanctity of the Social Contract and the laws: these are its positive dogmas. Its negative dogmas I confine to one, intolerance is to be forbidden.

Tolerance should be given to all religions that tolerate others, so long as their dogmas contain nothing contrary to the duties of citizenship. Whoever dares to say: "Outside the Church there is no salvation", ought to be driven from the State.

CONCLUSION

HAVING laid down the true principles of political right, and tried to give basis to the State, I ought next to look to the laws between nations. But this is too vast a subject.

An Inquiry into the Nature and Causes of the The Wealth of Nations
by Adam Smith
(Glasgow, 1776)

Before *The Wealth of Nations*, money came and money went, lands prospered or failed and no-one really had the faintest idea why. Adam Smith brought some science to the matter. He wasn't the first to realise that the only thing in the world which costs money is labour (everything else being provided free of charge) but he was among the first to realise that money is *not* wealth, to explain how the division of labour actually creates wealth and to see that money is a commodity and behaves just like any other commodity – if it is scarce it becomes more valuable, if it gets commonplace, it goes cheap. His theories invented economics, and even if it still doesn't work *perfectly* it *has* given us a more prosperous and much more stable society than the mere guesswork that went before.

Abridged: GH

OF THE CAUSES OF IMPROVEMENT IN THE PRODUCTIVE POWERS OF LABOUR

The division of labour has been the chief cause of improvement in the productiveness of labour. For instance. the making of a single pin involves eighteen separate operations, which are entrusted to eighteen separate workmen; and the result is, that whereas one man working alone could make perhaps only twenty pins in a day. several men working together, on the principle of division of labour, can make several thousands of pins per man in one day. Division of labour, in a highly developed state of society, is carried into almost every practical art: and its great benefits depend upon the increase of dexterity in each workman, upon the saving of time otherwise lost in passing from one kind of work to another and. finally, upon the use of many labour-saving machines.

This division of labour, from which so many advantages are derived, is not originally the effect of any human wisdom which foresees and intends the opulence to which it gives rise; it is rather the gradual result of the propensity in human nature to barter and exchange one thing for another. The power of exchanging their respective produce makes it possible for one man to produce only bread, and for another to produce only clothing.

The extent to which the division of labour can be carried is, therefore, limited by the extent of the market. There are some sorts of industry, even of the lowest kind, which can be carried on nowhere but in a great town- a porter, for example, cannot find employment and subsistence in a village. In the highlands of Scotland every farmer must be butcher, baker and brewer for his own family.

As water-carriage opens a more extensive market to every kind of industry than is afforded by land-carriage, it is on the sea-coast, and on the banks of navigable rivers, that industry begins to subdivide and improve itself, and it is not till long afterwards that these improvements extend to the inland parts. It was thus that the earliest civilized nations were grouped round the coasts of the Mediterranean Sea, and the extent arid easiness of its inland navigation was probably the chief cause of the early improvement of Egypt.

As soon as the division of labour is well established, every man becomes in some measure a merchant and the society becomes a commercial society, and the continual process of exchange leads inevitably to the origin of money. In the absence of money, or a general medium of exchange. society would be restricted to the cumbersome method of barter. Every man. therefore, would early endeavour to keep by him, besides the produce of his own industry, a certain quantity of some commodity such as other people will be likely to take in exchange for the produce of their particular industries.

Cattle, for example, have been widely used for this purpose in primitive societies, and Homer speaks of a suit of armour costing a hundred oxen.

But the durability of metals, as well as the facility with which they can be subdivided, has led to their employment, in all countries, as the means of exchange: and in order to obviate the necessity of weighing portions of the metals at every purchase, as well as to prevent fraud, it has been found necessary to affix a public stamp upon certain quantities of the metals commonly used to purchase goods. The value of commodities thus comes to be expressed in terms of coinage.

But labour is the real measure of the exchangeable value of all commodities: the value of any commodity to the person who possesses it is equal to the quantity of labour which it enables him to purchase or to command. What is bought with money or with goods is purchased by labour as much as what we require by the toil of our own body. Labour alone, never varying in its own value, is alone the ultimate and real standard by which the value of all commodities can at all times, and in all places, be estimated and compared. It is their real price; money is their nominal price only. Equal quantities of labour will at distant times he purchased more nearly with equal quantities of corn-the subsistence of the labourer-than with equal quantities of gold, or of any other commodity.

Several elements enter into the price of commodities. In a nation of hunters, if it costs twice the labour to kill a beaver which it costs to kill a deer, one beaver will be worth two deer. But if the one kind of labour be more severe than the other, some allowance will naturally he made for this superior hardship: and thirdly, if one kind of labour requires an uncommon degree of dexterity and ingenuity, it will command a higher value than that which would he due to the time employed in it.

So far the whole produce of labour belongs to the labourer. But as soon as stock has accumulated in the hands of particular persons, some of them will employ it in setting to work industrious workmen, whom they will supply with materials and subsistence, in order to make a profit by the sale of their work.

The profits of stock are not to be regarded as the wages of a particular sort of labour, the labour of inspection and direction; for they are regulated altogether by the value of the stock employed, and are greater or smaller in proportion to the extent of this stock.

There is in every society or neighbourhood an ordinary or average rate both of wages and profit in every different employment of labour and stock; and this rate is regulated partly by the general circumstances of the society, its riches or poverty, and partly by the peculiar nature of each employment.

There is also in every society or neighbourhood an ordinary or average rate of rent, which is regulated, too, by the general circumstances of the society or neighbourhood in which the land is situated, and partly by the natural or improved fertility of the land. What we may call the natural price of any commodity depends upon these natural rates of wages, profit and rent at the place where it is produced. But its market price may vary from its natural price, and depends upon the proportion between the supply and the demand.

Corn is an annual crop. Butcher's-meat, a crop which requires four or five years to grow. As an acre of land, therefore, will produce a much smaller quantity of the one species of food than of the other, the inferiority of the quantity must be compensated by the superiority of the price. If it was more than compensated, more corn land would be turned into pasture; and if it was not compensated, part of what was in pasture would be brought back into corn. Thus in France the proprietors of old vineyards obtained an order prohibiting the planting of new vineyards, under the pretence of a super-abundance of wine. But had this super-abundance been real, it would, without any order of council, have effectually prevented the plantation of new vineyards. Likewise tobacco planters and spice merchants have sometimes burned their crops in plentiful years.

The common people in Scotland, who are fed with oatmeal, are in general neither so strong nor so handsome as the same rank of people in England, who are fed with wheaten bread. But it seems to be otherwise with potatoes. The chairmen, porters, and coal-heavers in London, and those unfortunate women who live by prostitution, the strongest men and the most beautiful women perhaps in the British dominions, are, the greater part of them, from the lowest rank of people in Ireland, who are generally fed with this root.

APPENDIX TO BOOK I

Prices Of Wheat	Prices/Quarter	Average prices each year in money of 1776
Year	£ - s - d	£ - s - d
1202	0 - 12 - 0	1 - 16 - 0
1223	0 - 12 - 0	1 - 16 - 0
1237	0 - 3 - 4	0 - 10 - 0
1243	0 - 2 - 0	0 - 6 - 0
1257	1 - 4 - 0	3 - 12 - 0
1336	0 - 2 - 0	0 - 6 - 0
1361	0 - 2 - 0	0 - 4 - 8
1451	0 - 8 - 0	0 - 16 - 0
1457	0 - 7 - 8	1 - 15 - 4
1497	1 - 0 - 0	1 - 11 - 0
1521	1 - 0 - 0	1 - 10 - 0
1551	0 - 8 - 0	0 - 8 - 0
1600	1 - 17 - 8	1 - 17 - 8

Averaged prices of the quarter of nine bushels of the best or highest priced wheat at Windsor market:

1620	£1 - 10s - 4d
1640	2 - 4 - 8
1660	2 - 16 - 6
1680	2 - 5 - 0
1700	2 - 0 - 0
1720	1 - 17 - 0
1740	2 - 10 - 8
1760	1 - 16 – 6

NATURE, ACCUMULATION AND EMPLOYMENT OF STOCK

When the stock which a man possesses is no more than sufficient to maintain him for a few days or weeks, he seldom thinks of deriving any revenue from it, but, when he possesses enough to maintain him for months or years, he endeavours to derive a revenue from the greater part of it. The stock from which he derives revenue is called his capital.

There are two ways in which capital may be employed so as to yield a profit to its employer. First, it may he employed in raising, manufacturing, or purchasing goods, and selling them again with a profit; this is circulating capital.

Secondly, it may be employed in the improvement of land. or in the purchase of machines and instruments: and this capital, which yields a profit from objects which do not change masters, is called fixed capital.

The general stock of any country or society is the same as that of all its inhabitants or members and is, therefore, divided into three portions, each of which has a different function. The first is the portion which is reserved for immediate consumption, and so affords no revenue or profit. The second is the fixed capital, which consists of:

(a) All useful machines and instruments of trade which facilitate labour.

(b) All profitable buildings, which procure a revenue, not only to their owner, but also to the person who rents them, such as shops, warehouses, farmhouses, factories, etc.

(c) The improvements of land, and all that has been laid out in clearing, draining. enclosing, manuring and reducing it into a condition most proper for culture.

(d) The acquired and useful abilities of all the inhabitants or members of the society. The acquisition of such talents, and the maintenance of the learner during his training, costs a real expense, which is a capital fixed in his person.

The third and last of the three portions into which the general stock of society divides itself is the circulating capital, which affords a revenue only by changing masters. It includes:

(a) All the money by means of which the other three are circulated and distributed to their proper consumers.

(b) All the stock of provisions which are in the possession of the butcher, farmer, corn merchant, etc. and from the sale of which they expect to derive a profit.

(c) All the materials, whether altogether rude, or more or less manufactured, for clothes, furniture and building, which are not yet made up into any of these shapes, but remain in the hands of the growers, manufacturers and merchants.

(d) All the work which is made up and completed, but is not yet disposed of to the proper consumers.

The substitution of paper in the place of gold and silver money replaces a very expensive instrument of commerce by one much less costly, and sometimes equally convenient. Circulation comes to he carried on by a new wheel, which costs less both to erect and to maintain than the old one.

THE PROGRESS OF OPULENCE IN DIFFERENT NATIONS

The greatest commerce of every civilized society is that carried on between the inhabitants of the town and those of the country. It consists in the exchange of rude for manufactured produce, either immediately, or by the intervention of money, or of some sort of paper which represents money. The country supplies the town with the means of subsistence and the materials for manufactures. The town repays this supply by sending back a part of the manufactured produce to the inhabitants of the country. The town, in which there neither is nor can be any reproduction of substances, may very properly be said to gain its whole subsistence from the country. And in how great a degree the country is benefited by the commerce of the town may be seen from a comparison of the cultivation of the lands in the neighbourhood of any considerable town with that of those which lie at some distance from it.

As subsistence is, in the nature of things, prior to convenience and luxury, so the rural industries, which procure the former, must be prior to the urban industries, which minister to the latter. The greater part of the capital of every growing society is therefore directed first to agriculture, afterwards to manufactures, and last of all to foreign commerce.

But this natural order of things has, in all the modern states of Europe, been in many respects entirely inverted. The foreign commerce of some of their cities has given rise to their finer manufactures and manufactures and foreign commerce together have given birth to the principal improvements of agriculture.

The customs which their original government introduced, and which remained after that government was greatly altered, necessarily forced them into this unnatural and retrograde order.

In the ancient state of Europe, after the fall of the Roman Empire, agriculture was greatly discouraged by several causes. The rapine and violence which the barbarians exercised against the ancient inhabitants interrupted the commerce between towns and the country, the towns were deserted and the country was left uncultivated. The western provinces of Europe sank into the lowest state of poverty and the land, which was mostly uncultivated, was engrossed by a few great proprietors.

These lands might, in the natural course of events, have been soon divided again, and broken into small parcels by succession or by alienation: but the law of primogeniture hindered their division by succession, and the introduction of entails prevented their being divided by alienation. These hindrances to the division. and consequently to the cultivation. of the land were due to the fact that land was considered as the means not of subsistence merely, but of power and protection.

In the ancient state of Europe the occupiers of land were all tenants at will, and practically slaves. To these succeeded a kind of farmers known at present in France by the name of 'metayers.' whose produce was divided equally between the proprietor and the farmer, after setting aside what was judged necessary for keeping up the stock, which still belonged to the landlord. To these, in turn, succeeded farmers properly so called, who cultivated the land with their own stock, paying a fixed rent to the landlord and enjoying a certain degree of security of tenure. And every improvement in the position of the actual cultivation of the soil is attended by a corresponding improvement of the land and of its cultivation.

After the fall of the Roman Empire, the inhabitants of cities and towns were not more favoured than those of the country. The towns were inhabited chiefly by tradesmen and mechanics, who in those days were of servile, or nearly servile, condition. Yet the townsmen arrived at liberty and independence much earlier than the country population; their towns became 'free burghs,' and were erected into commonalties or corporations, with the privilege of having magistrates and a town council of their own, of making by-laws for their own government, and of building walls for their own defence. Order and good government, and the liberty and security of individuals, were thus established in cities at a time when the occupiers of land in the country were exposed to every sort of violence.

The increase and riches of commercial and manufacturing towns thenceforward contributed to the improvement and cultivation of the countries to which they belonged in three different ways. First, by affording a great and ready market for the rude produce of the country.

Secondly, the wealth acquired by the inhabitants of cities was employed in purchasing uncultivated lands and in bringing them under cultivation; for merchants are ambitious of becoming country gentlemen, and, when they do so, are generally the best of all improvers.

And, lastly, commerce and manufactures gradually introduced order and good government, and with them as a logical consequence the liberty and security of individuals among the inhabitants of the country.

THE MERCANTILE SYSTEM

From the mistaken theory that wealth consists in money, or in gold and silver, there has arisen an erroneous and harmful system of political economy and of legislation in the supposed interests of manufacture, of commerce and of the wealth of nations. A rich country is supposed to be a country abounding in money; and all the nations of Europe have consequently studied, though to little purpose, every possible means of accumulating gold and silver in their respective countries. For example, they have at times forbidden, or hindered by heavy duties, the export of these metals.

But all these attempts are vain, for, on the one hand, when the quantity of gold and silver imported into any country exceeds the effectual demand, no vigilance can prevent their exportation. The real inconvenience, which is commonly called 'scarcity of money' is not a shortness in the medium of exchange, but is a weakening and diminution of credit, due to over-trading.

The principle of the 'commercial system' or 'mercantile system is that wealth consists in money, or in gold and silver.

It is an utterly untrue principle. But once it had been established in general belief that wealth consists in gold and silver, and that these metals can be brought into a country which has no mines only by the 'balance of trade'-that is to say. by exporting to a greater value than it imports-it necessarily became the great object of political economy to diminish as much as possible the importation of foreign goods for .home consumption, and to increase as much as possible the exportation of the produce of domestic industry. Its great engines for enriching the country, therefore, were restraints upon importation and encouragements to exportation.

The restraints upon importation were of two kinds, First, restraints upon the importation of such foreign goods for home consumption as could be produced at home, from whatever country they were imported; and, secondly, restraints upon the importation of goods of almost all kinds from those particular countries with which the balance of trade was supposed to be disadvantageous. These restraints consisted sometimes in high duties, and sometimes in prohibitions.

Exportation was encouraged sometimes by drawbacks, sometimes by bounties, sometimes by advantageous treaties of commerce with sovereign states, and sometimes by the establishment of colonies in distant countries. The above two restraints, and these four encouragements to exportation, constitute the six principal means by which the commercial or mercantile system proposes to increase the quantity of gold and silver in any country by turning the balance of trade in its favour.

The entire system, in all its developments, is fallacious in theory and evil in its practical effect. It is not difficult to determine who have been the contrivers of this whole mercantile system--not the consumers, whose interest has been entirely neglected, but the producers, and especially the merchants and manufacturers, whose interest has been so carefully attended to.

It remains to be said, also, that the 'agricultural system' which represents the produce of land as the sole source of the revenue and wealth of every country, and as therefore justifying a special protection of it, is as fallacious and as harmful as the other.

THE REVENUE OF THE SOVEREIGN OR COMMONWEALTH

THE first duty of the sovereign--that of protecting the society from the violence and invasion of other independent societies--can be performed only by means of a military force. This may be effected either by obliging all the citizens of the military age, or a certain number of them, to join in some measure the trade of a soldier to whatever other trade or profession they may happen to carry on; or by maintaining a certain number of citizens in the constant practice of military exercises, thus rendering the soldier's occupation a special profession, distinct from

all others. A militia is the less expensive, but a standing army is by far the more efficient defence; and its cost falls to be borne by the sovereign or the commonwealth.

The second duty of government is to protect every member of the society from the violence or injustice of other members; and for this purpose courts and magistrates of justice have to be maintained, and officers must be appointed to preserve the internal peace of the community. Another duty is to maintain the means of education, among which we may include not only the universities, but also the Church. The building and maintenance of roads, bridges, canals and other communications, which cannot be undertaken by private enterprise, must also be reckoned among the duties of the sovereign.

The cost of all these functions of sovereignty is defrayed by taxation; and the great principles of taxation are that the taxes should be proportioned to the means of those who have to pay them, and that the collection of every tax should be as inexpensive and as little irksome or vexatious to the public as possible.

Voyages of Discovery
by Captain James Cook, Joseph Banks *et al.*
(London, 1784)

James Cook, son of a Yorkshire farm labourer, ran away to sea and rose to become a Captain in the Royal Navy, just as Europeans were at their busiest in searching the world. His first voyage in the *Endeavour* was to observe the transit of Venus from Tahiti and to record natural history under the supervision of the naturalist Joseph Banks. His second in 1772, was to verify reports of a Great South Land in the Pacific. His third and last voyage in the *Resolution* led him to explore the coast of North America as far as Icy Cape, and, returning to the Sandwich Islands, he met his death in Hawaii.

The original folio edition of the *Voyages* was published in 1784, compiled from journals of Cook, Banks, and others.

Abridged: JH/GH

TO THE SOUTH SEAS

We left Plymouth Sound on August 26, 1768, and spent five days at Madeira, where nature has been very liberal with her gifts, but the people lack industry. On reaching Rio de Janeiro, the captain met with much incivility from the viceroy, who would not let him land for a long time; but when we walked through the town, the females showed their welcome by throwing nose-gays from the windows. Dr. Solander and two other gentlemen of our party received so many of these love tokens that they threw them away by hatfuls.

When we came in sight of Tierra del Fuego, the captain went ashore to discourse with the natives, who rose up and threw away the small sticks which they held in their hands, as a token of amity. Snow fell thick, and we were warned by the doctor that 'whoever sits down will sleep, and whoever sleeps will wake no more.' But he soon felt so drowsy that he lay down, and we could hardly keep him awake.

Setting sail again, we passed the strait of Le Maire and doubled Cape Horn, and then, as the ship came near to Otaheite, where the transit of Venus was observed, the captain issued a new rule to this effect: 'That in order to prevent quarrels and confusion, every one of the ship's crew should endeavour to treat the inhabitants of Otaheite with humanity, and by all fair means to cultivate a friendship with them.' On New Year's Day, 1770, we passed Queen Charlotte's Sound, calling the point Cape Farewell. We found the natives of New Zealand modest and reserved in their behaviour, and, sailing northward for New Holland, we called a bay Botany Bay because of the number of plants discovered there, and another Trinity Bay because it was found on Trinity Sunday.

After much dangerous navigation, the ship was brought to in Endeavour River to be refitted. On a clear day, Mr. Green, the astronomer, and other gentlemen had landed on an island to observe the transit of Mercury, and for this reason this spot was called Mercury Bay.

Later, we discovered the mainland beyond York Islands, and here the captain displayed the English colours and called it New South Wales, firing three volleys in the name of the King of Great Britain. After we had left Booby Island in search of New Guinea, we came in sight of a small island, and some of the officers strongly urged the captain to send a party of men on shore to cut down the coconut trees for the sake of the fruit. This he peremptorily refused as unjust and cruel, sensible that the poor Indians, who could not brook even the landing of a small party on their coast, would have made vigorous efforts to defend their property.

Shortly afterwards, we were surprised at the sight of an island W.S.W., which we flattered ourselves was a new discovery. Before noon we had sight of houses, groves of trees, and flocks of sheep, and after the boat had put off to land, horsemen were seen from the ship, one of whom had a lace hat on, and was dressed in a coat and waistcoat of the fashion of Europe. The Dutch colours were hoisted over the town, and the rajah paid us a visit on board, accepting gifts of an English dog and a spying-glass.

During a short stay on shore for the purchase of provisions, we found that the Dutch agent, Mr. Lange, was not keeping faith with us. At his instigation the Portuguese were driving away such of the Indians as had brought palm syrup and fowls to sell.

At this juncture Captain Cook, happening to look at the old man who had been distinguished by the name of Prime Minister, imagined that he saw in his features a disapprobation of the present proceedings, and, willing to improve the advantage, he grasped the Indian's hand, and gave him an old broad-sword. The prime minister was enraptured at so great a mark of distinction, and, brandishing his sword over the head of the impertinent Portuguese, he made both him and the men who commanded the party sit down behind him on the ground, and the whole business was accomplished.

This island of Savu is between twenty and thirty miles long; the women wear a kind of petticoat held up by girdles of beads, the king and his minister a night gown of coarse chintz, carrying a silver-headed cane.

On October 10, 1770, the captain and the rest of the gentlemen went ashore on reaching the harbour of Batavia. Here the Endeavour had to be refitted; and intermittent fever laid many of our party low. Our surgeon, Dr. Monkhouse, died, our Indian boy, Tayeto, paid the debt to nature, and Captain Cook himself was taken ill.

We were glad to steer for Java, and on our way to the Cape of Good Hope the water was purified with lime and the decks washed with vinegar to prevent infection of fever. After a little stay at St. Helena we sighted Beachy Head, and landed at Deal, where the ship's company indulged freely in that mirth and social jollity common to all English sailors upon their return from a long voyage, who as readily forget hardships and dangers as with alacrity and bravery they encounter them.

ROUND THE WORLD BY THE ANTARCTIC

The King's expectation not being wholly answered, Captain Cook was appointed to the Resolution, and Captain Furneaux to the Adventure, both ships being fully equipped, with instructions to find Cape Circumcision, said to be in latitude 54° S. and about 11° 20' E. longitude from Greenwich. Captain Cook was to endeavour to discover whether this was part of the supposed continent or only the promontory\of an island, and then to continue his journey southward and then eastward.

On Monday, July 13, 1772, the two ships sailed from Plymouth, passing the Eddystone, and, after visiting the islands of Canaria, Teneriffe and others, reached the Cape of Good Hope on September 29. Here we stayed until November 22, when we directed our course towards the Antarctic circle, meeting on December 8 with a gale of such fury that we could carry no sails, and were driven by this means eastwards of our course, not the least hope remaining of our reaching Cape Circumcision.

We now encountered in 51° 50' S. latitude and 21° 3' E. longitude some ice islands. The dismal scene, a view to which we were unaccustomed, was varied as well by birds of the petrel kind as by several whales which made their appearance among the ice, and afforded us some idea of a southern Greenland. But though the appearance of the ice with the waves breaking over it might afford a few minutes' pleasure to the eye, yet it could not fail to fill us with horror when we reflected on our danger, for the ship would be dashed to pieces were she to get against the weather side of these islands, where the sea runs high.

Captain Cook had directed the Adventure, in case of separation, to cruise three days in that place, but in a thick fog we lost sight of her. This was a dismal prospect, for we now were exposed to the dangers of the frozen climate without the company of our fellow voyagers, which before had relieved our spirits when we considered we were not entirely alone in case we lost our vessel.

The spirits of our sailors were greatly exhilarated when we reached Dusky Bay, New Zealand. Landing a shooting party at Duck Cove, we found a native with his club and some women behind him, who would not move. His fears, however, were all dissipated by Captain Cook going up to embrace him. After a stay here we opened Queen Charlotte's Sound and found the Adventure at anchor; none can describe the joy we felt at this most happy meeting. They had experienced terrible weather and, having made no discovery of land, determined to bear away from Van Diemen's Land, which was supposed to join New Holland and was discovered by Tasman, in a.d. 1642.

Here they refitted their ship, and after three months' separation met us again. During all this arduous experience of seamanship it was astonishing that the crew of the Resolution should continue in perfect health. Nothing can redound more to the honour of Captain Cook than his paying particular attention to the preservation of health among his company.

After a lengthened stay with the New Zealanders, and all hopes of discovering a continent having now vanished, we were induced to believe that there is no southern continent between New Zealand and America, and steering clear the island, we made our way to Otaheite, where the Resolution lost her lower anchor in the bay.

On January 30, 1774, we sailed from New Zealand, and reaching latitude 67° 5' S., we found an immense field of ice with ninety-seven ice-hills glistening white in the distance. Captain Cook says: 'I will not say it was impossible anywhere to get farther to the south, but the attempting it would have been a dangerous and rash enterprise, and what I believe no man in any situation would have thought of.'

We therefore sailed northward again, meeting with heavy storms, and the captain, being taken ill with a colic, and in the extremity of the case, the doctor fed him with the flesh of a favourite dog.

On the discovery of Palmerston Island- named after one of the Lords of the Admiralty- and Savage Island, as appropriate to the character of the natives, we had some adventures with the Mallicos, who express their admiration by hissing like a goose.

We stayed some time in Tanna, with its vulcano furiously burning, and then steering south-west, we discovered an uninhabited island, which Captain Cook named Norfolk Island. We reached the Straits of Magalhaes, and, going north, the captain gave the names of Cumberland Bay and the Isle of Georgia, and then we found a land ice-bound and inhospitable. At last we reached home, landing at Portsmouth on July 30, 1775.

THE PACIFIC ISLES AND THE ARCTIC CIRCLE

Former navigators had returned to Europe by the Cape of Good Hope; the arduous task was now assigned to Captain Cook of attempting it by reaching the high northern latitudes between Asia and America. He was then ordered to proceed to Otaheite, or the Society Islands, and then, having crossed the Equator into the northern tropics, to hold such a course as might most probably give success to the attempt of finding out a northern passage.

On the afternoon of July n, 1776, Captain Cook set sail from Plymouth in the Resolution, giving orders to Captain Clerke to follow in the Discovery. After a short stay at Santa Cruz, in the island of Teneriffe, we were joined by the Discovery at Cape Town.

Leaving the Cape, we passed some islands, which Captain Cook named Princess Islands, and made for the land discovered by M. de Kerguelen. Here, in a bay, we celebrated our Christmas rejoicings amid desolate surroundings.

The captain named it Christmas Harbour, and wrote on the other side of a piece of parchment, found in a bottle, these words: Naves Resolution et Discovery de Rege Magnae Britanniae Decembris 1776, and buried the same beneath a pile of stones, waving above it the British flag.

Having failed to see a human being on shore, he sailed to Van Dieman's Land, and took the ships into Adventure Bay for water and wood. The natives, with whom we were conversant, seemed mild and cheerful, with little of that savage appearance common to people in their situation, nor did they discover the least reserve or jealousy in their intercourse with strangers.

On our landing at Annamooka, in the Friendly Islands, we were entertained with great civility by Toobou, the chief, who gave us much amusement by a sort of pantomime, in which some prize-fighters displayed their feats of arms, and this part of the drama concluded with the presentation of some laughable story which produced among the chiefs and their attendants the most immoderate mirth.

This friendly reception was also repeated in the island of Hapaee, where Captain Cook ordered an exhibition of fireworks, and in return the king, Feenou, gave us an exhibition of dances in which twenty women entered a circle, whose hands were adorned with garlands of crimson flowers, and many of their persons were decorate with leaves of trees, curiously scalloped, and ornamented at the edges. In the island of Matavai it is impossible to give an adequate idea of the joy of the natives on our arrival. The shores everywhere resounded with the name of Cook; not a child that could lisp 'Toote' was silent.

Before proceeding to the northern hemisphere we passed a cluster of isles which Captain Cook distinguished by the name of Sandwich Islands, in honour of the Earl of Sandwich. They are not inferior in beauty to the Friendly Islands, nor are the inhabitants less ingenious or civilized.

When in latitude 44° N., longitude 234° 30', the long expected coast of New Albion, so named by Sir Francis Drake, was described at a distance of ten leagues, and pursuing our course we reached the inlet which is called by the natives Nootka, but Captain Cook gave it the name of King George's Sound; here we moored our vessels for some time.

the inhabitants are short in stature, with limbs short in proportion to the other parts; they are wretched in appearance and lost to every idea of cleanliness. In trafficking with us some displayed a disposition to knavery, and the appellation of thieves is certainly applicable to. them.

Between the promontory which the captain named Cape Douglas after Dr. Douglas, the Dean of Windsor, and Point Banks is a large, deep bay, which received the name of Smoky Bay; and northward he discovered more land composed of a chain of mountains, the highest of which obtained the name of Mount St. Augustine.

Steering N.E., we discovered a passage of waves dashing against rocks; and, on tasting the water, it proved to be a river, and not a strait, as might have been imagined. This we traced to the latitude of 61° 30' and the longitude of

210°, which is upwards of 210 miles from its entrance, and saw no appearance of its source.

(Here the captain having left a blank in his journal, the Earl of Sandwich very properly directed it to be called Cook's River.)

The time we spent in the discovery of Cook's River ought not to be regretted if it should hereafter prove useful to the present or any future age, but the delay thus occasioned was an effectual loss to us, who had a greater object in view.

The season was far advanced, and it was now evident that the continent of North America extended much farther to the west than we had reason to expect from the most approved charts. A bottle was buried in the earth containing some English coins, and the point was called Point Possession, being taken under the flag in the name of His Majesty.

After passing Foggy Island, which we supposed from its situation to be the island on which Behring had bestowed the same appellation, we were followed by some natives in a canoe, who sent on board a small wooden box which contained a piece of paper in the Russian language. To this was prefixed the date 1778, and a reference made therein to the year 1776, from which we were convinced that others had preceded us in visiting these regions.

While staying at Oonalaska we observed to the north of Cape Prince of Wales neither tide nor current either on the cost of America or that of Asia. This circumstance gave rise to an opinion which some of our people entertained, that the two coasts were connected either by land or ice, and that opinion received some degree of strength from our never having seen any hollow waves from the northward, and from our seeing ice almost all the way across.

We were now by the captain's intention to proceed to Sandwich Islands to pass a few of the winter months there, if we should meet with the necessary refreshments, and then direct our course to Kamtchatka in the ensuing year.

LIFE'S VOYAGE SUDDENLY ENDED

We reached the island called by the natives Owhyhee with the summits of its mountains covered with snow.

Here an eclipse of the moon was observed. We discovered the harbour of Karakakooa, which we deemed a proper place for re-fitting the ships, our masts and rigging having suffered much.

On going ashore Captain Cook discovered the habitation of the Society of Priests, where he was present at some solemn ceremonies and treated with great civility. Afterwards the captain conducted the king, Terreeoboo, on to the ship with every mark of attention, giving him a shirt, and on our visits afterwards on shore we trusted ourselves among the natives without the least reserve.

Some time after, however, we noticed a change in their attitude. Following a short absence in search of a better anchorage, we found our reception very different, in a solitary and deserted bay with hardly a friend appearing or a canoe stirring. We were told that Terreeoboo was absent, and that the bay was tabooed. Our party on going ashore was met by armed natives, and a scuffle arose about the theft of some articles from the Discovery, and Pareea, our friendly native, was, through a misunderstanding, knocked down with an oar. Then Terreeoboo came and complained of our having killed two of his people.

On Sunday, February 14. 1779, that memorable day, very early in the morning, there was excitement on shore, and Captain Cook, taking his double-barrelled gun, went ashore to seize Terreeoboo and keep him on board, according to his usual practice, until the stolen boat should be returned. He ordered that every canoe should be prevented from leaving the bay, and the captain then awoke the old king and invited him to visit the ship.

After some disputation he set out with Captain Cook, when a woman near the waterside, the mother of the king's two boys, entreated him to go no farther, and two warriors obliged him to sit down.

The old king, filled with terror and dejection, refused to move, and Captain Cook, seeing further attempts would be risky, came to the shore. At the same time two principal chiefs were killed on the opposite side of the bay.

A native armed with a long iron spike threatened Captain Cook who at last fired a charge of small shot at him, but his mat prevented any harm. A general attack upon the marines in the boat was made, and with fury the natives rushed upon them, dangerously wounding several.

The last time the captain was distinctly seen he was standing at the water's edge, ordering the boats to cease firing and pull in, when a base assassin, coming behind him and striking him on the head with his club, felled him to the ground, where he lay with his face prone to the water.

A general shout was set up by the islanders on seeing the captain fall, and his body was dragged on shore, where he was surrounded by the enemy, who, snatching daggers from each other's hands, displayed a savage eagerness to join in his destruction. It would seem that vengeance was directed chiefly against our captain, by whom they supposed their king was to be dragged on board and punished at discretion; for, having secured his body, they fled without much regarding the rest of the slain, one of whom they threw into the sea.

Thus ended the life of the greatest navigator that this or any other nation could ever boast of, who led his crews of gallant British seamen twice round the world, reduced to a certainty the non existence of a southern continent, about which the learned of all nations were in doubt, settled the boundaries of the earth and sea, and demonstrated the impracticability of a north-west passage from the Atlantic to the great southern ocean, for which our ablest geographers had contended, and in pursuit of which vast sums had been spent in vain and many mariners had miserably perished.

Poems, Chiefly In The Scottish Dialect
by Robert Burns
(Kilmarnock, 1786)

Most lands have a national poet, but Rabbie Burns, the 'Ploughman Poet', the anti-clerical, egalitarian pioneer of the 'Romantic' movement, is much more; a part of the very fabric of Scottish identity. He is remembered by Scots the world over with 'Burns night' haggis suppers, usually on his birthday, January 25.

Abridged: GH

Address To The Deil

O Prince! O chief of many throned Pow'rs
That led th' embattl'd Seraphim to war—
Milton.[1]

O Thou! whatever title suit thee—
Auld Hornie, Satan, Nick, or Clootie,
Wha in yon cavern grim an' sootie,
Clos'd under hatches,
Spairges about the brunstane cootie,
To scaud poor wretches!

Hear me, auld Hangie, for a wee,
An' let poor damned bodies be;
I'm sure sma' pleasure it can gie,
Ev'n to a deil,
To skelp an' scaud poor dogs like me,
An' hear us squeel!

Great is thy pow'r an' great thy fame;
Far ken'd an' noted is thy name;
An' tho' yon lowin' heuch's thy hame,
Thou travels far;
An' faith! thou's neither lag nor lame,
Nor blate, nor scaur.

Whiles, ranging like a roarin lion,
For prey, a' holes and corners tryin;
Whiles, on the strong-wind'd tempest flyin,
Tirlin the kirks;
Whiles, in the human bosom pryin,
Unseen thou lurks.

I've heard my rev'rend graunie say,
In lanely glens ye like to stray;
Or where auld ruin'd castles grey
Nod to the moon,
Ye fright the nightly wand'rer's way,
Wi' eldritch croon.

When masons' mystic word an' grip
In storms an' tempests raise you up,
Some cock or cat your rage maun stop,
Or, strange to tell!
The youngest brither ye wad whip
Aff straught to hell.

Lang syne in Eden's bonie yard,
When youthfu' lovers first were pair'd,
An' all the soul of love they shar'd,
The raptur'd hour,
Sweet on the fragrant flow'ry swaird,
In shady bower;

Then you, ye auld, snick-drawing dog!
Ye cam to Paradise incog,
An' play'd on man a cursed brogue,
(Black be your fa'!)
An' gied the infant warld a shog,
'Maist rui'd a'.

An' now, auld Cloots, I ken ye're thinkin,
A certain bardie's rantin, drinkin,
Some luckless hour will send him linkin
To your black pit;
But faith! he'll turn a corner jinkin,
An' cheat you yet.

But fare-you-weel, auld Nickie-ben!
O wad ye tak a thought an' men'!
Ye aiblins might—I dinna ken—
Stil hae a stake:
I'm wae to think up' yon den,
Ev'n for your sake!

To A Mouse, On Turning Her Up In Her Nest With The Plough, November, 1785

Wee, sleekit, cow'rin, tim'rous beastie,
O, what a panic's in thy breastie!
Thou need na start awa sae hasty,
Wi' bickering brattle!
I wad be laith to rin an' chase thee,
Wi' murd'ring pattle!

---

1   **Milton:** see p185

I'm truly sorry man's dominion,
Has broken nature's social union,
An' justifies that ill opinion,
Which makes thee startle
At me, thy poor, earth-born companion,
An' fellow-mortal!

Still thou art blest, compar'd wi' me
The present only toucheth thee:
But, Och! I backward cast my e'e.
On prospects drear!
An' forward, tho' I canna see,
I guess an' fear!

Prayer, In The Prospect Of Death

O Thou unknown, Almighty Cause
Of all my hope and fear!
In whose dread presence, ere an hour,
Perhaps I must appear!

If I have wander'd in those paths
Of life I ought to shun,
As something, loudly, in my breast,
Remonstrates I have done;

Thou know'st that Thou hast formed me
With passions wild and strong;
And list'ning to their witching voice
Has often led me wrong.

Where human weakness has come short,
Or frailty stept aside,
Do Thou, All-Good—for such Thou art—
In shades of darkness hide.

Where with intention I have err'd,
No other plea I have,
But, Thou art good; and Goodness still
Delighteth to forgive.

To A Louse, On Seeing One On A Lady's Bonnet, At Church

Ha! whaur ye gaun, ye crowlin ferlie?
Your impudence protects you sairly;
I canna say but ye strunt rarely,
Owre gauze and lace;
Tho', faith! I fear ye dine but sparely
On sic a place.

Ye ugly, creepin, blastit wonner,
Detested, shunn'd by saunt an' sinner,
How daur ye set your fit upon her—
Sae fine a lady?
Gae somewhere else and seek your dinner
On some poor body.

I wad na been surpris'd to spy
You on an auld wife's flainen toy;
Or aiblins some bit dubbie boy,
On's wyliecoat;
But Miss' fine Lunardi! fye!
How daur ye do't?

O Jeany, dinna toss your head,
An' set your beauties a' abroad!
Ye little ken what cursed speed
The blastie's makin:
Thae winks an' finger-ends, I dread,
Are notice takin.

O wad some Power the giftie gie us
To see oursels as ithers see us!
It wad frae mony a blunder free us,
An' foolish notion:
What airs in dress an' gait wad lea'e us,
An' ev'n devotion!

Despondency: An Ode

Oppress'd with grief, oppress'd with care,
A burden more than I can bear,
I set me down and sigh;
O life! thou art a galling load,
Along a rough, a weary road,
To wretches such as I!
Dim backward as I cast my view,
What sick'ning scenes appear!
What sorrows yet may pierce me through,
Too justly I may fear!
Still caring, despairing,
Must be my bitter doom;
My woes here shall close ne'er
But with the closing tomb!

O, enviable, early days,
When dancing thoughtless pleasure's maze,
To care, to guilt unknown!
How ill exchang'd for riper times,
To feel the follies, or the crimes,
Of others, or my own!
Ye tiny elves that guiltless sport,
Like linnets in the bush,
Ye little know the ills ye court,
When manhood is your wish!
The losses, the crosses,
That active man engage;
The fears all, the tears all,
Of dim declining age!

Groundwork of the Metaphysic of Morals
by Immanuel Kant
(Königsburg, 1785)

Kant was born in Königsburg, Prussia, and stayed there all his life. His *Groundwork of the Metaphysic of Morals* tries to find the underlying principle which defines actions as good or bad, and ends up with a Categorical Rule (*you must act such that you expect everyone to act the same way*) and a Practical one (*we must treat others only as ends, not merely as means.*) They may not be perfect, but they remain one of the basic sets of standard by which 'good' and 'bad' are frequently officially judged.

Abridged: GH

Ancient Greek philosophy was divided into physics, ethics, and logic. The only improvement that can be made is to add the principle on which it is based.

FIRST SECTION

FROM COMMON KNOWLEDGE OF MORALITY TO THE PHILOSOPHICAL

Nothing can possibly be conceived in the world, or even out of it, which can be called good without qualification, except a good will. Intelligence, wit, judgement, courage, resolution, perseverance, power, riches, honour, even health, are undoubtedly good; but these gifts may also become extremely bad and mischievous if the will which makes use of them is bad. It is the coolness of a villain which not only makes him far more dangerous, but also more abominable in our eyes.

A good will is good not because of what it performs or effects, but simply by virtue of the volition; that is, it is good in itself. Even if, through the disfavor of fortune, or the niggardly provision of a step-motherly nature, good will should yet achieve nothing, then, still, like a jewel, it would shine by its own light. Its usefulness or fruitfulness can neither add nor take away anything from this value.

To be beneficent is a duty; and there are many minds so sympathetically constituted that they find a pleasure in spreading joy around them and take delight in the satisfaction of others so far as it is their own work. But I maintain that in such a case, however amiable it may be, has no true moral worth. It is in this manner, undoubtedly, that we are to understand those passages of Scripture in which we are commanded to love our neighbour.

A second proposition is: That an action done from duty derives its moral worth, not from the purpose which is to be attained by it, but from the maxim by which it is determined.

The third proposition, which is a consequence of the preceding, I would express thus: *Duty is the necessity of acting from respect for the law.*

But what sort of law can that be, that this will may be called good absolutely and without qualification? There remains nothing but the universal conformity of its actions to law in general, which alone is to serve the will as a principle, ie., *I am never to act otherwise than so that I could also will that my maxim should become a universal law.*

For example: May I, when in distress, make a promise with the intention not to keep it? The shortest way, and an unerring one, to answer this question, is to ask, "Should I be able to say to myself, "Every one may make a deceitful promise when he finds himself in a difficulty from which he cannot otherwise extricate himself?"" Then I presently become aware that while I can will the lie, I can by no means will that lying should be a universal law. For with such a law there would be no promises at all, since such would pay me back in my own coin. Hence my maxim, as soon as it should be made a universal law, would necessarily destroy itself.

SECOND SECTION

FROM POPULAR MORAL PHILOSOPHY TO THE METAPHYSIC OF MORALS

If we have hitherto drawn our notion of duty from the common use of our practical reason, it is by no means to be inferred that it as a concept of experience.

Even the Holy One of the Gospels must first be compared with our ideal of moral perfection before we can recognise Him as such; and so He says of Himself, "Why call ye Me (whom you see) good; none is good (the model of good) but God only (whom ye do not see)?" But whence have we the conception of God as the supreme good?

But in order to advance in natural steps in this study, we must follow and clearly describe the practical faculty of reason, from the general rules of its determination to the point where the notion of duty springs from it.

Everything in nature works according to laws. Rational beings alone have the faculty of acting according to the conception of laws, that is according to principles, ie., have a will. Since the deduction of actions from principles requires reason, the will is nothing but practical reason.

There is but one categorical imperative, namely, this: *Act only on that maxim whereby thou canst at the same time will that it should become a universal law.* Since the universality of the law according to which effects are produced constitutes what is properly called nature in the most general sense (as to form), the imperative of duty may be expressed thus: Act as if the maxim of thy action were to become by thy will a universal law of nature.

We will now enumerate a few duties, adopting the usual division of them into duties to ourselves and to others, and into perfect and imperfect duties.

1. A man reduced to despair by a series of misfortunes feels wearied of life, and asks himself whether it would not be contrary to his duty to take his own life. We see at once that a system of nature in which it should be a law to destroy life would contradict itself and, therefore, could not exist; hence that maxim cannot possibly exist as a universal law of nature.

2. Another finds himself forced by necessity to borrow money. He knows that he will not be able to repay it, but sees also that nothing will be lent to him unless he promises so. But supposing it to be a universal law that everyone when he thinks himself in a difficulty should be able to promise whatever he pleases, the promise itself would become impossible, since no one would consider that anything was promised to him, but would ridicule all such statements as vain pretences.

3. A third finds in himself a talent which, with the help of some culture, might make him useful. But he prefers to indulge in pleasure rather than to take pains in improving his happy natural capacities. He sees that a system of nature could indeed subsist with such a universal law where men (like the South Sea islanders) devote their lives to idleness, amusement, and propagation of their species; but he cannot possibly will that this should be a universal law of nature. For, as a rational being, he necessarily wills that his faculties be developed, since they serve him and have been given him, for all sorts of possible purposes.

4. A fourth, who is in prosperity, while he sees that others have to contend with great wretchedness, thinks: "What concern is it of mine? But it is impossible to will that such a principle should have the universal validity of a law of nature, for many cases might occur in which one would have need of the love and sympathy of others.

The question then is this: "Is it a necessary law for all rational beings that they should always judge of their actions by maxims of which they can themselves will that they should serve as universal laws?" But in order to discover this connexion we must, however reluctantly, take a step into a domain of metaphysic, namely, the metaphysic of morals. Here we are concerned with the relation of the will to itself so far as it is determined by reason alone.

The will is conceived as a faculty of determining oneself to action in accordance with the conception of certain laws.

Now I say: man, and generally any rational being, exists as an end in himself, not merely as a means to be arbitrarily used by this or that will, but in all his actions, whether they concern himself or other rational beings, must be always regarded at the same time as an end.

Man necessarily conceives his own existence as being so. But every other rational being regards its existence

similarly. Accordingly the practical imperative will be as follows: *So act as to treat humanity, whether in thine own person or in that of any other, in every case as an end withal, never as means only.*

We will now inquire whether this can be practically carried out. To abide by the previous examples:

Firstly, he who contemplates suicide should ask himself whether his action can be consistent with the idea of humanity as an end in itself. If he destroys himself in order to escape from painful circumstances, he uses a person merely as a mean to maintain a tolerable condition up to the end of life.

Secondly, as regards duties of strict obligation towards others: He who is thinking of making a lying promise to others will see at once that he would be using another man merely as a means, without the latter containing at the same time the end in himself.

Thirdly, as regards contingent (meritorious) duties to oneself: It is not enough that the action does not violate humanity in our own person as an end in itself, it must also harmonize with it.

Fourthly, as regards meritorious duties towards others: The ends of any subject which is an end in himself ought as far as possible to be my ends also, if that conception is to have its full effect with me.

Thus all maxims are rejected which are inconsistent with the will being itself universal legislator, and Thus the principle that every human will is a will which in all its maxims gives universal laws, would be very well adapted to be the categorical imperative because the idea of universal legislation is not based on any particular interest, and therefore it alone can be unconditional.

Looking back now on all previous attempts to discover the principle of morality, we need not wonder why they all failed. It was not seen that the laws to which man is subject are only those of his own giving, though at the same time they are universal.

The conception of the will of every rational being as one which must consider itself as giving in all the maxims of its will universal laws leads to a very fruitful conception, namely that of a *Kingdom of Ends*.

In the *Kingdom of Ends* everything has either value or dignity. Whatever has a value can be replaced by something else which is equivalent; whatever, on the other hand, is above all value, and therefore admits of no equivalent, has a dignity.

THE AUTONOMY OF THE WILL AS THE SUPREME PRINCIPLE OF MORALITY

Autonomy of the will is that property of it by which it is a law to itself (independently of any property of the objects of volition). The principle of autonomy then is: *"Always so to choose that the same volition shall comprehend the maxims of our choice as a universal law."* We cannot prove that this practical rule is an imperative by a mere analysis of the conceptions which occur in it, since it is a synthetical proposition. But that the principle of autonomy is the sole principle of morals can be readily shown by mere analysis of the conceptions of morality. For we find that its principle must be a categorical imperative and that what this commands is neither more nor less than this very autonomy.

HETERONOMY OF THE WILL AS THE SOURCE OF ALL SPURIOUS PRINCIPLES OF MORALITY

If the will seeks the law which is to determine it anywhere else than in the fitness of its maxims to be universal laws of its own creation, it goes out of itself and seeks this law in the character of any of its objects, there always results heteronomy. The will in that case does not give itself the law, but it is given by the object through its relation to the will. This relation, whether it rests on inclination or on conceptions of reason, only admits of hypothetical imperatives: "I ought to do something because I wish for something else." On the contrary, the moral, and therefore categorical, imperative says: "I ought to do so and so, even though I should not wish for anything else."

THIRD SECTION

FROM THE METAPHYSIC OF MORALS TO THE CRITIQUE OF PURE PRACTICAL REASON

THE CONCEPT OF FREEDOM IS THE KEY THAT EXPLAINS THE AUTONOMY OF THE WILL

The will is a kind of causality belonging to living beings in so far as they are rational, and freedom would be this property of such causality that it can be efficient, independently of foreign causes determining it. The preceding definition of freedom is negative and therefore unfruitful for the discovery of its essence, but it leads to a positive conception.

Since the conception of causality involves that of laws, what else then can freedom of the will be but autonomy, that is, the property of the will to be a law to itself? But the proposition: *"The will is in every action a law to itself,"* only expresses the principle: *"To act on no other maxim than that which can also have as an object itself as a universal law."* Now this is precisely the formula of the categorical imperative and is the principle of morality, so that a free will and a will subject to moral laws are one and the same.

However, that is a synthetic proposition, and such synthetic propositions are only possible in this way: that the two cognitions are connected together by a third in which they are both to be found. We cannot now at once show what this third is. Some further preparation is required.

FREEDOM MUST BE PRESUPPOSED AS A PROPERTY OF THE WILL OF ALL RATIONAL BEINGS

It is not enough to predicate freedom of our own will, if we have not grounds for predicating the same of all rational beings. Now I affirm that we must attribute to every rational being which has a will that it has also the idea of freedom and acts entirely under this idea.

It must be freely admitted that there is a sort of circle here from which it seems impossible to escape. In the order of efficient causes we assume ourselves free, in order that in the order of ends we may conceive ourselves as subject to moral laws: and we afterwards conceive ourselves as subject to these laws, because we have attributed to ourselves freedom of will.

One resource remains to us, namely, to inquire whether we do not occupy different points of view when by means of freedom we think ourselves as causes efficient *a priori*, and when we form our conception of ourselves from our actions as effects which we see before our eyes.

We can only attain to the knowledge of appearances, never to that of things in themselves. As soon as this distinction has once been made then it follows that we must admit and assume behind the appearance something else that is not an appearance, namely, the things in themselves. This must furnish a distinction, however crude, between a world of sense and the world of understanding.

Now man really finds in himself a faculty by which he distinguishes himself from everything else, even from himself as affected by objects, and that is reason. Hence he has two points of view from which he can regard himself, and recognise laws of the exercise of his faculties: first, so far as he belongs to the world of sense, he finds himself subject to laws of nature (heteronomy); secondly, as belonging to the intelligible world, under laws which, being independent of nature, have their foundation not in experience but in reason alone.

As a rational being, and consequently belonging to the intelligible world, man can never conceive the causality of his own will otherwise than on condition of the idea of freedom.

Now the suspicion is removed that there was a latent circle involved in our reasoning from freedom to autonomy. For now we see that, when we conceive ourselves as free, we transfer ourselves into the world of understanding as members of it and recognise the autonomy of the will with its consequence, morality; whereas, if we conceive ourselves as under obligation, we consider ourselves as belonging to the world of sense and at the same time to the world of understanding.

HOW IS A CATEGORICAL IMPERATIVE POSSIBLE?

Every rational being reckons himself, as intelligence, as belonging to the world of understanding, and also conscious of himself as a part of the world of sense in which his actions are displayed.

And thus what makes categorical imperatives possible is this, that the idea of freedom makes me a member of an intelligible world, in which all my actions would always conform to the autonomy of the will; but as I at the same time intuite myself as a member of the world of sense, they ought so to conform. It is this categorical "ought" which implies a synthetic *a priori* proposition, inasmuch as besides my will, as affected by sensible desires, there is added the further idea of the same will but as belonging to the world of the understanding. In this way synthetic a priori propositions become possible, on which all knowledge of physical nature rests.

The practical use of common human reason confirms this reasoning. There is no one, not even the most consummate villain, provided only that be is otherwise accustomed to the use of reason, who, when we set before him examples of honesty of purpose, of steadfastness in following good maxims, of sympathy and general benevolence, does not wish that he might also possess these qualities. Only on account of his inclinations and impulses he cannot attain this in himself, but at the same time he wishes to be free from such inclinations. What he morally "ought" is then what he necessarily "would," as a member of the world of the understanding, and is conceived by him as an "ought" only inasmuch as he likewise considers himself as a member of the world of sense.

OF THE EXTREME LIMITS OF ALL PRACTICAL PHILOSOPHY.

All men attribute to themselves freedom of will. Hence come all judgements upon actions as being such as ought to have been done, although they have not been done. However, this freedom is not a conception of experience, nor can it be so, since it still remains, even though experience shows the contrary.

There arises from this a dialectic of reason, since the freedom attributed to the will appears to contradict the necessity of nature. Philosophy must then assume that no real contradiction will be found between freedom and physical necessity.

Nevertheless, even though we should never be able to comprehend how freedom is possible, we must at least remove this apparent contradiction in a convincing manner.

The question then, "How a categorical imperative is possible," can be answered to this extent, that we can assign the only hypothesis on which it is possible, namely, the idea of freedom; but how this hypothesis itself is possible can never be discerned by any human reason. To explain how pure reason can be of itself practical is beyond the power of human reason, and all the labour and pains of seeking an explanation of it are lost.

Here now is the extreme limit of all moral inquiry, and it is of great importance to determine it in order that reason may not impotently flap its wings without being able to move in the empty space of transcendent concepts. For the rest, the idea of a pure world of understanding to which we as rational beings belong (while also being members of the sensible world), remains a useful and legitimate idea to produce in us a lively interest in the moral law.

CONCLUDING REMARK

It is no fault in our deduction of the supreme principle of morality, but an objection to human reason in general, that it cannot enable us to conceive the absolute necessity of an unconditional practical law (such as the categorical imperative). And thus while we do not comprehend the practical unconditional necessity of the moral imperative, we yet comprehend its incomprehensibility, and this is all that can be fairly demanded of a philosophy which strives to carry its principles up to the very limit of human reason.

The Decline and Fall of the Roman Empire
by Edward Gibbon
(London, 1787)

Edward Gibbon was a Hampshire gentleman and Member of Parliament. His *History of the Decline and Fall of the Roman Empire* is famous for the quality of its writing and Gibbon's care in trying to always check his sources has made it a model for every history book since. Winston Churchill said that "I devoured Gibbon. I rode triumphantly through it from end to end and enjoyed it all", and claimed to have modelled his own literary style on Gibbon's. But, above all, *Decline and Fall* is famous for being extraordinarily vast, more than 1.6 *million* words.

Abridged: JH

Rome, Mistress of the World

In the second century of the Christian era, the Empire of Rome comprehended the fairest part of the earth, and the most civilised portion of mankind. On the death of Augustus, that emperor bequeathed, as a valuable legacy to his successors, the advice of confining the empire within those limits which nature seemed to have placed as its permanent bulwarks and boundaries - on the west the Atlantic Ocean, the Rhine and Danube on the north, the Euphrates on the east, and towards the south the sandy deserts of Arabia and Africa.

By maintaining the dignity of the empire, without attempting to enlarge its limits, the early emperors caused the Roman name to be revered among the most remote nations of the earth. The terror of their arms added weight and dignity to their moderation. They preserved peace by a constant preparation for war. The soldiers, though drawn from the meanest of mankind, and no longer, as in the days of the ancient republic, recruited from Rome herself, were preserved in their allegiance to the emperor, and their invincibility before the enemy, by the influences of superstition, inflexible discipline, and the hopes of reward. The peace establishment of the Roman army numbered some 375,000 men, divided into thirty legions.

"Wheresoever the Roman conquers he inhabits," was a very just observation of Seneca. Colonies, composed for the most part of veteran soldiers, were settled throughout the empire. Rich and prosperous cities, adorned with magnificent temples and baths and other public buildings, demonstrated at once the magnificence and majesty of the Roman system. In Britain, York was the seat of government. London was already enriched by commerce, and Bath was celebrated for the salutary effects of its medicinal waters.

All the great cities were connected with each other, and with the capital, by the public highway, which, issuing from the Forum of Rome, traversed Italy, pervaded the provinces, and was terminated only by the frontiers of the empire. This great chain of communications ran in a direct line from city to city, and in its construction the Roman engineers snowed little respect for the obstacles, either of nature or of private property. Mountains were perforated and bold arches thrown over the broadest and most rapid streams. The middle part of the road, raised into a terrace which commanded the adjacent country, consisted of several strata of sand, gravel, and cement, and was paved with granite or large stones. Distances were accurately computed by milestones, and the establishment of post-houses, at a distance of five or six miles, enabled a citizen to travel with ease a hundred miles a day along the Roman roads.

This freedom of intercourse, which was established throughout the Roman world, while it extended the vices, diffused likewise the improvements of social life. Rude barbarians of Gaul laid aside their arms for the more peaceful pursuits of agriculture. Commerce flourished, and the products of Egypt and the East were poured out in the lap of Rome.

Though there still existed within the body of the Roman Empire an unhappy condition of men who endured the weight, without sharing the benefits of society, the position of a slave was greatly improved in the progress of Roman development. The power of life and death was taken from his master's hands and vested in the magistrate, to whom he had a right to appeal against intolerable treatment.

The Seeds of Dissolution

But while Roman society persisted in a state of peaceful security, it already contained within itself the seeds of dissolution. The long peace and uniform government of the Romans introduced a slow and secret poison into the vitals of the empire. The minds of men were gradually reduced to the same level, the fire of genius was extinguished, and even the military spirit evaporated. The citizens received laws and covenants from the will of their sovereign, and

trusted for their defence to a mercenary army. Of their ancient freedom nothing remained except the name, and that Augustus, sensible that mankind is governed by names, was careful to preserve.

It was by the will of the senate the emperor ruled. Moreover, the dependence of the emperor on the legions completely subverted the civil authority. To keep the military power, which had given him his position, from undermining it, Augustus had summoned to his aid whatever remained in the fierce minds of his soldiers of Roman prejudices, and interposing the majesty of the senate between the emperor and the army, boldly claimed their allegiance as the first magistrate of the republic. During a period of 220 years, the dangers inherent to a military government were in a great measure suspended by this artful system.

The emperors Caligula and Domitian were assassinated in their palace by their own domestics. The Roman world, it is true, was shaken by the events that followed the death of Nero, when, in the space of eighteen months, four princes perished by the sword. But, excepting this violent eruption of military licence, the two centuries from Augustus to Commodus passed away unstained with civil blood and undisturbed by revolution. The Roman citizens might groan under the tyranny, from which they could not hope to escape, of the unrelenting Tiberius, the furious Caligula, the profligate and cruel Nero, the beastly Vitellius, and the timid, inhuman Domitian; but order was maintained, and it was not until Commodus, the son of Marcus Aurelius Antoninus, the philosopher, succeeded to the authority that his father had exercised for the benefit of the Roman Empire that the army fully realised, and did not fail to exercise, the power it had always possessed.

During the first three years of his reign the vices of Commodus affected the emperor rather than the state. While the young prince revelled in licentious pleasures, the management of affairs remained in the hands of his father's faithful councillors; but, in the year 183, the attempt of his sister Lucilla to assassinate him produced fatal results. The assassin, in attempting the deed, exclaimed, "The senate sends you this!" and though the blow never reached the body of the emperor, the words sank deep into his heart.

He turned upon the senate with relentless cruelty. The possession of either wealth or virtue excited the tyrant's fury. Suspicion was equivalent to proof; trial to condemnation, and the noblest blood of the senate was poured out like water.

He has shed with impunity the noblest blood of Rome; he perished as soon as he was dreaded by his own domestics. A cup of drugged wine, delivered by his favourite concubine, plunged him in a deep sleep. At the instigation of Lætus, his Prætorian prefect, a robust youth was admitted into his chamber, and strangled him without resistance. With secrecy and celerity the conspirators sought out Pertinax, the prefect of the city, an ancient senator of consular rank, and persuaded him to accept the purple. A large donative secured them the support of the Prætorian guard, and the joyous senate eagerly bestowed upon the new Augustus all the titles of imperial power.

For eighty-six days Pertinax ruled the empire with firmness and moderation, but the strictness of the ancient discipline that he attempted to restore in the army excited the hatred of the Prætorian guards, and the new emperor was struck down on March 28, 193.

An Empire at Auction

The Prætorians had violated the sanctity of the throne by the atrocious murder of Pertinax; they dishonored the majesty of it with their subsequent conduct. They ran out upon the ramparts of the city, and with a loud voice proclaimed that the Roman world was to be disposed of to the best bidder by public auction. Sulpicianus, father-in-law of Pertinax, and Didius Julianus, bid against each other for the prize. It fell to Julian, who offered upwards of £1,000 sterling to each of the soldiers, and the author of this ignominious bargain received the insignia of the empire and the acknowledgments of a trembling senate.

The news of this disgraceful auction was received by the legions of the frontiers with surprise, with indignation, and, perhaps, with envy. Albinus, governor of Britain, Niger, governor of Syria, and Septimius Severus, a native of Africa, commander of the Pannonian army, prepared to revenge the death of Pertinax, and to establish their own claims to the vacant throne. Marching night and day, Severus crossed the Julian Alps, swept aside the feeble defences of Julian, and put an end to a reign of power which had lasted but sixty-six days, and had been purchased with such immense treasure. Having secured the supreme authority, Severus turned his arms against his two competitors, and within three years, and in the course of two or three battles, established his position and brought about the death of both Albinus and Niger.

The prosperity of Rome revived, and a profound peace reigned throughout the world. At the same time, Severus was guilty of two acts which were detrimental to the future interests of the republic. He relaxed the discipline of the army, increased their pay beyond the example of former times, re-established the Prætorian guards, who had been abolished for their transaction with Julian, and welded more firmly the chains of tyranny by filling the senate with his creatures. At the age of sixty-five in the year 211, he expired at York of a disorder which was aggravated by the labours of a campaign against the Caledonians.

Severus recommended concord to his sons, Caracalla and Geta, and his sons to the army. The government of the civilised world was entrusted to the hands of brothers who were implacable enemies. A latent civil war brooded in the city, and hardly more than a year passed before the assassins of Caracalla put an end to an impossible situation by murdering Geta. Twenty thousand persons of both sexes suffered death under the vague appellation of the friends of Geta. The fears of Macrinus, the controller of the civil

affairs of the Prætorian prefecture, brought about his death in the neighbourhood of Carrhæ in Syria on April 8, 217.

For a little more than a year his successor governed the empire, but the necessary step of reforming the army brought about his ruin. On June 7, 218, he succumbed to the superior fortune of Elagabulus, the grandson of Severus, a youth trained in all the superstitions and vices of the East.

Under this sovereign Rome was prostituted to the vilest vices of which human nature is capable. The sum of his infamy was reached when the master of the Roman world affected to copy the dress and manners of the female sex. The shame and disgust of the soldiers resulted in his murder on March 10, 222, and the proclamation of his cousin, Alexander Severus.

Again the necessity of restoring discipline within the army led to the ruin of the emperor, and, despite thirteen years of just and moderate government, Alexander was murdered in his tent on March 19, 235, on the banks of the Rhine, and Maximin, his chief lieutenant, a Thracian, reigned in his stead.

Tyranny and Disaster

Fear of contempt, for his origin was mean and barbarian, made Maximin one of the cruellest tyrants that ever oppressed the Roman world. During the three years of his reign he disdained to visit either Rome or Italy, but from the banks of the Rhine and the Danube oppressed the whole state, and trampled on every principle of law and justice. The tyrant's avarice ruined not only private citizens, but seized the municipal funds of the cities, and stripped the very temples of their gold and silver offerings.

Maximus and Balbinus, on July 9, 237, were declared emperors. The Emperor Maximus advanced to meet the furious tyrant, but the stroke of domestic conspiracy prevented the further eruption of civil war. Maximin and his son were murdered by their disappointed troops in front of Aquileia.

Three months later, Maximus and Balbinus, on July 15, 238, fell victims to their own virtues at the hands of the Prætorian guard, Gordian became emperor. At the end of six years, he, too, after an innocent and virtuous reign, succumbed to the ambition of the prefect Philip, while engaged in a war with Persia, and in March 244, the Roman world recognized the sovereignty of an Arabian robber.

Returning to Rome, Philip celebrated the secular games, on the accomplishment of the full period of a thousand years from the foundation of Rome. From that date, which marked the fifth time that these rites had been performed in the history of the city, for the next twenty years the Roman world was afflicted by barbarous invaders and military tyrants, and the ruined empire seemed to approach the last and fatal moment of its dissolution. Six emperors in turn succeeded to the sceptre of Philip and ended their lives, either as the victims of military licence, or in the vain attempt to stay the triumphal eruption of the Goths and the Franks and the Suevi. In three expeditions the Goths seized the Bosphorus, plundered the cities of Bithynia, ravaged Greece, and threatened Italy, while the Franks invaded Gaul, overran Spain and the provinces of Africa.

Some sparks of their ancient virtue enabled the senate to repulse the Suevi, who threatened Rome herself, but the miseries of the empire were not assuaged by this one triumph, and the successes of Sapor, king of Persia, in the East, seemed to foreshadow the immediate downfall of Rome. Six emperors and thirty tyrants attempted in vain to stay the course of disaster. Famine and pestilence, tumults and disorders, and a great diminution of the population marked this period, which ended with the death of the Emperor Gallienus on March 20, 268.

Restorers of the Roman World

The empire, which had been oppressed and almost destroyed by the soldiers, the tyrants, and the barbarians, was saved by a series of great princes, who derived their obscure origin from the martial provinces of Illyricum. Within a period of about thirty years, Claudius, Aurelian, Probus, Diocletian and his colleagues triumphed over the foreign and domestic enemies of the state, re-established, with a military discipline, the strength of the frontier, and deserved the glorious title of Restorers of the Roman world.

Claudius gained a crushing victory over the Goths, whose discomfiture was completed by disease in the year 269. And his successor, Aurelian, in a reign of less than five years, put an end to the Gothic war, chastised the Germans who invaded Italy, recovered Gaul, Spain, and Britain from the Roman usurpers, and destroyed the proud monarchy which Zenobia, Queen of Palmyra, had erected in the East on the ruins of the afflicted empire.

The murder of Aurelian in the East (January 275) led to a curious revival of the authority of the senate. During an interregnum of eight months the ancient assembly at Rome governed with the consent of the army, and appeared to regain with the election of Tacitus, one of their members, all their ancient prerogatives. Their authority expired, however, with the death of his successor, Probus, who delivered the empire once more from the invasions of the barbarians, and succumbed to the too common fate of assassination in August 282.

Carus, who was elected in his place, maintained the reputation of the Roman arms in the East; but his supposed death by lightning, by delivering the sceptre into the hands of his sons Carinus and Numerian (December 25, 283), once more placed the Roman world at the mercy of profligacy and licentiousness. A year later, the election of the Emperor Diocletian (September 17, 284) founded a new era in the history and fortunes of the empire.

It was the artful policy of Diocletian to destroy the last vestiges of the ancient constitution. Dividing his unwieldy power among three other associates - Maximian, a rough, brutal soldier, who ranked as Augustus; and Galerius and Constantius, who bore the inferior titles of Cæsar - the emperor removed the centre of government by gradual steps from Rome. Diocletian and Maximian held their courts in the provinces, and the authority of the senators was destroyed by spoliation and death.

Reign of the Six Emperors

For twenty-one years Diocletian held sway, establishing, with the assistance of his associates, the might of the Roman arms in Britain, Africa, Egypt, and Persia; and then, on May 1, 305, in a spacious plain in the neighborhood of Nicomedia, divested himself of the purple and abdicated the throne. On the same day at Milan, Maximian reluctantly made his resignation of the imperial dignity.

According to the rules of the new constitution, Constantius and Galerius assumed the title of Augustus, and nominated Maximin and Severus as Cæsars. The elaborate machinery devised by Diocletian at once broke down. Galerius, who was supported by Severus, intrigued for the possession of the whole Roman world. Constantine, the son of Constantius, on account of his popularity with the army and the people, excited his suspicion, and only the flight of Constantine saved him from death. He made his way to Gaul, and, after taking part in a campaign with his father against the Caledonians, received the title of Augustus in the imperial palace at York on the death of Constantius.

Civil war once more raged. Maxentius, the son of Maximian, was declared Emperor of Rome, and, with the assistance of his father, who broke from his retirement, defended his title against Severus, who was taken prisoner at Ravenna and executed at Rome in February 307. Galerius, who had raised Licinius to fill the post vacated by the death of Severus, invaded Italy to reestablish his authority, but, after threatening Rome, was compelled to retire.

There were now six emperors. Maximian and his son Maxentius and Constantine in the West; in the East, Gelerius, Maximin, and Licinius. The second resignation of Maximian, and his renewed attempt to seize the imperial power by seducing the soldiers of Constantine, and his subsequent execution at Marseilles in February 310, reduced the number to five. Galerius died of a lingering disorder in the following year, and the civil war that broke out between Maxentius and Constantine, culminating in a battle near Rome in 312, placed the sceptre of the West in the hands of the son of Constantius. In the East, the alliance between Licinius and Maximin dissolved into discord, and the defeat of the latter on April 30, 313, ended in his death three or four months later.

The empire was now divided between Constantine and Licinius, and the ambition of the two princes rendered peace impossible. In the years 315 and 323 civil conflict broke out, ending, after the battle of Adrianople and the siege of Byzantium, in a culminating victory for Constantine in the field of Chrysopolis, in September.

Licinius, taken prisoner, laid himself and his purple at the feet of his lord and master, and was duly executed.

By successive steps, from his first assuming the purple at York, to the resignation of Licinius, Constantine had reached the undivided sovereignty of the Roman world. His success contributed to the decline of the empire by the expense of blood and treasure, and by the perpetual increase as well of the taxes as of the military establishments. The foundation of Constantinople and the establishment of the Christian religion were the immediate and memorable consequences of this revolution.

Decay of the Empire under Constantine

The unfortunate Licinius was the last rival who opposed the greatness of Constantine. After a tranquil and prosperous reign, the conqueror bequeathed to his family the inheritance of the Roman Empire; a new capital, a new policy, and a new religion; and the innovations which he established have been embraced, and consecrated, by succeeding generations.

Byzantium, which, under the more august name of Constantinople, was destined to preserve the shadow of the Roman power for nearly a thousand years after it had been extinguished by Rome herself, was the site selected for the new capital. Its boundary was traced by the emperor, and its circumference measured some sixteen miles. In a general decay of the arts no architect could be found worthy to decorate the new capital, and the cities of Greece and Asia were despoiled of their most valuable ornaments to supply this want of ability. In the course of eight or ten years the city, with its beautiful forum, its circus, its imperial palace, its theatres, baths, churches, and houses, was completed with more haste than care. The dedication of the new Rome was performed with all due pomp and ceremony, and a population was provided by the expedient of summoning some of the wealthiest families in the empire to take up their residence within its walls.

The gradual decay of Rome had eliminated that simplicity of manners which was the just pride of the ancient republic. Under the autocratic system of Diocletian, a hierarchy of dependents had sprung up. The rank of each was marked with the most scrupulous exactness, and the purity of the Latin language was debased by the invention of the deceitful titles of your Sincerity, your Excellency, your Illustrious and Magnificent Highness.

The officials of the empire were divided into three classes of the Illustrious, Respectable, and Honourable. The consuls were still annually elected, but obtained the semblance of their ancient authority, not from the suffrages of the people, but from the whim of the emperor. On the morning of January 1 they assumed the ensigns of their dignity, and in the two capitals of the empire they celebrated their promotion to office by the annual games. As soon as they had discharged these customary duties, they retired into the shade of private life, to enjoy, during the remainder of the year, the undisturbed contemplation of their own greatness. Their names served only as the legal

date of the year in which they had filled the chair of Marius and of Cicero. The ancient title of Patrician became now an empty honour bestowed by the emperor. Four prefects held jurisdiction over as many divisions of the empire, and two municipal prefects ruled Rome and Constantinople. The proconsuls and vice-prefects belonged to the rank of Respectable, and the provincial magistrates to the lower class of Honourable. In the military system, eight master-generals exercised their jurisdiction over the cavalry and the infantry, while thirty-five military commanders, with the titles of counts and dukes, under their orders, held sway in the provinces. The army itself was recruited with difficulty, for such was the horror of the profession of a soldier which affected the minds of the degenerate Romans that compulsory levies had frequently to be made. The number of the barbarian auxiliaries enormously increased, and they were included in the legions and the troops that surrounded the throne. Seven ministers with the rank of Illustrious regulated the affairs of the palace, and a host of official spies and torturers swelled the number of the immediate followers of the sovereign.

The general tribute, or indiction, as it was called, was derived largely from the taxation of landed property. Every fifteen years an accurate census, or survey, was made of all lands, and the proprietor was compelled to state the true facts of his affairs under oath, and paid his contribution partly in gold and partly in kind. In addition to this land tax there was a capitation tax on every branch of commercial industry, and "free gifts" were exacted from the cities and provinces on the occasion of any joyous event in the family of the emperor. The peculiar "free gift" of the senate of Rome amounted to some sixteen hundred pounds of gold.

Constantine celebrated the twentieth year of his reign at Rome in the year 326. The glory of his triumph was marred by the execution, or murder, of his son Crispus, whom he suspected of a conspiracy, and the reputation of the emperor who established the Christian religion in the Roman world was further stained by the death of his second wife, Fausta. With a successful war against the Goths in 331, and the expulsion of the Sarmatians in 334, his reign closed. He died at Nicomedia on May 22, 337.

The Division of East and West

The unity of the empire was again destroyed by the three sons of Constantine. A massacre of their kinsmen preceded the separation of the Roman world between Constantius, Constans, and Constantine. Within three years, civil war eliminated Constantine. The conflict among the emperors resulted in a doubtful war with Persia, and the almost complete extinction of the Christian monarchy which had been founded for fifty-six years in Armenia.

Constantius was left sole emperor in 353. He associated with himself successively as Cæsars the two nephews of the great Constantine, Gallus and Julian. The first, being suspected, was destroyed in 354; the second succeeded to the purple in 361.

Trained in the school of the philosophers, and proved as a commander in a series of successful campaigns against the German hordes, Julian brought to the throne a genius which, in other times, might have effected the reformation of the empire. The sufferings of his youth had associated in a mind susceptible of the most lively impressions the names of Christ and of Constantius, the ideas of slavery and religion. At the age of twenty he renounced the Christian faith, and boldly asserted the doctrines of paganism. His accession to the supreme power filled the minds of the Christians with horror and indignation. But instructed by history and reflection, Julian extended to all the inhabitants of the Roman world the benefits of a free and equal toleration, and the only hardship which he inflicted on the Christians was to deprive them of the power of tormenting their fellow subjects, whom they stigmatised with the odious titles of idolaters and heretics.

While re-establishing and reforming the old pagan system and attempting to subvert Christianity, he held out a hand of succour to the persecuted Jews, asked to be permitted to pay his grateful vows in the holy city of Jerusalem, and was only prevented from rebuilding the Temple by a supposed preternatural interference. He suppressed the authority of George, Archbishop of Alexandria, who had infamously persecuted and betrayed the people under his spiritual care, and that odious priest, who has been transformed by superstition into the renowned St. George of England, the patron of arms, of chivalry, and of the Garter, fell a victim to the just resentment of the Alexandrian multitude.

The Persian system of monarchy, introduced by Diocletian, was distasteful to the philosophic mind of Julian; he refused the title of lord and master, and attempted to restore in all its pristine simplicity the ancient government of the republic. In a campaign against the Persians he received a mortal wound, and died on June 26, 363.

The election of Jovian, the first of the domestics, by the acclamation of the soldiers, resulted in a disgraceful peace with the Persians, which aroused the anger and indignation of the Roman world, and the new emperor hardly survived this act of weakness for nine months (February 17, 364). The throne of the Roman world remained ten days without a master. At the end of that period the civil and military powers of the empire solemnly elected Valentinian as emperor at Nice in Bithynia.

The new Augustus divided the vast empire with his brother Valens, and this division marked the final separation of the western and eastern empires. This arrangement continued, until the death of Valentinian in 375, when the western empire was divided between his sons, Gratian and Valentinian II.

His reign had been notable for the stemming of the invasion of the Alemanni of Gaul, the incursions of the Burgundians and the Saxons, the restoration of Britain from the attacks of the Picts and Scots, the recovery of Africa by the emperor's general, Theodosius, and the diplomatic settlement with the approaching hordes of the Goths, who already swarmed upon the frontiers of the empire.

Under the three emperors the Roman world began to feel more severely the gradual pressure exerted by the hordes of barbarians that moved westward. In 376 the Goths, pursued by the Huns, who had come from the steppes of China into Europe, sought the protection of Valens, who succoured them by transporting them over the Danube into Roman territory. They repaid his clemency by uniting their arms with those of the Huns, and defeating and killing him at the battle of Hadrianople in 378.

To save the provinces from the ravages of the barbarians, Gratian appointed Theodosius, son of his father's general, emperor of the East, and the wisdom of his choice was justified by the success of one who added a new lustre to the title of Augustus. By prudent strategy, Theodosius divided and defeated the Goths, and compelled them to submit.

The sons of Theodosius, Arcadius and Honorius succeeded respectively to the government of the East and the West in 395. The symptoms of decay, which not even the wise rule of Theodosius had been able to remove, had grown more alarming. The luxury of the Romans was more shameless and dissolute, and as the increasing depredations of the barbarians had checked industry and diminished wealth, this profuse luxury must have been the result of that indolent despair which enjoys the present hour and declines the thoughts of futurity.

The secret and destructive poison of the age had affected the camps of the legions. The infantry had laid aside their armour, and, discarding their shields, advanced, trembling, to meet the cavalry of the Goths and the arrows of the barbarians, who easily overwhelmed the naked soldiers, no longer deserving the name of Romans. The enervated legionaries abandoned their own and the public defence, and their pusillanimous indolence may be considered the immediate cause of the downfall of the empire.

Ruin by Goth, Vandal, and Hun

The genius of Rome expired with Theodosius. His sons within three months had once more sharply divided the empire. At a time when the only hope of delaying its ruin depended on the firm union of the two sections, the subject of Arcadius and Honorius were instructed by their respective masters to view each other in a hostile light, to rejoice in their mutual calamity, and to embrace as their faithful allies the barbarians, whom they incited to invade the territories of their countrymen.

Alarmed at the insecurity of Rome, Honorius about this time fixed the imperial residence within the naturally fortified city of Ravenna - an example which was afterwards imitated by his feeble successors, the Gothic kings and the Exarchs; and till the middle of the eighth century Ravenna was considered as the seat of government and the capital of Italy.

The reign of Arcadius in the East marked the complete division of the Roman world. His subjects assumed the language and manners of Greeks, and his form of government was a pure and simple monarchy. The name of the Roman republic, which so long preserved a faint tradition of freedom, was confined to the Latin provinces. A series of internal disputes, both civil and religious, marked his career of power, and his reign may be regarded as notable if only for the election of St. John Chrysostom to the head of the church of Constantinople. Arcadius died in May 408, and was succeeded by his supposed son, Theodosius, then a boy of seven, the reins of power being first held by the prefect Anthemius, and afterwards by his sister Pulcheria, who governed the eastern empire - in fact, for nearly forty years.

The wisdom of Honorius, emperor of the West, in removing his capital to Ravenna, was soon justified by events. Alaric, king of the Goths, advanced in 408 to the gates of Rome, and completely blockaded the city. In the course of a long siege, thousands of Romans died of plague and famine, and only a heavy ransom relieved the citizens from their terrible situation in the year 409. In the same year Alaric again besieged Rome, after fruitless negotiations with Honorius, and his attempt once more proving successful, he created Attilus, prefect of the city, emperor. But the imprudent measures of his puppet sovereign exasperated Alaric. Attilus was formally deposed in 410, and the infuriated Goth besieged and sacked Rome, and ravaged Italy. The spoil that the barbarians carried away with them comprised nearly all the movable wealth of the city.

The ancient capital was devastated, the exquisite works of art destroyed, and nearly all the monuments of a glorious past sacrificed to the insatiate greed of the conquerors. Fire helped to complete the ruin wrought by the Goths, and it is not easy to compute the multitude of citizens who, from an honourable station and a prosperous fortune, were suddenly reduced to the miserable condition of captives and exiles.

The complete ruin of Italy was prevented by the death of Alaric in 410.

During the reign of Honorius, the Goths, Burgundians, and Franks were settled in Gaul. The maritime countries, between the Seine and the Loire, followed the example of Britain in 409, and threw off the yoke of the empire. Aquitaine, with its capital at Aries, received, under the title of the seven provinces, the right of convening an annual assembly for the management of its own affairs.

Honorius died in 423, and was succeeded by Valentinian III. His long reign was marked by a series of disasters, which foretold the rapidly approaching dissolution of the western empire.

Genseric, king of the Vandals, in 429 crossed into Africa, conquered the province, and set up in the depopulated territory, with Carthage as his capital, a new rule and government. Italy was filled with fugitives from Africa, and a barbarian race, which had issued from the frozen regions of the north, established their victorious reign over one of the fairest provinces of the empire. Two years later, in 441, a new and even more terrible danger threatened the empire.

The Goths and Vandals, flying before the Huns, had oppressed the western World. The hordes of these barbarians, now gathering strength in their union under their king, Attila, threatened an attack upon the eastern empire. In appearance their chieftain was terrible in the extreme; his portrait exhibits the genuine deformity of a modern Calmuck: a large head, a swarthy complexion, small, deep-seated eyes, a flat nose, a few hairs in the place of a beard, broad shoulders, and a short, square body of nervous strength, though of a disproportionate form. He had a custom of fiercely rolling his eyes, as if he wished to enjoy the terror which he inspired.

This savage hero, who had subdued Germany and Scythia, and almost exterminated the Burgundians of the Rhine, and had conquered Scandinavia, was able to bring into the field 700,000 barbarians. An unsuccessful raid into Persia induced him to turn his attention to the eastern empire, and the enervated troops of Theodosius the Younger dissolved before the fury of his onset. He ravaged up to the very gates of Constantinople, and only a humiliating treaty preserved his dominion to the "invincible Augustus" of the East.

After the death of Theodosius the Younger, and the accession of Marcian, the husband of Pulcheria, Attila threatened, in 450, both empires. An incursion of his hordes into Gaul was rendered abortive by the conduct of the patrician, Ætius, who, uniting all the various troops of Gaul and Germany, the Saxons, the Burgundians, the Franks, under their Merovingian prince, and the Visigoths under their king, Theodoric, after two important battles, induced the Huns to retreat from the field of Chalons. Attila, diverted from his purpose, turned into Italy, and the citizens of the various towns fled before the savage destroyer. Many families of Aquileia, Padua, and the adjacent towns, found a safe refuge in the neighbouring islands of the Adriatic, where their place of refuge evolved, in time, into the famous Republic of Venice.

Valentinian fled from Ravenna to Rome, prepared to desert his people and his empire. The fortitude of Ætius alone supported and preserved the tottering state. Leo, Bishop of Rome, in his sacerdotal robes, dared to demand the clemency of the savage king, and the intervention of St. Peter and St. Paul is supposed to have induced Attila to retire beyond the Danube, with the Princess Honoria as his bride. He did not long survive this last campaign, and in 453 he died, and was buried amidst all the savage pomp and grief of his subjects. His death resolved the bonds that had united the various nations of which his subjects were composed, and in a very few years domestic discord had extinguished the empire of the Huns.

Genseric, king of the Vandals, sacked and pillaged the ancient capital in June 455.

The vacant throne was filled by the nomination of Theodoric, king of the Goths. The senate of Rome bitterly opposed the elevation of this stranger, and though Avitus might have supported his title against the votes of an unarmed assembly, he fell immediately he incurred the resentment of Count Ricimer, one of the chief commanders of the barbarian troops who formed the military defence of Italy. At a distance from his Gothic allies, he was compelled to abdicate (October 16, 456), and Majorian was raised to fill his place.

The Last Emperor of the West

The successor of Avitus was a great and heroic character, such as sometimes arise in a degenerate age to vindicate the honour of the human species. In the ruin of the Roman world he loved his people, sympathised with their distress, and studied by judicial and effectual remedies to allay their sufferings. He reformed the most intolerable grievances of the taxes, attempted to restore and maintain the edifices of Rome, and to establish a new and healthier moral code. His military abilities and his fortune were not in proportion to his merits. An unsuccessful attempt against the Vandals to recover the lost provinces of Africa resulted in the loss of his fleet, and his return from this disastrous campaign terminated his reign. He was deposed by Ricimer, and five days later died of a reported dysentery, on August 7, 461.

At the command of Ricimer, the senate bestowed the imperial title on Libius Severus, who reigned as long as it suited his patron. The increasing difficulties, however, of the kingdom of Italy, due largely to the naval depredation of the Vandals, compelled Ricimer to seek the assistance of the emperor Leo, who had succeeded Marcian in the East in 457. Leo determined to extirpate the tyranny of the Vandals, and solemnly invested Anthemius with the diadem and purple of the West (467).

In 472, Ricimer raised the senator Olybrius to the purple, and, advancing from Milan, entered and sacked Rome and murdered Anthemius (July 11, 472). Forty days after this calamitous event, the tyrant Ricimer died of a painful disease, and two months later death also removed Olybrius.

The emperor Leo nominated Julius Nepos to the vacant throne. After suppressing a rival in the person of Glycerius, Julius succumbed, in 475, to a furious sedition of the barbarian confederates, who, under the command of the patrician Orestes, marched from Rome to Ravenna. The troops would have made Orestes emperor, but when he declined they consented to acknowledge his son Augustulus as emperor of the West.

The ambition of the patrician might have seemed satisfied, but he soon discovered, before the end of the first year, that he must either be the slave or the victim of his barbarian mercenaries. The soldiers demanded a third part of the land of Italy. Orestes rejected the audacious demand, and his refusal was favourable to the ambition of Odoacer, a bold barbarian, who assured his fellow-soldiers that if they dared to associate under his command they might extort the justice that had been denied to their dutiful petition. Orestes was executed, and Odoacer, resolving to abolish the useless and expensive office of the emperor of the West, compelled the unfortunate Augustulus to resign.

So ended, in the year 476, the empire of the West, and the last Roman emperor lived out his life in retirement in the Lucullan villa on the promontory of Misenum.

The Life of Samuel Johnson, LL.D.
by James Boswell
(London, 1788)

Samuel Johnson was one of the wonders of his age, a journalist, historian, friend and advisor to the mighty and lowly alike. But his companion Boswell was an odd sort of biographer – a frivolous Scottish aristocrat, lawyer and hearty supporter of the slave trade. Yet this is often said to be the greatest biography ever written, huge, detailed and full of far more personal and human detail than any such work before.

Abridged: JH/GH

I. Parentage and Education

Samuel Johnson was born at Lichfield, in Staffordshire, on September 18,1709, and was baptised on the day of his birth. His father was Michael Johnson, a native of Derbyshire, who settled in Lichfield as a bookseller and stationer. His mother was Sarah Ford, descended of an ancient race of substantial yeomanry in Warwickshire. They were well advanced in years when they were married, and never had more than two children, both sons - Samuel, their first born, whose various excellences I am to endeavour to record, and Nathaniel, who died in his twenty-fifth year.

Young Johnson had the misfortune to be much afflicted with the scrofula, or king's evil, which disfigured a countenance naturally well formed, and hurt his visual nerves so much that he did not see at all with one of his eyes, though its appearance was little different from that of the other. Yet, when he and I were travelling in the Highlands of Scotland, and I pointed out to him a mountain, which, I observed, resembled a cone, he corrected my inaccuracy by showing me that it was indeed pointed at the top, but that one side of it was larger than the other. And the ladies with whom he was acquainted agree that no man was more nicely and minutely critical in the elegance of female dress.

He was first taught to read English by Dame Oliver, a widow, who kept a school for young children in Lichfield. From his earliest years Johnson's superiority was perceived and acknowledged. He was from the beginning a king of men. His schoolfellow, Mr. Hector, has assured me that he never knew him corrected at school but for talking and diverting other boys from their business. He was uncommonly inquisitive; and his memory was so tenacious that he never forgot anything that he either heard or read. Mr. Hector remembers having recited to him eighteen verses, which, after a little pause, he repeated verbatim.

At the age of fifteen, he was removed to the school of Stourbridge, in Worcestershire, of which Mr. Wentworth was then master. He had no settled plan of life, and though he read a great deal in a desultory manner, he read only as chance and inclination directed him. "What I read," he told me, "were not voyages and travels, but all literature, sir. I had looked into many books which were not known at the universities, where they seldom read any books but what are put into their hands by their tutors; so that when I came to Oxford, Dr. Adams, now Master of Pembroke College, told me I was the best qualified for the university that he had ever known come there."

II Marriage and Settlement in London

Johnson left Pembroke College in the autumn of 1731, without taking a degree, having been a member of it little more than three years. In December of this year his father died.

In this forlorn state of his circumstances, he accepted an offer to be employed as usher in the school of Market Bosworth, in Leicestershire. But relinquished after a few months a situation which all his life afterwards he recollected with the strongest aversion and even a degree of horror. Among the acquaintances he made at this period was Mr. Porter, a mercer at Birmingham, whose widow he afterwards married. Though Mrs. Porter, now a widow, was double the age of Johnson, and her person and manner, as described to me by the late Mr. Garrick, were by no means pleasing to others, she must have had a superiority of understanding and talents, as she certainly inspired him with a more than ordinary passion. The marriage took place at Derby, on July 9, 1736.

He now set up a private academy, for which purpose he hired a large house well situated near his native city. In the "Gentleman's Magazine" for 1736 there is the following advertisement:

> "At Edial, near Lichfield, in Staffordshire, young gentlemen are boarded and taught the Latin and Greek languages, by SAMUEL JOHNSON."

But the only pupils that were put under his care were the celebrated David Garrick, his brother George, and a Mr. Offely, a young gentleman of fortune, who died early.

III. Poverty Stricken in London

Johnson's first performance in the "Gentleman's Magazine," which for many years was his principal source of employment and support, was a copy of Latin verses, in March, 1738, addressed to the editor. Thus was Johnson employed during some of the best years of his life.

Johnson felt the hardships of writing for bread. He was therefore willing to resume the office of a schoolmaster, and, an offer being made to him of the mastership of a school, provided he could obtain the degree of Master of Arts, Dr. Adams was applied to by a common friend to know whether that could be granted to him as a favour from the university of Oxford. But it was then thought too great a favour to be asked.

During the next five years, 1739-1743, Johnson wrote largely for the "Gentleman's Magazine," and supplied the account of the Parliamentary Debates from 1740, to 1743. It does not appear that he wrote anything of importance for the magazine in 1744. But he produced one work this year, fully sufficient to maintain the high reputation which he had acquired. This was "The Life of Richard Savage," a man of whom it is difficult to speak impartially without wondering that he was for some time the intimate companion of Johnson; for his character was marked by profligacy, insolence, and ingratitude; yet, he undoubtedly had a warm and vigorous, though unregulated mind.

IV. Preparation of the "Dictionary"

The year 1747 is distinguished as the epoch when Johnson's arduous and important work, his "Dictionary of the English Language," was announced to the world, by the publication of its "Plan or Prospectus."

The "Plan" was addressed to Philip Dormer, Earl of Chesterfield, then one of his majesty's principal secretaries of state, a nobleman who was very ambitious of literary distinction, and who, upon being informed of the design, had expressed himself in terms very favourable to its success. The plan had been put before him in manuscript For the mechanical part of the work Johnson employed, as he told me, six amanuenses.

In the "Gentleman's Magazine" for May, 1748, he-wrote a "Life of Roscommon," with notes, which he afterwards much improved and inserted amongst his "Lives of the English Poets." And this same year he formed a club in Ivy Lane, Paternoster Row, with a view to enjoy literary discussion.

In January, 1749, he published "Vanity of Human Wishes, being the Tenth Satire of Juvenal Imitated"; and on February 6 Garrick brought out a tragedy of his at Drury Lane. Dr. Adams was present at the first night of "Irene," and gave me the following account. "Before the curtain drew up, there were catcalls and whistling, which alarmed Johnson's friends. The prologue, which was 'written by himself in a manly strain, soothed the audience, and the play went off tolerably till it came to the conclusion, when Mrs. Pritchard, the heroine of the piece, was to be strangled on the stage, and was to speak two lines with the bow-string around her neck. The audience cried out 'Murder! Murder!' She several times attempted to speak, but in vain. At last she was obliged to go off the stage alive." This passage was afterwards struck out, and she was carried off to be put to death behind the scenes, as the play now has it.

On occasion of his play being brought upon the stage, Johnson had a fancy that as a dramatic author his dress should be more gay than he ordinarily wore; he therefore appeared behind the scenes, and even in one of the side boxes, in a scarlet waistcoat, with rich gold lace and a gold laced hat.

V. "The Rambler" and New Acquaintance

In 1750 Johnson came forth in the character for which he was eminently qualified, a majestic teacher of moral and religious wisdom. The vehicle he chose was that of a periodical paper, which he knew had, upon former occasions - those of the "Tattler," "Spectator," and "Guardian" - been employed with great success.

The first paper of "The Rambler" was published on Tuesday, March 20, 1750, and its author was enabled to continue it without interruption, every Tuesday and Friday, till Saturday, March 17, 1752, on which day it closed. During all this time he received assistance on four occasions only.

Posterity will be astonished when they are told, upon the authority of Johnson himself, that many of these discourses, which we should suppose had been laboured with all the slow attention of literary leisure, were written in haste as the moments pressed, without even being read over by him before they were printed. Such was his peculiar promptitude of mind. He was wont to say, "A man may write at any time if he will set himself doggedly to it."

The circle of Johnson's friends, indeed, at this time was extensive and various. To trace his acquaintance with each particular person were unprofitable. But exceptions are to be made, one of which must be a friend so eminent as Sir Joshua Reynolds, with whom he maintained an uninterrupted intimacy to the last hour of his life.

VI. Lord Chesterfield and the "Dictionary"

In 1753 and 1754 Johnson relieved the drudgery of his "Dictionary" by taking an active part in the composition of "The Adventurer," a new periodical paper which his friends Dr. Hawkesworth and Dr. Bathurst had commenced.

Towards the end of the latter year, when the "Dictionary" was on the eve of publication, Lord Chesterfield, who, ever since the plan of this great work had been addressed to him, had treated its author with cold indifference, attempted to conciliate him by writing to papers in "The World" in recommendation of the undertaking. This courtly device failed of its effect, and Johnson, indignant that Lord Chesterfield should, for a moment, imagine that he could

be the dupe of such an artifice, wrote him that famous letter, dated February 7, 1755, which I have already given to the public. I will quote one paragraph.

> "Is not a patron, my lord, one who looks with unconcern on a man struggling for life in the water, and, when he has reached ground, encumbers him with help? The notice which you have been pleased to take of my labours, had it been early, had been kind; but it has been delayed till I am indifferent, and cannot enjoy it."

Thinking it desirable that the two letters intimating possession of the master's degree should, for the credit both of Oxford and of Johnson, appear after his name on the title page of his "Dictionary," his friends obtained for him from his university this mark of distinction by diploma; and the "Dictionary" was published on April 15 in two volumes folio.

It won him much honour at home and abroad; the Academy of Florence sent him their "Vocabulario," and the French Academy their "Dictionnaire." But it had not set him above the necessity of "making provision for the day that was passing over him," for he had spent during the progress of the work all the money which it had brought him.

He was compelled, therefore, to contribute to the monthly periodicals, and during 1756 he wrote a few essays for "The Universal Visitor," and superintended and contributed largely to another publication entitled "The Literary Magazine, or Universal Review."

His defence of tea was indeed made *con amore*. I suppose no person ever enjoyed with more relish the infusion of that fragrant leaf than Johnson. The quantities which he drank of it at all hours were so great that his nerves must have been uncommonly strong not to have been extremely relaxed by such an intemperate use of it.

On April 15, 1758, he began a new periodical paper entitled "The Idler," which came out every Saturday in a weekly newspaper called "The Universal Chronicle, or Weekly Gazette." In 1759, in the month of January, Johnson's mother died, at the great age of ninety, an event which deeply affected him, for his reverential affection for her was not abated by years. Soon after, he wrote his "Rasselas, Prince of Abyssinia," in order that with the profits he might defray the expenses of her funeral, and pay some little debts which she had left.

Early in 1762, having been represented to the king as a very learned and good person, without any certain provision, his majesty was pleased to grant him a pension of £300 a year.

VII. Boswell's First Meeting with Johnson

It was Mr. Thomas Davies, the actor, turned bookseller, who introduced me to Johnson. On Monday, May 16, 1763. I was sitting in Mr. Davies's back parlour at 8 Russell Street, Covent Garden, after having drunk tea with him and Mrs. Davies, when Johnson unexpectedly came into the shop. Mr. Davies mentioned my name, and respectfully introduced me to him. I was much agitated at my long-wished-for introduction to the sage, and recollecting his prejudice against the Scotch, of which I had heard much, I said to Davies, "Don't tell where I come from - - " "From Scotland!" cried Davies roguishly. "Mr. Johnson," said I, "I do, indeed, come from Scotland, but I cannot help it". But with that quickness of wit for which he was so known he remarked, "That, sir, I find, is what a very great many of your countrymen cannot help." This stroke, and another check which I subsequently received, stunned me a good deal; but eight days later I boldly repaired to his chambers on the first floor of No. 1, Inner Temple Lane, and he received me very courteously. His morning dress was sufficiently uncouth; his brown suit of clothes looked very rusty. He had on a little, old, shrivelled, unpowdered wig, which was too small for his head; his shirt-neck and knees of his breeches were loose; his black worsted stockings ill-drawn up; and he had a pair of unbuckled shoes by way of slippers. But all these slovenly particularities were forgotten the moment that he began to talk.

VIII. Tours in the Hebrides and in Wales

His friend, the Rev. Dr. Maxwell, speaks as follows on Johnson's general mode of life: "About twelve o'clock I commonly visited him, and frequently found him in bed, or declaiming over his tea, which he drank very plentifully. He generally had a levée of morning visitors, chiefly men of letters - Hawkesworth, Goldsmith, Murphy, etc., etc., and sometimes learned ladies, particularly I remember a French lady of wit and fashion doing him the honour of a visit. He seemed to me to be considered as a kind of public oracle, whom everybody thought they had a right to visit and to consult; and doubtless they were well rewarded."

On April 23, 1773, I was nominated by Johnson for membership of the Literary Club, and a week later I was elected to the society. There I saw for the first time Mr. Edmund Burke, whose splendid talents had made me ardently wish for his acquaintance.

This same year Johnson made, in my company, his visit to Scotland, which lasted from August 14, on which day he arrived, till November 22, when he set out on his return to London; and I believe one hundred days were never passed by any men in a more vigorous exertion. His various adventures, and the force and vivacity of his mind, as exercised during this peregrination, upon innumerable topics, have been faithfully, and to the best of my ability, displayed in my "Journal of a Tour to the Hebrides."

On his return to London his humane, forgiving dispositions were put to a pretty strong test by a liberty which Mr. Thomas Davies had taken, which was to publish two volumes, entitled "Miscellaneous and Fugitive Pieces," which he advertised in the newspapers, "By the Author of the Rambler." In some of these Johnson had no concern whatever. He was at first very angry, but, upon consideration of his poor friend's narrow circumstances, and that he meant no harm, he soon relented.

This year, too, my great friend again came out as a politician, for parliament having been dissolved in September, and Johnson published a short political pamphlet, entitled "The Patriot," addressed to the electors of Great Britain. It was written with energetic vivacity; and except those passages in which it endeavours to vindicate the glaring outrage of the House of Commons in the case of the Middlesex election and to justify the attempt to reduce our fellow-subjects in America to unconditional submission, it contained an admirable display of the properties of a real patriot, in the original and genuine sense.

IX. Johnson's Courage and Fear of Death

The "Rambler's" own account of our tour in the Hebrides was published in 1775 under the title of "A journey to the Western Islands of Scotland," and soon involved its author, who had expressed his disbelief in the authenticity of Ossian's poems, in a controversy with Mr. Macpherson. Johnson called for the production of the old manuscripts from which Mr. Macpherson said that he had copied the poems. Mr. Macpherson, exasperated by this scepticism, replied in words that are generally said to have been of a nature very different from the language of literary contest.

Mr. Macpherson knew little the character of Dr. Johnson if he supposed that he could be easily intimidated, for no man was ever more remarkable for personal courage. He had, indeed, an awful dread of death, or, rather, "of something after death"; and he once said to me, "The fear of death is so much natural to man that the whole of life is but keeping away the thoughts of it," and confessed that "he had never had a moment in which death was not terrible to him." But his fear was from reflection, his courage natural. Many instances of his resolution may be mentioned. One day, at Mr. Beauclerk's house in the country, when two large dogs were fighting, he went up to them and beat them till they separated.

My revered friend had long before indulged most unfavourable sentiments of our fellow-subjects in America. As early as 1769 he had said to them: "Sir, they are a race of convicts, and ought to be grateful for anything we allow them short of hanging." He had recently published, at the desire of those in power, a pamphlet entitled "Taxation no Tyranny; an Answer to the Resolutions and Address of the American Congress." Of this performance I avoided to talk with him, having formed a clear and settled opinion against the doctrine of its title.

In the autumn Dr. Johnson went to Ashbourne to France with Mr. and Mrs. Thrale and Mr. Baretti, which lasted about two months. But he did not get into any higher acquaintance; and Foote, who was at Paris at the time with him, used to give a description of my friend while there and of French astonishment at his figure, manner, and dress, which was abundantly ludicrous. He was now a Doctor of Laws of Oxford, his university having conferred that degree on him by diploma in the spring.

X. Johnson's "Seraglio"

A circumstance which could not fail to be very pleasing to Johnson occurred in 1777. The tragedy of "Sir Thomas Overbury," written by his early companion in London, Richard Savage, was brought out, with alterations, at Covent Garden Theatre; and the prologue to it, written by Mr. Richard Brinsley Sheridan, introduced an elegant compliment to Johnson on his "Dictionary." Johnson was pleased with young Mr. Sheridan's liberality of sentiment, and willing to show that though estranged from the father he could acknowledge the brilliant merit of the son, he proposed him, and secured his election, as a member of the Literary Club.

In the autumn Dr. Johnson went to Ashbourne to stop with his friend, the Rev. Dr. Taylor, and I joined him there. During this visit he put into my hands the whole series of his writings in behalf of the Rev. Dr. William Dodd, who, having been chaplain-in-ordinary to his majesty, and celebrated as a very popular preacher, was this year convicted and executed for forging a bond on his former pupil, the young Earl of Chesterfield. Johnson certainly made extraordinary exertions to save Dodd. He wrote several petitions and letters on the subject, and composed for the unhappy man his "Speech to the Recorder of London," at the Old Bailey, when sentence of death was about to be pronounced upon him.

In 1778, I arrived in London on March 18, and next day met Dr. Johnson at his old friend's, in Dean's Yard, for Dr. Taylor was a prebendary of Westminster. On Friday, March 2d, I found him at his own house, sitting with Mrs. Williams, and was informed that the room allotted to me three years previously was now appropriated to a charitable purpose, Mrs. Desmoulins, daughter of Johnson's godfather Dr. Swinfen, and, I think, her daughter, and a Miss Carmichael, being all lodged in it. Such was his humanity, and such his generosity, that Mrs. Desmoulins herself told me he allowed her half-a-guinea a week. Unfortunately his "Seraglio," as he sometimes suffered me to call his group of females, were perpetually jarring with one another. He thus mentions them, "Williams hates everybody; Levett hates Desmoulins, and does not love Williams - Desmoulins hates them both; Poll (Miss Carmichael) loves none of them."

On January 20, 1779, Johnson lost his old friend Garrick, and this same year he gave the world a luminous proof that the vigour of his mind in all its faculties, whether memory, judgement, and imagination, was not in the least abated, by publishing the first four volumes of his "Prefaces, Biographical and Critical, to the Most Eminent of the English Poets." The remaining volumes came out in 1781.

In 1780 the world was kept in impatience for the completion of his "Lives of the Poets," upon which he was employed so far as his indolence allowed him to labour.

This year - on March 11 - Johnson lost another old friend in Mr. Topham Beauclerk, of whom he said: "No man ever was so free when he was going to say a good thing, from a look that expressed that it was coming; or, when he had said it, from a look that expressed that it had come."

XI. Johnson's Humanity.

I was disappointed in my hopes of seeing Johnson in 1780, but I was able to come to London in the spring of 1781, and on Tuesday, March 20, I met him in Fleet Street, walking, or, rather, indeed, moving along - for his peculiar march is thus correctly described in a short life of him published very soon after his death: "When he walked the streets, what with the constant roll of his head, and the concomitant motion of his body, he appeared to make his way by that motion, independent of his feet." That he was often much stared at while he advanced in this manner may easily be believed, but it was not safe to make sport of one so robust as he was.

I waited on him next evening, and he gave me a great portion of his original manuscript of his "Lives of the Poets," which he had preserved for me.

I found on visiting his friend, Mr. Thrale, that he was now very ill, and had removed - I suppose by the solicitation of Mrs. Thrale - to a house in Grosvenor Square. I was sorry to see him sadly changed in his appearance. He died shortly after.

He told me I might now have the pleasure to see Dr. Johnson drink wine again, for he had lately returned to it. When I mentioned this to Johnson, he said: "I drink it now sometimes, but not socially." The first evening that I was with him at Thrale's, I observed he poured a large quantity of it into a glass, and swallowed it greedily. Everything about his character and manners was forcible and violent; there never was any moderation; many a day did he fast, many a year did he refrain from wine; but when he did eat, it was voraciously; when he did drink wine, it was copiously. He could practice abstinence, but not temperance.

"I am not a severe man," Johnson once said; "as I know more of mankind I expect less of them, and am ready now to call a man a good man upon easier terms than I was formerly."

This kind indulgence - extended towards myself when overcome by wine - had once or twice a pretty difficult trial, but on my making an apology, I always found Johnson behave to me with the most friendly gentleness. In fact, Johnson was not severe, but he was pugnacious, and this pugnacity and roughness he displayed most conspicuously in conversation. He could not brook appearing to be worsted in argument, even when, to show the force and dexterity of his talents, he had taken the wrong side. When, therefore, he perceived that his opponent gained ground, he had recourse to some sudden mode of robust sophistry. Once when I was pressing upon him with visible advantage, he stopped me thus: "My dear Boswell, let's have no more of this. You'll make nothing of it. I'd rather have you whistle a Scotch tune."

Goldsmith used to say, in the witty words of one of Cibber's comedies, "There is no arguing with Johnson, for when his pistol misses fire, he knocks you down with the butt end of it."

His love of little children, which he discovered upon all occasions, calling them "pretty dears," and giving them sweetmeats, was an undoubted proof of the real humanity and gentleness of his disposition. His uncommon kindness to his servants, and serious concern, not only for their comfort in this world, but their happiness in the next, was another unquestionable evidence of what all who were intimately acquainted with him knew to be true. Nor would it be just, under this head, to omit the fondness that he showed for animals which he had taken under his protection. I never shall forget the indulgence with which he treated Hodge, his cat, for whom he himself used to go out and buy oysters, lest the servants, having that trouble, should take a dislike to the poor creature.

XII. The Last Year

In April, 1783, Johnson had a paralytic stroke, which deprived him, for a time, of the powers of speech. But he recovered so quickly that in July he was able to make a visit to Mr. Langton, at Rochester, where he passed about a fortnight, and made little excursions as easily as at any time of his life. In August he went as far as the neighbourhood of Salisbury, to Heale, the seat of William Bowles, Esq.; and it was while he was here that he had a letter from his physician, Dr. Brocklesby, acquainting him of the death of Mrs. Williams, which affected him a good deal.

In the end of 1783, in addition to his gout and his catarrhous cough, he was seized with a spasmodic asthma of such violence that he was confined to the house in great pain, being sometimes obliged to sit all night in his chair, a recumbent posture being so hurtful to his respiration that he could not endure lying in bed; and there came upon him at the same time that oppressive and fatal disease of dropsy. His cough he used to cure by taking laudanum and syrup of poppies, and he was a great believer in the advantages of being bled. But this year the very severe winter aggravated

his complaints, and the asthma confined him to the house for more than three months; though he got almost complete relief from the dropsy by natural evacuation in February.

On Wednesday, May 5, 1784 - the last year of Dr. Johnson's life - I arrived in London for my spring visit; and next morning I had the pleasure to find him greatly recovered. He had now a great desire to go to Oxford, as his first jaunt after his illness; we talked of it for some days, and on June 3 the Oxford post-coach took us up at Bolt Court, and we spent an agreeable fortnight with Dr. Adams at Pembroke College.

The anxiety of his friends to preserve so estimable a life made them plan for him a retreat from the severity of a British winter to the mild climate of Italy; and, after consulting with Sir Joshua Reynolds, I wrote to Lord Thurlow, the Lord Chancellor, for such an addition to Johnson's income as would enable him to bear the expense. Lord Thurlow at first made a very favourable reply; but eventually he had to confess that his application had been unsuccessful.

On Wednesday, June 30, I dined with him, for the last time, at Sir Joshua Reynolds's, no other company being present; and on July 2 I left London for Scotland.

On December 8 and 9 he made his will; and on Monday, December 13, he expired about seven o'clock in the evening, with so little apparent pain that his attendants hardly perceived when his dissolution took place. A week later he was buried in Westminster Abbey, his old schoolfellow, Dr. Taylor, reading the service.

I trust I shall not be accused of affectation when I declare that I find myself unable to express all that I felt upon the loss of such a "Guide, Philosopher, and Friend." I shall, therefore, not say one word of my own, but adopt those of an eminent friend, which he uttered with an abrupt felicity: "He has made a chasm, which not only nothing can fill up, but which nothing has a tendency to fill up. Johnson is dead. Let us go to the next best: there is nobody; no man can be said to put you in mind of Johnson."

Introduction to the
Principles of Morals and Legislation
by Jeremy Bentham
(London, 1789)

Jeremy Bentham trained as a lawyer, but soon became disillusioned with the chicanery of legal practice and retired to Westminster, where, for nearly forty years he daily churned out manuscripts promoting the bold new ideas of individual freedom, separation of church and state, equality of the sexes, the abolition of slavery and physical punishment, the right to divorce, free trade, and the toleration of homosexuality. He made the phrase "*the greatest happiness to the greatest number*" (the 'principle of utility') into both an ethical formula and a political rallying-cry to lead the emerging movement for social reform. Bentham willed his body to be dissected and preserved at University College, London, where it was kept, dressed in his clothes, in a glass fronted mahogany case.

Abridged: GH

MANKIND is governed by pain and pleasure. Utility is that property in anything which tends to produce happiness in the party concerned, whether an individual or a community. The principle of utility makes utility the criterion for approval or disapproval of every kind of action. An act which conforms to this principle is one which ought to be done, or is not one which ought not to be done; is right, or, at least, not wrong. There is no other criterion possible which cannot ultimately be reduced to the personal sentiment of the individual.

The sources or sanctions of pleasure and pain are four - the physical, in the ordinary course of nature; political, officially imposed; moral or popular, imposed by public opinion; and religion. Pains under the first head are calamities; under the other three are punishments. Under the first three heads they concern the present life only. The second, third and the fourth, as concerns this life, operate through the first; but the first operates independently of the others.

Pleasures and pains, then, are the instruments with which the legislator has to work; he must, therefore, be able to gauge their relative values. These depend primarily and simply on four things - intensity, duration, certainty or uncertainty, propinquity or remoteness. Secondarily, on fecundity, the consequent probable multiplication of the like sensations; and purity, the improbability of consequent contrary sensations. Finally, on extent - the number of persons pleasurably or painfully affected. All these being weighed together, if the pleasurable tendency predominates, the act is good; if the painful, bad.

Pleasures and pains are either simple or complex - i.e., resolvable into several simple pleasures, and may be enumerated; as those of the senses, of wealth, of piety, of benevolence, of malevolence, of association, of imagination. Different persons are sensible to the same pleasure in different degrees, and the sensibility of the individual varies under different circumstances. Circumstances affecting sensibility are various - such as health, strength, sex, age, education; they may be circumstances of the body, of the mind, of the inclinations.

Their influence can be reckoned approximately, but should be taken into consideration so far as is practicable.

The legislator and the judge are concerned with the existing causes of pleasure and pain, but of pain rather than pleasure - the mischiefs which it is desired to prevent, and the punishments by which it is sought to prevent them - and for the due apportionment of the latter they should have before them the complete list of punishments and of circumstances affecting sensibility. By taking the two together - with one list or the other for basis, preferably the punishment list - a classification of appropriate penalties is attainable.

An analytical summary of the circumstances affecting sensibility will distinguish as secondary - i.e. as acting not immediately but mediately through the primary - sex, age, station in life, education, climate, religion. The others, all primary, are connate - viz. radical frame of mind and body - or adventitious. The adventitious are personal or exterior. The personal concern a man's disposition of body or mind, or his actions; exterior, the things or persons he is concerned with.

The business of government is to promote the happiness of society by rewarding and punishing, especially by punishing acts tending to diminish happiness. An act demands punishment in proportion to its tendency to diminish happiness - i.e. as the sum of its consequences does so. Only such consequences are referred to as influence the production of pain or pleasure. The intention, as involving other consequences, must also be taken into consideration. And the intention depends on the state of the will and of the understanding as to the circumstances - consciousness, unconsciousness, or false consciousness of them.

Hence with regard to each action we have to consider

(1) the act itself,
(2) the circumstances,
(3) the intentionality,
(4) the attendant consciousness, and also
(5) the motive, and
(6) the general disposition indicated.

Acts are positive and negative - i.e. of commission and omission, or forbearance; external or corporal, and internal or mental; transitive, affecting some body other than the agent's, or intransitive; transient or continued (mere repetition is not the same as habit). Circumstances are material when visibly related to the consequences in point of causality, directly or indirectly. They may be criminative, or exculpative, or aggravative, or evidential.

The intention may regard the act itself only, or its consequence also - for instance, you may touch a man intentionally and by doing so cause his death unintentionally. But you cannot intend the consequences - though you may desire them - without intending the action. The consequences may be intended directly or indirectly, and may or may not be the only thing intended. The intention is good or bad as the consequences intended are good or bad.

But these actually depend on the circumstances which are independent of the intention; here the important point is the man's consciousness of the circumstances, which are objects not of the will, but of the understanding. If he is conscious of the circumstances and of their materiality, the act is advised; if not, unadvised. Unadvisedness may be due either to heedlessness or to misapprehension.

And here we may remark that we may speak of a bad intention, though the motive was good, if the consequences intended were bad, and vice versa. In this sense also, the intention may be innocent - that is, not bad, without being positively good.

Of motives, we are concerned with practical motives only, not those which are purely speculative. Those are either internal or external; either events in esse, or events in prospect. The immediate motive is an internal motive in esse- -an awakened pleasure or pain at the prospect of pleasure or pain. All others are comparatively remote.

Now, since the motive is always primarily to produce some pleasure or prevent some pain, and since pleasure is identical with good and pain with evil, it follows that no motive is in itself bad. The motive is good if it tends to produce a balance of pleasure; bad, if a balance of pain. Thus any and every motive may produce actions good, indifferent, or bad. Hence, in cataloguing motives, we must employ only neutral terms, i.e. not such as are associated with goodness - as piety, honour - or with badness - as lust, avarice.

The motives, of course, correspond to the various pleasures as previously enumerated. They may be classified as good, bad, or indifferent according as their consequences are more commonly good, bad, or indifferent; but the dangers of such classification are obvious. In fact, we cannot affirm goodness, badness, or indifference of motive, except in the particular instance.

A better classification is into the social - including good will, love of reputation, desire of amity, religion; dissocial - displeasure; self-regarding - physical desire, pecuniary interest, love of power, self-preservation.

Of all these, the dictates of good will are the surest of coinciding with utility, since utility corresponds precisely to the widest and best-advised good will. Even here, however, there may be failure, since benevolence towards one group may clash with benevolence towards another. Next stands love of reputation, which is less secure, since it may lead to asceticism and to hypocrisy. Third comes the desire of amity, valuable as the sphere in which amity is sought is extended, but also liable to breed insincerity. Religion would stand first of all if we all had a correct perception of the divine goodness; but not when we conceive of God as malevolent or capricious; and, as a matter of fact, our conception of the Deity is controlled by our personal biases.

The self-regarding motives are, ex hypothesi, not so closely related to utility as the social motives, and the dissocial motives manifestly stand at the bottom of the scale. In respect to any particular action there may be a conflict of motives, some impelling towards it, others restraining from it; and any motive may come in conflict with any other motive.

It will be found hereafter that in the case of some offences the motive is material in the highest degree, and in others wholly immaterial; in some cases easy, and in others impossible to gauge.

Goodness or badness, then, cannot be predicated of the motive. What is good or bad in the man when actuated by one motive or another is his disposition, or permanent attitude of mind, which is good or bad as tending to produce effects beneficial to the community. It is to be considered in regard to its influence on (1) his own happiness; (2) other people's. The legislator is concerned with it so far as it is mischievous to others. A man is held to be of a mischievous disposition when it is presumed that he inclines to acts which appear to him mischievous. Here it is that 'intentionality' and 'consciousness' come in.

Where the tendency of the act is good and the motive is a social one, a good disposition is indicated; where the tendency is bad and the motive is self- regarding, a bad disposition is indicated. Otherwise, the indication of good or bad disposition may be very dubious or non-existent. Now, our problem is to measure the depravity of a man's disposition, which may be defined as the sum of his intentions. The causes of intentions are motives. The social motives may be called tutelary, as tending to restrain from mischievous intentions; but any motive may become tutelary on occasion. Love of ease, and desire of self-preservation, in the form of fear of punishment, are apt to be tutelary motives.

Now we can see that the strength of a temptation equals the sum of the impelling motives, minus the sum of the tutelary motives. Hence, the more susceptible a man is to the standing tutelary motives, the less likely is he to yield to temptation; in other words, the less depraved is his disposition. Hence, given the strength of the temptation, the mischievousness of the disposition is as the apparent mischievousness of the act. Given the apparent mischievousness of the act, the less the temptation yielded to the greater the depravity of disposition; but the stronger the temptation, the less conclusive is the evidence of depravity. It follows that the penalty should be increased - i.e. the fear of punishment should be artificially intensified, in proportion as, apart from that fear, the temptation is stronger.

We now come to consequences. The mischief of the act is the sum of its mischievous consequences, primary and secondary. The primary mischief sub- divides into original, i.e. to the sufferer in the first instance; and derivative, to the definite persons who suffer as a direct consequence, whether through their interest, or merely through sympathy.

The secondary mischiefs, affecting not specific persons but the community, are actual danger, or alarm - the apprehension of pain. For the occurrence of the act points to the possibility of its repetition; weakening the influence both of the political and of the moral sanction. An act of which the primary consequences are mischievous may have secondary beneficial consequences which altogether outweight the primary mischief - e.g. the legal punishment of crime. The circumstances influencing the secondary mischiefs of alarm and danger are the intentionality, the consciousness, the motive and the disposition; danger depending on the real, and alarm on the apparent, state of mind, though the real and the apparent coincide more commonly than not.

Between the completely intentional and completely unintentional act there are various stages, depending on the degree of consciousness, as explained above. The excellence of the motive does not obliterate the mischievousness of the act; nor vice versa; but the mischief may be aggravated by a bad motive, as pointing to greater likelihood of repetition.

Punishment, being primarily mischievous, is out of place when groundless, inefficacious, unprofitable, or needless. Punishment is inefficacious when it is ex post facto, or extra-legal, or secret; or in the case of irresponsible (including intoxicated) persons; and also so far as the intention of the act was incomplete, or where the act was actually or practically under compulsion. It is unprofitable when under ordinary circumstances the evils of the punishment outweigh those of the offence. It is needless when the end in view can be as well or better attained otherwise.

Now, the aim of the legislator is (1) to prevent mischief altogether; (2) to minimise the inclination to do mischief; (3) to make the prevention cheap. Hence (1) the punishment must outweigh the profit of the offence to the doer; (2) the greater the mischief, the greater the expense worth incurring to prevent it; (3) alternative offences which are not equally mischievous, as robbery and robbery with murder, must not be equally punished; (4) the punishment must not be excessive, and therefore should take into account the circumstances influencing sensibility; (5) so

also must the weakness of the punishment due to its remoteness, and the impelling force of habit.

The properties of punishment necessary to its adjustment to a particular offence are these: (1) variability in point of quantity, so that it shall be neither excessive nor deficient; (2) equality, so that when applied in equal degree it shall cause equal pain - e.g. banishment may mean much to one man, little to another; (3) commensurability with other punishments; (4) characteristicalness, or appropriateness; (5) exemplarity - it must not seem less than it is in fact; (6) frugality - none of the pain it causes is to be wasted. Minor desirable qualities are (7) subserviency to reformation of character; (8) efficiency in disabling from mischief; (9) subserviency to compensation; (10) popularity, i.e. accordant to common approbation; (11) remissibility.

An offence - a punishable act - is constituted such by the community; though it ought not to be an offence unless contrary to utility, it may be so. It is assumed to be a detrimental act; detrimental therefore to some person or persons, whether the offender himself or other assignable persons, or to persons not assignable.

Offences against assignable persons other than the offender form the first class; offences against individuals, or private offences, or private extra- regarding offences. The second class is formed by semi-public offences, i.e. not against assignable individuals, nor the community at large, but a separable group in the community, e.g. a class or a locality. The third class are those which are simply self-regarding; the fourth, against the community at large; the fifth, multiform or heterogeneous, comprising falsehood and breaches of trust.

The first class may be subdivided into offences against

(1) the person,

(2) reputation,

(3) to property,

(4) condition - i.e. the serviceableness to the individual or other persons,

(5) person and property together,

(6) person and reputation.

The second, semi-public, class, being acts which endanger a portion of the community, are those operating through calamity, or of mere delinquency. The latter are subdivided on the same lines as private offences. So with the third or self-regarding class.

In class four, public offences fall under eleven divisions:

(1) offences against external security - i.e. from foreign foes;

(2) against justice - i.e. the execution of justice;

(3) against the preventive branch of police;

(4) against the public force - i.e. military control;

(5) against increase of national felicity;

(6) against public wealth - i.e. the exchequer;

(7) against population;

(8) against national wealth - i.e. enrichment of the population;

(9) against sovereignty;

(10) against religion;

(11) against national interests in general.

In class five, falsehood comprises simple falsehoods, forgery, personation and perjury; again distributable like the private offences. In the case of trusts, there are two parties - the trustee and the beneficiary. Offences under this head cannot, for various reasons, be conveniently referred to offences against property or condition, which also must be kept separate from each other. As regards the existence of a trust: as against the trustee, offences are (1) wrongful non-investment of trust, and wrongful interception of trust, where the trusteeship is to his benefit; or (2) where it is troublesome, wrongful imposition of trust. Both may similarly be offences against the beneficiary. As regards the exercise of the trust, we have negative breach of trust, positive breach of trust, abuse of trust, disturbance of trust, and bribery.

We may now distribute class one - offences against the individual - into genera; to do so with the other classes would be superfluous. Simple offences against the person are actions referring to his actual person, body or mind, or external objects affecting his happiness. These must take effect either through his will, or not. In the former case, either by constraint, or restraint, confinement, or banishment. In any case the effect will be mortal or not mortal; if not mortal, reparable or irreparable injury when corporal, sufferance when mental. So the list stands - simple and irreparable corporal injuries, simple injurious restraint or constraint, wrongful confinement or banishment, homicide or menacement, actual or apprehended mental injuries.

Against reputation the genera of offences are (1) defamation, (2) vilification. Of offences against property, simple in their effects, whether by breach of trust or otherwise, the genera are: wrongful non-investment, interception, divestment, usurpation, investment of property; wrongful withholding of services, destruction, occupation, or detainment, embezzlement, theft, defraudment, extortion.

Of complex offences against person and reputation together: corporal insults, insulting menacement, seduction, and forcible seduction, simple lascivious injuries. Against person and property together: forcible interception, divestment, usurpation, investment, or destruction of property, forcible occupation of movables, forcible entry, forcible detainment of immovables robbery.

As to offences against condition: conditions are either domestic or civil; domestic relations are either purely natural, purely instituted, or mixed. Of the first, we are concerned only with the marital, parental and filial relations. Under the second head are the relations of master and servant, guardian and ward. In the case of master and servants, the headings of offences are much like those against property. Guardianship is required in the cases of infancy and insanity; again the list of offences is similar. The parental and filial relations, so far as they are affected by institutions, comprise those both of master and servant,

and of guardian and ward; so that the offences are correspondent.

The relation of husband and wife also comprises those of master and guardian to servant and ward. But there are further certain reciprocal services which are the subject of the marital contract, by which polygamy and adultery are constituted offences in Christian countries, and also the refusal of conjugal rights.

From domestic conditions we pass to civil.

Eliminating all those which can be brought under the categories of trusts and domestic conditions, there remain conditions constituted by beneficial powers over things, beneficial rights to things, rights to services, and by corresponding duties; and between these and property there is no clear line of demarcation, yet we can hit upon some such conditions as separable. Such are rank and profession which entail specific obligations and rights - these are not property but conditions; as distinguished from other exclusive rights bestowed by the law, concerned with saleable articles (e.g. copyright), which convey not conditions, but property. So, naturalisation conveys the conditions of a natural born subject.

Public offences are to be catalogued in a manner similar to private offences.

My object has been to combine intelligibility with precision; technical terms lack the former quality, popular terms the latter. Hence the plan of the foregoing analysis has been to take the logical whole constituted by the sum of possible offences, dissect it in as many directions as were necessary, and carry the process down to the point where each idea could be expressed in current phraseology. Thus it becomes equally applicable to the legal concerns of all countries or systems.

The advantages of this method are: it is convenient for the memory, gives room for general propositions, points out the reason of the law, and is applicable to the laws of all nations. Hence we are able to characterise the five classes of offences. Thus, of private offences, we note that they are primarily against assignable individuals, admit of compensation and retaliation, and so on; of semi-public offences, that they are not against assignable individuals and, with self-regarding offences, admit of neither compensation nor retaliation; a series of generalisations respecting each class can be added.

The relation between penal jurisprudence and private ethics must be clarified. Both are concerned with the production of happiness. A man's private ethics are concerned with his duty to himself and to his neighbour; prudence, probity and beneficence. Those cases described as unmeet for punishment are all within the ethical, but outside the legislative, sphere, except the 'groundless' cases, which are outside both. The special field of private ethics is among the cases where punishment is 'unprofitable' or 'inefficacious,' notably those which are the concern of prudence. So with the rules of beneficence; but beneficence might well be made compulsory in a greater degree than it is. The special sphere of legislation, however, lies in the field of probity.

A work of jurisprudence is either expository of what the law is, or censorial, showing what it should be. It may relate to either local or universal jurisprudence; but if expository can hardly be more than local. It may be internal, or international; if internal, it may be national or provincial, historical or living; it may be divided into statutory and customary, into civil and penal or criminal.

The Rights of Man
by Thomas Paine
(London, 1791)

Thomas Paine, son of a Norfolk corset-maker, published this book as a defence of the recent French and American Revolutions, in reply to the conservative Edmund Burke's *Reflections on the Revolution in France.* For it, Paine was tried in his absence and convicted of seditious libel. It has come to be seen as a seminal statement of liberty and equality, and a major influence on the spread of democracy.

Abridged: GH

DEDICATION

To George Washington: President Of The United States Of America

Sir,

I present you a small treatise in defence of those principles of freedom which your exemplary virtue hath so eminently contributed to establish. That the *Rights of Man* may become as universal as your benevolence can wish, and that you may enjoy the happiness of seeing the New World regenerate the Old, is the prayer of

Sir,

Your much obliged, and Obedient humble Servant,

Thomas Paine

RIGHTS OF MAN

Among the incivilities by which nations or individuals provoke and irritate each other, Mr. Burke's pamphlet on the French Revolution is an extraordinary instance. There is scarcely an epithet of abuse with which Mr. Burke has not loaded the French Nation. He calls the Declaration of the National Assembly of France, "paltry and blurred sheets of paper about the rights of man."

Does Mr. Burke mean to deny that man has any rights? If he does, then he must mean that there are no such things as rights anywhere, and that he has none himself? But if Mr. Burke means to admit that man has rights, the question then will be: What are those rights, and how man came by them originally?

Why then not trace the rights of man to the creation of man?

The Mosaic account of the creation, whether taken as divine authority or merely historical, is full to this point, the unity or equality of man. The expression admits of no controversy. "In the image of God created he him; male and female created he them." The distinction of sexes is pointed out, but no other distinction is even implied. If this be not divine, it is at least historical authority, and shows that the equality of man, so far from being a modern doctrine, is the oldest upon record.

His natural rights are the foundation of all his civil rights. Natural rights are those which appertain to man in right of his existence. Civil rights are those which appertain to man in right of his being a member of society.

In casting our eyes over the world, it is extremely easy to distinguish the governments which have arisen out of society, or out of the social compact, from those which have not; but to place this in a clearer light they may be all comprehended under three heads.

First, Superstition.

Secondly, Power.

Thirdly, The common interest of society and the common rights of man.

The first was a government of priestcraft, the second of conquerors, and the third of reason.

When a set of artful men pretended, through the medium of oracles, to hold intercourse with the Deity, as familiarly as they now march up the back-stairs in European courts, the world was completely under the government of superstition. The oracles were consulted, and whatever they were made to say became the law; and this sort of government lasted as long as this sort of superstition lasted.

After these a race of conquerors arose, whose government, like that of William the Conqueror, was founded in power, and the sword assumed the name of a sceptre. Governments thus established last as long as the power to support them lasts; but that they might avail themselves of every engine in their favor, they united fraud to force, and set up an idol which they called Divine Right, and which, in imitation of the Pope, who affects to be spiritual and temporal, and in contradiction to the Founder of the Christian religion, twisted itself afterwards into an idol of another shape, called Church and State. The key of St. Peter[1] and the key of the Treasury became quartered on one another, and the wondering cheated multitude worshipped the invention.

When I contemplate the natural dignity of man, when I feel (for Nature has not been kind enough to me to blunt my feelings) for the honour and happiness of its character, I become irritated at the attempt to govern mankind by force and fraud, as if they were all knaves and fools, and can scarcely avoid disgust at those who are thus imposed upon.

We have now to review the governments which arise out of society. In such, the fact must be that the individuals themselves, each in his own personal and sovereign right, entered into a compact with each other to produce a government: and this is the only mode in which governments have a right to arise, and the only principle on which they have a right to exist.

A constitution is not a thing in name only, but in fact. It has not an ideal, but a real existence; and wherever it cannot be produced in a visible form, there is none. Can, then, Mr. Burke produce the English Constitution?

The English Government is one of those which arose out of a conquest, and not out of society, and consequently it arose *over* the people; and though it has been much modified from the opportunity of circumstances since the time of William the Conqueror, the country has never yet regenerated itself, and is therefore without a constitution.

I now proceed to draw some comparisons between the French constitution and the governmental usages in England.

The constitution of France says that every man who pays a tax of sixty sous per annum (2s. 6d. English) is an elector. Can anything be more limited, and at the same time more capricious, than the qualification of electors is in England?

The French Constitution says that the number of representatives for any place shall be in a ratio to the number of taxable inhabitants or electors. In England, the old town of Sarum, which contains not three houses, sends two members; and the town of Manchester, which contains upward of sixty thousand souls, is not admitted to send any.

The French Constitution says that the National Assembly shall be elected every two years. What article will Mr. Burke place against this? Why, that the nation has no right at all in the case; that the government is perfectly arbitrary with respect to this point.

The French Constitution says that the right of war and peace is in the nation. Where else should it reside but in those who are to pay the expense? In England this right is said to reside in a metaphor shown at the Tower for sixpence: so are the lions; and it would be a step nearer to reason to say it resided in them, for any inanimate metaphor is no more than a hat or a cap.

The French Constitution says, There shall be no titles; and, of consequence, all that class of "aristocracy" and "nobility," is done away. Titles are but nicknames, and the thing is perfectly harmless in itself, but it marks a sort of foppery in the human character, which degrades it. It talks about its fine blue ribbon like a girl, and shows its new garter like a child. A certain writer, of some antiquity, says: "When I was a child, I thought as a child; but when I became a man, I put away childish things." It is from the elevated mind of France that the folly of titles has fallen. It has outgrown the baby clothes of Count and Duke, and breeched itself in manhood.

Let us then examine the grounds upon which the French Constitution has resolved against having a House of Peers in France.

Because, in the first place, aristocracy is kept up by family tyranny and injustice.

Secondly. Because there is an unnatural unfitness in an aristocracy to be legislators.

Thirdly. Because the idea of hereditary legislators is as inconsistent as that of hereditary judges, or hereditary juries; and as absurd as an hereditary mathematician, or an hereditary poet laureate.

Fourthly. Because a body of men, holding themselves accountable to nobody, ought not to be trusted by anybody.

Fifthly. Because it is continuing the uncivilised principle of governments founded in conquest, and the base idea of man having property in man, and governing him by personal right.

Sixthly. Because aristocracy has a tendency to deteriorate the human species.

The French Constitution hath abolished or renounced Toleration and Intolerance also, and hath established Universal Right Of Conscience. Toleration is not the opposite of Intolerance, but is the counterfeit of it. Both are despotisms.

Were a bill brought into any Parliament, entitled, "An Act to tolerate or grant liberty to the Almighty to receive the worship of a Jew or Turk," or "to prohibit the Almighty from receiving it," all men would startle and call it blasphemy. There would be an uproar. The presumption of toleration in religious matters would then present itself unmasked. Who then art thou, vain dust and ashes! by whatever name thou art called, whether a King, a Bishop, a Church, or a State, a Parliament, or anything else, that obtrudest thine insignificance between the soul of man and its Maker? Mind thine own concerns. If he believes not as thou believest, it is a proof that thou believest not as he believes, and there is no earthly power can determine between you.

The inquisition in Spain and the persecution of dissenters in England does not proceed from the religion originally professed, but from this mule-animal, engendered between the church and the state.

Persecution is not an original feature in any religion; but it is alway the strongly-marked feature of all law-religions, or religions established by law.

---

1   **St Peter:** See Gospels (p77), Matt. 17

One of the first works of the National Assembly in France, instead of vindictive proclamations against dissent, as has been the case with other governments, was to publish a declaration of the Rights of Man, as the basis on which the new constitution was to be built, and which is here subjoined:

Declaration
Of The Rights Of Man And Of Citizens
By The National Assembly Of France

The representatives of the people of France, formed into a National Assembly, doth recognize and declare, in the presence of the Supreme Being, and with the hope of his blessing and favor, the following sacred rights of men and of citizens:

One: Men are born, and continue, free and equal in respect of their Rights.

Two: The end of all Political associations is the Preservation of the Natural and Imprescriptible Rights of Man; Liberty, Property, Security, and Resistance of Oppression.

Three: The Nation is the source of all Sovereignty.

Four: Political Liberty consists in the power of doing whatever does not Injure another.

Five: The Law ought to Prohibit only actions hurtful to Society. What is not Prohibited should not be hindered.

Six: the Law is an expression of the Will of the Community. All Citizens have a right to concur, either personally or by their Representatives, in its formation.

Seven: No Man should be accused, arrested, or held in confinement, except in cases determined by the Law.

Eight: The Law ought to impose no other penalties but such as are absolutely and evidently necessary.

Nine: Every Man being presumed innocent till he has been convicted.

Ten: No Man ought to be molested on account of his opinions, not even on account of his Religious opinions, provided his avowal of them does not disturb the Public Order.

Eleven: Citizens may speak, write, and publish freely.

Twelve: A Public force is instituted for the benefit of the Community and not for the particular benefit of the persons to whom it is intrusted.

Thirteen: Contributions for defraying the expenses of Government ought to be divided equally among the Members of the Community, according to their abilities.

Fourteen: every Citizen has a Right, either by himself or his Representative, to a free voice in determining the necessity of Public Contributions.

Fifteen: every Community has a Right to demand of all its agents an account of their conduct.

Sixteen: every Community in which a Separation of Powers and a Security of Rights is not Provided for, wants a Constitution.

Seventeen: The Right to Property being inviolable and sacred, no one ought to be deprived of it, except in cases of evident Public necessity.

MISCELLANEOUS

The opinions of men with respect to government are changing fast in all countries. The Revolutions of America and France have thrown a beam of light over the world, which reaches into man.

The rights of men in society, are neither devisable or transferable, nor annihilable, but are descendable only, and it is not in the power of any generation to intercept finally, and cut off the descent. If the present generation, or any other, are disposed to be slaves, it does not lessen the right of the succeeding generation to be free. Wrongs cannot have a legal descent. When Mr. Burke attempts to maintain that the English nation did at the Revolution of 1688, most solemnly renounce and abdicate their rights for themselves, and for all their posterity for ever, he speaks a language which can only excite contempt for his prostitute principles, or pity for his ignorance.

When we survey the wretched condition of man, under the monarchical and hereditary systems of Government, dragged from his home by one power, or driven by another, and impoverished by taxes more than by enemies, it becomes evident that those systems are bad, and that a general revolution in the principle and construction of Governments is necessary.

As it is not difficult to perceive, that Revolutions on the broad basis of national sovereignty and Government by representation, are making their way in Europe, it would be an act of wisdom to anticipate their approach, and produce Revolutions by reason and accommodation, rather than commit them to the issue of convulsions.

PART SECOND

TO: M. DE LA FAYETTE

After an acquaintance of nearly fifteen years in difficult situations in America, and various consultations in Europe, I feel a pleasure in presenting to you this small treatise, in gratitude for your services to my beloved America, and as a testimony of my esteem for the virtues, public and private, which I know you to possess.

Your sincere, Affectionate Friend,

Thomas Paine

Independence is my happiness. When it shall be said in any country in the world, my poor are happy, my jails are empty of prisoners, my streets of beggars; the aged are not in want, the taxes are not oppressive; the rational world is my friend, because I am the friend of its happiness: then may that country boast its constitution and its government.

Never did so great an opportunity offer itself to England, and to all Europe, as is produced by the two Revolutions of America and France. By the former, freedom has a national champion in the western world; and by the latter, in Europe. When another nation shall join France, despotism and bad government will scarcely dare to appear. The insulted German and the enslaved Spaniard, the Russ and the Pole, are beginning to think.

The present age will hereafter merit to be called the Age of Reason, and the present generation will appear to the future as the Adam of a new world.

Why may we not suppose, that the great Father of all is pleased with variety of devotion; and that the greatest offence we can act, is that by which we seek to torment and render each other miserable? As to what are called national religions, we may, with as much propriety, talk of national Gods. It is either political craft or the remains of the Pagan system, when every nation had its separate and particular deity.

It is now towards the middle of February. Were I to take a turn into the country, the trees would present a leafless, wintery appearance. Yet people might by chance might observe that a single bud on a twig had begun to swell. I should reason very unnaturally to suppose this was the only bud in England which had this appearance. It is, however, not difficult to perceive that the spring is begun.

A Vindication of the Rights of Women
by Mary Wollstonecraft
(London, 1792)

Hard after the essays of revolutionists about the 'rights of man', came Mary Wollstonecraft - the "mother of feminism" – with her strange new ideas about rights for *women* too. Yet, for all that she was called a "hyena in petticoats" in her day, by the standards of now she seems somewhat prudish and rather modest in her aims; which means that she succeeded. (Mary's daughter was also a significant writer; see p290)

Abridged: GH

INTRODUCTION.

After considering the historic page, I have gained a profound conviction that women are rendered weak and wretched by a variety of causes. This barren blooming I attribute especially to a false system of education, gathered from books written by men who have been more anxious to make of women alluring mistresses than rational wives.

I wish to steer clear of the error of addressing only LADIES, but to pay particular attention to those in the middle class. I wish to persuade women to endeavour to acquire strength of mind and body, and to convince them that delicacy of sentiment and refinement of taste are almost synonymous with weakness, pity and contempt.

RIGHTS AND DUTIES OF MANKIND

It appears necessary to go back to first principles in search of the most simple truth. Thus, in what does man's pre-eminence over the brute creation consist? The answer is clear; in Reason. What acquirement exalts one being above another? Virtue.

Consequently, that the society is wisest whose constitution is founded on the nature of man, seems self-evident. Yet the desire of dazzling by riches, of commanding flattering sycophants, and doting self-love, have all contributed to overwhelm the mass of mankind, and make liberty a convenient handle for mock patriotism. Will men never be wise? will they never cease to expect corn from tares, and figs from thistles?

No man can acquire the strength of mind to discharge the duties of a king, where all feeling is stifled by flattery and power intoxicates weak men; but this simple piece of reason raises an outcry that its promoters are enemies of God and of man. After attacking the sacred majesty of kings, I shall scarcely excite surprise in declaring that every profession where rank and subordination constitutes power, is highly injurious to morality.

A standing army is incompatible with freedom, because subordination and despotism are the very sinews of military discipline. Besides, nothing is so prejudicial to the morality of garrison towns as those young idlers who conceal their deformity under gay drapery. Sailors come under the same description, only their vices assume a different and grosser cast. The clergy may have superior opportunities of improvement, but their colleges impose a blind submission.

A man of sense may have some individuality, but the weak, common, man has his opinions so steeped in the vat of consecrated authority, that the faint spirit which the grape of his own vine yields cannot be distinguished. It is this pestiferous purple which renders the progress of civilization a curse, and warps the understanding.

THE PREVAILING OPINION OF SEXUAL CHARACTER

To account for, and excuse the tyranny of man, it has been argued that the two sexes, in acquiring virtue, ought to aim at very different characters: or, to speak explicitly, women are not allowed to have sufficient strength of mind to acquire REAL virtue.

Women are told from their infancy, by the example of their mothers, that a little knowledge of human weakness, justly termed cunning, softness of temper, and OUTWARD obedience, will obtain for them the protection of man; and should they be beautiful, every thing else is needless.

Thus Milton[1] tells us that women are formed for softness and sweet attractive grace; I cannot comprehend his meaning, unless, in the true Mahometan strain, he meant to deprive us of souls. Children, I grant, should be innocent; but when the epithet is applied to men, or women, it is but a civil term for weakness.

As a proof that education gives this appearance of weakness to females, we may instance the example of military men, who are, like them, sent into the world before their minds have been stored with knowledge or fortified by principles. Like the FAIR sex, they were taught to please, and they only live to please. Yet they are still reckoned superior to women, though in what their superiority consists, it is difficult to discover.

Probably the prevailing opinion, that woman was created for man, may have risen from Moses's[2] poetical story; yet very few will seriously have supposed that Eve was, literally speaking, one of Adam's ribs, rather, the story proves that man, from the remotest antiquity, found it convenient to exert his strength to subjugate his companion.

To view the subject in another point of view. Do passive indolent women make the best wives? If they are really capable of acting like rational creatures, let them not be treated like slaves; let them attain conscious dignity by feeling themselves only dependent on God. I love man as my fellow; but his sceptre real or usurped, extends not to me.

Bodily strength, from being the distinction of heroes, is now sunk into such unmerited contempt, that men as well as women, seem to think it unnecessary. I will allow that bodily strength seems to give man a natural superiority over woman; and this is the only solid basis on which the superiority of the sex can be built. But women's limbs and faculties are cramped with worse than Chinese bands, and the sedentary life which they are condemned to live, whilst boys frolic in the open air, weakens the muscles and relaxes the nerves.

Taught from their infancy that beauty is woman's sceptre, the mind shapes itself to the body, and, roaming round its gilt cage, only seeks to adorn its prison. Women, deluded by this sentiment, sometimes boast of their weakness, cunningly obtaining power by playing on the WEAKNESS of men; and they may well glory in their illicit sway. The DIVINE RIGHT of husbands, like the divine right of kings, may, it is to be hoped, in this enlightened age, be contested without danger.

It is time to effect a revolution in female manners, time to restore to them their lost dignity, and make them, as a part of the human species, labour by reforming themselves to reform the world. It is time to separate unchangeable morals from local manners.

THE STATE OF DEGRADATION TO WHICH WOMAN IS REDUCED

That woman is degraded is, I think, clear. There is a power which has not only been denied to women; but writers have insisted is inconsistent with their sexual character. That power is knowledge.

Pleasure is the business of a woman's life, according to the present modification of society, and while it continues to be so, little can be expected from such weak beings. Confined in cages, like the feathered race, they have nothing to do but to plume themselves, and stalk with mock-majesty from perch to perch, systematically degraded by receiving trivial attentions. I scarcely am able to govern my muscles, when I see a man start with eager solicitude to lift a handkerchief, or shut a door, when the LADY could have done it herself, had she only moved a pace or two.

Men, in their youth, are prepared for professions, and marriage is not considered as the grand feature in their lives; whilst women, on the contrary, have no other scheme to sharpen their faculties. Yet, novels, music, poetry and gallantry, all tend to make women the creatures of sensation.

"Educate women like men," says Rousseau, "and the more they resemble our sex the less power will they have over us." This is the very point I aim at. I do not wish them to have power over men; but over themselves.

In the same strain have I heard men argue against instructing the poor. "Teach them to read and write," say they, "and you take them out of the station assigned them by nature." Ignorance is a frail base for virtue!

Polygamy, seduction and prostitution have long been the lot of woman always taught to look up to man for a maintenance, and to consider their persons as the proper return for his exertions to support them.

I have not here laid any great stress upon the example of a few women (Sappho, Eloisa, Mrs. Macaulay, the Empress of Russia, etc). These may be reckoned exceptions. I wish to see women neither heroines nor brutes; but reasonable creatures.

WRITERS WHO HAVE RENDERED WOMEN OBJECTS OF PITY

Sophia, says Rousseau in his novel, should be a perfect woman - weak and passive, because she has less bodily strength than man; and from hence infers, that she was formed to please and to be subject to him- this being the grand end of her existence.

Dr. Fordyce and Dr. Gregory's advice to women are full of old prejudices. Dr. Gregory's 'Legacy to his Daughters', asks that women modulate their behaviour to the level of fools. Mrs. Piozzi often repeated by rote what she did not understand. The Baroness de Stael speaks the same language, yet with more enthusiasm. Madame Genlis'

---

1   **Milton:** see p185
2   **Moses Story:** see p23

letters on Education afford many useful hints; but her views are narrow.

MODESTY

Modesty! Sacred offspring of sensibility and reason! may I unblamed presume to investigate thy nature!

It appears to me proper to discriminate that purity of mind, which is the effect of chastity, and modesty, that soberness of mind which teaches a man not to think more highly of himself than he ought, properly distinguished from humility. General Washington was modest; had he been humble, he would probably have shrunk from his enterprise.

The shameless behaviour of the prostitutes who infest the streets of London, raising alternate emotions of pity and disgust, tramples on virgin bashfulness with a sort of bravado, and they become more audaciously lewd than men. But these poor ignorant wretches never had any modesty to lose, they were only bashful, shame-faced innocents. Purity of mind, genuine delicacy, only resides in cultivated minds.

As a sex, women are more chaste than men, and must heartily disclaim that debauchery of mind which leads a man to bring forward indecent allusions, or obscene witticisms. How much more modest is the libertine who obeys the call of appetite, than the lewd joker who sets the table in a roar. Again; when men boast of their triumphs over women, what do they boast of?

To take another view of the subject; in nurseries, boarding schools and convents, I fear, girls are first spoiled. A number of them sleep in the same room, and wash together, acquiring immodest habits; and as many girls have learned very indelicate tricks from ignorant servants, the mixing of them indiscriminately is very improper. I cannot recollect without indignation the jokes and tricks which knots of young women indulge themselves in, they were almost on a par with the double meanings which shake the convivial table when the glass has circulated freely.

Personal reserve is ever the hand-maid of modesty. It is obvious that the reserve I mean has nothing sexual in it, I think it EQUALLY necessary in both sexes. If men and women took half as much pains to dress habitually neat, rather than to ornament and disfigure their persons, much would be done towards the attainment of purity of mind. But women only dress to gratify men; yet the lover is always best pleased with the simple garb that sits close to the shape.

Would ye, O my sisters, really possess modesty, ye must remember that the possession of any virtue is incompatible with ignorance and vanity!

MORALITY UNDERMINED BY THE IMPORTANCE OF REPUTATION.

It has long since occurred to me, that advice respecting behaviour, and all the various modes of preserving a good reputation, which have been so strenuously inculcated on the female world, were specious poisons, that incrusting morality eat away the substance.

I recollect a woman of quality, notorious for her gallantries, though as she still lived with her husband, who made a point of treating with the most insulting contempt a poor timid creature, whom a neighbouring gentleman had seduced and afterwards married.

Men are certainly more under the influence of their appetites than women; and their appetites are more depraved by unbridled indulgence. I will venture to assert, that all the causes of female weakness, as well as depravity, branch out of one grand cause- want of chastity in men.

But, surely nature never intended that women, by satisfying an appetite, should frustrate the very purpose for which it was implanted? Public spirit must be nurtured by private virtue, or it will resemble the factitious sentiment which makes women careful to preserve their reputation, and men their honour.

PERNICIOUS EFFECTS OF UNNATURAL DISTINCTIONS IN SOCIETY.

From the respect paid to property flow, as from a poisoned fountain, most of the evils and vices which render this world. One class presses on another, men neglect their duties, yet are treated like demi-gods, and religion is separated from morality by a ceremonial veil. There is a homely proverb, that whoever the devil finds idle he will employ. And what but idleness can hereditary wealth produce?

Women are more debased and cramped by this than men, because men may unfold their faculties as soldiers and statesmen. The whole system of British politics consists in multiplying dependants and contriving taxes which grind the poor to pamper the rich. The preposterous distinctions of rank corrupt, almost equally, every class of people. Still there are some loop-holes out of which a man may creep, and dare to think and act for himself; but for a woman it is an herculean task.

Though I consider that women in the common walks of life are called to fulfil the duties of wives and mothers, by religion and reason, I cannot help lamenting that women of a superior cast have not a road by which they can pursue usefulness and independence. I may excite laughter, by dropping an hint that I really think that women ought to have representatives, instead of being arbitrarily governed without having any share in the deliberations of government.

But, as the whole system of representation is now, in this country, only a convenient handle for despotism, they need not complain, for they are no better represented then the class of hard working mechanics who pay for royalty when they can scarcely stop their children's mouths with bread. Taxes on the very necessaries of life enable an endless tribe of idle princes and princesses to pass with stupid pomp before a gaping crowd. This is mere gothic grandeur, something like the barbarous, useless parade of having sentinels on horseback at Whitehall, which I could never view without a mixture of contempt and indignation.

Rather than all wanting to be ladies, which is simply to have nothing to do, women might certainly study the art of healing, and be physicians as well as nurses and midwives. They might, also study politics and business. Women would not then marry for a support; would men then not find us more observant daughters, more affectionate sisters, more faithful wives, more reasonable mothers- in a word, better citizens.

PARENTS

Parental affection is, perhaps, the blindest modification of perverse self-love; to many, it is but a pretext to tyrannize where it can be done with impunity. The rights of kings are deduced in a direct line from the King of kings; and that of parents from our first parent.

Children cannot be taught too early to submit to reason; for to submit to reason, is to submit to the nature of things, and to that God who formed them. It is unreasoned exercise of parental authority that first injures the mind, as when they see mamma's anger burst out- either her hair was ill-dressed, or she had lost more money at cards than she was willing to own to her husband. But, till society is better constituted, parents, I fear, will still insist on being obeyed, because they will be obeyed, and constantly endeavour to settle that power on a Divine right, which will not bear the investigation of reason.

NATIONAL EDUCATION

I think that schools, as they are now regulated, the hot-beds of vice and folly, and the knowledge of human nature, supposed to be attained there, merely cunning selfishness. There is not, perhaps, in the kingdom, a more dogmatical or luxurious set of men, than the pedantic tyrants who reside in colleges and preside at public schools. A few good scholars, I grant, may have been formed by emulation and discipline; but, to bring forward these clever boys, the health and morals of a number have been sacrificed.

Were boys and girls permitted to pursue the same studies together, those graceful decencies might early be inculcated which produce modesty. Day schools should be established by government, in which boys and girls might be educated together. Botany, mechanics, and astronomy, reading, writing, arithmetic, natural history, and experiments in natural philosophy, might fill up the day; but these pursuits should never encroach on gymnastic plays in the open air.

After the age of nine, girls and boys intended for domestic employments, or mechanical trades, ought to be removed to receive appropriate instruction, the two sexes being still together in the morning; but in the afternoon, the girls should attend a school and do plain work, millinery, etc. The young people of superior abilities, or fortune, might now be taught the dead and living languages, the elements of science, and continue the study of history and politics. Girls and boys still together?: yes.

Humanity to animals should be particularly inculcated as a part of national education, for it is not at present one of our national virtues. This habitual cruelty is first caught at school, where it is the sport of the boys to torment the miserable brutes that fall in their way. The transition from barbarity to brutes to domestic tyranny over wives, children, and servants, is very easy. The lady who sheds tears for the bird starved in a snare, will, nevertheless, keep her coachman and horses whole hours waiting for her, when the sharp frost bites.

Women should be taught the elements of anatomy and medicine, not only to enable them to take proper care of their own health, but to make them rational nurses of their infants, parents, and husbands. It is likewise proper to make women acquainted with the anatomy of the mind; never forgetting the science of morality, nor the study of the political history of mankind.

When I wish to see my sex become more like moral agents, my heart bounds with the anticipation of the general diffusion of that sublime contentment which only morality can diffuse.

SOME INSTANCES OF FOLLY

1: In this metropolis a number of lurking leeches gain a subsistence by practising on the credulity of women, pretending to cast nativities. O ye foolish women!

2: An instance of the SENTIMENTAL feminine weakness of character, is to be amused by the reveries of stupid novelists. The reading of novels makes women, and particularly ladies of fashion, very fond of using strong expressions and superlatives in conversation, which only mimick the dark the flame of passion.

3: An immoderate fondness for dress, for pleasure and for sway, are the passions of savages.

4: Women are supposed to possess more sensibility, compassion and stronger attachments, and even humanity, than men; but the clinging affection of ignorance has seldom any thing noble in it.

5: As the rearing of children has justly been insisted on as the peculiar destination of woman, the ignorance that incapacitates them must be contrary to the order of things. I have always found horses, an animal I am much attached to, very tractable when treated with humanity and steadiness, and children are likewise.

The majority of mothers leave their children entirely to the care of servants: or treat them as if they were little demi-gods, though I have always observed, that such women seldom show common humanity to servants. Nature has so wisely ordered things, that did women suckle their own children, they would preserve their own health, and there would be a reasonable interval between each child. But, visiting to display finery, card playing, and balls, not to mention the idle bustle of morning trifling, draw women from their duty.

6: That women at present are by ignorance rendered foolish or vicious, is, I think, not to be disputed; and, that the most salutary effects tending to improve mankind, might be expected from a REVOLUTION in female manners. From the tyranny of man, I firmly believe, the greater number of female follies proceed.

Let woman share the rights, and she will emulate the virtues of man; for she must grow more perfect when emancipated, or it will be expedient to open a fresh trade with Russia for whips; a present which a father should always make to his son-in-law on his wedding day, that a husband may keep his whole family in order.

Songs of Innocence and Experience
by William Blake
(London, 1794)

William Blake is as much known for his idiosyncratic mysticism as for his poetry and paintings. William Wordsworth said that, "There is something in the madness of this man which interests me more than the sanity of Lord Byron and Walter Scott." Blake's work is said to have been re-used by more than any other, including Philip Pullman, Monty Python, Ridley Scott, Billy Bragg, Emerson Lake & Palmer, Mike Westbrook, U2, Van Morrison, Bob Dylan, Allen Ginsberg and hundreds more.

Abridged: GH

SONGS OF INNOCENCE

THE SHEPHERD

How sweet is the shepherd's sweet lot!
From the morn to the evening he strays;
He shall follow his sheep all the day,
And his tongue shall be filled with praise.

For he hears the lambs' innocent call,
And he hears the ewes' tender reply;
He is watchful while they are in peace,
For they know when their shepherd is nigh.

THE LAMB

Little lamb, who made thee?
Does thou know who made thee,
Gave thee life, and bid thee feed
By the stream and o'er the mead;
Gave thee clothing of delight,
Softest clothing, woolly, bright;
Gave thee such a tender voice,
Making all the vales rejoice?
Little lamb, who made thee?
Does thou know who made thee?

Little lamb, I'll tell thee;
Little lamb, I'll tell thee:
He is called by thy name,
For He calls Himself a Lamb.
He is meek, and He is mild,
He became a little child.
I a child, and thou a lamb,
We are called by His name.
Little lamb, God bless thee!
Little lamb, God bless thee!

THE LITTLE BLACK BOY

My mother bore me in the southern wild,
And I am black, but O my soul is white!
White as an angel is the English child,
But I am black, as if bereaved of light.

My mother taught me underneath a tree,
And, sitting down before the heat of day,
She took me on her lap and kissed me,
And, pointing to the East, began to say:

'Look on the rising sun: there God does live,
And gives His light, and gives His heat away,
And flowers and trees and beasts and men receive
Comfort in morning, joy in the noonday.

'And we are put on earth a little space,
That we may learn to bear the beams of love;
And these black bodies and this sunburnt face
Are but a cloud, and like a shady grove.

'For, when our souls have learned the heat to bear,
The cloud will vanish, we shall hear His voice,
Saying, "Come out from the grove, my love and care,
And round my golden tent like lambs rejoice."'

Thus did my mother say, and kissed me,
And thus I say to little English boy.
When I from black, and he from white cloud free,
And round the tent of God like lambs we joy,

I'll shade him from the heat till he can bear
To lean in joy upon our Father's knee;
And then I'll stand and stroke his silver hair,
And be like him, and he will then love me.

THE CHIMNEY-SWEEPER

When my mother died I was very young,
And my father sold me while yet my tongue
Could scarcely cry 'Weep! weep! weep! weep!'
So your chimneys I sweep, and in soot I sleep.

There's little Tom Dacre, who cried when his head,
That curled like a lamb's back, was shaved; so I said,
'Hush, Tom! never mind it, for, when your head's bare,
You know that the soot cannot spoil your white hair.'

And so he was quiet, and that very night,
As Tom was a-sleeping, he had such a sight! -
That thousands of sweepers, Dick, Joe, Ned, and Jack,
Were all of them locked up in coffins of black.

And by came an angel, who had a bright key,
And he opened the coffins, and set them all free;
Then down a green plain, leaping, laughing, they run
And wash in a river, and shine in the sun.

Then naked and white, all their bags left behind,
They rise upon clouds, and sport in the wind:
And the angel told Tom, if he'd be a good boy,
He'd have God for his father, and never want joy.

And so Tom awoke, and we rose in the dark,
And got with our bags and our brushes to work.
Though the morning was cold, Tom was happy and warm:
So, if all do their duty, they need not fear harm.

SONGS OF EXPERIENCE

THE TIGER

Tiger, tiger, burning bright
In the forests of the night,
What immortal hand or eye
Could frame thy fearful symmetry?

In what distant deeps or skies
Burnt the fire of thine eyes?
On what wings dare he aspire?
What the hand dare seize the fire?

And what shoulder and what art
Could twist the sinews of thy heart?
And, when thy heart began to beat,
What dread hand and what dread feet?

What the hammer? what the chain?
In what furnace was thy brain?
What the anvil? what dread grasp
Dare its deadly terrors clasp?

When the stars threw down their spears,

And watered heaven with their tears,
Did He smile His work to see?
Did He who made the lamb make thee?

Tiger, tiger, burning bright
In the forests of the night,
What immortal hand or eye
Dare frame thy fearful symmetry?

LONDON

I wander through each chartered street,
Near where the chartered Thames does flow,
A mark in every face I meet,
Marks of weakness, marks of woe.

In every cry of every man,
In every infant's cry of fear,
In every voice, in every ban,
The mind-forged manacles I hear:

How the chimney-sweeper's cry
Every blackening church appals,
And the hapless soldier's sigh
Runs in blood down palace-walls.

But most, through midnight streets I hear
How the youthful harlot's curse
Blasts the new-born infant's tear,
And blights with plagues the marriage hearse.

THE HUMAN ABSTRACT

Pity would be no more
If we did not make somebody poor,
And Mercy no more could be
If all were as happy as we.

And mutual fear brings Peace,
Till the selfish loves increase;
Then Cruelty knits a snare,
And spreads his baits with care.

He sits down with holy fears,
And waters the ground with tears;
Then Humility takes its root
Underneath his foot.

Soon spreads the dismal shade
Of Mystery over his head,
And the caterpillar and fly
Feed on the Mystery.

And it bears the fruit of Deceit,
Ruddy and sweet to eat,
And the raven his nest has made
In its thickest shade.

The gods of the earth and sea
Sought through nature to find this tree,
But their search was all in vain:
There grows one in the human Brain.

A POISON TREE

I was angry with my friend:
I told my wrath, my wrath did end.
I was angry with my foe:
I told it not, my wrath did grow.

And I watered it in fears
Night and morning with my tears,
And I sunned it with smiles
And with soft deceitful wiles.

And it grew both day and night,
Till it bore an apple bright,
And my foe beheld it shine,
And he knew that it was mine, -

And into my garden stole
When the night had veiled the pole;

In the morning, glad, I see

A CRADLE SONG

Sleep, sleep, beauty bright,
Dreaming in the joys of night;
Sleep, sleep; in thy sleep
Little sorrows sit and weep.

Sweet babe, in thy face
Soft desires I can trace,
Secret joys and secret smiles,
Little pretty infant wiles.

As thy softest limbs I feel,
Smiles as of the morning steal
O'er thy cheek, and o'er thy breast
Where thy little heart doth rest.

O the cunning wiles that creep
In thy little heart asleep!
When thy little heart doth wake,
Then the dreadful light shall break.

Philosophy in The Boudoir
(*La Philosophie Dans le Boudoir*)
by le Marquis Alphonse Donatien de Sade
(Paris, 1795)

Sade is *the* champion of *absolute* freedom – in his case, freedom to indulge in the sexual violence which gives us the word *sadism*. And this aristocrat of pornographers *did* actually practice what he preached, which was why he spent much of his life in prison. Not too surprisingly, his books have been banned pretty much everywhere, but not always for the erotica - in the Soviet Union it was his politics of individual liberty which made them forbidden.

Abridged: GH

INTRODUCTION

TO LIBERTINES

Voluptuaries of all ages, of every sex, to you I offer this work. Nourish yourselves upon its principles. They favour your passions, which are naught but the means Nature employs to bring man to the ends she prescribes. For it is only by sacrificing everything to the senses' pleasure that this poor creature called Man may be able to sow a few roses by the thorny path of life.

THE DIALOGUE

Madame de Saint-Ange: You know, my dear brother, I begin to have misgivings about the obscene plans for today. At twenty-six, and resolved to take pleasure only with my own sex, I ought to be better behaved, but my imagination

is pricked the more. Tell me about your friend Dolmancé, before he arrives.

Le Chevalier: A little over thirty and six, tall, handsome, with a hint of the villain, and most philosophic.

Madame de Saint-Ange: And his fancies?

Le Chevalier: I think you know. He cares only for men.

Madame de Saint-Ange: Oh, my dear! Has he had you?

Le Chevalier: We've had our pleasures, but there's no need to belittle those with strange tastes, they are still as Nature meant.

Madame de Saint-Ange: Oh please, a few details!

Le Chevalier: They were naught beside the pleasures you offer, my dear.

Madame de Saint-Ange: Ah, what chivalry! Anyway, I intend to bring a virgin to the feast. Eugénie, a little thing I met last autumn at the convent, a few lessons will do her good.

Later, In an Elegant Boudoir

Young Eugénie and Madame de Saint-Ange are together embracing when M. Dolmancé enters...

Eugénie: God! We are betrayed!

Madame de Saint-Ange: Be at ease, my lovely Eugénie, this is Dolmancé, a most amiable man. Let us not be prudish! (She kisses him indecently.) Imitate me.

Eugénie: Oh, Most willingly! (they tongue Dolmancé, and each other)

Dolmancé: Ladies! It seems extraordinarily warm here (They undress, Dolmancé begins to inspect Eugenié.)

Madame de Saint-Ange: No, Dolmancé! Not yet! Our lessons first!

Dolmancé: Very well, Madame, I will recline on this couch, and you may begin instructing our student.

Madame de Saint-Ange: This sceptre - the member - Eugénie, is the agent of love's pleasure. It may settle here (She strokes Eugénie), or pursue a more mysterious sanctuary here (she indicates behind). Upon some agitation it may vent a viscous liquor, plunging the man into the sweetest pleasure of life.

Eugénie: I wish to see this liquor flow!

Madame de Saint-Ange: I may liberate it with my hand.

Eugénie: And the balls?

Madame de Saint-Ange: The testicles contain semen which produces the human species within the woman's womb. But a girl ought not to concern herself with that. Onto the couch, my sweet.

Eugénie: Dear God! And all these mirrors, how ingenious!

Madame de Saint-Ange: Examine my own Temple of Venus. The mound above gains hair at the age when a girl begins her periods. Here, above, is the little tongue-shaped clitoris, and all a woman's sensation. To tickle me there would make me swoon with delight. Try so. Ah, pretty bitch, how well you do it! Now, Eugénie, I will teach you how to drown in joy. Spread your thighs. Dolmancé, suck her behind while my tongue licks her. Let's make her swoon. What downy flesh! How you squirm!

Eugénie: Oh, I'm dying! (She discharges)

Eugénie: I begin to love whoredom, but is not virtue opposed to such misconduct?

Dolmancé: Ah, Eugénie, virtue is but a chimera whose worship consists exclusively in rebellion against the temperament. Can Nature recommend what offends her?

Eugénie: But what of pity as a virtue?

Dolmancé: What can that be for one with no religion? Come, let us use reason. The God who permits evils his omnipotence could prevent would be the most detestable of creatures.

Eugénie: You mean that God is an illusion?

Dolmancé: Fruit of the terror and of frailty. What does Christianity offer? The altars of Venus and Mars are changed to those of Jesus and Mary, his drivellings become the basis of a morality, and as this tale is preached to the poor, charity becomes its greatest virtue. Such, Eugénie, is the fable of God and religion.

Eugénie: But, Dolmancé, what of charity and benevolence?

Dolmancé: Be not deceived! Benevolence is naught but the vice of pride in the ostentatious almsgiver.

Eugénie: But surely there must be some actions so evil that they are known across al the earth as criminal.

Madame de Saint-Ange: There are none, my love, not even theft, nor incest, nor murder.

Eugénie: Extraordinary!

Dolmancé: Not at all! Nature made men with as many varieties of taste just as she made different their countenances.

Eugénie: Let us continue. Tell me how a girl may preserve herself from pregnancy.

Madame de Saint-Ange: Some women insert sponges, others have their lovers make use of little sacks of Venetian skin, called condoms. But of all the possibilities, that presented by the arse is without any doubt the most delicious. Dolmancé, is an expert!

Eugénie: How adorable!

Madame de Saint-Ange: 'Tis the filthiest and the most forbidden which best rouses the intellect. My brother and I often amused each other during our childhood years.

Eugénie: Is not incest a crime?

Dolmancé: Eugénie, a moment of reason- how did the human species perpetuate itself, if not through incest? By what other means could Adam's family and Noah's[1] have been preserved?

Eugénie: Oh! My divine teachers, I see full well that there are very few crimes in the world. But grant, you must, that murder is still a crime?

Dolmancé: Oh, Eugénie, 'tis our pride that elevates murder into a crime. Be frank, Eugénie, have you never wished the death of anyone?

Eugénie: Oh, I would glad see my mother dead, but alas, I lack the means.

Dolmancé: Come, my rascal, I can hold off no longer! I am going to enter you!

Eugénie: Oh! You tear me sir!

Dolmancé: Courage, Eugénie, courage!

Eugénie: Yet I feel the pain grows into pleasure. More, Dolmancé!

Dolmancé: God's holy fuck! Thrice bloody fuck of God!

Madame de Saint-Ange: How the wench has taken to it!

Dolmancé: 'Oh heavens! I'm spent!

Madame de Saint-Ange: Now is the time to return to our discussion- upon the libertine caprices.

---

1   **Adam and Noah:** see The Torah (p23)

Dolmancé: Of sodomy, assuredly the passive man who has himself buggered takes the greater pleasure, since he enjoys the sensations both before and behind. But do avoid acids before sodomite amusements- they aggravate haemorrhoids- and always wash out the juice of one man before taking another.

Eugénie: But if they were in my female organ, should not such purging be a crime?

Madame de Saint-Ange: Sweet fool! Propagation is not the objective of Nature; she merely tolerates it. If, however, some misfortune might occur, notify me within the first eight weeks, and I'll have it neatly remedied. Dread not infanticide- we are mistress of our womb, and we do no more harm in evacuating unwanted matter there than in evacuating another, by medicines, when we so need.

Dolmancé: As to cruelties, when we wish to be aroused, there is no doubt that we are much more keenly affected by pain than by pleasure. My dear Eugénie, cruelty, very far from being a vice, is the first sentiment Nature injects in us all. The infant breaks his toy, bites his nurse's breast, strangles his canary long before he is able to reason. Cruelty is stamped in animals. Cruelty is natural. Education may modify it, but education is as deforming to holy Nature as topiary is to trees. Nero, Tiberius, Heliogabolus, Charolais, Condé, all slaughtered to gain an erection. Queen Zingua of Angola killed her lovers when she was done with them.

Eugénie: Oh Christ! You drive me wild!

Dolmancé: Eugénie- in libertinage, nothing is frightful, because everything is inspired by nature, even the most extraordinary, the most bizarre.

Eugénie: But are not some manners necessary in a governed society?

Dolmancé: Why, by God, I have something here with me. I bought, outside the Palace of Equality, a little pamphlet, which ought surely to answer your question.

Madame de Saint-Ange: Chevalier, you possess a fine organ, read it to us.

Le Chevalier: YET ANOTHER EFFORT, FRENCHMEN, IF YOU WOULD BECOME REPUBLICANS !

RELIGION

I am about to put forward some major ideas; they will be heard and pondered. If not all of them please, surely a few will; in some sort, then, I shall have contributed to the progress of our age, and shall be content. Rome disappeared immediately Christianity was preached there, and France is doomed if she continues to revere it. Since we believe a cult necessary, let us imitate the Romans- actions, passions, heroes- those were the objects of their respect. Minerva's devotee coveted wisdom. Courage found its abode in Mars. What do we find in Christianity's futile gods? Does the grubby Nazarene fraud inspire any great thoughts? Does his repellent mother, the shameless Mary, excite any virtues? Do you discover in the saints any

example of greatness, of heroism or virtue? Lycurgus, Numa, Moses, Jesus Christ, Mohammed, all these great rogues, all these great thought-tyrants, knew how to fabricate divinities to serve their own interests. Let philosophers proclaim instead the wonderful sublimities of Nature, whose these laws are as wise as they are simple, and which are written in the hearts of all men. Let there be no doubt of it- at all times, in every century religions have been cradles of despotism. Massacres and expulsions, however, have no place in the enlightened mind. Let us condemn the charlatans to be jeered at. Let the most insulting blasphemy, the most atheistic works, be openly authorised, and, in six months, your infamous god will be as naught.

MANNERS

Frenchmen, you are too intelligent not to see that new government requires new manners. In every age, the duties of man have been considered under the following three categories- Those his conscience and his credulity impose upon him, with regards a supreme being; Those he is obliged to fulfil toward his brethren; Finally, those that relate only to himself. I cannot repeat it to you too often, Frenchmen, no more gods, lest their fatal influence plunge you back into despotism. As to the second class of man's duties, those which bind him to his fellows, the absurd Christian morality tells us to love our neighbour as ourselves- in defiance of all the laws of Nature. Since hers is the sole voice which must direct all our actions, it is only a question of loving others as brothers, as friends given us by Nature, and with whom we should be able to live much better in a republican State.

We cannot devise as many laws as there are men; but the laws can be lenient, and so few in number, that all men, of whatever character, can easily observe them. Especially we must get rid of the atrocity of capital punishment, because the law which attempts a man's life is impractical, unjust, inadmissible. It has never repressed crime- for a second crime is every day committed at the foot of the scaffold. The injuries we can work against our brothers may be reduced to four types- calumny or defamation, theft, crimes which may disagreeably affect others, and murder.

Here I address myself only to people capable of hearing me out; they will read me without any danger. If calumny attaches to a truly evil man, it makes little difference. If a virtuous man is calumniated, it is merely a test of purity whence his virtue emerges more resplendent than ever. As to theft, it is certain that stealing nourishes courage, strength, skill, tact, in a word, all the virtues useful to a republican system. Lay partiality aside, and answer me- is theft, whose effect is to distribute wealth more evenly- to be branded as a wrong under our government which aims at equality? There was once a people who punished not the thief but him who allowed himself to be robbed, in order to teach him to care for his property. A republic threated by despots outside can by no means preserve itself other than by war. Nothing is less moral than war, so how we ask, may the individual be required to be moral?

We may now consider modesty, that faint-hearted negative impulse of contradiction to impure affections. Were it among Nature's intentions that man be modest, assuredly she would not have caused him to be born naked. Lycurgus and Solon obliged girls to exhibit themselves naked at the theatre. We are persuaded that lust is not to be stifled or legislated against, but that it is, rather, a matter of arranging the means whereby passion may be satisfied in peace. We must thus introduce order into this sphere of affairs.

Various stations, cheerful, sanitary, spacious, properly furnished and safe, will be erected in each city; in them, all sexes, all ages, all creatures possible will be offered to the caprices of the libertines who shall come to divert themselves. Whenever you withhold from man the means to exhales the dose of despotism Nature instilled in the depths of his heart, he will seek other outlets for it. It is certain, in a state of Nature, that women are born vulguivaguous, that is to say, are born like other female animals- belonging, without exception, to all the males

There will then also be government houses intended for women's libertinage, and the more constantly they frequent them the higher they will be esteemed. Must the diviner half of humankind be laden with irons by the other? Ah, break those irons- Nature wills it. Amongst the Tartars, the profligate woman was honoured with jewels. In Peru, families rent their wives and daughters to visitors, like horses, or carriages! Every philosopher knows full well it is solely to the Christian impostors we are indebted for having puffed lewdness up into crime. The priests had excellent cause to forbid lechery- their power of absolution for private sins, gave them an incredible ascendancy over women. We know only too well how they took advantage of it.

Is incest more dangerous? Hardly. It loosens family ties so that the citizen has that much more love to lavish on his country; the primary laws of Nature dictate it to us, our feelings vouch for the fact; and nothing is so enjoyable as an object we have coveted over the years. If we traverse the world we will find incest everywhere established. The blacks of the Ivory Coast and Gabon prostitute their wives to their own children; in Judah, the eldest son must marry his father's wife; the people of Chile lie indifferently with their sisters and their daughters. I would venture, in a word, that incest ought to be every government's law- every government whose basis is fraternity.

As to sodomy, we wonder that savagery could ever reach the point where you condemn to death an unhappy person for the crime of not sharing your tastes. The greatest of men lean toward sodomy. Plutarch speaks with enthusiasm of the battalion of lovers who alone defended Greece's freedom. At the time it was discovered, the whole of America was found inhabited by people of this taste. In their letters, Martial, Catullus, Tibullus, Horace, and Virgil wrote to men as though to their mistresses; and we read in Plutarch that women must in no way figure in men's love. Amongst the Greeks, the female perversion was also supported by policy- so that women resorted to each other, and thus had less communication with men so that their detrimental influence in the republic's affairs was held to a minimum. In fine, these are perfectly inoffensive manias. Even if women were to go so far as caressing monsters and animals, no ill could possibly result therefrom. Of all the offences man may commit against his fellows, murder is without question the cruellest, since its loss is irreparable. But, from Nature's point of view, is murder a crime?

If Nature denies eternity to beings, it follows that their destruction is one of her laws. Little animals are formed immediately a large animal expires, and these little animals' lives are simply one of the necessary effects determined by the large animal's temporary sleep. Is it a political crime? Are wars, the unique fruit of political barbarism, anything but the means whereby a nation is nourished, strengthened, and buttressed? Is it not a strange blindness in man, who publicly teaches the art of killing, who rewards the most accomplished killer, and who punishes him who, with reason, does away with his enemy! Is murder then a crime against society? What difference does it make to society, whether it have one member more, or less? Will its laws, its manners, its customs be vitiated? No, alas.

What, then, must the attitude of a warlike and republican state be toward murder? Republican mettle calls for a touch of ferocity- if he grows soft, if his energy slackens in him, the republican will be subjugated in a trice. In Sparta, in Lacedaemon, they hunted Helots, just as we in France go on partridge shoots. In Mindanao, a man who wishes to commit a murder is raised to the rank of warrior brave and decorated with a turban. The inhabitants of Borneo believe all those they put to death will serve them when they themselves depart life. Devout Spaniards vow to St. James of Galicia to kill a dozen Americans every day. One sees it upon every page of their history. What people were at once greater and more bloodthirsty than the Romans, and what nation longer preserved its splendour and freedom? In the republics of Greece all the children who came into the world were carefully examined, and if they were found not to conform to the requirements determined by the republic's defence, they were sacrificed on the spot. In those days it was not deemed essential to build richly endowed houses for the preservation of mankind's scum. In China, one finds every morning an incredible number of children abandoned in the streets; a dung cart picks them up at dawn, and they are tossed into a moat.

Do you not prune the tree when it has overmany branches? And do not too many shoots weaken the trunk? To sum up: must murder be repressed by murder? Surely not. Let us never impose any other penalty upon the murderer than the one he may risk from the vengeance of the friends or family of him he has killed. Murder is a horror, but an often necessary horror, never criminal, which it is essential to tolerate in a republican State.

We have now but to speak of man's duties toward himself. The only offence of this order man can commit is suicide. I will not bother demonstrating here the imbecility of the people who make of this act a crime, they may read Rousseau's famous letter. In Greece, one killed oneself in public, and one made of one's death a spectacle of magnificence.

Let us create few laws, but let them be good; rather than multiplying hindrances, it is purely a question of giving an indestructible quality to the law we employ, of seeing to it that the laws we promulgate have, as ends, nothing but the citizen's tranquillity, his happiness, and the glory of the republic. But, Frenchmen, I should not like your zeal to broadcast your principles to lead you further afield. Remember the unsuccess of the crusades. Revive your trade, restore energy and markets to your manufacturing; cause your arts to flourish again, encourage agriculture. Leave the thrones of Europe to crumble.

Madame de Saint-Ange: Oh, my friend, fuck us, but let us have no sermons!

Pride and Prejudice
by Jane Austen
(London, written 1797, published 1813)

Jane Austen's famous novel, was the first to establish the format of a perceptive heroine (Elizabeth Bennet) and the aloof hunk (Mr Darcy) she comes to adore despite the surrounding pettiness of middle-class life.

Abridged: JH/GH

I: A Society Ball at Longbourn

It is a truth universally acknowledged, that a single man in possession of a good fortune, must be in want of a wife.

However little known the feelings or views of such a man may be on his first entering a neighbourhood, this truth is so well fixed in the minds of the surrounding families, that he is considered the rightful property of some one or other of their daughters.

Thus all Longbourn was agape with excitement when it became known that Netherfield Park, the great place of the neighbourhood, was let to a rich and handsome young bachelor called Bingley, and that Mr. Bingley and his party were to attend the forthcoming ball at the Assembly Rooms. Nowhere did the news create more interest and rouse greater hopes than in the household of the Bennets, the chief inhabitants of Longbourn.

Mr. Bennet, who was so odd a mixture of quick parts, sarcastic humour, reserve and caprice, that the experience of three-and-twenty years had been insufficient to make his wife understand his character, was the father of five unmarried daughters; Jane, Elizabeth, Mary, Kitty and Lydia. Mrs. Bennet, a still handsome woman, of mean understanding, little information, and uncertain temper, made the business of her life getting her daughters married, and its solace visiting and news.

The evening fixed for the ball came round at last; and when the Netherfield party entered the Assembly Rooms it was found to consist of five persons altogether; Mr. Bingley, his two sisters, the husband of the elder, and another young man.

Mr. Bingley was good-looking and gentleman-like; he had a pleasant countenance, and easy, unaffected manners. His sisters were fine women, with an air of decided fashion. His brother-in-law, Mr. Hurst, merely looked the gentleman; but his friend, Mr. Darcy, soon drew the attention of the room by his fine, tall person, handsome features, noble mien, and the report, which was in general circulation within five minutes after his entrance, of his having ten thousand a year. He was looked at with great admiration for about half the evening, till his manners gave a disgust which turned the tide of his popularity; for he was found to be proud, to be above his company, and above being pleased.

Mr. Bingley had soon made himself acquainted with all the principal people in the room. He was lively and unreserved, danced every dance, was angry that the ball closed so early, and talked of giving one himself at Netherfield. What a contrast between him and his friend! Mr. Darcy danced only once with Mrs. Hurst, and once with Miss Bingley, and declined being introduced to any other lady.

It so happened that Elizabeth, the second eldest of the Bennet girls, had been obliged, by the scarcity of gentlemen, to sit down for two dances; and during part of that time Mr. Darcy had been standing near enough for her to overhear a conversation between him and Mr. Bingley, who came from the dance for a few minutes.

"Come, Darcy," said he, "I must have you dance. I hate to see you standing about by yourself in this stupid manner. You had much better dance."

"I certainly shall not. You know how I detest it, unless I am particularly acquainted with my partner. At such an assembly as this it would be insupportable. Your sisters are engaged, and there is not another woman in the room whom it would not be a punishment to me to stand up with."

"I would not be so fastidious as you are," cried Bingley, "for a kingdom! Upon my honour, I never met with so many pleasant girls in my life as I have this evening, and there are several of them, you see, uncommonly pretty."

"You are dancing with the only handsome girl in the room," said Mr. Darcy, looking at the eldest Miss Bennet.

"Oh, she is the most beautiful creature I ever beheld! But there is one of her sisters sitting down just behind you who is very pretty, and I dare say very agreeable. Do let me ask my partner to introduce you."

"Which do you mean?" And turning round, he looked for a moment at Elizabeth, till, catching her eye, he withdrew his own, and coldly said: "She is tolerable, but not handsome enough to tempt me; and I am in no humour at present to give consequence to young ladies who are slighted by other men; You had better return to your partner and enjoy her smiles, for you are wasting your time with me."

Mr. Bingley followed his advice. Mr. Darcy walked off; and Elizabeth remained, with no very cordial feelings towards him. She told the story, however, with great spirit among her friends, for she had a lively, playful disposition, which delighted in anything ridiculous.

II-The Bennet Girls and their Lovers

Despite its rather unpromising commencement the course of a few days placed the acquaintance of the Bennets with the Bingleys on a footing approaching friendship; and soon matters began to stand somewhat as follow. It was obvious that Charles Bingley and Jane Bennet were mutually attracted, and this despite the latter's outward composure, which, like her amiability of manner and charity of view, was apt to mislead the superficial observer. On the other hand, while the Bingley ladies expressed themselves as willing to know the two elder Miss Bennets and pronounced Jane "a sweet girl", they found the other females of the family impossible.

Mrs. Bennet was intolerably stupid and tedious; Mary, who, being the only plain member of her family, piqued herself on the extent of her reading and the solidity of her reflections, was a platitudinous moralist; while Lydia and Kitty were loud, silly, giggling girls, who spent all their time in running after men.

As for Mr. Darcy, the indifference he at first felt to Elizabeth Bennet was gradually converted into a sort of guarded interest. Originally he had scarcely allowed her to be pretty, but now he admired the beautiful expression of her dark eyes. To this discovery succeeded some others equally mortifying. Though he had detected more than one failure of perfect symmetry in her form, he was forced to acknowledge her figure to be light and pleasing; and in spite of his asserting that her manners were not those of the fashionable world, he was caught by their easy playfulness. He began to wish to know more of her, and, as a step towards conversing with her himself, attended to her conversation with others, while, since both he and she were of a satirical turn, they soon began to exchange little rallying, challenging speeches, so that Caroline Bingley, who was openly angling for Darcy herself, said to him one night:

"How long has Miss Elizabeth Bennet been such a favourite? And pray when am I to wish you joy?"

To which remarks he merely replied: "That is exactly the question which I expected you to ask. A lady's imagination is very rapid; it jumps from admiration to love, from love to matrimony, in a moment. I knew you would be wishing me joy."

Meantime, the friendship subsisting between the two families was advanced by a visit of some days paid by the two Bennet sisters to the Bingleys, at whose house Jane, thanks to her mother's scheming, was laid up with a bad cold. On this occasion Jane was coddled and made much of by her dear friends Caroline and Mrs. Hurst; but Elizabeth was now reckoned too attractive by one sister, and condemned as too sharp-tongued by both.

"Elizabeth Bennet," said Miss Bingley, when the door was closed on her, "is one of those young ladies who seek to recommend themselves to the other sex by undervaluing their own; and with many men, I dare say, it succeeds. But in my opinion it is a very mean art."

"Undoubtedly," replied Darcy, to whom this remark was chiefly addressed, "there is meanness in all the arts which ladies sometimes condescend to employ for captivation. Whatever bears affinity to cunning is despicable."

Miss Bingley was not so entirely satisfied with this reply as to continue the subject.

Nevertheless, Darcy's growing attachment to Eliza was little dreamt of by that young lady. Indeed, her prejudice against him was strengthened by her pleasant intercourse with a handsome and agreeable young man called Wickham, an officer of the militia regiment quartered at Meryton, the nearest town to Longbourn. He told her how he was the son of a trusted steward of Darcy's father, and had been left by the old gentleman to his heir's liberality and care, and how Darcy had absolutely disregarded his father's wishes, and had treated his protégé, in cruel and unfeeling fashion.

On the top of this disclosure, and just at it seemed certain that Bingley was on the point of proposing to Jane, the whole Netherfield party suddenly abandoned Hertfordshire and returned to town, partly, as Elizabeth could not help thinking, in consequence of the behaviour of her family at a ball given at Netherfield Park, where it appeared to her that, had they made an agreement to expose themselves as much as they could during the evening, they could not have played their parts with more spirit or finer success.

III. Elizabeth Rejects the Rector

"I hope, my dear," said Mr. Bennet to his wife, "that you have ordered a good dinner to-day, because I have reason to expect an addition to our family party. My cousin, Mr. Collins, who, when I am dead, may turn you all out of this house as soon as he pleases."

"Oh! my dear," cried his wife, "Pray do not talk of that odious man." Mrs. Bennet continued to rail bitterly against the cruelty of settling an estate away from a family of five daughters, in favour of a man whom nobody cared anything about.

Thus, the Rev. Mr. Collins of Hunsford, the heir-presumptive to Longbourn, came to visit to the Bennets. He was a tall, heavy-looking young man of five-and-twenty. His air was grave and stately, and his manners were very formal. He was a strange mixture of pomposity, servility, and self-importance, a creature most abjectly, yet most amusingly, devoid of anything like tact, taste, or humour.

Being ready to make the Bennet girls every possible amends for the unwilling injury he must eventually do them, he thought first of all of offering himself to Jane; but hearing that her affections were pre-engaged, he had only to change from Jane to Elizabeth. It was soon done, done while Mrs. Bennet was stirring the fire. His proposal he made to the younger lady in a long, set speech, in which he explained, first of all, his general reasons for marrying, and then his reasons for directing his matrimonial views to Longbourn, finally assuring her that on the subject of the small portion she would bring him no ungenerous reproach should ever pass his lips when they were married.

It was absolutely necessary to interrupt him then, so Elizabeth told him he was too hasty, thanked him for his proposals, and declined them.

"I am not now to learn," replied Mr. Collins, with a formal wave of the hand, "that it is usual with young ladies to reject the addresses of the man whom they secretly mean to accept, when he first applies for their favour; and that sometimes the refusal is repeated a second, or even a third, time. I am, therefore, by no means discouraged by what you have said, and shall hope to lead you to the altar ere long."

"Upon my word, sir," cried Elizabeth, "your hope is rather an extraordinary one after my declaration! I do assure you that I am not one of those young ladies (if such young ladies there are) who are so daring as to risk their happiness on the chance of being asked a second time. I am perfectly serious in my refusal. You could not make me happy; and I am convinced that I am the last woman in the world who would make you so. Nay; were your patron, Lady Catherine, to know me, I am persuaded she would find me in every respect ill qualified for the situation."

Said Mr. Collins, very gravely. "I cannot imagine that her ladyship would at all disapprove of you. And you may be certain that when I have the honour of seeing her again, I shall speak in the highest terms of your modesty, economy, and other amiable qualifications."

Twice more was Mr. Collins refused, and even then he would not take "No" for an answer.

"You must give me leave to flatter myself, my dear cousin," said he, "that your refusals of my addresses are merely words, of course. My reasons for believing it are chiefly these. It does not appear to me that my hand is unworthy your acceptance, or that the establishment I can offer would be any other than highly desirable. My situation in life, my connections with the family of De Bourgh, and my relationship to your own, are circumstances highly in my favour; and you should take it into further consideration that, in spite of your manifold attractions, it is by no means certain that another offer of marriage may ever be made to you. Your portion is unhappily so small that it will, in all likelihood, undo the effects of your loveliness and amiable qualifications. As I must, therefore, conclude that you are not serious in your rejection of me, I shall choose to attribute it to your wish of increasing my love by suspense, according to the usual practice of elegant females."

"I do assure you, sir," said Elizabeth, "that I have no pretensions whatever to that kind of elegance which consists in tormenting a respectable man. I would rather be paid the compliment of being believed sincere. I thank you again and again for the honour you have done me in your proposals, but to accept them is absolutely impossible. My feelings in every respect forbid it. Can I speak plainer? Do not consider me now as an elegant female intending to plague you, but as a rational creature speaking the truth from her heart."

"You are uniformly charming," said he, with an air of awkward gallantry; "and I am persuaded that, when sanctioned by the express authority of both your excellent parents, my proposals will be acceptable."

IV. Darcy Loves and Loses

Rejected by Elizabeth, to the great satisfaction of her father and to the great indignation of her mother, the rector of Hunsford lost no time in betaking himself to Elizabeth's friend, Charlotte Lucas, who, being a girl with unromantic, not to say prosaic, views of marriage, readily accepted and married him, thereby moving to further disgust and anger poor Mrs. Bennet, who was already wondering and repining at Mr. Bingley's returning no more into Hertfordshire.

Jane suffered in silence, and despite Elizabeth's efforts to point out the duplicity of Caroline Bingley, was inclined to believe the protestations that the latter made in her letters from London of Bingley's growing attachment to Darcy's sister Georgiana.

Mr. Bennet treated the matter in his customary ironical way.

"So, Lizzy," said he, one day, "your sister is crossed in love, I find. I congratulate her. Next to being married, a girl likes to be crossed in love a little now and then. It is something to think of, and gives her a sort of distinction among her companions. When is your turn to come? You will hardly bear to be long outdone by Jane. Now is your time. Here are officers enough at Meryton to disappoint all the young ladies in the country. Let Wickham be your man. He is a pleasant fellow, and would jilt you creditably."

"Thank you, sir, but a less agreeable man would satisfy me. We must not all expect Jane's good fortune."

"True," said Mr. Bennet; "but it is a comfort to think that, whatever of that kind may befall you, you have a mother who will always make the most of it."

As it turned out, Wickham, though he had not arrived at an intimacy which enabled him to jilt Elizabeth, yet most certainly transferred his attentions very shortly from her to a Miss King, who, by the death of her grandfather, had come into £10,000. Elizabeth, however, was quite heartwhole; and she and her former admirer parted on friendly terms when she left Longbourn to pay her promised visit to Mr. and Mrs. Collins at Hunsford.

There she found Charlotte, managing her home and her husband with considerable discretion: and, as the rectory adjoined Rosings Park, the seat of Lady Catherine de Bourgh, the patroness of the living, she was introduced to that lady, in whom she could discover nothing but an insolent aristocratic woman, who dictated to everyone about her, meddled in everybody's business, aimed at marrying her sickly daughter to Darcy, and was, needless to say, slavishly adored by Mr. Collins.

In the third week of her visit Mr. Darcy and his cousin, Colonel Fitzwilliam, came down to see their aunt, and thus, to Elizabeth's indifference, an acquaintance was renewed which Darcy soon seemed to show a real desire to take up again. He sought her society at Rosings Park, he called familiarly at the rectory, he waylaid her in her favourite walk; and all the time, in all his intercourse with her, he revealed such a mixture of interest and constraint as demonstrated only too clearly that some internal struggle was going on within him.

Mrs. Collins began to hope for her friend; but Elizabeth, who had received from Colonel Fitzwilliam ample confirmation of her suspicion that it was Darcy who had persuaded Bingley to give up Jane, was now only more incensed against the man who had broken her sister's peace of mind.

On the very evening of the day on which she had extracted this piece of information from his cousin, Darcy, knowing her to be alone, called at the rectory, and, after a silence of several minutes, came towards her in an agitated manner.

"In vain have I struggled," he said. "It will not do. My feelings will not be repressed. You must allow me to tell you how ardently I admire and love you."

Elizabeth's astonishment was beyond expression. She stared, coloured, doubted, and was silent. This he considered sufficient encouragement; and the avowal of all that he felt, and had long felt, for her immediately followed. He spoke well; but there were feelings besides those of the heart to be detailed. His sense of her inferiority, of marriage with her being a degradation, of the family obstacles which judgement had always opposed to inclination, were dwelt on with a warmth which seemed due to the consequence he was wounding, but was very unlikely to recommend his suit. In truth, it was already lost, for though Elizabeth could not be insensible to the compliment of such a man's affection, her intentions did not vary for an instant. Accusing him of having ruined, perhaps for ever, the happiness of her sister Jane, and of having blighted the career of his former friend Wickham, she reproached him with the uncivil style of his declaration, and gave him her answer in the words:

"You could not have made me the offer of your hand in any possible way that would have tempted me to accept it."

Soon after, Darcy took his leave; but the next day he accosted Elizabeth in the park, and handed her a letter, which he begged her to read. She read it, and had the mortification to discover not only that Darcy made some scathing but perfectly justifiable comments on the objectionable members of her family, but that he was able to clear himself of both the charges she had brought against him. He maintained that in separating Bingley from Jane he had not the slightest notion that he was doing the latter any injury, since he never credited her with any strong attachment to his friend; and he assured Elizabeth that, though Wickham had always been an idle and dissipated person, he had more than fulfilled his father's intentions to him, and that Wickham had repaid him for his generosity by trying to elope with his young sister Georgiana, a girl of fifteen.

When Elizabeth returned to Longbourn, she found it a relief to tell Jane of Darcy's proposal, and of his revelation of Wickham's real character; but she thought it best to suppress every particular of the letter in which Jane herself was concerned.

V. An Elopement

Some two months later Elizabeth went on a tour in Derbyshire with her maternal uncle and aunt, Mr. and Mrs. Gardiner. The latter had lived for some years at a town called Lambton, and wished to revisit her old friends there; and as Pemberley, Mr. Darcy's seat, was only five miles off, and was a show-place, the Gardiners determined to see it, though their niece was reluctant to accompany them until she had learned that its owner was not at home. As they were being shown over the place, Elizabeth could not help reflecting that she might have been mistress of it, and she listened with surprise as the old housekeeper told them that she should never meet with a better master, that she had never had a cross word from him in her life, that as a child he was always the sweetest-tempered, most generous-hearted boy in the world, and that there was not one of his tenants or servants but would testify to his excellent qualities as a landlord and a master.

As they were walking across the lawn the owner of Pemberley himself suddenly came forward from the road, and as if to justify the praises of his housekeeper, and to show that he had taken to heart Elizabeth's former complaints of his behaviour, proceeded to treat the Gardiner party with the greatest civility, and even cordiality. He introduced his sister to them, asked them to dinner, invited Mr. Gardiner to fish at Pemberley as often as he chose, and, in answer to a spiteful remark of Miss

Bingley's to the effect that he had thought Elizabeth pretty at one time, made the crushing reply:

"Yes, but that was only when I first knew her; for it is many months since I have considered her as one of the handsomest women of my acquaintance."

But just when Elizabeth's growing esteem and gratitude might have deepened into affection for Darcy, circumstances were communicated to her in a letter from Jane which seemed to render it in the highest degree improbable that so proud and fastidious a man as he would ever make any further advances. Lydia, who had got herself invited by some friends to Brighton in order to be near the militia regiment which had been transferred there from Meryton, had eloped with Wickham, and the pair, instead of going to Scotland to be married, appeared, though their whereabouts could not yet be discovered, to be living together in London unmarried.

Darcy seemed to be staggered when he heard the news, and instantly acquiesced in the immediate return of the Gardiner party to Longbourn. They found on their arrival that Mr. Bennet was searching for his daughter in London, where Mr. Gardiner agreed to go to consult with him.

"Oh, my dear brother," said Mrs. Bennet, on hearing this, "that is exactly what I could most wish for! And now do, when you get to town, find them out wherever they may be; and if they are not married already, make them marry. And as for wedding clothes, do not let them wait for that; but tell Lydia she shall have as much money as she chooses to buy them after they are married. And, above all things, keep Mr. Bennet from fighting. Tell him what a dreadful state I am in, that I am frightened out of my wits, and have such tremblings, such flutterings all over me; such spasms in my side, and pains in my head, and such beatings at my heart that I can get no rest by day nor by night. And tell my dear Lydia not to give any directions about her clothes till she has seen me, for she does not know which are the best warehouses. Oh, brother, how kind you are! I know you will contrive it all."

Mr. Collins improved the occasion by writing a letter of condolence, in which he assured the distressed father that the death of Lydia would have been a blessing in comparison with her elopement. But, unfortunately, much of this instruction was wasted, the distress of the Bennets proving less irremediable than their cousin had anticipated or their neighbours feared-for, thanks, as it seemed, to the investigations and to the generosity of Mr. Gardiner, the eloping couple were discovered, and it was made worth Wickham's while to marry Lydia. Longbourn society bore the good news with decent philosophy, though, to be sure, it would have been more for the advantage of conversation had Miss Lydia Bennet come upon the town.

VI. Three Bennet Weddings

After arrangements had been made for Wickham's entering the regulars and joining a regiment at Newcastle, his marriage with Lydia took place, and the young couple were received at Longbourn. Their assurance was quite reassuring.

"Well, mamma," said Lydia, "and what do you think of my husband? Is not he a charming man? I am sure my sisters must all envy me. I only hope they may have half my good luck. They must all go to Brighton. That is the place to get husbands. What a pity it is, mamma, we did not all go!"

"Very true. And if I had my will we should. But, my dear Lydia, I don't at all like your going such a way off. Must it be so?"

"Oh, Lord, yes! There is nothing in that. I shall like it of all things. You and papa and my sisters must come down and see us. We shall be at Newcastle all the winter; and I dare say there will be some balls, and I will take care to get good partners for them all."

"I should like it beyond anything!" said her mother.

"And then, when you go away, you may leave one or two of my sisters behind you; and I dare say I shall get husbands for them before the winter is over."

"I thank you for my share of the favour," said Elizabeth; "but I do not particularly like your way of getting husbands!"

Indeed, from some remark which Lydia let slip about Darcy being at the wedding, Elizabeth soon began to think that it was only due to outside efforts that Mrs. Wickham had succeeded in getting her own husband.

An application for information which she made to her Aunt Gardiner confirmed this suspicion. Darcy, it seems, had hurried up to London immediately on hearing of the elopement; and he it was who, thanks to his knowledge of Wickham's previous history, found out where Lydia and he were lodging, and by dint of paying his debts to the tune of a thousand pounds, buying his commission, and settling another thousand pounds on Lydia, persuaded him to make her an honest woman. That is to say, thought Elizabeth, Darcy had met, frequently met, reasoned with, persuaded, and finally bribed the man whom he always most wished to avoid, and whose very name it was punishment to him to pronounce. Meantime, Bingley, accompanied by Darcy, made his reappearance at Netherfield Park and at the Bennets'; and Elizabeth had the mortification of seeing her mother welcome the former with the greatest effusiveness, and treat the latter coldly and almost resentfully. "Any friend of Mr. Bingley's will always be welcome here, to be sure; but else I must say that I hate the very sight of him," said Mrs. Bennet, as she watched the two men approaching the house to pay their first visit.

Despite, however, rather than by reason of, this surfeit of amiability on the part of the mother, the lovers quickly came to an understanding, and this, strangely enough, in the absence of Darcy, who had gone up to town. It was in Darcy's absence, also, that Lady Catherine de Bourgh came over to Longbourn, and helped to bring about what she most ardently wished to prevent by making an unsuccessful demand on Elizabeth that she should promise not to accept

Darcy for a husband, and by then reporting to him that Elizabeth had refused to give such a promise. The natural result followed. Elizabeth mustered up courage one day to thank Darcy for all he had done for Lydia; and this subject soon led him to affirm that in that matter he had thought only of Elizabeth, and to renew, and to renew successfully, his former proposals of marriage. When Mrs. Bennet first heard the great news she sat quite still, and unable to utter a syllable; and at first even Jane and her father were almost incredulous of the engagement, because they had seen practically nothing of the courtship.

But in the end they were all convinced, and Mr. Bennet's decisive comment was: "I admire all my three sons-in-law highly. Wickham, perhaps, is my favourite; but I think I shall like your husband quite as well as Jane's. If any young men come for Mary or Kitty, send them in, for I am quite at leisure."

The Rime of the Ancient Mariner
by Samuel Taylor Coleridge
(London, 1798)

The *'Ancyent Marinere'* was published in the collection *Lyrical Ballads* along with works by Wordsworth, its magical quality perhaps born of Coleridge's opium addiction. It is considered a foundation of "Romantic" literature, and of a whole sailship terror genre leading to *Pirates of the Caribbean*.

Abridged: GH, from the 1817 edition which modernised the pseudo-ancient English of the original.

IT IS an ancient Mariner,
And he stoppeth one of three.
"By thy long grey beard and glittering eye,
Now wherefore stopp'st thou me?

The Wedding-Guest sat on a stone:
He cannot chuse but hear;
And thus spake on that ancient man,
The bright-eyed Mariner.

The ship was cheered, the harbour cleared,
Merrily did we drop
Below the kirk, below the hill,
Below the light-house top.

And then the STORM-BLAST came, and he
Was tyrannous and strong:
He struck with his o'ertaking wings,
And chased south along.

And now there came both mist and snow,
And it grew wondrous cold:
And ice, mast-high, came floating by,
As green as emerald.

At length did cross an Albatross:
Thorough the fog it came;
As if it had been a Christian soul,
We hailed it in God's name.

"God save thee, ancient Mariner!
From the fiends, that plague thee thus!--
Why look'st thou so?"--With my cross-bow
I shot the ALBATROSS.

And I had done an hellish thing,

And it would work 'em woe:
For all averred, I had killed the bird
That made the breeze to blow.

Day after day, day after day,
We stuck, nor breath nor motion;
As idle as a painted ship
Upon a painted ocean.

Water, water, every where,
And all the boards did shrink;
Water, water, every where,
Nor any drop to drink.

The very deep did rot: O Christ!
That ever this should be!
Yea, slimy things did crawl with legs
Upon the slimy sea.

Ah! well a-day! what evil looks
Had I from old and young!
Instead of the cross, the Albatross
About my neck was hung.

With throats unslaked, with black lips baked,
We could not laugh nor wail;
I bit my arm, I sucked the blood,
And cried, A sail! a sail!

Alas! (thought I, and my heart beat loud)
How fast she nears and nears!
Are those her sails that glance in the Sun,
Like restless gossameres!

Are those her ribs through which the Sun
Did peer, as through a grate?

And is that Woman all her crew?
Is that a DEATH? and are there two?
Is DEATH that woman's mate?

The naked hulk alongside came,
And the twain were casting dice;
"The game is done! I've won! I've won!"
Quoth she, and whistles thrice.

Four times fifty living men,
(And I heard nor sigh nor groan)
With heavy thump, a lifeless lump,
They dropped down one by one.

The many men, so beautiful!
And they all dead did lie:
And a thousand thousand slimy things
Lived on; and so did I.

I looked to Heaven, and tried to pray:
And from my neck so free
The Albatross fell off, and sank
Like lead into the sea.

Oh sleep! it is a gentle thing,
Beloved from pole to pole!
To Mary Queen the praise be given!
She sent the gentle sleep from Heaven,
That slid into my soul.

Beneath the lightning and the Moon
The dead men gave a groan.
Their lifeless limbs 'gan work the ropes,
We were a ghastly crew.

I heard and in my soul discerned
Two VOICES in the air.
Quoth one, "The man hath penance done,
And penance more will do."

Swiftly, swiftly flew the ship,
Yet she sailed softly too:
Sweetly, sweetly blew the breeze--

On me alone it blew.

Oh! dream of joy! is this indeed
The light-house top I see?
Is this the hill? is this the kirk?
Is this mine own countree!

Each corse lay flat, lifeless and flat,
And, by the holy rood!
A man all light, a seraph-man,
On every corse there stood.

But soon I heard the dash of oars;
I heard the Pilot's cheer;
My head was turned perforce away,
And I saw a boat appear.

And now, all in my own countree,
I stood on the firm land!
The Hermit stepped forth from the boat,
And scarcely he could stand.

"O shrieve me, shrieve me, holy man!"
The Hermit crossed his brow.
"Say quick," quoth he, "I bid thee say--
What manner of man art thou?"

Since then I pass from land to land,
Till the agony returns,
And till my ghastly tale is told,
This heart within me burns.

Farewell, farewell! but this I tell
To thee, thou Wedding-Guest!
He prayeth well, who loveth well
Both man and bird and beast.

And now the Mariner is gone,
The Wedding-Guest forlorn,
A sadder and a wiser man,
He rose the morrow morn

I Wandered Lonely as a Cloud
by William Wordsworth
(1804)

Possibly the most famous poem in English. It is an evocation of the English Lake District around the future poet laureate's Dove Cottage at Grasmere, a landscape which came to be an inspiration for the 'Romanticism' of Thomas de Quincey (p299), Walter Scott, Samuel Taylor Coleridge (p285) and many, many others.

Unabridged

I wandered lonely as a cloud
That floats on high o'er vales and hills,
When all at once I saw a crowd,

A host of golden daffodils;
Beside the lake, beneath the trees,
Fluttering and dancing in the breeze.

Continuous as the stars
that shine and twinkle on the Milky Way,
They stretched in never-ending line
along the margin of a bay:
Ten thousand saw I at a glance,
tossing their heads in sprightly dance.

The waves beside them danced; but they
Out-did the sparkling waves in glee:
A poet could not but be gay,

in such a jocund company:
I gazed - and gazed - but little thought
what wealth the show to me had brought:

For oft, when on my couch I lie
In vacant or in pensive mood,
They flash upon that inward eye
Which is the bliss of solitude;
And then my heart with pleasure fills,
And dances with the daffodils.

A New System of Chemical Philosophy
by John Dalton
(Manchester, 1808)

The idea that absolutely every bit of matter is made from tiny atoms goes back to the ancient Greeks, but it was Dalton, despite being debarred from university for his refusal to acquiesce to the State religion, who showed how just a few different atom types or 'elements' can combine in fixed proportions to make seemingly quite different substances. He didn't get it quite right; he guessed that water was HO and ammonia was NH (they're actually H_2O and NH_3) and his theory of heat was plain wrong, but Dalton is still a 'Father' of 'The Central Science' of chemistry.

Abridged: GH

I. On Heat or Caloric

The most probable opinion concerning the nature of caloric, is, that of its being an elastic fluid of great subtility, the particles of which repel one another, but are attracted by all other bodies.

When all surrounding bodies are of one temperature, then the heat attached to them is in a quiescent state; the absolute quantities of heat in any two bodies in this case are not equal, whether we take the bodies of equal weights or of equal bulks. Each kind of matter has its peculiar affinity for heat, by which it requires a certain portion of the fluid, in order to be in equilibrium with other bodies at a certain temperature. Were the whole quantities of heat in bodies of equal weight or bulk, or even the relative quantities, accurately ascertained, for any temperature, the numbers expressing those quantities would constitute a table of specific heats, analogous to a table of specific gravities, and would be an important acquisition to science.

II. On the Constitution of Bodies.

There are three distinctions in the kinds of bodies, or three states, which have more especially claimed the attention of philosophical chemists; namely, those which are marked by the terms elastic fluids, liquids, and solids. A very famous instance is exhibited to us in water, of a body, which, in certain circumstances, is capable of assuming all the three states. In steam we recognise a perfectly elastic fluid, in water a perfect liquid, and in ice a complete solid. These observations have tacitly led to the conclusion which seems universally adopted, that all bodies of sensible magnitude, whether liquid or solid, are constituted of a vast number of extremely small particles, or atoms of matter bound together by a force of attraction, which is more or less powerful according to circumstances, and which as it endeavours to prevent their separation, is very properly called in that view, attraction of cohesion; but as it collects them from a dispersed state (as from steam into water) it is called, attraction of aggregation, or more simply affinity. Whatever names it may go by, they still signify one and the same power. It is not my design to call in question this conclusion, which appears completely satisfactory; but to shew that we have hitherto made no use of it, and that the consequence of the neglect, has been a very obscure view of chemical agency, which is daily growing more so in proportion to the new lights attempted to be thrown upon it.

The opinions I more particularly allude to, are those of Berthollet on the Laws of chemical affinity; such as that chemical affinity is proportional to the mass, and that in all chemical unions, there exist insensible gradations in the proportions of the constituent principles. The inconsistence of these opinions, both with reason and observation, cannot, I think, fail to strike every one who takes a proper view of the phenomena.

Whether the ultimate particles of a body, such as water, are all alike, that is, of the same figure, weight, &c. is a question of some importance. From what is known, we have no reason to apprehend a diversity in the particulars: if it does exist in water, it must equally exist in the elements constituting water, namely, hydrogen and oxygen. Now it is scarcely possible to conceive how the aggregates of dissimilar particles should be so uniformly the same. If some of the particles of water were heavier than others, if a parcel of the liquid on any occasion were constituted principally of these heavier particles, it must be supposed to affect the specific gravity of the mass, a circumstance not known. Similar observations may be made on other substances. Therefore we may conclude that the ultimate particles of all homogeneous bodies are perfectly alike in weight, figure, &c. In other words, every particle of water is like every other particle of water; every particle of hydrogen is like every other particle of hydrogen, &c.

Besides the force of attraction, which, in one character or another, belongs universally to ponderable bodies, we find another force that is likewise universal, or acts upon all matter which comes under our cognisance, namely, a force of repulsion. This is now generally, and I think properly, ascribed to the agency of heat. An atmosphere of this subtile fluid constantly surrounds the atoms of all bodies, and prevents them from being drawn into actual contact. This appears to be satisfactorily proved by the observation, that the bulk of a body may be diminished by abstracting some of its heat: But from what has been stated in the last section, it should seem that enlargement and diminution of bulk depend perhaps more on the arrangement, than on the size of the ultimate particles. Be this as it may, we cannot avoid inferring from the preceding doctrine on heat, and particularly from the section on the natural zero of temperature, that solid bodies, such as ice, contain a large portion, perhaps 4/5 of the heat which the same are found to contain in an elastic state, as steam.

We are now to consider how these two great antagonist powers of attraction and repulsion are adjusted, so as to allow of the three different states of elastic fluids, liquids, and solids. We shall divide the subject into four Sections; namely, first, on the constitution of pure elastic fluids; second, on the constitution of mixed elastic fluids; third, on the constitution of liquids, and fourth, on the constitution of solids.

III. On Chemical Synthesis.

When any body exists in the elastic state, its ultimate particles are separated from each other to a much greater distance than in any other state; each particle occupies the centre of a comparatively large sphere, and supports its dignity by keeping all the rest, which by their gravity, or otherwise are disposed to encroach up it, at a respectful distance. When we attempt to conceive the number of particles in an atmosphere, it is somewhat like attempting to conceive the number of stars in the universe; we are confounded with the thought. But if we limit the subject, by taking a given volume of any gas, we seem persuaded that, let the divisions be ever so minute, the number of particles must be finite; just as in a given space of the universe, the number of stars and planets cannot be infinite.

Chemical analysis and synthesis go no farther than to the separation of particles one from another, and to their reunion. No new creation or destruction of matter is within the reach of chemical agency. We might as well attempt to introduce a new planet into the solar system, or to annihilate one already in existence, as to create or destroy a particle of hydrogen. All the changes we can produce,

consist in separating particles that are in a state of cohesion or combination, and joining those that were previously at a distance.

In all chemical investigations, it has justly been considered an important object to ascertain the relative weights of the simples which constitute a compound. But unfortunately the enquiry has terminated here; whereas from the relative weights in the mass, the relative weights of the ultimate particles or atoms of the bodies might have been inferred, from which their number and weight in various other compounds would appear, in order to assist and to guide future investigations, and to correct their results. Now it is one great object of this work, to shew the importance and advantage of ascertaining the relative weights of the ultimate particles, both of simple and compound bodies, the number of simple elementary particles which constitute one compound particle, and the number of less compound particles which enter into the formation of one more compound particle.

If there are two bodies, A and B, which are disposed to combine, the following is the order in which the combinations may take place, beginning with the most simple: namely,

* 1 atom of A + 1 atom of B = 1 atom of C, binary.
* 1 atom of A + 2 atoms of B = 1 atom of D, ternary.
* 2 atoms of A + 1 atom of B = 1 atom of E, ternary.
* 1 atom of A + 3 atoms of B = 1 atom of F, quarternary.
* 3 atoms of A + 1 atom of B = 1 atom of G, quarternary.
* &c. &c.

The following general rules may be adopted as guides in all our investigations respecting chemical synthesis.

1st. When only one combination of two bodies can be obtained, it must be presumed to be a binary one, unless some other cause appear to the contrary.

2d. When two combinations are observed, they must be presumed to be a binary and a ternary.

3d. When three combinations are observed, they must be presumed to be a binary, and the other two ternary.

4th. When four combinations are observed, we should expect one binary, two ternary, and one quarternary, &c.

5th. A binary compound should always be specifically heavier than the mere mixture of its two ingredients.

6th. A ternary compound should be specifically heavier than the mixture of a binary and a simple, which would, if combined, constitute it; &c.

7th. The above rules and observations equally apply, when two bodies, such as C and D, D and E, &c. are combined.

From the application of these rules, to the chemical facts already well ascertained, we deduce the following conclusions; 1st. That water is a binary compound of hydrogen and oxygen, and the relative weights of the two elementary atoms are as 1:7, nearly; 2d. That ammonia is a binary compound of hydrogen and azote[1], and the relative weights of the two atoms are as 1:5, nearly; 3d. That nitrous gas is a binary compound of azote and oxygen, the

---

1   **Azote:** now called 'Nitrogen'

atoms of which weigh 5 and 7 respectively; that nitric acid is a binary or ternary compound according as it is derived, and consists of one atom of azote and two of oxygen, together weighing 19; that nitrous oxide is a compound similar to nitric acid, and consists of one atom of oxygen and two of azote, weighing 17; that nitrous acid is a binary compound of nitric acid and nitrous gas, weighing 31; that oxynitric acid is a binary compound of nitric acid with oxygen, weighing 26; 4th. That carbonic oxide is a binary compound, consisting of one atom of charcoal, and one of oxygen, together weighing nearly 12; that carbonic acid is a ternary compound, (but sometimes binary) consisting of one atom of charcoal, and two of oxygen, weighing 19; &c. &c. In all these cases the weights are expressed in atoms of hydrogen, each of which is denoted by unity.

ELEMENTS

Binary

Ternary

Quarternary

Quinquenary & Sextenary

Septenary

In the sequel, the facts and experiments from which these conclusions are derived, will be detailed; as well as a great variety of others from which are inferred the constitution and weight of the ultimate particles of the principal acids, the alkalis, the earths, the metals, the metallic oxides and

sulphurets, the long train of neutral salts, and in short, all the chemical compounds which have hitherto obtained a tolerably good analysis. Several of the conclusions will be supported by original experiments.

From the novelty as well as importance of the ideas suggested in this chapter, it is deemed expedient to give plates, exhibiting the mode of combination in some of the more simple cases. A specimen of these accompanies this first part. The elements or atoms of such bodies as are conceived at present to be simple, are denoted by a small circle, with some distinctive mark; and the combinations consist in the juxta-position of two or more of these; when three or more particles of elastic fluids are combined together in one, it is supposed that the particles of the same kind repel each other, and therefore take their stations accordingly.

Table of Atomic Weights

1.	Hydrogen, its relative weight	1
2.	Azote	5
3.	Carbone or charcoal	5
4.	Oxygen	7
5.	Phosphorous	9
6.	Sulphur	13
7.	Magnesia	20
8.	Lime	23
9.	Soda	28
10.	Potash	42
11.	Strontites	46
12.	Barytes	68
13.	Iron	38
14.	Zinc	56
15.	Copper	56
16.	Lead	95
17.	Silver	100
18.	Platina	100
19.	Gold	140
20.	Mercury	167

An atom of water or steam, composed of 1 of oxygen and 1 of hydrogen, retained in physical contact by a strong affinity, and supposed to be surrounded by a common atmosphere of heat; its relative weight = 8

An atom of ammonia, composed of 1 of azote and 1 of hydrogen = 6

An atom of nitrous gas, 1 of azote and 1 of oxygen = 12

An atom of nitrous oxide, 2 azote + 1 oxygen = 17

An atom of nitric acid, 1 azote + 2 oxygen = 19

An atom of carbonic acid, 1 carbone + 2 hydrogen = 19

An atom of sulphuric acid, 1 sulphur + 3 oxygen = 34

An atom of alcohol, 3 carbone, + 1 hydrogen = 16

An atom of nitrous acid, 1 nitric acid + 1 nitrous gas = 31

An atom of sugar, 1 alcohol + 1 carbonic acid = 35

Frankenstein
or, The Modern Prometheus
by Mary Shelley
(London, 1818)

1816 was the "Year Without a Summer", a long volcanic winter caused by the eruption of Mount Tambora. On holiday in Switzerland the 19 year-old Mary Godwin, (daughter of Mary Wollstonecraft, see p270) her lover the poet Percy Bysshe Shelley and Lord Byron amused themselves by inventing horror stories. Byron came up with *The Vampyre* and Mary with *Frankenstein.* Although precisely how Dr. Frankenstein gave life to a dead body is left to the imagination of future film-makers, it seems that Mary was influenced by Anton Mesmer's claims to have discovered a life-force of 'animal magnetism' and the attempts of Erasmus Darwin (Charles' (p360) grandfather) and others to animate dead matter using electricity. It is one of the great 'Gothic' novels and a continuing warning against human ambition in the industrial age.

Abridged: GH

Robert Walton's Letter

August 5, 17-; My Dear Sister. This letter will reach England by a merchantman now on its homeward voyage from Archangel; more fortunate than I, who may not see my native land, perhaps for many years. We have already reached a very high latitude, and it is the height of summer; but last Monday, July 31, we were nearly surrounded by ice which closed in the ship on all sides. Our situation was somewhat dangerous, especially as we were compassed round by a very thick fog. About two o'clock the mist cleared away, and we beheld in every direction, vast and irregular plains of ice. A strange sight suddenly attracted our attention. We perceived a low carriage, fixed on a sledge and drawn by dogs, pass on towards the North: a being which had the shape of a man, but apparently of gigantic stature, sat in the sledge and guided the dogs. We watched the rapid progress of the traveller until he was lost among the distant inequalities of the ice. Before night the ice broke and freed our ship.

In the morning, as soon as it was light, I went upon deck, and found all the sailors apparently talking to some one in the sea, it was, in fact, a sledge, like that we had seen before, which had drifted towards us in the night, on a large fragment of ice. Only one dog remained alive, but there was a human being whom the sailors were persuading to enter the vessel.

On perceiving me, the stranger addressed me in English. "Before I come on board your vessel," said he, "will you have the kindness to inform me whither you are bound?"

I replied that we were on a voyage of discovery towards the northern pole.

Upon hearing this he consented to come on board. His limbs were nearly frozen, and his body dreadfully emaciated. I never saw a man in so wretched a condition, and I often feel that his sufferings had deprived him of understanding.

Once the lieutenant asked why he had come so far upon the ice in so strange a vehicle. He replied, "To seek one who fled from me." "And did the man whom you pursued travel in the same fashion?"

"Yes."

"Then I fancy we have seen him; for the day before we picked you up, we saw some dogs drawing a sledge, with a man in it, across the ice."

From this time a new spirit of life animated the decaying frame of the stranger. He manifested the greatest eagerness to be upon deck, to watch for the sledge which had before appeared.

August 17; Yesterday the stranger said to me, "You may easily perceive, Capt. Walton, that I have suffered great and unparalleled misfortunes. My fate is nearly fulfilled. I wait but for one event, and then I shall repose in peace. Listen to my history, and you will perceive how irrevocably my destiny is determined."

Frankenstein's Story

I am by birth a Genevese; and my family is one of the most distinguished of that republic. My father has filled several public situations with honour and reputation. He passed his younger days perpetually occupied by the affairs of his country, and it was not until the decline of life that he became a husband and the father of a family.

When I was about five years old, my mother, whose benevolent disposition often made her enter the cottages of the poor, brought to our house a child fairer than pictured cherub, an orphan whom she found in a peasant's hut; the infant daughter of a nobleman who had died fighting for Italy. Thus Elizabeth became the inmate of my parents' house. Every one loved her, and I looked upon Elizabeth as mine, to protect, love, and cherish. We called each other familiarly by the name cousin, and were brought up together. No human being could have passed a happier childhood than myself.

While I followed the routine of education in the schools of Geneva, I was, to a great degree, self-taught. Under the guidance of my books I searched for the philosopher's stone and the elixir of life. Wealth was an inferior object, but what glory would attend the discovery if I could banish disease from the human frame! Nor were these my only visions. The raising of ghosts or devils was a promise liberally accorded by my favourite authors, the fulfilment of which I most eagerly sought, guided by an ardent imagination and childish reasoning, till an accident again changed the current of my ideas.

When I was about fifteen years old we witnessed a most violent and terrible thunderstorm as it advanced from behind the mountains of Jura. I beheld a stream of fire issue from an old oak about twenty yards from our house; and so soon as the dazzling light vanished, we found the tree entirely reduced to thin ribbons of wood. I never beheld anything so utterly destroyed. On this occasion a man of great research in natural philosophy was with us, and he entered on the explanation of a theory of electricity and galvanism, which was at once new and astonishing to me.

When I had attained the age of seventeen, my parents resolved that I should become a student at the University of Ingolstadt; I had hitherto attended the schools, of Geneva.

Before the day of my departure arrived, the first misfortune of my life occurred- an omen of my future misery. My mother attended Elizabeth in an attack of scarlet fever. Elizabeth was saved, but my mother sickened and died. On her deathbed she joined the hands of Elizabeth and myself:-"My children," she said, "my firmest hopes of future happiness were placed on the prospect of your union. This expectation will now be the consolation of your father."

The day of my departure for Ingolstadt, deferred for some weeks by my mother's death, at length arrived. I reached the town after a long and fatiguing journey, delivered my letters of introduction, and paid a visit to some of the principal professors.

M. Krempe, professor of Natural Philosophy, was an uncouth man. He asked me several questions concerning my progress in different branches of science, and informed me I must begin my studies entirely anew.

M. Waldman was very unlike his colleague. His voice was the sweetest I had ever heard. Partly from curiosity, and partly from idleness, I entered his lecture room, and his panegyric upon modern chemistry I shall never forget:-"The ancient teachers of this science," said he, "promised impossibilities, and performed nothing. The modern masters promise very little, and have, indeed, performed miracles. They have discovered how the blood circulates, and the nature of the air we breathe. They have acquired new and almost unlimited powers; they can command the thunders of the heaven, mimic the earthquake, and even mock the invisible world with its own shadows."

Such were the professor's words, words of fate enounced to destroy me. As he went on, I felt as if my soul were grappling with a palpable enemy. So much has been done, exclaimed the soul of Frankenstein. More, far more, will I achieve: I will pioneer a new way, explore unknown powers, and unfold to the world the deepest mysteries of creation. I closed not my eyes that night; and from this time natural philosophy, and particularly chemistry, became nearly my sole occupation. My progress was rapid, and at the end of two years I made some discoveries in the improvement of chemical instruments which procured me great esteem at the University.

I became acquainted with the science of anatomy, and often asked myself, Whence did the principle of life proceed? I observed the natural decay of the human body, and saw how the fine form of man was degraded and wasted. I examined and analysed all the minutiae of causation in the change from life to death and death to life, until from the midst of this darkness a sudden light broke in upon me. I became dizzy with the immensity of the prospect, and surprised that among so many men of genius I alone should be reserved to discover so astonishing a secret.

When I found so astonishing a power placed within my hands, I hesitated a long time concerning the manner in which I should employ it. Although I possessed the capacity of bestowing animation, yet to prepare a frame for the reception of it, with all its intricacies of fibres, muscles, and veins, still remained a work of inconceivable difficulty and labour. I doubted at first whether I should attempt the creation of a being like myself, or one of simpler organization; but my imagination was too much exalted by my first success to permit me to doubt of my ability to give life to an animal as complex and wonderful as man.

I collected bones from charnel houses, and the dissecting room and the slaughter house furnished many of my materials. Often my nature turned with loathing from my occupation, but the thought that if I could bestow animation upon lifeless matter I might in process of time renew life where death had apparently devoted the body to corruption, supported my spirits.

In a solitary chamber at the top of the house I kept my workshop of filthy creation. The summer months passed, but my eyes were insensible to the charms of nature. Winter, spring, and summer passed away before my work drew to a close, but now every day showed me how well I had succeeded. But I had become a wreck, so engrossing was my occupation, and nervous to a most painful degree. I shunned my fellow-creatures as if I had been guilty of a crime.

Frankenstein's Creation

It was on a dreary night of November that I beheld the accomplishment of my toil. With an anxiety that amounted to agony, I collected the instruments of life around me, that I might infuse a spark of being into the lifeless thing that lay at my feet. I saw the dull yellow eye of the creature open; it breathed hard; and a convulsive motion agitated its limbs.

How can I delineate the wretch whom with such infinite pains and care I had endeavoured to form? His yellow skin scarcely covered the work of muscles and arteries beneath; his hair was of a lustrous black, and flowing; his teeth of a pearly whiteness; but his watery eyes seemed almost of the same colour as the dun-white sockets in which they were set.

I had worked hard for nearly two years for the sole purpose of infusing life into an inanimate body. For this I had deprived myself of rest and health. But now that I had finished, breathless horror and disgust filled my heart. Unable to endure the aspect of the being I had created, I rushed out of the room. I tried to sleep, but disturbed by the wildest dreams, I started up. By the dim and yellow light of the moon I beheld the miserable monster whom I had created. He held up the curtains of the bed, and his eyes were fixed on me. He might have spoken, but I did not hear; one hand was stretched out, seemingly to detain me, but I escaped and rushed downstairs.

No mortal could support the horror of that countenance. I had gazed on him while unfinished; he was ugly then, but when those muscles and joints were rendered capable of motion, no mummy could be so hideous. I took refuge in the court-yard, and passed the night wretchedly.

For several months I was confined by a nervous fever, and on my recovery was filled with a violent antipathy even to the name of Natural Philosophy.

A letter from my father telling me that my youngest brother William had been found murdered, and bidding me return and comfort Elizabeth, made me decide to hasten home.

It was completely dark when I arrived in the environs of Geneva. The gates of the town were shut, and I was obliged to pass the night at a village outside. A storm was raging on the mountains, and I wandered out to watch the tempest and resolved to visit the spot where my poor William had been murdered.

Suddenly I perceived in the gloom a figure which stole from behind a clump of trees near me; I could not be mistaken. A flash of lightning illuminated the object, and discovered its shape plainly to me. Its gigantic stature, and the deformity of its aspect, more hideous than belongs to humanity, instantly informed me that it was the wretch to whom I had given life. What did he there? Could he be the murderer of my brother? No sooner did that idea cross my imagination than I became convinced of its truth. The figure passed me quickly, and I lost it in the gloom. I thought of pursuing, but it would have been in vain, for another flash discovered him to me hanging among the rocks, and he soon reached the summit and disappeared.

It was about five in the morning when I entered my father's house. It was a house of mourning, and from that time I lived in daily fear lest the monster I had created should perpetrate some new wickedness. I wished to see him again that I might avenge the death of William.

My wish was soon gratified. I had wandered off alone up the valley of Chamounix, and was resting on the side of the mountain, when I beheld the figure of a man advancing towards me, over the crevices in the ice, with superhuman speed. He approached: his countenance bespoke bitter anguish-it was the wretch whom I had created.

"Devil," I exclaimed, "do you dare approach me? Begone, vile insect! Or, rather, stay, that I may trample you to dust!"

"I expected this reception," said the monster. "All men hate the wretched: how, then, must I be hated, who am miserable beyond all living things. You purpose to kill me. Do your duty towards me and I will do mine towards you and the rest of mankind. If you will comply with my conditions I will leave them and you at peace; but if you refuse, I will glut the maw of death with the blood of your remaining friends."

My rage was without bounds, but he easily eluded me and said:

"Have I not suffered enough, that you seek to increase my misery? Remember that I am thy creature. Everywhere I see bliss, from which I alone am excluded. I was benevolent and good; misery made me a fiend. I have assisted the labours of man, I have saved human beings from destruction, and I have been stoned and shot at as a recompense. The feelings of kindness and gentleness have given place to rage. Mankind spurns and hates me. The desert mountains and dreary glaciers are my refuge, and the bleak sky is kinder to me than your fellow-beings. Shall I not hate them who abhor me? Listen to me, Frankenstein. I have wandered through these mountains consumed by a burning passion which you alone can gratify. You must create a female for me with whom I can live. I am alone and miserable; man will not associate with me; but one as deformed and horrible as myself would not deny herself to me.

"What I ask of you is reasonable and moderate. It is true, we shall be monstrous, cut off from all the world: but on that account we shall be more attached to one another. Our lives will not be happy, but they will be harmless, and free from the misery I now feel. If you consent, neither you nor any other human being shall ever see us again: I will go to the vast wilds of South America. We shall make our bed of dried leaves; the sun will shine on us as on man, and will ripen our foods. My evil passion will have fled, for I shall meet with sympathy. My life will flow quietly away, and in my dying moments I shall not curse my maker."

His words had a strange effect on me. I compassionated him, and concluded that the justest view both to him and my fellow-creatures demanded of me that I should comply with his request.

"I consent to your demand," I said, "on your solemn oath to quit Europe forever."

"I swear," he cried, "by the sun and by the fire of love which burns in my heart that if you grant my prayer, while they exist you shall never behold me again. Depart to your home, and commence your labours: I shall watch their progress with unutterable anxiety."

Saying this, he suddenly quitted me, fearful, perhaps, of any change in my sentiments.

The Doom of Frankenstein

I travelled to England with my friend Henry Clerval, and we parted in Scotland. I had fixed on one of the remotest of the Orkneys as the scene of my labours.

Three years before I was engaged in the same manner, and had created a fiend whose barbarity had desolated my heart. I was now about to form another being, of whose dispositions I was alike ignorant. He had sworn to quit the neighbourhood of man, and hide himself in deserts, but she had not. They might even hate each other, and she might quit him. Even if they were to leave Europe, a race of devils would be propagated upon the earth, who might make the very existence of man precarious and full of terror.

I was alone on a solitary island, when looking up, the monster whom I dreaded appeared. My mind was made up: I would never create another like to him.

"Begone," I cried, "I break my promise. Never will I create your equal in deformity and wickedness. Leave me; I am inexorable."

The monster saw my determination in my face, and gnashed his teeth in anger. "Shall each man," cried he, "find a wife for his bosom, and each beast have his mate, and I be alone? I had feelings of affection, and they were requited by detestation and scorn. Are you to be happy, while I grovel in the intensity of my wretchedness? I go, but remember, I shall be with you on your wedding night."

I started forward, but he quitted the house with precipitation. In a few moments I saw him in his boat, which shot across the waters with an arrowy swiftness.

The next day I set off to rejoin Clerval, and return home. But I never saw my friend again. The monster murdered him, and for a time I lay in prison on suspicion of the crime. On my release one duty remained to me. It was necessary that I should hasten without delay to Geneva, there to watch over the lives of those I loved, and to lie in wait for the murderer.

Soon after my arrival, my father spoke of my long-contemplated marriage with Elizabeth. I remembered the fiend's words, "I shall be with you on your wedding night," and if I had thought what might be the devilish intention of my adversary I would never have consented. But thinking it was only my own death I was preparing I agreed with a cheerful countenance.

Elizabeth seemed happy, and I was tranquil. In the meantime I took every precaution, carrying pistols and dagger, lest the fiend should openly attack me.

After the ceremony was performed, a large party assembled at my father's; it was agreed that Elizabeth and I should proceed immediately to the shores of Lake Como.

That night we stopped at an inn. I reflected how fearful a combat, which I momentarily expected, would be to my wife, and earnestly entreated her to retire. She left me, and

I walked up and down the passages of the house inspecting every corner that might afford a retreat to my adversary.

Suddenly I heard a shrill and dreadful scream. It came from the room into which Elizabeth had retired. I rushed in. There, lifeless and inanimate, thrown across the bed, her head hanging down, and her pale and distorted features half covered with her hair, was the purest creature on earth, my love, my wife, so lately living, and so dear.

And at the open window I saw a figure the most hideous and abhorred. A grin was on the face of the monster as with his fiendish finger he pointed towards the corpse.

Drawing a pistol I fired; but he eluded me, and running with the swiftness of lightning, plunged into the lake.

The report of the pistol brought a crowd into the room. I pointed to the spot where he had disappeared, and we followed the track with boats. Nets were cast, but in vain. On my return to Geneva, my father sank under the tidings I bore, for Elizabeth had been to him more than a daughter, and in a few days he died in my arms.

Then I decided to tell my story to a criminal judge in the town, and beseech him to assert his whole authority for the apprehension of the murderer. This Genevan magistrate endeavoured to soothe me as a nurse does a child, and treated my tale as the effects of delirium. I broke from the house angry and disturbed, and soon quitted Geneva, hurried away by fury. Revenge has kept me alive; I dared not die and leave my adversary in being.

For many months this has been my task. Guided by a slight clue, I followed the windings of the Rhone, but vainly. The blue Mediterranean appeared; and, by a strange chance, I saw the fiend hide himself in a vessel bound for the Black Sea.

Amidst the wilds of Tartary and Russia, although he still evaded me, I have ever followed in his track. Sometimes the peasants informed me of his path; sometimes he himself left some mark to guide me. The snows descended on my head, and I saw the print of his huge step on the white plain.

My life, as it passed thus, was indeed hateful to me, and it was during sleep alone that I could taste joy.

As I still pursued my journey to the northward, the snows thickened and the cold increased in the degree almost too severe to support. I found the fiend had pursued his journey across the frost-bound sea in a direction that led to no land, and exchanging my land sledge for one fashioned for the Frozen Ocean I followed him.

I cannot guess how many days have passed since then. I was about to sink under the accumulation of distress when you took me on board. But I had determined, if you were going southward, still to trust myself to the mercy of the seas rather than abandon my purpose-for my task is unfulfilled.

Walton's Letter, continued

A week has passed away while I have listened to the strangest tale that ever imagination formed.

The only joy that Frankenstein can now know will be when he composes his shattered spirit to peace and death.

September 12: I am returning to England. I have lost my hopes of utility and glory. September 9 the ice began to move, and we were in the most imminent peril. I had promised the sailors that should a passage open to the south, I would not continue my voyage, but would instantly direct my course southward. On the 11th a breeze sprung from the west, and the passage towards the south became perfectly free. Frankenstein bade me farewell when he heard my decision, and died pressing my hand.

At midnight I heard the sound of a hoarse human voice in the cabin where the remains of Frankenstein were lying. I entered, and there, over the body, hung a form gigantic, but uncouth and distorted, and with a face of appalling hideousness.

The monster uttered wild and incoherent self-reproaches. "He is dead who called me into being," he cried, "and the remembrance of us both will speedily vanish. Soon I shall die, and what I now feel be no longer felt."

He sprang from the cabin window as he said this, upon the ice-raft which lay close to the vessel, and was borne away by the waves, and lost in darkness and distance.

Ivanhoe
by Sir Walter Scott
(Edinburgh,1819)

Ivanhoe reinvented Robin Hood as the cheerful, patriotic rebel of Douglas Fairbanks and *Prince of Thieves*, provided the popular image of Normans and Saxons, of bold King Richard, sneaky Prince John (see p106), of knights in armour and ladies in towers. This book, despite, or probably because of, its suspect historical accuracy, heralded-in the century-long Victorian fascination with the medieval which spilled over into art, architecture and even religion.

Abridged: GH

IN that pleasant district of merry England which is watered by the river Don, there extended in ancient times a large forest, covering the greater part of the beautiful hills and valleys between Sheffield and Doncaster.

Such being our chief scene, the date of our story refers to a period when King Richard was a prisoner of the perfidious Duke of Austria, and when his return had become an event rather wished than hoped for by his despairing subjects. His brother, Prince John, was using every species of influence to prolong the captivity, and to strengthen his own faction in the kingdom.

The condition of the English nation was miserable. From the Conquest, by Duke William of Normandy, four generations had not sufficed to blend the hostile blood of the Normans and Anglo-Saxons.

* * *

The hall of Rotherwood was of the rude simplicity of the Saxon period; the walls were left bare, the rude earthen floor was uncarpeted and the board was uncovered by cloth.

In the centre of the upper table, were placed two chairs for the master and mistress of the family. One of these was occupied by Cedric the Saxon, who, though but in rank a thane, or, as the Normans called him, a Franklin, felt, at the delay of his evening meal, an irritable impatience at the absence of his faithful slaves, Wamba and Gurth. "I suppose, they are carried off, the Saxon fools, to serve the Norman lord. But I will be avenged," he added. "Haply

they think me old; but they shall find, alone and childless as I am, the blood of Hereward is in the veins of Cedric."

From his musing, Cedric was suddenly awakened by the blast of a horn at his gate followed by a warder announcing "The Prior Aymer of Jorvaulx, and the good knight Brian de Bois-Guilbert, commander of the Knights Templars, with a small retinue, requested hospitality and lodging for the night, being on their way to a tournament to be held not far from Ashby-de-la-Zouche, on the second day from the present."

Cedric muttered; "Normans both;- but Norman or Saxon, the hospitality of Rotherwood must not be impeached; they are welcome." He knit his brows, and fixed his eyes for an instant on the ground; as he raised them, the folding doors at the bottom of the hall were cast wide, and, preceded by the major-domo, or steward, with his wand, the guests of the evening entered the apartment.

The Prior Aymer wore a cope curiously embroidered, and his fingers, contrary to the canon, were loaded with precious gems. The Knight Templar was as rich in dress, and his appearance far more commanding.

These two were followed by their respective attendants, and at a more humble distance by their guide, whose figure wore the weeds of a pilgrim.

When the repast was about to commence the major-domo suddenly said aloud, "Forbear! for the Lady Rowena."

A side-door at the upper end of the hall opened and Rowena, followed by four female attendants, entered the apartment. Cedric hastened to meet his ward, and to conduct her, with respectful ceremony, to the seat at his own right hand. All stood up to receive her; as she moved gracefully forward to assume her place at the board.

Rowena perceived the Knight Templar's eyes bent on her with ardour, and drew with dignity the veil around her.

"Sir Prior," said the Saxon, "I drink to you, in this cup of wine, unless you be so rigid in adhering to monastic rule as to prefer your acid preparation of milk."

"Nay," said the Priest, laughing, "it is only in our abbey that we confine ourselves to the 'lac acidum'. Conversing with, the world, we use the world's fashions."

A servant whispered into Cedric's ear, "A Jew is at the gate, Isaac of York; should I marshal him into the hall?"

"St Mary," said the Abbot, "an unbelieving Jew!"

"A dog Jew," echoed the Templar, "my Saracen slaves are true Moslems, and scorn as much as any Christian to hold intercourse with a Jew."

"Hush," said Cedric, "let him enter."

As Isaac stood an outcast in the present society, like his people among the nations, the pilgrim who sat by the chimney took compassion upon him, and resigned his seat, saying briefly, "Old man, my garments are dried, my hunger is appeased, thou art both wet and fasting."

Meanwhile the Abbot and Cedric continued their discourse upon hunting. "Pledge me in a cup of wine, Sir Templar," said Cedric, "and fill another to the Abbot. To the strong in arms, Sir Templar, be their race or language what it will, who now bear them in Palestine among the champions of the Cross!"

"To the Knights Hospitallers," said the Abbot."

"Were there none in the English army," said the Lady Rowena, "worthy to be mentioned?"

"Forgive me, lady," replied De Bois-Guilbert; "the English warriors were second only to..."

"Second to NONE," said the Pilgrim, who had stood near enough to hear, "the English chivalry were second to NONE who ever drew sword in defence of the Holy Land. I say, for I saw it. King Richard and five of his knights held a tournament after the taking of St John-de-Acre, as challengers against all comers - and Sir Brian de Bois-Guilbert well knows the truth of what I tell you."

At Cedric's request the Pilgrim told out the names of the English knights, only pausing at the sixth to say- "he was a young knight- his name dwells not in my memory."

"Sir Palmer," said Sir Brian de Bois-Guilbert scornfully, I will myself tell the name - it was the Knight of Ivanhoe; nor was there one of the six that had more renown in arms. Were he in England, I would give him every advantage of weapons, and abide the result."

"If Ivanhoe ever returns from Palestine," replied the Palmer, "I will be his surety that he meets you."

"And what do you proffer as pledge?" said the Templar.

"This reliquary," said the Palmer, taking a small ivory box from his bosom, "containing a portion of the true cross, brought from the Monastery of Mount Carmel."

The Prior of Jorvaulx crossed himself, in which all devoutly joined, excepting the Jew, the Mahomedans, and the Templar. "Let Prior Aymer hold my pledge and that of this nameless vagrant, in token that when the Knight of Ivanhoe comes within the four seas of Britain, he underlies the challenge of Brian de Bois-Guilbert, which, if he answer not, I will proclaim him as a coward on the walls of every Temple Court in Europe."

"My voice shall be heard," said the Lady Rowen, "if no other in this hall is raised on behalf of the absent Ivanhoe. I affirm he will meet every honourable challenge."

The grace-cup was served round, and the guests, after making obeisance to their landlord, arose and mingled in the hall, before, by separate doors, they retired.

* * *

In a sleeping-chamber the Palmer stirred the Jew with his pilgrim's staff.

"Fear nothing from me, Isaac," said the Palmer, "I come as your friend. The Templar yesternight spoke to his Mussulman slaves, charging them to seize the Jew. You have cause for terror, considering how your brethren have been ill-used; but, I say, leave this mansion instantly, while its inmates sleep.

"In truth", said the Jew, "I am a plundered, man. Hard hands have wrung from me all that I possessed - Yet I can tell that thy wish is for a horse and armour."

The Palmer started, but the Jew delivered a scroll, in Hebrew characters, saying, "In the town of Leicester all men know Kirjath Jairam of Lombardy; give him this scroll, and he will give thee thy choice of armour and mount. Thy lance will be powerful as the rod of Moses[1]."

They parted, and took different roads towards Sheffield.

* * *

The Passage of Arms, as it was called, at Ashby, attracted universal attention, as champions of the first renown were to take the field in the presence of Prince John himself, whose quick eye instantly recognised the Jew among the crowds, but was more agreeably attracted by his beautiful daughter, Rebecca.

Waldemar Fitzurse, Prince John's favourite minister, gave signal to the heralds to proclaim the laws of the tournament, which were briefly as follows:

First, the five challengers were to undertake all comers. Secondly, any knight proposing to combat, might select an antagonist by touching his shield.

The lists presented a most splendid spectacle. The Wardour Manuscript records at great length their devices, colours, and the embroidery of their horse trappings. But, to borrow lines from a contemporary poet:

---

1   **Moses' rod:** see the Torah p23, Exodus 4 and 14

"The knights are dust,
And their good swords are rust,
Their souls are with the saints, we trust."

Their castles themselves are but green mounds and shattered ruins - the place that once knew them, knows them no more

The challengers, headed by Brian de Bois-Guilbert, were all Normans, and Cedric saw, with keen dissatisfaction, the advantage they gained. No less than four parties of knights had gone down before them, and Prince John began to talk about adjudging the prize to Bois-Guilbert.

At length, a solitary trumpet, breathed a note of defiance. All eyes were turned to see a new champion

His suit of armour was formed of steel, richly inlaid with gold, and the device on his shield was a young oak-tree pulled up by the roots, with the Spanish word Desdichado, signifying Disinherited. He struck with the sharp end of his spear the shield of Brian de Bois-Guilbert until it rang.

"Have you confessed yourself, brother," said the Templar, "for today you look your last upon the sun."

The champions closed with the shock of a thunderbolt. The Templar aimed at the centre of his antagonist's shield, while that champion directed the point of his lance towards Bois-Guilbert's helmet, as saddle, horse, and man, rolled on the ground under a cloud of dust.

The Templar drew his sword and waved it in defiance, as the marshals of the field spurred their horses between them, and reminded them, that the laws of the tournament did not permit this species of encounter.

The conqueror called for a bowl of wine, and opening the beaver, or lower part of his helmet, announced that he quaffed it, "To all true English hearts." He then commanded his trumpet to sound a defiance to challengers, and four Normans each in his turn retired discomfited.

The acclamations of thousands applauded the unanimous award of that day's honours to the Disinherited Knight.

Prince John, having placed upon his lance a coronet of green satin, the Disinherited Knight rode slowly around the lists and deposited the coronet at the feet of the fair Rowena, while the populace shouted "Long live the Lady Rowena, the chosen Queen of Love and of Beauty!

On the following morning the general tournament was proclaimed, and about fifty knights were ready upon each side. The Disinherited Knight led one body, and Brian de Bois-Guilbert the other, with the gigantic Front-de-Boeuf, and the ponderous Athelstane, who, though a Saxon, had enlisted as a Norman, to Cedric's disgust.

The masterly horsemanship of the Disinherited Knight, and his noble mount, enabled him for a few minutes to keep at sword's point his antagonists, until an unexpected incident changed the fortune of the day.

Among the ranks of the Disinherited Knight a champion in black armour, who bore on his shield no device of any kind, had hitherto evinced very little interest. At once this knight seemed to throw aside his apathy, and came like a thunderbolt, exclaiming, "Desdichado, to the rescue!" "Le Noir Faineant" then turned his horse upon Athelstane of Coningsburgh; and bestowed him such a blow upon the crest, that Athelstane lay senseless.

The knight returned calmly to the extremity of the lists, leaving his leader to cope as he best could with Brian de Bois-Guilbert. This was no longer matter of so much difficulty as formerly. The Templar's horse had bled much, and gave way under the shock of the Disinherited Knight's charge. Brian de Bois-Guilbert rolled on the field, encumbered with the stirrup, from which he was unable to draw his foot. His antagonist sprung from horseback, waved his fatal sword over the head of his adversary, and commanded him to yield himself. Prince John only saved him by casting down his warder, and putting an end to the conflict.

Thus ended the memorable field of Ashby. The Knight of the Black Armour, to the surprise of all present, was nowhere to be found, so that the Disinherited Knight was, therefore, named champion of the day.

The marshals conducted the Disinherited Knight across the lists to the foot of that throne of honour occupied by the Lady Rowena.

The knight muttered that his helmet might not be removed, but the marshals paid no attention and unhelmed him by cutting the laces of his casque, so that the well-formed, yet sun-burnt features of a young man of twenty-five were seen,

Rowena had no sooner beheld him than she uttered a faint shriek; as the knight stooped his head, and then, sinking forward, lay prostrate at her feet.

Cedric, who had been struck mute by the sudden appearance of none other than his banished son, now rushed forward, as the marshals of the field hastened to undo his armour, and found that the head of a lance had inflicted a wound in his side.

As the name of Ivanhoe reached the circle of the Prince, his brow darkened.

"Ay," said Fitzurse, "this gallant is likely to reclaim the castle and manor which Richard assigned to him, and which your Highness's generosity has since given to Front-de-Boeuf."

"Whatever becomes of him," said Prince John, "he is victor of the day. For now, we must begin the archery contest."

More than thirty yeomen at first presented themselves, but soon only Hubert, a forester in the service of Philip de Malvoisin, and one other remained.

"Fellow," said Prince John, "What is thy name?"

"Locksley," answered the yeoman.

"Then, Locksley," said Prince John, "If thou carriest the prize, I will add to it twenty nobles; but if thou losest, thou shalt be stript of thy Lincoln green

Hubert shot so successfully that his arrow alighted in the very centre of the target.

"Thou canst not mend that shot, Locksley," said the Prince, with an insulting smile.

Locksley let fly his arrow, it lighted right upon that of his competitor, which it split to shivers. "Such archery was never seen since bow was first bent in Britain," whispered the yeomen to each other.

A jubilee of acclamations followed; and even Prince John, was forced to admire Locksley's skill, "These twenty nobles, thou hast fairly won; we will make them fifty, if thou wilt take livery and service with us as a yeoman of our body guard,

"Pardon me, noble Prince," said Locksley; "but I have vowed, that if ever I take service, it should be with your royal brother King Richard", and Locksley, anxious to escape further observation, mixed with the crowd, and was seen no more.

* * *

But Cedric, Rowena, and Athelstane, returning home with their retinue from Ashby, were waylaid by Bois-Guilbert and his followers, and boldly carried off as prisoners to Torquilstone, Front-de-Boeuf's castle. In those lawless times these Norman nobles trusted thus to obtain a good ransom, and to win Rowena for a bride. Ivanhoe, who, enfeebled by his wound, lay concealed in a litter, unknown to his father, was also taken. It was not long before the Jew and his daughter were taken too.

The Black Knight, meanwhile, was holding course northward through the woodlands. The sun had sunk behind the Derbyshire hills when he reached an open plat of turf and a rude hut, the door of which he assailed with the butt of his lance.

The door was opened; and the hermit, a large man, in his sackcloth gown with two large shaggy dogs, spoke,

"Thou mayst call me, the Clerk of Copmanhurst. They add the epithet holy, but I stand not upon that."

"Truly," said the knight, "men call me the Black Knight, - many add the epithet of Sluggard, whereby I am no way ambitious to be distinguished."

After exchanging a mute glance or two, the hermit brought out a large pasty. "Sit thee down, Sir Knight, and fill thy cup; let us drink, sing, and be merry. Thou art welcome to a nook of pasty at Copmanhurst so long as I serve the chapel of St Dunstan, which, please God, shall be till I change my grey covering for one of green turf.

While they were speaking, loud and repeated knocks at length disturbed the anchorite and his guest.

"Mad priest," came a voice, "open to Locksley!"

The hermit speedily unbolted his portal.

"I tell thee, friar," said Locksley; "thou must lay down the rosary and take up the quarter-staff; we shall need every one of our merry men, whether clerk or layman."

* * *

The armed men by whom Cedric and his companions had been seized, hurried their captives along towards the place where they intended to imprison them. The Lady Rowena was separated from her train, and conducted, with courtesy, indeed, to a distant apartment. The old Jew was forcibly dragged off to a dungeon while his daughter Rebecca awaited her fate in a distant and sequestered turret where she was able to bring her knowledge of the healing arts to the aid of the stricken Ivanhoe.

A great noise was heard without; "Rebecca!" exclaimed Ivanhoe, "I lie here like a bedridden monk, Look from the window kind maiden, and tell me if they yet advance."

"I see a cloud of arrows flying so thick as to dazzle mine eyes!" She exclaimed, "He is down! - he is down!"

"Who is down?" cried Ivanhoe; "for our dear Lady's sake, tell me?"

"The Black Knight," answered Rebecca, faintly; "But no - but no! - he is on foot again, and fights as if there were twenty men's strength in his single arm - His sword is broken - he snatches an axe from a yeoman - he presses Front-de-Boeuf with blow on blow - The giant stoops and totters like an oak under the steel - he falls - he falls!"

"The assailants have won the barriers, have they not?" said Ivanhoe.

"They have - they have!" exclaimed Rebecca -

There the stout yeoman Locksley was seen hasting to the outwork. "Saint George!" he cried, "merry Saint George for England! - To the charge, bold yeomen!"

"The castle burns," said Rebecca; "it burns!

One turret was now in bright flames, which flashed out furiously from window and shot-hole. In the castle-yard, Athelstane snatched a mace from the pavement, to join the fray, but a silken bonnet keeps out no steel blade and he fell before the Templar's weapon.

Tower after tower crashed down, with blazing roof and rafter; and the combatants were driven from the court-yard. The voice of Locksley was then heard, "Shout, yeomen! - the den of tyrants is no more!

* * *

The daylight dawned upon the glades of the forest, within half a mile of the demolished castle. Here Locksley assumed his throne of turf under the twisted branches of a huge oak, and his silvan followers gathered around him. He assigned to the Black Knight a seat at his right hand, and to Cedric a place upon his left.

Cedric was oppressed with sadness for the loss of the noble Athelstane of Coningsburgh, and, ere they departed, expressed his gratitude to the Black Champion, and earnestly entreated him to accompany him to Rotherwood, "not as a guest, but as a son or brother."

"To Rotherwood will I come, brave Saxon; and when I come hither, I will ask such a boon as will put even thy generosity to the test."

"It is granted ere spoken out," said Cedric,

Rowena waved a graceful adieu to The Black Knight, and on they moved away through a wide glade of the forest.

"Thou bearest an English heart, Locksley," said the Black Knight, "and well dost judge thou art bound to obey my behest - for I am Richard of England!"

At these words, pronounced in a tone of majesty, the yeomen at once kneeled down before him.

"Rise, my friends," said Richard, "and thou, brave Locksley-"

"Call me no longer Locksley, my Liege, for I am Robin Hood of Sherwood Forest."

"King of Outlaws, and Prince of good fellows!" said the King, "be assured, brave Outlaw, that no deed done in our absence, and in the turbulent times to which it hath given rise, shall be remembered to thy disadvantage."

* * *

Preparing for the funeral rites of the noble Athelstane, all around the castle of Coningsburgh was a scene of busy commotion when the Black Knight, attended by Ivanhoe, who had muffled his face in his mantle, entered and was welcomed gravely by Cedric- chief of the distinguished Saxon families present.

"It seems to me fit" said the Knight, "that, when closing the grave on the noble Athelstane, we should deposit therein certain prejudices. As yet you have known me but as the Black Knight - know me now as Richard Plantagenet of England! Hast thou no knee for thy prince?"

"To Norman blood," said Cedric, "it hath never bended."

"Reserve thine homage then," said the King, "until I shall prove my equal protection of Normans and English."

"And now to my boon," said the King, "I require of thee to forgive thy good knight, Wilfred of Ivanhoe."

"My father! - my father!" said Ivanhoe

"Thou hast it, my son," said Cedric, raising him up. "The ghost of Athelstane himself would forbid such dishonour to his memory."

It seemed as if Cedric's words had raised a spectre; for, scarce had he uttered them ere the door flew open, and Athelstane, arrayed in the garments of the grave, stood before them, pale, haggard, and like something arisen from the dead!

"In the name of God!" said Cedric, "if thou art mortal, speak!"

"I will," said the spectre, "I am as much alive as he can be who has fed on bread and water for three days.

"Why, noble Athelstane," said the Black Knight, "I myself saw you struck down by the fierce Templar.

"You thought amiss," said Athelstane, "I went, stunned, indeed, but unwounded. I never recovered my senses until I found myself in a coffin, and would well have been kept there if that villain Abbot had held his way. I tell you, I will

be king in my own domains, and nowhere else; and my first act shall be to hang the Abbot."

"And my ward Rowena," said Cedric - "I trust you intend not to desert her?"

"Father Cedric," said Athelstane, "The Lady Rowena loves the little finger of my kinsman Wilfred's glove better than my whole person. Hey! by Saint Dunstan, Wilfred hath vanished!"

But King Richard was gone also. Summoned to the courtyard by a Jew, Ivanhoe had thrown himself upon a steed and set off at a rate.

Brian de Bois-Guilbert, had abducted Rebecca, and spurned by her, had only escaped condemnation by the Grand Master of the Templars for his offence by claiming Rebecca to be a sorceress. Thus our scene transfers to the Castle of Templestowe, where the bloody die was to be cast for the life or death of Rebecca.

* * *

In the courtyard a throne was erected for the Grand Master of the Templars, opposite a pile of faggots around a stake, ready for the unfortunate Rebecca.

Said the Grand Master. "Go, herald, and ask her whether she expects any champion to do battle in her cause."

At this instant a knight appeared. "My name," he said, raising his helmet, "is Wilfred of Ivanhoe. Does the Grand Master allow me the combat?"

"I may not deny it." said the Grand Master

But Ivanhoe was already at his post, and had closed his visor, and assumed his lance. Bois-Guilbert did the same, and the knights charged each other in full career. It was not log before Wilfred, placing his foot on his antagonists breast, and the sword's point to his throat, commanded him to yield. Bois-Guilbert returned no answer. Unscathed by the lance of his enemy, he had died a victim to the violence of his own contending passions.

"I will not despoil him of his weapons," said the Knight of Ivanhoe, "nor condemn his corpse to shame - he hath fought for Christendom in his time."

He was interrupted by a clattering of horses' feet, and the Black Knight galloped into the lists.

"Peace be with him," said Richard, "he was a gallant knight - Bohun, do thine office!"

A Knight stepped forward from the King's attendants, and, laying his hand on the shoulder of Albert de Malvoisin, said, "I arrest thee of High Treason."

* * *

The nuptials of Rowena and Ivanhoe, were celebrated in the noble Minster of York. The King himself attended, and the presence of high-born Normans, as well as Saxons, joined with the universal rejoicing of the lower orders, marked the marriage as a pledge of the future peace and harmony betwixt the two races.

And, after this happy bridal, a certain lady came to Rowena, saying; "The people of England are a fierce race, such is no safe abode for the children of my people. Ere I leave, accept these my jewels, to me they are valueless above my liberty."

"O, Rebecca," said Rowena, "remain with us - the counsel of holy men will wean you from your erring law, and I will be a sister to you."

"No, lady," answered Rebecca, "I may not change the faith of my fathers like a garment unsuited to the climate in which I dwell. Farewell, and may He, who made both Jew and Christian, shower down on you his choicest blessings!"

Confessions of an English Opium-Eater
Being an extract from the life of a scholar.
by Thomas de Quincey
(London, 1821)

For all his substantial literary output, this intimate of Wordsworth (p286) and Coleridge (p285) is remembered pretty much only for this record of his opium-fuelled descent from divine enjoyment to sunless misery, which remains famous as a warning about what those happy-making drugs can do.

Abridged: GH

PRELIMINARY CONFESSIONS

I HERE present you, courteous reader, with the record of a remarkable period in my life, and I trust that it will prove not merely an interesting record, but in a considerable degree useful and instructive. That must be my apology for breaking through the delicate and honourable reserve which, for the most part, restrains us from the public exposure of our own errors and infirmities, as if declining to claim fellowship with the great family of man, and wishing (in the affecting language of Mr. Wordsworth)

Humbly to express, A penitential loneliness.

If opium-eating be a sensual pleasure, and if I am bound to confess that I have indulged in it to an excess not yet *recorded* of any other man, it is no less true that I have struggled against this fascinating enthralment with a religious zeal, and have at length accomplished what I never yet heard attributed to any other man - have untwisted, almost to its final links, the accursed chain which fettered me.

I have often been asked how I first came to be a regular opium-eater, and have suffered, very unjustly, in the opinion of my acquaintances, from being reputed to have brought upon myself all the sufferings which I shall have to record, by a long course of indulgence in this practice purely for the sake of creating an artificial state of pleasurable excitement. This, however, is a misrepresentation of my case. It was not for the purpose of creating pleasure, but of mitigating pain in the severest degree, that I first began to use opium as an article of daily diet.

The calamities of my novitiate in London, when, as a runaway from school, I made acquaintance with starvation and horror, had struck root so deeply in my bodily constitution that afterwards they shot up and flourished afresh, and grew into a noxious umbrage that has overshadowed and darkened my latter years.

THE PLEASURES OF OPIUM

It is so long since I first took opium that, if it had been a trifling incident in my life, I might have forgotten its date; but, from circumstances connected with it, I remember that it must be referred to the autumn of 1804. During that season I was in London, having come thither for the first time since my entrance at college. And my introduction to opium arose in the following way. One morning I awoke with excruciating rheumatic pains of the head and face, from which I had hardly any respite.

On the twenty-first day, I think it was, and on a Sunday, I went out into the streets, rather to run away, if possible, from my torments than with any distinct purpose. By accident, I met a college acquaintance, who recommended opium. Opium! dread agent of unimaginable pleasure and pain! I had heard of it as I had of manna or of ambrosia, but no further. My road homewards lay through Oxford Street; and near *the stately Pantheon* I saw a druggist's shop, where I first became possessed of the celestial drug.

Arrived at my lodgings, I took it, and in an hour - oh, heavens! what a revulsion! what an unheaving, from its lowest depths, of the inner spirit! what an apocalypse of the world within me! That my pains had vanished was now a trifle in my eyes; this negative effect was swallowed up in the immensity of those *positive* effects which had opened before me, in the abyss of divine enjoyment thus suddenly revealed.

First one word with respect to its bodily effects. It is not so much affirmed as taken for granted that opium does, or can, produce intoxication. Now, reader, assure yourself that no quantity of the drug ever did, or could, intoxicate. The pleasure given by wine is always mounting and tending to a crisis, after which it declines; that from opium, when once generated, is stationary for eight or ten hours; the one is a flame, the other a steady and equable glow.

Another error is that the elevation of spirits produced by opium is necessarily followed by a proportionate depression. This I shall content myself with simply denying; assuring my readers that for ten years, during which I took opium at intervals, the day succeeding to that on which I allowed myself this luxury was always a day of unusually good spirits.

With respect to the torpor supposed to accompany the practice of opium-eating, I deny that also. The primary effects of opium are always, and in the highest degree, to excite and stimulate the system. But, that the reader may judge of the degree in which opium is likely to stupefy the faculties of an Englishman, I shall mention the way in which I myself often passed an opium evening in London during the period between 1804 and 1812. I used to fix beforehand how often within a given time, and when, I would commit a debauch of opium. This was seldom more than once in three weeks, and it was usually on a Tuesday or a Saturday night; my reason for which was this: in those days Grassini sang at the opera, and her voice was delightful to me beyond all that I had ever heard. The choruses were divine to hear, and when Grassini appeared and poured forth her passionate soul as *Andromache* at the tomb of Hector, etc., I question whether any Turk, of all that ever entered the paradise of opium-eaters, can have had half the pleasure I had.

Another pleasure I had which, as it could be had only on a Saturday night, occasionally struggled with my love of the opera. The pains of poverty I had lately seen too much of; but the pleasures of the poor, their consolations of spirit, and their reposes from bodily toil, can never become oppressive to contemplate. Now, Saturday night is the season for the chief, regular, and periodic return of rest for the poor. For the sake, therefore, of witnessing a spectacle with which my sympathy was so entire, I used often on Saturday nights, after I had taken opium, to wander forth, without much regarding the direction or the distance, to all the markets, and other parts of London to which the poor resort of a Saturday night for laying out their wages.

Sometimes in my attempts to steer homewards by fixing my eye on the Pole star, and seeking ambitiously for a north-west passage, instead of circumnavigating all the capes and headlands I had doubled in my outward voyage, I came suddenly upon such knotty problems of alleys, such enigmatical entries, and such sphinx's riddles of streets without thoroughfares, as must, I conceive, baffle the audacity of porters, and confound the intellects of hackney coachmen. For all this I paid a heavy price in distant years, when the human face tyrannised over my dreams, and the perplexities of my steps in London came back and haunted my sleep with the feeling of perplexities, moral and intellectual, that brought confusion to the reason, or anguish and remorse to the conscience.

Courteous reader, let me request you to move onwards for about eight years, to 1812. The years of academic life are now over and gone - almost forgotten. Am I married? Not yet. And I still take opium? On Saturday nights. And how do I find my health after all this opium-eating? In short, how do I do? Why, pretty well, I thank you, reader. In fact, though, to satisfy the theories of medical men I ought to be ill, I never was better in my life. I suppose, that as yet, at least, I am unsuspicious of the avenging terrors which opium has in store for those who abuse its lenity.

THE PAINS OF OPIUM

As when some great painter dips
His pencil in the gloom of earthquake and eclipse.
> *SHELLEY'S Revolt of Islam.*

But now comes a different era. In 1813 I was attacked by a most appalling irritation of the stomach, and I could resist no longer. Let me repeat, that at the time I began to take opium daily, I could not have done otherwise. From 1813, the reader is to consider me as a regular and confirmed opium-eater. Now, reader, from 1813 please walk forward about three years more, and you shall see me in a new character.

Now, farewell - a long farewell - to happiness, winter or summer! Farewell to smiles and laughter! Farewell to peace of mind! Farewell to hope and to tranquil dreams, and to the blessed consolations of sleep. For more than three years and a half I am summoned away from these. I am now arrived at an Iliad of woes.

It will occur to you to ask, why did I not release myself from the horrors of opium by leaving it off or diminishing it? The reader may be sure that I made attempts innumerable to reduce the quantity. It might be supposed that I yielded to the fascinations of opium too easily; it cannot be supposed that any man can be charmed by its terrors.

My studies have now been long interrupted. I cannot read to myself with any pleasure, hardly with a moment's endurance. This intellectual torpor applies more or less to every part of the four years during which I was under the Circean spells of opium. But for misery and suffering, I might, indeed, be said to have existed in a dormant state. I seldom could prevail on myself even to write a letter. The opium-eater loses none of his moral sensibilities or aspirations. He wishes and longs as earnestly as ever to realise what he believes possible, and feels to be exacted by duty; but his intellectual apprehension of what is possible infinitely outruns his power, not of execution only, but even of power to attempt.

I now pass to what is the main subject of these latter confessions, to the history of what took place in my dreams, for these were the immediate and proximate cause of my acutest suffering. I know not whether my reader is aware that many children, perhaps most, have a power of painting, as it were, upon the darkness all sorts of phantoms.

In the middle of 1817, I think it was, this faculty became positively distressing to me. At nights, when I lay awake in bed, vast processions passed along in mournful pomp; friezes of never-ending stories, that to my feelings were as sad and solemn as if they were stories drawn from times before *Aedipus* or *Priam*, before Tyre, before Memphis. And at the same time a corresponding change took place in my dreams; a theatre seemed suddenly opened and lighted up within my brain, which presented nightly spectacles of more than earthly splendour.

All changes in my dreams were accompanied by deep-seated anxiety and gloomy melancholy, wholly incommunicable by words. I seemed every night to descend, not metaphorically, but literally, to descend into chasms and sunless abysses, depths below depths, from which it seemed hopeless that I should ever re-ascend. Nor did I, even by waking, feel that I had re-ascended.

The sense of space, and, in the end, the sense of time, were both powerfully affected. Buildings, landscapes, etc., were exhibited in proportions so vast as the bodily eye is not fitted to receive. Space swelled, and was amplified to an extent of unutterable infinity. This, however, did not disturb me so much as the vast expansion of time; I sometimes seemed to have lived for 70 or 100 years in one night - nay, sometimes had feelings representative of a millennium passed in that time, or, however, of a duration far beyond the limits of any human experience.

The minutest incidents of childhood, or forgotten scenes of later years, were often revived. Of this, at least, I feel assured, that there is no such thing as forgetting possible to the mind. A thousand accidents may and will interpose a veil between our present consciousness and the secret inscriptions of the mind; accidents of the same sort will also rend away this veil; but alike, whether veiled or unveiled, the inscription remains for ever; just as the stars seem to withdraw before the common light of day, whereas, in fact, we all know that it is the light which is drawn over them as a veil, and that they are but waiting to be revealed when the obscuring daylight shall have withdrawn.

In the early stage of my malady the splendours of my dreams were indeed chiefly architectural; and I beheld such pomp of cities and palaces as was never yet beheld by the waking eye, unless in the clouds. To architecture succeeded dreams of lakes and silvery expanses of water. The waters then changed their character - from translucent lakes shining like mirrors they now became seas and oceans.

And now came a tremendous change, which, unfolding itself slowly like a scroll through many months, promised an abiding torment; and, in fact, it never left me until the winding up of my case. Hitherto the human face had mixed often in my dreams, but not despotically, nor with any special power of tormenting. But now that which I have called the tyranny of the human face began to unfold itself. Perhaps some part of my London life might be answerable for this. Be that as it may, now it was that upon the rocking waters of the ocean the human face began to appear; the sea appeared paved with innumerable faces upturned to the heavens - faces imploring, wrathful, despairing, surged upwards by thousands, by myriads, by generations, by centuries; my agitation was infinite, my mind tossed and surged with the ocean.

I know not whether others share in my feelings on this point; but I have often thought that if I were compelled to forego England and to live in China, and among Chinese manners and modes of life and scenery, I should go mad. Southern Asia in general is the seat of awful images and associations. As the cradle of the human race, it would alone have a dim and reverential feeling connected with it. But there are other reasons. No man can pretend that the wild, barbarous, and capricious superstitions of Africa, or of savage tribes elsewhere, affect him in the way that he is affected by the ancient, monumental, cruel, and elaborate religions of Indostan, etc. The mere antiquity of Asiatic things, of their institutions, histories, modes of faith, etc., is so impressive that, to me, the vast age of the race and name overpowers the sense of youth in the individual. A young Chinese seems to me an antediluvian man renewed.

All this, and much more than I can say or have time to say, the reader must enter into before he can comprehend the unimaginable horror which these dreams of Oriental imagery and mythological tortures impressed upon me. Under the connecting feeling of tropical heat and vertical sunlight, I brought together all creatures, birds, beasts, reptiles, all trees and plants, usages and appearances, that are found in all tropical regions, and assembled them together in China or Indostan. From kindred feelings I soon brought Egypt and all her gods under the same law. I was stared at, hooted at, grinned at, chattered at, by monkeys, by paroqueats, by cockatoos. I ran into pagodas, and was fixed for centuries, at the summit, or in secret rooms; I was the idol; I was the priest; I was worshipped; I was sacrificed. I fled from the wrath of Brahma through all the forests of Asia; Vishnu hated me; Siva laid wait for me. I came suddenly upon Isis and Osiris; I had done a deed, they said, which the ibis and the crocodile trembled at I was buried for a thousand years in stone coffins, with mummies and sphinxes, in narrow chambers at the heart of eternal pyramids. I was kissed by crocodiles; and laid, confounded with all unutterable slimy things, amongst reeds and Nilotic mud.

Over every form and threat and punishment brooded a sense of eternity and infinity that drove me into an oppression as of madness. Into these dreams only it was, with one or two slight exceptions, that any circumstances of physical horror entered. But here the main agents were ugly birds, or snakes, or crocodiles; especially the last. The cursed crocodile became to me the object of more horror than almost all the rest. I was compelled to live with him, and - as was almost always the case in my dreams - for centuries. And so often did this hideous reptile haunt my dreams that many times the very same dream was broken up in the very same way. I heard gentle voices speaking to me - I hear everything when I am sleeping - and instantly I awoke. It was broad noon, and my children were standing, hand in hand, at my bedside - come to show me their coloured shoes, or new frocks, or to let me see them dressed for going out. I protest that so awful was the transition from the detestable crocodile, and the other unutterable monsters and abortions of my dreams, to the sight of innocent human natures and of infancy that in the mighty and sudden revulsion of mind I wept, and could not forbear it, as I kissed their faces.

As a final specimen, I cite a dream of a different character, from 1820. The dream commenced with a music which now I often heard in dreams - a music of preparation and of awakening suspense, a music like the opening of the Coronation Anthem, and which, like that, gave the feeling of a vast march, of infinite cavalcades filing off, and the tread of innumerable armies. The morning was come of a mighty day - a day of crisis and of final hope for human nature, then suffering some mysterious eclipse, and labouring in some dread extremity. Somewhere, I knew not where - somehow, I knew not how - by some beings, I knew not whom - a battle, a strife, an agony, was conducting, was evolving like a great drama or piece of music, with which my sympathy was the more insupportable from my confusion as to its place, its cause, its nature, and possible issue.

I, as is usual in dreams - where, of necessity, we make ourselves central to every movement - had the power, and yet had not the power, to decide it. I had the power, if I could raise myself to will it, and yet again had not the power, for the weight of twenty Atlantics was upon me, or the oppression of inexpiable guilt. "Deeper than ever plummet sounded," I lay inactive. Then, like a chorus, the passion deepened. Some greater interest was at stake, some mightier cause than ever yet the sword had pleaded, or trumpet had proclaimed. Then came sudden alarms, hurryings to and fro, trepidations of innumerable fugitives - I knew not whether from the good cause or the bad - darkness and lights, tempest and human faces, and at last, with the sense that all was lost, female forms, and the features that were worth all the world to me, and but a moment allowed - and clasped hands, and heart-breaking partings, and then - everlasting farewells! And with a sigh such as the caves of hell sighed when the incestuous mother uttered the abhorred name of death, the sound was reverberated - everlasting farewells! And again and yet again reverberated - everlasting farewells! And I awoke in struggles, and cried aloud, "I will sleep no more."

* * *

It now remains that I should say something of the way in which this conflict of horrors was finally brought to a crisis. I saw that I must die if I continued the opium. I determined, therefore, if that should be required, to die in throwing it off. I triumphed. But, reader, think of me as one, even when four months had passed, still agitated, writhing, throbbing, palpitating, shattered. During the whole period of diminishing the opium I had the torments of a man passing out of one mode of existence into another. The issue was not death, but a sort of physical regeneration.

One memorial of my former condition still remains - my dreams are not yet perfectly calm; the dread swell and agitation of the storm have not wholly subsided; the legions that encamped in them are drawing off, but not all departed; my sleep is still tumultuous, and, like the gates of Paradise to our first parents when looking back from afar, it is still - in Milton's (p185) tremendous line -

With dreadful faces throng'd and fiery arms.

On War
(*Vom Kriege*)
by General Carl Von Clausewitz
(Prussia, 1832)

Just as Machiavelli (p139) 'spilled the beans' on how States *really* work, General Clausewitz did so for soldiery - pointing out how war, the mere continuation of politics, is not the precisely drilled ballet of popular myth, but a fog-bound mire where no one really knows what is going on. This work became a standard textbook for the military leaders of the 19th and early 20th centuries, and must therefore take some of the blame, thanks to Clausewitz's absolute disinterest in death or distress, for the twenty million fallen of the 1914-1918 war (p453) and what Churchill called "that mechanical scattering of death which the polite nations of the earth have brought to such monstrous perfection".

Abridged: GH, from the translation by Colonel James John Graham.

PREFACE

IT will naturally excite surprise that a preface by a female hand should accompany the present work. This work occupied the last twelve years of the life of my inexpressibly beloved husband, who has unfortunately been torn too soon from myself and his country. But it was not his intention that it should be published during his life, though I cannot consider myself as the real editress of the papers he left, a work far above my capacity.

May the dear little Prince now entrusted to my care by the Royal couple, some day read this book and be animated by it to deeds like those of his glorious ancestors.

MARIE VON CLAUSEWITZ

the Marble Palace, Potsdam

I: THE NATURE OF WAR

- War is nothing but a duel on an extensive scale, an act of violence intended to compel our opponent to fulfil our will. Self-imposed restrictions, almost imperceptible and hardly worth mentioning, termed usages of International Law, accompany it without essentially impairing its power.
- War is utmost use of force: Philanthropists may imagine there is a method of disarming an enemy without great bloodshed. This is an error. In War, errors from benevolence are the worst. It is to no purpose, even against one's own interest, to turn away from the real nature of the affair because its horror excites repugnance. To introduce into the philosophy of War a principle of moderation would be an absurdity.
- Even the most civilized peoples can be fired with passionate hatred for each other. This is a reciprocal action.
- The aim is to disarm the enemy: As long as the enemy is not defeated, he may defeat me. This is the second reciprocal action.
- If we desire to defeat the enemy, we must proportion our efforts to his powers of resistance. But the adversary does the same. This is the third case of reciprocal action.
- The human will does not derive its impulse from logical subtleties.
- War is never an isolated act.
- War does not consist of a single instantaneous blow.
- The result in war is never absolute. The conquered State often sees in it only a passing evil, which may be repaired by politics.
- The probabilities of real life replace any absolute conceptions.
- The political object: It is quite possible for such a state of feeling to exist between two States that a very trifling political motive may produce a perfect explosion.
- Strife can be brought to a standstill by one motive alone, which is, that one party waits for a more favourable moment for action.
- Each Commander can only fully know his own position; that of his opponent can only be known to him by uncertain reports.
- War is a game both objectively and subjectively.
- The Art of War has to deal with living and with moral forces, thus it can never attain the absolute and positive clarity of logic or mathematics.

- War is always a serious means for a serious object. But War is no mere passion for venturing and winning. The War of civilised Nations always starts from a political motive.
- War is a mere continuation of politics by other means. War is not merely a political act, but also a real political instrument. War is a political act.
- The greater and the more powerful the motives of a War, the more it affects the whole existence of a people.
- The first, and most decisive judgement of the Statesman and General is rightly to understand the kind of War on which they are embarking.
- War is not only chameleon-like, because it forever changes its colour, but it is always a wonderful trinity, of:
- The original violence of its elements, hatred and animosity, fruits of blind instinct;
- The play of probabilities and chance, which make it a free activity of the soul;
- The subordinate nature of a political instrument.
- The first of these three concerns more the people, the second, more the General and his Army; the third, more the Government. But the passions which break forth in War must already have a latent existence in the nation.

The object of War is as variable as its political objects. But, every case depends on overthrowing the military power, the country, and the will of the enemy. But this complete disarming is rarely attained in practice. Frederick the Great was never strong enough to overthrow the Austrian monarchy, but his skilful husbanding of his resources showed that his strength far exceeded what they had anticipated, so that they made peace. There are many ways to one's object in War; and the complete subjugation of the enemy is not essential in every case.

But the enemy acts on the same principle as us; and we must require the commander to remember that the God of War may surprise him; that he ought always to keep his eye on the enemy, in order that he may not have to defend himself with a dress rapier if the enemy takes up a sharp sword.

If every combatant was required to be endowed with military genius, then our armies would be very weak. War is the province of danger, and therefore courage, both physical and moral, is the first quality of a warrior. War is the province of physical exertion and suffering, so strength of body and mind is required. War is the province of chance, so resolution is needed. As long as his men are full of courage to fight with zeal, it is seldom necessary for the Chief to show great energy of purpose. But as soon as difficulties arise then things no longer move on like a well-oiled machine, the machine itself begins to offer resistance, and the Commander must have a great force of will.

Of all the noble feelings which fill the human heart in the exciting tumult of battle, none are so powerful and constant as the soul's thirst for honour and renown, though, in War the abuse of these proud aspirations must bring about shocking outrages. Other feelings, such as love of country, fanaticism or revenge may rouse the great masses, but they do not give the Leader a desire to will more than others.

Now in War, in the harrowing sight of danger and the twilight which surrounds everything, a change of opinion is more conceivable and more pardonable. It is, at all times, only conjecture or guesses at truth which we have to act upon. This is why differences of opinion are nowhere so great as in War. It is here that force of character is needed. Which leads us to a spurious variety of it - obstinacy, or resistance against our better judgement.

The Commander in War must use the mental gift known as Orisinn, or sense of locality, and make himself familiar with the geography. For each station, from the lowest upwards, to render distinguished services in War, there must be a particular genius, for Buonaparte was right when he said that many of the questions which come before a General would equal the mathematics of a Newton or an Euler. The military genius is the mind searching rather than inventive, comprehensive rather than specialist, cool rather than fiery. It is to these, in time of War, we should entrust the welfare of our women and children, the honour and the safety of our fatherland.

When we first hear of danger, before we know what it is, we find it attractive. To throw oneself, blinded by excitement, against cold death, uncertain whether we shall escape him, and all this close to the golden gate of victory, close to the rich fruit which ambition thirsts for- can this be difficult? Let us accompany the novice to the battle-field. Here, in the close striking of the cannon balls and the bursting of shells, the seriousness of life makes itself visible. We see a friend fall, and know that even the bravest is confused. We see the General, a man of acknowledged courage, keeping carefully behind a rising ground, a house, or a tree. A picture far short of that formed by the student in his chamber!

A great part of the information obtained in War is contradictory, a still greater part is false. Everyone is inclined to magnify the bad in some measure, and although the alarms thus propagated subside into themselves like the waves of the sea, still, like them, they rise again. Firm in his own convictions, the Chief must stand like a rock against which the sea breaks its fury in vain.

Everything is very simple in War, but the simplest thing is difficult. Activity in War is movement in a resistant medium. Just as a man immersed in water is unable to perform the simplest movement, that of walking, so in War, with ordinary powers, one cannot achieve even mediocrity. This is why absurd theorists, who have never plunged in themselves, teach only what every one knows- how to walk.

II: THE THEORY OF WAR

WAR means fighting. But fighting is a trial of moral as well as physical forces, and the condition of the mind has always the most decisive influence.

- The first "art of war" was merely the preparation of forces.
- True war as craft appears in the art of sieges.
- Then tactics appeared, and, at first, led to an army like an automaton with rigid formations and orders, intended to unwind like clockwork.
- The real conduct of war appeared only incidentally.
- Which showed the want of a military theory.
- There arose maxims, rules, and even systems for the conduct of war.
- Theoretical writers attempted to make war a matter of calculation, but directed their maxims only upon material things and one-sided activity.
- Superiority in numbers was chosen from amongst all the factors required to produce victory, because it could be brought under mathematical laws, a restriction overruled by the force of realities.
- Victualling of troops was systematised, but only through arbitrary and impractical calculations.
- An ingenious author tried to concentrate on a single conception, that of a base for the subsistence of the troops, the keeping them complete in numbers and equipment.
- The idea of 'interior lines' is purely geometrical; another one-sided theory.
- All these attempts are open to objection. They strive after determinate quantities, whilst in war all is undetermined.
- As a rule they exclude genius. Pity the theory which sets itself in opposition to the mind!
- The moral quantities must not be excluded in war. War is never directed solely against matter; but always against an intelligent force. Danger in war is like a crystalline lens through which all appearances pass before reaching the understanding. Every one knows the moral effect of a surprise, of an attack in flank or rear. Every one thinks less of the enemy's courage as soon as he turns his back. Every one judges the enemy's General by his reputation, and shapes his course accordingly. Every one casts a scrutinising glance at the spirit and feeling of his own and the enemy's troops.
- The first great moral force is the expression of hostile feeling, but in wars, this frequently resolves into merely a hostile view, with no innate hostile feeling residing in individual against individual. National hatred is some substitute for personal hostility, but where this is wanting, a hostile feeling is kindled by the combat itself.
- The combat begets danger. Courage is no mere counterpoise to danger, but a peculiar power in itself.
- A soldier must become unused to deceit, because it is of no avail against death, and so attain that soldierly

- simplicity of character which has always been the best representative of the military profession.
- The second peculiarity in war is the living reaction, and the reciprocal action resulting therefrom.
- Thirdly, the great uncertainty of all data in war is a peculiar difficulty. All action must be planned in a mere twilight, which, like fog or moonshine, gives things exaggerated dimensions.
- Thus it is a sheer impossibility to construct a theory of war.
- Theory must, therefore, be of the nature of observations, not of doctrine.
- There are certain circumstances which attend the combat throughout; the locality, the time of day, and the weather.
- Strategy deduces only from experience the ends and means to be examined.
- How far should theory go in its analysis of the means. The conduct of war is not making powder and cannon. Strategy makes use of maps without troubling itself about triangulations; it does not inquire how the country is subdivided, how the people are educated and governed; but it takes things as it finds them in the community of european states, and observes where different conditions have an influence on war.
- A great simplification of knowledge is required.
- As a rule, the most distinguished generals have never risen from the very learned or erudite class of officers.
- Knowledge must be suitable to the position. There are field marshals who would not have shone at the head of a cavalry regiment, and vice versa.

- The knowledge in war is very simple, but not, at the same time, very easy. It increases in difficulty with increase of rank, and in the highest position, in that of commander-in-chief, is to be reckoned among the most difficult which there is for the human mind.
- The commander of an army need not understand the harness of a battery horse, but he must know how to calculate exactly the march of a column. The necessary knowledge for high military position is only to be attained through a special talent which understands how to extract from the phenomena of life only the essence or spirit, as bees take honey from the flowers. Life alone will never bring about a Newton by its rich teachings, but it may bring forth great calculators in war, such as Frederick.
- Knowledge must be converted into real power. Science must become art.

War is part of the intercourse of the human race, and so belongs not to the Arts and Sciences, but to social life. War is no activity of the will exerted upon inanimate matter like the mechanical Arts, but against a living and reacting force.

There is a logical hierarchy through which the world of action is governed. Law is the relation of things and their effects to one another; as a subject of the will, equivalent to command or prohibition. Principle is objective when it is the result of objective truth, and consequently of equal value for all men; it is subjective, and called maxim, if it has value only for the person who makes it. Methodicism is determination by methods instead of principles or prescriptions, founded on the average probability of cases one with another.

Father Goriot
(*Le Père Goriot*)
by Honoré de Balzac
(Paris, 1835)

Balzac's great work was his sequence of almost 100 novels and plays *La Comédie humaine*, a panorama of French life - unpleasantly accurate in its portrayal of character, corruption and greed, so that Balzac is regarded as one of the founders of realism in literature. *Le Père Goriot* has been adapted for film and stage, and has inspired modern writers to the extent that the novelist Félicien Marceau's said, "We are all children of Le Père Goriot." It has even given the French language the word 'Rastignac', to mean an unprincipled social climber.

Abridged: JH/GH

I. In a Paris Boarding-House

Madame Vauquer, née *Conflans*, is an elderly lady who for forty years past has kept a Parisian middle-class boarding-house, situated in the Rue Neuve Sainte-Geneviève, between the Latin Quarter and the Faubourg Saint Marcel. This pension, known under the name of the *Maison Vauquer*, receives men as well as women - young men and old; but hitherto scandal has never attacked the moral principles on which the respectable establishment has been conducted. Moreover, for more than thirty years, no young woman has been seen in the house; and if any young man ever lived there, it was because his family were able to make him only a very slender allowance. Nevertheless, in 1819, the date at which this drama begins, a poor young girl was found there.

The Maison Vauquer is of three stories, with attic chambers, and a tiny garden at the back. The ground floor consists of a parlour lighted by two windows looking upon the street. Nothing could be more depressing than this chamber, which is used as the sitting-room. It is furnished with chairs, the seats of which are covered with strips of alternate dull and shining horsehair stuff, while in the centre is a round table with a marble top. The room exhales a smell for which there is no name, in any language, except that of *odour de pension*. And yet, if you compare it with the dining-room which adjoins, you will find the sitting-room as elegant and as perfumed as a lady's boudoir. There misery reigns without a redeeming touch of poesie - poverty, penetrating, concentrated, rasping. This room appears at its best when at seven in the morning Madame Vauquer, preceded by her cat, enters it from her sleeping chamber. She wears a tulle cap, under which hangs awry a front of false hair; her gaping slippers flop as she walks across the room. Her features are oldish and flabby; from their midst springs a nose like the beak of a parrot. Her small fat hands, her person plump as a church rat, her bust too full and tremulous, are all in harmony with the room. About fifty years of age, Madame Vauquer looks as most women do who say that they have had misfortunes.

At the date when this story opens there were seven boarders in the house. The first floor contained the two best suites of rooms. Madame Vauquer occupied the small, and the other was let to Madame Couture, the widow of a paymaster in the army of the French Republic. She had with her a very young girl, named Victorine Taillefer. On the second floor, one apartment was tenanted by an old gentleman named Poiret; the other by a man of about forty years of age, who wore a black wig, dyed his whiskers, gave out that he was a retired merchant, and called himself Monsieur Vautrin. The third story was divided into four single rooms, of which one was occupied by an old maid named Mademoiselle Michonneau, and another by an aged manufacturer of vermicelli, who allowed himself to be called "Old Goriot." The two remaining rooms were allotted to a medical student known as Bianchon, and to a law student named Eugène de Rastignac. Above the third story were a loft where linen was dried, and two attic rooms, in one of which slept the man of all work, Christophe, and in the other the fat cook, Sylvie.

The desolate aspect of the interior of the establishment repeated itself in the shabby attire of the boarders. Mademoiselle Michonneau protected her weak eyes with a shabby green silk shade mounted on brass wire, which would have scared the Angel of Pity. Although the play of passions had ravished her features, she retained certain traces of a fine complexion, which suggested that the figure conserved some fragments of beauty. Poiret was a human automaton, who had earned a pension by mechanical labour as a government functionary.

Mademoiselle Victorine Taillefer was of a sickly paleness, like a girl in feeble health; but her grey-black eyes expressed the sweetness and resignation of a Christian. Her dress, simple and cheap, betrayed her youthful form. Happy, she might have been beautiful, for happiness imparts a poetic charm to women, as dress is the artifice of it. If love had ever given sparkle to her eyes, Victorine would have been able to hold her own with the fairest of her compeers. Her father believed he had reason to doubt his paternity, though she loved him with passionate tenderness; and after making her a yearly allowance of six hundred francs, he disinherited her in favour of his only son, who was to be the sole successor to his millions. Madame Couture was a distant relation of Victorine's mother, who had died in her arms, and she had brought up the orphan as her own daughter in a strictly pious fashion, taking her with rigid regularity to mass and confession.

Eugène de Rastignac, the eldest son of a poor baron of Angoulême, was a characteristic son of the South. His complexion was clear, hair black, eyes blue. His figure, manner, and habitual poses proved that he was a scion of a noble family, and that his early education had been based on aristocratic traditions. The connecting link between these two individuals and the other boarders was Vautrin - the man of forty, with the dyed whiskers. He was one of that sort of men who are familiarly described as "jolly good fellows." His face, furrowed with premature wrinkles, showed signs of hardness which belied his insinuating address. He was invariably obliging, with a breezy cheerfulness, though at times there was a steely expression in the eyes which inspired his fellow-boarders with a sense of fear. He knew or guessed the affairs of everybody in the house, but no one could divine his real business or his most inmost thoughts.

II. The Beginnings of the Tragedy

Such a household ought to offer, and did present in miniature, the elements of a complete society. Among the inmates there was, as in the world at large, one poor discouraged creature - a butt on whom mocking pleasantries were rained. This patient sufferer was the old vermicelli maker, Goriot. Six years before, he had come to live at the Maison Vauquer, having, so he said, retired from business. He dressed handsomely, wore a gold watch, with thick gold chain and seals, flourished a gold snuff-box, and, when Madame Vauquer insinuated that he was a *gallant*, he smiled with the complacency of vanity tickled. Among the china and silver articles with which he decorated his sitting-room were a dish and porringer, on the cover of which were figures representing two doves billing and cooing.

"That," said Goriot, "is the present which my wife made to me on the first anniversary of our wedding-day. Poor dear, she bought it with the little savings she hoarded before our marriage. Look you, madame, I would rather scratch the ground with my nails for a living than part with that porringer. God be praised, however, I shall be able to drink my coffee out of this dish every morning during the rest of my days. I cannot complain. I have on the shelf, as the saying is, plenty of baked bread for a long time to come."

At the close of his first year Goriot began to practise little economies; at the end of the second he removed his rooms to the second floor, and did without a fire all the winter.

This although, as Madame Vauquer's prying eyes had seen, Goriot's name appeared in the list of state funds for a sum representing an income of from eight to ten thousand francs. Henceforth she denounced him to the other paying-guests as an unprincipled old libertine, who lavished his enormous income from the funds on unknown youthful charmers. The boarders agreed; and when two young ladies in the most fashionable and costly attire visited him in succession in a semi-stealthy manner, their suspicions, as they believed, were confirmed. On one occasion, Sylvie followed Old Goriot and his beautiful visitor to a side street, and saw that there was a splendid carriage waiting and that she got into it. When challenged upon the point, the old man meekly declared that they were his daughters, though he never disclosed that their occasional visits were paid only to wheedle money from him.

The years passed, and with the gentleness of a broken spirit, beaten down to the docility of misery, Goriot curtailed his personal expenses, and again removed his lodgings; this time to the third floor. His dress turned shabbier; with each ascending grade his diamonds, gold snuff-box, and jewels disappeared. He grew thinner in person; his face, which had once the beaming roundness of a well-to-do middle-class gentleman, became furrowed with wrinkles. Lines appeared in his forehead, his jaws grew gaunt and sharp; and at the end of the fourth year he bore no longer the likeness of his former self. He was now a wan, worn-out septuagenarian - stupid, vacillating.

Eugène de Rastignac had ambitions, not only to win distinction as a lawyer, but also to play a part in the aristocratic society of Paris. He observed the influence which women exert upon society; and at his suggestion his aunt, Madame de Marcillac, who lived with his father in the old family château near Angoulême, and who had been at court in the days before the French Revolution, wrote to one of her great relatives, the Viscomtesse de Beauséant, one of the queens of Parisian society, asking her to give kindly recognition to her nephew. On the strength of that letter Eugène was invited to a ball at the mansion of the viscomtesse in the Faubourg Saint-Germain. The viscomtesse became interested in him, especially as she was suffering from the desertion of the Marquis d'Ajuda-Pinto, a Portuguese nobleman who had been long her lover, and stood sponsor for him in society. At the Faubourg, Eugène met the Duchesse de Langeais, from whom he learned the history of Old Goriot.

"During the Revolution," said the duchesse, "Goriot was a flour and vermicelli merchant, and, being president of his section, was behind the scenes. When a great scarcity of food was at hand he made his fortune by selling his goods for ten times what they cost him. He had but one passion; he loved his daughters, and by endowing each of them with a dot of eight hundred thousand francs, he married the eldest, Anastasie, to the Count de Restaud, and the youngest, Delphine, to the Baron de Nucingen, a rich German financier. During the Empire, his daughters sometimes asked their father to visit them; but after the

Restoration the old man became an annoyance to his sons-in-law. He saw that his daughters were ashamed of him; he made the sacrifice which only a father can, and banished himself from their homes. There is," continued the duchesse, "something in these Goriot sisters even more shocking than their neglect of their father, for whose death they wish. I mean their rivalry to each other. Restaud is of ancient family; his wife has been adopted by his relatives and presented at court. But the rich sister, the beautiful Madame Delphine de Nucingen, is dying with envy, the victim of jealousy. She is a hundred leagues lower in society than her sister. They renounce each other as they both renounced their father. Madame de Nucingen would lap up all the mud between the Rue Saint-Lazare and the Rue de Crenelle to gain admission to my salon." What the duchesse did not reveal was that Anastasie had a lover, Count Maxime de Trailles, a gambler and a duellist. To pay the gambling losses of this unscrupulous lover, to the extent of two hundred thousand francs, the Countess de Restaud induced Old Goriot to sell out of the funds nearly all that remained of his great fortune, and give the proceeds to her.

Returning to his lodgings from a ball in the Faubourg Saint-Germain, Eugène saw a light in Goriot's room; and, without being noticed, watched the old man laboriously twisting two pieces of silver plate - his precious dish and porringer - into one lump.

"He must be mad," thought the student.

"The poor child!" groaned Goriot.

The next morning Goriot visited a silversmith, and the Countess de Restaud received the money to redeem a note of hand which she had given to a moneylender on behalf of her lover.

"Old Goriot is sublime," muttered Eugène when he heard of the transaction.

Delphine de Nucingen also had an admirer, Count de Marsay, through whose influence she expected to be introduced into the exclusive aristocratic society to which even the great wealth of her husband and his German patent of nobility could not secure an entry. Apart from her social aspirations, Delphine was personally extravagant; and as the baron was miserly and only gave her a very scanty allowance, she visited the gambling dens of the Palais Royale to try and raise the money which she could no longer coax from her old father.

III. A Temptation and a Murder

To be young, to thirst after a position in the world of fashion, to hunger for the smiles of beautiful women, to obtain an entry into the salons of the Faubourg, meant to Rastignac large expenditure. He wrote home asking for a loan of twelve hundred francs, which, he said, he must have at all costs. The Viscomtesse de Beauséant had taken him under her protection, and he was in a situation to make an immediate fortune. He must go into society, but had not a penny even to buy gloves. The loan would be returned tenfold.

The mother sold her jewels, the aunt her old laces, his sisters sacrificed their economies, and the twelve hundred francs were sent to Eugène. With this sum he launched into the gay life of a man of fashion, dressed extravagantly, and gambled recklessly. One day Vautrin arrived in high spirits, surprising Eugène conversing with Victorine. This was Vautrin's opportunity, for which he had been preparing. When Victorine retired, Vautrin pointed out how impossible it was to maintain a position in society as a law student, and if Eugène wished to get on quickly he must either be rich, or make believe to be so.

"In view of all the circumstances, therefore, I make a proposition to you," said Vautrin to Eugène, "which I think no man in your position should refuse. I wish to become a great planter in the Southern States of America, and need two hundred thousand francs. If I get you a dot of a million, will you give me two hundred thousand francs? Is twenty per cent, commission on such a transaction too much? You will secure the affection of a little wife. A few weeks after marriage you will seem distracted. Some night, between kisses, you can own a debt of two hundred thousand francs, and ask your darling to pay it. The farce is acted every day by young men of good family, and no amorous young wife will refuse the money to the man she adores. Moreover, you will not lose the money; you will easily get it back by judicious speculation!"

"But where can I find such a girl?" said Eugène.

"She is here, close at hand."

"Mademoiselle Victorine?"

"Precisely!"

"But how can that be?"

"She loves you; already she thinks herself the little Baroness de Rastignac."

"She has not a penny!" cried Eugène in amazement.

"Ah, now we are coming to the point," said Vautrin.

Thereupon, Vautrin insinuated that if papa Taillefer lost his son through the interposition of a wise Providence, he would take back his pretty and amiable daughter, who would inherit his millions. To this end he, Vautrin, frankly volunteered to play the part of destiny. He had a friend, a colonel in the army of the Loire, who would pick a quarrel with Frederic, the young blackguard son who had never sent a five-franc piece to his poor sister, and then "to the shades" - making a pass as if with a sword.

"Silence, monsieur! I will hear no more."

"As you please, my beautiful boy! I thought you were stronger."

A few days after this scene, Mademoiselle Michonneau and Poiret were sitting on a bench in the Jardin des Plantes, when they were accosted by the chief of the detective force. He told them that the minister of police believed that a man calling himself Vautrin, who lived with them in the Maison Vauquer, was an escaped convict from Toulon galleys, Jacques Collin, but known by the nickname of Trompe-la-Mort, and one of the most dangerous criminals in all France. In order to obtain certainty as to the identity of Vautrin with Collin he offered a bribe of three thousand francs if mademoiselle would administer a potion in his coffee or wine, which would affect him as if he were stricken with apoplexy. During his insensibility they could easily discover whether Vautrin had the convict's brand on his shoulder. The pair accepted the bribe, and the plot succeeded. Vautrin was identified as Collin and arrested, just as a messenger came to announce that Frederic Taillefer had been killed in a duel, and Victorine was carried off with Madame Couture to her father's home, the sole heir to his millions. When he was being pinioned to be conveyed back to the galleys, Collin looked upon his late fellow boarders with fierce scorn. "Are you any better than we convicts are?" said he. "We have less infamy branded on our shoulders than you have in your hearts - you flabby members of a gangrened society. There is some virtue here," exclaimed he, striking his breast. "I have never betrayed anyone. As for you, you old female Judas," turning to Mademoiselle Michonneau, "look at these people. They regard me with terror, but their hearts turn with disgust even to glance at you. Pick up your ill-gotten gains and begone." As Jacques Collin disappeared from the Maison Vauquer, and from our story, Sylvie, the fat cook, exclaimed: "Well, he was a man all the same!"

Although the way was now clear for Rastignac to marry the enormously wealthy Victorine, he paid court instead to Delphine, the Baroness de Nucingen, and dined with her every night. Old Goriot was informed of the intrigue by the baroness's maid. He did not resent but rather encouraged the liaison, and spent his last ten thousand francs in furnishing a suite of apartments for the young couple, on condition that he was to be allowed to occupy an adjoining room, and see his daughter every day.

IV. Old Goriot's Death-Bed

The Viscomtesse de Beauséant was broken-hearted when the marriage of her lover was accomplished, but to maintain a brave spirit in the face of society she gave a farewell ball before retiring to her country estate. Among those invited was the Countess de Restaud, who ordered a rich costume for the occasion, which, however, she was unable to pay for. Her husband, the count, insisted on her appearing at the ball and wearing the family diamonds, which she had pawned to discharge her lover's gambling debts, and which had been redeemed to save the family honour. Anastasie sent her maid to Old Goriot, who rose from a sick-bed, sold his last forks and spoons for six hundred francs, pledged his annuity for four hundred francs, and so raised a thousand, which enabled Anastasie to obtain the gown and shine at the ball. Through Rastignac's influence, Delphine, Baroness de Nucingen, received from the viscomtesse a ticket for the dance, and insisted on going, as Rastignac declared "even over the dead body of her father," to challenge her sister's social precedence at the supreme society function. The ball was the most brilliant of the Parisian season. Both Goriot's daughters satisfied their selfish ambitions and gave never a thought to their old parent in the wretched Maison Vauquer.

For Old Goriot was sick unto death. His garret was bare; the walls dripped with moisture; the floor was damp; the bed was comfortless, and the few faggots which made the handful of fire had been bought only by the money got from pawning Eugène's watch. Christophe, the man servant, was sent by Rastignac to tell the daughters of their father's condition.

"Tell them that I am not very well," said Old Goriot; "that I should like to see them, to kiss them before I die."

By and by, when the messenger had gone, the old man said: "I don't want to die. To die, my good Eugène, is - not to see them there, where I am going. How lonely I shall be! Hell, to a father, is to be without his children. Tell me, if I go to heaven, can I come back in spirit and hover near them? You saw them at the ball; they did not know that I was ill, did they?"

On the return of the messenger, Old Goriot was told that both his daughters refused to come and see him. Delphine was too tired and sleepy; Anastasie was discussing with her husband the future disposition of her marriage portion. Then alternately Goriot blamed his daughters and pardoned their unfilial and selfish behaviour.

"My daughters were my vice - my mistresses. Oh, they will come! Come, my darlings! A kiss, a last kiss, the viaticum of your father! I am justly punished; my children were good, and I have spoiled them; on my head be their sins. I alone am guilty; but guilty through love." Eugène tried to soothe the old man by saying that he would go himself to fetch his daughters; but Goriot kept muttering in his semi-delirium. "Here, Nasie! here Delphine, come to your father who has been so good to you, and who is dying! Are they coming? No? Am I to die like a dog? This is my reward; forsaken, abandoned! They are wicked; they are criminal. I hate them. I will rise from my coffin to curse them. Oh, this is horrible! Ah, it is my sons-in-law who keep them away from me!"

"My good Old Goriot," said Eugène, "be calm."

"Not to see them - it is the agony of death!"

"You shall see them."

"Ah! my angels!"

And with these feeble words, Old Goriot sank back on the pillow and breathed his last.

Anastasie did come to the death-chamber, but too late. "I could not escape soon enough," she said to Rastignac. The student smiled sadly, and Madame de Restaud took her father's hand and kissed it, saying, "Forgive me, my father."

Goriot had a pauper's funeral. The aristocratic sons-in-law refused to pay the expenses of the burial. These were scraped together with difficulty by Eugène de Rastignac, the law student, and Bianchon, the medical student, who had nursed him with loving tenderness to the last. At the graveside in Père Lachaise, Eugène and Christophe were the only mourners; Bianchon's duties detained him at the hospital. When the body of Old Goriot was lowered into the earth, the clergy recited a short prayer - all that could be given for the student's money. The pall of night was falling; the mist struck a chill on Eugène's nerves, and when he took a last glance at the shell containing all that was mortal of his old friend, he buried the last tear of his young manhood - a tear drawn by a sacred emotion from a pure heart.

Eugène wandered to the most elevated part of the cemetery, whence he surveyed that portion of the city between the Place Vendome and the dome of the Invalides, where lives that world of fashion which he had hungered to penetrate. With bitterness he muttered: "Now there is relentless war between us." And as the first act of defiance which he had sworn against society, Rastignac went to dine with Madame Nucingen!

The Adventures of Oliver Twist
Or, The Parish Boy's Progress
by Charles Dickens
(London, 1838)

The subtitle of Charles Dickens' second novel refers back to John Bunyan (p202) and draws attention to the social evils of the Poor Law, child labour and the criminal underworld. Oliver Twist has produced numerous TV, movie and stage adaptations, including the musical *Oliver!*

Abridged: GH

TREATS OF OLIVER TWIST'S BIRTH, GROWTH, EDUCATION AND BOARD

Oliver was born in the workhouse, and his mother died the same night. Not even a promised reward of £10 could produce any information as to the boy's father, or the name of his mother- a woman, young, frail, and delicate- a stranger to the parish.

"How comes he to have any name at all, then?" said Mrs. Mann (who was responsible for the early bringing up of the workhouse children) came to Mr. Bumble, the parish beadle.

The beadle drew himself up with great pride, and said, "I invented it. We name our foundings in alphabetical order. The last was a S; Swubble I named him. This was a T; Twist I named *him*. I have got names ready made to the end of the alphabet, and all the way through it again, when we come to Z."

"Why, you're quite a literary character, sir," said Mrs. Mann.

Oliver, being now nine years old, was removed from the tender mercies of Mrs. Mann, in whose wretched home not one kind word or look had ever lighted the gloom of his infant years, and was taken into the workhouse.

Now the members of the board, who were long-headed men, had just established the rule that all poor people should have the alternative (for they would compel nobody, not they) of being starved by a gradual process in the house, or by a quick one out of it. All relief was inseparable from the workhouse, and the thin gruel issued three times a day to its inmates.

The system was in full operation for the first six months after Oliver Twist's admission, and boys having generally excellent appetites, Oliver Twist and his companions suffered the tortures of slow starvation. Each boy had one porringer of gruel, and no more. At last the boys got so voracious and wild with hunger, that one, who was tall for his age and hadn't been used to that sort of thing (for his father had kept a small cook's shop), hinted darkly to his companions that unless he had another basin of gruel *per diem* he was afraid he might some night happen to eat the boy who slept next him, a weakly youth of tender age. He had a wild, hungry eye, and they implicitly believed him. A council was held, lots were cast who should walk up to the master after supper that evening and ask for more, and it fell to Oliver Twist.

The evening arrived, the boys took their places. The master, in his cook's uniform, stationed himself at the copper to ladle out the gruel; his pauper assistants ranged themselves behind him, the gruel was served out, and a long grace was said over the short commons.

The gruel disappeared, the boys whispered to each other, and winked at Oliver, while his next neighbours nudged him. Child as he was, he was desperate with hunger, and reckless with misery. He rose from the table, and advancing to the master, basin and spoon in hand, said, somewhat alarmed at his own temerity, "Please, sir, I want some more."

The master was a fat, healthy man, but he turned very pale. He gazed in stupefied astonishment on the small rebel for some seconds, and then said, "What!"

"Please, sir," replied Oliver, "I want some more."

The master aimed a blow at Oliver's head with the ladle, pinioned him in his arms, and shrieked aloud for the beadle.

The board were sitting in solemn conclave when Mr. Bumble rushed into the room in great excitement, and addressing a gentleman in a high chair, said, "Mr. Limbkins, I beg your pardon, sir! Oliver Twist has asked for more!"

There was a general start. Horror was depicted on every countenance.

"For *more*?" said the chairman. "Compose yourself, Bumble, and answer me distinctly. Do I understand that he asked for more, after he had eaten the supper allotted by the dietary?"

"He did, sir," replied Bumble.

"That boy will be hung," said a gentleman in a white waistcoat. "I know that boy will be hung."

Nobody disputed the opinion. Oliver was ordered into instant confinement, and a bill was next morning pasted on the outside of the workhouse gate, offering a reward of five pounds to anybody who would take Oliver Twist off their hands. In other words, five pounds and Oliver Twist were offered to any man or woman who wanted an apprentice to any trade, business, or calling.

Mr. Gamfield, the chimney sweep, was the first to respond to this offer.

"It's a nasty trade," said the chairman of the board.

"Young boys have been smothered in chimneys before now," said another member.

"That's because they damped the straw afore they lit it in the chimbley to make 'em come down again," said Gamfield. "That's all smoke, and no blaze; vereas smoke only sinds him to sleep, and that ain't no use in making a boy come down. Boys is wery obstinte and wery lazy, gen'l'men, and there's nothink like a good hot blaze to make 'em come down with a run. It's humane, too, gen'l'men, acause, even if they've stuck in the chimbley, roasting their feet makes 'em struggle to hextricate theirselves."

The board consented to hand over Oliver to the chimney-sweep (the premium being reduced to £3 10s.), but the magistrates declined to sanction the indentures, and it was Mr. Sowerberry, the undertaker, who finally relieved the board of their responsibility.

Mrs. Sowerberry, a squeezed-up woman with a vixenish countenance, who saw no saving in parish children, who "always cost more to keep, than they're worth." greeted Oliver with "There! Get downstairs, little bag o' bones.'" With this, she opened a side door, and pushed Oliver down a steep flight of stairs into a stone cell, damp and dark, wherein sat a slatternly girl, in broken shoes and ragged stockings.

Oliver left the house in the early morning before anyone was stirring, struck across fields, and gained the high road outside the town. A milestone intimated that it was seventy miles to London. In London he would be beyond the reach of Mr. Bumble; to London he would trudge.

A STRANGE YOUNG GENTLEMAN

It was on the seventh morning after he had left his native place that Oliver limped slowly into the town of Barnet. Tired and hungry he sat down on a doorstep, and presently was roused by the question "Hallo, my covey, what's the row?"

The boy who addressed this inquiry to the young wayfarer was about his own age, but one of the queerest-looking boys that Oliver had ever seen. He was short for his age, and dirty, and he had about him all the airs and manners of a man. He wore a man's coat which reached nearly to his heels, and he had turned the cuffs back half-way up his arm to get his hands out of the sleeves. Altogether he was as roystering and swaggering a young gentleman as ever stood four feet six in his bluchers.

"You want grub," said this strange boy, helping Oliver to rise; "and you shall have it.

I'm at low-watermark myself, only one bob and a magpie; but as far as it goes, I'll fork out and stump."

"Going to London?" said the strange boy, while they sat and finished a meal in a small public-house.

"Yes."

"Got any lodgings?"

"No."

"Money?"

"No."

The strange boy whistled.

"I suppose you want some place to sleep in to-night, don't you? Well, I've got to be in London to-night, and I know a 'spectable old genelman as lives there, wot'll give you lodgings for nothink, and never ask for the change- that is, if any genelman he knows interduces you."

This unexpected offer of shelter was too tempting to be resisted, and on the way to London, where they arrived at nightfall, Oliver learnt that his friend's name was Jack Dawkins, but that he was known among his intimates as "The Artful Dodger."

In Field Lane, in the slums of Saffron Hill, the Dodger pushed open the door of a house, and drew Oliver within.

"Now, then," cried a voice, in reply to his whistle.

"Plummy and slam," said the Dodger.

This seemed to be a watchword, for a man at once appeared with a candle.

"There's two on you," said the man. "Who's the t'other one, and where does he come from?"

"A new pal from Greenland," replied Jack Dawkins. "Is Fagin upstairs?"

"Yes, he's sortin the wipes. Up with you."

The room that Oliver was taken into was black with age and dirt. Several rough beds, made of old sacks, were huddled side by side on the floor. Seated round the table were four or five boys, none older than the Dodger,

smoking long clay pipes, and drinking spirits with the air of middle-aged men. An old shrivelled Jew, of repulsive face, was standing over the fire, dividing his attention between a frying-pan and a clothes-horse full of silk handkerchiefs.

The Dodger whispered a few words to the Jew, and then said aloud, "This is him, Fagin, my friend Oliver Twist."

The Jew grinned. "We are very glad to see you, Oliver-very."

A good supper Oliver had that night, and a heavy sleep, and a hearty breakfast next morning.

When the breakfast was cleared away, Fagin, who was quite a merry old gentleman, and the Dodger and another boy named Charley Bates, played at a very curious game.

The merry old gentleman, placing a snuffbox in one pocket of his trousers, a notebook in the other, and a watch in his waistcoat, and sticking a mock diamond pin in his shirt, and spectacle-case and handkerchief in his coat-pocket, trotted up and down the room in imitation of the manner in which old gentlemen walk about the streets; while the Dodger and Charley Bates had to get all these things out of his pockets without being observed. It was so very funny that Oliver laughed till the tears ran down his face.

A few days later, and he understood the full meaning of the game.

The Dodger and Charley Bates had taken Oliver out for a walk, and after sauntering along, they suddenly pulled up short on Clerkenwell Green, at the sight of an old gentleman reading at a bookstall. So intent was he over his book that he might have been sitting in an easy chair in his study.

To Oliver's horror, the Dodger plunged his hand into the gentleman's pocket, drew out a handkerchief, and handed it to Bates. Then both boys ran away round the corner at full speed. Oliver, frightened at what he had seen, ran off, too; the old gentleman, at the same moment missing his handkerchief, and seeing Oliver scudding off, concluded he was the thief, and gave chase, still holding his book in his hand.

The cry of "Stop thief!" was raised. Oliver was knocked down, captured, and taken to the police-station by a constable.

The magistrate was still sitting, and Oliver would have been convicted there and then but for the arrival of the bookseller.

"Stop, stop! Don't take him away! I saw it all! I keep the bookstall," cried the man. "I saw three boys, two others, and the prisoner here. The robbery was committed by another boy. I saw that this one was amazed by it."

Oliver was acquitted. But he had fainted. Mr. Brownlow, for that was the name of the old gentleman, shocked and moved at the boy's deathly whiteness, straightway carried the boy off in a cab to his own house in a quiet, shady street near Pentonville.

MR. FAGIN AND COMPANY

For many days Oliver remained insensible to the goodness of his new friends. But all that careful nursing could do was done, and he slowly and surely recovered. Mr. Brownlow, a kind-hearted old bachelor, took the greatest interest in his *protégé*, and Oliver implored him not to turn him out of doors to wander in the streets.

"My dear child," said the old gentleman, moved by the warmth of Oliver's appeal, "you need not be afraid of my deserting you. I have been deceived before in people I have endeavored to benefit, but I feel strongly disposed to trust you, nevertheless; and I am more interested in your behalf than I can well account for. Let me hear your story; speak the truth to me, and you shall not be friendless while I am alive."

A certain unmistakable likeness in Oliver to a lady's portrait that was on the wall of the room struck Mr. Brownlow. What connection could there be between the original of the portrait, and this poor child?

But before Mr. Brownlow had heard Oliver's story he had lost the boy. For Fagin, horribly uneasy lest Oliver should be the means of betraying his late companions, resolved to get him back as quickly as possible. To accomplish his evil purpose, Nancy, a young woman who belonged to Fagin's gang, and who had seen Oliver, was prevailed upon to undertake the commission.

Now, the very evening before Oliver was to tell his story to Mr. Brownlow, the boy, anxious to prove his honesty, had set out with some books on an errand to the bookseller at Clerkenwell Green.

"You are to say," said Mr. Brownlow, "that you have brought these books back, and that you have come to pay the four pound ten I owe him. This is a five-pound note, so you will have to bring me back ten shillings change."

"I won't be ten minutes, sir," replied Oliver eagerly.

He was walking briskly along, thinking how happy and contented he ought to feel, when he was startled by a young woman screaming out very loud, "Oh, my dear brother!" He had hardly looked up when he was stopped by having a pair of arms thrown tight round his neck.

"Don't!" cried Oliver, struggling. "Let go of me. Who is it? What are you stopping me for?"

The only reply to this was a great number of loud lamentations from the young woman who had embraced him.

"I've found him! Oh, Oliver, Oliver! Oh, you naughty boy to make me suffer such distress on your account! Come home, dear, come. Oh, I've found him! Thank gracious goodness heavens, I've found him!"

The young woman burst out crying, and a couple of women standing by asked what was the matter.

"Oh, ma'am," replied the young woman, "he ran away from his parents, and went and joined a set of thieves and bad characters, and almost broke his mother's heart."

"Young wretch!" said one woman.

"Go home, do, you little brute," said the other.

"I'm not," replied Oliver, greatly alarmed. "I don't know her. I haven't any sister or father or mother. I'm an orphan; I live at Pentonville."

"Oh, only hear him, how he braves it out," cried the young woman. "Make him come home, or he'll kill his dear mother and father, and break my heart!"

"What the devil's this?" said a man, bursting out of a beer-shop, with a white dog at his heels. "Young Oliver! Come home to your poor mother, you young dog!"

"I don't belong to them. I don't know them! Help, help!" cried Oliver, struggling in the man's powerful grasp.

"Help!" repeated the man. "Yes, I'll help you, you young rascal! What books are these? You've been a-stealin' 'em, have you? Give 'em here!"

With these words the man tore the volumes from his grasp, and struck him on the head.

Weak already, stupefied by the blows and the suddenness of the attack, terrified by the brutality of the man- who was none other than Bill Sikes, the roughest of all Fagin's pupils- what could one poor child do? Darkness had set in; it was a low neighbourhood; resistance was useless. Sikes and Nancy hurried the boy on between them through courts and alleys till, once more, he was within the dreadful house where the Dodger had first brought him. Long after the gas-lamps were lighted, Mr. Brownlow sat waiting in his parlour. The servant had run up the street twenty times to see if there were any traces of Oliver. The housekeeper had waited anxiously at the open door. But no Oliver returned.

OF OLIVER WITH HIS KIND FRIENDS

Mr. Bill Sikes having an important house-breaking engagement with his fellow robber, Mr. Toby Crackit, at Shepperton, decided that Oliver must accompany him.

It was a detached house, and the night was dark as pitch when Sikes and Crackit, dragging Oliver along, climbed the wall and approached a narrow, shuttered window.

In vain Oliver implored them to let him go.

"Listen, you young limb," whispered Sikes, when a crowbar had overcome the shutter, and the lattice had been opened. "I'm going to put you through there." Drawing a dark lantern from his pocket, he added, "Take this light; go softly up the steps straight afore you, and along the hall to the street door; unfasten it, and let us in."

The boy was put through the window, and Sikes, pointing to the door with his pistol, told him if he faltered he would shoot him.

Hardly had Oliver advanced a few yards before Sikes called out, "Back! back!"

Startled, the boy dropped the lantern, uncertain whether to advance or fly.

The cry was repeated- a light appeared- a vision of two terrified, half-dressed men at the top of the stairs swam before his eyes- a flash- a loud noise- and he staggered back.

Sikes got him out of the window before the smoke cleared away, and fired his pistol after the men, who were already in retreat.

"Clasp your arm tighter," said Sikes. "Give me a shawl here. They've hit him. Quick!

The boy is bleeding."

Then came the loud ringing of a bell, and the shouts of men, and the sensation of being carried over uneven ground at a rapid pace. And then the noises grew confused in the distance, and Oliver saw and heard no more.

Sikes, finding the chase too hot, was compelled to leave Oliver in a ditch and make his escape with his friend Crackit.

It was morning when Oliver awoke. His left arm was rudely bandaged in a shawl, and the bandage was saturated with blood. Weak and dizzy, he yet felt that if he remained where he was he would surely die, and so he staggered to his feet. The only house in sight was the one he had entered a few hours earlier, and he bent his steps towards it.

He pushed against the garden-gate- it was unlocked. He tottered across the lawn, climbed the steps, knocked faintly at the door, and, his whole strength failing him, sank down against the little portico.

Mr. Giles, the butler and general steward of the house, who had fired the shot and led the pursuit, was just explaining the exciting events of the night to his fellow-servants of the kitchen when Oliver's knock was heard. With considerable reluctance the door was opened, and then the group, peeping timorously over each other's shoulders, beheld no more formidable object than poor little Oliver Twist, speechless and exhausted.

"Here he is!" bawled Giles. "Here's one of the, thieves, ma'am! Wounded, miss! I shot him!"

They lugged the fainting boy into the hall, and then in the midst of all the noise and commotion, there was heard a sweet and gentle voice, which quelled it in an instant.

"Giles!" whispered the voice from the stairhead. "Hush! You frighten my aunt as much as the thieves did. Is the poor creature much hurt?"

"Wounded desperate, miss," replied Giles.

After a hasty consultation with her aunt, the same gentle speaker bade them carry the wounded person upstairs, and send to Chertsey at all speed for a constable and a doctor. The latter arrived when the young lady and her aunt, Mrs. Maylie, were at breakfast, and his visit to the sick-room changed the state of affairs. On his return he begged Mrs. Maylie and her niece to accompany him upstairs.

In lieu of the dogged, black-visaged ruffian they had expected to see, there lay a mere child, sunk in a deep sleep.

The ladies could not believe this delicate boy was a criminal, and when, on waking up, he told them his simple history, they were determined to prevent his arrest.

The doctor undertook to save the boy, and to that end entered the kitchen where Mr. Giles, Brittles, his assistant, and the constable were regaling themselves with ale.

"How is the patient, sir?" asked Giles.

"So-so," returned the doctor. "I'm afraid you've got yourself into a scrape there, Mr. Giles. Are you a Protestant? And what are *you*?" turning sharply on Brittles.

"Yes, sir; I hope so," faltered Mr. Giles, turning very pale, for the doctor spoke with strange severity.

"I'm the same as Mr. Giles, sir," said Brittles, starting violently.

"Then tell me this, both of you," said the doctor. "Are you going to take upon yourselves to swear that that boy upstairs is the boy that was put through the little window last night? Come, out with it! Pay attention to the reply, constable. Here's a house broken into, and a couple of men catch a moment's glimpse of a boy in the midst of gunpowder-smoke, and in all the distraction of alarm and darkness. Here's a boy comes to that very same house next morning, and because he happens to have his arm tied up, these men lay violent hands upon him, place his life in danger, and swear he is the thief. I ask you again," thundered the doctor, "are you, on your solemn oaths, able to identify that boy?"

Of course, under these circumstances, as Mr. Giles and Brittles couldn't identify the boy, the constable retired, and the attempted robbery was followed by no arrests.

Oliver Twist grew up in the peaceful and happy home of Mrs. Maylie, under the tender affection of two good women. Later on, Mr. Brownlow was found, and Oliver's character restored. It was proved, too, that the portrait Mr. Brownlow possessed was that of Oliver's mother, whom its owner had once esteemed dearly. Betrayed by fate, the unhappy woman had sought refuge in the workhouse, only to die in giving birth to her son.

In that same workhouse, where his authority had formerly been so considerable, Mr. Bumble came- as a pauper- to die.

Tragic was the fate of poor Nancy. Suspected by Fagin of plotting against her accomplices, the Jew so worked on Sikes that the savage housebreaker murdered her.

But neither Fagin nor Sikes escaped.

For the Jew was taken and condemned to death, and in the condemned cell came the recollection to him of all the men he had known who had died upon the scaffold, some of them through his means.

Sikes, when the news of Nancy's murder got abroad, was hunted by a furious crowd.

He had taken refuge in an old, disreputable uninhabited house, known to his accomplices, which stood right over the Thames, in Jacob's Island, not far from Dockhead; but the pursuit was hot, and the only chance of safety lay in getting to the river.

At the very moment when the crowd was forcing its way into the house, Sikes made a running noose to slip beneath his arm-pits, and so lower himself to a ditch beneath. He was out on the roof, and then, when the loop was over his head, the face of the murdered girl seemed to stare at him.

"The eyes again!" he cried, in an unearthly screech, and threw up his arms in horror.

Staggering, as if struck by lightning, he lost his balance and tumbled over the parapet.

The noose was on his neck. It ran up with his weight, tight as a bowstring. He fell for five-and-thirty feet, and then, after a sudden jerk, and a terrible convulsion of the limbs, swung lifeless against the wall.

A Christmas Carol,
in Prose, Being a Ghost Story of Christmas
by Charles Dickens
(London, 1843)

Dickens has been called 'The Man Who Invented Christmas' as this story's huge popularity played a significant role in redefining the spirit of the holiday during a time when old traditions were declining. "If Christmas, with its ancient and hospitable customs, its social and charitable observances, were in danger of decay, this is the book that would give them a new lease," said the poet Thomas Hood.

Based on an Dickens' own abridgement, for his public readings.

I have endeavoured in this Ghostly little book, to raise the Ghost of an Idea, which shall not put my readers out of humour with themselves or with each other, with the season, or with me. May it haunt their houses pleasantly. - C.D.

STAVE ONE

Old Marley was as dead as a door-nail. There was no doubt whatever about that.

Scrooge knew he was dead? Of course he did. Scrooge and he were partners for I don't know how many years. Scrooge never painted out old Marley's name, however. There it yet stood, years afterwards, above the warehouse door, - Scrooge and Marley.

Oh! But he was a tight-fisted hand at the grindstone, was Scrooge! a squeezing, wrenching, grasping, scraping, clutching, covetous old sinner! Nobody ever stopped him in the street to say, with gladsome looks, "My dear Scrooge, how are you? No beggars implored him to bestow a trifle.

Once upon a time upon a Christmas eve old Scrooge sat busy in his counting-house. It was cold, bleak, biting, foggy weather; and the city clocks had only just gone three, but it was quite dark already.

The door of Scrooge's counting-house was open, that he might keep his eye upon his clerk, in a dismal little cell beyond. Scrooge had a very small fire, but the clerk's fire was so very much smaller that it looked like one coal. Wherefore the clerk put on his white comforter, and tried to warm himself at the candle; in which effort, not being a man of a strong imagination, he failed.

"A merry Christmas, uncle! God save you!" cried a cheerful voice. It was the voice of Scrooge's nephew, who came upon him so quickly that this was the first intimation Scrooge had of his approach.

"Bah!" said Scrooge; "humbug! If I had my will, every idiot who goes about with 'Merry Christmas' on his lips should be boiled with his own pudding, and buried with a stake of holly through his heart! He should!"

"Uncle! I am sure I have always thought of Christmas time, apart from the veneration due to its sacred origin, though it has never put a scrap of gold or silver in my pocket, I believe that it has done me good, and will do me good; and I say, God bless it!"

The clerk in the tank involuntarily applauded.

"Let me hear another sound from you " said Scrooge, "and you'll keep your Christmas by losing your situation!

"Don't be angry, uncle. Come! Dine with us, to-morrow."

"Why did you get married?"

"Because I fell in love."

"Because you fell in love!" growled Scrooge, as if that were the only one thing in the world more ridiculous than a merry Christmas. "Good afternoon!"

His nephew left the room without an angry word, notwithstanding. The clerk, in letting Scrooge's nephew out, had let two portly gentlemen in.

"Have I the pleasure of addressing Mr. Scrooge, or Mr. Marley?" said one of the gentlemen, referring to a list.

"Mr. Marley died seven years ago, this very night."

"At this festive season, Mr. Scrooge," said the gentleman, taking up a pen, "it is more than usually desirable that we should make some slight provision for the poor and destitute, sir. What shall I put you down for?"

"Nothing! I don't make merry myself at Christmas, and I can't afford to make idle people merry. I help to support the prisons and the workhouses, - they cost enough, - and those who are badly off must go there."

"Many would rather die."

"If they would rather die, they had better do it, and decrease the surplus population."

At length the hour of shutting up the counting-house arrived.

"You'll want all day to-morrow, I suppose?"

"It's only once a year, sir."

"A poor excuse for picking a man's pocket every twenty-fifth of December! Be here all the earlier next morning."

Scrooge took his melancholy dinner and went home to bed. He lived in a gloomy suite of rooms which had once belonged to his deceased partner.

Now it is a fact, that there was nothing at all particular about the knocker on the door of this house, except that it was very large; also, that Scrooge had as little of what is called fancy about him as any man in the city of London. And yet Scrooge, having his key in the lock of the door, saw in the knocker, not a knocker, but Marley's face. As Scrooge looked fixedly at this phenomenon, it was a knocker again. He said, "Pooh, pooh!" and closed the door with a sound like thunder.

Quite satisfied, he closed his door, and locked himself in; double-locked himself in, which was not his custom. Thus secured against surprise, he sat down before the very low fire to take some gruel.

As he threw his head back in the chair, his glance happened to rest upon a disused bell, that hung in the room, and communicated, for some purpose now forgotten, with a chamber in the highest story of the building. It begin to swing. Soon it rang out loudly, and so did every bell in the house. This was succeeded by a clanking noise as if some person were dragging a heavy chain over the casks in the wine-merchant's cellar below.

Through the heavy door a spectre passed into the room before his eyes. His body was transparent; so that Scrooge, looking through his waistcoat, could see the two buttons on his coat behind.

"How now!" said Scrooge, caustic and cold as ever. "What do you want with me?"

"In life I was your partner, Jacob Marley."

"Can you - can you sit down?"

"I can. Why do you doubt your senses?"

"Because a little thing affects them. A slight disorder of the stomach makes them cheats. You may be an undigested bit of beef, a fragment of an underdone potato. There's more of gravy than of grave about you, whatever you are!"

"Hear me! My time is nearly gone. I am here to-night to warn you that you have yet a chance and hope of escaping my fate. A chance and hope of my procuring, Ebenezer. You will be haunted by Three Spirits."

"Jacob? I - I think I'd rather not."

"Expect the first to-morrow night, when the bell tolls One."

It walked backward from him; and at every step it took, the window raised itself a little, so that, when the apparition reached it, it was wide open.

Scrooge closed the window, and examined the door by which the Ghost had entered. It was double-locked, and the bolts were undisturbed. Scrooge tried to say, "Humbug!" but stopped at the first syllable, and fell asleep on the instant.

STAVE TWO

When Scrooge awoke, it was so dark, and the church clock tolled a deep, dull, hollow, melancholy ONE.

Light flashed up in the room upon the instant, and the curtains of his bed were drawn aside by a strange figure,- like a child: yet not so like a child as like an old man. Its hair was white, yet the face had not a wrinkle in it. It held a branch of fresh green holly in its hand; yet had its dress trimmed with summer flowers. But the strangest thing about it was, that from the crown of its head there sprung a bright clear jet of light, by which all this was visible

"Who and what are you?"

"I am the Ghost of Christmas Past. Rise, and walk!"

It would have been in vain for Scrooge to plead that the weather and the hour were not adapted to pedestrian purposes.

"Bear but a touch of my hand there," said the Spirit, laying it upon his heart, "and you shall be upheld!"

As the words were spoken, they passed through the wall, and stood in the busy thoroughfares of a city. It was made plain enough by the dressing of the shops that here, too, it was Christmas time. The Ghost stopped at a certain warehouse door, and asked Scrooge if he knew it.

"Know it! Was I apprenticed here!"

They went in. At sight of an old gentleman in a Welsh wig, sitting behind such a high desk, Scrooge cried in great excitement: "Why, it's old Fezziwig, alive again!"

Old Fezziwig rubbed his hands and called out in a jovial voice, "Yo ho, there! Ebenezer! Dick!"

"Dick Wilkins, to be sure!" said Scrooge to the Ghost. "My old fellow-'prentice, bless me, yes!"

"Yo ho!" said Fezziwig. "No more work to-night. Christmas eve, Dick, Ebenezer! Clear away, my lads!"

Every movable was packed off, the floor was swept, the lamps were trimmed, fuel was heaped upon the fire. In came a fiddler with a music-book. In came Mrs. Fezziwig, one vast substantial smile. In came the three Miss Fezziwigs, the six young followers whose hearts they broke. In came all the young men and women employed in the business, the housemaid. In came the baker, the cook and the milkman.

There were dances, and there were forfeits, and there was cake, and there was negus, and there was a great piece of Cold Roast, and there was a great piece of Cold Boiled, and there were mince-pies, and plenty of beer.

When the clock struck eleven this domestic ball broke up. Mr. and Mrs. Fezziwig took their stations, one on either side the door, and, shaking hands with every person wished him or her a Merry Christmas.

"A small matter," said the Ghost, "to make these silly folks so full of gratitude. He has spent but a few pounds of your mortal money."

Scrooge felt the Spirit's glance.

"My time grows short," observed the Spirit. "Quick!"

Again he saw himself. He was older now; a man in the prime of life. He was sat by the side of a fair young girl in a black dress, in whose eyes there were tears.

"Spirit! remove me from this place."

"I told you these were shadows of the things that have been," said the Ghost. "That they are what they are, do not blame me!"

"Remove me!" Scrooge exclaimed. "I cannot bear it!"

As he struggled with the Spirit he was conscious of being exhausted. He had barely time to reel to bed before he sank into a heavy sleep.

STAVE THREE

Scrooge awoke in his own bedroom. But the walls and ceiling were so hung with living green, that it looked a perfect grove. Heaped upon the floor, to form a kind of throne, were turkeys, geese, game, great joints of meat, sucking pigs, long wreaths of sausages, mince-pies, plum-puddings, barrels of oysters, red-hot chestnuts, juicy oranges, immense twelfth-cakes, and great bowls of punch. In easy state upon this couch there sat a Giant glorious to see; who bore a glowing torch, in shape not unlike Plenty's horn, and who raised it high to shed its light on Scrooge, as he came peeping round.

"Come in,- come in! I am the Ghost of Christmas Present. Have never walked with my elder brothers?"

"I don't think I have. Have you many brothers, Spirit?"

"More than eighteen hundred."

"Spirit, conduct me where you will. I went forth last night on compulsion. To-night, if you have aught to teach me, let me profit by it."

"Touch my robe!"

Scrooge did as he was told, and held it fast. The room and its contents all vanished instantly, and they stood in the city streets upon a snowy Christmas morning.

Scrooge and the Ghost passed on, invisible, straight to Scrooge's clerk's; and on the threshold of the door the Spirit smiled, and stopped to bless Bob Cratchit's dwelling with the sprinklings of his torch.

Then up rose Mrs. Cratchit, Cratchit's wife and laid the cloth, assisted by Belinda Cratchit, second of her daughters, while Master Peter Cratchit plunged a fork into the saucepan of potatoes. And now two smaller Cratchits, boy and girl, came tearing in, screaming that outside the baker's they had smelt the goose, and known it for their own; and, basking in luxurious thoughts of sage and onion, these young Cratchits danced about the table, and exalted Master Peter Cratchit to the skies, while he blew the fire, until the slow potatoes, bubbling up, knocked loudly at the saucepan-lid to be let out and peeled.

"What has ever got your precious father, then?" said Mrs. Cratchit.

And in came little Bob, the father, with at least three feet of comforter, exclusive of the fringe, hanging down before him; and his threadbare clothes darned up and brushed, to look seasonable; and Tiny Tim upon his shoulder. Alas for Tiny Tim, he bore a little crutch, and had his limbs supported by an iron frame!

"Why, where's our Martha?" cried Bob Cratchit.

"Not coming," said Mrs. Cratchit.

"Not coming!" said Bob.

Martha didn't like to see him disappointed, if it were only in joke; so she came out prematurely from behind the closet door, and ran into his arms, while the two young Cratchits hustled Tiny Tim, and bore him off into the wash-house that he might hear the pudding singing in the copper.

"And how did little Tim behave?" asked Mrs. Cratchit. "As good as gold," said Bob, "and better. Somehow he gets thoughtful, sitting by himself so much, and thinks the strangest things you ever heard. He told me, coming home, that he hoped the people saw him in the church, because he was a cripple, and it might be pleasant to them to remember, upon Christmas day, who made lame beggars walk and blind men see."

His active little crutch was heard upon the floor, and back came Tiny Tim before another word was spoken, escorted by his brother and sister to his stool beside the fire. Master Peter and the two ubiquitous young Cratchits went to fetch the goose, with which they soon returned in high procession.

Bob said he didn't believe there ever was such a goose cooked. Its tenderness and flavor, size and cheapness, were the themes of universal admiration. Eked out by apple-sauce and mashed potatoes, it was a sufficient dinner for the whole family; indeed, as Mrs. Cratchit said with great delight (surveying one small atom of a bone upon the dish), they hadn't ate it all at last! Yet every one had had enough, and the youngest Cratchits in particular were steeped in sage and onion to the eyebrows! But now, the plates being changed by Miss Belinda, Mrs. Cratchit left the room alone,- too nervous to bear witnesses,- to take the pudding up, and bring it in.

Hallo! A great deal of steam! The pudding was out of the copper. A smell like a washing-day! That was the cloth. A smell like an eating-house and a pastry-cook's next door to each other, with a laundress's next door to that! That was the pudding! In half a minute Mrs. Cratchit entered,- flushed but smiling proudly,- with the pudding, like a speckled cannon-ball, so hard and firm, blazing in half of half a quartern of ignited brandy, and bedight with Christmas holly stuck into the top.

O, a wonderful pudding! Bob Cratchit said, and calmly, too, that he regarded it as the greatest success achieved by Mrs. Cratchit since their marriage.

At last the dinner was all done, the cloth was cleared, the hearth swept, and the fire made up. The compound in the jug being tasted and considered perfect, apples and oranges were put upon the table, and a shovelful of chestnuts on the fire.

Then all the Cratchit family drew round the hearth, in what Bob Cratchit called a circle, and at Bob Cratchit's elbow stood the family display of glass,- two tumblers, and a custard-cup without a handle.

These held the hot stuff from the jug, however, as well as golden goblets would have done; and Bob served it out with beaming looks, while the chestnuts on the fire sputtered and crackled noisily. Then Bob proposed:-

"A Merry Christmas to us all, my dears. God bless us!"

"God bless us every one!" said Tiny Tim, the last of all.

"Mr. Scrooge!" said Bob; "I'll give you Mr. Scrooge, the Founder of the Feast!"

"The Founder of the Feast, indeed!" cried Mrs. Cratchit, reddening. "The odious, stingy, hard, unfeeling man. Nobody knows it better than you do, poor fellow!"

"My dear," was Bob's mild answer, "Christmas day."

Scrooge was the Ogre of the family. The mention of his name cast a dark shadow on the party, which was not dispelled for full five minutes.

After it had passed away, they were ten times merrier than before, from the mere relief of Scrooge the Baleful being done with. The chestnuts and the jug went round and round; and by and by they had a song, about a lost child travelling in the snow, from Tiny Tim, who had a plaintive little voice, and sang it very well indeed.

They were not a handsome family; they were not well dressed; their shoes were far from being water-proof; their clothes were scanty; and Peter might have known, and very likely did, the inside of a pawnbroker's. But they were happy, grateful, pleased with one another, and contented with the time.

It was a great surprise to Scrooge, as this scene vanished, to hear a hearty laugh. It was a much greater surprise to Scrooge to recognize it as his own nephew's, and to find himself in a bright, dry, gleaming room, with the Spirit standing smiling by his side, and looking at that same nephew.

"He said that Christmas was a humbug, as I live!" cried Scrooge's nephew. "He believed it too!"

"More shame for him, Fred!" said Scrooge's niece.

"He's a comical old fellow," said Scrooge's nephew, "Who suffers by his ill whims? Himself, always. Here he takes it into his head to dislike us, and he won't come and dine with us. What's the consequence? He don't lose much of a dinner."

After tea they had some music. Then they set to a game called Yes and No, where Scrooge's nephew had to think of something, and the rest must find out what; he only answering to their questions yes or no. The fire of questioning elicited from him that he was thinking of an animal, rather a disagreeable animal, an animal that growled and grunted sometimes, and talked sometimes, and lived in London, and was not a horse, or a cow, or a cat, or a bear. At last the plump sister cried out, -

" I know what it is, Fred! I know what it is! It's your uncle Scro-o-o-o-oge!"

Suddenly, as they stood together in an open place, the bell struck twelve. Scrooge looked about him for the Ghost, and saw it no more. As the last stroke ceased to vibrate, he beheld a solemn Phantom, draped and hooded, coming like a mist along the ground towards him.

STAVE FOUR

The Phantom was shrouded in a deep black garment, which concealed its head.

"I am in the presence of the Ghost of Christmas Yet To Come? Ghost of the Future! I fear you more than any spectre I have seen. Will you not speak to me?"

It gave him no reply. The hand was pointed straight before them.

"I know. Lead on, Spirit!"

The city seemed to spring up about them as the Spirit stopped beside one little knot of business men. Scrooge advanced to listen to their talk.

"No," said a great fat man with a monstrous chin, "I don't know much. I only know he's dead."

"What has he done with his money?" asked a red-faced gentleman.

Scrooge was at first inclined to be surprised that the Spirit should attach importance to conversation apparently so trivial; they left this busy scene, and went into an obscure part of the town, to a low shop where iron, old rags, bottles, bones, and greasy offal were bought. A gray-haired rascal, of great age, sat smoking his pipe.

A woman with a heavy bundle slunk into the shop.

"What do you call this? Bed-curtains!"

"His blankets?"

"They'd have wasted it by dressing him up in it, if it hadn't been for me."

Scrooge listened to this dialogue in horror.

"Spirit! I see, I see. The case of this unhappy man might be my own. My life tends that way now. Merciful Heaven, what is this?"

The scene had changed. The Ghost conducted him to poor Bob Cratchit's house, and found the mother and the children seated round the fire.

Quiet. Very quiet. The noisy little Cratchits were as still as statues in one corner.

"'And he took a child, and set him in the midst of them.'"

Where had Scrooge heard those words? He had not dreamed them. The boy must have read them out, as he and the Spirit crossed the threshold.

The mother laid her work upon the table, and put her hand up to her face.

"The colour hurts my eyes," she said. "I wouldn't show weak eyes to your father when he comes home. It must be near his time."

"Past it, rather," Peter answered, shutting up his book. "But I think he has walked a little slower than he used, these few last evenings, mother."

"I have known him walk with - - I have known him walk with Tiny Tim upon his shoulder, very fast indeed."

"And so have I," cried Peter. "Often."

"But he was very light to carry, and his father loved him so, that it was no trouble, - no trouble. And there is your father at the door!"

She hurried out to meet him; and little Bob in his comforter - he had need of it, poor fellow - came in. His tea was ready for him on the hob, and they all tried who should help him to it most. Then the two young Cratchits got upon his knees and laid, each child, a little cheek against his face, as if they said, "Don't mind it, father. Don't be grieved!"

Bob was very cheerful with them, and spoke pleasantly to all the family. He looked at the work upon the table, and praised the industry and speed of Mrs. Cratchit and the girls. They would be done long before Sunday, he said.

"Sunday! You went to-day, then, Robert?"

"Yes, my dear," returned Bob. "I wish you could have gone. It would have done you good to see how green a place it is. But you'll see it often. I promised him that I would walk there on a Sunday. My little, little child! My little child!"

He broke down all at once. He couldn't help it.

The Ghost of Christmas Yet To Come conveyed him to a dismal, wretched, ruinous churchyard. The Spirit stood among the graves, and pointed down to One.

"Before I draw nearer, answer me one question. Are these the shadows of the things that Will be, or are they shadows of the things that May be only?"

Still the Ghost pointed downward to the grave by which it stood. "Men's courses will foreshadow certain ends."

Scrooge, trembling as he went, followed the finger, and read upon the stone of the neglected grave his own name, - EBENEZER SCROOGE.

No, Spirit! O no, no! Spirit! hear me! I am not the man I was. I will honour Christmas in my heart, and try to keep it all the year. Holding up his hands, he saw an alteration in the Phantom's hood and dress. It shrunk, collapsed, and dwindled down into a bedpost.

Yes, and the bedpost was his own. The bed was his own, the room was his own. Best and happiest of all, the Time before him was his own, to make amends in!

He was checked in his transports by the churches ringing out the lustiest peals he had ever heard. Running to the window, he opened it, and put out his head. "What's to-day?" cried Scrooge, calling downward to a boy.

"To-day! Why, CHRISTMAS DAY."

"It's Christmas day! I haven't missed it. Do you know the Poulterer's, in the next street but one, at the corner?"

"I should hope I did."

"An intelligent boy! A remarkable boy! Do you know whether they've sold the prize Turkey that was hanging up there? Go and buy it, and tell 'em to bring it here, and I'll give you half a crown!"

The boy was off like a shot.

"I'll send it to Bob Cratchit's! He sha'n't know who sends it. It's twice the size of Tiny Tim.

In the afternoon, he turned his steps towards his nephew's house. He passed the door a dozen times, before he had the courage to go up and knock.

"Is your master at home, my dear?" said Scrooge to the girl. Nice girl! Very.

"He's in the dining-room, sir, along with mistress."

"He knows me," said Scrooge, with his hand already on the dining-room lock. "I'll go in here, my dear."

"Why, bless my soul!" cried Fred, "who's that?"

"It's I. Your uncle Scrooge. I have come to dinner. Will you let me in, Fred?"

Let him in! It is a mercy he didn't shake his arm off. He was at home in five minutes. Nothing could be heartier. Wonderful party, wonderful games, wonderful unanimity, won-der-ful happiness!

But he was early at the office next morning. O, he was early there! If he could only be there first, and catch Bob Cratchit coming late! And he did it. Bob was full eighteen minutes and a half behind his time.

"Hallo!" growled Scrooge in his accustomed voice, as near as he could feign it. "What do you mean by coming here at this time of day?"

"I am very sorry, sir. I am behind my time."

"You are? Yes. Step this way, if you please."

"It's only once a year, sir. It shall not be repeated. I was making rather merry yesterday, sir."

"Now, I'll tell you what, my friend. I am not going to stand this sort of thing any longer. And therefore I am about to raise your salary! "A merry Christmas, Bob!" said Scrooge, with an earnestness that could not be mistaken, as he clapped him on the back. "We will discuss your affairs this very afternoon, over a bowl of smoking bishop!

Scrooge was better than his word. He did it all, and infinitely more; and to Tiny Tim, who did NOT die, he was a second father. He had no further intercourse with spirits, and it was always said of him, that he knew how to keep Christmas well, if any man alive possessed the knowledge. May that be truly said of us, and all of us! And so, as Tiny Tim observed, God bless us every one!

Fairy Tales
by Hans Christian Andersen
(Copenhagen, 1835-52)

Hans Christian Andersen suffered the early loss of his father, bullying at school in Elsinore (p 155), and rejection by all his loves including the opera singer Jenny Lind and Edvard Collin, the son of his benefactor. Yet he was honoured by Royalty and acclaimed by authors the world over. His, nearly 200, tales are still published in their millions and his birthday, 2nd April, is celebrated as International Children's Book Day.

Abridged: GH

THE EMPEROR'S NEW CLOTHES

Many years ago, there was an Emperor who was quite excessively fond of new clothes. He did not trouble himself about his soldiers, or care for the theatre or the chase.

One day, two rogues calling themselves weavers appeared and gave out that they knew how to make the most beautiful stuffs with the wonderful property of remaining *invisible* to everyone who was unfit for the office he held, or who was stupid.

Thought the Emperor, "Had I such a suit of such stuff, I would find out what men in my realms are unfit for their office!"

So the two set up looms, and affected to work very busily, though in reality they did nothing at all. They asked for the most delicate silk and the purest gold thread, and put both into their own knapsacks.

"I should like to know how the weavers are getting on," said the Emperor after some time, and sent off his faithful old minister to them, thinking "he will be best able to see how the cloth looks, for he is a man of sense, and entirely suitable for *his* office."

So the old minister went, and the knaves asked him to look at their looms, pointing to the empty frames. The poor minister looked and looked, but he could not see anything, for a very good reason, viz: there was nothing there. "What!" thought he, "is it possible that I am a simpleton?"

"Minister!" said one of the knaves, "Does it please you?"

"Oh, it is excellent!" replied the old minister, "I will tell the Emperor without delay."

And then the Emperor himself wished to see the costly manufacture, and went to the crafty impostors. "Is not the work absolutely magnificent?" said his officers.

Said the Emperor to himself. "I can see nothing! Perhaps I am a simpleton, or unfit to be an Emperor? "Oh! the cloth is charming," said he, aloud, and presented the impostors with a riband of knighthood.

When the day came to prepare a suit from the fabulous cloth, the rogues pretended to roll it off the looms, they cut the air with their scissors, and sewed with needles without any thread in them. "See!" cried they, "The Emperor's new clothes are ready!"

The Emperor was dressed, and walked out under his high canopy in the midst of a procession through the streets of his capital. All the people stood by crying out, "Oh! How beautiful are our Emperor's new clothes!" No one would allow that he could not see these clothes, because he would have declared himself either a simpleton or unfit for his office. None of the Emperor's various suits had ever made so great an impression as these invisible ones.

"But the Emperor has nothing at all on!" said a little child.

"Listen to the voice of innocence!" exclaimed his father. But what the child said was whispered from one to another.

"But he has nothing at all on!" at last cried out all the people. The Emperor was vexed, for he knew that the people were right, but he thought the procession must go on now! And the lords of the bedchamber took greater pains than ever, to appear holding up a train, although, in reality, there was no train to hold.

THE UGLY DUCKLING

In the midst of the summer sunshine, by the moat of an old manor house, a duck sat on her nest, hatching her ducklings.

At last the eggshells began to crack, and, one after another, the little things poked out their heads.

"How wide the world is," said all the young ducks.

"Do you think this is the whole world?" their mother asked. "Why the world extends on and on, clear across to the other side of the garden and right on into the parson's field."

"How goes it?" asked an old duck who came by.

"This last egg won't crack, but the others are the cutest little ducklings ever. They look exactly like their father, the wretch! He hasn't come to see me at all."

"That's a turkey egg," the old duck said. "Let it lie, and go teach your other children to swim."

"Oh, I'll sit a little longer," she said.

At last the big egg did crack. "Peep," said the young one, and out he tumbled, but he was so big and ugly.

Next day the mother duck led her family down to the moat. Splash! And the other ducks looked at the ugly one and said out loud, "What an ugly fellow! We won't stand for him." One duck charged up and bit his neck.

The poor duckling was sad because he was so desperately ugly, and because he was the laughing stock of the whole yard. So he ran away over the fence to the great marsh. There he lay all night long, weary and disheartened.

When morning came, the wild ducks flew up to have a look at their new companion. "What sort of creature are you?" they asked, "You are terribly ugly."

Then, Bing! Bang! Shots rang in the air, and those two ducks fell dead among the reeds. The bird dog came, splash, splash! He opened his wide jaws, flashed his sharp teeth, and - splash, splash - on he went without touching the duckling.

"Thank heavens," he sighed, "I'm so ugly that the dog won't even bother to bite me." He scurried away from that marsh as fast as he could go.

It grew winter and so bitterly cold that the duckling had to swim to and fro in the water to keep it from freezing over. At last, too tired to move, he was frozen fast in the ice.

Then, early next morning a farmer came by, and broke away the ice with his wooden shoe, and carried the duckling home to his wife. But when the children wished to play with him he thought they meant to hurt him. Luckily the door was open, and the duckling escaped.

It would be too sad to tell of all the hardships he had to endure during this cruel winter. But, when the warm sun of springtime shone once more, the duckling was still alive among the reeds.

Then, quite suddenly, he lifted his wings. They swept through the air much more strongly than before and soon he found himself in a great garden where apple trees bloomed, and from the thicket before him came three lovely white swans.

"I shall fly near these royal birds, and they will peck me to bits because I am so very ugly. But I don't care."

The splendid swans saw him, and swept down upon him. "Kill me!" said the poor creature. But what did he see there,

mirrored in the clear stream? He beheld his own image, not a clumsy, dirty, grey bird, ugly and offensive. He himself was a swan! Being born in a duck yard does not matter, if only you are hatched from a swan's egg.

Several little children came into the garden and threw bread and cake upon the water, while they all agreed, "The new one is the most handsome of all." The old swans bowed in his honour.

He felt so very happy, but he wasn't at all proud, for a good heart never grows proud. He rustled his feathers and held his slender neck high, as he cried out with full heart: "I never dreamed there could be so much happiness, when I was the ugly duckling."

THE SNOW QUEEN

FIRST STORY. The Mirror and the Splinters

You should listen to this story, for when we get to the end we shall know more than we do now.

Once upon a time there was a mischievous sprite who made a mirror with the power of causing everything reflected in it to look poor and mean and ugly In this mirror the most beautiful landscapes looked like boiled spinach, and the best persons were turned into terrors.

All the little sprites who went to his school -for he kept a sprite school- thought it would now be possible to see how the world really looked. So they flew up into the sky with it, but it fell out of their hands to earth and was dashed in a hundred million pieces. And some of these pieces were hardly so large as a grain of sand, and they got into people's eyes. And now we shall hear what happened next.

SECOND STORY. A Little Boy and Girl

Above the roofs of a large town there lived two little children. They were not brother and sister; but they cared for each other as much as if they were. Their garrets were exactly opposite and had some tubs in which vegetables and little rose trees were planted.

His name was Kay, hers was Gerda, and today there was quite a snow-storm. They heated coins on the stove and pressed them to the icy glass, so they could see out through round peep-holes.

"The white bees are swarming," said Kay's grandmother.

"Do the white bees choose a queen?" asked the little boy.

"Yes," said the grandmother. And then she patted his head and told him other stories.

And then the spring came; the sun shone, and the little children sat in their pretty garden, high up at the top of the house. The little girl had learned a hymn, and she sang the verse to the little boy, who then sang it with her:

"The rose in the valley is blooming so sweet,
And angels descend there the children to greet."

And the children held each other by the hand, kissed the roses, looked up at the clear sunshine, and spoke as though they really saw angels there. What lovely summer-days those were!

It was then that Kay said, "Oh! I feel such a sharp pain in my heart; and now something has got into my eye!"

"I think it is out now," said he; but it was not. It was one of those pieces of glass from the magic mirror.

He said, "You look so ugly! These roses are ugly! And he pulled the roses up and he hastened away.

In the market-place, the boys used to tie their sledges to carts as they passed by, and so they were pulled along. As they were playing, a large sledge came along, painted quite white, with someone in it wrapped up in a white fur. Kay tied his sledge on to the white one and they drove off. Quicker and quicker they went, into the next street, and on beyond the gates of the town. He was quite frightened, and he tried to repeat the Lord's Prayer; but he was only able to remember the multiplication table.

Suddenly the large sledge stopped, and the person who drove rose up. It was a lady; her cloak and cap of snow. She was tall and slender, and of a dazzling whiteness. It was the Snow Queen.

"It is freezingly cold," she said, "come under my bearskin." Ah! it was colder than ice. The Snow Queen kissed Kay, and then he forgot little Gerda, grandmother, and all he had left at his home, and the Snow Queen appeared beautiful and wise. They flew over woods and lakes, over seas, beneath them the chilling storm rushed fast, the wolves howled, and Kay slept at the feet of the Snow Queen.

THIRD STORY. Of the Old Woman Who Understood Witchcraft

At last spring came, with its warm sunshine.

"Is Kay dead and gone!" said little Gerda.

"That I don't believe," said the Sunshine and the Swallows.

"I'll ask the river where he is. I will give the river my red shoes as a gift," said she. So she clambered into a boat which lay among the rushes, and went to the farthest end, and threw out her shoes. But before she could return, the boat was gliding quickly onward.

She sailed by a cherry-orchard, by a little thatched cottage and by two wooden soldiers who presented arms when anyone went past.

Gerda called out and an old woman came out of the cottage, leaning upon a crooked stick. She had a large broad-brimmed hat on, painted with splendid flowers.

"Poor child!" said the old woman, and caught hold of the boat with her crooked stick, and drew it to the bank.

"Tell me who you are, and how you came here," said she.

Gerda told her all; and the old woman gave her cherries and, as she combed little Gerda's hair, the child forgot her Kay, for the old practised witchcraft a little for her own private amusement, and now she wanted very much to keep little Gerda. So Gerda stayed.

Then one morning Gerda went to play with the flowers, and kissed the roses, and thought of her own dear roses at home, and with them of little Kay.

"Oh, how long I have stayed!" said the little girl. "Don't you know where Kay is?" she asked of the roses.

"Dead he certainly is not," said the Roses. "We have been in the earth where the dead are, but Kay was not there."

"Many thanks!" said little Gerda; and she went and she asked the other flowers.

The Tiger-Lily told her of the drum that goes Bum! Bum! and of a Hindoo woman in her long robe upon the funeral pyre of her dead husband, whose loving heart burns hotter than the flames which will burn her to ashes.

The Convolvulus told her of a mountain-path and an old castle. The Snowdrops told her of two little girls and of a boy and a pipe of bubbes. The Narcissus told her of a littler dancer in a white dress.

But none of them told of Kay.

So Gerda ran to the very, very end of the garden, and shook the rusted gate open; and little Gerda ran off barefooted into the wide world.

FOURTH STORY. The Prince and Princess

It became winter and Gerda was obliged to rest, when a large Raven came hopping over the white snow and said, "Caw! Caw! Good day!"

Gerda asked if he had seen Kay.

Said the Raven. "In this kingdom the Princess is so extraordinarily clever that she has read all the newspapers in the whole world. With her your Kay lives, I will take you there."

That evening the Raven led Gerda to the palace and along a little back stair and into a great bedchamber. The ceiling of the resembled a large palm-tree with leaves of glass, and from a thick golden stem hung two beds, like lilies. In one lay the Princess; in the other Gerda was to look for little Kay. She called him quite loud by name, he awoke, turned his head, and - it was not little Kay!

The Princess awoke, and asked what was the matter. Then little Gerda cried, and told her her whole history.

"Poor little thing!" said the Prince and the Princess. And the Prince let Gerda sleep in his bed, and she folded her little hands and thought, "How good men and animals are!" and then fell asleep and slept soundly.

The next day they dressed her from head to foot in silk and velvet, and gave her a little carriage with a horse in front, and a small pair of shoes, to go forth again in the wide world and look for Kay.

"Farewell! Farewell!" cried Prince and Princess; and Gerda wept, and the Raven wept.

FIFTH STORY. The Little Robber Maiden

As they drove through the dark wood the bright carriage caught the eyes of robbers, who pulled little Gerda out.

"She shall play with me," said a little robber child. "Doubtless she is a Princess?"

"No," said little Gerda; who then related all that had happened to her, and about little Kay.

At length the carriage stopped at the robber's castle.

"You shall sleep here with me to-night, and with my animals," said the little robber maiden, taking her in.

Her pets were wood-pigeons and a reindeer called Bac, with a bright copper ring round its neck.

"Every evening I tickle his neck with my sharp knife", said the robber maiden, "he is so frightened at it!" And she pulled Gerda into bed with her and fell asleep.

The Wood-pigeons spoke softly to Gerda; "Coo! Coo! We have seen little Kay! He is with the Snow Queen, who passed here. She blew upon us young ones; and all died except we two. Coo! Coo!"

Cried little Gerda. "Where did the Snow Queen go to?"

The Reindeer said, "She is gone to Lapland. Her summer-tent there; but her real home is towards the North Pole, on the Island of Spitzbergen."

"Oh, poor little Kay!" sighed Gerda.

In the morning Gerda told the robber maiden all that the Wood-pigeons had said; and the little maiden looked very serious, and said to the reindeer, "I will untether you. You may go home to Lapland, and you must take this little girl to the palace of the Snow Queen"

SIXTH STORY. The Lapland Woman and the Finland Woman

After many miles they stopped before a miserable little house. The roof reached to the ground and the door was so low, that the family were obliged to creep in and out upon their stomachs. At home was an old Lapland woman, dressing fish; the Reindeer told her the whole of Gerda's history, but first of all his own.

"Poor thing," said the Lapland woman, and she gave Gerda a few words written on a dried cod-skin, she having no paper.

At last they came to Finland. They knocked at the chimney of the Finland woman; for a door, she had none.

The Finland woman was diminutive and dirty. She loosened little Gerda's clothes, laid a piece of ice on the Reindeer's head, and read what was written on the fish-skin.

"Little Kay is at the Snow Queen's, and he thinks it the very best place in the world; but the reason is, he has a splinter of glass in his eye, and in his heart. "

Asked the reindeer, "Can you not give little Gerda some special power to help her on her way?"

"I can give her no more power than what she has already. Don't you see how great it is? Don't you see how men and animals serve her; how well she gets through the world barefooted? Her power lies in her heart, because she is a sweet and innocent child! Carry her to the bush with red berries, for there garden of the Snow Queen begins.

Gerda spoke out the Lord's Prayer, and they set off.

But now we shall see how Kay fared.

SEVENTH STORY. In The Palace of the Snow Queen, and what Happened Afterwards.

The hundred halls of the palace were of driving snow, and the windows and doors of cutting winds. Each hall was many miles long, each lit by the Aurora Borealis, and all so icy cold, and so magnificent! Mirth never reigned there; nor was there ever a dance for the polar bears nor a little tea-party of white young lady foxes.

In the middle of the empty, endless halls was a frozen lake, cracked in a thousand pieces. In the middle of this lake sat the Snow Queen.

Little Kay was quite blue with cold; but he did not know it, for she had kissed away all feeling from his body, and his heart was a lump of ice. Kay spent his days arranging ice pieces into all sorts of shapes, which seemed to him, with the grain of glass in his eye, to be a gtreat and important work. But he never could manage to represent "eternity", for the Snow Queen had said, "If you can discover that figure, you shall be your own master, and I will make you a present of the whole world and a pair of new skates."

"I am going now to warm lands," said the Snow Queen. "I must give the volcanoes of Vesuvius and Etna a coating of white, which is good for the oranges and the grapes." And then away she flew, and Kay sat benumbed and motionless, quite alone in the empty halls of ice.

Suddenly little Gerda stepped through the great portal into the cold palace and the little maiden beheld Kay, She flew to embrace him, and cried out, "Kay, sweet little Kay! Have I then found you at last?"

But he sat quite still and cold. Then little Gerda shed burning tears; and they fell on his bosom, they penetrated to his heart, they thawed the lumps of ice, and consumed the splinters of the looking-glass; he looked at her, and she sang the hymn:

"The rose in the valley is blooming so sweet,
And angels descend there the children to greet."

Hereupon Kay burst into tears; he wept so much that the splinter rolled out of his eye, and he recognised her, and shouted, "Gerda, sweet little Gerda! And he held fast by Gerda, who laughed and wept for joy. It was so beautiful, that even the blocks of ice danced about for joy.

And Kay and Gerda looked in each other's eyes, and all at once they understood the old hymn:

"The rose in the valley is blooming so sweet,
And angels descend there the children to greet."

There sat the two grown-up persons; grown-up, and yet children; children at least in heart; and it was summer-time; summer, glorious summer!

THE LITTLE MATCH GIRL

Most terribly cold it was, on the last evening of the year. Along in the darkness there went a poor little girl, bareheaded, and with naked feet. When she left home she had slippers on, very large slippers of her mother's, but one had been lost and the other taken by an urchin as a cradle for his one-day children. She carried some matches in an old apron, but nobody had bought anything of her the whole livelong day.

The snow covered her beautiful long fair hair, while, from all the windows the candles were gleaming, and it smelt so deliciously of roast goose, for you know it was New Year's Eve.

In a corner by two houses, she sat down and pulled her little feet close up to her. She dared not go home for she had taken no money, which would certainly mean blows from her father, and at home it was cold too, even though the largest cracks in the roof were stopped up with rags.

Her little hands were almost numbed with cold. Oh! a match might afford a little comfort, so she drew one out. "Rischt!" how it blazed! It seemed as though she were sitting before an iron stove with burnished brass feet. which warmed so delightfully! But too quickly the small flame went out, and the stove vanished.

She rubbed another against the wall: it burned brightly, and the wall became transparent like a veil, so that she could see into the room to a table loaded with roasted goose and stuffing. And, wonder! The goose hopped down from the dish, reeled about on the floor with knife and fork in its breast, when the match went out.

She lighted another match. Now there she was sitting under the most magnificent Christmas tree: larger than the one she had seen through the glass door in the rich merchant's house. Thousands of lights were burning on the green branches, and gaily-coloured pictures looked down upon her. Then the match went out.

But the lights of the Christmas tree rose higher and higher, like the stars of heaven. Then one fell down with a long trail of fire.

"Someone has just died!" said the little girl; for her old grandmother, the only person who had loved her, and who was now no more, had told her that when a star falls, a soul ascends to God.

She drew another match against the wall, and in the lustre there stood the old grandmother, bright and radiant, with such an expression of love.

"Grandmother!" cried the little one. "Oh, take me with you!" And she rubbed the whole bundle of matches quickly against the wall, as grandmother took the little maiden on her arm, and both flew off in brightness and in joy so high, to where there was neither cold, nor hunger.

In the cold dawn they found the girl, smiling and frozen to death, with a bundle of burned matches in her hand. "She wanted to warm herself," they said. But they did not know what beautiful things she had seen, nor how, with her grandmother, she had entered into the joys of a new year.

The Communist Manifesto
by Karl Marx
(London, 1846)

This little paper is the most influential political pamphlet of all time. Nations of millions, from Russia to Cuba have tried to follow its plan for a proletarian revolution to overthrow the bourgeois social order and create a classless society without private property. Although ostensibly the work of a people's committee, *The Manifesto* is in Marx's handwriting and his colleague Friedrich Engels said that its ideas "belong solely and exclusively to Marx."

Abridged: GH, from the English edition of 1888.

A spectre is haunting Europe- the spectre of Communism. All the Powers of old Europe have entered into a holy alliance to exorcise this spectre: Pope and Czar, French Radicals and German police-spies. Where is the party in opposition that has not been decried as Communistic by its opponents?

Two things result from this fact.

I. Communism is already acknowledged by all European Powers to be itself a Power.

II. It is high time that Communists should openly publish their aims, and meet this nursery tale of the Spectre.

To this end, Communists of various nationalities have assembled in London, and sketched the following Manifesto.

I. BOURGEOIS AND PROLETARIANS

The history of all hitherto existing societies is the history of class struggles.

Freeman and slave, patrician and plebeian, lord and serf, guild-master and journeyman, in a word, oppressor and oppressed, stood in constant opposition to one another, carried on an uninterrupted, now hidden, now open fight. A fight that each time ended, either in a revolutionary re-constitution of society at large, or in the common ruin of the contending classes.

The modern bourgeois society that has sprouted from the ruins of feudal society has not done away with class antagonisms. Our epoch has simplified the class antagonisms. Society as a whole is more and more splitting up into two great hostile camps, into two great classes, directly facing each other: Bourgeoisie and Proletariat.

From the serfs of the Middle Ages sprang the chartered burghers of the earliest towns. From these burgesses the first elements of the bourgeoisie were developed. The discovery of America and the rounding of the Cape, opened up fresh ground for the rising bourgeoisie. The feudal system of industry, under which industrial production was monopolised by closed guilds, now no longer sufficed for the growing wants of the new markets. The manufacturing system took its place. The corporate guilds vanished in the face of division of labour in each single workshop.

Meantime the markets kept ever growing, the demand ever rising. Even manufacture no longer sufficed. Thereupon, steam and machinery revolutionised industrial production. The place of manufacture was taken by the giant, Modern Industry, the place of the industrial middle class, by industrial millionaires, the leaders of whole industrial armies, the modern bourgeois.

The executive of the modern State is but a committee for managing the common affairs of the bourgeoisie.

The bourgeoisie has pitilessly torn asunder the feudal ties that bound man to his "natural superiors," and has left no other nexus between man and man than naked self-interest, the callous "cash payment." It has drowned the most heavenly ecstasies of religious fervour, of chivalrous enthusiasm, in the icy water of egotistical calculation. It has resolved personal worth into exchange value, and, in place of the numberless chartered freedoms, has set up that single, unconscionable freedom - Free Trade. In one word; naked, shameless, direct, brutal exploitation.

The bourgeoisie has stripped of its halo every occupation hitherto honoured and looked up to with reverent awe. It has converted the physician, the lawyer, the priest, the poet, the man of science, into its paid wage labourers. The bourgeoisie has reduced the family relation to a mere money relation.

The need of a constantly expanding market for its products chases the bourgeoisie over the whole surface of the globe. In place of the old wants, satisfied by the productions of the country, we find new wants, requiring for their satisfaction the products of distant lands and climes. The bourgeoisie has subjected the country to the rule of the towns. It has created enormous cities, and has made barbarian and semi-barbarian countries dependent on the civilised ones, nations of peasants on nations of bourgeois, the East on the West.

Modern bourgeois society with its relations of production, of exchange and of property, is like the sorcerer, who is no longer able to control his spells. It is enough to mention the commercial crises that by their periodical return put on its trial, each time more threateningly, the existence of the entire bourgeois society. In these crises a great part of the previously created productive forces are periodically destroyed. In these crises there breaks out an epidemic that, in all earlier epochs, would have seemed an absurdity - the epidemic of over-production. Why? Because there is too much civilisation, too much means of subsistence, too much industry, too much commerce.

But not only has the bourgeoisie forged the weapons that bring death to itself; it has also called into existence the men who are to wield those weapons - the modern working class - the proletarians. These labourers, who must sell themselves piece-meal, are a commodity, like every other article of commerce, and are consequently exposed to all the vicissitudes of competition, to all the fluctuations of the market.

Owing to the extensive use of machinery and to division of labour, the work of the proletarians has lost all individual character, and consequently, all charm for the workman. He becomes an appendage of the machine. Hence, the cost of production of a workman is restricted, almost entirely, to the means of subsistence that he requires for his maintenance, and for the propagation of his race. In proportion therefore, as the repulsiveness of the work increases, the wage decreases.

No sooner does the labourer receive his wages in cash, than he is set upon by the other portions of the bourgeoisie, the landlord, the shopkeeper, the pawnbroker, etc. The lower strata of the middle class - the small tradespeople, shopkeepers, retired tradesmen generally, the handicraftsmen and peasants - all these sink gradually into the proletariat, partly because their diminutive capital does not suffice for the scale on which Modern Industry is carried on.

The proletariat goes through various stages of development. With its birth begins its struggle with the bourgeoisie. The workers begin to form combinations (Trades Unions) against the bourgeois; they club together in order to keep up the rate of wages. Here and there the contest breaks out into riots. At every disappointment the proletariat rises up again, stronger, firmer, mightier. It compels legislative recognition of particular interests of the workers, by taking advantage of the divisions among the bourgeoisie itself.

Finally, in times when the class struggle nears the decisive hour, the process of dissolution is going on within the ruling class. A small section of the ruling class cuts itself adrift, and joins the revolutionary class, the class that holds the future in its hands. Just as, at an earlier period, a section of the nobility went over to the bourgeoisie.

Of all the classes that stand face to face with the bourgeoisie today, the proletariat alone is a really revolutionary class. The lower middle class, the small manufacturer, the shopkeeper, the artisan, the peasant, all these fight against the bourgeoisie, but they are not revolutionary, but conservative.

All the preceding classes that got the upper hand sought to fortify their acquired status by subjecting society at large to their conditions of appropriation. The proletarians cannot become masters of the productive forces of society, except by abolishing their own previous mode of appropriation, and thereby also every other previous mode of appropriation. They have nothing of their own to secure and to fortify; their mission is to destroy all previous securities for, and insurances of, individual property.

All previous historical movements were movements of minorities. The proletarian movement is the self-conscious, independent movement of the immense majority, in the interests of the immense majority.

In depicting the most general phases of the development of the proletariat, we trace the more or less veiled civil war, raging within existing society, up to the point where that war breaks out into open revolution, and where the violent overthrow of the bourgeoisie lays the foundation for the sway of the proletariat.

The essential condition for the existence, and for the sway of the bourgeois class, is the formation and augmentation of capital; the condition for capital is wage-labour. Wage-labour rests exclusively on competition between the labourers. The advance of industry, whose involuntary promoter is the bourgeoisie, replaces the isolation of the labourers, due to competition, by their revolutionary combination, due to association. The development of Modern Industry, therefore, cuts from under its feet the very foundation on which the bourgeoisie produces and appropriates products. What the bourgeoisie, therefore, produces, above all, is its own grave-diggers. Its fall and the victory of the proletariat are equally inevitable.

II. PROLETARIANS AND COMMUNISTS

The Communists do not form a separate party opposed to other working-class parties. They have no interests separate and apart from those of the proletariat as a whole.

The immediate aim of the Communist is the same as that of all the other proletarian parties: formation of the proletariat into a class, overthrow of the bourgeois supremacy, conquest of political power by the proletariat.

All property relations have continually been subject to change consequent upon the change in historical conditions. The French Revolution, for example, abolished feudal property in favour of bourgeois property. The theory of the Communists may be summed up in the single sentence: Abolition of private property.

We Communists have been reproached with the desire of abolishing the right of personally acquiring property as the fruit of a man's own labour, which property is alleged to be the groundwork of all personal freedom, activity and independence.

Hard-won, self-acquired, self-earned property! Do you mean the property of the petty artisan and of the small peasant, a form of property that preceded the bourgeois form? There is no need to abolish that; the development of industry has to a great extent already destroyed it, and is still destroying it daily.

Or do you mean modern bourgeois private property?

Does wage-labour create any property for the labourer? Not a bit. It creates capital, i.e., that kind of property which exploits wage-labour. Capital is not a personal, it is a social power, for when capital is converted into common property personal property is not thereby transformed into social property. It is only the social character of the property that is changed. It loses its class-character.

The average price of wage-labour is the minimum wage, i.e., that means of subsistence which is absolutely requisite in bare existence as a labourer. All that we want to do away with is the miserable character of this appropriation. In Communist society, labour is but a means to widen, to enrich, to promote the existence of the labourer.

The abolition of this state of things is called by the bourgeois, abolition of individuality and freedom! You are horrified at our intending to do away with private property. But in your existing society, private property is already done away with for nine-tenths of the population; its existence for the few is solely due to its non-existence in the hands of those nine-tenths. You reproach us with intending to do away with your property. Precisely so; that is just what we intend.

It has been objected that upon the abolition of private property all work will cease, and universal laziness will overtake us.

According to this, bourgeois society ought long ago to have gone to the dogs through sheer idleness; for those of its members who work, acquire nothing, and those who acquire anything, do not work.

Abolition of the family! Even the most radical flare up at this infamous proposal of the Communists.

On what foundation is the present family, the bourgeois family, based? On capital, on private gain. The bourgeois family will vanish as a matter of course when its complement vanishes, and both will vanish with the vanishing of capital. Do you charge us with wanting to stop the exploitation of children by their parents? To this crime we plead guilty.

The bourgeois clap-trap about the family and education, about the hallowed co-relation of parent and child, becomes all the more disgusting, the more, by the action of Modern Industry, all family ties among the proletarians are torn asunder, and their children transformed into simple articles of commerce and instruments of labour.

But you Communists would introduce community of women, screams the whole bourgeoisie in chorus.

He has not even a suspicion that the real point is to do away with the status of women as mere instruments of production. The Communists have no need to introduce community of women; it has existed almost from time immemorial. Our bourgeois, not content with having the wives and daughters of their proletarians at their disposal, not to speak of common prostitutes, take the greatest pleasure in seducing each other's wives.

The Communists are further reproached with desiring to abolish countries and nationality.

The working men have no country. We cannot take from them what they have not got.

The charges against Communism made from a religious, philosophical, and an ideological standpoint, are not deserving of serious examination. But let us have done with the bourgeois objections to Communism.

The first step in the revolution by the working class, is to raise the proletariat to the position of political supremacy to wrest, by degrees, all capital from the bourgeoisie, to centralise all instruments of production in the hands of the State, i.e., of the proletariat organised as the ruling class; and to rapidly increase the total of productive force.

Of course, in the beginning, this cannot be effected except by means of despotic inroads on the rights of property. These measures will of course be different in different countries. Nevertheless in the most advanced countries, the following will be pretty generally applicable.

1. Abolition of property in land and application of all rents of land to public purposes.

2. A heavy progressive or graduated income tax.

3. Abolition of all right of inheritance.

4. Confiscation of the property of all emigrants and rebels.

5. Centralisation of credit in the hands of the State, by means of a national bank with State capital and an exclusive monopoly.

6. Centralisation of the means of communication and transport in the hands of the State.

7. Extension of factories and instruments of production owned by the State; the bringing into cultivation of waste-lands, and the improvement of the soil generally in accordance with a common plan.

8. Equal liability of all to labour. Establishment of industrial armies, especially for agriculture.

9. Combination of agriculture with manufacturing industries; gradual abolition of the distinction between town and country, by a more equable distribution of the population over the country.

10. Free education for all children in public schools. Abolition of children's factory labour in its present form. Combination of education with industrial production, &c., &c.

In place of the old bourgeois society, with its classes and class antagonisms, we shall have an association, in which the free development of each is the condition for the free development of all.

III. SOCIALIST AND COMMUNIST LITERAT- URE

1. REACTIONARY SOCIALISM

A. Feudal Socialism: It became the vocation of the aristocracies of France and England to write pamphlets against bourgeois society. Thus arose Feudal Socialism: half lamentation, half lampoon, but always ludicrous. As the parson has ever gone hand in hand with the landlord, so Christian Socialism is but the holy water with which the priest consecrates the heart-burnings of the aristocrat.

B. Petty-Bourgeois Socialism: In countries where modern civilisation has become fully developed, a new class of petty bourgeois has been formed, fluctuating between proletariat and bourgeoisie. Petty-bourgeois Socialism aims either at restoring the old means of production and of exchange, and the old property relations, and the old society, or to cramping the modern means of production and of exchange. It is both reactionary and Utopian.

C. German, or "True," Socialism: German philosophers, eagerly seized on French Socialist literature, forgetting that French social conditions had not immigrated along with them. German Socialists proclaimed the German nation to be the model nation, and the German petty Philistine to be the typical man - merely foul and enervating literature.

2. CONSERVATIVE, OR BOURGEOIS, SOCIALISM

A part of the bourgeoisie is desirous of redressing social grievances, in order to secure the continued existence of bourgeois society; philanthropists, humanitarians, organisers of charity, societies for the prevention of cruelty to animals, fanatics and reformers of every kind.

Free trade and protective duties: for the benefit of the working class. The bourgeois; for the benefit of the working class.

3. CRITICAL-UTOPIAN SOCIALISM

They reject all political, and especially all revolutionary, action; they wish to attain their ends by peaceful means, by small experiments, necessarily doomed to failure.

4. COMMUNISTS AND EXISTING PARTIES

The Communists fight for the interests of the working class. In France the Communists ally themselves with the Social-Democrats. In Switzerland they support the Radicals. In Poland they support the party of agrarian revolution. But they never cease, for a single instant, to instil into the working class the clearest possible recognition of the hostile antagonism between bourgeoisie and proletariat. They labour everywhere for the union and agreement of the democratic parties of all countries.

The Communists disdain to conceal their views and aims. They openly declare that their ends can be attained only by the forcible overthrow of all existing social conditions. Let the ruling classes tremble at a Communistic revolution. The proletarians have nothing to lose but their chains. They have a world to win.

WORKERS OF THE WORLD, UNITE !

Jane Eyre
by Charlotte Brontë
(London, 1847)

Charlotte, who first published under the pseudonym Currer Bell, was one of the novelist daughters of Irish churchman Patrick Brontë, of the romantically wild Haworth parsonage in Yorkshire. As well as having produced dozens of TV, stage and ballet versions, the story of *Jane Eyre* has inspired works as diverse as the Daphne du Maurier's *Rebecca*, the 1940's movie *I Walked with a Zombie,* and Jean Rhys' *Wide Sargasso Sea.*

Abridged: JH/GH

I

Thornfield, my new home after I left school, was, I found, a fine old battlemented hall, and Mrs. Fairfax, who had answered my advertisement, a mild, elderly lady, related by marriage to Mr. Rochester, the owner of the estate and the guardian of Adela Varens, my little pupil.

It was not till three months after my arrival there that my adventures began. One day Mrs. Fairfax proposed to show me over the house, much of which was unoccupied. The third storey especially had the aspect of a home of the past- a shrine of memory. I liked its hush and quaintness.

"If there were a ghost at Thornfield Hall this would be its haunt," said Mrs. Fairfax, as we passed the range of apartments on our way to see the view from the roof.

I was pacing through the corridor of the third floor on my return, when the last sound I expected in so still a region struck my ear-a laugh, distinct, formal, mirthless. At first it was very low, but it passed off in a clamorous peal that seemed to wake an echo in every lonely chamber.

"Mrs. Fairfax," I called out, "did you hear that laugh? Who is it?"

"Some of the servants very likely," she answered; "perhaps Grace Poole."

The laugh was repeated in a low tone, and terminated in an odd murmur.

"Grace!" exclaimed Mrs. Fairfax.

I didn't expect Grace to answer, for the laugh was preternatural.

Nevertheless, the door nearest me opened, and a servant came out-a set, square-made figure, with a hard, plain face.

"Too much noise, Grace," said Mrs. Fairfax. "Remember directions!"

Grace curtseyed silently, and went in.

Not unfrequently after that I heard Grace Poole's laugh and her eccentric murmurs, stranger than her laugh.

Late one fine, calm afternoon in January I volunteered to carry to the post at Hay, two miles distant, a letter Mrs. Fairfax had just written. The lane to Hay inclined uphill all the way, and having reached the middle, I sat on a stile till the sun went down, and on the hill-top above me stood the rising moon. The village was a mile distant, but in the absolute hush I could hear plainly its murmurs of life.

A rude noise broke on the fine ripplings and whisperings of the evening calm, a metallic clatter, a horse was coming. The windings of the lane hid it as it approached. Then I heard a rush under the hedge, and close by glided a great dog, not staying to look up. The horse followed- a tall steed, and on its back a rider. He passed; a sliding sound, a clattering tumble, and man and horse were down. They had slipped on the sheet of ice which glased the causeway. The dog came bounding back, sniffed round the prostrate group, and then ran up to me; it was all he could do. I obeyed him, and walked down to the traveller struggling himself free of his steed. I think he was swearing, but am not certain.

"Can I do anything?" I asked.

"You can stand on one side," he answered as he rose. Whereupon began a heaving, stamping process, accompanied by a barking and baying, and the horse was re-established and the dog silenced with a "Down, Pilot!"

"If you are hurt and want help, sir," I remarked, "I can fetch someone, either from Thornfield Hall or from Hay."

"Thank you, I shall do. I have no broken bones, only a sprain." And he limped to the stile.

He had a dark face, with stern features and a heavy brow. His eyes and gathered eyebrows looked ireful and thwarted; he was past youth, but had not reached middle age-perhaps he might be thirty-five. I felt no fear of him and but little shyness. His frown and roughness set me at ease.

He waved me to go, but I said:

"I cannot think of leaving you in this solitary lane till you are fit to mount your horse."

"You ought to be at home yourself," said he. "Where do you come from?"

"From just below."

"Do you mean that house with the battlements?"

"Yes, sir."

"Whose house is it?"

"Mr. Rochester's."

"Do you know Mr. Rochester?"

"No, I have never seen him."

"You are not a servant at the Hall, of course. You are-"

"I am the governess."

"Ah, the governess!" he repeated. "Deuce take me if I had not forgotten! Excuse me," he continued, "necessity compels me to make you useful."

He laid a heavy hand on my shoulder, limped to his horse, caught the bridle, and, grimacing grimly, sprang into the saddle and, with a "Thank you," bounded away.

When I returned from Hay, after posting Mrs. Fairfax's letter, I went to her room. She was not there, but sitting upright on the rug was a great black-and-white long-haired dog. I went forward and said, "Pilot," and the thing got up, came to me, sniffed me, and wagged his great tail. I rang the bell.

"What dog is this?"

"He came with master, who has just arrived. He has had an accident, and his ankle is sprained."

The next day I was summoned to take tea with Mr. Rochester and my pupil. When I entered he was looking at Adela, who knelt on the hearth beside Pilot.

"Here is Miss Eyre, sir," said Mrs. Fairfax, in her quiet way.

Mr. Rochester bowed, still not taking his eyes from the group of the dog and the child.

I sat down, disembarrassed. Politeness might have confused me; caprice laid me under no obligation.

Mrs. Fairfax seemed to think someone should be amiable, and she began to talk.

"Madam, I should like some tea," was the sole rejoinder she got.

"Come to the fire," said the master, when the tray was taken away. "When you came on me in Hay lane last night I thought unaccountably of fairy tales, and had half a mind to demand whether you had bewitched my horse. I am not sure yet. Who are your parents?"

"I have none."

"I thought not. And so you were waiting for your people when you sat on that stile?"

"For whom, sir?"

"For the men in green. Did I break through one of your rings that you spread that ice on the causeway?"

I shook my head.

"The men in green all forsook England a hundred years ago. I don't think either summer or harvest or winter moon will ever shine on their revels more."

Mrs. Fairfax dropped her knitting, wondering what sort of talk this was, and remarked that Miss Eyre had been a kind and careful teacher.

"Don't trouble yourself to give her a character," returned Mr. Rochester. "I shall judge for myself. She began by felling my horse."

"You said Mr. Rochester was not peculiar, Mrs. Fairfax," I remonstrated, when I rejoined her in her room after putting Adela to bed.

After a time my master's manner towards me changed. It became more uniform. I never seemed in his way. He did not take fits of chilling hauteur. When he met me, the encounter seemed welcome; he always had a word, and sometimes a smile. I felt at times as if he were my relation rather than my master, and so happy did I become that the blanks of existence were filled up. He had now been resident eight weeks, though Mrs. Fairfax said he seldom stayed at the Hall longer than a fortnight.

II

One night, I hardly know whether I had been sleeping or musing, I started wide awake on hearing a vague murmur, peculiar and lugubrious. It ceased, but my heart beat anxiously; my inward tranquillity was broken. The clock, far down in the hall, struck two. Just then my chamber-door was touched as if fingers swept the panels groping a way along the dark gallery outside. I was chilled with fear. Then I remembered that it might be Pilot, and the idea calmed me. But it was fated I should not sleep that night, for at the very keyhole of my chamber, as it seemed, a demoniac laugh was uttered. My first impulse was to rise and fasten the bolt, my next to cry: "Who is there?" Ere long steps retreated up the gallery towards the third floor staircase, and then all was still.

"Was it Grace Poole?" thought I. I hurried on my frock, and with a trembling hand opened the door. There, burning outside, left on the matting of the gallery, was a candle; and the air was filled with smoke, which rushed in a cloud from Mr. Rochester's room. In an instant I was within the chamber. Tongues of fire darted round the bed; the curtains were on fire, and in the midst lay Mr. Rochester, in deep sleep. I shook him, but he seemed stupefied. Then I rushed to his basin and ewer, and deluged the bed with water. He woke with the cry: "Is there a flood? What is it?"

I briefly related what had transpired. He was now in his dressing-gown, and, warning me to stay where I was and call no one, he added: "I must pay a visit to the third floor." A long time elapsed ere he returned, pale and gloomy.

"I have found it all out," said he; "it is as I thought. You are no talking fool. Say nothing about it."

He held out his hand as we parted. I gave him mine; he took it in both his own.

"You have saved my life. I have a pleasure in owing you so immense a debt. I feel your benefits no burden, Jane."

Strange energy was in his voice, strange fire in his look.

Till morning I was tossed on a buoyant, but unquiet sea. In the morning I heard the servants exclaim how providential that master thought of the water-jug when he had left the candle alight; and passing the room, I saw, sewing rings on the new curtains, no other than-Grace Poole.

Company now came to the hall, including the beautiful Miss Ingram, whom rumour associated with Mr. Rochester, as I heard from Mrs. Fairfax.

One day Mr. Rochester had been called away from home, and on his return, as I was the first inmate of the house to meet him, I remarked: "Oh, are you aware, Mr. Rochester, that a stranger has arrived since you left this morning?"

"A stranger! no; I expected no one; did he give his name?"

"His name is Mason, sir, and he comes from the West Indies."

Mr. Rochester was standing near me, and as I spoke he gave my wrist a convulsive grip, while a spasm caught his breath, and he turned whiter than ashes.

"Do you feel ill, sir?" I inquired.

"Jane, I've got a blow; I've got a blow, Jane!" he staggered.

Then he sat down and made me sit beside him.

"My little friend," said he, "I wish I were in a quiet island with only you; and trouble and danger and hideous recollections were removed from me."

"Can I help you, sir? I'd give my life to serve you."

"Jane, if aid is wanted, I'll seek it at your hands."

"Thank you, sir; tell me what to do."

"Go back into the room; step quietly up to Mason, tell him Mr. Rochester has come and wishes to see him; show him in here, and then leave me."

At a late hour that night I heard the visitors repair to their chambers and Mr. Rochester saying: "This way, Mason; this is your room."

He spoke cheerfully, and the gay tones set my heart at ease.

Awaking in the dead of night I stretched my hand to draw the curtain, for the moon was full and bright. Good God! What a cry! The night was rent in twain by a savage, shrilly sound that ran from end to end of Thornfield Hall.

The cry died and was not renewed. Indeed, whatever being uttered that fearful shriek could not soon repeat it; not the widest-winged condor on the Andes could, twice in succession, send out such a yell from the cloud shrouding his eyrie.

It came out of the third storey. And overhead-yes, in the room just above my chamber, I heard a deadly struggle, and a half-smothered voice shout, "Help! help!"

A chamber door opened; someone rushed along the gallery. Another step stamped on the floor above, and something fell. Then there was silence.

The sleepers were all aroused and gathered in the gallery, which but for the moonlight would have been in complete darkness. The door at the end of the gallery opened, and Mr. Rochester advanced with a candle. He had just descended from the upper storey.

"All's right!" he cried. "A servant has had a nightmare, that is all, and has taken a fit with fright. Now I must see you all back to your rooms." And so by dint of coaxing and commanding he contrived to get them back to their dormitories.

I retreated unnoticed and dressed myself carefully to be ready for emergencies. About an hour passed, and then a cautious hand tapped low at my door.

"Are you up and dressed?"

"Yes."

"Then come out quietly."

Mr. Rochester stood in the gallery holding a light.

"Bring a sponge and some volatile salts," said he.

I did so, and followed him.

"You don't turn sick at the sight of blood?"

"I think not; I have never been tried yet."

We entered a room with an inner apartment, from whence came a snarling, snatching sound. Mr. Rochester went forward into this apartment, and a shout of laughter greeted his entrance. Grace Poole, then, was there. When he came out he closed the door behind him.

"Here, Jane!" he said.

I walked round to the other side of the large bed in the outer room, and there, in an easy-chair, his head leaned back, I recognised the pale and seemingly lifeless face of the stranger, Mason. His linen on one side and one arm was almost soaked in blood.

Mr. Rochester took the sponge, dipped it in water, moistened the corpse-like face, and applied my smelling-bottle to the nostrils.

Mr. Mason unclosed his eyes and murmured: "Is there immediate danger?"

"Pooh!- a mere scratch! I'll fetch a surgeon now, and you'll be able to be removed by the morning."

"Jane," he continued, "you'll sponge the blood when it returns, and put your salts to his nose; and you'll not speak to him on any pretext- and, Richard, it will be at the peril of your life if you speak to her."

Two hours later the surgeon came and removed the injured man.

In the morning I heard Rochester in the yard, saying to some of the visitors, "Mason got the start of you all this morning; he was gone before sunrise. I rose to see him off."

III

A splendid midsummer shone over England. In the sweetest hour of the twenty-four, after the sun had gone down in simple state, and dew fell cool on the panting plain, I had walked into the orchard, to the giant horse-chestnut, near the sunk fence that separates the Hall grounds from the lonely fields, when there came to me the warning fragrance of Mr. Rochester's cigar. I was about to retreat when he intercepted me, and said: "Turn back, Jane; on so lovely a night it is a shame to sit in the house." I did not like to walk alone with my master at this hour in the shadowy orchard, but could find no reason for leaving him.

"Jane," he recommenced, as we slowly strayed down in the direction of the horse-chestnut, "Thornfield is a pleasant place in summer, is it not?"

"Yes, sir."

"And you must have become in some degree attached to it?"

"I am attached to it, indeed."

"Pity!" he said, and paused.

"Must I move on, sir?" I asked.

"I believe you must, Jane."

This was a blow, but I did not let it prostrate me.

"Then you are going to be married, sir?"

"In about a month I hope to be a bridegroom. We have been good friends, Jane, have we not?"

"Yes, sir."

"Here is the chestnut-tree; come, we will sit here in peace to-night." He seated me and himself.

"Jane, do you hear the nightingale singing in the wood? Listen!"

In listening, I sobbed convulsively, for I could repress what I endured no longer, and when I did speak, it was only to express an impetuous wish that I had never been born, or never come to Thornfield.

"Because you are sorry to leave it?"

The vehemence of emotion was claiming mastery, and struggling for full sway-to overcome, to live, rise, and reign at last; yes-and to speak.

"I grieve to leave Thornfield. I love Thornfield, because I have lived in it a full and delightful life. I have not been trampled on; I have not been petrified. I have talked face to face with what I delight in-an original, a vigorous and expanded mind. I have known you, Mr. Rochester. I see the necessity of departure, but it is like looking on the necessity of death."

"Where do you see the necessity?" he asked suddenly.

"Do you think I can stay to become nothing to you?" I retorted, roused to something like passion. "Do you think, because I am poor, obscure, plain, and little, I am soulless and heartless? You think wrong! I have as much soul as you- and full as much heart! I am not talking to you now through the medium of custom, conventionalities, nor even mortal flesh. It is my spirit that addresses your spirit, just as if both had passed through the grave, and we stood at God's feet, equal- as we are!"

"As we are!" repeated Mr. Rochester, gathering me to his heart and pressing his lips on my lips. "So, Jane!"

"Yes, so, sir!" I replied. "I have spoken my mind, and can go anywhere now. Let me go!"

"Jane, be still; don't struggle so, like a wild, frantic bird, rending its own plumage in its desperation."

"I am no bird, and no net ensnares me. I am a free human being, with an independent will, which I now exert to leave you."

Another effort set me at liberty, and I stood erect before him.

"And your will shall decide your destiny," he said. "I offer you my hand, my heart, and a share in all my possessions."

A waft of wind came sweeping down the laurel walk and trembled through the boughs of the chestnut; it wandered away-away to an infinite distance-it died. The nightingale's song was then the only voice of the hour; in listening to it again, I wept.

Mr. Rochester sat looking at me gently, and at last said, drawing me to him again: "My bride is here, because my equal is here, and my likeness. Jane, will you marry me? Give me my name- Edward. Say, 'I will marry you.'"

"Are you in earnest? Do you love me? Do you sincerely wish me to be your wife?"

"I do. I swear it!"

"Then, sir, I will marry you."

"God pardon me, and man meddle not with me. I have her, and will hold her!"

But what had befallen the night? And what ailed the chestnut-tree? It writhed and groaned, while the wind roared in the laurel walk.

"We must go in," said Mr. Rochester; "the weather changes."

He hurried me up the walk, but we were wet before we could pass the threshold.

IV

There were no groomsmen, no bridesmaids, no relatives to wait for or marshal; none but Mr. Rochester and I. I wonder what other bridegroom looked as he did- so bent up to a purpose, so resolutely grim. Our place was taken at the communion rails. All was still; two shadows only moved in a remote corner of the church.

As the clergyman's lips unclosed to ask, "Wilt thou have this woman for thy wedded wife?" a distinct and near voice said: "The marriage cannot go on. I declare the existence of an impediment."

"What is the nature of the impediment?" asked the clergyman.

"It simply consists in the existence of a previous marriage," said the speaker. "Mr. Rochester has a wife now living."

My nerves vibrated to those low-spoken words as they had never vibrated to thunder. I looked at Mr. Rochester; I made him look at me. His face was colourless rock; his eye both spark and flint; he seemed as if he would defy all things.

"Mr. Mason, have the goodness to step forward," said the stranger.

"Are you aware, sir, whether or not this gentleman's wife is still living?" inquired the clergyman.

"She is now living at Thornfield Hall," said Mason, with white lips. "I saw her there last April. I am her brother."

I saw a grim smile contract Mr. Rochester's lip.

"Enough," said he. "Wood"- to the clergyman-"close your book; John Green"- to the clerk- "leave the church; there will be no wedding to-day."

"Bigamy is an ugly word," he continued, "but I meant to be a bigamist. This girl thought all was fair and legal, and never dreamt she was going to be entrapped into a feigned union with a defrauded wretch already bound to a bad, mad, and embruted partner. Follow me. I invite you all to visit Grace Poole's patient and my wife!"

We passed up to the third storey, and there, in the deep shade of the inner room beyond the room where I had watched over the wounded Mason, ran backward and forward, seemingly on all fours, a figure, whether beast or human one could not at first sight tell. It snatched and growled like some wild animal. It was covered with clothing; but a quantity of dark, grizzled hair, wild as a mane, hid its head and face.

"That is my wife," said Mr. Rochester, "whom I was cheated into marrying fifteen years ago- a mad woman and a drunkard, of a family of idiots and maniacs for three generations. And this is what I wished to have"- laying his hand on my shoulder- "this young girl who stands so grave and quiet, at the mouth of hell. Jane," he continued, in an agonised tone, "I never meant to wound you thus."

Reader! I forgave him at the moment, and on the spot. I forgave him all; yet not in words, not outwardly; only at my heart's core.

That night I never thought to sleep, but a slumber fell on me as soon as I lay down in bed, and in my sleep a vision spoke to my spirit: "Daughter, flee temptation!" I rose with the dim dawn. One word comprised my intolerable duty- Depart!

After three days wandering and starvation on the north-midland moors, for hastily and secretly I had travelled by coach as far from Thornfield as my money would carry me, I found a temporary home at the vicarage of Morton, until the clergyman of that moorland parish, Mr. St. John Rivers, secured for me- under the assumed name of Jane Elliott- the mistresship of the village school.

At Christmas I left the school. As the spring advanced St. John Rivers, who, with an icy heroism, was possessed by the idea of becoming a missionary, urged me strongly to accompany him to India as his wife, on the grounds that I was docile, diligent, and courageous, and would be very useful. I felt such veneration for him that I was tempted to cease struggling with him-to rush down the torrent of his will into the gulf of his existence, and there lose my own.

V

The time came when he called on me to decide. I fervently longed to do what was right, and only that. "Show me the path, show me the path!" I entreated of Heaven.

My heart beat fast and thick; I heard its throb. Suddenly it stood still to an inexpressible feeling that thrilled it through. My senses rose expectant; ear and eye waited, while the flesh quivered on my bones. I saw nothing; but I heard a voice, somewhere, cry "Jane! Jane! Jane!"- nothing more.

"Oh, God! What is it?" I gasped. I might have said, "Where is it?" for it did not seem in the room, nor in the house, nor in the garden, nor from overhead. And it was the voice of a human being- a loved, well-remembered voice- that of Edward Fairfax Rochester; and it spoke in pain and woe, wildly, eerily, urgently.

"I am coming!" I cried. "Wait for me!" I ran out into the garden; it was void.

"Down, superstition!" I commented, as that spectre rose up black by the black yew at the gate.

I mounted to my chamber, locked myself in, fell on my knees, and seemed to penetrate very near a Mighty Spirit; and my soul rushed out in gratitude at His feet.

Then I rose from the thanksgiving, took a resolve, and lay down, unscared, enlightened, eager but for the daylight.

Thirty-six hours later I was crossing the fields to where I could see the full front of my master's mansion, and, looking with a timorous joy, saw-a blackened ruin.

Where, meantime, was the hapless owner?

I returned to the inn, where the host himself, a respectable middle-aged man, brought my breakfast into the parlour. I scarcely knew how to begin my questions.

"Is Mr. Rochester living at Thornfield Hall now?"

"No, ma'am-oh, no! No one is living there. It was burnt down about harvest time. The fire broke out at dead of night."

"Was it known how it originated?"

"They guessed, ma'am; they guessed. There was a lady- a-a lunatic kept in the house. She had a woman to take care of her called Mrs. Poole, an able woman but for one fault-she kept a private bottle of gin by her; and the mad lady would take the keys out of her pocket, let herself out of her chamber, and go roaming about the house doing any wild mischief that came into her head. Mr. Rochester was at home when the fire broke out, and he went up to the attics and got the servants out of their beds, and then went back to get his mad wife out of her cell. And then they called out to him that she was on the roof, where she was waving her arms and shouting till they could hear her a mile off. She was a big woman, and had long, black hair; and we could see it streaming against the flames as she stood. We saw Mr. Rochester approach her and call 'Bertha!' And then, ma'am, she yelled and gave a spring, and the next minute lay dead, smashed on the pavement."

"Were any other lives lost?"

"No. Perhaps it would have been better if there had. Poor Mr. Edward! He is stone-blind."

I had dreaded he was mad.

"As he came down the great staircase it fell, and he was taken out of the ruins with one eye knocked out and one hand so crushed that the surgeon had to amputate it directly. The other eye inflamed, and he lost the sight of that also."

"Where does he live now?"

"At Ferndean, a manor house on a farm he has- quite a desolate spot. Old John and his wife are with him; he would have none else."

To Ferndean I came just ere dusk, walking the last mile. As I approached, the narrow front door of the grange slowly opened, and a figure came out into the twilight; a man without a hat. He stretched forth his hand to feel whether it rained. It was my master, Edward Fairfax Rochester.

He groped his way back to the house, and, re-entering it, closed the door. I now drew near and knocked, and John's wife opened for me.

"Mary," I said, "how are you?"

She started as if she had seen a ghost. I calmed her, and followed her into the kitchen, where I explained in a few words that I should stay for the night, and that John must fetch my trunk from the turnpike house. At this moment the parlour bell rang.

Mary proceeded to fill a glass with water and place it on a tray, together with candles.

"Give the tray to me; I will carry it in."

The old dog Pilot pricked up his ears as I entered the room; then he jumped up with a yelp, and bounded towards me, almost knocking the tray from my hands.

"What is the matter?" inquired Mr. Rochester.

He put out his hand with a quick gesture. "Who is this?" he demanded imperiously.

"Will you have a little more water, sir? I spilt half of what was in the glass," I said.

"What is it? Who speaks?"

"Pilot knows me, and John and Mary know I am here," I answered.

He groped, and, arresting his wandering hand, I prisoned it in both mine.

"Her very fingers! Her small, slight fingers! Is it Jane-Jane Eyre?" he cried.

"My dear master, I am Jane Eyre. I have found you out; I am come back to you!"

Reader, I married him.

Wuthering Heights
by Emily (Jane) Brontë
(London, 1847)

Here is Emily Brontë's only novel, published in 1847 under the pseudonym Ellis Bell. The story of the all-encompassing, passionate, and thwarted, love between Heathcliff and Catherine Earnshaw is considered a classic of English literature, and has given rise to many adaptations and inspired works, including films, radio, television dramatisations, a musical, songs, notably by Kate Bush, ballet and opera.

Abridged: JH/GH

1801. I have just returned from a visit to my landlord—the solitary neighbour that I shall be troubled with in this beautiful country! He little imagined how my heart warmed towards him when I beheld his black eyes withdraw so suspiciously under their brows, as I rode up;

"Mr. Heathcliff?"

A nod was the answer.

"Mr. Lockwood, your new tenant at Thrushcross Grange, sir."

"Walk in." But the invitation, uttered with closed teeth, expressed the sentiment "Go to the deuce!" And it was not till my horse's breast fairly pushed the barrier that he put out his hand to unchain it. I felt interested in a man who seemed more exaggeratedly reserved than myself as he preceded me up the causeway, calling, "Joseph, take Mr. Lockwood's horse; and bring up some wine."

Joseph was an old man, very old, though hale and sinewy. "The Lord help us!" he soliloquised in an undertone as he relieved me of my horse.

Wuthering Heights, Mr. Heathcliff's dwelling, is a farmhouse on an exposed and stormy edge, its name being a provincial adjective of atmospheric tumult. Its owner is a dark-skinned gipsy in aspect, in dress and manners a gentleman, with erect and handsome figure, but morose demeanour. One step from the outside brought us into the family living-room, the recesses of which were haunted by a huge liver-coloured bitch pointer, with a swarm of squealing puppies, and other dogs. As the bitch sneaked wolfishly to the back of my legs I attempted to caress her, an action that provoked a long, guttural growl.

"You'd better let the dog alone," growled Mr. Heathcliff in unison, as he checked her with a punch of his foot. "She's not accustomed to be spoiled."

As Joseph was mumbling indistinctly in the depths of the cellar, and gave no sign of ascending, his master dived down to him, leaving me vis-a-vis with the ruffianly bitch and half a dozen four-footed fiends that suddenly broke into a fury, while I parried off the attack with a poker and called aloud for assistance.

"What the devil is the matter?" asked Heathcliff, as he returned.

"What the devil, indeed!" I muttered. "You might as well leave a stranger with a brood of tigers!"

"They won't meddle with persons who touch nothing," he remarked. "The dogs are right to be vigilant. Take a glass of wine."

Before I went home I determined to volunteer another visit to my sulky landlord, though evidently he wished for no repetition of my intrusion.

* * *

Yesterday I again visited Wuthering Heights, my nearest neighbours to Thrushcross Grange. On that bleak hill-top the earth was hard with a black frost, and the air made me shiver through every limb. As I knocked for admittance, till my knuckles tingled and the dogs howled, vinegar- faced Joseph projected his head from a round window of the barn, and shouted to me.

"What are ye for? T'maister's down i' t' fowld. There's nobbut t' missis. I'll hae no hend wi't," muttered the head, vanishing.

Then a young man, without coat and shouldering a pitchfork, hailed me to follow him, and showed me into the apartment where I had been formerly received with a gruff "Sit down; he'll be in soon."

In the room sat the "missis," motionless and mute. She was slender, scarcely past girlhood, with the most exquisite little face I have ever had the pleasure of beholding; and her eyes, had they been agreeable in expression, would have been irresistible. But the only sentiment they evinced hovered between scorn and a kind of desperation. As for the young man who had brought me in, he slung on his person a shabby jacket, and, erecting himself before the fire, gazed down on me from the corner of his eyes as if there was some mortal feud unavenged between us. The entrance of Heathcliff relieved me from an uncomfortable state.

I found in the course of the tea which followed that the lady was the widow of Heathcliff's son, and that the rustic youth who sat down to the meal with us was Hareton Earnshaw. Now, before passing the threshold, I had noticed over the principal door, among a wilderness of crumbling griffins and shameless little boys, the name "Hareton Earnshaw" and the date "1500." Evidently the place had a history.

The snow had fallen so deeply since I entered the house that return across the moor in the dusk was impossible.

Spending that night at Wuthering Heights on an old-fashioned couch that filled a recess, or closet, in a disused chamber, I found, scratched on the paint many times, the names "Catherine Earnshaw," "Catherine Heathcliff," and again "Catherine Linton." There were many books in the room in a dilapidated state, and, being unable to sleep, I examined them. Some of them bore the inscription "Catherine Earnshaw, her book"; and on the blank leaves and margins, scrawled in a childish hand, was a regular diary. I read: "Hindley is detestable. Heathcliff and I are going to rebel.... How little did I dream Hindley would ever make me cry so! Poor Heathcliff! Hindley calls him a vagabond, and won't let him sit or eat with us any more."

When I slept I was harrowed by nightmare, and next morning I gladly left the house; and, piloted by my landlord across the billowy white ocean of the moor, I reached the Grange benumbed with cold and as feeble as a kitten from fatigue.

When my housekeeper, Mrs. Nelly Dean, brought in my supper that night I asked her why Heathcliff let the Grange and preferred living in a residence so much inferior.

"He's rich enough to live in a finer house than this," said Mrs. Dean; "but he's very close-handed. Young Mrs. Heathcliff is my late master's daughter- Catherine Linton was her maiden name, and I nursed her, poor thing. Hareton Earnshaw is her cousin, and the last of an old family."

"The master, Heathcliff, must have had some ups and downs to make him such a churl. Do you know anything of his history?"

"It's a cuckoo's, sir. I know all about it, except where he was born, and who were his parents, and how he got his money. And Hareton Earnshaw has been cast out like an unfledged dunnock."

I asked Mrs. Dean to bring her sewing, and continue the story. This she did, evidently pleased to find me companionable.

* * *

Before I came to live here (began Mrs. Dean), I was almost always at Wuthering Heights, because my mother nursed Mr. Hindley Earnshaw, that was Hareton's father, and I used to run errands and play with the children. One day, old Mr. Earnshaw, Hareton's grandfather, went to Liverpool, and promised Hindley and Cathy, his son and daughter, to bring each of them a present. He was absent three days, and at the end of that time brought home, bundled up in his arms under his great-coat, a dirty, ragged, black-haired child, big enough both to walk and talk, but only able to talk gibberish nobody could understand. He had picked it up, he said, starving and homeless in the streets of Liverpool. Mrs. Earnshaw was ready to fling it out of doors, but Mr. Earnshaw told her to wash it, give it clean things, and let it sleep with the children. The children's presents were forgotten. This was how Heathcliff, as they called him, came to Wuthering Heights.

Miss Cathy and he soon became very thick; but Hindley hated him. He was a patient, sullen child, who would stand blows without winking or shedding a tear. From the beginning he bred bad feeling in the house. Old Earnshaw took to him strangely, and Hindley regarded him as having usurped his father's affections. As for Heathcliff, he was insensible to kindness. Cathy, a wild slip, with the bonniest eye, the sweetest smile, and the lightest foot in the parish, was much too fond of Heathcliff.

Old Mr. Earnshaw died quietly in his chair by the fireside one October evening.

Mr. Hindley, who had been to college, came home to the funeral, and set the neighbours gossiping right and left, for he brought a wife with him. What she was and where she was born he never informed us. She evinced a dislike to Heathcliff, and drove him to the company of the servants, but Cathy clung to him, and the two promised to grow up together as rude as savages. Once Hindley shut them out for the night and they came to Thrushcross Grange, where the Lintons took Cathy in, but would not have anything to do with Heathcliff, the Spanish castaway, as they called him. She stayed five weeks with the Lintons, and became very friendly with the children, Edgar and Isabella, and when she came back was a dignified little person, and quite a beauty.

Soon after, Hindley's son, Hareton, was born, the mother died, and the child fell wholly into my hands, for the father grew desperate in his sorrow, and gave himself up to reckless dissipation. His treatment of Heathcliff now was enough to make a fiend of a saint, and daily the lad became more savagely sullen. I could not half-tell what an infernal house we had, till at last nobody decent came near us, except that Edgar Linton called to see Cathy, who at fifteen was the queen of the countryside- a haughty and headstrong creature.

One day after Edgar Linton had been over from the Grange, Cathy came into the kitchen to me and said, "Nelly, will you keep a secret for me? To-day Edgar Linton has asked me to marry him, and I've given him an answer. I accepted him, Nelly. Be quick and say whether I was wrong."

"First and foremost," I said sententiously, "do you love Mr. Edgar?"

"I love the ground under his feet, and the air over his head, and everything he touches, and every word he says. I love his looks, and all his actions, and him entirely and altogether. There now!"

"Then," said I, "all seems smooth and easy. Where is the obstacle?"

"Here, and here!" replied Catherine, striking one hand on her forehead, and the other on her breast. "In my soul and in my heart I'm convinced I'm wrong! I've no more business to marry Edgar Linton than I have to be in heaven; and if the wicked man in there, my brother, had not brought Heathcliff so low I shouldn't have thought of it. It would degrade me to marry Heathcliff now; so he shall never know how I love him, and that not because he's handsome, Nelly, but because he's more myself than I am. Whatever

our souls are made of, his and mine are the same, and Linton's is as different as a moonbeam from lightning, or frost from fire. Nelly, I dreamed I was in heaven, but heaven did not seem to be my home, and I broke my heart with weeping to come back to earth; and the angels were so angry that they flung me out into the middle of the heath on the top of Wuthering Heights, where I woke sobbing for joy."

Ere this speech was ended, Heathcliff, who had been lying out of sight on a bench by the kitchen wall, stole out. He had heard Catherine say it would degrade her to marry him, and he had heard no further.

That night, while a storm rattled over the heights in full fury, Heathcliff disappeared. Catherine suffered uncontrollable grief, and became dangerously ill. When she was convalescent she went to Thrushcross Grange. But Edgar Linton, when he married her, three years subsequent to his father's death, and brought her here to the Grange, was the happiest man alive. I accompanied her, leaving little Hareton, who was now nearly five years old, and had just begun to learn his letters.

On a mellow evening in September, I was coming from the garden with a basket of apples I had been gathering, when, as I approached the kitchen door, I heard a voice say, "Nelly, is that you?"

Something stirred in the porch, and, moving nearer, I saw a tall man, dressed in dark clothes, with dark hair and face.

"What," I cried, "you come back?"

"Yes, Nelly. You needn't be so disturbed. I want one word with your mistress."

I went in, and explained to Mr. Edgar and Catherine who was waiting below.

"Oh, Edgar darling," she panted, flinging her arms round his neck, "Heathcliff's come back- he is!"

"Well, well," he said, "don't strangle me for that. There's no need to be frantic. Try to be glad without being absurd!"

When Heathcliff came in, she seized his hands and laughed like one beside herself.

It seemed that he was staying at Wuthering Heights, invited by Mr. Earnshaw! When I heard this I had a presentiment that he had better have remained away.

Later, we learned from Joseph that Heathcliff had called on Earnshaw, whom he found sitting at cards, had joined in the play, and, seeming plentifully supplied with money, had been asked by his ancient persecutor to come again in the evening. He then offered liberal payment for permission to lodge at the Heights, which Earnshaw's covetousness made him accept.

Heathcliff now commenced visiting Thrushcross Grange, and gradually established his right to be expected. A new source of trouble sprang up in an unexpected form-Isabella Linton evincing a sudden and irresistible attraction towards Heathcliff. At that time she was a charming young lady of eighteen. I tried to persuade her to banish him from her thoughts.

"He's a bird of bad omen, miss," I said, "and no mate for you. How has he been living? How has he got rich? Why is he staying at Wuthering Heights in the house of the man whom he abhors? They say Mr. Earnshaw is worse and worse since he came. They sit up all night together continually, and Hindley has been borrowing money on his land, and does nothing but play and drink."

"You are leagued with the rest," she replied, "and I'll not listen to your slanders." The antipathy of Mr. Linton towards Heathcliff reached a point at last at which he called on his servants one day to turn him out of the Grange, whereupon Heathcliff's revenge took the form of an elopement with Linton's sister. Six weeks later I received a letter of bitter regret from Isabella, asking me distractedly whether I thought her husband was a man or a devil, and how I had preserved the common sympathies of human nature at Wuthering Heights, where they had returned.

On receiving this letter, I obtained permission from Mr. Linton to go to the Heights to see his sister, and Heathcliff, on meeting me, urged me to secure for him an interview with Catherine.

"Nelly," said he, "you know as well as I do that for every thought she spends on Linton she spends a thousand on me. If he loved her with all the powers of his puny being, he couldn't love as much in eighty years as I could in a day. And Catherine has a heart as deep as I have. The sea could be as readily contained in that horse-trough as her whole affection be monopolised by him."

Well, I argued, and refused, but in the long run he forced me to agree to put a missive into Mrs. Linton's hand.

When he met her, I saw that he could hardly bear, for downright agony, to look into her face, for he was stricken with the conviction that she was fated to die.

"Oh, Cathy, how can I bear it?" was the first sentence he uttered.

"You and Edgar have broken my heart, Heathcliff," was her reply. "You have killed me and thriven on it, I think."

"Are you possessed with a devil," he asked, "to talk in that manner to me when you are dying? You know you lie to say I have killed you, and you know that I could as soon forget my existence as forget you. Is it not sufficient that while you are at peace, I shall be in the torments of hell?"

"I shall not be at peace," moaned Catherine.

"Why did you despise me? Why did you betray your own heart? You loved me. What right had you to leave me?"

"Let me alone!" sobbed Catherine. "I've done wrong, and I'm dying for it! Forgive me!"

That night was born the Catherine you, Mr. Lockwood, saw at the Heights, and her mother's spirit was at home with God.

When in the morning I told Heathcliff, who had been watching near all night, he dashed his head against the knotted trunk of the tree by which he stood and howled, not like a man, but like a savage beast, as he besought her ghost to haunt him. "Be with me always-take any form!" he cried. "Only do not leave me in this abyss, where I cannot find you!"

Life with Heathcliff becoming impossible to Isabella, she left the neighbourhood, never to revisit it, and lived near London; and there her son, whom she christened Linton, was born a few months after her escape. He was an ailing, peevish creature. When Linton was twelve, or a little more, and Catherine thirteen, Isabella died, and the boy was brought to Thrushcross Grange. Hindley Earnshaw drank himself to death about the same time, after mortgaging every yard of his land for cash; and Heathcliff was the mortgagee. So Hareton Earnshaw, who should have been the first gentleman in the neighbourhood, was reduced to dependence on his father's enemy, in whose house he lived, ignorant that he had been wronged.

The motives of Heathcliff now became clear. Under the influence of a passionate but calculating revenge, allied with greed, he was planning the destruction of the Earnshaw family, and the union of the Wuthering Heights and Thrushcross Grange estates. To this end, having brought his weakly son home to the Heights and terrorised him into a pitiable slavery, he schemed a marriage between him and young Catherine Linton, who was induced to accept the arrangement through sympathy with her cousin, and the hope of removing him from the paralysing influence of his father. The marriage was almost immediately followed by the death of both Catherine's father and her boyish husband, who, it was afterwards found, had been coaxed or threatened into bequeathing all his property to his father. Thus ended Mrs. Dean's story of how the strangely assorted occupants of Wuthering Heights had come together, my landlord Heathcliff, the disinherited, poor Hareton Earnshaw, and Catherine Heathcliff, who had been Catherine Linton and the daughter of Catherine Earnshaw. I propose riding over to Wuthering Heights to inform my landlord that I shall spend the next six months in London, and that he may look out for another tenant for the Grange.

* * *

Yesterday was bright, calm, and frosty, and I went to the Heights as I proposed. My housekeeper entreated me to bear a little note from her to her young lady, and I did not refuse, for the worthy woman was not conscious of anything odd in her request. Hareton Earnshaw unchained the gate for me. The fellow is as handsome a rustic as need be seen, but he does his best, apparently, to make the least of his advantages. Catherine, who was preparing vegetables for a meal, looked more sulky and less spirited than when I had seen her first.

"She does not seem so amiable," I thought, "as Mrs. Dean would persuade me to believe. She's a beauty, it is true, but not an angel."

I approached her, pretending to desire a view of the garden, and dropped Mrs. Dean's note on her knee unnoticed by Hareton. But she asked aloud, "What is that?" and chucked it off.

"A letter from your old acquaintance, the housekeeper at the Grange," I answered. She would gladly have gathered it up at this information, but Hareton beat her. He seized and put it in his waistcoat, saying Mr. Heathcliff should look at it first; but later he pulled out the letter, and flung it on the floor as ungraciously as he could. Catherine perused it eagerly, and then asked, "Does Ellen like you?"

"Yes, very well," I replied hesitatingly.

Whereupon she became more communicative, and told me how dull she was now Heathcliff had taken her books away.

When Heathcliff came in, looking restless and anxious, he sent her to the kitchen to get her dinner with Joseph; and with the master of the house, grim and saturnine, and Hareton absolutely dumb, I made a cheerless meal, and bade adieu early.

* * *

Next September, when going north for shooting, a sudden impulse seized me to visit Thrushcross Grange and pass a night under my own roof, for the tenancy had not yet expired. When I reached the Grange before sunset I found a girl knitting under the porch, and an old woman reclining on the house-steps, smoking a meditative pipe.

"Is Mrs. Dean within?" I demanded.

"Mistress Dean? Nay!" she answered. "She doesn't bide here; shoo's up at th' Heights."

"Are you housekeeper, then?"

"Eea, aw keep th' house," she replied.

"Well, I'm Mr. Lockwood, the master. Are there any rooms to lodge me in, I wonder? I wish to stay all night."

"T' maister!" she cried in astonishment. "Yah sud ha' sent word. They's nowt norther dry nor mensful abaht t' place!"

Leaving her scurrying about making preparations, I climbed the stony by-road that branches off to Mr. Heathcliff's dwelling. On reaching it I had neither to climb the gate nor to knock-it yielded to my hand. "This is an improvement," I thought. I noticed, too, a fragrance of flowers wafted on the air from among the homely fruit-trees.

"Con-trary!" said a voice as sweet as a silver bell "That for the third time, you dunce! I'm not going to tell you again."

"Contrary, then," answered another in deep but softened tones. "And now kiss me for minding so well."

The male speaker was a young man, respectably dressed and seated at a table, having a book before him. His handsome features glowed with pleasure, and his eyes kept impatiently wandering from the page to a small white hand over his shoulder. So, not to interrupt Hareton Earnshaw and Catherine Heathcliff, I went round to the kitchen, where my old friend Nelly Dean sat sewing and singing a song.

Mrs. Dean jumped to her feet as she recognised me. "Why, bless you, Mr. Lockwood!" she exclaimed. "Pray step in! Have you walked from Gimmerton?"

"No, from the Grange," I replied; "and while they make me a lodging room there I want to finish my business with your master."

"What business, sir?" said Nelly.

"About the rent," I answered.

"Oh, then it is Catherine you must settle with, or rather me, as she has not learned to arrange her affairs yet."

I looked surprised.

"Ah! You have not heard of Heathcliff's death, I see," she continued.

"Heathcliff dead!" I exclaimed. "How long ago?"

"Three months since; but sit down, and I'll tell you all about it."

"I was summoned to Wuthering Heights," she said, "within a fortnight of your leaving us, and I went gladly for Catherine's sake. Mr. Heathcliff, who grew more and more disinclined to society, almost banished Earnshaw from his apartment, and was tired of seeing Catherine-that was the reason why I was sent for-and the two young people were thrown perforce much in each other's company in the house, and presently Catherine began to make it clear to her obstinate cousin that she wished to be friends. The intimacy ripened rapidly, and, Mr. Lockwood, on their wedding day there won't be a happier woman in England than myself. Joseph was the only objector, and he appealed to Heathcliff against 'yon flaysome graceless quean, that's witched our lad wi' her bold een and her forrad ways.' But after a burst of passion at the news, Mr. Heathcliff suddenly calmed down and said to me, 'Nelly, there is a strange change approaching; I'm in its shadow.'

"Soon after that he took to wandering alone, in a state approaching distraction. He could not rest; he could not eat; and he would not see the doctor. One morning as I walked round the house I observed the master's window swinging open and the rain driving straight in. 'He cannot be in bed,' I thought, 'those showers would drench him through.' And so it was, for when I entered the chamber his face and throat were washed with rain, the bed-clothes dripped, and he was perfectly still- dead and stark. I called up Joseph. 'Eh, what a wicked 'un he looks, girning at death,' exclaimed the old man, and then he fell on his knees and returned thanks that the ancient Earnshaw stock were restored to their rights.

"I shall be glad when they leave the Heights for the Grange," concluded Mrs. Dean.

"They are going to the Grange, then?"

"Yes, as soon as they are married; and that will be on New Year's Day."

My walk home was lengthened by a diversion in the direction of the kirk. I sought, and soon discovered, three headstones on the slope next the moor: on middle one grey, and half buried in the heath; Edgar Linton's only harmonized by the turf and moss creeping up its foot; Heathcliff's still bare.

I lingered round them, under that benign sky: watched the moths fluttering among the heath and harebells, listened to the soft wind breathing through the grass, and wondered how any one could ever imagine unquiet slumbers for the sleepers in that quiet earth.

Moby-Dick
or, The Whale
by Herman Melville
(New York, 1851)

Melville's strange, vast, tale, founded on his own experience as schoolmaster-turned-whaler, was far from well-received initially. Now, it tends to be seen as one of the glories of American Romanticism and among the greatest stories ever told.

Abridged: GH

"WHALE: This animal is named from roundness or rolling" - *Webster's Dictionary*

"So be cheery, my lads, let your hearts never fail, While the bold harpooneer is striking the whale!" - *Nantucket song.*

Call me Ishmael.

Some years ago- never mind how long precisely- having little or no money in my purse, and nothing particular to interest me on shore, I thought I would sail about a little and see the watery part of the world.

There is nothing surprising in this. Landsmen, pent up in lath and plaster, tied to counters, nailed to benches, clinched to desks, if they but knew it, almost all in their degree, some time or other, cherish very nearly the same feelings towards the ocean with me.

Yes, as every one knows, meditation and water are wedded for ever. It is the image of the ungraspable phantom of life; and this is the key to it all.

Now, when I say that I am in the habit of going to sea, I do not mean as a passenger. Passengers get sea-sick. No, when I go to sea, I go as a simple sailor, right before the mast. The transition is a keen one, I assure you, from a schoolmaster to a sailor, and requires a strong decoction of Seneca and the Stoics[1] to enable you to grin and bear it.

I am tormented with an everlasting itch for things remote. I love to sail forbidden seas, and land on barbarous coasts.

I stuffed a shirt or two into my old carpet-bag, tucked it under my arm, and started for Cape Horn and the Pacific. Quitting the good city of old Manhatto, I duly arrived in New Bedford. It was a Saturday night in December.

With halting steps I paced the streets, and passed the sign of 'The Crossed Harpoons'- it looked too expensive and jolly there. At the sign of 'The Trap' I found a negro church. Wretched entertainment!

I at last came to a forlorn swinging sign over a door with a painting upon it faintly representing a jet of misty spray, and these words- "The Spouter Inn:- Peter Coffin." Coffin?- Spouter?- Rather ominous, thought I. But it is a common name in Nantucket.

Entering, it reminding one of the bulwarks of some condemned old craft. On one side hung a very large oilpainting so thoroughly besmoked, that it was only by diligent study and careful inquiry of the neighbors, that you could determine its faint resemblance to a gigantic fish. The opposite wall was hung all over with a heathenish array of monstrous clubs and spears mixed with rusty old whaling lances and harpoons.

I sought the landlord, and discovered that his house was full- not a bed unoccupied. "But you haint no objections to sharing a harpooneer's blanket, have ye? I s'pose you are goin' a-whalin', so you'd better get used to that sort of thing."

I told him that I would put up with the half of any decent man's blanket.

"Take a seat. Supper'll be ready directly."

It was cold as Iceland- no fire but two dismal tallow candles- but the fare was of the most substantial kind- not only meat and potatoes, but dumplings! Dumplings!

But though the other boarders kept coming in by ones, twos, and threes, and going to bed, yet no sign of this harpooneer fellow.

"Landlord! said I, "what sort of a chap keeps such late hours?" It was now hard upon twelve o'clock.

The landlord chuckled. "To-night he went out a peddling, you see, to sell his head."

"Please unsay that story, for I've no idea of sleeping with a madman."

"Wall," said the landlord, "be easy, this here harpooneer has just arrived from the south seas, where he bought up a

---

1   **Stoicism** (see p84)

lot of 'balmed New Zealand heads (great curios, you know), and he's sold all on 'em but one, and that one he's trying to sell to-night, cause to-morrow's Sunday, and it would not do to be sellin' human heads about the streets."

I considered the matter a moment, and then up stairs we went, and I was ushered into a small room, cold as a clam, and furnished with a prodigious bed, almost big enough indeed for any four harpooneers to sleep abreast. Though none of the most elegant, it yet stood the scrutiny tolerably well.

At last I slid off into a light doze, when I heard a heavy footfall in the passage. Lord save me, thinks I, that must be the harpooneer, the infernal head-peddler. The stranger entered the room, and without looking towards the bed, placed his candle on the floor. I was all eagerness to see his face, but he kept it averted for some time while employed in unlacing his bag's mouth. This accomplished, he turned round- when, good heavens! what a sight! There was no hair on his head but a small scalp-knot on his forehead. His bald purplish head looked for all the world like a mildewed skull, and completely covered in squares of tattooing. Ignorance is the parent of fear, I confess I was now as much afraid of him as if the devil himself had thus broken into my room.

"Who-e debel you?"- he at last said.

"Peter Coffin!" shouted I. "Angels! save me!"

"Don't be afraid now," said he, grinning, "Queequeg here wouldn't harm a hair of your head."

"You gettee in," he added, in not only a civil but a really kind and charitable way. For all his tattooings he was on the whole a clean, comely looking cannibal. Better sleep with a sober cannibal than a drunken Christian.

I turned in, and never slept better in my life.

Upon waking next morning about daylight, I found Queequeg's tattooed arm, almost indistinguishable from the patchwork counterpane, thrown over me in the most loving and affectionate manner. He commenced dressing at top by donning his beaver hat, a very tall one, by the by, and then- still minus his trowsers- he hunted up his boots.

I was watching to see where he kept his razor, when lo and behold, he takes his harpoon from the corner, whets it a little on his boot, and striding up to the bit of mirror against the wall, begins a vigorous scraping of his cheeks. The rest of his toilet achieved, he proudly marched out of the room, sporting his harpoon like a marshal's baton.

If I had been astonished at first catching a glimpse of so outlandish an individual as Queequeg, that astonishment soon departed upon taking my first daylight stroll through the streets of New Bedford. Besides the Feegeeans, Tongatobooarrs and Brighggians, and the wild specimens of the whaling-craft which reel about the streets, you will see other sights still more curious, certainly more comical.

In New Bedford there stands a Whaleman's Chapel, and few are the moody fishermen, shortly bound for the Indian Ocean or Pacific, who fail to make a Sunday visit to the spot. Entering, I found the chaplain had not yet arrived; and silent islands of men and women sat steadfastly eyeing marble tablets, with black borders, commemorating this captain, or that whole crew, killed by this whale or lost to that other one.

Oh! ye whose dead lie buried beneath the green grass; ye know not the desolation that broods in bosoms like these. How it is that we still refuse to be comforted for those who we nevertheless maintain are dwelling in unspeakable bliss? But Faith, like a jackal, feeds among the tombs, and even from these dead doubts she gathers her most vital hope. Methinks that what they call my shadow here on earth is my true substance.

Father Mapple entered, climbed the rope ladder to his high pulpit.

"Shipmates, WHAT is this lesson that the book of Jonah teaches? If we obey God, we must disobey ourselves; and it is in this disobeying ourselves, wherein the hardness of obeying God consists. Woe to him who seeks to pour oil upon the waters when God has brewed them into a gale! Oh! shipmates!"

* * *

Returning to the Inn, I found Queequeg sitting before the fire, holding a little idol, humming, and with a jack-knife gently whittling away at its nose.

I proposed a social smoke; and, producing his pouch he quietly offered me a puff. He seemed to take to me quite as naturally and unbiddenly as I to him; and when our smoke was over, he pressed his forehead against mine, clasped me round the waist, and said that henceforth we were married; meaning, in his country's phrase, that we were bosom friends; he would gladly die for me.

After supper he went about his evening prayers, and I deliberated a moment whether I would join him or otherwise. I was a good Christian; born and bred in the bosom of the infallible Presbyterian Church. But what is worship?- to do the will of God. And what is the will of God?- to do to my fellow man what I would have my fellow man to do to me. Consequently, I kindled the shavings; helped prop up the innocent little idol; offered him burnt biscuit, salamed before him twice or thrice; and that done, we undressed and went to bed, at peace with our own consciences and all the world. In our hearts' honeymoon, lay I and Queequeg- a cosy, loving pair.

* * *

We talked. Queequeg was a native of Rokovoko, an island where his father was High Chief. It is not down in any map; true places never are. He had first sought passage to learn wisdom among the Christians. But, alas! the practices of whalemen soon convinced him that even Christians could be both miserable and wicked. I told him that whaling was my own design, and informed him of my intention to sail out of Nantucket. He at once resolved to accompany me, embraced me, pressed his forehead against mine, and blowing out the light, we rolled over, and very soon were sleeping.

Next morning, Monday, after disposing of the embalmed head to a barber, for a block, we went down to the *Moss,* the little packet schooner, and, after a fine run, we safely arrived in Nantucket.

I learnt that there were three ships up for three-years' voyages. I peered and pryed about the *Devil-dam*; from her hopped over to the *Tit-bit*; and finally, going on board the *Pequod*, looked around her for a moment, and decided that this was the very ship for us.

"Is this the Captain of the *Pequod*?" said I, "I was thinking of shipping."

"Want to see what whaling is, eh? Thou art speaking to Captain Peleg. It belongs to me and Captain Bildad, we are part owners and agents. Clap eye on Captain Ahab, young man, thou wilt find that he has only one leg."

"What do you mean, sir? Was the other one lost by a whale?"

"Lost by a whale! Young man, come nearer to me: it was devoured, chewed up, crunched by the monstrousest parmacetty that ever chipped a boat!- ah, ah!

Bildad, like Peleg, and indeed many other Nantucketers, was a Quaker. They are fighting Quakers; they are Quakers with a vengeance. Nor will it at all detract from him, dramatically regarded, if he seems to have a half willful overruling morbidness at the bottom of his nature. For all men tragically great are made so through a certain morbidness. Be sure of this, O young ambition, all mortal greatness is but disease.

After signing the papers, I inquired of Captain Peleg, where Captain Ahab was to be found.

"Any how, young man, he won't always see me, so I don't suppose he will thee. Oh, thou'lt like him well enough; no fear, no fear. He's a grand, ungodly, god-like man, Captain Ahab; doesn't speak much; but, when he does speak, then you may well listen. No, no, my lad; stricken, blasted, if he be, Ahab has his humanities!"

* * *

At last it was given out that some time next day the ship would certainly sail. So next morning, Queequeg and I took a very early start there, while Captain Ahab remained invisibly enshrined within his cabin.

Among landsmen, this business of whaling has somehow come to be regarded as a rather unpoetical and disreputable pursuit. Doubtless the world thinks that our vocation amounts to a butchering sort of business. But what disordered slippery decks of a whale-ship are comparable to the unspeakable carrion of those battle-fields from which so many soldiers return to drink in all ladies' plaudits?

Whaling not respectable? Whaling is imperial! By old English law, the whale is "a royal fish."

* * *

The chief mate of the *Pequod* was Starbuck, a native of Nantucket, and a Quaker by descent. "I will have no man in my boat," said Starbuck, "who is not afraid of a whale." By this, he seemed to mean, that an utterly fearless man is a far more dangerous comrade than a coward.

Stubb was the second mate, a native of Cape Cod; a happy-go-lucky; neither craven nor valiant; taking perils as they came with an indifferent air.

The third mate was Flask, a native of Tisbury, in Martha's Vineyard. A short, stout, ruddy young fellow, very pugnacious concerning whales, who somehow seemed to think that the great leviathans had personally and hereditarily affronted him.

Now each mate, like a Gothic Knight of old, is always accompanied by his boat-steerer or harpooneer, who in certain conjunctures provides him with a fresh lance, when the former one has been badly twisted. The *Pequod*'s harpooneers were, first of all Queequeg, whom Starbuck, the chief mate, had selected for his squire. Next was Tashtego, an unmixed Indian from Gay Head, Stubb the second mate's squire. Third was Daggoo, a gigantic, coal-black negro, with a lion-like tread and golden hoops in his ears. Curious to tell, he was the Squire of little Flask, who looked like a chess-man beside him.

As for the residue of the *Pequod*'s company, know that not one in two of the men before the mast in the American whale fishery are Americans born, though pretty nearly all the officers are.

And then Little Black Pip, poor Alabama boy! On the grim *Pequod*'s forecastle, beating his tambourine.

For several days after leaving Nantucket, nothing above hatches was seen of Captain Ahab.

It was one of those less lowering, but still grey and gloomy enough mornings that as I mounted to the deck at the call of the forenoon watch, so soon as I levelled my glance towards the taffrail, foreboding shivers ran over me. Reality outran apprehension; Captain Ahab stood upon his quarter-deck.

His whole high, broad form, seemed made of solid bronze, and shaped in an unalterable mould, like Cellini's cast Perseus. Upon each side of the *Pequod*'s quarter deck, and pretty close to the mizzen shrouds, there was an auger hole, bored into the plank. His bone leg steadied in that hole; one arm elevated; Captain Ahab stood erect, looking straight out beyond the ship's ever-pitching prow. Ahab stood before all with a crucifixion in his face; in all the nameless regal overbearing dignity of some mighty woe.

Ahab stood for a while leaning over the bulwarks. Lighting the pipe at the binnacle lamp and planting the stool on the weather side of the deck, he sat and smoked.

"How now," he soliloquized at last, withdrawing the tube, "this smoking no longer soothes. I'll smoke no more- "

He tossed the still lighted pipe into the sea.

Cetology.

The uncertain, unsettled condition of this science of Cetology is attested by the fact, that in some quarters it still remains a moot point whether a whale be a fish. Be it known that I take the good old fashioned ground that the whale is a fish, and call upon holy Jonah to back me. Next: how shall we define the whale?

To be short, then, a whale is A SPOUTING FISH WITH A HORIZONTAL TAIL. There you have him.

I divide the whales into three primary BOOKS:

Book I. (Folio): Sperm Whale, Right Whale, Fin-Back, Hump-Back, Razor-Back, Sulphur-Bottom

Book II. (Octavo): Grampus, Black Fish, Narwhale (or, Nostril Whale), Killer

Book III. (Duodecimo): The Huzza, The Algerine, and the Mealy-Mouthed Porpoises.

But I now leave my cetological System, thus unfinished. God keep me from ever completing anything.

* * *

The Quarter-Deck. (ENTER AHAB: THEN, ALL)

It was not a great while after the affair of the pipe, that one morning shortly after breakfast, Ahab, as was his wont, ascended the cabin-gangway to the deck. Soon his steady, ivory stride was heard, as to and fro he paced his old rounds, upon planks so familiar to his tread, that they were all over dented, like geological stones, with the peculiar mark of his walk.

"D'ye mark him, Flask?" whispered Stubb; "the chick that's in him pecks the shell. 'Twill soon be out."

"What do ye do when ye see a whale, men?"

"Sing out for him!" rejoined a score of voices.

"And what do ye next, men?"

"Lower away, and after him!"

"Look ye! d'ye see this Spanish ounce of gold? Mr. Starbuck, hand me yon top-maul."

Receiving the top-maul from Starbuck, he advanced towards the main-mast with the hammer uplifted in one hand, exhibiting the gold with the other: "Whosoever of ye raises me a white-headed whale with a wrinkled brow and a crooked jaw; shall have this gold ounce, my boys!"

"Huzza! huzza!" cried the seamen, as they hailed the act of nailing the gold to the mast.

"Captain Ahab," said Tashtego, "that white whale must be the same that some call Moby Dick."

"Captain Ahab," said Starbuck, "Was not Moby Dick that took off thy leg?"

"Who told thee that?" cried Ahab; then pausing, "Aye, Starbuck; aye, my hearties all round; it was Moby Dick that dismasted me. Aye, aye! it was that accursed white whale that made a poor pegging lubber of me for ever and a day! I'll chase him round the Horn, and round the Norway Maelstrom, and round perdition's flames before I give him

up. And this is what ye have shipped for, men! to chase that white whale over all sides of earth, till he spouts black blood and rolls fin out. What say ye, men, will ye splice hands on it, now? I think ye do look brave."

"Aye, aye!" shouted the harpooneers and seamen.

"Steward! go draw the great measure of grog. But what's this long face, Mr. Starbuck; wilt thou not chase the white whale?"

"Vengeance on a dumb brute!" cried Starbuck, "that simply smote thee from blindest instinct! Madness! To be enraged with a dumb thing, Captain Ahab, seems blasphemous."

"Talk not to me of blasphemy, man; I'd strike the sun if it insulted me. Who's over me? Stand up amid the general hurricane, thy one tost sapling cannot! Starbuck now is mine; cannot oppose me now, without rebellion."

"God keep me!- keep us all!" murmured Starbuck, lowly.

I, Ishmael, was one of that crew; my shouts had gone up with the rest; Ahab's quenchless feud seemed mine.

* * *

Of the wild superstitions linked with the White Whale, was the unearthly conceit that Moby Dick was ubiquitous; that he had been encountered in opposite latitudes at one and the same instant of time. Some went further, declaring Moby Dick immortal (for immortality is but ubiquity in time). Already several fatalities had attended his chase, and such seemed the White Whale's ferocity, that every dismembering or death was not wholly regarded as having been inflicted by an unintelligent agent.

And there was another thought; it was the whiteness of the whale that, above all things, appalled me.

* * *

Perhaps the only formal whaling code was that of Holland in 1695. The American fishermen have been their own legislators, whose simple laws might be engraven on a Queen Anne's forthing, or the barb of a harpoon, and worn round the neck, so small are they.

I. A Fast-Fish belongs to the party fast to it.

II. A Loose-Fish is fair game for anybody who can soonest catch it.

What are the souls of Russian serfs and Republican slaves but Fast-Fish? What was America in 1492 but a Loose-Fish? What was Poland to the Czar? What India to England? All Loose-Fish. What are the Rights of Man and the Liberties of the World but Loose-Fish?

And what are you, reader, but a Loose-Fish and a Fast-Fish, too?

* * *

A week or two and we were slowly sailing over a sleepy, vapoury, mid-day sea, and the many noses on the *Pequod*'s deck proved more vigilant discoverers than the three pairs of eyes aloft. A peculiar and not very pleasant smell was smelt in the sea.

As we glided nearer, the stranger showed French colors, we saw that the *Bouton-Rose* held alongside what the fishermen call a blasted whale, that is, a whale that has died unmolested on the sea. Stubb was soon on the case and, informed the French captain that "Only yesterday his ship spoke to a vessel, whose captain and chief-mate, with six sailors, had all died of a fever caught from a blasted whale." His tale was believed, and thanks given for his offer to help them divest themselves of the unhappy carcass.

As the Frenchman gained some distance, the *Pequod* slid in and Stubb quickly pulled to the floating corpse. Seizing his sharp boat-spade, he commenced an excavation in the body, a little behind the side fin.

"I have it," cried Stubb, with delight, striking something in the subterranean regions, "a purse!"

Dropping his spade, he thrust both hands in, and drew out handfuls of something that looked like ripe Windsor soap, or rich mottled old cheese; very unctuous and savory withal. And this, good friends, is ambergris, worth a gold guinea an ounce to any druggist.

Ambergris is largely used in perfumery. The Turks use it in cooking, and also carry it to Mecca, as frankincense is carried to St. Peter's in Rome. Some wine merchants drop a few grains into claret, to flavor it. Who would think, then, that such fine ladies and gentlemen should regale themselves with an essence found in the inglorious bowels of a sick whale! Yet so it is.

I cannot conclude the chapter without repelling a charge often made against whalemen, that whales always smell bad. The truth is, that living or dead, if but decently treated, whales are by no means creatures of ill odor.

* * *

It was but some few days after encountering the Frenchman, that a most significant event befell the most insignificant of the *Pequod*'s crew. Poor Pip! the little negro ye have heard of him before; ye must remember his tambourine.

It came to pass, that Stubb's after-oarsman chanced to sprain his hand, and, temporarily, Pip was put into his place. Now the boat paddled upon a whale; and as the fish received the darted iron, it gave its customary rap, which caused Pip to leap out of the boat with the line entangled around him. "Damn him, cut!" roared Stubb; and so the whale was lost and Pip was saved.

Stubb then cursed Pip officially; and unofficially gave him much wholesome advice. "Stick to the boat, Pip, or by the Lord, I won't pick you up if you jump; mind that. We can't afford to lose whales; a whale would sell for thirty times what you would, Pip, in Alabama."

But we are all in the hands of the Gods; and Pip jumped again, under very similar circumstances. Alas! Stubb was but too true to his word.

By the merest chance the ship itself at last rescued him; but from that hour the little negro went about the deck an idiot.

The sea had jeeringly kept his finite body up, but drowned the infinite of his soul.

Look not too long in the face of the fire, O man! Never dream with thy hand on the helm! There is a wisdom that is woe; but there is a woe that is madness. And there is a Catskill eagle in some souls that can alike dive down into the blackest gorges, and soar out of them again and become invisible in the sunny spaces.

* * *

According to usage they were pumping the ship next morning; and lo! no inconsiderable oil came up with the water; the casks below must have sprung a bad leak. Starbuck went down into the cabin to report this unfavourable affair.

"Captain Ahab, sir. We must up Burtons and break out."

"Up Burtons and break out? Now that we are nearing Japan; heave-to here for a week to tinker a parcel of old hoops?"

"Either do that, sir, or waste in one day more oil than we may make good in a year. What we come twenty thousand miles to get is worth saving, sir."

"Begone! Let it leak! "

"What will the owners say, sir?"

"Let the owners stand on Nantucket beach and outyell the Typhoons. What cares Ahab?

"Captain Ahab..." said the reddening mate.

Ahab seized a loaded musket from the rack, and pointing it towards Starbuck, exclaimed: "There is one God that is Lord over the earth, and one Captain that is lord over the *Pequod*!"

Mastering his emotion, Starbuck half calmly rose, and as he quitted the cabin, paused for an instant and said: "Thou hast outraged, not insulted me, sir; but for that I ask thee not to beware of Starbuck; let Ahab beware of Ahab; beware of thyself, old man."

* * *

Now, at this time it was that my poor pagan companion, and fast bosom-friend, Queequeg, was seized with a fever. Poor Queequeg! His cheek-bones grew sharper. Not a man of the crew but gave him up; and, as for Queequeg himself, his only desire was that his final rest be in one of the wooden canoes he had heard of made for those who died in Nantucket; it being not unlike the custom of his own race to float out to the stars. He shuddered at the thought of being buried in his hammock, according to the usual sea-custom.

Thus was the carpenter called and a coffin made.

"He'll have to die now," ejaculated the Long Island sailor.

In good time my Queequeg gained strength, suddenly leaped to his feet, gave himself a good stretching, yawned a bit, and pronounced himself fit for a fight.

With a wild whimsiness, he now used his coffin for a sea-chest; and his spare hours he spent in carving the lid with all manner of grotesque figures taken from the twisted tattooing on his body, the work of a departed prophet and seer of his island, who had written out on his body a complete theory of the heavens and the earth, and a mystical treatise on the art of attaining truth.

* * *

Penetrating further and further into the heart of the Japanese cruising ground, the *Pequod* was soon all astir in the fishery. These are the times of dreamy quietude, when beholding the tranquil beauty and brilliancy of the ocean's skin, one forgets the tiger heart that pants beneath it; and would not willingly remember, that this velvet paw but conceals a remorseless fang.

But the mingled, mingling threads of life are woven by warp and woof: calms crossed by storms, a storm for every calm. Where lies the final harbor, whence we unmoor no more? Let faith oust fact; let fancy oust memory; I look deep down and do believe.

* * *

At sun-rise this man went from his hammock to his mast-head at the fore; and had not been long at his perch, when a cry was heard and a rushing- and looking up, they saw a falling phantom in the air; and looking down, a little tossed heap of white bubbles in the blue of the sea.

The life-buoy- a long slender cask- was dropped from the stern, where it always hung obedient to a cunning spring; but no hand rose to seize it, and the sun having long beat upon this cask it had shrunken, so that it slowly filled, and followed the sailor to the bottom, as if to yield him his pillow.

The lost life-buoy was now to be replaced; but no cask of sufficient lightness could be found, when by certain strange signs and inuendoes Queequeg hinted a hint concerning his coffin.

"A life-buoy of a coffin!" cried Starbuck, starting.

"Rather queer, that, I should say," said Stubb.

"It will make a good enough one," said Flask, "the carpenter here can arrange it easily."

* * *

Next day, a large ship, the *Rachel*, was descried, bearing directly down upon the *Pequod*, her spars thickly clustering with men.

"Bad news; she brings bad news," muttered the old Manxman. But ere her commander, with trumpet to mouth, could hopefully hail, Ahab's voice was heard.

"Hast seen the White Whale?"

"Aye, yesterday. Have ye seen a whale-boat adrift?"

Throttling his joy, Ahab negatively answered this unexpected question. "Where was he?- not killed!- not killed!" cried Ahab, closely advancing. "How was it?"

It seemed that the day previous, while three of the stranger's boats were engaged with a shoal of whales, the white hump and head of Moby Dick had suddenly loomed up out of the water, and, in the confusion of pursuit, one of their boats had been lost from sight. The stranger Captain desired the *Pequod* to unite with his own in the search.

"My boy, my own boy is among them. For God's sake- I beg, I conjure"- exclaimed the stranger Captain to Ahab. "For eight-and-forty hours let me charter your ship- I will gladly pay for it, and roundly pay for it- you must, oh, you must, and you SHALL do this thing."

"His son!" cried Stubb, "We must save that boy."

"YOU too have a boy, Captain Ahab, nestling safely at home now, a child of your old age too."

"Avast," cried Ahab- then in a voice that molded every word- "Captain Gardiner, I will not do it. Even now I lose time. Good-bye. God bless ye, man, and may I forgive myself. Mr. Starbuck, let the ship sail as before."

Soon the two ships diverged their wakes. But you plainly saw that this ship that so wept with spray, still remained without comfort. She was *Rachel*, weeping for her children, because they were not.

* * *

(*Pip catches Ahab by the hand to follow*.) "Lad, lad, thou must not follow Ahab now. The hour is coming."

In this foreshadowing interval all humor, forced or natural, vanished. Alike, joy and sorrow, hope and fear, seemed ground to finest dust, and powdered, for the time, in the clamped mortar of Ahab's iron soul. Like machines, they dumbly moved about the deck, ever conscious that the old man's despot eye was on them.

At the first faintest glimmering of the dawn, his iron voice was heard from aft,- "Man the mast-heads!"- and all through the day, till after sunset and after twilight, the same voice every hour, at the striking of the helmsman's bell, was heard- "What d'ye see?- sharp! Sharp!"

"I will have the first sight of the whale myself,"- he said. "Aye! Ahab must have the doubloon!" And with his own hands he rigged a nest of basketed bowlines; and had his person hoisted to the highest perch. Now, the first time Ahab was aloft, one of those red-billed sea-hawks came wheeling and screaming round his head. But Ahab's eyes were elsewhere.

"Your hat, sir!" cried the Sicilian seaman.

But already the black hawk darted away with his prize.

The intense *Pequod* sailed on; the rolling waves and days went by; the life-buoy-coffin still lightly swung; and another ship, miserably misnamed the *Delight*, was descried. Upon the stranger's shears were beheld the shattered, white ribs, and some few splintered planks, of what had once been a whale-boat; now more like to the peeled and bleaching skeleton of a horse.

"Hast seen the White Whale?"

"Look!" replied the hollow-cheeked captain.

"Hast killed him?"

"The harpoon is not yet forged that ever will do that."

As Ahab glided from the dejected *Delight*, the strange life-buoy hanging at the *Pequod*'s stern came into conspicuous relief. "Ha! look yonder, men!" cried a foreboding voice. "Ye turn us your taffrail to show us your coffin!"

* * *

It was a clear steel-blue day. Oh, immortal infancy, and innocency of the azure! How oblivious were ye of old Ahab's close-coiled woe! From beneath his slouched hat Ahab dropped a tear into the sea; nor did all the Pacific contain such wealth as that one wee drop.

Is Ahab, Ahab? Is it I, God, or who, that lifts this arm? But if the great sun move not of himself; but is as an errand-boy in heaven; how then can this one small heart beat; this one small brain think thoughts; unless God does that and not I.

That night, in the mid-watch, the old man went to his pivot-hole, snuffing up the sea air as a sagacious ship's dog will, he declared that a whale must be near. Ahab rapidly ordered the ship's course to be slightly altered, and the sail to be shortened.

* * *

"There she blows!- there she blows! A hump like a snow-hill! It is Moby Dick!"

Soon the boats were dropped; all the boat-sails set- all the paddles plying; and Ahab heading the onset. A death-glimmer lit up Fedallah's sunken eyes. White birds were wheeling round and round, with joyous, expectant cries.

Their vision was keener than man's; Ahab could discover no sign in the sea. But suddenly as he peered down and down into its depths, he profoundly saw a white living spot no bigger than a white weasel. It was Moby Dick's open mouth and scrolled jaw; his vast, shadowed bulk still half blending with the blue of the sea.

Seizing a harpoon, he commanded his crew to grasp their oars. But as if perceiving this stratagem, Moby Dick, with that malicious intelligence ascribed to him raised his pleated head lengthwise beneath the boat. The bluish pearl-white of the inside of the jaw was within six inches of Ahab's head. Ripplingly withdrawing from his prey, Moby Dick swam swiftly round and round the wrecked crew; sideways churning the water in his vengeful wake.

Dragged into Stubb's boat with blood-shot eyes, Ahab lay crushed, like one trodden under herds of elephants.

"The harpoon," said Ahab, half way rising, "Lay it before me;- any missing men?"

"There were five oars, sir, and here are five men."

Soon, it was almost dark, but the look-out men still remained unset.

* * *

At day-break, the mast-heads were punctually manned afresh, and soon "There she breaches!" was the cry, as the White Whale tossed himself salmon-like to Heaven.

"Aye, breach your last to the sun, Moby Dick!" cried Ahab, "thy hour and thy harpoon are at hand!"

"Lower away," he cried, so soon as he had reached his boat- a spare one, rigged the afternoon previous.

But ere close limit was gained, the White Whale churned himself into furious speed, rushing among the boats with open jaws and a lashing tail; and heedless of the irons darted at him. But skilfully manoeuvred, the boats for a while eluded him; though, at times, but by a plank's breadth. A maze of the lines, loose harpoons and lances, with all their bristling barbs and points, came flashing and dripping up to the chocks in the bows of Ahab's boat.

The White Whale made a sudden rush among the tangles; dashing together the boats of Stubb and Flask, and then, diving down into the sea, disappeared in a boiling maelstrom, in which, for a space, the odorous cedar chips of the wrecks danced round and round, like the grated nutmeg in a swiftly stirred bowl of punch.

Ahab's yet unstricken boat seemed drawn up towards Heaven by invisible wires, as, arrow-like, shooting perpendicularly from the sea, the White Whale dashed his broad forehead against its bottom, and sent it, turning over and over, into the air.

As before, the attentive ship came bearing down to the rescue, and dropping a boat, picked up the floating mariners, tubs and oars. Ahab was found grimly clinging to his boat's broken half, his ivory leg had been snapped off, leaving but one short sharp splinter.

"But no bones broken, sir, I hope," said Stubb.

Mustering the company, the Parsee sailor was not there.

"Great God!" cried Starbuck; "never, never wilt thou capture him, old man- Jesus, this is worse than devil's madness. Shall we keep chasing this murderous fish till he we be dragged by him to the bottom of the sea?

* * *

The morning of the third day dawned fair and fresh, daylight look-outs dotted every mast.

"D'ye see him?" cried Ahab.

"Nothing, sir."

"I've oversailed him. Aye, he's chasing ME now; not I, HIM. Fool! the lines- the harpoons he's towing. About! about! Come all of ye! Forehead to forehead I meet thee, this third time, Moby Dick!"

In due time the boats were lowered; and Ahab paused upon the point of the descent;

"Starbuck!"

"Sir?"

"For the third time my soul's ship starts upon this voyage, Starbuck."

"Aye, sir, thou wilt have it so."

"Some ships sail from their ports, and ever afterwards are missing, Starbuck!"

"Truth, sir: saddest truth."

"Some men die at ebb tide; some at low water; some at the full of the flood. Starbuck. I am old; shake hands with me, man."

Their hands met; their eyes fastened; Starbuck's tears the glue.

"The sharks! the sharks!" cried a voice from the low cabin-window; "O master, my master, come back!"

The voice spake true; for numbers of sharks, seemingly rising from out the dark waters beneath the hull, maliciously snapped at the blades of the oars. Ahab knew that the whale had sounded. Suddenly the waters around them slowly swelled in broad circles.

"Give way!" cried Ahab to the oarsmen, and the boats darted forward to the attack; but maddened by yesterday's irons, Moby Dick seemed combinedly possessed by all the angels that fell from heaven. He rose, and showed one entire flank as he shot by them. Lashed round and round to the fish's back; pinioned in the turns of lines around him, the half torn body of the Parsee was seen; his distended eyes turned full upon old Ahab. The harpoon dropped from his hand.

"Oh! Ahab," cried Starbuck, "not too late is it, even now, to desist. See! Moby Dick seeks thee not. It is thou, thou, that madly seekest him!"

"Pull on!"

Moby Dick sideways writhed and, so suddenly canted the boat over, that had it not been for the gunwale to which he then clung, Ahab would once more have been tossed into the sea. The whale wheeled round, and catching sight of the black hull of the ship, the source of all his persecutions, he bore down upon its advancing prow amid fiery showers of foam.

"I spit my last breath at thee. THUS, I give up the spear!"

The harpoon was darted; the stricken whale flew forward; the line ran foul. Ahab stooped to clear it; but the flying turn caught him round the neck, and voicelessly as Turkish mutes bowstring their victim, he was shot out of the boat, and smiting the sea, disappeared in its depths.

For an instant, the tranced boat's crew stood still; then turned. "The ship? Great God, where is the ship?"

And now, concentric circles seized the lone boat itself, and all its crew, and each floating oar, and spinning all round and round in one vortex, carried the smallest chip of the *Pequod* out of sight.

"I only am escaped alone to tell thee" - Job.

The drama's done. Why then here does any one step forth?- Because one did survive the wreck. Buoyed up by a coffin, the unharming sharks glided by as if with padlocks on their mouths. On the second day, a sail drew near, nearer, and picked me up at last. It was the Rachel, that in her retracing search after her missing children, only found another orphan.

Uncle Tom's Cabin
by Harriet Beecher Stowe
(Cleveland, Ohio, 1852)

This book had such a profound effect on attitudes toward slavery in the United States that it is often credited with having contributed to Civil War. Indeed, when when Harriet Elizabeth Beecher Stowe, daughter of a Connecticut preacher, met President Lincoln he said, "Is this the little woman who brought on so great a war?" *Uncle Tom* was one one of the most successful books ever, selling some 300,000 copies in its first year.

Abridged: GH/JH

Humane Dealing

Late in the afternoon of a chilly day in February two gentlemen were sitting over their wine, in a well-furnished parlour in the town of P---- in Kentucky in the midst of an earnest conversation.

"That is the way I should arrange the matter," said Mr. Shelby, the owner of the place. "The fact is, Tom is an uncommon fellow; he is certainly worth that sum anywhere; steady, honest, capable, manages my farm like a clock."

"You mean honest, as niggers go," said Haley.

"You ought to let him cover the whole of the debt. He got religion at a camp-meeting, four years ago, and I've trusted him ever since."

"Some folks don't believe there is pious niggers Shelby," said Haley

"Well, I've got just as much conscience as any man in business can afford to keep," said Haley, "and I'm willing to do anything to 'blige friends; but this yer, ye see, is too hard on a feller, it really is. Haven't you a boy or gal you could thrown in with Tom?"

"Hum! - none that I could well spare; to tell the truth, it's only hard necessity makes me sell at all." Here the door opened, and a small quadroon boy, remarkably beautiful and engaging, entered with a comic air of assurance which showed he was used to being petted and noticed by his master. "Hulloa, Jim Crow," said Mr. Shelby, snapping a bunch of raisins towards him, "pick that up, now!" The child scampered, with all his little strength after the prize, while his master laughed. "Tell you what," said Haley, "fling in that chap, and I'll settle the business, I will."

At this moment a young woman, obviously the child's mother, came in search of him, and Haley, as soon as she had carried him away, turned to Mr. Shelby in admiration.

"By Jupiter!" said the trader, "there's an article now! You might make your fortune on that one gal in Orleans, any way. What shall I say for her? What'll you take?"

"Mr. Haley, she is not to be sold. I say no, and I mean no," said Mr. Shelby, decidedly.

"Well, you'll let me have the boy, though."

"I would rather not sell him," said Mr. Shelby; "the fact is, I'm a humane man, and I hate to take the boy from his mother, sir."

"Oh, you do? La, yes, I understand perfectly. It is mighty unpleasant getting on with women sometimes. I al'ays hates these yer screechin' times. As I manages business, I generally avoids 'em, sir. Now, what if you get the gal off for a day or so? then the thing's done quietly. It's always best to do the humane thing, sir; that's been my experience." "I'd like to have been able to kick the fellow down the steps," said Mr. Shelby to himself, when the trader had bowed himself out. "And Eliza's child, too! I know I shall have some fuss with the wife about that, and for that matter, about Tom, too! So much for being in debt, heigho!"

* * *

The prayer-meeting at Uncle Tom's Cabin had been protracted to a very late hour, and Tom and his worthy helpmeet were not yet asleep, when between twelve and one there was a light tap on the window pane.

"Good Lord! what's that?" said Aunt Chloe, starting up. "My sakes alive, if it aint Lizzy! Get on your clothes, old man, quick. I'm gwine to open the door." And suiting the action to the word, the door flew open, and the light of the candle which Tom had hastily lighted, fell on the face of Eliza. "I'm running away, Uncle Tom and Aunt Chloe - carrying off my child. Master sold him."

"Sold him?" echoed both, holding up their hands in dismay.

"Yes, sold him!" said Eliza firmly. "I crept into the closet by mistress's door to-night, and I heard master tell missus that he had sold my Harry and you, Uncle Tom, both to a trader, and that the man was to take possession to-day."

Slowly, as the meaning of this speech came over Tom, he collapsed on his old chair, and sunk his head on his knees.

"The good Lord have pity on us!" said Aunt Chloe. "What has he done that mas'r should sell him?"

"He hasn't done anything - it isn't for that. I heard Master say there was no choice between selling these two, and selling all, the man was driving him so hard. Master said he was sorry; but, oh! missis! you should have heard her talk! If she ain't a Christian and an angel, there never was one. I'm a wicked girl to leave her so - but then I can't help it, the Lord forgive me, for I can't help doing it."

"Well, old man," said Aunt Chloe, "why don't you go too? Will you wait to be toted down river, where they kill niggers with hard work and starving? There's time for ye; be off with Lizzy, you've got a pass to come and go any time."

Tom slowly raised his head, and sorrowfully said, "No, no: I aint going. Let Eliza go - it's her right. 'Tan't in natur for her to stay, but you heard what she said. If I must be sold, or all the people on the place and everything to go to rack, why let me be sold. Mas'r aint to blame, Chloe; and he'll take care of you and the poor-." Here he turned to the rough trundle-bed full of little woolly heads and fairly broke down.

"And now," said Eliza, "do try, if you can, to get a word to my husband. He told me this afternoon he was going to run away. Tell him why I went, and tell him, I'm going to try and find Canada. Give my love to him, and tell him, if I never see him again - tell him to be as good as he can, and try and meet me in the kingdom of heaven."

A few last words and tears, a few simple adieus and blessings, and she glided noiselessly away.

Eliza's Escape

It is impossible to conceive of a human being more wholly desolate and forlorn than Eliza as she left the only home she had ever known. Her husband's sufferings and danger, and the danger of her child, all blended in her mind, she trembled at every sound, and every quaking leaf quickened her steps. She felt the weight of her boy as if it had been a feather, he was old enough to have walked by her side, but now she strained him to her bosom as she went rapidly forward; and every flutter of fear seemed to increase the supernatural strength that bore her on, while from her pale lips burst forth, in frequent ejaculations, "Lord help me."

Still she went, leaving one familiar object after another, till reddening daylight found her many a long mile, upon the open highway, on the way to the village of T---- upon the Ohio river, when she constrained herself to walk regularly and composedly, quickening the speed of her child, by rolling an apple before him, when the boy would run with all his might after it; this ruse often repeated carried them over many a half-mile.

An hour before sunset she came in sight of the river, which lay between her and liberty. Great cakes of floating ice were swinging heavily to and fro in the turbid waters. Eliza turned into a small public house to ask if there was no ferry boat.

"No, indeed," said the hostess, stopping her cooking as Eliza's sweet, plaintive voice fell on her ear; "the boats has stopped running." Eliza's look of dismay struck her and she said, "Maybe you're wanting to get over? anybody sick? Ye seem mighty anxious."

"I've got a child that's very dangerous," said Eliza, "I never heard of it till last night, and I've walked quite a piece to-day, in hopes to get to the ferry."

"Well, now, that's unlucky" said the woman, her motherly sympathies aroused; "I'm rilly concerned for ye. Solomon!" she called from the window. "I say Sol, is that ar man going to tote them bar'ls over to-night?"

"He said he should try, if 'twas any ways prudent," replied a man's voice.

"There's a man going over to-night, if he durs' to; he'll be in to supper, so you'd better sit down and wait. That's a sweet little fellow" added the woman, offering him a cake.

But the child, wholly exhausted, cried with weariness.

"Take him into this room," said the woman opening into a small bedroom, and Eliza laid the weary boy on the comfortable bed, and held his hands till he was fast asleep. For her there was no rest, the thought of her pursuers urged her on, and she gazed with longing eyes on the swaying waters between her and liberty.

She was standing by the window as Haley and two of Mr. Shelby's servants came riding by. Sam, the foremost, catching sight of her, contrived to have his hat blown off, and uttered a loud and characteristic ejaculation. She drew back and the whole train swept by to the front door. A thousand lives were concentrated in that moment to Eliza. Her room opened by a side door to the river. She caught her child and sprang down the steps. The trader caught a glimpse of her as she disappeared down the bank, and calling loudly to Sam and Andy, was after her like a hound after a deer. Her feet scarce seemed to touch the ground, a moment brought her to the water's edge. Right on behind they came, and nerved with strength such as God gives only to the desperate, with one wild and flying leap, she vaulted sheer over the current by the shore, on to the raft of ice beyond. It was a desperate leap - impossible to anything but madmen and despair. The huge green fragment of ice pitched and creaked as her weight came on it, but she stayed there not a moment. With wild cries and desperate energy she leaped to another and still another cake; stumbling, leaping, slipping, springing upwards again. Her shoes were gone - her stockings cut from her feet - while blood marked every step; but she saw nothing, felt nothing, till dimly she saw the Ohio side, and a man helping her up the bank.

"Yer a brave girl, now, whoever ye are!" said he. Eliza recognised a farmer from near her old home. "Oh, Mr. Symmes! save me! do save me! do hide me!" said Eliza.

"Why, what's this?" said the man, "why, if 'taint Shelby's gal!"

"My child! - this boy - he'd sold him! There is his mas'r," said she, pointing to the Kentucky shore. "Oh, Mr. Symmes, you've got a little boy."

"So I have," said the man, as he roughly but kindly helped her up the bank. "Besides, you're a right brave gal. I'd be glad to do something for you. The best thing I can do is to tell you to go there," pointing to a large white house, standing by itself, "they're kind folks. There's no kind o'

danger but they'll help you - they're up to all that sort of thing."

"The Lord bless you!" said Eliza earnestly, and folding her child to her bosom, walked firmly away.

* * *

Late that night the fugitives were driven to the house of a man who had once been a considerable shareholder in Kentucky; but, being possessed of a great, honest, just heart, he had witnessed for years with uneasiness the workings of a system equally bad for oppressors and oppressed, and one day bought some land in Ohio, made out free passes for all his people, and settled down to enjoy his conscience. He conveyed Eliza to a Quaker settlement, where by the help of these good friends she was joined by her husband and soon landed in Canada. Free!

The Property Is Carried Off

An unceremonious kick pushed open the door of Uncle Tom's cabin, and Mr. Haley stood there in very ill humour after his hard riding and ill success.

"Come, ye nigger, ye'r ready. Servant, ma'am!" said he, taking off his hat as he saw Mrs. Shelby, who detained him a few moments. Speaking in an earnest manner, she made him promise to let her know to whom he sold Tom; while Tom rose up meekly, and his wife took the baby in her arms, her tears seeming suddenly turned to sparks of fire, to go with him to the wagon: "Get in," said Haley, and Tom got in, when Haley made fast a heavy pair of shackles round each ankle; a groan of indignation ran round the crowd of servants gathered to bid Tom farewell. Mr. Shelby had gone away on business, hoping all would be over before he returned.

"Give my love to Mas'r George," said Tom earnestly, as he was whirled away, fixing a steady, mournful look to the last on the old place. Tom insensibly won his way far into the confidence of such a man as Mr. Haley, and on the steamboat was permitted to come and go freely where he pleased. Among the passengers was a young gentleman of New Orleans whose little daughter often and often walked mournfully round the place where Haley's gang of men and women were chained. To Tom she appeared almost divine; he half believed he saw one of the angels stepped out of his New Testament, and they soon got on confidential terms. As the steamer drew near New Orleans Mr. St. Clare, carelessly putting the tip of his finger under Tom's chin, said good-humouredly, "Look up, Tom, and see how you like your new master."

It was not in nature to look into that gay, handsome young face without pleasure, and Tom said heartily, "God bless you, Mas'r."

Eva's fancy for him had led her to petition her father that Tom might be her special attendant in her walks and rides. He was called coachman, but his stable duties were a sinecure; struck with his good business capacity, his master confided in him more and more, till gradually all the providing for the family was entrusted to him. Tom regarded his airy young master with an odd mixture of fealty, reverence and fatherly solicitude, and his friendship with Eva grew with the child's growth; but his home yearnings grew so strong that he tried to write a letter - so unsuccessfully that St. Clare offered to write for him, and. Tom had the joy of receiving an answer from Master George, stating that Aunt Chloe had been hired out, at her own request, to a confectioner, and was gaining vast sums of money, all of which was to be laid by for Tom's redemption.

About two years after his coming, Eva began to fail rapidly, and even her father could no longer deceive himself. Eva was about to leave him. It was Tom's greatest joy to carry the frail little form in his arms, up and down, into the veranda, and to him she talked, what she would not distress her father with, of these mysterious intimations which the soul feels ere it leaves its clay for ever. He lay, at last, all night in the veranda ready to rouse at the least call, and at midnight came the message. Earth was passed and earthly pain; so solemn was the triumphant brightness of that face it checked even the sobs of sorrow. A glorious smile, and she said, brokenly, "Oh-love-joy-peace" and passed from death unto life.

Week after week glided by in the St. Clare mansion and the waves of life settled back to their usual flow where that little bark had gone down. St. Clare was in many respects another man; he read his little Eva's Bible seriously and honestly; he thought soberly of his relations to his servants, and he commenced the legal steps necessary to Tom's emancipation as he had promised Eva he would do. But, one evening while Tom was sitting thinking of his home, feeling the muscles of his brawny arms with joy as he thought how he would work to buy his wife and boys; his master was brought home dying. He had interfered in an affray in a cafe and been stabbed.

He reached out and took Tom's hand; he closed his eyes, but still retained his hold; for in the gates of eternity the black hand and the white hold each other with an equal grasp, and softly murmured some words he had been singing that evening - words of entreaty to Infinite Pity.

Freedom

Mrs. St. Clare decided at once to sell the place and all the servants, except her own personal property, and although she was told of her husband's intention of freeing Tom, he was sold by auction with the rest. His new master, Mr. Simon Legree, came round to review his purchases as they sat in chains on the lower deck of a small mean boat, on their way to his cotton plantation, on the Red River. "I say, all on ye," he said, "look at me - look me right in the eye - straight, now!" stamping his foot. "Now," said he, doubling his great heavy fist, "d'ye see this fist? Heft it," he said, bringing it down on Tom's hand. "Look at these yer bones! Well, I tell ye this yer fist has got as hard as iron knocking down niggers. I don't keep none of yer cussed overseers; I does my own overseeing and I tell ye things is seen to. You won't find no soft spot in me, nowhere. So, now, mind

yourselves; for I don't show no mercy!" The women drew in their breath; and the whole gang sat with downcast, dejected faces.

Trailing wearily behind a rude wagon, and over a ruder road, Tom and his associates came to their new home. The whole place looked desolate, everything told of coarse neglect and discomfort. Three or four ferocious looking dogs rushed out and were with difficulty restrained from laying hold of Tom and his companions.

"Ye see what ye'd get!" said Legree. "Ye see what ye'd get if you tried to run off. They'd just as soon chaw one on ye up as eat their supper. So mind yourself. How now, Sambo!" to a ragged fellow, who was officious in his attentions, "How have things been goin' on?"

"Fust rate, mas'r."

"Quimbo," said Legree to another, "ye minded what I tell'd ye?"

"Guess I did, didn't I?"

Legree had trained these two men in savagery as systematically as he had his bulldogs, and they were in admirable keeping with the vile character of the whole place.

Tom's heart sank as he followed Sambo to the quarters. They had a forlorn, brutal air. He had been comforting himself with the thought of a cottage, rude indeed but one which he might keep neat and quiet and read his Bible in out of his labouring hours. They were mere rude sheds with no furniture but a heap of straw, foul with dirt. "Spec there's room for another thar'," said Sambo, "thar's a pretty smart heap o' niggers to each on 'em, now. Sure, I dunno what I's to do with more."

* * *

Tom looked in vain, as the weary occupants of the shanties came flocking home, for a companionable face; he saw only sullen, embruted men and feeble, discouraged women; or, those who, treated in every way like brutes, had sunk to their level.

"Thar you!" said Quimbo throwing down a coarse bag containing a peck of corn, "thar, nigger, grab, you won't get no more dis yer week."

Tom was faint for want of food, but moved by the utter weariness of two women, whom he saw trying to grind their corn, he ground for them; and then set about getting his own supper. An expression of kindness came over their hard faces - they mixed his cake for him, and tended the baking, and Tom drew out his Bible by the light of the fire - for he had need of comfort.

Tom saw enough of abuse and misery in his new life to make him sick and weary; but he toiled on with religious patience, committing himself to Him that judgeth righteously. Legree took silent note, and rating him as a first-class hand, made up his mind that Tom must be hardened; he had bought him with a view to making him a sort of overseer, so one night he told him to flog one of the women. Tom begged him not to set him at that. He could not do it, "no way possible." Legree struck him repeatedly with a cowhide. "There," said he stopping to rest, "now will ye tell me ye can't do it?"

"Yes, mas'r," said Tom, wiping the blood from his face. "I'm willin' to work, night and day; but this yer thing I can't feel it right to do; and mas'r, I never shall do it, never!"

Legree looked stupefied - Tom was so respectful - but at last burst forth:

"What, ye blasted black beast! tell me ye don't think it right to do what I tell ye. So ye pretend it's wrong to flog the girl?"

"I think so, mas'r," said Tom. "'Twould be downright cruel, the poor critter's sick and feeble. Mas'r, if you mean to kill me, kill me; but as to my raising my hand against anyone here, I never will - I'll die first." Legree shook with anger. "Here, Sambo! - Quimbo!" he shouted, "give this dog such a breakin' in as he won't get over this month."

The two seized Tom with fiendish exultation, and dragged him unresistingly from the place.

* * *

For weeks and months Tom wrestled, in darkness and sorrow - crushing back to his soul the bitter thought that God had forgotten him. One night he sat like one stunned when everything around him seemed to fade, and a vision rose of One crowned with thorns, buffeted and bleeding; and a voice said, "He that overcometh shall sit down with Me on My throne, even as I also overcame, and am set down with My Father upon His throne."

From this time an inviolable peace filled the lowly heart of the oppressed one; life's uttermost woes fell from him unharming.

* * *

Scenes of blood and cruelty are shocking to our ear and heart. What man has nerve to do, man has not nerve to hear.

Tom lay dying at last; not suffering, for every nerve was blunted and destroyed; when George Shelby found him, and his voice reached his dying ear.

"Oh, Mas'r George, he ain't done me any real harm: only opened the gate of Heaven for me. Who - who shall separate us from the love of Christ?" and with a smile he fell asleep.

* * *

As George knelt by the grave of his poor friend, "Witness, eternal God," said he, "Oh, witness that, from this hour, I will do what one man can to drive out the curse of slavery from my land!"

Walden
or, A Life in the Woods
by Henry D. Thoreau
(Boston, 1854)

Henry David Thoreau, of Concord, Massachusetts, became entranced with the philosopher Ralph Waldo Emerson's ideas of self-reliance. Ideas that led, on a parcel of Emerson's land, to the *Walden* project, to prison for refusing to pay his poll tax, to helping runaway slaves to freedom, and to voluminous writings. Though now seen as a centrepiece of American Transcendentalism, what Martin Luther King called Thoreau's "legacy of creative protest" against governments led to his writings being officially removed from US libraries in the 1950's.
Abridged: GH

The Simple Life

When I wrote the following pages, I lived alone, in the woods, a mile from any neighbor, in a house I had built for myself, on the shore of Walden Pond, in Concord, Massachusetts, and earned my living by the labor of my hands only. I lived there two years and two months. At present I am a sojourner in civilized life again.

Men labor under a mistake. By a seeming fate, commonly called necessity, they are employed laying up treasures which moth and rust will corrupt. It is a fool's life, as they will find when they get to the end of it if not before.

But it is never too late to give up our prejudices. What old people say you cannot do, you try and find that you can. I have lived some thirty years and I have yet to hear the first syllable of valuable advice from my seniors.

To many creatures, there is but one necessity of life - food. None of the brute creation require more than food and shelter. The necessaries of life for man in this climate may be distributed under the several heads of food, shelter, clothing, and fuel. I find by my own experience a few implements, a knife, an ax, a spade, a wheelbarrow, etc., and for the studious, lamplight, stationery, and access to a few books, rank next to necessaries, and can all be obtained at a trifling cost. Most of the luxuries, and many of the so-called comforts of life, are positive hindrances to the elevation of mankind. None can be an impartial or wise observer of human life but from the vantage ground of voluntary poverty.

Ideals

If I should attempt to tell how I have desired to spend my life in years past it would probably astonish those who know nothing about it.

I long ago lost a hound, a bay horse, and a turtle dove, and am still on their trail. Many are the travelers I have spoken, concerning them, describing their tracks and what calls they answered to. I have met one or two who had heard the hound, and the tramp of the horse, and even seen the dove disappear behind a cloud, and they seemed as anxious to recover them as if they had lost them themselves.

How many mornings, summer and winter, before any neighbor was stirring about his business, have I been about mine! So many autumn, aye, and winter days, spent outside the town trying to hear what was in the wind, to hear and carry it. At other times waiting at evening on the hill-tops for the sky to fall that I might catch something, though I never caught much, and that, manna-wise, would dissolve again in the sun.

For many years I was self-appointed inspector of snow storms and rain storms, and did my duty faithfully; surveyor, if not of highways, then of forest paths. I looked after the wild stock of the town. I have watered the red huckleberry, the sand cherry and the nettle tree, the red pine and the black ash, the white grape and the yellow violet, which might have withered else in dry seasons.

My purpose in going to Walden Pond was not to live cheaply nor to live dearly there, but to transact some private business with the fewest obstacles.

House Building

When I consider my neighbors, the farmers of Concord, I find that for the most part they have been toiling twenty, thirty, or forty years, that they may become the real owners of their farms; and we may regard one-third of that toil as the cost of their houses. And when the farmer has got his house he may not be the richer but the poorer for it, and it be the house that has got him. The very simplicity and nakedness of men's life in the primitive ages imply that they left him still a sojourner in nature. When he was refreshed with food and sleep he contemplated his journey again. He dwelt as it were in the tent of this world. We now no longer camp as for a night, but have settled down on earth and forgotten Heaven.

Near the end of March, 1845, I borrowed an axe and went down to the woods by Walden Pond, nearest to where I intended to build my house, and began to cut down some tall, arrowy, white pines, still in their youth, for timber. It was a pleasant hillside where I worked, covered with pine woods, through which I looked out on the pond, and a small open field in the woods where pines and hickories were springing up. Before I had done I was more the friend than the foe of the pine tree, having become better acquainted with it.

By the middle of April my house was framed and ready for raising. At length, in the beginning of May, with the help of some of my acquaintances, rather to improve so good an occasion for neighborliness than from any necessity, I set up the frame of my house. I began to occupy it on the 4th of July, as soon as it was boarded and roofed, for the boards were carefully feather-edged and lapped, so that it was perfectly impervious to rain, but before boarding I laid the foundation of a chimney. I built the chimney after my hoeing in the fall, before a fire became necessary for warmth, doing my cooking in the meantime out of doors on the ground, early in the morning. When it stormed before my bread was baked I fixed a few boards over the fire, and sat under them to watch my loaf, and passed some pleasant hours in that way.

The exact cost of my house, not counting the work, all of which was done by myself, was just over twenty-eight dollars. I thus found that the student who wishes for a shelter can obtain one for a lifetime at an expense not greater than the rent which he now pays annually.

Farming

Before I finished my house, wishing to earn ten or twelve dollars by some honest and agreeable method, in order to meet my unusual expenses, I planted about two acres and a half of light and sandy soil near it, chiefly with beans, but also a small part with potatoes, corn, peas, and turnips. I was obliged to hire a team and a man for the plowing, though I held the plow myself. My farm outgoes for the first season were, for employment, seed, work, etc., 14 dollars 72½ cents. I got twelve bushels of beans and eighteen bushels of potatoes, besides some peas and sweet corn. My whole income from the farm was 23 dollars 43 cents, a profit of 8 dollars 71½ cents, besides produce consumed.

The next year I did better still, for I spaded up all the land that I required, about a third of an acre, and I learned from the experience of both years, not being in the least awed by many celebrated works on husbandry, that if one would live simply and eat only the crop which he raised, he would need to cultivate only a few rods of ground, and that it would be cheaper to spade up that than to use oxen to plow it, and he could do all his necessary farm work, as it were, with his left hand at odd hours in the summer.

My food for nearly two years was rye and Indian meal without yeast, potatoes, rice, a very little salt pork, molasses and salt, and my drink water. I learned from my two years' experience that it would cost incredibly little trouble to obtain one's necessary food even in this latitude, and that a man may use as simple a diet as the animals and yet retain health and strength.

Bread I at first made of pure Indian meal and salt, genuine hoe-cakes, which I baked before my fire out of doors, but at last I found a mixture of rye and Indian meal most convenient and agreeable. I made a study of the ancient and indispensable art of bread-making, going back to the primitive days. Leaven, which some deem to be the soul of bread, I discovered was not indispensable.

Thus I found I could avoid all trade and barter, so far as my food was concerned, and having a shelter already, it would only remain to get clothing and fuel. My furniture, part of which I made myself, consisted of a bed, a table, a desk, three chairs, a looking-glass, three inches in diameter, a pair of tongs and andirons, a kettle, a skillet, and a frying pan, a dipper, a wash bowl, two knives and forks, three plates, one cup, one spoon, a jug for oil, a jug for molasses, and a japanned lamp. When I have met an immigrant tottering under a bundle which contained his all, I have pitied him, not because it was his all, but because he had all that to carry.

Earning a Living

For more than five years I maintained myself solely by the labor of my hands, and I found that by working for about six weeks in the year I could meet all the expenses of living. The whole of my winters, as well as most of my summers, I had free and clear for study. I have thoroughly tried school-keeping, and found that my expenses were out of proportion to my income, for I was obliged to dress and train, not to say think and believe accordingly; and I lost my time into the bargain. I have tried trade; but I have learned that trade curses everything it handles; and though you trade in messages from Heaven, the whole curse of trade attaches to the business. I found that the occupation of day-laborer was the most independent of any, especially as it required only thirty or forty days in the year to support me. The laborer's day ends with the going down of the sun, and he is then free to devote himself to his chosen pursuit, independent of his labor; but his employer, who speculates from month to month, has no respite from one end of the year to the other.

But all this is very selfish, I have heard some of my townsmen say. I confess that I have hitherto indulged very little in philanthropic enterprises. However, when I thought to indulge myself in this respect by maintaining certain poor persons as comfortably as I maintain myself, and even ventured so far as to make them the offer, they one and all unhesitatingly preferred to remain poor. The Life with Nature

When I took up my abode in the woods I found myself suddenly neighbor to the birds, not by having imprisoned one, but having caged myself near them. I was not only nearer to some of those which commonly frequent the garden and orchard, but to those wilder and more thrilling songsters of the forest which never, or rarely, serenade a villager.

Every morning was a cheerful invitation to make my life of equal simplicity, and I may say, innocence, with Nature herself. I have been as sincere a worshiper of Aurora as the Greeks. Morning brings back the heroic ages. Then, for an hour at least, some part of us awakes which slumbers all the rest of the day and night.

Why should we live with such hurry and waste of life? As for work, we haven't any of any consequence. We have the Saint Vitus' dance, and cannot possibly keep our heads still.

Hardly a man takes a half hour's nap after dinner, but when he wakes he holds up his head and asks: "What's the news?" as if the rest of mankind had stood his sentinels. "Pray tell me anything new that has happened to a man anywhere on this globe." And he reads over his coffee and rolls that a man has had his eyes gouged out this morning on the Wachito River, never dreaming the while that he lives in the dark, unfathomed mammoth cave of this world, and has but the rudiment of an eye himself.

Let us spend our day as deliberately as Nature. Let us rise early and fast, or break fast, gently and without perturbation. Let us not be upset and overwhelmed in that terrible rapid and whirlpool called a dinner situated in the meridian shadows.

Time is but the stream I go a-fishing in. I drink at it, but while I drink I see the sandy bottom, and detect how shallow it is. Its thin current glides away, but eternity remains. I would drink deeper, fish in the sky, whose bottom is pebbly with stars.

Reading

My residence was more favorable, not only to thought but to serious reading, than a university; and though I was beyond the range of the morning circulating library I had more than ever come within the influence of those books which circulate round the world. I kept Homer's 'Iliad' on my table through the summer, though I looked at his pages only now and then. To read well - that is to read true books in a true spirit - is a noble exercise and one that will task the reader more than any exercise which the customs of the day esteem. Books must be read as deliberately and reservedly as they were written. No wonder that Alexander carried the 'Iliad' with him on his expeditions in a precious casket. A written word is the choicest of relics.

That age will be rich indeed when those relics which we call Classics, and the even less known Scriptures of the nations, shall have still further accumulated, when the Vaticans shall be filled with Vedas and Zendavestas and Bibles, with Homers and Dantes and Shakespeares[1], and all the centuries to come shall have successively deposited their trophies in the forum of the world. By such a pile we may hope to scale heaven at last.

In the Sun

I did not read books the first summer; I hoed beans. Nay, I often did better than this. There were times when I could not afford to sacrifice the bloom of the present moment to any work, whether of the head or hands. I love a broad margin to my life. Sometimes on a summer morning, having taken my accustomed bath, I sat in my sunny doorway from sunrise till noon, rapt in a reverie, amidst the pines and hickories and sumachs in undisturbed solitude and stillness, while the birds sang around or flitted noiseless through the house, until by the sun falling in at my west window, or the noise of some traveler's wagon on

1   Vedas p16, Bible p23, p77, Homer p35, Dante p112 Shakespeare p149

the distant highway, I was reminded of the lapse of time. I grew in those seasons like corn in the night, and they were far better than any work of the hands would have been. They were not time subtracted from my life, but so much over and above my usual allowance. I realized what the Orientals mean by contemplation and the forsaking of works. Instead of singing like the birds I silently smiled at my incessant good fortune. This was sheer idleness to my fellow townsmen, no doubt, but if the birds and flowers had tried me by their standard I should not have been found wanting.

Night Sounds

Regularly at half past seven, in one part of the summer, the whip-poor-wills chanted their vespers for half an hour, sitting on a stump by my door, or upon the ridge pole of the house. When other birds were still the screech owls took up the strain, like mourning women their ancient u-lu-lu. Wise midnight hags! I love to hear their wailing, their doleful responses, trilled along the woodside. They give me a new sense of the variety and capacity of that nature which is our common dwelling. Oh-o-o-o-o that I had never been bor-r-r-r-n! sighs one on this side of the pond, and circles, with the restlessness of despair to some new perch on the gray oaks. Then: That I had never been bor-r-r-r-n! echoes another on the further side with tremulous sincerity, and bor-r-r-r-n! comes faintly from far in the Lincoln woods. I require that there are owls. They represent the stark twilight and unsatisfied thoughts which all have.

I am not sure that ever I heard the sound of cock crowing from my clearing, and I thought that it might be worth the while to keep a cockerel for his music merely, as a singing bird. The note of this once wild Indian pheasant is certainly the most remarkable of any bird's, and if they could be naturalized without being domesticated it would soon become the most famous sound in our woods.

I kept neither dog, cat, cow, pig, nor hens, so that you would have said there was a deficiency of domestic sounds, neither the churn nor the spinning wheel, nor even the singing of the kettle, nor the hissing of the urn, nor children crying, to comfort me; only squirrels on the roof, a whip-poor-will on the ridge pole, a bluejay screaming beneath the window, a woodchuck under the house, a laughing loon on the pond, and a fox to bark in the night.

This is a delicious evening, when the whole body is one sense and imbibes delight through every pore. I go and come with a strange liberty in Nature, a part of herself. Sympathy with the fluttering alder and poplar leaves almost takes away my breath; yet, like the lake, my serenity is rippled, but not ruffled. Though it is now dark the wind still blows and roars in the woods, the waves still dash, and some creatures lull the rest with their notes. The repose is never complete. The wildest animals do not repose but seek their prey now. They are Nature's watchmen - links which connect the days of animated life.

I find it wholesome to be alone the greater part of the time. I never found the companion that was never so companionable as solitude. A man thinking or working is always alone, let him be where he will. I am no more lonely than the loon in the pond that laughs so loud. God is alone, but the devil, he is far from being alone; he sees a great deal of company; he is legion. I am no more lonely than a single dandelion in a pasture, or a humble bee, or the North Star, or the first spider in a new house.

In the morning I bathe my intellect in the stupendous and cosmogonal philosophy of the Bhagvat-Geeta[2], since whose composition years of the gods have elapsed. I lay down the book and go to my well for water, and lo! there I meet the servant of the Bramin. The pure Walden water is mingled with the sacred water of the Ganges. With favoring winds it is wafted past the site of the fabulous islands of Atlantis and the Hesperides, makes the periplus of Hanno, and, floating by Ternate and Tidore and the mouth of the Persian Gulf, melts in the tropic gales of the Indian seas, and is landed in ports of which Alexander only heard the names.

Visitors

In my house I have three chairs: one for solitude, two for friendship, three for society. My best room, however - my withdrawing room - always ready for company, was the pine wood behind my house. Thither in Summer days, when distinguished guests came, I took them, and a priceless domestic swept the floor and kept the things in order.

I could not but notice some of the peculiarities of my visitors. Girls and boys, and young women generally, seemed glad to be in the woods. They looked in the pond and at the flowers, and improved their time. Men of business, even farmers, thought only of solitude and employment, and of the great distance at which I dwelt from something or other; and though they said that they loved a ramble in the woods occasionally, it was obvious that they did not. Restless, committed men, whose time was all taken up in getting a living, or keeping it, ministers, who spoke of God as if they enjoyed a monopoly of the subject, and who could not bear all kinds of opinions, doctors, lawyers, and uneasy housekeepers, who pried into my cupboard and bed when I was out, young men who had ceased to be young, and had concluded that it was safest to follow the beaten track of the professions - all these generally said that it was not possible to do as much good in my position.

Interference

After hoeing, or perhaps reading and writing in the forenoon, I usually bathed again in the pond, washed the dust of labor from my person, and for the afternoon was absolutely free. Every day or two I strolled to the village. As I walked in the woods to see the birds and the squirrels, so I walked in the village to see the men and the boys. Instead of the wind among the pines I heard the carts rattle.

---

2   **Bhagvat-Geeta:** see p16

One afternoon near the end of the first summer, when I went to the village to get a shoe from the cobbler's, I was seized and put into jail, because I did not pay a tax to, or recognize the authority of, the State. I had gone down to the woods for other purposes. But wherever a man goes men will pursue and paw him with their dirty institutions, and, if they can, constrain him to belong to their desperate Odd Fellows society. However, I was released the next day, obtained my mended shoe, and returned to the woods in season to get my dinner of huckleberries on Fair Haven Hill. I was never molested by any person but those who represented the State. I had no lock nor bolt but for the desk which held my papers, not even a nail to put over my latch or window. I never fastened my door night or day, and though I was absent several days my house was more respected than if it had been surrounded by a file of soldiers.

Exhausted Experience

I left the woods for as good a reason as I went there. Perhaps it seemed to me that I had several more lives to live and could not spare any more time for that one. It is remarkable how easily and insensibly we fall into a particular route, and make a beaten track for ourselves. I had not lived there a week before my feet wore a path from my door to the pond side, and though it is five or six years since I trod it, it is still quite distinct. So with the paths which the mind travels. How worn and dusty then must be the highways of the world - how deep the ruts of tradition and conformity. I learned this, at least by my experiment, that if one advances confidently in the direction of his dreams, and endeavors to live the life which he has imagined, he will meet with a success unexpected in common hours. In proportion as he simplifies his life the laws of the Universe will appear less complex, and solitude will not be solitude, nor poverty poverty, nor weakness weakness.

Love your life, poor as it is. The setting sun is reflected from the windows of the almshouse as brightly as from the rich man's abode. It is life near the bone where it is sweetest.

Rather than love, than money, than fame, give me truth. I sat at a table where were rich food and wine in abundance, and obsequious attendance, but sincerity and truth were not; and I went away hungry from the inhospitable board. The hospitality was as cold as the ices.

This generation inclines a little to congratulate itself, and in Boston and London and Paris and Rome, it speaks of its progress in art and science and literature with satisfaction. Yet there is not one of my readers who has lived a whole human life.

There is more day to dawn. The sun is but a morning star.

Tom Brown's Schooldays
by Thomas Hughes
(London, 1857)

The loosely-autobiographical *Tom Brown* pretty much invented the genre of British school novels, and so led to *St. Trinian's*, Billy Bunter's *Greyfriars*, Mr Chips' *Brookfield* and to *Hogwarts*, as well as whole series of books based on the Flashman character.

Abridged: JH

I. Tom Goes to Rugby

Squire Brown, J.P. for the county of Berks, dealt out justice and mercy, in a thorough way, and begat sons and daughters, and hunted the fox, and grumbled at the badness of the roads and the times. And his wife dealt out stockings and shirts and smock frocks, and comforting drinks to the old folks with the "rheumatiz," and good counsel to all.

Tom was their eldest child, a hearty, strong boy, from the first given to fighting with and escaping from his nurse, and fraternising with all the village boys, with whom he made expeditions all round the neighbourhood.

Squire Brown was a Tory to the backbone; but, nevertheless, held divers social principles not generally supposed to be true blue in colour; the foremost of which was the belief that a man is to be valued wholly and solely for that which he is himself, apart from all externals whatever. Therefore, he held it didn't matter a straw whether his son associated with lords' sons or ploughmen's sons, provided they were brave and honest. So he encouraged Tom in his intimacy with the village boys, and gave them the run of a close for a playground. Great was the grief among them when Tom drove off with the squire one morning, to meet the coach, on his way to Rugby, to school.

It had been resolved that Tom should travel down by the Tally-ho, which passed through Rugby itself; and as it was an early coach, they drove out to the Peacock Inn, at Islington, to be on the road. Towards nine o'clock, the squire, observing that Tom was getting sleepy, sent the little fellow off to bed, with a few parting words, the result of much thought.

"And now, Tom, my boy," said the squire, "remember you are going, at your own earnest request, to be chucked into this great school, like a young bear, with all your troubles before you - earlier than we should have sent you, perhaps. You'll see a great many cruel blackguard things done, and hear a deal of foul, bad talk. But never fear. You tell the truth, and keep a brave, kind heart, and never listen to or say anything you wouldn't have your mother or sister hear, and you'll never feel ashamed to come home, or we to see you."

The mention of his mother made Tom feel rather choky, and he would have liked to hug his father well, if it hadn't been for his recent stipulation that kissing should now cease between them, so he only squeezed his father's hand, and looked up bravely, and said, "I'll try, father!"

At ten minutes to three Tom was in the coffee-room in his stockings, and there was his father nursing a bright fire; and a cup of coffee and a hard biscuit on the table.

Just as he was swallowing the last mouthful, Boots looks in, and says, "Tally-ho, sir!" And they hear the ring and rattle as it dashes up to the Peacock.

"Good-bye, father; my love at home!" A last shake of the hand. Up goes Tom, the guard holding on with one hand, while he claps the horn to his mouth. Toot, toot, toot! Away goes the Tally-ho into the darkness.

Tom stands up, and looks back at his father's figure as long as you can see it; and then comes to an anchor, and finishes his buttonings and other preparations for facing the cold three hours before dawn. The guard muffles Tom's feet up in straw, and puts an oat-sack over his knees, but it is not until after breakfast that his tongue is unloosed, and he rubs up his memory, and launches out into a graphic history of all the performances of the Rugby boys on the roads for the last twenty years.

"And so here's Rugby, sir, at last, and you'll be in plenty of time for dinner at the schoolhouse, as I tell'd you," says the old guard.

Tom's heart beat quick, and he began to feel proud of being a Rugby boy when he passed the school gates, and saw the boys standing there as if the town belonged to them.

One of the young heroes ran out from the rest, and scrambled up behind, where, having righted himself with, "How do, Jem?" to the guard, he turned round short to Tom, and began, "I say, you fellow, is your name Brown?"

"Yes," said Tom, in considerable astonishment.

"Ah, I thought so; my old aunt, Miss East, lives somewhere down your way in Berkshire; she wrote that you were coming to-day and asked me to give you a lift!"

Tom was somewhat inclined to resent the patronising air of his new friend, a boy of just about his own age and height, but gifted with the most transcendent coolness and assurance, which Tom felt to be aggravating and hard to bear, but couldn't help admiring and envying, especially when my young lord begins hectoring two or three long loafing fellows, and arranges with one of them to carry up Tom's luggage.

"You see," said East, as they strolled up to the school gates, "a good deal depends on how a fellow cuts up at first. You see I'm doing the handsome thing by you, because my father knows yours; besides, I want to please the old lady - she gave me half-a-sov. this half, and perhaps'll double it next if I keep in her good books."

Tom was duly placed in the Third Form, and found his work very easy; and as he had no intimate companion to make him idle (East being in the Lower Fourth), soon gained golden opinions from his master, and all went well with him in the school. As a new boy he was, of course, excused fagging, but, in his enthusiasm, this hardly pleased him; and East and others of his young friends kindly allowed him to indulge his fancy, and take their turns at night, fagging and cleaning studies. So he soon gained the character of a good-natured, willing fellow, ready to do a turn for anyone.

II. The War of Independence

The Lower Fourth was an overgrown Form, too large for any one man to attend to properly, consequently the elysium of the young scamps who formed the staple of it. Tom had come up from the Third with a good character, but he rapidly fell away, and became as unmanageable as the rest. By the time the second monthly examination came round, his character for steadiness was gone, and for years after, he went up the school without it, and regarded the masters, as a matter of course, as his natural enemies. Matters were not so comfortable in the house, either. The new praeposters of the Sixth Form were not strong, and the big Fifth Form boys soon began to usurp power, and to fag and bully the little boys.

One evening Tom and East were sitting in their study, Tom brooding over the wrongs of fags in general and his own in particular.

"I say, Scud," said he at last, "what right have the Fifth Form boys to fag us as they do?"

"No more right than you have to fag them," said East, without looking up from an early number of "Pickwick" Tom relapsed into his brown study, and East went on reading and chuckling.

"Do you know, old fellow, I've been thinking it over, and I've made up my mind I won't fag except for the Sixth."

"Quite right, too, my boy," cried East. "I'm all for a strike myself; it's getting too bad."

"I shouldn't mind if it were only young Brooke now," said Tom; "I'd do anything for him. But that blackguard Flashman-"

"The cowardly brute!" broke in East.

"Fa-a-ag!" sounded along the passage from Flashman's study.

The two boys looked at one another.

"Fa-a-ag!" again. No answer.

"Here, Brown! East! You young skulks!" roared Flashman. "I know you're in! No shirking!"

Tom bolted the door, and East blew out the candle.

"Now, Tom, no surrender!"

Then the assault commenced. One panel of the door gave way to repeated kicks, and the besieged strengthened their defences with the sofa. Flashman & Co. at last retired, vowing vengeance, and when the convivial noises began again steadily, Tom and East rushed out. They were too quick to be caught, but a pickle-jar, sent whizzing after them by Flashman narrowly missed Tom's head. Their story was soon told to a knot of small boys round the fire in the hall, who nearly all bound themselves not to fag for the Fifth, encouraged and advised thereto by Diggs - a queer, very clever fellow, nearly at the top of the Fifth himself. He stood by them all through and seldom have small boys had more need of a friend.

Flashman and his associates united in "bringing the young vagabonds to their senses," and the whole house was filled with chasings, sieges, and lickings of all sorts.

One evening, in forbidden hours, Brown and East were in the hall, chatting by the light of the fire, when the door swung open, and in walked Flashman. He didn't see Diggs, busy in front of the other fire; and as the boys didn't move for him, struck one of them, and ordered them all off to their study.

"I say, you two," said Diggs, rousing up, "you'll never get rid of that fellow till you lick him. Go in at him, both of you! I'll see fair play."

They were about up to Flashman's shoulder, but tough and in perfect training; while he, seventeen years old, and big and strong of his age, was in poor condition from his monstrous habits of stuffing and want of exercise.

They rushed in on him, and he hit out wildly and savagely, and in another minute Tom went spinning backwards over a form; and Flashman turned to demolish East, with a savage grin. But Diggs jumped down from the table on which he had seated himself.

"Stop there!" shouted he. "The round's over! Half minute time allowed! I'm going to see fair. Are you ready, Brown? Time's up!"

The small boys rushed in again; Flashman was wilder and more flurried than ever. In a few moments over all three went on the floor, Flashman striking his head on a form. But his skull was not fractured, as the two youngsters feared it was, and he never laid a finger on them again. But whatever harm a spiteful tongue could do them, he took care should be done. Only throw dirt enough, and some will stick. And so Tom and East, and one or two more, became a sort of young Ishmaelites. They saw the praeposters cowed by or joining with the Fifth and shirking their own duties; and so they didn't respect them, and rendered no willing obedience, and got the character of sulky, unwilling fags. At the end of the term they are told the doctor wants to see them. He is not angry only very grave. He explains that rules are made for the good of the school and must and shall be obeyed! He should be sorry if they had to leave, and wishes them to think very seriously in the holidays over what he has said. Good-night!

III. The Turn of the Tide

The turning point of our hero's school career had now come, and the manner of it was as follows.

Tom and East and another Schoolhouse boy rushed into the matron's room in high spirits when they got back on the first day of the next half-year. She sent off the others, but kept Tom to tell him Mrs. Arnold wished him to take a new boy to share the study he had hoped to share with East. She had told Mrs. Arnold she thought Tom would be kind to him, and see that he wasn't bullied.

In the far corner of the room he saw a slight, pale boy, who looked ready to sink through the floor. The matron watched Tom for a minute, and saw what was passing in his mind.

"Poor little fellow," she said, almost in a whisper. "His father's dead, and his mamma - such a sweet, kind lady - almost broke her heart at leaving him. She said one of his sisters was like to die of a decline- "

"Well, well," burst in Tom, "I suppose I must give up East. Come along, young 'un! What's your name? We'll go and have supper, and then I'll show you our study."

"His name's George Arthur," said the matron. "I've had his books and things put into the study, which his mamma has had new papered, and the sofa covered, and new curtains. And Mrs. Arnold told me to say she'd like you both to come up to tea with her."

Here was an announcement for Master Tom! He was to go up to tea the first night, just as if he were of importance in the school world instead of the most reckless young scapegrace among the fags. He felt himself lifted on to a higher moral platform at once; and marched off with his young charge in tow in monstrous good humour with himself and all the world. His cup was full when Dr. Arnold, with a warm shake of the hand, seemingly oblivious of all the scrapes he had been getting into, said, "Ah, Brown, you here! I hope you left all well at home. And this is the little fellow who is to share your study? Well, he doesn't look as we should like to see him. You must take him some good long walks, and show him what little pretty country we have about here."

The tea went merrily off, and everybody felt that he, young as he was, was of some use in the school world, and had a work to do there. When Tom was recognised coming out of the private door which led from the doctor's house, there was a great shout of greeting, and Hall at once began to question Arthur.

"What a queer chum for Tom Brown," was the general comment. And it must be confessed that so thought Tom himself as he lighted the candle in their study, and surveyed the new curtains with much satisfaction.

"I say, Arthur, what a brick your mother is to make us so cosy! But look here now, you must answer straight up when the fellows speak to you. If you're afraid, you'll get bullied. And don't you ever talk about home or your mother or sisters."

Poor little Arthur looked ready to cry.

"But please, mayn't I talk about home to you?"

"Oh, yes, I like it. But not to boys you don't know. What a jolly desk!"

And soon Tom was deep in Arthur's goods and chattels, and hardly thought of his friends outside till the prayer-bell rang.

He thought of his own first night there when he was leading poor little Arthur up to No. 4, and showing him his bed. The idea of sleeping in a room with strange boys had clearly never crossed his mind before. He could hardly bare to take his jacket off. However, presently off it came, and he paused and looked at Tom, who was sitting on his bed, talking and laughing.

"Please, Brown," he whispered, "may I wash my face and hands?"

"Of course, if you like," said Tom, staring. "You'll have to go down for more water if you use it all." On went the talk and laughter. Arthur finished his undressing, and looked round more nervously than ever. The light burned clear, the noise went on. This time, however, he did not ask Tom what he might or might not do, but dropped on his knees by his bedside to open his heart to Him who heareth the cry of the tender child, or the strong man.

Tom was unlacing his boots with his back towards Arthur, and looked up in wonder at the sudden silence. Then two or three boys laughed, and one big, brutal fellow picked up a slipper and shied it at the kneeling boy. The next moment the boot Tom had just taken off flew straight at the head of the bully.

"If any other fellow wants the other boot," said Tom, stepping on to the floor, "he knows how to get it!"

At this moment the Sixth Form boy came in, and not another word could be said. Tom and the rest rushed into bed, and finished unrobing there. Sleep seemed to have deserted the pillow of poor Tom. The thought of his promise to his mother came over him, never to forget to kneel at his bedside and give himself up to his Father before he laid his head on the pillow from which it might never rise; and he lay down gently, and cried as if his heart would break. He was only fourteen years old.

Next morning he was up and washed and dressed just as the ten-minutes bell began, and then in the face of the whole room knelt down to pray. Not five words could he say; he was listening for every whisper in the room. What were they all thinking of him? At last, as it were from his inmost heart, a still, small voice seemed to breathe: "God be merciful to me, a sinner." He repeated the words over and over again, and rose from his knees comforted and humbled, and ready to face the whole school. It was not needed; two other boys had already followed his example. Before either Tom or Arthur left the Schoolhouse there was no room in which it had not become the regular custom.

IV. Tom Brown's Last Match

The curtain now rises on the last act of our little drama. Eight years have passed, and it is the end of the summer half-year at Rugby. The boys have scattered to the four winds, except the Eleven, and a few enthusiasts who are permitted to stay to see the result of the cricket matches. For this year the return matches are being played at Rugby, and to-day the great event of the year, the Marylebone match, is being played. I wish I had space to describe the whole match; but I haven't, so you must fancy it all, and let me beg to call your attention to a group of three eagerly watching the match. The first, evidently a clergyman, is carelessly dressed, and looks rather used up, but is bent on enjoying life as he spreads himself out in the evening sun. By his side, in white flannel shirt and trousers, and the captain's belt, sits a strapping figure near six feet high, with ruddy, tanned face and a laughing eye. He is leaning forward, dandling his favourite bat, with which he has made thirty or forty runs to-day. It is Tom Brown, spending his last day as a Rugby boy. And at their feet sits Arthur, with his bat across his knees. He is less of a boy, in fact, than Tom, if one may judge by the thoughtfulness of his face, which is somewhat paler than we could wish, but his figure is well-knit and active, and all his old timidity has disappeared, and is replaced by silent, quaint fun, as he listens to the broken talk, and joins in every now and then. Presently he goes off to the wicket, with a last exhortation from Tom to play steady and keep his bat straight.

"I'm surprised to see Arthur in the Eleven," says the master.

"Well, I'm not sure he ought to be for his play," said Tom; "but I couldn't help putting him in. It will do him so much good, and you can't think what I owe him!"

The master smiled. Later he returned to the subject

"Nothing has given me greater pleasure," he said, "than your friendship for him. It has been the making of you both."

"Of me, at any rate," answered Tom. "It was the luckiest chance in the world that sent him to Rugby and made him my chum."

"There was neither luck nor chance in that matter," said the master. "Do you remember when the Doctor lectured you and East when you had been getting into all sorts of scrapes?"

"Yes; well enough," said Tom. "It was the half-year before Arthur came."

"Exactly so," said the master. "He was in great distress about you both, and after some talk, we both agreed that you in particular wanted some object in the school beyond games and mischief. So the Doctor looked out the best of the new boys, and separated you and East in the hope that when you had somebody to lean on you, you'd be steadier yourself, and get manliness and thoughtfulness. He has watched the experiment ever since with great satisfaction."

Up to this time Tom had never fully given in to, or understood, the Doctor. He had learnt to regard him with love and respect, and to think him a very great and wise and good man. But as regarded his own position in the school, he had no idea of giving anyone credit but himself.

It was a new light to Tom to find that besides teaching the Sixth, and governing and guiding the whole school, editing classics, and writing histories, the great headmaster had found time to watch over the career even of him, Tom Brown, and his particular friends. However, the Doctor's

victory was complete from that moment. It had taken eight long years to do it, but now it was done thoroughly.

The match was over.

Tom said good-bye to his tutor, and marched down to the Schoolhouse.

Next morning he was in the train and away for London, no longer a schoolboy.

On Liberty
by John Stuart Mill
(London, 1859)

This book, by a modest clerk to the East India Company, is the great defence of a bold new idea - that individual people, as long as they don't harm others, ought to be free to do as they wish, to invent and show the world their ideas, without from interference by either State or Society. It is a text which has profoundly influenced the form of governments the whole world over.

Abridged: GH

To the beloved memory of her that was the inspirer, and in part the author – the friend and wife whose approbation was my strongest reward, and whose great thoughts and noble feelings are buried in her grave – I dedicate this volume.

1: Introductory

THE subject of this Essay is not the so-called 'Liberty of the Will', but Civil, or Social Liberty. A subject hardly ever discussed in general terms, but of profound importance.

The struggle between liberty and authority is the most conspicuous feature of the history of Greece, Rome and England. But in old times liberty meant protection against the tyranny of the political rulers. They consisted of a governing One, or a governing tribe or caste, who derived their authority from inheritance or conquest. To prevent the weaker members of society from being preyed upon by innumerable vultures it was thought that there should be an animal of prey stronger than the rest. The aim of patriots was to set limits to the power of the ruler.

As human affairs progressed, there came a time when what was wanted was that rulers should be identified with the people, that their interests should be the interests of the whole nation. But, like other tyrannies, the tyranny of the majority was, at first (and still commonly is) held in dread. Society as a whole can issue wrong mandates and practice a tyranny more formidable than many kinds of political oppression.

Protection, therefore, against the tyranny of the magistrate is not enough: there also needs to be protection against the tyranny of prevailing opinion. But some rules of conduct must be imposed - by either law or public opinion.

No two ages, and scarcely any two countries, have decided it alike. People are accustomed to believe (encouraged by

some philosophers) their feelings on such subjects are better than reasons, and render reasons unnecessary.

Whenever there is an ascendant class, the morality of the country emanates from its class interests - consider the Spartans and the Helots, the Negroes and the planters, men and women. Another grand principle has been the servility of mankind towards their gods. It has made men burn witches and magicians, yet remember that those who first broke away from the yoke of the so-called Universal Church were usually as unwilling to permit difference of religious opinion as that church itself. The majority have not yet learned to feel the power of the government to be their power, or its opinions their opinions.

The object of this essay is to assert one simple principle, as entitled to govern absolutely the dealings of society with the individual. That principle is that the sole end for which mankind are warranted in interfering with the liberty of action of any of their number is to prevent harm to others. His own good, either physical or moral, is not sufficient warrant. Over himself, over his own body and mind, the individual is sovereign.

2: Of Liberty of Thought and Discussion

Let us suppose that the government is entirely at one with the people, and never thinks of exerting coercion unless in agreement with their voice. I deny the right of the people to exercise such coercion.

The particular evil of silencing the expression of opinion is that it is robbing the human race, posterity as well as the existing generation - those who dissent as well as hold the opinion. If the opinion is right, they are deprived of the opportunity to exchange error for truth, if wrong they loose what is almost as great a benefit, the clearer perception and livelier impression of truth produced by its collision with error.

It is necessary to consider two hypotheses.

First, the opinion which it is attempted to suppress may possibly be true. Those who desire to suppress it, of course, deny its truth: but they are not infallible. The silencing of discussion is an assumption of infallibility, for while everyone knows himself to be fallible, few think it necessary to take any precautions against their own fallibility. Few care that it is mere accident which has decided their opinions, like the devout churchman in London, who would be a Buddhist or a Confucian[1] in Peking.

Mankind can hardly be too often reminded that there was once a man called Socrates[2], who was put to death for denying the gods recognized by the state. Then there was the event on Calvary more than eighteen hundred years ago[3] - the man who has left such an impression of moral grandeur that subsequent centuries have done homage to him as the Almighty in person, was ignominiously put to death, as what? As a blasphemer. Men did not merely mistake their benefactor, they took him for the exact contrary of what he was.

The enemies of religious freedom occasionally say, with Dr Johnson[4], that persecution is an ordeal through which truth must pass, legal penalties being, in the end, powerless against truth. This argument is, I believe, mostly confined to the sort of persons who think that new truths may have been desirable once, but that we have had enough of them now.

The dictum that truth always triumphs over persecution is a pleasant falsehood which experience refutes. To speak only of religious opinions: Arnold of Brescia, Fra Dolcino, Savonarola, The Albigeois, The Lollards, The Hussites and many others were all put down before the Reformation succeeded. We do not now put to death the introducers of new opinions, but let us not flatter ourselves that we are free from legal persecution.

In 1857 a Cornish man was sentenced to twenty-one months in prison for using some offensive words concerning Christianity. These are, indeed, but rags and remnants of persecution. Our mere intolerance kills no one, roots out no opinions but induces men to disguise them or to abstain from any active effort to diffuse them.

Second: let us assume received opinions to be true and examine in what manner they are likely to be held when their truth is not freely and openly canvassed. However unwilling a person is to admit that his opinion may be false, he ought to consider that if it is not fully and fearlessly discussed it will be held as a dead dogma, not a living truth.

Those who know that they are right think that no good, and some harm, comes from it being allowed to be questioned. But he who know only his own side, knows little of that. His reasons may be good, but if he is unable to refute the reasons of the other side he has no grounds for preferring either opinion. Ninety-nine in a hundred 'educated men' are in this condition, even those who can fluently argue for their opinion. Their conclusion may be true, but it might be false for anything they know.

The Catholic Church has a way of dealing with this problem. The clergy may acquaint themselves with the arguments of their opponents, in order to answer them, and may therefore read heretical books. The laity must accept opinions on trust; instead of a vivid conception of a living belief, there remains only a few phrases learned by rote.

We have now recognized the necessity to the mental well being of mankind (on which all other well-being depends) of freedom of opinion, and freedom of the expression of opinion,on, on, four distinct grounds:

(1) If any opinion is compelled to silence, that opinion may, for aught we know, be true.

(2) Though the silenced opinion be an error, it may, and commonly does, contain a portion of truth.

(3) Even if the received opinion be the whole truth: unless it is vigorously and earnestly contested it will be held in the manner of a prejudice with little comprehension or feeling of its rational grounds.

(4) The meaning of a doctrine will be in danger of being lost.

Before quitting the subject of freedom of opinion it is fit to point out that unmeasured vituperation really does deter people from learning contrary opinions.

3: On Individuality

Let us next examine whether the same reasons require that men should be free to act upon their opinions - so long as it is at their own risk and peril. The last proviso is indispensable. No one pretends that actions should be as free as opinions. An opinion that corn dealers are starvers of the poor ought to be unmolested in the press, but may justly incur punishment when delivered to an excited mob assembled before the house of a corn dealer. The liberty of the individual must be thus far limited: he must not make himself a nuisance to other people. But if he refrains from molesting others in what concerns them, and merely acts according to his own inclination in things which concern himself he should be allowed to carry his opinions into practice at his own cost.

While mankind are fallible, their truths only half-truths, it is useful that there should be different opinions and different experiments of living: that free scope should be given to varieties of character, short of injury to others, so that the worth of different modes of life can be proved in practice, when anyone thinks fit to try them.

The majority, being satisfied with the ways of mankind as they are now cannot comprehend why those ways should not be good enough for everybody. He who lets the world choose his plan of life for him has no need of any faculty other than ape-like imitation.

1   **Confucian:** See p42
2   **Socrates:** See p.55
3   **Calvary:** See p.77
4   **Dr Johnson:** See p.257

We are assuredly but starved specimens of what nature can and will produce. Human nature is not a machine doing exactly the work prescribed for it, but like a tree which requires to grow and develop on all sides.

In proportion to the development of his individuality, each person becomes more valuable to himself, and is therefore capable of being more valuable to others. It is essential that different persons be allowed to lead different lives - even despotism does not produce its worst effects so long as individuality exists under it: and whatever crushes individuality is despotism, by whatever name it be called, whether it professes to be enforcing the will of God or the injunctions of men.

There is always need of persons to discover new truths, to commence new practices. These few are the salt of the earth.

Persons of genius, it is true, are always likely to he a small minority: but in order to have them it is necessary to preserve the soil in which they grow. Persons of genius are by definition more individual than other people- less capable of fitting into any of the small number of moulds which society provides.

Originality is the one thing which unoriginal minds cannot feel the use of. The first service which originality has to render them, is to open their eyes. In this age the mere example of non-conformity, the mere refusal to bend the knee to custom, is itself a service. Precisely because the tyranny of opinion is such as to make eccentricity a reproach, it is desirable, in order to break through that tyranny, that people should be eccentric.

Eccentricity has always abounded when and where strength of character has abounded; and the amount of eccentricity in a society has generally been proportional to the amount of genius, mental vigour, and moral courage which it contained. That so few now dare to be eccentric, marks the chief danger of the time.

Nothing was ever done which someone was not first to do, and all good things which exist are the fruits of originality.

In sober truth the general tendency of mankind is to mediocrity. At present, individuals are lost in the crowd. Public opinion rules the world, though not always the same sort of public. In America it is the whole white population: in England the middle class. But they are always a mass, a collective mediocrity.

The popular idea of character is to be without any marked character- to maim by compression like a Chinese lady's foot.

Much of the world has, properly speaking, no history because the despotism of Custom is complete. We have as a warning example China - a nation of much talent and wisdom who ought to have kept themselves at the head of the development of the world. Yet they have become stationary, and if they are to be improved it must be by foreigners. A people, it appears, may be progressive for a certain length of time, and then stop: when does it stop? When it ceases to possess individuality.

What is it that has preserved Europe from this lot? What has made the European family of nations an improving, instead of a stationary, portion of mankind? Not any superior excellence in themselves, but their remarkable diversity of character and culture, their striking out in such a variety of paths.

4: Of The Limits to The Authority of Society

What then is the rightful limit to the sovereignty of the individual over himself? How much of human life should be assigned to individuality, and how much to society? To individuality should belong the part of life in which the individual is interested: to society, the part which chiefly interests society.

Though society is not founded on a contract[5], everyone who receives the protection of society owes a return for the benefit.

I do not mean that our feelings toward others should not be affected by their self-regarding qualities. A person who shows rashness, obstinacy, self-conceit- who cannot live within moderate means or who pursues animal pleasures at the expense of those of feeling and intellect must expect to be lowered in the opinion of others. We are not bound to seek his society: we have a right to avoid it and a right, maybe a duty, to caution others against him.

The distinction here between the part of a person's life which concerns only himself and that which concerns others, many will refuse to admit. How can the conduct of a member of society be a matter of indifference to the rest of society? No person is entirely isolated. If he injures his property, he does harm to those who derived support from it. If he deteriorates his bodily faculties, he becomes a burden on others. Even if his follies do no direct harm to others, he is nevertheless injurious by example.

If protection against themselves is due to children, is not society equally bound to afford it to those mature persons who are incapable of self-government? If gambling, drunkenness or idleness are injurious to happiness, why should the law not repress them? There is no question here about restricting individuality. The only things it is sought to prevent are things which have been tried and condemned from the beginning of the world.

So no person should be punished for being drunk: but a soldier or policeman should be punished for being drunk on duty. Whenever, in short, there is a definite damage, or risk of damage, either to an individual or the public, the case is out of the provenance of liberty and placed in that of morality or law.

But the strongest argument against public interference with personal conduct is that when it does interfere, the odds are that it interferes wrongly. There are many who consider as an injury to themselves any conduct they have a distaste

---

5   **Society and Contract:** See p.233

for- like the religious bigot when charged with disregarding the religious feelings of others has been known to retort that they disregard his feelings by persisting in their abominable worship. Examples will show that this principle is of serious and practical moment.

Nothing in the creed of Christians does more to envenom hatred of the Mohammedans than their practice of eating pork, which they think to be forbidden and abhorred by the Deity. But to forbid the eating of pork, even in a Mohammedan country would be interfering with the personal tastes of individuals.

Under the name of preventing intemperance, the people of one English colony and nearly half the United States have been interdicted by law from making any use whatever of fermented drinks. The claim is that "strong drink destroys my primary right of security by creating social disorder". A theory of "social rights" like this says that 'it is the right of every individual to require every other individual to act as he ought'

Polygamy: permitted to Mohammedans, Hindus and Chinese seems to excite unquenchable animosity when practised by persons who speak English and profess to be a kind of Christians - the Mormons.

Let them send missionaries if they please, but I am not aware that any community has a right to force another to be civilized. So long as the sufferers from a bad law do not ask for assistance, I cannot admit that persons entirely unconnected with them have any right to step in.

5: Applications

I now offer not so much applications as specimens of applications which may serve to bring into greater clearness the principles asserted in these pages. The maxims being followed are:

(1) The individual is not accountable to society for his actions in so far as these concern the interests of no person but himself.

(2) The individual is accountable for such actions as are prejudicial to the interests of others, and may be subject to social or legal punishment if society is of the opinion that this is necessary for its protection.

In many cases the individual pursuing a legitimate object necessarily causes pain or loss to others. Whoever succeeds in an overcrowded profession or in competitive examinations reaps benefit from the loss of others. But, by common admission, society admits no right to the disappointed competitors to immunity from this kind of suffering, and feels called to interfere only when means of success contrary to the general interest have been employed- namely fraud, force or treachery.

Trade is a social act. It is now recognized, though not till after a long struggle, that both the cheapness and good quality of commodities are most effectually provided for by leaving the producers and sellers perfectly and equally free. This is the doctrine of 'free-trade'.

With the sale of poisons- labelling as dangerous can be enforced without violation of liberty. But to require, in all cases, the certificate of a medical practitioner would make it sometimes impossible or expensive to obtain the article for legitimate use.

Drunkenness is not a fit subject for legislative interference, but I consider it perfectly legitimate that a person who had once been convicted of an act of violence to others under the influence of drink should be placed under a special restriction.

So again, idleness (except in a person receiving public support, or when it constitutes a breach of contract) cannot without tyranny be made a subject of legal punishment: but if due to idleness a man fails to, for instance, support his children, it is no tyranny to force him to fulfil that obligation by compulsory labour, if no other means are available.

Again, there are acts which, being directly injurious only to the agents themselves ought not to be prevented, but which if done publicly, are a violation of good manners and, as offences against others may be rightly prohibited. Of this kind are offences against decency: on which it is unnecessary to dwell.

All persons should be free to assemble in each other's houses- yet public gambling houses should not be permitted. It is true that the prohibition is never effectual: but they may be compelled to conduct their operations with secrecy, so that only those who seek them know anything about them.

An arrangement by which someone sells themselves as a slave would be null and void as he would defeat his own case for liberty.

Baron Von Humboldt states that engagements which involve personal relations or services should never be legally binding beyond a certain duration of time- and that the most important of these, marriage, should be dissolvable by nothing more than the declared will of the parties. The present almost despotic power of husbands over wives need hardly be enlarged upon here.

At an early age every child must be examined to see if he (or she) is able to read. If unable, the father might be subject to a moderate fine, to be worked out, if necessary, by his labour. Higher examinations should be voluntary, granted to all who pass the exam and conferring no authority other than that granted by public opinion.

Laws on the Continent which forbid marriage unless the parties can show that they have means to support a family are not objectionable as violations of liberty.

Objections to government interference (when it does not infringe liberty) are of three kinds:

(1) When a thing is better done by individuals than by government. Generally there are none so fit to conduct any business as those who are personally interested in it.

(2) Even if individuals do not do things so well, it is better to let them take care of their own affairs in, for instance,

jury trials, industrial and philanthropic organizations, voluntary associations, allowing each to learn from the experiments of others.

(3) The most cogent reason is to prevent the evil of too great a power. If roads, railways and companies all became departments of central administration then not all the freedom of the press or a popular legislature would make the country free in any but name.

Where people are accustomed to expect everything to be done by the state, they hold the state responsible for all evil which befalls them. Should the evil exceed their patience, they make revolution- whereupon someone else, with or without legitimate authority, vaults into the seat and all continues much as before.

The central organ should have a right to know all that is done, and a duty to disseminate that knowledge- but limited to compelling local officers to obey the law. Like the Poor Law Boards superintending the administrators of the Poor Rate, such powers as the Board exercises are for the cure of maladministration in matters affecting the wider community, for no locality has a moral right to make itself a nest of pauperism overflowing into neighbouring communities to impair their moral and physical condition.

The worth of the state is the worth of the individuals comprising it. A state which dwarfs its men will find that with small men no great thing can be accomplished.

On The Origin of Species
by Means of Natural Selection,
or The Preservation of Favoured Races in the Struggle for Life.
by Charles Darwin
(London, 1859)

This scientific treatise not only revolutionized every branch of the natural sciences, but has profoundly influenced the literary, philosophical and religious thinkers who followed. With it the established Western view that creatures had been created independently by a God (see p23), and indeed the whole supernatural explanation of the universe, had competition. At first, denunciation by the likes of Bishop Wilberforce was complete. But religious views gradually evolved, through Philip Grosse's theory that fossils had been planted by God to give the earth a coherent history, to today's position where only a remnant population of creationists remains.

This is what the modern philosopher Daniel Dennett called 'Darwin's dangerous idea'- that natural selection governs, not only the world's flora and fauna, but its history, economics and beliefs. Even religious ideas, it seems, are subject to the same laws of advancement as all other things, "multiply, vary, let the strongest live and the weakest die."

The Origin was banned from Trinity College, Cambridge in 1859; in Yugoslavia (1935) and Greece (1937). In 1925 in the USA, John Scopes was famously convicted of teaching from it, and it remained banned from some American schools until 1967.

Abridged: GH

"Let no man out of a weak conceit of sobriety, or an ill-applied moderation, think or maintain, that a man can search too far or be too well studied in the book of God's word, or in the book of God's works; divinity or philosophy; but rather let men endeavour an endless progress or proficience in both".- Bacon: Advancement of Learning.[1]

When on board H.M.S. 'Beagle,' as naturalist, I was struck with certain facts, which seemed to throw light on the origin of species, that mystery of mysteries, as it has been called by one of our greatest philosophers. On my return home in 1837, I began patiently accumulating and reflecting on all sorts of facts which could have any bearing on it. After five years' work I drew up some short notes; enlarged in 1844 into a sketch of the conclusions. From

that period to the present I have steadily pursued this object. I have not been hasty in coming to a decision.

Although much remains obscure, I can entertain no doubt that the idea which I formerly entertained- namely, that each species has been independently created- is erroneous. I am convinced that Natural Selection has been the main, but not exclusive, means of modification.

Charles Darwin, October 1st, 1859.

VARIATION UNDER DOMESTICATION

When we look at individuals of cultivated plants and animals, we are struck by how they differ much more from each other, than do individuals in nature. Our oldest cultivated plants, such as wheat, still yield new varieties.

Some organisms breed freely under most unnatural conditions (for instance, rabbits or ferrets kept in hutches), showing that their reproductive system has not been

---

1   **Bacon:** see p.167

affected; so will some animals and plants withstand domestication or cultivation, and vary very slightly-perhaps hardly more than in a state of nature.

Gardeners are aware of 'sporting' buds, which suddenly assume a new and sometimes very different character from that of the rest of the plant. Such buds can be propagated by grafting, &c., and sometimes by seed, showing that variation is not necessarily connected, as some authors have supposed, with the act of generation.

He who breeds animals knows how strong is the tendency to inheritance: like produces like is his fundamental belief. Breeders know too that one characteristic accompanies another; long limbs go with an elongated head, hairless dogs have imperfect teeth; pigeons with feathered feet have skin between their toes. But the number and diversity of inheritable deviations of structure, whether of slight or considerable physiological importance, is endless. The laws governing inheritance are quite unknown; no one can say why the child often reverts in certain characters to its remote ancestor; why a peculiarity is often transmitted from one sex to both sexes or to one sex alone.

Here I may comment on the matter of reversion, that domestic varieties, when run wild, gradually but certainly revert to their aboriginal character. Hence it has been argued that no deductions can be drawn from domestic races to species in a state of nature. Certainly, when under nature the conditions of life change, variations and reversions of character probably do occur; but natural selection, as will hereafter be explained, will determine how far the new characters thus arising shall be preserved.

Believing that it is always best to study some special group, I have joined two of the London Pigeon Clubs. The diversity of the breeds is something astonishing. The short-faced tumbler has a beak like a finch; the runt is a bird of great size; the turbit has a line of reversed feathers down the breast. Such are the variations that an ornithologist would certainly rank them as well-defined species. Yet I am fully convinced that the common opinion of naturalists is correct, namely, that all have descended from the wild rock-pigeon (*Columba livia*).

Such variability may be attributed to the conditions of life, to use and disuse. But I am convinced that Selection is by far the predominant Power.

VARIATION UNDER NATURE

Before considering variation in nature, we must briefly discuss whether variation occurs in that state.

The terms 'species' and 'variety' are difficult to define, but a distinct act of creation and a community of descent is implied. We have also what are called monstrosities; but they graduate into varieties. Again, we have the slight, individual differences as appear in offspring from the same parents. These individual differences generally affect what naturalists consider unimportant parts; but I could show by a long catalogue of facts, that even important parts sometimes vary in the individuals of the same species.

There is one extremely perplexing point connected with individual differences: those 'protean' or 'polymorphic,' genera which present such an inordinate amount of variation that hardly two naturalists can agree which forms are species and which varieties. We may instance, among the plants, Rubus and Rosa. I am inclined to suspect that we see in these polymorphic genera variations which are of no service or disservice to the species, so have not been seized on and rendered definite by natural selection, as hereafter will be explained.

Compare the floras of Great Britain, of France or of the United States, drawn up by different botanists, and see what a surprising number of forms have been ranked by one botanist as species, and by another as mere varieties. Certainly no clear line of demarcation has as yet been drawn between species and sub-species. I look at varieties which are in any degree distinct and permanent, as steps leading to more strongly marked and more permanent varieties; and at these latter, as leading to sub-species, and to species. The passage from one stage to another may sometimes be due to long-continued different physical conditions in different regions; but I am more inclined to attribute the changes to the action of natural selection.

Hence it is the most flourishing, or, as they may be called, the dominant species,- those which range widely over the world, are the most diffused in their own country, and are the most numerous in individuals,- which oftenest produce well-marked varieties. It seems to me that only natural selection can account for this. On the other hand, if we look at each species as a special act of creation, there is no apparent reason why more varieties should occur in a group having many species, than in one having few.

STRUGGLE FOR EXISTENCE

It has never been disputed that there is variation amongst organic beings in a state of nature. It is immaterial for us whether a multitude of doubtful forms be called species or sub-species or varieties. But how have all those exquisite adaptations been perfected?

All these results, as we shall more fully see in the next chapter, follow inevitably from the struggle for life. The elder De Candolle and Lyell have philosophically shown that all organic beings are exposed to severe competition. Nothing is easier than to admit in words the truth of the universal struggle for life. We behold the face of nature bright with gladness, we often see superabundance of food; we do not see, or we forget, that the birds which are idly singing round us mostly live on insects or seeds, and are thus constantly destroying life; or we forget how largely these songsters, or their eggs, or their nestlings, are destroyed by birds and beasts of prey; we do not always bear in mind, that though food may be now superabundant, it is not so at all seasons of each recurring year. Two canine animals in a time of dearth, may be truly said to struggle with each other which shall get food and live. A plant which annually produces a thousand seeds, of which on an average only one comes to maturity, may be more truly said to struggle with the plants of the same and other kinds which already clothe the ground. The missletoe depends on other trees, but can only in a far-fetched sense be said to struggle with these trees, for if too many of these parasites grow on the same tree, it will languish and die. But several seedling missletoes, growing close together on the same branch, may truly be said to struggle with each other. This struggle for life must be most severe between individuals and varieties of the same species who compete for precisely the same resources.

Linnaeus has calculated that if an annual plant produced only two seeds- and there is no plant so unproductive- and their seedlings next year produced two, and so on, then in twenty years there would be a million plants. One fly deposits hundreds of eggs, and another, like the hippobosca, a single one; but this difference does not determine how many individuals of the two species can be supported in a district. Climate plays an important part in determining the average numbers of a species, and periodical seasons of extreme cold or drought, I believe to be the most effective of all checks.

NATURAL SELECTION

Can the principle of selection, so potent in the hands of man, apply in nature? I think it can. Let it be borne in mind how infinitely complex and close-fitting are the mutual relations of all organic beings to each other and to their physical conditions of life. Since variations useful to man have undoubtedly occurred, could not other variations useful in some way to each being in the great and complex battle of life, have sometimes occurred in the course of thousands of generations? This preservation of favourable variations and the rejection of injurious variations, I call Natural Selection. Variations neither useful nor injurious would not be affected by natural selection, and would be left a fluctuating element, as perhaps we see in the species called polymorphic.

We know that changes in a creature's neighbours, and changes in climate can most seriously affect survival. Man keeps creatures of many climates in the same country; yet seldom treats each in their accustomed manner; he feeds long and short beaked pigeons the same food; he exposes sheep with long and short wool to the same climate. He does not allow the most vigorous males to struggle for the females. In such ways man preserves differences which would run out in nature.

In plants, the down on the fruit skin, and its colour, are considered by botanists as of trifling importance: yet that excellent horticulturist, Downing, shows that smooth-skinned fruits suffer more from beetle; that purple plums suffer more from disease than yellow plums. If such slight differences make a great difference in cultivating varieties, then assuredly, in a state of nature, where trees have to struggle with other trees and a host of enemies, such differences would effectually settle which variety should succeed. In all cases, natural selection will ensure that modifications shall not be in the least degree injurious: for

if they became so, they would cause the extinction of the species.

In social animals, natural selection will adapt the structure of each individual for the benefit of the community. This depends, not on a struggle for existence, but on a struggle between the males for possession of the females; the result is not death to the unsuccessful competitor, but few or no offspring.

Consider the case of wolves. It is possible that a cub might be born with a slight innate tendency to pursue a particular prey, and we know from Mr St.John that the tendency to capture particular prey is inherited. If that were followed by some slight change in the climate and in the availability of prey, then that animal would be advantaged. Some of its young would probably inherit the same habits, and by the repetition of this process, a new variety might be formed. Indeed we know, according to Mr. Pierce, that in the Catskill Mountains in the United States, there exists a greyhound-like wolf, which pursues deer, and another more bulky one which attacks sheep.

In man's methodical selection, a breeder selects for some definite object. Thus it will be in nature; when some place is not so perfectly occupied as might be, natural selection will tend to preserve all the individuals varying in the right direction, so as better to fill the vacancy.

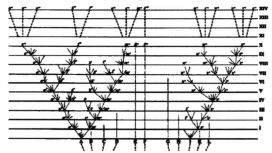

The affinities of creatures have sometimes been represented by a great tree. I believe this simile largely speaks the truth. In the diagram, each horizontal line may be supposed to represent a thousand, or a million or hundred million generations, and likewise a section of the strata of the earth's crust containing extinct remains. The green and budding twigs may represent existing species; and those produced during each former year may represent the long succession of extinct species.

LAWS OF VARIATION

I have hitherto sometimes spoken as if the variations in organic beings had been due to chance. Some authors believe it to be as much the function of the reproductive system to produce individual differences. But the greater variability, as well as the greater frequency of monstrosities, under domestication, than under nature, leads me to believe that deviations are in some way due to the conditions of life to which the parents have been exposed.

How much direct effect difference of climate, food, &c., produces on any being is extremely doubtful. My impression is, that the effect is extremely small in the case of animals, but perhaps rather more in that of plants. The fact that varieties of one species, when they range into the habitation of other species, often acquire in a very slight degree some of the characters of such species, accords with our view that species are merely well-marked varieties.

Natural selection will accumulate all profitable variations, however slight, until they become plainly developed and appreciable by us. For instance, when a new insect first arrived on an island, selection will enlarge or reduce the wings, depending on whether a greater number of individuals were saved by battling with the winds, or by rarely or never flying.

When a part has been developed in an extraordinary manner in any one species, we may conclude that this part has undergone an extraordinary amount of modification, since the period when the species branched off from the common progenitor.

Distinct species present analogous variations; and a variety of one species often assumes some of the characters of an allied species, or reverts to some of the characters of an early progenitor. After twelve generations, the proportion of blood, to use a common expression, of any one ancestor, is only 1 in 2048; and yet it seems that a tendency to reversion is retained by this very small proportion of foreign blood.

DIFFICULTIES ON THEORY

Difficulties and objections may be classed under the following heads:- Firstly, why, if species have descended from other species by minuscule gradations, do we not everywhere see innumerable transitional forms? Secondly, is it possible that an animal having, for instance, the structure and habits of a bat, could have been formed by the modification of some animal with wholly different habits? Can we believe that natural selection could produce, on the one hand, organs of trifling importance, such as the tail of a giraffe, which serves as a fly-flapper, and, on the other hand, such wonderful structures as the eye, of which we hardly as yet understand the inimitable perfection? Thirdly, can instincts be acquired and modified through natural selection?

As to the rarity of transitional varieties, as natural selection acts solely by the preservation of profitable modifications, each new form will tend to take the place of, and finally to exterminate, its less improved parent. Hence, if we look at each species as descended from some other unknown form, both the parent and all the transitional varieties will generally have exterminated by the very process of formation and perfection of the new form. Furthermore, forms existing in larger numbers will always have a better chance, within any given period, of presenting further favourable variations for natural selection to seize on, than will the rarer forms which exist in lesser numbers. So that, in any one region and at any one time, we ought only to see

a few species presenting slight modifications of structure in some degree permanent; and this assuredly we do see. Consequently evidence of the existence of earlier forms could be found only amongst fossil remains which are preserved, and as we shall in a future chapter attempt to show, these form an extremely imperfect and intermittent record.

In considering how animals of precise and perfected structure might arise from quite different forms, look at the family of squirrels. Here we have fine gradation from animals with their tails only slightly flattened, and others, as Sir J. Richardson has remarked, with the posterior part of their bodies and the skin on their flanks rather full, to the so-called flying squirrels with their limbs united by a broad expanse of skin, which serves as a parachute and allows them to glide through the air from tree to tree. I can see no difficulty in the continued preservation of individuals with fuller and fuller flank-membranes, each useful modification being propagated, until the accumulated effects of this process of natural selection produced a perfect so-called flying squirrel. When we see any structure perfected for any particular habit, as the wings of a bird for flight, we should bear in mind that animals displaying transitional grades of the structure will seldom continue to exist, having been supplanted by the very process of perfection through natural selection.

He who believes in separate and innumerable acts of creation will say that it has pleased the Creator to cause a being of one type to take the place of one of another type. He who believes in the struggle for existence and in the principle of natural selection, will acknowledge that every organic being is constantly endeavouring to increase in numbers; and that if any one being varies ever so little in habits or structure, and thus gains an advantage over some other inhabitant of the country, it will seize on the place of that inhabitant. Hence, it will cause him no surprise that there should be geese and frigate-birds with webbed feet living away from water; long-toed corncrakes living in meadows instead of in swamps; or woodpeckers where not a tree grows.

Organs of extreme perfection and complication. - To suppose that the eye could have been formed by natural selection, seems absurd. Yet reason tells me, that if gradations from a perfect and complex eye to one very imperfect and simple, can be shown to exist; if further, the eye does vary ever so slightly, and the variations be inherited, which is certainly the case; and if any variation or modification in the organ be ever useful to an animal under changing conditions of life, then the difficulty of believing that a perfect and complex eye could be formed by natural selection, though insuperable by our imagination, can hardly be considered real.

In the Articulata we see an optic nerve merely coated with pigment, and without any other mechanism. In certain crustaceans, there is a double cornea, with a lens-shaped swelling. In other crustaceans the transparent cones which are coated by pigment, are convex at their upper ends and must act by convergence; and at their lower ends there seems to be an imperfect vitreous substance. These facts, here far too briefly and imperfectly given, show that there is much graduated diversity in the eyes of living crustaceans.

He who will go thus far ought not to hesitate to go further, and to admit that a structure even as perfect as the eye of an eagle might be formed by natural selection. His reason ought to conquer his imagination. It is scarcely possible to avoid comparing the eye to a telescope. We know that this instrument has been perfected by the long-continued efforts of the highest human intellects; and we naturally infer that the eye has been formed by a somewhat analogous process. Is it not presumptuous to assume that the Creator works by intellectual powers like those of man?

INSTINCT

I will treat the subject of instinct separately, especially as such wonderful instincts as those of the hive-bee will probably have occurred to many readers. I am not explaining the origin of mental powers, any more than of life itself. 'Instinct' embraces many mental actions; but every one understands what is meant when it is said that instinct impels the cuckoo to migrate and to lay her eggs in other birds' nests. A little dose, as Huber says, of judgement or reason, is apparent, even in the lowliest of animals.

Instincts are certainly as important as corporeal structure for the welfare of each species. Under changed conditions of life, it is at least possible that slightly changed instincts might be profitable; and if it can be shown that instincts do vary ever so little, then I can see no difficulty in natural selection preserving and accumulating their variations.

But, as with corporeal structures, we ought to find in nature, not the actual transitional gradations by which each complex instinct has been acquired, but only the collateral lines of descent; or we ought at least to be able to show that gradations are possible. But I am well aware that these general statements, without detailed facts, can produce but a feeble effect on the reader's mind.

Mozart played the pianoforte at three years old with wonderfully little practice, only if he had played with no practice at all could we say he did so instinctively.

Familiarity alone prevents our seeing how universally the minds of our domestic animals have been modified by domestication. How rarely do our civilised dogs, even when young, require to be taught not to attack livestock! When occasionally they do attack, they are then beaten; and if not cured, are destroyed; so that habit, with some degree of selection, has probably civilised our dogs.

Domestic instincts are sometimes thought to be inherited from long-continued habit, but this, I think, is not true. No one would ever have thought of teaching, or probably could have taught, the tumbler-pigeon to tumble, an action which, as I have witnessed, is performed by young birds, that have never seen a pigeon tumble. We may believe that some one pigeon showed a slight tendency to this strange habit, and that selection in successive generations made tumblers what they now are.

Huber has observed an ant (*Formica polyerges*) in which both males and fertile females do no work other than capturing slaves. They are incapable of making their own nests, or of feeding their own larvae. So utterly helpless are the masters, that when Huber shut up thirty of them without a slave, but with ample food, and their larvae to stimulate them to work, they did nothing; they could not even feed themselves, and many perished of hunger. Huber then introduced a single slave (*F. fusca*), and she instantly set to work, fed and saved the survivors; made cells, tended the larvae, and put all to rights. Are these facts not extraordinary?

By what steps the slave-making instinct originated I will not pretend to conjecture. But as ants will, as I have seen, carry off pupae of other species, it is possible that pupae originally stored as food might become developed; and the ants thus unintentionally reared would then follow their instincts to work. If their presence proved useful to the species which had seized them, then the habit of collecting pupae originally for food might by natural selection be strengthened and rendered permanent for the purpose of raising slaves.

The hive bee has perfected the art of making its cells the proper shape to hold the greatest possible amount of honey, with the least possible consumption of precious wax. Indeed, the geometer Professor Miller, of Cambridge, tells me that the shape could not be bettered. Natural selection of each tiny modification profitable to the individual seems the only possible explanation.

Finally, it may not be a logical deduction, but I feel that such instincts as the young cuckoo ejecting its foster-brothers, ants making slaves, ichneumonidae larvae feeding within live caterpillars, are not specially created instincts, but are small consequences of one general law, leading to the advancement of all organic beings, namely; multiply, vary, let the strongest live and the weakest die.

THE IMPERFECTION OF THE GEOLOGICAL RE-CORD

In a previous chapter I endeavoured to show that intermediate varieties, from existing in lesser numbers than the forms which they connect, will generally be beaten out and exterminated during the course of further modification and improvement.

It is hardly possible for me even to recall to one who is not a practical geologist, the facts leading the mind feebly to comprehend the lapse of time. It is not enough to study the principles of geology, a man must for years examine for himself great piles of superimposed strata, and watch the sea at work grinding down old rocks, before he can hope to comprehend anything of the lapse of time, the monuments of which we see around us.

To give a small example, consider the denudation of the Weald, though this is but a mere trifle. Standing on the North Downs one can safely picture to oneself the great dome of rocks which must have covered up the Weald. The distance from the northern to the southern Downs is about 22 miles, and the thickness of the several formations is on an average about 1100 feet, says Prof. Ramsay. If their denudation had proceeded at a rate of one inch per century, which would be an ample allowance, the denudation of the Weald must have required 306,662,400 years; or say three hundred million years.

That our palaeontological collections are very imperfect, is admitted by every one. The late Edward Forbes noted that many of our fossil species are known and named from single and often broken specimens, or from specimens collected on one spot. Only a small portion of the surface of the earth has been geologically explored, and no part with sufficient care. Further even shells and bones will decay and disappear when left on the bottom of the sea. Such as is preserved is held only when sediment is deposited over it, yet the bright purity of much of the seas tells that this but rarely happens. For instance, only one single land shell is known in the whole carboniferous strata of North America. The consideration of these facts impresses my mind almost in the same manner as does the vain endeavour to grapple with the idea of eternity.

Those who think the natural geological record in any degree perfect, and who do not attach much weight to the facts and arguments given in this volume, will reject my theory. For my part, following Lyell's metaphor, I look at the natural geological record, as a history of the world imperfectly written in a changing dialect; of this history we possess the last volume alone, and that of only two or three countries. Of this volume, only here and there a short chapter has been preserved; and of each page, only here and there a few lines.

ON THE GEOLOGICAL SUCCESSION

Let us now see whether the facts of geological succession better accord with the common view of the immutability of species, or with that of gradual modification.

In the oldest tertiary beds a few living shells may still be found among a multitude of extinct forms. But, when a species has once disappeared from the face of the earth, we have reason to believe that the same identical form never reappears.

This whole subject of extinction has been involved in the most gratuitous mystery. Some authors have even supposed that as the individual has a definite length of life, so have species a definite duration. When I found in La Plata the tooth of a horse along with the remains of Mastodon, Megatherium, and other extinct monsters, which all co-existed, I was filled with astonishment. Seeing that the horse, since its introduction by the Spaniards into South America, has run wild over the whole country, I asked myself what could so recently have exterminated the former horse under conditions of life apparently so favourable. My astonishment was groundless, for we cannot tell what unfavourable conditions checked its increase.

It is worth noting that the improved and modified descendants of a species will generally cause the extermination of their nearest allies. Therefore, the utter extinction of a group is generally a slower process than its production.

On the Affinities of extinct Species to each other, and to living forms- As Buckland remarked, all fossils belong either in still existing groups, or between them. Some writers have objected to extinct species being considered intermediate between living species. This objection may have some validity, yet if we compare the older Reptiles and Batrachians, the older Fish, the older Cephalopods, and the eocene Mammals, with the more recent, we must admit that there is some truth in the remark.

On this theory, it is evident that the fauna of any great period in the earth's history will be intermediate in general character between that which preceded and that which succeeded it. I need give only one instance, namely, the manner in which the fossils of the Devonian system were at once recognised by palaeontologists as intermediate in character between those of the overlying carboniferous, and underlying Silurian system.

On the state of Development of Ancient Forms-. In one particular sense the more recent forms must, on my theory, be higher than the more ancient; for each new species is formed by having had some advantage in the struggle for life over preceding forms. If the eocene inhabitants were put into competition with the existing inhabitants, the eocene fauna or flora would certainly be beaten and exterminated; as would a secondary fauna by an eocene, and a palaeozoic fauna by a secondary fauna.

Mr. Agassiz insists that ancient animals partly resemble recent animals of the same classes. The embryo seems a sort of picture, preserved by nature, of the ancient and less modified form of each animal. This view may be true, and yet it may never be capable of full proof.

On the Succession of the same Types within the same areas - Mr. Clift many years ago showed that fossil mammals from the Australian caves were closely allied to the living marsupials. In South America, a similar relationship is manifest, even to an uneducated eye, in the gigantic pieces of armadillo-like armour, found in La Plata. On the theory of descent with modification, the great law of the long enduring, but not immutable, succession of the same types within the same areas, is at once explained.

If then the geological record be as imperfect as I believe it to be, and it cannot be proved more perfect, then the main objections to the theory of natural selection are greatly diminished or disappear.

GEOGRAPHICAL DISTRIBUTION

In considering the distribution of organic beings over the face of the globe, the first fact which strikes us is, that the similarity and dissimilarity of the inhabitants of various regions cannot be accounted for by their climatal and other physical conditions. The case of America alone would almost suffice to prove its truth. If we travel over the vast American continent, we find deserts, mountains, grassy plains, forests, marshes, lakes, and great rivers, under almost every temperature. There is hardly a climate or condition in the Old World which cannot be paralleled in the New. Yet how widely different are their living productions!

A second great fact which strikes us is, that barriers of any kind, or obstacles to free migration, are related in a close and important manner to the differences between the productions of various regions. On each continent we find different productions in different regions; though as mountain chains, deserts, &c., are not as impassable as the oceans separating continents, the differences are less than those of distinct continents.

Beyond the westward shores of America, a wide space of open ocean extends, with not an island as a halting-place for emigrants. Here we have a barrier of another kind, and as soon as this is passed we meet in the eastern islands of the Pacific, with another and totally distinct fauna. Proceeding still further westward we come to the shores of Africa, where we meet with quite different productions. The plains near the Straits of Magellan are inhabited by a species of Rhea (American ostrich), and northward the plains of La Plata by another species of the same genus; but not by the true ostrich or emeu found in Africa and Australia. We see in these facts some deep organic bond, prevailing throughout space and time, over the same areas of land and water, and independent of their physical conditions.

We are thus brought to the question as to whether species have been created at one or more points of the earth's surface. The conditions of life are so nearly the same that a multitude of European animals and plants have become naturalised in America and Australia; and some of the aboriginal plants are identical at distant points of the northern and southern hemispheres. If the existence of similar species at distant and isolated points of the earth's surface can in many instances be explained by species having migrated from a single birthplace we must then ask if such transport is possible.

 Seeds may be occasionally transported on drift timber, in the carcasses of birds or, indeed, through living birds.

For myself, I am disposed to the view that much dispersal occurred during the Glacial period. The very wide distribution of alpine species seems to attest to this. We have evidence of almost every kind, organic and inorganic, that within a very recent geological period, central Europe and North America suffered an Arctic climate. The ruins of a house burnt by fire do not tell their tale more plainly, than do the mountains of Scotland, with their scored flanks, and perched boulders, of the icy streams with which their valleys were lately filled. As each southern zone became fitted for arctic beings and ill-fitted for their former more temperate inhabitants, the latter would be supplanted by arctic productions. The inhabitants of the temperate regions would at the same time travel southward where they could.

The many cases we find of relationship, without identity, of the inhabitants of seas now disjoined, and likewise of the past and present inhabitants of the temperate lands of North America and Europe, are inexplicable on the theory of creation.

As lakes and river-systems are separated from each other by barriers of land, it might have been thought that fresh-water productions would not have ranged widely within the same country, yet alone would have extended to distant countries. But not only have many fresh-water species, an enormous range, but allied species prevail in a remarkable manner throughout the world. I well remember, when first collecting in the fresh waters of Brazil, feeling much surprise at the similarity of the fresh-water insects, shells, &c., and at the dissimilarity of the surrounding terrestrial beings, compared with those of Britain.

But this wide range, can, I think, in most cases be explained by their having become fitted, in a manner highly useful to them, for short and frequent migrations from pond to pond, or from stream to stream. Sir Charles Lyell informs me that a Dyticus has been caught with an Ancylus (a shell like a limpet) firmly adhering to it; and a Colymbetes water-beetle once flew on board the 'Beagle,' when forty-five miles distant from the nearest land. I have myself germinated 537 plants from as much pond-mud as would be contained in a breakfast cup! Nature, like a careful gardener, thus takes her seeds from a bed of a particular nature, and drops them in another equally well fitted for them.

On the Inhabitants of Oceanic Islands- The most striking and important fact for us in regard to the inhabitants of islands, is their affinity to those of the nearest mainland, without being actually the same species. I will give the example of the Galapagos Archipelago, situated under the equator, some 550 miles off South America.

There is nothing in the land or climate of the islands, which resembles closely the conditions of the South American coast: in fact there is a considerable dissimilarity. On the other hand, there is considerable resemblance between the Galapagos and Cape de Verde Archipelagos: but what an entire and absolute difference in their inhabitants! The inhabitants of the Cape de Verde Islands are related to those of Africa, those of the Galapagos to America. I believe this grand fact can receive no sort of explanation on the ordinary view of independent creation; whereas on the view here maintained, it is obvious that the Galapagos Islands would be likely to receive colonists, whether by occasional means of transport or by formerly continuous land, from America; and the Cape de Verde Islands from Africa; and that such colonists would be liable to modification;- the principle of inheritance still betraying their original birthplace. Many facts could be given to support an almost universal rule that the endemic productions of islands are related to those of the nearest continent, or near islands.

MUTUAL AFFINITIES OF ORGANIC BEINGS

From the first dawn of life, all organic beings are found to resemble each other in descending degrees, so that they can be classed in groups. The existence of groups would have been of simple signification, if one group had been exclusively fitted to inhabit the land, and another the water; one to feed on flesh, another on vegetable matter, and so on; but the case is that even the same subgroup have different habits.

Morphology is the very soul of natural history. What can be more curious than that the hand of a man, formed for grasping, that of a mole for digging, the leg of the horse, the paddle of the porpoise, and the wing of the bat, should all be constructed on the same pattern, of the same bones, in the same relative positions?

We see the same great law in the construction of the mouths of insects: what can be more different than the long spiral proboscis of a sphinx-moth, the curious folded one of a bee or bug, and the great jaws of a beetle? - yet all these organs, serving for such different purposes, are formed by modifications of an upper lip, mandibles and maxillae. So it is with the flowers of plants, with the limbs of crustaceans and many others.

The ordinary view of creation can only say that;- it has so pleased the Creator to construct each animal and plant. On the theory of the natural selection, it can be said that each modification has little or no tendency to modify the original pattern, or to transpose parts. Bones might be shortened and widened, become gradually enveloped in thick membrane, so as to serve as a fin; or a webbed foot might have its bones lengthened, and the membrane connecting them increased, so as to serve as a wing: yet in all this great amount of modification there will be no tendency to alter the framework of bones or the relative connexion of the several parts.

Embryology- How can we explain these several facts in embryology,- namely of the striking similarity between embryos of different species. I believe that all these facts can be explained only on the view of descent with modification.

Rudimentary, atrophied, or aborted organs- These are extremely common throughout nature. For instance, rudimentary mammae are very general in the males of mammals. Nothing can be plainer than that wings are formed for flight, yet in how many insects do we see wings so reduced in size as to be utterly incapable of flight, and not rarely lying under wing-cases, firmly soldered together!

Every one must be struck with astonishment: for the same reasoning which tells us that most parts and organs are exquisitely adapted for certain purposes, tells us with equal plainness that these rudimentary or atrophied organs, are imperfect and useless. In works on natural history rudimentary organs are generally said to have been created 'for the sake of symmetry,' or in order 'to complete the scheme of nature;' but this seems to me no explanation, merely a restatement of the fact. On the view of descent with modification, we may conclude that the existence of organs in a rudimentary, imperfect, and useless condition, far from presenting a strange difficulty, as they assuredly do on the ordinary doctrine of creation, might even have been anticipated and accounted for by the laws of inheritance.

Finally, the several classes of facts which have been considered in this chapter, seem to me to proclaim so plainly, that the innumerable species, genera, and families of organic beings, with which this world is peopled, have all descended, each within its own class or group, from common parents, and have all been modified in the course of descent.

RECAPITULATION AND CONCLUSION

That many and grave objections may be advanced against the theory of descent with modification through natural selection, I do not deny. Nothing at first can appear more difficult to believe than that complex organs and instincts should have been perfected, not by means analogous with human reason, but by the accumulation of innumerable slight variations. Nevertheless, this difficulty cannot be considered real if we admit the following propositions, namely; that there are gradations in the perfection of any organ or instinct, - that all organs and instincts are, in ever so slight a degree, variable, - and, lastly, that there is a struggle for existence leading to the preservation of each profitable deviation of structure or instinct. The truth of these propositions cannot, I think, be disputed.

In the distant future I see this understanding opening fields for far more important researches. Psychology will be based on a new foundation, that of the necessary acquirement of each mental power and capacity by gradation. Light will be thrown on the origin of man and his history.

Authors of the highest eminence seem to be fully satisfied with the view that each species has been independently created. To my mind it accords better with what we know of the laws impressed on matter by the Creator, that the production and extinction of the past and present inhabitants of the world should have been due to secondary causes, like those determining the birth and death of the individual. When I view all beings not as special creations, but as the lineal descendants of some few beings which lived long before the first Silurian age, they seem to me to become ennobled. And as natural selection works solely by and for the good of each being, all corporeal and mental endowments will tend to progress towards perfection.

It is interesting to contemplate an entangled bank, clothed with many plants of many kinds, with birds singing on the bushes, insects flitting about and worms crawling through the damp earth, and to reflect that these forms, so different yet so dependent on each other in so complex a manner, have all been produced by simple laws. There is grandeur in this view of life, with its several powers, having been originally breathed by the Creator into a few forms or into one; and that, whilst this planet has gone circling on according to the fixed law of gravity, from so simple a beginning endless forms most beautiful and most wonderful have been, and are being evolved.

Les Misérables
by Victor (Marie) Hugo
(Paris, 1862)

This essay on generosity, one of the best-known novels of the 19th century, has generated numerous stage and screen adaptations, of which the most famous is the opera known simply as *'Les Mis'*.
Abridged: JH/GH

Jean Valjean, Galley-Slave

Early in October 1815, at the close of the afternoon, a man came into the little town of D-. He was on foot, and the few people about looked at him suspiciously. The traveller was of wretched appearance, though stout and robust, and in the full vigour of life. He was evidently a stranger, and tired, dusty, and wearied with a long day's tramp.

But neither of the two inns in the town would give him food or shelter, though he offered good money for payment.

He was an ex-convict - that was enough to exclude him.

In despair he went to the prison, and asked humbly for a night's lodging, but the jailer told him that was impossible unless he got arrested first.

It was a cold night and the wind was blowing from the Alps; it seemed there was no refuge open to him.

Then, as he sat down on a stone bench in the marketplace and tried to sleep, a lady coming out of the cathedral noticed him, and, learning his homeless state, bade him knock at the bishop's house, for the good bishop's charity and compassion were known in all the neighbourhood.

At the man's knock the bishop, who lived alone with his sister, Madame Magloire, and an old housekeeper, said "Come in;" and the ex-convict entered.

He told them at once that his name was Jean Valjean, that he was a galley-slave, who had spent nineteen years at the hulks, and that he had been walking for four days since his release. "It is the same wherever I go," the man went on. "They all say to me, 'Be off!' I am very tired and hungry. Will you let me stay here? I will pay."

"Madame Magloire," said the bishop, "please lay another knife and fork. Sit down, monsieur, and warm yourself. We shall have supper directly, and your bed will be got ready while we are supping."

Joy and amazement were on the man's face; he stammered his thanks as though beside himself.

The bishop, in honour of his guest, had silver forks and spoons placed on the table. The man took his food with frightful voracity, and paid no attention to anyone till the meal was over. Then the bishop showed him his bed in an alcove, and an hour later the whole household was asleep.

Jean Valjean soon woke up again. For nineteen years he had been at the galleys. Originally a pruner of trees, he had broken a baker's window and stolen a loaf one hard winter when there was no work to be had, and for this the sentence was five years. Time after time he had tried to escape, and had always been recaptured; and for each offence a fresh sentence was imposed.

Nineteen years for breaking a window and stealing a loaf! He had gone into prison sobbing and shuddering. He came out full of hatred and bitterness.

That night, at the bishop's house, for the first time in nineteen years, Jean Valjean had received kindness. He was moved and shaken. It seemed inexplicable.

He got up from his bed. Everyone was asleep, the house was perfectly still. Jean Valjean seized the silver plate-basket which stood in the bishop's room, put the silver into his knapsack, and fled out of the house.

In the morning, while the bishop was breakfasting, the gendarmes brought in Jean Valjean. The sergeant explained that they had met him running away, and had arrested him, because of the silver they found on him.

"I gave you the candlesticks, too!" said the bishop; "they are silver. Why did not you take them with the rest of the plate?" Then, turning to the gendarmes, "It is a mistake."

"We are to let him go?" said the sergeant.

"Certainly," said the bishop.

The gendarmes retired.

"My friend," said the bishop to Jean Valjean, "here are your candlesticks. Take them with you." He added in a low voice, "Never forget that you have promised me to use this silver to become an honest man. My brother, you belong no longer to evil, but to good."

Jean Valjean never remembered having promised anything. He left the bishop's house and the town dazed and stupefied. It was a new world he had come into.

He walked on for miles, and then sat down by the roadside to think.

Presently a small Savoyard boy passed him, and as he passed dropped a two-franc piece on the ground. Jean Valjean placed his foot upon it. In vain the boy prayed him for the coin. Jean Valjean sat motionless, deep in thought.

Only when the boy had gone on, in despair, did Jean Valjean wake from his reverie.

He shouted out, "Little Gervais, little Gervais!" for the boy had said his name. The lad was out of sight and hearing, and no answer came.

The enormity of his crime came home to him, and Jean Valjean fell on the ground, and for the first time in nineteen years he wept.

Father Madeleine

On a certain December night in 1815 a stranger entered the town of M-, at the very time when a great fire had just broken out in the town hall.

This man at once rushed into the flames, and at the risk of his own life saved the two children of the captain of gendarmes. In consequence of this act no one thought of asking for his passport.

The stranger settled in the town; by a happy invention he improved the manufacture of the black beads, the chief industry of M-, and in three years, from a very small capital, he became a rich man, and brought prosperity to the place.

In 1820, Father Madeleine, for so the stranger was called, was made Mayor of M- by unanimous request, an honour he had declined the previous year. Before he came everything was languishing in the town, and now, a few years later, there was healthy life for all.

Father Madeleine employed everybody who came to him. The only condition he made was - honesty. From the men he expected good-will, from the women, purity.

Prosperity did not make Father Madeleine change his habits. He performed his duties as mayor, but lived a solitary and simple life, avoiding society. His strength, although he was a man of fifty, was enormous. It was noticed that he read more as his leisure increased, and that as the years went by his speech became gentler and more polite.

One person only in all the district looked doubtfully at the mayor, and that was Javert, inspector of police.

Javert, born in prison, was the incarnation of police duty – implacable, resolute, fanatical. He arrived in M- when Father Madeleine was already a rich man, and he felt sure he had seen him before.

One day in 1823 the mayor interfered to prevent Javert sending a poor woman, named Fantine, to prison. Fantine had been dismissed from the factory without the knowledge of M. Madeleine; and her one hope in life was in her little girl, whom she called Cosette. Now, Cosette was boarded out at the village of Montfermeil, some leagues distance from M-, with a family grasping and dishonest, and to raise money for Cosette's keep had brought Fantine to misery and sickness.

The mayor could save Fantine from prison, he could not save her life; but before the unhappy woman died she had delivered a paper to Mr. Madeleine authorising him to take her child, and Mr. Madeleine had accepted the trust.

It was when Fantine lay dying in the hospital that Javert, who had quite decided in his own mind who M. Madeleine was, came to the mayor and asked to be dismissed from the service.

"I have denounced you, M. le Maire, to the prefect of police at Paris as Jean Valjean, an ex-convict, who has been wanted for the robbery of a little Savoyard more than five years ago."

"And what answer did you receive?"

"That I was mad, for the real Jean Valjean has been found."

"Ah!"

Javert explained that an old man had been arrested for breaking into an orchard; that on being taken to the prison he had been recognised by several people as Jean Valjean, and that he, Javert, himself recognised him. To-morrow he was to be tried at Arras, and, as he was an ex-convict, his sentence would be for life.

Terrible was the anguish of M. Madeleine that night. He had done all that man could do to obliterate the past, and now it seemed another was to be taken in his place. The torture and torment ended. In the morning M. Madeleine set out for Arras.

M. Madeleine arrived before the orchard-breaker was condemned. He proved to the court's astonishment that he, the revered and philanthropic Mayor of M-, was Jean Valjean, and that the prisoner had merely committed a trivial theft. Then he left the court, returned to M-, removed what money he had, buried it, and arranged his affairs.

A few days later Jean Valjean was sent back to the galleys at Toulon, and with his removal the prosperity of M- speedily collapsed. This was in July 1823. In November of that year the following paragraph appeared

in the Toulon paper: "Yesterday, a convict, on his return from rescuing a sailor, fell into the sea and was drowned. His body has not been found. His name was registered as Jean Valjean."

A Hunted Man

At Christmas, in the year 1823, an old man came to the village of Montfermeil, called at the inn, paid money to the rascally innkeeper, Thenardier, and carried off little Cosette to Paris.

The old man rented a large garret in an old house, and Cosette became inexpressibly happy with her doll and with the good man who loved her so tenderly.

Till then Jean Valjean had never loved anything. He had never been a father, lover, husband, or friend. When he saw Cosette, and had rescued her, he felt his heart strangely moved. All the affection he had was aroused, and went out to this child. Jean Valjean was fifty-five and Cosette eight, and all the love of his life, hitherto untouched, melted into a benevolent devotion.

Cosette, too, changed. She had been separated from her mother at such an early age that she could not remember her. And the Thenardiers had treated her harshly. In Jean Valjean she found a father, just as he found a daughter in Cosette.

Weeks passed away. These two beings led a wonderfully happy life in the old garret; Cosette would chatter, laugh, and sing all day. Jean Valjean was careful never to go out in the daytime, but he began to be known in the district as "the mendicant who gives away money." There was one old man who sat by some church steps, and who generally seemed to be praying, whom Jean Valjean always liked to relieve. One night when Jean Valjean had dropped a piece of money into his hand as usual, the beggar suddenly raised his eyes, stared hard at him, and then quickly dropped his head. Jean Valjean started, and went home greatly troubled.

The face which he fancied he had seen was that of Javert.

A few nights later Jean Valjean found that Javert had taken lodgings in the same house where he and Cosette lived. Taking the child by the hand, he at once set out for fresh quarters. They passed through silent and empty streets, and crossed the river, and it seemed to Jean Valjean that no one was in pursuit. But soon he noticed four men plainly shadowing him, and a shudder went over him. He turned from street to street, trying to escape from the city, and at last found himself entrapped in a *cul-de-sac*. What was to be done?

There was no time to turn back. Javert had undoubtedly picketed every outlet. Fortunately for Jean Valjean, there was a deep shadow in the street, so that his own movements were unseen.

While he stood hesitating, a patrol of soldiers entered the street, with Javert at their head. They frequently halted. It was evident that they were exploring every hole and corner, and one might judge they would take a quarter of an hour before they reached the spot where Jean Valjean was. It was a frightful moment. Capture meant the galleys, and Cosette lost for ever. There was only one thing possible - to scale the wall which ran along a wide portion of the street. But the difficulty was Cosette; there was no thought of abandoning her.

First, Jean Valjean procured a rope from the lamppost. This he fastened round the child, taking the other end between his teeth. Half a minute later he was on his knees on the top of the wall. Cosette watched him in silence. All at once she heard Jean Valjean saying in a very low voice, "Lean against the wall. Don't speak, and don't be afraid."

She felt herself lifted from the ground, and before she had time to think where she was she found herself on the top of the wall.

Jean Valjean grasped her, put the child on his back, and crawled along the wall till he came to a sloping roof. He could hear the thundering voice of Javert giving orders to the patrol to search the *cul-de-sac* to the end.

Jean Valjean slipped down the roof, still carrying Cosette, and leaped on the ground. It was a convent garden he had entered.

On the other side of the wall the clatter of muskets and the imprecations of Javert resounded; from the convent came a hymn.

Cosette and Jean Valjean fell on their knees. Presently Jean Valjean discovered that the gardener was an old man whose life he had saved at M-, and who, in his gratitude, was prepared to do anything for M. Madeleine.

It ended in Cosette entering the convent school as a pupil, and Jean Valjean being accepted as the gardener's brother. The good nuns never left the precincts of their convent, and cared nothing for the world beyond their gates.

As for Javert, he had delayed attempting an arrest, even when his suspicions had been aroused, because, after all, the papers said the convict was dead. But once convinced, he hesitated no longer.

His disappointment when Jean Valjean escaped him was midway between despair and fury. All night the search went on; but it never occurred to Javert that a steep wall of fourteen feet could be climbed by an old man with a child.

Several years passed at the convent.

Jean Valjean worked daily in the garden, and shared the hut and the name of the old gardener, M. Fauchelevent. Cosette was allowed to see him for an hour every day.

The peaceful garden, the fragrant flowers, the merry cries of the children, the grave and simple women, gradually brought happiness to Jean Valjean; and his heart melted into gratitude for the security he had found.

Higher than Duty

For six years Cosette and Jean Valjean stayed at the convent; and then, on the death of the old gardener, Jean Valjean, now bearing the name of Fauchelevent, decided that as Cosette was not going to be a nun, and as recognition was no longer to be feared, it would be well to remove into the city.

So a house was taken in the Rue Plumet, and here, with a faithful servant, the old man dwelt with his adopted child. But Jean Valjean took other rooms in Paris, in case of accidents.

Cosette was growing up. She was conscious of her good looks, and she was in love with a well-connected youth named Marius, the son of Baron Pontmercy.

Jean Valjean learnt of this secret love-making with dismay. The idea of parting from Cosette was intolerable to him.

Then, in June 1832, came desperate street fighting in Paris, and Marius was in command of one of the revolutionary barricades.

At this barricade Javert had been captured as a spy, and Jean Valjean, who was known to the revolutionaries, found his old, implacable enemy tied to a post, waiting to be shot. Jean Valjean requested to be allowed to blow out Javert's brains himself, and permission was given.

Holding a pistol in his hand, Jean Valjean led Javert, who was still bound, to a lane out of sight of the barricade, and there with his knife cut the ropes from the wrists and feet of his prisoner.

"You are free," he said. "Go; and if by chance I leave this place alive, I am to be found under the name of Fauchelevent, in the Rue de l'Homme-Arme, No. 7."

Javert walked a few steps, and then turned back, and cried, "You worry me. I would rather you killed me!"

"Go!" was the only answer from Jean Valjean.

Javert moved slowly away; and when he had disappeared Jean Valjean discharged his pistol in the air.

Soon the last stand of the insurgents was at an end, and the barricade destroyed. Jean Valjean, who had taken no part in the struggle, beyond exposing himself to the bullets of the soldiers, was unhurt; but Marius lay wounded and insensible in his arms.

The soldiers were shooting down all who tried to escape. The situation was terrible.

There was only one chance for life - underground. An iron grating, which led to the sewers, was at his feet. Jean Valjean tore it open, and disappeared with Marius on his shoulders.

He emerged, after a horrible passage through a grating by the bank of the river, only to find there the implacable Javert!

Jean Valjean was quite calm.

"Inspector Javert," he said, "help me to carry this man home; then do with me what you please."

A cab was waiting for the inspector. He ordered the man to drive to the address Jean Valjean gave him. Marius, still unconscious, was taken to his grandfather's house.

"Inspector Javert," said Jean Valjean, "grant me one thing more. Let me go home for a minute; then you may take me where you will."

Javert told the driver to go to Rue de l'Homme-Arme, No. 7. When they reached the house, Javert said, "Go up; I will wait here for you!"

But before Jean Valjean reached his rooms Javert had gone, and the street was empty.

Javert had not been at ease since his life had been spared. He was now in horrible uncertainty. To owe his life to an ex-convict, to accept this debt, and then to repay him by sending him back to the galleys was impossible. To let a malefactor go free while he, Inspector Javert, took his pay from the government, was equally impossible. It seemed there was something higher and above his code of duty, something he had not come into collision with before. The uncertainty of the right thing to be done destroyed Javert, to whom life had hitherto been perfectly plain. He could not live recognising Jean Valjean as his saviour, and he could not bring himself to arrest Jean Valjean.

Inspector Javert made his last report at the police-station, and then, unable to face the new conditions of life, walked slowly to the river and plunged into the Seine, where the water rolls round and round in an endless whirlpool.

Marius recovered, and married Cosette; and Jean Valjean lived alone. He had told Marius who he was - Jean Valjean, an escaped convict; and Marius and Cosette gradually saw less and less of the old man.

But before Jean Valjean died Marius learnt the whole truth of the heroic life of the old man who had rescued him from the lost barricade. For the first time he realised that Jean Valjean had come to the barricade only to save him, knowing him to be in love with Cosette.

He hastened with Cosette to Jean Valjean's room; but the old man's last hour had come.

"Come closer, come closer, both of you," he cried. "I love you so much.

It is good to die like this! You love me too, my Cosette. I know you've always had a fondness for the poor old man. And you, M. Pontmercy, will always make Cosette happy. There were several things I wanted to say, but they don't matter now. Come nearer, my children. I am happy in dying!"

Cosette and Marius fell on their knees, and covered his hands with kisses.

Jean Valjean was dead.

Alice's Adventures in Wonderland
by Lewis Carroll (Rev. Charles Lutwidge Dodgson)
(London, 1865)

Dodgson was a mathematics lecturer at Oxford University, a logician and pioneer photographer who delighted in puzzles and nonsense stories. This, probably the most popular children's story of all time, is said to have been invented for Alice Liddell, daughter of the Dean of Christ Church, during a rowing trip on 4th July 1862. Its hallucinogenic style, along with much of Dodgson's private life, remains puzzling.

Abridged: GH. The first illustration is from Dodgson's self-published original, others are by the leading illustrator John Tenniel.

Down the Rabbit-Hole

Alice was beginning to get very tired of sitting by her sister on the bank, and of having nothing to do; once or twice she had peeped into the book her sister was reading, but it had no pictures or conversations in it, "and what is the use of a book," thought Alice, "without pictures or conversations?"

Suddenly a White Rabbit with pink eyes ran close by her. There was nothing so very remarkable in that; nor did Alice think it so very much out of the way to hear the Rabbit say to himself: "Oh, dear! Oh, dear! I shall be too late!" But when the Rabbit actually took a watch out of his waistcoat pocket, Alice started to her feet, for she had never before seen a rabbit with either a waistcoat pocket or a watch to take out of it, and, burning with curiosity, she ran across the field after him, just in time to see him pop down a large rabbit-hole under the hedge.

In another moment down went Alice after him.

The rabbit-hole went straight on like a tunnel for some way, and then dipped suddenly down, so that Alice found herself falling down what seemed to be a very deep well. Down, down, down. Then suddenly, thump! thump! down she came upon a heap of sticks and dry leaves, and the fall was over.

The White Rabbit was still in sight, and away went Alice like the wind, and was just in time to hear him say, as he turned a corner, "Oh, my ears and whiskers, how late it is getting!" She turned the corner, but the Rabbit was no longer to be seen. She found herself in a long narrow hall, which was lit up by lamps hanging from the roof.

In the hall she came upon a little three-legged table, all made of solid glass. There was nothing on it but a tiny golden key. Behind a low curtain, she came upon a little door about fifteen inches high. She tried the little golden key in the lock, and, to her great delight, it fitted.

Alice opened the door, and knelt down and looked along the passage into the loveliest garden you ever saw. But she could not even get her head through the doorway.

So she went back to the table, half hoping she might find a book of rules for shutting people up like telescopes. This time she found a little bottle on it ("which certainly was not here before," said Alice), and tied round the neck of the bottle was a paper label, with the words DRINK ME in large letters. Alice tasted it, and very soon finished it off.

"What a curious feeling!" said Alice. "I must be shutting up like a telescope."

And so it was, indeed; she was now only ten inches high, and soon her eye fell on a little glass box that was lying under the table. She opened it, and found in it a very small cake, on which the words EAT ME were beautifully marked in currants.

She very soon finished off the cake.

"Curiouser and curiouser!" cried Alice. "Now I'm opening out like the largest telescope that ever was. Good-by feet!"

Just at this moment her head struck against the roof of the hall; in fact, she was now more than nine feet high, and she at once took up the little golden key, and hurried off to the garden door.

Poor Alice! To get through was more hopeless than ever. She sat down and began to cry, shedding gallons of tears, until there was a large pool all round her.

After a time she heard a little pattering of feet in the distance, and she hastily dried her eyes to see what was coming. It was the White Rabbit returning, splendidly dressed, with a pair of white kid gloves in one hand and a large fan in the other. He came trotting along in a great hurry, muttering to himself as he came, "Oh, the Duchess! the Duchess!"

Alice felt so desperate that she was ready to ask help of anyone; so, when the Rabbit came near her, she began, in a timid voice: "If you please, sir -"

The Rabbit started violently, dropped the gloves and the fan, and scurried away into the darkness.

The pool, by now, was getting quite crowded with the birds and animals that had fallen into it; there were a duck and a dodo, a lory and an eaglet, and other curious creatures. Alice led the way, and the whole party swam to the shore.

A very queer-looking party of dripping birds and animals now gathered on the bank of the Pool of Tears. The Mouse, tried to dry them by telling them frightfully dry stories from history. Then the Dodo proposed a Caucus race. They all started off when they liked, and stopped when they liked. The Dodo said everybody had won, and Alice had to give the prizes. Luckily she had some sweets, which were not wet, and there was just one for each of them. The party were anxious she, too, should have a prize, and as she happened to have a thimble, the Dodo commanded her to hand it to him, and then, with great ceremony, the Dodo presented it to her, saying, "We beg your acceptance of this elegant thimble," and they all cheered.

The Mouse began to tell Alice why it hated C- and D-, but when Alice mentioned Dinah, her cat, the birds got uneasy, and one by one the whole party gradually went off and left her all alone. Just when she was beginning to cry, she heard a pattering of little feet.

It was the White Rabbit, trotting slowly back again, and looking anxiously about as he went, as if he had lost something and she heard him muttering to himself, "The Duchess! The Duchess!"

Very soon the Rabbit noticed Alice, and called out to her in an angry tone, "Why, Mary Ann, what are you doing out here? Run home this moment, and fetch me a pair of gloves and a fan. Quick, now!"

Alice ran off as hard as she could, and soon found herself safe in a thick wood.

Alice took up the fan and gloves, and, as the hall was very hot, she kept fanning herself all the time she went on talking.

"Dear, dear! How queer everything is to-day! How puzzling it all is!" But presently on looking down at her hands, she was surprised to see that she had put on one of the rabbit's little white kid gloves while she was talking.

"How can I have done that?" she thought. "I must be growing small again."

She soon found out that the cause of this was the fan she was holding, and she dropped it hastily, just in time to save herself from shrinking away altogether. Now she hastened to the little door, but alas, it was shut again. "I declare it's too bad, that it is!" she said aloud, and just as she spoke her foot slipped, and in another moment, splash! she was up to her chin in salt water. It was the pool of tears she had wept when she was nine feet high!

The Pool of Tears

Just then she heard something splashing about in the pool a little way off, and she swam nearer to make out what it was. She soon made out that it was only a mouse that had slipped in like herself.

She began, "O Mouse, do you know the way out of this pool?" The Mouse said nothing.

"Perhaps it doesn't understand English," thought Alice; "I daresay it's a French mouse, come over with William the Conqueror." So she began again, "ou est ma chatte?" which was the first sentence in her French lesson book. The Mouse seemed to quiver all over with fright. "Oh, I beg your pardon!" cried Alice, "I quite forgot you don't like cats."

Advice from a Caterpillar

Peeping over a mushroom, she beheld a large blue caterpillar sitting on the top with its arms folded, quietly smoking a long hookah, and taking not the smallest notice of her or of anything else. At length, in a sleepy sort of way, it began talking to her, and she told it what she wanted so much - to grow to her right size again.

"Three inches" she said, "is such a wretched height to be."

"It is a very good height indeed," said the Caterpillar angrily, (it was exactly three inches high).

"You'll get used to it in time," said the Caterpillar; and it put the hookah into its mouth and began smoking again.

Then it got down off the mushroom, and crawled away into the grass, merely remarking as it went, "One side will make you grow taller, and the other side will make you grow shorter."

"The other side of what?" thought Alice to herself.

"Of the mushroom," said the Caterpillar, just as if she had asked it aloud and in another moment it was out of sight.

Alice broke off a bit of the edge with each hand, and nibbled a little of the right-hand bit to try the effect. The next moment she felt a violent blow underneath her chin; it had struck her foot!

She managed to swallow a morsel of the left-hand bit. The next minute she had grown so tall that her neck rose like a stalk out of a sea of green leaves, and these green leaves were the trees of the wood. But, by nibbling bits of mushroom, she at last succeeded in bringing herself down to her usual height. But, oh dear, in order to get into the first house she saw, she had to eat some more of the mushroom from her right hand and bring herself down to nine inches. Outside the house she saw a Fish-footmen and a Frog-footmen with invitations from the Queen to the Duchess, asking her to play croquet. The Duchess lived in the house, and a terrible noise was going on inside, and when the door was opened a plate came crashing out. But Alice got in at last, and found the Duchess and her cook quarrelling because there was too much pepper in the soup.

The Duchess had the baby in her lap, and tossed it about ridiculously, finally throwing it in the most heartless way to Alice. She took it out of doors, and behold, it turned into a little pig, jumped out of her arms, and ran away into the wood.

"If it had grown up," she said, "it would have made a dreadfully ugly child; but it makes rather a handsome pig, I think."

She was a little startled now by seeing a Cheshire-Cat sitting on a bough of a tree. The Cat grinned when it saw Alice. She felt that it ought to be treated with respect.

"Cheshire Puss," she said, "what sort of people live about here?"

"In that direction," the Cat said, waving its right paw round, "lives a Hatter; and in that direction" - waving the other paw - "lives a March Hare. Visit either you like; they're both mad."

A Mad Tea Party

There was a table set out under a tree in front of the house, and the March Hare and the Hatter were having tea at it; a Dormouse was sitting between them fast asleep, and the other two were using it as a cushion, resting their elbows on it, and talking over its head.

The table was a large one, but the three were all crowded together at one corner.

"No room! No room!" they cried out when they saw Alice coming.

"There's plenty of room!" said Alice indignantly. And she sat down in a large armchair at one end of the table.

"What day of the month is it?" asked the Hatter, turning to Alice.

He had taken his watch out of his pocket and was looking at it uneasily, shaking it every now and then, and holding it to his ear.

Alice considered a little, and said, "The fourth."

"Two days wrong," sighed the Hatter. "I told you butter wouldn't suit the works," he added, looking angrily at the March Hare.

"It was the best butter," the March Hare meekly replied.

"It's always tea-time with us here," explained the Hatter, "and we've no time to wash the things between whiles."

"Then you keep moving round, I suppose?" said Alice.

"Exactly so," said the Hatter; "as the things get used up."

"But when you come to the beginning again?" Alice

ventured to ask.

The March Hare interrupted, yawning. "I vote the young lady tells us a story."

"I'm afraid I don't know one," said Alice, rather alarmed at the proposal.

"Then the Dormouse shall!" they both cried. "Wake up the Dormouse!" And they pinched it on both sides.

The Dormouse slowly opened its eyes. "I wasn't asleep," it said, in a hoarse, feeble voice.

"Tell us a story," said the March Hare.

"Yes, please do!" pleaded Alice.

"Once upon a time there were three little sisters," the Dormouse began, "and their names were Elsie, Lacie, and Tillie and they lived at the bottom of a well - "

"What did they live on?" said Alice.

"They lived on treacle," said the Dormouse, after thinking a minute or two.

Alice gently remarked, "They'd have been ill."

"So they were very ill."

"I want a clean cup," interrupted the Hatter. "Let's all move one place on."

"They were learning to draw," the Dormouse went on, yawning and rubbing its eyes, "and they drew all manner of things - everything that begins with an M. such as mouse-traps, and the moon, and memory, and muchness - you know you say things are 'much of a muchness' - did you ever see such a thing as a drawing of a muchness?"

"Really," said Alice, confused, "I don't think- "

"Then you shouldn't talk," said the Hatter.

This piece of rudeness was more than Alice could bear; she got up in disgust, and walked off. The Dormouse fell asleep instantly, and the last time she saw them, they were trying to put the Dormouse into the teapot.

The Mock Turtle's Story

Alice got into the beautiful garden at last, but she had to nibble a bit of the mushroom again to bring herself down to twelve inches, so as to get through the little door. It was a lovely garden, and in it was the Queen's croquet-ground. The Queen of Hearts was very fond of ordering heads to be cut off. "Off with his head!" was her favourite phrase whenever anybody displeased her. She asked Alice to play croquet with her, but they had no rules; they had live flamingoes for mallets, and the soldiers had to stand on their hands and feet to form the hoops. It was extremely awkward, especially as the balls were hedgehogs, who sometimes rolled away without being hit. The Queen had a great quarrel with the Duchess, and wanted to have her head off.

After the game of croquet, the Queen said to Alice, "Have you seen the Mock Turtle yet?"

Said Alice. "I don't even know what a mock turtle is."

"It's the thing mock turtle soup is made from," said the Queen, "and he shall tell you his history."

They came upon a gryphon, lying fast asleep in the sun.

"Up, lazy thing!" said the Queen; "and take this young lady to see the Mock Turtle. I must go back and see after some executions I have ordered."

Alice and the Gryphon had not gone far before they saw the Mock Turtle in the distance, sitting sad and lonely on a little ledge of rock, and, as they came nearer, Alice could hear him sighing as if his heart would break.

"This here young lady," said the Gryphon, "she wants for to know your history."

"Once," said the Mock Turtle at last, with a deep sigh, "I was a real turtle. When we were little, we went to school in the sea. The master was an old turtle - we used to call him Tortoise."

'Why 'Tortoise', if he wasn't one?' Alice asked.

"Because he taught us," said the Mock Turtle angrily: "really you are very dull!"

We had the best of educations. Reeling and Writhing, of course, to begin with, and then the different branches of Arithmetic - Ambition, Distraction, Uglification, and Derision."

"I never heard of 'Uglification,'" Alice ventured to say.

"Well, then," the Gryphon went on, "if you don't know what to uglify is, you are a simpleton."

Alice said, "What else had you to learn?"

"Well, there was Mystery," the Mock Turtle replied, counting out the subjects on his flappers - "Mystery, ancient and modern, with Seaography; then Drawling - the Drawling-master was an old conger-eel, that used to come once a week; he taught us Drawling, Stretching, and Fainting in Coils. The Classical master taught Laughing and Grief."

"And how many hours a day did you do lessons?" said Alice, in a hurry to change the subject.

"Ten hours the first day, nine the next, and so on."

"What a curious plan!" exclaimed Alice.

"That's the reason they're called lessons," the Gryphon remarked; "because they lessen from day to day."

"That's enough about lessons," the Gryphon interrupted, "Tell her something about the games."

The Mock Turtle sighed deeply, and drew the back of one flapper across his eyes.

"Would you like to see a little of a Lobster Quadrille?" said he to Alice.

"Very much indeed," said Alice.

"Let's try the first figure," said the Mock Turtle to the Gryphon. "We can do without lobsters, you know. Which shall sing?"

"Oh, you sing!" said the Gryphon. "I've forgotten the words."

So they began solemnly dancing round and round Alice, every now and then treading on her toes, and waving their fore-paws to mark the time while the Mock Turtle sang this, very slowly and sadly.

> *"Will you walk a little faster?" said a whiting to a snail,*
> *"There's a porpoise close behind us, and he's treading on my tail.*
> *See how eagerly the lobsters and the turtles all advance!*
> *They are waiting on the shingle-will you come and join the dance?*
> *Will you, won't you, will you, won't you, will you join the dance?*
> *Will you, won't you, will you, won't you, won't you join the dance?"*

"Now, come, let's hear some of your adventures," said the Gryphon to Alice, after the dance.

So Alice began telling them her adventures from the time when she first saw the White Rabbit. After a while a cry of "The Trial's beginning!" was heard in the distance.

"Come on!" cried the Gryphon. And, taking Alice by the hand, it hurried off.

"What trial is it?" Alice panted, as she ran, but the Gryphon only answered, "Come on!" and ran the faster.

Who Stole the Tarts?

The King and Queen of Hearts were seated on their throne when they arrived, with a great crowd assembled about them - all sorts of little birds and beasts, as well as the whole pack of cards. The Knave was standing before them, in chains, with a soldier on each side to guard him; and near the King was the White Rabbit, with a trumpet in one hand, and a scroll of parchment in the other. In the very middle of the court was a table, with a large dish of tarts upon it. They looked so good that it made Alice quite hungry to look at them. "I wish they'd get the trial done," she thought, "and hand round the refreshments." But there seemed to be no chance of this, so she began looking at everything about her to pass away the time.

"Herald, read the accusation!" said the King.

On this the White Rabbit blew three blasts on the trumpet, and then unrolled the parchment scroll, and read as follows.

The Queen of Hearts, she made some tarts,
All on a summer's day;
The Knave of Hearts, he stole those tarts,
And took them quite away.

"Consider your verdict," the King said to the jury.

"Not yet, not yet!" the Rabbit hastily interrupted. "There's a great deal to come before that!"

"Call the first witness," said the King.

The first witness was the Hatter. He came in with a teacup in one hand and a piece of bread-and-butter in the other. "I beg pardon, your Majesty," he began, "I hadn't quite finished my tea when I was sent for."

"Take off your hat," the King said to the Hatter.

"It isn't mine," said the Hatter.

"Stolen!" the King exclaimed.

"I keep them to sell," the Hatter added; "I'm a hatter."

"Give your evidence," said the King, "and don't be nervous, or I'll have you executed on the spot."

Just at this moment Alice felt a very curious sensation, which puzzled her a good deal until she made out what it was. She was beginning to grow larger again.

"I'm a poor man, your Majesty," the Hatter began in a trembling voice, "only the March Hare said- "

"I deny it!" said the March Hare.

"Just take his head off outside," the Queen said to one of the officers; but the Hatter was out of sight before the officer could get to the door.

"Call the next witness!" said the King.

Imagine her surprise when the White Rabbit read out, at the top of his shrill little voice, the name "Alice!"

"Here!" cried Alice, quite forgetting how large she had grown in the last few minutes, she jumped up in such a hurry that she tipped over the jury-box with the edge of her skirt, upsetting all the jurymen on to the heads of the crowd below, and there they lay sprawling about, reminding her very much of a globe of gold-fish she had accidentally upset the week before.

"Oh, I beg your pardon!" she exclaimed, and began picking them up again as quickly as she could.

"What do you know about this business?" the King said.

"Nothing," said Alice.

"That's very important," the King said, turning to the jury. They were just beginning to write this down on their slates, when the White Rabbit interrupted.

"Unimportant, your Majesty means, of course," he said, in a very respectful tone.

Presently the King, who had been for some time busily writing in his notebook, called out "Rule Forty-two. All persons more than a mile high to leave the court."

Everybody looked at Alice.

"I'm not a mile high," said Alice.

"You are," said the King.

"Nearly two miles high," added the Queen.

"Well, I shan't go, at any rate," said Alice. "Besides, that's not a regular rule; you invented it just now."

"It's the oldest rule in the book," said the King.

"Then it ought to be Number One," said Alice.

The King turned pale, and shut his notebook hastily. "Consider your verdict," he said to the jury, in a low, trembling voice.

"No, no!" said the Queen. "Sentence first - verdict afterwards."

"Stuff and nonsense!" said Alice loudly. "The idea of having the sentence first!"

"Hold your tongue!" said the Queen.

"I won't!" said Alice.

"Off with her head!" the Queen shouted at the top of her voice. Nobody moved.

"Who cares for you?" said Alice (she had grown to her full size by this time). "You're nothing but a pack of cards!"

At this the whole pack rose up into the air, and came flying down upon her; she gave a little scream, and tried to beat them off, and found herself lying on the bank, with her head in the lap of her sister, who was gently brushing away some dead leaves that had fluttered down from the trees on her face.

"Oh, I've had such a curious dream!" said Alice.

Crime and Punishment
(Преступление и Наказание)
by Fyodor Dostoyevsky
(Moscow, 1866)

Dostoevsky is repeatedly lauded as the writer with the greatest understanding of human psychology - perhaps borne from his upbringing as the son of an alcoholic military physician, and his four years in Siberia with hard labour for anti-state activity. The subtleties of Russian names don't really make much sense in English translation, which misses, too, the joke that Raskolnikov means something like 'Mr. Separate', Marmeladova is 'Mr. Sweetlady', and so on, marking this story out as a fantastical morality tale.

Abridged: GH, based on the translation by Constance Garnett

I

On an exceptionally hot evening early in July a young man came out of the garret in which he lodged in S-- Place and walked slowly towards K-- bridge. He was hopelessly in debt to his landlady, and successfully avoided meeting her on the staircase.

In fact, he had lately become so completely absorbed in himself, that he dreaded meeting anyone and he had given up attending to matters of practical importance. This evening, however, he became acutely aware of his fears.

"I want to attempt a thing like that and am frightened by trifles," he thought, with an odd smile. "It would be interesting to know what it is men are most afraid of. Taking a new step, uttering a new word? But I am talking too much. I've learned to chatter this last month, lying for days together in my den thinking of Jack the Giant-killer. Why am I going there? Am I capable?"

With a sinking heart and a nervous tremor, he went up to a huge house by the canal, a house let out in tiny tenements to working people of all kinds - tailors, locksmiths, cooks, Germans, girls picking up a living as best they could.

"If I am so scared now, what would it be if I were really going to do it?" he asked himself as he reached the fourth storey. There his progress was barred by some porters moving furniture. "That's a good thing anyway," he thought to himself, as he rang the bell of the old woman's flat. The bell gave a faint tinkle as though it were made of tin and not of copper.

He started, his nerves were terribly overstrained by now. The door was opened, the young man stepped into the dark entry, and the diminutive, withered old woman stood looking inquiringly at him.

"Raskolnikov, a student, I came here a month ago," the young man muttered with a half bow, remembering that he ought to be polite. "Here I am again."

The old woman paused: "Step in, my good sir."

The little room was brightly lit up by the setting sun. Everything was very clean; the floor and the furniture were brightly polished. "Lizaveta's work," thought the young man. There was not a speck of dust to be seen in the whole flat. "It's in the houses of spiteful old widows that one finds such cleanliness."

"I've brought something to pawn, how much will you give me for the watch, Alyona Ivanovna?"

"My good sir, it's scarcely worth anything. A rouble and a half, and interest in advance, if you like!"

"It is worth...!" cried the young man. "Oh, hand it over."

The old woman fumbled in her pocket for her keys, and disappeared into the other room, where the young man could hear her unlocking a chest of drawers.

The old woman came back.

"Here, sir. Ten copecks the rouble a month in advance, and you owe me for last time, so I must give you a rouble and fifteen copecks for the watch. Here it is."

The young man took the money, but hesitated, as if there was still something he wanted to say or to do.

"I may be bringing you something else in a day or two, Alyona Ivanovna - a valuable thing - silver - a cigarette-box, as soon as I get it back from a friend ..." he broke off in confusion.

"Well, we will talk about it then, sir."

"Good-bye - are you always at home alone, your sister Lizaveta is not here with you?" He asked her as casually as possible as he went out into the passage.

"What business is she of yours, my good sir?"

"Oh, nothing particular. Good-day, Alyona Ivanovna."

Raskolnikov went out in complete confusion. When he was in the street he cried out, "Oh, God, how loathsome it all is! How could such an atrocious thing come into my head? Loathsome!"

At that instant two drunken men came out at a door. Raskolnikov at once went to the door end entered. Till that moment he had never been into a tavern, but now he felt tormented by a burning thirst. He sat down at a sticky little table in a dark and dirty corner; ordered some beer, and eagerly drank off the first glassful. At once he felt easier; and his thoughts became clear.

"All that's nonsense," he said hopefully, "there is nothing at all to worry about! How utterly petty it all is!"

There are chance meetings that interest us from before a word is spoken. Such was the impression made on Raskolnikov by the person sitting a little distance from him, who looked like a retired clerk. He was a man over fifty, bald and grizzled, his beardless face bloated from continual drinking. At last he looked straight at Raskolnikov, and said loudly:

"May I venture, honoured sir, to engage you in polite conversation? Marmeladov is my name."

"No, I am studying," answered the young man.

"A student then, or formerly a student," cried the clerk. He got up, staggered, took up his jug and glass, and sat down beside the young man. He was drunk, but spoke fluently and boldly.

"Honoured sir," he began almost with solemnity, "poverty is not a vice, and drunkenness is not a virtue, and that's true. Allow me to ask you a question: have you ever spent a night on a hay barge, on the Neva?"

He emptied his glass, and paused. Bits of hay were clinging to his clothes and sticking to his hair.

"Have you ever had to petition hopelessly for a loan? Do you know, sir, that I have a wife - Katerina Ivanovna? And do you know that I have sold my wife's very stockings for drink? We live in a cold room and she has begun coughing and spitting blood. We have three little children and she works from morning till night. Do you suppose I don't feel it? That's why I drink. I drink so that I may suffer twice as much!"

"Young man," he went on, "in your face I seem to read some trouble of mind. My daughter by my first wife has grown up. What she has had to put up with from her step-mother! Katerina Ivanovna is a grand and spirited lady, but it's no use going over that! Sonia has had no education, though I did try, so do you think she can make a living in a respectable way? I have seen Sonia, when the children are crying from hunger, put on her cape, and go out, and later, come back, and lay thirty roubles on the table. Do you understand, sir? Do you understand what it means when you have absolutely nowhere to turn?

The tavern, the degraded appearance of the man, and yet this sort-of love for his wife and children bewildered his listener.

"This morning I went to see Sonia, for a pick-me-up! He-he-he! This very quart was bought with her thirty copecks yes! And maybe she needs them, eh? For she's got to keep up her appearance. It costs money, petticoats, starched ones, shoes, too, real jaunty ones to show off her foot, that special smartness, you know? Do you understand? Are you sorry for me, sir, or not?"

"Let us go, sir," said Marmeladov all at once, addressing Raskolnikov- "come along with me. I'm going back to Katerina, time I did."

The home, when they reached it, was one poor room, a mere corridor, littered with rags and lighted by a half-candle.

"He's drunk it! he's drunk it all," Ivanovna screamed, "and his clothes are gone! And they are hungry, hungry!" - she pointed to the children. "Are you not ashamed?"- she pounced upon Raskolnikov - "Have you been drinking with him? You have! Go away!"

As he went out, Raskolnikov put his hand into his pocket, to snatch up the coppers he had received in exchange for his rouble in the tavern and to lay them unnoticed on the window.

Outside he sank into thought. "They have Sonia, digging for gold. Man grows used to everything, the scoundrel!"

He woke late next day after a broken sleep, bilious, irritable, ill-tempered, and looked with hatred at his tiny cupboard of a room with the old sofa which served Raskolnikov as a bed.

It was the landlady's maid, Nastasya, who finally roused him with tea.

"Praskovya Pavlovna means to complain to the police about you," she said.

"What!"

"You don't pay her rent, she wants you gone."

"The devil, that's the last straw," he muttered.

"What are you doing now?"

"Work."

"What sort of work?"

"I am thinking," he answered seriously after a pause.

"And have you made much money by your thinking?"

"Oh I know, I can give lessons, but what's the use of a few copecks?" he answered.

"You want to get a fortune all at once?"

"Yes, I want a fortune," he answered firmly.

"Ah, I forgot! A letter came for you when you were out."

It was from his mother. "My dear Rodya," she wrote, "it's two months since I last had a talk with you by letter ... You know how we all look to you ... your sister Dounia has at last escaped from service with the dreadful Svidrigailovs ... at least she managed to save the sixty roubles we sent to you ... soon she will be married, God be thanked, to a lawyer, to Pyotr Petrovitch Luzhin! ... the fifteen roubles I sent you I had borrowed from a merchant against my pension ... perhaps you and her new husband might become partners … true, he is older, and might seem rather self-possessed ... what grief it was to me when I heard that you had given up the university ... best of all, we shall soon come to visit you in Petersburg ... Rodya, you are everything to us ... Do say your prayers, and believe in the mercy of our Creator and Redeemer. Yours till death, Pulcheria Raskolnikov."

As he finished reading, Raskolnikov's face was wet with tears. He took up his hat and went out towards Vassilyevsky Prospect, muttering to himself. Many a passer-by took him to be drunk.

Dounia, he thought, will have to live with the man. She will have to 'keep up appearance,' too. Do you understand what that smartness means? Like Sonia, but viler, baser.

It was clear that he must do something, do it at once, and do it quickly.

"I know, to Vasilievsky Island, to my old university comrade Razumihin." he thought suddenly. "What for, though?"

But Razumihin looked almost as poor as himself. Yes, he did have some work, but three roubles for translating a ridiculous pamphlet, 'Is Woman a Human Being?', from German was not to Raskolnikov's taste.

He went into a miserable little tavern on his way home. He asked for tea, sat down and sank into deep thought. A strange idea was pecking at his brain like a chicken in the egg, and it very, very much absorbed him.

Almost beside him at the next table there was sitting a student and a young officer. All at once he heard the student mention the pawnbroker Alyona Ivanovna.

"She is as rich as a Jew. She can give you five thousand roubles at a time. Her sister Lizaveta is sweet-natured and not without admirers, but a mere slave. The old woman is stupid, senseless, worthless, spiteful, not simply useless but doing actual mischief. You understand?"

"Kill her, take her money and with the help of it devote oneself to the service of humanity and the good of all. For one life thousands would be saved from corruption and decay. She does not deserve to live."

Of course, it was all idle youthful talk. But why had he heard such ideas at the very moment his own brain was conceiving the very same?

Back in his flat, Raskolnikov got to work. He made a noose of cord and slung it underneath his arm, below his threadbare coat. He wrapped a piece of old iron in paper to look like something valuable. Downstairs, the caretaker's room was empty, he slipped in and borrowed an axe, which he slung beneath his arm.

At the old woman's flat, she held out her hand.

"But how pale you are, and your hands are trembling."

"You can't help getting pale if you've nothing to eat," he answered. "Here, a thing, a cigarette case, silver."

"But what has he tied it up like this for?" the old woman cried with vexation.

The old woman was as always bareheaded, and the axe blow fell on the very top of her skull. She cried out, but very faintly, and sank on the floor. The blood gushed as from an overturned glass. He stepped back, and bent over her face; she was dead.

He saw clearly that the skull was broken. He was about to feel it with his finger, but drew back his hand. He remembered to snatch the full purse from her neck.

Then, suddenly, he heard steps. In the middle of the room stood Lizaveta with a big bundle in her arms.

The second murder was quick, and a sort of blankness, even dreaminess, began to take possession of him. "Good God!" he muttered "I must fly, fly," and he rushed into the entry. But here a shock of terror awaited him such as he had never known before.

The outer door from the stairs was standing unfastened. No lock, no bolt, all the time, all that time!

He dashed to the door and fastened the latch.

"But no, the wrong thing again! I must get away."

He unfastened the latch, opened the door and began listening on the staircase.

Two voices were loudly and shrilly shouting, quarrelling and scolding. "What are they about? Coming here!"

He suddenly started, slipped quickly back into the flat and closed the door behind him. He crouched down, holding his breath.

The first visitor took hold of the bell, rang it loudly, and the began to speak.

"What's up? Are they asleep or murdered?" he bawled in a thick voice, "Hey, Alyona Ivanovna, old witch! Lizaveta Ivanovna, my beauty! open the door!"

"Stay!" cried the younger visitor suddenly. "Listen how the hook clanks? It must be locked from inside There is something wrong. Either they've both fainted or..."

"Let's go fetch the porter, let him wake them up."

"All right."

Both were going down.

Raskolnikov stood keeping tight hold of the axe. He was in a sort of delirium. "Only make haste!" was the thought that flashed through his mind.

He waited, went out on tiptoe and ran down.

No one was on the stairs, nor in the gateway. Then – voices. He slipped through an open doorway into an empty flat, decorator's brushes and pots on the floor. The voices passed and he was quickly into the street.

Almost falling from fatigue, he went a long way round so as to get home from quite a different direction.

At his house, the caretaker was out, and he succeeded in putting the axe back as before. When he was in his room, he flung himself on the sofa just as he was - he did not sleep, but sank into blank forgetfulness.

II

He rushed to the window. There was light enough, and he began hurriedly looking himself all over; were there no traces?

Some thick drops of congealed blood were clinging to the frayed edge of his trousers. He picked up a big claspknife and cut off the frayed threads.

Suddenly he remembered the purse, and turned it inside-out on the table. There were trinkets as well as money. He had not reckoned on needing to hide things, and began stuffing everything into a hole where the wallpaper had come away.

"My God!" he whispered in despair: "Is that the way to hide things?"

He sat down on the sofa in exhaustion and was at once shaken by an unbearable fit of shivering.

And for a long while, for some hours, he was haunted by the impulse to go off somewhere and fling it all away, out of sight and done with!

He was thoroughly brought round at last by a violent knocking at his door.

"Open, do, are you dead or alive!" shouted Nastasya."

He half rose, stooped forward and unlatched the door.

The porter and Nastasya were standing there.

The porter held out a grey paper sealed with bottle-wax.

"A summons from the office," he announced.

"What office?"

"The police office, of course."

"The police?... What for?..."

"How can I tell? You're sent for, so you go."

"He's ill!" observed Nastasya. "He's been in a fever since yesterday," she added, and followed the porter out, giggling.

The police office was easy, they asked for no more than he sign an IOU to the landlady.

As he left he thought; did they suspect him? What if they search? How could he have left all those things in the hole?

At home, he rushed to the corner, pulled the things out from under the paper and stuffed them into his pockets.

Back outside, the canal was too obvious, too many people about, and what if the things floated?

In the end he buried them under a big stone lying by a house wall. He scraped the earth about it with his foot. Nothing could be noticed.

An intense, almost unbearable joy overwhelmed him for an instant. "I have buried my tracks! And who, who can think of looking under that stone? It is all over! No clue!" And he laughed.

Raskolnikov walked straight to X-- Bridge, and leaning both elbows on the rail, stared into the distance.

"A woman drowning! A woman drowning!" shouted dozens of voices; people ran up, and crowded about Raskolnikov, pressing up behind him.

"Very well then!" A decision seemed to be made for him. He moved from the bridge and began in the direction of the police office. His heart felt hollow. Absolute nothingness overwhelmed him.

He took the second turning to the left.

There, an elegant carriage stood in the middle of the road, the coachman holding the horses nearby. A mass of people had gathered round, the police standing in front.

Raskolnikov pushed his way in. On the ground a man who had been run over lay unconscious, covered with blood.

"I know him!" Raskolnikov shouted. "It's Marmeladov. He lives close by. Make haste for a doctor! I will pay!"

The police were glad enough to have found out who the man was, and happy to help the unconscious Marmeladov to his lodging.

The room became so full of people that you couldn't have dropped a pin. The policemen left, all except one, and Katerina Ivanovna flew into a fury.

"You might let him die in peace, at least, is it a spectacle for you to gape at? With cigarettes! (Cough, cough, cough!) You should respect the dead, at least!"

Katerina Ivanovna walked to the window: "Oh, cursed life!"

The doctor arrived and shook his head. A moment later the priest, a little, grey old man, appeared in the doorway bearing the sacrament.

At that moment, timidly and noiselessly a young girl made her way through the crowd, and strange indeed was her appearance in the midst of want, rags, death and despair. She, too, was in rags, but decked out in gutter finery, unmistakably betraying its shameful purpose. Sonia was a small thin girl of eighteen with fair hair, rather pretty, with wonderful blue eyes. She looked intently at the bed.

The priest began a few words of consolation to Katerina Ivanovna.

"God is merciful," he began.

"Ach! Not to us. This man wasted these children's lives and mine for drink! "

"That's a sin, a sin, madam," observed the priest, "You must forgive in the hour of death, madam."

"He's already dead," said Raskolnikov, strangely pleased to notice that he had been splattered with blood, and turned round to be met by a child's thin but pretty little face.

"My name is Polenka. Sister Sonia sent me," said the girl, smiling brightly. "I'll pray for you all the rest of my life."

Raskolnikov left his name and address and in five minutes he was standing again on the bridge.

III

The next day, his mother and sister arrived. They sat, not at all comfortably, in his flat, especially so as a rather frosty letter from Dounia's intended, Pyotr Petrovitch, had made it clear that he well knew about Raskolnikov's dissolute lifestyle.

As Raskolnikov told the story of yesterday's events, the door was softly opened, and a young girl walked into the room. It was Sofya Semyonovna Marmeladov, now modestly and poorly-dressed, very young, candid but somewhat frightened-looking.

"I. . . I. . . have come for one minute."

"Mother," he said, "this is Sonia, daughter of the unfortunate Mr. Marmeladov, of whom I was just telling you."

"My mother begs you to do us the honour to be in the church to-morrow for the service, and then to be present at the funeral lunch."

"You gave us everything yesterday," Sonia whispered. A silence followed. There was a light in Dounia's eyes, and even his mother Pulcheria Alexandrovna looked kindly at Sonia.

"Come, that's capital," he said to Sonia, going back and looking brightly at her. "God give peace to the dead, the living have still to live. That is right, isn't it?"

Sonia was extremely glad to escape, unconscious to the whole new world which was opening before her.

IV

The next day Raskolnikov had another summons to the police office. The detective Porfiry, "Just wanted to establish a few facts," about a recent murder, "and make sure any pledged property got back to its rightful owner." But he seemed to know more.

"He knows," flashed through Raskolnikov's mind like lightning.

He left and hurried to the house on the canal bank where Sonia lived. It was an old green house of three storeys.

"I've come to you for the last time," Raskolnikov said, although this was the first time. "How thin you are! Well, I can understand, with your living like this."

Sonia smiled faintly.

"Katerina Ivanovna has consumption; she will soon die." Raskolnikov said.

"Oh, no, no, no!"

"But it will be better if she does die."

"No, not better! God will not let it be!"

"But, perhaps, there is no God," Raskolnikov answered with a sort of malignance.

Sonia's face suddenly changed; a tremor passed over it.

Five minutes passed. All at once he bent down and kissed her foot.

"What are you doing?" she muttered, turning pale.

"I bowed down to all the suffering of humanity," he said wildly and walked away to the window. "What does God do for you?"

There was a book lying on the chest of drawers. It was a New Testament, bound in leather, old and worn.

"Where did you get that?" he asked.

"From Lizaveta."

Everything about Sonia seemed to him stranger and more wonderful every moment.

"The story of Lazarus?" he asked suddenly. "Find it and read it to me. Were you friends with Lizaveta?"

"Yes. She was killed with an axe. We used to read together. She will see God."

Sonia opened the book and found the place. Her hands were shaking, her voice failed her.

"Now a certain man was sick named Lazarus of Bethany... Jesus said, I am the resurrection and the life: he that believeth in Me though he were dead, yet shall he live."

She closed the book and got up from her chair.

"Today, I have abandoned my family," he said, "and I have chosen you. And if I come tomorrow, I'll tell you who killed the old woman and her sister. Good-bye, don't shake hands. To-morrow!"

Sonia spent the whole night feverish and delirious. She jumped up from time to time, wept and wrung her hands, then sank again into feverish sleep.

V

As the day came and he made his way to Sonia's lodging, he felt a sudden impotence and fear. He stood still in hesitation at the door, asking himself the question: "Must he tell her who killed Lizaveta?" To cut short his suffering, he quickly opened the door and looked at Sonia from the doorway.

"You'd better say straight out what you want!" Sonia cried in distress. "You are leading up to something. Have you discovered who murdered Lizaveta?"

"You can't guess, then?" he asked suddenly.

"N-no." whispered Sonia.

"Take a good look."

"Good God!" broke in an awful wail from her bosom. "What have you done to yourself?" she said in despair, flinging herself on his neck.

"Sonia, I must speak, but I don't know how to begin."

"But perhaps it is just that?" he said, as though reaching a conclusion. "I wanted to become a Napoleon, that is why I killed her. Do you understand now?"

"N-no," Sonia whispered naïvely and timidly.

"It was like this: I asked myself, what if a great man, Napoleon for instance, had not had Toulon nor Egypt to begin his career with, but instead there had simply been some ridiculous old hag, a pawnbroker, who had to be murdered to get the money to begin his great work. Would he have done that? That is exactly how it was! Perhaps that's just how it was."

"You had better tell me straight out," she begged, timidly and scarcely audibly.

"You are right, Sonia. Of course that's nonsense! It is like this, all my family have put all their hopes on me, but I couldn't keep myself at the university. And even if I had stayed, what of it? In in ten years, with luck, I might have made some sort of teacher or clerk. So I resolved to get the old woman's money and use it to make something worthwhile of myself. Well, of course, I did wrong. But I've only killed a louse, Sonia, a useless, loathsome, harmful creature."

"A human being!"

"I am talking nonsense, Sonia," he added. "My head aches dreadfully. Closed up in that cramped room, lying alone for days. I had dreams, and I kept asking myself this, am I not at least a little less stupid than others? Shouldn't the man with some strength of spirit have some power over others? He who despises most things will be the lawgiver, and he who dares most of all will be most in the right! So it has always been. "

"Then an idea took shape in my mind - an idea which no one had ever thought of before me - no one! I saw clear as daylight how strange it is that not a single person in this mad world is ever brave enough to go straight for it all and send care flying to the devil! I, I wanted to be brave - and I killed her. That was the whole cause of it!"

"Oh hush, hush," cried Sonia. "You turned away from God and God has given you over to the devil!"

"Well, what am I to do now?" he asked.

"What are you to do?" she cried, jumping up, her eyes full of tears. "Stand up!" She seized him by the shoulders. "You are to go at once, this very minute, stand at the cross-roads, bow down, and kiss the earth which you have defiled. Then go and say to all men aloud, 'I am a murderer!' Then God will send you life again. Will you go?" she asked him, with eyes full of fire.

"You mean I must give myself up?" he asked gloomily.

"Suffer and atone by it, that's what you must do."

"Don't be a child, Sonia," he said softly. "What wrong have I done them? Why should I go to them? They destroy men by millions themselves and look on it as a virtue. I won't. Don't be a child, Sonia."

They sat side by side, both mournful and dejected. He looked at Sonia and felt a great love for him, and strange to say he felt it suddenly burdensome and painful to be so loved.

"Sonia," he said, "you'd better not come and see me when I am in prison."

Sonia did not answer, she was crying. Several minutes passed.

"Have you a cross on you?" she asked, as though suddenly thinking of it.

He did not at first understand the question.

"No, of course not. Here, take this one, of cypress wood. I have another, a copper one that belonged to Lizaveta. I will wear that now and give you this. Take it it's mine! It's mine, you know," she begged him. "We will go to suffer together, and together we will bear our cross!"

EPILOGUE

Siberia. On the banks of a broad solitary river stands a town; in the town there is a prison where the second-class convict Rodion Raskolnikov has been confined for nine months.

The criminal had not tried to justify himself, and he had made no use of what he had stolen. Witnesses told how he had once been generous and kindly. So, the sentence was more merciful than could have been expected - penal servitude in the second class for a term of eight years only.

At first he had been indifferent to Sonia's visits. But it was she who brought him news from outside, she who had brought him the news when his mother died. She who had waited while he was ill in the prison hospital.

Then, on one warm bright day, early in the morning, Raskolnikov sat outside gazing at the river, while his guard went to get some tools.

Suddenly he found Sonia beside him; she had come up noiselessly and sat down. How it happened he did not know, but all at once something seemed to seize him and fling him at her feet. They both wanted to speak, but could not; tears stood in their eyes. They were pale and thin; but those sick pale faces were bright with the dawn of a new future, of a full resurrection into a new life. They were renewed by love; the heart of each held infinite sources of life for the heart of the other.

They had another seven years to wait, but he had risen again and he knew it and felt it in all his being, while she - she only lived in his life. Life had stepped into the place of theory.

But that is the beginning of a new story.

Twenty Thousand Leagues Under the Sea
(*Vingt mille lieues sous les mers*)
by Jules Verne
(Paris, 1873)

One of the most translated authors of all time, Verne, a 'Father of Science Fiction', wrote about space, air, and submarine travel long before such means had been invented. Yet many of his books, and especially this one, suffer from a poor reputation in English, often due to biased translations which tried to make them seem *British*. It has been adapted for film and TV many times, and provided the inspiration for dozens of works, including the 2003 film *The League of Extraordinary Gentlemen* which did at least restore Captain Nemo as an Indian nobleman.
Abridged: JH.

I Join a Strange Expedition

In the year 1866 the whole seafaring world of Europe and America was greatly disturbed by an ocean mystery which baffled the wits of scientists and sailors alike. Several vessels, in widely different regions of the seas, had met a long and rapidly moving object, much larger than a whale, and capable of almost incredible speed. It had also been seen at night, and was then phosphorescent, moving under the water in a glow of light.

There was no doubt whatever as to the reality of this unknown terror of the deep, for several vessels had been struck by it, and particularly the Cunard steamer *Scotia*, homeward bound for Liverpool. It had pierced a large triangular hole through the steel plates of the Scotia's hull, and would certainly have sunk the vessel had it not been divided into seven water-tight compartments, any one of which could stand injury without danger to the vessel. It was three hundred miles off Cape Clear that the Scotia encountered this mysterious monster. Arriving after some days' delay at Liverpool, the vessel was put into dock, when the result of the blow from the unknown was thoroughly investigated. So many vessels having recently been lost from unknown causes, the narrow escape of the Scotia directed fresh attention to this ocean mystery, and both in Europe and America there was a strong public agitation for an expedition to be sent out, prepared to do battle with, and if possible destroy, this narwhal of monstrous growth, as many scientists believed it to be.

Now I, Pierre Arronax, assistant professor in the Paris Museum of Natural History, was at this time in America, where I had been engaged on a scientific expedition into the disagreeable region of Nebraska. I had arrived at New York in company of my faithful attendant, Conseil, and was devoting my attention to classifying the numerous specimens I had gathered for the Paris Museum. As I had already some reputation in the scientific world from my book on "The Mysteries of the Great Submarine Grounds," a number of people did me the honour of consulting me concerning the one subject then exercising the minds of all interested in ocean travel.

An expedition was also being fitted out by the United States government, the fastest frigate of the navy, the *Abraham Lincoln*, under command of Captain Farragut, being in active preparation, with the object of hunting out this wandering monster which had last been seen three weeks before by a San Francisco steamer in the North Pacific Ocean. I was invited to join this expedition as a representative of France, and immediately decided to do so. The faithful Conseil said he would go with me wherever I went, and thus it came about that my sturdy Flemish companion, who had accompanied me on scientific expeditions for ten years was with me again on the eventful cruise which began when we sailed from Brooklyn for the Pacific and the unknown.

The crew of the frigate and the various scientists on board were all eagerness to meet the great cetacean, or sea-unicorn. My own opinion was that it would be found to be a narwhal of monstrous growth, for these creatures are armed with a kind of ivory sword, or tusk, as hard as steel, and sometimes nearly seven feet long by fifteen inches in diameter at the base. Supposing one to exist ten times as large as any that had ever been captured, with its tusk proportionately powerful, it was conceivable that such a gigantic creature, moving at a great rate, could do all the damage that had been reported.

There was among our crew one Ned Land, a gigantic Canadian of forty, who was considered to be the prince of harpooners. Many a whale had received its deathblow from him, and he was eager to flesh his harpoon in this redoubtable cetacean which had terrified the marine world.

Week after week passed without any sign that our quest would be successful. Indeed, after nearly four months had gone, and we had explored the whole of the Japanese and Chinese coasts, the captain reached the point of deciding to return, when one night the voice of Ned Land was heard calling:

"Look out there! The thing we are looking for on our weather-beam!"

At this cry the entire crew rushed towards the harpooner-captain, officers, masters, sailors, and cabin-boys; even the engineers left their engines, and the stokers their furnaces. The frigate was now moving only by her own momentum, for the engines had been stopped.

My heart beat violently. I was sure the harpooner's eyes had not deceived him. Soon we could all see, about two cables' length away, a strange and luminous object, lying some fathoms below the surface, just as described in many of the reports. One of the officers suggested that it was merely an enormous mass of phosphorous particles, but I replied with conviction that the light was electric. And even as I spoke the strange thing began to move towards us!

The captain immediately reversed engines and put on full speed, but the luminous monster gained on us and played round the frigate with frightful rapidity. Its light would go out suddenly and reappear again on the other side of the vessel. It was clearly too great a risk to attack the thing in the dark, and by midnight it disappeared, dying out like a huge glow-worm. It appeared again, about five miles to the windward, at two in the morning, coming up to the surface as if to breathe, and it seemed as though the air rushed into its huge lungs like steam in the vast cylinders of a 2,000 horse-power engine.

"Hum!" said I. "A whale with the strength of a cavalry regiment would be a pretty whale!"

The Attack and After

Everything was in readiness to attack with the coming of the dawn, and Ned Land was calmly sharpening his great harpoon, but by six in the morning the thing had again disappeared, and a thick sea-fog made it impossible to observe its further movements. At eight o'clock, however, the mist had begun to clear, and then, as suddenly as on the night before, Ned Land's voice was heard calling: "The thing on the port-quarter!"

There it was, surely enough, a mile and a half away, now a large black body showing above the waves, and leaving a track of dazzling white as its great tail beat the water into foam.

Moving rapidly, it approached within twenty feet of the frigate. Ned stood ready at the bow to hurl his harpoon, and the monster was now shining again with that strange light which dazzled our eyes. All at once he threw the harpoon. It struck on a hard body.

Instantly the light went out and two enormous water-spouts fell on our deck. A frightful shock followed, and the next moment I found myself struggling in the sea. Though a good swimmer, I kept afloat with some difficulty, and great was my joy when I heard the voice of the faithful Conseil, who had jumped in after me. Much stronger than myself, he helped me to remove some of my clothes, and thus we kept afloat until I fainted.

When I regained consciousness, I found myself on the top of what seemed to be a floating island, and there was Ned Land as well as Conseil. We were on the back of the mysterious monster, and it was made of metal! Presently it began to move, and we were afraid it might go below the surface.

Indeed, it seemed to be on the point of submerging, when Land hammered loudly on the metal plates, and in a moment an opening was made and the three of us were drawn inside by eight masked men. A door banged on us, and for half an hour we lay in utter darkness. Then a brilliant electric light flooded the cabin, a room of about twenty feet by ten, and two men entered. One was tall, pale, and dark-eyed, but magnificently proportioned.

Though we spoke to them in French, German, English, and Latin, they did not seem to understand, while their own speech was unintelligible to us. But they gave us clothes and food. After eating the food, which was strange but delicious, we all lay down and slept the sleep of sheer exhaustion.

Next day the tall man, whom I afterwards came to know as Captain Nemo, master of his marvellous submarine boat, came to me, and, speaking in French, said:

"I have been considering your case, and did not choose to speak till I had weighed it well. You have pursued me to destroy me. I have done with society for reasons of my own. I have decided. I give you choice of life or death. If you grant me a passive obedience, and submit to my consigning you to your cabin for some hours or days, as occasion calls, you are safe. You, Monsieur Arronax, have least cause to complain, for you have written on the life of the sea-I have your book in my library here-and will benefit most when I show you its marvels. I love it. It does not belong to despots."

Clearly we could do nothing but submit, and afterwards Captain Nemo showed me his wondrous craft.

Our Life on the Nautilus

It was indeed a thing of marvels; for, besides the dining-room, it contained a large library of twelve thousand volumes, a drawing-room measuring thirty feet by eighteen, and fifteen high. The walls of this apartment were adorned with masterpieces of the great painters, and beautiful marbles and bronzes. A large piano-organ stood in one corner, and there were glass cases containing the rarest marine curiosities which a naturalist could wish to see. A collection of enormous pearls in a cabinet must have been worth millions, and Captain Nemo told me he had rifled every sea to find them.

The room assigned to me was fitted up with every luxury, yet the captain's own apartment was as simply furnished as a monastic cell, but in it were contained all the ingenious instruments that controlled the movements of the *Nautilus*, as his submarine was named. The electricity was manufactured by a process of extracting chloride of sodium from the sea-water, but the fresh air necessary for the life of the crew could only be obtained by rising to the surface. The engine-room was sixty-five feet long, and in it was the machinery for producing electricity as well as that for applying the power to the propeller.

The *Nautilus*, Captain Nemo explained, was capable of a speed of fifty miles an hour, and could be made to sink or rise with precision by flooding or emptying a reservoir. In a box, raised somewhat above the hull and fitted with glass ten inches thick, the steersman had his place, and a powerful electric reflector behind him illuminated the sea for half a mile in front.

The submarine also carried a small torpedo-like boat, fitted in a groove along the top, so that it could be entered from the *Nautilus* by opening a panel, and, after that was closed, the boat could be detached from the submarine, and would then bob upwards to the surface like a cork. The importance of this and its bearing on my story will appear in due time.

It was on a desert island that Captain Nemo had carried out the building of the *Nautilus*, and from many different places he had secured the various parts of the hull and machinery, in order to maintain secrecy.

Deeply interested as I was in every detail of this extraordinary vessel, and excited beyond measure at the wonders which awaited me in exploring the world beneath the waves, I had still the feeling of a prisoner who dared scarcely hope that liberty might some day be obtained. But when the metal plates which covered the windows of the saloon were rolled back as we sailed under the water, and on each hand I could see a thronging army of many-coloured aquatic creatures swimming around us, attracted by our light, I was in an ecstasy of wonder and delight.

Then days would pass without Captain Nemo putting in an appearance, and none of the crew were ever to be seen. But the *Nautilus* kept on its journey, which, I learned, took us to the Torres Strait, the Papuan coast, through the Red Sea, through a subterranean strait, under the Isthmus of Suez, to the island of Santorin, the Cretan Archipelago, to the South Pole, on whose sterile wastes Captain Nemo reared his black flag with a white "N" upon it, and through the Gulf Stream.

Of the wonders of the deep, those amazing and beautiful specimens of unknown life that passed before my vision on this strange journey, never before seen by the eye of any naturalist, I cannot here enter into particulars. But it must not be supposed, prisoners though we were, that we never emerged from the interior of the *Nautilus*.

One of my first surprises, indeed, was to be invited by Captain Nemo to accompany him on a hunting expedition in the marine forest that grew about the base of the little island of Crespo, in the North Pacific Ocean. We were told to make a hearty breakfast, as the jaunt would be a long one. This we did, for we had soon become accustomed to the strange food, every item of which was produced by the sea.

For our submarine excursion we were furnished with diving dresses of seamless india-rubber, fitted on the shoulders with a reservoir of stored air, its tubes opening into the great copper helmet. We even had powerful air-guns and electric bullets, which proved weapons of deadly precision. When inside our diving dresses, we could not move our feet on account of the enormous leaden soles, so that we had to be pushed into a compartment at the bottom of the vessel, and the iron doors secured behind us. Water was then pumped in, and we could feel it rising around us, until the compartment was full, when an outer door opened and we stepped on to the floor of the sea.

For some considerable distance we walked along sands of the most perfect smoothness, and then had to make our way over slimy rocks and treacherous masses of seaweed, before we reached the fairy-like forest under the sea, where all the branches of the marvellous growths ascended perpendicularly.

It was indeed a rare experience for me, who had written "The Mysteries of the Great Submarine Grounds," thus to see, at first hand, the life which I had only been able to speculate on before. We captured many rare specimens, and shot a fine sea-otter, the only known quadruped that inhabits the rocky depths of the Pacific. It was five feet long, and its skin was worth a hundred pounds.

Captain Nemo and the Avenger

So constantly was I enchanted with the wonders of our journey that day succeeded day without my taking note of them; but Captain Nemo, for all his kindness, still remained as mysterious as the Sphinx. One day he became violently agitated after looking through the glass at a point indicated by his lieutenant, and I and my companions were immediately imprisoned in darkness, as we had been when first taken into the *Nautilus*. When I awoke next morning the captain took me to see a wounded Englishman whose head had been shattered, and on my stating that the man could not live for two hours, the dark eyes of the captain

seemed to fill with tears. I thought that night I heard sounds of a funeral hymn, and next day I was taken to a submarine forest of coral, where they buried the man. This was really a little cemetery beneath the sea, as I gathered from the coral cross which had been erected there. Ned Land, unlike me, was soon satisfied with what he had seen of the submarine world, and had now but one thought of escape. We were sailing up the eastern coast of South America, and by May 17 were some five hundred miles from Heart's Content. There I saw, at a depth of more than fifteen hundred fathoms, the great electric cable lying at the bottom of the ocean. The restlessness of poor Ned Land was at its height when he had a glimpse of the American shore; but Captain Nemo bent his course towards Ireland, and then southward, passing within sight of Land's End on May 30.

All the next day the vessel seemed to be making a series of circular movements, in some endeavour to locate a particular spot, and the captain was gloomier than I had ever seen him, having no word for me. The following day, which was beautifully clear, we could make out, some eight miles to the eastward, a large steam vessel flying no flag. Suddenly, after using his sextant, the captain exclaimed: "It is here!"

Presently the *Nautilus* sank to the bottom of the sea. When at rest the lights were put out and the sliding panels opened. We could now see on our starboard the remains of a sunken vessel, so encrusted with shells that it must have lain there a great many years. As I stood there wondering what might be Captain Nemo's reason for his manoeuvres, he came to my side and, speaking slowly, said:

"That was the *Marseillais*, launched in 1772. It carried seventy-four guns, and fought gallantly against the *Preston*, was in action again at the siege of Granada, and in Chesapeake Bay. Then in 1794 the French Republic changed the vessel's name, and it joined a squadron at Brest to escort a cargo of corn coming from America. The squadron fell in with an English man-o'-war, and seventy-two years ago to this very day, on this very spot, after fighting heroically, until its masts were shot away, its hold full of water, and a third of its crew disabled, this vessel preferred sinking, with its 356 sailors, to surrendering. Nailing its colours to the mast, it sank beneath the waves to the cry of 'Long live the Republic!'"

"The *Avenger*!" I exclaimed.

"Yes, the *Avenger*. A good name!" said the captain, with a strange seriousness, as he crossed his arms.

I was deeply impressed with his whole bearing while he recalled these facts. It was clearly no common spite against his fellow-men that had shut up Captain Nemo and his crew in the *Nautilus*.

Already we were ascending, fast leaving the grave of the old *Avenger*. When we had reached the surface we could see another vessel steaming towards us. A low boom greeted the *Nautilus* as its upper part showed above the water. Ned Land, aflame once more with hope of escape, made out the vessel to be a two-decker ram, but she showed no flag at her mizzen. It seemed for a moment there might just be some chance of escape for us three prisoners, and Ned declared he would jump into the sea if the man-o'-war came within a mile of us. Just then another gun boomed out. She was firing at us.

It flashed across my mind at that moment that as those on board the *Abraham Lincoln,* having once seen the effect of Ned Land's harpoon when it struck the *Nautilus,* could not but have concluded their enemy was no monster of the deep-though indeed a monster of man's contriving - the warships of all nations would now be on the look-out for the *Nautilus,* and we on board it could scarcely hope for mercy.

The shot rattled about us as we stood on the opened upper deck of the submarine, and Ned Land, in a mad moment, waved his handkerchief to the enemy, only to be instantly felled by the iron hand of Captain Nemo. Then, frightfully pale, the captain turned towards the approaching man-o'-war, and, in a voice terrible to hear, cried: "Ah, ship of an accursed nation, you know who I am! I do not need to see your colours to know you. Look, and see mine!"

So saying, he unfurled his black flag, and then sternly bade us go below, just as a shell struck the *Nautilus,* and rebounded into the sea. "You have seen the attack," he said calmly. "I shall sink yonder ship, but not here - no, not here. Her ruins shall not mingle with those of the Avenger."

The Doom of the Oppressor

Having no choice but to obey, we all went below, and the propeller of the *Nautilus* was soon lashing the water into creamy foam, taking us beyond the range of fire. I held my peace for a time, but, after some deliberation, ventured to go up in the hope of dissuading Captain Nemo from his destructive plans. His vessel was now coursing round the other ship like a wild beast manoeuvring to attack its prey, and I had scarcely spoken when the captain turned on me fiercely, commanding silence.

"Here I am the law and the judge," he said, almost in a shriek. "There is the oppressor. Through him I have lost all that I have loved, cherished, and venerated - country, wife, children, father, and mother. I saw all perish! All that I hate is represented by that ship! Not another word!"

In the face of such fierce hatred it was useless to try persuasion. I and my companions resolved to attempt escape when the *Nautilus* made the attack. At six the next morning, being the second day of June, the two vessels were less than a mile and a half apart. Suddenly, as the three of us were preparing to rush on deck and jump overboard, the upper panel closed sharply. Our chance was gone!

Next moment the noise of the water rushing into the reservoir indicated that we were sinking, and in a moment more the machinery throbbed at its greatest speed as the *Nautilus* shot forward under the sea. Then the whole submarine trembled; there was a shock, and then a rending

jar above. The terror of the seas had cut its way through the other vessel like a needle through sailcloth! Horror-stricken, I rushed into the saloon and found Captain Nemo, mute and gloomy, standing by the port panel, which had instantly been slid back, watching with a terrible satisfaction the injured vessel sinking with all its crew beneath the waves. The *Nautilus* sank with it, so that its terrible captain might lose nothing of the fascinating horror presented by the spectacle of his victims descending to their ocean grave. When we had seen all, he went to his room, and, following him, I saw on the wall the portraits of a woman, still young, and two little children. He looked at them, and as he stretched his arms toward them the fierce expression of hate died away from his face. He sank down on his knees, and burst into deep sobs. I felt a strange horror for this man, who, though he might have suffered terribly, had no right to exact so terrible a vengeance.

The *Nautilus* was now making its top speed, and the instruments indicated a northerly direction. Whither was it flying? That night we covered two hundred leagues of the Atlantic. Onward we kept our course, the speed never lessening, and for fifteen or twenty days, during which we prisoners never saw the captain or his lieutenant, this headlong race continued.

Our Escape from the Nautilus

Poor Ned Land was in despair, and Conseil and I had to watch him carefully lest he might kill himself. One morning he said to me:

"We are going to fly to-night. I have taken the reckoning, and make out that twenty miles or so to the east is land. I have got a little food and water, and Conseil and I will be near the opening into the small boat at ten. Meet us there. If we do not escape, they sha'n't take me alive."

"I will go with you," I said. "At least we can die together."

Wishing to verify the direction of the *Nautilus,* I went to the saloon. We were going N.N.E. with frightful speed at a depth of twenty-five fathoms. I took a last look at all the natural marvels and art treasures collected in this strange museum, a collection doomed to perish in the depths of the ocean with the man who had made it. Back in my own room I donned my sea garments, and placed all my notes carefully about my clothing. My heart was beating so loudly that I feared my agitation might betray me if I met Captain Nemo. I decided it was best to lie down on my bed in the hope of calming my nerves, and thus to pass the time till the hour determined upon for our attempt. Ten o'clock was on the point of striking, when I heard Captain Nemo playing a weird and sad melody, and I was struck with the sudden terror of having to pass through the saloon while he was there. I must make the attempt, and softly I crept to the door of the saloon and softly opened it. Captain Nemo was still playing his subdued melody; but the room was in darkness, and slowly I made my way across it to the library door. I had almost opened this when a sigh from him made me pause.

He had risen from the organ, and, as some rays of light were now admitted from the library, I could see him coming toward me with folded arms, gliding like a ghost rather than walking. His breast heaved with sobs, and I heard him murmur these words, the last of his I heard: "Enough! O God, enough!" Was it remorse escaping thus from the conscience of this mysterious being? Had I not seen it begin with the tears in his eyes at the death of the Englishman whom he had buried in the coral cemetery, and who was doubtless a victim of one of his acts of destruction?

Now rendered desperate, I rushed into the library, up the central staircase, and so gained the opening to the boat where my companions were awaiting me. Quickly the panel through which we went was shut and bolted by means of a wrench which Ned Land had secured. The opening of the boat was also quickly fastened after we had got inside, and the harpooner had begun to undo from the inside the screws that still fastened the boat to the *Nautilus*. Suddenly a great noise was heard within the submarine. We thought we had been discovered, and were prepared to die defending ourselves. Ned Land stopped his work for the moment, and the noise grew louder. It was a terrible word, twenty times repeated, that we heard. "The Maelstrom! The Maelstrom!" was what they were crying. Was it to this, then, that the *Nautilus* had been driven, by accident or design, with such headlong speed? We heard a roaring noise, and could feel ourselves whirled in spiral circles. The steel muscles of the submarine were cracking, and at times in the awful churning of the whirlpool it seemed to stand on end. "We must hold on," cried Land, "and we may be saved if we can stick to the *Nautilus*."

His anxiety now was to make fast the screws that bound the boat to the submarine, but he had scarcely finished speaking when, with a great crash, the bolts gave way, and the boat shot up, released from the larger vessel, into the midst of the whirlpool. My head struck on its iron framework and I lost all consciousness.

How we escaped from that hideous gulf, where even whales of mighty strength have been tossed and battered to death, none of us will ever know! But I was in a fisherman's hut on the Lofoden Isles when I regained consciousness. My two companions were by my side, safe and sound, and we all shook hands heartily. There we had to wait for the steamer that runs twice a month to Cape North, and in the interval I occupied myself revising this record of our incredible expedition in an element previously considered inaccessible to man, but to which progress will one day open up a way.

I may be believed or not, but I know that I have made a journey of twenty thousand leagues under the sea.

Does the *Nautilus* still exist? Is Captain Nemo still alive? Was that night in the Maelstrom his last, or is he still pursuing a terrible vengeance? Will the confessions of his life, which he told me he had written, and which the last survivor of his fellow-exiles was to cast into the sea in an air-tight case, ever be found?

This I know, that only two men could have a right to answer the question asked in the Ecclesiastes three thousand years ago: "That which is far off and exceeding deep, who can find it out?" These two men are Captain Nemo and I.

Anna Karenina
(*Анна Каренина*)
by Count Leo Tolstoy
(Moscow, 1877)

Tolstoy's 'realist' novel was said to have been inspired by the life of Maria Hartung, a daughter of the poet Alexander Pushkin. The Russian writers Fyodor Dostoevsky and Vladimir Nabokov both declared it to be "flawless", while *Time* magazine's 2007 survey of novelists chose it as the greatest book ever written.

Abridged: JH

I

Happy families are all alike; every unhappy family is unhappy in its own way.

The Oblonsky family was plunged into miserable confusion. The wife had discovered that the husband was carrying on an intrigue with the French governess, and had announced to her husband that she could not go on living in the same house with him. She remained in her rooms, and the husband had not shown himself at home for three days. Some of the servants quarrelled and others demanded their wages.

Prince Stepan Arkadyevitch Oblonsky - Stiva, as he was called - had on returning one evening from the theatre found his Dolly sitting with a letter in her hand, and an expression of terror and despair on her countenance. "What is this? This?" she asked. Instead of attempting a reply, Stepan smiled good-humouredly and stupidly; and Dolly, after a flow of passionate reproaches, rushed from the room.

Stepan had never imagined that any such discovery would have such an effect on his wife. "How delightfully we were living till this happened!" said he, as on the third morning after the outbreak he awoke in his library, where he had rested on the lounge. "I never interfered with Dolly, and she did as she pleased with the household and children. What can be done?" He rose and put on his dressing gown and rang for his valet, who came in response to the summons, followed by the barber. The valet handed him a telegram, which announced that his loving sister, Anna Arkadyevna, was coming on a visit. He was pleased to receive the intelligence, for it might mean that she would effect a reconciliation.

Prince Stepan tranquilly partook of breakfast over his newspaper, and became absorbed in thought. Suddenly two children's voices roused him from his reverie. They were those of Grisha, his youngest boy, and Tania, his eldest daughter. The little girl, his favourite, ran in and laughingly and fondly embraced him. "What is mamma doing? Is she all right?" he asked of the girl.

"I don't know," was the reply. "She told us we were not to have lessons to-day but were to go to grandmamma's." He told the children to run along, and then said to himself, "To go, or not to go - but it has to be done, sooner or later," and straightening himself and lighting a cigarette, he opened the door into his wife's room. She was standing in the room removing the contents of a drawer, and turned her worn face on Stepan with a look of terror. She had dreaded this moment, for though she felt she could not stay, yet she knew she loved him and that it was impossible to leave him.

"What do you want? Go away, go away," she cried. He broke into sobs and began to beg forgiveness. "Dolly, think for the love of God of the children. They are not to blame. I alone am to blame. Now, Dolly, forgive me." But as the voice of one of the children was heard, she went out from him and slammed the door.

II

Stepan Arkadyevitch was naturally idle, yet his gifts had enabled him to do well at school, and he had gained an excellent position at Moscow as natchalnik, or president of one of the courts, through the influence of Aleksei Alexandrovitch Karenin, husband of his sister Anna, one of the most important members of the ministry. In this office Stepan enjoyed a salary of 6,000 roubles. Everyone who knew Oblonsky liked him, for his amiability, honesty, and brilliance, qualities which rendered him a most attractive character.

Going to his office after his unpleasant interview with his wife, he attended to matters in the court for some time, and on suspending business for lunch found his friend Levin waiting to see him - a fair-complexioned, broad-shouldered man whom he often saw in Moscow. Levin frequently came in from the country, full of enthusiasm about great things he had been attempting, at the reports of which Stepan was apt to smile in his good-humoured style. That Levin was in love with his sister Kitty was well enough known to Stepan.

When Oblonsky on this occasion, after chatting over some rural concerns in Levin's district, asked his friend what had specially brought him to Moscow, Levin blushed and was vexed with himself for blushing. He could not bring himself to reply that he had come to ask for the hand of Stepan's sister-in-law Kitty, though that was really his errand. As a student and a friend of the Shcherbatsky family, belonging like his own to the old nobility of Moscow, Konstantin Levin at first thought himself in love with Dolly, the eldest, but she married Oblonsky; then with Natalie, who married Lyof, a diplomat; and finally his passion settled on Kitty, who had been only a child when he left the University. He was now thirty-two, was wealthy, would surely have been reckoned an acceptable suitor, but had a most exalted opinion of Kitty, and to a corresponding degree depreciated himself.

He feared that probably Kitty did not love him, and he knew that his friends only looked upon him as a country proprietor, occupied with farming, or amusing himself with hunting. He was not what is understood as a society man. But he felt that he could no longer rest without seeking to get the question settled whether she would or would not be his wife.

III

Levin made his way to the gate of the Zoological Gardens and followed the path to the ice-mountains, where he knew that he should find the Shcherbatskys there, Kitty among them. He had seen their carriage at the gate. It was a lovely day, and the gaily-clad fashionable people, the Russian izbas with their carved woodwork, the paths gleaming with snow, and the old birch-trees, brilliant with icicles, combined to render the whole scene one of fascination.

Drawing near the ice-mountains, where the sledges rushed down the inclines, he soon discovered Kitty, who was on the opposite side, standing in close conversation with a lady. For him her presence filled the place with light and glory. He asked himself whether he was brave enough to go and meet her on the ice. The spot where she was seemed to him like a sanctuary, and all the persons privileged to be near her seemed to be the elect of heaven. This day the ice was the common meeting-ground for fashionable people, the masters in the art of skating being among them. Nikolai Shcherbatsky, Kitty's cousin, catching sight of Levin, exclaimed, "There is the best skater in Russia." Kitty cordially invited Levin to skate with her. He did so, and the faster they went together, the closer Kitty held his hand. And when after a spin they rested, and she asked how long he was going to stay in St. Petersburg, he astonished her by replying, "It depends on you." Either she did not understand, or did not wish to understand, his words, for she at once made an excuse to leave him.

At this moment Stepan came up and took Levin's arm, and the two went to the restaurant. Here Levin opened his soul to Stepan, and Stepan assured him that Kitty would become his wife. "But," said Levin, "it is shocking that we who are already getting old dare not approach a pure and innocent being. I look on my life with dismay, and mourn over it bitterly."

Said Stepan, "You have not much cause for self-reproach. What can you do? The world is thus constituted."

"There is only one comfort," replied Levin. "That is in the prayer I have always delighted in: 'Pardon me not according to my deserts, but according to Thy loving kindness.' Thus only can she forgive me."

IV

Kitty had another suitor, Count Vronsky, on whom she looked with the favour that she could not accord to Levin. He was rich, intelligent, of good birth, with a brilliant career before him in court and navy. He was charming, and in him the Princess Shcherbatsky saw an admirable match for her youngest daughter. Princess Kitty was now eighteen. She was the favourite child of her father. It was manifest to both parents that she was in love with Vronsky. Yet when at length Levin ventured on an actual declaration of his love, she was deeply agitated. Lifting her sincere glance to him, she said hastily, "This cannot be. Forgive me."

Anna Karenina arrived in the home of Stepan Arkadyevitch, where she was received with cordial kisses by Dolly, who remembered that Stepan's sister was not to blame, and that she was a grande dame of St. Petersburg, wife of one of the important personages of the city. She was delighted to think that at last she could open her mind and tell her troubles. And she was not disappointed, for in a lengthy and sympathetic colloquy Dolly's heart was touched with the sentiment of forgiveness.

Anna was one of the most beautiful and graceful of women. And she was as tactful as she was lovely. Before many hours she had successfully played the part of peacemaker, and thanked God in her heart that she had been able to effect complete reconciliation between Stepan and his wife. That same evening Anna went to a grand ball with Kitty and her mother, where the three were quickly saluted by Vronsky. It was a most brilliant affair. But next morning Anna telegraphed to her husband that she was leaving Moscow for home. It happened that Vronsky travelled by the same train, and thus the two were thrown together for the long journey.

V

Aleksei Alexandrovitch, though he affectionately met his wife, found but little time to spend with her. The next day several visitors came to dine with the Karenins. Every moment of Aleksei's life was fully occupied with his official duties, and he was forced to be strictly regular and punctual in his arrangements. He was an excellent man, and an intellectual one, delighting in art, poetry, and music, and loving to talk of Shakespeare, Raphael, and Beethoven.

Society in St. Petersburg is very united, and Anna Karenina had very friendly relations with the gay world of fashion, with its dinner parties and balls. She met Vronsky at several of these brilliant reunions. He, deeply impressed

with her, notwithstanding his connection with Kitty, went everywhere that he was likely to meet her, and her joy at meeting him easily betrayed itself in her eyes and her smile. And he did not refrain from actually making love to Anna on the occasions when they were able to engage in tête-à-tête conversations. Nor was he positively repelled. Soon the acquaintance became more and more intimate. Meantime, Aleksei as usual would come home and, instead of seeking his wife's society, would bury himself in his library amongst his books. But suddenly the idea that his wife could form an attachment to another man filled him with terror. He resolved to remonstrate with her, but she received his expostulations with laughing and good-humoured mockery, which entirely frustrated his purpose. He dropped the subject; yet from that moment a new life began for the husband and wife. There was no outward sign of the change. Anna continued to meet Vronsky, and Aleksei felt himself powerless to intervene.

While Vronsky was thus entangling himself with Anna Karenina at St. Petersburg, the Shcherbatskys at Moscow were growing anxious about the health of Princess Kitty, their beautiful daughter who was so deeply in love with him. She was ill, and after a consultation of physicians it was decided that travelling abroad would be advisable. But the girl said to herself that her trouble was one that they could not fathom, that her supposed illness and the remedies she had to endure were nonsense. What did they amount to? Nothing more than the gathering up of the fragments of a broken vase to patch it up again. Her heart was broken, and could it be healed by pills and powders?

VI

Absorbed by his passion, Vronsky yet proceeded in his regular manner of life, sustaining as usual his social and military relations. He loved his regiment and was very popular in it. Naturally, he spoke not a syllable to anyone about his passion. He drank moderately, and not an indiscreet word escaped him. But his mother was not a little disturbed when she discovered that his infatuation for Madame Karenina had impelled him to refuse an excellent promotion which would have necessitated his removal from the metropolis. She feared that instead of being a flirtation of which she might not disapprove, this passion might develop into a Werther-like tragedy and lead her son to commit some imprudence.

Many fashionable young ladies who were jealous of Anna and were weary of hearing her praised, were malignantly pleased to hear rumours to her disparagement and to feel justified in alluding scornfully to her. Vronsky received a message from his mother in Moscow. She desired him to come to her. His elder brother, though not himself by any means a pattern of perfect propriety, strongly expressed his dissatisfaction, because he felt that the unpleasant rumours would be likely to cause displeasure in certain high quarters.

Early in the spring, Anna Karenina's husband went abroad, according to his annual custom, to take the water-cure after the toils of winter. Returning in July to St. Petersburg, he at once resumed his official duties with the usual vigour. Anna had already gone into the country, not far from the capital, to the summer datcha at Peterhof. Since the pair had failed to come to a mutual understanding coolness had existed, but it was simply a cloud, not an actual alienation.

He resolved for the sake of appearances to visit his wife once a week. To his astonishment, his doctor called voluntarily on him, to ask if he might examine into the condition of his health. The secret reason of this was that a kind friend, the Countess Lidia, had begged the doctor to do so, as she had noticed that Aleksei did not look well. The medical man after the diagnosis was perturbed with the result, for Aleksei's liver was congested and his digestion was out of order. The waters had not benefited him. He was ordered to take more physical exercise and to undergo less mental strain, and above all to avoid all worry.

It was not with real pleasure, but with an affectation of cordiality that Anna received her husband when he reached the datcha. She was gay and animated. He was somewhat constrained, and the conversation was without any special interest. But Anna afterwards could only recall it with real pain. The crisis came on a racecourse. One of Vronsky's chief pleasures was horse-racing, and at the brilliant races that season he himself rode his own splendid horse. But the occasion was a most disastrous one, for at the hurdle races more than half the riders were thrown, Vronsky being one of them. He was picked up uninjured, but the horse had its back broken.

Aleksei and his wife and several friends were amongst the gay crowd, and he noted with deep displeasure that his wife turned pale when the accident happened and was strangely excited throughout the occasion. In the carriage, as the pair returned, he taxed her with her unseemly demeanour, and a violent quarrel ensued, in which she exclaimed, "I love him. I fear you. I hate you. Do as you please with me." And Anna flung herself to the bottom of the carriage, covering her face with her hands and sobbing convulsively.

Aleksei sat in silence during the rest of the journey home, but as they came near the house he said, "I insist that from this moment appearances be preserved for the sake of my honour, and I will communicate my decision to you after I have considered what measures I shall take." He assisted her to alight at the datcha, shook hands with her in the presence of the servants, and returned to St. Petersburg.

"Thank God, it is all over between us," said Anna to herself. But, notwithstanding this reflection, she had felt strangely impressed by the aspect of deathlike rigidity in her husband's face, though he gave no sign of inward agitation. As he rode off alone he felt a keen pain in his heart. But, curiously enough, he also experienced a sensation of deep relief of soul now that a vast load of doubt and jealousy had been lifted from him.

"I always knew she was without either heart or religion," said he to himself. "I made a mistake when I united my life with hers, but I should not be unhappy, for my error was not my fault. Henceforth for me she does not exist." He pondered over the problem whether he should challenge Vronsky, but he soon decided against the idea of fighting a duel. No one would expect it of him, so his reputation would not be injured by abstaining from such a proceeding. At length he came to the conclusion that an open separation would not be expedient and that the status quo alone was advisable, on the condition that Anna should obey his will and break off her acquaintance with Vronsky.

"Only thus," thought Aleksei, "can I conform to the requirements of religion. I give her another chance, and consecrate my powers to her salvation." He wrote his wife a letter saying that for his own sake, for her sake, and the sake of her son, their lives must remain unchanged, the family must not be sacrificed, and as he was sure she felt penitent, he hoped at their next interview to come to a complete understanding.

Though, when she received this communication, Anna felt her anger rising, yet her heart told her that she was in a false position from which she longed to escape. A new sensation had taken possession of her soul, and she seemed to be a double kind of personality. At length, after long agitation she wrote to her husband, telling him that she could no longer remain in his house, but was going away, taking their boy Serosha with her. "Be generous; let me have him," were the last words in the letter. She wrote a little note to Vronsky, but her cheeks burned as she wrote, and presently she tore the note to tatters. Then she made her preparations for going to Moscow.

VII

Anna returned to the home in St. Petersburg. Husband and wife met with a silent greeting, and the silence lasted some time. Then ensued an interview in which each side coldly accused the other, but which ended in Aleksei's demand that his wife should so comport herself that neither the world nor the servants could accuse her, on which condition she could enjoy the position and fulfil the duties of an honourable wife.

And so the Kareninas continued to live in the same house, to meet daily, and yet to remain strangers to each other. Vronsky was never seen near the place, yet Anna met him elsewhere and Aleksei knew it.

Meanwhile, a change was coming over the prospect for Kitty and Levin. He had never renounced the hope of possessing the beautiful girl, and at length she had come to understand his nobility of character and to feel that she could reciprocate his affection. During a conversation with her, he watched as she mechanically drew circles with chalk on the table-cloth.

"I have waited for a long time to ask you a question," said he, looking fondly at her.

"What is it?" said Kitty.

"This is it," said Levin, taking the chalk and writing the letters w, y, s, i, i, i, w, i, i, t, o, a? The letters were the initials of the words, "When you said 'It is impossible,' was it impossible then, or always?"

Kitty studied the letters long and attentively, and at length took the chalk and, blushing deeply, wrote the letters: t, I, c, n, a, d. Levin's face soon beamed with joy. He comprehended that the reply was: "Then I could not answer differently." Everything was settled. Kitty had acknowledged her love for him, and Levin at last was happy.

VIII

Aleksei sat alone in his room, pondering events, when he was startled by a telegram from his wife - "I am dying. I beg you to come; I shall die easier if I have your forgiveness." He read the words with momentary scorn, imagining that some scheme of deceit was being practised. But presently he reflected that it might be true, and, if so, it would be cruel and foolish to refuse to go, and besides, everybody would blame him.

He travelled all night and arrived, tired and dusty, in the morning at St. Petersburg. Reaching his house, he went into the drawing-room, and the nurse quickly led him into the bedroom, saying, "Thank God, you have come. She talks only of you."

"Bring ice at once," the doctor's voice was heard saying. Aleksei was startled to see in the boudoir, seated on a low chair, Vronsky, weeping with his hands over his face. And the latter was startled in turn as, disturbed by the doctor's words, he looked up and caught sight of the husband. He rose and seemed desiring to disappear, but with an evident effort said, "She is dying and the doctors say there is no hope. I am in your power, but allow me to stay and I will conform to your wishes."

Aleksei turned without replying and went to the door. Anna was talking clearly and gaily. Her cheeks were bright and her eyes gleamed. Rattling on incoherently, she suddenly recognised her husband, and looking terrified, raised her hands as if to avert a blow; but she said the next moment, "No, no, I am not afraid of him, I am afraid of dying. Aleksei, I have but a few moments to live. Soon the fever will return and I shall know nothing more, but now I understand everything. There is another being in me, who loved him and hated you, but now I am my real self. But no, you cannot forgive me. Go away, you are too good."

With one burning hand she pushed him away, with the other she held him. Aleksei's emotion became uncontrollable. His soul was filled with love and forgiveness. Kneeling by the bed, he sobbed like a child. The doctors said that there was not one chance in a hundred of her living.

Vronsky returned to his home in an agony of soul. He tried in vain to sleep. Visions of the faces of Aleksei and Anna rose before him. Suddenly his brain seemed to receive a shock. He rose, paced the room, went to the table, took from it a revolver, which he examined and loaded. Presently he held it to his breast and without flinching pulled the trigger. The blow knocked him down, but he had failed to kill himself The valet, who had heard the report, ran in, but was so frightened at the sight of his master lying on the floor wounded that he rushed out again for help. In an hour came Varia, Vronsky's sister-in-law, who sent for three doctors. They managed to put the wounded man to bed, and Varia stayed to nurse him.

IX

Vronsky's wound, though the heart was not touched, was so dangerous that for several days his life was in the balance. But gradually the crisis passed, and as he recovered he felt calmed with the conviction that he had now effected redemption from his faults. He accepted without hesitation an appointment to a position in Tashkend. But the nearer the time came, the more irrepressible grew the desire to see Anna for a farewell. He sent her a message, and she waited for his coming. The visit was fatal. Anna had made up her mind what to say, but the presence of Vronsky instantly overcame her resolution, and when she could find words she said, "Yes, you have conquered me. I am yours."

A month later Aleksei was left alone with his son, and Anna went abroad with Vronsky.

The marriage of Levin and Kitty was a brilliant occasion. A difficulty for Levin before the marriage was the necessity of attending confession. Like the majority of his fellows in society, he cherished no decided views on religion. He did not believe, nor did he positively disbelieve. But there could be no wedding without a certificate of confession. To the priest he frankly acknowledged his doubts, that doubt was his chief sin, that he was nearly always in doubt. But the gentle and kindly priest exhorted him to cultivate the practice of prayer, and then pronounced the formula of absolution.

In presence of a great assembly the wedding took place. The same priest who had heard the confession ministered for the marriage. He handed to each of the couple a lighted candle decorated with flowers. The chanting of an invisible choir resounded richly through the church, and when the liturgy was finished, the solemn benediction was read over the bridal pair. It was a great event in the fashionable world of Moscow.

X

Anna and Vronsky had been travelling for three months in Europe. As for Anna, she had revelled in the exuberance of her freedom from a disagreeable past, the events of which seemed like some frightful nightmare. She appeased her conscience to some extent by saying to herself: "I have done my husband an irreparable injury, but I also suffer, and I shall suffer." The prediction was soon fulfilled. Vronsky soon began to feel dissatisfied. He grew weary of lack of occupation in foreign cities for sixteen hours a day. Life soon became intolerable in little Italian cities, and Anna, though astonished at this speedy disillusionment, agreed to return to Russia and to spend the summer on his estate. They travelled home, but neither of them was happy.

Vronsky perceived that Anna was in a strange state of mind, evidently tormented by something which she made no attempt to explain. By degrees she, on her part, realized that Vronsky was willing to absent himself from her society on various excuses. Quarrels became frequent, and at length alienation was complete.

* * *

A tragedy happened on the railway. A woman went along the platform of the station and walked off on to the line.

Like a madman a short time afterwards Vronsky rushed into the barracks where Anna's body had been carried. Her head was untouched, with its heavy braids of hair and light curls gathered about the temples. Her eyes were half closed and her lips were slightly opened as if she was about to speak, and to repeat the last words she had uttered to him: "You will repent."

The war with Turkey had broken out, and Vronsky, disgusted with his whole life, left for Servia.

Strange Case of Dr Jekyll and Mr Hyde
by Robert Louis Stevenson
(London, 1886)

At least since Descartes (p175) the apparent dual nature of humans has been a puzzle. Stevenson gave it solid form in this story which, by one account, he discovered in a dream, then burned his first draft, only to re-write it with the help of a considerable quantity of cocaine. Jekyll and Hyde has provided the basis for *The Hulk*, *The Nutty Professor* and the whole superhero genre, as well as more than 120 stage and film adaptations.

Abridged: GH

STORY OF THE DOOR

MR. UTTERSON the lawyer was a man of a rugged countenance that was never lighted by a smile; cold and embarrassed in discourse, yet somehow lovable.

It was a nut to crack for many, the bond that united him to Mr. Richard Enfield, his distant kinsman. It was reported by those who encountered them in their Sunday walks, that they said nothing and looked singularly dull.

It chanced on one of these rambles that their way led down a by-street in a busy quarter of London.

Two doors from one corner a sinister block of building thrust forward its gable on the street. It was two stories high; showed no window, nothing but a blistered door on the lower story. Tramps slouched into the recess and struck matches on the panels.

Mr Enfield lifted up his cane and pointed. "Did you ever remark that door?" he asked; "It is connected in my mind," added he, "with a very odd story."

"I was coming home about three o'clock of a black winter morning, and I saw a little man stumping along eastward at a good walk, and a girl of maybe eight or ten who was running as hard as she was able down a cross street. Well, sir, the two ran into one another at the corner; and then came the horrible part of the thing; for the man trampled calmly over the child's body and left her screaming on the ground. It sounds nothing to hear, but it was hellish to see. It wasn't like a man; it was like some damned Juggernaut. I gave a view-halloa, took to my heels, collared my gentleman, and brought him back to where there was already quite a group about the screaming child.

'If you choose to make capital out of this accident,' said he, 'I am naturally helpless. Name your figure.' Well, we screwed him up to a hundred pounds for the child's family.

The next thing was to get the money; and where do you think he carried us but to that place with the door? - whipped out a key, went in, and presently came back with ten pounds in gold and a cheque for the balance on Coutts's.

His name was Hyde. He is not easy to describe. I never saw a man I so disliked, and yet I scarce know why.

Let us make a bargain never to refer to this again."

"With all my heart," said the lawyer.

SEARCH FOR MR. HYDE

That evening Mr. Utterson took up a candle and went into his business-room. There he opened his safe, took from the most private part of it a document endorsed on the envelope as 'Dr. Jekyll's Will', and sat down with a clouded brow to study its contents.

The will was holograph, for Mr. Utterson had refused to lend assistance in the making of it. It provided that, in case of the decease, disappearance or unexplained absence of Henry Jekyll, M.D., all his possessions were to pass into the hands of his "friend and benefactor Edward Hyde."

With that he blew out his candle, put on a great-coat, and set forth in the direction of Cavendish Square, that citadel of medicine, where his friend, the great Dr. Lanyon, had his house and received his crowding patients.

The hearty, healthy, dapper, red-faced gentleman, at sight of Mr. Utterson, sprang up from his chair and welcomed him with both hands.

"I suppose, Lanyon," said he "you and I must be the two oldest friends that Henry Jekyll has?"

"We were," was the reply. "But it is more than ten years since Henry Jekyll became too fanciful for me. Such unscientific balderdash," added the doctor.

"Did you ever come across a protégé of his - one Hyde?" he asked.

"No. Never heard of him."

That was the amount of information that the lawyer carried back with him to the great, dark bed on which he tossed to and fro, until the small hours of the morning began to grow large.

From that time forward, Mr. Utterson began to haunt the door in the by-street. "If he be Mr. Hyde," he had thought, "I shall be Mr. Seek."

And at last his patience was rewarded. The man was small and very plainly dressed, and the look of him, even at that distance, went somehow strongly against the watcher's inclination. Mr. Utterson stepped out and touched him on the shoulder as he passed.

"Mr. Hyde, I think? I am an old friend of Dr. Jekyll's, I thought you might admit me."

"You will not find Dr. Jekyll; he is from home," replied Mr. Hyde."But it is as well we have, met; and you should have my address." And he gave a number of a street in Soho.

Mr. Hyde was pale and dwarfish, he gave an impression of deformity without any nameable malformation, he had a displeasing smile, but these could not explain the disgust, loathing, and fear with which Mr. Utterson regarded him.

The other snarled aloud into a savage laugh; and the next moment, with extraordinary quickness, he had unlocked the door and disappeared into the house.

Round the corner there was a square of ancient, handsome houses, now for the most part decayed from their high estate and let in flats and chambers. One house, however, was still occupied entire; and at the door of this, Mr. Utterson stopped and knocked. A well-dressed, elderly servant opened the door.

"Is Dr. Jekyll at home, Poole?" asked the lawyer.

"Dr. Jekyll" said Poole, "Has gone out."

"I saw Mr. Hyde go in by the old dissecting-room door, Poole," he said. "Is that right, when Dr. Jekyll is from home?"

"Quite right, Mr. Utterson, sir," replied the servant. "Mr. Hyde has a key. We have all orders to obey him. Good-night, Mr. Utterson."

And the lawyer set out homeward with a very heavy heart. "Poor Harry Jekyll," he thought, "he is in deep waters."

THE CAREW MURDER CASE

Nearly a year later, in the month of October, 18--, London was startled by a crime of singular ferocity.

A maid servant became aware from her window of an aged and beautiful gentleman with white hair, and a very small gentleman she was surprised to recognise as a certain Mr. Hyde, who had once visited her master and for whom she had conceived a dislike. Next moment, with ape-like fury, Hyde was trampling his victim under foot and hailing down a storm of blows, under which the bones were audibly shattered. She called the police.

The stick with which the deed had been done had broken in the middle under the stress of this insensate cruelty; and one splintered half had rolled in the neighbouring gutter - the other, without doubt, had been carried away by the murderer.

A purse and a gold watch were found upon the victim: but no cards or papers, except a sealed and stamped envelope, which bore the name and address of Mr. Utterson.

Thus it was Mr Utterson who had the sad task of identifying the body as that of his client, the Member of Parliament Sir Danvers Carew. He quailed at the name of Hyde, and showed his police hosts to the dingy address in Soho, but Hyde was long gone and the servants tight-lipped.

INCIDENT OF THE LETTER

It was late that afternoon, when Mr. Utterson found his way to Dr. Jekyll's door, where he was at once admitted by Poole, and carried down by the kitchen offices and across a yard which had once been a garden, to the dingy, windowless building which was indifferently known as the laboratory or the dissecting-rooms.

A fire burned in the grate; a lamp was set lighted on the chimney shelf, for even in the houses the fog began to lie thickly; and there, close up to the warmth, sat Dr. Jekyll, looking deadly sick.

"And now," said Mr. Utterson, as soon as Poole had left them, "you have heard the news?"

The doctor shuddered.

"You have not been mad enough to hide this fellow?"

"I bind my honour to you that I am done with him in this world." replied Jekyll; "But I have received a letter; and I should like to leave it in your hands, Utterson; I have great trust in you."

The letter was written in an odd, upright hand and signed 'Edward Hyde'. The lawyer liked this letter well enough; it put a better colour on the intimacy than he had looked for; and he blamed himself for some of his past suspicions.

Presently Utterson sat on one side of his own hearth, with Mr. Guest, his head clerk, upon the other, and midway between them a bottle of old wine that had long dwelt unsunned in the foundations of his house, the glow of hot autumn afternoons on hillside vineyards ready to be set free and to disperse the fogs of London.

Guest was a great student and critic of handwriting. The clerk, besides, was a man of counsel.

"This is a sad business about Sir Danvers," he said. "The man, of course, was mad."

"I should like to hear your views on that," replied Utterson. "I have a document here in his handwriting. Here it is; a murderer's autograph. And beside it a second note, from my friend Dr. Jekyll."

The clerk laid the two sheets of paper alongside and sedulously compared their contents.

"Well, sir," he said, "there's a rather singular resemblance; the two hands are in many points identical: only differently sloped."

"Rather quaint," said Utterson.

"What!" he thought. "Henry Jekyll forge for a murderer!" And his blood ran cold in his veins.

THE LAST NIGHT

Some days later, Mr. Utterson was sitting by his fireside one evening after dinner, when he was surprised to receive a visit from Poole.

"What brings you here?" he cried; "is the doctor ill?"

"I think there's been foul play," said Poole, hoarsely.

Mr. Utterson's only answer was to rise and get his hat and great-coat.. It was a wild, cold, seasonable night of March, with a pale moon, lying on her back as though the wind had tilted her. Mr. Utterson thought he had never seen that part of London so deserted. Soon he found himself in front of Jekyll's door

The servant knocked in a very guarded manner; and a voice asked from within, "Is that you, Poole?"

"It's all right," said Poole. "Open the door."

"Jekyll," cried Utterson, with a loud voice, "I demand to see you." He paused a moment.

"Utterson," said the voice, "for God's sake, have mercy!"

"Ah, that's not Jekyll's voice - it's Hyde's!" cried Utterson. "Down with the door, Poole!"

A blow shook the building, and the red baize door leaped against the lock and hinges.

And there lay the cabinet before their eyes in the quiet lamplight, a good fire glowing on the hearth, the kettle singing its thin strain, and the things laid out for tea: the quietest room, you would have said, and, but for the glazed presses full of chemicals, the most commonplace in London.

Right in the midst there lay the body of a man sorely contorted and still twitching.

They drew near on tiptoe, turned it on its back and beheld the face of Edward Hyde. He was dressed in clothes far too large for him, life was quite gone; and by the crushed phial in the hand and the strong smell of kernels that hung upon the air, Utterson knew that he was looking on the body of a self-destroyer.

"We have come too late." he said sternly, "Hyde is gone to his account; and it only remains for us to find the body of your master."

Nowhere was there any trace of Henry Jekyll, dead or alive.

At one table, there were traces of chemical work, and, among the neat array of papers, a large envelope was uppermost, and bore, in the doctor's hand, the name of Mr. Utterson.

It was a brief note in the doctor's hand and dated at the top. "O Poole!" the lawyer cried, "he was alive and here this day."

And with that he brought the paper to his eyes and read as follows:

HENRY JEKYLL'S STATEMENT

I WAS born in the year 18-- to a large fortune, endowed with excellent parts, inclined by nature to industry, fond of the respect of the wise and good among my fellow-men, and thus with every guarantee of an honourable and distinguished future.

It was rather the exacting nature of my aspirations than any particular degradation in my faults, that severed in me those provinces of good and ill which divide and compound man's dual nature. And it chanced that the direction of my scientific studies, which led toward the mystic and the transcendental, shed a strong light on this consciousness of the perennial war among my members.

With every day I drew steadily nearer to that truth: that man is not truly one, but truly two. I began to perceive more deeply than it has ever yet been stated, the trembling immateriality, the mist-like transience of this seemingly so solid body in which we walk attired.

I not only recognised my natural body for the mere aura and effulgence of the powers that made up my spirit, but managed to compound a drug by which these powers should be dethroned from their supremacy. I hesitated long before I put this theory to the test of practice. I knew well that I risked death; but the temptation of a discovery so singular and profound, at last overcame the suggestions of alarm.

I purchased a large quantity of a particular salt which I knew, from my experiments, to be the last ingredient required; and late one accursed night, I compounded the elements, watched them boil and smoke together in the glass, and when the ebullition had subsided, with a strong glow of courage, drank off the potion.

The most racking pangs succeeded: a grinding in the bones, deadly nausea, and a horror of the spirit that cannot be exceeded at the hour of birth or death. Then these agonies began swiftly to subside, and I came to myself as if out of a great sickness.

I felt younger, lighter, happier in body; within I was conscious of a heady recklessness, an unknown but not an innocent freedom of the soul. I knew myself, at the first breath of this new life, to be more wicked, tenfold more wicked, sold a slave to my original evil; and the thought braced and delighted me like wine.

I stretched out my hands and was suddenly aware that I had lost in stature. The evil side of my nature was less robust and less developed than the good which I had just deposed. And hence, as I think, it came about that Edward Hyde was so much smaller, slighter, and younger than Henry Jekyll.

And yet when I looked upon that ugly idol in the glass, I was conscious of no repugnance, rather of a leap of welcome. This, too, was myself. It seemed natural and human.

That night I had come to the fatal cross-roads.

I would still be merrily disposed at times; and as my pleasures were (to say the least) undignified, I had but to drink the cup, to doff at once the body of the noted professor, and to assume, like a thick cloak, that of Edward Hyde.

I took and furnished that house in Soho, and engaged as housekeeper a creature whom I well knew to be silent and unscrupulous. On the other side, I announced to my servants that a Mr. Hyde (whom I described) was to have full liberty and power about my house in the square.

I next drew up that will to which you so much objected; so that if anything befell me in the person of Dr. Jekyll, I could enter on that of Edward Hyde without pecuniary loss. And thus fortified, as I supposed, on every side, I began to profit by the strange immunities of my position.

Think of it - I did not even exist! Let me but escape into my laboratory door, give me but a second or two to mix and swallow the draught that I had always standing ready; and whatever he had done, Edward Hyde would pass away like the stain of breath upon a mirror; and there in his stead, quietly at home, trimming the midnight lamp in his study, a man who could afford to laugh at suspicion, would be Henry Jekyll.

The pleasures which I made haste to seek in my disguise were, as I have said, undignified; I would scarce use a harder term. But in the hands of Edward Hyde, they soon began to turn toward the monstrous.

Some while before the murder of Sir Danvers, I had been out for one of my adventures, had returned at a late hour, and woke the next day in bed with somewhat odd sensations. My waking eyes fell upon my hand. The hand which I now saw in the yellow light of a mid-London morning, lying half shut on the bed-clothes, was lean, corded, knuckly, of a dusky pallor and thickly shaded with a swart growth of hair.

Yes, I had gone to bed Henry Jekyll, I had awakened Edward Hyde.

The next day, came the news that a murder had been seen, that the guilt of Hyde was patent to the world, and that the victim was a man high in public estimation. It was not only a crime, it had been a tragic folly.

I resolved to abjure Hyde, and in my future conduct to redeem the past; and I can say with honesty that my resolve was fruitful of some good.

It was a fine, clear, January day, wet under foot where the frost had melted, but cloudless overhead; and the Regent's Park was full of winter chirrupings and sweet with spring odours. I sat in the sun on a bench; the animal within me licking the chops of memory. I was, I reflected, like my neighbours; and then I smiled, comparing my active goodwill with the lazy cruelty of their neglect.

And at the very moment of that vain-glorious thought, a qualm came over me, a horrid nausea and the most deadly shuddering. I looked down; my clothes hung formlessly on my shrunken limbs; the hand that lay on my knee was corded and hairy. I was once more Edward Hyde, a known murderer, thrall to the gallows.

My drugs were in one of the presses of my cabinet; how was I to reach them? If I sought to enter by the house, my own servants would consign me to the gallows.

Thereupon, I arranged my clothes as best I could, and summoning a passing hansom, drove to an hotel. At the inn, the attendants trembled at my appearance, but obsequiously took my orders. In a private room the creature composed his important letters.

He dined alone with his fears, the waiter visibly quailing before his eye; and, when the night was fully come, he set forth in the corner of a closed cab.

He - I cannot say, I - thinking the driver had begun to grow suspicious, discharged the cab and ventured on foot, attired in his misfitting clothes. Once a woman spoke to him, offering, I think, a box of lights. He smote her in the face, and she fled.

I came home to my own house and got into bed. I awoke in the morning shaken, weakened, but refreshed. I was once more at home, in my own house and close to my drugs. It took on this occasion a double dose to recall me to myself; and alas! Six hours after, as I sat looking sadly in the fire, the pangs returned, and the drug had to be re-administered.

In short, from that day forth it seemed only by a great effort as of gymnastics, and only under the immediate stimulation of the drug, that I was able to wear the countenance of Jekyll. At all hours of the day and night, I would be taken with the premonitory shudder; above all, if I slept, or even dozed for a moment in my chair, it was always as Hyde that I awakened.

Under the strain of this continually-impending doom and sleeplessness I became a creature weak both in body and mind, and solely occupied by one thought: the horror of my other self.

My provision of the salt, which had never been renewed since the date of the first experiment, began to run low. I sent out for a fresh supply; I drank it and it was without efficiency, and I am now persuaded that my first supply was impure, and that it was that unknown impurity which lent efficacy to the draught.

I am now finishing this statement under the influence of the last of the old powders. Half an hour from now I shall again and for ever re-indue that hated personality. Will Hyde die upon the scaffold? or will he find courage to release himself at the last moment? Here then, as I lay down the pen and proceed to seal up my confession, I bring the life of that unhappy Henry Jekyll to an end.

Beyond Good and Evil
Prelude to a Philosophy of the Future
by Friedrich Nietzsche,
(Leipzig, 1886)

Nietzsche turned away from his life as a professor of Greek to devote himself to producing a whole series of, in his own time, unsold and unread books arguing that 'God is dead', that new thinkers are needed, free to create their own values. His ideal Übermensch, or 'Overman', would rise above the 'slave morality' of European Christianity to impose his will on the weak and worthless.

Was Nietzsche the philosopher of Nazism? Was Nietzsche mad? Or just the sort of genius which looks mad when viewed from below? Well, he only *officially* went insane in 1889, but, then, Nietzsche being Nietzsche, who knows?

Abridged: GH

PREFACE

Supposing that Truth is a woman - what then? Is there not ground for suspecting that all dogmatic philosophers, just as they have failed to understand women, have failed to woo truth?

The struggle against Plato[1], the struggle for the 'people', the struggle against Christian oppression (for Christianity is Platonism for the 'people'), has produced in Europe a magnificent tension of soul, such as had not existed anywhere previously. With such a tensely strained bow one can now aim at the furthest goals..

FN

Part One: On the Prejudices of Philosophers

1 The will to truth tempts us to many a venture. We want truth: why not rather untruth? Truth out of error or the pure and sunlike gaze of the sage out of lust? To be sure, among scientific men, you may find something like a drive for knowledge, a clockwork that, once wound, works without any participation from the other drives of the scholar.

8 There is a point in every philosophy when the philosopher's "conviction" appears on the stage.

9 Live "according to nature" said the ancient Stoics![2] What words these are! How can one not live according to nature? One must first, give the finishing stroke to that calamitous atomism which Christianity has taught best and longest, soul atomism - the belief that the soul is something indestructible.

13 Physiologists should think before taking the instinct of self-preservation as the cardinal instinct of organic beings.

A living thing seeks above all to discharge its strength - life itself is will to power; self-preservation is only one of the results.

We sail right over morality! Psychology is become again the path to fundamental problems.

Part Two: The Free Spirit

25 Take care, philosophers and friends of knowledge, beware of martyrdom! Of suffering "for the truth's sake"! You of all people, you knights of the sorrowful countenances[3], idlers and cobweb-spinners of the spirit, you know well enough that it cannot be of any consequence if you are proved right. You know that no philosopher so far has been proved right. Choose a good solitude, the free, playful, easy solitude that gives you, too, the right, to remain in some sense good!

27 It is hard to be understood, especially when one thinks and lives gangasrotogati among men who think and live kurmagati, or at best "the way frogs walk," mandeikagati - I do try to make myself hard to understand!

30 Our highest insights must, and should, sound like follies or even crimes when they are heard without permission by those they are not intended for. The virtues of the common man might perhaps signify vices and weaknesses in a philosopher. It might even be that only by degenerating into the lower spheres would the man of high type be there venerated as a saint. There are books that have opposite values for soul and health, depending on whether the sluggish lower soul, or the higher and more vigorous ones turn to them: in the former case, these books are dangerous and lead to crumbling and disintegration; in the latter, they are herald's cries calling the bravest to courage. Books for everybody are always foul-smelling books: the smell of small people clings to them. Where the people eat and

---

1 **Plato:** see p55
2 **Stoicism** (see p84)

3 **Knights of the Sorrow..** ie, pursuers of nothing see p163

drink and worship, there is usually a stink. One should not go to church if one wants to breathe pure air.

32 In the "pre-moral" period of mankind the imperative "know thyself!" was unknown; the value of an action was derived from its consequences.

33 Those feelings of devotion, self-sacrifice for one's neighbour, and the whole morality of self-denial must be questioned mercilessly and taken to court.

34 Shouldn't philosophers be permitted to rise above faith in grammar? All due respect for governesses but hasn't the time come for philosophy to renounce the faith of governesses?

Perhaps hardness and cunning furnish more favourable conditions for the strong, independent spirit and philosopher than that light-hearted good-naturedness which people prize in a scholar.

40 Whatever is profound loves masks, and hates image and parable. A questionable question: it would be odd if some mystic had not risked thinking it. A man whose sense of shame has some profundity encounters delicate decisions, of whose mere existence his closest intimates must not know. Not to cleave to a fatherland - not even if it suffers and needs help. Not to cleave to pity - not even when we see the torture of noble men. Not to cleave to a science - even if it lures us with precious discoveries.

42 A new species of philosophers is coming up: I venture to baptise them with a name that is not free of danger, and rightly or wrongly, call them attempters. Great things for the great, abysses for the profound, all that is rare for the rare.

44 These philosophers of the future will certainly be free spirits. In Europe and America, there are those 'levellers', so-called "free spirits", the eloquent scribbling slaves of democratic taste and "modern ideas", who have some courage, but are unfree and ridiculously superficial. They strive for the universal green pasture, happiness of the herd, security without danger, and an easier life for everyone. We opposite men, see how the plant "man" has grown most vigorously under the opposite conditions. We think that hardness, slavery, danger, experimentation, devilry, everything evil, tyrannical in man, everything akin to beasts of prey and serpents, serves to enhance the species as much as its opposite does. You new philosophers?

Part Three : The Religious Nature

46 The faith of primitive Christianity, surrounded by the sceptical southerly free-spirited world with its centuries-long struggle between philosophical schools, plus the education in tolerance of the Imperium Romanum, is not that gruff, true-hearted liegeman's faith with which a Luther, or a Cromwell, or some other northern barbarian, cleaved to his God. Christianity is a faith of sacrifice; sacrifice of all freedom, pride, self-confidence, and enslavement, self-mockery and self-mutilation.

51 Hitherto the mightiest men have bowed down reverently before the saint as the enigma of self-constraint and

voluntary renunciation: why? Moreover, the saint aroused a suspicion: such an enormity of denial, of anti-nature, could not have been desired for nothing. The mighty of the world sensed a new power, a strange enemy, it was the 'will to power' which constrained them to halt before the saint and question him.

One stands in reverence and trembling before these remnants of what man once was. At one time one sacrificed human beings to one's god, perhaps precisely those most loved. Then, in the moral epoch of mankind, one sacrificed to one's god the strongest instincts one possessed; one's 'nature'. Did one not have to sacrifice God himself, and worship nothingness?.

58 Has it been observed that genuine religious life requires leisure, I mean a leisure not unlike the aristocratic idea that work degrades? Perhaps there has up till now been no finer way of making man himself more beautiful than piety.

61 The philosophers, we free spirits, who take responsibility for the evolution of mankind, will make use of the religions, and the politics, for the work of education and breeding, so as to be able to rule. To ordinary men, the great majority, who exist only for service and general utility, religion gives an invaluable contentment with their station, peace of heart, an ennobling of obedience, a piece of joy and sorrow more to share with their fellows. Christianity and Buddhism, especially, have shed sunshine over these perpetual drudges, as an Epicurean[4] philosophy does on sufferers of a higher rank.

62 Among men, as among every other species, there is a surplus of failures, of the sick, the degenerate, the fragile, of those who are bound to suffer. The successful cases are, too, always the exception, and, in man as the animal whose nature has not yet been fixed, the rare exception. Men not high or hard enough for the refashioning of mankind, have allowed the law of thousandfold failure to prevail. Men, with their 'equal before God' have hitherto ruled the destiny of Europe, until at last a shrunken, almost ludicrous species, a herd-animal, something full of good will, sickly and mediocre has been bred, the European of today.

Part Four : Maxims and Interludes

108 There are no moral phenomena at all, only moral interpretations of phenomena.

134 All evidence of truth comes only from the senses.

137 Behind a remarkable scholar one often finds a mediocre man, and behind a mediocre artist, often, a very remarkable man.

156 Madness is something rare in individuals - but in groups, parties, peoples, ages it is the rule.

162 'Our neighbour is not our neighbour but our neighbour's neighbour' - thus thinks every people.

164 Jesus said to his Jews: 'The law was made for servants - love God as I love him, as his son! What have we sons of God to do with morality!'

---

4   **Epicurean Philosophy:** see p68

169 To talk about oneself a great deal can be a means of concealing oneself.

175 Ultimately one loves one's desires and not that which is desired.

176 The vanity of others offends our taste only when it offends our vanity.

Part Five : On the Natural History of Morals

186 Moral sensibility is as subtle, sensitive and refined in Europe today as the 'science of morals' is still young, clumsy and coarse-fingered.

188 Every morality is against 'nature' and 'reason': which is no objection unless another morality decrees tyranny and unreason impermissible. Morality is constraint.

195 The Jews - a people 'born for slavery' as Tacitus and the whole ancient world says, 'the chosen people' as they themselves say - achieved that miracle of inversion of values which gave two millennia a new and dangerous fascination. It is with them there begins the slave revolt in morals.

199 As long as there have been human beings there have been human herds (families, tribes, nations, states, churches), and always very many who obey and very few who command. Nothing has been cultivated among men better than obedience; 'thou shalt unconditionally do this, unconditionally not do that'. Those commanding have to deceive themselves that they too are only obeying; I call it the moral hypocrisy of commanders. The herd-man in Europe today glorifies his qualities of timidity, modesty, industriousness, and peace which make him useful to the herd. And when leaders seem to be indispensable, the clever herd-men gather together; this is the origin of all parliamentary constitutions.

200 Lofty spiritual independence, the will to stand alone, even great intelligence, are felt to be dangerous; everything that raises the individual above the herd and makes his neighbour quail is called evil. Eventually, under very peaceful conditions, every kind of severity, even severity in justice, begins to trouble the conscience; 'the lamb', even more 'the sheep', is held in higher and higher respect. One day everywhere in Europe the will to that day is now called 'progress'.

202 We know how offensive it sounds to say that man is an animal; and almost criminal to talk of 'herd' and 'herd instinct'. But we must insist: that which calls itself good, is the instinct of the herd-animal man. Europe seems threatened with a new Buddhism; a faith of mutual pity, with faith in the community, the herd, as the saviour.

203 We, who have a different faith - we, to whom the democratic movement is not merely politics in decay but also man in decay - whither is our hope? Towards new philosophers; towards spirits strong and original enough to revalue and reverse 'eternal values'. Towards men of the future who will compel the will of millennia on to new paths. The collective degeneration of man to the pygmy animal of equal rights and equal pretensions is certainly possible!

Part Six: We Scholars

204 The Declaration of Independence of science, its emancipation from philosophy, is one of the more subtle after-effects of the democratic formlessness of life. It is the colour blindness of the utility man who sees in philosophy nothing but refuted systems and wasteful expenditure which 'benefits' nobody. How our world is lacking royal and splendid hermits in the mould of Heraclitus, Plato or Empedocles! Philosophy reduced to 'theory of knowledge' is philosophy at its last gasp. How could such a philosophy rule!

206 Unlike genius, which always begets or bears, the scholar, the average man of science, has, like the old maid, some respectability, but no acquaintanceship with the two most valuable functions of mankind. So, what is the man of science? A species with ignoble virtues; subservient, unauthoritative and un-self-sufficient.

208 When a philosopher today gives us to understand that he is not a sceptic, all the world is offended. Our new philosophers will say: critics are philosophers' instruments and not philosophers themselves! Even the Chinaman of Königsberg[5] was only a great critic.

211 The philosopher must traverse the whole range of human value-feelings and be able to gaze from the heights into every distance, from the depths into every height. More - he must create values. Must there not be such philosophers?

Part Seven: Our Virtues

214 Our virtues? We Europeans of the day after tomorrow, we first-born of the twentieth century with all our dangerous curiosity, our multiplicity and art of disguise, our mellow and sugared cruelty in spirit and senses - if we are to have virtues we shall presumably have only such virtues as have learned to get along with our most secret and heartfelt inclinations. Alas! The fact emerges that the great majority of things which interest and stimulate every higher nature and refined taste appear altogether 'uninteresting' to the average man. There have been philosophers who have failed to state obvious truth that the 'disinterested' act is a very interesting and interested act, provided that ... But here truth prefers to stifle her yawns.

224 The historical sense, that Europeans speciality, has come to us through the mad and fascinating semi-barbarism into which Europe has been plunged through the democratic mingling of classes and races.

227 Honesty is our only virtue, we free spirits - let us labour at it with love and malice to 'perfect' ourselves in our virtue: may its brightness one day overspread this ageing culture like a gilded azure mocking evening glow!

228 May I be forgiven the discovery that all moral philosophy hitherto has been boring. Fear not! I see no one

5 **Chinaman:** Kant (p247), being as obscure as Confucius (p42)

in Europe who sees any danger in thinking about morality! In 'the common good', ultimately, they want English morality to prevail. It is here that the spirit lets itself be deceived, it enjoys the sense of being safe.

232 Woman wants to be independent, and so she is beginning to enlighten men about 'woman as such' - this is one of the worst developments in the general uglification of Europe. Is it not in the worst of taste when woman tries to adorn herself with science? But what is truth to a woman! Her great art is the lie, her supreme concern is appearance and beauty. Let us confess it, we men: it is precisely this art and this instinct in woman which we love and honour: which makes our seriousness appear to us almost as folly.

234 Woman does not understand what food means. It is the complete absence of reason in the kitchen, that the evolution of man has been most harmed.

237 Proverbs for Women

How the slowest tedium flees when a man comes on his knees!

Sober garb and total muteness dress a woman with astuteness.

God! Noble name, a leg that's fine, man as well: oh were he mine!

Men have hitherto treated women like beautiful, delicate, birds strayed down from the heights: but which must be caged to stop them escaping.

239 The weak sex has in no age been treated by men with such respect as it is in ours: is it any wonder if this respect is immediately abused? She wants more, she unlearns fear of man: and sacrifices her most womanly instincts. Wherever the spirit of industry has triumphed over the military and aristocratic, woman now aspires to economic and legal independence. As she looks to the 'progress' of women, the reverse is happening: woman is retrogressing. There is stupidity in this 'emancipation of women', an almost masculine stupidity, of which real woman - clever woman - will be ashamed from the very heart. Is woman slowly being made boring? O Europe! Europe!

Part Eight: Peoples and Fatherlands

240 A genuine token of the German soul, at once young and aged, over-mellow and still too rich in future.

245 Wagner's music for Manfred is a mistake to the point of injustice, his quiet lyricism merely a German event in music, not a European event. In him German music was losing the voice for the soul of Europe and sinking into mere nationality.

248 There are two kinds of genius: the kind which begets and the kind which likes to give birth. Likewise there are among peoples of genius those upon whom has fallen the woman's problem of pregnancy and the secret task of forming, maturing - the Greeks were a people of this kind, and so were the French, the Jews, the Romans and, I ask, the Germans? These two kinds of genius seek one another, as man and woman do; but they also misunderstand one another, as man and woman do.

251 If a people is suffering from nationalistic nervous fever, it must be expected that little attacks of stupidity will pass over its spirit. The Jews are wishing to be assimilated into Europe, they are longing to put an end to the nomadic life of the 'Wandering Jew'. European noblesse of feeling, taste, of custom, is the work and invention of France; European vulgarity, the plebeianism of modern ideas, that of - England.

254 France is still the seat of Europe's most spiritual and refined culture - and there are things which the French can still exhibit with pride. Their ancient, manifold, moralistic culture, by virtue of which even boulevardiers de Paris have a psychological sensitivity and curiosity of which Germans have no conception. The south preserves them from dreary northern grey-on-grey and makes in France a kind of patriotism, which knows how to love the south in the north and the north in the south - the born Midlanders, the 'good Europeans'.

256 Thanks to the morbid estrangement which the lunacy of nationality has produced between the peoples of Europe, and thanks to the shortsighted politicians who have used it - the obvious sign is being overlooked - Europe wants to become one. The more profound and comprehensive men of this century have anticipated the European of the future: only in their foreground hours of weakness were they 'patriots'. I think of men such as Napoleon, Goethe, Beethoven, Schopenhauer; and I include Richard Wagner.

Part Nine : What Is Noble?

257 Every elevation of the type "man," has hitherto been the work of an aristocratic society - a society believing in differences of worth among human beings, and requiring slavery in some form or other. The truth is hard.

260 There is master-morality and slave-morality; though in higher civilisations, there are some attempts to reconcile the two. When moral values have originated with the ruling caste, when the rulers have determined the conception 'good,' then 'good' and 'bad' means practically the same as 'noble' and 'despicable'. Here is the seat of the origin of the famous antithesis 'good' and 'evil': According to slave-morality, the 'evil' man arouses fear; according to master-morality, it is the 'good' man who arouses fear. And one fundamental difference: the desire for liberty necessarily belongs to slave-morals, just as reverence and devotion are symptoms of aristocratic thinking. Hence we can understand why love as passion - our European speciality - must necessarily be of noble origin.

261 Vanity, trying to arouse a good opinion of oneself, and even to try to believe in it, seems, to the noble man, such bad taste, so self-disrespectful, so grotesquely unreasonable, that he would like to consider vanity a rarity. The man of noble character must learn that in all social strata in any way dependent, the ordinary man has only

ever valued himself as his master dictates (it is the peculiar right of masters to create values). Vanity is an atavism.

262 A species originates, and becomes strong, in the long struggle with unfavourable conditions. The old morality is out of date. Danger is again present, the mother of morality, great danger.

263. There is an instinct for rank, which is itself a sign of a high rank. He who investigates souls will test each one by its instinct for reverence.

264 It cannot be effaced from a man's soul what his ancestors did: whether they were diligent economisers attached to desk and a cash-box; or whether they were accustomed to commanding from morning to night; or whether they sacrificed all for their "God". This is the problem of race.

265 At the risk of displeasing innocent ears, I submit that egoism belongs to the essence of a noble soul. He might call it "justice", and, once he has settled questions of rank he moves among his equals with respect.

267 Chinese mothers still teach their children "Siao-sin" ("make thy heart small"). Such self-dwarfing of latter civilisations would, no doubt, make an ancient Greek shudder at today's Europe.

268 When people have lived long together under similar conditions there grows an entity that "understands itself" - a nation. The greater their common danger, the greater the need of agreeing words about necessities. We discover how love and friendship falters when we realise that we understand words in ways unalike. Whenever a man finishes building his house, he discovers what he needed to know to begin.

278 Wanderer, rest here: there is hospitality for everyone. What refreshes? Speak out! 'Another mask! A second mask!'...

287 What is noble? How does the noble man betray himself, how is he recognised in the gloom of the new plebeianism? The noble soul has reverence for itself.

294 The Olympian Vice - Despite the, very English, philosopher who said; "Laughing is a bad infirmity of human nature, which every thinking mind will strive to overcome" (Hobbes), - I might rank philosophers according to the quality of their laughter.

295 The genius of the heart of the hidden tempter god, the pied-piper of consciences, whose voice can descend into the underworld of every soul. Have I forgotten to name who I talk about? I mean the God Dionysus, the great equivocator and tempter. I, his last disciple; might I give you, a little taste of his philosophy? The very fact that Dionysus, a god, is a philosopher, might arouse suspicion among you philosophers - loth nowadays to believe in God and gods. Here, you see, is a divinity lacking not only shame, but among gods who might learn from we humans. We humans are more - humane...

296 Alas! what are you, my written and my painted thoughts! Not long ago you were young and malicious and full of thorns and secret spices - you made me sneeze and laugh - and now? You have doffed your novelty, and some of you, I fear, are ready to become truths, so immortal do they look, so tediously honest! What then do we write and paint, we mandarins with Chinese brush? Alas, only that which is about to fade and lose its scent! Alas, only birds exhausted by flight, which let themselves be caught with our hand! We immortalise things exhausted and mellow! And it is only for your afternoon, my written and painted thoughts, for which alone I have many colours; but nobody will divine how you looked in your morning, you sudden sparks and marvels of my solitude, you, my old, beloved - wicked thoughts!

From High Mountains: Epode

Oh life's midday! Oh garden of summer!
I wait restless in ecstasy, I stand and watch and wait.
Where are you, friends?
Now is the time!
Let the old go! If once you were young, now you are
*   younger!*
The feast of feasts:
Friend Zarathustra has come, the guest of guests!
Now the world is laughing, the dread curtain is rent.

A Study in Scarlet
by Arthur Conan Doyle
(London, 1887)

This is the book which invented the modern crime novel by introducing the world to Sherlock Holmes. As of today there are some *four thousand* different books, films and plays featuring him, by far the most popular character in all fiction.

Abridged: GH

(From the reminiscences of JOHN H. WATSON, M.D)

IN the year 1878 I took my degree of Doctor of Medicine of the University of London, and joined the Northumberland Fusiliers as Assistant Surgeon, just as the second Afghan war had broken out. The campaign brought honours and promotion to many, but for me it had nothing but misfortune and disaster. At the fatal battle of Maiwand I was struck on the shoulder by a Jezail bullet, and sent back to England.

I naturally gravitated to London, that great cesspool into which all the loungers and idlers of the Empire are irresistibly drained. Thus it was that I found myself standing at the Criterion Bar, when some one tapped me on the shoulder, and I recognized young Stamford, who had been a dresser under me at Barts.

"Whatever have you been doing with yourself, Watson?"

"Looking for lodgings." I answered.

"That's a strange thing. A fellow up at the hospital was bemoaning himself this morning because he could not get someone to go halves with him in some nice rooms."

"By Jove!" I cried, "I am the very man for him."

Stamford looked rather strangely at me over his wine-glass. "You don't know Sherlock Holmes yet. He is a little queer in his ideas."

* * *

After luncheon we drove round to the chemical laboratory, a lofty chamber, lined and littered with countless bottles. There was only one student in the room, absorbed in his work. At the sound of our steps he glanced round and sprang to his feet with a cry of pleasure. "I've found it!" he shouted. "a re-agent which is precipitated by hoemoglobin, and by nothing else."

"Dr. Watson, Mr. Sherlock Holmes," said Stamford, introducing us.

"How are you?" he said, gripping my hand. "You have been in Afghanistan, I perceive."

"How on earth did you know that?" I asked in astonishment.

"Never mind," said he, chuckling to himself. "The question now is about hoemoglobin. Don't you see that it gives us an infallible test for blood stains. Ha! ha!"

"My friend here," said Stamford, "wants to take diggings, and I thought that I had better bring you together."

Sherlock Holmes seemed delighted. "I have my eye on a suite in Baker Street," he said, "You don't mind the smell of strong tobacco, I hope?"

"I always smoke 'ship's' myself," I answered.

* * *

No. 221B, Baker Street, consisted of a couple of comfortable bed-rooms and a single large airy sitting-room, illuminated by two broad windows. That very evening I moved my things round from the hotel.

Holmes was certainly not a difficult man to live with. He was quiet and his habits were regular. In height he was rather over six feet, and so excessively lean that he seemed to be considerably taller. His eyes were sharp and piercing, and his thin, hawk-like nose gave his whole expression an air of alertness.

He was not studying any course of reading which might fit him for a degree in any recognized portal, and his ignorance was as remarkable as his knowledge. Of contemporary literature, philosophy and politics he appeared to know next to nothing. My surprise reached a climax, however, when I found that he was ignorant of the Copernican Theory[1]. That any civilized human being in this nineteenth century should not be aware that the earth travelled round the sun!

"Now that I do know it," he said, smiling, "I shall do my best to forget it. You see, I consider that a man's brain originally is like a little empty attic. It is a mistake to think that that little room has elastic walls. It is of the highest importance, therefore, not to have useless facts elbowing out the useful ones. You say that we go round the sun, if we went round the moon it would not make a pennyworth of difference to me or to my work."

I was on the point of asking him what that work might be, but I saw that the question would not be welcome.

During the first week or so we had no callers, and I had begun to think that my companion was as friendless as I was myself. Presently, however, there was one little rat-faced fellow who was introduced to me as Mr. Lestrade. One morning a young girl called, fashionably dressed, and stayed for half an hour or more. The same afternoon brought a grey-headed Jew pedlar, a slip-shod elderly woman, and a railway porter in his velveteen uniform.

When any of these individuals put in an appearance, Sherlock Holmes used to beg for the use of the sitting-room. "I have to use this room as a place of business," he said, "and these people are my clients."

It was upon the 4th of March, when I picked up a magazine to while away the time with an article entitled "The Book of Life." It attempted to show how much an observant man might learn by an accurate and systematic examination of all that came in his way. "From a drop of water," said the writer, "a logician could infer the possibility of an Atlantic or a Niagara. All life is a great chain, the nature of which is known whenever we are shown a single link of it. Let the enquirer begin by mastering some elementary problems. Let him, on meeting a fellow-mortal, learn at a glance to distinguish the history of the man. By a man's finger nails, by his coat-sleeve, by his boot, by his shirt cuffs - by each of these things a man's calling is plainly revealed."

"What ineffable twaddle!" I cried, slapping the magazine down on the table.

Holmes remarked calmly. "I wrote that article myself."

"You!"

"Yes. The theories which I have expressed there, I depend upon for my bread and cheese."

"And how?" I asked involuntarily.

---

1   **Copernican Theory:** see p144

"Well, I have a trade. I suppose I am the only one in the world. I'm a consulting detective. People come, I listen to their story, they listen to my comments, and then I pocket my fee."

"But do you mean to say," I said, "that without leaving your room you can unravel some knot which other men can make nothing of?"

"Quite so. You appeared to be surprised when I told you, on our first meeting, that you had come from Afghanistan."

"You were told, no doubt."

"Nothing of the sort. I knew you came from Afghanistan. A gentleman of a medical type, but with the air of a military man. His face, dark. His left arm, injured. Where in the tropics could an English army doctor have got his arm wounded? Clearly in Afghanistan. The whole train of thought did not occupy a second."

"You remind me," I said, smiling, "Of Edgar Allen Poe's Dupin.

Sherlock Holmes rose and lit his pipe. "Dupin was a very inferior fellow. No man lives or has ever lived who has brought the same amount of study and of natural talent to the detection of crime which I have done."

I thought it best to change the topic.

"I wonder what that fellow is looking for?" I asked, pointing to a stalwart individual walking slowly down the other side of the street, looking anxiously at the numbers.

"You mean the retired sergeant of Marines," said Sherlock Holmes.

"Brag and bounce!" thought I to myself. "He knows that I cannot verify his guess."

The thought had hardly passed through my mind when we heard a loud knock, and heavy steps on the stair.

"For Mr. Sherlock Holmes," said the very same fellow, stepping into the room and handing my friend a letter.

"May I ask, my lad," I said, in the blandest voice, "what your trade may be?"

"Commissionaire, sir," he said, gruffly.

"And you were?" I asked, with a slightly malicious glance at my companion.

"A sergeant, sir, Royal Marine Light Infantry, sir."

"How in the world did you deduce that?" I asked Holmes as the visitor left.

"I have no time for trifles, look at this!" He threw me over the note which the commissionaire had brought.

MY DEAR MR. SHERLOCK HOLMES, - There has been a bad business during the night at 3, Lauriston Gardens, off the Brixton Road. Our man on the beat discovered the body of a gentleman, well dressed, and having cards in his pocket bearing the name of 'Enoch J. Drebber, Cleveland, Ohio, U.S.A.' There had been no robbery, nor is there any evidence as to how the man met his death. We are at a loss as to how he came into the empty house; indeed, the whole affair is a puzzler. I would esteem it a great kindness if you would favour me with your opinion. Yours faithfully, TOBIAS GREGSON.

"Gregson is the smartest of the Scotland Yarders," my friend remarked; "he and Lestrade are the pick of a bad lot. Get your hat."

A minute later we were both in a hansom, driving furiously for the Brixton Road, Holmes discoursing on Cremona fiddles.

"You don't seem to give much thought to the matter in hand," I said at last.

"It is a capital mistake," he answered, "to theorize before you have all the evidence. So it is. Stop, driver, stop!"

We were still a hundred yards away, but he insisted upon our alighting, and we finished our journey upon foot.

Number 3, Lauriston Gardens wore an ill-omened and minatory look. A small garden sprinkled over with sickly plants separated each of these houses from the street, and was traversed by a pathway of clay and gravel.

I had imagined that Sherlock Holmes would at once have hurried into the house. Nothing appeared to be further from his intention. With an air of nonchalance he lounged up and down the pavement, and gazed at the ground, the sky, the opposite houses and the line of railings.

At the door of the house we were met by a tall man, with a notebook in his hand. "It is indeed kind of you to come," he said, "I have had everything left untouched."

"Except that!" my friend answered, pointing at the pathway. "If a herd of buffaloes had passed along there could not be a greater mess."

Gregson rubbed his hands in a self-satisfied way. "I think we have done all that can be done,"

Holmes walked in, and I followed. A vulgar flaring paper adorned the walls, blotched in places with mildew, and here and there great strips had become detached and hung down, exposing the yellow plaster beneath.

My attention was centred upon the single grim motionless figure which lay stretched upon the boards. It was that of a man about forty-three years of age, middle-sized, broad shouldered, with crisp curling black hair, and a short stubbly beard. On his rigid face there stood an expression of horror, and hatred, such as I have never seen upon human features.

Lestrade, lean and ferret-like, greeted my companion.

Sherlock Holmes approached the body, and, kneeling down, examined it intently. "You are sure that there is no wound?" he asked, pointing to numerous splashes of blood which lay all round.

"Positive!" cried both detectives.

"Then, of course, this blood belongs to a second individual. It reminds me of the death of Van Jansen, in Utrecht, in the year '34."

"You can take him to the mortuary now," he said. "There is nothing more to be learned."

As Gregson's men raised the body, a ring tinkled down and rolled across the floor.

"This complicates matters." said Gregson.

"You're sure it doesn't simplify them?" observed Holmes, and appeared to be about to make some remark, when Lestrade, who had been in the front room, reappeared, rubbing his hands in a self-satisfied manner.

"Mr. Gregson," he said, "I have just made a discovery."

In a corner of the room a large piece of paper had peeled off. Across this bare space there was scrawled in blood-red letters a single word - RACHE

"And what does it mean?" asked Gregson in a depreciatory voice. "Why, it means that the writer was going to put the female name Rachel, but was disturbed before he or she had time to finish."

"I really beg your pardon!" said my companion, as he whipped a tape measure and a large round magnifying glass from his pocket. With these two implements he trotted noiselessly about the room, sometimes stopping, occasionally kneeling, and once lying flat upon his face.

"If you will let me know how your investigations go," he continued, "I shall be happy to give you any help I can. In the meantime I should like to speak to the constable who found the body."

Lestrade glanced at his note-book. "John Rance," he said. "You will find him at 46, Audley Court."

"Come along, Doctor," he said; "I'll tell you one thing which may help you in the case," turning to the two detectives. "There has been murder done, and the murderer was a man. He was more than six feet high, was in the prime of life, had small feet for his height, wore coarse, square-toed boots and smoked a Trichinopoly cigar. He came here with his victim in a four-wheeled cab, which was drawn by a horse with three old shoes and one new one on his off fore leg. In all probability the murderer had a florid face, and the finger-nails of his right hand were remarkably long. These are only a few indications, but they may assist you."

Lestrade and Gregson glanced at each other with an incredulous smile.

"Poison," said Sherlock Holmes curtly, and strode off. "One other thing," he added, turning round at the door: "'Rache,' is the German for 'revenge;' so don't lose your time looking for Miss Rachel."

He walked away, leaving the two rivals open-mouthed behind him.

* * *

"You amaze me, Holmes," said I. "Surely you are not as sure as you pretend to be."

"I observed on arriving that a cab had made two ruts with its wheels close to the curb. There were the marks of the horse's hoofs, too. The height of a man, in nine cases out of ten, can be told from the length of his stride. I had this fellow's stride both on the clay outside and on the dust within. It was child's play."

"The finger nails and the Trichinopoly," I suggested.

"The writing on the wall was slightly scratched, which would not have been the case if the man's nail had been trimmed. I gathered up some scattered ash from the floor. I have made a special study of cigar ashes - in fact, I have written a monograph upon the subject. As to poor Lestrade's discovery, the style of script tells me that it was not done by a German. It was simply a ruse to divert inquiry by suggesting Socialism and secret societies. I'm not going to tell you much more of the case, Doctor. You know a conjurer gets no credit when once he has explained his trick. We must hurry up, for I want to go to Halle's concert to hear Norman Neruda this afternoon."

Our cab had been threading its way through a long succession of dingy streets and dreary by-ways. Audley Court was not an attractive locality, and the constable a little irritable at being disturbed in his slumbers. "I made my report at the office," he said.

Holmes took a half-sovereign from his pocket and played with it pensively. "We should like to hear from your own lips," he said.

"My time is from ten at night to six in the morning. At eleven there was a fight at the 'White Hart'; but bar that all was quiet enough. Now, I knew that them two houses in Lauriston Gardens was empty on account of him that owns them won't have the drains seed to, though the very last tenant what lived in them died o' typhoid fever. I was knocked all in a heap at seeing a light in the window, and I suspected as something was wrong. When I got to the door ..."

"You stopped, and then walked back to the garden gate." my companion interrupted.

Rance stared at Sherlock Holmes with the utmost amazement upon his features.

"Where was you hid to see all that?"

Holmes laughed and threw his card across the table. "I am one of the hounds and not the wolf. Go on, what did you do next?"

"I went back to the gate and sounded my whistle. That brought Murcher and two more to the spot."

"Was the street empty then?"

"Well, it was, as far as anybody that could be of any good goes."

"What do you mean?"

The constable's features broadened into a grin. "I've seen many a drunk chap in my time," he said, "but never anyone so cryin' drunk as that cove a-leanin' up agin the railings, a-singin' at the pitch o' his lungs about Columbine's New-fangled Banner."

"His face - his dress - didn't you notice them?" Holmes broke in impatiently.

"We'd enough to do without lookin' after him," the policeman said. "I'll wager he found his way home all right."

"There's a half-sovereign for you," my companion said, standing up and taking his hat. "I am afraid, Rance, that you will never rise in the force. The man whom you saw is the man who holds the clue of this mystery. Come along, Doctor."

"The blundering fool," Holmes said, bitterly, as we drove back to our lodgings.

"I am rather in the dark still. If it is true that this man tallies with your idea of the second party in this mystery, why should he come back to the house?"

"The ring, man, the ring: that was what he came back for. There's the scarlet thread of murder running through the colourless skein of life, and our duty is to unravel it. And now for lunch, and then for Norman Neruda."

* * *

Homes was very late in returning - so late, that I knew that the concert could not have detained him all the time.

"Have you seen the evening paper?" he asked.

He threw the paper across to me and I glanced at the place he indicated. It was the "Found" column. "In Brixton Road, this morning," it ran, "a plain gold wedding ring, in the roadway between the 'White Hart' Tavern and Holland Grove. Apply Dr. Watson, 221B, Baker Street."

"Excuse my using your name," he said.

"And who do you expect will answer this advertisement."

"Why, our florid friend. If my view of the case is correct, this man would rather risk anything than lose the ring. You had better clean your old service revolver. He will be a desperate man."

I went to my bedroom and followed his advice. When I returned Holmes was engaged in his favourite occupation of scraping upon his violin.

There was a sharp ring at the bell. "Come in," I cried.

Instead of the man of violence whom we expected, a very old and wrinkled woman hobbled into the apartment. The crone drew out a paper, and pointed at our advertisement.

"It belongs to my Sally, married this time twelvemonth."

"Here is your ring, Mrs. Sawyer," I interrupted, "I am glad to be able to restore it to the rightful owner."

With many mumbled blessings and protestations of gratitude the old crone packed it away in her pocket, and shuffled off down the stairs.

Sherlock Holmes sprang to his feet and rushed into his room. He returned in a few seconds enveloped in an ulster. "I'll follow her," he said; Wait up for me."

* * *

It was past midnight when I heard the sharp sound of his latch-key. The instant he entered I saw by his face that he had not been successful.

"What is it then?" I asked.

"That creature had gone a little way when she began to limp, and hailed a cab. I perched myself behind and hopped off before we came to the address, and strolled down the street. I saw the driver jump down, and when I reached him he was groping about in the empty cab."

"You don't mean to say," I cried, in amazement, "that that tottering, feeble old woman was able to get out of the cab while it was in motion?"

"Old woman be damned!" said Sherlock Holmes, sharply. "We were the old women to be so taken in. It must have been a young man, and an active one, too, besides being an incomparable actor. Take my advice and turn in."

I was certainly feeling very weary, so I obeyed his injunction. I left Holmes seated in front of the smouldering fire, and long into the watches of the night I heard the low, melancholy wailings of his violin.

* * *

THE papers next day were full of the "Brixton Mystery." Sherlock Holmes and I read these notices over together at breakfast, and they appeared to afford him considerable amusement.

"What on earth is this?" I cried, for at this moment there came the pattering of many steps in the hall.

"It's the Baker Street division of the detective police force," said my companion, gravely; and as he spoke there rushed into the room half a dozen of the dirtiest and most ragged street Arabs that ever I clapped eyes on.

"'Tention!" cried Holmes, "Have you found it, Wiggins?"

"No, sir, we hain't," said one of the youths.

He presented a shilling, waved his hand, and they scampered away downstairs like so many rats..

"These youngsters go everywhere and hear everything; all they want is organisation. Here is Gregson coming down the road, bound for us, I know."

In a few seconds the detective burst into our sitting-room.

"My dear fellow," he cried, "congratulate me! We have the man under lock and key."

"Let us hear how you arrived at this gratifying result."

"You remember a hat beside the dead man?"

"Yes," said Holmes; "Underwood and Sons, 129, Camberwell Road."

"I had no idea that you noticed that," he said. "Well, I went to Underwood, he looked over his books, and came on it at once. He had sent the hat to a Mr. Drebber, residing at Charpentier's Boarding Establishment, Torquay Terrace. Thus I got at his address."

"Smart - very smart!" murmured Sherlock Holmes.

"I called upon Madame Charpentier. When I asked if they had heard about the mysterious death of Enoch J. Drebber, her features turned perfectly livid."

"Mr. Drebber had been staying there with his secretary, Mr. Stangerson. It seems that Drebber had returned drunk and made to force himself upon young Alice Charpentier. Alice's brother, a most violent man, had gone off after Drebber. I soon found out where Lieutenant Charpentier was, took two officers with me, and arrested him."

"Really, Gregson," said Holmes, "we shall make something of you yet."

What amuses me is to think of Lestrade, who had started off upon the wrong scent. Why, by Jove, here's the very man himself!"

"Mr. Lestrade!" cried Gregson, triumphantly. "Have you managed to find the Secretary, Mr. Joseph Stangerson?"

"Joseph Stangerson," said Lestrade gravely, "was murdered about six o'clock this morning."

"Are you - are you sure?" stammered Gregson.

Lestrade answered, seating himself. "I set myself to find out what had become of the Secretary, calling upon all the hotels and lodging-houses in the vicinity. This morning I reached Halliday's Private Hotel. On my enquiry as to whether a Mr. Stangerson was living there, they at once answered, 'No doubt you are the gentleman whom he was expecting. He is upstairs in bed.' The Boots pointed out the door to me, when I saw something that made me feel sickish. From under the door there curled a little red ribbon of blood. The door was locked on the inside, but we put our shoulders to it, and knocked it in. Beside the open window, all huddled up, lay the body of a man in his nightdress. The cause of death was a deep stab, which must have penetrated the heart. What do you suppose was above the murdered man?"

I felt a creeping of the flesh, and a presentiment of coming horror, even before Sherlock Holmes answered.

"The word RACHE, written in letters of blood," he said.

Lestrade continued "The milk boy had seen a man descend a ladder raised against one of the windows of the second floor. The boy imagined him to be some carpenter or joiner at work. He has an impression that the man was tall, had a reddish face. There were no papers in the murdered man's pocket, except a single telegram, dated from Cleveland about a month ago, and containing the words, 'J. H. is in Europe.' "

"And there was nothing else?" Holmes asked.

"Nothing of any importance. There was a small box containing a couple of pills."

Sherlock Holmes sprang from his chair.

"The last link," he cried, exultantly. "Could you lay your hand upon those pills?

"I have them," said Lestrade.

"Give them here," said Holmes. "Now, Doctor," turning to me, "would you mind going down and fetching that poor little devil of a terrier which has been bad so long."

I went downstairs and carried the dog upstairs.

"I will now cut one of these pills in two," said Holmes, "and on presenting it to the dog we find that he laps it up readily enough."

The unfortunate creature's tongue seemed hardly to have been moistened before it gave a convulsive shiver in every limb, and lay rigid and lifeless.

Mr. Gregson, could contain himself no longer. "Look here, Mr. Sherlock Holmes," he said, "we are all ready to acknowledge that you are smart. Can you name the man who did it?"

Neither of them had time to speak, however, before there was a tap at the door, and the spokesman of the street Arabs, young Wiggins, introduced his unsavoury person.

"Please, sir," he said, touching his forelock, "I have the cab downstairs."

"Very good, very good," said Holmes, smiling. "The cabman may as well help me with my boxes. Just ask him to step up, Wiggins."

The cabman entered the room, and put down his hands to assist. At that instant there was a sharp click, the jangling of handcuffs, and Sherlock Holmes sprang to his feet.

"Gentlemen," he cried, with flashing eyes, "let me introduce you to Mr. Jefferson Hope, the murderer of Enoch Drebber and of Joseph Stangerson."

The Country of the Saints.

Upon the fourth of May, eighteen hundred and forty-seven, a solitary man and a little girl-child lay dying, lost in the arid and repulsive desert of the great North American Continent. John Ferrier and his adopted daughter, Lucy, were saved by the pilgrim band of Mormons under their resolute holy prophet Brigham Young, in return for John promising to adopt their religion. John prospered in Mormon Utah, and kept his promise. Apart from one thing; he steadfastly refused to enter into a polygamous marriage as Mormonism demands, and equally refused to hand his daughter over to the Mormon Elders Stangerson or Drebber when she had her heart set on marrying the young prospector Jefferson Hope. Threatened by Brigham Young's sinister 'Danite Band', of 'Avenging Angels' who ruthlessly suppressed dissenters, John, Lucy and Jefferson tried to escape. Ferrier was murdered. Lucy was captured and forced into a multiple marriage with Elder Drebber. She died soon afterwards, though Jefferson Hope, now fugitive, managed to prevent her being buried with her sham wedding ring.

At Scotland Yard a police Inspector read the charge and said; "Mr. Jefferson Hope, have you anything that you wish to say? I must warn you that your words will be taken down, and may be used against you."

"I've got a good deal to say," our prisoner said slowly. "I have an aortic aneurism, I'm on the brink of the grave. If I die to-morrow, as is likely enough, I die knowing that my work in this world is done. I followed those fiends here, and got employment as a cab driver. Murder? Who talks of murdering a mad dog? He cowered away with prayers for mercy, but I drew my knife and held it to his throat until he obeyed me. He swallowed the poison, and I laughed, and held Lucy's ring in front of his eyes. The blood had been streaming from my nose, and I had the mischievous idea of setting the police upon a wrong track. I remembered a German being found in New York with RACHE written up above him, I guessed that what puzzled the New Yorkers would puzzle the Londoners. Then I walked down to my cab and put my hand into the pocket in which I usually kept Lucy's ring, and found that it was not there. I had to go on to do much the same for Stangerson. You may consider me to be a murderer; but I hold that I am as much an officer of justice as you are."

Jefferson Hope was led off by a couple of warders, while my friend and I took a cab back to Baker Street.

* * *

WE had all been warned to appear before the magistrates upon the Thursday; but there was no occasion for our testimony. A higher Judge had taken the matter in hand.

"Gregson and Lestrade will be wild about his death," Holmes remarked, as we chatted it over next evening. "Where will their grand advertisement be now? What you do in this world is a matter of no consequence, the question is, what can you make people believe that you have done. Never mind, simple as the investigation was, there were several most instructive points about it."

"Simple!" I ejaculated.

"I naturally began by examining the roadway, as I have already explained to you. There was no wound upon the dead man's person, but the agitated expression upon his face assured me that he had foreseen his fate before it came upon him. Having sniffed the dead man's lips I detected a slightly sour smell, and I came to the conclusion that he had had poison forced upon him. Robbery had not been the object, for nothing was taken. Was it politics, or was it a woman? The ring settled the question. I had already come to the conclusion that the blood which covered the floor had burst from the murderer's nose in his excitement, hence a ruddy-faced man. I telegraphed to the police at Cleveland, enquiring about the marriage of Enoch Drebber. The answer was conclusive; Drebber had already applied for the protection of the law against an old rival named Jefferson Hope, and that Hope was at present in Europe. I had already determined that the man who had walked into the house with Drebber, was none other than the man who had driven the cab. The marks in the road showed me that the horse had wandered on in a way which would have been impossible had there been anyone in charge of it. All these considerations led me to the irresistible conclusion that Jefferson Hope was to be found among the jarveys of the Metropolis. There was no reason to suppose that he was going under an assumed name. Why should he change his name in a country where no one knew his original one? I therefore organized my Street Arab detective corps, and sent them systematically to every cab proprietor in London until they ferreted out the man that I wanted.

"It is wonderful!" I cried. "You should publish an account of the case. If you won't, I will for you."

Tess of the d'Urbervilles
by Thomas Hardy
(London, 1891)

Hardy, son of a stonemason, created an imaginary version of the then disappearing old-time rural West of England; 'Wessex' His melodramatic stories, generally of people failing to escape their destiny, are among the most popular novels of all time, *Tess* alone has been filmed at least seven times. They challenged and often outraged the sexual and religious conventions of his day to the point where one book was solemnly burned by a bishop.

Abridged: GH

Phase the First: The Maiden

On an evening in the latter part of May, a middle-aged man was walking homeward from Shaston to the village of Marlott, in the Vale of Blakemore. The pair of legs that carried him were rickety, and there was a bias in his gait which inclined him somewhat to the left of a straight line. Presently he was met by an elderly parson astride on a gray mare, who, as he rode, hummed a wandering tune.

"Good night, Sir John," said the parson.

The pedestrian halted, and turned round.

"What might your meaning be in calling me 'Sir John', when I be plain Jack Durbeyfield, the haggler?"

Parson Tringham rode a step or two nearer.

"I am an antiquarian. Throw up your chin a moment. Yes, that's the d'Urberville nose and chin - a little debased. Your ancestors held manors over all this part of England; their names appear in the Pipe Rolls of King Stephen. Aye, there have been generations of Sir Johns among you."

"Ye don't say so! And where be our family mansions and estates?"

"You are extinct - as a county family."

"And shall we ever come into our own again?"

"Ah - that I can't tell!"

Concluding thus, the parson rode on his way, leaving Durbeyfield in a profound reverie with the faint notes of a band the only human sounds audible within the rim of blue hills.

* * *

The village of Marlott lay amid the tract of country, known in former times as the Forest of the White Hart. The forests have departed, but some old customs remain. The Women's May-Day dance, or "club-walking," had been walked for hundreds of years as a votive sisterhood of some sort; and it walked still. In addition to the distinction of a white frock, every woman and girl carried in her right hand a peeled willow wand, and in her left a bunch of white flowers.

As they came round by The Pure Drop Inn, one of the women said -

"The Load-a-Lord! Why, Tess Durbeyfield, if there isn't thy father!"

A young member of the band turned her head at the exclamation to see Durbeyfield moving along the road in a chaise belonging to The Pure Drop, leaning back, his eyes closed luxuriously, and singing -

"I've-got-a-gr't-family-vault-at-Kingsbere - and knighted-forefathers-in-lead-coffins-there!"

"He's tired, that's all," said Tess hastily.

"Bless thy simplicity, Tess," said her companions.

Among the on-lookers were three young men of a superior class, brethren spending their Whitsun holidays in a walking tour. The younger unstrapped his knapsack and opened the gate.

"What are you going to do, Angel?" asked the eldest, "Go dancing in public with a troop of country hoydens!"

But the young man took the first that came to hand. Their eyes met, but pedigree, ancestral skeletons and the d'Urberville lineaments, did not help Tess in her life's battle as yet.

* * *

Tess Durbeyfield remained with her comrades till dusk came and then bent her steps towards the parental cottage.

"Well, I'm glad you've come," her mother, Jane, said, "I want to tell 'ee what have happened! We've been found to be the greatest gentlefolk in the whole county - reaching all back long before Oliver Grumble's time - to the days of the Pagan Turks - with monuments, and vaults, and crests, and the Lord knows what all. Don't that make your bosom plim?"

"Will it do us any good, mother?"

"O yes! 'Tis thoughted that great things may come o't. Your father learnt it on his way hwome."

"Where is father now?" asked Tess suddenly.

Her mother put on a deprecating look. "He went up to Rolliver's half an hour ago. He do want to get up his strength for his journey to-morrow with that load of beehives, which must be delivered, family or no."

"Get up his strength!" said Tess impetuously.

"O, Tess. I will go," she said. "You hide the *Compleat Fortune-Teller* in the outhouse."

At Rolliver's inn Mrs Durbeyfield was welcomed with a mug and glances and nods by the conclave.

"He's told 'ee what's happened to us, I suppose?"

"Yes - in a way. D'ye think there's any money hanging by it?" said the landlady.

"Ah," said Joan Durbeyfield sagely. "There's a great rich lady out by Trantridge, of the name of d'Urberville. My projick is to send Tess to claim kin with her. I tried her fate in the *Fortune-Teller*, and it brought out that very thing!"

The conversation became inclusive, and presently other footsteps were heard. The newcomer was Tess; and hardly was a reproachful flash from her dark eyes needed to make her father and mother rise from their seats, hastily finish their ale, and descend the stairs behind her.

It was eleven o'clock before the family were all in bed, and two o'clock next morning was the latest hour for starting with the beehives if they were to be delivered to Casterbridge before the Saturday market. Her father was clearly in no proper state, so Tess hastily dressed herself; and went out to the stable.

Tess was not skilful in the management of a horse, but Prince required only slight attention, lacking energy for superfluous movements of any sort. Tess fell deeply into reverie, until a sudden jerk shook her in her seat.

The morning mail-cart, speeding along these lanes like an arrow, had driven into her slow and unlighted equipage. The pointed shaft of the cart had entered the breast of the unhappy Prince like a sword, and he suddenly sank down in a heap. The knacker and tanner offered only a very few shillings for his carcase, so, like a knight's charger of old, he was buried in the family garden. Tess regarded herself in the light of a murderess.

The haggling business, which had mainly depended on the horse, became disorganized forthwith. Tess, as the one who had dragged her parents into this quagmire, was silently wondering what she could do to help them out of it when her mother broached her scheme.

* * *

At Mrs d'Urberville's seat, The Slopes, simple Tess Durbeyfield stood at gaze, in a half-alarmed attitude, on the edge of the gravel sweep.

"I thought we were an old family; but this is all new!" she said, in her artlessness.

Parson Tringham had spoken truly - our shambling John Durbeyfield was the only lineal representative of the old d'Urberville family. Mr Simon Stoke, latterly deceased, had, on retiring, felt the necessity of a name that would not too readily identify him with the smart tradesman of the past. An hour of study in the British Museum discovered "d'Urberville", which, accordingly was annexed for himself and his heirs eternally.

Tess still stood hesitating like a bather about to make his plunge, when a tall young man came forth.

"Well, my Beauty, what can I do for you?" said he, "I am Alec d'Urberville. What is your business?"

"It is so very foolish," she stammered; "I came, sir, to tell you that we are of the same family as you."

"Ho! Poor relations?"

"Yes."

"Stokes?"

"No; d'Urbervilles."

"Ay, ay; I mean d'Urbervilles."

"Our names are worn away to Durbeyfield; but we have an old seal, marked with a ramping lion on a shield, and a castle over him. And we have a very old silver spoon, which mother uses to stir the pea-soup."

"Supposing we walk round the grounds to pass the time, my pretty coz?"

Tess wished to abridge her visit as much as possible; but the young man was pressing, and asked her if she liked strawberries.

"Yes," said Tess, "when they come."

"They are already here." D'Urberville began gathering specimens of the fruit, and holding one by the stem to her mouth.

"No - no!" she said quickly, putting her fingers between his hand and her lips. "I would rather take it in my own hand."

"Nonsense!" he insisted; and in a slight distress she parted her lips and took it in.

"I must think if I cannot do something for you. My mother must find a berth for you. But, no nonsense about 'd'Urberville'; - 'Durbeyfield' only, you know - quite another name."

"I wish for no better, sir," said she with something of dignity.

* * *

So it was that Tess found herself at The Slopes, mistress of a community of fowls, and a familiarity with Alec d'Urberville's presence - which that young man carefully cultivated in her by playful dialogue.

Then there came a Saturday in September, on which a fair and a market coincided; and the pilgrims from Trantridge sought double delights at the inns on that account. After the jigs were over, Tess and her companions began to make their way home.

Passing through a field-gate, an argument broke out. Fists were about to be raised at Tess, when a horseman emerged almost silently from the corner of the hedge, and Alec d'Urberville looked round upon them.

"What the devil is all this row about?" he asked.

Tess was standing apart from the rest, near the gate. "Jump up behind me," he whispered, "and we'll get shot of the screaming cats in a jiffy!"

At almost any other moment of her life she would have refused, but she scrambled into the saddle behind him.

"Heu-heu-heu!" laughed one of the girls: "Out of the frying-pan into the fire!"

The twain cantered along for some time, until Tess begged him to slow the animal to a walk.

"Neatly done, was it not, dear Tess?" he said by and by.

"Where be we?" she exclaimed.

"A bit of The Chase - the oldest wood in England. It is a lovely night, why not prolong our ride a little?"

"Put me down, I beg you, sir, please!"

"Very well, then, I will. But as to your getting to Trantridge without assistance, it is quite impossible."

She accepted these terms, and slid off on the near side, though not till he had stolen a cursory kiss. He sprang down on the other side.

He took a few steps away from her, but, returning, said, "By the bye, Tess, your father has a new cob to-day. Somebody gave it to him."

He touched her with his fingers, which sank into her as into down. "You have only that puffy muslin dress on - how's that?"

Doubtless some of Tess d'Urberville's mailed ancestors rollicking home from a fray had dealt the same measure even more ruthlessly towards peasant girls of their time. But though to visit the sins of the fathers upon the children may be a morality good enough for divinities, it is scorned by average human nature; and it does not mend the matter.

Phase the Second: Maiden No More

It was a Sunday morning in late October when Tess returned home, and by reaping time her new baby's offence against society in coming into the world was forgotten. However, it soon grew clear that the hour of emancipation for that little prisoner of the flesh was to arrive earlier than her worst misgiving had conjectured. And her baby had not been baptized.

Like all village girls, she was well grounded in the Holy Scriptures, and she thought of the child consigned to the nethermost corner of hell, as its double doom for lack of baptism and lack of legitimacy; saw the arch-fiend tossing it with his three-pronged fork, to which picture she added many other quaint and curious details of torment sometimes taught the young in this Christian country.

One night the infant's breathing grew more difficult. She lit a candle, and awoke her young sisters and brothers. Pulling out the washing-stand, she poured some water from a jug, and made them kneel around, putting their hands together with fingers exactly vertical; and thus the girl set about baptizing her child.

"Be you really going to christen him, Tess?"

The girl-mother replied in a grave affirmative.

"What's his name going to be?"

She had not thought of that, but a name suggested by a phrase in the book of Genesis came into her head:

"SORROW, I baptize thee in the name of the Father, and of the Son, and of the Holy Ghost."

She sprinkled the water, and there was silence.

In the blue of the morning that fragile soldier and servant breathed his last. So passed away Sorrow the Undesired - that intrusive creature, that bastard gift of shameless Nature; a waif to whom eternal Time had been a matter of days merely, to whom the cottage interior was the universe, and the instinct to suck human knowledge.

Even if the parson assured her that amateur efforts were doctrinally sufficient to secure salvation, that did not, it seemed, extend to a Christian burial. So the baby was buried by lantern-light, at the cost of a shilling and a pint of beer to the sexton, in that shabby corner of God's allotment where He lets the nettles grow, and where all unbaptized infants, notorious drunkards, suicides, and others of the conjecturally damned are laid. Tess bravely made a little cross of two laths and a piece of string, putting at the foot also a bunch of flowers in a little jar of water to keep them alive. What matter was it that on the outside of the jar the eye of mere observation noted the words "Keelwell's Marmalade"? The eye of maternal affection did not see them in its vision of higher things.

She - and how many more - might have ironically said to God with Saint Augustine: "Thou hast counselled a better course than Thou hast permitted."[1]

Almost at a leap Tess thus changed from simple girl to complex woman. On one point she was resolved: there should be no more d'Urberville air-castles. She would be the dairymaid Tess, and nothing more.

Phase the Third: The Rally

On a thyme-scented, bird-hatching morning in May, between two and three years after the return from Trantridge, Tess Durbeyfield left her home for the second time. In good heart, and full of zest for life, she descended the Egdon slopes towards the dairy of her pilgrimage. The master-dairyman, Mr Crick, was glad to get a new hand,

and he received her warmly, with his vague recollection of "some such name as yours in Blackmoor Vale that 'twere a old ancient race."

Two or three of the maids, blooming young women, Tess learnt, slept in the dairy-house besides herself and by bedtime one of her fellows insisted upon relating various particulars of the homestead into which she had entered.

"Mr Angel Clare - he that is here learning farming - is too much taken up wi' his own thoughts to notice girls. His father is the Reverent Mr Clare at Emminster - a very earnest clergyman."

At breakfast that Mr. Angel Clare noticed Tess, and seemed to discern in this virginal daughter of Nature something that was familiar, something which carried him back into a joyous and unforeseeing past.

The season developed and matured. Another year's instalment of flowers, leaves, nightingales, thrushes, finches, and such ephemeral creatures, took up their positions where only a year ago others had stood in their place when these were nothing more than germs and inorganic particles. Tess and Clare unconsciously studied each other, ever balanced on the edge of a passion, yet apparently keeping out of it. All the while they were converging, under an irresistible law, as surely as two streams in one vale.

One morning, there was a great stir in the milk-house. The churn revolved as usual, but the butter would not come. The dairy was paralyzed.

"'Tis years since I went to Conjuror Trendle's son in Egdon - years!" said the dairyman bitterly. "I don't believe in en; though 'a do cast folks' waters very true. But I shall have to go to 'n, if this sort of thing continnys!"

"Perhaps somebody in the house is in love," said Mrs Crick tentatively. "I've heard tell that will cause it."

Tess, pale-faced, had gone to the door.

"How warm 'tis to-day!" she said, almost inaudibly.

Izz Huett and Retty Priddle giggled,

"'Tis only one who is in love here," said jolly-faced Marian.

* * *

It was the hot of July when the rush of juices could almost be heard below the hiss of fertilization, that Angel Clare's reticences, prudences, fears, fell back like a defeated battalion. He jumped up from his seat at milking, and, leaving his pail, went quickly towards the desire of his eyes, and, kneeling down beside her, clasped her in his arms.

"Forgive me, Tess dear!" he whispered. "I am devoted to you, Tessy, dearest, in all sincerity!"

Tess's eyes, fixed on distance, began to fill.

"Why do you cry, my darling?" he said.

"O - I don't know!" she murmured.

---

1   **Augustine:** see p88, book X

A veil had been whisked aside; the tract of each one's outlook was to have a new horizon thenceforward - for a short time or for a long.

Phase the Fourth: The Consequence

Angel Clare spent a less than comfortable few days at his father's house in Emminster. His brothers were now returned from University and settled in holy orders, his parents expecting the same of Angel, and with an eye to their neighbour Mercy Chant as a pious wife. But he was set upon life as a farmer, which must needs a farmer's wife.

Back at the Talbothays dairy he came upon Tess skimming milk.

"I wish to ask you something of a very practical nature. I shall soon want to marry, and, being a farmer, you see I shall require for my wife a woman who knows all about the management of farms. Will you be that woman, Tessy?"

Driven to subterfuge, she stammered -

"I feel I cannot - never, never! Your father is a parson, and your mother will want you to marry a lady."

Her refusal, though unexpected, did not permanently daunt Clare, but it was some weeks before, while taking the milk cart up by Egdon Heath, that he asked her again. This time she found a different reason to refuse;

"But my history. You will not like me so well! I - I was -"

At the last moment her courage had failed her.

"I - I - am not a Durbeyfield, but a d'Urberville! I was told that you hated grand old families."

He laughed. "Now then, Mistress Teresa d'Urberville, I have you. Take my name, and so you will escape yours! You will?"

He clasped her close and kissed her.

"Yes!"

She had no sooner said it than she burst into a dry hard sobbing, so violent that it seemed to rend her.

"I must write to my mother," she said. "You don't mind my doing that?"

"Of course not, dear child. Where does she live?"

"At Marlott. On the further side of Blackmoor Vale."

"Ah, then I have seen you before this summer - "

"Yes; at that dance on the green; but you would not dance with me. O, I hope that is of no ill-omen for us now!"

By the end of the week Tess had a response to her communication in Joan Durbeyfield's wandering last-century hand.

Dear Tess, we are all glad to Hear that you are going really to be married soon. But, Tess, J say between ourselves, quite private but very strong, that on no account do you say a word of your Bygone Trouble to him. Keep up your Spirits, and we mean to send you a Hogshead of Cyder for you Wedding, knowing there is not much in your parts, and thin Sour Stuff

what there is. So with kind love to your Young Man.
- From your affectte. Mother, J. Durbeyfield

* * *

The wedding was held on new year's day, and as they came out of church and the ringers swung the bells off their rests, Tess stepped into the carriage.

"I am so anxious to talk to you - I want to confess all my faults and blunders!" she said with attempted lightness.

"No, no," he cried. "we shall both have plenty of time, hereafter, I hope, to talk over our failings."

"I tremble at many things. Among other things I seem to have seen this carriage before. It is very odd."

"Oh - you have heard the legend of the d'Urberville Coach?"

"What is the legend?"

"Well - a certain d'Urberville committed a dreadful crime in his family coach; and since that time members of the family see or hear the old coach whenever - But I'll tell you another day."

They drove to the house wherein they had engaged lodgings; once portion of a fine manorial residence, the property and seat of a d'Urberville, but since its partial demolition a farmhouse. But the mouldy old habitation, full of gloomy portraits, somewhat depressed the bride. Even the arrival of Clare's godmothers' jewels, a wedding gift from his parents, little raised her mood.

"Do you remember what we said about telling our faults?" he asked. "I want to make a confession to you, Love."

He then told her of his life in London, and an eight-and-forty hours' dissipation with a stranger.

"Do you forgive me?"

"O, Angel - I am almost glad - because now you can forgive me! I have a confession, too, 'tis just the same!"

Their hands were still joined. Before the fire, pressing her forehead against his temple, she entered on her story of her acquaintance with Alec d'Urberville.

Phase the Fifth: The Woman Pays

Her narrative ended, Clare performed the irrelevant act of stirring the fire.

"Tess! Am I to believe this?"

"I have forgiven you for the same!" she whispered.

"Tess," he said, as gently as he could speak, "I cannot stay - in this room. I will walk out a little way."

"Angel! - Angel! I was a child - a child when it happened! I knew nothing of men."

"You were more sinned against than sinning, that I admit. I do forgive you, but forgiveness is not all."

"And love me?"

To this question he did not answer, and that night he spent on his couch in the sitting-room, as the night came in and swallowed up his happiness. At breakfast the pair were, in truth, but the ashes of their former fires.

The day went. Midnight came and passed silently, for there was nothing to announce it in the Valley of the Froom. Not long after one o'clock Tess saw the door of her bedroom open, and the figure of her husband crossed the stream of moonlight with his eyes fixed in an unnatural somnambulistic stare. Clare came close, bent lower, enclosed her in his arms, and, lifting her from the bed, he carried her across the room, murmuring

"My wife - dead, dead!" he said. "My dearest, darling Tess! So sweet, so good, so true!"

Soon they were within the Abbey grounds. Clare carefully laid Tess in the ancient stone coffin of an abbot, when he immediately fell into the deep dead slumber of exhaustion.

Tess soon had him back on his own sofa bed, covered up warmly, and, the next morning divined that Angel knew little or nothing of the nocturnal proceeding.

He had ordered a vehicle from the nearest town, and soon after breakfast it arrived. The luggage was put on the top, and the man drove them off, by the dairy from which they had started, by the mead which had been the scene of their first embrace. The gold of the summer picture was now gray, and the river cold.

"Now, let us understand each other," he said gently. "There is no anger between us. Until I come to you, you must not try to come to me."

He handed her a packet containing a fairly good sum of money, he bade her goodbye; and they parted there and then.

A few days were all that Tess allowed herself back in her family house, while, for his part, Clare observed a red-and-blue placard setting forth the Empire of Brazil as a field for the emigrating agriculturist.

Let us press on to an October day, more than eight months subsequent. We discover a lonely woman, holding but a nominal sum, and reluctant to seek help of her, or her husband's, parents. Meanwhile her husband was lying ill of fever in the clay lands near Curitiba in Brazil.

Tess was now bound towards an upland farm west of the River Brit, a region where she might at last go unrecognized. All was, alas, worse than vanity - injustice, punishment, exaction, death. Resting among leaves she heard a new strange sound. Under the trees several pheasants lay about, their rich plumage dabbled with blood; all of them writhing in agony, the remnants of some shooting-party.

"Poor darlings - to suppose myself the most miserable being on earth in the sight o' such misery as yours!" she exclaimed, her tears running down as she killed the birds tenderly.

Tess went onward with fortitude, the birds' silent endurance impressing upon her the tolerable nature of her own. There is no sign of young passion in her now - she is set for

swede-hacking at Flintcomb-Ash, a poor starve-acre farm, along with Izz Huett and Retty Priddle and Marian.

* * *

When the snow had gone, she took advantage of the state of the roads to try an experiment. Sunday being the only day off for a farm worker, she started early. By a brisk walk she reached the edge of the vast escarpment above the loamy Vale of Blackmoor, in which Emminster and its Vicarage lay. Arriving there she took off the thick walking boots, put on her pretty thin ones of patent leather, and, stuffing the former into the hedge by the gatepost where she might readily find them again, descended the hill. At the Vicarage she nerved herself by an effort, entered the swing-gate, and rang the door-bell. The thing was done; there could be no retreat.

Nobody answered to her ringing. Ah - they were all at church, every one, and as she reached the churchyard-gate Tess found herself in the midst of them. Among them were two youngish men, in whose voices she did not fail to recognize the quality of her husband's tones. They were his two brothers.

"Here's a pair of old boots, thrown away," one said. "I'll carry them home for some poor person."

Thereupon our heroine resumed her walk. Tears, blinding tears, were running down her face. It was impossible to think of returning to the Vicarage.

Her journey back was rather a meander than a march. Sitting down at a cottage, while the woman fetched her some milk, Tess perceived that the street seemed quite deserted.

"The people are gone to hear the ranter preacher, my dear," said the old woman. "An excellent, fiery, Christian man, they say."

Tess went onward into the village, and soon heard the animated enthusiasm of the preacher. He had, he said, wantonly associated with the reckless and the lewd. But by the grace of Heaven a change had come. But more startling to Tess than the doctrine had been the voice, which, impossible as it seemed, was that of Alec d'Urberville.

Phase the Sixth: The Convert

There was the same handsome unpleasantness of mien, but now he wore neatly trimmed, old-fashioned whiskers and and his dress was half-clerical. The moment he recognized her the effect was electric;

"Tess!" he said. "It is I - Alec d'Urberville."

"Have you saved yourself?" she rejoined.

"I have done nothing!" said he indifferently. "Heaven has done all. My conversion was brought about by old Mr Clare; one of the few intense men left in the Church; You have heard of him?"

"I don't believe in you!", she cried passionately.

He stepped down and walked along with her. At length the road touched the spot called 'Cross-in-Hand', where an old stone pillar stands desolate and silent.

"I think I must leave you now," he remarked. "You upset me somewhat Tessy. I must go away and get strength. How is it that you speak so well now?"

"I have learnt things in my troubles," she said evasively.

"What troubles have you had?"

She told him of the first one - the one that related to him.

"I knew nothing of this!" he murmured. "Why didn't you write to me? Well - you will see me again?"

"No," she answered. "Do not again come near me!"

"I will think. But before we part come here." He stepped up to the pillar. "This was once a Holy Cross. Put your hand upon that stone hand, and swear that you will never tempt me - by your charms or ways."

"Good God - how can you ask what is so unnecessary!"

"Yes - but swear it."

Tess, half frightened, gave way; placed her hand upon the stone and swore.

"I am sorry you are not a believer," he continued, "At home at least I can pray for you. Goodbye!"

She kept along the edge of the hill by which lay her nearest way home. Within the distance of a mile she met a solitary shepherd.

"What is the meaning of that old stone I have passed?" she asked of him. "Was it ever a Holy Cross?"

"Cross - no! 'Tis a thing of ill-omen, Miss. 'Twas for a malefactor who was tortured there. They say his soul walks at times."

* * *

But Alec did not stay away. It was but a few days before he came to Tess as she worked in the fields.

"Will you not marry me, Tess, and make me a self-respecting man?"

"Never! I love somebody else. I have married him."

"And where is he? You are a deserted wife, my fair Tess. He will never come back, you know."

Farmer Groby espied the two figures, and inquisitively rode across.

"Go - I do beg you!" she said.

"What! And leave you to that tyrant?"

"He won't hurt me. He's not in love with me. I can leave at Lady-Day."

"But - well, goodbye! Pray for me, Tess!"

"How can I pray for you," she said, "when I am forbidden to believe that the great Power who moves the world would alter His plans on my account?"

"Tess?" he asked. "You seem to have no religion."

"But I have. Though I don't believe in anything supernatural. I believe in the spirit of the Sermon on the Mount, and so did my dear husband."

"The fact is," said d'Urberville drily, "whatever your dear husband believed you accept. That's just like you women. Your mind is enslaved to his."

"I have arranged to preach, and I shall not be there. You have been the cause of my backsliding," he continued, stretching his arm towards her waist; "you should be willing to leave that mule you call husband for ever."

"Punish me!" she said, turning up her eyes to him with the hopeless defiance of the sparrow's gaze before its captor twists its neck. "Whip me, crush me. I shall not cry out. Once victim, always victim - that's the law!"

That very night she began an appealing letter to Clare.

My own Husband, -

Let me call you so - I must - even if it makes you angry to think of such an unworthy wife as I. I have no one else! I am so exposed to temptation, Angel. I fear to say who it is, and I do not like to write about it at all. Can you not come to me now, at once, before anything terrible happens? Angel, I live entirely for you. Only come back to me. I would be content, ay, glad, to live with you as your servant, if I may not as your wife; so that I could only be near you, and get glimpses of you, and think of you as mine.

Your faithful heartbroken, Tess

* * *

Something happened which made Tess think of far different matters. Before long her father was dead. The news meant even more than it sounded. Her father's life had a value apart from his personal achievements. It was the last of the three lives for whose duration the house and premises were held under a lease.

Thus the Durbeyfields, once d'Urbervilles, saw descending upon them the destiny which, no doubt, when they were among the Olympians of the county, they had caused to descend many a time, and severely enough, upon the heads of such landless ones as they themselves were now.

* * *

Come the eve of Old Lady-Day, and the work-folk, as they used to call themselves, who wish to remain no longer in old places are moving to new farms, and Tess, back with her mother prepares to do the same.

She hardly at first took note of a man in a white mackintosh whom she saw riding down the street.

"Didn't you see me?" asked d'Urberville. "Where are you going to?"

"Kingsbere. We have taken rooms there."

"Why not come to my garden-house at Trantridge? Your mother can live there quite comfortably; and I will put the children to a good school. Really I ought to do something for you!"

Tess shook her head.

"I owe you something for the past, you know," he resumed. "And you cured me, too, of that craze; so I am glad - "

Whatever her sins, why should she have been punished so persistently?

* * *

As they arrived with their rented waggon at the half-dead townlet of their pilgrimage, Kingsbere, where lay those ancestors of whom her father had spoken and sung to painfulness, a man could be seen advancing.

"You be Mrs Durbeyfield, I reckon?" he said.

"Widow of the late Sir John d'Urberville, poor nobleman." She said.

"Oh? Well, I know nothing about that; I am sent to tell 'ee that the rooms you wanted be let. No doubt you can get other lodgings somewhere."

"What shall we do now, Tess?" she said bitterly. "Here's a welcome to your ancestors' lands!"

An hour later, when a search for accommodation had been fruitless, the waggon left them and their poor heap of household goods up under the churchyard wall, hard by the green foundations that showed where the d'Urberville mansion once had stood.

"Isn't your family vault your own freehold?" said Tess's mother, as she returned from a reconnoitre of the church and graveyard. "That's where we will camp, girls, till the place of your ancestors finds us a roof!

The door of the church was unfastened, and Tess entered it for the first time in her life.

On the dark stone of a canopied tomb were the words:

SEPULCHRI D'URBERVILLE

As Tess mused on her ancestral sepulchre, one of the effigies moved. Alec d'Urberville leapt off a slab.

"A family gathering, is it not?" he said smiling.

"Go away!" she murmured.

"I will - I'll look for your mother," said he blandly.

When he was gone she bent down upon the entrance to the vaults, and said -

"Why am I on the wrong side of this door!"

Phase the Seventh: Fulfilment

Angel Clare left the home of his parents, he went to the inn and hired a trap. Travelling and asking, Clare learned that John Durbeyfield was dead; that his widow and children had left Marlott, declaring that they were going to live at Kingsbere. His way was by the field in which he had first beheld her at the dance, and on through the churchyard, where, amongst the new headstones, he saw one of a somewhat superior design to the rest:

In memory of John Durbeyfield, rightly d'Urberville, 'How Are the Mighty Fallen.'

Finding Mrs Durbeyfield's tenement, he was awkwardly obliged to explain that he was Tess's husband, "Do you think Tess would wish me to try and find her? If not - "

"I don't think she would."

"I am sure she would!" he retorted passionately. "I know her better than you do."

"That's very likely, sir; for I have never really known her. She is at Sandbourne."

The next morning he walked out into this fashionable watering-place, and, from enquiries of the postman, arrived at a house called The Herons. There, the landlady herself opened the door. Clare inquired for Teresa d'Urberville or Durbeyfield.

"Will you kindly tell her that a relative is anxious to see her?"

"What name shall I give, sir?"

"Angel. She'll understand."

He was shown into the front room and looked out through the spring curtains at the little lawn, and the rhododendrons. Obviously her position was by no means so bad as he had feared.

Tess appeared on the threshold - not at all as he had expected to see her - bewilderingly otherwise, indeed.

"Tess!" he said huskily, "can you forgive me for going away?"

"It is too late," said she.

"But don't you love me, my dear wife?"

"I waited and waited for you," she went on. "But you did not come! And I wrote to you, and you did not come! He kept on saying you would never come any more, and that I was a foolish woman. He was very kind to me, and to mother. He - "

"I don't understand."

"He has won me back to him."

Clare looked at her keenly, then, gathering her meaning.

"He is upstairs. I hate him now, because he told me a lie - he said that you would not come again; and you have come! But - will you go away, Angel, please, and never come any more?"

They stood fixed, their baffled hearts looking out of their eyes with a joylessness pitiful to see. A few instants passed, and Tess was gone. A minute or two after, he found himself in the street.

Mrs Brooks, the landlady, sat in her back room, sewing. She heard the floorboards slightly creak, and saw the form of Tess passing through the gate and into the street.

Mrs Brooks pondered these events and leant back in her chair. As she did so her eyes were arrested by a spot in the middle of the ceiling which she had never noticed there before. She got upon the table, and touched the spot in the ceiling with her fingers. It was damp, and she fancied that it was a blood stain. Drip, drip, drip.

Within a quarter of an hour the news that a gentleman had been stabbed to death in his bed, spread through every street and villa of the popular watering-place.

Meanwhile Angel Clare had walked automatically to the station; reaching it, he sat down to wait, and as he gazed at the road a moving spot intruded on the white vacuity of its perspective. It was Tess.

"Angel," she said, breathless, "do you know what I have been running after you for? To tell you that I have killed him!" A pitiful white smile lit her face as she spoke.

"But how do you mean? What, bodily? Is he dead?"

"Yes. He heard me crying about you, and called you by a foul name; and then I did it."

Unable to realize the gravity of her conduct, she seemed at last content; and he looked at her as she lay upon his shoulder, weeping with happiness, and wondered what obscure strain in the d'Urberville blood had led to this aberration - if it were an aberration.

"I will not desert you! I will protect you, dearest love, whatever you may have done!"

"Where are we going?"

"Well, we might walk a few miles, and when it is evening find lodgings in a lonely cottage, perhaps. Can you walk well, Tessy?"

On the first night they found some rest in a deserted mansion-house. As they left for another night journey, Tess paused a moment ; "Happy house - goodbye!" she said. "My life can only be a question of a few weeks."

"Don't say it, Tess! We'll keep straight north, get to a port and away."

They had proceeded gropingly some miles when on a sudden Clare became conscious of a vast erection close in his front, rising sheer from the grass. They had almost struck themselves against it in the dark.

"What monstrous place is this?" said Angel.

"It hums," said she. "Hearken!"

He listened. The wind, playing upon the edifice, produced a booming tune, like the note of some gigantic one-stringed harp.

"A Temple of the Winds," he said. "It is Stonehenge!"

"The heathen temple, you mean?"

"Yes. Older than the centuries; older than the d'Urbervilles!"

"And you used to say at Talbothays that I was a heathen. So now I am at home."

He knelt down and put his lips upon hers.

"Sleepy are you, dear? I think you are lying on an altar."

"I like very much to be here," she murmured. "It seems as if there were no folk in the world but we two."

Clare flung his coat upon her, and sat down by her side.

"Angel, if anything happens to me, will you watch over 'Liza-Lu for my sake?" she asked.

"I will."

"I wish you would marry her if you lose me, as you will do shortly. Did they sacrifice to God here?" asked she.

"No," said he. "I believe to the sun."

"This reminds me, dear," she said. "Do you think we shall meet again after we are dead? I want to know."

He kissed her to avoid a reply.

"I fear that means no!" said she. "Not even you and I, Angel, who love each other so well?"

They slept with the great flame-shaped Sun-stone beyond them; and the Stone of Sacrifice midway. Presently the night wind died out, the dawn shone and figures came straight towards the circle of pillars in which they were.

"What is it, Angel?" she said, starting up. "Have they come for me?"

"Yes, dearest," he said. "They have come."

"It is as it should be," she murmured. "Angel, I am almost glad - yes, glad! This happiness could not have lasted. It was too much. I have had enough; and now I shall not live for you to despise me!"

She stood up, shook herself, and went forward.

"I am ready," she said quietly.

* * *

Up on a hill above the fine old city of Wintoncester Angel Clare and 'Liza-Lu watched a black flag raised above a large red-brick building, whose rows of short barred windows bespoke captivity.

"Justice" was done, and the President of the Immortals had ended his sport with Tess. And the d'Urberville knights and dames slept on in their tombs unknowing.

My Confession

(*Исповедь*)

by Count Leo Tolstoy

(Moscow, 1892)

His novels (p387) brought Count Lev Nikolayevich Tolstoy great success, and his position in the Russian Aristocracy brought great wealth. Yet he came to reject both for a fervent anarchist and pacifist interpretation of the teachings of Jesus (p77). This did not endear him to either government or church (he was excommunicated in 1901), but thousands tried to practice his principles in Tolstoyan communes throughout Russia and his ideas had a profound impact on such pivotal twentieth-century figures as Gandhi and Martin Luther King Jr.

Abridged: JH

I

Though reared in the faith of the Orthodox Church, I had by the time I left university ceased to believe what I had been taught. My faith could never have been well grounded in conviction. I not only ceased to pray, but also to attend the services and to fast. Without denying the existence of God, I cherished no ideas either as to the nature of God or the teaching of Christ.

I found that my wish to become a good and virtuous man, whenever the aspiration was in any way expressed, simply exposed me to ridicule; while I instantly gained praise for any vicious behaviour. Even my excellent aunt declared that she wished two things for me. One was that I should form a liaison with some married lady; the other that I should become an adjutant to the Tsar.

I look back with horror on the years of my young manhood, for I was guilty of slaying men in battle, of gambling, of riotous squandering of substance gained by the toil of serfs, of deceit, and of profligacy. That course of life lasted ten years. Then I took to writing, but the motive was grovelling, for I aimed at gaining money and flattery.

My aims were gratified, for, coming to St. Petersburg at the age of 26, I secured the flattering reception I had coveted from the authors most in repute. The war, about which I had written much from the field of conflict, had just closed. I found that a theory prevailed amongst the "Intelligentsia" that the function of writers, thinkers, and poets was to teach; they were to teach not because they knew or understood, but unconsciously and intuitively. Acting on this philosophy, I, as a thinker and poet, wrote and taught I knew not what, received large remuneration for my efforts with the pen, and lived loosely, gaily, and extravagantly.

Thus I was one of the hierarchs of the literary faith, and for a considerable time was undisturbed by any doubts as to its soundness; but when three years had been thus spent, serious suspicions entered my mind. I noted that the devotees of this apparently infallible principle were at variance amongst themselves, for they disputed, deceived, abused, and swindled each other. And many were grossly selfish, and most immoral.

Disgust supervened, both with myself and with mankind in general. My error now was that though my eyes were opened to the vanity and delusion of the position, yet I retained it, imagining that I, as thinker, poet, teacher, could teach other men while not at all knowing what to teach. To my other faults an inordinate pride had been added by my intercourse with these littérateurs. That period viewed retrospectively seems to me like one of a kind of madness. Hundreds of us wrote to teach the people, while we all abused and confuted one another. We could teach nothing, yet we sent millions of pages all over Russia, and we were unspeakably vexed that we seemed to gain no attention whatever, for nobody appeared to listen to us.

II

I travelled in Europe at this period, before my marriage, still cherishing in my mind the idea of general perfectibility, which was so popular at that time with the "Intelligentsia." Cultured circles clung to the theory of what we call "progress," vague though are the notions attaching to the term. I was horrified with the spectacle of an execution in Paris, and my eyes were opened to the fallacy underlying the theory of human wisdom. The doctrine of "progress" I now felt to be a mere superstition, and I was further confirmed in my conviction by the sad death of my brother after a painful illness of a whole year.

My brother was kind, amiable, clever, and serious; but he passed away without ever knowing why he had lived or what his death meant for him. All theories were futile in the face of this tragedy. Returning to Russia I settled in my rural home and began to organise schools for the peasants, feeling real enthusiasm for the enterprise. For I still clung to a great extent to the idea of progress by development. I thought that though highly cultured men all thought and taught differently and agreed about nothing, yet in the case of the children of the mujiks the difficulty could easily be surmounted by permitting the children to learn what they liked.

I also tried through my own newspaper to indoctrinate the people, but my mind grew more and more embarrassed. At length I fell sick, rather mentally than physically. I went off to the Steppes to breathe the pure air and to take mare's milk and to live the simple life. I married soon after my return to my estate. As time passed on I became happily absorbed in the interests of wife and children, largely forgetting during a happy interval of fifteen years the old anxiety for individual perfection. For this desire was superseded by that of promoting the welfare of my family.

All this time, however, I was writing busily, and was gaining much money as well as winning great applause. And in everything I wrote I persistently taught what was for me the sole truth - that our chief object in life should be to secure our own happiness and that of our family. Then, five years ago, supervened a mood of mental lethargy. I grew despondent; my perplexity increased, and I was tormented by the constant recurrence of such questions as-"Why?" and "What afterwards?" And by degrees the questions took a more concrete form. "I now possess six thousand desyatins of land in the government of Samara, and three hundred horses - what then?" I could find no answer. Then came the question, "What if I could excel Shakespeare, and Molière, and Gogol, and become the most celebrated the world has ever seen-what then?" Answer, there was none; yet I felt that I must find one in order to go on living.

Life had now lost its meaning, and was no longer real to me. I was a healthy and happy man, and yet so empty did life seem to me that I was afraid of being tempted to commit suicide, even though I had not the slightest intention to perpetrate such a deed. But, fearing lest the temptation might come upon me I hid a rope away out of my sight, and ceased carrying a gun in my walks.

III

It was in my 50th year that the question "What is life" had reduced me to utter despair. Various queries clustered round this central interrogation. "Why should I live? Why should I do anything? Is there any signification in life that can overcome inevitable death?" I found that in human knowledge no real answer was forthcoming to such yearnings. None of the theories of the philosophers gave any satisfaction. In my search for a solution of life's problem I felt like a traveller lost in a forest, out of which he can find no issue.

I found that not only did Solomon declare that he hated life, for all is vanity and vexation of spirit; but that Sakya Muni, the Indian sage, equally decided that life was a great evil; while Socrates[1] and Schopenhauer agree that annihilation is the only thing to be wished for. But neither these testimonies of great minds nor my own reasoning could induce me to destroy myself. For a force within me, combined with an instinctive consciousness of life, counteracted the feeling of despair and drew me out of my misery of soul. I felt that I must study life not merely as it was amongst those like myself, but as it was amongst the millions of the common people. I reflected that knowledge based on reason, the knowledge of the cultured, imparted no meaning to life, but that, on the other hand, amongst the masses of the common people there was an unreasoning consciousness of life which gave it a significance.

This unreasoning knowledge was the very faith which I was rejecting. It was faith in things I could not understand; in God, one yet three; in the creation of devils and angels. Such things seemed utterly contrary to reason. So I began to reflect that perhaps what I considered reasonable was after all not so, and what appeared unreasonable might not really be so.

I discovered one great error that I had perpetrated. I had been comparing life with life, that is, the finite with the finite, and the infinite with the infinite. The process was vain. It was like comparing force with force, matter with matter, nothing with nothing. It was like saying in mathematics that A equals A, or O equals O. Thus the only answer was "identity."

Now I saw that scientific knowledge would give no reply to my questions. I began to comprehend that though faith seemed to give unreasonable answers, these answers certainly did one important thing. They did at least bring in the relation of the finite to the infinite. I came to feel that in addition to the reasoning knowledge which I once reckoned to be the sole true knowledge, there was in every man also an unreasoning species of knowledge which makes life possible. That unreasoning knowledge is faith.

What is this faith? It is not only belief in God and in things unseen, but it is the apprehension of life's meaning. It is the force of life. I began to understand that the deepest source of human wisdom was to be found in the answers given by faith, that I had no reasonable right to reject them, and that they alone solved the problem of life.

IV

Nevertheless my heart was not lightened. I studied the writings of Buddhism, Islam, and Christianity[2]. I also studied actual religious life by turning to the orthodox, the monks, and the Evangelicals who preach salvation through faith in a Redeemer. I asked what meaning was given for them to life by what they believed. But I could not accept the faith of any of these men, because I saw that it did not explain the meaning of life, but only obscured it. So I felt a return of the terrible feeling of despair.

Being unable to believe in the sincerity of men who did not live consistently with the doctrines they professed, and feeling that they were self-deceived, and, like myself, were satisfied with the lusts of the flesh, I began to draw near to the believers amongst the poor, simple, and ignorant, the pilgrims, monks, and peasants. I found that though their faith was mingled with much superstition, yet with them the whole life was a confirmation of the meaning of life which their faith gave them.

The more I contemplated the lives of these simple folk, the more deeply was I convinced of the reality of their faith, which I perceived to be a necessity for them, for it alone gave life a meaning and made it worth living. This was in direct opposition to what I saw in my own circle, where I marked the possibility of living without faith, for not one in

---

1 **Socrates:** see p55

2 **Buddhism p16, Islam p92, and Christianity** p77

a thousand professed to be a believer, while amongst the poorer classes not one in thousands was an unbeliever. The contradiction was extreme. In my class a tranquil death, without terror or despair, is rare; in that lower class, an uneasy death is a rare exception. I found that countless numbers in that lower mass of humanity had so understood the meaning of life that they were able both to live bearing contentedly the burdens of life, and to die peacefully.

The more I learned of these men of faith the more I liked them, and the easier I felt it so to live. For two years I lived in their fashion. Then the life of my own wealthy and cultured class became repellent to me, for it had lost all meaning whatever. It seemed like empty child's play, while the life of the working classes appeared to me in its true significance.

Now I began to apprehend where I had judged wrongly. My mistake was that I had applied an answer to my question concerning life which only concerned my own life, to life in general. My life had been but one long indulgence of my passions. It was evil and meaningless. Therefore such an answer had no application to life at large, but only to my individual life.

I understood the truth which the Gospel subsequently taught me more fully, that men loved darkness rather than light, because their deeds were evil. I understood that for the comprehension of life, it was essential that life should be something more than an evil and meaningless thing revealed by reason. Life must be considered as a whole, not merely in its parasitic excrescences. I felt that to be good was more important than to believe. I loved good men. I hated myself. I accepted truth. I understood that we were all more or less mad with the love of evil.

I looked at the animals, saw the birds building nests, living only to fly and to subsist. I saw how the goat, hare, and wolf live, but to feed and to nurture their young, and are contented and happy. Their life is a reasonable one. And man must gain his living like the animals do, only with this great difference, that if he should attempt this alone, he will perish. So he must labour for the good of all, not merely for himself.

I had not helped others. My life for thirty years had been that of a mere parasite. I had been contented to remain ignorant of the reason why I lived at all.

There is a supreme will in the universe. Some one makes the universal life his secret care. To know what that supreme will is, we must obey it implicitly. No reproaches against their masters come from the simple workers who do just what is required of them, though we are in the habit of regarding them as brutes. We, on the contrary, who think ourselves wise, consume the goods of our master while we do nothing willingly that he prescribes. We think that it would be stupid for us to do so.

What does such conduct imply? Simply that our master is stupid, or that we have no master.

V

Thus I was led at last to the conclusion that knowledge based on reason is fallacious, and that the knowledge of truth can be secured only by living. I had come to feel that I must live a real, not a parasitical life, and that the meaning of life could be perceived only by observation of the combined lives of the great human community.

The feelings of my mind during all these experiences and observations were mingled with a heart-torment which I can only describe as a searching after God. This search was a feeling rather than a course of reasoning. For it came from my heart, and was actually opposed to my way of thinking. Kant[3] had shown the impossibility of proving the existence of God, yet I still hoped to find Him, and I still addressed Him in prayer. Yet I did not find Him whom I sought.

At times I contended against the reasoning of Kant and Schopenhauer, and argued that causation is not in the same category with thought and space and time. I argued that if I existed, there was a cause of my being, and that cause was the cause of all causes. Then I pondered the idea that the cause of all things is what is called God, and with all my powers I strove to attain a sense of the presence of this cause.

Directly I became conscious of a power over me I felt a possibility of living. Then I asked myself what was this cause, and what was my relation to what I called God? Simply the old familiar answer occurred to me, that God is the creator, the giver of all. Yet I was dissatisfied and fearful, and the more I prayed, the more convinced I was that I was not heard. In my despair I cried aloud for mercy, but no one had mercy on me, and I felt as if life stagnated within me.

Yet the conviction kept recurring that I must have appeared in this world with some motive on the part of some one who had sent me into it. If I had been sent here, who sent me? I had not been like a fledgling flung out of a nest to perish. Some one had cared for me, had loved me. Who was it? Again came the same answer, God. He knew and saw my fear, my despair, and so I passed from the consideration of the existence of God, which was proved, on to that of our relation towards him as our Redeemer through His Son. But I felt this to be a thing apart from me and from the world, and this God vanished like melting ice from my eyes. Again I was left in despair. I felt there was nothing left but to put an end to my life; yet I knew that I should never do this.

Thus did moods of joy and despair come and go, till one day, when I was listening to the sounds in a forest, and was still on that day in the early springtide seeking after God in my thoughts, a flash of joy illumined my soul. I realised that the conception of God was not God Himself. I felt that I had only truly lived when I believed in God. God is life. Live to seek God and life will not be without Him. The

---

3   **Kant:** see p247

light that then shone never left me. Thus I was saved from self-destruction. Gradually I felt the glow and strength of life return to me. I renounced the life of my own class, because it was unreal, and its luxurious superfluity rendered comprehension of life impossible. The simple men around me, the working classes, were the real Russian people. To them I turned. They made the meaning of life clear. It may thus be expressed:-

Each of us is so created by God that he may ruin or save his soul. To save his soul, a man must live after God's word by humility, charity, and endurance, while renouncing all the pleasures of life. This is for the common people the meaning of the whole system of faith, traditionally delivered to them from the past and administered to them by the pastors of the Church.

If -
by Rudyard Kipling
(London, 1895)

This evocation of the supposed British Virtues was said by its author to have been inspired by the failed military adventure of 'Lanner' Jameson in 1895 against the Boers of South Africa. The poem has repeatedly been voted Britain's favourite, and the line "If you can meet with Triumph and Disaster..." is inscribed over the player's entrance to the Wimbledon Tennis courts.

Unabridged

IF you can keep your head when all about you
Are losing theirs and blaming it on you,
If you can trust yourself when all men doubt you,
But make allowance for their doubting too;
If you can wait and not be tired by waiting,
Or being lied about, don't deal in lies,
Or being hated, don't give way to hating,
And yet don't look too good, nor talk too wise:

If you can dream - and not make dreams your master;
If you can think - and not make thoughts your aim;
If you can meet with Triumph and Disaster
And treat those two impostors just the same;
If you can bear to hear the truth you've spoken
Twisted by knaves to make a trap for fools,
Or watch the things you gave your life to, broken,
And stoop and build 'em up with worn-out tools:

If you can make one heap of all your winnings
And risk it on one turn of pitch-and-toss,
And lose, and start again at your beginnings
And never breathe a word about your loss;
If you can force your heart and nerve and sinew
To serve your turn long after they are gone,
And so hold on when there is nothing in you
Except the Will which says to them: 'Hold on!'

If you can talk with crowds and keep your virtue,
Or walk with Kings - nor lose the common touch,
If neither foes nor loving friends can hurt you,
If all men count with you, but none too much;
If you can fill the unforgiving minute
With sixty seconds' worth of distance run,
Yours is the Earth and everything that's in it,
And - which is more - you'll be a Man, my son!

The Ballad of Reading Gaol
by C.3.3
(London, 1897)

The great Irish poet and playwright Oscar Wilde (see p51) wrote this poem while incarcerated for the crime of homosexuality, disguising his authorship under his prison number.

Abridged: GH

In Memoriam
C.T.W. Sometime Trooper of the Royal Horse Guards.
Obiit H.M. Prison, Reading, Berkshire, July 7th, 1896

He did not wear his scarlet coat,
For blood and wine are red,
And blood and wine were on his hands
When they found him with the dead,
The poor dead woman whom he loved,
And murdered in her bed.

But I never saw a man who looked
    With such a wistful eye
Upon that little tent of blue
    Which prisoners call the sky

And wondering if the man had done
    A great or little thing
When a voice behind me whispered low
    'That fellow's got to swing'

Dear Christ! the very prison walls
    Suddenly seemed to reel,
And the sky above my head became,
    Like a casque of scorching steel;

And, though I was a soul in pain,
    My pain I could not feel
The man had killed the thing he loved
    And so he had to die

Yet each man kills the thing he loves,
    By each let this be heard
Some do it with a bitter look,
    Some with a flattering word.

The coward does it with a kiss,
    The brave man with a sword!
For Man's grim Justice goes its way,
    And will not swerve aside:

It slays the weak, it slays the strong,
    It has a deadly stride
For he who lives more lives than one
    More deaths than one must die

I know not whether Laws be right,
    Or whether laws be wrong;
All that we know who lie in gaol
    Is that the wall is strong;
And that each day is like a year,
    A year whose days are long

Heart of Darkness
by Joseph Conrad
(London, 1899)

King Leopold of Belgium, the man for whom the phrase 'crimes against humanity' was invented, murderously plundered his private African Congo for ivory and rubber under the pretence of promoting civilisation. It was there that the Polish-Ukrainian Conrad served, briefly, as a riverboat captain, for, as he said, "Heart of Darkness is experience, pushed only very little beyond the actual facts." The book has been adapted into the movie *Apocalypse Now*, and is one of the most discussed and the most admired of all stories.

Abridged: GH

I

The Nellie, a cruising yawl, was at rest. The sea-reach of the Thames stretched before us like the beginning of an interminable waterway. The air was dark above Gravesend, and farther back still seemed condensed into a mournful gloom, brooding motionless over the biggest, and the greatest, town on earth.

The Director of Companies was our captain and our host, there was the Lawyer, and the Accountant, and Marlow, leaning against the mizzen-mast. We exchanged a few words lazily. The sun set; the dusk fell on the stream, and lights began to appear along the shore.

"And this also," said Marlow suddenly, "has been one of the dark places of the earth." Marlow was a seaman still, his home the ship and his country the sea. "I was thinking of very old times, when the Romans first came here. Imagine the feelings of a commander ordered suddenly to the very end of the world. Land in a swamp, march through the woods, no proper food, and in some inland post, feel the savagery, the utter savagery, had closed round him."

He paused.

"Mind," he began again, "What saves us is the devotion to efficiency. They grabbed what they could get for the sake of what was to be got. It was just robbery with violence, aggravated murder on a great scale, and men going at it blind - as is very proper for those who tackle a darkness. The conquest of the earth, which mostly means the taking it away from those who have a different complexion or slightly flatter noses than ourselves, is not a pretty thing when you look into it too much. What redeems it is the idea only."

"I don't want to bother you much with what happened to me personally," he began, "yet, you ought to know how I got out there, what I saw, how I went up that river to the place where I first met the poor chap."

"I had just returned to London after a regular dose of the East and began to look for a ship. Now when I was a little chap I had a passion for maps. And there was one mighty big river, that you could see on the map, resembling an immense snake uncoiled, with its head in the sea, in a land still blank. Then I remembered there was a Company for trade on that river. Dash it all! Why shouldn't I? The snake had charmed me.

"Thanks to my aunt, who knew the wife of a very high personage in the Administration, I got my appointment.

"It appears that one of their captains - a Dane called Fresleven - had got a spear between the shoulder-blades after hammering a village chief over some trivial argument about two black hens. Oh, it didn't surprise me in the least to hear this, and at the same time to be told that Fresleven was the gentlest, quietest creature that ever walked on two legs. No doubt he was; but a couple of years out there engaged in the noble cause, you know, and he probably felt the need of asserting his self-respect. Months later, when an opportunity offered at last to meet my predecessor, the grass growing through his ribs was tall enough to hide his bones. The supernatural being had not been touched after he fell. And the village was deserted, mad terror had scattered them, men, women, and children, through the bush, and they had never returned. What became of the hens I don't know.

"Before forty-eight hours I was crossing the Channel to sign the contract and arrived in a city that always makes me think of a whited sepulchre. Prejudice no doubt. I had no difficulty in finding the Company's offices. It was the biggest thing in the town, and everybody I met was full of it. They were going to run an over-sea empire, and make no end of coin by trade.

"In the outer room two women knitted black wool feverishly. The secretary seemed uncanny and fateful. *Morituri te salutant*[1]. Not many of those she looked at ever saw her again - not half, by a long way.

"The old doctor felt my pulse, and produced a thing like callipers and got the dimensions of my head. 'In the interests of science.' he said. 'Ever any madness in your family?' I felt very annoyed. 'Adieu.' He lifted a warning forefinger. 'Keep calm, *du calme*. Adieu.'

"I left in a French steamer, which called at places with farcical names along coasts of monotonous grimness, in and out of rivers, streams of death in life, whose banks were rotting into mud that seemed to writhe at us in the extremity of an impotent despair.

"At last a rocky cliff appeared, mounds of turned-up earth by the shore, houses on a hill, others, with iron roofs, amongst a waste of excavations. A lot of people, mostly black and naked, moved about like ants. A jetty projected into the river. 'There's your Company's station,' said the Swedish captain, pointing to three wooden barrack-like structures on the rocky slope. 'So. Farewell.'

"A slight clinking behind me made me turn my head. Six black men advanced in a file, toiling up the path. Each had an iron collar on his neck, and all were connected together with a chain, rhythmically clinking. They passed me within six inches, with that complete, deathlike indifference of unhappy savages. Behind this raw matter one of the reclaimed, the product of the new forces at work, strolled despondently, and seeing a white man, hoisted his weapon

to his shoulder. For a moment I stood appalled, as though by a warning. Finally I descended the hill, obliquely, towards the trees I had seen.

"Black shapes crouched, lay, sat between the trees, leaning against the trunks, clinging to the earth, half coming out, half effaced within the dim light, in all the attitudes of pain, abandonment, and despair. A mine on the cliff went off. The work was going on. The work! And this was the place where some of the helpers had withdrawn to die.

"Brought from all the recesses of the coast, lost in uncongenial surroundings, fed on unfamiliar food, they sickened, became inefficient, and were then allowed to crawl away and rest. I found nothing else to do but to offer one of my good Swede's ship's biscuits I had in my pocket. Fingers closed slowly on it and held - there was no other movement and no other glance.

"I didn't want any more loitering, and made haste towards the station.

"When near the buildings I met a white man, in such an unexpected elegance of get-up that in the first moment I took him for a sort of vision. I saw a high starched collar, white cuffs, a light alpaca jacket, snowy trousers, a clear necktie, and varnished boots. He was amazing, and had a penholder behind his ear.

"I shook hands with this miracle, and I learned he was the Company's chief accountant. Everything else in the station was in a muddle, - heads, things, buildings. Strings of dusty niggers with splay feet arrived and departed; a stream of manufactured goods, rubbishy cottons, beads, and brass-wire, and in return came a precious trickle of ivory.

"I had to wait in the station for ten days - an eternity. I lived in a hut in the yard, but to be out of the chaos I would sometimes get into the accountant's office. One day he remarked, 'In the interior you will no doubt meet Mr. Kurtz. He is a very remarkable person. Sends in as much ivory as all the others put together ... .' He began to write again. The flies buzzed in a great peace; and fifty feet below the doorstep I could see the still tree-tops of the grove of death.

"Next day I left that station at last, with a caravan of sixty men, for a two-hundred-mile tramp.

"I passed through several abandoned villages. There's something pathetically childish in the ruins of grass walls. Now and then a carrier dead in harness, at rest in the long grass near the path. A great silence around and above. Perhaps on some quiet night the tremor of far-off drums, sinking, swelling, a tremor vast, faint; a sound weird, appealing, suggestive, and wild - and perhaps with as profound a meaning as the sound of bells in a Christian country. Once a white man in an unbuttoned uniform, very hospitable and festive - not to say drunk. Was looking after the upkeep of the road, he declared. Can't say I saw any road or any upkeep, unless the body of a middle-aged negro, with a bullet-hole in the forehead, upon which I absolutely stumbled three miles farther on, may be considered as a permanent improvement. On the fifteenth

---

1   *Morituri...*"Those who are about to die salute you", the supposed cry of ancient Roman gladiators before the fight.

day I came in sight of the big river again, and hobbled into the Central Station. White men with long staves in their hands appeared languidly. One of them, a stout, excitable chap with black moustaches, informed me with great volubility and many digressions, that my steamer was at the bottom of the river. I was thunderstruck.

"Still, it presented itself simply as a confounded nuisance. I had to set about it the very next day.

"My first interview with the manager was curious. He was a common trader - nothing more. He was obeyed, yet he inspired neither love nor fear, nor even respect. He inspired uneasiness. Not a definite mistrust - just uneasiness - nothing more. You have no idea how effective such a ... a ... faculty can be.

"He began to speak as soon as he saw me. The up-river stations had to be relieved. There were rumours that a very important station was in jeopardy, and its chief, Mr. Kurtz, was ill. Hoped it was not true. He was a chattering idiot.

"Oh, these months! Well, never mind. Various things happened. One evening a grass shed full of calico, cotton prints, beads, and I don't know what else, burst into a blaze.

"I strolled up. A nigger was being beaten. As I approached the glow I found myself at the back of two men, talking. I heard the name of Kurtz pronounced, then the words, 'take advantage of this unfortunate accident.' One of the men was a first-class agent, young, gentlemanly, a bit reserved, with a forked little beard and a hooked nose. He asked me to his room, which was in the main building of the station. He struck a match, and I perceived that this young aristocrat had not only a silver-mounted dressing-case but also a whole candle all to himself. Native mats covered the clay walls; a collection of spears, assegais, shields, knives was hung up in trophies. I noticed a small sketch in oils, on a panel, representing a woman, draped and blindfolded, carrying a lighted torch. 'Tell me, pray,' said I, 'who is this Mr. Kurtz?'

"'The chief of the Inner Station,' he answered in a short tone. 'He is a prodigy, an emissary of pity, and science, and progress' he began to declaim, 'for the guidance of the cause intrusted to us by Europe, so to speak.'

Mr. Kurtz was a 'universal genius,' but even a genius would find it easier to work with 'adequate tools - intelligent men.' Did I see it? I saw it. What more did I want? What I really wanted was rivets, by heaven!

"But instead of rivets there came an invasion of white men on donkeys calling themselves the Eldorado Exploring Expedition. To tear treasure out of the bowels of the land was their desire, with no more moral purpose than there is in burglars breaking into a safe.

II

"One evening as I was lying flat on the deck of my steamboat, I heard voices approaching. I laid my head on my arm when somebody said in my ear, as it were: 'Am I the manager - or am I not? ... I was ordered to send him there. - It is unpleasant. - He sent his assistant down the river with a note to me in these terms: "Clear this poor devil out of the country, and don't bother sending more of that sort'. Then silence. They had been talking about Kurtz. 'We will not be free from unfair competition till one of these fellows is hanged for an example,' 'Each station should be like a beacon on the road towards better things, a centre for trade of course, but also for humanizing, improving, instructing.'

"They swore aloud together, then turned back to the station.

"In a few days the Eldorado Expedition went into the patient wilderness, that closed upon it as the sea closes over a diver.

"Going up that river was like travelling back to the earliest beginnings of the world, when vegetation rioted on the earth and the big trees were kings. The air was warm, thick, heavy, sluggish. On silvery sandbanks hippos and alligators sunned themselves side by side.

"I don't pretend to say that steamboat floated all the time. More than once she had to wade for a bit, with twenty cannibals splashing around and pushing. We had enlisted some of these chaps on the way for a crew, and I am grateful to them. And, after all, they did not eat each other before my face: they had brought along a provision of hippo-meat, which went rotten and stank. I had the manager on board and three or four pilgrims with their staves - all complete. The earth seemed unearthly. And we crept on, towards Kurtz.

"Some fifty miles below the Inner Station we came upon a hut of reeds, an inclined and melancholy pole, with the unrecognisable tatters of what had been a flag of some sort flying from it. This was unexpected. We came to the bank, and on a stack of firewood found a flat piece of board with some faded pencil-writing on it. It said: 'Hurry up. Approach cautiously.' Where? Up the river? 'Approach cautiously.' We had not done so. The bush around said nothing. By the door I picked up a book; 'An Inquiry into some Points of Seamanship' by Tower, Towson - some such name. Such a book being there was wonderful enough; but still more astounding were the notes pencilled in the margin, and plainly referring to the text. They were in cipher! It was an extravagant mystery.

"I started the lame engine ahead. 'It must be some miserable trader - an intruder,' exclaimed the manager, looking back malevolently at the place we had left.

"Towards the evening of the second day we judged ourselves about eight miles from Kurtz's station. I wanted to push on; but the manager looked grave, and told me the navigation up there was so dangerous that it would be advisable to wait till next morning. This was sensible enough, but sleep seemed unnatural, like a state of trance.

When the sun rose there was a white fog, very warm and clammy, and more blinding than the night. Then - I don't know how it struck the others - to me it seemed as though the mist itself had screamed. A hurried outbreak of almost intolerably excessive shrieking. 'Good God! What is the meaning - ?' What we could see was just the steamer we were on, her outlines blurred as though she had been on the point of dissolving, and a misty strip of water, perhaps two feet broad, around her - and that was all. 'Will they attack, do you think?' asked the manager, in a confidential tone.

"I was looking down at the sounding-pole, when I saw my poleman give up the business suddenly, and stretch himself flat on the deck. At the same time the fireman, sat down abruptly before his furnace. I was amazed. Then, sticks, little sticks, were flying about - thick: they were whizzing before my nose, dropping below me. Arrows, by Jove! We were being shot at! With one hand I felt above my head for the line of the steam-whistle, and jerked out screech after screech hurriedly. The tumult of angry and warlike yells was checked instantly, and then from the depths of the woods went out such a tremulous and prolonged wail of mournful fear and utter despair as may be imagined to follow the flight of the last hope from the earth.

"My helmsman lay dead, and, by the way, I supposed Mr. Kurtz to be dead as well by this time.

"The original Kurtz had been educated partly in England, and by-and-by I learned that the *International Society for the Suppression of Savage Customs* had intrusted him with the making of a report, for its future guidance. I've read it. It was eloquent, vibrating with eloquence. He began with the argument that we whites, from the point of development we had arrived at, 'must necessarily appear to them [savages] in the nature of supernatural beings - we approach them with the might as of a deity. By the simple exercise of our will we can exert a power for good practically unbounded,' &c., &c. From that point he soared, and took me with him. It made me tingle with enthusiasm. There were no practical hints to interrupt the magic current of phrases, except a kind of note at the foot of the last page, scrawled evidently much later, in an unsteady hand. It was very simple, and at the end of that moving appeal to every altruistic sentiment it blazed at you, luminous and terrifying, like a flash of lightning in a serene sky: 'Exterminate all the brutes!' He won't be forgotten.

"'The station!' cried the manager, and on the water-side I saw a white man under a hat like a cart-wheel beckoning persistently with his whole arm. The fellow looked like a harlequin. His clothes were covered with patches all over, with bright patches, blue, red, and yellow; and the sunshine made him look extremely wonderfully neat withal.

"When the manager, escorted by the pilgrims, all of them armed to the teeth, had gone to the house, this chap came on board. He rattled away at such a rate he seemed to be trying to make up for lots of silence. 'Don't you talk with Mr. Kurtz?' I said. 'You don't talk with that man - you listen to him,' he exclaimed with severe exaltation. 'But now ... Brother sailor ... honour ... pleasure ... delight ... introduce myself ... Russian ... son of an arch-priest ... Government of Tambov ... What? Excellent English tobacco!'

"I gave him Towson's book. 'I thought I had lost it,' he said, looking at it ecstatically. 'You made notes in Russian?' I asked. He nodded. 'I thought they were written in cipher,' I

said. He laughed, then became serious. 'Why did they attack us?' I asked. He hesitated, then said shamefacedly, 'They are simple people, they don't want him to go. I tell you,' he cried, 'this man has enlarged my mind.'

III

"I looked at him, lost in astonishment. 'You take Kurtz away quick - quick - I tell you.'

"I suppose Kurtz wanted an audience, because on a certain occasion, when encamped in the forest, it seems they had talked all night, or more probably Kurtz had talked. 'We talked of everything,' he said, quite transported at the recollection. 'I forgot there was such a thing as sleep. Everything! Of love too.' 'Ah, he talked to you of love!' I said, much amused. 'It isn't what you think,' he cried, almost passionately. 'It was in general. He made me see things - things.' 'And, ever since, you have been with him, of course?' I said.

"He had, as he informed me proudly, managed to nurse Kurtz through two illnesses, but as a rule Kurtz wandered alone, far in the depths of the forest. There he had discovered lots of villages, a lake too - but mostly his expeditions had been for ivory. 'But he had no goods to trade with,' I objected. 'There's a good lot of cartridges left even yet,' he answered, looking away. 'To speak plainly, he raided the country,' I said. He nodded. 'Not alone, surely!' He muttered something about the villages round that lake. 'Kurtz got the tribe to follow him, did he?' I suggested. He fidgeted a little. 'They adored him,' he said. The tone of these words was so extraordinary that I looked at him searchingly. It was curious to see his mingled eagerness and reluctance to speak of Kurtz. The man filled his life, occupied his thoughts, swayed his emotions.

I had taken up my binoculars while we talked and was looking at the shore. I directed my glass to the house. I had been struck at the distance by certain attempts at ornamentation, rather remarkable in the ruinous aspect of the place. Now I saw my mistake. These round knobs were not ornamental but symbolic; they were expressive and puzzling, striking and disturbing - food for thought and also for the vultures if there had been any looking down from the sky. They would have been even more impressive, those heads on the stakes, if their faces had not been turned to the house.

"The admirer of Mr. Kurtz was a bit crestfallen. In a hurried, indistinct voice he began to assure me he had not dared to take these - say, symbols - down. He was not afraid of the natives; they would not stir till Mr. Kurtz gave the word. His ascendency was extraordinary. The chiefs came every day to see him. They would crawl. ... 'I don't want to know anything of the ceremonies used when approaching Mr. Kurtz,' I shouted. I suppose it did not occur to him Mr. Kurtz was no idol of mine. 'I am a simple man. I don't understand,' he groaned. 'I've been doing my best to keep him alive, and that's enough'

"Suddenly round the corner of the house a group of men appeared, as though they had come up from the ground, bearing an improvised stretcher in their midst. Instantly, in the emptiness of the landscape, a cry arose whose shrillness pierced the still air; and, as if by enchantment, streams of naked human beings were poured into the clearing by the dark-faced and pensive forest.

"'Now, if he does not say the right thing to them we are all done for,' said the Russian at my elbow. The knot of men with the stretcher had stopped too, half-way to the steamer, as if petrified. I saw the man on the stretcher sit up and fall back suddenly.

"Some of the pilgrims behind the stretcher carried his arms - two shot-guns, a heavy rifle, and a light revolver-carbine - the thunderbolts of that pitiful Jupiter. The manager bent over him murmuring as he walked beside his head. They laid him down in one of the little cabins - just a room for a bed-place and a camp-stool or two, you know.

"Dark human shapes could be made out in the distance, leaning on tall spears, and from along the lighted shore moved a wild and gorgeous apparition of a woman. She carried her head high; her hair was done in the shape of a helmet; innumerable necklaces of glass beads, charms, gifts of witch-men, that hung about her, glittered and trembled at every step. She must have had the value of several elephant tusks upon her. She was savage and superb, wild-eyed and magnificent. She looked at us all as if her life had depended upon the unswerving steadiness of her glance. She turned away slowly, walked on, following the bank, and passed into the bushes to the left.

"At this moment I heard Kurtz's deep voice behind the curtain, 'Save me! - save the ivory, you mean. Sick! Not so sick as you would like to believe. I will return. I ... '

"The manager came out. 'He is very low, very low,' he said. 'We have done all we could for him - haven't we? I said with emphasis.

"The Russian tapped me on the shoulder. I heard him mumbling something about 'brother seaman - couldn't conceal - thinking of Mr. Kurtz's reputation' 'All right,' said I. 'Mr. Kurtz's reputation is safe with me.' I did not know how truly I spoke.

"He informed me, lowering his voice, that it was Kurtz who had ordered the attack to be made on the steamer. 'He hated sometimes the idea of being taken away - and then again. ... But I don't understand these matters. I am a simple man.

"I woke up shortly after midnight, and got up for the purpose of having a look round. One of the agents with a picket of a few of our blacks, armed for the purpose, was keeping guard over the ivory; but deep within the forest, red gleams that wavered, that seemed to sink and rise from the ground amongst confused columnar shapes of intense blackness, showed the exact position of the camp where Mr. Kurtz's adorers were keeping their uneasy vigil. The monotonous beating of a big drum filled the air with muffled shocks and a lingering vibration. I glanced casually into the little cabin. A light was burning within, but Mr. Kurtz was not there.

"As soon as I got on the bank I saw a trail - a broad trail through the grass. I remember the exultation with which I said to myself, 'He can't walk - he is crawling on all-fours - I've got him.'

"I came upon him, and, he rose, unsteady, long, pale, indistinct, like a vapour exhaled by the earth, and swayed slightly, misty and silent before me; while at my back the fires loomed between the trees, and the murmur of many voices issued from the forest. I glanced back. A black figure stood up, strode on long black legs, waving long black arms, across the glow. It had horns - antelope horns, I think - on its head. Some sorcerer, some witch-man. 'Do you know what you are doing?' I whispered. 'Perfectly,' he answered.

"'I had immense plans,' he muttered irresolutely. Confound the man! Believe me or not, his intelligence was perfectly clear, but his soul was mad.

When I had him at last stretched on the couch, my legs shook under me as though I had carried half a ton on my back down that hill. And yet I had only supported him, his bony arm clasped round my neck - and he was not much heavier than a child.

"When next day we left at noon, the crowd, of whose presence behind the curtain of trees I had been acutely conscious all the time, flowed out of the woods again, filled the clearing, covered the slope with a mass of naked, breathing, quivering, bronze bodies. In front of the first rank, three men, plastered with bright red earth from head to foot, strutted to and fro restlessly. They shouted periodically together strings of amazing words that resembled no sounds of human language; and the deep murmurs of the crowd, interrupted suddenly, were like the response of some satanic litany.

"We had carried Kurtz into the pilot-house: there was more air there. There was an eddy in the mass of human bodies, and the woman with helmeted head and tawny cheeks rushed out to the very brink of the stream. She put out her hands, shouted something, and all that wild mob took up the shout in a roaring chorus of articulated, rapid, breathless utterance.

"The brown current ran swiftly out of the heart of darkness, bearing us down towards the sea with twice the speed of our upward progress; and Kurtz's life was running swiftly too, ebbing, ebbing out of his heart into the sea of inexorable time.

"Sometimes he was contemptibly childish. He desired to have kings meet him at railway-stations on his return from some ghastly Nowhere, where he intended to accomplish great things. '

"We broke down - as I had expected - and had to lie up for repairs at the head of an island. This delay was the first thing that shook Kurtz's confidence. One morning he gave me a packet of papers and a photograph, - the lot tied together with a shoe-string. 'Keep this for me,' he said. 'This noxious fool' (meaning the manager) 'is capable of prying into my boxes when I am not looking.'

"One evening coming in with a candle I was startled to hear him say a little tremulously, 'I am lying here in the dark waiting for death.' The light was within a foot of his eyes. I forced myself to murmur, 'Oh, nonsense!' and stood over him as if transfixed.

"It was as though a veil had been rent. I saw on that ivory face the expression of sombre pride, of ruthless power, of craven terror - of an intense and hopeless despair. He cried out twice, a cry that was no more than a breath -

"'The horror! The horror!'

"I blew the candle out and left the cabin. The pilgrims were dining in the mess-room, and I took my place opposite the manager, who lifted his eyes to give me a questioning glance. Suddenly the manager's boy put his insolent black head in the doorway, and said in a tone of scathing contempt -

"'Mistah Kurtz - he dead.'

"All the pilgrims rushed out to see. I remained, and went on with my dinner. I believe I was considered brutally callous. But I am of course aware that next day the pilgrims buried something in a muddy hole.

"Thus I was left at last with a slim packet of letters and the girl's portrait. She struck me as beautiful - I mean she had a beautiful expression. I concluded I would go and give her back her portrait and those letters myself. Curiosity? I don't know. I can't tell. But I went.

"I rang the bell before a mahogany door on the first floor, and she came forward, all in black. It was more than a year since his death, more than a year since the news came; she seemed as though she would remember and mourn for ever.

"'You were his friend,' she said. 'I feel I can speak to you - and oh! I am proud to know I understood him better than anyone on earth - he told me so himself.'

"'We shall always remember him,' I said, hastily.

"'No!' she cried. 'It is impossible that such a life should be sacrificed to leave nothing. You know what vast plans he had. Men looked up to him - his goodness shone in every act. His example...You were with him - to the last?'

"'To the very end,' I said, shakily. 'I heard his very last words ...' I stopped in a fright.

"'Repeat them,' she said in a heart-broken tone.

"I was on the point of crying at her, 'Don't you hear them? The horror! The horror!'

"I pulled myself together and spoke slowly.

"'The last word he pronounced was - your name.'

"The heavens do not fall for such a trifle. But I couldn't tell her. It would have been too dark - too dark altogether ..."

Marlow ceased, and sat apart, indistinct and silent, in the pose of a meditating Buddha. Nobody moved for a time. "We have lost the first of the ebb," said the Director, suddenly. The offing was barred by a black bank of clouds, and the tranquil waterway seemed to lead into the heart of an immense darkness.

The Wind in The Willows
by Kenneth Grahame
(London, 1908)

Written by an official at the Bank of England, this is one of the most popular books of all time, having produced at least *thirty* different illustrated editions, more than a dozen plays and movies and inspired creators as far apart as AA Milne, Pink Floyd, Disney, Van Morrison and the heavy metal band Iron Maiden.

It is often thought of as a whimsical hymn to nature, yet its presentation of Pan the God is still seen as sufficiently anti-Christian to require censorship in some quarters, while others find in the story a set of undemocratic and highly paternalistic Edwardian values which need keeping well away from children.

Abridged: GH.

THE RIVER BANK

The Mole had been working very hard all the morning, spring-cleaning his little home, till he had dust in his throat and eyes, and splashes of whitewash all over his black fur. Spring was moving in the air above and in the earth below and around him, penetrating even his dark and lowly little house with its spirit of divine discontent and longing. It was small wonder that he suddenly flung down his brush, said 'Hang spring-cleaning!' and made for the steep little tunnel which answered in his case to the gravelled carriage-drive owned by animals whose residences are nearer to the sun and air. So he scraped and scratched and scrabbled and scrooged till at last, pop! his snout came out into the sunlight, and he found himself rolling in the warm grass of a great meadow.

He thought his happiness was complete when suddenly he stood by the edge of a full-fed river. Never in his life had he seen a river before, and the Mole was bewitched, entranced, fascinated. By the side of the river he trotted as one trots, when very small, by the side of a man who holds one spell-bound by exciting stories; and when tired at last, he sat on the bank and looked across the river.

A dark hole in the bank opposite, just above the water's edge, caught his eye, and dreamily he fell to considering what a nice snug dwelling-place it would make for an animal with few wants and fond of a bijou riverside residence. As he gazed, something bright and small seemed to twinkle down in the heart of it, like a tiny star.

A brown little face, with whiskers. Small neat ears and thick silky hair.

It was the Water Rat!

'Hullo, Mole!' said the Water Rat! 'Would you like to come over?'

The Rat then lightly stepped into a little boat, sculled smartly across and made fast. Then he held up his forepaw as the Mole stepped gingerly down and found himself actually seated in the stern of a real boat.

'Do you know,' said Mole, as the Rat shoved off, 'I've never been in a boat before in all my life.'

'What?' cried the Rat, open-mouthed: 'Believe me, my young friend, there is NOTHING - absolute nothing - half so much worth doing as simply messing about in boats. Simply messing - .' Look here! If you've really nothing else on hand this morning, supposing we drop down the river together, and have a long day of it? I have coldtonguecoldhamcoldbeefpickledgherkinssaladfrenchroll scresssandwichespottedmeatgingerbeerlemonadesodawater - -'

'O stop, stop,' cried the Mole in ecstasies: This is so new to me. So-this-is-a-River!'

'THE River,' corrected the Rat. 'I live on it and in it. It's brother and sister to me, and food and drink, and (naturally) washing. It's my world, and I don't want any other.'

'What lies over THERE' asked the Mole, waving a paw towards a background of woodland.

'That? O, that's just the Wild Wood,' said the Rat shortly. 'We don't go there very much, we river-bankers. Weasels-and-stoats-and foxes-and so on. They're all right in a way - but - well, you can't really trust them, and that's the fact.'

'And beyond the Wild Wood again?' Mole asked: 'Where it's all blue and dim, and one sees what may be hills or perhaps they mayn't, and something like the smoke of towns, or is it only cloud-drift?'

'Beyond the Wild Wood comes the Wide World,' said the Rat. 'And that's something that doesn't matter, either to you or me. I've never been there, and I'm never going, nor you either, if you've got any sense at all. Don't ever refer to it again, please.'

This day was only the first of many similar ones for the emancipated Mole, each of them longer and full of interest as the ripening summer moved onward. He learned about weirs, and sudden floods, and leaping pike, and steamers that flung hard bottles - at least bottles were certainly flung, and FROM steamers, so presumably BY them; and

about herons, and how particular they were whom they spoke to; and night-fishings with Otter, excursions far a-field with the Badger. He heard about the grand and jovial Toad, he learnt to swim and to row, and entered into the joy of running water; and with his ear to the reed-stems he caught, at intervals, something of what the wind went whispering so constantly among them.

THE OPEN ROAD

The Rat was sitting on the river bank, singing a little song he had just composed;

'DUCKS' DITTY.'
All along the backwater,
Through the rushes tall,
Ducks are a-dabbling,
Up tails all!

'Won't you take me to call on Mr. Toad?' asked the Mole cautiously, 'I've heard so much about him.'

'Why, certainly,' said the good-natured Rat, abandoning poetry and jumping to his feet. 'Get the boat out, and we'll paddle up there at once. It's never the wrong time to call on Toad.'

Rounding a bend in the river, they came in sight of a handsome, dignified old house of mellowed red brick, with well-kept lawns reaching down to the water's edge.

'There's Toad Hall,' said the Rat; 'Toad is rather rich, you know. No rowing-boats in the water any more, so I just wonder what new fad he has taken up?'

They disembarked, and found Toad in a wicker garden-chair, with a large map spread out on his knees.

'Hooray!' he cried, jumping up, 'You don't know how lucky it is, your turning up just now!'

'It's about your rowing, I suppose,' said the Rat, with an innocent air. 'With a great deal of coaching, you may--'

'O, pooh! boating!' interrupted the Toad, in great disgust. 'Silly boyish amusement. No, I've discovered the real thing. I can only regret the wasted years that lie behind me, squandered in trivialities. Come with me, dear Ratty, and your amiable friend, just as far as the stable-yard!'

He led the way, and there they saw a gipsy caravan, shining with newness, painted a canary-yellow picked out with green, and red wheels.

'There you are!' cried the Toad, straddling and expanding himself. 'There's real life for you. The open road, the dusty highway, the heath! Here to-day, up and off to somewhere else to-morrow! You see- little sleeping bunks-a little table that folded up against the wall, lockers, bookshelves; you'll find that nothing what ever has been forgotten, when we make our start this afternoon.'

'I beg your pardon,' said the Rat slowly, as he chewed a straw, 'but did I overhear you say something about "WE," and "START," and "THIS AFTERNOON?"'

But to the loyal Mole, the Life Adventurous was so new a thing, and the Rat hated disappointing people. So, the old grey horse was caught and harnessed, and they set off.

It was a golden afternoon. The smell of the dust they kicked up was rich and satisfying; out of thick orchards on either side the road, birds called and whistled to them cheerily and good-natured wayfarers gave them 'Good-day'.

They were strolling along the high-road easily, the Mole by the horse's head, when they saw a small cloud of dust advancing on them at incredible speed. In an instant the peaceful scene was changed, and with a blast of wind and a whirl of sound that made them jump for the nearest ditch, it was on them! The 'Poop-poop' rang with a brazen shout in their ears, they had a moment's glimpse of glittering plate-glass and rich morocco, and the magnificent motor-car then dwindled to a droning speck in the far distance.

The old grey horse simply abandoned himself to his natural emotions, he reared, plunged, and the canary-coloured cart, their pride and their joy, lay on its side in the ditch, an irredeemable wreck.

The Rat danced up and down in the road, simply transported with passion. 'You villains!' he shouted, shaking both fists, 'You scoundrels! - I'll have the law on you!'

Toad sat straight down in the middle of the dusty road, his legs stretched out before him, and stared fixedly in the direction of the disappearing motor-car. His face wore a placid satisfied expression, and at intervals he faintly murmured 'Poop-poop! O bliss! O poop-poop! O my! All those wasted years that lie behind me! '

They left the horse at an inn stable, gave what directions they could about the cart, took a slow train back to a station near Toad Hall, put the still-dazed Toad in the care of his housekeeper, sculled down the river home, and at a very late hour sat down to supper in their own cosy riverside parlour, to the Rat's great joy and contentment.

The following evening the Mole, who had risen late and taken things very easy all day, was sitting on the bank fishing, when the Rat, came strolling along to find him. 'Heard the news?' he said. 'There's nothing else being talked about, all along the river bank. Toad went up to Town by an early train this morning. And he has ordered a large and very expensive motor-car.'

THE WILD WOOD

The Mole had long wanted to make the acquaintance of the Badger, who seemed, by all accounts, to be an important personage, though rarely visible. 'Couldn't you ask him here to dinner or something?' he asked.

'He wouldn't come,' replied the Rat, 'and calling on him is out of the question, because he lives in the very middle of the Wild Wood.'

But the Badger never came along, and, so, when winter arrived and the Rat took to spending much of his time asleep, the Mole formed the resolution to go by himself.

It was a cold still afternoon with a hard steely sky overhead, when he slipped out of the warm parlour into the open air, and with great cheerfulness of spirit he pushed towards the Wild Wood. There was nothing to alarm him at first entry. Twigs crackled under his feet, logs tripped him, funguses on stumps resembled caricatures; but that was all fun, and exciting.

Then the faces began. It was over his shoulder, and indistinctly, that he first thought he saw a little evil wedge-shaped face, looking out at him from a hole. When he turned and confronted it, the thing had vanished.

Then the pattering began. He thought it was only falling leaves at first, so slight and delicate was the sound of it. Then it increased till it sounded like sudden hail on the dry leaf-carpet spread around him.

Meantime the Rat, warm and comfortable by his fireside, woke with a start, and looked round for the Mole to ask him if he knew a good rhyme for something or other. Receiving no answer, he got up and went out into the hall. The Mole's cap was missing from its accustomed peg. His galoshes, which always lay by the umbrella-stand, were also gone.

The Rat looked very grave, he re-entered the house, strapped a belt round his waist, shoved a brace of pistols into it, and set off for the Wild Wood.

It was already getting towards dusk when he heard, from a hole in an old beech tree, a feeble voice, saying 'Ratty! Is that you?'

Mole was greatly cheered by the sound of the Rat's careless laughter, as well as the sight of his pistols. The Rat climbed in, and the two friends pulled the dry leaves over themselves to rest.

When they awoke, the moon was high and it was snowing hard.

'Snow's UP. Well, well, it can't be helped,' said the Rat. 'We must make a start, I suppose. The worst of it is, I don't exactly know where we are. This snow makes everything look so very different.'

They set off to investigate, when suddenly the Mole tripped up and fell forward with a squeal.

'O my shin!' he cried.

'It's a very clean cut,' said the Rat, examining it attentively. 'Looks as if it was made by a sharp edge of something metal. Funny!'

The Rat started scratching and shovelling busily, till he suddenly cried 'Hooray-oo-ray-oo-ray-oo-ray! A door-scraper!'

'What!' cried The Mole, 'Well, when I get home I shall go and complain about it to - to somebody or other, see if I don't!'

'O, dear!' cried the Rat, in despair. 'You-you thick-headed beast. Not another word!'

The Rat attacked a snow-bank beside them with ardour, probing and digging with fury. Ten minutes hard work revealed the companions of a door-scraper - a door-mat, and a door.

Mole sprang up at the bell-pull, and from quite a long way off they could faintly hear a deep-toned bell respond.

MR. BADGER

The Badger, who wore a long dressing-gown, opened the door and patted both their heads. 'This is not the sort of night for small animals to be out,' he said paternally. 'But come along; come into the kitchen. There's a first-rate fire there, and supper and everything.'

The floor was well-worn red brick, and on the wide hearth burnt a fire of logs. In the middle of the room stood a long table, rows of spotless plates winked from the shelves of the dresser, and from the rafters hung hams, bundles of dried herbs, nets of onions, and baskets of eggs.

When their meal was finished, the Badger said heartily, 'Now then! tell us the news. How's old Toad going on?'

'Oh, from bad to worse,' said the Rat gravely. 'Another smash-up only last week, and a bad one.'

'How many has he had?' inquired the Badger gloomily.

'Smashes, or machines?' asked the Rat. 'Oh, well, after all, it's the same thing-with Toad. This is the seventh. Killed or ruined - it's got to be one of the two things, sooner or later. Badger! we're his friends-oughtn't we to do something?'

The Badger went through a bit of hard thinking. 'Of course you know I can't do anything NOW?'

His two friends assented. No animal, according to the rules of animal-etiquette, is ever expected to do anything even moderately active during the off-season of winter. All are sleepy-some actually asleep.

'Well, THEN,' went on the Badger, 'we - that is, you and me and our friend the Mole here - we'll take Toad seriously in hand. We'll bring him back to reason, by force if need be. We'll - you're asleep, Rat!'

And as the Rat slumbered, the Badger led his fellow underground-dweller around the many tunnels of his home. The Mole was staggered at its size, the length, the solid vaultings of the crammed store-chambers. 'How on earth, Badger,' he said at last, 'did you ever find time and strength to do all this?'

As a matter of fact,' said the Badger simply, 'I did none of it. Very long ago, on the spot where the Wild Wood waves now, before ever it had planted itself, there was a city - a city of people, you know. They were a powerful people, and rich, and great builders. They built to last, for they thought their city would last for ever.'

'But what has become of them all?' asked the Mole.

'Who can tell?' said the Badger. 'People come - they stay for a while, they flourish, they build - and they go. It is their way. But we remain. And so it will ever be.'

MR. TOAD

It was a bright morning in the early part of summer when the hour came for Badger to appear to Rat and Mole, and for the confrontation with Toad to begin.

At Toad Hall, the chauffeur was dismissed and Toad denuded of his driving-clothes. At first, kind words were tried. Then stern ones, and, all sorts of words failing, the Toad, no longer the Terror of the Highway, was locked into his room and his three friends took turns to sit sentry at his door pending some believable promise that Toad would henceforth avoid motor-cars.

But, with the aid of some knotted sheets, the rather resourceful Toad made good his escape and soon found himself marching into 'The Red Lion,' and ordering the best luncheon that could be provided at so short a notice.

'Smart piece of work that!' he remarked to himself chuckling. 'Brain against brute force - and brain came out on the top - as it's bound to do.'

He was about half-way through his meal when an only too familiar sound made him start and fall a-trembling all over. The poop-poop! drew nearer and nearer, the car could be heard to turn into the inn-yard and come to a stop, and Toad had to hold on to the leg of the table to conceal his over-mastering emotion. Presently the party entered the coffee-room, and Toad slipped out quietly, paid his bill at the bar, and sauntered round quietly to the inn-yard. 'There cannot be any harm,' he said to himself, 'in my only just LOOKING at it!'

'I wonder,' he said to himself presently, 'I wonder if this sort of car STARTS easily?'

* * * * * *

The Clerk of the Bench of Magistrates scratched his nose with his pen. 'Some people would consider,' he observed, 'that stealing the motor-car was the worst offence; and so it is. But cheeking the police undoubtedly carries the severest penalty; and so it ought. You had better make it a round twenty years and be on the safe side.'

'An excellent suggestion!' said the Chairman approvingly.

Then the brutal minions of the law fell upon the hapless Toad; loaded him with chains, and dragged him from the Court House, shrieking, praying, protesting; across the marketplace, where the playful populace, always as severe upon detected crime as they are sympathetic and helpful when one is merely 'wanted,' assailed him with jeers, carrots, and popular catch-words.

The rusty key creaked in the lock, the great door clanged behind them; and Toad was a helpless prisoner in the remotest dungeon of the best-guarded keep of the stoutest castle in all the length and breadth of Merry England.

THE PIPER AT THE GATES OF DAWN

The Water Rat had returned from an evening with his friends, bringing grave news. 'Young Portly has been missing for some days now', he explained, 'Otter dotes on that son of his, and now he IS nervous. There are - well, traps and things - YOU know. '

So, they got the boat out, and followed the clear, narrow track that faintly reflected the sky; the night full of small noises, song and chatter and rustling. A bird piped suddenly, and was still; and a light breeze sprang up and set the reeds and bulrushes rustling. Rat sat up suddenly and listened with a passionate intentness. Mole looked at him with curiosity.

'It's gone!' sighed the Rat, sinking back in his seat again. 'So beautiful and strange and new. Since it was to end so soon, I almost wish I had never heard it. No! There it is again! O Mole! the beauty of it! Such music I never dreamed of! Row on, Mole, row! For the music and the call must be for us.'

Slowly the two animals moored their boat at the flowery margin of an island.

'This is the place of my song-dream, the place the music played to me,' whispered the Rat, as if in a trance.

Then suddenly the Mole felt a great Awe fall upon him, an awe that turned his muscles to water, bowed his head, and rooted his feet to the ground. He knew it could only mean that some august Presence was very, very near.

Trembling he raised his humble head; and then, in that utter clearness of the imminent dawn, while Nature, flushed with fullness of incredible colour, seemed to hold her breath for the event, he looked in the very eyes of the Friend and Helper; saw the backward sweep of the curved horns, saw the stern, hooked nose between the kindly eyes, the bearded mouth and the long supple hand still holding the pan-pipes only just fallen away from the parted lips; saw, last of all, nestling between his very hooves, sleeping soundly in entire peace and contentment, the little, round, podgy, childish form of the baby otter.

'Rat!' he found breath to whisper, shaking. 'Are you afraid?'

'Afraid?' murmured the Rat, his eyes shining with unutterable love. 'Afraid! Of HIM? O, never, never! And yet - and yet - O, Mole, I am afraid!'

Then the two animals, crouching to the earth, bowed their heads and did worship.

Sudden and magnificent, the sun's broad golden disc showed itself over the horizon, took the animals full in the eyes and dazzled them, and with its soft touch came the end of the vision, instant oblivion and the kindly demi-god's gift of forgetfulness, lest the awful remembrance should remain and grow, and overshadow mirth and pleasure.

Mole rubbed his eyes and stared at Rat, who was looking about him in a puzzled sort of way. 'Why, there he is, the little fellow!' And with a cry of delight he ran towards the slumbering Portly.

TOAD'S ADVENTURES

When Toad found himself immured in a dank and noisome dungeon, he shed bitter tears, and abandoned himself to dark despair. 'This is the end of everything' (he said), 'at least it is the end of the career of Toad, which is the same thing; the popular and handsome Toad, the rich and hospitable Toad!

Now, it so happened that the gaoler's daughter was extraordinarily fond of animals. Over the weeks, somewhat under the influence of the Toad's natural charm, she came to see that his crimes were trivial and his incarceration clearly unjust. A certain financial arrangement was made, with the result that Toad simply walked out of the prison gates, in the dress and the guise of a washerwoman.

Dizzy with the easy success of his daring exploit, he made his way to the nearby railway station, and found to his horror, that he had left both his coat and waistcoat behind him in his cell, and with them his pocket-book, money, keys, watch, matches, pencil-case - all that makes life worth living, all that distinguishes the many-pocketed animal, the lord of creation, from the inferior one-pocketed or no-pocketed productions that hop or trip about permissively, unequipped for the real contest.

Fortune, however, smiled again on the Toad, as the engine-driver took pity on, what appeared to him, to be a sobbing washerwoman, and provided a free ride to the point where Toad could jump from the train into an unknown wood.

Free! The road, when he reached it, seemed like a stray dog, to be looking anxiously for company. Toad, however, was looking for something that could talk, and tell him clearly which way he ought to go. Help arrived first in the shape of a bargewoman and then of a gypsy, so that the afternoon found Toad tramping along gaily, thinking of his adventures and escapes, and how when things seemed at their worst he had always managed to find a way out. 'Ho, ho!' he said to himself as he marched along with his chin in the air...'

> The world has held great Heroes,
> As history-books have showed;
> But never a name to go down to fame
> Compared with that of Toad!

After some miles of country lanes he reached the high road, and saw approaching him a speck that turned into a dot and then a double note of warning, only too well known, fell on his delighted ear. He stepped confidently out into the road to hail the motor-car, when suddenly he became very pale; for the approaching car was the very one he had stolen out of the yard of the Red Lion Hotel.

He sank down in a shabby, miserable heap in the road, as the terrible motor-car stopped just short of him. Two gentlemen got out and walked round the trembling heap of crumpled misery lying in the road, and one of them said, 'O dear! this is very sad! A washerwoman who has fainted in the road! They tenderly lifted Toad into the motor-car and propped him up with soft cushions, and proceeded on their way.

When Toad knew that he was not recognised, his courage began to revive.

'Thank you kindly, Sirs,' said Toad in a feeble voice. 'Please, Sir,' he said, 'I wish you would kindly let me try and drive the car for a little. I've been watching you carefully, and it looks so easy and so interesting, and I should like to be able to tell my friends that once I had driven a motor-car!'

The gentleman said, to Toad's delight, 'Bravo, ma'am! I like your spirit. Let her have a try.'

But, once in the driver's seat, Toad, the motor-car snatcher, the prison-breaker soon revealed himself, shortly followed by the car crashing through the low hedge that ran along the roadside. One mighty bound, a violent shock, and the wheels were churning up the thick mud of a horse-pond.

Toad found himself flying through the air with the strong upward rush and delicate curve of a swallow. He liked the motion, and was just beginning to wonder whether it would go on until he developed wings and turned into a Toad-bird, when he landed on his back with a thump, in the soft rich grass of a meadow.

He picked himself up, and was about to burst into song again when he observed, about two fields off, a chauffeur in his leather gaiters and two large rural policemen running towards him as hard as they could go!

Poor Toad struggled on blindly and wildly, when suddenly the earth failed under his feet, he grasped at the air, and, splash! He found himself head over ears straight into the river!

As he sighed and blew and stared before him into the dark hole, some bright small thing shone and twinkled in its depths, moving towards him. As it approached, a face grew up gradually around it, and it was a familiar face!

Brown and small, with whiskers.

It was the Water Rat!

'LIKE SUMMER TEMPESTS CAME HIS TEARS'

The Rat gripped Toad firmly by the scruff of the neck, and pulled him onto the bank.

'Toad,' he said, gravely and firmly, 'you go off upstairs at once, and take off that old cotton rag that looks as if it might formerly have belonged to some washerwoman, put on some of my clothes, and try and come down looking like a gentleman if you CAN!'

By the time he came down, luncheon was on the table, and very glad Toad was to see it. 'Oh Ratty', Toad said, 'I've been a conceited old ass; but now I'm going to be a good Toad. I'm done with motor-cars. I had a sudden brilliant idea - connected with motor-boats. We'll have our coffee, AND a smoke, and then I'm going to stroll quietly down to Toad Hall.'

'What are you talking about?' cried the Rat, greatly excited. 'Do you mean to say you haven't HEARD? About the Stoats and Weasels?'

Toad leaned his elbows on the table, and a large tear welled up in each of his eyes.

'While you were in that trouble of yours,' said the Rat, slowly and impressively, 'one dark night, a band of weasels crept up to the front entrance, a body of desperate ferrets possessed themselves of the backyard and offices, and the Wild Wooders have been living in Toad Hall ever since,

eating your grub, and drinking your drink, making bad jokes about you, and telling everyone they're there to stay.'

There came a heavy knock at the door, the Rat opened it, and in walked Mr. Badger and the Mole.

'Hooray! Here's old Toad!' cried the Mole, his face beaming. 'You clever, ingenious, intelligent Toad!'

Toad puffed and swelled. 'Clever? O, no!' he said. 'I've only broken out of the strongest prison in England, that's all! And captured a railway train and escaped on it, that's all!'

'Toad!' said the Badger, severely. 'You bad, troublesome little animal!' Then; 'Now I'm going to tell you a great secret. There-is-an-underground-passage that leads from the river-bank, right up into the middle of Toad Hall.'

'Aha! that squeaky board in the butler's pantry!' said Toad.

'We shall creep out quietly-' cried the Mole.

'-with our pistols and swords and sticks-' shouted the Rat.

'-and rush in upon them,' said the Badger.

'-and whack 'em, and whack 'em, and whack 'em!' cried the Toad in ecstasy, running round and round the room, and jumping over the chairs.

'Very well, then,' said the Badger, resuming his usual dry manner, 'our plan is settled. We will make all the necessary arrangements in the course of the to-morrow.'

THE RETURN OF ULYSSES

When it began to grow dark, the Rat summoned them back into the parlour, provided each with a cutlass, a pair of pistols, some bandages, and a sandwich-case. When all was quite ready, the Badger took a dark lantern in one paw, grasped his great stick with the other, and said, 'Now then, follow me!'

At last they were in the secret passage, and the cutting-out expedition had really begun!

Such a tremendous noise was going on in the banqueting-hall that there was little danger of their being overheard. The four of them put their shoulders to the trap-door and heaved it back. Hoisting each other up, they found themselves standing in the pantry.

'Hold hard a minute!' said the Badger. 'Get ready, all of you!'

'-Let me sing you a little song,' came the voice of the chief weasel, 'which I have composed' - (applause).

'Toad he went a-pleasuring
Gaily down the street-'

The Badger drew himself up, took a firm grip of his stick with both paws, glanced round, and cried-

'The hour is come! Follow me!'

My! What a squealing and a squeaking and a screeching filled the air! Well might the terrified weasels dive under the tables and spring madly up at the windows!

The affair was soon over. Up and down, the whole length of the hall, strode the four Friends, whacking with their sticks at every head that showed itself; and in five minutes the room was cleared.

The following morning, Toad, who had overslept himself as usual, came down to breakfast disgracefully late, to be told by Badger that he was to arrange a banquet as some little thanks to the good animals all around who had helped him. A modest banquet, with no songs by and about Mr Toad and no speeches by Mr Toad either.

When the evening arrived, Toad was melancholy and thoughtful. Alone in his room, to a circle of chairs, he did allow one last little song...

The Toad-came-home!
There was panic in the parlours and howling in the halls,

There was crying in the cow-sheds and shrieking in the stalls,
When the Toad-came-home!

Then he heaved a deep sigh; a long, long, long sigh. He dipped his hairbrush in the water-jug, parted his hair in the middle, and went quietly down the stairs to greet his guests.

The Badger had ordered everything of the best, and the banquet was a great success. There were some knockings on the table and cries of 'Toad! Speech! Mr. Toad's song!' But Toad only shook his head gently, raised one paw in mild protest, and managed to convey to them that this dinner was being run on strictly conventional lines.

He was indeed an altered Toad!

The Origin and Development of Psychoanalysis
by Sigmund Freud
(Worcester, Massachusetts, 1910)

The Austrian Freud was was the 'Father of Psychoanalysis' whose attempts to help 'hysterics' led to the idea that unconscious forces influence people's thoughts and actions, and that repression of infantile sexuality and aggression can be the root of adult neuroses. Even though his theories are now widely seen as unscientific nonsense, they did bring about a much more open approach to sexual matters and changed the way people think about human nature so that irrationality, crime, love, hate and fear are seen as the product of deep, internal, drives.

Abridged: GH from the lectures given by Freud at Clark University in September 1909

FIRST LECTURE

Ladies and Gentlemen: I assume that you have invited me to talk of psychoanalysis. So, I shall attempt to give you a brief history of this new method of research and cure.

If creating psychoanalysis is a merit, it is not my merit. I was a busy student, when another Viennese physician, Joseph Breuer, first applied this method to the case of a hysterical girl.

Dr. Breuer's patient was an intelligent girl of twenty one, who had developed paralysis of her extremities, impairment of vision, intense *Tussis nervosa*, nausea on trying to take nourishment, and, at one time, an inability to drink. She lost speech and was subject to 'absences', delirium, and alteration of her whole personality.

There is clearly an injury here, probably to the brain. As her vital organs seemed normal, physicians will expect that there is a state of hysteria, known since the ancient Greeks. We should know that the illness first appeared while she was caring for her beloved dying father.

The physician, who has learned much anatomy and physiology and pathology, can understand alterations of the brain in apoplexy or dementia, but he cannot understand hysteria. He is reduced to the layman's position, which is very disagreeable to one who sets a high value on his own knowledge. Hystericals, accordingly, tend to lose his sympathy; he blames them for exaggerations, deceit and

"simulation," and punishes them by withdrawing his interest.

Now Dr. Breuer did offer sympathy and interest. He noticed that in her states of "absence," she mumbled words to herself. He used a sort of hypnosis in which he repeated these words, in order to bring up any associations that they might have.

The patient yielded up certain fancies, deeply sad, often poetically beautiful, daydreams, commonly centered on a girl beside her father's sickbed. In relating them, she seemed to be freed and restored to normal mental life, until the next day a new "absence" arose, which was removed in the same way. The patient herself, who strangely enough understood and spoke only English, called this "the talking cure," or jokingly, "chimney sweeping." Symptoms would disappear when, in hypnosis, she could be made to remember the situation under which they first appeared, provided free vent was given to the emotions that they aroused.

It was a hot summer, yet the patient developed an extreme fear of drinking water, eating only fruit to relieve her tormenting thirst. After about six weeks, she was talking in hypnosis of how she had once met with her despised English governess, to find that lady's dog had drunk out of a glass. After she had energetically expressed her restrained anger, she was easily able to drink. The symptom thereupon vanished permanently. Breuer found that almost all symptoms originated as remnants, as precipitates, of affectively toned experiences, which we came to call "psychic traumata."

There was one curiosity; it was usually several experiences which seemed to co-operate in bringing about the trauma, and it was impossible to reach the first and most essential one, without first clearing away those coming later.

When I began to use Breuer's methods, my experiences coincided with his. There was the case of a woman who developed a peculiar smacking tic whenever she was excited. It had its origin in two experiences where she had tried to suppress all sound, once in putting her sick child to sleep, and once in trying to remain calm during a thunderstorm. To generalize: Hysterical patients suffer from symptoms which are the remnants of traumatic experiences.

We are now on the way to a purely psychological theory of hysteria. A further observation by Breuer will compel us to ascribe much of the disease to an altered condition of consciousness.

Our patient was normally quite unaware of her "absences," and alteration of character, which were only revealed under hypnosis. It is through the study of hypnotic phenomena that we have come to see that in the same individual several mental groupings are possible. Cases of such spit consciousness, known as "double personality" ("double conscience"), occasionally appear spontaneously. Where consciousness remains constantly bound up with one of the two states, this is called the conscious mental state, and the other the unconscious. Breuer concluded that hysterical symptoms originated in such a mental state, which he called "hypnoidal state." Emotional experiences during such hypnoidal states easily become pathogenic, since such states do not allow for a normal draining off of emotion. Consequently, the products of the exciting process are projected as symptoms, like a foreign body, into the normal state, which then has no conception of their significance. Where a symptom arises, we also find amnesia, a memory gap, and the filling of this gap includes the removal of the conditions under which the symptom originated.

So far, it may seem that our knowledge in this field is not very far advanced. Indeed, Breuer's idea of the hypnoidal states has been shown to hinder further investigation. But complete theories do not fall from Heaven. Indeed, to present a perfectly rounded explanation from the beginning could only be seen as the child of speculation and not the fruit of unprejudiced investigation of the facts

SECOND LECTURE

When I began to follow-on from Breuer's investigations, I soon came to a different view of the origin of hysterical dissociation (or splitting of consciousness). Practical needs urged me on. Breuer's cathartic treatment required deep hypnosis. But I came to dislike that fanciful, almost mystical, aid, when I discovered that I could not hypnotize by any means all of my patients.

Since I could not alter the psychic state of most of my patients, I directed my efforts to working with them in their normal state. This seems at first sight to be a particularly senseless undertaking. The problem was this: to find out something from the patient that the doctor did not know and the patient himself did not know. I was helped by recalling Bernheim's experience at his clinic at Nancy. He found that persons put in a condition of hypnotic somnambulism, stated afterwards that they had no memory of their experiences during somnambulism, but if he persisted, urged and assured them that they did know, then every time the forgotten memory came back

Accordingly, I did this with my patients. When I had reached with them a point at which they declared that they knew nothing more, I would assure them that they did know, asserting that the memory would emerge at the moment that I laid my hand on the patient's forehead. This was an exhausting procedure, but it substantiated the fact that the forgotten memories were but hindered from becoming conscious by some resisting forces.

But what were those forces? It seemed that a wish had been aroused, which was incompatibility with the "ego" of the patient. His ethical and other pretensions were the repressing forces. The mental pain of incompatible wishes was avoided by repression.

I will give you the history of a single one of my cases. It is that of a young girl whose sister fell ill and died, leaving her with a desire to marry her brother-in-law. This love, of which she had not been conscious, was rapidly repressed by her revolted feelings. The girl fell ill with severe hysterical symptoms, and, when I came to treat her, she had entirely forgotten that scene at her sister's bedside and the unnatural, egoistic desire which had arisen in her. She remembered it during the treatment, reproduced the pathogenic moment with every sign of intense emotional excitement, and was cured. I can make this process of repression more concrete by a rough illustration.

Suppose that here in this hall and in this audience, whose exemplary stillness and attention I cannot sufficiently commend, an individual is creating a disturbance. He is expelled, or "repressed," and strong men at the door keep up the repression. Now, if you call this "consciousness," and the outside the "unconscious," you have a tolerably good illustration of the process of repression.

It may very well happen that the repressed man, now embittered and quite careless of consequences, makes a terrible uproar outside, and interferes with my lecture even more. Perhaps our honored president, Dr. Stanley Hall, might speak with the rowdy on the outside, and then turn to us with the recommendation that we let him in again, provided he would guarantee to behave himself better. On Dr. Hall's authority we decide to stop the repression, and peace reigns again. This is a fairly good presentation of the task of psychoanalytic therapy.

In driving matters out of consciousness and out of memory, a great amount of psychic pain is saved. But the suppressed wish still exists, only waiting for its chance to become active, and finally succeeds in sending into consciousness, instead of the repressed idea, a disguised and unrecognizable surrogate creation (Ersatzbildung). The psychic conflict which then arises, is made capable of a happier termination, under the guidance of the physician, than is offered by repression. Either the personality of the patient may be convinced to wholly or partly accept the pathogenic wish; or this wish may be directed to a less objectionable goal, by what is called sublimation (Sublimierung); or the rejection may be recognized as rightly motivated, and the automatic and therefore insufficient mechanism of repression be reinforced by the higher, more characteristically human mental faculties, the patient succeeds in mastering his wishes by conscious thought.

THIRD LECTURE

Ladies and Gentlemen: It is not always easy to tell the truth, but I must correct a statement that I made in my last lecture. I told you how when I gave up hypnosis I pressed my patients to remember what they had apparently forgotten. But, often, ideas emerged which could not be the right ones. In this state of perplexity, I clung to a prejudice, which was later proved by my friend Dr. Jung of Zürich to have a scientific justification. I must confess that it is often of great advantage to have prejudices. I could not believe that any idea occurring to the patient could be quite arbitrary and out of all relation to the idea we sought. These surrogates must be related to the repressed thought as a sort of allusion, as a statement of the same thing in indirect terms

We know of analogous situations in ordinary experience, such as instances of wit. Such as that story about the art critic asked to pass judgment on two portraits of famously unscrupulous businessmen who just asked "And where is the Saviour?" He meant, "You are a couple of malefactors, like those crucified beside the Saviour." But he expresses himself through allusion, a surrogate, to the insult. The same constellation comes into play, according to our hypothesis, when our patient produces the irruptive idea as a surrogate for the forgotten idea which is the object of the quest.

Ladies and gentlemen, the Zürich School of Bleuler, Jung and others usefully designate a group of ideas belonging together and having a common emotive tone, as a "complex." We have every prospect of discovering a repressed complex, if only the patient will communicate a sufficient number of the ideas which come into his head. So we let the patient speak as he desires, and cling to the hypothesis that nothing can occur to him except what has some indirect bearing on the complex we are seeking. If this method of discovering the repressed complexes seems too circumstantial, I can assure you that it is the only available one.

One is further bothered by the fact that the patient often arrives at a point where he considers that he has nothing more to say. He must be encouraged to lay aside any critical choice, although he may think his ideas irrelevant, nonsensical, or especially unpleasant. In this way, we secure the material which sets us on the track of the repressed complex

These irruptive ideas, which the patient himself values little, are for the psychologist like the ore, which by interpretation, he reduces to valuable metal.

Two other methods are available, the interpretation of dreams and the evaluation of acts which he bungles or does without intending to (Fehl und Zufallshandlungen).

The interpretation of dreams, old-fashioned as it seems, is in fact the *via regia* to the interpretation of the unconscious, the surest ground of psychoanalysis. If I were asked how one could become a psychoanalyst, I should answer, through the study of one's own dreams.

You must remember that our nightly dream productions show the greatest outer similarity to the creations of the insane, yet are compatible with full health during waking life.

In our waking state, we usually reject dreams, forget them quickly, and consider them foreign to our personality. Our rejection derives support from the unrestrained shamelessness and immoral longings in many dreams. Yet, antiquity, and still today the lower classes of our people, value dreams highly, expecting from them some revelation of the future. Yet, dreams are wonderful enough, without having to hypothesize any prophetic nature.

Consider the dreams of young children from the age of a year and a half on. They always present the fulfillment of wishes aroused from the previous day's experiences.

But adult dreams generally have an incomprehensible content; they have become disguised, so that we must differentiate between the manifest dream content and the latent dream-thoughts, whose presence in the unconscious we must assume.

This disguising, the work of the defensive forces of the ego, prevents repressed wishes from entering consciousness during waking life. The dreamer knows just as little of the sense of his dream as the hysterical knows of the significance of his symptoms. Discovering, through analysis, the relation between the manifest and latent dream-content is exactly the technique of psychoanalysis.

Through this "dream-work" (Traumarbeit) it is possible to get some insight into the process which has brought about the disguise of unconscious thoughts. You will furthermore discover in dreams, especially your own, the unsuspected importance of experiences from early childhood. In the dream life, the child, as it were, continues his existence in the man. We have also discovered from the analysis of dreams that the unconscious makes use of a symbolism, especially in presenting sexual complexes. This symbolism partly varies with the individual, but is partly is of a typical nature, and seems to be identical with the symbolism of our myths and legends.

Finally, I must remind you that the occurrence of anxiety-dreams (Angsttraüme) does not contradict our idea of dreams as a wish fulfillment. Anxiety is just one of the ways in which the ego relieves itself of repressed wishes.

I may now pass from dreams to a group of everyday mental phenomena whose study has become a technical help for psychoanalysis.

These are the bungling of acts (Feldhandlungen) among normal men as well as among neurotics, to which no significance is ordinarily attached; the forgetting of things (such as proper names); mistakes in speaking (Versprechen), which occur so frequently; mistakes in writing (Verschreiben) and in reading (Verlesen), the automatic execution of purposive acts in wrong situations (Vergreifen) and the loss or breaking of objects, etc.

These trifles have passed unchallenged as chance consequences of absent-minded inattention. Likewise playing with objects, humming melodies, handling one's person and clothing and the like are not chance, but meaningful acts. That meaning is generally easy and sure to interpret from the situation in which they occur, and their observation, like that of dreams, can reveal hidden complexes in the psychic life. With their help, one will usually betray the most intimate of secrets

For the psychoanalyst there is in the expressions of the psyche nothing trifling, nothing arbitrary and lawless, he expects everywhere a clear psychic motivation.

Seeing our ability to discover repressed things in the soul life, you will come with me to the conclusion that our technique can show how pathogenic psychic material enters into consciousness, and so to do away with the suffering brought on by surrogate symptoms.

You may have gained the impression that psychoanalysis is peculiarly difficult On the contrary, once learned, its is easy. But it must be learned, just as much as histological or surgical techniques. You may surprised to learn that in Europe there have been frequently judgements passed on psychoanalysis by persons who knew nothing of its technique and had never practiced it.

It is not difficult to substantiate in our opponents the same impairment of intelligence produced by emotivity which we may observe every day with our patients. The arrogance of that consciousness which, for example, rejects dreams so lightly, generally belongs to the strongest protective apparatus which guards us against the breaking through of unconscious complexes. Consequently, it is hard to convince people of the reality of the unconscious, and to teach them anew, what their conscious knowledge contradicts.

FOURTH LECTURE

Ladies and Gentlemen, at this point you will be asking what the psychoanalysis has taught us of the nature of repressed wishes. One thing in particular is surprising; the regularity of impressions from the sexual life in both men and women.

I know that this assertion will not willingly be credited. Some think that I overestimate sexuality, and ask why other mental excitations should not equally lead to the phenomena of repression and surrogate-creation. I can only answer that experience has clearly shown it so. You will find that my co-workers were equally sceptical, until their own analytic labors forced them to the same conclusion.

The conduct of the patients does not make it any easier to convince one's self of the correctness of this view. Instead of willingly giving us information concerning their sexual life, they wear a thick overcoat, a fabric of lies, as though it were bad weather in the world of sex. And they are not wrong; sun and wind are not favorable in our civilized society to any demonstration of sex life.

But when your patients are assured that they may disregard conventional restraints, they lay aside this veil of lies, and leave you in a position to formulate a judgment. Unfortunately, physicians are not favored above the rest of the children of men in questions of the sex life. Many of them are under that ban of prudery and lasciviousness which determines the behaviour of most Kulturmenschen in affairs of sex.

It is only in recovering the wishes of adolescence and early childhood that we hit upon the circumstances which determine the later sickness. These mighty wishes of childhood are very generally sexual.

Now I can be sure of your astonishment. You ask, is not childhood distinguished by the lack of the sexual impulse? No, gentlemen, it is not at all true that the sexual impulse enters the child at puberty, as the biblical devils entered the swine. The child has sexual impulses and activities from the beginning, and from these the so-called normal sexuality of adults emerges. As fate would have it, I am in a position to call a witness from your own midst; Dr. Sanford Bell, a fellow of Clark University, the same institution within whose walls we now stand. In his "A Preliminary Study of the Emotion of Love between the Sexes".

A short time ago from the analysis of a five-year-old boy who was suffering from anxiety, an analysis undertaken with correct technique by his own father, I succeeded in getting a fairly complete picture of the bodily expressions of an early stage of childish sexual life. My friend, Dr. Jung, read to you a few hours ago in this room an observation on a still younger girl. Accordingly, I hope that you may feel this idea of infantile sexuality not so strange. If it is true that most men do not want to know anything about the sexual life of the child, a fact which is explained all too easily.

The sexual impulse of the child is complex, and entirely disconnected from reproduction. It permits the child to gain different sorts of pleasure sensations, notably in the auto-excitation of the genitals, the rectum, the opening of the urinary canal, the skin and other sensory surfaces. We call this early phase after a word coined by Havelock Ellis, "auto-eroticism." The parts of the body significant in giving sexual pleasure we call "erogenous zones." The passionate sucking of very young children has been correctly interpreted by Dr Lindner of Budapest, as sexual satisfaction. Another sexual satisfaction of this time of life is masturbation, which has such a great significance for later life and, in many individuals, is never fully overcome. Besides auto-erotic manifestations, we see very early in the child the impulse-components of sexual pleasure, of the libido, which presupposes a second person as its object. These impulses appear in opposed pairs, as active and passive, most importantly as pleasure in inflicting pain (sadism) with its passive opposite (masochism).

The difference between the sexes plays, however, no very great rôle so that one may attribute to every child, without wronging him, a bit of the homosexual disposition.

Even before puberty certain impulses undergo energetic repression under the impulse of education, and mental forces like shame, disgust and morality are developed, which, like sentinels, keep the repressed wishes in subjection. The most important of these repressed impulses are koprophilism, that is, taking pleasure in excrement; and, further, the tendencies attaching themselves to the persons of the primitive object-choice.

The development of the sexual function is not always smoothly completed, and may leave behind either abnormalities or disposition to later diseases. It may happen that not all the partial impulses subordinate themselves to the rule of the genital zone, bringing about what we call a perversion, as when the auto-erotism is not fully overcome. The originally equal value of both sexes as sexual objects may be maintained and give rise to exclusive homosexuality.

The primitive object-choice of the child, which is derived from his need of help, at first attaches to all familiar persons, but gives way in favor of his parents. This relation is not at all free from a sexual component. The child takes both parents, and especially one, as an object of his erotic wishes. Usually this follows the stimulus given by his parents, whose tenderness has the character of a sex manifestation, though inhibited. As a rule, the father prefers the daughter, the mother the son. The child reacts to this situation, since, as son, he wishes himself in the place of his father, as daughter, in the place of the mother. The complex built up in this way is quickly repressed, but still exerts a great and lasting effect from the unconscious. We must express the opinion that this presents the nuclear complex of every neurosis. The myth of King Oedipus, who kills his father and wins his mother as a wife, or Shakespeare's Hamlet[1], are only a slightly altered presentations of these infantile wishes.

The child arrives at a number of "infantile sexual theories"; that the same male genitals belong to both sexes, that children are conceived by eating, and that sexual intercourse is to be regarded as an inimical act, a sort of overpowering.

But the unfinished nature of his sexual constitution and the gaps in his knowledge about by the hidden feminine sexual canal, cause the infant investigator to abandon his search. The invention of infant sex theories are of determinative significance in building the child's character, and in the content of his later neuroses.

It is quite normal that the child should make his parents his first object-choice. But his libido must not remain fixed on them, it is merely a prototype for a transfer to other persons. The breaking loose (Ablösung) of the child from his parents is necessary if the social virtue of the young individual is not to be impaired. This presents a great task for education, which at present certainly does not always solve it in the most intelligent way.

FIFTH LECTURE

The deeper you investigate neurotic diseases, the more the relation of neuroses to normal mentality becomes apparent. You will be reminded that we men, with the high claims of our civilization and under the pressure of our repressions, find reality generally quite unsatisfactory, and so keep up a life of fancy to compensate for what is lacking. These phantasies often contain much of the essence of personality, repressed in real life. The successful man is he who can transform his wish-fancies into reality. Under favorable conditions, he may find another link between fancies and reality, as where those with artistic talent, (still psychologically puzzling) can transform fancies into artistic creations.

Let me give at this point the main result of the psychoanalytic investigation of neurotics, namely, that neuroses have no peculiar psychic content which is not also found in healthy states; or, as Jung has expressed it, neurotics fall ill of the same complexes with which we sound people struggle.

Ladies and gentlemen, I have withheld from you the most remarkable experience which corroborates our assumptions of the sexual impulse-forces of neurotics. Whenever we treat a neurotic psychoanalytically, there occurs the phenomenon of transfer (Uebertragung), where the patient applies to the physician much tender emotion, often mixed with enmity, which has no foundation in any real relation, and must be derived from unconscious wish-fancies.

One is afraid of doing harm by psychoanalysis, of calling up repressed sexual impulses. One can see that the patient has sore places in his soul life, but one is afraid to touch them, lest his suffering be increased. But nobody thinks of blaming the surgeon for temporarily making a condition worse on the way to restoring lasting health. The consequence which is feared, the disturbance of the cultural character, is wholly impossible. Our experience has shown that the power of a wish is incomparably stronger when it is unconscious than when it is conscious. By being made conscious, it can only be weakened.

The neurotic has lost, by his repressions, many valuable sources of mental energy. The components of the sexual

---

1   **Hamlet:** see p155

instinct, in particular, have a capacity for sublimation into ones more socially valuable. The mental energy won in such a way has probably had the highest cultural consequences.

However, a certain part of the suppressed libidinous excitation deserves satisfaction. We should remember that individual happiness ought to be one of the aims of our culture. If the narrowing of sexuality is pushed too far it will have all the evil effects of a robbery.

Perhaps you regard that exhortation as presumptuous? Consider the old tale of the citizens of Schilda who tried to make their horse work without fodder, only to be amazed when it died. Without a certain ration of oats, no work could be expected from any animal.

I thank you for calling me here to speak, and for your attention.

Antarctic Journals
by Capt. Robert Falcon Scott
(Antarctica, 1910-13)

Scott wanted to be first to reach the South Pole, which fellow Englishman Ernest Shackleton had come very close to a year before. With the 'right attitude' of boundless enthusiasm, the 'right chaps' of the officer class and more than a year's preparation at the edge of Antarctica, what could possibly go wrong?

Abridged: GH

Sunday, September 10: My whole time has been occupied in making detailed plans for the Southern journey. It would be impossible to imagine a more vigorous community, and there does not seem to be a single weak spot in the twelve good men and true who are chosen for the Southern advance. All are now experienced sledge travellers, knit together with a bond of friendship that has never been equalled under such circumstances. It is good to have arrived at a point where one can run over facts and figures again and again without detecting a flaw or foreseeing a difficulty. We had two lectures last week - the first dealing with General Geology and the second was given by Ponting. This time we had pictures of the Great Wall and other stupendous monuments of North China. It is a really satisfactory state of affairs all round. If the Southern journey comes off, nothing, not even priority at the Pole, can prevent the Expedition ranking as one of the most important that ever entered the polar regions.

Thursday, September 14: I held forth on the 'Southern Plans' yesterday; everyone was enthusiastic. To-morrow Bowers, Simpson, Petty Officer Evans, and I are off to the west.

Wednesday, October 3: We have had a very bad weather spell. Time simply flies and the sun steadily climbs the heavens. Breakfast, lunch, and supper are now all enjoyed by sunlight, whilst the night is no longer dark.

'When they after their headstrong manner, conclude that it is their duty to rush on their journey all weathers' - 'Pilgrim's Progress.[1]

Sunday, October 8: A very beautiful day. Everyone out and about after Service, all ponies going well. Went to Pressure Ridge with Ponting and took a number of photographs. So far good.

Thursday, November 2: The plan of further advance has now been evolved. We shall start in three parties - the very slow ponies, the medium paced, and the fliers.

Saturday, December 2: The ponies went poorly on the first march, when there was little or no wind and a high temperature. It was so warm when we camped that the snow melted as it fell, and everything got sopping wet. The lists now: Self, Wilson, Oates, and Keohane. Bowers, P.O. Evans, Cherry and Crean. Man-haulers: E. R. Evans, Atkinson, Wright, and Lashly. We have all taken to horse meat and are so well fed that hunger isn't thought of.

Tuesday, December 5: Camp 30. Noon. There are pools of water on everything, the tents are wet through, also the wind clothes, night boots, &c.; water drips from the tent poles and door, lies on the floorcloth, soaks the sleeping-bags, and makes everything pretty wretched.

Friday, December 8: Camp 30. All tents had been reduced to the smallest volume by the gradual pressure of snow. Evans and his man-haulers tried to pull a load this afternoon. They managed to move a sledge with four people on it.

Saturday, December 9: At 8 P.M. the ponies were quite done, one and all. We camped, and the ponies have been shot. Poor beasts! The scenery is most impressive; three huge pillars of granite form the right buttress of the Gateway, and a sharp spur of Mount Hope the left. In spite of some doubt in our outlook, everyone is very cheerful to-night and jokes are flying freely around.

Wednesday, December 20: 6500 feet about. Just got off our last best half march - 10 miles. All day we have been admiring a wonderful banded structure of the rock; to-night it is beautifully clear on Mount Darwin. I have just told off the people to return to-morrow night: Atkinson, Wright, Cherry-Garrard, and Keohane. All are disappointed - poor

---

1   **Pilgrim's Progress:** see p202

Wright rather bitterly, I fear. I dread this necessity of choosing.

A FRESH MS. BOOK: On the Flyleaf : Ages: Self 43, Wilson 39, Evans (P.O.) 37, Oates 32, Bowers 28. Average 36.

Monday, December 25. CHRISTMAS: Night. Camp No. 47. Bar. 21.18. T: 7°. I am so replete that I can scarcely write. I must write a word of our supper last night. We had four courses. The first, pemmican[2], full whack, with slices of horse meat flavoured with onion and curry powder and thickened with biscuit; then an arrowroot, cocoa and biscuit hoosh[3] sweetened; then a plum-pudding; then cocoa with raisins, and finally a dessert of caramels and ginger. Wilson and I couldn't finish our share of plum-pudding.

Thursday, December 28: The marches are terribly monotonous. One's thoughts wander occasionally to pleasanter scenes and places, but necessity to, or some hitch in the surface, quickly brings them back.

Monday, January 1, 1912: NEW YEAR'S DAY. We are very comfortable in our double tent. Stick of chocolate to celebrate the New Year. Prospects seem to get brighter - only 170 miles to go and plenty of food left.

Wednesday, January 3: Minimum -18.5°. Within 150 miles of our goal. Last night I decided to reorganise, and this morning told off Teddy Evans, Lashly, and Crean to return. They are disappointed, but take it well. Bowers is to come into our tent, and we proceed as a five man unit to-morrow. We have 5½ units of food - practically over a month's allowance for five people - it ought to see us through. I think it's going to be all right. We have a fine party going forward and arrangements are all going well.

Friday, January 5: A dreadfully trying day. The sastrugi[4] seemed to increase as we advanced and they have changed direction from S.W. to S. by W. What lots of things we think of on these monotonous marches! What castles one builds now hopefully that the Pole is ours.

Monday, January 8: Min. for night -25°. It is quite impossible to speak too highly of my companions. Wilson, first as doctor, ever on the lookout to alleviate the small pains and troubles incidental to the work. Evans, a giant worker with a really remarkable headpiece. Little Bowers remains a marvel. Oates had his invaluable period with the ponies; now he is a foot slogger. So our five people are perhaps as happily selected as it is possible to imagine.

Tuesday, January 9: We made a very steady afternoon march, covering 6½, miles. This should place us in Lat. 88° 25', beyond the record of Shackleton's walk. All is new ahead.

Night, January 15: It is wonderful to think that two long marches would land us at the Pole. We left our depot to-day with nine days' provisions, so that it ought to be a certain thing now, and the only appalling possibility the

sight of the Norwegian flag forestalling ours. Only 27 miles from the Pole. We ought to do it now.

Tuesday, January 16: The worst has happened, or nearly the worst. We marched well in the morning and covered 7½ miles. Noon sight showed us in Lat. 89° 42' S., and we started off in high spirits, feeling that to-morrow would see us at our destination. About the second hour of the March Bowers' sharp eyes detected what he thought was a cairn. We marched on, found that it was a black flag tied to a sledge bearer; near by the remains of a camp. This told us the whole story. The Norwegians have forestalled us and are first at the Pole. It is a terrible disappointment, and I am very sorry for my loyal companions. It will be a wearisome return.

Wednesday, January 17: The Pole. Yes, but under very different circumstances from those expected. To-night little Bowers is laying himself out to get sights in terrible difficult circumstances; the wind is blowing hard, T: 21°, and there is that curious damp, cold feeling in the air which chills one to the bone in no time. Great God! this is an awful place and terrible enough for us to have laboured to it without the reward of priority. Well, it is something to have got here, and the wind may be our friend to-morrow. We have had a fat Polar hoosh in spite of our chagrin, and feel comfortable inside - added a small stick of chocolate and the queer taste of a cigarette brought by Wilson.

Thursday morning, January 18: We have just arrived at this tent, 2 miles from our camp, therefore about 1½ miles from the Pole. In the tent we find a record of five Norwegians having been here: Roald Amundsen, Olav Olavson Bjaaland, Hilmer Hanssen, Sverre H. Hassel, Oscar Wisting. 16 Dec. 1911. A note from Amundsen asks me to forward a letter to King Haakon! The following articles have been left in the tent: 3 half bags of reindeer containing a miscellaneous assortment of mits and sleeping socks, very various in description, a sextant, a Norwegian artificial horizon and a hypsometer. We built a cairn, put up our poor slighted Union Jack, and photographed ourselves - mighty cold work all of it - less than ½ a mile south we saw stuck up an old underrunner of a sledge. This we commandeered as a yard for a floorcloth sail. I imagine it was intended to mark the exact spot of the Pole as near as the Norwegians could fix it. Well, good-bye to most of the daydreams!

Monday, January 22: We got away sharp at 8 and marched a solid 9 hours, and thus we have covered 14.5 miles but, by Jove! it has been a grind.

Wednesday, January 24: Things beginning to look a little serious. This is the second full gale since we left the Pole. I don't like the look of it. I don't like the easy way in which Oates and Evans get frostbitten.

Thursday, January 25: Thank God we found our Half Degree Depôt. We are not without ailments: Oates suffers from a very cold foot; Evans' fingers and nose are in a bad state, and to-night Wilson is suffering tortures from his eyes.

---

2   **Pemmican:** Cake of dried meat, fruit and fat
3   **Hoosh:** Stew
4   **Sastrugi:** Wind-blown snow ridges

Monday, January 29: Excellent march of 19½ miles, 10.5 before lunch. Wind helping greatly, considerable drift; tracks for the most part very plain. We are only 24 miles from our depôt - an easy day and a half.

Tuesday, January 30: Thank the Lord, another fine march - 19 miles. Evans has dislodged two finger-nails to-night; his hands are really bad, and to my surprise he shows signs of losing heart over it.

Thursday, February 1: It ought to be easy to get in with a margin, having 8 days' food in hand (full feeding). Wilson's leg much better. Evans' fingers now very bad, two nails coming off, blisters burst.

Friday, February 2: -19°. We started well on a strong southerly wind. Soon got to a steep grade, when the sledge overran and upset us one after another. We got off our ski, and pulling on foot reeled off 9 miles by lunch at 1.30. Started in the afternoon on foot, going very strong. Pray God another four days will see us pretty well clear of it. Our bags are getting very wet and we ought to have more sleep.

Monday, February 5: A good forenoon, few crevasses; we covered 10.2 miles. We may be anything from 25 to 30 miles from our depot, but I wish to goodness we could see a way through the disturbances ahead. Our faces are much cut up by all the winds we have had, mine least of all; the others tell me they feel their noses more going with than against the wind. Evans' nose is almost as bad as his fingers. He is a good deal crocked up.

Wednesday, February 7: Mount Darwin Depot. Soon after 6.30 we saw our depot easily and camped next it at 7.30.

Thursday, February 8: Started from the depot rather late owing to weighing biscuit, &c., and rearranging matters. Had a beastly morning. Wind very strong and cold. Steered in for Mt. Darwin to visit rock. Bowers obtained several specimens, a close-grained granite rock which weathers red. Wilson, with his sharp eyes, has picked several plant impressions, the last a piece of coal with beautifully traced leaves in layers. There is a good deal of pure white quartz. Altogether we have had a most interesting afternoon. A lot could be written on the delight of setting foot on rock after 14 weeks of snow and ice and nearly 7 out of sight of aught else. It is like going ashore after a sea voyage. We hope to get a chance to dry our sleeping-bags and generally make our gear more comfortable.

Saturday, February 10: The fallen snow crystals are quite feathery like thistledown. We have two full days' food left, and though our position is uncertain, we are certainly within two outward marches from the middle glacier depot.

Sunday, February 11: Supper -3.5°. The worst day we have had during the trip and greatly owing to our own fault. I think we are on or about the right track now, but we are still a good number of miles from the depôt, so we reduced rations to-night. We had three pemmican meals left and decided to make them into four.

Monday, February 12: Two hours before lunch we were cheered by the sight of our night camp of the 18th December, the day after we made our depôt - this showed we were on the right track. In the afternoon, refreshed by tea, we struck uphill and, tired and despondent, arrived in a horrid maze of crevasses and fissures.

Tuesday, February 13: Temp: 10°. Last night we all slept well in spite of our grave anxieties. Evans raised our hopes with a shout of depot ahead, but it proved to be a shadow on the ice. Then suddenly Wilson saw the actual depot flag. It was an immense relief, and we were soon in possession of our 3½ days' food. The relief to all is inexpressible; needless to say.

Wednesday, February 14: There is no getting away from the fact that we are not going strong. Probably none of us: Wilson's leg still troubles him and he doesn't like to trust himself on ski; but the worst case is Evans, who is giving us serious anxiety. This morning he suddenly disclosed a huge blister on his foot. Sometimes I fear he is going from bad to worse, but I trust he will pick up again when we come to steady work on ski like this afternoon. He is hungry and so is Wilson. We can't risk opening out our food again, and as cook at present I am serving something under full allowance. The next depot some 30 miles away and nearly 3 days' food in hand.

Thursday, February 15: We don't know our distance from the depot, but imagine about 20 miles. Heavy march - did 13¾. In the afternoon it was overcast; land blotted out for a considerable interval. We have reduced food, also sleep; feeling rather done. Trust 1½ days or 2 at most will see us at depot.

Friday, February 16: A rather trying position. Evans has nearly broken down in brain, we think. This morning and this afternoon he stopped the march on some trivial excuse. Perhaps all will be well if we can get to our depot.

Saturday, February 17: A very terrible day. Evans looked a little better after a good sleep, and declared, as he always did, that he was quite well. The surface was awful, the sky overcast, and the land hazy. We stopped after about one hour, and Evans came up again, but very slowly. Half an hour later he dropped out again on the same plea. He asked Bowers to lend him a piece of string. I cautioned him to come on as quickly as he could, and he answered cheerfully as I thought. We had to push on, and the remainder of us were forced to pull very hard, sweating heavily. Abreast the Monument Rock we stopped, and seeing Evans a long way astern, I camped for lunch. There was no alarm at first, and we prepared tea and our own meal, consuming the latter. After lunch, and Evans still not appearing, we looked out, to see him still afar off. By this time we were alarmed, and all four started back on ski. I was first to reach the poor man and shocked at his appearance; he was on his knees with clothing disarranged, hands uncovered and frostbitten, and a wild look in his eyes. Asked what was the matter, he replied with a slow speech that he didn't know, but thought he must have fainted. He showed every sign of complete collapse. We returned him into the tent quite comatose. He died quietly at 12.30 A.M. Wilson thinks it certain he must have injured his brain by a fall. It is a terrible thing to lose a companion in this way, but calm reflection shows that there could not have been a better ending to the terrible anxieties of the past week. Discussion of the situation at lunch yesterday shows us what a desperate pass we were in with a sick man on our hands at such a distance from home. At 1 A.M. we packed up and came down over the pressure ridges, finding our depôt easily.

Sunday, February 18: R. 32. Temp: 5.5°. At Shambles Camp. We gave ourselves 5 hours sleep at the lower glacier depot after the horrible night, and came on at about 3 to-day to this camp, coming fairly easily over the divide. Here with plenty of horsemeat we have had a fine supper, to be followed by others such, and so continue a more plentiful era if we can keep good marches up. New life seems to come with greater food almost immediately, but I am anxious about the Barrier surfaces.

Monday, February 19: Lunch T: 16°. We have struggled out 4.6 miles in a short day over a really terrible surface - it has been like pulling over desert sand, not the least glide in the world. If this goes on we shall have a bad time. To-night we had a sort of stew fry of pemmican and horseflesh, and voted it the best hoosh we had ever had on a sledge journey. The absence of poor Evans is a help to the commissariat, but if he had been here in a fit state we might have got along faster.

Monday, February 20: 13°. Same terrible surface; four hours' hard plodding in morning brought us to our Desolation Camp, where we had the four-day blizzard. We looked for more pony meat, but found none.

Wednesday, February 22: To-night we had a pony hoosh so excellent and filling that one feels really strong and vigorous again.

Thursday, February 23: This afternoon we marched on and picked up another cairn; then on and camped only 2½ miles from the depot. We cannot see it, but, given fine weather, we cannot miss it.

Friday, February 24: Lunch. Beautiful day - too beautiful - an hour after starting loose ice crystals spoiling surface. Saw depot and reached it middle forenoon. Found store in order except shortage oil - shall have to be very saving with fuel - otherwise ten full days' provision from to-night and less than 70 miles to go.

Sunday, February 26: Lunch Temp: 17°. Sky overcast. Nine hours' solid marching has given us 11½ miles. Only 43 miles from the next depôt. Wonderfully fine weather but cold, very cold. Nothing dries and we get our feet cold too often. We want more food yet and especially more fat. Fuel is woefully short.

Monday, February 27: Desperately cold last night: -33° when we got up, with -37° minimum. We talk of little but food, except after meals. Land disappearing in satisfactory manner. Pray God we have no further set-backs. We are naturally always discussing possibility of meeting dogs,

where and when, &c. It is a critical position. 31 miles to depot, 3 days' fuel at a pinch, and 6 days' food. Things begin to look a little better; we can open out a little on food from to-morrow night, I think. Very curious surface - soft recent sastrugi which sink underfoot, and between, a sort of flaky crust with large crystals beneath.

Tuesday, February 28: Lunch. Thermometer went below -40° last night; it was desperately cold for us, but we had a fair night. Only 24½ miles from the depot. The sun shines brightly, but there is little warmth in it. There is no doubt the middle of the Barrier is a pretty awful locality.

Wednesday, February 29: Frightfully cold. Next camp is our depot and it is exactly 13 miles. It ought not to take more than 1½ days; we pray for another fine one. The oil will just about spin out in that event, and we arrive 3 clear days' food in hand. The increase of ration has had an enormously beneficial result. Wind still very light from west - cannot understand this wind.

Thursday, March 1: There is a bright and comparatively warm sun. All our gear is out drying.

Friday, March 2: Lunch. Misfortunes rarely come singly. We marched to the (Middle Barrier) depot fairly easily yesterday afternoon, and since that have suffered three distinct blows which have placed us in a bad position. First we found a shortage of oil; with most rigid economy it can scarce carry us to the next depot on this surface (71 miles away). Second, Titus Oates disclosed his feet, the toes showing very bad indeed, evidently bitten by the late temperatures. Worse was to come - the surface is simply awful. In spite of strong wind and full sail we have only done 5½ miles.

Sunday, March 4: Things looking very black indeed. As usual we forgot our trouble last night, got into our bags, slept splendidly on good hoosh, woke and had another, and started marching. We are about 42 miles from the next depot and have a week's food, but only about 3 to 4 days' fuel - we are as economical of the latter as one can possibly be, and we cannot afford to save food and pull as we are pulling. We are in a very tight place indeed, but none of us despondent yet. I fear that Oates at least will weather such an event very poorly.

Monday, March 5: Lunch. Regret to say going from bad to worse. We went to bed on a cup of cocoa and pemmican solid with the chill off. We talk of all sorts of subjects in the tent, not much of food now, since we decided to take the risk of running a full ration.

Wednesday, March 7: A little worse I fear. One of Oates' feet very bad this morning; he is wonderfully brave. We only made 6½ miles yesterday. We are 16 from our depot. If we only find the correct proportion of food there and this surface continues, we may get to the next depot.

Saturday, March 10: Things steadily downhill. Oates' foot worse. I practically ordered Wilson to hand over the means of ending our troubles to us, so that anyone of us may know how to do so. We have 30 opium tabloids apiece and he is left with a tube of morphine.

Wednesday, March 14: It is only with greatest pains rest of us keep off frostbites. Truly awful outside the tent. Must fight it out to the last biscuit, but can't reduce rations.

Friday, March 16 or Saturday 17: Lost track of dates, but think the last correct. Tragedy all along the line. At lunch, the day before yesterday, poor Titus Oates said he couldn't go on; he proposed we should leave him in his sleeping-bag. That we could not do, and induced him to come on, on the afternoon march, and we made a few miles. At night he was worse and we knew the end had come. Should this be found I want these facts recorded. Oates' last thoughts were of his Mother, but immediately before he took pride in thinking that his regiment would be pleased with the bold way in which he met his death. He was a brave soul. He slept through the night before last, hoping not to wake; but he woke in the morning. It was blowing a blizzard. He said, "I am just going outside and may be some time." He went out into the blizzard and we have not seen him since. We knew that poor Oates was walking to his death, but though we tried to dissuade him, we knew it was the act of a brave man and an English gentleman. We all hope to meet the end with a similar spirit, and assuredly the end is not far. I can only write at lunch and then only occasionally. The cold is intense, -40° at midday. My companions are unendingly cheerful, but we are all on the verge of serious frostbites, and though we constantly talk of fetching through I don't think anyone of us believes it in his heart.

Sunday, March 18: To-day, lunch, we are 21 miles from the depot. We have had more wind and drift from ahead yesterday; had to stop marching; wind N.W., force 4, temp: 35°. My right foot has gone, nearly all the toes - two days ago I was proud possessor of best feet.

Monday, March 19: We camped with difficulty last night, and were dreadfully cold till after our supper of cold pemmican and biscuit and a half a pannikin of cocoa cooked over the spirit. Sledge dreadfully heavy. We are 15½ miles from the depot and ought to get there in three days. We have two days' food but barely a day's fuel.

Wednesday, March 11: Got within 11 miles of depôt Monday night; had to lay up all yesterday in severe blizzard. To-day forlorn hope, Wilson and Bowers going to depot for fuel.

Thursday, March 22 and 23: Blizzard bad as ever - Wilson and Bowers unable to start - to-morrow last chance - no fuel and only one or two of food left - must be near the end. Have decided it shall be natural - we shall march for the depot with or without our effects and die in our tracks.

Thursday, March 29: Since the 21st we have had a continuous gale. We had fuel to make two cups of tea apiece and bare food for two days on the 20th. Every day we have been ready to start for our depot 11 miles away, but outside the door of the tent it remains a scene of whirling drift. We shall stick it out to the end, but we are getting weaker, of course, and the end cannot be far. It seems a pity, but I do not think I can write more.

R. SCOTT.

For God's sake look after our people.

[*Note found with the diary:*]

MESSAGE TO THE PUBLIC

The causes of the disaster are not due to faulty organisation, but to misfortune in all risks which had to be undertaken. As I have said elsewhere we got into frightfully rough ice and Edgar Evans received a concussion of the brain - he died a natural death, but left us a shaken party with the season unduly advanced.

Had we lived, I should have had a tale to tell of the hardihood, endurance, and courage of my companions which would have stirred the heart of every Englishman. These rough notes and our dead bodies must tell the tale, but surely, surely, a great rich country like ours will see that those who are dependent on us are properly provided for.

R. SCOTT.

Le Répertoire de La Cuisine
by Louis Saulnier
(Paris, 1914)

The magnificent French *haute cuisine* we know now was substantially created and codified in the 19th Century by Antoine Carême and Auguste Escoffier. It was Escoffier's student Louis Saulnier who prepared this list of quick definitions of their dishes in the book known to cooks the world over as 'Le Répertoire'.

Abridged: GH. This version gives a mere 300 or so of Saulnier's 7000 short definitions, but most are complete as written.

To The Master of Modern Cookery
AUGUSTE ESCOFFIER

A - FONDS DE CUISINE
FUNDAMENTAL ELEMENTS OF COOKING

Appareil Maintenon - Two parts of onion sauce and one part mushroom sauce cohered with yolks of eggs; add minced mushrooms.

Aspic - Mould lined with aspic jelly, decorated to taste, ingredients placed in the interior.

Consommé Blanc - (White Consommé) - Shin of beef, veal knuckles, water, carrots, turnips, leeks, parsnips, celery-stick, onion with clove stuck in it, cook 5 hours, strain.

Consommé Clarifié - (Clarified Consommé) Lean beef chopped or passed through a mincing machine, and put in a pan with white of eggs previously beaten with water, add to the above white consommé, minced carrots and leeks, and bring quickly to the boil. Simmer gently for two or three hours.

Court-Bouillon - A: White or red wine, fish stock and aromatic herbs, for matelots. B: Salt water, milk, lemon juice, for white sea fish. C: Salt water, vinegar and aromatic herbs, for shellfish and river-fish.

Croûtons - Bread, cut different shapes and fried in butter.

Farce à l'Américaine - (American Stuffing) Chopped onions tossed with smoked bacon, add bread crumbs, salt and pepper.

Farce de Poisson - (Fish Forcemeat) Fillets of fish, pounded with white of eggs, pass through a sieve and gradually add cream until the proper consistency.

Fonds Blanc - (White Stock) Veal bones and shin of veal, fowls' carcasses, carrots, onion stuck with clove, leek, celery, faggot of herbs, water, salt. Boil 3 to 5 hours and strain.

Fonds Brun ou Estouffade - (Brown Stock or Estouffade) Whole shin of beef, shin of veal, raw ham, fresh pork rind, carrots and minced onions, browned in butter. Break the bones and colour in oven, moisten with water, add vegetables and Bouquet Garni. Cook 8 hours, strain.

Mirepoix - Cubes of carrot, onions, raw ham, bay leaf, thyme, tossed in butter.

Roux Brun - (Brown Roux) Clarified butter mixed with flour and cooked slowly in oven until light brown.

BEURRES COMPOSES
COMPOUND BUTTERS

Ail - (Garlic) Blanched garlic cloves pounded in a mortar with butter – sieved.

Maitre-d'hôtel - Butter softened to a cream, mixed with chopped parsley, salt, black pepper, lemon juice.

Meunière - Nut brown cooked butter with lemon juice, chopped parsley.

Montpellier - Watercress, parsley, chervil, chives, spinach, chopped shallots, boiled 2 minutes, drained and pressed, add gherkins, capers, garlic, anchovy fillets, pounded with butter, yolk of raw eggs and hard. Add oil by degrees, cayenne pepper, sieved.

Noir - (Black) Cook butter until black, strain, add vinegar.

Raifort - (Horseradish) Scraped horseradish pounded with butter and sieved.

GARNITURES - GARNISHES

Algérienne - Small tomatoes, peeled an cooked in oil, croquettes of sweet potato.

Ambassadeur - Duchesse potatoes, artichoke bottoms filled with mushroom purée, scraped horseradish.

Américaine - Slices of lobster tail and slices of truffle.

Ancienne - Small braised onions without colouring, and mushrooms.

Anglaise - Carrots, turnips, cauliflowers, French beans, plain boiled potatoes. All cooked in salt water.

Béatrix - Morels tossed in butter, new carrots, artichoke bottoms, fondante new potatoes.

Belle-Hélène - Grilled mushrooms filled with concassed tomatoes, new peas, new carrot and potato croquettes.

Bohémienne - Pilaf rice, concassed tomatoes, roundels of fried onions.

Boulangère - Onions and potatoes, salt and pepper, cook with the joint.

Bourgeoise - Shaped carrots, glazed onions, dice of bacon

Bourguignonne - Glazed onions, mushrooms tossed in butter, dice of bacon.

Bretonne - Haricot beans cohered with Bretonne sauce, chopped parsley.

Bruxelloise - Braised chicory, Brussels sprouts and château potatoes.

Cardinal - Collops of lobster and slices of truffles. Cardinal sauce mixed with dice of truffles and lobster.

Catalane - Artichoke bottoms and grilled tomatoes.

Daumont - Large mushroom heads cooked in butter, garnished with crayfish tails cohered with Nantua sauce, fish quenelles, fried soft roes.

Dauphine - Croquettes of Dauphine potatoes.

Dubarry - Cauliflower moulded into balls with a serviette, coated with Mornay sauce, glazed, château potatoes.

Favorite - Thick slices of fois gras, slices of truffles, asparagus heads.

Figaro - Small nests of duchesse potato, Vermicelli fried, garnish with small balls of carrots.

Financière - Quenelles, cockscombs and kidneys, slices of truffles, mushroom heads and stoned olives.

Florentine - Spinach leaves.

Forestière - Morels in butter, diced bacon, Parmentier potato.

Française - Spinach leaves, Anna potatoes.

Hongroise - Cauliflower moulded into balls, coated with Mornay sauce and paprika, glazed, chopped ham, glazed potatoes.

Jardinière - Carrots, turnips, French beans, flageolets, green peas, and cauliflower coated in Hollandaise sauce.

Lorraine - Braised red cabbage and fondant potatoes.

Louisiane - Sweet corn creamed, moulded rice on slices of fried sweet potato, roundels of fried banana.

Macédoine - Vegetables mixed and served in artichoke bottoms.

Matelote - Glazed onions, mushroom heads, heart-shaped croutons, trussed crayfish.

Montmorency - Artichoke bottoms garnished with carrot balls, noisette potatoes.

Napolitaine - Spaghetti cohered with butter, tomato sauce and cheese; small heaps of tomatoes concassed.

Provençale - Small tomatoes, stuffed mushrooms with duxelles and garlic.

Rossini - Collops of foe gras tossed in butter, slices of truffles. Meat glaze.

Samaritaine - Timbales of rice, Dauphin potatoes, braised lettuces.

Talleyrand - Macaroni cohered with butter and cheese, garnished with julienne of truffles and slices of fois gras.

Victoria - Macaroni, tomatoes, lettuces and mashed potatoes.

B - SAUCES - SAUCES

Aïoli - Garlic cloves pounded with boiled potato, egg yolk, salt, pepper, lemon juice and oil.

Béarnaise - Reduction of chopped shallots, mignonnette pepper, tarragon, salt and vinegar. Add yolks of eggs and finish as Hollandaise sauce, add crayfish, butter and cream. Garnished with crayfish tails.

Béchamel - White roux moistened with milk, salt, onion stuck with cloves, cook for 20 minutes.

Cardinal - Béchamel sauce with fish stock, truffle essence and lobster butter, cayenne pepper.

Hollandaise - Reduction of vinegar with mignonnette pepper. Add yolk of eggs and whisk in gradually some melted butter and a little water or cream, strain and finish with lemon juice, (Must not boil)

Mayonnaise - Put some yolk of eggs in a basin. Season with salt, pepper, cayenne, pour some vinegar on the yolks while whisking briskly, add oil gradually, finish the sauce with lemon juice and a little boiling water to prevent turning.

Mornay - Béchamel sauce mixed with butter, grated gruyère and parmesan.

Oignons - (Onion Sauce) Minced onions cooked in milk, seasoned with salt, pepper and nutmeg.

Persil - (Parsley) Butter sauce with blanched, chopped parsley.

Velouté - White roux. Moisten with white stock.

C - HORS D'ŒUVRES
SIDE DISHES or APPETISERS

Barquettes - Small boat-shaped crusts, garnished in any way, chicken, vegetables, oysters, etc.

Canapés - Toast, cut into various shapes, round, square, oval, etc.

Frivolités - Hors d'œuvres composed of moulded cream, barquettes, tartlets, etc.

Fruits de Mer - All sorts of raw sea shell fish except oysters, served with bread and butter.

Huitres - Oysters served on crushed ice, with brown bread and butter, lemon quarters or shallot sauce.

Salade de Pieds de Mouton - Sheep's feet, cooked and boned, cut into small fillets, seasoned with oil and vinegar.

Tartelettes - Are garnished with mousse or compound butters, and finished according to taste or fancy.

Variantes - Assortment of blanched artichoke bottoms, French beans, cauliflowers etc, marinated in oil, vinegar, coriander and English mustard.

D - POTAGES – SOUPS
CONSOMMES CLAIRS - CLEAR SOUPS

Aurore - Consommé thickened with tapioca and tomato purée. Garnished with Julienne of Chicken.

Brunoise - Consommé garnished with small cubes of carrots, turnips, leeks, celery, peas and chervil.

Floréal - Chicken consommé garnished with carrots, turnips, peas, asparagus heads, small quenelles with pistachio powder and chervil shreds.

Milanaise - Chicken in consommé with tomato flavour, garnished with mushrooms, ham, truffles, spaghetti. Cheese.

Parisienne - Consommé with leek flavour, garnished with julienne of potato and leek.

SOUPES - SOUPS

Ail - Thin slices of French bread sprinkled with grated cheese and gratinated. Boil some garlic, sage, bay leaves, cloves, salt, pepper and pour over the toasted bread dressed in a soup bowl.

Bonne Femme - Minced leeks and potatoes fried in butter and moistened with white consommé; garnished with French bread, finished with butter and cream

Laboureur - Marmite with beef, mutton and chicken, garnished with vegetables and rice with saffron.

Savoyarde - Celery, leeks, onions and minced potatoes, tossed in minced lard moistened with water and milk. Slices of toast with cheese.

VELOUTES - CREAM or THICK SOUPS

Bisque d'écrevisses - Mirepoix of vegetables tossed in Butter with crayfishes, peppercorns, moistened with white wine, fish stock, consommé, and burned brandy; add tomato, faggot, rice. Cook 30 minutes. Pound and sieve. Butter and cream.

Céleri - Veloute with celery purée. Cream.

Crécy - Carrots puréed with rice. Butter and cream.

Flamande - Potato purée and Brussels sprouts. Cream or yolk of eggs.

Garbure - Vegetable purée, butter and cream (Separately). Fried croûtons.

Impérial - Tapioca cohered with yolk of eggs and cream, passed through a tammy, garnished with large sago.

Lamballe - ½ fresh peas purée and ½ tapioca. Butter.

Reine - Chicken purée with rice, garnished with rice. Liaison with cream or eggs.

Vuillemot - Haricot bean purée, garnished with shredded sorrel and rice, fried croutons, butter and cream.

POTAGES ÉTRANGERS - FOREIGN SOUPS

Bortsch Koop - Julienne of leeks, carrots, onions, celery, beef, moistened with water. The consommé garnished with minced beetroot. (Separately): serve small pies in puff paste stuffed with chicken forcemeat and beetroot juice.

Mock Turtle - Thin half-glaze with celery and mushroom flavour, infusion of turtle herbs.

Selinka - Consommé with ham fumet, garnished with sauerkraut and blanched parsley.

E – ŒUFS – EGGS
BROUILLES - SCRAMBLED

Aumale - Mixed with tomatoes, dice of kidneys sautés with Madeira.

Leuchtemberg - Mixed with blanched chives, caviare in the centre.

Orloff - In cocottes: garnished with crayfish tails, slice of truffle on top.

EN COCOTTE - IN COCOTTE

Bergère - Interior garnished with minced mutton and mushrooms a thread of meat glaze around.

Parisienne - Interior coated with chicken forcemeat mixed with tongue, mushrooms and truffles, a thread of half-glaze

Zingara - With a thread of Zingar sauce around.

DURS - HARD BOILED

Aurore - Coated with tomato béchamel, grated cheese glaze.

Granville - Cut into quarters and mixed with Bordelaise sauce.

Portugaise - In half tomatoes cooked in oil, coated with tomato sauce.

Tripe (à la) - Cut into roundels and mix with onion sauce, chopped parsley.

FRITS - FRIED

Américaine - Dressed on rashers of grilled bacon, fried parsley. Tomato sauce.

Diable - Cooked in butter, both sides, pour over some nut-brown butter and vinegar.

Romaine - Poach egg, coated in Villeroy sauce, egg and crumb, fry deep fat, tomato sauce.

COQUE, MOLLETS, MOULES ET POCHES - BOILED, SOFT-BOILED, MOULDED AND POACHED.

Coque - Plunge the egg in boiling water and cook two or three minutes.

Mollets - Boil for 5½ minutes, cool and shelled.

Moulés - Break the egg into buttered moulds, cook 5½ minutes, let stand a while and unmould.

Pochés - Break the eggs in boiling water and poach 2½ minutes, when done dip in cold water. Note: Add salt and vinegar before poaching.

Bénédictine - (A) In tartlets garnished with brandade of salt codfish with truffles coated with cream sauce. (B) On muffin toasted, with slice of tongue and the egg on it, coated with Hollandaise sauce.

Duchesse - On croutons of duchesse potatoes, coated with thickened gravy.

Florentine - In croustades garnished with spinach in leaves tossed in butter, coated with Mornay sauce and glazed.

Gratin - (or Mornay) In croustades, with Mornay sauce, glazed.

Verdi - In buttered moulds decorated with truffles and filled with scrambled eggs mixed with Parmesan, chopped truffles and beaten eggs, poached, dressed on croutons,

surround base with half-glaze.

OMELETTES - OMELETS

Bénédictine - Stuffed with brandade of morue and truffles, a thread of supreme sauce around.

Bonne-Femme - Mix with the beaten eggs, some dice of bacon, minced mushrooms and slices of onion tossed in butter.

Fines-Herbes - Mix with the eggs chopped parsley, chives, tarragon leaves, chervil.

Limousine - Mix with the eggs some dice of potatoes and ham tossed in butter.

Rognons - Stuffed with dice of kidneys tossed in butter and cohered with Madeira sauce.

F – POISSIONS - FISH

Aigrefin Flamande - (Haddock) Poach in white wine in a buttered dish, garnish with onions and mushrooms. Dress, reduce the liquor, add parsley and coat the fish.

Alose Grille - (Shad) Season, marinade with oil, lemon juice, parsley, thyme, bay. Grill. Separately – melted butter.

Anguilles Orly - Eel fillets, season egg and crumb, fry deep fat. Tomato sauce.

Bouillabaisse (Marseillaise) - Fish to employ: racasses, John Dory, whiting, conger-eel, red mullets, langoustines (all from Mediterranean). Large fishes cut, others whole. Preparation – Fried in oil, minced onions, leek, add crushed garlic, bay leaf, fennel, dice of tomato. Set some fried slices of bread in a deep dish, pour over cooking liquor, serve fish in another dish.

Brochet Anglaise - Fillets of pike, seasoned, bread crumbed baked in oven in a gratin dish, serve in the dish.

Coquilles Saint-Jacques Gratin - (Scallops) Blanch, slice, braise in white wine and mushrooms cooking liquor, place in the shells and coat with gratin sauce, sprinkle with breadcrumbs and set in oven to gratin.

Crevettes Frittes - Alive, toss shrimps in clarified butter or oil, cayenne pepper.

Escargots Vigneronne - (Snails) Toss the snails in butter with chopped shallots, garlic, salt and pepper, dip them in batter and fry in walnut oil.

Nymphes (Grenouilles) - (Frogs) Poach in white wine, let cool, coat with paprika, chaud-froid sauce, dress and decorate with tarragon leaves and sprigs of chervil, glaze with aspic jelly.

Harengs Grillés - (Herrings) Oiled and grilled, serve mustard sauce.

Homard Newburg - (Lobster) Cut up the live lobster, season and toss in butter and oil, swill with brandy and Marsala, reduce, add cream and fish stock, cook 15 minutes, dish the fillets in timbale, thicken the sauce with the creamy parts and coral, finish with butter, strain and coat.

Homard Thermidor - (Lobster) Dress the collops in halved carapaces and coat with Bercy reduction and mustard cohered with Mornay sauce, glaze.

Moules Marinière - (Mussels) Stewed in their shells with shallots and white wine, cohere with beeurre manié, and lemon juice, serve in timbale, chopped parsley.

Potted Char - Poach in white wine with mirepoix, remove the fillets and lay them in an earthen pot, cover with clarified butter, cook in oven 15 minutes, keep in cool place.

Sole Bercy - Poached with shallots and chopped parsley, white wine and fish stock. Reduce the stock, add butter and coat the fish, glaze.

Sole Boitelle - As Bercy, with sliced mushrooms

Sole Bonne-Femme - As Boitelle with a border of slices of steamed potatoes.

Sole Vin Blanc - Poached in white wine, coated in the reduced cooking liquor mixed with white wine sauce.

Tortue Baltimore - (Turtle) Cooked pieces of turtle, tossed in nut brown cooked butter, dressed in cocotte, with thickened gravy, and a glass of Xérès wine [sherry].

Truite George Sand - (Trout) Filleted, poached, skinned, coated in shrimp sauce, garnished with quenelles and shrimps, slices of truffle.

G – ENTRÉES D'ABATS
PREPARATIONS OF OFFAL

Boudions blanc et noirs - (Black and white puddings) Are served grilled

Cervelles Bourguignonne - (Brains) Poach. Dress with garnish and Bourguignonne sauce.

Foie à l'Anglaise - (Liver) Cut in slices, grilled, dressed alternately with grilled rashers of bacon.

Oreilles Frites - (Ears) Calves ears, blanch, braise in Madeira, cut in shreds, dip in batter and fry deep fat. Serve with tomato sauce.

Queue de Bœuf Cavour - (Oxtail) In sections, braise with brown stock and white wine, place in a cocotte and add the braising stock, strain and thicken. Serve with chestnut purée.

Rognons Marchand de Vin - (Kidneys) Tossed in butter, cohered with red wine Bercy sauce.

Tripes a la Mode de Caen - (Tripe) Carrots, onions, ox feet, tripe with beef fat and herbs, moistened with white wine, cider, brandy, cooked 10 hours.

ENTRECÔTES - BEEFSTEAKS

Américaine - Grilled. Fried egg on top, serve with tomato sauce.

Forestière - Fry in butter, coat with mushroom sauce and mushroom heads. Garnish with sautéed morels, dice of bacon and Parmentier potatoes.

Hambourg or Bismark - Chopped raw, seasoned with salt, pepper and nutmeg and raw egg, chopped onions, tossed in butter, mix together, divided and shaped like a Tournedos, flour and cook in clarified butter.

Lyonnaise - Cook in butter, garnish with sliced onions, coat with half-glaze.

Vert-Pré - Grilled, garnish with straw potatoes and water-cress.

COTES - CHOPS

Cotes Bergère - Egg and bread crumbs, cook in clarified butter, dress in a circle alternately with slices of grilled

ham, garnish centre with straw potatoes, surround with cooked morels or Mousserons and glazed onions (small).

Mouton Bretonne - Egg and bread crumbs, cook, dish in the form of a crown, garnish centre with beans a la Bretonne, serve with thickened gravy.

Mouton Minute - Cut thin, fry quickly in butter, add chopped parsley and lemon juice to the cooking butter.

Mouton Réforme - Egg and bread crumbs, with chopped ham added to the bread crumbs. Serve with Réforme sauce.

Veau Belle-Vue - (Veal) Braise, decorate with truffles and cooked vegetables, garnish with aspic.

Veau Marigny - (Veal) Cooked in butter, garnish with tartlets filled with peas and French beans alternately. Serve with thickened gravy.

NOISETTES, TOURNEDOS, FILETS MIGNONS

Alexandra - Cook in butter, garnish with slices of truffles and artichoke bottoms

Choisy - Cooked in butter, dressed on croutons, cover with white wine half-glaze sauce, garnish with braised lettuces and Château potatoes.

Dubarry - Cooked in butter, surround with small cauliflowers covered with Mornay sauce and glazed. Sauce Madeira half-glaze.

Marie-Thérèse - Cook in butter, coat with tomatoed half-glaze, garnish with timbales filled with rizotto and sliced truffle on top.

Nichette - Cook in butter, garnish with grilled mushrooms filled with small balls of carrots, coat with marrow sauce combined with cockscombs and kidneys.

Romanoff - Covered with cream sauce mixed with chopped cèpes, cover the top with Béchamel sauce finished with crayfish butter, surround the borders with braised half fennels, serve stock separately.

H - ENTRÉES et RELEVÉS
BUTCHERS MEATS

Pieces de Bœuf - Lard rump of beef, season and pickle in brandy and wine 4 hours, dry. Brown in hot fat, moisten with pickle and brown stock, add herbs and mushroom peelings, cook in oven. Pass and reduce sauce, thin glaze.

Bœuf Bourguignonne - As above, with Bourguignonne garnish.

Porc Choucroute - Roasted, served with braised sauerkraut and gravy.

ENTRÉES DIVERSES - VARIOUS ENTRÉES

Carbonnades - Scallops of beef tossed in butter or lard nicely browned, then cooked in a sauté dish with finely chopped onion, drop of beer and brown stock mixed with brown roux, add a little demerara sugar, cook in over 3 hours.

Cassoulet - (1) Haricot beans cooked with onions, carrots, garlic, herbs, fresh pork rind, blanched and tied together, when half cooked add a piece of breast of pork and a garlic sausage. (2) Cut into squares shoulder of mutton or goose, fry with chopped onions and garlic, moisten with the bean stock, cook, garnish dish or cocotte with alternate layers of mutton or goose, beans, bacon cut into dice, and slices of sausage, sprinkle with crumbs, browned in the oven.

Daube Provençale - (Stew) Pieces of beef larded with fat bacon, rolled in chopped parsley and crushed garlic, pickled with white wine and brandy, oil, to be cooked in a braising pan with alternate layers of beef, pork rind, carrots, chopped onions, thyme, bay leaf, tomatoes, mushrooms, stoned black olives, herbs, orange peel.

Goulache - (Goulash) Cubes of beef, chopped onions, garlic, paprika, smoked bacon, water, put in stew pan and cook slowly, garnish with boiled potatoes.

Lièvre a la Royale - (Royal Jugged Hare) Line a braising pan with bacon, place hare in it, add carrots, 4 onions stuck with cloves, 20 cloves of garlic, 40 shallots, herbs, ½ bottle red wine, a little vinegar, braise in oven 5 hours.

Galantine - Skin and bone fowl or game, season, marinade with tongue, truffles, lardons, pistachios, brandy, Madeira. Forcemeat made from the meat, and rolled inside the skin, wrapped in bacon and cooked. Served cold and sliced.

Pâtè - Flour and butter paste to line mould, filled with scallops of meat and lardons, cover with fat bacon, paste on top, egg wash, decorate and cook.

VOLAILLE - POULTRY

Canard Bigarde - (Duck) Cooked underdone, remove the fillets and slice lengthways. Bigarde sauce.

Canard à l'orange - (Duck) Braised, add orange and lemon and julienne of zest, surround with quarters of oranges skinned raw.

Poulet Châtelaine - (Chicken) Cooke in cocotte, add white wine and half-gaze, garnish with artichoke quarters, truffles, cocotte potatoes.

Poulet Alexandra - Lard with tongue and truffles, poach, remove the suprêmes, replace with mousseline forcemeat, reshape the bird, coat with Mornay sauce, glaze, garnish with tartlets filled with asparagus heads, place a scallop of supreme on each, surround with a thread of pale glaze.

Poulet Carmelite - (Cold) Scallop the suprêmes, coat with Chaud-froid sauce flavoured with mushroom essence, surround with grooved mushroom heads.

Poulet Élysée - Stuff with chicken mousseline and foie gras purée, truffles, poach, surround with Régence garnish, Suprême sauce.

Poulet Reine - Poach, cover with Suprême sauce, surround with timbales of chicken purée.

Poulet Rossini - Rinse with Madeira and half-glaze, dress in terrine, garnish with slices of foie gras and quarters of truffles, seal lid with thin paste, finish in the oven.

Poulet Vichy - Poach, cover with Suprême sauce, finish with purée of carrots, garnish with tartlets crusts filled with Vichy carrots.

Oie - (Goose) Is roasted and stuffed the English way, with apple sauce and gravy.

I - SALADES - SALADS

Américaine - Curly chicory, tomatoes and sliced artichoke bottoms, julienne of green pimentos and whites of hard-boiled eggs, cover with hard yolks, sieved, vinaigrette with mustard.

Châtelaine - Hard-boiled eggs, truffles, artichoke bottoms, potatoes, vinaigrette with chopped tarragon.

Impériale - French beans, carrots, apples and truffles cut in Julienne, vinaigrette and chopped parsley.

Monte-Carlo - Dice of pineapple and oranges, grains of pomegranate, lemon juice and cream, dressed in tangerine skins, served on crushed ice, hearts of lettuce between each.

Niçoise - French beans, tomato quarters, potatoes, decorate with fillets of anchovy. Olives and capers. Vinaigrette sauce.

Tosca - Dice of chicken with truffles, celery and parmesan cheese, mayonnaise with anchovy essence thinned with mustard vinaigrette.

Waldorf - Dice of celeriac, russet apples, halved peeled walnuts, thin mayonnaise.

POMMES DE TERRE - POTATOES

Anglaise - Shape, cook in steamer and season.

Anna - Cut in cylinders, slice in rounds, wash and dry, set in layers on a special pan with clarified butter, cook in oven, when half done turn over to colours both sides.

Château - Shape like a large olive, blanched, roasted nice brown, in butter.

Chips - Slices very thin, fry in deep fat.

Croquettes - Purée, shape as you fancy, egg and bread crumb, fry deep fat.

Dauphine - One part choux paste without sugar, two parts Duchesse Potato, shape as corks, egg and bread crumb.

Dauphinoise - Cut in raw slices, cook in oven with milk and grated Gruyère cheese.

Duchesse - Cook as purée, thicken with yolks of eggs.

Fondantes - Château potatoes, cooked in covered pan with a little white wine consommé.

Gratinées - Mashed potatoes well buttered, put into a gratin dish, sprinkle with cheese and browned.

Lyonnaise - Sauté potatoes, mixed with onions.

Marquise - Pommes Duchess mixed with tomato sauce.

Parmentier - Cut into ½ inch cubes, cook in clarified butter.

Rissolées - As château, well browned.

MACARONI, SPAGHETTI

Bolonaise - With slices of fillet of beef, cooked with chopped onions, veal stock and herbs.

Italienne - Cook, strain, season, add butter, cream and grated cheese. Mix together.

Napolitaine - As Italienne, add tomatoes in dice and tomato sauce.

K – ENTREMENTS - SWEETS

Crème Anglaise - 16 yolks of eggs, 1 lb sugar. Beat together. Add 1 quart boiling milk, vanilla. Cook slowly until thick.

Crème Frangipane - 1lb sugar. Work in gradually 8 eggs and 16 yolks. Add 10 oz flour, 5 pints milk. Boil a few minutes. Vanilla.

Crème Pâtissière - 12 yolks, work with 1 lb sugar. Add 4 oz flour. Mix in a quart of milk. Let boil. Vanilla.

Sauce Framboises - Raspberry jam thinned with syrup, flavoured with kirsch.

Sauce Noisette - Crème Anglaise, mix with powder of aveline toffee.

Bavarois - 16 oz sugar work with 16 yolks, add quart of milk cook like a custard, add 1 oz gelatine, vanilla, let cool and mix 1 quart whipped cream.

Blanc-manger - (Blancmange) 1 lb sweet almonds pounded with a glass of water. Strain the liquid, mix with 8 oz sugar and 1 oz gelatine. Flavour to taste.

Charlotte de Pommes - Line in a well-buttered mould some oblong slices of bread. Fill the interior with quarters of apples partly cooked in butter. Cook in oven. Dish up. Pour apricot sauce over.

Charlotte Chantilly - Mould lined with finger biscuits, filled with whipped cream.

Crème Caramel - Moulds lined with caramel sugar, filled with Crème reversée custard, cook in oven in bain-marie.

Crème Mont-Blanc - Whipped cream with chestnut purée.

Crêpes Gil-Blas - Spread pancake with 4 oz butter worked with 4 oz sugar and aveline powder.

Crêpes Suzette - As Gil-Blas, flavoured with curaçao and tangerine.

Omelette Célestine - Small omelette with marmalade in centre, another larger spread with jam. Roll together, sprinkle sugar, glaze with red iron.

Albert Pudding - 1 lb butter, 1 lb sugar, 16 yolks, 1 lb flour, 16 whites beaten stiff, 1 lb candied cherries, cut in dice, custard, Madeira.

Bread-and-Butter Pudding - Slices of bread and butter in a pie dish, Sultanas and currants, fill dish with custard preparation.

Cabinet Pudding - Pieces of finger biscuits in a Charlotte mould, mixed peel, sultanas and currants, fill with custard, flavour vanilla.

Souffles - Crème pâtissière, yolk of eggs, mix the whites whipped in a firm froth.

Fruits Cardinal - Strawberries, Peaches, Pears – poached, dressed on vanilla ice, covered with raspberry purée. Sprinkle with sliced grilled almonds.

Fruits Compote - All kinds of fruits peeled and poached in light syrup, flavour to taste.

Hélène - Pears, Apples, poached, dressed on vanilla ice and candied violets. Serve with hot chocolate sauce.

Marguerite - Wild strawberries soaked in kirsch and maraschino, mix with grenadine sorbet, decorate whipped cream, flavour maraschino.

Melba - Strawberries, nectarines, peaches, pears – dressed on vanilla ice, cover with raspberry purée.

Sarah Bernhardt - Nectarines, peaches – poached, dressed on pineapple ice, covered with mousse of strawberries and curaçao.

Metamorphosis
(*Die Verwandlung*)
by Franz Kafka
(Leipzig, 1915)

As this might be the most famous 'existentialist' or 'surrealist' novel, explanation is neither possible or necessary.

Abridged: GH

I

One morning, as Gregor Samsa woke from troubled dreams, he found himself transformed in his bed into a very large creepy-crawly. He lay on his armour-like back, and lifting his head a little, he could see his belly, brown and divided into stiff sections. His many, pitifully thin, legs waved about helplessly.

"What has happened to me?" he thought. It wasn't a dream. This was his room, a proper human room although a little small, and there was his collection of textile samples, for Samsa was a travelling salesman. Gregor looked out the window at the grey skies. "Perhaps I might I sleep a little longer and forget all this nonsense". What about if he reported sick? But that would be extremely suspicious, Gregor had never once been ill in his fifteen years of service

There was a gentle knock at the door. "Gregor", - it was his mother - "it's quarter to seven. Didn't you want to go somewhere?" Gregor wanted to explain everything, but in the circumstances contented himself with saying: "Yes, mother, yes, thank-you."

It was a simple matter for him to throw off the bed covers. But, after that, it became rather difficult, especially as he had become so exceptionally wide. He would have used his arms and his hands to push himself up, but instead of them he only had all those little legs, forever moving in different directions. He wanted to get out of the bed, but he had never yet seen the lower part of his new body, and it turned out to be rather hard to move; it went so slowly; he bounced against the bedpost, and learned from the burning pain that the new body might well be rather sensitive.

"Seven o'clock, already", he said to himself when the clock struck. But then he said, "Before it strikes quarter past, I'll definitely have to be out of bed. And by then somebody will have come round from work to ask what's happened to me." And so he set himself to the task of swinging his body out of the bed. His back seemed to be pretty tough, so might well withstand falling onto the carpet. He would have to just risk the loud noise it would make.

It occurred to him how simple everything would be if somebody came to help, perhaps his father and the maid. After a while he had worked so far across the bed that a simple rocking motion was ready to dislodge him.

Then there was a ring at the door of the flat. "That'll be someone from work", he said to himself, and froze very still, although his little legs became all the more lively as they danced around. Gregor only needed to hear the visitor's first words and he knew who it was - the chief clerk himself.

There was a loud thump, and his fall was softened a little by the carpet. Gregor's back was more elastic than he had thought. "Something's fallen down in there", said the chief clerk whose footsteps in his highly polished boots could now be heard in the adjoining room. "Gregor", said his father from the room to his left, "please open up this door. I'm sure he'll be good enough to forgive the untidiness of your room." Then the chief clerk called "Good morning, Mr. Samsa". "He isn't well", said his mother. "Mrs. Samsa", said the chief clerk, "I hope it's nothing serious. But, you know, we business people do have to try and overcome these little things." "Can the chief clerk come in to see you now?", asked his father. "No", said Gregor. In the room on his left his sister Grete began to cry.

The chief clerk now raised his voice, "Mr. Samsa", he called, "what is wrong? You barricade yourself in your room, your employer did suggest that your failure to appear might not be unconnected with the money that was recently entrusted to you - but I doubt that that could be right." "Sir", called Gregor, "I'm just getting out of bed. It's not as easy as I'd thought. No need to wait, sir; I'll be in the office soon". "Did he understand a word of that?" the chief clerk asked his parents. "Oh, God!" called his mother, in tears, "he could be seriously ill."

But Gregor had become much calmer. So they couldn't understand his words any more, although they seemed clear enough to him, it had become very quiet in the next room. Perhaps his parents were whispering with the chief clerk, or perhaps they were pressed against the door, listening.

Gregor slowly pushed his way over to the door, using the adhesive on the tips of his legs. He then set himself to the task of turning the key in the lock with his mouth. He seemed, unfortunately, to have no proper teeth.

"Listen", said the chief clerk in the next room, "he's turning the key." Gregor was greatly encouraged, though would have preferred "Well done, Gregor". Then he lay his head on the handle of the door, and opened it.

He heard the chief clerk exclaim a loud "Oh!", like a sigh of the wind. Gregor's mother looked at his father, then she sank onto the floor into her skirts. His father clenched his fists. Then he looked uncertainly round the living room. Gregor leant against the inside of the other door, so that only half of his body could be seen, along with his head.

"Well, then", said Gregor, aware that he was the only one to have kept calm, "I'll get dressed straight away."

But the chief clerk turned away as soon as Gregor started to speak, and only stared back at him over his trembling shoulders as he left. Gregor realised that it was out of the question to let the chief clerk go away in this mood if his position in the firm was not to be put into extreme danger. That was something his parents simply did not understand, they had become convinced that this job would provide for Gregor for life. The chief clerk had to be calmed, convinced and finally won over; the future of Gregor and his family depended on it!

The chief clerk had already reached the stairs when Gregor made a run for him; he wanted to be sure of reaching him; but the chief leapt down several steps at once and disappeared; his shouts resounding all around the staircase. Gregor's appeals to his father were of no help. His appeals were simply not understood.

Now nothing would stop Gregor's father as he drove him back, hissing at him like a wild man. Gregor was as yet unskilled in moving backwards and was only able to go very slowly. If Gregor had only been allowed to turn round he would have been back in his room quite quickly, but his father seemed impatient. He lay at an angle in the doorway, one flank scraped on the door and was painfully injured, leaving vile brown flecks behind. Then his father gave him a hefty shove from behind which sent him flying, and heavily bleeding, deep into his room. The door was slammed shut with the stick, then, all was quiet.

II

It was not until that evening that Gregor awoke from his deep sleep. The light from the electric street lamps shone palely here and there onto the ceiling and glistened on the furniture, but down below, where Gregor was, it was dark. He pushed himself over to the door, feeling his way clumsily with his antennae - of which he was now beginning to learn the value. One of the legs had been badly injured in the events of that morning, and dragged along lifelessly.

By the door he discovered a bowl filled with sweetened milk with little pieces of bread floating in it. He was even hungrier than he had been that morning, so immediately dipped in. but the milk did not taste nice. Milk was normally his favourite drink, and his sister had certainly left it there for him because of that. But he turned away from the dish and crawled back into the centre of the room.

He spent the whole night there, barely sleeping from fear and hunger. He knew, however, that he must remain calm, show patience and consideration so that his family could bear the unpleasantness of his condition. Gregor soon had the opportunity to test the strength of his decisions.

Early next morning his sister opened the door and looked anxiously in. Gregor pushed his head forward to the edge of the couch, and watched. His sister noticed the full dish and immediately picked it up - using a rag, not her bare hands - and carried it out. Gregor never could have guessed what his sister, in her goodness, actually did bring. She brought him a whole selection of things, spread out on an old newspaper. Half-rotten vegetables, bones from the evening meal, covered in white sauce gone hard, raisins and almonds and some cheese that Gregor himself had declared inedible two days before. She poured some water into the dish, and placed it beside them. Then, out of consideration for Gregor's feelings, she hurried out.

Gregor's little legs whirred, at last he could eat. "Am I less sensitive than I used to be, then?", he thought, sucking greedily at the cheese which, almost compellingly, attracted him much more than the other foods. His eyes watering with pleasure, he consumed the cheese, the vegetables and the sauce. The fresh foods, on the other hand, he found not to his taste at all.

From now on Gregor received his food once in the morning while his parents and the maid were still asleep, and again after everyone had eaten their meal at midday As nobody could understand him, not even his sister, though he could understand them, he had to be content to hear his sister's sighs and appeals to the saints as she moved about his room.

Gregor would sometimes catch a friendly comment, "He's enjoyed his dinner today", or if he left most of it, which was becoming more frequent, she would say, sadly, "Everything's just been left again".

Although Gregor wasn't able to hear any news directly, he did listen to what was said in the next rooms. All the talk was about what they should do now, and how the maid had fallen to her knees and begged Gregor's mother to let her go without delay. She left within a quarter of an hour, tearfully thanking Gregor's mother for her dismissal as if she had done her an enormous service. She even swore emphatically not to tell anyone about what had happened.

For the first fourteen days, Gregor's parents could not bring themselves to come into the room to see him. His father and mother would wait outside the door while his sister tidied up, and as soon as she went out she would tell them how everything looked, how Gregor had behaved and whether any improvement could be seen. His mother wanted to go in and visit Gregor relatively soon but his father and sister persuaded her against it.

Out of consideration for his parents, Gregor tried to avoid being seen at the window during the day. But it was hard to just lie quietly, so, to entertain himself, he took to crawling up and down the walls and ceiling. He especially liked hanging from the ceiling- his body had a swing to it up there, he was almost happy. Now, of course, he had far better control of his body.

Soon his sister noticed the traces of the adhesive from his feet as he crawled about - and thought to make it as easy as possible for him by removing the furniture- not something that she could do by herself, but she did not dare ask for help from her father. So she had no choice but to choose some time when Gregor's father was absent, and fetch mother to help.

First, his sister came in and looked round to see that everything in the room was alright, and only then did she let her mother enter. Gregor hurriedly pulled a sheet over himself, and refrained from spying out from under it. The old chest of drawers was too heavy for a pair of feeble women, and Gregor listened as they pushed it. Did he really want his room transformed into a cave? They were taking away everything that was dear to him. So, while the women were catching their breath, he sallied out, not knowing what he should save first, until his attention was caught by the picture on the wall. He hurried up and pressed himself against its glass. This picture at least, now totally covered by Gregor, would certainly be taken away by no-one.

Then there was someone at the door, his father had arrived home. "What's happened?" were his first words. Sister Grete's appearance must have made everything clear, " Gregor got out." "Ah!", he shouted as he came in, both angry and glad at the same time. Gregor ran up to his father, stopped when his father stopped, scurried forwards again when he moved, even slightly. In this way they went round the room several times without anything decisive happening, until something rolled in front of him. It was an apple, then another one. Gregor froze in shock. His father had filled his pockets with fruit from the bowl on the sideboard and now threw one apple after another. One glanced against Gregor's back without doing any harm. Another one however, immediately following it, hit squarely and lodged in his body.

III

No-one dared to remove the apple lodged in Gregor's flesh, so it remained there for more than a month. Because of his injuries, he was now reduced to the condition of an ancient invalid - crawling over the ceiling was out of the question. But this deterioration, he thought, was fully made up for by the door to the living room now being left open in the evenings.

He got into the habit of lying in the darkness of his room to listen to their evening conversation - with everyone's permission, in a way, and so quite differently from before.

Who, in this tired and overworked family, would have had time to give attention to Gregor? The household budget was now considerably shrunken, so the maid was dismissed, to be replaced each morning and evening by an enormous, thick-boned charwoman. Gregor even learned that several items of family jewellery had been sold. But the loudest complaint was that although the flat was much too big for their present circumstances, they could not move out, there being no imaginable way of transferring Gregor to a new address.

He hardly slept at all, either night or day. Gregor's sister no longer thought about how she could please him but would hurriedly push some food or other into his room with her foot before she rushed out to work in the morning. She still cleared up the room in the evening, but now smudges of dirt were left on the walls, and here and there were little balls of dust and fluff. Gregor's mother did once thoroughly clean his room, using buckets of water, but the dampness made Gregor ill. Gregor's sister was exhausted from going out to work, and looking after Gregor was even more work for her.

Just by chance one day, the charwoman opened the door to Gregor's room and found herself face to face with him. He was taken entirely by surprise, and began to rush to and fro while she just stood there in amazement. From then on she never failed to open the door slightly every evening and morning and look briefly in on him. At first she would call to him with words that she probably considered friendly, such as " Hey! old dung-beetle!". If only they had told this charwoman to clean up his room instead of just disturbing him!

By now Gregor had almost entirely stopped eating. If he happened to find himself next to the food he might take some of it into his mouth to play with it, leave it there a few hours and then, more often than not, spit it out again.

They had got into the habit of putting things into this room that they had no place for anywhere else, and there were now many such things- for one of the other rooms had been rented out to three gentlemen with full beards. And then the charwoman, being always in a hurry, would just chuck anything she couldn't use in there. At first he moved the stuff about, because he was forced to, to make some space for himself. But later he came to enjoy it, though the exercise left him immobile, sad and tired to death for hours afterwards.

The new gentlemen would take their evening meal up at the table where, formerly, Gregor had taken his meals with his family, who now ate in the kitchen. And above all the noises of eating Gregor could still hear their chewing teeth, as if they wanted to show Gregor that you need teeth to eat and it was not possible to perform anything with jaws that are toothless however nice they might be. "I'd like to eat something", said Gregor anxiously, "but not anything like they're eating."

Throughout all this time, Gregor could not remember having heard the violin being played, but this evening it began to be heard from the kitchen. Hearing, too, the middle gentleman said, "Would the young lady like to come and play for us here in the room?" "Oh yes, we'd love to", Gregor's father called back. His sister began to play, and, drawn in by the playing, Gregor dared to come forward, pushing his head a little into the living room. No-one noticed him. Yet Gregor's sister was playing so beautifully, so Gregor crawled a little further forward, keeping his head close to the ground so that he could meet her eyes if the chance came.

"Mr. Samsa!", shouted the middle gentleman, pointing with his forefinger. The violin went silent, the middle of the three gentlemen first smiled at his two friends, shook his head, and then looked back at Gregor. His father rushed up to the gentlemen, his arms spread out and attempted to drive them back into their room, while trying to block their view of Gregor with his body. Gregor's father forgot all the respect he owed to his tenants, and the middle gentlemen shouted like thunder and stamped his foot, "I give immediate notice on my room". His two friends joined in. With that, he took hold of the door handle and slammed the door.

Gregor's father staggered back to his seat. "Father, Mother", said his sister, banging the table, "we can't carry on like this. I don't want to call this monster my brother, all I can say is: we have to try and get rid of it. We've done all anyone could to look after it. No one could accuse us of doing anything wrong."

"My child", said her father with sympathy, "what are we to do? If he could just understand us, but as it is..."

"It's got to go", shouted his sister. "We've got to rid ourselves of the idea that that's Gregor. If it were Gregor he would have seen long ago that it's not possible for human beings to live with an animal like that and he would have gone of his own free will. But this animal is persecuting us, it's driven out our tenants, and now it clearly want to drive us out onto the streets."

But Gregor had had no wish to cause fear, least of all to his sister. He concentrated on crawling as fast as he could until he had reached the doorway to his room. He was hardly inside before the door was shut and locked. "What now, then?", Gregor asked himself as he looked round in the darkness. If it was possible, he felt that he must go away even more strongly than his sister. He remained in this state of empty and peaceful rumination until he heard the clock tower strike three in the morning. He watched as it slowly began to get light everywhere outside the window. Then, without his willing it, his head sank down completely, and his last breath flowed weakly from his nostrils.

When the cleaner came in early in the morning she poked at him a little, and only when she found she could shove him across the floor with no resistance at all did she start to pay attention. She soon realised what had happened; "Come and 'ave a look at this, it's dead, just lying there, stone dead!"

Mr. and Mrs. Samsa sat upright there in their marriage bed. Mr. Samsa threw a blanket over his shoulders, Mrs. Samsa just came out in her nightdress; and that is how they went into Gregor's room. On the way they opened the door to the living room where Grete had been sleeping since the three gentlemen had moved in, she was already fully dressed, her face as pale as one who has not slept. "Dead?", asked Mrs. Samsa. "That's what I said", replied the cleaner, and to prove it she gave Gregor's body another shove with the broom, sending it sideways across the floor.

They decided that they were in serious need of relaxation. So they sat at the table and wrote three letters of excusal, Mr. Samsa to his employers, Mrs. Samsa to her contractor and Grete to her principal. The cleaner came in while they were writing to say "That thing in there, you needn't worry about how you're going to get rid of it. That's all been sorted out." Mr. Samsa saw that the cleaner wanted to start describing everything in detail but, with outstretched hand, he made it quite clear that she was not to. So, she called out "Cheerio, everyone", turned round and left, slamming the door fiercely as she went.

After that, the three of them left the flat together, which was something they had not done for months, and took the tram out to the open country outside the town. They had the tram, filled with warm sunshine, all to themselves. All the time, Grete was becoming livelier. With all the worry they had been having of late her cheeks had become pale, but, while they were talking, Mr. and Mrs. Samsa were struck, almost simultaneously, with the thought of how their daughter was blossoming into a well built and beautiful young lady.

Relativity
by Albert Einstein
(1916)

The life of Albert Einstein from Ulm, in Germany has become the stuff of legend. Either he theorised about magnetism at the age of five and played the violin at six, or else he showed little ability and left school without a diploma. Or possibly both. Either way, after studying in Zürich, and working at the Swiss Patent Office he produced his theories of relativity with their astonishing discovery that the progress of time is *not* fixed as Newton (p198), and everyone else, had always assumed.

This is a condensed version of the explanation of Einstein's Relativity by JWN Sullivan, first published in 1920.

Abridged: JH

THE famous Einstein theory was published in two parts. The first part, the so-called 'Special' theory, was published in 1905, when Einstein was only twenty-six years of age. The 'General' theory which, besides greatly extending the special theory, gave also a solution of the problem of gravitation, was published ten years later. It is this theory that attracted the attention of the whole world, as well as the strictly scientific portion of it, by the dramatic verification, at the total solar eclipse of May 29, 1919, of one of the most startling predictions of the theory.

The book under consideration is Einstein's own exposition, for the general public, of both theories. It may be said at once that, judging from this book, Einstein had a rather exalted opinion of the intelligence of the general public. His exposition is superb, but it demands very close attention. He says what he has to say so compactly that the reader is in danger of missing the full significance of his statements.

He begins with a question which is fundamental for his whole theory, and that is the status of the axioms of geometry. His own words are:

> We cannot ask whether it is true that only one straight line goes through two points. We can only say that Euclidean[1] geometry deals with things called 'straight lines' to each of which is ascribed the property of being uniquely determined by two points situated on it. The concept 'true' does not tally with the assertions of pure geometry, because by the word 'true' we are eventually in the habit of designating always the correspondence with a 'real' object; geometry, however, is not concerned with the

relation of the ideas involved in it to objects of experience, but only with the logical connexion of these ideas among themselves.

This estimate of the status of Euclidean geometry is justified by the fact that any number of non-Euclidean geometries exist. For two thousand years Euclid's axioms were regarded as necessities of thought. But early in the nineteenth century it was discovered that certain of Euclid's axioms could be denied and others substituted for them, and yet that perfectly self-consistent systems of geometry could be constructed. It follows that Euclid's axioms are not necessary truths. They are 'conventions.' We may adopt them or not, as we please. Consequently, in applying geometry to the real world, we are at liberty to apply that system of geometry we find most convenient. All systems of geometry are equally logical and no one is more 'true' than another, just as it is no more true that there are three feet in a yard than it is that there are one hundred centimetres in a metre. Which system we employ is a matter of convenience. In his general theory of relativity Einstein finds it convenient to use a non-Euclidean geometry.

After some preliminary remarks dealing with our methods of measuring the positions of bodies Einstein enunciates his 'special' theory of relativity which is to the effect that two observers in uniform translatory motion with respect to one another find the same laws for natural phenomena. By uniform translatory motion is meant motion at a constant speed in a straight line, i.e. without rotation or acceleration of any kind. Now, Newton had said, long ago, that two such observers will find the same laws for mechanics. But will they find the same laws for optics and for electricity? Einstein says that they will, but this statement, when we

---

1   **Euclidian Geometry:** see p 66

come to think about it, is a very puzzling one. Consider, for instance, the fact that light travels at 186,000 miles per second for a given observer. Could it have the same velocity for a second observer moving relatively to the first? It seems obvious that it could not.

An aeroplane does not pass a moving train at the same pace that it passes one at rest. Nevertheless, Einstein asserts that light will have the same velocity for two observers, whatever their relative motion. He says:

> As a result of an analysis of the physical conceptions of time and space, it became evident that in reality there is not the least incompatibility between the principle of relativity and the law of propagation of light, and that by systematically holding fast to both these laws a logically rigid theory could be arrived at.

He then proceeds to show that the notion of simultaneity is a relative one. Events which are simultaneous for one observer are not simultaneous for an observer moving relatively to the first. Two such observers will not agree in their estimates of the time-lapse between two events. Neither will their distance measurements agree. What are the relations between the space and time measurements of such observers, supposing them to get the same velocity for light? This is a purely mathematical problem, and Einstein gives the solution, which we need not quote. But we must realize clearly what he has done here, for this is the basis of the whole theory.

He has shown that observers in uniform relative motion will obtain the same laws of nature for phenomena provided they use different space and time measurements, and he has shown just what these differences would be. Now it is a fact of experiment that such observers do obtain the same laws of nature. Not only the famous Michelson-Morley experiment on light, described by Einstein, but many other experiments bear out this statement. It follows that observers in relative motion naturally adopt space and time measurements which differ in the way described by Einstein. In other words, each observer has his own space-time framework. There is no absolute space and time, the same for all observers.

If an observer B, carrying a clock and also carrying a yard measure pointing in the direction of his motion moves past an observer A then, from A's point of view, B's yard measure is short of a yard and his clock is going slow. And the discrepancy is greater the greater B's velocity relative to A. If B passed A with the velocity of light then we reach the highly astonishing result that from A's point of view B's yard measure would be of zero length and his clock would not be going at all! This means that the velocity of light is a limiting velocity. No object in the universe can possibly move at a speed greater than the speed of light.

Einstein proceeds to work out some of the consequences of this theory: The most important result of a general character to which the special theory of relativity has led is concerned with the conception of mass. Before the advent of relativity, physics recognized two conservation laws of fundamental importance, namely, the law of the conservation of energy and the law of the conservation of mass; these two fundamental laws appeared to be quite independent of each other. By means of the theory of relativity they have been united into one law.

Mass and energy have become, in fact, interchangeable terms. A body radiating energy thereby loses mass; a body receiving energy thereby gains mass. As a body moves faster its energy, and therefore its mass, increases. At the velocity of light its mass would be infinite. We may mention that these deductions from Einstein's theory have been verified by experiment.

Thus the swiftest electrons we can produce artificially have speeds within a few per cent. of that of light, and their mass is found to increase to just the extent calculated by Einstein. The reader should remember, in reading this book, that he is not dealing with speculations 'in the air.' Countless experiments have confirmed Einstein's conclusions.

Einstein concludes this part of his exposition with an account of Minkowski's 'four-dimensional space.' The central idea of this must be understood before the general theory can be tackled. It is thus described by Einstein:

> Space is a three-dimensional continuum. By this we mean that it is possible to describe the position of a point (at rest) by means of three numbers (co-ordinates) x, y, z, and that there is an indefinite number of points in the neighbourhood of this one, the position of which can be described by coordinates such as Xi, yi, Zi, which may be as near as we choose to the respective values of the co-ordinates x, y, z, of the first point. In virtue of the latter property we speak of a 'continuum,' and owing to the fact that there are three co-ordinates we speak of it as being 'three-dimensional.' Similarly, the world of the physical phenomena which was briefly called 'world' by Minkowski is naturally four-dimensional in the space-time sense. For it is composed of individual events, each of which is described by four numbers, namely, three space coordinates x, y, z, and a time co-ordinate, the time-value t. The 'world' is in this sense also a continuum; for to every event there are as many 'neighbouring' events (realized or at least thinkable) as we care to choose, the co-ordinates Xi yi Zi ti of which differ by an indefinitely small amount from those of the event x y z t originally considered.

That we have not been accustomed to regard the world in this sense as a four-dimensional continuum is due to the fact that in physics, before the advent of the theory of relativity, time played a different and more independent role, as compared with the space co-ordinates. It is for this reason that we have been in the habit of treating time as an independent continuum.

As a matter of fact, according to classical mechanics, time is absolute, i.e. it is independent of the position and the condition of motion of the system of co-ordinates

The four-dimensional mode of consideration of the 'world' is natural on the theory of relativity, since according to this theory time is robbed of its independence.

We say that space has three dimensions because we require three measurements to specify the position of a point in space. For instance, to specify the position in a room of the tip of an electric light bulb we would have to give its distances from two walls and its distance from the floor or the ceiling. Whatever method we adopted we should have to give at least three measurements. That is why we call space three-dimensional. And space is continuous because we can have points in space as close together as we like. The three distances of a point from our frame of reference (such a frame, for instance, as the two walls and the ceiling) are called the 'co-ordinates' of the point.

But if we are specifying an event we want to say when as well as where it happened. We must give, therefore, the moment of time of its occurrence. This is called its time co-ordinate. In calculations the space co-ordinates are usually denoted by x, y, z, and the time co-ordinate by t.

Now Minkowski showed that the space and time co-ordinates of an event are not independent of one another. Two flashes of light may be separated by ten yards for one observer and occur at an interval of ten seconds. But for a second observer, moving relatively to the first, they may be more than ten yards apart and occur at an interval of more than ten seconds. A certain combination of distance and time will be the same for both observers, but the distances and times taken separately will not be the same. That particular combination of distance and time that all observers will find to be the same is called the 'interval'. Minkowski showed that the interval could be regarded as a 'distance in a four-dimensional space.' This four-dimensional space we split up into a three-dimensional space and a one-dimensional time-and each observer splits it up differently. The actual four-dimensional quantity involved- the 'interval'- is the same for all of them. but they split it up differently into so much of space and so much of time. This result is very interesting, but there is one particular aspect of it which is of the greatest importance for the relativity theory. This aspect is described by Einstein as follows:

> But the discovery of Minkowski, which was of importance for the formal development of the theory of relativity, does not lie here. It is to be found rather in the fact of his recognition that the four-dimensional space-time continuum of the theory of relativity, in its most essential formal properties, shows a pronounced relationship to the three-dimensional continuum of Euclidean geometrical space.

That is to say the geometry of this four-dimensional space of Minkowski's is a Euclidean geometry. The whole 'special' theory of relativity can be explained as the geometry of a four-dimensional 'Euclidean' space. This fact gave Einstein a very important clue for developing his theory. For Einstein was dissatisfied with his special theory. We have pointed out that that theory says that the laws of nature are the same for observers in uniform translatory motion with respect to one another, and only for such observers. Einstein comments:

> But no person whose mode of thought is logical can rest satisfied with this condition of things. He asks: 'How does it come that certain reference-bodies (or their states of motion) are given priority over other reference-bodies (or their states of motion)? What is the reason for this preference?

Einstein wants to know why the laws of nature should not be the same for all observers, whatever their state of motion. We have found that uniform motion makes no difference. What difference does non-uniform motion make? His solution of this question is Einstein's most dazzling achievement. We begin with his famous account of the man in the box.

> As reference-body let us imagine a spacious chest resembling a room with an observer inside who is equipped with apparatus. Gravitation naturally does not exist for this observer. (Einstein imagines the man in the chest to be right away in empty space.) He must fasten himself with strings to the floor, otherwise the slightest impact against the floor will cause him to rise slowly towards the ceiling of the room. To the middle of the lid of the chest is fixed externally a hook with rope attached, and now a 'being' (what kind of a being is immaterial to us) begins pulling at this with a constant force. The chest, together with the observer, begin to move 'upwards' with a uniformly accelerated motion. In course of time their velocity will reach unheard-of values - provided that we are viewing all this from another reference-body which is not being pulled with a rope. But how does the man in the chest regard the process. The acceleration of the chest will be transmitted to him by the reaction of the floor of the chest. He must therefore take up this pressure by means of his legs if he does not wish to be laid out full length on the floor. He is then standing in the chest in exactly the same way as anyone stands in a room of a house on our earth. If he release a body which he previously had in his hand, the acceleration of the chest will no longer be transmitted to this body, and for this reason the body will approach the floor of the chest with an accelerated relative motion. The observer will further convince himself that the acceleration of the body towards the floor of the chest is always of the same magnitude, whatever kind of body he may happen to use for the experiment.

The point Einstein is leading up to is clear from the above passage in italics. For it is characteristic of the gravitational force, and of the gravitational force alone, that it is entirely independent of the physical or chemical constitution of the bodies on which it operates. The man in the chest will naturally conclude that he and his chest are in a gravitational field.

Einstein goes on:

> Of course he will be puzzled for a moment as to why the chest does not fall in this gravitational field. Just then, however, he discovers the hook in the middle of the lid of the chest and the rope which is attached to it, and he consequently comes to the conclusion that the chest is suspended at rest in the gravitational field.

From this illustration we can grasp Einstein's conception of the essential difference between uniform and non-uniform motion. An observer in non-uniform motion may be regarded as existing in a gravitational field. The laws of phenomena for observers in non-uniform motion, therefore, are the laws of phenomena in gravitational fields. But we must be careful in reading this example not to suppose that Einstein means to say that a gravitational field is always merely apparent. There is a gravitational field for the man in the chest although there is no gravitational field from the point of view of an observer outside the chest. But there is no possible observer for whom the gravitational field of the earth does not exist.

Let us imagine the man looking through a window in his moving chest and observing the passage of a ray of light outside. Since the man's motion is an accelerated motion the ray of light would appear to him curved. But since, according to Einstein, there is no essential difference between accelerated motion and a gravitational field, it follows that light passing through a gravitational field should follow a curved path. Einstein prophesied, therefore, that this would be so and, as all the world knows, the prophecy was verified at the eclipse expedition of May 29, 1919

This case exemplified a procedure which is pretty general in the theory. We imagine an artificial gravitational field and find what would happen to phenomena in that field. We then use this result to say what would happen to phenomena in a real gravitational field. Also, by finding the laws obeyed by these artificial fields themselves we can deduce the laws obeyed by real gravitational fields. This is what Einstein has done, and it is perhaps the most celebrated part of his achievement. He has found the true laws for gravitation and shown that Newton's law is only approximate.

But, to do this, he had greatly to extend Minkowski's idea, mentioned above. He found that if Minkowski's four-dimensional space was permeated by a gravitational field, then its geometry was not Euclidean. He had to apply non-Euclidean geometry. Einstein, in his desire to omit no steps from the argument, gives the reader an outline of the method by which he did this. The reader will probably find this the most obscure part of his book.

There would be no point in quoting it and still less in summarising it. It is best for the reader who is not a mathematician to take this part of the argument for granted. Suffice it to say that the laws of motion in a non-Euclidean space can be worked out, and that they are found to give just the motions we observe in the case of the planets. Thus the actual motion of Mercury had never been satisfactorily explained on Newton's theory. The difference between observation and calculation was slight, but it was there, and the greatest mathematicians had exerted themselves in vain to explain it. Einstein's theory, in a perfectly natural and unforced way, clears up the whole mystery. Einstein's own words are:

> Since the time of Leverrier, it has been known that the ellipse corresponding to the orbit of Mercury ... is not stationary with respect to the fixed stars, but that it rotates exceedingly slowly in the plane of the orbit and in the sense of the orbital motion. The value obtained for this rotary movement of the orbital ellipses was 43 seconds of arc per century, an amount ensured to be correct to within a few seconds of arc. This effect can be explained by means of classical mechanics only on the assumption of hypotheses which have little probability, and which were devised solely for this purpose. On the basis of the general theory of relativity, it is found that the ellipse of every planet round the sun must necessarily rotate in the manner indicated above; that for all the planets, with the exception of Mercury, this rotation is too small to be detected with the delicacy of observation possible at the present time; but that in the case of Mercury it must amount to 43 seconds of arc per century, a result which is strictly in agreement with observation.

This result, the deflection of light mentioned above, and the shift of the lines of the sun's spectrum towards the red, are the three great experimental confirmations of Einstein's general theory.

It may help the reader to grasp the central idea of Einstein's general theory if it be put in the following way. The natural motion of a body, left to itself, is, in Euclidean space, motion in a straight line and with a constant velocity. Now the planets do not move in straight lines with uniform velocity. Why? Newton said because there is a force of gravitation emanating from the sun and pulling them out of the straight line. Einstein says, No, there is no force of gravitation at all. The planets do not move in straight lines because they are not moving in a Euclidean space at all, but in a non-Euclidean space, where their actual motions are their natural motions. And his general conditions for this non Euclidean space are what he calls the law of gravitation. His law of gravitation, therefore, is not the law of a force; it is a set of geometrical conditions. As a matter of fact, Einstein does not need the notion of 'force' at all.

In the last part of his book Einstein deals with his notion of a finite universe. We are accustomed to think of the universe as consisting of matter (in the form of stars) distributed pretty uniformly throughout infinite space. It can be shown that, on Newton's law of gravitation, such a universe is impossible. The gravitational force would be infinite. And there are grave objections to such a universe also on relativity theory. Einstein therefore supposes that our universe is finite. But, although finite, it is unbounded. He illustrates the idea by asking us to consider perfectly flat creatures living on the surface of a sphere. Such creatures could wander forward on this sphere for ever without meeting any boundary. Nevertheless their space, that is the area of their sphere, is of finite size. Analogously, the mathematics of a sort of three-dimensional spherical surface can be worked out. It will be of finite size but it will have no boundaries.

Einstein supposes that the space we live in is of this kind. We can get a rough idea of the size of this universe. A ray of light would go all round this spherical universe in about one thousand million years. Light sent out a thousand million years ago would come back to the place it started from and, if it had not become too scattered by passing through gravitational fields en route, would unite again in a focus at that point. It may be, therefore, that some of the stars we see are really ghosts-the images of stars that were there a thousand million years ago, but which have since moved on to other parts of the universe, or which have even become extinct or perished in a collision.

But this part of Einstein's theory, although it solves certain difficulties, must not be taken as on the same level of evidence as the rest of his theory. The rest of the theory may fairly be regarded as proved. The theory of the finite universe is still only a speculation. Even as it stands, however, the theory has been justly described by a great mathematician as 'the greatest synthetic achievement of the human mind.'

Dulce et Decorum Est
by Wilfred Owen
(1918)

Wilfred Owen was a soldier in the Great War of 1914-18. Like thousands of his fellow-soldiers he wrote poems, and like millions more he was killed, in his case at the Battle of the Sambre, just a week before the war ended. The last lines (and the title) are from the Roman poet Horace meaning "Sweet and proper it is, to die for your county".

Unabridged

Bent double, like old beggars under sacks,
Knock-kneed, coughing like hags, we cursed through sludge,
Till on the haunting flares we turned our backs
And towards our distant rest began to trudge.
Men marched asleep. Many had lost their boots
But limped on, blood-shod. All went lame; all blind;
Drunk with fatigue; deaf even to the hoots
Of tired, outstripped Five-Nines that dropped behind.

Gas! Gas! Quick, boys!-- An ecstasy of fumbling,
Fitting the clumsy helmets just in time;
But someone still was yelling out and stumbling
And flound'ring like a man in fire or lime...
Dim, through the misty panes and thick green light,
As under a green sea, I saw him drowning.

In all my dreams, before my helpless sight,
He plunges at me, guttering, choking, drowning.

If in some smothering dreams you too could pace
Behind the wagon that we flung him in,
And watch the white eyes writhing in his face,
His hanging face, like a devil's sick of sin;
If you could hear, at every jolt, the blood
Come gargling from the froth-corrupted lungs,
Obscene as cancer, bitter as the cud
Of vile, incurable sores on innocent tongues,--
My friend, you would not tell with such high zest
To children ardent for some desperate glory,
The old Lie: *Dulce et decorum est*
Pro patria mori.

Ulysses

by James Joyce
(New York, 1918)

James Joyce's attempt at writing Ireland's National Epic has repeatedly been chosen, by literary experts, as simply the best book of all time. Which is strange, as ordinary people tend to denounce it as pretentious and unreadable twaddle. Why the difference? Apart from its odd, fragmented, form, *Ulysses* makes *very* little sense unless the reader is already familiar with its many references to earlier books, including the general outline of the ancient (p 35) tale on which it is *vaguely* based. Anyone who has read *The Hundred Books* this far, shouldn't have *too* much trouble.

Abridged: GH

1: Telemachus

STATELY, plump Buck Mulligan came from the stairhead, bearing a bowl of lather on which a mirror and a razor lay crossed. A yellow dressinggown, ungirdled, was sustained gently behind him by the mild morning air. He held the bowl aloft and intoned: *Introibo ad altare Dei.[1]* Come up, Kinch! Come up, you fearful jesuit!

Stephen Dedalus stepped up, and sat down on the edge of the gunrest.

- Tell me, Mulligan, Stephen said quietly. How long is Haines going to stay in this tower?

- God, these bloody English! Bursting with money and indigestion. Lend us your noserag to wipe my razor.

Stephen suffered him to pull out a dirty crumpled handkerchief.

- The bard's noserag! A new art colour for our Irish poets: snotgreen. You can almost taste it, can't you?

He mounted to the parapet again and gazed out over Dublin bay, his fair oakpale hair stirring slightly.

- God! The snotgreen sea. The scrotumtightening sea. *Epi oinopa ponton.* Ah, Dedalus, the Greeks! You must read them in the original.

He turned abruptly his grey eyes to Stephen's face.

- To think of your mother begging you with her last breath to kneel down and pray for her. And you refused. How are the secondhand breeks?

- Thanks, Stephen said. I can't wear them if they are grey.

- He can't wear them, Buck Mulligan told his face in the mirror. He kills his mother but he can't wear grey trousers. Look at yourself!

Stephen peered at the mirror held out to him.

- It is a symbol of Irish art. The cracked looking-glass of a servant.

- A voice within the tower called loudly: Dedalus, come down. Breakfast is ready.

In the gloomy domed livingroom of the tower Buck Mulligan's gowned form moved briskly to and fro.

- The grub is ready. Bless us, O Lord, and these thy gifts. Where's the sugar? O, jay, there's no milk.

- We can drink it black, Stephen said thirstily. There's a lemon in the locker.

- O, damn you and your Paris fads! Buck Mulligan said. I want Sandycove milk.

Haines came in from the doorway and said quietly:

- That woman is coming up with the milk.

- Come in, ma'am, Mulligan said. Kinch, get the jug.

An old woman came forward and stood by Stephen's elbow. He watched her pour into the measure and thence into the jug rich white milk, not hers. Old shrunken paps.

- Are you a medical student, sir? the old woman asked.

- I am, ma'am, Buck Mulligan answered.

Haines spoke to her, confidently.

- Is it French you are talking, sir? the old woman said.

- Irish, Buck Mulligan said.

- I thought it was Irish, she said, by the sound of it. Are you from the west, sir?

- I am an Englishman, Haines answered.

- He's English, Buck Mulligan said, and he thinks we ought to speak Irish in Ireland.

She curtseyed and went out.

- That reminds me, Haines said, rising, that I have to visit your national library today.

- Our swim first, Buck Mulligan said. Are you coming, you fellows?

Stephen, taking his ashplant from its leaningplace, followed them out and down the ladder. At the foot of the ladder Haines asked:

- Do you pay rent for this tower?

- Twelve quid, Buck Mulligan said.

- Bleak in wintertime, I should say. Martello you call it?

- Billy Pitt had them built, when the French were on the sea. But ours is the *omphalos[2]*.

- What is your idea of Hamlet?[3] Haines asked Stephen. This tower and these cliffs remind me of Elsinore.

- I read a theological interpretation of it somewhere. The Father and the Son idea.

- You're not a believer, are you? Haines asked. You are your own master, it seems to me.

- I am a servant of two masters, Stephen said, an English and an Italian.

- Italian? Haines said.

---

1   **Introibo...:** First words of the Christian Mass ceremony

2   **Omphalos:** Navel of the world
3   **Hamlet:** See p155

- The imperial British state, Stephen answered, and the holy Roman catholic and apostolic church.

- I can quite understand that, Haines said calmly. We feel in England that we have treated you rather unfairly. It seems history is to blame.

They followed the winding path down to the creek. Buck Mulligan stood on a stone, in shirtsleeves, his unclipped tie rippling over his shoulder.

- My twelfth rib is gone, he cried. I'm the Ubermensch.[4]

- Are you going in here, Malachi?

- We'll see you again, Haines said, turning as Stephen walked up the path and smiling at wild Irish.

Horn of a bull, hoof of a horse, smile of a Saxon.

2: Nestor

- YOU, ARMSTRONG, Stephen said. What was the end of Pyrrhus?

A bag of figrolls lay snugly in Armstrong's satchel.

- Pyrrhus, sir? Pyrrhus, a pier.

All laughed. Mirthless high malicious laughter.

- Tell me now, Stephen said, poking the boy's shoulder with the book, what is a pier.

- A pier, sir, Armstrong said. A thing out in the water. A kind of a bridge. Kingstown pier, sir.

- Kingstown pier, Stephen said. Yes, a disappointed bridge.

A stick struck the door and a voice in the corridor called:

- Hockey!

Quickly they were gone. Sargent who alone had lingered came forward slowly, showing an open copybook. The word SUMS was written on the headline. Beneath were sloping figures and at the foot a crooked signature and a blot. Cyril Sargent: his name and seal.

- Mr Deasy told me to write them out all again, he said, and show them to you, sir.

Stephen touched the edges of the book. Ugly and futile. Yet someone had loved him, borne him in her arms and in her heart. But for her the race of the world would have trampled him underfoot, a squashed boneless snail. Sitting at his side Stephen solved out the problem. He proves by algebra that Shakespeare's ghost is Hamlet's grandfather.

- Can you work the second for yourself?

- Call into my study for a moment, Mr Deasy said.

Blowing out his rare moustache Mr Deasy halted at the table.

- First, our little financial settlement, he said.

A sovereign fell, bright and new, on the soft pile of the tablecloth.

- Thank you, sir, Stephen said, gathering the money.

- No thanks at all, Mr Deasy said. You have earned it.

The same room and hour, the same wisdom.

- He knew what money was, Mr Deasy said. He made money. Do you know what is the pride of the English? I

will tell you, he said solemnly. I paid my way. I never borrowed a shilling in my life. Can you feel that?

Mulligan, nine pounds, three pairs of socks, one pair brogues. McCann, one guinea. Temple, two lunches, Cousins, ten shillings, Koehler, three guineas, Mrs MacKernan, five weeks' board.

- For the moment, no, Stephen answered.

- That reminds me, Mr Deasy said. You can do me a favour, Mr Dedalus, with some of your literary friends. I have a letter here for the press. It's about the foot and mouth disease. Just look through it. There can be no two opinions on the matter.

May I trespass on your valuable space. That doctrine of Laissez Faire which so often in our history. Pardoned a classical allusion. Known as Koch's preparation. In every sense of the word take the bull by the horns.

- I want that to be printed and read, Mr Deasy said.

He raised his forefinger and beat the air oldly before his voice spoke.

- Mark my words, Mr Dedalus, he said. History shows that England is in the hands of the jews.

- History, Stephen said, is a nightmare from which I am trying to awake.

- The ways of the Creator are not our ways, Mr Deasy said.

Stephen jerked his thumb towards the window, saying:

- That is God.

Hooray! Ay! Whrrwhee!

- What? Mr Deasy asked.

- A shout in the street, Stephen answered.

3: Proteus

INELUCTABLE modality of the visible: at least that if no more, thought through my eyes. Signatures of all things I am here to read, seaspawn and seawrack, the nearing tide, that rusty boot. Snotgreen, bluesilver, rust: coloured signs. Shut your eyes and see. Stephen closed his eyes to hear his boots crush crackling wrack and shells.

Am I walking into eternity along Sandymount strand? Crush, crack, crick, crick. I have passed the way to aunt Sara's. Am I not going there? Seems not. He turned northeast and crossed the firmer sand towards the Pigeonhouse. A woman and a man. The bloated carcass of a dog. Under the upswelling tide he saw the writhing weeds lift languidly and sway reluctant arms, hising up their petticoats. He laid the dry snot picked from his nostril on a ledge of rock, carefully. For the rest let look who will.

4: Calypso

MR LEOPOLD BLOOM ate with relish the inner organs of beasts and fowls. Most of all he liked grilled mutton kidneys which gave to his palate a fine tang of faintly scented urine. The coals were reddening. Another slice of bread and butter: three, four: right.

- Mkgnao!

- Milk for the pussens, he said.

On quietly creaky boots he went up the staircase to the hall, paused by the bedroom door.

---

4   **Ubermensch:** the 'overman', see Nietzsche, p396

- You don't want anything for breakfast?

A sleepy soft grunt answered. No. She didn't want anything. Pity. All the way from Gibraltar.

His hand took his hat from the peg over his initialled heavy overcoat and his lost property office secondhand waterproof. On the doorstep he felt in his hip pocket for the latchkey.

Not there. In the trousers I left off. Must get it. Potato I have. No use disturbing her. He crossed to the bright side, avoiding the loose cellarflap of number seventyfive. Be a warm day I fancy. He halted before Dlugacz's window, staring at the hanks of sausages, polonies, black and white. A final kidney oozed bloodgouts on the willowpatterned dish: the last. Girl in front. Quick.

- Threepence, please.

His hand accepted the moist tender gland and slid it into a sidepocket.

- Thank you, sir. Another time.

He walked back along Dorset street, with newspaper, reading gravely. Agendath Netaim: planters' company. To purchase waste sandy tracts from Turkish government. You pay eighty marks and they plant a dunam of land for you with olives, oranges, almonds or citrons. Can pay in yearly instalments. Bleibtreustrasse 34, Berlin. Quiet long days: pruning, ripening. Oranges in tissue paper packed in crates. No, not like that. A barren land, bare waste. Sodom[5], Gomorrah, Edom. All dead names. The oldest people. Folding the page into his pocket he turned into Eccles street, hurrying homeward.

Two letters and a card lay on the hallfloor. He stooped and gathered them. Mrs Marion Bloom. His quickened heart slowed at once. Bold hand. Entering the bedroom he halfclosed his eyes and walked through warm yellow twilight towards her tousled head.

- Who are the letters for?

- A letter for me from our Milly, he said carefully, and a card to you. And a letter for you.

As he went down the kitchen stairs she called:

- Poldy!

- What?

- Scald the teapot.

He scalded and rinsed out the teapot and crushed the pan flat on the live coals and watched the lump of butter slide and melt. While he unwrapped the kidney the cat mewed hungrily against him. He prodded a fork into the kidney and slapped it over: then fitted the teapot on the tray. Everything on it? Bread and butter, four, sugar, spoon, her cream. Yes. He carried it upstairs, his thumb hooked in the teapot handle.

- Who was the letter from? he asked.

- O, Boylan, she said. He's bringing the programme.

- What are you singing?

- *La Ci Darem* with J. C. Doyle, she said, and *Love's Old Sweet Song.*

---

5   **Sodom:** see Genesis 19 p23

She doubled a slice of bread into her mouth, asking:

- What time is the funeral? There's a smell of burn, she said. Did you leave anything on the fire?

- The kidney! he cried suddenly.

5: The Lotus Eaters

BY LORRIES along sir John Rogerson's quay Mr Bloom walked soberly with newspaper to glance through the door of the postoffice. No-one. In.

- Are there any letters for me? he asked.

The postmistress handed him back through the grill a letter. He glanced at the typed envelope.

Henry Flower Esq, c/o P. O. Westland Row, City.

He strolled out and turned to the right. He unrolled his newspaper baton idly and read idly:

> *What is home without*
> *Plumtree's potted meat?*
> *Incomplete*
> *With it an abode of bliss.*

He drew the letter from his pocket and folded it into the newspaper. Might just walk into her here. The lane is safer. He passed the cabman's shelter and opened the letter within the newspaper. A flower. I think it's a. A yellow. Not annoyed then? What does she say?

> Dear Henry
>
> I am sorry you did not like my last letter. I am awfully angry with you. Are you not happy in your home you poor little naughty boy? Dear Henry, when will we meet? Remember if you do not reply I will punish you. Henry dear, do not deny my request before my patience are exhausted. Goodbye now, write by return to your longing
>
> Martha
>
> P. S. Do tell me what kind of perfume does your wife use. I want to know.

Going under the railway arch he took the envelope, tore it swiftly in shreds and scattered them towards the road. He had reached the open backdoor of All Hallows. Same notice on the door. Sermon by the very reverend John Conmee S.J. on the African Mission. Save China's millions. Buddha their God taking it easy with hand under his cheek. Josssticks burning. He walked southward along Westland row. Sweny's in Lincoln place. Chemists rarely move.

- Sweet almond oil and tincture of benzoin, Mr Bloom said, and then orangeflower water...

- Yes, sir, the chemist said. Have you brought a bottle?

- No, Mr Bloom said. Make it up, please. I'll call later in the day and I'll take one of these soaps.

- Fourpence, sir.

Mr Bloom raised a cake to his nostrils. Sweet lemony wax. He strolled out of the shop, newspaper baton under his arm, the coolwrapped soap in his left hand. At his armpit Bantam Lyons' voice and hand said:

- Hello, Bloom. What's the best news? Is that today's?

Bantam Lyons's blacknailed fingers unrolled the baton.

- I want to see that French horse that's running today.

- Keep it, Mr Bloom said. I was going to throw it away.

- *Throwaway*. I'll risk it, he said. Here, thanks.

He sped off towards Conway's corner. Silly lips of that chap. Betting. Regular hotbed of it lately. He walked cheerfully towards the mosque of the baths. Enjoy a bath now: clean trough of water, cool enamel, the gentle tepid stream. This is my body. He foresaw his pale body reclined in it at full, naked, in a womb of warmth, oiled by scented melting soap, softly laved. He saw the dark tangled curls of his bush floating, floating hair of the stream around the limp father of thousands, a languid floating flower.

6: Hades

THE BLACK carriage creaked and swayed past Watery lane. Mr Bloom smiled joylessly on Ringsend road. Wallace Bros: the bottleworks: Dodder bridge. Nelson's pillar.

- Better look a little serious, Martin Cunningham said.

- The Lord forgive me! Mr Power said, wiping his wet eyes. Poor Paddy! He's gone from us.

Too much John Barleycorn. Cure for a red nose. A lot of money he spent colouring it.

- As decent a little man as ever wore a hat, Mr Dedalus said. He went very suddenly.

- The best Death, Mr Bloom said.

No-one spoke. A tiny coffin flashed by. A mourning coach. A baby. Mistake of nature. Rattle his bones. Over the stones. Only a pauper. Nobody owns.

- But the worst of all, Mr Power said, is the man who takes his own life.

- It is not for us to judge, Martin Cunningham said.

Mr Bloom, about to speak, closed his lips again. Martin Cunningham's large eyes. Looking away now. Sympathetic human man he is. Intelligent. He looked away from me. He knows. Rattle his bones. That afternoon of the inquest. Verdict: overdose. Death by misadventure. The letter. For my son Leopold. No more pain.

The carriage rattled swiftly along Blessington street. Over the stones. Crossguns bridge: the royal canal.

The felly harshed against the curbstone: stopped. Martin Cunningham stepped out. Mr Power and Mr Dedalus followed. Mr Bloom's hand unbuttoned his hip pocket swiftly and transferred the paperstuck soap to his inner handkerchief pocket.

Coffin now. Got here before us, dead as he is. Do they know what they cart out here every day? Funerals all over the world everywhere every minute. Thousands every hour.

The mutes shouldered the coffin and bore it in through the gates and into the mortuary chapel. Which end is his head? They halted by the bier and the priest began to read out of his book with a fluent croak. Father Coffey. With a belly on him like a poisoned pup. Makes them feel more important to be prayed over in Latin. What swells him up that way? Molly gets swelled after cabbage.

- *Non intres in judicium cum servo tuo, domine.*

The priest took a stick with a knob at the end of it out of the boy's bucket and shook it over the coffin.

Holy water that was, I expect. Every mortal day a fresh batch: middleaged men, old women, children, women dead in childbirth, men with beards, bald businessmen, consumptive girls with little sparrows' breasts.

- *In paradisum.*

The priest closed his book and went off, followed by the server. Corny Kelleher opened the sidedoors and the gravediggers came in, hoisted the coffin again, carried it out and shoved it on their cart.

Broken heart. A pump after all, pumping thousands of gallons of blood every day. One fine day it gets bunged up: and there you are. Lots of them lying around here: lungs, hearts, livers. Old rusty pumps. The resurrection and the life. Once you are dead you are dead. That last day idea. Come forth, Lazarus! And he came fifth and lost the job. Get up! Last day! Then every fellow mousing around for his liver and his lights and the rest of his traps.

Corny Kelleher fell into step at their side.

- What is he? he asked. Wasn't he in the stationery line?

Ned Lambert smiled.

- Yes, Wisdom Hely's. A traveller for blottingpaper.

Poor Dignam! Lay me in my native earth. Bit of clay from the holy land. The Irishman's house is his coffin.

An obese grey rat toddled along the side of the crypt, moving the pebbles. A corpse is meat gone bad. Well and what's cheese? Corpse of milk. Cremation better. Ashes to ashes. Where is that Parsee tower of silence? Eaten by birds. Enough of this place. Brings you a bit nearer every time. Poor papa. They are not going to get me this innings. Warm beds: warm fullblooded life.

7: Aeolus
A NEWSPAPER OF THE METROPOLIS

- THERE IT IS, Red Murray said. Alexander Keyes.

- Just cut it out, will you? Mr Bloom said, and I'll take it round to the *Telegraph* office.

WE SEE THE CANVASSER AT WORK

Nature notes. Cartoons. Phil Blake's weekly Pat and Bull story. Uncle Toby's page for tiny tots. Country bumpkin's queries. Dear Mr Editor, what is a good cure for flatulence? Mr Bloom laid his cutting on Mr Nannetti's desk.

- Excuse me, councillor, he said. This ad, you see. Keyes, you remember? He wants it in for July.

The foreman moved his pencil towards it.

- But he wants it changed. Keyes, you see. He wants two keys at the top. Like that, Mr Bloom said, crossing his forefingers at the top.

The doorknob hit Mr Bloom in the small of the back as the door was pushed in.

- Excuse me, J. J. O'Molloy said, entering. Is the editor to be seen?

- Very much so, MacHugh said. Seen and heard.

EXIT BLOOM

- I'm just running round to the library, Mr Bloom said, about this ad of Keyes's. Want to fix it up.

The editor, leaning against the mantelshelf, stretched forth an arm amply.

- Begone! he said. The world is before you.

THE GRANDEUR THAT WAS ROME

- We think of Rome, imperial, imperious, imperative, Professor MacHugh said. What was their civilisation? Vast, I allow: but vile. The Jews in the wilderness and on the mountaintop said: *It is meet to be here. let us build an altar to Jehovah.* The Roman, like the Englishman who follows in his footsteps, gazed about him in his toga and he said: *It is meet to be here. Let us construct a watercloset.*

- Which they accordingly did do, Lenehan said.

Mr O'Madden Burke, tall in copious grey of Donegal tweed, came in from the hallway. Stephen Dedalus, behind him, uncovered as he entered.

- I escort a suppliant, Mr O'Madden Burke said melodiously. Youth led by Experience visits Notoriety.

- Good day, Stephen, the professor said, coming to peer over their shoulders. Foot and mouth? Are you turned...?

Bullockbefriending bard.

8: The Lestrygonians

A PROCESSION of whitesmocked sandwichmen marched slowly along the gutter, scarlet sashes across their boards. He read the scarlet letters on their five tall white hats: H. E. L. Y. S. Wisdom Hely's. Y lagging behind drew a chunk of bread from under his foreboard, crammed it into his mouth and munched as he walked.

- O, Mr Bloom, how do you do?

- O, how do you do, Mrs Breen?

- How is Molly those times? Haven't seen her for ages.

- Milly has a position down in Mullingar, you know. Yes. In a photographer's there.

- And your lord and master? Said Bloom.

She took a folded postcard from her handbag.

- Read that, she said. He got it this morning.

- What is it? Mr Bloom asked, taking the card. U.P.?

- U.P.: up, she said. Someone taking a rise out of him. And now he's going round to Mr Menton's office. He's going to take an action for ten thousand pounds, he says. She folded the card into her untidy bag and snapped the catch.

Change the subject.

- Do you see anything of Mrs Beaufoy? Bloom asked.

- She's in the lying-in hospital in Holles street. Dr Horne got her in. She's three days bad now.

- O, Mr Bloom said. I'm sorry to hear that. Poor thing! Three days! That's terrible for her.

A bony form strode along the curbstone. Tight as a skullpiece a tiny hat gripped his head.

- Watch him, Mr Bloom said. He always walks outside the lampposts. Watch!

- Is he dotty? Mrs Breen asked.

His name is Cashel Boyle O'Connor Fitzmaurice Tisdall Farrell, Mr Bloom said smiling. Watch!

- Denis will be like that one of these days, she said. Goodbye. Remember me to Molly, won't you?

A squad of constables debouched from College street, marching in Indian file. Foodheated faces, sweating helmets. Policeman's lot is oft a happy one.

Duke street. Here we are. Must eat. Feel better then.

His heart astir he pushed in the door of the Burton restaurant. Stink gripped his trembling breath: pungent meatjuice, slush of greens. See the animals feed. Men, men, men. Perched on high stools by the bar, hats shoved back, at the tables calling for more bread no charge, swilling, wolfing gobfuls of sloppy food, their eyes bulging, wiping wetted moustaches. A man spitting halfmasticated gristle. Get out of this. Out. I hate dirty eaters. Get a light snack in Davy Byrne's. Stopgap. Keep me going. He came out into clearer air and turned back towards Grafton street.

He entered Davy Byrne's. Moral pub.

- Hello, Bloom, Nosey Flynn said from his nook. How's things?

- Tiptop... Let me see. I'll take a glass of burgundy and... let me see.

Sardines on the shelves. Almost taste them by looking. Sandwich? Ham and his descendants musterred and bred there. Potted meats. What is home without Plumtree's potted meat? Incomplete. What a stupid ad! Dignam's potted meat. Kosher. No meat and milk together.

- Wife well?

- Quite well, thanks... A cheese sandwich, then. Gorgonzola, have you?

Mr Bloom cut his sandwich into slender strips.

- Mustard, sir?

Feel better. Burgundy. Good pick me up. *Kilkenny People* in the national library now I must. Mr Bloom passed the reverend Thomas Connellan's bookstore. *Why I Left The Church Of Rome*? A blind stripling stood tapping the curbstone with his slender cane. No tram in sight.

- Do you want to cross? Mr Bloom asked.

The blind stripling did not answer.

9: Scylla and Charybdis

URBANE, to comfort them, the quaker librarian purred:

- Our young Irish bards have yet to create a figure which the world will set beside Saxon Shakespeare's Hamlet.

- The deepest poetry of Shelley, Russell oracled out of his shadow, the words of Hamlet bring our minds into contact with the eternal wisdom, Plato's[6] world of ideas. All the rest is the speculation of schoolboys for schoolboys.

- The schoolmen were schoolboys first, Aristotle[7] was once Plato's schoolboy. Stephen said superpolitely.

Mr Best came forward, amiable, towards his colleague.

---

6   **Plato's world of ideas:** See p55
7   **Aristotle:** was indeed a pupil of Plato, see p62

- Haines is gone, he said. He's quite enthusiastic, don't you know, about Hyde's *Lovesongs of Connacht.* I couldn't bring him in to hear the discussion. He's gone to Gill's to buy it.

- The peatsmoke is going to his head, John Eglinton opined.

We feel in England. Penitent thief. Gone.

- He will have it that Hamlet is a ghoststory, John Eglinton said for Mr Best's behoof.

- Young Hamnet was son of Shakespere's body. Is it possible that that player Shakespeare did not draw the conclusion: I am the murdered father: your mother is the guilty queen, Ann Shakespeare, born Hathaway?

- Ann Hathaway? Mr Best's quiet voice said forgetfully. Yes, we seem to be forgetting her as Shakespeare himself forgot her.

- The world believes that Shakespeare made a mistake

- Bosh! Stephen said rudely. A man of genius makes no mistakes. His errors are volitional and are the portals of discovery.

Portals of discovery opened to let in the quaker librarian, softcreakfooted, bald, eared and assiduous.

- Reminds one of Don Quixote[8] and Sancho Panza. Our national epic has yet to be written, Dr Sigerson says. We are becoming important, it seems.

- Mr Lyster, an attendant said from the door ajar. There's a gentleman here, sir. He wants to see the files of the *Kilkenny People* for last year.

A patient silhouette waited, listening.

- If you just follow the atten... Or, please allow me... This way... Please, sir...

- What's his name? Buck Mulligan cried. Ikey Moses[9]? Bloom. The wandering jew. I fear thee, ancient mariner.[10]

- We want to hear more, John Eglinton decided with Mr Best's approval. We begin to be interested in Mrs S, and other lady friends as Lawn Tennyson, gentleman poet, sings.

10: Wandering Rocks

THE SUPERIOR, the very reverend John Conmee S.J. reset his smooth watch in his interior pocket as he came down the presbytery steps. Five to three. Just nice time to walk to Artane.

* * *

A onelegged sailor crutched himself round MacConnell's corner, skirting Rabaiotti's icecream car, and jerked himself up Eccles street. Towards Larry O'Rourke, in shirtsleeves in his doorway, he growled unamiably:

- *For England, Home and beauty.*

A stout lady stopped, took a copper coin from her purse and dropped it into the cap held out to her.

* * *

Katey and Boody Dedalus shoved in the door of the closesteaming kitchen. Maggy at the range rammed down a greyish mass beneath bubbling suds twice with her potstick and wiped her brow.

* * *

Blazes Boylan walked here and there in new tan shoes about the fruitsmelling shop, lifting fruits, young juicy crinkled and plump. H. E. L. Y.'S filed before him, tallwhitehatted, past Tangier lane, plodding towards their goal.

The blond girl handed him a docket and pencil.

- Send it at once, will you? he said. It's for an invalid.

- Yes, sir. I will, sir.

Blazes Boylan looked into the cut of her blouse. A young pullet.

* * *

Mr Bloom turned over idly pages of *The Awful Disclosures of Maria Monk.* Crooked botched print. The shopman let two volumes fall on the counter.

- Them are two good ones, he said.

Mr Bloom, alone, looked at the titles. *Fair Tyrants* by James Lovebirch. Know the kind that is. Had it? Yes. No: she wouldn't like that much. He read the other title: *Sweets Of Sin.* Let us see. He read where his finger opened.

- All the dollarbills her husband gave her were spent in the stores on wondrous gowns and costliest frillies. For him! For Raoul!

Mastering his troubled breath, he said:

- I'll take this one.

The shopman lifted eyes bleared with old rheum.

- *Sweets Of Sin*, he said, tapping on it. That's a good one.

* * *

As they trod across the thick carpet Buck Mulligan and Haines chose a small table near the window, opposite a longfaced man whose beard and gaze hung intently down on a chessboard. Haines opened his newbought book.

* * *

Almidano Artifoni walked past Holles street, past Sewell's yard. Distantly behind him a blind stripling tapped his way by the wall of College park.

* * *

William Humble, earl of Dudley, and lady Dudley, accompanied by lieutenantcolonel Heseltine, drove out after luncheon from the viceregal lodge. The viceroy was most cordially greeted on his way through the metropolis. By the provost's wall came jauntily Blazes Boylan, stepping in tan shoes and socks with skyblue clocks to the refrain of *My Girl's a Yorkshire Girl.* His Excellency acknowledged punctually salutes from rare male walkers, the salute of two small schoolboys at the garden gate of the house said to have been admired by the late queen when visiting the Irish capital with her husband, the prince consort, in 1849.

---

8   **Don Quixote:** See p163
9   **Moses:** See p23
10   **Ancient Mariner:** See p285

11: The Sirens

BRONZE by gold, miss Douce's head by miss Kennedy's head, over the crossblind of the Ormond bar heard the viceregal hoofs go by, ringing steel. A man. Bloom. Bloowho went by bearing in his breast the sweets of sin, by Wine's antiques, for Raoul.

Where eat? The Clarence, Dolphin. On. For Raoul. Eat. If I net five guineas with those ads. The violet silk petticoats. Not yet. The sweets of sin. To Martha I must write. Two sheets cream vellum paper one reserve two envelopes when I was in Wisdom Hely's wise Bloom Henry Flower bought. For Raoul.

Blazes Boylan's smart tan shoes creaked on the barfloor where he strode. See the conquering hero comes. Horn. Have you the? Horn. Haw haw horn.

By the window, warily walking, went Bloom, unconquered hero.

See me he might. Avoid. What is he doing in the Ormond? Something to eat? I too was just. Ormond? Best value in Dublin. Diningroom. Sit tight there. Pat, deaf waiter. See, not be seen. Come on. Dinner fit for a prince.

- Let me see. Let me see. Cider. Yes Pat, bottle of cider. Liver and bacon. Right, sir.

Bloom ate liv. Clean here at least. Best value in Dub. Piano music. Piano players. Numbers it is. All music when you come to think.. Two multiplied by two divided by half is twice one. Musemathematics.

Bald deaf Pat brought quite flat pad ink. Pat went.

Bloom dipped, Bloo mur: dear sir. Dear Henry wrote: dear Mady. Got your lett and flow.

Folly am I writing? Husbands don't. That's marriage does, their wives. Sauce for the gander.

- Answering an ad? keen Richie's eyes asked Bloom.

- Yes, Mr Bloom said.

Blot over the other so he can't read. Something detective read off blottingpad. Poor Mrs Purefoy. Done anyhow.

Postal order, stamp. Postoffice lower down. Walk now. Gassy thing that cider: binding too. Music. Gets on your nerves. Up the quay went Lionelleopold, naughty Henry with letter for Mady, with sweets of sin with frillies for Raoul went Poldy on.

Tap blind walked tapping by the tap the curbstone tapping, tap by tap. Tap. Tap. A stripling, blind, with a tapping cane.

Prrprr. Must be the bur. Fff! Oo. Rrpr. Pprrpffrrppffff. DONE.

12: The Cyclops

I WAS just passing the time of day at the corner of Arbour hill when I see Joe Hynes.

- Are you a strict t.t? says Joe.

- Not taking anything between drinks, says I.

- Come around to Barney Kiernan's, says Joe. I want to see the Citizen.

So we turned into Barney Kiernan's and there, sure enough, was the Citizen up in the corner having a great confab with himself and that bloody mangy mongrel, Garryowen.

- Three pints, Terry, says Joe. And how's the old heart, Citizen? says he.

- Never better, says he.

The figure seated on a large boulder at the foot of a round tower was that of a broadshouldered deepchested shaggybearded ruddyfaced sinewyarmed hero. From his girdle hung a row of seastones graven with rude tribal images of Irish heroes of antiquity, Cuchulin, Conn of hundred battles, Brian of Kincora, Father John Murphy, Captain Boycott, Charlemagne, the Last of the Mohicans, the Rose of Castile, Benjamin Franklin, Napoleon Bonaparte, sir Thomas Lipton, Michelangelo Hayes, Muhammad, Patrick W. Shakespeare, Brian Confucius, Dolly Mount, Sidney Parade, Herodotus, Jack the Giantkiller, Gautama Buddha.[11]

- Ah, well, says Joe, handing round the boose. Drink that, Citizen.

Ah! I was blue mouldy for the want of that pint.

Old Garryowen started growling again it was that Bloom that was skeezing round the door.

- Come in, come on, he won't eat you, says the Citizen.

- And Joe has these letters from hangmen and starts reading; Sir I beg to offer my services in the abovementioned painful case I hanged Joe Gann in Bootle jail on the 12 of febuary 1900 and I hanged...

- The dirty scrawl of the wretch, says Joe. Here, says he, take them to hell out of my sight. Hello, Bloom, says he, what will you have?

Bloom saying he wouldn't and he'd just take a cigar.

- They're all barbers, says he, from the black country that would hang their own fathers for five quid down and travelling expenses.

So they started talking about capital punishment and of course Bloom comes out with the why and the wherefore and the old dog smelling him all the time I'm told those Jewies does have a sort of a queer odour coming off them for dogs about I don't know what all deterrent effect and so forth and so on.

- Sinn Fein! says the Citizen. The friends we love are by our side and the foes we hate before us.

So then the Citizen begins talking about the Irish language and all the shoneen games like lawn tennis and about hurley. And of course Bloom had to have his say too. I declare to my antimacassar that Bloom could talk steady an hour about a straw on the floor.

- Persecution, says he, all the history of the world is full of it. Perpetuating national hatred among nations.

- Do you know what a nation means? says John Wyse.

- A nation? says Bloom. A nation is the same people living in the same place.

- What is your nation if I may ask? says the Citizen.

---

11 Alleged Irish heroes are found at pages 92, 149and 42

- Ireland, says Bloom. I was born here. Ireland. And I belong to a race that is hated and persecuted. This very moment.

- Are you talking about the new Jerusalem? says Citizen.

- The Saviour was a Jew, his father was a Jew. Your God.

- Whose God? says the Citizen.

- Your God was a Jew. Christ was a Jew like me.

Gob, the Citizen made a plunge back into the shop.

- By Jesus, says he, I'll brain that bloody Jewman for using the holy name. By Jesus, I'll crucify him so I will. Give us that biscuitbox here.

The departing guest was the recipient of a hearty ovation, many of those who were present being visibly moved when the select orchestra of Irish pipes struck up the wellknown strains of *Come Back To Erin.*

Begob he drew his hand and made a swipe and let fly, the old tinbox clattering along the street. And the last we saw was a car rounding the corner and old sheepsface on it gesticulating and the bloody mongrel after it.

When, lo, there came about them all a great brightness and they beheld the chariot wherein He stood ascend to heaven. And they beheld Him even Him, ben Bloom Elijah, amid clouds of angels ascend to the glory of the brightness like a shot off a shovel.

13: Nausicaa

THE SUMMER evening had begun to fold the world in its mysterious embrace. Far away in the west the sun was setting on the weedgrown rocks along Sandymount shore. The three girl friends were seated there, enjoying the evening scene. Cissy Caffrey and Edy Boardman with the baby in the pushcar and Tommy and Jacky, two little curlyheaded boys, dressed in sailor suits with caps to match.

- O, look, Cissy!

And they all looked was it sheet lightning but Tommy saw it too over the trees beside the church, blue and then green and purple.

- It's fireworks, Cissy Caffrey said. Come on, Gerty.

But Gerty leaned back far to look up where the fireworks were and she caught her knee in her hands so as not to fall back looking up and there was no-one to see only him and her when she revealed all, and she seemed to hear the panting of his heart, his hoarse breathing, because she knew too about the passion of men like that. Besides there was absolution so long as you didn't do the other thing before being married and there ought to be women priests that would understand.

And then a rocket sprang and bang shot blind blank and O! then the Roman candle burst and it was like a sigh of O! and everyone cried O! O! in raptures and it gushed out of it a stream of rain. O, soft, sweet, soft!

Ah! She glanced at him as she bent forward quickly. He was leaning back against the rock behind. Leopold Bloom (for it is he) stands silent, with bowed head before those young guileless eyes. What a brute he had been! At it

again? Should a girl tell? No, a thousand times no. That was their secret, only theirs.

Tight boots? No. She's lame! O! Mr Bloom watched her as she limped away. Poor girl! A defect is ten times worse in a woman. Hot little devil all the same. I wouldn't mind. Curiosity like a nun or a negress or a girl with glasses.

Mr Bloom with careful hand recomposed his wet shirt. O Lord, that little limping devil. Begins to feel cold and clammy. Aftereffect not pleasant. Still you have to get rid of it someway. They don't care. Complimented perhaps. Drained all the manhood out of me, little wretch. Do fish ever get seasick? Mr Bloom with his stick gently vexed the thick sand at his foot. Write a message for her. Might remain. What?

I AM A

Mr Bloom effaced the letters with his slow boot. Thanks. Made me feel so young. O sweety all your little girlwhite up I saw dirty bracegirdle made me do love sticky we two naughty Grace darling she him half past the bed met him pike hoses frillies for Raoul.

Cuckoo Cuckoo

14: The Oxen of the Sun

DESHIL Holles Eamus. Send us bright one, light one, Horhorn, quickening and wombfruit. Before born bliss babe had. Within womb won he worship. Seventy beds keeps he there teeming mothers are wont that they lie for to bring forth bairns hale.

Watchers tway there walk, white sisters in ward sleepless. Therefore, everyman, look to that last end that is thy Death and the dust that gripeth on every man that is born of woman for as he came naked forth from his mother's womb so naked shall he wend him at the last for to go as he came.

The man that was come in to the house then spoke to the nursingwoman and he asked her how it fared with the woman that lay there in childbed. She said thereto that she had seen many births of women but never was none so hard as was that woman's birth.

And whiles they spake the door of the castle was opened and there came the traveller Leopold.

And the learning knight let pour for childe Leopold a draught and halp thereto the while all they that were there drank every each. This meanwhile a good sister stood by the door and begged them at the reverence of Jesu our alther liege Lord to leave their wassailing. For they were right witty scholars, saying, greater love than this, he said, no man hath that a man lay down his wife for his friend. Go thou and do likewise. Thus, or words to that effect, saith Zarathustra, sometime regius professor of French letters to the university of Oxtail.

15: Circe

THE MABBOT street entrance of Nighttown. Rows of grimy houses with gaping doors. Rare lamps with faint rainbow fins. Round Rabaiotti's halted icecream gondola stunted men and women squabble. A deafmute idiot with goggle eyes, his shapeless mouth dribbling, jerks past, shaken in saint vitus' dance. Private Carr and Private

Compton turn and counterretort, their tunics bloodbright in a lampglow.

Stephen Dedalus and Lynch pass through the crowd close to the redcoats.

Bloom appears, flushed, panting, cramming bread and chocolate into a sidepocket. He disappears into Olhausen's, the porkbutcher's, under the downcoming rollshutter. A few moments later he emerges from under the shutter, puffing poldy, blowing bloohoom. In each hand he holds a parcel, one containing a lukewarm pig's crubeen, the other a cold sheep's trotter, sprinkled with wholepepper. He stands at Cormack's corner, watching. Two cyclists, with lighted paper lanterns aswing, swim by him, grazing him, their bells rattling

THE BELLS: Haltyaltyaltyall.

(*A stooped bearded figure appears garbed in the long caftan of an elder in zion and a smokingcap with tassels. Yellow poison streaks are on the drawn face.*)

BLOOM: (*hides the crubeen and trotter behind his back*) Papachi?

RUDOLPH: Have you no soul? Are you not my dear son Leopold who left the house of his father and left the God of his fathers Abraham[12] and Jacob?

A VOICE: (*sharply*) Poldy!

BLOOM: I was just going back for that lotion whitewax, orangeflower water. (*he pats divers pockets*)

(*A cake of new clean lemon soap arises, diffusing light and perfume.*)

THE SOAP: We're a capital couple are Bloom and I. He brightens the earth. I polish the sky.

Followed by whining dog he walks on towards hellsgates.

THE WHORES: How's your middle leg? Got a match on you? Eh, come here till I stiffen it for you.

Gaudy dollwomen loll in the lighted doorways, in window embrasures, smoking birdseye cigarettes.

THE CRIER: (*loudly*) Whereas Leopold Bloom of no fixed abode is a wellknown dynamitard, forger, bigamist, bawd and cuckold ...

Zoe Higgins, a young whore in a sapphire slip, trips down steps and accosts him.

ZOE: How's the nuts?

Her hand slides into his left trouser pocket and brings out a hard black shrivelled potato.

BLOOM: Are you a Dublin girl?

ZOE: (*curling a stray hair*) No bloody fear. I'm English. Have you a swaggerroot?

BLOOM: Rarely smoke, dear. Cigar now and then.

Midnight chimes from distant steeples.

THE CHIMES: Turn again, Leopold! Lord mayor of Dublin!

BLOOM: My subjects! The keys of Dublin, crossed on a crimson cushion, are given to him. He shows all that he is

wearing green socks. (*shaking hands with a blind stripling*) My more than Brother! Roygbiv. 32 feet per second.

DAUGHTERS OF ERIN: Kidney of Bloom, pray for us

BLOOM: Where are you from? London?

ZOE: I'm Yorkshire born. (*she holds his hand which is feeling for her nipple*) I say, Tommy Tittlemouse. Stop that and begin worse. Are you coming into the musicroom to see our new pianola? Come and I'll peel off.

Zoe and Bloom reach the doorway where two sister whores are seated. Lynch squats crosslegged on the hearthrug of matted hair, his cap back to the front. With a wand he beats time slowly.

ZOE: More limelight, Charley. (*she goes to the chandelier and turns the gas full cock*)

STEPHEN: God, the sun, Shakespeare, a commercial traveller. Wait a moment. Wait a second. Damn that fellow's noise in the street.

Stephen turns and sees Bloom. Reuben I Antichrist, wandering jew.

THE GRAMOPHONE: Whorusalaminyourhighhohhhh...

VIRAG: My name is Virag Lipoti. (*coughs*) Promiscuous nakedness, eh?

FLORRY: Sing us something. *Love's old sweet song.*

ZOE: There was a priest down here two nights ago. You needn't try to hide, I says to him. I know you've a Roman collar.

VIRAG: Perfectly logical from his standpoint. Why I left the church of Rome.

His eminence Simon Stephen cardinal Dedalus, primate of all Ireland, appears in the doorway, followed by Bella Cohen, a massive whoremistress. She is dressed in a threequarter ivory gown, and cools herself flirting a black horn fan. She has a sprouting moustache and large pendant beryl eardrops.

BELLA: My word! I'm all of a mucksweat.

THE FAN: (*flirting quickly, then slowly*) Married, I see.

BLOOM: (*cowed*) Exuberant female. Enormously I desiderate your domination. I stand, so to speak, with an unposted letter.

BELLO: (*laughs loudly*) Holy smoke! You little know what's in store for you. Hold him down, girls, till I squat on him. What else are you good for, an impotent thing like you? Up! Up! It's as limp as a boy of six's doing his pooly behind a cart. Can you do a man's job?

BLOOM: (*quickly*) Yes, yes. Frailty, thy name is marriage. O, I have been a perfect pig. Enemas too I have administered. Up the fundament. With Hamilton Long's syringe, the ladies' friend.

STEPHEN: To have or not to have that is the question.

BELLA: Here. This isn't a musical peepshow. Who's paying here?

Stephen fumbles in his pocket and, taking out a banknote by its corner, hands it to her.

BELLA: Do you want three girls? It's ten shillings here.

BLOOM: (*lays a half sovereign on the table*) Allow me.

---

12 **Abraham:** see The Torah (p23), Genesis 17

STEPHEN: Thanks.

STEPHEN: Cigarette, please.

LYNCH: You would have a better chance of lighting it if you held the match nearer.

BOYLAN: You can apply your eye to the keyhole and play with yourself while I go through her a few times.

BLOOM: Thank you, sir. I will, sir. May I bring two men chums to witness the deed and take a snapshot?

LYNCH: The mirror up to nature.

(*Stephen and Bloom gaze in the mirror. William Shakespeare, beardless, appears there, crowned by the reflection of the reindeer antlered hatrack in the hall.*)

SHAKESPEARE: (*in dignified ventriloquy*) 'Tis the loud laugh bespeaks the vacant mind.

THE PIANOLA: *My girl's a Yorkshire girl. And wears no fancy clothes.*

STEPHEN: Nothung!

THE MOTHER: (*Dying in agony*) Have mercy on Stephen, Lord, for my sake!

He lifts his ashplant high with both hands and smashes the chandelier.

THE GASJET: Pwfungg!

BELLA: Police!

Stephen, abandoning his ashplant, beats the ground and flies from the room, past the whores at the door.

BELLA: Who pays for the lamp? (*she seizes Bloom's coattail*) Here, you were with him. The lamp's broken.

BLOOM: O, I know. But he's a Trinity student. (*He makes a masonic sign*) You don't want a scandal.

He hurries out through the hall. The Whores Point. They Blow Ickylickysticky Yumyum Kisses.

THE HUE AND CRY: (*helterskelterpelterwelter*) He's Bloom! Stop Bloom! Stopabloom! Stopperrobber! Hi! Hi! Stophim on the corner!

At the corner of Beaver street beneath the scaffolding Bloom panting stops on the fringe of the noisy quarrelling knot.

STEPHEN: (with elaborate gestures, breathing deeply and slowly) History to blame. Fabled by mothers of memory.

LORD TENNYSON: (*Gentleman poet in union jack blazer and cricket flannels, bareheaded, flowingbearded*) Their's not to reason why.

PRIVATE COMPTON: Biff him, Harry.

STEPHEN: How? Noble art of selfpretence. Personally, I detest action.

BLOOM: (*plucks stephen's sleeve*) Come now, professor, that carman is waiting.

Edward the seventh appears in an archway. He is robed as a grand elect perfect and sublime mason with trowel and apron, marked made in Germany. In his left hand he holds a plasterer's bucket on which is printed *defense d'uriner.*

EDWARD THE SEVENTH: (*slowly, solemnly but indistinctly*) Peace, perfect peace. He shakes hands with private Carr, private Compton, Stephen, Bloom and Lynch.

(*levitates over heaps of slain, in the garb and with the halo of joking Jesus.*)

VOICES: Police!

FATHER MALACHI O'FLYNN: *Introibo ad altare diaboli.*

BLOOM: (*runs to Stephen*) Come along with me now before worse happens. Here's your stick.

STEPHEN: Stick, no. Reason. This feast of pure reason.

FIRST WATCH: Here, what are you all gaping at?

CORNY KELLEHER: Leave it to me, sergeant.

BLOOM: Father is a wellknown highly respected citizen. Just a little wild oats, you understand.

STEPHEN: (*Murmurs*) Sshadows... the woods... white breast... dim sea.

Against the dark wall a figure appears slowly, a fairy boy of eleven, dressed in an eton suit with a book in his hand. He reads from right to left inaudibly, smiling, kissing the page.

BLOOM: (*Wonderstruck, calls inaudibly*) Rudy!

RUDY: (*Gazes, unseeing, into bloom's eyes and goes on reading, kissing, smiling.*)

16: Eumaeus

HIS (Stephen's) mind being a bit unsteady, Bloom and his new friend took to the cabman's shelter, and a boiling swimming cup of a choice concoction labelled coffee, possibly delivered by the once infamous Skin-the-Goat Fitzharris. From thence by loud Italians they sang their tracks arm-in-arm across Beresford place.

17: Ithaca

OF WHAT did the duumvirate deliberate during their itinerary? - Music, literature, Ireland, Dublin, Paris, prostitution, diet, the influence of gaslight, the Roman catholic church, the Irish nation, jesuit education, the study of medicine, Stephen's collapse.

What act did Bloom make on their arrival at their destination? - At the housesteps of number 7 Eccles street, he inserted his hand mechanically into the back pocket of his trousers to obtain his latchkey.

Was it there? - No.

Bloom's decision? - A stratagem. Resting his feet on the dwarf wall, he climbed over the area railings, raised the latch of the area door, gained retarded access to the kitchen through the subadjacent scullery.

What did Bloom do? - He drew two spoonseat deal chairs to the hearthstone, one for Stephen, the other for himself. Carried the iron kettle to the sink in order to tap the current by turning the faucet to let it flow.

Did it flow? - Yes. From Roundwood reservoir in county Wicklow of a cubic capacity of 2400 million gallons, percolating through a subterranean aqueduct by way of the Dargle, Rathdown, Glen of the Downs and Callowhill, a distance of 22 statute miles.

How did Bloom prepare a collation for a gentile? - He poured into two teacups two level spoonfuls, four in all, of Epps's soluble cocoa.

Did he find four separating forces between his temporary guest and him? - Name, age, race, creed.

What anagrams had he made on his name in youth? - Leopold Bloom, Ellpodbomool, Old Ollebo, M.P.

What two temperaments did they individually represent? - The scientific. The artistic.

What also stimulated him in his cogitations? - The financial success achieved by Ephraim Marks by his 1d bazaar and the infinite possibilities hitherto unexploited of the modern art of advertisement.

Such as not? - What is home without Plumtree's Potted Meat? Peatmot. Trumplee. Moutpat. Plamtroo.

What did each do at the door of egress? - Bloom set the candlestick on the floor. Stephen put the hat on his head.

For what creature was the door of egress a door of ingress? - For a cat.

What spectacle confronted them? - The heaventree of stars hung with humid nightblue fruit.

How did they take leave, one of the other? - Standing perpendicular at the same door and on different sides of its base, the lines of their valedictory arms meeting at any point and forming any angle less than the sum of two right angles.

Did he remain? - With deep inspiration he returned, retraversing the garden, reclosing the door.

What suddenly arrested his ingress? - The right temporal lobe of his cranium came into contact with a solid timber angle where, a sensible fraction of a second later, a painful sensation was registered.

Compile the budget for 16 June 1904 - DEBIT: £2.19.3.

In what ultimate ambition had all ambition now coalesced? - To purchase by private treaty in fee simple a thatched bungalowshaped 2 storey dwellinghouse of southerly aspect, surmounted by vane and lightning conductor, with porch covered by ivy or Virginia creeper, halldoor, olive green, with smart carriage finish and neat doorbrasses

What might be the name of this erigible or erected residence? - Bloom Cottage. Saint Leopold's. Flowerville.

What rapid but insecure means to opulence might facilitate immediate purchase? - A prepared scheme based on a study of the laws of probability to break the bank at Monte Carlo.

What did his drawer, unlocked, contain? - A Vere Foster's handwriting copybook, property of Milly (Millicent) Bloom, certain pages of which bore diagram drawings, marked Papli, which showed a large globular head with 5 hairs erect, the trunk full front with 3 large buttons, 1 triangular foot: 2 fading photographs of queen Alexandra of England and of Maud Branscombe, actress: a Yuletide card, bearing on it a pictorial representation of a parasitic plant, the legend Mizpah, the date Xmas 1892: a butt of red sealing wax, obtained from Messrs Hely's, Ltd., Dame street: a sealed prophecy written by Leopold Bloom in 1886 concerning the consequences of the passing into law of William Ewart Gladstone's Home Rule bill: 3 typewritten letters, addressee, Henry Flower, c/o P.O.

Westland Row: 2 coupons of the Royal Hungarian Lottery: a magnifying glass: 2 erotic photocards showing a) coition between nude señorita and nude torero b) anal violation by male religious (fully clothed, eyes abject) of female religious: a press cutting of recipe for renovation of old tan boots: 1 prospectus of The Wonderworker, the world's greatest remedy for rectal complaints, recommend it to your lady and gentlemen friends, lasts a lifetime. Insert long round end: A bank passbook issued by the Ulster Bank, College Green, balance in depositor's favour: £18-14-6: a local press cutting concerning change of name by deedpoll whereas Rudolph Virag, formerly of Szombathely in the kingdom of Hungary, hereby gives notice that I have assumed the name of Rudolph Bloom: A note... it is no use Leopold to be... with your dear mother... that is not more to stand... all for me is out... be kind to Athos, Leopold... my dear son... always... of me... das Herz... Gott... dein...

Why did Bloom experience a sentiment of remorse? - Because in immature impatience he had treated with disrespect certain beliefs and practices, as the prohibition of the use of fleshmeat and milk at one meal: the sanctity of the sabbath.

Bloom's acts? - He deposited the articles of clothing on a chair, took a folded white nightshirt, inserted his head and arms into the proper apertures, and entered the bed.

What did his limbs encounter? - The presence of a human form, female, hers, the imprint of a human form, male, not his, some crumbs, some flakes of potted meat.

Then? - He kissed the plump mellow yellow smellow melons of her rump, with obscure prolonged provocative melonsmellonous osculation.

Womb? Weary? - He rests. He has travelled.

18: Penelope

YES because he never did a thing like that before as ask to get his breakfast in bed with a couple of eggs since the City Arms hotel when he used to be pretending to be laid up with a sick voice doing his highness to make himself interesting for that old faggot Mrs Riordan if they only knew him as well as I do yes because the day before yesterday he was scribbling a letter when I came into the front room he covered it up with the blottingpaper pretending to be thinking about business not that I care two straws now who he does it with so long as I dont have the two of them under my nose all the time like that slut that Mary we had in Ontario Terrace padding out her false bottom to excite him he was with a dirty barefaced liar and sloven like that one denying it up to my face yes and the last time he came on my bottom when was it the night Boylan gave my hand a great squeeze singing the young May Moon shes beaming love I wish some man or other would take me sometime when hes there and kiss me in his arms theres nothing like a kiss long and hot down to your soul almost paralyses you then I hate that confession when I used to go to Father Corrigan he touched me father and what harm if he did where and I said on the canal bank like a fool but whereabouts on your person my child it never entered my head what kissing meant till he put his tongue in my mouth his mouth O yes I pulled him off perhaps hes dead or killed or a Captain or admiral its nearly 20 years I never thought that would be my name Bloom youre looking blooming Josie used to say after I married him thats 11 year yes I often felt I wanted to kiss him all over also his lovely young cock so clean and white he looks with his boyish face O move over your big carcass out of that for the love of Mike listen to him the winds that waft my sighs to thee I suppose theyre just getting up in China now combing out their pigtails well I must clean the keys of the piano with milk I liked him because I saw he understood or felt what a woman is and I knew I could always get round him and I gave him all the pleasure I could leading him on till he asked me to say yes and I wouldnt answer first only looked out over the sea and the sky and the old castle thousands of years old yes and those handsome Moors all in white and turbans like kings asking you to sit down in their little bit of a shop and the rosegardens and Gibraltar as a girl where I was a Flower of the mountain yes when I put the rose in my hair like the Andalusian girls or shall I wear a red yes and how he kissed me under the Moorish wall and I thought well as well him as another and then I asked him with my eyes to ask again yes and then he asked me would I yes to say yes my mountain flower and first I put my arms around him yes and drew him down to me so he could feel my breasts all perfume yes and his heart was going like mad and yes I said yes I will Yes.

The Great Gatsby
by F Scott Fitzgerald
(New York, 1925)

This is *the* novel of the American inter-war 'Jazz Age', a term invented by Fitzgerald himself. The book was only modestly successful when first released, but gained huge popularity after the Armed Services Editions gave away some 150,000 copies to the American military in World War II.

Abridged: GH.

Then wear the gold hat, if that will move her;
If you can bounce high, bounce for her too,
Till she cry "Lover, gold-hatted, high-bouncing lover,
I must have you!"
— *Thomas Parke D'Invilliers.*

In my younger and more vulnerable years my father gave me some advice that I've been turning over in my mind ever since. "Whenever you feel like criticizing any one," he told me, "just remember that all the people in this world haven't had the advantages that you've had."

I understood that he meant a great deal more than that. Conduct may be founded on the hard rock or the wet marshes but after a certain point I don't care what it's founded on. When I came back from the East last autumn I wanted no more riotous excursions with privileged glimpses into the human heart. Only Gatsby, the man who gives his name to this book, was exempt from my reaction - Gatsby who represented everything for which I have an unaffected scorn. Gatsby turned out all right at the end; it is what preyed on Gatsby, what foul dust floated in the wake of his dreams that temporarily closed out my interest in the abortive sorrows and short-winded elations of men.

My family, the Carraway clan, have been well-to-do people in a middle-western city since my grandfather's brother started his wholesale hardware business. I graduated from New Haven in 1915, and a little later I participated in that delayed Teutonic migration known as the Great War.

It was a matter of chance that I should have rented a house in one of the strangest communities in North America.

Twenty miles from New York city a pair of enormous eggs, separated only by a courtesy bay, jut out into the great wet barnyard of Long Island Sound. I lived at West Egg, the - well, the less fashionable of the two. My own small eye-sore of a house was squeezed between two huge places, the one on my right was a colossal imitation of some Hôtel de Ville in Normandy with a marble swimming pool. It was Gatsby's mansion. I had the consoling proximity of millionaires for eighty dollars a month.

The history of the summer really begins on the evening I drove over to have dinner with two old friends whom I scarcely knew at all, the Tom Buchanans. Daisy was my second cousin once removed and I'd known Tom in college. He had played football at New Haven, and his family were enormously wealthy. Now he was a sturdy, straw haired man of thirty with a rather hard mouth and a supercilious manner. "Now, don't think my opinion is final," he seemed to say, "just because I'm stronger and more of a man than you are."

At his elaborate house, on an enormous couch two young women in white dresses were fluttering.

I told cousin Daisy how desolate Chicago was without her. "All the cars have the left rear wheel painted black as a mourning wreath."

She laughed, and murmured that the other girl was Baker, the golfer.

"You live in West Egg," Miss Baker remarked contemptuously to me. "You must know Gatsby."

"Gatsby?" demanded Daisy. "What Gatsby?"

Before I could reply, dinner was announced; and Tom Buchanan compelled me from the room as though he were moving a checker to another square, out onto a rosy-colored porch open toward the sunset where four candles flickered on the table.

Daisy snapped out the candles. "In two weeks it'll be the longest day in the year."

"Civilization's going to pieces," broke out Tom violently. "Have you read 'The Rise of the Colored Empires' by this man Goddard?"

"Why, no," I answered, rather surprised by his tone.

"The idea is if we don't look out the white race will be - will be utterly submerged. It's all scientific stuff."

Almost immediately, the telephone rang inside and the butler came and murmured something close to Tom's ear whereupon Tom frowned, pushed back his chair and without a word went inside. As if his absence quickened something within her Daisy suddenly threw her napkin on the table and went into the house.

Miss Baker and I exchanged a short glance.

She said hesitantly, "Tom's got some woman in New York."

Then, with a flutter of a dress and the crunch of leather boots, Tom and Daisy were back at the table. I her asked some sedative questions about her little girl.

She looked at me absently. "Listen, Nick; I hope she'll be a fool - that's the best thing a girl can be in this world, a beautiful little fool. And I KNOW. I've been everywhere and seen everything and done everything. Sophisticated - God, I'm sophisticated!"

As I left that night Daisy asked if I didn't have a girl out West.

Their interest rather touched me and made them less remotely rich - nevertheless, I was confused and a little disgusted as I drove away.

When I reached my estate at West Egg I saw that I was not alone - fifty feet away Mr. Gatsby himself had come out to determine what share was his of our local heavens. When I looked once more for Gatsby he had vanished, and I was alone again in the unquiet darkness.

2

About half way between West Egg and New York the motor-road runs beside a valley of ashes - a fantastic farm where ashes take the forms of houses and chimneys and rising smoke. There, above the gray land, you perceive the eyes of Doctor T. J. Eckleburg - their retinas are one yard high – looking out from a pair of enormous yellow spectacles over a nonexistent nose. Evidently some wild wag of an oculist set them there, before sinking himself into eternal blindness .

I went up to New York with Tom on the train one afternoon and when we stopped by the ashheaps he jumped to his feet and literally forced me from the car.

"We're getting off!" he insisted. "I want you to meet my girl."

I followed him over a low white-washed fence to a garage - Repairs. GEORGE B. WILSON. Cars Bought and Sold - and I followed Tom inside.

The proprietor himself appeared in the door, a blonde, spiritless man, anaemic, and faintly handsome.

"Hello, Wilson, old man," said Tom. "How's business?"

"I can't complain," answered Wilson unconvincingly.

Then I heard footsteps on a stair and in a moment the thickish figure of a woman smiled slowly and walking through her husband as if he were a ghost, shook hands with Tom, looking him flush in the eye. Then she wet her lips and without turning around spoke to her husband in a soft, coarse voice:

"Get some chairs, why don't you, so somebody can sit down."

Wilson hurried toward the little office. His wife moved close to Tom.

"I want to see you, Myrtle" said Tom intently. "Get on the next train."

She nodded and moved away from him just as George Wilson emerged with two chairs from his office door.

So, we waited for her down the road and out of sight, and Tom Buchanan and his girl and I went up together to New York - or not quite together, for Mrs. Wilson sat discreetly in another car.

Tom helped her to the platform in New York. At the newsstand she bought a copy of "Town Tattle" and a moving-picture magazine and, in the station drug store, some cold cream and a small flask of perfume, and, on a whim, a small dog from a street-seller. At 158th Street our cab stopped at one slice in a long white cake of apartment houses, where Mrs. Wilson gathered up her dog and her other purchases and went haughtily in.

After the first drink, company commenced to arrive at the apartment door. There was McKee, the photographer, and Myrle's sister, Catherine, who sat down beside me on the couch.

"Do you live down on Long Island, too?" she inquired.

"I live at West Egg."

"Really? I was down there at a party about a month ago. At a man named Gatsby. They say he's a nephew of Kaiser Wilhelm's."

Catherine looked at Myrtle and then at Tom, leaned close to me and whispered in my ear: "Neither of them can stand the person they're married to. If I was them I'd get a divorce and get married to each other right away."

A bottle of whiskey - a second one - was now in constant demand by all present. I wanted to get out, but each time I tried to go I became entangled in some wild strident argument which pulled me back, as if with ropes, into my chair.

Some time toward midnight Tom Buchanan and Mrs. Wilson stood face to face discussing in impassioned voices whether Mrs. Wilson had any right to mention Daisy's name.

"Daisy! Daisy! Daisy!" shouted Mrs. Wilson. "I'll say it whenever I want to! Daisy! Dai - "

Making a short deft movement Tom Buchanan broke her nose with his open hand.

Then there were bloody towels upon the bathroom floor, and women's voices scolding, and high over the confusion a long broken wail of pain. Then Mr. McKee turned and moved on out the door. Taking my hat from the chandelier I followed.

3

I believe that on the first night I went to Gatsby's house I was one of the few guests who had actually been invited. People were not invited - they went there. Dressed up in white flannels I went over to his lawn a little after seven and was on my way to get roaring drunk when Jordan Baker came over.

"I thought you might be here," she said. "Let's find our host."

The bar was crowded but Gatsby was not there. She couldn't find him from the top of the steps, and he wasn't on the veranda. The high Gothic library, paneled with carved English oak, contained only a stout, owl-eyed man, anxious to express his amazement that the books were not sham cardboard.

There was dancing on the canvas in the garden, a celebrated tenor had sung in Italian while happy vacuous bursts of laughter rose toward the summer sky. A pair of stage "twins" did a baby act in costume and champagne was served in glasses bigger than finger bowls. I was enjoying myself.

At a lull in the entertainment a man looked at me and smiled.

"Your face is familiar," he said, politely. "Weren't you in the Third Division during the war?"

"Why, yes." I replied. "This is an unusual party for me. I haven't even seen the host."

"I'm Gatsby," he said.

He smiled much more than understandingly. It was one of those rare smiles with a quality of eternal reassurance in it, that you may come across four or five times in life. It understood you just so far as you wanted to be understood, believed in you as you would like to believe in yourself and precisely at that point it vanished - and I was looking at an elegant young rough-neck, a year or two over thirty, whose elaborate formality of speech just missed being absurd.

Almost at the moment Mr. Gatsby excused himself with a small bow, and I turned to Jordan.

"Who is he?" I demanded.

"Well, - he told me once he was an Oxford man. However, I don't believe it. Anyhow he gives large parties," said Jordan. "And I like large parties."

There was the boom of a bass drum, and the voice of the orchestra leader rang out suddenly above the echolalia of the garden.

"Ladies and gentlemen," he cried. "At the request of Mr. Gatsby - 'Vladimir Tostoff's Jazz History of the World.' "

Gatsby's butler was suddenly standing beside us.

"Miss Baker?" he inquired. "I beg your pardon but Mr. Gatsby would like to speak to you alone."

"With me?"

She got up slowly, raising her eyebrows at me in astonishment, and followed the butler toward the house.

I looked around. Most of the remaining women were now having fights with men said to be their husbands. Time to leave.

As I waited for my hat in the hall the door of the library opened and Jordan Baker and Gatsby came out together.

"I've just heard the most amazing thing," she whispered. "But I swore I wouldn't tell it and here I am tantalizing you." She yawned gracefully in my face. "Please come and see me. . . . Phone book. . . . " Her brown hand waved a jaunty salute as she melted into her party at the door.

But all these were merely casual events in a crowded summer. Most of the time I worked down the white chasms of lower New York at the Probity Trust. I knew the other clerks and young bond-salesmen by their first names and I even had a short affair with a girl who lived in Jersey City. I lost sight of Jordan Baker, and then in midsummer I found her again.

We were on a house-party together up in Warwick, she left a borrowed car out in the rain with the top down, and then lied about it - and suddenly I remembered the story about her – that at her first big golf tournament there was a suggestion that she had moved her ball from a bad lie.

Jordan Baker was incurably dishonest, but dishonesty in a woman is a thing you never blame deeply. She was a rotten driver, too, and I told her so.

"They'll keep out of my way," she insisted. "It takes two to make an accident."

"Suppose you met somebody just as careless as yourself."

"I hope I never will," she answered. "I hate careless people. That's why I like you."

For a moment I thought I loved her. Every one suspects himself of at least one of the cardinal virtues, and this is mine: I am one of the few honest people that I have ever known.

4

"Gatsby's a bootlegger," said the young ladies, moving somewhere between his cocktails and his flowers. "One time he killed a man."

Once I wrote down on the empty spaces of a time-table the names of those who came to Gatsby's house that summer. Gulick the state senator and James B. ("Rot-Gut") Ferret came to gamble. Klipspringer was there so long that he became known as "the boarder". There were theatrical people and business people and Henry L. Palmetto who killed himself, and Benny McClenahan, who arrived always with four girls, and a prince of something whom we called Duke and whose name, if I ever knew it, I have forgotten.

At nine o'clock, one morning late in July Gatsby's gorgeous cream-colored car, bright with nickel, swollen here and there in its monstrous length with triumphant hatboxes and tool-boxes, and terraced with a labyrinth of windshields that mirrored a dozen suns, lurched up to my door and gave out a burst of melody from its three noted horn.

"Good morning, old sport. You're having lunch with me today and I thought we'd ride up together."

Sitting down behind many layers of glass in a sort of green leather conservatory we started that disconcerting ride to town.

"Look here, old sport," he broke out surprisingly. "I'm going to tell you something about my life, I don't want you to get a wrong idea of me."

He told me about his education, about how his parents had died and left him money, how he'd been decorated for his bravery in the war. In case I might harbor any foolish doubts, he produced a Montenegran war medal and a photograph of himself in Trinity Quad. Then it was all true.

"I thought you ought to know something about me." He hesitated. "Miss Baker has kindly consented to speak to you about this matter."

I hadn't the faintest idea what "this matter" was, but I was more annoyed than interested.

We passed Port Roosevelt, then the valley of ashes, Gatsby dismissed a motor cycle policeman with a wave of some white card, and then, in a well-fanned Forty-second Street cellar I joined Gatsby for lunch.

"Mr. Carraway this is my friend Mr. Wolfshiem."

"This is a nice restaurant here," said Mr. Wolfshiem looking at the Presbyterian nymphs on the ceiling. "But I like the old Metropole, across the street better! I can't forget so long as I live the night they shot Rosy Rosenthal there."

His luxuriously haired nostrils turned to me in an interested way. "I understand you're looking for a business gonnegtion."

Gatsby answered for me:

"Oh, no," he exclaimed, "this isn't the man! This is just a friend."

A succulent hash arrived, and Mr. Wolfshiem began to eat with ferocious delicacy.

Gatsby, suddenly looked at his watch, jumped up and hurried from the room leaving me with Mr. Wolfshiem at the table.

"He has to telephone," said Mr. Wolfshiem, "Fine fellow, isn't he? He went to Oggsford College in England. It's one of the most famous colleges in the world."

"Have you known Gatsby for a long time?" I inquired.

"Several years," He paused. "I see you're looking at my cuff buttons."

I hadn't been looking at them, but I did now. They were composed of oddly familiar pieces of ivory.

"Finest specimens of human molars," he informed me.

Mr. Wolfshiem drank his coffee with a jerk and got to his feet.

"I have enjoyed my lunch," he said, "and I'm going to run off from you two young men before I outstay my welcome."

As he shook hands and turned away his tragic nose was trembling.

"He becomes very sentimental sometimes," explained Gatsby. "He's quite a character around New York - He's the man who fixed the World's Series back in 1919."

"Fixed the World's Series?" I repeated. "Why isn't he in jail?"

"They can't get him, old sport. He's a smart man."

***

Jordan Baker, sitting up very straight in the tea-garden at the Plaza Hotel, told me how of how she and Daisy had shared a white girlhood, how Daisy had met a lieutenant called Jay Gatsby, but married Tom Buchanan of Chicago.

Half an hour later we were driving in a Victoria through Central Park. The sun had gone down behind the tall apartments of the movie stars and the clear voices of girls, already gathered like crickets on the grass, rose through the hot twilight:

"I'm the Sheik of Araby,
Your love belongs to me.
At night when you're are asleep,
Into your tent I'll creep--"

"It was a strange coincidence," I said.

"But it wasn't a coincidence at all. Gatsby bought that house so that Daisy would be just across the bay."

Then he came alive to me, delivered suddenly from the womb of his purposeless splendor.

"He wants to know - " continued Jordan " - if you'll invite Daisy to your house some afternoon and then let him come over."

The modesty of the demand shook me. He had waited five years and bought a mansion where he dispensed starlight to casual moths so that he could "come over" some afternoon to a stranger's garden.

"She's not to know about it. Gatsby doesn't want her to know. You're just supposed to invite her to tea."

I drew up the girl beside me, tightening my arms. Her wan, scornful mouth smiled and so I drew her up again, closer, this time to my face.

5

When I came home that night I found Gatsby's house lit like fire from tower to cellar. As my taxi groaned away I saw Gatsby walking toward me across his lawn.

"I talked with Miss Baker," I said after a moment. "I'm going to call up Daisy tomorrow and invite her over here to tea."

"Oh, that's all right," he said carelessly. "Oh - " He fumbled with a series of beginnings. "Why, I thought - why, look here, old sport, you don't make much money, do you? I thought, if - you see, I carry on a little business on the side, you understand. And I thought - ? You wouldn't have to do any business with Wolfshiem."

"I've got my hands full," I said. He went unwillingly home.

I called up Daisy from the office next morning and invited her to come to tea. "Don't bring Tom," I warned her.

So, the meeting happened, at my place.

"We haven't met for many years," said Daisy, her voice as matter-of-fact as it could ever be.

"Five years next November," said a nervous Gatsby. "I want you to come over to my house," he said, "I'd like to show her around."

"That huge place THERE?" she cried pointing.

"Do you like it?"

"I love it, but I don't see how you live there all alone."

"I keep it always full of interesting people, night and day. People who do interesting things. Celebrated people. If it wasn't for the mist we could see your home across the bay," said Gatsby. "You always have a green light that burns all night at the end of your dock."

In his own house room Gatsby turned on a solitary lamp beside the piano. He lit Daisy's cigarette from a trembling match, and sat down with her on a couch far across the room where there was no light save what the gleaming floor bounced in from the hall.

Gatsby found someone, Klipspringer, to play the piano.

> One thing's sure and nothing's surer
> The rich get richer and the poor get - children.
> In the meantime,
> In between time -

As I went over to say goodbye I saw that the expression of bewilderment had come back into Gatsby's face. Almost five years! There must have been moments even that afternoon when Daisy tumbled short of his dreams - not through her own fault but because of the colossal vitality of his illusion. It had gone beyond her, beyond everything. No amount of fire or freshness can challenge what a man will store up in his ghostly heart.

6

About this time an ambitious young reporter from New York arrived one morning at Gatsby's door and asked him if he had anything to say.

"Anything to say about what?" inquired Gatsby politely.

It transpired that the man had heard Gatsby's name around his office in a connection which he either wouldn't reveal or didn't fully understand. It was a random shot, and yet the reporter's instinct was right. Gatsby's notoriety had increased all summer until he fell just short of being news.

In reality the seventeen year old James Gatz - that was really, or at least legally, his name – son of shiftless and unsuccessful farm people, had chanced upon the silver tycoon Dan Cody's yacht on Lake Superior and helped him out of a storms way. Cody employed Gatsby in a vague personal capacity, and it was from Cody that he inherited money - a legacy of twenty-five thousand dollars.

He told me all this very much later, and he told me too about the autumn night, five years before, when Daisy's white face first came up to his own. He knew that when he kissed this girl, and forever wed his unutterable visions to her perishable breath, his mind would never romp again like the mind of God.

7

Some days later Gatsby called me on the phone.

"Daisy comes over quite often - in the afternoons." Would I come to lunch at her house tomorrow? Miss Baker would be there.

I remember I went, I remember we had beer, and we all took the inexplicable step of driving over to the city in the two cars and engaging the parlor of a suite in the Plaza Hotel. The prolonged and tumultuous argument that ended by herding us into that room eludes me, though.

"Open the whiskey, Tom," Daisy ordered. "And I'll make you a mint julep. Then you won't seem so stupid to yourself."

"Wait a minute," snapped Tom, "I want to ask Mr. Gatsby one question."

They were out in the open at last and Gatsby was content.

Daisy looked desperately from one to the other. "Please have a little self control."

"Your wife doesn't love you," said Gatsby. "She's never loved you. She loves me."

Daisy turned to me, and her voice, dropping an octave lower, filled the room with thrilling scorn: "Do you know why we left Chicago? I'm surprised that they didn't treat you to the story of that little spree."

"Daisy, that's all over now," Tom said earnestly. "It doesn't matter any more. Just tell him the truth - that you never loved him - and it's all wiped out forever."

The words seemed to bite physically into Gatsby.

"Daisy's leaving you."

"Nonsense."

"I am, though," she said with a visible effort. "PLEASE, Tom! I can't stand this any more."

"You two start on home, Daisy," said Tom. "In Mr. Gatsby's car."

She looked at Tom, alarmed now, but he insisted with magnanimous scorn.

"Go on. He won't annoy you. I think he realizes that his presumptuous little flirtation is over."

They were gone, without a word, snapped out, made accidental, isolated, like ghosts even from our pity.

After a moment Tom got up and began wrapping the unopened bottle of whiskey in the towel.

"Want any of this stuff? Jordan? . . . Nick?"

"No . . . I just remembered that today's my birthday."

I was thirty. Before me stretched the portentous menacing road of a new decade.

It was seven o'clock when we got into the coupé with him and started for Long Island. So we drove on toward death through the cooling twilight.

The young Greek, Michaelis, who ran the coffee joint beside the ashheaps was the principal witness at the inquest. He had strolled over to the garage and found George Wilson sick in his office - really sick, and a violent racket going on overhead.

"I've got my wife locked in up there," explained Wilson calmly. "She's going to stay there till the day after tomorrow and then we're going to move away."

Michaelis was astonished, and tried to find out what had happened. When he came outside again a little after seven he heard Mrs. Wilson's voice, loud and scolding, downstairs in the garage.

"Beat me!" he heard her cry. "Throw me down and beat me, you dirty little coward!"

A moment later she rushed out into the dusk, waving her hands and shouting; before he could move from his door the business was over.

The "death car" as the newspapers called it, didn't stop; it came out of the gathering darkness, wavered tragically for a moment and then disappeared around the next bend. The other car, the one going toward New York, came to rest a hundred yards beyond, and its driver hurried back to where Myrtle Wilson, her life violently extinguished, knelt in the road and mingled her thick, dark blood with the dust.

Michaelis and this man reached her first but when they had torn open her shirtwaist, still damp with perspiration, they saw that her left breast was swinging loose like a flap and there was no need to listen for the heart beneath. The mouth was wide open and ripped at the corners as though she had choked a little in giving up the tremendous vitality she had stored so long.

We saw the three or four automobiles and the crowd when we were still some distance away.

"Wreck!" said Tom. "That's good. Wilson'll have a little business at last. We'll take a look, just a look."

"O, my Ga-od! O, my Ga-od! Oh, Ga-od! Oh, my Ga-od!"

"What happened - that's what I want to know!"

"She ran out ina road. Son-of-a-bitch didn't even stopus car."

A pale, well-dressed Negro stepped near.

"It was a yellow car," he said, "big yellow car. New."

Tom helped Wilson into the office, and we drove slowly away until we were beyond the bend - then his foot came down hard and the coupé raced along through the night. In a little while I heard a low husky sob and saw that the tears were overflowing down his face.

"The God Damn coward!" he whimpered. "He didn't even stop his car."

At the Buchanans' house I declined their offer to come inside and walked slowly down the drive intending to wait by the gate for a taxi. I hadn't gone twenty yards when I heard my name, and Gatsby stepped from between two bushes into the path.

"Did you see any trouble on the road?" he asked.

"Yes."

He hesitated.

"Was she killed?"

"Yes."

"I thought so; I told Daisy I thought so. It's better that the shock should all come at once. She stood it pretty well."

He spoke as if Daisy's reaction was the only thing that mattered.

"Who was the woman?" he inquired.

"Her name was Wilson. Her husband owns the garage. How the devil did it happen?"

"Well, I tried to swing the wheel - " He broke off, and suddenly I guessed at the truth.

"Was Daisy driving?"

"Yes," he said after a moment, "but of course I'll say I was."

"It ripped her open - "

"Don't tell me, old sport." He winced.

"You'd better come home and get some sleep."

He shook his head. "I want to wait here till Daisy goes to bed. Good night, old sport."

He put his hands in his coat pockets and turned back eagerly to his scrutiny of the house, as though my presence marred the sacredness of the vigil. So I walked away and left him standing there in the moonlight - watching over nothing.

8

I couldn't sleep all night; a fog-horn was groaning incessantly on the Sound. Toward dawn I crossed the lawn to find Gatsby leaning against a table in the hall, heavy with dejection or sleep.

"You ought to go away," I said. "It's pretty certain they'll trace your car."

He wouldn't consider it. He couldn't possibly leave Daisy until he knew what she was going to do. He was clutching at some last hope and I couldn't bear to shake him free.

"Of course she might have loved him, just for a minute, when they were first married - and loved me more even then, do you see? In any case, it was just personal."

What could you make of that, except to suspect some intensity in his conception of the affair that couldn't be measured?

"I'll call you up," I said finally.

"I suppose Daisy'll call too." He looked at me anxiously.

"I suppose so."

"Well - goodbye."

We shook hands and I started away.

"They're a rotten crowd," I shouted across the lawn. "You're worth the whole damn bunch put together."

I've always been glad I said that. It was the only compliment I ever gave him, because I disapproved of him from beginning to end.

Now I want to go back a little and tell what happened at the garage the night before.

Until long after midnight a changing crowd lapped up against the front of the garage while George Wilson rocked himself back and forth on the couch inside. He announced that he had a way of finding out whom the yellow car belonged to, and then he blurted out that a couple of months ago his wife had come from the city with her face bruised and her nose swollen. She had bought a dog leash, he knew it was something funny.

"He murdered her."

"It was an accident, George."

"You may fool me," he muttered, after a long silence. "but you can't fool God!' "

At two o'clock Gatsby gave instructions that the open car wasn't to be taken out under any circumstances - and this was strange because the front right fender needed repair. He shouldered a pneumatic mattress and started for the pool.

The chauffeur - he was one of Wolfshiem's protégés - heard the shots. I drove from the station directly to Gatsby's house and four of us, the chauffeur, butler, gardener and I, hurried down to the pool.

There was a faint, barely perceptible movement of the water as the laden mattress revolved slowly, tracing, like the leg of compass, a thin red circle in the water.

It was after we started with Gatsby toward the house that the gardener saw Wilson's body a little way off in the grass, and the holocaust was complete.

9

After two years I remember the rest of that day only as an endless drill of police and photographers and newspaper men in and out of Gatsby's front door.

I called up Daisy half an hour after we found him, but she and Tom had gone away early that afternoon, and left no address.

When the phone rang at Gatsby's that afternoon it was a man's voice, very thin and far away.

"This is Slagle speaking. Get my wire? Young Parke's in trouble," he said rapidly. "They picked him up when he handed the bonds over the counter - "

"Hello!" I interrupted breathlessly. "Look here - this isn't Mr. Gatsby. Mr. Gatsby's dead."

There was a long silence . . . then a quick squawk as the connection was broken.

I think it was on the third day that Henry C. Gatz arrived from a town in Minnesota. Gatsby's father was a solemn old man, very helpless and dismayed, bundled up in a long cheap ulster against the warm September day.

"I saw it in the Chicago newspaper," he said.

"I didn't know how to reach you." I said.

The morning of the funeral I went up to New York to see Meyer Wolfshiem; I couldn't seem to reach him any other way. I found him at his "Swastika Holding Company."

"You were his closest friend," I said, "so I know you'll want to come to his funeral this afternoon."

"I can't do it - I can't get mixed up in it," he said.

For a moment I thought he was going to suggest a "gonnegtion" but he only nodded and shook my hand.

I spent my Saturday nights in New York because those gleaming, dazzling parties of his were with me so vividly that I could still hear the music and the laughter faint and incessant from his garden and the cars going up and down his drive. One night I did hear a material car stop at his front steps. Probably some final guest who didn't know that the party was over.

On the last night, with my trunk packed, I wandered down to the beach and sprawled out on the sand. And as I sat there brooding on the old, unknown world, I thought of Gatsby's wonder when he first picked out the green light at the end of Daisy's dock. He had come a long way to this blue lawn and his dream must have seemed so close that he could hardly fail to grasp it. He did not know that it was already behind him.

Gatsby believed in the green light, the orgastic future that year by year recedes before us. It eluded us then, but that's no matter - tomorrow we will run faster, stretch out our arms farther. . . . And one fine morning -

So we beat on, boats against the current, borne back ceaselessly into the past.

Lady Chatterley's Lover
by D H Lawrence
(Florence, 1928)

There is nothing new about the erotic in fiction (see p51, p276 etc). What shocked genteel English society in *Lady Chatterley* was an aristocratic woman having a relationship with a social inferior, the indecent exposure of upper-class sexual habits with their preference for dynasty above love, and, worst of all, that in a new, affordable 'Penguin' paperback, the lower orders could read about it. Prosecuted in England for obscenity in 1960, the jury were asked if this was a book they would wish their servants to read. They decided that, now, it was.

Abridged: GH.

Ours is essentially a tragic age, so we refuse to take it tragically. The cataclysm has happened, we are among the ruins, we start to build up new little habitats, to have new little hopes. We've got to live, no matter how many skies have fallen.

This was more or less Constance Chatterley's position. The war had brought the roof down over her head. She married Clifford Chatterley in 1917, when he was home for a month on leave. They had a month's honeymoon. Then he went back to Flanders: to be shipped over to England again six months later, more or less in bits, with the lower half of his body, from the hips down, paralysed for ever. Constance, was then twenty-three years old, and he was twenty-nine.

This was in 1920. They returned, Clifford and Constance, to his home, Wragby Hall, the family 'seat'. His father had died, Clifford was now a baronet, Sir Clifford, and Constance was Lady Chatterley. Crippled for ever, knowing he could never have any children, Clifford came home to the smoky Midlands to keep the Chatterley name alive while he could.

He was not really downcast. He could wheel himself about in a wheeled chair, and he had a bath-chair with a small motor attachment, so he could drive himself slowly round the garden and into the melancholy park, of which he was really so proud.

Constance was a ruddy, country-looking girl with soft brown hair and sturdy body, and slow movements, full of unusual energy. Her father was the once well-known R.A., her mother one of the cultivated Fabians in the palmy, rather pre-Raphaelite days. Constance and her sister Hilda had been taken to Paris and Florence and Rome to breathe in art, and they had been taken also to the Hague and Berlin, to great Socialist conventions.

Both Hilda and Constance had had their tentative love-affairs by the time they were eighteen. And however one might sentimentalize it, this sex business was one of the most ancient, sordid connexions and subjections. Poets who glorified it were mostly men. Women had always known there was something better, something higher, than mere crisis and orgasm.

* * *

Wragby was a long low old house in brown stone, a warren of a place without much distinction. It stood on an eminence in a rather old park of oak trees, but alas, one could see in the near distance the chimney of Tevershall pit, with its clouds of steam and smoke, and on the damp, hazy distance of the hill the raw straggle of Tevershall village, a village which began almost at the park gates, and trailed in utter hopeless ugliness for a long and gruesome mile.

Connie was accustomed to Kensington or the Scotch hills. With the stoicism[1] of the young she took in the utter, soulless ugliness of the coal-and-iron Midlands at a glance.

Connie and Clifford were attached to one another, in the aloof modern way. He was a hurt thing. And as such Connie stuck to him passionately. But she could not help feeling how little connexion he really had with people. The miners were, in a sense, his own men; but he saw them as objects rather than men, parts of the pit rather than parts of life.

He had taken to writing stories; curious, very personal stories about people he had known. Clever, rather spiteful, and yet, in some mysterious way, meaningless. They appeared in the most modern magazines, and were praised and blamed as usual.

Connie's father, where he paid a flying visit to Wragby, said to her: 'I hope you won't let circumstances force you into being a demi-vierge - a half virgin. Why don't you get yourself a beau, Connie? Do you all the good in the world.'

Time went on. Whatever happened, nothing happened. Time went on as the clock does, half past eight instead of half past seven.

* * *

Connie was aware of a growing restlessness. And she was getting thinner. Vaguely she knew herself that she was going to pieces in some way.

That winter Michaelis came for a few days. He was a young Irishman who had made a large fortune by his plays in America. He arrived in a very neat car, with a chauffeur and a manservant. He was absolutely Bond Street, this Dublin mongrel!

---

1   **Stoicism** (see p84)

He sent a servant to ask, could he be of any service to Lady Chatterley: he thought of driving into Sheffield. The answer came, would he care to go up to Lady Chatterley's sitting-room.

Connie had a sitting-room on the third floor, the top floor of the central portion of the house. Clifford's rooms were on the ground floor, of course. She and Michaelis sit on opposite sides of the fire and talked.

He was a curious and very gentle lover, very gentle with the woman, trembling uncontrollably, and yet at the same time detached, aware, aware of every sound outside.

To her it meant nothing except that she gave herself to him.

'And now, I suppose you'll hate me, they mostly do,' he said; then he caught himself up. 'I mean...a woman is supposed to.'

'No, I don't hate you,' she said. 'I think you're nice.'

* * *

Connie always had a foreboding of the hopelessness of her affair with Mick, as people called him. Yet she was attached to Clifford.

Clifford was making strides into fame, and even money. People came to see him. Connie nearly always had somebody at Wragby. But if they weren't mackerel they were herring, with an occasional cat-fish, or conger-eel.

There were a few regular men, constants; men who had been at Cambridge with Clifford. There was Tommy Dukes, who had remained in the army, and was a Brigadier-General. 'The army leaves me time to think, and saves me from having to face the battle of life,' he said.

There was Charles May, an Irishman, who wrote scientifically about stars. There was Hammond, another writer. All were about the same age as Clifford; the young intellectuals of the day. They all believed in the life of the mind. What you did apart from that was your private affair, and didn't much matter.

There was a gorgeous talk on Sunday evening, when the conversation drifted to love.

'The whole point about the sexual problem,' said Hammond, 'is that there is no point to it. We don't want to follow a man into the w.c., so why should we want to follow him into bed with a woman?'

'Quite, Hammond, quite! But if someone starts making love to Julia, you begin to simmer.'...Julia was Hammond's wife.

'Blest be the tie that binds', said Tommy Dukes. 'The tie that binds us just now is mental friction on one another. And, apart from that, there's damned little tie between us. We bust apart, and say spiteful things about one another, like all the other damned intellectuals in the world. Always has been so! Look at Socrates and his bunch round him! And Jesus, telling his disciples little Sunday stories. No, there's something wrong with the mental life, radically. It's rooted in spite and envy, envy and spite.'

* * *

On a frosty morning with a little February sun, Clifford and Connie went for a walk across the park to the wood. That is, Clifford chuffed in his motor-chair, and Connie walked beside him.

The sheep coughed in the rough, sere grass of the park, where frost lay bluish in the sockets of the tufts. Clifford loved the wood; he loved the old oak-trees. He felt they were his own through generations. He wanted to protect them. He wanted this place inviolate, shut off from the world.

'I consider this is really the heart of England,' said Clifford to Connie, 'I mind more, not having a son, when I come here, than any other time,' he said.

'I'm sorry we can't have a son,' she said.

'It would almost be a good thing if you had a child by another man, he said. 'If we brought it up at Wragby, it would belong to us and to the place.'

'But what about the other man?' she asked.

'Does it matter very much? Do these things really affect us very deeply?'

She was watching a brown spaniel that had run out of a side-path, and was looking towards them with lifted nose, making a soft, fluffy bark. A man with a gun strode swiftly, softly out. It was only the new game-keeper, but he had frightened Connie, he seemed to emerge with such a swift menace. That was how she had seen him, like the sudden rush of a threat out of nowhere. He was a man in dark green velveteens and gaiters...the old style, with a red face and red moustache and distant eyes.

'Mellors!' called Clifford.

The man faced lightly round, and saluted with a quick little gesture, a soldier!

'Will you turn the chair round and get it started?' said Clifford.

'Connie, this is the new game-keeper, Mellors.'

He gave another slight bow, turned, put his hat on, and strode to take hold of the chair. Clifford started the little engine, the man carefully turned the chair, and set it nose-forwards to the incline that curved gently to the dark hazel thicket.

'Thanks for the help, Mellors,' said Clifford casually.

'Good morning, Sir.'

'Good morning!' said Connie, looking back at the keeper.

His eyes came to hers in an instant, as if wakened up. He was aware of her.

Then his voice dropped again into the broad sound of the vernacular: 'Good mornin' to your Ladyship!'

* * *

The next afternoon she went to the wood again. The place was a little sinister, cold, damp. And she noticed a narrow track between young fir-trees, a track that seemed to lead nowhere. She saw a secret little clearing, and a secret little hut made of rustic poles. And she had never been here before! She realized it was the quiet place where the growing pheasants were reared; the keeper in his shirt-sleeves was kneeling, hammering.

He straightened himself and saluted, watching her in silence, as she came forward with weakening limbs. He resented the intrusion; he cherished his solitude as his only and last freedom in life.

'I wondered what the hammering was,' she said, feeling weak and breathless, and a little afraid of him, as he looked so straight at her.

'Ah'm gettin' th' coops ready for th' young bods,' he said, in broad vernacular.

'I should like to sit down a bit,' she said.

'Come and sit 'ere i' th' 'ut,' he said. 'Am Ah t' light yer a little fire?'

'Oh, don't bother,' she replied.

'Sit 'ere then a bit, and warm yer,' he said.

She obeyed him. The hut was quite cosy, panelled with unvarnished deal, having a little rustic table and stool beside her chair, and a carpenter's bench, then a big box, tools, new boards, nails.

'It is so nice here, so restful,' she said. 'Do you lock the hut when you're not here?'

'Yes, your Ladyship.'

'Do you think I could have a key too, so that I could sit here sometimes?'

Their eyes met. His had a cold, ugly look of dislike and contempt, and indifference to what would happen. Hers were hot with rebuff.

'Afternoon, my Lady!' She had wakened the sleeping dogs of old voracious anger in him, anger against the self-willed female. And he was powerless, powerless. He knew it!

She looked at him.

'Why don't you speak ordinary English?' she said coldly.

'Me! AH thowt it wor ordinary.'

* * *

Connie was surprised at her own feeling of aversion from Clifford. And Clifford the same. All that talk! All that writing! But at least, Clifford was shifting his grip from her on to his nurse, Mrs Bolton.

Mrs Bolton was admirable in many ways. But she had that queer sort of bossiness, endless assertion of her own will, which is one of the signs of insanity in modern woman. She thought she was utterly subservient and living for others.

Nevertheless, one got a new vision of Tevershall village from Mrs Bolton's talk. A terrible, seething welter of ugly life it seemed: not at all the flat drabness it looked from outside. Clifford of course knew by sight most of the people mentioned, Connie knew only one or two. But it sounded really more like a Central African jungle than an English village.

'Is there much Socialism, Bolshevism, among the people?' Clifford asked.

'Oh!' said Mrs Bolton, 'you hear a few loud-mouthed ones. But I don't believe you'll ever turn our Tevershall men into reds. They're too decent for that.'

Under Mrs Bolton's influence, Clifford began to take a new interest in the mines. He began to feel he belonged.

* * *

Connie was a good deal alone now, fewer people came to Wragby. Clifford no longer wanted them. He had turned against even the cronies. She fled as much as possible to the wood. One afternoon, as she sat brooding, the keeper had strode up to her.

'I got you a key made, my Lady!' he said, saluting, and he offered her the key.

'But I didn't want you to trouble!' she said.

'I am setting the hens in about a week. But they won't be scared of you.'

He seemed kindly, but distant. But at least he was sane, and wholesome, if even he looked thin and ill. A cough troubled him.

'You have a cough,' she said.

'Nothing - a cold! The last pneumonia left me with a cough, but it's nothing.'

He had made the hut tidy, put the little table and chair near the fireplace, left a little pile of kindling and small logs, and put the tools and traps away as far as possible, effacing himself. And, one day when she came, she found two brown hens sitting alert and fierce in the coops, sitting on pheasants' eggs, and fluffed out so proud and deep in all the heat of the pondering female blood. This almost broke Connie's heart. She, herself was so forlorn and unused, not a female at all, just a mere thing of terrors.

One evening, guests or no guests, she escaped after tea. She arrived at the clearing flushed and semi-conscious. The keeper was there, in his shirt-sleeves, just closing up the coops for the night, so the little occupants would be safe.

'I had to come and see the chickens!' she said, panting, glancing shyly at the keeper, almost unaware of him. 'Are there any more?'

'Thurty-six so far!' he said. 'Not bad!'

'I'd love to touch them,' she said, putting her fingers gingerly through the bars of the coop.

The man standing above her laughed, and crouched down beside her, knees apart, and put his hand with quiet confidence slowly into the coop. And slowly, softly, with sure gentle fingers, he felt among the old bird's feathers and drew out a faintly-peeping chick in his closed hand.

'There!' he said, holding out his hand to her. She took the little drab thing between her hands, and there it stood, on its impossible little stalks of legs, its atom of balancing life trembling through its almost weightless feet into Connie's hands.

The keeper, squatting beside her, saw a tear fall on to her wrist.

And he stood up, and stood away, moving to the other coop. For suddenly he was aware of the old flame shooting and leaping up in his loins, that he had hoped was quiescent for ever.

'You shouldn't cry,' he said softly.'Shall you come to the hut?'

His face was pale and without expression, like that of a man submitting to fate.

'You lie there,' he said softly, and he shut the door, so that it was dark, quite dark.

With a queer obedience, she lay down on the blanket. Then she felt the soft, groping, helplessly desirous hand touching her body, feeling for her face. The hand stroked her face softly, softly, with infinite soothing and assurance, and at last there was the soft touch of a kiss on her cheek.

She lay quite still, in a sort of sleep, in a sort of dream. Then she quivered as she felt his hand groping softly, yet with queer thwarted clumsiness, among her clothing. Yet the hand knew, too, how to unclothe her where it wanted. Then with a quiver of exquisite pleasure he touched the warm soft body, and touched her navel for a moment in a kiss. And he had to come in to her at once, to enter the peace on earth of her soft, quiescent body. It was the moment of pure peace for him, the entry into the body of the woman.

She lay still, in a kind of sleep, always in a kind of sleep. The activity, the orgasm was his, all his; she could strive for herself no more. Even the tightness of his arms round her, even the intense movement of his body, and the springing of his seed in her, was a kind of sleep, from which she did not begin to rouse till he had finished and lay softly panting against her breast.

Then she wondered, just dimly wondered, why? Why was this necessary? Was it real? Was it real? She was old; millions of years old, she felt. She was to be had for the taking. To be had for the taking.

She saw a very brilliant little moon shining above the afterglow over the oaks. Quickly she got up and arranged herself she was tidy. Then she went to the door of the hut.

'You aren't sorry, are you?' he asked, as he went at her side.

'No! No! Are you?' she said.

'In a way!' he replied, looking up at the sky. 'I thought I'd done with it all. Now I've begun again.'

'Begun what?'

'Life.'

'Life!' she re-echoed, with a queer thrill.

He kissed her softly, softly, with the kisses of warmth.

'Shall I come again?' she asked wistfully.

'Yes! Yes!'

* * *

The next day she did not go to the wood. She went instead with Clifford to Uthwaite to see his godfather, Leslie Winter, who lived at Shipley Hall. Towards Connie the Squire was always rather gallant; he himself had no heir.

Connie wondered what he would say if he knew that Clifford's game-keeper had been having intercourse with her, and saying to her 'tha mun come to th' cottage one time.' He would detest and despise her, for he had come almost to hate the shoving forward of the working classes. A man of her own class he would not mind.

She did not go to the wood that day nor the next, nor the day following. She did not go so long as she felt, or imagined she felt, the man waiting for her, wanting her. But the fourth day she was terribly unsettled and uneasy. She called at Marehay Farm, the Flints were Chatterley tenants, and was persuaded in to admire Mrs Flint's new baby.

Connie climbed the fence into the narrow path between the dense, bristling young firs. Yes, Mrs Flint had flaunted her motherhood. And Connie had been just a bit, just a little bit jealous. She couldn't help it.

She started out of her muse, and gave a little cry of fear. A man was there.

It was the keeper. He stood in the path like Balaam's ass, barring her way.

'And were you going to the hut now?' he asked rather sternly.

'No! I mustn't. I stayed at Marehay. No one knows where I am. I'm late. I've got to run.'

'Giving me the slip, like?' he said, with a faint ironic smile. 'No! No. Not that. Only - '

'Oh, not now, not now,' she cried, trying to push him away.

'Why not? It's only six o'clock. You've got half an hour. Nay! Nay! I want you.'

He held her fast and she felt his urgency. He looked around.

He led her through the wall of prickly trees, that were difficult to come through, to a place where was a little space and a pile of dead boughs. He threw one or two dry ones down, put his coat and waistcoat over them, and she had to lie down there under the boughs of the tree, like an animal, while he waited, standing there in his shirt and breeches, watching her with haunted eyes.

He bared the front part of his body and she felt his naked flesh against her as he came into her. Then as he began to move, in the sudden helpless orgasm, there awoke in her new strange thrills rippling inside her. Rippling, rippling, rippling, like a flapping overlapping of soft flames, soft as feathers, running to points of brilliance, exquisite, exquisite and melting her all molten inside. She lay unconscious of the wild little cries she uttered at the last. But it was over too soon, too soon, and she could no longer force her own conclusion with her own activity.

But he drew away at last, and kissed her and covered her over.

She turned and looked at him. 'We came off together that time,' he said.

She did not answer.

'It's good when it's like that. Most folks live their lives through and they never know it,' he said, speaking rather dreamily.

'Don't people often come off together?' she asked with naive curiosity.

'A good many of them never. You can see by the raw look of them.' He spoke unwittingly, regretting he had begun.

'Have you come off like that with other women?'

He looked at her amused.

'I don't know,' he said, 'I don't know.'

He put on his waistcoat and his coat, and pushed a way through to the path again.

Connie went slowly home, realizing the depth of the other thing in her. Another self was alive in her, burning molten and soft in her womb and bowels, and with this self she adored him. In her womb and bowels she was flowing and alive now and vulnerable, and helpless in adoration of him as the most naive woman. It feels like a child, she said to herself it feels like a child in me. And so it did, as if her womb, that had always been shut, had opened and filled with new life, almost a burden, yet lovely.

* * *

Connie was sorting out one of the Wragby lumber rooms. Wrapped up carefully to preserve it from damage and dry-rot was the old family cradle, of rosewood.

'It's thousand pities it won't be called for,' sighed Mrs Bolton, who was helping.

'It might be called for. I might have a child,' said Connie casually, as if saying she might have a new hat.

'You mean if anything happened to Sir Clifford!' stammered Mrs Bolton.

'No! I mean as things are. It's only muscular paralysis with Sir Clifford - it doesn't affect him,' said Connie, lying as naturally as breathing.

'Well, my Lady, I only hope and pray you may. It would be lovely for you: and for everybody. My word, a child in Wragby, what a difference it would make!'

But oh my dear! Mrs Bolton was thinking to herself. Is it Oliver Mellors' child you're preparing us for? Oh my dear, that would be a Tevershall baby in the Wragby cradle, my word! Wouldn't shame it, neither!

* * *

'I had a letter from Father this morning,' Connie said. 'He wants to know if I am aware he has accepted Sir Alexander Cooper's Invitation for me for July and August, to the Villa Esmeralda in Venice.'

'Well,' said Clifford slowly, and a little gloomily. 'I suppose I could stand it for three weeks: if I were absolutely sure you'd want to come back.'

'I should want to come back,' she said, with a quiet simplicity, heavy with conviction. She was thinking of the other man.

She went away gloomily. But she was going as a sort of discipline: and also because, if she had a child, Clifford could think she had a lover in Venice.

It was already May, and in June they were supposed to start. Always these arrangements! The car ploughed uphill through the long squalid straggle of Tevershall, the blackened brick dwellings, the black slate roofs glistening their sharp edges, the mud black with coal-dust, the pavements wet and black. What could possibly become of such a people, a people in whom the living intuitive faculty was dead as nails, and only queer mechanical yells and uncanny will-power remained?

Merrie England! Shakespeare's England! No, but the England of today, as Connie had realized since she had come to live in it. Half-corpses, all of them: but with a terrible insistent consciousness in the other half. Yet Mellors had come out of all this! - Yes, but he was as apart from it all as she was.

Children from such men! Oh God, oh God!

* * *

Connie went to the wood directly after lunch. It was really a lovely day, the first dandelions making suns, the first daisies so white. Everywhere the bud-knots and the leap of life!

The keeper was not at the hut. Connie walked on towards the cottage, because she wanted to find him.

The cottage stood in the sun, off the wood's edge. He rose, and came to the door, wiping his mouth with a red handkerchief still chewing.

'May I come in?' she said.

'Come in!'

On the table was his plate, with potatoes and the remains of the chop; also bread in a basket, salt, and a blue mug with beer. The table-cloth was white oil-cloth, he stood in the shade.

'I'm going away for a while next month,' she said.

'You are! Where to?'

'Venice! For a month or so,' she replied. 'Clifford won't go. He hates to travel as he is.'

'Ay, poor devil!' he said, with sympathy.

'I might have a love-affair in Venice,' she said.

'You might,' he replied slowly. 'So that's why you're going?'

'Not to have the love-affair,' she said, looking up at him, pleading.

'Just the appearance of one,' he said.

There was silence. He sat staring out the window, with a faint grin, half mockery, half bitterness, on his face. She hated his grin.

'That was why you wanted me, then, to get a child? 'Well,' he said at last. 'It's as your Ladyship likes. If you get the baby, Sir Clifford's welcome to it. I shan't have lost anything. On the contrary, I've had a very nice experience, very nice indeed!'

'But I didn't make use of you,' she said, pleading. 'I liked your body.'

'Did you?' he replied, and he laughed. 'Well, then, we're quits, because I liked yours.'

'Shall us go i' th' 'ut?' he asked.

'Do you want me?' she asked, in a sort of mistrust.

'Ay, if you want to come.'

She was silent.

'Come then!' he said.

He spread the blankets, putting one at the side for a coverlet. She took off her hat, and shook her hair. He sat down, taking off his shoes and gaiters, and undoing his cord breeches.

'Eh, but tha'rt nice, tha'rt nice!' he said, suddenly rubbing his face with a snuggling movement against her warm belly.

And she put her arms round him under his shirt, but she was afraid, afraid of his thin, smooth, naked body, that seemed so powerful, afraid of the violent muscles. She began to weep.

'What's amiss?' he said. 'It's once in a while that way.'

'I...I can't love you,' she sobbed, suddenly feeling her heart breaking.

'Canna ter? Well, dunna fret! There's no law says as tha's got to. Ta'e it for what it is.'

* * *

'How strange!' she said slowly. 'How strange he stands there! So big! and so dark and cock-sure! Is he like that?'

'So proud!' she murmured, uneasy. 'And so lordly! Now I know why men are so overbearing! But he's lovely, really. Like another being! A bit terrifying! But lovely really!'

'Ay!' he said at last, in a little voice. 'Ay ma lad! Theer on thy own, eh? Art boss? of me? Dost want her? Dost want my lady Jane? Ay, th' cheek on thee! Cunt, that's what tha're after. Tell lady Jane tha wants cunt.'

'Oh, don't tease him,' said Connie, crawling on her knees on the bed towards him and putting her arms round his white slender loins.

'Lie down!' he said. 'Lie down! Let me come!' He was in a hurry now.

'John Thomas! John Thomas!' and she quickly kissed the soft penis, that was beginning to stir again.

There was silence through the lovely dewy wood. But they were together in a world of their own.

* * *

Connie had been at Venice a fortnight, and was in a sort of stupor of well-being. From which a letter of Clifford roused her.

We too have had our mild local excitement. It appears the truant wife of Mellors, the keeper, turned up. He beat a retreat and retired, it is said, to his mother's house in Tevershall. This Bertha Coutts has blown off an amazing quantity of poison-gas. She has aired in detail all those incidents of her conjugal life which are usually buried down in the deepest grave of matrimonial silence. Humanity has always had a strange avidity for unusual sexual postures, and if a man likes to use his wife, as Benvenuto Cellini says, 'in the Italian way', well that is a matter of taste. The execrable Bertha Coutts has discovered, at the top of her voice, that her husband has been 'keeping' women down at the cottage, and has made a few random shots at naming the women. Meanwhile, my dear Connie, if you would enjoy to stay in Venice or in Switzerland till the beginning of August, I should be glad to think you were out of all this buzz of nastiness.

The irritation, and the lack of any sympathy in any direction, of Clifford's letter, had a bad effect on Connie. But she understood it better when she received the following from Mellors:

The cat is out of the bag, along with various other pussies. You have heard that my wife Bertha came back to my unloving arms, and took up her abode in the cottage. Unfortunately, she found one of your books, with your name on the front page. I shall go to London, and my old landlady, Mrs Inger, 17 Coburg Square, will either give me a room or will find one for me.

* * *

In London on the Monday following, they walked together by the remoter streets to Coburg Square, where he had a room at the top of the house, an attic room where he cooked for himself on a gas ring. It was small, but decent and tidy.

'Say you're glad about the child,' she said.

'I've a dread of puttin' children i' th' world,' he said. 'I've such a dread o' th' future for 'em.'

* * *

So Connie left Wragby, and went on with Hilda to Scotland. Mellors went into the country and got work on a farm. The idea was, he should get his divorce, if possible, whether Connie got hers or not. And for six months he should work at farming, so that eventually he and Connie could have some small farm of their own, into which he could put his energy. So they would have to wait till spring was in, till the baby was born, till the early summer came round again.

The Grange Farm Old Heanor 29 September: Here I get thirty shillings a week as labourer. Patience, always patience. This is my fortieth winter. But I'll stick to my little Pentecost flame, and have some peace. And if you're in Scotland and I'm in the Midlands, and I can't put my arms round you, and wrap my legs round you, yet I've got something of you. We fucked a flame into being. So I love chastity now, because it is the peace that comes of fucking. I love being chaste now. I love it as snowdrops love the snow.

Well, so many words, because I can't touch you. If I could sleep with my arms round you, the ink could stay in the bottle. We could be chaste together just as we can fuck together. But we have to be separate for a while, and I suppose it is really the wiser way. But a great deal of us is together, and we can but abide by it, and steer our courses to meet soon. John Thomas says good-night to Lady Jane, a little droopingly, but with a hopeful heart.

The Remembrance of Times Past
(*À la recherche du temps perdu / In Search of Lost Time*)
by Marcel Proust
(Paris, 1913-31)

The wealthy Proust spent the later years of his life largely confined to a cork-lined room, writing this extraordinary semi-autobiography, a truly vast narrative across seven volumes. Here is the better-known first part, 'Combray' - his evocation of how our past experiences can return to life, in what psychology calls the 'Proust effect'.

Abridged: GH, from the translation by C.K. Scott Moncrieff.

OVERTURE

For a long time I used to go to bed early. Sometimes, when I had put out my candle, my eyes would close so quickly that I had not even time to say "I'm going to sleep." And half an hour later the thought that it was time to go to sleep would awaken me.

When a man is asleep, he has in a circle round him the chain of the hours, the sequence of the years, the order of the heavenly host. At the moment of waking, he will have no idea of the time, but will conclude that he has just gone to bed. But for me it was enough if, in my own bed, my sleep was so heavy as completely to relax my consciousness; for I had only the most rudimentary sense of existence, such as may lurk and flicker in the depths of an animal's consciousness; but then the memory, not yet of the place in which I was, but of various other places where I had lived, and might now very possibly be, would come like a rope let down from heaven to draw me up out of the abyss of not-being, from which I could never have escaped by myself.

As a rule, I would not attempt to go to sleep again at once, but used to spend the greater part of the night recalling our life in the old days at Combray with my great-aunt, at Balbec, Paris, Doncières, Venice, and the rest. At Combray, as every afternoon ended, long before the time when I should have to go up to bed, and to lie there, unsleeping, far from my mother and grandmother, my bedroom became the fixed point on which my melancholy and anxious thoughts were centred.

Some one had had the happy idea of giving me, to distract me, a magic lantern, which used to be set on top of my lamp while we waited for dinner-time to come: in the manner of the master-builders and glass-painters of gothic days it substituted for the opaqueness of my walls an impalpable iridescence, supernatural phenomena of many colours, in which legends were depicted, as on a shifting and transitory window. I found plenty of charm in these bright projections, which seemed to have come straight out of a past of Merovingian castles, and to shed around me the reflections of such ancient history. And as soon as the dinner-bell rang I would run down to the dining-room, to the dish of stewed beef; and I would fall into the arms of my mother.

But after dinner, alas, I was soon obliged to leave Mamma, who stayed talking with the others, in the garden if it was fine, or in the little parlour when it was wet. Everyone except my grandmother, who held that "It is a pity to shut oneself indoors in the country," and was only borough in by my great-aunt calling out to her: "Bathilde! Come in and stop your husband from drinking brandy!"

My sole, brief, consolation when I went upstairs for the night was that Mamma would come in and kiss me after I was in bed. But on those evenings on which we had guests to dinner, she did not come at all.

Our 'guests' were practically limited to M. Swann, who came (now less frequently since his unfortunate marriage, as my family did not care to receive his wife) sometimes after dinner, uninvited. Although a far younger man, M. Swann was very much attached to my grandfather, who had been an intimate friend, in his time, of Swann's father. My great-aunt and grandparents never suspected that in Swann they were harbouring one of the smartest members of the Jockey Club, a particular friend of the Comte de Paris and of the Prince of Wales. Our utter ignorance of the brilliant part which Swann was playing in the world of fashion was due in part to his own reserve, but also to that middle-class, almost Hindu, view of society, which held to sharply defined castes, so that everyone at his birth found himself called to that station in life which his parents already occupied, from which nothing, except the chance of a brilliant career or of a 'good' marriage, could extract you.

But on one occasion my grandfather read in a newspaper that M. Swann was one of the most faithful attendants at the Sunday luncheons given by the Duc de X--. Now my grandfather was curious to learn all the little details. And so, on the day that Swann next arrived, we all sat down round the iron table, and conversations began. And then, before the dinner, my father said with unconscious cruelty: "Run along; to bed with you, little man. "Leave your mother alone. You've said good night quite enough. Go on upstairs."

Once in my room I had to stop every loophole, to close the shutters, to dig my own grave as I turned down the bed-clothes, to wrap myself in the shroud of my nightshirt. But before burying myself in the iron bed I was stirred to revolt, and attempted the desperate stratagem of a condemned prisoner. I wrote a note to my mother begging her to come upstairs, and sent it to her, by way of Françoise, my aunt's cook who used to be put in charge of me at Combray.

I lay down and shut my eyes, and realised that, by writing that line to Mamma, I had cut myself off from the possibility of going to sleep until I actually had seen her. In time, I heard my father saying: "Well, shall we go up to bed?", and I went quietly into the passage; my heart beating so violently that I could hardly move with terror and with joy. I saw in the well of the stair a light coming upwards, from Mamma's candle. Then I saw Mamma herself: I threw myself upon her, and her face assumed an expression of anger. "We must not make him accustomed," said my father, with a shrug of the shoulders; "but you can see that the child is unhappy. After all, we aren't gaolers.

Mamma spent that night in my room. It struck me that if I had just scored a victory it was over her; that I had succeeded, as sickness or sorrow or age might have succeeded, in relaxing her will, in altering her judgement; that this evening opened a new era, must remain a black date in the calendar.

Many years had elapsed during which nothing of Combray, save what was comprised in the theatre and the drama of my going to bed there, had any existence for me, when one day in winter, as I came home, my mother, seeing that I was cold, offered me some tea, a thing I did not ordinarily take. I declined at first, and then, for no particular reason, changed my mind. She sent out for one of those short, plump little cakes called 'madeleines,' which look as though they had been moulded in the fluted scallop of a pilgrim's shell. And soon, mechanically, weary after a dull day with the prospect of a depressing morrow, I raised to my lips a spoonful of the tea in which I had soaked a morsel of the cake. No sooner had the warm liquid, and the crumbs with it, touched my palate than a shudder ran through my whole body, and I stopped, intent upon the extraordinary changes that were taking place. At once the vicissitudes of life had become indifferent to me, its disasters innocuous, its brevity illusory - this new sensation having had on me the effect which love has of filling me with a precious essence; or rather this essence was not in me, it was myself. I had ceased now to feel mediocre, accidental, mortal. Whence could it have come to me, this all-powerful joy? I was conscious that it was connected with the taste of tea and cake, but that it infinitely transcended those savours, could not, indeed, be of the same nature as theirs. Whence did it come? What did it signify? How could I seize upon and define it?

And suddenly the memory returns. The taste was that of the little crumb of madeleine which on Sunday mornings at Combray, when I went to say good day to her in her bedroom, my aunt Léonie used to give me, dipping it first in her own cup of real or of lime-flower tea. The sight of the little madeleine had recalled nothing to my mind before I tasted it, but when from a long-distant past nothing subsists, after the people are dead, after the things are broken and scattered, still, alone, more fragile, but with more vitality, more unsubstantial, more persistent, more faithful, the smell and taste of things remain poised a long time, like souls, ready to remind us, waiting and hoping for their moment, amid the ruins of all the rest; and bear unfaltering, in the tiny and almost impalpable drop of their essence, the vast structure of recollection.

Just as the Japanese amuse themselves by filling a porcelain bowl with water and steeping in it little crumbs of paper which, the moment they become wet, stretch themselves and bend, become flowers or houses or people, so in that moment all the flowers in our garden and in M. Swann's park, and the water-lilies on the Vivonne and the good folk of the village and their little dwellings and the parish church and the whole of Combray sprang into being from my cup of tea.

COMBRAY

To live in, Combray was a trifle depressing, like its streets of blackened stone. Streets with the solemn names of Saints; the Rue Saint-Hilaire, and the Rue Saint-Jacques, in which my aunt's house stood. My grandfather's cousin - by courtesy my great-aunt - with whom we used to stay, had gradually declined to leave, first Combray, then her house in Combray, then her bedroom, and finally her bed; and who now never 'came down,' but lay perpetually in an indefinite condition of grief, physical exhaustion, illness, obsessions, and religious observances. At one side of her bed stood a big yellow chest-of-drawers of lemon-wood, and a table which served at once as pharmacy and as high altar, on which, beneath a statue of Our Lady and a bottle of Vichy-Célestins, might be found her service-books and her medical prescriptions, everything that she needed for the performance, in bed, of her duties to soul and body, to keep the proper times for pepsin and for vespers.

Everyone was so well known in Combray, animals as well as people, that if my aunt had happened to see a dog go by which she 'didn't know at all' she would think about it incessantly, devoting to the solution of the incomprehensible problem all her inductive talent and her leisure hours. "That will be Mme. Sazerat's dog," Françoise would suggest, without any real conviction, but in the hope of peace. "I can't afford to stay here amusing myself; look, it's nearly ten o'clock and I've still to dress the asparagus." "What, Françoise, more asparagus! It's a regular disease of asparagus you have got this year: you will make our Parisians sick of it."

While my aunt gossiped on in this way with Françoise I would have accompanied my parents to mass. How I loved it: how clearly I can see it still, our church at Combray! Blackened and worn down by the gentle grazing touch of peasant-women, its memorial stones, beneath which lay the noble dust of the Abbots of Combray, furnished the choir with a sort of spiritual pavement. Two tapestries of high warp represented the coronation of Esther, in which tradition would have it that the weaver had given to Ahasuerus the features of one of the kings of France and to Esther those of a lady of Guermantes whose lover he had been.

All these things and, more than these, made of the church for me something entirely different from the rest of the town; a building which occupied, so to speak, four dimensions of space - the name of the fourth being Time - which had sailed the centuries with that old nave, where bay after bay, chapel after chapel, seemed to stretch across and hold down and conquer not merely a few yards of soil, but each successive epoch from which the whole building had emerged triumphant. It was the steeple of Saint-Hilaire which shaped and crowned and consecrated every occupation, every hour of the day, every point of view in the town.

On our way home from mass we would often meet M. Legrandin, a Parisian engineer, with more than some skill as a 'man of letters'. "Well met, my friends!" he would say. "Always try to keep a patch of sky above your life, little boy," he added, turning to me. You have a soul in you of rare quality, an artist's nature; never let it starve for lack of what it needs."

When, on our reaching the house, my aunt would send to ask us whether Mme. Goupil had indeed arrived late for mass, not one of us could inform her. "Ah!" my aunt would sigh, "I wish it were time for Eulalie to come. She is really the only person who will be able to tell me."

Eulalie was a limping, energetic, deaf spinster who had retired from the service of Mme. de la Bretonnerie, and had then taken a room beside the church. Eulalie knew that her visits, which took place regularly every Sunday, were for my aunt a pleasure the prospect of which kept her in days of expectation, appetising enough to begin with, but at once changing to an agony of a hunger too long unsatisfied if Eulalie were a minute late in coming.

Our Sundays there were built by Françoise upon the permanent foundation of eggs, cutlets, potatoes, preserves, and biscuits, whose appearance on the table she no longer announced to us, to which Françoise would add - as the labour of fields and orchards, the harvest of the tides, the luck of the markets, the kindness of neighbours, and her own genius might provide; so effectively that our bill of fare, like the quatrefoils that were carved on the porches of cathedrals in the thirteenth century, reflected to some extent the march of the seasons and the incidents of human life - a brill, because the fish-woman had guaranteed its freshness; a turkey, because she had seen a beauty in the market at Roussainville-le-Pin; cardoons with marrow, because she had never done them for us in that way before; apricots, because they were still hard to get; raspberries, which M. Swann had brought specially; an almond cake, because she had ordered one the evening before; a fancy loaf, because it was our turn to 'offer' the holy bread. And when all these had been eaten, a work composed expressly for ourselves, but dedicated more particularly to my father, who had a fondness for such things, a cream of chocolate, inspired in the mind, created by the hand of Françoise, would be laid before us, light and fleeting as an 'occasional piece' of music, into which she had poured the whole of her talent. Anyone who refused to partake of it, saying: "No, thank you, I have finished; I am not hungry," would at once have been lowered to the level of the Philistines who, when an artist makes them a present of one of his works, examine its weight and material, whereas what is of value is the creator's intention and his signature. To have left even the tiniest morsel in the dish would have shewn as much discourtesy as to rise and leave a concert hall under the composer's very eyes while the 'piece' was still being played.

In earlier days I would steal into the little sitting-room which my uncle Adolphe, a brother of my grandfather and an old soldier who had retired from the service as a major, used to occupy on the ground floor, a room which suggesting at once an open-air and an old-fashioned kind of existence, which sets and keeps the nostrils dreaming when one goes into a disused gun-room. But for some years now I had not gone into my uncle Adolphe's room, since he no longer came to Combray on account of a quarrel which had arisen between him and my family.

At this date I was a lover of the theatre: a Platonic[1] lover, of necessity, since my parents had not yet allowed me to enter one. All my conversations with my playfellows bore upon actors, Got, Delaunay, Sarah Bernhardt, Berma, Bartet, Madeleine Brohan, and so on. Now my uncle knew many of them personally, and also ladies of another class, not

1   **Plato:** see p55

clearly distinguished from actresses in my mind. My uncle's fatal readiness to pay pretty widows (who had perhaps never been married) and countesses (whose high-sounding titles were probably no more than *noms de guerre*) the compliment of presenting them to my grandmother or even of presenting to them some of our family jewels, had already embroiled him more than once with my grandfather.

And so, taking advantage of the fact that my parents had had luncheon earlier than usual; I slipped out unaccompanied, and ran all the way to his house. As I climbed the staircase I could hear laughter and a woman's voice, and, as soon as I had rung, silence and the sound of shutting doors. The man-servant who let me in appeared embarrassed, and said that my uncle was extremely busy and probably could not see me; he went in, however, to announce my arrival, and the same voice I had heard before said: "Oh, yes! Do let him come in; just for a moment; it will be so amusing. On the table was the plate of marchpanes that was always there; my uncle wore the same alapca coat as on other days; but opposite to him, in a pink silk dress with a great necklace of pearls about her throat, sat a young woman who was just finishing a tangerine.

Two hours later, after a string of mysterious utterances, I found it simpler to let my parents have a full account, omitting no detail, of the visit I had paid that afternoon. Unfortunately my parents had recourse to principles entirely different from those which I suggested they should adopt when they came to form their estimate of my uncle's conduct. A few days later, passing my uncle in the street as he drove by in an open carriage, I turned my head away. My uncle thought that, in doing so I was obeying my parents' orders; he never forgave them; and though he did not die until many years later, not one of us ever set eyes on him again.

And so I no longer used to go into the little sitting-room (now kept shut) of my uncle Adolphe; instead, after Françoise announced: "I am going to let the kitchen-maid serve the coffee; it is time I went off to Mme. Octave." I would go straight upstairs to my room, to read.

The kitchen-maid was an abstract personality; for we never found the same girl there two years running. In the year in which we ate those quantities of asparagus, the kitchen-maid was a poor sickly creature, some way 'gone' in pregnancy, whose splendid outline could be detected through the folds of her ample smocks, recalling the cloaks in which Giotto shrouds some of the allegorical figures in his paintings.

I would be lying stretched out on my bed, a book in my hand, in my room which trembled with the effort to defend its frail, transparent coolness against the afternoon sun. But my grandmother would come up and beg me to go outside. And I would take my book, and go under the chestnut-tree to a little sentry-box of canvas and matting, in the farthest recesses of which I used to sit and feel that I was hidden from all eyes.

And then my thoughts, did not they form a similar sort of hiding-hole, in the depths of which I felt that I could bury myself and remain invisible even when I was looking at what went on outside? When I saw any external object, my consciousness that I was seeing it would remain between me and it, enclosing it in a slender, incorporeal outline which prevented me from ever coming directly in contact with the material form; for it would volatilise itself in some way before I could touch it, just as an incandescent body which is moved towards something wet never actually touches moisture, since it is always preceded, itself, by a zone of evaporation. Upon the sort of screen, patterned with different states and impressions, my consciousness would quietly unfold while I was reading.

In this way, for two consecutive summers I used to sit in the heat of our Combray garden, sick with a longing inspired by the book I was then reading for a land of mountains and rivers, where I could see an endless vista of sawmills, where beneath the limpid currents fragments of wood lay mouldering in beds of watercress; and nearby, rambling and clustering along low walls, purple flowers and red. And since there was always lurking in my mind the dream of a woman who would enrich me with her love, that dream in those two summers used to be quickened with the freshness and coolness of running water; and whoever she might be, the woman whose image I called to mind, purple flowers and red would at once spring up on either side of her like complementary colours.

This was not only because an image of which we dream remains for ever distinguished, is adorned and enriched by the association of colours not its own which may happen to surround it in our mental picture; for the scenes in the books I read were to me not merely scenery more vividly portrayed by my imagination than any which Combray could spread before my eyes but otherwise of the same kind.

Sometimes I would be torn from my book by the gardener's daughter, who came running like a mad thing, overturning an orange-tree in its tub, cutting a finger, breaking a tooth, and screaming out "They're coming, they're coming!" so that Françoise and I should run too and not miss anything of the show. That was on days when the cavalry stationed in Combray went out for some military exercise, going as a rule by the Rue Sainte-Hildegarde. While our servants, sitting in a row on their chairs outside the garden railings, stared at the people of Combray taking their Sunday walks and were stared at in return. "Poor children," Françoise would exclaim, in tears almost before she had reached the railings; "poor boys, to be mown down like grass in a meadow"[2]. Then Françoise would hasten back to my aunt, and I would return to my book, and the servants would take their places again outside the gate to watch the dust settle on the pavement, and the excitement caused by the passage of the soldiers subside.

---

2   **Mown down:** see p453

I discovered Bergotte for the first time from a friend older than myself, for whom I had a strong admiration, a precious youth of the name of Bloch. Hearing me confess my love of the Nuit d'Octobre, he had burst out in a bray of laughter, warning: "You must conquer your vile taste for these things". Bloch was not invited to the house again.

My grandfather made out that, whenever I formed a strong attachment to any one of my friends and brought him home with me, that friend was invariably a Jew; to which he would not have objected on principle - indeed his own friend Swann was of Jewish extraction - had he not found that the Jews whom I chose as friends were not usually of the best type. And so I was hardly ever able to bring a new friend home without my grandfather's humming "Israel, break thy chain".

While I was reading in the garden, my aunt Léonie would be gossiping with Françoise until it was time for Eulalie to arrive. Scarcely had she been admitted to the presence when Françoise reappeared: "His reverence the Curé would be delighted, enchanted, if Mme. His reverence is downstairs; I told him to go into the parlour." Had the truth been known, the Curé's visits gave my aunt no such ecstatic pleasure as Françoise supposed. His wordy descriptions of his church were erudite and accurate, but to an ear unused to history in any form, only suffered out of respect for the office of the teller.

The day had yet another characteristic feature, namely, that during May we used to go out on Saturday evenings after dinner to the 'Month of Mary' devotions. We were liable, there, to meet M. Vinteuil, who held very strict views on "the deplorable untidiness of young people, which seems to be encouraged in these days". It was in these services that I can remember having first fallen in love with hawthorn-blossom. The hawthorn was not merely in the church, for there, holy ground as it was, we had all of us a right of entry; but, arranged upon the altar itself, inseparable from the mysteries in whose celebration it was playing a part, it thrust in among the tapers and the sacred vessels its rows of branches, tied to one another horizontally in a stiff, festal scheme of decoration. Though I dared not look at them save through my fingers, I could feel that the formal scheme was composed of living things, and that it was Nature herself who, by trimming the shape of the foliage, and by adding the crowning ornament of those snowy buds, had made the decorations worthy of what was at once a public rejoicing and a solemn mystery.

When, before turning to leave the church, I made a genuflection before the altar, I felt suddenly, as I rose again, a bitter-sweet fragrance of almonds steal towards me from the hawthorn-blossom, and I then noticed that on the flowers themselves were little spots of a creamier colour, in which I imagined that this fragrance must lie concealed, as the taste of an almond cake lay in the burned parts, or the sweetness lay beneath the freckled cheeks of M. Vinteuil's daughter. Gusts of fragrance came to me like the murmuring of an intense vitality, with which the whole altar was quivering like a roadside hedge explored by living antennae, of which I was reminded by seeing some stamens, almost red in colour, which seemed to have kept the springtime virulence, the irritant power of stinging insects now transmuted into flowers.

* * *

One Sunday, my father said, "I am afraid we are in M. Legrandin's bad books; he would hardly say 'How d'ye do' to me this morning." But my father's fears were dissipated no later than the following evening. As we returned from a long walk we saw, near the Pont-Vieux, Legrandin himself. He came up to us with outstretched hand: "Do you know, master book-lover," he asked me, "this line of Paul Desjardins? *Now are the woods all black, but still the sky is blue.* Is not that a fine rendering of a moment like this? Read him, my boy, read him. Goodbye, friends!" he exclaimed, and left us.

At the hour when I usually went downstairs to find out what there was for dinner, its preparation would already have begun, and Françoise, a colonel with all the forces of nature for her subalterns, as in the fairy-tales where giants hire themselves out as scullions, would be stirring the coals, putting the potatoes to steam, and, at the right moment, finishing over the fire those culinary masterpieces which had been first got ready in some of the great array of vessels, triumphs of the potter's craft.

Poor Giotto's Charity, as Swann had named her, charged by Françoise with the task of preparing them for the table, would have the asparagus lying beside her in a basket; sitting with a mournful air, as though all the sorrows of the world were heaped upon her; and the light crowns of azure which capped the asparagus shoots above their pink jackets would be finely and separately outlined, star by star, as in Giotto's fresco are the flowers banded about the brows. I felt that these celestial hues indicated the presence of exquisite creatures who had been pleased to assume vegetable form, who, through the disguise which covered their firm and edible flesh, allowed me to discern in this radiance of earliest dawn, these hinted rainbows, these blue evening shades, that precious quality which I should recognise again when, all night long after a dinner at which I had partaken of them, they played (lyrical and coarse in their jesting as the fairies in Shakespeare's Dream) at transforming my humble chamber pot into a bower of aromatic perfume.

But the day on which, while my father took counsel with his family upon our strange meeting with Legrandin, I went down to the kitchen, was one of those days when Giotto's Charity, still very weak and ill after her recent confinement, had been unable to rise from her bed; Françoise, being without assistance, had fallen into arrears. When I went in, I saw her in the back-kitchen in process of killing a chicken; by its desperate and quite natural resistance, which Françoise, beside herself with rage as she attempted to slit its throat beneath the ear, accompanied with shrill cries of "Filthy creature! Filthy creature!" I crept out of the kitchen and upstairs, trembling all over; I could have prayed, then, for the instant dismissal of Françoise. But who would have baked me such hot rolls, boiled me such fragrant coffee, and even-roasted me such chickens?

M. Legrandin had asked my parents to send me to dine with him on this same Sunday evening. "Come and bear your aged friend company," he had said to me. "Like the nosegay which a traveller sends us from some land to which we shall never go again, come and let me breathe from the far country of your adolescence the scent of those flowers of spring among which I also used to wander, many years ago". So, after sole little discussion, I dined with Legrandin on the terrace of his house, by moonlight. "There is a charming quality, is there not," he said to me, "in this silence; for hearts that are wounded, as mine is, a novelist, whom you will read in time to come, claims that there is no remedy but silence and shadow. And see you this, my boy, there comes in all lives a time, towards which you still have far to go, when the weary eyes can endure but one kind of light, the light which a fine evening like this prepares for us in the stillroom of darkness, when the ears can listen to no music save what the moonlight breathes through the flute of silence."

I could hear what M. Legrandin was saying; like everything that he said, it sounded attractive; but knowing that Legrandin was on friendly terms with several of the local aristocracy, I summoned up all my courage and said to him: "Tell me, sir, do you know the Guermantes family?" and I felt glad because, in pronouncing the name, I had secured a sort of power over it. But, at the sound of the word Guermantes, I saw in the middle of each of our friend's blue eyes a little brown dimple appear, as though they had been stabbed by some invisible pin-point. Legrandin the talker would reply, "No, I have never cared to know them." But unfortunately the talker was subordinated to another Legrandin, who might say "Oh, how you hurt me! Do not remind me of the great sorrow of my life."

* * *

There were, in the environs of Combray, two 'ways' which we used to take for our walks, so diametrically opposed that we would actually leave the house by a different door, according to the way we had chosen: the way towards Méséglise-la-Vineuse, which we called also 'Swann's way,' because, to get there, one had to pass along the boundary of M. Swann's estate, and the 'Guermantes way.'

One day my grandfather said to my 'father: "Don't you remember Swann telling us that his wife and daughter had gone off to Rheims and that he was spending a day or two in Paris? We might go along by his park, since the ladies are not at home."

We stopped for a moment by the fence. I should have liked to see, by a miracle, Mlle. Swann appear, with her father, so close to us that we should not have time to escape, and should therefore be obliged to make her acquaintance. And so, when I suddenly noticed a straw basket lying forgotten on the grass by the side of a line whose float was bobbing in the water, I made a great effort to keep my father and grandfather looking in another direction, away from this sign that she might, after all, be in residence. I found the whole path throbbing with the fragrance of hawthorn-blossom. The hedge resembled a series of chapels, whose walls were no longer visible under the mountains of flowers that were heaped upon their altars. How simple and rustic, in comparison with these, would seem the dog-roses which, in a few weeks' time, would be climbing the same hillside path in the heat of the sun, dressed in the smooth silk of their blushing pink bodices, which would be undone and scattered by the first breath of wind. Suddenly I stood still, unable to move, as happens when something appears that requires not only our eyes to take it in, but involves a deeper kind of perception and takes possession of the whole of our being. A little girl, with fair, reddish hair, who appeared to be returning from a walk, and held a trowel in her hand, was looking at us, raising towards us a face powdered with pinkish freckles. "Gilberte, come along; what are you doing?" called out in a piercing tone of authority a lady in white, whom I had not seen until that moment.

And so was wafted to my ears the name of Gilberte, uttered across the heads of the stocks and jasmines, pungent and cool as the drops which fell from the green watering-pipe; impregnating and irradiating the zone of pure air through which it had passed, which it set apart and isolated from all other air, with the mystery of the life of her whom its syllables designated to the happy creatures that lived and walked and travelled in her company; unfolding through the arch of the pink hawthorn, which opened at the height of my shoulder, the quintessence of their familiarity - so exquisitely painful to myself - with her, and with all that unknown world of her existence, into which I should never penetrate.

* * *

That year my family fixed the day of their return to Paris rather earlier than usual, but found ourselves returning to Combray in autumn to settle my aunt Léonie's estate; for she had died at last, leaving both parties among her neighbours triumphant in the fact of her demise - those who had insisted that her mode of life was enfeebling and must ultimately kill her, and, equally, those who had always maintained that she suffered from some disease not imaginary, but organic.

During that time my parents, finding the days so fully occupied with the legal formalities that they had little time for walks, began to let me go, without them, along the 'Méséglise way,' wrapped up in a huge Highland plaid which protected me from the rain. I felt that the stripes of its gaudy tartan scandalised Françoise, whom it was impossible to convince that the colour of one's clothes had nothing whatever to do with one's mourning for the dead. But the moment that Françoise herself approached, some evil spirit would urge me to attempt to make her angry, and I would avail myself of the slightest pretext to say to her that I regretted my aunt's death because she had been a good woman in spite of her absurdities. And if Françoise then were to plead her inability to rebut my theories, saying: "I don't know how to *espress* myself"; and if she went on: "All the same she was a *geological* relation; there is always the respect due to your *geology*," I would shrug my shoulders and say: "It is really very good of me to discuss the matter with an illiterate old woman who cannot speak her own language," adopting the mean outlook of the pedant, whom those who are most contemptuous of, are only too prone to copy when they are obliged to play a part upon the vulgar stage of life.

My walks, that autumn, were all the more delightful because I used to take them after long hours spent over a book. And it is perhaps from an impression which I received years later at Montjouvain that there arose my idea of that cruel side of human passion called 'sadism.'

It was during a spell of very hot weather, when, having woken from a sleep in the shade, I saw Mlle. Vinteuil, now growing into a young woman only a few feet away, in a room where I could watch her every movement without her being able to see me. She was in deep mourning, for her father had but lately died.

At the far end of Mlle. Vinteuil's sitting-room, on the mantelpiece, stood a small photograph of her father which she went briskly to fetch, and placed it on a little table beside her sofa. The sound of carriage wheels was heard from the road outside, then her friend came in. Mlle. Vinteuil greeted her and rose and came to the window, where she pretended to be trying to close the shutters. "Leave them open," said her friend. "I am hot." "But people will see us," Mlle. Vinteuil answered. "And what if they do? said her friend, "Your ladyship's thoughts seem to be rather hot this evening". In the V-shaped opening of her crepe bodice Mlle. Vinteuil felt the sting of her friend's sudden kiss; she gave a little scream and ran away; and then they began to chase one another about the room, their wide sleeves fluttering like wings, clucking and crowing like a pair of amorous fowls. At last Mlle.Vinteuil fell down exhausted upon the sofa, where she was screened from me by the stooping body of her friend. Mlle. Vinteuil exclaimed: "Oh! there's my father's picture looking at us; that is not the proper place for it." The response seemed liturgical: "Let him stay there. He can't trouble us any longer, the ugly monkey? I should like to spit on the old horror." she said, taking up the photograph. I heard no more, for Mlle. Vinteuil, drew the shutters close. A 'sadist'[3] of her kind is an artist in evil, which a wholly wicked person could not be.

When we took the 'Guermantes way,' we had beside us, almost all the time, the course of the river Vivonne. We crossed it first, ten minutes after leaving the house, by a foot-bridge called the Pont-Vieux to a tow-path overhung in summer by the bluish foliage of a hazel, under which a fisherman in a straw hat seemed to have taken root. I would

amuse myself by watching the carafes which the boys used to lower into the waters, to catch minnows, and which, filled by the current of the stream, in which they themselves also were enclosed, at once 'containers' whose transparent sides were like solidified water and 'contents' plunged into a still larger container of liquid.

Never did we penetrate as far as the source of the Vivonne, nor could we ever reach that other goal, to which I longed so much to attain, Guermantes itself. I knew that it was the residence of its proprietors, the Duc and Duchesse de Guermantes, I knew that they were real personages who did actually exist, but whenever I thought about them I pictured them to myself either in that tapestry of the 'Coronation of Esther' which hung in our church.

I used to dream that Mme. de Guermantes, taking a sudden capricious fancy for myself, invited me there, that all day long she stood fishing for trout by my side. She would make me tell her all about the poems that I meant to compose. And these dreams reminded me that, since I wished, some day, to become a writer, it was high time to decide what sort of books I was going to write.

One day my mother said: "You are always talking about Mme. de Guermantes. Well, Dr. Percepied did a great deal for her when she was ill, four years ago, and so she is coming to Combray for his daughter's wedding. You will be able to see her in church."

During the nuptial mass, the beadle, by moving to one side, enabled me to see, sitting in a chapel, a lady with fair hair and a large nose, and piercing blue eyes. I said to myself: "This lady is the Duchesse de Guermantes." I can see again to-day the almost timid smile of a sovereign lady who seems to be making an apology for her presence among the vassals whom she loves. This smile rested upon myself, who had never ceased to follow her with my eyes, and at once I fell in love with her. Her eyes waxed blue as a periwinkle flower, wholly beyond my reach, yet dedicated by her to me.

How often, after that day, in the course of my walks along the 'Guermantes way,' and with what an intensified melancholy did I reflect on my lack of qualification for a literary career, and that I must abandon all hope of ever becoming a famous author. Once, however, we had been very glad to encounter, half way home, Dr. Percepied in his carriage, who made us jump in beside him. We were going like the wind, and at a bend in the road I experienced, suddenly, that special pleasure, which bore no resemblance to any other, when I caught sight of the twin steeples of Martinville, on which the setting sun was playing. I borrowed a pencil and some paper from the Doctor, and composed, in spite of the jolting of the carriage, the following little fragment, which I have since discovered, and now reproduce, with only a slight revision here and there.

> Alone, rising from the level of the plain, and seemingly lost in that expanse of open country, climbed to the sky the twin steeples of Martinville.

---

3   **Sadist:** see p276

Presently we saw three: springing into position confronting them by a daring volt, a third, a dilatory steeple, that of Vieuxvicq, was come to join them. Then the steeple of Vieuxvicq withdrew, took its proper distance, and the steeples of Martinville remained alone, gilded by the light of the setting sun, which, even at that distance, I could see playing and smiling upon their sloped sides. They made me think of three maidens in a legend, abandoned in a solitary place over which night had begun to fall; and while we drew away from them at a gallop, I could see them timidly seeking their way, and, after some awkward, stumbling movements of their noble silhouettes, drawing close to one another, slipping one behind another, shewing nothing more, now, against the still rosy sky than a single dusky form, charming and resigned, and so vanishing in the night.

When I had finished writing it, I found such a sense of happiness that I began to sing at the top of my voice.

So the 'Méséglise way' and the 'Guermantes way' remain for me linked with many of the little incidents of that one of all the divers lives along whose parallel lines we are moved, which is the most abundant in sudden reverses of fortune, the richest in episodes; I mean the life of the mind.

The scent of hawthorn which strays plundering along the hedge, a sound of footsteps followed by no echo, upon a gravel path, a bubble formed at the side of a waterplant - my exaltation of mind has succeeded in making them traverse all these successive years, while all around them the one-trodden ways have vanished, while those who thronged those ways, and even the memory of those who thronged those trodden ways, are dead.

And so I would often lie until morning, dreaming of the old days at Combray, the memory of which had been lately restored to me by the taste - by what would have been called at Combray the 'perfume' - of a cup of tea.

The Hundred Books

Done and read ...
by

....

on...

....

Made in United States
Orlando, FL
12 June 2022

18727358R00267